Poole's Casebook on Contract Law

Poole's Casebook on
Contract Law

15th Edition

ROBERT MERKIN QC

Professor of Commercial Law
Universities of Reading and Exeter

SÉVERINE SAINTIER

Maitrise, LLM, PhD
Associate Professor in Commercial Law
Exeter Law School,
University of Exeter

Earlier editions of this book were produced by the late Professor Jill Poole.

JILL POOLE

LLB, LLM, FHEA, FRSA, FCI Arb, Barrister
50th Anniversary Professor of Commercial Law and Head of Aston Law
Deputy Dean, Aston Business School,
Aston University

OXFORD
UNIVERSITY PRESS

OXFORD
UNIVERSITY PRESS

Great Clarendon Street, Oxford, OX2 6DP,
United Kingdom

Oxford University Press is a department of the University of Oxford.
It furthers the University's objective of excellence in research, scholarship,
and education by publishing worldwide. Oxford is a registered trade mark of
Oxford University Press in the UK and in certain other countries

Twelfth edition 2014
Thirteenth edition 2016
Fourteenth edition 2019

Impression: 1

Published in the United States of America by Oxford University Press
198 Madison Avenue, New York, NY 10016, United States of America

British Library Cataloguing in Publication Data
Data available

Library of Congress Control Number: 2021940027

ISBN 978–0–19–886998–6

Printed in Great Britain by
Bell & Bain Ltd., Glasgow

Dedicated to the memory of Professor Jill Poole: Scholar, teacher, and inspiration.

ABOUT THE AUTHORS

Professor Robert Merkin QC

Robert Merkin is Professor of Law at the University of Reading, Emeritus Professor of Law at the University of Exeter and Special Counsel to Duncan Cotterill. He has taught the Law of Contract for many years. Robert has written a number of texts and articles on contract, insurance, and arbitration. He is co-editor of the Lloyd's Law Reports. He was appointed Queen's Counsel (honoris causa) in 2015 and was awarded a higher doctorate by Cardiff University in the same year. In 2018, Robert became Honorary Life President of the International Association of Insurance Law (AIDA). Robert and Jill Poole were colleagues at Cardiff for a number of years, and Robert worked with Jill on an informal advisory basis on earlier editions of both the *Textbook* and *Casebook*. He has co-edited the book *Essays in Memory of Professor Jill Poole: Coherence, Modernisation and Integration in Contract, Commercial and Corporate Laws.*

Dr Séverine Saintier

Séverine Saintier is Associate Professor in Commercial Law at the University of Exeter where she teaches contract, commercial, and French contract law. She has authored publications such as *Commercial Agency Law: A Comparative Analysis* and written a number of articles for leading journals including the *Journal of Business Law* and the *European Review of Private Law*. Séverine is co-author with Robert of the Privity chapter in *Essays in Memory of Professor Jill Poole.*

Professor Jill Poole LLB, LLM, FHEA, FRSA, FCI Arb, Barrister

Jill Poole was Deputy Dean, Head of Aston Law and 50th Anniversary Professor of Commercial Law, Aston Business School, Aston University. Before her appointment at Aston she was a lecturer at Cardiff Law School. She was co-author of *Contract Formation and Letters of Intent* and also authored *Casebook on Contract Law*, to be used alongside this textbook, and *Contract Law Concentrate*, a law revision and study guide. Jill also authored and co-authored a series of important articles on contract law, particularly remedies for breach.

PREFACE

Professor Jill Poole was taken from us in 2016 at a tragically young age. She left a rich legacy of published work, a superb Law School at Aston, a generation of students who were fortunate enough to receive the benefit of her teaching and of course admiration and deep affection from everyone who worked with her. She was immensely proud of the *Casebook on Contract Law*, which she intended to be used in conjunction with her *Textbook on Contract Law*. In a relatively short period both texts became some of the most popular student works on the Law of Contract. The academic world owes Jill a great debt, and on a personal note we will both miss her wisdom and friendship.

As with the fourteenth edition, the first to appear under our names, we have aimed to follow closely in Jill's footsteps when preparing the present edition of the *Casebook*. We have sought to emulate her approach to the *Casebook*, which she described in her preface to the thirteenth edition as 'intended to provide a readable, detailed and structured account of relevant principles as developed through case law'. We have retained as much as Jill's own work as has been possible, but rapid developments in pretty much all areas of contract law have required us to replace her thoughts with our own. Reviewers of the fourteenth edition have been generous in their reception of our efforts, and we hope that as the work continues to change the importance of Jill's influence will not have been lost.

Similarly to the support obtained in preparing for Jill's Textbook, for the Casebook, we were also greatly assisted. We therefore wish to note the help of a number of anonymous reviewers, both teachers and students, who pointed out to us where we might amend the text in the light of new developments. We also wish to reiterate our thanks to the team at Oxford University Press, particularly Sarah Stephenson and Elakkia Bharathi, for their considerable efforts in the production of this edition.

In her final preface, Jill thanked all those tutors and students who had recommended and used the Casebook. We echo that thanks, and repeat her receptiveness to comments and questions from readers irrespective of their level of experience.

Rob Merkin: r.m.merkin@exeter.ac.uk
Séverine Saintier: s.saintier@exeter.ac.uk
School of Law, University of Exeter

GUIDE TO USING *POOLE'S CASEBOOK ON CONTRACT LAW*

All the cases you need, together with the tools to understand them.

Poole's Casebook on Contract Law includes a range of features to support your learning. The progression of case law through each chapter provides a logical account of the development of the legal principles. This guide shows you how to utilize your casebook fully to get the most out of your studies.

Guidance on reading cases

An introductory chapter provides valuable guidance on how to use a casebook, developing essential academic and practical skills. It is designed to give you confidence in reading and understanding case reports and to help you to study more effectively.

 You will find further guidance and exercises on the **online resources**: www.oup.com/he/poole15e/

Case extracts

Extracts from case reports and legislation are highlighted for easy identification.

Case summaries

Brief synopses of cases and the *ratio decidendi* (reasons upon which a case is decided) are provided, so you can easily pick out the salient facts and details in order to contextualize the extracts.

Notes

Extracts are followed by notes explaining the key points of the extracts in more detail. They might highlight the significance of the judgment or particular points made, explain how the decision relates to earlier case law, or provide details of further reading and academic analysis of the point of law under consideration.

Questions

Many extracts are followed by questions concerning the impact and significance of the decisions. Taking some time to pause and consider the questions will help you to develop a fuller understanding of the specific issues, as well as the wider context in which each decision was made.

Poole's Casebook on Contract Law can be used as a stand-alone text or in conjunction with *Poole's Textbook on Contract Law*. There are cross-references to the *Textbook* throughout and more analysis alongside further reading can be found in the companion book.

stal rule apply to acceptance messages sent by

ussion see *Poole's Textbook on Contract Law*, pages 70–1.
visable to avoid the postal rule expressly and to require a
rs (a firm) [2010] EWHC 306 (Ch), [2010] All ER (D) 306 (F
eed, considering that where contracts are made by excha
by analogy with the telex case law and *Entores v Miles Far*

NEW TO THIS EDITION

This case law list represents the most important new cases included in this book:

- Chapter 2: *Astra Asset Management v Co-operative Bank* [2019] EWHC 897 (Comm)
- Chapter 3: *Simantob v Yacob Shayleyan* [2019] EWCA Civ 1105
- Chapter 5: *Merthyr (South Wales) Ltd v Merthyr Tydfil County Borough Council* [2019] EWCA Civ 526; *Wells v Devani* [2019] UKSC 4
- Chapter 7: *BV Nederlandse Industrie Van Eiprodukten v Rembrandt Entreprises Inc.* [2019] EWCA Civ 596
- Chapter 8: *FSHC Group Holdings Ltd v GLAS Trust Corp. Ltd* [2019] EWCA Civ 1361
- Chapter 9: *BV Nederlandse Industrie Van Eiprodukten v Rembrandt Entreprises Inc.* [2019] EWCA Civ 596
- Chapter 10: *Times Travel (UK) LTD v Pakistan International Airlines Corp.* [2019] EWCA Civ 828
- Chapter 11: *Peninsula Securities Ltd v Dunnes Stores (Bangor) Ltd (Northern Ireland)* [2020] UKSC 36; *Tillman v Egon Zehnder Ltd* [2019] UKSC 32
- Chapter 12: *Canary Wharf (BP4) T1 Ltd v European Medicines Agency* [2019] EWHC 921 (Ch)
- Chapter 13: *Ark Shipping Co. LLC v Silverburn Shipping (IoM) Ltd* [2019] EWCA Civ 1161
- Chapter 14: *Classic Maritime Inc. v Limbungan Maknur SDN BHD* [2019] EWCA Civ 1102
- Chapter 15: *Priyanka Shipping Ltd v Glory Bulk Carriers Pte Ltd* [2019] EWHC 2804 (Comm)

OUTLINE CONTENTS

DETAILED CONTENTS

ACKNOWLEDGEMENTS

Grateful acknowledgement is made to all the authors and publishers of copyright material which appears in this book, and in particular to the following for permission to reprint material from the sources indicated:

Canada Law Book—Extract from *London Drugs Ltd v Kuehne & Nagel International Ltd* (1992), 1992 CarswellBC 913, 1992 CarswellBC 315, 97 D.L.R. (4th) 261 (S.C.C.), reproduced by permission of Thomson Reuters Canada Limited.

DSP Publishing Ltd—Extracts from the *Commercial Law Cases* reproduced by kind permission of DSP Publishing Ltd.

The Estates Gazette Ltd—Extracts from *The Estates Gazette Law Reports* are reproduced by kind permission of The Estates Gazette Ltd.

The High Court of Australia—Extracts from cases reported in *The Commonwealth Law Reports* are reproduced by kind permission of the High Court of Australia.

The Incorporated Council of Law Reporting for England and Wales—*The Law Reports*, the *Business Law Reports*, the *Weekly Law Reports*, and the *Industrial Cases Reports*. The special permission to reproduce in Chapter 1 extracts from the headnotes of *Carlill v Carbolic Smoke Ball Company* [1893] 1 QB 256 and *Howard Marine and Dredging Co. Ltd v A. Ogden and Sons (Excavations) Ltd* [1978] QB 574, is gratefully acknowledged.

Informa Law—Extracts from cases reported in *Lloyd's Law Reports* and the *Building Law Reports* are reproduced by kind permission of Informa Law, Informa House, 30–32 Mortimer Street, London W1W 7RE, Tel: +44 (0)20 7017 5048, Fax: +44 (0)20 7017 5274.

LexisNexis—Extracts from *The All England Law Reports, The All England Law Reports Commercial Cases, English Reports,* reproduced by permission of RELX (UK) Limited, trading as LexisNexis.

New Zealand Council of Law Reporting—Extracts from *Antons Trawling Co Ltd v Smith* [2003] 2 NZLR 23 reproduced by kind permission of the New Zealand Council of Law Reporting.

The Singapore Academy of Law—Extracts from *Chwee Kin Keong v Digilandmall.com Pte Ltd* [2004] 2 SLR(R) 594 reproduced with permission from the Singapore Academy of Law. All rights reserved. No portion of the case may be used or reproduced without the prior written consent of the Singapore Academy of Law.

Thomson Reuters, Sweet and Maxwell Limited—Extracts from *R v Attorney General of England and Wales* [2003] UKPC 22, [2003] EMLR 24, and *Office of Fair Trading v Ashbourne Management Services Ltd* [2011] EWHC 1237 (Ch), [2011] ECC 31, are reproduced by kind permission of Sweet & Maxwell Ltd. *Hochster v De La Tour* (1853) 2 E & B 678, 118 ER 922 (QB) Reproduced with permission of the Licensor through PLSclear.

Every effort has been made to trace and contact copyright holders prior to publication. Where this has not proved possible, if notified, the publisher will undertake to rectify any errors or omissions at the earliest opportunity.

TABLE OF CASES

TABLE OF LEGISLATION

Chapter 1
Guidance on reading cases

1.1 A guiding principle

For legal research, knowing how to read a case is essential as it will help you to understand how it relates to the legal principles learned in lectures. It is important, therefore, to know what issue you should find in the case, and then use this to give your case reading some direction and context.

Read a case with either a broad heading or a specific principle in mind. The principle or heading will be indicated on your lecture outline, in the lecture itself, or in a textbook. If you need to read a recent case and are not sure about the issues involved, help is provided by the catchwords and headnote at the top of the report. An individual case may well be concerned with many different issues that you are not currently studying and, while it is interesting to read about them, the pressures of time mean that it is necessary to be selective.

Of course, the casebook helps as it provides the headings and highlights the relevant parts of decisions and judgments to illustrate the principle. This guides you whilst you acquire the necessary skills.

1.2 Useful notes

To understand a case, you may wish to make notes of it. To be helpful, avoid merely copying *verbatim* (except the facts and specific statements in the judgments that you may wish to use later) and aim to explain the case in your own words. This will ensure that you understand what you are writing and can rely on it later. Of particular importance in doing so is to appreciate the significance of the case in relation to the legal issue involved, i.e. does it reverse or confirm a previous decision, does it clarify a previously unclear point, etc.

1.3 The basics of reading a case

1.3.1 Decide which case(s) to read

The more cases you read entirely, the better, but the most important ones are indicated by your lecturer.

1.3.2 Use the citation to find the report of the case

In January 2001, neutral citations were introduced for decisions of the Court of Appeal and the then House of Lords, e.g. '[2001] EWCA Civ 12': see *Practice Direction (Form of Judgments, Paragraph Marking and Neutral Citation)* [2001] 1 WLR 194 and extended (*Practice Direction (Judgments: Neutral Citation)* [2002] 1 WLR 346) to all judgments given by the High Court in London after 14 January 2002, i.e. 'EWHC [number] (Ch)' for the Chancery Division, 'EWHC [number] (QB)' for the Queen's Bench Division, and 'EWHC [number] (Comm)' for the Commercial Court. Such changes aim to facilitate the publication of judgments on the Internet, and assist in identifying individual judgments on issues involving the same parties. There is a difference between those cases that were reported before 2001–2 and those reported after. (Note, the retrospective neutral citation for cases before these dates invented by the British and Irish Legal Information Institute—online at www.bailii.org—is not authoritative and you should avoid using it in written work.) When in doubt about case citation, always consult the case index of a practice volume (e.g. *Chitty on Contracts*) or a reputable student textbook for the correct citations of cases, particularly for historic case law.

1.3.3 Note the full case name and court

The full case name and the court in which it was heard are given at the top of the report (for older cases in the English Reports, you may have to look back to the first among the cases reported by the particular reporter to identify the court in which they were heard). The court deciding the case is significant, and you must be familiar with the structure of the courts (the civil courts, for contract cases) and the doctrine of precedent.

Note the citation for the case, since you will need to include this in the footnotes of any written work. Following the 2001 and 2002 Practice Directions (*page 2, 1.3.2*), all judgments must list the appropriate neutral citation before that of any law report series, e.g. '*Watford Electronics Ltd v Sanderson CFL Ltd* [2001] EWCA Civ 317, [2001] 1 All ER (Comm) 696, [2001] BLR 143'. For a neutral citation, pinpoints should be to paragraphs rather than to page numbers, e.g. '[2001] EWCA Civ 317, [31]–[34]'.

Under *Practice Direction: Citation of Authorities* [2012] 1 WLR 780 where a case is reported in the official Law Reports published by the Incorporated Council of Law Reporting for England and Wales (ICLR)—whether Appeal Cases (AC), or cases before the Queen's Bench Division (QB), the Chancery Division (Ch), or the Family Division (Fam)—that source must be used before the name of the court. It is crucial for you to adopt this practice. Where a case is not reported in the official Law Reports, any report in the Weekly Law Reports (WLR) or All England Law Reports (All ER) should be used. Only where there is no report in any of these law report series should other reports be cited.

1.3.4 **Consider the presentation of case reports**

The presentation of case reports is fairly standardized.

1.3.4.1 **Catchwords**

At the top of the headnote, a section identifies the issues in the case (so-called 'catchwords'). These should correspond at some point with the legal issues given in the heading or principle in your lecture notes or outline. No need to note them.

1.3.4.2 **Headnote facts**

The headnote facts can be very brief and too general or comprise full case facts and details of the decision at first instance or previous appeals.

Make notes on whatever facts are relevant to the principle that you are using as your guide. If the headnote facts are brief, then look for further facts in the judgments.

Each case is a decision on its particular facts, so the facts are crucial.

1.3.4.3 **Statement of the decision of the court**

The headnote may not be detailed enough on the reasons for the decision; if so, you need to look at the judgments themselves to find out.

1.3.4.4 **More detailed facts**

A more detailed statement of the facts may follow the headnote. Some judgments will also contain details of the facts. Lord Denning was particularly adept at setting out the facts in a readable form, and used headings to helpful effect. It is common practice to find headings and subheadings within judgments in order to separate and identify issues both of fact and of law.

1.3.4.5 **Details of the grounds of any appeal and the arguments of each set of counsel**

It is useful, especially for moot preparation, to read the arguments of each set of counsel in light of the actual decision given in the headnote.

1.3.4.6 **A judgment or number of judgments**

The headnote is helpful in indicating the majority, the judgments that require particular attention, and the principles for which you will need to look in reading the judgments. It should also indicate any dissenting judgments.

With appeal cases, the headnote may indicate relevant page numbers (or paragraphs, in the case of neutral citation) within judgments, as you will see shortly when we look at the headnote in *Howard Marine & Dredging Co. Ltd v A. Ogden & Sons (Excavations) Ltd* [1978] QB 574 (*pages 16–17, 1.5*).

If there is any difference of opinion on the reasons for a decision or an actual dissent, these judgments require particular examination to determine the reasons given for the differences and dissents.

Ensure that the judgments do, in fact, correspond with the decision stated in the headnote, and use the comments in the judgments to explain and illustrate the decision.

1.3.4.7 **Case law applied and distinguished**

The names of the important previous cases that the court is purporting to apply and on which it is relying as justification for part or all of its decision should be given. If the court purports to distinguish any case authority, this should also be noted.

1.4 **Reading a case in practice**

You are required to read *Carlill v Carbolic Smoke Ball Co.* [1893] 1 QB 256, on offer and acceptance.

Find the report of the case in the first volume of the Law Reports Queen's Bench Division for 1893, at p. 256. (There are numerous other reports of this case, e.g. at 62 LJQB 257 or 67 LT 837.)

Make a note of the full case name and the fact that this is a decision of the Court of Appeal. (It may be preferable to list the members of the court when stating the decision.) Remember to note the citation used.

An extract from the judgment follows and the issues are highlighted and explained alongside the relevant text.

❶ The catchwords help to show that this case about a contract is concerned with an offer by advertisement. This is within your guiding principle of offer and acceptance.

❷ This case also raises two other issues that are not within your guiding principle of offer and acceptance— namely, wager and insurance. Do not worry about these for the present.

❸ The facts given in the headnote are very brief. More details of the facts follow the headnote.

❹ The facts are followed by a brief statement of what was decided.

❺ We are told that the Court of Appeal affirmed the first instance decision of Hawkins J (the citation for this decision is given at the bottom of p. 256 in note (2) as [1892] 2 QB 484). If you are mooting, it is advisable to have full details of this first instance decision to know the arguments presented and those that were accepted on that occasion.

❻ The headnote states that the Court of Appeal held that the defendants (the Smoke Ball Company) agreed to pay the plaintiff £100 conditional upon a certain event that subsequently occurred—namely, contracting influenza after having used one of the smoke balls in the specified manner and for the specified period.

[IN THE COURT OF APPEAL]

CARLILL V CARBOLIC SMOKE BALL COMPANY

Contract—Offer by Advertisement—Performance of Condition in Advertisement—Notification of Acceptance of Offer ❶ *—Wager—Insurance—*❷ *8&9 Vict. c. 109—14 Geo. 3, c. 48, s. 2*

The defendants, the proprietors of a medical preparation called 'The Carbolic Smoke Ball', issued an advertisement in which they offered to pay 100*l.* to any person who contracted influenza after having used one of their smoke balls in a specified manner and for a specified period. The plaintiff on the faith the advertisement bought one of the balls, and used it in the manner and for the period specified, but nevertheless contracted the influenza:—❸

*Held,*❹ affirming the decision of Hawkins, J ❺ that the above facts established a contract by the defendants to pay the plaintiff 100*l.* in the event which had happened❻; that such contract was neither a contract by way of wagering within 8 & 9 Vict c. 109, nor a policy within 14 Geo 3, c. 48, s. 2; and that the plaintiff was entitled to recover.❼

❼ We are also told that it was decided that it was not a wagering contract or a policy of insurance, the plaintiff was therefore entitled to the £100. Although, under the Civil Procedure Rules 1998, the term 'claimant' (person bringing the claim) is now used in place of 'plaintiff', this case predates this change, so the term 'plaintiff' remains appropriate.

1.4.1 Note the facts

The facts will help you to understand the judgments. Because the headnote facts are too brief for this purpose, the statement of facts on pp. 256–7 of the report is used:

Carlill v Carbolic Smoke Ball Co.
[1893] 1 QB 256 (CA)

The defendants, who made and sold a medical preparation called 'The Carbolic Smoke Ball', issued an advertisement in a number of newspapers in the following terms:

> £100 reward will be paid by the Carbolic Smoke Ball Company to any person who contracts the increasing epidemic influenza, colds, or any disease caused by taking cold, after having used the ball three times daily for two weeks according to the printed directions supplied with each ball. £1,000 is deposited with the Alliance Bank, Regent Street, shewing our sincerity in the matter.

Relying on this advertisement, the claimant bought one of the balls at a chemist and used it as directed three times a day from 20 November 1891 to 17 January 1892, when she contracted influenza.

She sought payment of the £100, the defendants refused.

1.4.2 Decision at first instance

Hawkins J at first instance held that the claimant was entitled to recover, since the advertisement was intended to attract custom and was supported by the deposit with the Company's bank. The Company should not have been surprised if it was held to its promise (this information is only found in the report of the first instance decision).

The Court of Appeal purport to affirm the first instance decision; it is therefore unnecessary to make detailed notes on the earlier decision.

1.4.3 Decision of the Court of Appeal

Making a note of the Court of Appeal's decision in this case is difficult since the headnote is a broad statement of result without giving reasons. You must therefore look at the judgments. (There is no indication in the headnote of any dissent, so that the three judgments should be saying the same thing.)

On occasions it can be helpful to look at the counsel's arguments. In this case the defendants put forward a number of arguments as to why there should be no binding contract. However, since the Court of Appeal members identify and answer these points in their judgments, it is unnecessary to duplicate them by making notes on the arguments of counsel.

1.4.4 Judgments

Read each judgment and make notes.

1.4.4.1 Judgment of lindley lj

Lindley LJ rejects the two arguments that are outside the scope of our directing issue—namely, that it was an unenforceable wagering contract and insurance policy.

LINDLEY LJ: [The Lord Justice stated the facts, and proceeded:] I will begin by referring to two points which were raised in the Court below. I refer to them simply for the purpose of dismissing them. First, it is said no action will lie upon this contract because it is a policy. You have only to look at the advertisement to dismiss that suggestion. Then it was said that it is a bet. Hawkins, J., came to the conclusion that nobody ever dreamt of a bet, and that the transaction had nothing whatever in common with a bet. I so entirely agree with him that I pass over this contention also as not worth serious attention.

. . .

Lindley LJ considered that there was no doubt that the language used indicated that a binding promise was being made. To be enforceable, the promise must have been intended to give rise to legal relations (*page* 145, 4.1). One of the arguments put by counsel for the defendants was that this advertisement was not intended to create legal relations. It was a 'mere puff', or advertising gimmick, which was not intended to be taken literally and which therefore could not be enforced by the plaintiff.

Was it a mere puff? My answer to that question is No, and I base my answer upon this passage: '1000/. is deposited with the Alliance Bank, shewing our sincerity in the matter.' Now, for what was that money deposited or that statement made except to negative the suggestion that this was a mere puff and meant nothing at all? The deposit is called in aid by the advertiser as proof of his sincerity in the matter—that is, the sincerity of his promise to pay this 100/. in the event which he has specified. I say this for the purpose of giving point to the observation that we are not inferring a promise; there is the promise, as plain as words can make it.

. . .

He then identified this advertisement as an offer to the world.
The advertisement is an offer to pay a reward to anybody who performs the stipulated act, and performance of that act constitutes the acceptance of the offer. Lindley LJ states that this is a unilateral offer, i.e. a promise to pay money in exchange for an act.

Now that point is common to the words of this advertisement and to the words of all other advertisements offering rewards. They are offers to anybody who performs the conditions named in the advertisement, and anybody who does perform the condition accepts the offer. In point of law this advertisement is an offer to pay 100/. to anybody who will perform these conditions, and the performance of the conditions is the acceptance of the offer.

. . .

A further argument for the defendants was that any acceptance had to be communicated to the offeror, and Mrs Carlill did not notify the Company that she intended to use the smoke ball.

But then it is said, 'Supposing that the performance of the conditions is an acceptance of the offer, that acceptance ought to have been notified.' Unquestionably, as a general proposition, when an offer is made, it is necessary in order to make a binding contract, not only that it should be accepted, but that the acceptance should

Thus, Lindley LJ stated that the nature of the transaction indicated that the offeror had waived the normal requirement of communication of acceptance (although it was necessary, having performed, to notify the offeror of this fact in order to claim the reward).

The advertisement's language was so vague, as argued, that it could not possibly amount to a promise.

be notified. But is that so in cases of this kind? . . . [I] think that the true view, in a case of this kind, is that the person who makes the offer shews by his language and from the nature of the transaction that he does not expect and does not require notice of the acceptance apart from notice of the performance.

. . .

The language is vague and uncertain in some respects, and particularly in this, that the 100*l*. is to be paid to any person who contracts the increasing epidemic after having used the balls three times daily for two weeks. It is said, When are they to be used? According to the language of the advertisement no time is fixed, and, construing the offer most strongly against the person who has made it, one might infer that any time was meant. I do not think that was meant, and to hold the contrary would be pushing too far the doctrine of taking language most strongly against the person using it. I do not think that business people or reasonable people would understand the words as meaning that if you took a smoke ball and used it three times daily for two weeks you were to be guaranteed against influenza for the rest of your life, and I think it would be pushing the language of the advertisement too far to construe it as meaning that. But if it does not mean that, what does it mean? It is for the defendants to shew what it does mean; and it strikes me that there are two, and possibly three, reasonable constructions to be put on this advertisement, any one of which will answer the purpose of the plaintiff. Possibly it may be limited to persons catching the 'increasing epidemic' (that is, the then prevailing epidemic), or any colds or diseases caused by taking cold, during the prevalence of the increasing epidemic. That is one suggestion; but it does not commend itself to me. Another suggested meaning is that you are warranted free from catching this epidemic, or colds or other diseases caused by taking cold, whilst you are using this remedy after using it for two weeks. If that is the meaning, the plaintiff is right, for she used the remedy for two weeks and went on using it till she got the epidemic. Another meaning, and the one which I rather prefer, is that the reward is offered to any person who contracts the epidemic or other disease within a reasonable time after having used the smoke ball.

. . .

Lindley LJ considered that the offer could be construed to apply to any person who contracted influenza within a reasonable time of having used the smoke ball. Clearly, this covered the claimant, who had contracted influenza while using the smoke ball.

The Company's promise had to be supported by consideration (*Chapter 3*) provided by Mrs Carlill (i.e. Mrs Carlill had to give something of value in exchange for the Company's promise). Consideration was seen as being either a benefit to the offeror (the Smoke Ball Company) and/or a detriment to the offeree (Mrs Carlill). Lindley LJ considered that consideration was present in the sense of a benefit to the offeror company and/or a detriment to the offeree (Mrs Carlill).

It has been argued that this is nudum pactum—that there is no consideration. We must apply to that argument the usual legal tests. Let us see whether there is no advantage to the defendants. It is said that the use of the ball is no advantage to them, and that what benefits them is the sale; and the case is put that a lot of these balls might be stolen, and that it would be no advantage to the defendants if the thief or other people used them. The answer to that, I think, is as follows. It is quite obvious that in the view of the advertisers a use by the public of their remedy, if they can only get the public to have confidence enough to use it, will react and produce a sale which is directly beneficial to them. Therefore, the advertisers get out of the use an advantage which is enough to constitute a consideration.

Lindley LJ states that the performance of the act specified in the unilateral offer constitutes both the acceptance of the promise and the consideration for it.

But there is another view. Does not the person who acts upon this advertisement and accepts the offer put himself to some inconvenience at the request of the defendants? Is it nothing to use this ball three times daily for two weeks according to the directions at the request of the advertiser? Is that to go for nothing? It appears to me that there is a distinct inconvenience, not to say a detriment, to any person who so uses the smoke ball. I am of opinion, therefore, that there is ample consideration for the promise.

. . .

Lindley LJ concludes his judgment.

It appears to me, therefore, that the defendants must perform their promise, and, if they have been so unwary as to expose themselves to a great many actions, so much the worse for them.

1.4.4.2 Judgment of Bowen LJ

Bowen LJ's judgment is the clearest and most frequently cited judgment, with a most logical order presentation of the issues.

Was the advertisement too vague to be enforced?

BOWEN LJ: The defendants contend, that it is an offer the terms of which are too vague to be treated as a definite offer, inasmuch as there is no limit of time fixed for the catching of the influenza, and it cannot be supposed that the advertisers seriously meant to promise to pay money to every person who catches the influenza at any time after the inhaling of the smoke ball . . . It seems to me that in order to arrive at a right conclusion we must read this advertisement in its plain meaning, as the

Bowen LJ adopted the correct approach of looking at the statement objectively to see what the reasonable man would consider was intended.

public would understand it. It was intended to be issued to the public and to be read by the public. How would an ordinary person reading this document construe it? It was intended unquestionably to have some effect, and I think the effect which it was intended to have, was to make people use the smoke ball, because the suggestions and allegations which it contains are directed immediately to the use of the smoke ball as distinct from the purchase of it. It did not follow that the smoke ball was to be purchased from the defendants directly, or even from agents of theirs directly. The intention was that the circulation of the smoke ball should be promoted, and that the use of it should be increased. The advertisement begins by saying that a reward will be paid by the Carbolic Smoke Ball Company to any person who contracts the increasing epidemic after using the ball. It has been said that the words do not apply only to persons who contract the epidemic after the publication of the advertisement, but include persons who had previously contracted the influenza. I cannot so read the advertisement. It is written in colloquial and popular language, and I think that it is equivalent to this: '100/. will be paid to any person who shall contract the increasing epidemic after having used the carbolic smoke ball three times daily for two weeks.' And it seems to me that the way in which the public would read it would be this, that if anybody, after the advertisement was published, used three times daily for two weeks the carbolic smoke ball, and then caught cold, he would be entitled to the reward.

Bowen LJ differs from Lindley LJ on the question of the length of the immunity. Lindley LJ considered that it should last for a reasonable time after use of the smoke ball, while Bowen LJ confined it to protection during the use of the smoke ball. It did not affect the decision on these facts, since Mrs Carlill had been using the smoke ball when she contracted influenza.

. . . Then again it was said: 'How long is this protection to endure? Is it to go on forever, or for what limit of time?' I think that there are two constructions of this document, each of which is good sense, and each of which seems to me to satisfy the exigencies of the present action. It may mean that the protection is warranted to last during the epidemic, and it was during the epidemic that the plaintiff contracted the disease. I think, more probably, it means that the smoke ball will be a protection while it is in use. That seems to me the way in which an ordinary person would understand an advertisement about medicine, and about a specific against influenza. It could not be supposed that after you have left off using it you are still to be protected for ever, as if there was to be a stamp set upon your forehead that you were never to catch influenza because you had once used the carbolic smoke ball. I think the immunity is to last during the use of the ball . . . I therefore, have myself no hesitation in saying that I think, on the construction of this advertisement, the protection was to enure during the time that the carbolic smoke ball was being used. My brother, the Lord Justice who preceded me, thinks that the contract would be sufficiently definite if you were to read it in the sense that the protection was to be warranted during a reasonable period after use. I have some difficulty myself on that point; but it is not necessary for me to consider it further, because the disease here was contracted during the use of the carbolic smoke ball.

Bowen LJ then addressed the contention that this was a 'mere puff' and that there was no intention to create legal relations.

He then went on to address the argument that this would amount to a contract with the whole world, which was impossible.

Bowen LJ states that *this* advertisement was an offer, whereas advertisements are normally invitations to treat. The unilateral contract is therefore an exception to the general rule in *Partridge v Crittenden* [1968] 1 WLR 1204 (page 26, 2.3.1), since an advertisement that requests the performance of an act will be an offer. To construe such advertisements to pay rewards as an invitation to treat would have been illogical since the offeror would have the benefit of seeing the stipulated conditions performed without being bound to pay the reward.

. . . Was it intended that the 100*l*. should, if the conditions were fulfilled, be paid? The advertisement says that 1000*l*. is lodged at the bank for the purpose. Therefore, it cannot be said that the statement that 100*l*. would be paid was intended to be a mere puff. I think it was intended to be understood by the public as an offer which was to be acted upon.

. . . It is not a contract made with all the world. There is the fallacy of the argument. It is an offer made to all the world; and why should not an offer be made to all the world which is to ripen into a contract with anybody who comes forward and performs the condition? It is an offer to become liable to any one who, before it is retracted, performs the condition, and, although the offer is made to the world, the contract is made with that limited portion of the public who come forward and perform the condition on the faith of the advertisement. It is not like cases in which you offer to negotiate, or you issue advertisements that you have got a stock of books to sell, or houses to let, in which case there is no offer to be bound by any contract. Such advertisements are offers to negotiate—offers to receive offers—offers to chaffer . . . If this is an offer to be bound, then it is a contract the moment the person fulfils the condition.

Was it necessary that the acceptance be notified?

. . . One cannot doubt that, as an ordinary rule of law, an acceptance of an offer made ought to be notified to the person who makes the offer, in order that the two minds may come together. Unless this is done the two minds may be apart, and there is not that consensus which is necessary according to the English law . . . to make a contract. But there is this clear gloss to be made upon that doctrine, that as notification of acceptance is required for the benefit of the person who makes the offer, the person who makes the offer may dispense with notice to himself if he thinks it desirable to do so, and I suppose there can be no doubt that where a person in an offer made by him to another person, expressly or impliedly intimates a particular mode of acceptance as sufficient to make the bargain binding, it is only necessary for the other person to whom such offer is made to follow the indicated method of acceptance; and if the person making the offer, expressly or impliedly intimates in his offer that it will be sufficient to action the proposal without communicating acceptance of it to himself, performance of the condition is a sufficient acceptance without notification . . .

Now, if that is the law, how are we to find out whether the person who makes the offer does intimate that notification of acceptance will not be necessary in order to constitute a binding bargain? In many cases you look to the offer itself. In many cases you extract from the character of the transaction that notification is not required, and in the advertisement cases it seems to me to follow as an inference to be drawn from the transaction itself that a person is not to notify his acceptance of the offer before he performs the condition, but that if he performs the condition notification is dispensed with. It seems to me that from the point of view of common sense no other idea could be entertained. If I advertise to the world that my dog is lost, and that anybody who brings the dog to a particular place will be paid some money, are all the police or other persons whose business it is to find lost dogs to be expected to sit down and write me a note saying that they have accepted my proposal? Why, of course, they at once look after the dog, and as soon as they find the dog they have performed the condition. The essence of the transaction is that the dog should be found, and it is not necessary under such circumstances, as it seems to me, that in order to make the contract binding there should be any notification of acceptance. It follows from the nature of the thing that the performance of the condition is sufficient acceptance without the notification of it, and a person who makes an offer in an advertisement of that kind makes an offer which must be read by the light of that common sense reflection. He does, therefore, in his offer impliedly indicate that he does not require notification of the acceptance of the offer.

Finally, in answer to the argument that, since catching influenza was only a condition, the Company's promise was not supported by any consideration from Mrs Carlill, Bowen LJ agreed with Lindley LJ that there was both a benefit to the Company and a detriment to Mrs Carlill.

. . . Can it be said here that if the person who reads this advertisement applies thrice daily, for such time as may seem to him tolerable, the carbolic smoke ball to his nostrils for a whole fortnight, he is doing nothing at all—that it is a mere act which is not to count towards consideration to support a promise (for the law does not require us to measure the adequacy of the consideration). Inconvenience sustained by one party at the request of the other is enough to create a consideration. I think, therefore, that it is consideration enough that the plaintiff took the trouble of using the smoke ball. But I think also that the defendants received a benefit from this user, for the use of the smoke ball was contemplated by the defendants as being indirectly a benefit to them, because the use of the smoke balls would promote their sale.

1.4.4.3 Judgment of A. L. Smith LJ

This judgment is more general in its presentation of the issues. His Lordship examined the vagueness of the promise.

A. L. SMITH LJ: It comes to this: 'In consideration of your buying my smoke ball, and then using it as I prescribe, I promise that if you catch the influenza within a certain time I will pay you 100/.' It must not be forgotten that this advertisement states that as security for what is being offered, and as proof of the sincerity of the offer, 1000/. is actually lodged at the bank wherewith to satisfy any possible demands which might be made in the event of the conditions contained therein being fulfilled and a person catching the epidemic so as to entitle him to the 100/. How can it be said that such a statement as that embodied only a mere expression of confidence in the wares which the defendants had to sell? I cannot read the advertisement in any such way. In my judgment, the advertisement was an offer intended to be acted upon, and when accepted and the conditions performed constituted a binding promise on which an action would lie, assuming there was consideration for that promise . . .

His Lordship neatly avoided having to choose between the construction of Lindley LJ or that of Bowen LJ by stating that it was not necessary for him to do so. There is therefore no clear interpretation of the promise by the Court of Appeal.

... [I]t was said that the promise was too wide, because there is no limit of time within which the person has to catch the epidemic. There are three possible limits of time to this contract. The first is, catching the epidemic during its continuance; the second is, catching the influenza during the time you are using the ball; the third is, catching the influenza within a reasonable time after the expiration of the two weeks during which you have used the ball three times daily. It is not necessary to say which is the correct construction of this contract, for no question arises thereon. Whichever is the true construction, there is sufficient limit of time so as not to make the contract too vague on that account.

There was no express requirement that acceptance be notified.

This helps since it indicates that if a unilateral offeror does wish to know who is attempting to accept his offer, he must include an express provision requiring this. Interestingly, there is no mention of the need to catch influenza as being the act required for acceptance (see the discussion of condition imposed on a recipient of a gift, at page 90, 3.1.2). The other members of the Court of Appeal referred only to performance of the 'conditions named'.

... Then it was argued, that if the advertisement constituted an offer which might culminate in a contract if it was accepted, and its conditions performed, yet it was not accepted by the plaintiff in the manner contemplated, and that the offer contemplated was such that notice of the acceptance had to be given by the party using the carbolic ball to the defendants before user, so that the defendants might be at liberty to superintend the experiment. All I can say is, that there is no such clause in the advertisement, and that, in my judgment, no such clause can be read into it; and I entirely agree with what has fallen from my Brothers, that this is one of those cases in which a performance of the condition by using these smoke balls for two weeks three times a day is an acceptance of the offer.

A. L. Smith LJ also recognized that to perform the conditions specified constituted the acceptance and concluded by agreeing that consideration had been provided, since it was a detriment to the offeree to use the smoke ball as requested and a benefit to the Company.

... Lastly, it was said that there was no consideration, and that it was nudum pactum. There are two considerations here. One is the consideration of the inconvenience of having to use this carbolic smoke ball for two weeks three times a day; and the other more important consideration is the money gain likely to accrue to the defendants by the enhanced sale of the smoke balls, by reason of the plaintiff's user of them. There is ample consideration to support this promise ...

Counsel for the defendants argued that the terms of the advertisement would enable someone who stole the smoke ball to claim the reward when, clearly, the actions of any thief would not have benefited the defendants by way of increased sales. Lindley and Bowen LJJ considered that the benefit was the general increase in sales through improved public confidence, and that this was a sufficient consideration. This definition would allow a thief to claim the reward. Of course, a thief would suffer a detriment in using the smoke ball in the stipulated manner.

1.4.5 Notes on the decision and the judgments

Let us now use the judgments to make a note on the decision and explain it.

> The Court of Appeal (Lindley, Bowen, and A. L. Smith LJJ) held that the defendants' promise in their advertisement was sufficiently certain and constituted a unilateral offer.
>
> This offer was a promise to pay £100 to anyone who performed the stipulated act, i.e. using the smoke ball three times a day as directed for two weeks and still catching influenza.
>
> The promise was intended to have legal effects, since the defendants had demonstrated their sincerity by depositing £1,000 with their bank.
>
> The claimant when performing the specified act had accepted the offer. In a unilateral contract, the offeror will normally have impliedly waived the requirement communication of the acceptance to be effective. Notification of acceptance is therefore not required.
>
> The performance of the act also constituted the consideration to support the defendants' promise: it was a detriment to the claimant to have to use the smoke ball in accordance with these directions; and it was a benefit to the defendants, since the claimant's use of the smoke ball would indirectly improve its sales through increased public confidence in the product.
>
> Since there was a binding contract, the claimant was entitled to be paid the £100.

Note You may wish to add to these notes by including important statements from the judgments and by filling out the notes on the law concerning unilateral contracts. For example, you may wish to record Bowen LJ's statement that this was an offer to the world and his statement that, in a unilateral contract, there is no requirement to notify the offeror of your intention to accept. Bowen LJ's example of the lost dog is particularly famous and worth noting.

1.4.6 General notes on the legal principles in the case

You should always assess how the case you are reading fits into the general body of case law principles. If it appears out of line with previous authority, you need to question whether the court in question realized this, and if not, why not. If the court did realize the inconsistency, you will need to examine in detail the explanation for the decision in each judgment. You should also ask whether the case adds to the development of principle, and if so, in what way. Is this development a broad one or is it very fact-specific? This is important in terms of precedent.

Carlill v Carbolic Smoke Ball Co. [1893] 1 QB 256 is valuable in explaining that a unilateral contract is a contract whereby the offeror makes a promise (in this case, to pay £100) in return for the performance of a stipulated act. Mrs Carlill makes no promise and can decide not to continue her use of the smoke ball at any time.

To summarize, a number of exceptional rules apply to unilateral contracts for which *Carlill v Carbolic Smoke Ball Co.* is authority.

(a) The general rule is that an advertisement is an invitation to treat (i.e. an invitation to make an offer), so a response to an advertisement can at best be only an offer and there is no binding contract at that stage. However, if the advertisement requests the performance of an act (unilateral), then the advertisement will be an offer. On performance of the requested act, the offer is accepted and a binding contract follows.

(b) Whereas the general rule is that an acceptance must be communicated to the offeror, the offeror may impliedly waive this requirement and is taken to have done so when the offer is unilateral, unless an express indication of the fact that notification is required.

(c) In a unilateral contract, the requested act is both the acceptance and the consideration for the promise.

Other legal principles applicable to unilateral contracts must be considered at this point.

(a) You can only accept a unilateral offer of a reward if you know that it has been made and if you accept in response to it: *R v Clarke* (1927) 40 CLR 227 (*page 45*, 2.4.3). The act that is the purported acceptance cannot have been performed before any promise of a reward was made.

(b) Since the acceptance is the performance of the stipulated act and performing this act may be a continuing act (as in *Carlill*), the general principle should be that the offer may be revoked at any time before the act is completely performed. However, it may not be possible to revoke a unilateral offer once the offeree has started to perform: *Errington v Errington & Woods* [1952] 1 KB 290 (*page 63*, 2.5.2).

(c) The general rule that a revocation of an offer must be communicated to the offeree is impractical in the case of a unilateral offer to the whole world, since it is not possible to identify the potential offerees. The American case *Shuey v United States*, 23 L Ed 697, (1875) 92 US 73 (*page 67*, 2.5.3), is authority for the fact that it is sufficient if the revocation is communicated using the same channel used to communicate the original offer, and that if this is done, it is irrelevant if particular offerees did not see or know about the revocation.

? QUESTIONS

1. What was the stipulated act in *Carlill v Carbolic Smoke Ball*? Was it merely using the smoke ball as specified so that catching influenza was only a condition of entitlement to enforce the promise? Or was it using the ball as specified and catching influenza (*page 90*, *3.1.2* and *page 91*, *3.1.3*)?

2. What do you think the position would have been if, at the time of using the smoke ball, Mrs Carlill's only reason for doing so was to avoid catching influenza?

3. Did the smoke ball have to be purchased by Mrs Carlill?

4. What would the legal position be if, when Mrs Carlill had been using the smoke ball for one week, the Company had issued another advertisement withdrawing its offer, but, because Mrs Carlill did not see this, she had carried on using the smoke ball for the full two weeks and caught influenza?

NOTES

1. For further discussion of the background to the decision in *Carlill v Carbolic Smoke Ball*, see A. W. B. Simpson (1985) 14 JLS 345.

2. In *Bowerman v Association of British Travel Agents Ltd* [1996] CLC 451 (*page 149*, 4.1.2), the Court of Appeal majority, relying on *Carlill*, held that a notice would reasonably have been read by the public as an offer by ABTA to give protection to the customer if the

ABTA member were to fail financially. This unilateral offer was accepted by the customer when booking a holiday with the ABTA member.

3. It is increasingly common for the courts to 'imply' unilateral contracts in order to recognize contractual liability: see e.g. *Blackpool & Fylde Aero Club Ltd v Blackpool Borough Council* [1990] 1 WLR 1195 (at *page 32*, 2.3.3.2).

1.5 Exercise

Read the judgment and make quick, rough notes. Once you have read the judgment, test your learning by trying to answer the question and compare your comments to the notes that appear at the end of this extract.

Howard Marine and Dredging Co. Ltd v A. Ogden & Sons (Excavations) Ltd
[1978] QB 574 (CA)

See *page 478*, *9.3.2.2*. The catchwords and headnote facts in this case are far more detailed than those in *Carlill v Carbolic Smoke Ball Co.* [1893] 1 QB 256, and the headnote decision is divided into four distinct issues: collateral warranty, damages for misrepresentation, the exemption clause, and the possibility of an action in negligence at common law.

Held, (1) that the contractors could not establish any claim in contract for there was nothing in the pre-contract negotiations which could amount to a collateral warranty.

(2) (*Per* Bridge and Shaw LJJ) That the plaintiff owners were liable in tort for damages under section 2(1) of the Misrepresentation Act 1967, for the misrepresentation by their marine manager at the pre-contract meeting on July 11, 1974, as the deadweight capacity of the barges was a most material matter on which the contractors had relied in concluding the contract, and was one in respect of which the representor would have been liable had it been made fraudulently; that to avoid liability under the statutory terms the owners had to prove that their marine manager had had reasonable ground to believe and did believe up to the time the contract was made that the facts he represented were true; that on an analysis of the evidence that burden had not been discharged for the marine manager had not shown any objectively reasonable ground for disregarding the figure of deadweight capacity in the ship's documents and for preferring the Lloyd's Register incorrect figure; and accordingly the contractors' appeal should be allowed.

Per Bridge LJ. In the course of negotiations leading to a contract the Act of 1967 imposes an absolute obligation not to state facts which the representor cannot prove he had reasonable ground to believe (post, p. 596F).

(3) (*Per* Bridge and Shaw LJJ) That the owners could not escape liability by reliance on the exception clause, for, as the judge had held, it was a provision in an agreement which would exclude or restrict any liability to which a party to a contract might be subject by reason of any misrepresentation made by him within section 3 of the Act of 1967, and should therefore be of no effect unless the court in its discretion allowed reliance on it as being 'fair and reasonable in the circumstances of the case'; and accordingly, as it was not 'fair and reasonable' to allow the owners to rely on it, the owners' cross appeal should be dismissed.

Per Shaw LJ. The contractors also have a cause of action in negligence at common law, for in a business transaction whose nature made clear the importance and influence of the answer to the question as to the vessel's carrying capacity, the owners were under a duty of care in giving information on matters peculiarly within their knowledge (post, pp. 600F–601D).

Per Lord Denning MR. The trial judge's decision that the misrepresentation at the July 11 meeting was not negligent showed that he was satisfied that the representor had discharged the burden of proof imposed by section 2(1) and there was no reason for disturbing that decision (post, p. 593C–G). Nor was there any reason why the court should not allow the owners to rely on the exception clause as 'fair and reasonable' under section 3 of the Act of 1967, since the parties to the contract were of equal bargaining power and the contractors could easily have obtained advice that the barges were not fit for the use for which they were intended before concluding the contract (post, p. 594B–F). Further, there was no special relationship between the parties which gave rise to the duty of care at common law; the only duty of the owners' marine manager was to be honest when asked about the dead-weight capacity; he had answered as best he could from memory and the contractors should not have acted on his oral answers without further inquiry (post, pp. 591H–592C).

Decision of Bristow J reversed in part.

NOTES

1. The first part of the Court of Appeal's judgment relates to the contention that the pre-contractual statement was a collateral warranty, so that its inaccuracy was a breach of contract. All of the members of the Court of Appeal rejected this, but we do not know the reasons without looking at the judgments.

2. Secondly, the majority (Bridge and Shaw LJJ) held that the claimants were liable in damages under s. 2(1) of the Misrepresentation Act 1967, and this time full reasons are given. The claimants had failed to show that they had reasonable grounds to believe, and that they did believe up to the time at which the contract was made, that the facts represented were true. They had failed to show any 'objectively reasonable ground' for their actions. We are informed of a statement by Bridge LJ which goes further and imposes an absolute obligation not to state facts that you cannot prove you had reasonable grounds to believe.

3. Lord Denning MR (dissenting) considered that the burden in s. 2(1) had been discharged.

4. Examine Lord Denning's judgment in this case to discover that, having explained the facts in a very clear and readable way, he then deals with each of the issues under an appropriate heading. At pp. 590–5 of the report, he examines first the collateral warranty argument, and then the claim based on the tort of negligent misstatement and the claim under the Misrepresentation Act 1967, before discussing the exemption clause. Look for these same issues in the judgments of Bridge and Shaw LJJ.

Top TIP: The headnote contains references to pages and letters in the judgment, which are very useful in directing the reader to those parts of the judgments dealing with the major points of the decision. The same is true of paragraph numbers following *Practice Direction* [2001] 1 WLR 194 (*page 2*, 1.3.2).

? QUESTION

There were two other arguments addressed by the Court of Appeal—namely, the claim in tort based on breach of a duty of care and the question of whether the exemption clause applied to allow the owners to escape liability. What did the majority of the Court of Appeal decide on these issues and what did Lord Denning decide?

Further exercises, and guidance, relating to *Williams v Roffey Bros. and Nicholls (Contractors) Ltd* [1991] 1 QB 1 (*Chapter 3*) and *Great Peace Shipping Ltd v Tsavliris Salvage (International) Ltd* [2002] EWCA Civ 1407, [2003] QB 679 (*Chapter 8*), are available in the online resources that accompany this book: www.oup.com/he/poole15e/.

Formation

Chapter 2

Agreement

A contract is an agreement that is legally enforceable. This chapter deals with how we determine the existence of the agreement.

2.1 Judicial assessment of agreement: subjectivity versus objectivity

2.1.1 Objectivity prevails

Smith v Hughes
(1871) LR 6 QB 597

> BLACKBURN J: If, whatever a man's real intention may be, he so conducts himself that a reasonable man would believe that he was assenting to the terms proposed by the other party, and that other party upon that belief enters into the contract with him, the man thus conducting himself would be equally bound as if he had intended to agree to the other party's terms . . .

Robert Goff LJ, in *Allied Marine Transport Ltd v Vale do Rio Doce Navegacao SA, The Leonidas D* [1985] 1 WLR 925, 936G–H, put the matter thus:

> [I]f one party, O, so acts that his conduct, objectively considered, constitutes an offer, and the other party, A, believing that the conduct of O represents his actual intention, accepts O's offer, then a contract will come into existence, and on those facts it will make no difference if O did not in fact intend to make an offer, or if he misunderstood A's acceptance, so that O's state of mind is, in such circumstances, irrelevant.

2.1.2 Subjectivity has some relevance

Although the offeror's subjective intentions are irrelevant if the offer is reasonably, and objectively, understood in a particular way by the offeree, the offeree must believe that the offer represents the actual intentions of the offeror. To this extent, the offeree's subjective intentions are relevant. If the offeree *knows or ought reasonably to have known* at the time of the purported acceptance that the offeror made a mistake on the terms of the offer, the offeree cannot purport to accept that offer.

Hartog v Colin & Shields
[1939] 3 All ER 566

The defendants contracted to sell 30,000 Argentine hare skins to the claimant, but by mistake offered them at a price per pound instead of per piece. In the pre-sale negotiations, reference had always been made to the price per piece and never to the price per pound, and there was expert evidence that Argentine hare skins were generally sold at prices per piece.

Held: Since the claimant could not reasonably have supposed that the offer contained the offerors' real intention, there was no binding contract.

NOTES

1. It is first necessary to examine how the offeror's words and conduct might reasonably have appeared to the offeree. The offeree cannot then accept if he knew, or ought reasonably to have known, that the offeror was making a mistake. In *Chwee Kin Keong v Digilandmall.com Pte Ltd* [2005] 1 SLR(R) 502, the Singapore Court of Appeal regarded what the offeree 'ought reasonably to have known' as evidential factors or reasoning processes in reaching the conclusion that there was, in fact, knowledge of the mistake in the sense of actual knowledge, e.g. if the price of goods on an Internet site 'is so absurdly low in relation to its known market value, it stands to reason that a reasonable man would harbour a real suspicion that the price may not be correct or that there may be some troubling underlying basis for such a pricing' (quoting the judge at first instance: [2004] SLR(R) 594, [145]). In *Commission for the New Towns v Cooper (GB) Ltd* [1995] Ch 259, actual knowledge was considered to extend to 'wilfully and recklessly failing to make such inquiries as an honest and reasonable man would make' (category (iii) actual knowledge or 'Nelsonian blindness').

2. In *Centrovincial Estates plc v Merchant Investors Assurance Co. Ltd* [1983] Com LR 158, the defendants accepted a figure of £65,000 per annum during a rent review, where the original rent had been £68,320 and the rent review clause stated that in no circumstances should the rent be reduced below the rent payable immediately before the review. This figure had been offered in error and the correct figure offered should have been £126,000. The defendants sought to hold the claimants to the £65,000 figure, claiming that there was a binding agreement based on this figure. The Court of Appeal agreed that there was a binding agreement at £65,000, since there was no proof that the defendants either knew or ought reasonably to have known of the claimants' error at the time when they purported to accept it.

Although we might think that the defendants should have known of the claimants' (offerors') mistake given the terms of the rent review clause, the burden of proving the defendants' subjective intentions and that the defendants knew that the claimants did not intend to be bound by the £65,000 figure rested with the claimants, and that burden had not been discharged on the facts. It also appears that this burden would not be discharged if the defendants had simply not addressed any thought to the question of what the claimants intended at the time.

This burden of proof was also explained at first instance in *Maple Leaf Macro Volatility Master Fund v Rouvroy* [2009] EWHC 257 (Comm), [2009] 1 Lloyd's Rep 475 where, on an objective assessment, the parties had indicated an intention to be bound to a funding agreement. The defendants failed to show that the claimants did not believe that the defendants intended to be bound.

ANDREW SMITH J: 228. However, there are circumstances in which the parties to what would objectively be held to be contractual are not legally bound by it under English law. If the other parties actually and reasonably believed that the defendants intended to make a contract, there would be a concluded contract, but not if the other parties knew or would reasonably have believed that that was not the defendants' intention and not, in my judgment, if the other parties had simply formed no view one way or the other as to whether the defendants so intended. That is the opinion expressed by Professor Sir Gunter Treitel in *Chitty on Contracts*, (2008) 30th Ed at para 2-004, and I agree with it. The defendants submit that they are not contractually bound even if on an objective assessment they and the claimants evinced an intention to be bound.

229. Thus the defendants' argument depends upon them showing that the claimants did not believe that the defendants intended to be bound . . . or at least that they would not reasonably have so believed. They have not shown this . . .

2.2 The criteria to determine agreement

Traditionally, the courts have required that agreement be demonstrated by an offer made by one party and by complete acceptance of that offer by the other party. However, Lord Denning, in particular, took the view that the circumstances as a whole should be examined in an attempt to discover whether there was agreement: *Butler Machine Tool Co. Ltd v Ex-Cell-O Corporation (England) Ltd* [1979] 1 WLR 401 (see *2.4.1.4*).

The majority of the Court of Appeal (Lord Denning and Ormrod LJ) in the following case had also adopted this approach.

Gibson v Manchester City Council
[1978] 1 WLR 520 (CA)

The facts of this case appear at *2.3*.

LORD DENNING MR: To my mind it is a mistake to think that all contracts can be analysed into the form of offer and acceptance. I know in some of the text books it has been the custom to do so: but, as I understand the law, there is no need to look for a strict offer and acceptance. You should look at the correspondence as a whole and at the conduct of the parties and see therefrom whether the parties have come to an agreement on everything that was material. If by their correspondence and their conduct you can see an agreement on all material terms—which was intended thenceforward to be binding—then there is a binding contract in law even though all the formalities have not been gone through: see *Brogden v Metropolitan Railway Co.* (1877) 2 App Cas 666.

It seems to me that on the correspondence I have read—and, I may add, on what happened after—the parties had come to an agreement in the matter which they intended to be binding . . .

NOTE The House of Lords rejected this approach, [1979] 1 WLR 294, Lord Diplock stated at 297:

My Lords, there may be certain types of contract, though I think they are exceptional, which do not fit easily into the normal analysis of a contract as being constituted by offer and acceptance; but a contract alleged to have been made by an exchange of correspondence between the parties in which the successive communications other than the first are in reply to one another, is not one of these. I can see no reason in the instant case for departing from the conventional approach of looking at the handful of documents relied upon as constituting the contract sued upon and seeing whether upon their true construction there is to be found in them a contractual offer by the corporation to sell the house to Mr Gibson and an acceptance of that offer by Mr Gibson. I venture to think that it was by departing from this conventional approach that the majority of the Court of Appeal was led into error.

In *New Zealand Shipping Co. Ltd v A. M. Satterthwaite & Co. Ltd, The Eurymedon* [1975] AC 154 (PC), 167E, Lord Wilberforce expressed some dissatisfaction with the traditional approach when he stated:

English law, having committed itself to a rather technical and schematic doctrine of contract, in application takes a practical approach, often at the cost of forcing the facts to fit uneasily into the marked slots of offer, acceptance and consideration.

A contract may be found to exist, despite the fact that it cannot be analysed precisely into an offer and corresponding acceptance, where the terms are fully agreed and executed by the parties.

Trentham Ltd v Archital Luxfer
[1993] 1 Lloyd's Rep 25 (CA)

Trentham was a main contractor employed to design and build industrial units. This work included 'window works', i.e. the supply and installation of aluminium windows and doors. The defendants, Archital, were manufacturers, suppliers, and installers of these products, and had carried out this work for Trentham and been paid. Trentham then alleged that the defendants' work was defective and that they were therefore in breach of binding subcontracts between them. The defendants denied that any binding subcontracts ever came into existence.

Held: Binding subcontracts had been concluded for the window works.

STEYN LJ: Before I turn to the facts it is important to consider briefly the approach to be adopted to the issue of contract formation in this case. It seems to me that four matters are of importance. The first is the fact that English law generally adopts an objective theory of contract formation. That means that in practice our law generally ignores the subjective expectations and the unexpressed mental reservations of the parties. Instead the governing criterion is the reasonable expectations of honest men. And in the present case that means that the yardstick is the reasonable expectations of sensible business-men. Secondly, it is true that the coincidence of offer and acceptance will in the vast majority of cases represent the mechanism of contract formation. It is so in the case of a contract alleged to have been made by an exchange of correspondence. But it is not necessarily so in the case of a contract alleged to have come into existence during and as a result of performance. See *Brogden v Metropolitan Railway* (1877) 2 AC 666; *New Zealand Shipping Co. Ltd v A.M. Satterthwaite & Co. Ltd* [1974] 1 Lloyd's Rep 534 at p. 539, col. 1; [1975] AC 154 at p. 167 D–E; *Gibson v Manchester City Council* [1979] 1 WLR 294. The third matter is the impact of the fact that the transaction is executed rather than executory. It is a consideration of the first importance on a number of levels. See *British Bank for Foreign Trade Ltd v Novinex* [1949] 1 KB 628, at p. 630. The fact that the transaction was performed on both sides will often make it unrealistic to argue that there was no intention to enter into legal relations. It will often make it difficult to submit that the contract is void for vagueness or uncertainty. Specifically, the fact that the transaction is executed makes it easier to imply a term resolving any uncertainty, or, alternatively, it may make it possible to treat a matter not finalised in negotiations as inessential. In this case fully executed transactions are under consideration. Clearly, similar considerations may sometimes be relevant in partly executed transactions. Fourthly, if a contract only comes into existence during and as a result of performance of the transaction it will frequently be possible to hold that the contract impliedly and retrospectively covers pre-contractual performance. See *Trollope & Colls Ltd v Atomic Power Constructions Ltd* [1963] 1 WLR 333 . . . The contemporary exchanges, and the carrying out of what was agreed in those exchanges, support the view that there was a course of dealing which on Trentham's side created a right to performance of the work by Archital, and on Archital's side it created a right to be paid on an agreed basis. What the parties did in respect of phase 1 is only explicable on the basis of what they had agreed in respect of phase 1. The Judge analysed the matter in terms of offer and acceptance. I agree with his conclusion. But I am, in any event, satisfied that in this fully executed transaction a contract came into existence during performance even if it cannot be precisely analysed in terms of offer and acceptance. And it does not matter that a contract came into existence after part of the work had been carried out and paid for. The conclusion must be that when the contract came into existence it impliedly governed pre-contractual performance . . .

NOTES

1. Significantly, the arrangement was executed by the parties. Steyn LJ (with whose judgment Ralph Gibson and Neill LJJ agreed) accepted the judge's decision at first instance, which was based on offer and acceptance. He was also prepared to conclude, relying on *Brogden v Metropolitan Railway Co.* (1877) 2 App Cas 666 (see *page 37*, *2.4.1.2*), that a contract can come into existence following performance of an executed contract.

2. Compare this with *British Steel Corporation v Cleveland Bridge & Engineering Co. Ltd* [1984] 1 All ER 504 (see *page 82*, *2.6.4*), in which, in spite of performance, it was concluded that there was no binding contract.

? QUESTION

Can the distinction in result between *Trentham v Luxfer* and *BSC v Cleveland Bridge* be explained on the basis of the different remedies being sought and the certainty or uncertainty of terms?

In *RTS Flexible Systems Ltd v Molkerei Alois Müller GmbH & Co. KG (UK Production)* [2010] UKSC 14, [2010] 1 WLR 753, [2010] Bus LR 776 (SC) (*page 82*, *2.6.4*), the Supreme Court noted that performance does not always equate with a finding that there is a binding contract. However, it is an important factor in supporting such a finding in instances in which there is agreement on all material terms.

2.3 Offer distinguished from invitation to treat

If the statement maker clearly intends to be bound by acceptance of the stated terms, the statement will amount to an offer and, on acceptance, there will be a binding contract. However, if there is no such intention, the statement will be part of the negotiating process (an invitation to treat) and any response to it will at best be no more than an offer.

Much depends upon whether the language used indicates 'a definite promise to be bound' without more.

Gibson v Manchester City Council
[1979] 1 WLR 294 (HL)

The Council adopted a policy of selling council houses to tenants. The respondent tenant applied on a printed form for details of the price and mortgage terms. The city treasurer wrote to the respondent that the Council '*may be prepared to sell the house to you* at the purchase price of £2,725 less 20% = £2,180'. The letter gave details of the mortgage likely to be made available and stated: 'If you would like to make a formal application to buy . . . please complete the enclosed application form and return it to me as soon as possible.' The respondent completed the application form and returned it. Before contracts were prepared and exchanged, political control of the Council changed and the Council decided to proceed only with those sales for which contracts had already been exchanged. The respondent sought specific performance of an alleged contract to purchase his council house, claiming that he had accepted the offer in the city treasurer's letter.

Held: There was no binding contract because no offer capable of acceptance had been made by the Council. The statements in the city treasurer's letter that the Council '*may be prepared to sell*' and inviting Mr Gibson 'to *make a formal application to buy*' did not constitute an offer to sell, but only an invitation to treat.

LORD DIPLOCK: My Lords, the words I have italicised [see the facts above] seem to me, as they seemed to Geoffrey Lane LJ, to make it quite impossible to construe this letter as a contractual offer capable of being converted into a legally enforceable open contract for the sale of land by Mr Gibson's written acceptance of it. The words 'may be prepared to sell' are fatal to this; so is the invitation, not, be it noted, to accept the offer, but 'to make formal application to buy' upon the enclosed application form. It is, to quote Geoffrey Lane LJ, a letter setting out the financial terms on which it may be the council will be prepared to consider a sale and purchase in due course.

NOTE As a practical point, there was no firm offer of a mortgage by the Council, and it is unlikely that Mr Gibson would have intended to bind himself in the absence of a firm commitment on this matter.

2.3.1 Advertisements

Generally, advertisements are invitations to treat.

Partridge v Crittenden
[1968] 1 WLR 1204 (QB)

The claimant had placed an advertisement in a periodical, which read 'Bramblefinch cocks, Bramblefinch hens, 25s each'. He was charged with unlawfully offering for sale a wild live bird contrary to s. 6(1) of and Sch. 4 to the Protection of Birds Act 1954.

Held: The advertisement was an invitation to treat, not an offer for sale. The claimant could therefore not be guilty of the offence charged.

? QUESTION

It is argued that if an advertisement is an offer, then the trader will have to supply the quantity ordered when the stock available to do so is limited. In *Grainger & Son v Gough* [1896] AC 325, 334, Lord Herschell said:

> The transmission of such a price-list does not amount to an offer to supply an unlimited quantity of the wine described at the price named, so that as soon as an order is given there is a binding contract to supply that quantity. If it were so, the merchant might find himself involved in any number of contractual obligations to supply wine of a particular description which he would be quite unable to carry out, his stock of wine of that description being necessarily limited.

What would the position be if the advertisement were specifically to state that supplies were limited, e.g. goods in a sale?

NOTES

1. A unilateral advertisement (requesting performance of an act as the acceptance) is an offer: see *Carlill v Carbolic Smoke Ball Co.* [1893] 1 QB 256 (see page 5, 1.4.1). If a shop advertises 'Sale—15 Sat Navs at the knock-down price of £40 each. First come first served', the wording may convert this advertisement into a unilateral offer requiring the performance of an act—namely, being the first person at the sale to offer to purchase one of these Sat Navs at the knock-down price. In US law, this type of advertisement amounts to an offer: *Lefkowitz v Great Minneapolis Surplus Store*, 86 NW 2d 689 (1957). The advertisement was in the

following terms: 'Saturday 9 a.m. sharp: 3 brand new fur coats, worth $100. First come first served, $1 each.'

2. A notice that detailed the Association of British Travel Agents (ABTA) scheme of protection was held by the Court of Appeal majority in *Bowerman v Association of British Travel Agents Ltd* [1996] CLC 451 (see *page 149*, 4.1.2), to be a unilateral offer that customers accepted by booking a holiday with an ABTA member (performance of an act). The result was a unilateral contract between the customer and ABTA.

3. In *O'Brien v MGN Ltd* [2001] EWCA Civ 1279, [2002] CLC 33, the advertisement of a newspaper scratch card game with a prize of £50,000 was held to be a contractual offer, which was accepted when those with eligible cards rang the telephone hotline (performance of an act).

4. The question of how to determine whether the advertisement is unilateral is discussed in *Poole's Textbook on Contract Law,* 15th edn (Oxford University Press, 2021), 2.3.2.1.2.

2.3.2 Display of goods

Fisher v Bell
[1961] 1 QB 394 (QB)

A shopkeeper displayed a flick knife in his shop window with a ticket stating 'Ejector knife—4s'. He was charged with offering the knife for sale contrary to s. 1(1) of the Restriction of Offensive Weapons Act 1959.

Held: A display of goods in a shop window with a price ticket attached was merely an invitation to treat and not an offer for sale, so that no offence had been committed.

Pharmaceutical Society of Great Britain v Boots Cash Chemists (Southern) Ltd
[1952] 2 QB 795 (Court of Queen's Bench)

Boots was charged with an offence under the Pharmacy and Poisons Act 1933, s. 18, which required that sales of poisons in Part I of the Poisons List take place under the supervision of a registered pharmacist. Boots operated a self-service system and a pharmacist at the cash desk was authorized to prevent the removal of any drug from the premises. The factor determining whether an offence had been committed was the point at which the sale in this self-service shop took place. The Court of Appeal agreed with Lord Goddard CJ.

Held: Boots had not committed the offence. The display of goods on a supermarket's shelves was merely an invitation to customers to make offers to buy.

LORD GODDARD CJ: I think that it is a well-established principle that the mere exposure of goods for sale by a shopkeeper indicates to the public that he is willing to treat but does not amount to an offer to sell. I do not think I ought to hold that that principle is completely reversed merely because there is a self-service scheme, such as this, in operation. In my opinion it comes to no more than that the customer is informed that he may himself pick up an article and bring it to the shopkeeper with a view to buying it, and if, but only if, the shopkeeper then expresses his willingness to sell, the contract for sale is completed. In fact, the offer is an offer to buy, and there is no offer to sell; the customer brings the goods to the shopkeeper to see whether he will sell or not. In 99 cases out of a 100 he will sell and, if so, he accepts the customer's offer, but he need not do so. The very fact that the supervising pharmacist is at the place where the money has to be paid is an indication to the purchaser that the shopkeeper may not be willing to complete a contract with anybody who may bring the goods to him.

Ordinary principles of common sense and of commerce must be applied in this matter, and to hold that in the case of self-service shops the exposure of an article is an offer to sell, and that a person can accept the offer by picking up the article, would be contrary to those principles and might entail serious results.

On the customer picking up the article the property would forthwith pass to him and he would be able to insist upon the shopkeeper allowing him to take it away, though in some particular cases the shopkeeper might think that very undesirable. On the other hand, if a customer had picked up an article, he would never be able to change his mind and to put it back; the shopkeeper could say, 'Oh no, the property has passed and you must pay the price.'

It seems to me, therefore, that the transaction is in no way different from the normal transaction in a shop in which there is no self-service scheme. I am quite satisfied it would be wrong to say that the shopkeeper is making an offer to sell every article in the shop to any person who might come in and that that person can insist on buying any article by saying 'I accept your offer.' I agree with the illustration put forward during the case of a person who might go into a shop where books are displayed. In most book-shops customers are invited to go in and pick up books and look at them even if they do not actu-ally buy them. There is no contract by the shopkeeper to sell until the customer has taken the book to the shopkeeper or his assistant and said 'I want to buy this book' and the shopkeeper says 'Yes.' That would not prevent the shopkeeper, seeing the book picked up, saying: 'I am sorry I cannot let you have that book; it is the only copy I have got and I have already promised it to another customer.' Therefore, in my opinion, the mere fact that a customer picks up a bottle of medicine from the shelves in this case does not amount to an acceptance of an offer to sell. It is an offer by the customer to buy and there is no sale effected until the buyer's offer to buy is accepted by the acceptance of the price. The offer, the acceptance of the price, and therefore the sale, take place under the supervision of the pharmacist.

[1953] 1 QB 401 (CA)

SOMERVELL LJ: I agree with the Lord Chief Justice in everything that he said, but I will put the matter shortly in my own words. Whether the view contended for by the plaintiffs is a right view depends on what are the legal implications of this layout—the invitation to the customer. Is a contract to be regarded as being completed when the article is put into the receptacle, or is this to be regarded as a more organ-ised way of doing what is done already in many types of shops—and a bookseller is perhaps the best example—namely, enabling customers to have free access to what is in the shop, to look at the different articles, and then, ultimately, having got the ones which they wish to buy, to come up to the assistant saying 'I want this'? The assistant in 999 times out of 1,000 says 'That is all right,' and the money passes and the transaction is completed. I agree with what the Lord Chief Justice has said, and with the reasons which he has given for his conclusion, that in the case of an ordinary shop, although goods are displayed and it is intended that customers should go and choose what they want, the contract is not completed until, the customer having indicated the articles which he needs, the shopkeeper, or someone on his behalf, accepts that offer. Then the contract is completed. I can see no reason at all, that being clearly the normal position, for drawing any different implication as a result of this layout.

The Lord Chief Justice, I think, expressed one of the most formidable difficulties in the way of the plaintiffs' contention when he pointed out that, if the plaintiffs are right, once an article has been placed in the receptacle the customer himself is bound and would have no right, without paying for the first article, to substitute an article which he saw later of a similar kind and which he perhaps preferred. I can see no reason for implying from this self-service arrangement any implication other than that which the Lord Chief Justice found in it, namely, that it is a convenient method of enabling customers to see what there is and choose, and possibly put back and substitute, articles which they wish to have, and then to go up to the cashier and offer to buy what they have so far chosen. On that conclusion the case fails, because it is admitted that there was supervision in the sense required by the Act and at the appropriate moment of time.

NOTES

1. Lord Goddard and the Court of Appeal assumed that if they held that the display were an offer, the acceptance would be the customer's act of placing the goods selected in the wire basket. However, the acceptance might be the customer's act of handing the goods to the cashier. See Jackson (1979) 129 NLJ 775 and the American case *Lasky v Economy Grocery Stores*, 163 ALR 235 (1946), in which it was held that the display was an offer, but that acceptance did not take place until the goods were handed to the cashier.

2. Incorrect pricing may give rise to criminal liability under the Consumer Protection from Unfair Trading Regulations 2008, SI 2008/1277, reg. 5 (actions misleading consumers). Following the Consumer Protection (Amendment) Regulations 2014, SI 2014/870, which added a new Part 4A to the CPRs 2008, SI 2008/1277 (effective 1 October 2014), consumers now have the ability, in this situation, to bring civil proceedings to enforce those rights, assuming that the misleading price is a significant factor in the consumer's decision to purchase the goods. In practical terms, the remedy would be restricted to the right to a refund (which shops tend to offer anyway in this situation) where the consumer has paid more for the goods as a result of the misleading pricing. It is difficult to envisage a situation in which, additionally, damages would be payable, since there would need to be additional financial losses (i.e. not remedied by the refund) that would not have occurred had the misleading pricing not taken place. In any event, no damages would be payable if the mispricing resulted from a mistake that the retailer had taken all reasonable precautions to avoid.

? QUESTIONS

1. Both Lord Goddard and the Court of Appeal considered that the offer must come from the customer and that acceptance must be by or on behalf of the shopkeeper, but what did they say would constitute the offer and what act would be the acceptance? Montrose (1955) 4 Am J Comp Law 235 argued that the offer occurs when the customer hands the goods to the cashier, as opposed to when they are placed in the wire basket, because until that point the customer has not evinced a definite intention to be bound.

2. What is the position if there is a non-self-service counter inside a supermarket? For example, if I request that a joint of meat be cut to my specifications, but before I reach the cash desk, I change my mind, has a contract of sale already been concluded? (*Poole's Textbook on Contract Law*, page 44, 2.3.2.2.1).

3. In *Chapelton v Barry Urban District Council* [1940] 1 KB 532 (*page 192*, 5.3.1.1), the Court of Appeal held that a pile of deck chairs accompanied by a notice indicating the hire charge and stating that tickets should be obtained from the attendants amounted to an offer. If automatic machines represent standing offers—*Thornton v Shoe Lane Parking Ltd* [1971] 2 QB 163 (*page 195*, 5.3.1.3)—why are goods on supermarket shelves not classified as a standing offer? See Unger (1953) 16 MLR 369.

4. Modern shopping practices raise a further question: would a self-service checkout in a supermarket alter the traditional analysis? Is this position similar to an ordinary vending machine? It would seem that the traditional position must remain since it is the customer who is making the offer when presenting the goods to the self-service checkout and it is the machine that is accepting the customer's offer on behalf of the supermarket.

5. If goods are advertised or displayed on a retailer's website, does this website constitute an invitation to treat or an offer? See the detailed discussion in *Poole's Textbook on Contract Law*, 2.3.2.3.

Regulation 12 of the Electronic Commerce (EC Directive) Regulations 2002, SI 2002/2013, suggests that a website may be an invitation to treat, since it provides that an order 'may be but need not be the contractual offer'. Regulation 9 requires the online retailer to communicate in advance 'the different technical steps to follow to conclude the contract' and it is common practice for online retailers to delay acceptance of the customer's offer until the point at which the goods are dispatched.

2.3.3 Tenders

A request for tenders is an invitation to treat and each tender is an offer. The requestor is free to accept or reject any tender to purchase goods, even if it is the highest bid.

Spencer v Harding
(1870) LR 5 CP 561 (CP)

WILLES J: The action is brought against persons who issued a circular offering a stock for sale by tender, to be sold at a discount in one lot. The plaintiffs sent in a tender which turned out to be the highest, but which was not accepted. They now insist that the circular amounts to a contract or promise to sell the goods to the highest bidder, that is, in this case, to the person who should tender for them at the smallest rate of discount; and reliance is placed on the cases as to rewards offered for the discovery of an offender. In those cases, however there never was any doubt that the advertisement amounted to a promise to pay the money to the person who first gave information. The difficulty suggested was that it was a contract with all the world. But that, of course, was soon overruled. It was an offer to become liable to any person who before the offer should be retracted should happen to be the person to fulfil the contract of which the advertisement was an offer or tender. That is not the sort of difficulty which presents itself here. If the circular had gone on, 'and we undertake to sell to the highest bidder,' the reward cases would have applied, and there would have been a good contract in respect of the persons. But the question is, whether there is here any offer to enter into a contract at all, or whether the circular amounts to anything more than a mere proclamation that the defendants are ready to chaffer for the sale of the goods, and to receive offers for the purchase of them. In advertisements for tenders for buildings it is not usual to say that the contract will be given to the lowest bidder, and it is not always that the contract is made with the lowest bidder. Here there is a total absence of any words to intimate that the highest bidder is to be the purchaser. It is a mere attempt to ascertain whether an offer can be obtained within such a margin as the sellers are willing to adopt.

2.3.3.1 What if the invitation to tender contains an express undertaking to accept the highest (or lowest) bid?

Harvela Investments Ltd v Royal Trust Co. of Canada (CI) Ltd
[1986] AC 207 (HL)

The claimant (Harvela) and the second defendant (Sir Leonard) were rival offerors for a parcel of shares belonging to the first defendants (Royal Trust). Royal Trust invited both parties to submit a sealed offer or confidential telex by a stipulated date and stated in the invitation to tender that it bound itself to accept the highest offer received that complied with the terms of the invitation. The claimant tendered a bid of $2,175,000, and the second defendant's bid was $2,100,000 or $101,000 in excess of any other offer. Royal Trust accepted the second defendant's bid as being $2,276,000 and entered into a sale contract. The claimant argued that the second defendant's bid was invalid. At first instance, Peter Gibson J held ([1985] Ch 103) that the invitation to bid constituted an offer to be bound by the highest bid. This offer was unilateral in that it requested the performance of an act—submitting the highest bid—and performance of this act constituted the acceptance of that offer. The claimant's bid was the only valid bid, so that there was a contract with the claimant. The Court of Appeal agreed, but refused to imply a term excluding referential bids.

Held: Referential bids were invalid, so that the only valid bid was the claimant's and Royal Trust was bound to accept it. Lord Diplock confirmed the analysis of Peter Gibson J on the effect of the invitation to tender.

LORD DIPLOCK: The construction question turns upon the wording of the telex of 15 September 1981 referred to by Lord Templeman as 'the invitation' and addressed to both Harvela and Sir Leonard. It was not a mere invitation to negotiate for the sale of the shares . . . Its legal nature was that of a unilateral or 'if' contract, or rather of two unilateral contracts in identical terms to one of which the vendors and Harvela were the parties as promisor and promisee respectively, while to the other the vendors were promisor and Sir Leonard was promisee. Such unilateral contracts were made at the time when the invitation was received by the promisee to whom it was addressed by the vendors; under neither of them did the promisee, Harvela and Sir Leonard respectively, assume any legal obligation to anyone to do or refrain from doing anything.

The vendors, on the other hand, did assume a legal obligation to the promisee under each contract. That obligation was conditional upon the happening, after the unilateral contract had been made, of an event which was specified in the invitation; the obligation was to enter into a synallagmatic contract to sell the shares to the promisee, the terms of such synallagmatic contract being also set out in the invitation. The event upon the happening of which the vendors' obligation to sell the shares to the promisee arose was the doing by the promisee of an act which was of such a nature that it might be done by either promisee or neither promisee but could not be done by both. The vendors thus did not by entering into the two unilateral contracts run any risk of assuming legal obligations to enter into conflicting synallagmatic contracts to sell the shares to each promisee.

The two unilateral contracts were of short duration; for the condition subsequent to which each was subject was the receipt by the vendors' solicitors on or before 3 pm on the following day, 16 September 1981, of a sealed tender or confidential telex containing an offer by the promisee to buy the shares for a single sum of money in Canadian dollars. If such an offer was received from each of the promisees under their respective contracts, the obligation of the promisor, the vendors, was to sell the shares to the promisee whose offer was the higher; and any obligation which the promisor had assumed to the promisee under the other unilateral contract came to an end, because the event the happening of which was the condition subsequent to which the vendors' obligation to sell the shares to that promisee was subject had not happened before the unilateral contract with that promisee expired.

Since the invitation in addition to containing the terms of the unilateral contract also embodied the terms of the synallagmatic contract into which the vendors undertook to enter upon the happening of the specified event, the consequence of the happening of that event would be to convert the invitation into a synallagmatic contract between the vendors and whichever promisee had offered, by sealed tender or confidential telex, the higher sum . . .

NOTE This is an example of an 'implied' unilateral contract based on the express promise to accept the highest bid. The invitation to tender was a unilateral offer to accept the highest bid. This was accepted by everyone who bid. It was then followed by a synallagmatic (bilateral) contract with whoever was the highest bidder. If the person inviting tenders did not comply with the offer terms, then he would be in breach of the unilateral contract and would be liable in damages.

2.3.3.2 In some circumstances, there may be a binding contractual obligation to consider tenders conforming to the bid conditions

Blackpool & Fylde Aero Club Ltd v Blackpool Borough Council
[1990] 1 WLR 1195 (CA)

The Council invited the claimant club and six other parties to tender for a concession to operate pleasure flights from Blackpool airport. Tenders would not be considered if received after 12 noon on 17 March 1983. The club's tender was put in the town hall letterbox at 11 a.m. on 17 March, but the letterbox was not cleared, as it should have been, at 12 noon. The club's tender was not considered on the basis that it was received too late. On discovering what had happened, the Council decided to carry out the tendering exercise again. However, when the successful tenderer threatened to sue, the Council retracted. The club sought damages for breach of warranty, arguing that the Council had warranted (promised) that the tender would be considered if it was received by the deadline. However, there was no express promise to this effect.

Held: An invitation to tender could give rise to an implied binding contractual obligation to consider tenders conforming to the conditions of tender when the tenders had been solicited by the Council from specified parties who were known to the Council, and there were absolute conditions governing submission including an absolute deadline.

BINGHAM LJ: During the hearing the questions were raised: what if, in a situation such as the present, the council had opened and thereupon accepted the first tender received, even though the deadline had not expired and other invitees had not yet responded? Or if the council had considered and accepted a tender admittedly received well after the deadline? [Counsel] answered that although by so acting the council might breach its own standing orders, and might fairly be accused of discreditable conduct, it would not be in breach of any legal obligation because at that stage there would be none to breach. This is a conclusion I cannot accept. And if it were accepted there would in my view be an unacceptable discrepancy between the law of contract and the confident assumptions of commercial parties, both tenderers . . . and invitors (as reflected in the immediate reaction of the council when the mishap came to light).

A tendering procedure of this kind is, in many respects, heavily weighted in favour of the invitor. He can invite tenders from as many or as few parties as he chooses. He need not tell any of them who else, or how many others, he has invited. The invitee may often, although not here, be put to considerable labour and expense in preparing a tender, ordinarily without recompense if he is unsuccessful. The invitation to tender may itself, in a complex case, although again not here, involve time and expense to prepare, but the invitor does not commit himself to proceed with the project, whatever it is; he need not accept the highest tender; he need not accept any tender; he need not give reasons to justify his acceptance or rejection of any tender received. The risk to which the tenderer is exposed does not end with the risk that his tender may not be the highest or, as the case may be, lowest. But where, as here, tenders are solicited from selected parties all of them known to the invitor, and where a local authority's invitation prescribes a clear, orderly and familiar procedure—draft contract conditions available for inspection and plainly not open to negotiation, a prescribed common form of tender, the supply of envelopes designed to preserve the absolute anonymity of tenderers and clearly to identify the tender in question and an absolute deadline—the invitee is in my judgment protected at least to this extent: if he submits a conforming tender before the deadline he is entitled, not as a matter of mere expectation but of contractual right, to be sure that his tender will after the deadline be opened and considered in conjunction with all other conforming tenders or at least that his tender will be considered if others are. Had the club, before tendering, inquired of the council whether it could rely on any timely and conforming tender being considered along with others, I feel quite sure that the answer would have been 'of course'. The law would, I think, be defective if it did not give effect to that . . .

I readily accept that contracts are not to be lightly implied. Having examined what the parties said and did, the court must be able to conclude with confidence both that the parties intended to create contractual relations and that the agreement was to the effect contended for . . . [Counsel for the club] was in my view right to contend for no more than a contractual duty to consider. I think it plain that the council's invitation to tender was, to this limited extent, an offer, and the club's submission of a timely and conforming tender an acceptance.

? QUESTION

If the remedy for breach of such a contractual obligation to consider tenders is damages, how might those damages be measured? Should damages be limited to the recovery of wasted expenses or would loss of chance damages be more appropriate? See the discussion of measures of damages at 14.1–14.4, and the case law discussed in Note 4 below.

NOTES

1. This decision can be analysed as an example of an implied unilateral contract, i.e. an offer to consider conforming tenders, which is accepted by submitting a conforming tender. However, it differs from *Harvela* where the obligation forming the basis for the implied unilateral contract was an express promise rather than one implied from the circumstances. *Blackpool* is therefore the more radical decision.

2. Bingham LJ refers to this decision as avoiding 'an unacceptable discrepancy between the law of contract and the confident assumptions of commercial parties', i.e. the club would not have bothered to tender unless its tender was to be considered and, on discovering its failure to consider the club's tender, the Council had declared the tendering process invalid until the successful tenderer had threatened legal action.

3. For further discussion of this case, see Adams and Brownsword (1991) 54 MLR 281, McKendrick [1991] LMCLQ 31, or Phang (1991) 4 JCL 46.

4. In *Fairclough Building Ltd v Port Talbot Borough Council* (1992) 62 Build LR 82, 33 Con LR 24, the Court of Appeal also recognized the existence of a contractual obligation to consider tenders from contractors on a council shortlist 'unless there were reasonable grounds for not doing so'. On the facts in Fairclough, the Council did have reasonable grounds for removing the claimants from the shortlist, so that there was no breach of contract and Blackpool was therefore distinguished. The Court of Appeal in Fairclough also suggested that, had there been a breach, damages would be based on the loss of a chance to be considered. By comparison, in the Northern Ireland High Court decision in *J. & A. Developments Ltd v Edina Manufacturing Ltd* [2006] NIQB 85, the court awarded full expectation loss to the claimant on the basis that but for the defendant's breach of the unilateral contract, it would otherwise have been awarded the contract, i.e. that this was a loss of a certainty rather than a loss of a chance.

2.3.4 Auction sales

An auctioneer's request for bids is an invitation to treat. The bid is the offer, which the auctioneer can accept or reject. The Sale of Goods Act 1979, s. 57(2), provides that acceptance occurs on the fall of the hammer and that any bidder may withdraw its bid before that time.

Harris v Nickerson
(1873) LR 8 QB 286 (QB)

The defendant auctioneer advertised that lots, including certain office furniture, would be sold by him at Bury St Edmunds on specified days. The claimant had a commission to buy this furniture and travelled from London for the sale. However, the lots were withdrawn from sale. The claimant brought an action against the defendant to recover for his loss of time and expenses.

Held: He had no such right of action. The advertisement was only an invitation to treat and did not amount to a promise that all of the articles advertised would be put up for sale.

What if the auction is advertised as being 'without reserve' (i.e. there is to be no reserve price and the property will be sold to the highest bidder)?

Warlow v Harrison
(1859) 1 E & E 309, 120 ER 925 (Exchequer Chamber)

The defendant, an auctioneer, advertised the sale without reserve of a horse by public auction. The claimant attended the sale and bid 60 guineas. The horse's owner bid 61 guineas. The claimant refused to make any further bid and the defendant (who, it appears, did not know that the bidder was the owner) knocked down the horse to the owner for 61 guineas. The claimant claimed that the horse was his since he was the highest bona fide (genuine) purchaser at an unreserved sale. In his pleadings, the claimant alleged that the defendant was the claimant's agent to complete this contract.

Held: On the pleadings, the claimant had no claim, since there was no agency relationship between the claimant and the defendant. The pleadings required amendment.

MARTIN B [*obiter*]: The sale was announced . . . to be 'without reserve.' This, according to all the cases both at law and equity, means that neither the vendor nor any person in his behalf shall bid at the auction, and that the property shall be sold to the highest bidder, whether the sum bid be equivalent to the real value or not. We cannot distinguish the case of an auctioneer putting up property for sale upon such a condition from the case of the loser of property offering a reward . . . Upon the same principle, it seems to us that the highest bona fide bidder at an auction may sue the auctioneer as upon a contract that the sale shall be without reserve. We think the auctioneer who puts the property up for sale upon such a condition pledges himself that the sale shall be without reserve; or, in other words, contracts that it shall be so; and that this contract is made with the highest bona fide bidder; and, in case of a breach of it, that he has a right of action against the auctioneer.

NOTE There were two agreements. First, there was the bilateral sale agreement determining the purchaser of the goods. In this context, the claimant's bid was an offer, but since his bid was not accepted, he was not entitled to the horse that was knocked down to the owner. However, there was a second agreement, since the advertisement of an auction sale without reserve is a unilateral offer by the auctioneer that no reserve will be applied. Martin B indicates that only the highest bona fide bidder can accept this unilateral offer. The claimant clearly accepted this offer and the auctioneer would be liable in damages for breach of his promise that there would be no reserve. (Compare this with the analysis of invitations to tender agreeing to accept the highest bid in *Harvela Investments Ltd v Royal Trust Co. of Canada Ltd*, at *page 30*, 2.3.3.1.)

The two contracts are explained in the summary in *Poole's Textbook on Contract Law*, 2.7.3.3.

? QUESTIONS

1. Could we argue that the unilateral offer to hold an auction without reserve could be accepted by all those who bid at such an auction, but that only the highest bona fide bidder would suffer loss in the event of breach and be entitled to recover damages? See the discussion in the notes relating to the Court of Appeal decision in *Barry v Davies* [2000] 1 WLR 1962 (below).

2. The *obiter* statement in *Warlow v Harrison* was set in relation to the position of the highest genuine bidder at an auction without reserve where the owner is permitted to bid. However, what is the position if the auctioneer, having received one or more bids at an auction without reserve, then withdraws those goods and does not allow the hammer to fall? The Court of Appeal applied *Warlow v Harrison* in answering this question in the following case.

Barry v Davies (t/a Heathcote Ball & Co.)
[2000] 1 WLR 1962 (CA)

At an auction without reserve, the claimant had made the only bid (of £200 each) for two engine analysers. The auctioneer considered the bid too low (on the basis that each machine was worth about £14,000) and withdrew the engine analysers from the sale. They were sold privately a few days later for £750 each.

The claimant sought damages alleging breach of contract by the auctioneer, since the claimant was the highest bidder at an auction without reserve. The claimant claimed damages of £27,600, being the difference between the value of both machines (£28,000) less the total amount of his bid (£400).

Held: The auctioneer was liable. Following *Warlow v Harrison*, at an auction without reserve there was a collateral contract between the auctioneer and the highest bidder based on the auctioneer's undertaking to sell to the highest bidder. By withdrawing the machines from the auction, the auctioneer was in breach of this contract, and was liable to pay the highest bidder the difference between the bid amount and the market price at the date of the auction of the goods withdrawn. The only evidence of market price was the manufacturer's list price for new machines—namely, £14,000 each.

SIR MURRAY STUART SMITH LJ: The judge held that it would be the general and reasonable expectation of persons attending at an auction sale without reserve that the highest bidder would and should be entitled to the lot for which he bids. Such an outcome was in his view fair and logical. As a matter of law he held that there was a collateral contract between the auctioneer and the highest bidder constituted by an offer by the auctioneer to sell to the highest bidder which was accepted when the bid was made. In so doing he followed the views of the majority of the Court of Exchequer Chamber in *Warlow v Harrison* (1859) 1 E & E 309 . . .

[Counsel] on behalf of the defendant criticised this conclusion on a number of grounds. First, he submitted that the holding of an auction without reserve does not amount to a promise on the part of the auctioneer to sell the lots to the highest bidder. There are no express words to the effect, merely a statement of fact that the vendor has not placed a reserve on the lot. Such an intention, he submitted, is inconsistent with two principles of law, namely that the auctioneer's request for bids is not an offer which can be accepted by the highest bidder (*Payne v Cave* (1789) 3 Durn & E 148) and that there is no completed contract of sale until the auctioneer's hammer falls and the bidder may withdraw his bid up until that time (Sale of Goods Act 1979, s. 57(2), which reflects the common law). There should be no need to imply such a promise into a statement that the sale is without reserve, because there may be other valid reasons why the auctioneer should be entitled to withdraw the lot, for example if he suspected an illegal ring or that the vendor had no title to sell.

Secondly, [counsel] submitted that there is no consideration for the auctioneer's promise. He submitted that the bid itself cannot amount to consideration because the bidder has not promised to do anything, he can withdraw the bid until it is accepted and the sale completed by the fall of the hammer. At most the bid represents a discretionary promise, which amounts to illusory consideration, for example promising to do something 'if I feel like it'. The bid only had real benefit to the auctioneer at the moment the sale is completed by the fall of the hammer. Furthermore, the suggestion that consideration is provided because the auctioneer has the opportunity to accept the bid or to obtain a higher bid as the bidding is driven up depends upon the bid not being withdrawn . . .

The authorities, such as they were, do not speak with one voice. The starting point is s. 57 of the Sale of Goods Act 1979 . . .

Subsections (3) and (4) are . . . important. They provide:

> (3) A sale by auction may be notified to be subject to a reserve or upset price, and a right to bid may also be reserved expressly by or on behalf of the seller.
> (4) Where a sale by auction is not notified to be subject to the right to bid by or on behalf of the seller, it is not lawful for the seller to bid himself or to employ any person to bid at the sale, or for the auctioneer knowingly to take any bid from the seller or any such person.

Although the Act does not expressly deal with sales by auction without reserve, the auctioneer is the agent of the vendor and, unless subsection (4) has been complied with, it is not lawful for him to make a bid. Yet withdrawing the lot from the sale because it has not reached the level which the auctioneer considers appropriate is tantamount to bidding on behalf of the seller. The highest bid cannot be rejected simply because it is not high enough . . .

[Sir Murray Stuart Smith LJ then discussed *Warlow v Harrison* as being authoritative on the question of the collateral contract and continued:]

As to consideration, in my judgment there is consideration both in the form of detriment to the bidder, since his bid can be accepted unless and until it is withdrawn, and benefit to the auctioneer as the bidding is driven up. Moreover, attendance at the sale is likely to be increased if it is known that there is no reserve . . .

For these reasons I would uphold the judge's decision on liability.

NOTES

1. The second (unilateral) contract is referred to as a collateral contract.

2. It appears from this decision that a bid at an auction without reserve can be withdrawn at any time before the hammer falls. This suggests that the unilateral (collateral) offer—to apply the reserve and not to allow the owner to bid—cannot be accepted by every bidder at an auction without reserve. If the acceptance can be made only by the highest bona fide bidder, that person's identity will not be revealed and acceptance will not occur until the hammer falls or the goods are withdrawn from the sale. Such an

analysis preserves the ability to withdraw bids at an auction without reserve.

 3. The Court of Appeal rejected the argument that the measure of damages should be restricted to £1,500, which the defendant alleged was the value of the machines, having sold them for this figure. In his judgment, Pill LJ makes it clear that the claimant was 'fortunate' in relation to the damages award, because there was no evidence of value other than the manufacturer's list price. Normally, there will be evidence of second-hand market value, which will be applied in fixing the damages award.

2.4 Acceptance

2.4.1 The mirror-image rule

2.4.1.1 Counter-offers

Hyde v Wrench
(1840) 3 Beav 334, 49 ER 132 (Rolls Court)

On 6 June, the defendant offered to sell his farm for £1,000 and, in reply, the claimant offered to buy it for £950. On 27 June, the defendant refused the claimant's offer of £950 and, on 29 June, the claimant, by letter, agreed to pay £1,000. However, the defendant did not indicate any agreement to the offer to pay £1,000.

 Held: There was no binding contract for the purchase of the farm.

> LORD LANGDALE MR: I think there exists no valid binding contract between the parties for the purchase of the property. The defendant offered to sell it for £1,000, and if that had been at once unconditionally accepted, there would undoubtedly have been a perfect binding contract; instead of that, the plaintiff made an offer of his own to purchase the property for £950, and he thereby rejected the offer previously made by the defendant. I think that it was not afterwards competent for him to revive the proposal of the defendant, by tendering an acceptance of it; and that, therefore, there exists no obligation of any sort between the parties . . .

2.4.1.2 A counter-offer (or offer) can be accepted by conduct

---

Brogden v Metropolitan Railway Co.
(1877) 2 App Cas 666 (HL)

Brogden had suggested that the Railway Company should enter into a formal contract for the supply and purchase of coal. The Company sent terms of agreement. Brogden added the name of an arbitrator to settle any differences, before writing 'approved' and signing the document. The agreement was returned to the Company's manager, who put it in his desk. The manager then ordered and received coal on the basis of the arrangements in this document. When disputes arose, Brogden denied that there was any binding contract.

 Held: By inserting the name of an arbitrator, Brogden had rejected the offer and made a counter-offer. This counter-offer had been accepted by the Company when it ordered and had taken delivery of coal upon the terms of the agreement; acceptance by conduct.

LORD BLACKBURN: I have always believed the law to be this, that when an offer is made to another party, and in that offer there is a request express or implied that he must signify his acceptance by doing some particular thing, then as soon as he does that thing, he is bound. If a man sent an offer abroad saying: I wish to know whether you will supply me with goods at such and such a price, and, if you agree to that, you must ship the first cargo as soon as you get this letter, there can be no doubt that as soon as the cargo was shipped the contract would be complete, and if the cargo went to the bottom of the sea, it would go to the bottom of the sea at the risk of the orderer . . .

But when you come to the general proposition which [the judge at first instance] seems to have laid down, that a simple acceptance in your own mind, without any intimation to the other party, and expressed by a mere private act, such as putting a letter into a drawer, completes a contract, I must say I differ from that . . .

But my Lords, while, as I say, this is so upon the question of law, it is still necessary to consider this case farther upon the question of fact. I agree, and I think every Judge who has considered the case does agree, certainly Lord Chief Justice Cockburn does, that though the parties may have gone no farther than an offer on the one side, saying, Here is the draft,—(for that I think is really what this case comes to,)—and the draft so offered by the one side is approved by the other, everything being agreed to except the name of the arbitrator, which the one side has filled in and the other has not yet assented to, if both parties have acted upon that draft and treated it as binding, they will be bound by it . . .

NOTE In *Pickfords Ltd v Celestica Ltd* [2003] EWCA Civ 1741, the Court of Appeal considered that an 'acceptance' fax was, in fact, a counter-offer since it purported to accept the first-price offer, although this first-price offer had been revoked by a second-price offer on different terms. The 'acceptance' fax therefore represented an offer on the terms of the first-price offer with the addition of a cap of £100,000 (a material new term added in the counter-offer). This counter-offer had then been accepted by conduct when the claimant carried out the removal work under the contract.

Acceptance by conduct, provided that it is clear and unequivocal, can even trump an earlier prescribed mode of acceptance as illustrated by *Reveille Independent LLC v Anotech International (UK) Ltd* [2016] EWCA Civ 443, where the Court of Appeal held that acceptance had occurred by conduct even though the parties had originally prescribed signature as the only mode of acceptance. Cranston J (at [40]–[53]) considered that, in this instance, acceptance by conduct had occurred and this therefore meant that the offeree had waived the signature requirement. Conduct can only trump a prescribed mode of acceptance in the following manner:

40. There are a number of rules of English contract law which, in combination, bear on the resolution of this appeal. First, classical analysis finds the parties' consent to a contract in the acceptance of an offer, and it is well accepted that acceptance can be by the conduct of the offeree so long as that conduct, as a matter of objective analysis, is intended to constitute acceptance: *Brogden* v. *Metropolitan Railway Co* (1877) 2 App Cas 666. Secondly, as in *Brogden*, acceptance can be of an offer on the terms set out in a draft agreement drawn up between the parties but never signed. Thirdly, if a party has a right to sign a contract before being bound, it is open to it by clear and unequivocal words or conduct to waive the requirement and to conclude the contract without insisting on its signature: *Oceanografia SA de CV* v. *DSND Subsea AS (The Botnica)* [2006] EWHC 1360 (Comm); [2007] 1 All E.R. (Comm) 28 at [94], per Aikens J.

41. Fourthly, if signature is the prescribed mode of acceptance an offeror will be bound by the contract if it waives that requirement and acquiesces in a different mode of acceptance. In my view it follows that where signature as the prescribed mode of acceptance is intended for the benefit of the offeree, and the offeree accepts in some other way, that should be treated as effective unless it can be shown that the failure to sign has prejudiced the offeror: see *Chitty on Contracts*, 32nd ed, 2015, §§2-066, 2-067; *MSM Consulting Ltd* v. *United Republic of Tanzania* [2009] EWHC 121 (QB), at [119] per Christopher Clarke J. Fifthly, a draft agreement can have contractual force, although the parties do not comply with a requirement that to be binding it must be signed, if essentially all the terms have been agreed and their subsequent conduct indicates this, albeit a court will not reach this conclusion lightly: *RTS Flexible Systems* v. *Molkeroi Alois Muller GmbH* [2010] UKSC 14, [2010] 1 WLR 753, at [54]–[56]. Finally, the subsequent conduct of the parties is admissible to prove the existence of a contract, and its terms, although not as an aid to its interpretation: *Chitty on Contracts*, 32nd ed, 2015, §13-129.

42. These rules take effect against the background of legal policies recognised in the case law . . . In my view the same realistic approach must be taken in deciding whether a party has accepted an offer through its conduct.

2.4.1.3 Does the correspondence amount to a counter-offer?

(a) A request for further information before the offeree makes up his mind is not a counter-offer.

Stevenson, Jacques & Co. v McLean
(1880) 5 QBD 346 (QB)

The defendant wrote to the claimants giving 40s. net cash per ton as the lowest price at which he could sell iron and stating that he would hold the offer open until the following Monday. The claimants telegraphed: 'Please wire whether you would accept forty for delivery over two months, or, if not, the longest limit you could give.' The defendant did not reply. One of the issues before Lush J was whether this telegram amounted to a counter-offer, thereby rejecting the defendant's offer to sell at 40s. net cash per ton.

Held: The telegram was not a rejection of the defendant's offer, but merely an inquiry as to whether the defendant would modify the terms of his offer.

LUSH J: [T]he form of the telegram is one of inquiry. It is not 'I offer forty for delivery over two months,' which would have likened the case to *Hyde v Wrench* (1840) 3 Beav 334, where one party offered his estate for 1,000*l.*, and the other answered by offering 950*l.* Lord Langdale, in that case, held that after the 950*l.* had been refused, the party offering it could not, by then agreeing to the original proposal, claim the estate, for the negotiation was at an end by the refusal of his counter proposal. Here there is no counter proposal. The words are, 'Please wire whether you would accept forty for delivery over two months, or, if not, the longest limit you would give.' There is nothing specific by way of offer or rejection, but a mere inquiry, which should have been answered and not treated as a rejection of the offer.

(b) What is the position if the offeree purports to accept in one document, but attaches a covering letter asserting that he will not be in a position to comply with the terms of that acceptance? Does this make the acceptance conditional and hence ineffective as an acceptance?

2.4.1.4 Battle of forms and the counter-offer analysis

Butler Machine Tool Co. Ltd v Ex-Cell-O Corporation (England) Ltd
[1979] 1 WLR 401 (CA)

On 23 May 1969, the sellers issued a quotation offering to sell a machine tool to the buyers for £75,535, delivery to be in ten months' time. The offer was stated to be subject to certain terms and conditions, which 'shall prevail over any terms and conditions in the buyer's order'. The conditions included a price variation clause providing for the goods to be charged at the price on the date of delivery. On 27 May, the buyers replied by placing an order for the machine. The order was stated to be subject to certain terms and conditions, which were materially different from those put forward by the sellers and which, in particular, made no provision for a variation in price. At the foot of the buyers' order, there was a tear-off acknowledgement of receipt of the order stating: 'We accept your order on the Terms and Conditions stated thereon.' On 5 June, the sellers completed and signed the acknowledgement, and returned it to the buyers along with a letter stating that the buyers' order was being entered in accordance with the sellers' quotation of 23 May. When the sellers came to deliver the machine, they claimed that the price had increased by £2,892. The buyers refused to pay the difference and the sellers brought an action claiming that the price variation clause contained in their offer entitled them to the increased price. The buyers contended that the contract had been concluded on the buyers' terms and was therefore a fixed price contract.

Held: The contract had been concluded on the buyers' terms. The majority, Lawton and Bridge LJJ, held that the buyers' order was a counter-offer, which the sellers had accepted by completing and returning the acknowledgement.

LAWTON LJ: The modern commercial practice of making quotations and placing orders with conditions attached, usually in small print, is indeed likely, as in this case to produce a battle of forms. The problem is how should that battle be conducted? . . . In my judgment, the battle has to be conducted in accordance with set rules. It is a battle more on classical 18th century lines when convention decided who had the right to open fire first rather than in accordance with the modern concept of attrition.

The rules relating to a battle of this kind have been known for the past 130-odd years. They were set out by Lord Langdale MR in *Hyde v Wrench*, 3 Beav 334, 337, . . . and, if anyone should have thought they were obsolescent, Megaw J in *Trollope & Colls Ltd v Atomic Power Constructions Ltd* [1963] 1 WLR 333, 337 called attention to the fact that those rules are still in force.

When those rules are applied to this case, in my judgment, the answer is obvious. The sellers started by making an offer. That was in their quotation. The small print was headed by the following words:

> General. All orders are accepted only upon and subject to the terms set out in our quotation and the following conditions. These terms and conditions shall prevail over any terms and conditions in the buyer's order.

That offer was not accepted. The buyers were only prepared to have one of these very expensive machines on their own terms. Their terms had very material differences in them from the terms put forward by the sellers. They could not be reconciled in any way. In the language of article 7 of the Uniform Law on the Formation of Contracts for the International Sale of Goods (see Uniform Laws on International Sales Act 1967, Schedule 2) they did 'materially alter the terms' set out in the offer made by the plaintiffs.

As I understand *Hyde v Wrench*, 3 Beav 334, and the cases which have followed, the consequence of placing the order in that way, if I may adopt Megaw J's words [*Trollope & Colls Ltd v Atomic Power Constructions Ltd* [1963] 1 WLR 333, 337], was 'to kill the original offer.' It follows that the court has to look at what happened after the buyers made their counter-offer. By letter dated June 4, 1969, the plaintiffs acknowledged receipt of the counter-offer, and they went on in this way:

> Details of this order have been passed to our Halifax works for attention and a formal acknowledgment of order will follow in due course.

That is clearly a reference to the printed tear-off slip which was at the bottom of the buyers' counteroffer. By letter dated June 5, 1969, the sales office manager at the plaintiffs' Halifax factory completed that tear-off slip and sent it back to the buyers.

It is true, [counsel for the plaintiffs] has reminded us, that the return of that printed slip was accompanied by a letter which had this sentence in it: 'This is being entered in accordance with our revised quotation of May 23 for delivery in 10/11 months.' I agree with Lord Denning MR that, in business sense, that refers to the quotation as to the price and the identity of the machine, and it does not bring into the contract the small print conditions on the back of the quotation. Those small print conditions had disappeared from the story. That was when the contract was made. At that date it was a fixed price contract without a price escalation clause.

Lord Denning also allowed the appeal, but came to his conclusion by a different route.

LORD DENNING: In many of these cases our traditional analysis of offer, counter-offer, rejection, acceptance and so forth is out of date. This was observed by Lord Wilberforce in *New Zealand Shipping Co. Ltd v A.M. Satterthwaite & Co. Ltd* [1975] AC 154, 167. The better way is to look at all the documents passing between the parties—and glean from them, or from the conduct of the parties, whether they have reached agreement on all material points—even though there may be differences between the forms and conditions printed on the back of them. As Lord Cairns said in *Brogden v Metropolitan Railway Co.* (1877) 2 App Cas 666, 672:

> . . . there may be a *consensus* between the parties far short of a complete mode of expressing it, and that *consensus* may be discovered from letters or from other documents of an imperfect and incomplete description; . . .

Applying this guide, it will be found that in most cases when there is a 'battle of forms', there is a contract as soon as the last of the forms is sent and received without objection being taken to it. That is well observed in *Benjamin* [*on Sale of Goods*]. The difficulty is to decide which form, or which part of which form, is a term or condition of the contract. In some cases the battle is won by the man who fires the last shot. He is the man who puts forward the latest terms and conditions: and, if they are not objected to by the other party, he may be taken to have agreed to them. Such was *British Road Services Ltd v Arthur V. Crutchley & Co. Ltd* [1968] 1 Lloyd's Rep 271, 281–2, per Lord Pearson; and the illustration given by Professor Guest in *Anson's Law of Contract* when he says that 'the terms of the contract consist of the terms of the offer subject to the modifications contained in the acceptance'. In some cases the battle is won by the man who gets the blow in first. If he offers to sell at a named price on the terms and conditions stated on the back: and the buyer orders the goods purporting to accept the offer—on an order form with his own different terms and conditions on the back—then if the difference is so material that it would affect the price, the buyer ought not to be allowed to take advantage of the difference unless he draws it specifically to the attention of the seller. There are yet other cases where the battle depends on the shots fired on both sides. There is a concluded contract but the forms vary. The terms and conditions of both parties are to be construed together. If they can be reconciled so as to give a harmonious result, all well and good. If differences are irreconcilable—so that they are mutually contradictory—then the conflicting terms may have to be scrapped and replaced by a reasonable implication.

In the present case the judge [at first instance] thought that the sellers in their original quotation got their blow in first: especially by the provision that 'these terms and conditions shall prevail over any terms and conditions in the buyer's order'. It was so emphatic that the price variation clause continued through all the subsequent dealings and that the buyers must be taken to have agreed to it. I can understand that point of view. But I think that the documents have to be considered as a whole. And, as a matter of construction, I think the acknowledgment of June 5 1969, is the decisive document. It makes it clear that the contract was on the buyers' terms and not on the sellers' terms: and the buyers' terms did not include a price variation clause.

? QUESTIONS

1. Lord Denning's approach separates the issue of formation from the question of content of the contract and so challenges the traditional mirror-image rule governing acceptances. Is there any empirical evidence to support Lord Denning's assessment that businessmen pay no attention to fine print and consider that they have a deal when the major terms are agreed? See Beale and Dugdale (1975) 2 Br J Law & Soc 45, 49–51.

2. What does Lord Denning mean when he refers to the parties reaching agreement 'on all material points'? What difficulties exist with his categorization of terms? See Rawlings (1979) 42 MLR 715.

NOTE The contemporary relevance of Lord Denning's approach in *Butler Machine Tool* of separating the formation of a contract from a determination of its content has been considered in some recent decisions. First, in *Sterling Hydraulics Ltd v Dichtomatik Ltd* [2006] EWHC 2004 (QB), [2007] 1 Lloyd's Rep 8, the judge concluded that there was a binding contract on the basis of all of the correspondence passing between the parties. Secondly, in *GHSP Inc. v AB Electronic Ltd* [2010] EWHC 1828 (Comm), [2011] 1 Lloyd's Rep 432, Burton J was faced with parties who were agreed that they had contracted and the goods that were the subject of their contract had been manufactured and supplied. However, both parties had been equally clear during negotiations that they were not prepared to agree to the terms of the other; the seller's terms contained a limitation of liability and the seller had not been prepared to contract without a cap on its liability. The judge applied Lord Denning's 'formation and content' analysis and accepted the solution, advocated by counsel for both parties, that the terms of the parties' contract should be those implied by the Sale of Goods Act 1979 rather than the terms of any one party. Thirdly, in *Tekdata Interconnections Ltd v Amphenol Ltd* [2009] EWCA Civ 1209, [2009] 2 CLC 866, [2010] 2 All ER (Comm) 302, the judge at first instance, relying on Lord Denning's approach, had analysed the parties' relationship, and concluded that the buyer's terms prevailed because that had been the parties' intention all along. It was left to the Court of Appeal to restore and apply the traditional approach.

Tekdata Interconnections Ltd v Amphenol Ltd
[2009] EWCA Civ 1209, [2009] 2 CLC 866, [2010] 1 Lloyd's Rep 357 (CA)

In a long-term contracting arrangement, Tekdata bought parts for its cable harnesses from Amphenol. Tekdata (the buyer) would send purchase orders containing its terms and conditions, and Amphenol (the seller) would acknowledge these orders by sending a statement that its own terms and conditions, which included an exemption clause, would prevail. Tekdata alleged a breach of contract of an order, but Amphenol claimed that its terms governed, so that it could rely on exemption clauses to protect it from liability.

Held (in the Court of Appeal, allowing the appeal): Amphenol's terms governed. The Court of Appeal considered that, in general, the traditional analysis would prevail and, on these facts, this meant that Amphenol's acknowledgement was the last shot, which had been accepted by conduct when the goods were delivered and accepted by Tekdata.

LONGMORE LJ: 1. This appeal raises the question whether in what is sometimes called 'the battle of forms', there can be circumstances in which a traditional offer and acceptance analysis can be displaced by reference to the conduct of the parties over a long-term relationship. An offer to buy containing the purchaser's terms which is followed by an acknowledgement of purchase containing the seller's terms which is followed by delivery will (other things being equal) result in a contract on the seller's terms. If, however, it is clear that the neither party ever intended the seller's terms to apply and always intended the purchaser's terms to apply, it is conceptually possible to arrive at the conclusion that the purchaser's terms are to apply. It will be a rare case where that happens. Do the facts of this appeal amount to that rare case? . . .

20. In paras 2–110 and 111 of *Chitty on Contracts* (30th ed) Professor Sir Guenther Treitel points out that the traditional offer and acceptance analysis is not always without its difficulties. Having referred to three specific cases of (1) multilateral contracts, (2) references to third parties and (3) sale of land, he cites the words of Lord Denning MR in *Butler* and his similar words in the earlier case of *Gibson v Manchester City Council* [1978] 1 WLR 520, 523. He then says of these comments:

But such an outright rejection of the traditional analysis is open to the objection that it provides too little guidance for the courts (or their parties or their legal advisers) in determining whether an agreement has been reached and I might add 'on what terms'. The fact that *Gibson* was reversed by the House of Lords [1979] 1 WLR 294 adds considerable force to this comment . . .

21. So, although I am not saying that the context of a long term relationship and the conduct of the parties can never be so strong as to displace the result which a traditional offer and acceptance analysis would dictate, I do not consider the circumstances are sufficiently strong to do so in this present case. Indeed I think it will always be difficult to displace the traditional analysis, in a battle of forms case, unless it can be said there was a clear course of dealing between the parties. That was never proved . . .

DYSON LJ [expressing agreement with the judgment of Longmore LJ]: 23. The so-called 'last shot' doctrine has been explained in *Chitty on Contracts* (30th edition) at para 2–037 as meaning that where conflicting communications are exchanged, each is a counter-offer, so that if a contract results at all (eg from an acceptance by conduct) it must be on the terms of the final document in the series leading to the conclusion of the contract. This doctrine has been criticised in *Anson's Law of Contract* (28th edition) at p 39 as depending on chance and being potentially arbitrary as well as on the ground that, unless and until the counter-offer is accepted, there is no contract even though both buyer and seller may firmly believe that a contract has been made . . .

25. In my judgment, it is not possible to lay down a general rule that will apply in all cases where there is a battle of the forms. It always depends on an assessment of what the parties must objectively be taken to have intended. But where the facts are no more complicated than that A makes an offer on its conditions and B accepts that offer on its conditions and, without more, performance follows, it seems to me that the correct analysis is what Longmore LJ has described as the 'traditional offer and acceptance analysis', ie that there is a contract on B's conditions. I accept that this analysis is not without its difficulties in circumstances of the kind to which Professor Treitel refers in the passage quoted at [20] above. But in the next sentence of that passage, Professor Treitel adds: 'For this reason the cases described above are best regarded as exceptions to a general requirement of offer and acceptance'. I also accept the force of the criticisms made in *Anson*. But the rule s which govern the formation of contracts have been long established and they are grounded in the concepts of offer and acceptance. So long as that continues to be the case, it seems to me that the general rule should be that the traditional offer and acceptance analysis is to be applied in battle of the forms cases. That has the great merit of providing a degree of certainty which is both desirable and necessary in order to promote effective commercial relationships.

Pill LJ agreed with both Longmore and Dyson LJJ.

NOTE Following the statement to this effect by Longmore LJ in Tekdata (at [21] above), in *Trebor Bassett Holdings Ltd v ADT Fire and Security plc* [2011] EWHC 1936 (TCC), [2011] BLR 661, Coulson J confirmed that the traditional analysis would be applied unless there was a clear course of dealing indicating a common intention that other terms should prevail. No such course of dealing existed on the facts. ADT had sent a quotation to design, supply, and install a fire suppression system on its own terms, which contained a limitation of liability, but the 'last shot' (Trebor's purchase order referring to its terms, which did not contain any limitation of liability) had been accepted by conduct when ADT had commenced the contract work without objecting to Trebor's terms. It followed that the total loss of £110 million could be recovered. Nevertheless, Coulson J accepted that all of the communications need to be considered and not merely 'the last shot':

154 *Butler* is often cited as authority for the proposition that, where there is a battle of forms, the critical act may be the so-called firing of the last shot, the last letter or communication in the series. But some care is needed with that analysis. The court has to construe all the relevant communications.

2.4.2 Offeror prescribes the method of acceptance

Manchester Diocesan Council for Education v Commercial & General Investments Ltd
[1970] 1 WLR 241 (Ch D)

Condition 4 of a request for tenders stated that the person whose tender was accepted would be informed by letter sent to him at the address given in the tender. On 15 September 1964, the claimant wrote to the defendant company's surveyor, stating that the sale to the company had been approved, but it was not until 7 January 1965 that the claimant's solicitors wrote to the defendant company at the address given in the tender giving formal notification of acceptance of its offer. It was alleged that the offer in the tender had lapsed, so that it was necessary to decide when the contract had been concluded.

BUCKLEY J: Condition 4, however, does not say that that shall be the sole permitted method of communicating an acceptance. It may be that an offeror, who by the terms of his offer insists on acceptance in a particular manner, is entitled to insist that he is not bound unless acceptance is effected or communicated in that precise way, although it seems probable that, even so, if the other party communicates his acceptance in some other way, the offeror may by conduct or otherwise waive his right to insist on the prescribed method of acceptance. Where, however, the offeror has prescribed a particular method of acceptance, but not in terms insisting that only acceptance in that mode shall be binding, I am of opinion that acceptance communicated to the offeror by any other mode which is no less advantageous to him will conclude the contract. Thus in *Tinn v Hoffman & Co.* (1873) 29 LT 271, where acceptance was requested by return of post, Honeyman J, said at p. 274:

> That does not mean exclusively a reply by letter by return of post, but you may reply by telegram or by verbal message or by any means not later than a letter written and sent by return of post.

If an offeror intends that he shall be bound only if his offer is accepted in some particular manner, it must be for him to make this clear. Condition 4 in the present case has not, in my judgment, this effect.

Moreover, the inclusion of condition 4 in the defendant's offer was at the instance of the plaintiff, who framed the conditions and the form of tender. It should not, I think, be regarded as a condition or stipulation imposed by the defendant as offeror upon the plaintiff as offeree, but as a term introduced into the bargain by the plaintiff and presumably considered by the plaintiff as being in some way for the protection or benefit of the plaintiff. It would consequently be a term strict compliance with which the plaintiff could waive, provided the defendant was not adversely affected. The plaintiff did not take advantage of the condition which would have resulted in a contract being formed as soon as a letter of acceptance complying with the condition was posted, but adopted another course, which could only result in a contract when the plaintiff's acceptance was actually communicated to the defendant.

For these reasons, I have reached the conclusion that in accordance with the terms of the tender it was open to the plaintiff to conclude a contract by acceptance actually communicated to the defendant in any way; and, in my judgment, the letter of September 15 constituted such an acceptance . . .

Yates Building Co. Ltd v Pulleyn & Sons (York) Ltd
(1975) 237 EG 183, (1975) 119 SJ 370 (CA)

The defendants granted the claimants an option to buy building plots for £18,900 'exercisable by notice in writing . . . between 6 April and 6 May 1973 . . . to be sent by registered or recorded delivery post' to the defendants or their solicitors. The option was exercised by a letter of 30 April 1973 sent by ordinary post, but the defendants refused to accept it as a valid acceptance.

Held: Because the method was not clearly stated to be mandatory, any acceptance that was communicated to the offeror by any other no less advantageous method would conclude the contract. The provision for registered or recorded post was for the benefit of the claimants, and they could waive the requirement and take the risk of ordinary post.

NOTE In *A Ltd v B Ltd* [2015] E WHC 137 (Comm), A Ltd sought to avoid an agreement to purchase cotton from B Ltd by arguing that, since it had not signed and returned a copy of the draft contract, it had not followed the prescribed method of communicating acceptance. In rejecting this argument, Phillips J held, following a similar comment by Longmore LJ in *Maple Leaf Macro Volatility Master Fund v Rouvroy* [2009] EWHC 257 (Comm), [2009] 1 Lloyd's Rep 475 at [15], that the insertion of a signature block (or space for a signature) in the draft contract did not mean that signature became a prescribed method of acceptance, even if the block was headed with the word 'Acceptance' and there was a request for the signed contract to be returned. In any event, the judge held that any signature prescription would have been to benefit B Ltd, as offeror, and B Ltd was free to waive, and had waived, this stipulation for its benefit.

2.4.3 Acceptance must be made in response to the offer

An offer is not 'accepted' by doing the required act in ignorance of the offer. However, if the offeree responds with knowledge, his motive in so doing is irrelevant.

R v Clarke
(1927) 40 CLR 227 (High Court of Australia)

A reward was offered by the government of Western Australia for information leading to the arrest and conviction of the persons who committed the murders of two police officers. Clarke gave this information after he had been arrested for the crime, and it was found as a fact that his only intention was to save himself from an unfounded charge, so that he had not acted on the faith of, or in reliance upon, the offer. In reaching the conclusion that he could not recover, the High Court had to distinguish *Williams v Carwardine* (1833) 5 C & P 566, 172 ER 1101, in which the claimant had given the information requested because she thought that she was dying. It was held in that case that she could recover the reward that had been offered, because she knew about the reward. Her motive in supplying the information was not material because she had acted on the offer.

HIGGINS J: That case [*Williams v Carwardine*] seems to me not to deal with the essential elements for a contract at all: it shows merely that the *motive* of the informer in accepting the contract offered (and the performing the conditions is usually sufficient evidence of acceptance) has nothing to do with his right to recover under the contract. The reports show (as it was assumed by the Judges after the verdict of the jury in favour of the informer), that the informer *knew* of the offer when giving the information, and meant to accept the offer though she had also a *motive* in her guilty conscience.

. . . The reasoning of Woodruff J in *Fitch v Snedaker* [38 NY 248 (1868)] seems to me to be faultless; and the decision is spoken of in *Anson* as being undoubtedly correct in principle:—'The motive inducing consent may be immaterial, but the consent is vital. Without that there is no contract. How then can there be consent or assent to that of which the party has never heard?' Clarke had seen the offer, indeed; but it was not present to his mind—he had forgotten it, and gave no consideration to it, in his intense excitement as to his own danger. There cannot be assent without knowledge of the offer; and ignorance of the offer is the same thing whether it is due to never hearing of it or to forgetting it after hearing. But for this candid confession of Clarke's it might fairly be presumed that Clarke, having once seen the offer, acted on the faith of it, in reliance on it; but he has himself rebutted that presumption.

Gibbons v Proctor
(1891) 64 LT 594

On 29 May, the defendant had offered a reward of £25 to the person who gave information, leading to the conviction of the perpetrator of a particular crime, to police Superintendent Penn. The claimant, a police officer, had already communicated the required information to a colleague, named Coppin, with instructions to forward it to Superintendent Penn. Coppin had communicated the information to his superior, Inspector Lennan, who had passed it on to Superintendent Penn. The information reached Penn on 30 May.

Held: The claimant was entitled to the reward. Coppin and Lennan were the claimant's agents for the purposes of conveying the information. The terms of the offer required the information to be given to Penn. The acceptance was the supply of the information to Penn, and at that time the claimant knew that a reward had been offered.

NOTES

1. Hudson (1968) 84 LQR 503 argued that, on grounds of policy, the law should encourage rather than penalize people who do not know about a reward and who act under a sense of moral duty.

2. It is objectionable to allow the offeror of a reward to escape liability on his promise when he has had the benefit of seeing his conditions fulfilled. (Avoidance of this situation is the very reason for holding such a promise to be an offer and not an invitation to treat.)

2.4.4 Communication of the acceptance to the offeror

2.4.4.1 Implied waiver of the need to communicate

Carlill v Carbolic Smoke Ball Co. [1893] 1 QB 256 (*Chapter 1*) is authority for the general principle that, in a unilateral contract, the performance of the act is the acceptance and there is no need to communicate the attempt to perform it.

The circumstances may also indicate that there is a waiver of the need to communicate acceptance. For example, in *Dresdner Kleinwort Ltd v Attrill* [2013] EWCA Civ 394, [2013] 3 All ER 607, the employer had announced that it would pay a guaranteed employment bonus to its employees. This promise was clearly beneficial to the employees and nobody hearing the announcement would expect that an employee could benefit only if he positively accepted the offer. The usual requirement to notify acceptance was therefore dispensed with.

As a general rule, however, silence in a bilateral contract will not constitute acceptance.

Felthouse v Bindley
(1862) 11 CB (NS) 869, 142 ER 1037 (CP)

During negotiations for the sale of a horse, the claimant wrote to his nephew stating: 'If I hear no more about him, I consider the horse is mine at £30 15s.' The nephew did not respond, but did instruct the defendant, an auctioneer, to reserve the horse in question because it had already been sold. By mistake, the defendant put the horse up for sale and it was sold. The claimant sued the auctioneer for the conversion of the horse (which meant that he had to show that the horse was his property at the time that it was sold).

Held: The claimant did not have property in the horse.

> WILLES J: [I]t is clear that the uncle had no right to impose upon the nephew a sale of his horse for 30/.15s. unless he chose to comply with the condition of writing to repudiate the offer. The nephew might, no doubt, have bound his uncle to the bargain by writing to him: the uncle might also have retracted his offer at any time before acceptance. It stood an open offer: and so things remained until the 25th of February, when the nephew was about to sell his farming stock by auction. The horse in question being catalogued with the rest of the stock, the auctioneer (the defendant) was told that it was already sold. It is clear, therefore, that the nephew in his own mind intended his uncle to have the horse at the price which he (the uncle) had named,—30/.15s.: but he had not communicated such his intention to his uncle, or done anything to bind himself. Nothing, therefore, had been done to vest the property in the horse in the plaintiff down to the 25th of February, when the horse was sold by the defendant. It appears to me that, independently of the subsequent letters, there had been no bargain to pass the property in the horse to the plaintiff . . .

? QUESTIONS

1. Why had the nephew not accepted by his act of informing the auctioneer that the horse had been sold?

2. What would the position have been had the nephew been trying to enforce the sale contract against his uncle based upon the uncle's statement that silence would constitute acceptance?

NOTE For a discussion of exceptional situations in which silence may constitute acceptance in a bilateral contract, (discussion in *Poole's Textbook on Contract Law*, 2.4.5.1.1.

2.4.4.2 The postal rule of acceptance

If the post is the proper method to communicate acceptance, then the acceptance is deemed complete as soon as the letter of acceptance is posted.

Adams v Lindsell
(1818) 1 B & Ald 681, 106 ER 250 (KB)

On 2 September, the defendants wrote to the claimants offering to sell them certain fleeces of wool and requiring an answer by post. The defendants misdirected this letter, so that the claimants did not receive it until 5 September. The claimants posted their acceptance on the same day, but it was not received until 9 September. Meanwhile, on 8 September, the defendants, not having received an answer by 7 September as they had expected, sold the wool to someone else.

Held: There was a contract on 5 September when the claimants posted their acceptance. In answer to the argument that the acceptance had to be communicated, the court said that if that were so, no contract could ever be completed by post. If the defendants were not bound by their offer when accepted by the claimants until the answer was received, then the claimants ought not to be bound until after they had received the notification that the defendants had received their answer and assented to it, and so it might go on *ad infinitum*. The court stressed the fact that the delay in notifying the acceptance was solely the result of the defendants' mistake and 'it therefore must be taken as against them, that the plaintiffs' answer was received in course of post'.

The following case considers the question of when the post is a proper method for communicating acceptance.

Henthorn v Fraser
[1892] 2 Ch 27 (CA)

The facts of this case appear at *page 60*, 2.5.1.

> LORD HERSCHELL: Where the circumstances are such that it must have been within the contemplation of the parties that, according to the ordinary usages of mankind, the post might be used as a means of communicating the acceptance of an offer, the acceptance is complete as soon as it is posted.

NOTE The offer in this case had not been made by post. The offeree had been handed an option to purchase by the offeror in Liverpool. The offeree lived in Birkenhead. Therefore, it was held that acceptance by post must have been within the parties' contemplation. The method need only be 'a' possible method given the context and circumstances.

Household Fire and Carriage Accident Insurance Co. (Ltd) v Grant
(1879) 4 Ex D 216 (CA)

The defendant applied for shares in the claimant company. The company allotted the shares to the defendant and posted a letter addressed to him containing the notice of allotment, but he never received the letter.

    Held (Thesiger and Baggally LJJ; Bramwell LJ dissenting): The defendant had become a shareholder. Acceptance was complete when the letter of allotment was posted and it was irrelevant that it never arrived.

> THESIGER LJ: An acceptance, which only remains in the breast of the acceptor without being actually and by legal implication communicated to the offerer, is no binding acceptance. How then are these elements of law to be harmonised in the case of contracts formed by correspondence through the post? I see no better mode than that of treating the post office as the agent of both parties, and it was so considered by Lord Romilly in *Hebb's Case* (1867) LR 4 Eq 9, when in the course of his judgment he said: '*Dunlop v Higgins* (1848) 1 HLC 381 decides that the posting of a letter accepting an offer constitutes a binding contract, but the reason of that is, that the post office is the common agent of both parties.' Alderson, B., also in *Stocken v Collin* (1841) 7 M &W 515, a case of notice of dishonour, . . . says: 'If the doctrine that the post office is only the agent for the delivery of the notice were correct no one could safely avail himself of that mode of transmission.' But if the post office be such common agent, then it seems to me to follow that, as soon as the letter of acceptance is delivered to the post office, the contract is made as complete and final and absolutely binding as if the acceptor had put his letter into the hands of a messenger sent by the offerer himself as his agent to deliver the offer and receive the acceptance. What other principle can be adopted short of holding that the contract is not complete by acceptance until and except from

the time that the letter containing the acceptance is delivered to the offerer, a principle which has been distinctly negatived? . . . The acceptor, in posting the letter, has, to use the language of Lord Blackburn, in *Brogden v Directors of Metropolitan Ry. Co.* (1877) 2 App Cas 666, 'put it out of his control and done an extraneous act which clenches the matter, and shews beyond all doubt that each side is bound.' How then can a casualty in the post, whether resulting in delay, which in commercial transactions is often as bad as no delivery, or in non-delivery, unbind the parties or unmake the contract? To me it appears that in practice a contract complete upon the acceptance of an offer being posted, but liable to be put an end to by an accident in the post, would be more mischievous than a contract only binding upon the parties to it upon the acceptance actually reaching the offerer, and I can see no principle of law from which such an anomalous contract can be deduced.

There is no doubt that the implication of a complete, final, and absolutely binding contract being formed, as soon as the acceptance of an offer is posted, may in some cases lead to inconvenience and hardship. But such there must be at times in every view of the law. It is impossible in transactions which pass between parties at a distance, and have to be carried on through the medium of correspondence, to adjust conflicting rights between innocent parties, so as to make the consequences of mistake on the part of a mutual agent fall equally upon the shoulders of both. At the same time I am not prepared to admit that the implication in question will lead to any great or general inconvenience or hardship. An offerer, if he chooses, may always make the formation of the contract which he proposes dependent upon the actual communication to himself of the acceptance. If he trusts to the post he trusts to a means of communication which, as a rule, does not fail, and if no answer to his offer is received by him, and the matter is of importance to him, he can make inquiries of the person to whom his offer was addressed. On the other hand, if the contract is not finally concluded, except in the event of the acceptance actually reaching the offerer, the door would be opened to the perpetration of much fraud, and, putting aside this consideration, considerable delay in commercial transactions, in which despatch is, as a rule, of the greatest consequence, would be occasioned; for the acceptor would never be entirely safe in acting upon his acceptance until he had received notice that his letter of acceptance had reached its destination.

Bramwell LJ delivered an important dissenting judgment.

BRAMWELL LJ [dissenting]: That because a man, who may send a communication by post or otherwise, sends it by post, he should bind the person addressed, though the communication never reaches him, while he would not so bind him if he had sent it by hand, is impossible. There is no reason in it; it is simply arbitrary. I ask whether any one who thinks so is prepared to follow that opinion to its consequence; suppose the offer is to sell a particular chattel, and the letter accepting it never arrives, is the property in the chattel transferred? Suppose it is to sell an estate or grant a lease, is the bargain completed? The lease might be such as not to require a deed, could a subsequent lessee be ejected by the would-be acceptor of the offer because he had posted a letter? Suppose an article is advertised at so much, and that it would be sent on receipt of a post office order. Is it enough to post the letter? If the word 'receipt' is relied on, is it really meant that that makes a difference? If it should be said let the offerer wait, the answer is, maybe he may lose his market meanwhile. Besides, his offer may be by advertisement to all mankind. Suppose a reward for information, information posted does not reach, some one else gives it and is paid, is the offerer liable to the first man?

It is said that a contrary rule would be hard on the would-be acceptor, who may have made his arrangements on the footing that the bargain was concluded. But to hold as contended would be equally hard on the offerer, who may have made his arrangements on the footing that his offer was not accepted; his non-receipt of any communication may be attributable to the person to whom it was made being absent. What is he to do but to act on the negative, that no communication has been made to him? Further, the use of the post office is no more authorised by the offeror than the sending an answer by hand, and all these hardships would befall the person posting the letter if he sent it by hand. Doubtless in that case he would be the person to suffer if the letter did not reach its destination. Why should his sending it by post relieve him of the loss and cast it on the other party. It was said, if he sends it by hand it is revocable, but not if he sends it by post, which makes the difference. But it is revocable when sent by post, not that the letter can be got back, but its arrival might be anticipated by a letter by hand or telegram, and there is no case to shew that such anticipation would not prevent the letter from binding. It would be a most alarming thing to say that it would. That a letter honestly but mistakenly written and posted must bind the writer if hours before its arrival he informed the person addressed that it was coming, but was wrong and recalled; suppose a false but honest character given, and the mistake found out after the letter posted, and notice that it was wrong given to the person addressed.

NOTES

1. Evans (1966) 15 ICLQ 553 and Winfield (1939) 55 LQR 499 contain criticisms and justifications of the postal rule (discussed in *Poole's Textbook on Contract Law*, 2.4.5.2. See also Gardner (1992) 12 OJLS 170.

2. The postal rule does prevent the offeror revoking her offer once the offeree has posted an acceptance. However, the UNIDROIT Principles of International Commercial Contracts (PICC) advocate a 'receipt' rule for any postal acceptance (Art. 2.1.6(2)), but provide protection for the offeree who posts his acceptance, since a revocation will be effective only if it reaches the offeree before the offeree has posted his acceptance (Art. 2.1.4(1)). This is also the position in the Principles of European Contract Law (PECL), Arts 2:205 and 2:202.

2.4.4.3 Avoiding the postal rule

To avoid the postal rule, the offeror can always require actual communication of the acceptance to him. This leads to fine distinctions between words requiring actual communication and those that do not.

Holwell Securities Ltd v Hughes
[1974] 1 WLR 155 (CA)

On 19 October 1971, the claimants were granted an option by the defendant 'exercisable by notice in writing to [the defendant] at any time within six months from the date hereof'. On 14 April 1972, the claimants wrote to the defendant, giving notice of the exercise of the option, but the letter did not arrive. The claimants sought specific performance of the option agreement, arguing that it was complete on 14 April when the acceptance was posted.

Held: The option had not been validly exercised because actual communication was required.

RUSSELL LJ: It is the law in the first place that, prima facie, acceptance of an offer must be communicated to the offeror. Upon this principle the law has engrafted a doctrine that, if in any given case the true view is that the parties contemplated that the postal service might be used for the purpose of forwarding an acceptance of the offer, committal of the acceptance in a regular manner to the postal service will be acceptance of the offer so as to constitute a contract, even if the letter goes astray and is lost. Nor, as was once suggested, are such cases limited to cases in which the offer has been made by post. It suffices I think at this stage to refer to *Henthorn v Fraser* [1892] 2 Ch 27. In the present case, as I read a passage in the judgment below . . ., Templeman J concluded that the parties here contemplated that the postal service might be used to communicate acceptance of the offer (by exercise of the option); and I agree with that.

But that is not and cannot be the end of the matter. In any case, before one can find that the basic principle of the need for communication of acceptance to the offeror is displaced by this artificial concept of communication by the act of posting, it is necessary that the offer is in its terms consistent with such displacement and not one which by its terms points rather in the direction of actual communication . . .

The relevant language here is, 'The said option shall be exercisable by notice in writing to the intending vendor . . .', a very common phrase in an option agreement. There is, of course, nothing in that phrase to suggest that the notification to the defendant could not be made by post. But the requirement of 'notice . . . to', in my judgment, is language which should be taken expressly to assert the ordinary situation in law that acceptance requires to be communicated or notified to the offeror, and is inconsistent with the theory that acceptance can be constituted by the act of posting, referred to by *Anson's Law of Contract* . . . as 'acceptance *without notification*'.

It is of course true that the instrument could have been differently worded. An option to purchase within a period given for value has the characteristic of an offer that cannot be withdrawn. The instrument might have said 'The offer constituted by this option may be accepted in writing within six months': in which case no doubt the posting would have sufficed to form the contract. But that language was not used, and, as indicated, in my judgment, the language used prevents that legal outcome . . .

LAWTON LJ: Does the [postal] rule apply in *all* cases where one party makes an offer which both he and the person with whom he was dealing must have expected the post to be used as a means of accepting it? In my judgment, it does not. First, it does not apply when the express terms of the offer specify that the acceptance must reach the offeror. The public nowadays are familiar with this exception to the general rule through their handling of football pool coupons. Secondly, it probably does not operate if its application would produce manifest inconvenience and absurdity. This is the opinion set out in Cheshire and Fifoot, *Law of Contract* . . . It was the opinion of Lord Bramwell as is seen by his judgment in *British & American Telegraph Co. v Colson* (1871) LR 6 Exch 108, and his opinion is worthy of consideration even though the decision in that case was overruled by this court in *Household Fire and Carriage Accident Insurance Co. v Grant* (1879) 4 Ex D 216. The illustrations of inconvenience and absurdity which Lord Bramwell gave are as apt today as they were then. Is a stockbroker who is holding shares to the orders of his client liable in damages because he did not sell in a falling market in accordance with the instructions in a letter which was posted but never received? Before the passing of the Law Reform (Miscellaneous Provisions) Act 1970 (which abolished actions for breach of promise of marriage), would a young soldier ordered overseas have been bound in contract to marry a girl to whom he had proposed by letter, asking her to let him have an answer before he left and she had replied affirmatively in good time but the letter had never reached him? In my judgment, the factors of inconvenience and absurdity are but illustrations of a wider principle, namely, that the rule does not apply if, having regard to all the circumstances, including the nature of the subject matter under consideration, the negotiating parties cannot have intended that there should be a binding agreement until the party accepting an offer or exercising an option had in fact communicated the acceptance or exercise to the other. In my judgment, when this principle is applied to the facts of this case it becomes clear that the parties cannot have intended that the posting of a letter should constitute the exercise of the option.

1. What form of wording will suffice to oust the postal rule and ensure that any acceptance must be actually communicated? Will 'let me know your answer' suffice?

2. For Lawton LJ, the postal rule will not apply where its application 'would produce manifest inconvenience and absurdity'. What situations would this cover and are the examples he gives appropriate?

NOTE The Contracts (Rights of Third Parties) Act 1999, s. 2(2)(b), requires actual receipt and expressly ousts the postal rule for third party assent to a term that will operate to prevent the parties from cancelling or varying that contract term without that third party's consent.

2.4.4.4 May a postal acceptance be retracted or overtaken before it reaches the offeror?

Countess of Dunmore v Alexander
(1830) 9 S 190 (Court of Session)

The Countess wrote to Lady Agnew asking for a reference for Alexander. Lady Agnew replied. On 5 November, the Countess wrote to Lady Agnew, asking her to engage Alexander. This was forwarded to Alexander. Meanwhile, on 6 November, the Countess wrote another letter to Lady Agnew, stating that she no longer needed Alexander. The second letter was forwarded to Alexander by express and both were delivered at the same moment to Alexander. Alexander argued that there was a concluded contract.

Held: There was no concluded contract.

LORD BALGRAY: The admission that the two letters were simultaneously received puts an end to the case. Had the one arrived in the morning and the other in the evening of the same day, it would have been different. Lady Dunmore conveys a request to Lady Agnew to engage Alexander, which request she recalls by a subsequent letter, that arrives in time to be forwarded to Alexander as soon as the first. This, therefore, is just the same as if a man had put an order into the Post Office, desiring his agent to buy stock for him. He afterwards changes his mind, but cannot recover his letter from the Post Office. He therefore writes a second letter countermanding the first. They both arrive together, and the result is, that no purchase can be made to bind the principal.

LORD CRAIGIE [dissenting]: Every letter between the principals, relative to an offer or an acceptance respectively was, as soon as it reached Lady Agnew, the same as delivered for behoof of the party on whose account it was written. I hold, therefore, that when Lady Dunmore's letter reached Lady Agnew, the contract of hiring Alexander was complete,—the offer on the part of Alexander being met by an intimated acceptance on the part of the Countess. No subsequent letter from the Countess to Lady Agnew could annul what had passed by the mere circumstance of its being delivered, at the same time with the first, into the hands of Alexander. I do not think the servant could have retracted after the first letter reached Lady Agnew; and if she was bound, it seems clear that the Countess could not be free.

NOTES

1. The case is of questionable authority in support of the proposition that it is possible to overtake a postal acceptance because the court appears to treat the letter from the Countess on 5 November as an offer and the letter of 6 November as a valid revocation of that offer.

2. Allowing a letter of acceptance to be withdrawn once posted is contrary to the postal 'rule' and would give the offeree the best of both worlds, i.e. on posting, he could decide whether to hold the offeror to the contract or to recall his acceptance. However, Evans (1966) 15 ICLQ 553 argued in favour of allowing a revocation to overtake a postal acceptance, and it is clear that Bramwell LJ in *Household Fire* (*page 47, 2.4.4.2*) supported this position. See also Hudson (1966) 82 LQR 169, for whom there is no disadvantage to the offeror, since the offeror will act on the first communication that he receives.

2.4.4.5 Instantaneous methods of communicating and non-instantaneous messages

2.4.4.5.1 *Are acceptances by telephone, telex, and fax subject to the postal rule?*

Where an acceptance is instantaneous, receipt is required and the postal rule does not apply. Defining exactly what is meant by 'receipt' is problematic.

Entores Ltd v Miles Far East Corporation
[1955] 2 QB 327 (CA)

An English company received a telex offer from a Dutch company and made a counter-offer, which the Dutch company accepted by telex. The English company needed to establish that the contract was made within the English jurisdiction.

Held: Since the acceptance was received in England, the contract was made within the jurisdiction.

DENNING LJ: Let me first consider a case where two people make a contract by word of mouth in the presence of one another. Suppose, for instance, that I shout an offer to a man across a river or a courtyard but I do not hear his reply because it is drowned by an aircraft flying overhead. There is no contract at that moment. If he wishes to make a contract, he must wait till the aircraft is gone and then shout back his acceptance so that I can hear what he says. Not until I have his answer am I bound . . .

Now take a case where two people make a contract by telephone. Suppose, for instance, that I make an offer to a man by telephone and, in the middle of his reply, the line goes 'dead' so that I do not hear his words of acceptance. There is no contract at that moment. The other man may not know the precise moment when the line failed. But he will know that the telephone conversation was abruptly broken off: because people usually say something to signify the end of the conversation. If he wishes to make a contract, he must therefore get through again so as to make sure that I heard. Suppose next, that the line does not go dead, but it is nevertheless so indistinct that I do not catch what he says and I ask him to repeat it. He then repeats it and I hear his acceptance. The contract is made, not on the first time when I do not hear, but only the second time when I do hear. If he does not repeat it, there is no contract. The contract is only complete when I have his answer accepting the offer.

Lastly, take the Telex. Suppose a clerk in a London office taps out on the teleprinter an offer which is immediately recorded on a teleprinter in a Manchester office, and a clerk at that end taps out an acceptance. If the line goes dead in the middle of the sentence of acceptance, the teleprinter motor will stop. There is then obviously no contract. The clerk at Manchester must get through again and send his complete sentence. But it may happen that the line does not go dead, yet the message does not get through to London. Thus the clerk at Manchester may tap out his message of acceptance and it will not be recorded in London because the ink at the London end fails, or something of that kind. In that case, the Manchester clerk will not know of the failure but the London clerk will know of it and will immediately send back a message 'not receiving'. Then, when the fault is rectified, the Manchester clerk will repeat his message. Only then is there a contract. If he does not repeat it, there is no contract. It is not until his message is received that the contract is complete.

In all the instances I have taken so far, the man who sends the message of acceptance knows that it has not been received or he has reason to know it. So he must repeat it. But suppose that he does not know that his message did not get home. He thinks it has. This may happen if the listener on the telephone does not catch the words of acceptance, but nevertheless does not trouble to ask for them to be repeated: or if the ink on the teleprinter fails at the receiving end, but the clerk does not ask for the message to be repeated: so that the man who sends an acceptance reasonably believes that his message has been received. The offeror in such circumstances is clearly bound, because he will be estopped from saying that he did not receive the message of acceptance. It is his own fault that he did not get it. But if there should be a case where the offeror without any fault on his part does not receive the message of acceptance—yet the sender of it reasonably believes it has got home when it has not—then I think there is no contract.

My conclusion is that the rule about instantaneous communications between the parties is different from the rule about the post. The contract is only complete when the acceptance is received by the offeror: and the contract is made at the place where the acceptance is received.

NOTE *JSC Zestafoni G Nikoladze Ferroalloy Plant v Ronly Holdings Ltd* [2004] EWHC 245 (Comm), [2004] 2 Lloyd's Rep 335, confirms that, by analogy with *Entores v Miles Far East Corporation* (telex machine), the same principle applies in the case of an acceptance sent by facsimile (fax), so that the contract was made in the jurisdiction where the fax acceptance was received. Colman J noted, at [75]:

A fax is a form of instantaneous communication: if a message has not been received, the sender is informed by his machine. Most machines also indicate to the sender whether the message has been effectively, as distinct from only partly, received.

However, it does not necessarily follow that the fax message received will be legible.

2.4.4.5.2 *Is an acceptance sent by an instantaneous method actually 'received' (communicated) when it is received by the machine or does it have to be read by the intended recipient?*

Where the message is sent to a business, this depends on whether it is sent within or outside office hours, since the recipient business can be expected to supervise its machines during office hours.

In *Tenax Steamship Co. Ltd v The Brimnes (Owners), The Brimnes* [1975] QB 929, a telex withdrawal had appeared on the charterers' telex machine between 17:30 and 18:00 (held to be within office hours) on 2 April, but it was not noted until the following day. The Court of Appeal held that the withdrawal was received when it appeared on the machine rather than when it was actually read the following day. The owners, having sent their message within office hours, had done all that they could be expected to do to transmit their message, and they would not know that it was not actually read until the following day. Megaw LJ said, at 966H–967A:

I think that the principle which is relevant is this: if a notice arrives at the address of the person to be notified, at such a time and by such a means of communication that it would in the normal course of business come to the attention of that person on its arrival, that person cannot rely on some failure of himself or his servants to act in a normal businesslike manner in respect of taking cognisance of the communication so as to postpone the effective time of the notice until some later time when it in fact came to his attention.

By analogy, if an acceptance were sent during office hours, it would be received when it was received by the telex or fax machine. There is support for this view in the judgment of Lord Fraser in *Brinkibon Ltd v Stahag Stahl GmbH* [1983] 2 AC 34 (HL) (see below).

It appears that the position will be different if the communication is sent *outside office hours*. Such a communication will inevitably be 'non-instantaneous'.

Brinkibon Ltd v Stahag Stahl GmbH
[1983] 2 AC 34 (HL)

A telex acceptance was sent from London to Vienna. The English company could commence a claim for breach of contract against the Austrian company only if the contract was made in England.

Held: Approving *Entores v Miles Far East*, the contract in question had been concluded where the telex acceptance had been received: in Vienna.

LORD FRASER: I have reached the opinion that, on balance, an acceptance sent by telex directly from the acceptor's office to the offeror's office should be treated as if it were an instantaneous communication between principals, like a telephone conversation. One reason is that the decision to that effect in *Entores v Miles Far East Corporation* [1955] 2 QB 327 seems to have worked without leading to serious difficulty or complaint from the business community. Secondly, once the message has been received on the offeror's telex machine, it is not unreasonable to treat it as delivered to the principal offeror, because it is his responsibility to arrange for prompt handling of messages within his own office. Thirdly, a party (the acceptor) who tries to send a message by telex can generally tell if his message has not been received on the other party's (the offeror's) machine, whereas the offeror, of course, will not know if an unsuccessful attempt has been made to send an acceptance to him. It is therefore convenient that the acceptor, being in the better position, should have the responsibility of ensuring that his message is received. For these reasons I think it is right that in the ordinary simple case, such as I take this to be, the general rule and not the postal rule should apply. But I agree with both my noble and learned friends that the general rule will not cover all the many variations that may occur with telex messages.

LORD WILBERFORCE [*obiter*]: Since 1955 the use of telex communication has been greatly expanded, and there are many variants on it. The senders and recipients may not be the principals to the contemplated contract. They may be servants or agents with limited authority. The message may not reach, or be intended to reach, the designated recipient immediately: messages may be sent out of office hours, or at night, with the intention, or upon the assumption, that they will be read at a later time. There may be some error or default at the recipient's end which prevents receipt at the time contemplated and believed in by the sender. The message may have been sent and/or received through machines operated by third persons. And many other variations may occur. No universal rule can cover all such cases: they must be resolved by reference to the intentions of the parties, by sound business practice and in some cases by a judgment where the risks should lie . . .

NOTE Lord Brandon expressed agreement with Lord Wilberforce on this point, and Lord Wilberforce's *obiter* comment was relied on by Gatehouse J in the following case.

Mondial Shipping and Chartering BV v Astarte Shipping Ltd
[1995] CLC 1011

The issue in the case was whether a telex notice of intention to withdraw the vessel for non-payment of hire, sent by the shipowners to the charterers late on the evening of

Friday 2 December 1994 (at 23:41 hours), was received instantaneously or at the start of business on the next working day. This was important on the facts because payment of the hire could lawfully have been made at any time before midnight on Friday 2 December and, if the notice took effect at 23:41 on Friday 2 December, the charterers would not have been in default at the time that the notice was served. On the other hand, the notice would have been valid if it had not taken effect until the next working day, Monday 5 December.

Held: The notice was communicated at the start of business on the next working day—namely, Monday 5 December. Accordingly, it was not served before the charterers were in breach of the charterparty, which occurred at midnight on the Friday night. (However, the notice was nevertheless invalid because it did not indicate the action required of the charterers.)

GATEHOUSE J: It was not in dispute in the present case that a notice under cl. 27 is not effective until it is actually received by the charterer—the 'postal rule' referable to the conclusion of a contract has no application. The crucial question is what is meant by 'received'? The charterers contended that this must be the moment when it was printed out on their telex machine; that this occurred before the time when they would be in default under cl. 7, and accordingly the notice was premature and invalid for that reason, apart from its want of proper form. The owners contended that the moment of receipt was when the telex message was, or must be taken to have been, first read by a responsible member of the charterers' organisation, i.e., at or shortly after 9 am on Monday 5 December; that the charterers were by then in default of their duty of punctual payment: accordingly the notice was not then premature . . .

There is no authority on this. The question has not arisen in any reported decision. In *The Afovos* [*Afovos Shipping Co. SA v R. Pagnan and F. Illi, The Afovos* [1983] 1 Lloyd's Rep 335] and other similar cases of instantaneous transmission the message was sent during ordinary business hours so the time of sending the notice by the owners and its receipt by the charterers was identical. It is therefore not significant that various judges have referred to the time when the notice was 'sent', or 'issued' . . .

What matters is not when the notice is given/sent/despatched/issued by the owners but when its content reaches the mind of the charterer. If the telex is sent in ordinary business hours, the time of receipt is the same as the time of despatch because it is not open to the charterer to contend that it did not in fact then come to his attention (see *The Brimnes* per Brandon J [1973] 1 WLR 386 at p. 406, and per the Court of Appeal [1975] QB 929).

The problem has, of course, been referred to. See the well-known passage in the speech of Lord Wilberforce in *Brinkibon Ltd v Stahag Stahl and Stahlwarenhandelsgesellschaft mbH* [1983] 2 AC 34 at p. 42. [Gatehouse J went on to consider this *obiter* statement (*page 55*, earlier in this section).] Brandon J also referred, in passing, to an out-of-hours telex in *The Brimnes* . . .

The charterers in order to found their contention that the telex message was premature, are in fact contending for a universal rule for telex communications which, they say, has the commercial advantage of certainty. But I propose to follow Lord Wilberforce's words and resolve this issue by reference to the particular circumstances. His Lordship's words, . . . were spoken with reference to where a contract is to be regarded as having been concluded: hence, as I think, his reference to the intentions of the parties and in some cases, where the risks should lie (both the cases cited were concerned with the risks which arise from a postal acceptance). A notice such as the one with which I am concerned is clearly of a quite different type and does not involve any consideration of the mutual intentions of contracting parties or of where the risks should lie. But I think the tribunal were entitled to find . . . that a notice which arrives at 23.41 on a Friday night is not to be expected to be read before opening hours on the following Monday, and that was a conclusion of fact arrived at by the arbitrators as a matter of commercial common sense.

Why the telex was sent when it was is not explained. It may be that the owners or their agents, forgetful of the midnight rule (or, more likely, wholly ignorant of it) assumed that as the vessel had been delivered at 23.00 hours that was the moment each successive 15 days after which hire became overdue. If they had waited a further 20 minutes this problem would not have arisen.

In my judgment the tribunal were right to find that the notice under cl. 31 was not received by charterers until the opening of business on 5 December, and was not premature.

? QUESTIONS

1. This decision clarifies the position on communication where the message is obviously sent 'outside ordinary business hours'. However, this expression is not defined. In *The Brimnes* [1975] QB 929, a message received between 17:30 and 18:00 was considered to be received within 'ordinary business hours'. Blair J, in *Thomas v BPE Solicitors (a firm)* [2010] EWHC 306 (Ch), [2010] All ER (D) 306 (Feb), [90], considered that an email sent at 18:00 was sent within office hours given the context of the parties' negotiations. On the basis of the previous emails, the transaction could have been completed that evening. In fact, the recipient had gone home at 17:45 on a Friday evening in late August and the office did not reopen until the following Tuesday because of the bank holiday. It is also possible to imagine a situation arising in which a message is sent within the communicator's business hours, but outside the recipient's official business hours. Blair J returned to the issue in *Lehman Brothers International (Europe) (In administration) v Exxonmobil Financial Services BV* [2016] EWHC 2699 (Comm), [2017] 2 All ER (Comm) 959 in relation to the meaning of 'close of business' in para. 14(b) of standard form Global Master Repurchase Agreement (version 2000) (GMRA 2000). The issue is discussed in *Poole's Textbook on Contract Law*, page 68, 2.4.5.3.1.

Do expressions such as 'ordinary business hours' or 'close of business' really help?

2. Would it be preferable to adopt a clear and certain definition of what will constitute receipt? The PICC contain a definition of 'receipt' for non-oral communications, such as fax, telex, or computer, as occurring when there is delivery at the offeror's place of business or mailing address (Art. 1.10(3)). See also Art. 1:303 PECL, which also states that electronic mail 'or other individual communication' is received when it can be accessed by the addressee (Art. 10(4) (c)). In *Pickfords Ltd v Celestica Ltd* [2003] EWCA Civ 1741, Arden LJ considered that where the communication was intended for an organization, it would be sufficient if notice was received by the organization, as opposed to an individual employee.

3. When are messages left on telephone answering machines communicated? See the arguments of Coote (1971) 4 New Zealand UL Rev 331.

2.4.4.6 Does the postal rule apply to acceptance messages sent by electronic mail?

For an in-depth discussion, see *Poole's Textbook on Contract Law*, 2.4.5.2. It is advisable to avoid the postal rule expressly by requiring actual receipt. In *Thomas v BPE Solicitors (a firm)* [2010] EWHC 306 (Ch), [2010] All ER (D) 306 (Feb), [86], in *obiter* comments, Blair J agreed, considering that where contracts are made by exchange of email, the receipt rule applies (by analogy with the telex case law and *Entores v Miles Far East Corporation* [1955] 2 QB 327). Responsibility for getting the message through to its destination should lie with the communicator.

There is further support for the receipt rule High Court of Singapore decision in *Chwee Kin Keong v Digilandmall.com Pte Ltd* [2005] 1 SLR(R) 502.

V. K. RAJAH JC: 97 Different rules may apply to e-mail transactions and worldwide web transactions. When considering the appropriate rule to apply, it stands to reason that as between sender and receiver, the party who selects the means of communication should bear the consequences of any unexpected events. An e-mail, while bearing some similarity to a postal communication, is in some aspects fundamentally different. Furthermore, unlike a fax or a telephone call, it is not instantaneous. E-mails are processed through servers, routers and Internet service providers. Different protocols may result in messages arriving in an incomprehensible form. Arrival can also be immaterial unless a recipient accesses the e-mail, but in this respect e-mail does not really differ from mail that has to be opened. Certain Internet service providers provide the technology to inform a sender that a message has not been properly routed. Others do not.

98 Once an offer is sent over the Internet, the sender loses control over the route and delivery time of the message. In that sense, it is akin to ordinary posting. Notwithstanding some real differences with posting, it could be argued cogently that the postal rule should apply to e-mail acceptances; in other words, that the acceptance is made the instant the offer is sent . . . acceptance would be effective the moment the offer enters that node of the network outside the control of the originator. There are, however, other sound reasons to argue against such a rule in favour of the recipient rule. It should be noted that while the common law jurisdictions continue to wrestle over this vexed issue, most civil law jurisdictions lean towards the recipient rule. In support of the latter it might be argued that unlike a posting, e-mail communication takes place in a relatively short time frame. The recipient rule is therefore more convenient and relevant in the context of both instantaneous or near instantaneous communications. Notwithstanding occasional failure, most e-mails arrive sooner rather than later.

99 . . . Like the somewhat arbitrary selection of the postal rule for ordinary mail, in the ultimate analysis, a default rule should be implemented for certainty, while accepting that such a rule should be applied flexibly to minimise unjustness. In these proceedings, it appears that the purchases made by the sixth plaintiff were not accompanied by a corresponding receipt of acceptances, as his e-mail inbox was full. Notwithstanding, the defendant does not take issue with this as the sixth plaintiff's orders were received and the appropriate automated responses generated. In light of this, the parties did not address me on the issue of when the contract was formed, though this appears to be a relevant issue depending on which rule is adopted. In the absence of proper and full arguments on the issue of which rule is to be preferred, I do not think it is appropriate for me to give any definitive views in these proceedings on this very important issue . . .

100 . . . The Vienna Sales Convention ('the Convention') applies in Singapore . . . Article 24 of the Convention states:

> For the purposes of this Part of the Convention, an offer, declaration of acceptance or any other indication of intention 'reaches' the addressee when it is made orally to him or delivered by any other means to him personally, to his place of business or mailing address or, if he does not have a place of business or mailing address, to his habitual residence.

It appears that in Convention transactions, the receipt rule applies unless there is a contrary intention. Offer and acceptances have to 'reach' an intended recipient to be effective. It can be persuasively argued that e-mails involving transactions embraced by the Convention are only effective on reaching the recipient. If this rule applies to international sales, is it sensible to have a different rule for domestic sales?

101 The applicable rules in relation to transactions over the worldwide web appear to be clearer and less controversial. Transactions over websites are almost invariably instantaneous and/or interactive. The sender will usually receive a prompt response. The recipient rule appears to be the logical default rule. Application of such a rule may however result in contracts being formed outside the jurisdiction if

not properly drafted. Web merchants ought to ensure that they either contract out of the receipt rule or expressly insert salient terms within the contract to deal with issues such as a choice of law, jurisdiction and other essential terms relating to the passing of risk and payment. Failure to do so could also result in calamitous repercussions. Merchants may find their contracts formed in foreign jurisdictions and therefore subject to foreign laws.

102 Inevitably mistakes will occur in the course of electronic transmissions. This can result from human interphasing, machine error or a combination of such factors. Examples of such mistakes would include (a) human error (b) programming of software errors and (c) transmission problems in the communication systems. Computer glitches can cause transmission failures, garbled information or even change the nature of the information transmitted. This case is a paradigm example of an error on the human side. Such errors can be magnified almost instantaneously and may be harder to detect than if made in a face to face transaction or through physical document exchanges. Who bears the risk of such mistakes? It is axiomatic that normal contractual principles apply but the contractual permutations will obviously be sometimes more complex and spread over a greater magnitude of transactions. The financial consequences could be considerable. The court has to be astute and adopt a pragmatic and judicious stance in resolving such issues.

103 The amalgam of factors a court will have to consider in risk allocation ought to include:

(a) the need to observe the principle of upholding rather than destroying contracts,

(b) the need to facilitate the transacting of electronic commerce, and

(c) the need to reach commercially sensible solutions while respecting traditional principles applicable to instances of genuine error or mistake.

It is essential that the law be perceived as embodying rationality and fairness while respecting the commercial imperative of certainty.

In Singapore, if the receipt solution is adopted, it may also be helpful to define what will constitute 'receipt' for this purpose. This might be when the recipient is able to access the message—by analogy with the position under reg. 11(2)(a) of the Electronic Commerce Regulations 2002.

NOTES

1. What suffices for receipt is also determined by relevant contract terms which make clear the parties' expectations in the circumstances. In *Greenclose Ltd v National Westminster Bank plc* [2014] EWHC 1156 (Ch), [2014] 2 Lloyd's Rep 169, [2014] 1 CLC 562, the issue was whether the defendant bank had validly exercised its contractual right to give notice to extend the term of a five-year interest rate collar (or hedging) transaction. This notice needed to be given to Greenclose by 11 a.m. on 30 December 2011. The bank alleged that it had given this notice by sending an email at 9.45 a.m. on that date. However, the email had not been opened or seen until after the deadline had passed. Andrews J held the notice ineffective because email was not a permissible means of giving the notice in accordance with the contractual prescribed methods. Nevertheless, in *obiter* statements, the judge considered that even if email had been a permitted method, the notice would have been invalid on the

facts because notice had to be given to Greenclose, i.e. actual communication was required by the terms of the contract. *The Brimnes* was distinguished on the facts and the specific contractual terms.

ANDREWS J: 138 An e-mail is not subject to the postal acceptance rule. It is a form of near-instantaneous communication. I do not accept that, on an objective analysis, the parties to this contract can be taken to have agreed at the time of entry into the collar, that in five years' time, sending an e-mail to the computer of someone who is not a named contact in the Schedule to the Master Agreement, and who would not be expecting notice to be given in that way, would suffice in and of itself to bring to Greenclose's attention the exercise of the bank's unilateral right to extend the term by a further two years . . . There would have to be actual communication . . . It is irrelevant that advance warning may have been given to the recipient to expect some form of written notice that morning . . .

140 The burden on the sender is not particularly onerous. Modern technology easily enables the sender to find out when the e-mail has been opened by setting up the computer to

generate the appropriate message. However, as I have said, [the sender] did not ask for a 'read receipt' . . .

141 There was nothing unbusiness-like about an 'out of office' auto reply being set up on Mr Leach's [the recipient's] computer in these circumstances; quite the reverse. The bank knew full well that it was the Christmas holiday period and having dealt with Greenclose for five years, it would have been aware that it closed the office between Christmas and New Year . . .

Andrews J was therefore clear that in these circumstances the onus was on the communicator to get their message through.

2. Contracts made by exchange of email messages are expressly excluded from the operation of the Electronic Commerce (EC Directive) Regulations 2002, regs. 9(4) and 11(3), which apply to Internet contracts made via websites.

2.5 Revocation of an offer

An offer can be revoked at any time before it is accepted.

2.5.1 Communication of the revocation

A revocation of an offer must be received by the offeree in order to take effect. The postal rule applies only to acceptances and not to revocations.

Henthorn v Fraser
[1892] 2 Ch 27 (CA)

A withdrawal of an offer had been posted at midday, but it was not received until 5 p.m. In the meantime, an acceptance had been posted at 3.50 p.m.

Held: There was a binding contract at 3.50 p.m. on posting the acceptance.

LORD HERSCHELL: If the acceptance by the Plaintiff of the Defendants' offer is to be treated as complete at the time the letter containing it was posted, I can entertain no doubt that the society's attempted revocation of the offer was wholly ineffectual. I think that a person who has made an offer must be considered as continuously making it until he has brought to the knowledge of the person to whom it was made that it is withdrawn . . .

KAY LJ: Then what was the effect of the withdrawal by the letter posted between 12 and 1 the same day, and received in the evening? Did that take effect from the time of posting? It has never been held that this doctrine applies to a letter withdrawing the offer. Take the cases alluded to by Lord Bramwell in the *Household Fire and Carriage Accident Insurance Company v Grant* (1879) 4 ExD 216. A notice by a tenant to quit can have no operation till it comes to the actual knowledge of the person to whom it is addressed. An offer to sell is nothing until it is actually received. No doubt there is the seeming anomaly pointed out by Lord Bramwell that the same letter might contain an acceptance, and also such a notice or offer as to other property, and that when posted it would be effectual as to the acceptance, and not as to the notice or offer. But the anomaly, if it be one, arises from the different nature of the two communications. As to the acceptance, if it was contemplated that it might be sent by post, the acceptor . . ., has done all that he was bound to do by posting the letter, but this cannot be said as to the notice of withdrawal. That was not a contemplated proceeding. The person withdrawing was bound to bring his change of purpose to the knowledge of the said party, and as this was not done in this case till after the letter of acceptance was posted, I am of opinion that it was too late.

Byrne & Co. v Van Tienhoven & Co.
(1880) 5 CPD 344 (CP)

On 1 October, the defendants in Cardiff wrote to the claimants in New York offering to sell goods. The claimants received this offer letter on 11 October and accepted it by telegram on the same day. On 8 October, the defendants posted a revocation of their offer, which reached the claimants on 20 October. The claimants brought an action for non-delivery.

Held: A revocation of an offer is not effective until it is communicated to the offeree. The offer was therefore available for acceptance until 20 October. Since the postal rule applied to the telegram acceptance, a binding contract was entered into on 11 October when the acceptance telegram was sent.

LINDLEY J: It may be taken as now settled that where an offer is made and accepted by letters sent through the post, the contract is completed the moment the letter accepting the offer is posted: *Harris' Case* (1872) LR 7 Ch App 587; *Dunlop v Higgins* (1848) 1 HLC 381, even although it never reaches its destination. When, however, these authorities are looked at, it will be seen that they are based upon the principle that the writer of the offer has expressly or impliedly assented to treat an answer to him by a letter duly posted as a sufficient acceptance and notification to himself, or, in other words, he has made the post office his agent to receive the acceptance and notification of it. But this principle appears to me to be inapplicable to the case of the withdrawal of an offer. In this particular case I can find no evidence of any authority in fact given by the plaintiffs to the defendants to notify a withdrawal of their offer by merely posting a letter; and there is no legal principle or decision which compels me to hold, contrary to the fact, that the letter of the 8th of October is to be treated as communicated to the plaintiff on that day or on any day before the 20th, when the letter reached them. But before that letter had reached the plaintiffs they had accepted the offer, both by telegram and by post; and they had themselves resold the tin plates at a profit. In my opinion the withdrawal by the defendants on the 8th of October of their offer of the 1st was inoperative; and a complete contract binding on both parties was entered into on the 11th of October, when the plaintiffs accepted the offer of the 1st, which they had no reason to suppose had been withdrawn. Before leaving this part of the case it may be as well to point out the extreme injustice and inconvenience which any other conclusion would produce. If the defendants' contention were to prevail no person who had received an offer by post and had accepted it would know his position until he had waited such a time as to be quite sure that a letter withdrawing the offer had not been posted before his acceptance of it. It appears to me that both legal principles, and practical convenience require that a person who has accepted an offer not known to him to have been revoked, shall be in a position safely to act upon the footing that the offer and acceptance constitute a contract binding on both parties.

Stevenson, Jacques & Co. v McLean
(1880) 5 QBD 346

The defendant had made an offer to sell iron at 40s. net cash per ton to the claimants and stated that he would hold the offer open until the following Monday. On the Monday, the defendant sold the iron and informed the claimants of this by a telegram sent at 1.25 p.m. Before this arrived (at 1.46 p.m.), the claimants sent an acceptance telegram to the defendant at 1.34 p.m. The claimants brought an action for non-delivery.

Held: Although the defendant was free to revoke his offer before the close of the day on Monday, any revocation would not have effect until it reached the claimants. Consequently, the defendant's offer was still open when the claimants accepted it at 1.34 p.m. (on sending the acceptance telegram).

The revocation need not be communicated by the offeror himself.

Dickinson v Dodds
(1876) 2 Ch D 463 (CA)

On Wednesday 10 June 1874, the defendant offered to sell his house to the claimant, stating that: 'This offer to be left over until Friday 9 am.' On the Thursday afternoon, the claimant was informed by Berry that the defendant had been offering or agreeing to sell the property to Allan. The claimant therefore went to the house where the defendant was staying and left a formal written acceptance there (the evidence was that the defendant did not receive this document). On the Friday, at 7 a.m., Berry, who was acting as the claimant's agent, found the defendant at the railway station, handed him a copy of the claimant's acceptance, and stated its contents. In fact, the defendant had sold the property to Allan on Thursday 11 June.

Held: The offer might be withdrawn at any time before acceptance, since there was no consideration for the promise to keep the offer open until 9 a.m. on the Friday. Had it, in fact, been withdrawn?

JAMES LJ: [I]t is said that the only mode in which Dodds could assert that freedom was by actually and distinctly saying to Dickinson, 'Now I withdraw my offer.' It appears to me that there is neither principle nor authority for the proposition that there must be an express and actual withdrawal of the offer, or what is called a retraction. It must, to constitute a contract, appear that the two minds were at one, at the same moment of time, that is, that there was an offer continuing up to the time of the acceptance. If there was not such a continuing offer, then the acceptance comes to nothing. Of course it may well be that the one man is bound in some way or other to let the other man know that his mind with regard to the offer has been changed; but in this case, beyond all question, the Plaintiff knew that Dodds was no longer minded to sell the property to him as plainly and clearly as if Dodds had told him in so many words, 'I withdraw the offer.'

. . . It is to my mind quite clear that before there was any attempt at acceptance by the Plaintiff, he was perfectly well aware that Dodds had changed his mind, and that he had in fact agreed to sell the property to Allan. It is impossible, therefore, to say there was ever that existence of the same mind between the two parties which is essential in point of law to the making of an agreement. I am of opinion, therefore, that the Plaintiff has failed to prove that there was any binding contract between Dodds and himself.

NOTES

1. Unless the promise to keep an offer open for a stated period is supported by consideration, the offeror is free to revoke the offer at any time before acceptance: *Routledge v Grant* (1828) 4 Bing 653, 130 ER 920. This may be harsh where the offeree has relied on this 'firm offer' promise. See the proposals of the Law Commission Working Paper No. 60, Firm Offers (1975).

2. Peel, *Treitel's The Law of Contract*, cites *Dickinson v Dodds* as authority for the proposition that there is sufficient communication if the offeree knows from 'any reliable source' that the offeror no longer intends to contract with him. What problems might exist in deciding who is a 'reliable source'?

3. Although this decision appears to suggest that it is not necessary to communicate a revocation, it is based on a subjective approach to contract formation and is now incorrect on this point.

4. In *Pickfords Ltd v Celestica Ltd* [2003] EWCA Civ 1741, [32], Arden LJ noted that '[t]he revocation of an offer must be communicated to the offeree, but where the offeree is an organisation, it is sufficient if the organisation receives notice of the withdrawal', as opposed to an individual employee.

2.5.2 Revocation of a unilateral offer

Since the acceptance in unilateral contracts is the complete performance of the act, if—to use the classical example of a unilateral contract quoted by Brett J in *Great Northern Railway Co. v Witham* (1873) LR 9 CP 16, 19—I offer you £100 if you will walk to York, I could revoke my offer at any time before you reached York.

It is now accepted that, in English law, the offer *may* contemplate that it is not possible to revoke once the offeree has started to perform.

Errington v Errington & Woods
[1952] 1 KB 290 (CA)

A father purchased a house, and promised his son and daughter-in-law that if they continued in occupation and paid all of the mortgage instalments for the house, he would transfer the house to them. They duly paid the instalments, but when the father died, he left the house to his widow who sought possession. The issue in the judgments is whether the couple were tenants at will or had a contractual licence to occupy.

Held: They were contractual licensees.

DENNING LJ: It is to be noted that the couple never bound themselves to pay the instalments to the building society; and I see no reason why any such obligation should be implied. It is clear law that the court is not to imply a term unless it is necessary; and I do not see that it is necessary here. Ample content is given to the whole arrangement by holding that the father promised that the house should belong to the couple as soon as they paid off the mortgage. The parties did not discuss what was to happen if the couple failed to pay the instalments to the building society, but I should have thought it clear that, if they did fail to pay the instalments, the father would not be bound to transfer the house to them. The father's promise was a unilateral contract—a promise of the house in return for their act of paying the instalments. It could not be revoked by him once the couple entered on performance of the act, but it would cease to bind him if they left it incomplete and unperformed, which they have not done. If that was the position during the father's lifetime, so it must be after his death. If the daughter-in-law continues to pay all the building society instalments, the couple will be entitled to have the property transferred to them as soon as the mortgage is paid off; but if she does not do so, then the building society will claim the instalments from the father's estate and the estate will have to pay them. I cannot think that in those circumstances the estate would be bound to transfer the house to them, any more than the father himself would have been.

. . . [I]t is clear that the father expressly promised the couple that the property should belong to them as soon as the mortgage was paid, and impliedly promised that so long as they paid the instalments to the building society they should be allowed to remain in possession. They were not purchasers because they never bound themselves to pay the instalments, but nevertheless they were in a position analogous to purchasers. They have acted on the promise, and neither the father nor his widow, his successor in title, can eject them in disregard of it . . .

NOTES

1. What do you think is the basis of the decision in *Errington*? Are the words 'acted on the promise' significant? (See the discussion of promissory estoppel at *pages 122–144, 3.2*.) What difficulties would exist in using promissory estoppel as the basis of this principle?

2. McGovney (1914) 27 Harv L Rev 644, 659, suggested that there are two separate offers in the unilateral offeror's statement—namely, an express offer to pay on performance of the act, and an implied offer not to revoke once the offeree starts to perform.

This implied offer is accepted by beginning performance, and if the offeror were to attempt to revoke, he would be liable for breach of this promise. The problem with this analysis is that it would not prevent revocation, but would mean only that damages would be payable for breach of the implied offer not to revoke. *Errington*, however, appears to be based on the view that revocation is not possible once the offeree has started to perform.

3. In *Soulsbury v Soulsbury* [2007] EWCA Civ 969, [2008] 2 WLR 834, there was an agreement that if the ex-wife did not seek to enforce the county court order for maintenance, the ex-husband would leave her £100,000 on his death. Longmore LJ (with whose judgment Ward and Smith LJJ agreed) considered this to be a unilateral offer.

LONGMORE LJ: 48 . . . [A]ny enforcement of the order of the court would not have been a breach of contract. It would just mean that she would not be entitled to the £100,000 which her husband had promised to leave her by will.

49 This is a classic unilateral contract of the *Carlill v Carbolic Smoke Ball Co* [1893] 1 QB 256 or the 'walk to York' kind. Once the promisee acts on the promise by inhaling the smoke ball, by starting the walk to York or (as here) by not suing for the maintenance to which she was entitled, the promisor cannot revoke or withdraw his offer. But there is no obligation on the promisee to continue to inhale, to walk the whole way to York or to refrain from suing. It is just that if she inhales no more, gives up the walk to York or does sue for her maintenance, she is not entitled to claim the promised sum.

50 . . . [Longmore LJ considered the facts to be analogous to *Errington v Errington* and continued:] The present case is stronger than *Errington's* case since on Mr Soulsbury's death, Mrs Soulsbury had completed all possible performance of the act required for enforcement of Mr Soulsbury's promise.

4. The other suggested explanation (*Pollock on Contract*) is based on the fact that, in a unilateral contract, performance of the act requested is both the acceptance and the consideration. Acceptance is stated to occur when the offeree starts to perform so that revocation is no longer possible, but the consideration is the completion of the act and, until that time, no reward is payable. This is somewhat difficult to justify since, at the point of starting to perform, the offeree would also be bound to perform, which defeats the very nature of the unilateral contract. Lord Denning may well have supported this approach (i.e. acceptance on starting to perform). See his comments in *Ward v Byham* [1956] 1 WLR 496 (*page 98, 3.1.3.5*). However, in his judgment in *Errington*, Lord Denning very clearly states that the couple were not under any obligation.

The *Pollock* explanation (acceptance on starting to perform) has also received recent support in *obiter* comments in *Schweppe v Harper* [2008] EWCA Civ 442, [2008] BPIR 1090 (CA), in which there was a proposal by the defendant to pay the claimant a fee

of £50,000 if the claimant secured an annulment of the defendant's bankruptcy and secured finance to rescue properties held by the trustee in bankruptcy. The claimant had been acting to secure this aim when the defendant instructed him to stop. On appeal, the claimant alleged that the judge had been wrong to conclude that the defendant had been free to revoke the offer at any time. However, the majority of the Court of Appeal (Waller LJ dissenting) considered that it was not necessary to consider whether this was a unilateral offer that was capable of being revoked before acceptance, because the terms of the 'offer' were too uncertain. Accordingly, only Waller LJ (dissenting) considered this question. He appeared to equate 'starting performance' with 'part performance' and treated it as acceptance that precluded withdrawal of the unilateral offer. Waller LJ went further on the facts, considering (at [48]) the part performance to give rise to 'a contract' entitling the claimant to the fee.

WALLER LJ: 29 . . . . I propose first to consider whether on the basis that Mr Schweppe did not promise to do anything there came into existence what is called a unilateral contract.

30. If Mr Schweppe was not promising to do anything then his entitlement to a fee would depend on whether there was an offer by Mr Harper to pay a fee if Mr Schweppe performed some task, and either he had performed that task or, if not, [and this does not appear to have been considered as a possibility by the judge] whether he had by conduct performed the task to such an extent that a contract came into existence precluding Mr Harper from withdrawing the offer.

31. That requires to be considered first, precisely for what task Mr Harper was offering to pay £50,000 to Mr Schweppe and second, since it is common ground that Mr Schweppe did not complete performance following termination of his instructions, whether a contract ever came into being as a result of part performance, so as to preclude Mr Harper being entitled to withdraw the offer other than for breach or abandonment of the task by Mr Schweppe . . .

36. It would not, I think, be disputed that if Mr Schweppe achieved the annulment he would be entitled to his fee. I would furthermore add that I do not think it would be disputed that if it was a condition precedent that Mr Schweppe obtain third party finance, if he did so he would be entitled to his fee. Thus an offer was being made which was capable of acceptance.

37. However that leaves the critical question as to whether whatever offer was being made for whatever task it could be withdrawn at any time prior to completion of the task, i.e. whether there came into existence prior to completion of any task a unilateral contract . . .

[Waller LJ considered relevant paragraphs of *Chitty on Contracts*, 29th edn, including para. 2–077, supporting the *Pollock* approach that there is acceptance when the offeree has 'made an unequivocal beginning on the requested performance'.]

43. The real point which seems to me to arise is whether the parties would have intended that Mr Harper would have

a '*locus poenitentiae*', i.e. a right to withdraw his offer at any time, even if Mr Schweppe had performed much work towards achieving completion of the task or tasks. I say that is 'the real point' because the arguments for there being intended to be such a right encompass other points which could be said to arise. In order for Mr Schweppe to achieve the annulment he needed the co-operation of Mr Harper. If Mr Schweppe negotiated third party finance it still had to be acceptable to Mr Harper. If it was contemplated that Mr Harper was to be completely free to turn down third party finance however good the offer obtained by Mr Schweppe and/or if it was contemplated that at any time right up to the moment of obtaining the annulment he could act in a way which prevented the annulment being obtained, there would be some force in the argument that he was at all times to be free to withdraw instructions and thus the offer.

44. If Mr Schweppe had not in fact done any work and thus not provided any consideration for the offer, I can accept that Mr Harper should be entitled to withdraw the offer, but what I cannot accept is that Mr Harper should be free to watch Mr Schweppe work once the offer has been made, take advantage of the work done, continue to seek an annulment and in those circumstances withdraw the offer . . .

45. The law surely should not countenance what would in effect be sharp practice unless driven to do so. If one takes the simple example, if A offers to pay £1000 if B walks from London to York, A should not be entitled to withdraw that offer once it is realised B is within very few miles of York. Furthermore, if as part of the offer A says 'once within 10 miles you will have to paint the mile stones in a colour acceptable to me', A should not be entitled to act unreasonably in relation to the selection of colours so as to make completion of the task impossible.

46. Where there is an offer to pay for the performance of a certain task, part performance can produce a contract under which that offer cannot be withdrawn. That should be the more so where there has not only been part performance but there is a real benefit being accepted by the offeror from that part performance. In such a case the court should be reluctant to find that the offeror has reserved a right to withdraw the offer after part performance.

47. It seems to me that in this case Mr Schweppe had performed much of the work required to achieve annulment by February 2004; he was within a very few miles of York. Even if in addition it was a condition that he should find finance, he had not been given an opportunity to provide finance, i.e. finance which, if acting reasonably, Mr Harper would have been bound to accept. In my view therefore even if there was no bilateral contract as at November 2003 there was thus by February 2004 a contract under which Mr Schweppe was entitled to continue do what he could to achieve the annulment of Mr Harper's bankruptcy and under which Mr Harper was bound to cooperate to enable that to be done.

48. If it were necessary to do so I would find that even if the obtaining of finance was a condition precedent to receipt of a fee that Mr Harper was not free to withdraw instructions and terminate what by then was a contract as at February 2004.

49. It follows, as it seems to me that Mr Harper's conduct in seeking to terminate at will was a repudiatory breach of contract.

5. The crucial question is how the courts will determine when an offeree 'enters on performance of the act'. Will it cover preparation to perform, e.g. when walking shoes are purchased in preparation for the walk to York?

There is *obiter* support for the decision in *Errington* in the Court of Appeal's decision in the next case, although the approach taken appears to support McGovney's analysis.

Daulia v Four Mill Bank Nominees Ltd
[1978] Ch 231 (CA)

The claimants wished to purchase property. They were told by the defendants that if they attended the next day at 10 a.m. with a banker's draft for the deposit, and a signed and engrossed contract, the defendants would exchange contracts. The claimants did this, but the defendants refused to exchange because they had found another purchaser at an increased price.

Held: The promise amounted to a unilateral offer, and since the claimants had fulfilled the conditions, they had accepted the offer.

GOFF LJ: Was there a concluded unilateral contract by the . . . defendants to enter into a contract for sale on the agreed terms? The concept of a unilateral or 'if contract' is somewhat anomalous, because it is clear that, at all events until the offeree starts to perform the condition, there is no contract at all, but merely an offer which the offeror is free to revoke.

Doubts have been expressed whether the offeror becomes bound so soon as the offeree starts to perform or satisfy the condition, or only when he has fully done so.

In my judgment, however, we are not concerned in this case with any such problem, because in my view the plaintiffs had fully performed or satisfied the condition when they presented themselves at the time and place appointed with a banker's draft for the deposit, and their part of the written contract for sale duly engrossed and signed and there tendered the same, which I understand to mean preferred it for exchange. Actual exchange, which never took place, would not in my view have been part of the satisfaction of the condition but something additional which was inherently necessary to be done by the plaintiffs to enable, not to bind, the . . . defendants to perform the unilateral contract.

Accordingly, in my judgment, the answer to the . . . question must be in the affirmative.

Even if my reasoning so far be wrong the conclusion in my view is still the same for the following reasons. Whilst I think the true view of a unilateral contract must in general be that the offeror is entitled to require full performance of the condition which he has imposed and short of that he is not bound, that must be subject to one important qualification, which stems from the fact that there must be an implied obligation on the part of the offeror not to prevent the condition becoming satisfied, which obligation it seems to me must arise as soon as the offeree starts to perform. Until then the offeror can revoke the whole thing, but once the offeree has embarked on performance it is too late for the offeror to revoke his offer.

Does the offer contemplate that the unilateral offeror should be free to revoke at any time before the complete performance of the act? If so, no restriction can be implied on the offeror's ability to revoke before that time.

Luxor (Eastbourne) Ltd v Cooper
[1941] AC 108 (HL)

The owners of two cinemas orally agreed with the agent that if he were to introduce someone who purchased these cinemas for at least £185,000, they would each pay him £5,000 *on the completion of the sale*. He produced purchasers who were willing to pay the price, but a sale did not take place. The agent brought an action claiming the £10,000 commission, or alternatively £10,000 in damages for breach of the implied term by which the owners undertook not to do anything to prevent him from earning his commission.

Held: Because the commission was payable only on completion, the nature of the offer contemplated that the offeror reserved the right to revoke at any time before completion. The House of Lords refused, in the circumstances of the case, to imply a term that the owners had undertaken not to prevent the sale.

LORD RUSSELL: A few preliminary observations occur to me. (1) Commission contracts are subject to no peculiar rules or principles of their own; the law which governs them is the law which governs all contracts and all questions of agency. (2) No general rule can be laid down by which the rights of the agent or the liability of the principal under commission contracts are to be determined. In each case these must depend upon the exact terms of the contract in question, and upon the true construction of those terms. And (3) contracts by which owners of property, desiring to dispose of it, put it in the hands of agents on commission terms, are not (in default of specific provisions) contracts of employment in the ordinary meaning of those words. No obligation is imposed on the agent to do anything. The contracts are merely promises binding on the principal to pay a sum of money upon the happening of a specified event, which involves the rendering of some service by the agent. There is no real analogy between such contracts, and contracts of employment by which one party binds himself to do certain work, and the other binds himself to pay remuneration for the doing of it.

I do not assent to the view, which I think was the view of the majority in the first *Trollope* case [1934] 2 KB 436, that a mere promise by a property owner to an agent to pay him a commission if he introduces a purchaser for the property at a specified price, or at a minimum price, ties the owner's hands, and compels him (as between himself and the agent) to bind himself contractually to sell to the agent's client who offers that price, with the result that if he refuses the offer he is liable to pay the agent a sum equal to or less than the amount of the commission either (a) on a quantum meruit or (b) as damages for breach of a term to be implied in the commission contract. As to the claim on a quantum meruit, I do not see how this can be justified in the face of the express provision for remuneration which the contract contains. This must necessarily exclude such a claim . . .

As to the claim for damages, this rests upon the implication of some provision in the commission contract, the exact terms of which were variously stated in the course of the argument, the object always being to bind the principal not to refuse to complete the sale to the client whom the agent has introduced.

I can find no safe ground on which to base the introduction of any such implied term. Implied terms, as we all know, can only be justified under the compulsion of some necessity. No such compulsion or necessity exists in the case under consideration. The agent is promised a commission if he introduces a purchaser at a specified or minimum price. The owner is desirous of selling. The chances are largely in favour of the deal going through, if a purchaser is introduced. The agent takes the risk in the hope of a substantial remuneration for comparatively small exertion. In the case of the plaintiff his contract was made on September 23, 1935; his client's offer was made on October 2, 1935. A sum of 10,000*l.* (the equivalent of the remuneration of a year's work by a Lord Chancellor) for work done within a period of eight or nine days is no mean reward, and is one well worth a risk. There is no lack of business efficacy in such a contract, even though the principal is free to refuse to sell to the agent's client.

? QUESTIONS

1. On the facts, the House of Lords refused to imply a promise not to revoke (prevent the sale). Does this support McGovney's analysis and indicate that the implication of a promise will turn on what is contemplated by the wording of the offer?

2. Is Lord Russell suggesting that if the reward is great compared to the actual effort needed to earn it, then the offeree must take the risk of the offer being withdrawn?

NOTE Waller LJ in *Schweppe v Harper* [2008] EWCA Civ 442, stated that a court 'should be reluctant' to find that the offer contemplates the ability to revoke at any time before acceptance in circumstances under which the offeree has gone beyond starting performance and there is 'part performance', with a 'real benefit being accepted by the offeror from that part performance'.

2.5.3 Communication of revocation of unilateral offers

A unilateral offer *to unascertained offerees* can be revoked through the same channel as the offer was made.

Shuey v United States
23 L Ed 697 (1875), 92 US 73 (US Supreme Court)

A proclamation dated 20 April 1865 had been published offering a reward of $25,000 for the apprehension of a particular criminal. On 24 November 1865, a notice revoking the offer was published. In 1866, the claimant discovered the criminal and informed the authorities. He was unaware that the offer of the reward had been revoked.

Held: He had not actually apprehended the criminal as required by the terms of the offer. Strong J also made the following statement on the revocation.

> STRONG J: The offer of a reward for the apprehension of Surratt was revoked on the twenty-fourth day of November, 1865; and notice of the revocation was published. It is not to be doubted that the offer was revocable at any time before it was accepted, and before anything had been done in reliance upon it. There was no contract until its terms were complied with. Like any other offer of a contract, it might, therefore, be withdrawn before rights had accrued under it; and it was withdrawn through the same channel in which it was made. The same notoriety was given to the revocation that was given to the offer; and the findings of fact do not show that any information was given by the claimant, or that he did anything to entitle him to the reward offered, until five months after the offer had been withdrawn. True, it is found that then, and at all times until the arrest was actually made, he was ignorant of the withdrawal; but that is an immaterial fact. The offer of the reward not having been made to him directly, but by means of a published Proclamation, he should have known that it could be revoked in the manner in which it was made.

? QUESTIONS

1. What do you think would be covered by the expression 'withdrawn through the same channel in which it was made'? If I were to advertise a reward in a particular national newspaper, but issue a notice of revocation in a different national newspaper, would this be revocation through the same channel?

2. Could this authority be distinguished where the offeree has taken steps to perform (i.e. has relied upon the offer) before the publication of the revocation? See Strong J's reference to 'before anything had been done in reliance upon' the offer. Does this amount to an acceptance of Pollock's analysis (*page 63, 2.5.2, note 4*)?

2.6 Reaching an (uncertain or incomplete) agreement: curable uncertainty?

Traditionally, the courts considered their function to be limited to interpreting the words that the parties used, so that if an agreement were uncertain, they would not construct a binding contract for the parties. Where the courts do intervene to provide certainty, they can do so only as a process of construction, starting with the words used by the parties (*Arnold v Britton* [2015] UKSC 36, [2015] 2 WLR 1593), where there is sufficient context to provide an objectively clear meaning for what must have been the parties' intentions: *Chartbrook Ltd v Persimmon Homes Ltd* [2009] UKHL 38, [2009] 2 WLR 267 (5.5.5). If the reasonable person could not interpret the words that the parties have used as having a clear meaning, even in the light of the background knowledge, the courts should not create agreement by filling the gaps.

2.6.1 Vagueness

Scammell & Nephew Ltd v Ouston
[1941] AC 251 (HL)

The respondents agreed to purchase a van on hire purchase terms over a two-year period. Before the hire purchase agreement could be entered into (and terms settled), the appellants refused to proceed. The respondents brought an action claiming damages for breach of contract, the appellants argued there was no contract because the agreement was void for uncertainty.

Held: There was no enforceable contract because the clause relating to the hire purchase terms was too vague and uncertain, and required further agreement to be reached between the parties.

VISCOUNT MAUGHAM: In order to constitute a valid contract the parties must so express themselves that their meaning can be determined with a reasonable degree of certainty. It is plain that unless this can be done it would be impossible to hold that the contracting parties had the same intention; in other words the consensus ad idem would be a matter of mere conjecture. This general rule, however, applies somewhat differently in different cases. In commercial documents connected with dealings in a trade with which the parties are perfectly familiar the court is very willing, if satisfied that the parties thought that they made a binding contract, to imply terms and in particular terms as to the method of carrying out the contract which it would be impossible to supply in other kinds of contract: see *Hile & Co. v Arcos, Ltd* . . .

. . . [W]hat do the words as to 'hire-purchase terms' mean in the present case? They may indicate that the hire-purchase agreement was to be granted by the appellants or on the other hand by some finance company acting in collaboration with the appellants; they may contemplate that the appellants were to receive by instalments a sum of 168*l*. spread over a period of two years upon delivering the new van and receiving the old car, or, on the other hand, that the appellants were to receive from a third party a lump sum of 168*l*. and that the third party, presumably a finance company, was to receive from the respondents a larger sum than 168*l*. to include interest and profit spread over a period of two years. Moreover, nothing is said (except as to the two years period) as to the terms of the hire-purchase agreement, for instance, as to the interest payable, and as to the rights of the letter whoever he may be in the event of default by the respondents in payment of the instalments at the due dates. As regards the last matters there was no evidence to suggest that there are any well known 'usual terms' in such a contract; and I think it is common knowledge that in fact many letters though by no means all of them insist on terms which the legislature regards as so unfair and unconscionable that it was recently found necessary to deal with the matter in the recent Act entitled the Hire-Purchase Act, 1938.

These, my Lords, are very serious difficulties, and when we find as we do in this curious case that the trial judge and the three Lords Justices, and even the two counsel who addressed your Lordships for the respondents, were unable to agree upon the true construction of the alleged agreement, it seems to me that it is impossible to conclude that a binding agreement has been established by the respondents.

NOTE In a hire purchase contract, the supplier hires the goods to the customer, but on payment of a specified number of 'hire instalments', the hirer has the option to buy the goods. Many different types of hire purchase agreement with different terms exist, and it was not clear what type of hire purchase contract was envisaged here.

Hillas & Co. Ltd v Arcos Ltd
(1932) 147 LT 503 (HL)

By an agreement made on 21 May 1930, the claimants agreed 'to buy 22,000 standards of softwood goods of fair specification over the season 1930'. Clause 9 also stated that 'the buyers shall also have the option of entering into a contract with the sellers for the purchase of 100,000 standards for delivery during 1931' at a 5 per cent discount on the 1931 official price list. The option clause did not specify what qualities or type of goods were to be supplied. On 22 December 1930, the claimants purported to exercise the option, but the defendants could not perform because they had already sold their supply to a third party. The claimants sued for damages for breach and the defendants argued that the agreement was void for uncertainty.

Held: The agreement was binding and was not dependent on any future agreement for its validity.

LORD TOMLIN: First, the parties were both intimately acquainted with the course of business in the Russian softwood timber trade and had without difficulty carried out the sale and purchase of 22,000 standards under the first part of the document of the 21st May 1930. Secondly, although the question here is whether clause 9 of the document of the 21st May 1930, with the letter of the 22nd Dec. 1930, constitutes a contract, the validity of the whole of the document of the 21st May 1930 is really in question so far as the matter depends upon the meaning of the phrase 'of fair specification'. Thirdly, it is indisputable, having regard to clause 11, which provides that 'this agreement cancels all previous agreements,' that the parties intended by the document of the 21st May 1930 to make, and believed that they had made, some concluded bargain.

. . . [I]t is said that there is in clause 9 no sufficient description of the goods to be sold . . . it is plain that something must necessarily be implied in clause 9. The words '100,000 standards' without more do not even indicate that timber is the subject-matter of the clause. The implication at the least of the words 'of softwood goods' is, in my opinion, inevitable, and if this is so I see no reason to separate the words 'of fair specification' from the words 'of softwood goods.' In my opinion there is a necessary implication of the words 'of softwood goods of fair specification' after the words '100,000 standards' in clause 9.

What then is the meaning of '100,000 standards of softwood goods of fair specification for delivery during 1931'?

If the words 'of fair specification' have no meaning which is certain or capable of being made certain, then not only can there be no contract under clause 9 but there cannot have been a contract with regard to the 22,000 standards mentioned at the beginning of the document of the 21st May 1930. This may be the proper conclusion; but before it is reached it is, I think, necessary to exclude as impossible all reasonable meanings which would give certainty to the words. In my opinion this cannot be done.

The parties undoubtedly attributed to the words in connection with the 22,000 standards, some meaning which was precise or capable of being made precise . . .

Reading the document of the 21st May 1930 as a whole, and having regard to the admissible evidence as to the course of the trade, I think that upon their true construction the words 'of fair specification over the season, 1930,' used in connection with the 22,000 standards, mean that the 22,000 standards are to be satisfied in goods distributed over kinds, qualities, and sizes in the fair proportions having regard to the output of the season 1930, and the classifications of that output in respect of kinds, qualities, and sizes. That is something which if the parties fail to agree can be ascertained just as much as the fair value of a property.

NOTES

1. In *Hillas v Arcos*, the contract had been performed and the option had been exercised by the claimants. In *Scammell v Ouston*, the respondents were asking the court to enforce an executory contract (one that had not yet been performed). In addition, in *Hillas v Arcos* the court was able to imply terms based on commercial practice, whereas in *Scammell v Ouston* there were no such common terms.

2. Lord Wright made clear in *Hillas v Arcos*, at p. 514, how important it was to find the certainty that businessmen intended, but had not included in their agreement:

The document of the 21st May 1930 cannot be regarded as other than inartistic, and may appear repellent to the trained sense of an equity draftsman. But it is clear that the parties both intended to make a contract and thought they had done so. Business men often record the most important agreements in crude and summary fashion; modes of expression sufficient and clear to them in the course of their business may appear to those unfamiliar with the business far from complete or precise. It is accordingly the duty of the court to construe such documents fairly and broadly, without being too astute or subtle in finding defects; but, on the contrary, the court should seek to apply the old maxim of English law, *verba ita sunt intelligenda ut res magis valeat quam pereat*. That maxim, however, does not mean that the court is to make a contract for the parties, or to go outside the words they have used, except in so far as there are appropriate implications of law, as for instance, the implication of what is just and reasonable to be ascertained by the court as matter of machinery where the contractual intention is clear, but the contract is silent on some detail. Thus in contracts for future performance over a period, the parties may neither be able nor desire to specify many matters of detail, but leave them to be adjusted in the working out of the contract. Save for the legal implication I have mentioned, such contracts might well be incomplete or uncertain; with that implication in reserve they are neither incomplete nor uncertain. As obvious illustrations I may refer to such matters as prices or times of delivery in contracts for the sale of goods, or times for loading or discharging in a contract of sea carriage. Furthermore, even if the construction of the words used may be difficult, that is not a reason for holding them too ambiguous or uncertain to be enforced if the fair meaning of the parties can be extracted.

3. In *Durham Tees Valley Airport Ltd v bmibaby Ltd* [2010] EWCA Civ 485, [2011] 1 All ER (Comm) 731, [2011] 1 Lloyd's Rep 68, the contract required the airline to base and fly two aircrafts from a particular airport over a ten-year term. When the airline shut its base at the airport, the claimant sought damages. The Court of Appeal held that the agreement was not void for uncertainty, since it contained sufficient terms to enable a court to give the agreement a practical meaning and determine whether the airline was in breach. It was not necessary for the contract to specify a minimum number of flights or passengers. It followed that the alleged implied term (to operate from the airport in a manner that was reasonable in all of the circumstances) did not need to be found. The express terms sufficed.

TOULSON LJ: 88. Where parties intend to create a contractual obligation, the court will try to give it legal effect. The court will only hold that the contract, or some part of it, is void for uncertainty, if it is legally or practically impossible to give to the agreement (or that part of it) any sensible content. (See *Scammell v Dicker* [2005] EWCA Civ 405, [2005] 3 All ER 838, para 30, per Rix LJ.).

4. In *Baird Textile Holdings Ltd v Marks & Spencer plc* [2001] EWCA Civ 274, [2002] 1 All ER (Comm) 737, [2001] CLC 999, *Hillas & Co. Ltd v Arcos Ltd* could be distinguished since the claim in *Baird* was based on an implied contract and there was no evidence on which to determine the essential terms of the contract.

MORRITT VC: 26 . . . The distinction between those cases in which the implication of reasonableness provides for certainty and those in which it does not appears most clearly from the speech of Lord Thankerton [in *Hillas v Arcos Ltd*]. He distinguished (p. 513) between cases where the contract provides for an objective standard which the court applies by ascertaining what is reasonable and those where, there being no such standard, the test of reasonableness is being used to make an agreement for the parties which they have not made for themselves. He was impressed by the consideration that a commercial matter was involved and the parties themselves thought that they had made a contract . . .

29. The issue of certainty arises, not with regard to the alleged obligation to give reasonable notice of termination, but with the allegation that

. . . during the subsistence of the relationship Marks & Spencer would acquire garments from BHT in quantities and at prices which in all the circumstances were reasonable . . .

Counsel for Baird accepted that this involved an obligation on Baird to supply such garments irrespective of whether it had accepted the order. It is not alleged that there was some objective criteria by which to assess what was a reasonable quantity or price. Counsel disclaimed any contention that M&S in fact allocated business from year to year in accordance with some formula of its own. The annual allocation was separately determined in each year in the light of the circumstances then prevailing.

30. I agree with the conclusion of the judge. The alleged obligation on M&S to acquire garments from Baird is insufficiently certain to found any contractual obligation because there are no objective criteria by which the court could assess what would be reasonable either as to quantity or price. This is not a case in which, the parties having evidently sought to make a contract, the court seeks to uphold its validity by construing the terms to produce certainty. Rather it is a case in which the lack of certainty confirms the absence of any clear evidence of an intention to create legal relations . . .

2.6.2 Severing a meaningless clause

Nicolene Ltd v Simmonds
[1953] 1 QB 543 (CA)

The acceptance of an offer to sell a quantity of steel bars stated: 'I assume that we are in agreement that the usual conditions of acceptance apply.' There were no 'usual conditions' operating between the parties. The defendant failed to deliver and the claimants brought an action for breach of contract.

Held: The clause specifying 'usual conditions' was meaningless and could be severed from the rest of the contract without impairing the sense or reasonableness of the contract as a whole.

DENNING LJ: In my opinion a distinction must be drawn between a clause which is meaningless and a clause which is yet to be agreed. A clause which is meaningless can often be ignored, whilst still leaving the contract good; whereas a clause which has yet to be agreed may mean that there is no contract at all, because the parties have not agreed on all the essential terms.

I take it to be clear law that if one of the parties to a contract inserts into it an exempting condition in his own favour, which the other side agrees, and it afterwards turns out that that condition is meaningless, or what comes to the same thing, that it is so ambiguous that no ascertainable meaning can be given to it, that does not mean that the whole contract is a nullity. It only means that the exempting condition is a nullity and must be rejected. It would be strange indeed if a party could escape from every one of his obligations by inserting a meaningless exception from some of them.

2.6.3 Incompleteness

2.6.3.1 Agreements to negotiate

Where the parties simply agree to negotiate a matter between themselves, such an agreement to agree will be unenforceable. In *Courtney & Fairbairn Ltd v Tolani Brothers (Hotels) Ltd* [1975] 1 WLR 297 (CA), 301H, Lord Denning MR explained:

If the law does not recognise a contract to enter into a contract (when there is a fundamental term yet to be agreed) it seems to me it cannot recognise a contract to negotiate. The reason is because it is too uncertain to have any binding force. No court could estimate the damages because no one can tell whether the negotiations would be successful or would fall through: or if successful, what the result would be. It seems to me that a contract to negotiate, like a contract to enter into a contract, is not a contract known to the law . . .

Walford v Miles
[1992] 2 AC 128 (HL)

The defendants, owners of a company, were negotiating for the sale of the company to the claimants. On 17 March 1987, they had entered into an agreement whereby, in return for the provision of a comfort letter from the claimants' bank (indicating that loan facilities had been granted to cover the price of £2 million), the defendants agreed to terminate any negotiations with third parties, agreed not to entertain offers from any other prospective purchasers, and agreed to deal exclusively with the claimants. Although the claimants complied with their side of the agreement, the defendants withdrew from the negotiations and decided to sell to a third party.

The claimants claimed damages for breach of this collateral agreement. The Court of Appeal held that the collateral agreement alleged was only an agreement to negotiate and was therefore unenforceable. The claimants appealed.

Held (dismissing the appeal):

(a) A lock-out agreement (not to negotiate with any other person) could be enforceable if it were made for good consideration and covered a fixed period of time. However, where, as here, it covered an unspecified period of time, it was unenforceable.

(b) There could be no *implied* term to negotiate in good faith for a reasonable period of time.

LORD ACKNER: I believe it is helpful to make these observations about a so-called 'lock-out' agreement. There is clearly no reason in the English contract law why A, for good consideration, should not achieve an enforceable agreement whereby B, agrees for a specified period of time, not to negotiate with anyone except A in relation to the sale of his property. There are often good commercial reasons why A should desire to obtain such an agreement from B. B's property, which A contemplates purchasing, may be such as to require the expenditure of not inconsiderable time and money before A is in a position to assess what he is prepared to offer for its purchase or whether he wishes to make any offer at all. A may well consider that he is not prepared to run the risk of expending such time and money unless there is a worthwhile prospect, should he desire to make an offer to purchase, of B, not only then still owning the property, but of being prepared to consider his offer. A may wish to guard against the risk that, while he is investigating the wisdom of offering to buy B's property, B may have already disposed of it or, alternatively, may be so advanced in negotiations with a third party as to be unwilling or for all practical purposes unable, to negotiate with A. But I stress that this is a negative agreement—B by agreeing not to negotiate for this fixed period with a third party, locks himself out of such negotiations. He has in no legal sense locked himself *into* negotiations with A. What A has achieved is an exclusive opportunity, for a fixed period, to try and come to terms with B, an opportunity for which he has, unless he makes his agreement under seal, to give good consideration . . .

The agreement alleged . . . contains the essential characteristics of a basic valid lock-out agreement, save one. It does not specify for how long it is to last. Bingham LJ [in the Court of Appeal] sought to cure this deficiency by holding that the obligation upon [the respondents] not to deal with other parties should continue to bind them 'for such time as is reasonable in all the circumstances'. He said:

> the time would end once the parties acting in good faith had found themselves unable to come to mutually acceptable terms . . . the defendants could not . . . bring the reasonable time to an end by procuring a bogus impasse, since that would involve a breach of the duty of reasonable good faith which parties such as these must, I think, be taken to owe to each other.

However, as Bingham LJ recognised, such a duty, if it existed, would indirectly impose upon [the respondents] a duty to negotiate in good faith. Such a duty, for the reasons which I have given [see next extract], cannot be imposed . . .

NOTES

1. It was also held that any *lock-in* agreement (to negotiate only with a particular party) was unenforceable because it was inherently uncertain: approving *Courtney & Fairbairn Ltd v Tolani Bros. (Hotels) Ltd.*

2. The Court of Appeal decision in *Pitt v PHH Asset Management Ltd* [1994] 1 WLR 327 is an example of an enforceable *lock-out* agreement for good consideration because the duration of the agreement was fixed at 14 days. This may indicate that the fixed period will itself need to be fairly short. As on the facts of *Pitt*, this device may prove popular with prospective purchasers of land who fear that they may be 'gazumped' and so seek some protection. However, if there is a breach of an enforceable lock-out agreement, the remedy appears to be damages, so that the device will not secure the eventual purchase of that property.

? QUESTIONS

1. Should an injunction be available to prevent a vendor from considering offers from third parties during the period of the lock-out agreement?

2. Is there any real difference in terms of practical effect between a lock-in and a lock-out agreement?

2.6.3.2 Can there ever be a duty to negotiate in good faith?

The House of Lords in *Walford v Miles* [1992] 2 AC 128 rejected the argument that it was necessary to imply a term that the defendants were obliged to negotiate in good faith in order to reach agreement and to terminate those negotiations only for subjectively assessed 'proper reasons'.

LORD ACKNER: The reason why an agreement to negotiate, like an agreement to agree, is unenforceable, is simply because it lacks the necessary certainty . . . This uncertainty is demonstrated in the instant case by the provision which it is said has to be implied in the agreement for the determination of the negotiations. How can a court be expected to decide whether, *subjectively*, a proper reason existed for the termination of negotiations? The answer suggested depends upon whether the negotiations have been determined 'in good faith'. However, the concept of a duty to carry on negotiations in good faith is inherently repugnant to the adversarial position of the parties when involved in negotiations. Each party to the negotiations is entitled to pursue his (or her) own interest, so long as he avoids making misrepresentations. To advance that interest he must be entitled, if he thinks it appropriate, to threaten to withdraw from further negotiations or to withdraw in fact, in the hope that the opposite party may seek to reopen the negotiations by offering him improved terms. [Counsel for the plaintiffs] of course, accepts that the agreement upon which he relies does not contain a duty to complete the negotiations. But that still leaves the vital question—how is a vendor ever to know that he is entitled to withdraw from further negotiations? How is the court to police such an 'agreement'? A duty to negotiate in good faith is as unworkable in practice as it is inherently inconsistent with the position of a negotiating party. It is here that the uncertainty lies. In my judgment, while negotiations are in existence either party is entitled to withdraw from those negotiations, at any time and for any reason. There can be thus no obligation to continue to negotiate until there is a 'proper reason' to withdraw. Accordingly a bare agreement to negotiate has no legal content.

2.6.3.3 Express provision to negotiate in good faith or to use reasonable endeavours

The decision in *Walford v Miles* that there could be no *implied* duty to negotiate in good faith was made in the context of negotiations that were expressly 'subject to contract'. Unlike in *Walford v Miles*, in which the argument had been to *imply* a duty to negotiate in good faith, in *Petromec Inc. v Petroleo Brasileiro SA Petrobas (No. 3)* [2005] EWCA Civ 891, [2006] 1 Lloyd's Rep 121, the Court of Appeal had to consider whether the courts should enforce an *express provision in a commercial contract* requiring the parties to negotiate in good faith in respect of the cost of certain contractual extras.

In *Petromec*, Longmore LJ set out the issues as follows:

> 116. The traditional objections to enforcing an obligation to negotiate in good faith are (1) that the obligation is an agreement to agree and thus too uncertain to enforce, (2) that it is difficult, if not impossible, to say whether, if negotiations are brought to an end, the termination is brought about in good or in bad faith, and (3) that, since it can never be known whether good faith negotiations would have produced an agreement at all or what the terms of any agreement would have been if it would have been reached, it is impossible to assess any loss caused by breach of the obligation.

Longmore LJ discounted objections (1) and (3) on these facts, since the obligation was an express clause in an enforceable contract and it would have been possible to assess the costs of contractual extras that were subject to the clause in question, or reasonable costs could have been calculated. He accepted that (2) posed the greatest difficulties, but did not consider that the concept of bringing negotiations to an end in bad faith was reason in itself to impose a blanket ban on enforceability of a provision requiring the parties to negotiate in good faith.

He added:

> 121 . . .. It would be a strong thing to declare unenforceable a clause into which the parties have deliberately and expressly entered. I have already observed that it is of comparatively narrow scope. To decide that it has 'no legal content' to use Lord Ackner's phrase [*Walford v Miles*, see the extract at *page 74*, 2.6.3.2] would be for the law deliberately to defeat the reasonable expectations of honest men, to adapt slightly the title of Lord Steyn's Sultan Azlan Shah lecture . . . (113 LQR 433 (1977)). At page 439 Lord Steyn hoped that the House of Lords might reconsider *Walford v Miles* with the benefit of fuller argument. That is not an option open to this court. I would only say that I do not consider that *Walford v Miles* binds us to hold that the express obligation to negotiate . . . is completely without legal substance.

It would seem to follow that the concept of 'good faith' negotiating cannot be inherently uncertain; rather, enforceability is unlikely to be denied where the obligation is an express obligation contained in an enforceable contract between the parties and where that good faith obligation is limited in scope, as opposed to an abstract good faith obligation.

Consequently, there must be criteria on which the assessment of good faith can be assessed, i.e. it must be possible for the court to conduct the exercise of fixing the cost or price in question. In *Shaker v Vistajet Group Holdings SA* [2012] EWHC 1329 (Comm), [2012] 2 All ER (Comm) 1010, [2012] 2 Lloyd's Rep 93, in relation to an agreement to use reasonable endeavours to agree, Teare J distinguished *Petromec* on the basis that, in that case, there were objective criteria by which to assess the extra costs in the absence of agreement:

> 17 [Counsel for the defendant] submitted that an obligation to negotiate in good faith can be enforceable and in that context relied on *Petromec v Petroleo Brasileiro* [2006] 1 Lloyd's Rep. at paragraphs 115–121. However, what had to be negotiated in that case was the cost to Petromec of upgrading a vessel in accordance with an amended specification over and above the cost of upgrading the vessel in accordance with the original specification. There were therefore objective criteria by which the extra costs could be assessed in the absence of agreement. That is a different case from the present. I recognise that Longmore LJ said that it is 'a strong thing to declare unenforceable a clause into which the parties have deliberately and expressly entered' but an agreement to negotiate the terms of four further agreements and secure

written confirmation from a financier contains no objective criteria by which such agreements or written confirmation could be produced for the parties by the court in the absence of agreement. Where there are no objective criteria the court is unable to enforce the parties' agreement to agree; see *Dhanani v Crasnianski* [2011] EWHC 926 (Comm).

The general acceptance of such clauses, provided that they are expressly provided is now clear. If broken, they will give rise to compensation: *Knatchbull-Hugessen and others v SISU Capital Ltd* [2014] EWHC 1194 (Comm).

2.6.3.4 The Price

Sale of Goods Act 1979

8. Ascertainment of price

(1) The price in a contract of sale may be fixed by the contract, or may be left to be fixed in a manner agreed by the contract, or may be determined by the course of dealing between the parties.

(2) Where the price is not determined as mentioned in subsection (1) above the buyer must pay a reasonable price.

(3) What is a reasonable price is a question of fact dependent on the circumstances of each particular case.

NOTE Section 8 of the Sale of Goods Act (SGA) 1979 appears applicable in both B2B (business to business) and B2C (trader and consumer) contractual contexts.

Supply of Goods and Services Act 1982

15. Implied term about consideration

(1) Where, under a relevant contract for the supply of a service, the consideration for the service is not determined by the contract, left to be determined in a manner agreed by the contract or determined by the course of dealing between the parties, there is an implied term that the party contracting with the supplier will pay a reasonable charge.

(2) What is a reasonable charge is a question of fact.

Consumer Rights Act 2015

51 Reasonable price to be paid for a service

(1) This section applies to a contract to supply a service if—

   (a) the consumer has not paid a price or other consideration for the service,

   (b) the contract does not expressly fix a price or other consideration, and does not say how it is to be fixed, and

   (c) anything that is to be treated under section 50 as included in the contract does not fix a price or other consideration either.

(2) In that case the contract is to be treated as including a term that the consumer must pay a reasonable price for the service, and no more.

(3) What is a reasonable price is a question of fact.

NOTE Supply of Goods and Services Act (SGSA) 1982, s. 15 applies only to 'relevant' contracts of service, and relevant in this context means in a B2B (business to business) contract given the scope of s. 51 of the Consumer Rights Act (CRA) 2015 and its application in the B2C context (i.e. trader and consumer contract).

For consumer contracts, s. 51 CRA 2015 implies that the court can interfere only if there is no price *and* no mechanism for fixing the price. Given this wording, the existing case law governing failure of mechanisms therefore remains relevant.

If the contract provides a mechanism for fixing the price, but it has not been implemented, s. 8(2) SGA 1979 will not allow the implication of a reasonable price.

May and Butcher Ltd v R
[1934] 2 KB 17 (HL)

The parties entered into a contract under which the government was to sell 'the whole of the tentage which might become available in the UK for disposal up to 31 March 1923'. The relevant terms were:

(3) The price or prices to be paid, and the date or dates on which payment is to be made by the purchasers to the Commission for such old tentage shall be agreed upon from time to time between the Commission and the purchasers as the quantities of the said old tentage become available for disposal, and are offered to the purchasers by the Commission . . .

(10) It is understood that all disputes with reference to or arising out of this agreement will be submitted to arbitration in accordance with the provisions of the Arbitration Act, 1889.

The parties failed to agree on the prices to be paid. The appellants argued that the agreement should be construed as an agreement to sell at a fair or reasonable price, or alternatively at a price to be fixed under the arbitration clause in the agreement.

Held: Because there was no agreement on price and dates, the contractual mechanism having failed, there was no concluded contract.

VISCOUNT DUNEDIN: To be a good contract there must be a concluded bargain, and a concluded contract is one which settles everything that is necessary to be settled and leaves nothing to be settled by agreement between the parties. Of course it may leave something which still has to be determined, but then that determination must be a determination which does not depend upon the agreement between the parties. In the system of law in which I was brought up, that was expressed by one of those brocards of which perhaps we have been too fond, but which often express very neatly what is wanted: '*Certum est quod certum reddi potest.*' Therefore, you may very well agree that a certain part of the contract of sale, such as price, may be settled by someone else. As a matter of the general law of contract all the essentials have to be settled. What are the essentials may vary according to the particular contract under consideration. We are here dealing with sale, and undoubtedly price is one of the essentials of sale, and if it is left still to be agreed between the parties, then there is no contract. It may be left to the determination of a certain person, and if it was so left and that person either would not or could not act, there would be no contract because the price was to be settled in a certain way and it has become impossible to settle it in that way, and therefore there is no settlement. No doubt as to goods, the Sale of Goods Act, 1893, says that if the price is not mentioned and settled in the contract it is to be a reasonable price. The simple answer in this case is that the Sale of Goods Act provides for silence on the point and here there is no silence, because there is a provision that the two parties are to agree . . . Here there was clearly no contract. There would have been a perfectly good settlement of price if the contract had said that it was to be settled by arbitration by a certain man, or it might have been quite good if it was said that it was to be settled by arbitration under the Arbitration Act so as to bring in a material plan by which a certain person could be put in action. The question then arises, has anything of that sort been done? I think clearly not. The general arbitration clause is one in very common form as to disputes arising out of the arrangements. In no proper meaning of the word can this be described as a dispute arising between the parties; it is a failure to agree, which is a very different thing from a dispute.

Where the price is to be fixed by agreement between the parties, it may make a difference that the agreement has been executed.

Foley v Classique Coaches Ltd
[1934] 2 KB 1 (CA)

The defendants entered into an agreement to purchase all of their petrol requirements from the claimant 'at a price to be agreed by the parties in writing and from time to time'. An arbitration clause was included. After purchasing their petrol from the claimant for three years, the defendants purported to repudiate the agreement on the ground that there was no agreement in writing as to the price.

Held: The agreement was valid and binding, and if any dispute arose as to the reasonable price, the parties had provided for it to be determined by arbitration. After considering *May & Butcher* and *Hillas v Arcos*, Scrutton LJ continued as follows.

SCRUTTON LJ: In the present case the parties obviously believed they had a contract and they acted for three years as if they had; they had an arbitration clause which relates to the subject-matter of the agreement as to the supply of petrol, and it seems to me that this arbitration clause applies to any failure to agree as to the price. By analogy to the case of a tied house there is to be implied in this contract a term that the petrol shall be supplied at a reasonable price and shall be of reasonable quality. For these reasons I think the Lord Chief Justice was right in holding that there was an effective and enforceable contract, although as to the future no definite price had been agreed with regard to the petrol.

NOTES

1. Since the parties had acted on this agreement for three years, the court was unwilling to undo it simply to serve the defendants' commercial interests (they had obtained better terms elsewhere). Moreover, the petrol agreement was linked to a contract for the sale of land by the claimant to the defendants and, arguably, was part of the consideration for that sale.

2. In *British Bank for Foreign Trade Ltd v Novinex Ltd* [1949] 1 KB 623, an agreement provided that 'an agreed commission' would be payable if the claimants put the defendants in direct contact with a supplier. The claimants did this, but were not paid any commission. The Court of Appeal held that the defendants were bound to pay a 'reasonable sum' and stressed the fact that the claimants had executed

their part of the agreement. Cohen LJ said, at pp. 629–30:

[I]f there is an essential term which has yet to be agreed and there is no express or implied provision for its solution, the result in point of law is that there is no binding contract. In seeing whether there is an implied provision for its solution, however, there is a difference between an arrangement which is wholly executory on both sides, and one which has been executed on one side or the other. In the ordinary way, if there is an arrangement to supply goods at a price 'to be agreed,' or to perform services on terms 'to be agreed,' then although, while the matter is still executory, there may be no binding contract, nevertheless, if it is executed on one side, that is, if the one does his part without having come to an agreement as to the price or the terms, then the law will say that there is necessarily implied, from the conduct of the parties a contract that, in default of agreement, a reasonable sum is to be paid . . .

3. In *Mamidoil-Jetoil Greek Petroleum Co. SA v Okta Crude Oil Refinery (No. 1)* [2001] EWCA Civ 406, [2001] 2 Lloyd's Rep 76, a term for price fixing was held not to mount to an 'agreement to agree' where this agreement on price is not required for the conclusion of the contract. The fee was fixed for the first two years of the ten-year term of the contract (1993 and 1994), but left open for the remaining eight years. The Court of Appeal, stressing the history of commercial dealings between these parties and the need to uphold an existing contract, held that in the event that there was a failure to fix the fee in the remaining period of the contract, a term would be implied providing for a reasonable fee to be fixed.

RIX LJ [with whose judgment Schiemann LJ and Sir Ronald Waterhouse agreed]: 69 In my judgment the following principles relevant to the present case can be deduced from [the] authorities, but this is intended to be in no way an exhaustive list:

(i) Each case must be decided on its own facts and on the construction of its own agreement. Subject to that:

(ii) Where no contract exists, the use of an expression such as 'to be agreed' in relation to an essential term is likely to prevent any contract coming into existence, on the ground of uncertainty. This may be summed up by the principle that 'you cannot agree to agree'.

(iii) Similarly, where no contract exists, the absence of agreement on essential terms of the agreement may prevent any contract coming into existence, again on the ground of uncertainty.

(iv) However, particularly in commercial dealings between parties who are familiar with the trade in question, and particularly where the parties have acted in the belief that they had a binding contract, the Courts are willing to imply terms, where that is possible, to enable the contract to be carried out.

(v) Where a contract has once come into existence, even the expression 'to be agreed' in relation to future executory obligations is not necessarily fatal to its continued existence.

(vi) Particularly in the case of contracts for future performance over a period, where the parties may desire or need to leave matters to be adjusted in the working out of their contract, the Courts will assist the parties to do so, so as to preserve rather than destroy bargains, on the basis that what can be made certain is itself certain. Certum est quod certum reddi potest.

(vii) This is particularly the case where one party has either already had the advantage of some performance which reflects the parties' agreement on a long term relationship, or has had to make an investment premised on that agreement.

(viii) For these purposes, an express stipulation for a reasonable or fair measure or price will be a sufficient criterion for the courts to act on. But even in the absence of express language, the Courts are prepared to imply an obligation in terms of what is reasonable.

(ix) Such implications are reflected but not exhausted by the statutory provision for the implication of a reasonable price now to be found in s. 8(2) of the Sale of Goods Act, 1979 (and, in the case of services, in s. 15(1) of the Supply of Goods and Services Act, 1982).

(x) The presence of an arbitration clause may assist the Courts to hold a contract to be sufficiently certain or to be capable of being rendered so, presumably as indicating a commercial and contractual mechanism, which can be operated with the assistance of experts in the field, by which the parties, in the absence of agreement, may resolve their dispute . . .

73 In my judgment, the 1993 contract should be viewed as a contract for a fixed period of at least 10 years and a term should be implied that in the absence of agreement reasonable fees should be determined for the period after 1994. I would seek to put the matter in the following way.

(i) The context is that of a long term (10 year) commercial agreement between parties who have had long familiarity with the subject matter of agreement and with each other.

(ii) The agreement in question undoubtedly arises out of a contract, the 1993 contract. This is not, therefore, one of those cases where the initial issue is whether the parties have ever reached the stage of contractual relations. If the question is whether any contract has ever been arrived at, lack of certainty in essential terms may well make it difficult or impossible to say that the parties ever intended to have legal relations, or even if they did, whether they had reached sufficient certainty to enable a Court to find a contract. If they never achieved a contract in the first place, then there is no assistance to be gained from agreement of an arbitration clause, or from statutory or any other implications. That is not to say, however, that the possibility of such implications or the presence of such an arbitration clause may not assist the Court in the overall question of whether a contract can be found. However, once a contract exists, it not only needs to be construed for its terms, but the Courts will seek to make it work, as the parties must have intended, in accordance with its terms, that it should . . .

(v) The contract does not expressly state that the fee after the end of 1994 is 'to be agreed'. It is simply silent as to what is to happen in that period. Therefore, this case is simply not presented with the difficulties which arise, in the face of 'to be agreed' language, where it is uncertain whether there is any contract at all. It cannot be said, as was said in *May and Butcher v The King*, that the statutory implication of a reasonable price, or an implication that the fee should be such reasonable fee as the arbitrator may decide, is excluded by express agreement that the parties were to agree the figure.

(vi) There is no evidence that the resolution of a reasonable fee would cause any difficulty at all. On the contrary, the evidence is the other way . . . In the absence of evidence to the contrary, I would infer that it was perfectly possible to derive from the agreements of price and price increases over the years objective criteria for working out a reasonable fee. Thus, although it is true to say that the contract itself contained no mechanism or guidance (other than the arbitration clause) as to how a reasonable fee would be derived, I do not consider that the contract should fail on that ground. Contractually derived criteria or guidance may be of assistance in finding an implied term for a reasonable price: but the authorities indicate that the Courts are well prepared to make the implication even in their absence.

Compare *May & Butcher Ltd v R* [1934] 2 KB 17 (*page 78*, earlier in this section), with the next case.

Sudbrook Trading Estate Ltd v Eggleton
[1983] 1 AC 444 (HL)

Lessees were granted the option of purchasing the reversion of the lease:

> at such price not being less than £12,000 as may be agreed by two valuers, one to be nominated by the lessor and the other by the lessee and in default of such agreement by an umpire appointed by . . . valuers.

The lessees exercised the option, but the lessors refused to appoint a valuer and claimed that the option was void for uncertainty.

Held: Where machinery was in place that had broken down and that machinery was simply a means of ensuring that a fair price was paid as opposed to an essential factor in determining the price, then the court could substitute its own machinery to ascertain a fair and reasonable price.

> LORD FRASER OF TULLYBELTON: [The courts have] laid down the principle that where parties have agreed on a particular method of ascertaining the price, and that method has for any reason proved ineffective, the court will neither grant an order for specific performance to compel parties to operate the agreed machinery, nor substitute its own machinery to ascertain the price, because either of these clauses would be to impose upon parties an agreement that they had not made . . .
>
> I recognise the logic of the reasoning which has led to the courts' refusing to substitute their own machinery for the machinery which has been agreed upon by the parties. But the result to which it leads is so remote from that which parties normally intend and expect, and is so inconvenient in practice, that there must in my opinion be some defect in the reasoning. I think the defect lies in construing the provisions for the mode of ascertaining the value as an essential part of the agreement. That may have been perfectly true early in the 19th century, when the valuer's profession and the rules of valuation were less well established than they are now. But at the present day these provisions are only subsidiary to the main purpose of the agreement which is for sale and purchase of the property at a fair or reasonable value. In the ordinary case parties do not make any substantial distinction between an agreement to sell at a fair value, without specifying the mode of ascertaining the value, and an agreement to sell at a value to be ascertained by valuers appointed in the way provided in these leases. The true distinction is between those cases where the mode of ascertaining the price is an essential term of the contract, and those cases where the mode of ascertainment, though indicated in the contract, is subsidiary and non-essential . . .
>
> The present case falls, in my opinion, into the latter category. Accordingly when the option was exercised there was constituted a complete contract for sale, and the clause should be construed as meaning that the price was to be a fair price. On the other hand where an agreement is made to sell at a price to be fixed by a valuer who is named, or who, by reason of holding some office such as auditor of a company

whose shares are to be valued, will have special knowledge relevant to the question of value, the prescribed mode may well be regarded as essential. Where, as here, the machinery consists of valuers and an umpire, none of whom is named or identified, it is in my opinion unrealistic to regard it as an essential term. If it breaks down there is no reason why the court should not substitute other machinery to carry out the main purpose of ascertaining the price in order that the agreement may be carried out.

LORD RUSSELL OF KILLOWEN [dissenting]: Basically the assumption is made that the parties intended that the exercise of the option should involve payment of a 'fair price' or a 'fair value.' Of course parties to such a contract could in terms so agree, and I am not concerned to deny that in such a case a court could enforce the contract by ascertainment of a fair price or fair value, treating specific provisions in the contract for methods (which proved to be unworkable) of ascertaining that fair price or valuation as being inessential. But that is not this case. Why should it be thought that potential vendor and purchaser intended the price to be 'fair'? The former would intend the price to be high, even though 'unfairly' so. And the latter vice versa. Vendors and purchasers are normally greedy.

? QUESTIONS

1. Is it possible to distinguish an agreement whereby the price will be fixed by the parties themselves and an agreement whereby the price will be fixed by valuers appointed by the parties?

2. Is it correct to say that the parties intended to sell and buy at a fair price? Whose approach is the more realistic: Lord Fraser's or Lord Russell's?

NOTE *Sudbrook v Eggleton* was distinguished by the Court of Appeal in *Gillatt v Sky Television Ltd* [2000] 1 All ER (Comm) 461.

Sky had acquired shares in Tele-Aerials Satellite Ltd (TAS) by an agreement that provided (in clause 6) that, if Sky were to sell or dispose of this shareholding, Sky would pay Mallard Ltd '55 per cent of the open market value of such shares . . . as determined by an independent chartered accountant'. Mallard Ltd had subsequently assigned (transferred) this right to Gillatt. When Sky transferred the shares to a wholly owned subsidiary, Gillatt claimed to be entitled to the payment under clause 6. However, there had been no attempt to appoint an independent accountant to determine the value of the shares and, since a reasonable time had elapsed, it was no longer possible to do so. Gillatt sought to rely on *Sudbrook* to argue that this was not an essential element of the machinery for fixing the value of the shareholding and, since this machinery had failed, the court could substitute its own machinery. The court held that it would not interfere. The machinery specified was both integral and essential. In any event, the machinery failed through the claimant's own inaction (not making the necessary appointment).

Gillatt indicates that *Sudbrook* may be limited to instances in which a joint appointment is required and one party is obstructing the other's attempts to appoint in an effort to avoid the application of the agreed machinery. Having failed to follow the agreed procedure of appointing an independent chartered accountant, Mr Gillatt could not argue that the provision meant nothing and should be replaced by a determination of the court.

Similarly, in *Infiniteland Ltd v Artisan Contracting Ltd* [2005] EWCA Civ 758, [2006] 1 BCLC 6323, the court concluded that the machinery for price adjustment was essential and had not broken down; rather, as in *Gillatt*, the machinery had failed to operate following the failure of the party seeking the adjustment to operate the machinery in the clause. Chadwick LJ stated:

59. I can see no reason, in principle, why a party, say 'A', who chooses not to allow the contractual machinery to operate, should be able to ask the court, nevertheless, to enforce the contract against the other party, say 'B'. It is no answer, in such a case, to say that the machinery is non-essential. It is the machinery upon which the parties agreed when they made their bargain. A cannot be heard to insist on the agreed machinery—as a defence to a claim made against him—if it is he who has not allowed it to operate. But, equally, as it seems to me, in such a case A cannot insist on imposing on B other machinery to which B has never agreed. B is not to be denied the benefit of the machinery to which he has agreed—in resisting a claim made against him—by A's unilateral refusal to allow that machinery to operate.

2.6.4 Conclusion of 'no contract' and payment for performance

British Steel Corporation v Cleveland Bridge & Engineering Co. Ltd
[1984] 1 All ER 504

The defendants entered into negotiations with the claimants whereby the claimants would manufacture steel nodes. The defendants sent the claimants a letter of intent stating their intention to place an order for the nodes and proposing that the contract be on the defendants' standard terms (providing for unlimited liability of the claimants in respect of consequential loss from late delivery). The letter of intent requested that the claimants commence work immediately pending the issue of the formal contract. The claimants refused to contract on the proposed terms and, although detailed negotiations took place, no agreement was reached on the question of losses following late delivery and no formal contract was concluded. In the meantime, the claimants had gone ahead with the manufacture of the nodes as requested. All but one of the nodes had been delivered, but the last one was delayed by an industrial dispute at the claimants' plant. The defendants refused to pay and sought damages as there had been a breach of a binding contract. The claimants sued for the value of the nodes on a *quantum meruit* (reasonable value) basis, contending that there was no binding contract.

Held: Because the parties had not reached agreement, it was impossible to say what the material terms were; there was no formal contract. Consequently, the work performed under the letter of intent was not referable to any contractual terms as to payment and performance. However, because the defendants had requested the claimants to deliver the nodes and had therefore received a benefit at the expense of the claimants, it would be unjust for them to retain that benefit without recompensing the claimants for the reasonable value of the nodes.

ROBERT GOFF J: No doubt it was envisaged by CBE at the time they sent the letter that negotiations had reached an advanced stage, and that a formal contract would soon be signed; but, since the parties were still in a state of negotiation, it is impossible to say with any degree of certainty what the material terms of that contract would be. I find myself quite unable to conclude that, by starting work in these circumstances, BSC bound themselves to complete the work. In the course of argument, I put to counsel for CBE the question whether BSC were free at any time, after starting work, to cease work. His submission was that they were not free to do so, even if negotiations on the terms of the formal contract broke down completely. I find this submission to be so repugnant to common sense and the commercial realities that I am unable to accept it . . .

I therefore reject CBE's submission that a binding executory contract came into existence in this case.

In my judgment, the true analysis of the situation is simply this. Both parties confidently expected a formal contract to eventuate. In these circumstances, to expedite performance under that anticipated contract, one requested the other to commence the contract work, and the other complied with that request. If thereafter, as anticipated, a contract was entered into, the work done as requested will be treated as having been performed under that contract; if, contrary to their expectation, no contract was entered into, then the performance of the work is not referable to any contract the terms of which can be ascertained, and the law simply imposes an obligation on the party who made the request to pay a reasonable sum for such work as has been done pursuant to that request, such an obligation sounding in quasi contract or, as we now say, in restitution.

NOTES

1. Similarly, in *Whittle Movers Ltd v Hollywood Express Ltd* [2009] EWCA Civ 1189, [2009] CLC 771, although performance had commenced, there could be no contract because the parties were still negotiating on important terms.

2. In *Regalian Properties plc v London Dockland Development Corporation* [1995] 1 WLR 212, Rattee J held that there could be no recovery of pre-contractual expenses when a contract did not result between the parties. With the expression 'subject to contract' in their negotiations, the parties had accepted that any pre-contract costs were incurred at that party's own expense. There could also be no recovery on a *quantum meruit* since (distinguishing *British Steel Corporation v Cleveland Bridge & Engineering*) the costs that Regalian (a property development company) wanted to recover were costs that it had incurred for the purpose of putting itself into a position from which it could obtain and perform a proposed contract to build—namely, the costs of professional fees, site investigations, and detailed costings. These were not costs incurred 'by way of accelerated performance of the anticipated contract at the request of LDDC': see McKendrick [1995] RLR 100.

? QUESTION

In what circumstances will a *quantum meruit* be appropriate to recover expenditure incurred when a contract fails to materialize?

In *Countrywide Communications Ltd v ICL Pathway Ltd* [2000] CLC 324, Nicholas Strauss QC accepted that, in 'exceptional cases' in which a contract failed to materialize, a claimant would be able to recover on a *quantum meruit* for expenditure incurred in anticipation of such a contract. This was such a case since the claimant had been persuaded to carry out work on a bid on the basis of an assurance that if its bid were successful, the claimant would be awarded the work on the contract. The bid had succeeded, but another consultant had been appointed. The claimant was able to recover the costs of its work on the bid.

NICHOLAS STRAUSS QC: I have found it impossible to formulate a clear general principle which satisfactorily governs the different factual situations which have arisen, let alone those which could easily arise in other cases. Perhaps, in the absence of any recognition in English law of a general duty, of good faith in contractual negotiations, this is not surprising. Much of the difficulty is caused by attempting to categorise as an unjust enrichment of the defendant, for which an action in restitution is available, what is really a loss unfairly sustained by the plaintiff. There is a lot to be said for a broad principle enabling either to be recompensed, but no such principle is clearly established in English law. Undoubtedly the court may impose an obligation to pay for benefits resulting from services performed in the course of a contract which is expected to, but does not, come into existence. This is so, even though, in all cases, the defendant is *ex hypothesi* free to withdraw from the proposed contract, whether the negotiations were expressly made 'subject to contract' or not. Undoubtedly, such an obligation will be imposed only if justice requires it or, which comes to much the same thing, if it would be unconscionable for the plaintiff not to be recompensed.

Beyond that, I do not think that it is possible to go further than to say that, in deciding whether to impose an obligation and if so its extent, the court will take into account and give appropriate weight to a number of considerations which can be identified in the authorities. The first is whether the services were of a kind which would normally be given free of charge. Secondly, the terms in which the request to perform the services was made may be important in establishing the extent of the risk (if any) which the plaintiffs may fairly be said to have taken that such services would in the end be unrecompensed. What may be important here is whether the parties are simply negotiating, expressly or impliedly 'subject to contract', or whether one party has given some kind of assurance or indication that he will not withdraw, or that he will not withdraw except in certain circumstances. Thirdly, the nature of the benefit which has resulted to the defendants is important, and in particular whether such benefit is real (either 'realised' or 'realisable') or a fiction . . . Plainly, a court will at least be more inclined to impose an obligation to pay for a real benefit, since otherwise the abortive negotiations will leave the defendant with a windfall and the plaintiff out of pocket. However, the judgment of Denning LJ in [*Brewer Street Investments Ltd v Barclays Woollen Co. Ltd* [1954] 1 QB 428] suggests that the performance of services requested may of itself suffice [*sic*] amount to a benefit or enrichment. Fourthly, what may often be decisive are the circumstances in which the anticipated contract does not materialise and in particular whether they can be said to involve 'fault' on the part of the defendant, or (perhaps of more relevance) to be outside the scope of the risk undertaken by the plaintiff at the outset. I agree with the view of Rattee J [in *Regalian plc v LDDC*] that the law should be flexible in this area, and the weight to be given to each of these factors may vary from case to case.

There is in my view considerable doubt whether an obligation can be imposed in a case in which the plaintiff has not provided a benefit of any kind, even of the 'fictional' kind discussed earlier of performing services at the request of the defendant albeit without enriching him in any real sense. Thus I doubt whether an obligation can be imposed on a contracting party to repay a plaintiff for expense incurred, reasonably or even necessarily, in anticipation of a contract which does not materialise, where this is not in the course of providing services requested by the defendant. Such an obligation would not be restitutionary . . .

Performance under an anticipated contract was insufficient to conclude that there was a contract in *British Steel Corporation v Cleveland Bridge & Engineering Co. Ltd* [1984] 1 All ER 504. However, this case was distinguished in *RTS Flexible Systems Ltd v Molkerei Alois Müller GmbH & Co. (UK Production)*.

RTS Flexible Systems Ltd v Molkerei Alois Müller GmbH & Co. (UK Production)
[2010] UKSC 14, [2010] 1 WLR 753, [2010] Bus LR 776 (SC)

The parties had entered negotiations for the manufacture of automated packaging machinery by the claimant. Work had initially been undertaken under a letter of intent (or intention to contract and hence was 'subject to contract'). This letter of intent (LOI) had set out a draft contract, which incorporated a standard form in the industry containing liquidated damages and limitation of liability provisions. Clause 48 provided that the contract would not be binding unless signed and executed by the parties. The parties did not sign or execute that agreement, but proceeded with the project, although some matters remained unresolved. The work was completed and 70 per cent of the agreed price paid when a dispute arose over whether the equipment supplied complied with the specifications. The defendant refused to make any further payments, so the claimant commenced proceedings for payment of the balance of the purchase price on the basis that there was a continuing contract on the terms of the LOI contract or, alternatively, that it had been replaced by a new contract that incorporated the standard form conditions, or that no contract had been formed after the expiry of the LOI, but it was entitled to a *quantum meruit*. The defendant counterclaimed for damages of £3 million alleging that, since the standard form had not been signed, the limitations of liability did not apply. The Court of Appeal had held that there was no contract.

Held (on appeal to the Supreme Court): Allowing the appeal, the Supreme Court held that even if certain terms had not been finalized, where an objective appraisal of the parties' words and conduct led to the conclusion that they had not intended agreement on the terms outstanding to preclude agreement, but had reached agreement on all terms of 'economic significance', and where work had begun and there had been performance on both sides, it was possible to conclude that there was a legally binding agreement that was sufficiently certain. The conduct of the parties, including the fact that there had been 'substantial works carried out', led to the conclusion that the parties were proceeding with a contract on the basis of all of the essential terms that they had agreed. This contract was not 'subject to contract' (as to the meaning of this term, see *Astra Asset Management v Co-operative Bank* [2019] EWHC 897 (Comm), *Poole's Textbook on Contract Law*, 2.3.1.2), since this had been waived, and included the standard terms, which therefore applied to govern the dispute.

LORD CLARKE OF STONE-CUM-EBONY JSC [delivering the judgment of the Court]: 45 The general principles are not in doubt. Whether there is a binding contract between the parties and, if so, upon what terms depends upon what they have agreed. It depends not upon their subjective state of mind, but upon a consideration of what was communicated between them by words or conduct, and whether that leads objectively to a conclusion that they intended to create legal relations and had agreed upon all the terms which they regarded or the law requires as essential for the formation of legally binding relations. Even if certain terms of economic or other significance to the parties have not been finalised, an objective appraisal of their words and conduct may lead to the conclusion that they did not intend agreement of such terms to be a precondition to a concluded and legally binding agreement.

46 The problems that have arisen in this case are not uncommon, and fall under two heads. Both heads arise out of the parties agreeing that the work should proceed before the formal written contract was executed in accordance with the parties' common understanding. The first concerns the effect of the parties' understanding (here reflected in clause 48 of the draft written contract) that the contract would not become effective until each party has executed a counterpart and exchanged it with the other which never occurred. Is that fatal to a conclusion that the work done was covered by a contract? The second frequently arises in such circumstances and is this. Leaving aside the implications of the parties' failure to execute and exchange any agreement in written form, were the parties agreed upon all the terms which they objectively regarded or the law required as essential for the formation of legally binding relations? Here, in particular, this relates to the terms on which the work was being carried out. What, if any, price or remuneration was agreed and what were the rights and obligations of the contractor or supplier?

47 We agree with [counsel for the respondent's] submission that, in a case where a contract is being negotiated subject to contract and work begins before the formal contract is executed, it cannot be said that there will always or even usually be a contract on the terms that were agreed subject to contract. That would be too simplistic and dogmatic an approach. The court should not impose binding contracts on the parties which they have not reached. All will depend upon the circumstances. This can be seen from a contrast between the approach of Steyn LJ in the *Percy Trentham* case [1993] 1 Lloyd's Rep 25 . . . and that of Robert Goff J in *British Steel Corpn v Cleveland Bridge and Engineering Co Ltd* [1984] 1 All ER 504 . . .

48 These principles apply to all contracts, including both sales contracts and construction contracts, and are clearly stated in *Pagnan SpA v Feed Products Ltd* [1987] 2 Lloyd's Rep 601, both by Bingham J at first instance and by the Court of Appeal. In the *Pagnan* case it was held that, although certain terms of

economic significance to the parties were not agreed, neither party intended agreement of those terms to be a precondition to a concluded agreement. The parties regarded them as relatively minor details which could be sorted out without difficulty once a bargain was struck. The parties agreed to bind themselves to agreed terms, leaving certain subsidiary and legally inessential terms to be decided later.

49 In his judgment in the Court of Appeal in *Pagnan* Lloyd LJ (with whom O'Connor LJ and Stocker LJ agreed) summarised the relevant principles in this way, at p 619:

> (1)   In order to determine whether a contract has been concluded in the course of correspondence, one must first look to the correspondence as a whole . . . (2) Even if the parties have reached agreement on all the terms of the proposed contract, nevertheless they may intend that the contract shall not become binding until some further condition has been fulfilled. That is the ordinary 'subject to contract' case. (3) Alternatively, they may intend that the contract shall not become binding until some further term or terms have been agreed . . . (4) Conversely, the parties may intend to be bound forthwith even though there are further terms still to be agreed or some further formality to be fulfilled . . . (5) If the parties fail to reach agreement on such further terms, the existing contract is not invalidated unless the failure to reach agreement on such further terms renders the contract as a whole unworkable or void for uncertainty. (6) It is sometimes said that the parties must agree on the essential terms and it is only matters of detail which can be left over. This may be misleading, since the word 'essential' in that context is ambiguous. If by 'essential' one means a term without which the contract cannot be enforced then the statement is true: the law cannot enforce an incomplete contract. If by 'essential' one means a term which the parties have agreed to be essential for the formation of a binding contract, then the statement is tautologous. If by 'essential' one means only a term which the court regards as important as opposed to a term which the court regards as less important or a matter of detail, the statement is untrue. It is for the parties to decide whether they wish to be bound and if so, by what terms, whether important or unimportant. It is the parties who are, in the memorable phrase coined by the judge [at p 611] 'the masters of their contractual fate'. Of course the more important the term is the less likely it is that the parties will have left it for future decision. But there is no legal obstacle which stands in the way of the parties agreeing to be bound now while deferring important matters to be agreed later. It happens every day when parties enter into so-called 'heads of agreement'.

The same principles apply where, as here, one is considering whether a contract was concluded in correspondence as well as by oral communications and conduct.

50 Before the judge much attention was paid to the *Percy Trentham* case [1993] 1 Lloyd's Rep 25, where, as Steyn LJ put it at p 26, the case for Trentham (the main contractor) was that the sub-contracts came into existence, not simply from an exchange of contracts, but partly by reason of written exchanges, partly by oral discussions and partly by performance of the transactions. In the passage from the judgment of Steyn LJ, at p 27, . . . he identified these four particular matters which he regarded as of importance. (1) English law generally adopts an objective theory of contract formation, ignoring the subjective expectations and the unexpressed mental reservations of the parties. Instead the governing criterion is the reasonable expectations of honest sensible businessmen. (2) Contracts may come into existence, not as a result of offer and acceptance, but during and as a result of performance. (3) The fact that the transaction is executed rather than executory can be very relevant. The fact that the transaction was performed on both sides will often make it unrealistic to argue that there was no intention to enter into legal relations and difficult to submit that the contract is void for vagueness or uncertainty. Specifically, the fact that the transaction is executed makes it easier to imply a term resolving any uncertainty, or, alternatively, it may make it possible to treat a matter not finalised in negotiations as inessential. This may be so in both fully executed and partly executed transactions. (4) If a contract only comes into existence during and as a result of performance it will frequently be possible to hold that the contract impliedly and retrospectively covers pre-contractual performance.

51 By contrast, in the Court of Appeal much attention was paid to the decision of Robert Goff J in the *British Steel* case [1984] 1 All ER 504, which had not been cited to the judge.

[Lord Clarke referred to this decision and continued:]

54 There is said to be a conflict between the approach of Steyn LJ in the *Percy Trentham* case [1993] 1 Lloyds Rep 25 and that of Robert Goff J in the *British Steel* case [1984] 1 All ER 504. We do not agree. Each case depends upon its own facts. We do not understand Steyn LJ to be saying that it follows from the fact that the work was performed that the parties must have entered into a contract. On the other hand, it is plainly a very relevant factor pointing in that direction. Whether the court will hold that a binding contract was made depends upon all the circumstances of the case, of which that is but one. The decision in the *British Steel* case was simply one on the other side of the line. Robert Goff J was struck by the likelihood that parties would agree detailed provisions for matters such as liability for defects and concluded on the facts that no binding agreement had been reached. By contrast, in the *Pagnan* case [1987] 2 Lloyd's Rep 601 Bingham J and the Court of Appeal reached a different conclusion, albeit in a case of sale not construction.

55 We note in passing that the *Percy Trentham* case was not a 'subject to contract' or 'subject to written contract' type of case. Nor was the *Pagnan* case, whereas part of the reasoning in the *British Steel* case . . . was that the negotiations were throughout conducted on the basis that, when reached, the agreement would be incorporated in a formal contract . . . In our judgment, in such a case, the question is whether the parties have nevertheless agreed to enter into contractual relations on particular terms notwithstanding their earlier understanding or agreement . . .

[Lord Clarke then explained the Supreme Court's conclusions:]

58 We agree with the judge that it is unrealistic to suppose that the parties did not intend to create legal relations. This can be tested by asking whether the price of £1,682,000 was agreed. Both parties accept that it was. If it was, as we see it, it must have formed a part of a contract between the parties. Moreover, once it is accepted (as both parties now accept) that the LOI contract expired and was not revived, the contract containing the price must be contained in some agreement other than the LOI contract. If the price is to be a term binding on the parties, it cannot, at any rate on conventional principles, be a case of no contract. Although it did not address this question, the Court of Appeal's solution involves holding that there was no binding agreement as to price or anything else and that evidence of the agreed price is no more than some evidence of what a reasonable price would have been for *quantum meruit* purposes. The difficulty with that analysis seems to us to be threefold. First, neither party suggested in the course of the project that the price was not agreed and RTS invoiced for percentages of the price and Müller paid sums so calculated as described above. Second, the price of £1,682,000 was agreed and included in the LOI contract on the footing that there would be a detailed contract containing many different provisions including, as expressly recognised in the LOI contract, the MF/1 terms. Third, there was an agreed variation on 25 August which nobody suggested was not a contractual variation.

59 In these circumstances the no contract solution is unconvincing. Moreover, it involves RTS agreeing to proceed with detailed work and to complete the whole contract on a non-contractual basis subject to no terms at all . . .

60 We entirely agree with the judge that the parties initially intended that there should be a written contract between them which was executed by each and exchanged between them. We further accept that, if the matter were tested on, say, 5 July, the correct conclusion may well have been that that remained the position and that there was no binding agreement between them. However, that is not on the basis that the parties had not reached agreement (or sufficient agreement) but because the agreement they had reached remained (in the traditional language) 'subject to contract' . . . Müller correctly submitted that the

question was, objectively speaking, whether the parties' intentions took a new turn at some stage such that they intended to be bound by the final draft contract without the need for its formal execution . . .

61 The striking feature of this case which makes it very different from many of the cases which the courts have considered is that essentially all the terms were agreed between the parties and that substantial works were then carried out and the agreement was subsequently varied in important respects. The parties treated the agreement of 25 August as a variation of the agreement that they had reached by 5 July. Nobody suggested in August that there was no contract and thus nothing to vary. It was not until November, by which time the parties were in dispute, that points were taken as to whether there was a contract.

62 We have reached the firm conclusion that by 25 August at the latest the parties' communications and actions lead to the conclusion that they had agreed that RTS would perform the work and supply the materials on the terms agreed between them up to and including 5 July as varied by the agreement of 25 August . . . As stated above, it does not seem to us to make commercial sense to hold that the parties were agreeing to the works being carried out without any relevant contract terms.

Chapter 3

Enforceability of promises: consideration and promissory estoppel

In addition to any requirements of form—*Poole's Textbook on Contract Law*, 15th edn (Oxford University Press, 2021), 4.4.2–4.4.2.4.2—a promise must either be expressed in the form of a deed or be supported by consideration to be enforceable. Indeed, English contract law assumes that only bargains should be enforced (i.e. that the promisor must get something in exchange for his promise).

Case law is concerned with identifying what can constitute consideration and whether it is possible to enforce a promise in the absence of consideration.

3.1 Consideration

3.1.1 What is consideration?

Traditionally, consideration is identified as a detriment to the promisee and/or a benefit to the promisor. See e.g. *Currie v Misa* (1875) LR 10 Ex 153, 162, in which Lush J said:

> A valuable consideration, in the sense of the law, may consist either in some right, interest, profit, or benefit accruing to the one party, or some forbearance, detriment, loss, or responsibility, given, suffered, or undertaken by the other . . .

Another approach is to define consideration as the price requested by the promisor, in exchange for which the promisor's promise was bought. Lord Dunedin, in *Dunlop Pneumatic Tyre Co. Ltd v Selfridge & Co. Ltd* [1915] AC 847, 855, expressed this as:

> An act or forbearance of one party, or the promise thereof, is the price for which the promise of the other is bought, and the promise thus given for value is enforceable.

3.1.2 Consideration distinguished from a condition imposed on recipients of gifts

Thomas v Thomas
(1842) 2 QB 851, 114 ER 330 (QB)

Shortly before his death, the testator had stated that he wished his wife to have their house during her lifetime and while she remained his widow, or £100 instead. There was no provision to this effect in his will. The executors of the will, to comply with the testator's intentions, agreed with the claimant widow 'in consideration of such desire' to convey the house to her for her life 'provided nevertheless and it is further agreed' that, during that time, the claimant would pay £1 yearly towards the ground rent for the property and keep the house 'in good and tenantable repair'. The defendant executors later refused to convey the house and ejected her. The issue was whether any consideration had been provided for the executors' promise.

Held: Although the testator's desire was only the motive for the agreement and a motive could not be consideration, the widow's promise to pay £1 towards the ground rent and to keep the house in repair was good consideration to support the promise to convey the house to her. The promise to perform these acts had some value in the eyes of the law, and the court did not have to inquire as to the adequacy of the widow's promise.

PATTERSON J: Motive is not the same thing with consideration. Consideration means something which is of some value in the eye of the law, moving from the plaintiff: it may be some benefit to the plaintiff, or some detriment to the defendant; but at all events it must be moving from the plaintiff. Now that which is suggested as the consideration here, a pious respect for the wishes of the testator, does not in any way move from the plaintiff; it moves from the testator; therefore, legally speaking, it forms no part of the consideration. Then it is said that, if that be so, there is no consideration at all, it is a mere voluntary gift: but when we look at the agreement we find that this is not a mere proviso that the donee shall take the gift with the burthens; but it is an express agreement to pay what seems to be a fresh apportionment of a ground rent, and which is made payable not to a superior landlord but to the executors. So that this rent is clearly not something incident to the assignment of the house; for in that case, instead of being payable to the executors, it would have been payable to the landlord. Then as to the repairs: these houses may very possibly be held under a lease containing covenants to repair; but we know nothing about it: for any thing that appears, the liability to repair is first created by this instrument. The proviso certainly struck me at first . . . that the rent and repairs were merely attached to the gift by the donors; and, had the instrument been executed by the donors only, there might have been some ground for that construction; but the fact is not so . . .

NOTES

1. Consideration must move from the promisee: *Tweddle v Atkinson* (1861) B & S 393 (*page 307, 7.1*). Therefore, the testator's desire could not have amounted to consideration in any event, because it did not move from the promisee (the recipient of the promise)—here, the widow.

2. Since the Contracts (Rights of Third Parties) Act 1999, consideration need not be provided by a claimant, but must be provided by someone (the promisee) if the promise is to be enforceable.

3. Since any benefit to the promisor must move from the promisee, and the person whose promise it was sought to enforce on the facts in *Thomas v Thomas* was the defendant, the true statement should be that the consideration must be 'some benefit to the defendant or some detriment to the claimant'.

4. Provided that the promisee suffers a detriment at the request of the promisor, it is unnecessary for a corresponding benefit to the promisor. This can occur where the promisee enters into a contract with a third party at the request of the promisor; e.g. in *Hunt v Optima (Cambridge) Ltd* [2014] EWCA Civ 714, [2015] 1 WLR 1346, Optima sold flats to purchasers and Strutt & Parker (S&P), who were employed by Optima for this purpose, issued architects' certificates attesting to the satisfactory construction of the flats. The purchasers of the flats received the certificates after exchange of contracts and execution of the leases on the flats. Did the certificates constitute binding contractual promises supported by consideration provided by the purchasers? It was argued that any consideration, interpreted as promising to pay for the flat in exchange for the promise to convey the flat and supply the certificate, did not move to S&P as the promisor of the certificates. However, the Court of Appeal rejected this since the only requirement was that the consideration should move from the purchasers (as promisees). (Compare this definition of the consideration requirements with that in the alteration context in *Williams v Roffey Bros. & Nicholls (Contractors) Ltd* [1991] 1 QB 1 (*page 107, 3.1.3.7*).

5. In practice, it is difficult to distinguish a party's motive from the consideration provided. It may be preferable to regard a motive as consideration, provided that it is of economic value rather than purely sentimental (*page 93, 3.1.3.2*).

? QUESTIONS

1. Why did the court consider that this was not a gratuitous promise to convey the house *conditional* on the promise to make this £1 payment and to carry out repairs?

2. Peel, *Treitel's The Law of Contract*, 14th edn (Sweet & Maxwell, 2015), [3-011], argues that, in *Carlill v Carbolic Smoke Ball Co.* [1893] 1 QB 256, the consideration was using the smoke ball in accordance with the instructions, but the promise was conditional on the user contracting influenza. Should a wider interpretation be used so that consideration consists of whatever has been requested by the promisor in exchange for their promise? See *Chappell & Co. Ltd v Nestlé Co. Ltd* [1960] AC 87 (*page 91, 3.1.3.1*).

3.1.3 Consideration must be sufficient, but need not be adequate

3.1.3.1 Adequacy

If what is given in exchange for the promise has value in the eyes of the law, the court will not question whether that value is adequate and will not interfere with the fairness of the bargain made by the parties.

Trivial acts have been held to amount to consideration because they have been requested by the promisor.

Chappell & Co. Ltd v Nestlé Co. Ltd
[1960] AC 87 (HL)

The claimants owned the copyright in a piece of music, 'Rockin' Shoes'. The defendants, Nestlé, arranged for copies of this tune to be manufactured into records, and offered these records to the public for 1s. 6d. plus three wrappers from their 6d. chocolate bars. Section 8 of the Copyright Act 1956 permitted the making of records for retail sale, provided that a royalty of

6¼ per cent on 'the ordinary retail selling price' was paid to the claimants. The claimants were informed that 1s. 6d. was the ordinary retail selling price. They sought an injunction claiming breach of copyright.

Held (Viscount Simonds and Lord Keith dissenting): The wrappers were part of the consideration for the sale of the records, even though of very trivial economic value and thrown away by Nestlé. Section 8 of the Copyright Act 1956 was intended to apply where a money sum was the entire consideration for the sale; since this sale was outside s. 8, there was a breach of copyright.

LORD SOMERVELL: The question, then, is whether the three wrappers were part of the consideration or, as Jenkins LJ held, a condition of making the purchase, like a ticket entitling a member to buy at a co-operative store.

I think they are part of the consideration. They are so described in the offer. 'They,' the wrappers, 'will help you to get smash hit recordings.' They are so described in the record itself—'all you have to do to get such new record is to send three wrappers from Nestlé's 6d. milk chocolate bars, together with postal order for 1s. 6d.' This is not conclusive but, however described, they are, in my view, in law part of the consideration. It is said that when received the wrappers are of no value to Nestlé's. This I would have thought irrelevant. A contracting party can stipulate for what consideration he chooses. A peppercorn does not cease to be good consideration if it is established that the promisee does not like pepper and will throw away the corn. As the whole object of selling the record, if it was a sale, was to increase the sales of chocolate, it seems to me wrong not to treat the stipulated evidence of such sales as part of the consideration.

LORD REID: The respondents [submit] that acquiring and delivering the wrappers was merely a condition which gave a qualification to buy and was not part of the consideration for sale. Of course, a person may limit his offer to persons qualified in a particular way, e.g., members of a club. But where the qualification is the doing of something of value to the seller, and where the qualification only suffices for one sale and must be re-acquired before another sale, I find it hard to regard the repeated acquisitions of the qualification as anything other than parts of the consideration for the sales. The purchaser of records had to send three wrappers for each record, so he had first to acquire them. The acquisition of wrappers by him was, at least in many cases, of direct benefit to the Nestlé Co., and required expenditure by the acquirer which he might not otherwise have incurred. To my mind the acquiring and delivering of the wrappers was certainly part of the consideration in these cases, and I see no good reason for drawing a distinction between these and other cases.

NOTES

1. For Lord Somervell there was a benefit to Nestlé through increased chocolate sales by requiring the wrappers (although Professor Atiyah has argued that this was only the motive that inspired the promise). He also considered that the wrappers were part of the consideration because they were asked for. In *Carlill v Carbolic Smoke Ball Co.* [1893] 1 QB 256 (*page 4, 1.4*), catching influenza was a stipulated act and arguably, therefore, should form part of the consideration for the promise of the reward.

2. Viscount Simonds (dissenting) in *Chappell & Co. Ltd v Nestlé Co. Ltd*, at p. 104, did not think the wrappers were part of the consideration:

In my opinion, my Lords, the wrappers are not part of the selling price. They are admittedly themselves valueless and are thrown away and it was for that reason, no doubt, that Upjohn J was constrained to say that their value lay in the evidence they afforded of success in an advertising campaign. That is what they are. But what, after all, does that mean? Nothing more than that someone, by no means necessarily the purchaser of the record, has in the past bought not from Nestlé's but from a retail shop three bars of chocolate and that the purchaser has thus directly or indirectly acquired the wrappers. How often he acquires them for himself, how often through another, is pure speculation. The only thing that is certain is that, if he buys bars of chocolate from a retail shop or acquires the wrappers from another who has bought them, that purchase is not, or at the lowest is not necessarily, part of the same transaction as his subsequent purchase of a record from the manufacturers. I conclude, therefore, that the objection fails, whether it is contended that (in the words of Upjohn J) the sale 'bears no resemblance at all to the transaction to which the section . . . is pointing' or that the three wrappers form part of the selling price and are incapable of valuation. Nor is there any need to take what, with respect, I think is a somewhat artificial view of a simple transaction. What can be easier than for a manufacturer to limit his sales to those members of the public who fulfil the qualification of being this or doing that? It may be assumed that the manufacturer's motive is his own advantage. It is possible that he achieves his object. But that does not mean that the sale is not a retail sale to which the section applies or that the ordinary retail selling price is not the price at which the record is ordinarily sold, in this case 1s. 6d.

Under the Consumer Rights Act (CRA) 2015 s 64, the 'fairness' of the price may be assessed (and the term not binding on the consumer) where the term in question is not presented in a way that satisfies the requirements of transparency and prominence (discussion at *page 295, 6.5.3*). Terms in small print will not be transparent or prominent.

3.1.3.2 Sufficiency ('of value in the eyes of the law')

The consideration provided must be capable of expression in economic terms.

White v Bluett
(1853) 23 LJ Ex 36 (Court of Exchequer)

Bluett's father had lent him some money. Bluey had given his father a promissory note (a promise to pay contained in a written document, e.g. a banknote). His father's executor sued Bluett on the note, and he claimed in his defence that his father had promised to discharge him from the obligation if he would stop complaining about the father's distribution of his property among his children.

Held: Bluett had provided no consideration for such a promise by his father; Bluett was under no legal duty to refrain from complaining and therefore his forbearance could not amount to consideration.

POLLOCK CB: If such a plea as this could be supported, the following would be a binding promise: A man might complain that another person used the public highway more than he ought to do, and that other might say, do not complain, and I will give you five pounds. It is ridiculous to suppose that such promises could be binding. So, if the holder of a bill of exchange were suing the acceptor, and the acceptor were to complain that the holder had treated him hardly, or that the bill ought never to have been circulated, and the holder were to say, Now, if you will not make any more complaints, I will not sue you. Such a promise would be like that now set up. In reality, there was no consideration whatever. The son had no right to complain, for the father might make what distribution of his property he liked; and the son's abstaining from doing what he had no right to do can be no consideration.

White v Bluett can be contrasted with the following American case in which the court recognized forbearance for activities in which the claimant had a lawful right to engage.

Hamer v Sidway
27 NE 256 (1891) (Court of Appeals of New York)

An uncle promised his nephew $5,000 if the nephew would refrain from 'drinking liquor, using tobacco, swearing and playing cards or billiards for money until he should become 21 years of age'. The nephew complied, but the defendant, the uncle's executor, refused to make the payment.

Held: The promise was enforceable because the nephew had provided consideration for the uncle's promise by restricting his lawful freedom of action.

> PARKER J: The defendant contends that the contract was without consideration to support it, and therefore invalid. He asserts that the promisee, by refraining from the use of liquor and tobacco, was not harmed, but benefited; that that which he did was best for him to do, independently of his uncle's promise,—and insists that it follows that, unless the promisor was benefited, the contract was without consideration,—a contention which, if well founded, would seem to leave open for controversy in many cases whether that which the promisee did or omitted to do was in fact of such benefit to him as to leave no consideration to support the enforcement of the promisor's agreement. Such a rule could not be tolerated, and is without foundation in the law . . . '"Consideration" means not so much that one party is profiting as that the other abandons some legal right in the present, or limits his legal freedom of action in the future, as an inducement for the promise of the first.' Now, applying this rule to the facts before us, the promisee used tobacco, occasionally drank liquor, and he had a legal right to do so. That right he abandoned for a period of years upon the strength of the promise of the testator that for such forbearance he would give him $5,000. We need not speculate on the effort which may have been required to give up the use of those stimulants. It is sufficient that he restricted his lawful freedom of action within certain prescribed limits upon the faith of his uncle's agreement, and now, having fully performed the conditions imposed, it is of no moment whether such performance actually proved a benefit to the promisor, and the court will not inquire into it; but, were it a proper subject of inquiry, we see nothing in this record that would permit a determination that the uncle was not benefited in a legal sense . . .

NOTES

1. It is difficult to see how this consideration could be classified as having 'economic value'. The decision may rest on policy, in that it is more socially acceptable to enforce this promise than to enforce the father's promise in *White v Bluett*. It may also be explained on the nephew's detrimental reliance.

2. Arguably, there is a benefit to the uncle from ensuring that his nephew refrains from these activities—see *Shadwell v Shadwell* (1860) 9 CBNS 139 (*page 99, 3.1.3.6*)—although some commenta-tors would argue that this is the uncle's motive rather than a benefit to him.

3. An important point on the facts was that the nephew had used tobacco and had drunk liquor in the past. In *Arrale v Costain Civil Engineering Ltd* [1976] 1 Lloyd's Rep 98, Geoffrey Lane LJ stated that consideration was not provided by refraining from a course of conduct that the subject never intended to pursue.

3.1.3.3 **Past consideration is not a good (sufficient) consideration**

Any act carried out *before* a promise is made cannot be sufficient consideration to support the promise, because it is not carried out in exchange for the promise.

Re McArdle
[1951] Ch 669 (CA)

The testator's widow had a life interest in a property held upon trust for the testator's five children. In 1943, improvements were carried out to the property and paid for by the wife of one of the beneficiaries. (She had not been requested to do this.) In 1945, after this work had been completed, the five children signed a document addressed to the wife providing:

> [I]n consideration of your carrying out certain alterations and improvements to the property . . . We the beneficiaries under the will of [the testator] hereby agree that the executors . . . shall repay to you from the said estate when so distributed the sum of £488 in settlement of the amount spent on the improvements.

When the testator's widow died, the wife claimed this sum under the agreement.

Held: Since the work had been completed before the agreement of 1945, the consideration for the agreement was past consideration and unenforceable.

3.1.3.3.1 *Prior request device*

However, a device can be employed by the courts to avoid the literal nature of the past consideration rule and to allow such promises to be enforced: there must be a prior request to carry out the act, which carries with it a promise to pay or benefit the performer of the act in some way. The later express promise merely fixes the reward; for the earlier promise, the act is not past consideration.

Pao On v Lau Yiu Long
[1980] AC 614 (PC)

The claimants owned shares in a private company, Shing On, the principal asset of which was a building under construction. The defendants were the majority shareholders in the Fu Chip Investment Company, which wished to acquire the building. In February 1973, the claimants agreed with the Fu Chip Company to sell their shares in Shing On to Fu Chip in return for shares in Fu Chip. To avoid depressing the market for shares in Fu Chip, the defendants requested that the claimants retain 60 per cent of their shares until after 30 April 1974, and it was agreed that the defendants would protect the claimants against any loss from a fall in the value of those shares during that period. A subsidiary agreement was entered into under which the defendants agreed to buy, and the claimants agreed to sell, 60 per cent of the shares on or before 30 April 1974 at $2.50 a share. The claimants realized, however, that such an agreement meant that they would lose the benefit of any possible rise in the market price of that 60 per cent holding, and they refused to complete the sale of the shares in Shing On to Fu Chip unless the defendants agreed to replace the subsidiary agreement with an indemnity. The defendants signed an indemnity in consideration of the claimants having agreed to sell their shares in Shing On. The claimants later sought to rely on the indemnity and one issue before the court was whether the claimants had provided any consideration for the indemnity. The Privy Council applied *Re Casey's Patents* [1892] 1 Ch 104.

Held: The consideration was the claimants' promise not to sell 60 per cent of their Fu Chip shares for one year. Although this promise had been made before the indemnity was given, it had been made at the request of the defendants and on the understanding that the claimants were to be protected against the risk that the value of their shareholding might fall in this period.

LORD SCARMAN: The first question is whether upon its true construction the written guarantee of May 4, 1973, states a consideration sufficient in law to support the defendants' promise of indemnity against a fall in value of the Fu Chip shares . . . [C]ounsel for the plaintiffs before their Lordships' Board . . . contends that the consideration stated in the agreement is not in reality a past one. It is to be noted that the consideration was not on May 4, 1973, a matter of history only. The instrument by its reference to the main agreement with Fu Chip incorporates as part of the stated consideration the plaintiffs' three promises to Fu Chip: to complete the sale of Shing On, to accept shares as the price for the sale, and not to sell 60 per cent of the shares so accepted before April 30, 1974. Thus, on May 4, 1973, the performance of the main agreement still lay in the future. Performance of these promises was of great importance to the defendants, and it is undeniable that, as the instrument declares, the promises were made to Fu Chip at the request of the defendants. It is equally clear that the instrument also includes a promise by the plaintiffs to the defendants to fulfil their earlier promises given to Fu Chip.

The Board agrees with [counsel for the plaintiffs'] submission that the consideration expressly stated in the written guarantee is sufficient in law to support the defendants' promise of indemnity. An act done before the giving of a promise to make a payment or to confer some other benefit can sometimes be consideration for the promise. The act must have been done at the promisors' request: the parties must have understood that the act was to be remunerated either by a payment or the conferment of some other benefit: and payment, or the conferment of a benefit, must have been legally enforceable had it been promised in advance. All three features are present in this case. The promise given to Fu Chip under the main agreement not to sell the shares for a year was at the first defendant's request. The parties understood at the time of the main agreement that the restriction on selling must be compensated for by the benefit of a guarantee against a drop in price: and such a guarantee would be legally enforceable. The agreed cancellation of the subsidiary agreement left, as the parties knew, the plaintiffs unprotected in a respect in which at the time of the main agreement all were agreed they should be protected.

[Counsel for the plaintiffs'] submission is based on *Lampleigh v Brathwait* (1615) Hobart 105. In that case the judges said, at p. 106:

> First . . . a meer voluntary courtesie will not have a consideration to uphold an assumpsit. But if that courtesie were moved by a suit or request of the party that gives the assumpsit, it will bind, for the promise, though it follows, yet it is not naked, but couples itself with the suit before, and the merits of the party procured by that suit, which is the difference.

The modern statement of the law is in the judgment of Bowen LJ in *In re Casey's Patents* [1892] 1 Ch 104, 115–116; Bowen LJ said:

> Even if it were true, as some scientific students of law believe, that a past service cannot support a future promise, you must look at the document and see if the promise cannot receive a proper effect in some other way. Now, the fact of a past service raises an implication that at the time it was rendered it was to be paid for, and, if it was a service which was to be paid for, when you get in the subsequent document a promise to pay, that promise may be treated either as an admission which evidences or as a positive bargain which fixes the amount of that reasonable remuneration on the faith of which the service was originally rendered. So that here for past services there is ample justification for the promise to give the third share.

. . . [Counsel] for the defendants, does not dispute the existence of the rule but challenges its application to the facts of this case. He submits that it is not a necessary inference or implication from the terms of the written guarantee that any benefit or protection was to be given to the plaintiffs for their acceptance of the restriction on selling their shares. Their Lordships agree that the mere existence or recital of a prior request is not sufficient in itself to convert what is prima facie past consideration into sufficient consideration in law to support a promise as they have indicated, it is only the first of three necessary preconditions. As for the second of those preconditions, whether the act done at the request of the promisor raises an implication of promised remuneration or other return is simply one of the construction of the words of the contract in the circumstances of its making. Once it is recognised, as the Board considers it inevitably must be, that the expressed consideration includes a reference to the plaintiffs' promise not to sell the shares before April 30, 1974—a promise to be performed in the future, though given in the past—it is not possible to treat the defendants' promise of indemnity as independent of the plaintiffs' antecedent promise, given at the first defendant's request, not to sell. The promise of indemnity was given because at the time of the main agreement the parties intended that the first defendant should confer upon the plaintiffs the benefit of his protection against a fall in price. When the subsidiary agreement was cancelled, all were well aware that the plaintiffs were still to have the benefit of his protection as consideration for the restriction on selling . . . Their Lordships, therefore, accept the submission that the contract itself states a valid consideration for the promise of indemnity.

NOTE To imply an earlier promise to remunerate, it must be asked every time whether it was reasonable in the circumstances for the parties to assume that the act would be remunerated.

There is some strength in the argument that such an implication of remuneration is more likely to arise in commercial cases or cases involving professional services (such as *Re Casey's Patents* and *Pao On v Lau Yiu Long*) than in arrangements between friends and family (*Re McArdle*) or in which the services are not professional.

If you are drowning and I rescue you, although a request might be inferred from your call for help, because of the nature of the service that I provide in rescuing you it is most unlikely that the request carries with it any understanding that the rescue will be remunerated. The act of rescue cannot be consideration for any promise of reward.

3.1.3.4 Performance of existing duties

If a person either does or promises to do what he is already legally bound to do in exchange for a promise made, then that person suffers no legal detriment and the act confers no legal benefit so that, traditionally, this has not been accepted as constituting sufficient consideration.

Prior to the Court of Appeal decision in *Williams v Roffey Bros. & Nicholls (Contractors) Ltd* [1991] 1 QB 1 (*page 106*, 3.1.3.7), it was generally held to be insufficient that a factual detriment had been incurred or that a factual benefit had been conferred. Lord Denning had been alone in accepting this as sufficient consideration in itself. The device employed to avoid the rule in practice was to hold that a promisee had *gone beyond the scope of his existing duty* and had thereby provided the necessary consideration.

3.1.3.5 Performance of a duty imposed by law is not a good (sufficient) consideration

In *Collins v Godefroy* (1831) 1 B & Ad 950, 109 ER 1040, the Court of King's Bench held that a promise by Godefroy to pay Collins, whom he had subpoenaed, six guineas for attending as a witness was unenforceable because if a person was subpoenaed, he was under a duty imposed by law to attend and give evidence, and therefore performance of that duty could not support a promise to pay.

If a promisee has done more than he was legally obliged to do, that will constitute consideration for a promise to pay.

Ward v Byham
[1956] 1 WLR 496 (CA)

The father of an illegitimate child made the following promise to the child's mother:

> I am prepared to let you have [the child] and pay you up to £1 a week allowance for her providing you can prove that she will be well looked after and happy and also that she is allowed to decide for herself whether or not she wishes to come and live with you.

The father later stopped making these payments and the mother sought to enforce his promise.

Held: The promise was supported by consideration and therefore enforceable. The majority (Morris and Parker LJJ) considered that, although the mother was required by statute to maintain her child, she had gone beyond that statutory duty by complying with the father's request, and this was a sufficient consideration for the father's promise to pay.

Denning LJ considered that the factual benefit to the father was sufficient.

> DENNING LJ: I approach the case . . . on the footing that the mother, in looking after the child, is only doing what she is legally bound to do. Even so, I think that there was sufficient consideration to support the promise. I have always thought that a promise to perform an existing duty, or the performance of it, should be regarded as good consideration, because it is a benefit to the person to whom it is given. Take this very case. It is as much a benefit for the father to have the child looked after by the mother as by a neighbour. If he gets the benefit for which he stipulated, he ought to honour his promise, and he ought not to avoid it by saying that the mother was herself under a duty to maintain the child.
>
> I regard the father's promise in this case as what is sometimes called a unilateral contract, a promise in return for an act, a promise by the father to pay £1 a week in return for the mother's looking after the child. Once the mother embarked on the task of looking after the child, there was a binding contract. So long as she looked after the child, she would be entitled to £1 a week.

? QUESTION

How realistic is the view of the majority that the mother had suffered 'extra detriment'? It could be argued that the mother's promise to ensure that the child was happy was not capable of expression in economic terms.

Lord Denning also repeated his view of the correct principles in the next case.

Williams v Williams
[1957] 1 WLR 148 (CA)

In January 1952, a wife deserted her husband; in March of that year, the parties signed an agreement whereby the husband promised to pay the wife £1 10s. a week for their joint lives so long as the wife led 'a chaste life'. The wife promised to use this sum to support and maintain herself, 'and promised not to pledge her husband's credit and to indemnify him against any debts she incurred'. The wife later claimed arrears of this maintenance, but the husband argued that she had provided no consideration for his promise to pay, since a husband was not bound to maintain a wife who had deserted him and a wife who had deserted her husband was not entitled to pledge her husband's credit.

Held: The wife's promise did constitute good consideration, since she could return at any time and had therefore only suspended her right to be maintained by her husband.

DENNING LJ: Now I agree that, in promising to maintain herself whilst she was in desertion, the wife was only promising to do that which she was already bound to do. Nevertheless, a promise to perform an existing duty is, I think, sufficient consideration to support a promise, so long as there is nothing in the transaction which is contrary to the public interest. Suppose that this agreement had never been made, and the wife had made no promise to maintain herself and did not do so. She might then have sought and received public assistance or have pledged her husband's credit with tradesmen: in which case the National Assistance Board might have summoned him before the magistrates, or the tradesmen might have sued him in the county court. It is true that he would have an answer to those claims because she was in desertion, but nevertheless he would be put to all the trouble, worry and expense of defending himself against them. By paying her 30s. a week and taking this promise from her that she will maintain herself and will not pledge his credit, he has an added safeguard to protect himself from all this worry, trouble and expense. That is a benefit to him which is good consideration for his promise to pay maintenance . . .

NOTE Denning LJ's qualification 'so long as there was nothing in the transaction which was contrary to the public interest' refers to public policy reasons why a promise should not be enforced: see e.g. *Collins v Godefroy* (1831) 1 B & Ad 950 (at *pages 97–99, 3.1.3.5*). This might now encompass situations covered by the operation of the doctrine of economic duress (*page 511, 10.1.3*).

3.1.3.6 Performance of an existing contractual duty owed to a third party is a good (sufficient) consideration

If B is already bound under a contractual promise to C, B can use that promise in favour of C (or B's performance of the promise to C) as consideration for a promise by A, e.g. involving payment for that very same performance—the assumption being that the promise or performance of the contract B/C is a benefit to A.

Shadwell v Shadwell
(1860) 9 CB NS 159, 142 ER 62 (Court of Common Bench)

After his engagement to Ellen Nicholl, the claimant received the following letter from his uncle:

I am glad to hear of your intended marriage with Ellen Nicholl; and, as I promised to assist you at starting, I am happy to tell you that I will pay to you £150 yearly during my life and until your annual income derived from your profession of a Chancery barrister shall amount to 600 guineas.

The claimant claimed arrears in these yearly sums from the uncle's executors, alleging the consideration for the promise to be his marriage to Ellen Nicholl.

Held (Erle CJ and Keating J; Byles J dissenting): The promise was binding, since it was supported by good consideration.

ERLE CJ [giving his own judgment and that of Keating J]: Now, do these facts shew that the promise was in consideration either of a loss to be sustained by the plaintiff or a benefit to be derived from the plaintiff to the uncle, at his, the uncle's request? My answer is in the affirmative.

First, do these facts shew a loss sustained by the plaintiff at his uncle's request? When I answer this in the affirmative, I am aware that a man's marriage with the woman of his choice is in one sense a boon, and in that sense the reverse of a loss: yet, as between the plaintiff and the party promising to supply an income to support the marriage, it may well be also a loss. The plaintiff may have made a most material change in his position, and induced the object of his affection to do the same, and may have incurred pecuniary liabilities resulting in embarrassments which would be in every sense a loss if the income which had been promised should be withheld; and, if the promise was made in order to induce the parties to marry, the promise so made would be in legal effect a request to marry.

Secondly, do these facts shew a benefit derived from the plaintiff to the uncle, at his request? In answering again in the affirmative, I am at liberty to consider the relation in which the parties stood and the interest in the settlement of his nephew which the uncle declares. The marriage primarily affects the parties thereto; but in a secondary degree it may be an object of interest to a near relative, and in that sense a benefit to him. This benefit is also derived from the plaintiff at the uncle's request. If the promise of the annuity was intended as an inducement to the marriage, and the averment that the plaintiff, relying on the promise, married, is an averment that the promise was one inducement to the marriage, this is the consideration averred in the declaration; and it appears to me to be expressed in the letter, construed with the surrounding circumstances.

. . . [T]he decision turns upon the question of fact, whether the consideration for the promise is proved as pleaded. I think it is; and therefore my judgment . . . is for the plaintiff.

BYLES J [dissenting]: I am of opinion that the defendant is entitled to the judgment of the court . . . The inquiry . . . narrows itself to this question,—Does the letter itself disclose any consideration for the promise? the consideration relied on by the plaintiff's counsel being the subsequent marriage of the plaintiff. I think the letter discloses no consideration . . .

It is by no means clear that the words 'at starting' mean 'on marriage with Ellen Nicholl,' or with anyone else. The more natural meaning seems to me to be, 'at starting in the profession;' for, it will be observed that those words are used by testator in reciting a prior promise made when the testator had not heard of the proposed marriage with Ellen Nicholl, or, so far as appears, heard of any proposed marriage. This construction is fortified by the consideration that the annuity is not in terms made to begin from the marriage, but, as it should seem, from the date of the letter: neither is it in terms made defeasible if Ellen Nicholl should die before marriage . . .

Marriage of the plaintiff at the testator's express request would be no doubt an ample consideration. But marriage of the plaintiff without the testator's request is no consideration to the testator. It is true that marriage is or may be a detriment to the plaintiff: but detriment to the plaintiff is not enough, unless it either be a benefit to the testator, or be treated by the testator as such by having been suffered at his request. Suppose a defendant to promise a plaintiff,—'I will give you 500l. if you break your leg,'—would that detriment to the plaintiff, should it happen, be any consideration? If it be said that such an accident is an involuntary mischief, would it have been a binding promise if the testator had said,—'I will give you 100l. a year while you continue in your present chambers'? I conceive that the promise would not be binding, for want of a previous request by the testator.

Now, the testator in the case before the court derived, so far as appears, no personal benefit from the marriage. The question, therefore, is still further narrowed to this point,—Was the marriage at the testator's request? Express request there was none. Can any request be implied? The only words from which it can be contended that it is to be implied, are the words 'I am glad to hear of your intended marriage with Ellen Nicholl.' But it appears from the fourth plea that the marriage had already been agreed on, and that the testator knew it. These words, therefore, seem to me to import no more than the satisfaction of the testator at the engagement,—an accomplished fact. No request can, as it seems to me, be inferred from them. And, further, how does it appear that the testator's implied request, if it could be implied, or his promise, if that promise alone would suffice, or both together, were intended to cause the marriage or did cause it, so that the marriage can be said to have taken place at the testator's request? or, in other words, in consequence of that request?

It seems to me not only that this does not appear, but that the contrary appears; for, the plaintiff before the letter had already bound himself to marry, by placing himself not only under a moral but under a legal objection to marry; and the testator knew it.

The well-known cases which have been cited at the bar in support of the position that a promise based on the consideration of doing that which a man is already bound to do is invalid, apply in this case . . . The reason why the doing what a man is already bound to do is no consideration, is, not only because such a consideration is in judgment of law of no value, but because a man can hardly be allowed to say that the prior legal obligation was not his determining motive. But, whether he can be allowed to say so or not, the plaintiff does not say so here. He does, indeed, make an attempt to meet this difficulty by alleging in the replication to the fourth plea that he married relying on the testator's promise: but he shrinks from alleging, that, though he had promised to marry before the testator's promise to him, nevertheless he would have broken his engagement, and would not have married without the testator's promise. A man may rely on encouragements to the performance of his duty, who yet is prepared to do his duty without those encouragements. At the utmost the allegation that he relied on the testator's promise seems to me to import no more than that he believed the testator would be as good as his word.

It appears to me, for these reasons, that this letter is no more than a letter of kindness, creating no legal obligation.

NOTES

1. It is questionable whether the majority judgments support the principle that the nephew's performance of his contractual duty owed to Ellen Nicholl (a third party) to marry her was a good consideration for the uncle's promise. The majority judgments do not refer to the fact that the nephew was already contractually bound to his fiancée to marry her (at this time, an action existed for breach of a promise to marry).

2. Erle CJ states that the marriage could be seen as a detriment to the nephew and stresses that the nephew might well have relied upon this promise in incurring additional expenses. Erle CJ also considered that there was a benefit to the uncle in seeing his nephew well settled. This so-called benefit is, of course, purely sentimental and cannot be expressed in economic terms.

3. Byles J (dissenting) considered that, on the construction of the letter, the marriage was not the intended consideration for the uncle's promise since there was no request to marry. In any event, he considered that there was no intention to create legal relations (*page 145, 4.1*). This dissenting judgment was approved by Salmon LJ in *Jones v Padavatton* [1969] 1 WLR 328.

? QUESTIONS

1. Is the true reason for enforcement the fact that the nephew had relied on his uncle's promise?

2. Byles J, dissenting, was clearly of the opinion that a detriment could be a sufficient consideration only if it was requested by the promisor. Is this a necessary requirement?

However, the principle that performance of an existing contractual duty owed to a third party can be a good consideration has been approved by the Privy Council in two further cases—namely, *New Zealand Shipping Co. Ltd v A. M. Satterthwaite, The Eurymedon* [1975] AC 154 (PC) (below) and *Pao On v Lau Yiu Long* [1980] AC 614 (PC) (*page 95, 3.1.3.3.1*).

New Zealand Shipping Co. Ltd v A. M. Satterthwaite, The Eurymedon
[1975] AC 154 (PC)

The shipper entered into a contract with the carrier for the carriage of a drilling machine from Liverpool to Wellington in New Zealand. This contract of carriage exempted the carrier from all liability for loss or damage unless the action was brought within one year, and this immunity was extended to the carrier's servants, agents, or independent contractors:

It is hereby expressly agreed that no servant or agent of the carrier (including every independent contractor from time to time employed by the carrier) shall in any circumstances whatsoever be under any liability whatsoever to the shipper, consignee or owner of the goods or to any holder of this bill of lading for any loss or damage or delay of whatsoever kind arising or resulting directly or indirectly from any act neglect or default on his part while acting in the course of or in connection with his employment and, without prejudice to the generality of the foregoing provisions in this clause, every exemption, limitation, condition and liberty herein contained and every right, exemption from liability, defence and immunity of whatsoever nature applicable to the carrier or to which the carrier is entitled hereunder shall also be available and shall extend to protect every such servant or agent of the carrier acting as aforesaid and for the purpose of all the foregoing provisions of this clause the carrier is or shall be deemed to be acting as agent or trustee on behalf of and for the benefit of all persons who are or might be his servants or agents from time to time (including independent contractors as aforesaid) and all such persons shall to this extent be or be deemed to be parties to the contract in or evidenced by this bill of lading.

The carrier was a wholly owned subsidiary company of the stevedores, who were employed to unload the machine at Wellington. While unloading the machine, the stevedores were negligent and damaged it. The claimant cargo owner brought an action against the stevedores for the cost of repairing the drill. The stevedores pleaded the time limit in the contract of carriage between the shipper and the carrier. The Privy Council analysed the clause in the contract of carriage as a promise of exemption made to the stevedores through the carrier as their agent. In order to accept this promise, the stevedores had to provide consideration for the promise, and this was held to be the services of unloading, which were of benefit to the shipper. The stevedores were already bound to perform these services under their contract with the carrier, and this could be a good consideration to support the shipper's promise.

LORD WILBERFORCE: If the choice, and the antithesis, is between a gratuitous promise, and a promise for consideration, as it must be in the absence of a tertium quid, there can be little doubt which, in commercial reality, this is. The whole contract is of a commercial character, involving service on one side, rates of payment on the other, and qualifying stipulations as to both. The relations of all parties to each other are commercial relations entered into for business reasons of ultimate profit. To describe one set of promises, in this context, as gratuitous, or nudum pactum, seems paradoxical and is prima facie implausible. It is only the precise analysis of this complex of relations into the classical offer and acceptance, with identifiable consideration, that seems to present difficulty, but this same difficulty exists in many situations of daily life, e.g., sales at auction; supermarket purchases; boarding an omnibus; purchasing a train ticket; tenders for the supply of goods; offers of rewards; acceptance by post; warranties of authority by agents; manufacturers' guarantees; gratuitous bailments; bankers' commercial credits. These are all examples which show that English law, having committed itself to a rather technical and schematic doctrine of contract, in application takes a practical approach, often at the cost of forcing the facts to fit uneasily into the marked slots of offer, acceptance and consideration . . .

There is possibly more than one way of analysing this business transaction into the necessary components; that which their Lordships would accept is to say that the bill of lading brought into existence a bargain initially unilateral but capable of becoming mutual, between the shipper and the appellant, made through the carrier as agent. This became a full contract when the appellant performed services by discharging the goods. The performance of these services for the benefit of the shipper was the consideration for the agreement by the shipper that the appellant should have the benefit of the exemptions and limitations contained in the bill of lading. The conception of a 'unilateral' contract of this kind was recognised in *Great Northern Railway Co. v Witham* (1873) LR 9 CP 16 and is well established. This way of regarding the matter is very close to if not identical to that accepted by Beattie J in the Supreme Court: he analysed the transaction as one of an offer open to acceptance by action such as was found in *Carlill v Carbolic Smoke Ball Co.* [1893] 1 QB 256 . . .

The following points require mention. 1. In their Lordships' opinion, consideration may quite well be provided by the appellant, as suggested, even though (or if) it was already under an obligation to discharge to the carrier. (There is no direct evidence of the existence or nature of this obligation, but their Lordships are prepared to assume it.) An agreement to do an act which the promisor is under an existing obligation to a third party to do, may quite well amount to valid consideration and does so in the present case: the promisee obtains the benefit of a direct obligation which he can enforce. This proposition is illustrated and supported by *Scotson v Pegg* (1861) 6 H & N 295 which their Lordships consider to be good law . . .

NOTES

1. The principle was extended to *promises* to perform an existing contractual duty owed to a third party, not only the performance of that duty, in *Pao On v Lau Yiu Long* (*page 95, 3.1.3.3.1*). The Privy Council held the consideration for the defendants' promise to be the claimants' promise to the Fu Chip Company (the third party) to retain 60 per cent of their shares for one year. Lord Scarman said, at p. 632B: 'Their Lordships do not doubt that a promise to perform, or the performance of, a pre-existing contractual obligation to a third party can be valid consideration.'

2. In *Scotson v Pegg* (1861) 6 H & N 295, 158 ER 121, the Court of Exchequer held that it was necessary for the promisee's action, which he was contractually bound to the third party to perform, also to be a benefit to the promisor. Clearly, the defendants in *Pao On v Lau Yiu Long*, as majority shareholders,

benefited from seeing the main agreement with the company performed. The Privy Council in *The Eurymedon* also appeared to treat it as a benefit to the shipper to have the goods unloaded by the stevedores. If the stevedores failed to unload the goods, that would inevitably cause loss to the shipper, but the only party with a remedy in breach of contract would be the carrier. It might be argued that, in all of these cases, the promisor does get a benefit from the performance of a contractual duty owed to a third party, but it is a *factual benefit*. Should this be sufficient? (*page 103, 3.1.3.7.*)

3. The difficulty is to find additional detriment to the promisee, who is already bound by this promise. If there is none, does it matter? See the discussion of *Williams v Roffey Bros. & Nicholls (Contractors) Ltd* [1991] 1 QB 1 at *pages 106, 3.1.3.7.*

3.1.3.7 Performance of a contractual duty owed to the promisor

This arises in relation to *a promise to alter an existing contract between the parties.*

Stilk v Myrick

The two reports of this case—Campbell's Report and Espinasse's Report—give different explanations of why the claim was unenforceable.

(1809) 2 Camp 317, 170 ER 1168 (Campbell's Report)

On a voyage from London to the Baltic, two of the seamen deserted and, because the captain could not find replacements at Cronstadt, he promised the remaining crew that he would divide the wages of the deserters between them if they were to sail the ship back to London. Was this promise enforceable?

Garrow for the defendant insisted that this agreement was contrary to public policy and utterly void. In West India voyages, crews are often thinned greatly by death and desertion; if a promise of advanced wages were valid, exorbitant claims would be set up on all such occasions. This ground was strongly taken by Lord Kenyon in *Harris v Watson* (1791) Peake 102, in which that learned judge held that no action would lie at the suit of a sailor on a promise of a captain to pay him extra wages, in consideration of his doing more than the ordinary share of duty in navigating the ship—his Lordship saying that, if such a promise could be enforced, sailors would in many cases suffer a ship to sink unless the captain would accede to any extravagant demand that they might think it proper to make.

LORD ELLENBOROUGH: I think *Harris v Watson* was rightly decided; but I doubt whether the ground of public policy, upon which Lord Kenyon is stated to have proceeded, be the true principle on which the decision is to be supported. Here, I say, the agreement is void for want of consideration. There was no consideration for the ulterior pay promised to the mariners who remained with the ship. Before they sailed from London they had undertaken to do all that they could under all the emergencies of the voyage. They had sold all their services till the voyage should be completed. If they had been at liberty to quit the vessel at Cronstadt, the case would have been quite different; or if the captain had capriciously discharged the two men who were wanting, the others might not have been compellable to take the whole duty upon themselves, and their agreeing to do so might have been a sufficient consideration for the promise of an advance of wages. But the desertion of a part of the crew is to be considered an emergency of the voyage as much as their death; and those who remain are bound by the terms of their original contract to exert themselves to the utmost to bring the ship in safety to her destined port. Therefore, without looking to the policy of this agreement, I think it is void for want of consideration . . .

NOTES

1. Campbell's Report stresses that the desertions were covered by the agreed terms of the contract, so that, by sailing the ship home shorthanded, the sailors had done no more than they were already bound to do. Consequently, the master's promise was not supported by any consideration and was unenforceable.

2. Espinasse's Report—(1809) 6 Esp 129, 170 ER 851—stresses the policy grounds for refusing enforcement: see the comments of Garrow, who argued that a sea captain could be held to ransom on the High Seas if such promises of additional payment were to be held to be enforceable.

3. If Espinasse's Report were to be accepted as the correct basis for the decision that the promise was unenforceable, then it might be argued that, in the absence of circumstances of extortion, there would be no reason why such a promise should not be enforced. However, Mocatta J in *North Ocean Shipping v Hyundai Construction Co. Ltd* [1979] QB 705 accepted Campbell's Report as the correct one; such acceptance is also implicit in the judgment of the Court of Appeal in *Williams v Roffey Bros.* (*pages 106–110, 3.1.3.7*), since the court did not question the need to establish consideration, although there was

no extortion on the facts. There also appears to be no evidence of extortion on the facts of *Stilk v Myrick* itself, since the initiative for the payment came from the ship's captain and not the crew.

4. In *Stilk v Myrick*, although there was a factual benefit to the captain from the sailors' promise to sail the ship home, this was not accepted as sufficient consideration.

5. The principle in *Stilk v Myrick* applies to variations, but not to instances of rescission (termination) and replacement. The question facing the Court of Appeal in *Compagnie Noga D'Importation et D'Exportation v Abacha (No. 4)* [2003] EWCA Civ 1100, [2003] 2 All ER (Comm) 915, related to an agreement to settle a claim. Under the first agreement (13 August), the Federal Government of Nigeria (FGN) had waived all claims against SJ Berwin (SJB) in return for a specified payment. However, this agreement was rescinded and replaced by an agreement of 16 August under which only certain clauses were waived. The agreement of 16 August expressly provided that it superseded the earlier agreement. The FGN sought to rely on the 16 August agreement, but SJB argued that it was not supported by consideration, since it amounted to no more than a promise to perform an

existing contractual obligation (in the agreement of 13 August) and was therefore unenforceable (*Stilk v Myrick*). However, the Court of Appeal held that the agreement of 13 August, under which both parties had unperformed obligations, had been terminated by mutual release and that the obligations under it had ended. It followed that the principle in *Stilk* did not apply, since it depended on the continuation of the obligations in the old agreement (13 August). The mutual release and the mutual promises in the new agreement were construed as the consideration for the new agreement of 16 August.

It has always been accepted that if a promisee has done more than he was contractually obliged to do, then the extra performance is consideration to support the promisor's promise.

North Ocean Shipping Co. Ltd v Hyundai Construction Co. Ltd, The Atlantic Baron
[1979] QB 705

The full facts of this case appear at *page 511, 10.1.3.1.*

A shipbuilding company agreed to build a tanker for the owners and opened a letter of credit to provide security for repayment of the instalments paid by the owners in the event of the shipbuilding company's default. The owners promised to pay an additional 10 per cent in the instalments when the US dollar was devalued and asked the shipbuilding company to make a corresponding increase in the letter of credit, which it did.

Held (although with some hesitation): In agreeing to increase the letter of credit, the shipbuilding company had undertaken an additional contractual obligation that rendered it liable to an increased detriment, and this constituted consideration for the promise by the owners to increase the instalment payments.

MOCATTA J: [Counsel for the owners'] argument that the agreement to pay the extra 10 per cent was void for lack of consideration was based upon the well-known principle that a promise by one party to fulfil his existing contractual duty towards his other contracting party is not good consideration; he relied upon the well-known case of *Stilk v Myrick* (1809) 2 Camp 317; 6 Esp 129 for this submission. Accordingly there was no consideration for the owner's agreement to pay the further 10 per cent, since the Yard were already contractually bound to build the ship and it is common ground that the devaluation of the dollar had in no way lessened the Yard's legal obligation to do this. There has of course been some criticism in the books of the decision in *Stilk v Myrick*, which is somewhat differently reported in the two sets of reports, but Campbell's Reports have the better reputation and what I have referred to as being the law on this point is referred to as 'the present rule' in *Chitty on Contracts, General Principles*, 24th ed. (1977), p. 86: see, also, *Cheshire and Fifoot, Law of Contract*, 9th ed. (1976), p. 83 . . .

[Counsel for the shipbuilding company] relied upon what Denning LJ said in two cases dealing with very different subject matters [*Ward v Byham* (*page 98, 3.1.3.5*) and *Williams v Williams* (*pages 98–99, 3.1.3.5*] . . . I do not . . . think either of these cases successfully enables [counsel] to avoid the rule in *Stilk v Myrick*, 2 Camp 317.

What I have, however, found more difficult is whether the Yard did not give some consideration for the extra 10 per cent on the contract price, on which they insisted, in the form of their agreement to increase pro tanto what was for short called in argument 'the return letter of credit.' . . . I remain unconvinced . . . that by merely securing an increase in the instalments to be paid of 10 per cent the Yard automatically became obliged to increase the return letter of credit pro tanto and were therefore doing no more than undertaking in this respect to fulfil their existing contractual duty. I think that here they were undertaking an additional obligation or rendering themselves liable to an increased detriment. I therefore conclude, though not without some doubt, that there was consideration for the new agreement.

The decision of the Court of Appeal in *Williams v Roffey Bros.* demonstrates that, since the recognition of a doctrine of economic duress (*page 511*, 10.1.3) as the protection against extortion, it is no longer necessary to adopt a rule requiring legal benefit or detriment and that consideration may be found where there is a factual benefit to the promisor or avoidance of a disbenefit arising from a promise to pay more money (or to undertake other additional obligations) under an existing contract.

Williams v Roffey Bros. & Nicholls (Contractors) Ltd
[1991] 1 QB 1 (CA)

The defendant building contractors had entered into a contract to refurbish a block of 27 flats. They subcontracted the carpentry work to the claimant carpenter for a price of £20,000. When the claimant had completed the carpentry work on the roof and only nine of the flats, and had carried out only preliminary work on the others, the claimant found that he was in financial difficulties, despite the fact that he had already received interim payments of £16,200. The difficulties were a result partly of the fact that he had underestimated the cost of doing the work and partly of his failure to supervise the work properly. The defendants were liable under a 'penalty clause' in the main contract if the flats were not completed on time. They were aware of the claimant's difficulties and that the subcontract had been under-priced. The defendants agreed to pay the claimant an extra £10,300 at the rate of £575 on completion of each flat. The claimant completed eight further flats and the defendants made one further payment of £1,500. The claimant stopped work and sued the defendants on their promise, which the defendants claimed was unenforceable because it was not supported by any consideration.

Held: Although the claimant was doing no more than he was already legally obliged to do, since the defendants had obtained a benefit in making this promise, the promise was enforceable against them (in the absence of economic duress or fraud). The Court of Appeal stated that this did not overrule or contravene the principle in *Stilk v Myrick* (1809) 2 Camp 317, 6 Esp 129.

GLIDEWELL LJ: In his address to us [counsel for the defendants] outlined the benefits to his clients, the defendants, which arose from their agreement to pay the additional £10,300 as: (i) seeking to ensure that the plaintiff continued work and did not stop in breach of the sub-contract; (ii) avoiding the penalty for delay; and (iii) avoiding the trouble and expense of engaging other people to complete the carpentry work.

However, [counsel] submits that, though his clients may have derived, or hoped to derive, practical benefits from their agreement to pay the 'bonus', they derived no benefit in law, since the plaintiff was promising to do no more than he was already bound to do by his subcontract, i.e. continue with the carpentry work and complete it on time. Thus there was no consideration for the agreement.

[Counsel for the defendants] relies on the principle of law which, traditionally, is based on the decision in *Stilk v Myrick* . . .

In *North Ocean Shipping Co. Ltd v Hyundai Construction Co. Ltd* [1979] QB 705, Mocatta J regarded the general principle of the decision in *Stilk v Myrick* as still being good law . . .

It was suggested to us in argument that, since the development of the doctrine of promissory estoppel, it may well be possible for a person to whom a promise has been made, on which he has relied, to make an additional payment for services which he is in any event bound to render under an existing contract or by operation of law, to show that the promisor is estopped from claiming that there was no consideration for his promise. However, the application of the doctrine of promissory estoppel to facts such as those of the present case has not yet been fully developed: see e.g. the judgment of Lloyd J in *Syros Shipping*

Co. SA v Elaghill Trading Co. [1980] 2 Lloyd's Rep 390, 392. Moreover, this point was not argued in the court below, nor was it more than adumbrated before us. Interesting though it is, no reliance can in my view be placed on this concept in the present case.

There is, however, another legal concept of relatively recent development which is relevant, namely that of economic duress. Clearly, if a subcontractor has agreed to undertake work at a fixed price, and before he has completed the work declines to continue with it unless the contractor agrees to pay an increased price, the subcontractor may be held guilty of securing the contractor's promise by taking unfair advantage of the difficulties he will cause if he does not complete the work. In such a case an agreement to pay an increased price may well be voidable because it was entered into under duress. Thus this concept may provide another answer in law to the question of policy which has troubled the courts since before *Stilk v Myrick* . . . and no doubt led at the date of that decision to a rigid adherence to the doctrine of consideration.

. . . [T]he present state of the law on this subject can be expressed in the following proposition: (i) if A has entered into a contract with B to do work for, or to supply goods or services to, B in return for payment by B; and (ii) at some stage before A has completely performed his obligations under the contract B has reason to doubt whether A will, or will be able to, complete his side of the bargain; and (iii) B thereupon promises A an additional payment in return for A's promise to perform his contractual obligations on time; and (iv) as a result of giving his promise, B obtains in practice a benefit, or obviates a disbenefit; and (v) B's promise is not given as a result of economic duress or fraud on the part of A; then (vi) the benefit to B is capable of being consideration for B's promise, so that the promise will be legally binding.

As I have said, [counsel for the defendants] accepts that in the present case by promising to pay the extra £10,300 his client secured benefits. There is no finding, and no suggestion, that in this case the promise was given as a result of fraud or duress. If it be objected that the propositions above contravene the principle in *Stilk v Myrick*, I answer that in my view they do not; they refine, and limit the application of that principle, but they leave the principle unscathed e.g. where B secures no benefit by his promise. It is not in my view surprising that a principle enunciated in relation to the rigours of seafaring life during the Napoleonic wars should be subjected during the succeeding 180 years to a process of refinement and limitation in its application in the present day. It is therefore my opinion that on his findings of fact in the present case, the judge was entitled to hold, as he did, that the defendants' promise to pay the extra £10,300 was supported by valuable consideration, and thus constituted an enforceable agreement.

As a subsidiary argument, [counsel for the defendants] submits that on the facts of the present case the consideration, even if otherwise good, did not 'move from the promisee'. This submission is based on the principle illustrated in the decision in *Tweddle v Atkinson* (1861) 1 B & S 393. My understanding of the meaning of the requirement that 'consideration must move from the promisee' is that such consideration must be provided by the promisee, or arise out of his contractual relationship with the promisor. It is consideration provided by somebody else, not a party to the contract, which does not 'move from the promisee'. This was the situation in *Tweddle v Atkinson*, but it is, of course, not the situation in the present case. Here the benefits to the defendants arose out of their agreement of 9 April 1986 with the plaintiff, the promisee. In this respect I would adopt the following passage from *Chitty on Contracts*, 26th ed. (1989), p. 126, para. 183, and refer to the authorities there cited:

> The requirement that consideration must move from the promisee is most generally satisfied where some detriment is suffered by him e.g. where he parts with money or goods, or renders services, in exchange for the promise. But the requirement may equally well be satisfied where the promisee confers a benefit on the promisor without in fact suffering any detriment.

That is the situation in this case.

RUSSELL LJ: Speaking for myself—and I notice it is touched on in the judgment of Glidewell LJ—I would have welcomed the development of argument, if it could have been properly raised in this court, on the basis that there was here an estoppel and that the defendants, in the circumstances prevailing, were precluded from raising the defence that their undertaking to pay the extra £10,300 was not binding. For example, in *Amalgamated Investment and Property Co Ltd v Texas Commerce International Bank Ltd* [1982] QB 84 Robert Goff J said, at p. 105:

> [I]t is in my judgment not of itself a bar to an estoppel that its effect may be to enable a party to enforce a cause of action which, without the estoppel, would not exist. It is sometimes said that an estoppel cannot create a cause of action, or that an estoppel can only act as a shield, not as a sword. In a sense this is true—in the sense that estoppel is not, as a contract is, a source of legal obligation. But, as Lord Denning MR pointed out in *Crabb v Arun District Council* [1976] Ch 179, 187, an estoppel may have the effect that a party can enforce a cause of action which, without the estoppel, he would not be able to do.

Brandon LJ said, at pp. 131–132:

> while a party cannot in terms found a cause of action on an estoppel, he may, as a result of being able to rely on an estoppel, succeed on a cause of action on which, without being able to rely on that estoppel, he would necessarily have failed.

. . . [W]hile consideration remains a fundamental requirement before a contract not under seal can be enforced, the policy of the law in its search to do justice between the parties has developed considerably since the early nineteenth century when *Stilk v Myrick* 2 Camp 317 was decided by Lord Ellenborough CJ. In the late 20th century I do not believe that the rigid approach to the concept of consideration to be found in *Stilk v Myrick* is either necessary or desirable. Consideration there must still be but in my judgment the courts nowadays should be more ready to find its existence so as to reflect the intention of the parties to the contract where the bargaining powers are not unequal and where the finding of consideration reflects the true intention of the parties.

. . . The plaintiff has got into financial difficulties. The defendants, through their employee Mr Cottrell, recognised that the price that had been agreed originally with the plaintiff was less than what Mr Cottrell himself regarded as a reasonable price. There was a desire on Mr Cottrell's part to retain the services of the plaintiff so that the work could be completed without the need to employ another subcontractor. There was further a need to replace what had hitherto been a haphazard method of payment by a more formalised scheme involving the payment of a specified sum on the completion of each flat. These were all advantages accruing to the defendants which can fairly be said to have been in consideration of their undertaking to pay the additional £10,300. True it was that the plaintiff did not undertake to do any work additional to that which he had originally undertaken to do but the terms on which he was to carry out the work were varied and, in my judgment, that variation was supported by consideration which a pragmatic approach to the true relationship between the parties readily demonstrates.

For my part I wish to make it plain that I do not base my judgment on any reservation as to the correctness of the law long ago enunciated in *Stilk v Myrick*. A gratuitous promise, pure and simple, remains unenforceable unless given under seal. But where, as in this case, a party undertakes to make a payment because by so doing it will gain an advantage arising out of the continuing relationship with the promisee the new bargain will not fail for want of consideration.

PURCHAS LJ: The point of some difficulty which arises on this appeal is whether the judge was correct in his conclusion that the agreement reached on 9 April did not fail for lack of consideration because the principle established by the old cases of *Stilk v Myrick* 2 Camp 317, approving *Harris v Watson* Peake 102, did not apply. [Counsel] for the plaintiff, was bold enough to submit that . . . this court was bound by neither authority. I feel I must say at once that, for my part, I would not be prepared to overrule two cases of such veneration involving judgments of judges of such distinction except on the strongest possible grounds since they form a pillar stone of the law of contract which has been observed over the years and is still recognised in principle in recent authority: see the decision of *Stilk v Myrick* to be found in *North Ocean Shipping Co Ltd v Hyundai Construction Co Ltd* [1979] QB 705, 712 *per* Mocatta J. With respect, I agree with his view of the two judgments of Denning LJ in *Ward v Byham* [1956] 1 WLR 496 and *Williams v Williams* [1957] 1 WLR 148 in concluding that these judgments do not provide a sound basis for avoiding the rule in *Stilk v Myrick*. Although this rule has been the subject of some criticism it is still clearly recognised in current textbooks of authority: see *Chitty on Contracts*, 28th ed. (1989) and *Cheshire Fifoot and Furmston's Law of Contract*, 11th ed. (1986) . . .

In my judgment, therefore, the rule in *Stilk v Myrick* remains valid as a matter of principle, namely that a contract not under seal must be supported by consideration . . . The modern cases tend to depend more on the defence of duress in a commercial context rather than lack of consideration for the second agreement. In the present case the question of duress does not arise. The initiative in coming to the agreement of 9 April came from Mr Cottrell and not from the plaintiff. It would not, therefore, lie in the defendants' mouth to assert a defence of duress. Nevertheless, the court is more ready in the presence of this defence being available in the commercial context to look for mutual advantages which would amount to sufficient consideration to support the second agreement under which the extra money is paid. Although the passage cited below from the speech of Lord Hailsham LC in *Woodhouse AC Israel Cocoa Ltd SA v Nigerian Produce Marketing Co Ltd* [1972] AC 741 was strictly obiter dicta I respectfully adopt it as an indication of the approach to be made in modern times . . .

> . . . Business men know their own business best even when they appear to grant an indulgence, and in the present case I do not think that there would have been insuperable difficulty in spelling out consideration from the earlier correspondence.

. . . The question must be posed: what consideration has moved from the plaintiff to support the promise to pay the extra £10,300 added to the lump sum provision? In the particular circumstances . . . there was clearly a commercial advantage to both sides from a pragmatic point of view in reaching the agreement of 9 April. The defendants were on risk that as a result of the bargain they had struck the plaintiff would not or indeed possibly could not comply with his existing obligations without further finance. As a result of the agreement the defendants secured their position commercially. There was, however, no obligation added to the contractual duties imposed on the plaintiff under the original contract. Prima facie this would appear to be a classic *Stilk v Myrick* case. It was, however, open to the plaintiff to be in deliberate breach of the contract in order to 'cut his losses' commercially. In normal circumstances the suggestion that a contracting party can rely on his own breach to establish consideration is distinctly unattractive. In many cases it obviously would be and if there was any element of duress brought upon the other contracting party under the modern development of this branch of the law the proposed breaker of the contract would not benefit. With some hesitation and comforted by the passage from the speech of Lord Hailsham of St. Marylebone LC in *Woodhouse AC Israel Cocoa Ltd SA v Nigerian Produce Marketing Co Ltd* [1972] AC 741, 757–758 to which I have referred, I consider that the modern approach to the question of consideration would be that where there were benefits derived by each party to a contract of variation even though one party did not suffer a detriment this would not be fatal to the establishing of sufficient consideration to support the agreement. If both parties benefit from an agreement it is not necessary that each also suffers a detriment. In my judgment, on the facts as found by the judge, he was entitled to reach the conclusion that consideration existed and in those circumstances I would not disturb that finding . . .

NOTES

1. The Court of Appeal affirmed the need for consideration to support such a promise, but made it much easier to establish its existence, at least for alteration promises to pay more. There are other signs of relaxation of the strict rules relating to consideration: see e.g. Law Commission Report No. 242, *Privity of Contract: Contracts for the benefit of third parties* (Cm. 3329, 1996), paras. 6.13–6.17 (discussed at *page 312, 7.2.1*).

2. The 'penalty clause' was, in fact, an enforceable liquidated damages clause rather than a true penalty clause. The term 'penalty clause' is often used in a very general sense. (For a discussion of liquidated damages and penalty clauses, *page 753, 14.10.1*.)

3. If factual benefits are assessed subjectively, they will be relatively easy to establish since, as Coote (1990) 3 JCL 23 argued, no voluntary promise of further payment would be made if it were not perceived to benefit the promisor; no one would throw good money after bad.

4. The factual benefit in *Williams v Roffey* arose from the fact that the promisor agreed to pay more money to secure completion on time and it was not conferred by anything that the promisee did. The Court of Appeal held that the benefit could be generated by the compromise itself. This is the case e.g. with agreements to discharge a contract, where both parties get the benefit of not having to fulfil their obligations under the contract.

5. The apparent disregard of the Court of Appeal in *Roffey* for the principle that *consideration must move from the promisee* led to strong criticism by Colman J in *obiter* remarks in *South Caribbean Trading v Trafalgar Beheer BV* [2004] EWHC 2676 (Comm), [2005] 1 Lloyd's Rep 128. The comments were *obiter* because the extension of the letter of credit amounted to an agreement to deliver at a later date and to accept that late delivery, i.e. it was a binding variation by exchange of mutual promises. The judge concluded that if there had been no mutual promises, the seller's promise to release the cargo (to deliver) could not be consideration for the buyer's promise to accept delivery because this was no more than the performance required under the existing contract (*Stilk v Myrick*). *Williams v Roffey* was held to be inapplicable on these facts because the factual benefit that would have resulted from this delivery could not operate as

consideration as a result of the threat not to comply with the delivery obligation, which had led to the variation agreement—and which was seen as analogous to economic duress. In other words, having threatened not to deliver the fuel oil, the later promise to deliver could not be treated as enforceable in the sense of providing its own consideration despite the benefit in securing eventual performance. More significantly, perhaps, the judge noted:

COLMAN J: 108. But for the fact that *Williams v Roffey Bros Ltd . . .* was a decision of the Court of Appeal, I would not have followed it. That decision is inconsistent with the long-standing rule that consideration, being the price of the promise sued upon, must move *from* the promisee. The judgment of Glidewell LJ was substantially based on *Pao On v Lau You Long* [1980] AC 614 in which the Judicial Committee of the Privy Council had held a promise by A to B to perform a contractual obligation owed by A to X could be sufficient consideration as against B. At page 15 Glidewell LJ regarded Lord Scarman's reasoning in relation to such tripartite relationships as applicable in principle to a bipartite relationship. But in the former case by the additional promise to B, consideration has moved from A because he has made himself liable to an additional party, whereas in the latter case he has not undertaken anything that he was not already obliged to do for the same party. Glidewell LJ substituted for the established rule as to consideration moving from the promisee a completely different principle—that the promisor must by his promise have conferred a benefit on the other party. Purchas LJ at pages 22–23 clearly saw the nonsequitur but was 'comforted' by observations from Lord Hailsham LC in *Woodhouse AC Israel Cocoa Ltd v Nigerian Product Marketing Co Ltd* [1972] AC 741 at pages 757–758. Investigation of the correspondence referred to in those observations shows that the latter are not authority for the proposition advanced 'with some hesitation' by Purchas LJ.

This comment appears to overlook the acceptance that conferring a benefit can constitute sufficient consideration—particularly where there are reasons for seeking to give effect to a promise (see note 4). Insistence upon compliance with consideration technicalities seems to run counter to the reasoning in *Roffey*, and to the developments in Australia and New Zealand (discussed at *page 137, 3.2.3.1*).

6. For the *Roffey* principle to apply, it is necessary to ensure that the alteration promise was not obtained under duress and to ascertain whether there is any factual benefit to the promisor arising from the making of this promise. It would seem from the principles in the judgment of Glidewell LJ that it

is necessary to establish both to succeed with a *Roffey* argument and to establish consideration (i.e. establishing that there is no duress may be an element of a 'single integrated principle').

Nevertheless, it is commonplace to see comments suggesting that duress has replaced consideration when determining the enforceability of certain alteration promises. In *Adam Opel GmbH v Mitras Automotive (UK) Ltd* [2007] EWHC 3205 (QB) (*page 515*, 10.1.3.2 for the facts), there were alternative claims based on duress and absence of consideration to seek to avoid a compromise agreement whereby Mitras had agreed to continue its supply of products under a notice period in an existing contract in return for an additional payment. The duress argument succeeded, so that the compromise agreement was voidable.

DAVID DONALDSON QC [sitting as a deputy High Court judge]:

Absence of consideration

38 GMR's case is that under the agreement of 15 March 2006 Mitras did no more than promise continued supply, which it was already contractually obliged to effect. GMR submits that such a promise is void for lack of consideration under a long-established rule going back at least to *Stilk v Myrik*, [*sic*] (1809) 2 Camp. 317; 6 Esp 129, where the master of a vessel promised to divide the wages of two deserters among the remaining members of the crew and Lord Ellenborough CJ rejected a claim by one of promisees on the return of the vessel for his share of the extra wages . . . .

40 A more fundamental submission by Mitras is that a promise to perform an existing contractual obligation can be legal consideration. Its argument relies heavily on *Williams v Roffey Bros. & Nicholls (Contractors) Ltd.*, [1991] 1 QB 1 (C.A.) . . . [The judge then gave the facts of *Roffey*.] The defendants contended that their undertaking to pay the additional sums was void for absence of consideration, an argument rejected by the judge and on appeal.

41 Glidewell LJ said (at 15G–16C) that—absent economic duress or fraud—where (1) there was doubt whether the promisor would complete his side of the bargain and promised in return for the further payment that he would complete on time, and (2) the promisee thereby obtained a benefit, that would constitute good consideration, and counsel for the defendant had accepted that his clients derived a practical benefit from the new promise. Russell LJ (at 19D–E) spoke of the defendant having gained an advantage out of the continuing relationship with the plaintiff. And Purchas LJ referred (at 22H) to a commercial advantage. Though all three judges claimed to accept the rule in *Stilk v Myrik*, it is wholly unclear how the decision in *Williams v Roffey* can be reconciled with it. On analysis, the benefit or advantage lay in an act or promise wholly coincident with the plaintiff's existing contractual obligation.

42 In terms of its result and the reasons advanced by the judges, however, *Williams v Roffey* would seem to permit any variation of a contract, even if the benefits and burdens of the variation move solely in one direction, and I am bound to apply the decision accordingly, whatever view I might take of its logical coherence. *The law of consideration is no longer to be used to protect a participant in such a variation. That role has passed to the law of economic duress, which provides a more refined control mechanism, and renders the contract voidable rather than void.* [Emphasis added]

43 Accordingly, GMR cannot rely on absence of consideration, whether as a supplement or an alternative to economic duress.

This approach—and in particular the passage of the judgment emphasized in the extract—suggests that establishing the absence of any duress is a necessary first hurdle, although among Glidewell LJ's principles it is but one component when establishing the existence of consideration.

7. The Court of Appeal in *Roffey* seemed quite willing to relieve the carpenter from the consequences of his own inaccurate tender. Once a contract has been made at a fixed price, the courts are not normally as willing to disturb it where there is no evidence of duress, mistake, or misrepresentation.

8. The thorny issue of whether *Roffey* applies to alteration promises to accept less is discussed below to take account of *MWB Business Exchange*.

3.1.4 Part payment of a debt

Where a creditor promises to accept a smaller sum than is due from a debtor and promises not to sue for the balance, this is a promise to alter an existing contract (the debt contract). In *Pinnel's Case* (1602) 5 Co Rep 117a, the Court of Common Pleas held that, in such circumstances, the debtor must provide consideration for the creditor's promise to release him. Simply paying a smaller sum than that owed will not be sufficient, since the debtor has done only what he was legally obliged to do anyway under the debt contract. Traditionally, the factual benefit that might accrue to the creditor from securing some payment rather than nothing at all was not regarded as sufficient and some separate consideration was required. However, the 'gift of a horse, hawk or robe' (property other than money) would be good consideration for a promise to forgo the balance if accepted by the creditor as full payment, since the court will not inquire into the adequacy of the consideration.

Payment before the due date is a good consideration, as is payment at a different place—provided that the change of venue is at the creditor's request and not the debtor's, since if it were at the debtor's request, there would be neither a benefit to the creditor, nor a detriment to the debtor: *Vanbergen v St Edmunds Properties Ltd* [1933] 2 KB 223.

The principle in *Pinnel's Case* was confirmed by the House of Lords in the next case.

Foakes v Beer
(1884) 9 App Cas 605 (HL)

In August 1875, Julia Beer had obtained a High Court judgment against Dr Foakes for £2,090 19s. It was agreed in writing, in December 1876, that if Dr Foakes were to pay £500 immediately and pay £150 on two occasions each year until the whole sum of £2,090 19s. had been paid, then Julia Beer 'would not take any proceedings whatever on the said judgment'. (As a judgment debtor, Dr Foakes was liable for the interest that had accrued on the judgment debt, but the agreement had not mentioned this.) Dr Foakes paid the judgment debt in accordance with the agreement, but Julia Beer then brought an action claiming the interest on the debt. The House of Lords was divided on the question of whether the agreement amounted to a promise to excuse Dr Foakes from payment of the interest.

Held: In any event, Dr Foakes had not provided any consideration for Julia Beer's promise not to take any proceedings on the judgment and therefore the promise was unenforceable. He had done only what he was legally bound to do anyway.

EARL OF SELBORNE LC: [T]he question remains, whether the agreement is capable of being legally enforced. Not being under seal, it cannot be legally enforced against the respondent, unless she received consideration for it from the appellant, or unless, though without consideration, it operates by way of accord and satisfaction, so as to extinguish the claim for interest. What is the consideration? On the face of the agreement none is expressed, except a present payment of £500, on account and in part of the larger debt then due and payable by law under the judgment. The appellant did not contract to pay the future instalments of £150 each, at the times therein mentioned; much less did he give any new security; in the shape of negotiable paper, or in any other form. The promise de futuro was only that of the respondent, that if the half-yearly payments of £150 each were regularly paid, she would 'take no proceedings whatever on the judgment.' No doubt if the appellant had been under no antecedent obligation to pay the whole debt, his fulfilment of the condition might have imported some consideration on his part for that promise. But he was under that antecedent obligation; and payment at those deferred dates, by the forbearance and indulgence of the creditor, of the residue of the principal debt and costs, could not (in my opinion) be a consideration for the relinquishment of interest and discharge of the judgment, unless the payment of the £500, at the time of signing the agreement, was such a consideration. As to accord and satisfaction, in point of fact there could be no complete satisfaction, so long as any future instalment remained payable; and I do not see how any mere payments on account could operate in law as a satisfaction ad interim, conditionally upon other payments being afterwards duly made, unless there was a consideration sufficient to support the agreement while still unexecuted. Nor was anything, in fact, done by the respondent in this case, on the receipt of the last payment, which could be tantamount to an acquittance, if the agreement did not previously bind her.

The question, therefore, is nakedly raised by this appeal, whether your Lordships are now prepared, not only to overrule, as contrary to law, the doctrine stated by Sir Edward Coke to have been laid down by all the judges of the Common Pleas in *Pinnel's Case* (1602) 5 Co Rep 117a, . . . but to treat a prospective agreement, not under seal, for satisfaction of a debt, by a series of payments on account to a total amount less than the whole debt, as binding in law, provided those payments are regularly made; the case not being one of a composition with a common debtor, agreed to, inter se, by several creditors . . . The doctrine itself, as laid down by Sir Edward Coke, may have been criticised, as questionable in principle, by some persons whose opinions are entitled to respect, but it has never been judicially overruled; on the contrary I think it has always, since the sixteenth century, been accepted as law. If so, I cannot think that your Lordships would do right, if you were now to reverse, as erroneous, a judgment of the Court of Appeal, proceeding upon a doctrine which has been accepted as part of the law of England for 280 years . . .

The distinction between the effect of a deed under seal, and that of an agreement by parol, or by writing not under seal, may seem arbitrary, but it is established in our law; nor is it really unreasonable or practically inconvenient that the law should require particular solemnities to give to a gratuitous contract the force of a binding obligation. If the question be (as, in the actual state of the law, I think it is), whether consideration is, or is not, given in a case of this kind, by the debtor who pays down part of the debt presently due from him, for a promise by the creditor to relinquish, after certain further payments on account, the residue of the debt, I cannot say that I think consideration is given, in the sense in which I have always understood that word as used in our law. It might be (and indeed I think it would be) an improvement in our law, if a release or acquittance of the whole debt, on payment of any sum which the creditor might be content to receive by way of accord and satisfaction (though less than the whole), were held to be, generally, binding, though not under seal; nor should I be unwilling to see equal force given to a prospective agreement, like the present, in writing though not under seal; but I think it impossible, without refinements which practically alter the sense of the word, to treat such a release or acquittance as supported by any new consideration proceeding from the debtor.

. . . What is called 'any benefit, or even any legal possibility of benefit,' . . . is not (as I conceive) that sort of benefit which a creditor may derive from getting payment of part of the money due to him from a debtor who might otherwise keep him at arm's length, or possibly become insolvent, but is some independent benefit, actual or contingent, of a kind which might in law be a good and valuable consideration for any other sort of agreement not under seal . . .

Lord Blackburn, however, accepted that, in practice, agreements to accept part payment in full satisfaction often have factual benefits for the creditor. His position recognizes the practical realities.

LORD BLACKBURN: [Lord Blackburn referred to the decision in *Pinnel's Case* and continued:] There are two things here resolved. First, that where a matter paid and accepted in satisfaction of a debt certain might by any possibility be more beneficial to the creditor than his debt, the Court will not inquire into the adequacy of the consideration. If the creditor, without any fraud, accepted it in satisfaction when it was not a sufficient satisfaction it was his own fault. And that payment before the day might be more beneficial, and consequently that the plea was in substance good, and this must have been decided in the case.

There is a second point stated to have been resolved, viz.: 'That payment of a lesser sum on the day cannot be any satisfaction of the whole, because it appears to the judges that by no possibility a lesser sum can be a satisfaction to the plaintiff for a greater sum.' This was certainly not necessary for the decision of the case; but though the resolution of the Court of Common Pleas was only a dictum, it seems to me clear that Lord Coke deliberately adopted the dictum, and the great weight of his authority makes it necessary to be cautious before saying that what he deliberately adopted as law was a mistake, and though

I cannot find that in any subsequent case this dictum has been made the ground of the decision . . . yet there certainly are cases in which great judges have treated the dictum in *Pinnel's Case* as good law.

. . . I doubt much whether any judge sitting in a Court of the first instance would be justified in treating the question as open. But as this has very seldom, if at all, been the ground of the decision even in a Court of the first instance, and certainly never been the ground of a decision in the Court of Exchequer Chamber, still less in this House, I did think it open in your Lordships' House to reconsider this question. And, notwithstanding the very high authority of Lord Coke, I think it is not the fact that to accept prompt payment of a part only of a liquidated demand, can never be more beneficial than to insist on payment of the whole. And if it be not the fact, it cannot be apparent to the judges . . .

What principally weighs with me in thinking that Lord Coke made a mistake of fact is my conviction that all men of business, whether merchants or tradesmen, do every day recognise and act on the ground that prompt payment of a part of their demand may be more beneficial to them than it would be to insist on their rights and enforce payment of the whole. Even where the debtor is perfectly solvent, and sure to pay at last, this often is so. Where the credit of the debtor is doubtful it must be more so. I had persuaded myself that there was no such long-continued action on this dictum as to render it improper in this House to reconsider the question. I had written my reasons for so thinking; but as they were not satisfactory to the other noble and learned Lords who heard the case, I do not now repeat them nor persist in them.

I assent to the judgment proposed, though it is not that which I had originally thought proper.

? QUESTIONS

1. Was the House of Lords, in fact, bound to follow the *obiter dictum* in *Pinnel's Case*?

2. Do you consider that the creditor should be able to sue for the balance where the debtor has relied on the promise to forgo the balance and has spent it or incurred other obligations in the belief that he was no longer bound to pay it? (See the discussion of promissory estoppel at *pages 122–144, 3.2*.)

NOTE Julia Beer clearly secured a factual benefit in ensuring payment of the judgment debt and avoiding enforcement proceedings. However, the Court of Appeal has stated that *Williams v Roffey* cannot apply in this context.

In *Re Selectmove*, below, it was held that a factual benefit will not constitute consideration for an alteration promise to accept less. This decision must however now be seen in relation to *MWB Business Exchange Centres Ltd v Rock Advertising Ltd*.

Re Selectmove Ltd
[1995] 1 WLR 474 (CA)

In July 1991, a company that owed the (then) Inland Revenue considerable sums in income tax and National Insurance contributions had made a proposal at a meeting with the collector of taxes that, in future, it should pay the tax as it fell due and repay the arrears in instalments (commencing in February 1992). The collector stated that he would have to seek the approval of his superiors and would advise the company if the proposal was unacceptable. The company heard nothing, but the Revenue later demanded payment of the arrears in full and eventually presented a petition for winding-up. The company argued that the petition should be dismissed on the ground that the proposal of July 1991 had been accepted by the Revenue, or that the Revenue was estopped from relying on this debt as being due. The judge ordered compulsory winding-up on the basis that there was no such agreement and, in any event, no consideration to support it. The judge also rejected the claim based on estoppel because there was no promise that could give rise to an estoppel. On appeal, the company argued, inter alia, that its promise to pay an existing debt was a good consideration because it amounted to a practical (or factual) benefit to the Revenue.

Held: There was no agreement by the Revenue to accept the company's proposal, since the official in question did not have the authority to bind the Revenue. The comments relating to the arguments based on consideration and promissory estoppel were therefore *obiter*.

PETER GIBSON LJ [with whose judgment Balcombe and Stuart-Smith LJJ agreed]: The judge held that the case fell within the principle of *Foakes v Beer* (1884) 9 App Cas 605. In that case a judgment debtor and creditor agreed that in consideration of the debtor paying part of the judgment debt and costs immediately and the remainder by instalments the creditor would not take any proceedings on the judgment. The House of Lords held that the agreement was nudum pactum, being without consideration, and did not prevent the creditor, after payment of the whole debt and costs, from proceeding to enforce payment of the interest on the judgment. Although their Lordships were unanimous in the result, that case is notable for the powerful speech of Lord Blackburn, who made plain his disagreement with the course the law had taken in and since *Pinnel's Case* (1602) 5 Co Rep 117a and which the House of Lords in *Foakes v Beer* 9 App Cas 605 decided should not be reversed . . . Yet it is clear that the House of Lords decided that a practical benefit of that nature is not good consideration in law.

Foakes v Beer has been followed and applied in numerous cases subsequently . . . [Peter Gibson LJ referred to *Vanbergen v St Edmunds Properties Ltd* [1933] 2 KB 223 and *D. & C. Builders Ltd v Rees* [1966] 2 QB 617 as examples.] [Counsel] however submitted that an additional benefit to the revenue was conferred by the agreement in that the revenue stood to derive practical benefits therefrom: it was likely to recover more from not enforcing its debt against the company, which was known to be in financial difficulties, than from putting the company into liquidation. He pointed to the fact that the company did in fact pay its further PAYE and NIC liabilities and £7,000 of its arrears. He relied on the decision of this court in *Williams v Roffey Bros. & Nicholls (Contractors) Ltd* [1991] 1 QB 1 for the proposition that a promise to perform an existing obligation can amount to good consideration provided that there are practical benefits to the promisee.

[Peter Gibson LJ referred to the propositions expressed by Glidewell LJ in that case, and continued:] [Counsel] submitted that although Glidewell LJ in terms confined his remarks to a case where B is to do the work for or supply goods or services to A, the same principle must apply where B's obligation is to pay A, and he referred to an article by Adams and Brownsword 'Contract, Consideration and the Critical Path' (1990) 53 MLR 536, 539–540 which suggests that *Foakes v Beer* might need reconsideration. I see the force of the argument, but the difficulty that I feel with it is that if the principle of *Williams v Roffey Bros. & Nicholls (Contractors) Ltd* is to be extended to an obligation to make payment, it would in effect leave the principle in *Foakes v Beer* without any application. When a creditor and a debtor who are at arm's length reach agreement on the payment of the debt by instalments to accommodate the debtor, the creditor will no doubt always see a practical benefit to himself in so doing. In the absence of authority there would be much to be said for the enforceability of such a contract. But that was a matter expressly considered in *Foakes v Beer* yet held not to constitute good consideration in law. *Foakes v Beer* was not even referred to in *Williams v Roffey Bros. & Nicholls (Contractors) Ltd*, and it is in my judgment impossible, consistently with the doctrine of precedent, for this court to extend the principle of *Williams'* case to any circumstances governed by the principle of *Foakes v Beer*. If that extension is to be made, it must be by the House of Lords or, perhaps even more appropriately, by Parliament after consideration by the Law Commission.

In my judgment, the judge was right to hold that if there was an agreement between the company and the revenue it was unenforceable for want of consideration.

NOTES

1. Although this result was inevitable given the doctrine of precedent, it is nevertheless difficult to justify the arbitrary distinction that now exists between alteration promises to pay more and alteration promises to accept less.

2. In *Re C (A Debtor)* [1996] BPIR 535, The Times, 11 May 1994, a differently constituted Court of Appeal, in *obiter* remarks, also confirmed this restrictive approach to part payments of debts. In *Re C (A debtor)*, Bingham MR had stressed the fact that the relevant case law had not been referred to in *Williams v Roffey* and he also appeared to consider that there are important differences between alteration promises to pay more and alteration promises to accept less. See also O'Sullivan (1996) 55 CLJ 219, although compare Adams and Brownsword (1990) 53 MLR 536, 540; Carter, Phang, and Poole (1995) 8 JCL 248, 266–7; and (in Australia) the judgment of Santow J in *Musumeci v Winadell Pty Ltd* (1994) 34 NSWLR 723, 747. The question was recently revisited in *MWB Business Exchange Centres Ltd v Rock Advertising Ltd* [2016] EWCA Civ 553, [2016] 2 Lloyd's rep 391 (see below).

3. In *Collier v P. & M. J. Wright (Holdings) Ltd* [2007] EWCA Civ 1329, [2008] 1 WLR 643 (*page 133, 3.2.2.5*), the Court of Appeal applied *Foakes v Beer* in relation to an agreement by a creditor with a joint debtor whereby the creditor had agreed to accept only the proportionate share from that debtor and not to sue him for the remainder of the debt. It appears to have been implicitly accepted that *Roffey* could not apply in this context.

4. In *Re Selectmove*, counsel for the company had argued that, even if consideration did not exist, promissory estoppel operated to prevent the Revenue from going back on its implied promise not to enforce the debt, since the company had acted on this promise and it would be inequitable for the Revenue to go back on it. The Court of Appeal rejected this argument on the basis that the official in question had no authority to make such a promise and, since the company had not complied with the terms of any such 'promise', it was not inequitable for the Revenue to insist on payment.

5. *Roffey*, although initially criticized for its refusal to accept that, in reality, it was striking at the heart of *Stilk v Myrick*, was nevertheless welcomed as a pragmatic means of enabling alteration promises to be enforced: see Adams and Brownsword (1990) 53 MLR 536 and Coote (1990) 3 JCL 23. It has subsequently—particularly following the decision in *Re Selectmove*—become the subject of more vocal academic criticism suggesting that the decision is wrong and that alteration promises should instead be enforceable by extending the doctrine of estoppel, following the approach taken in the Australian decision of *Waltons Stores v Maher* (1988) 164 CLR 387 (*page 137, 3.2.3.1*): see Carter, Phang, and Poole (1995) 8 JCL 248; Chen-Wishart, 'Consideration: Practical benefit and the emperor's new clothes', in Beatson and Friedmann (eds.), *Good Faith and Fault in Contract Law* (Oxford University Press, 1995); and Hird and Blair [1996] JBL 254. The Court of Appeal of New Zealand in *Antons Trawling Co. Ltd v Smith* [2003] 2 NZLR 23 (*page 142, 3.2.3.2*) preferred to accept that variations that have been relied upon should be binding despite the absence of consideration, unless affected by 'duress or other policy factors'. *Roffey* must of course be now appreciated in the light of *MWB Business Exchange*.

MWB Business Exchange Centres Ltd v Rock Advertising Ltd
[2016] EWCA Civ 553, [2017] QB 604, CA

Rock Advertising Ltd rented out serviced offices in central London from the claimant. By February 2012, the defendant had accumulated significant arrears. The defendant's managing director claimed that, following negotiations with the claimant's credit-controller, a revised payment schedule was agreed whereby February and March payments would be deferred and the accumulated arrears would be spread over the remaining term, allowing all the arrears to be paid by the end of the calendar year. The claimant denied having entered into this agreement and asserted that, in any case, it was unenforceable for lack of consideration. The court of appeal held that there was consideration.

Considering first whether practical benefit can be good consideration [77–81], Arden LJ turned to the question of part payment of debt.

Pinnel's case does not have to be considered where there is good consideration

82. The argument for MWB amounts to this: the variation agreement was a promise to pay a smaller amount than originally agreed in that the time value of money has the effect that an agreement to defer payment of a due debt is in effect an agreement to pay a smaller sum. MWB invokes the well-known rule in *Pinnel's case* for the proposition that in those circumstances there is no good conclusion in law: see *Foakes v Beer* (above, [38]).

83. Furthermore in *re Selectmove*, this Court drew a distinction between obligations to perform work and obligations to pay money and it held that the practical benefit to the creditor of (my words) 'a bird in the hand rather than two in the bush' did not mean that a contract to pay a lesser sum than originally agreed was enforceable. The critical passage in the judgment of Peter Gibson LJ, with whom Stuart Smith and Balcombe LJJ agreed, is set out in [44] above.

84. In my judgment, *Selectmove* is distinguishable from the present case and decides only that the benefit which a creditor obtains from a promise to pay an existing debt by instalments is not good consideration in law. In that case, there was no finding by the trial judge that there was any extra benefit to the Inland Revenue in having an instalment agreement with the taxpayer. The question of practical benefit only arose in this Court in *Selectmove* because counsel for the taxpayer argued that there was consideration because the instalment agreement was beneficial to the Inland Revenue in the sense that it had a promise to make payments in discharge of the existing debt in accordance with an agreed schedule, which would obviate the need for it to take steps to enforce payment of the amount owed to it. It was that argument that Peter Gibson LJ rejected. Peter Gibson LJ could not reject the general principle that, where there was other consideration, which the law recognised was sufficient to support a contract, that was good consideration for a promise. There can be no coherent distinction between agreement to pay debts and agreements to do work in this context. The strength of that general principle may well explain why in *Roffey* this Court did not refer to *Foakes v Beer*.

85. My conclusion that *Selectmove* can be distinguished in this case is not inconsistent with *Foakes v Beer*, where the only suggested consideration was the debtor's promise to pay part of his existing debt. Nor is it inconsistent with the dictum of Lord Coke LC in *Pinnel's case* itself. After stating that 'payment of a lesser sum . . . in satisfaction of a greater, cannot be any satisfaction for the whole,' Lord Coke had added a rider that 'the gift of a horse, hawk or robe, etc in satisfaction is good for it shall be intended that a horse, hawk, or robe, etc might be more beneficial to the plaintiff than the money.' The House of Lords in *Foakes v Beer* approved both the statement of general rule and the rider. As the law of consideration now stands, the gift of the horse, hawk or robe is no different in principle from the conferral of a benefit or advantage, a point in fact made by Lefroy CJ in *Corporation of Drogheda v Fairclough* 8 Ir. C. L. R. 98, 110, 114, cited with approval by Lord Fitzgerald in *Foakes v Beer* (at 629). In accepting that a practical benefit can be good consideration for part payment of a debt, all I am doing is replacing the words 'the gift of a horse, hawk or robe' with a more modern equivalent in line with the responsibility which Glidewell LJ in *Roffey* (at 16) described as refining and limiting the common law but leaving the principle (the actual Rule in *Pinnel's case*) unscathed.

86. The judge held that MWB did not enter into the variation agreement simply to accommodate Rock. I accept that in the light of *Selectmove* it may be difficult for any benefit solely of that kind to

constitute a practical benefit for the purposes of the law of consideration. On the judge's findings it did so in its own interests in order to, as I put it above, avoid a void and that this was a practical benefit to MWB. In those circumstances there was in my judgment on the judge's findings a binding contract in law.

87. As I explained in *Collier v Wright*, the Rule in *Pinnel's case* is controversial . . . If my Lords agree that I have correctly stated the law, the necessary result of this is that there will be cases in the future, of which this is one, where agreements to pay a lesser sum than was due under a previous contract will be held to be enforceable because there has been shown to have been consideration in the form of a practical benefit to the creditor which he sought and which is an identifiable benefit over and above the mere fact of accommodating the debtor and not having to enforce payment of the debt. This may well strike a satisfactory balance between on the one hand enforcing promises and enabling debtors to rely on their creditors' promises and on the other hand of protecting creditors from debtors who seek unfairly to gain an advantage from their creditors.

88. . . . to the question whether MWB was bound to accept the deferred payments provided for in the variation agreement as soon as Rock paid the sum of £3,500 and even if it made no further payment. That would not have been a sensible commercial agreement. Accordingly it is unlikely that the parties made an agreement in those terms. (The case was argued on the basis that the payment of £3,500 had to be made before the agreement became binding: it was not argued that the variation agreement became binding merely on the exchange of promises and so I do not need to deal with that still less sensible result). Lord Justice Kitchin has addressed this problem by holding that the variation agreement contained a term that the rescheduling arrangement would be binding on MWB only so long as Rock performed its side of the bargain (paragraph 49 above). I agree that that is one interpretation and analysis which addresses the problem. But there is another possible interpretation and analysis which would lead to the same result that Rock would have to perform the whole of its side of the bargain. That would be the case if the variation agreement took effect as a collateral unilateral contract (binding on MWB once the sum of £3,500 was paid), and accordingly that is the question which I next consider.

NOTE Reversed on a different ground in the Supreme Court, [2018] UKSC 24, Lord Sumption giving the leading judgment, stated, *obiter*, (at [18]) that the issue of practical benefit was 'ripe for re-examination' and that 'any decision on this point is likely to involve a re-examination of the decision of *Foakes v Beer*'. The situation therefore remains extremely complicated. The decision of the CA and its impact is discussed in *Poole's Textbook on Contact Law*.

The consequences of *Foakes v Beer* will be avoided where the part payment is made by a third party and the creditor promises to accept this in full satisfaction. The creditor cannot then go back on its promise to the third party and sue the debtor for the balance.

Hirachand Punamchand v Temple
[1911] 2 KB 330 (CA)

Lieutenant Temple had borrowed money from the claimants, money lenders, and had given them a promissory note. The claimants had pressed Lieutenant Temple for payment on the note, but, having had no success, they had informed his father. The father had sent a draft for a smaller sum than that due on the promissory note in full satisfaction of his son's debt. The claimants cashed the draft, but then brought an action on the note against Lieutenant Temple seeking the balance on the debt.

Held: This action could not be maintained.

VAUGHAN WILLIAMS LJ: The learned judge [Scrutton J] dealt with the case largely on the footing that the question was whether the effect of the transaction between the plaintiffs and the father was that there had been an accord and satisfaction in respect of the debt due upon the note, and he came to the conclusion that there had been no such accord and satisfaction. Personally, I am inclined to agree that prima facie such an accord and satisfaction must be by virtue of an agreement made between a person who is under an obligation to another person, which he ought to have and has not performed, and that other person. I should hesitate to say that there can, properly speaking, be an accord and satisfaction in respect of a contractual obligation as between one of the parties to the contract, who ought to have but has not performed that obligation, and a stranger to the contract . . . I shall assume that there was such an agreement as I have mentioned entered into between Sir Richard Temple and the plaintiffs by reason of their keeping the draft. They not only kept it, but they cashed it, and, if they changed their minds afterwards, it was too late. Under these circumstances, assuming that there was no accord and satisfaction, what form of defence, if any, could be pleaded by the defendant? In my judgment it would be that the plaintiffs had ceased really to be holders of the negotiable instrument on which they sued. They had ceased to be such holders, because, in effect, in their hands the document had ceased to be a negotiable instrument quite as much as if there had been on the acceptance of the draft by the plaintiffs an erasure of the writing of the signature to the note. There was not in fact such an erasure, but to my mind the case must be considered as standing on the same footing as if there been an erasure of the signature, and a cancellation by reason of that erasure of the promissory note, in which case, I think, the maker of the note would have had a defence, though he was not a party to the transaction in pursuance of which the note was cancelled, in the sense of being a contracting party. His defence would then have been that the document in the circumstances had ceased to be a promissory note. But, alternatively, assuming that this was not so, and that the instrument did not cease to be a negotiable instrument, then, in my judgment, from the moment when the draft sent by Sir Richard Temple was cashed by the plaintiffs a trust was created as between Sir Richard Temple and the money-lenders in favour of the former, so that any money which the latter might receive upon the promissory note, if they did receive any, would be held by them in trust for him. I wish to say here that I do not think that it makes any difference under the circumstances that the amount of the draft sent by Sir Richard Temple was not the full amount of the promissory note, but a smaller amount, because, as between Sir Richard Temple and these plaintiffs, there was an agreement by the plaintiffs for good consideration to receive that amount in satisfaction of the note, which agreement arose from their having retained and cashed the draft . . .

Having said thus much, I desire to add a word or two with regard to the case of *Cook v Lister* (1863) 13 CBNS 543 in the Common Pleas. If the judgments in that case are looked at, it will be found that Willes J said, in explaining the grounds of his judgment, that, under circumstances like those of the present case, the debt is gone, because it would be a fraud upon the stranger who pays part of a debt in discharge of the whole, that an action should be brought for the debt. I have founded my judgment upon the grounds which I have already expressed, but I do not wish to be understood as thereby negativing the proposition that a defence might be set up on the alternative basis mentioned by Willes J.

FLETCHER MOULTON LJ: I am of opinion that by that transaction between the plaintiffs and Sir Richard Temple the debt on the promissory note became extinct. I agree with the view expressed by Willes J in *Cook v Lister* (1863) 13 CBNS 543. The effect of such an agreement between a creditor and a third party with regard to the debt is to render it impossible for the creditor afterwards to sue the debtor for it. The way in which this is worked out in law may be that it would be an abuse of the process of the Court to allow the creditor under such circumstances to sue, or it may be, and I prefer that view, that there is an extinction of the debt; but, whichever way it is put, it comes to the same thing, namely that, after acceptance by the creditor of a sum offered by a third party in settlement of the claim against the debtor, the creditor cannot maintain an action for the balance . . .

FARWELL LJ: In my opinion, it is clear that in the events that have happened the debt became extinguished. Assuming that an accord and satisfaction must be by agreement between the debtor and the creditor, it occurs to me from what was said by Willes J in *Cook v Lister* (1863) 13 CBNS 543 that the facts in this case might support such a plea. That learned judge there said, 'if a stranger pays a part of a debt in discharge of the whole, the debt is gone because it would be a fraud on the stranger to proceed. So, in the case of a composition made with a body of creditors, the assent to receive the composition discharges the debt, because otherwise fraud would be committed against the rest of the creditors' . . . We were pressed with *Day v McLea* (1889) 22 QBD 610, where the debtor himself sent a cheque for an amount smaller than that of the debt to the creditor on the terms that it should be in satisfaction of the debt. In that case, there being no consideration for the discharge of the balance of the debt, it was held that the creditor could retain the money, and sue for the balance. The same reasoning does not apply where the money is sent by a stranger, in which case it can only be accepted on the terms upon which it is sent. In the former case the creditor can reply to the debtor, 'you owe me more than this, and, if you sue for a return of this, I shall set off my larger claim against it.' In the latter case, the creditor has no excuse or justification for retaining the stranger's money, unless he complies with the condition on which it was paid. I agree with Fletcher Moulton LJ that the plaintiffs cannot be heard to say that they have acted dishonestly when an honest construction can be put upon their conduct by treating their acceptance and retention of the money as being upon the terms on which it was offered. If there be any difficulty in formulating a defence at common law in such case, I have no hesitation in saying that a Court of Equity would have regarded the plaintiffs as disentitled to sue except as trustees for the father, and would have restrained them from suing under such circumstances as existed in the present case.

NOTES

1. The precise reason for this decision is unclear. The Court of Appeal appeared to consider that, in cashing the draft, the claimants accepted the father's terms and this had the effect of extinguishing the promissory note. It was also considered to be a fraud on the father for the claimants to go back on their promise, but breach of contract will not normally constitute a fraud.

2. If the test of enforceability in s. 1 of the Contracts (Rights of Third Parties) Act 1999 is satisfied (*page 312, 7.2.1*), the debtor (as third party) may rely on a contractual term in the contract between the creditor and the person making part payment that excludes the debtor's liability for the balance. In such a situation, it would be sufficient that the consideration was provided by the person making the part payment (*page 307, 7.1*), rather than the debtor.

It is also now clear that a forbearance to raise a defence can provide consideration to support a compromise to accept less as a full settlement of a debt.

Simantob v Yacob Shavleyan t/a Yacob's Gallery
[2019] EWCA Civ 1105

The parties were both dealers in Islamic antiquities. Following Shavleyan owing substantial amount of money to Simantob, in May 2010, the parties entered into an agreement whereby Shavleyan would pay Simantob, in full and final settlement, the sum of US$1.5 million. Failing to do so would trigger an 'interest clause' of US$1,000 per late day. Although Shavleyan started to repay some money, he failed to repay the sum in its entirety and the interest clause was triggered. With the debt mounting substantially, in 2014, a new agreement was entered into, whereby Shavleyan agreed to pay, in full settlement of the debt, US$800,000.

In 2016, Simantob sued for the rest of the money. In defence, Shavleyan argued that the claim is void on the ground that the interest clause is a penalty and that the 2014 agreement varies the 2010 agreement, with fresh consideration having been provided by Shavleyan by forbearing a claim that the clause is a penalty clause.

In a summary judgment, McCloud rejected the penalty defence and gave summary judgment to Simantob, but the only sums to be claimed were those under the 2014 agreement. In the High Court, Kerr upheld the 2014 agreement. Shavleyan's forbearance of pursuing the penalty defence was valid consideration as it represented a benefit to Simantob. Simantob appealed, amongst other things, on a point of public policy, that forbearance of a defence that has no real prospect of success cannot be good consideration. Simon LJ, for the Court of Appeal, dismissed the appeal. Simon LJ's judgment clarified two important points.

First, on the public policy element, his Lordship stated that it has to be balanced by another public policy, that of holding the parties to their bargain:

48. Mr Ramsden's public policy point was somewhat different from that suggested by Chitty. It is one thing for a person to threaten a claim or defence in which that person has no confidence at all. It is a quite different thing for a person to intimate a claim or defence which, whilst the person recognises that it raises a doubtful or undecided point, he or she also believes in and intends to pursue it in court if necessary. On the Judge's findings, this case fell squarely into the second category. The respondent had raised his concerns about the $1,000 per day clause, had intimated the penalty defence and plainly intended to raise it in any proceedings brought by the appellant. By entering into the April/May 2014 variation agreement, he agreed that he would no longer be able to raise that defence and the debt would be consolidated at $800,000. The fact that the appellant subsequently sued for the whole amount allegedly due under the Settlement Agreement, denying the existence of the April/May 2014 variation agreement in the process, can have no effect on the legal position at the time that when that agreement was made in April/May 2014; and the fact that the respondent then pleaded and relied on the penalty defence, having agreed to compromise the point is equally irrelevant.

49. Furthermore, there is another countervailing public policy that must also be taken into account in this context: namely, the public policy in favour of holding people to their commercial bargains. This element of public policy provides a limitation on the public policy discouraging parties from threatening unreasonable claims or defences. There cannot be any sensible public policy against encouraging parties to raise claims or defences that they reasonably believe may succeed, even if they eventually turn out to fail. It may be noted that the suggestion that the $1,000 per day clause was a penalty was made at a time when there was considerable uncertainty in the law, and before the Supreme Court ruled in *Cavendish Square Holding BV v. Makdessi, ParkingEye Ltd v. Beavis.*

50. See also, Cheshire, Fifoot and Furmston (above) at p.115:

In the modern law, the consideration in [cases where the promise is not to pursue a claim or defence] is said to be the surrender, not of a legal right, which may or may not exist and whose existence, at the time of the compromise remains untested, but of the claim to such a right.

This attitude is sensible. It is true that if the claim is baseless, the claimant may appear to have got something for nothing, or that contrariwise, if a claimant settles a good claim for less than its true value, he may appear to have given up something for nothing but this is to ignore the cost, both monetary and psychic, of litigation. It is in the public interest to encourage reasonable settlements.

The second point that Simon LJ makes is to reiterate that the assessment of the existence of consideration is the time the contract was made.

51. It is in the light of these considerations that the decision of Master McCloud must be seen. In our view, whether she was right or wrong is immaterial. The question of the validity of the consideration for the April/May 2014 variation agreement must be judged at the time that it was made.

[Finally, it is also worth noting the parting comment of his Lordship on the impact of MWB.]

52. Finally, the uncertainty alluded to by Lord Sumption in *MWB Business Exchange Centres Ltd v. Rock Advertising Ltd* [2018] UKSC 24 at [18] is not engaged on the facts of this case. The consideration alleged here was the forbearance to rely on a penalty defence, not the expectation of some commercial advantage as a result of accepting a less advantageous series of payments. As Chitty makes clear '[t]he compromise of a claim which is doubtful in law is binding as a contract' (paragraph 4-052 above). It cannot seriously be suggested that there was not genuine doubt as to whether the $1,000 per day clause was or was not a penalty, when that clause could have resulted in the respondent paying $1,000 per day in interest, even if only $1 remained outstanding by way of principal. This case has little to do with the correctness or otherwise of the decision in *Foakes v. Beer* (1884) 9 App Cas 605, which may arise in another case.

3.2 Promissory estoppel

If a creditor promises to accept a smaller sum in full settlement, intending the debtor to rely on that promise and the debtor does rely on it, the debtor may have a *defence* of promissory estoppel when sued for the balance by the creditor. The promise will, in this limited way, be enforced despite the absence of consideration to support it.

3.2.1 Origins of the doctrine

Central London Property Trust Ltd v High Trees House Ltd
[1947] KB 130

In September 1937, the claimants let a block of flats in London to the defendants for a term of 99 years at a rent of £2,500 a year. In 1940, owing to the wartime conditions and bombing raids over London, only a few of the flats were actually let to tenants, and it became apparent that the defendants would not be able to pay the rent under the main lease. Following discussions, the claimants agreed to reduce the rent from £2,500 to £1,250, and thereafter the defendants paid the reduced rent. By the beginning of 1945, all of the flats were let, but the defendants continued to pay the reduced rent. In September 1945, the claimants wrote to the defendants claiming rent at the rate of £2,500 a year and brought an action claiming the full rent for the last two quarters of 1945.

Held: Since the claimants knew that their promise would be acted upon and it had been acted upon, it was enforceable despite the absence of consideration while the conditions giving rise to it continued to exist—but since they had ceased to do so in 1945, the claimants were entitled to claim the full rent from that time.

DENNING J: If I were to consider this matter without regard to recent developments in the law, there is no doubt that had the plaintiffs claimed it, they would have been entitled to recover ground rent at the rate of 2,500*l.* a year from the beginning of the term, since the lease under which it was payable was a lease under seal which, according to the old common law, could not be varied by an agreement by parol (whether in writing or not), but only by deed. Equity, however stepped in, and said that if there has been a variation of a deed by a simple contract (which in the case of a lease required to be in writing would have to be evidenced by writing), the courts may give effect to it . . . That equitable doctrine, however, could hardly apply in the present case because the variation here might be said to have been made without consideration. With regard to estoppel, the representation made in relation to reducing the rent, was not a representation of an existing fact. It was a representation, in effect, as to the future, namely, that payment of the rent would not be enforced at the full rate but only at the reduced rate. Such a representation would not give rise to an estoppel, because, as was said in *Jorden v Money* (1854) 5 HL 185, 10 ER 868, a representation as to the future must be embodied as a contract or be nothing.

But what is the position in view of developments in the law in recent years? The law has not been standing still since *Jorden v Money*. There has been a series of decisions over the last fifty years which, although they are said to be cases of estoppel are not really such. They are cases in which a promise was made which was intended to create legal relations and which, to the knowledge of the person making the promise, was going to be acted on by the person to whom it was made, and which was in fact so acted on. In such cases the courts have said that the promise must be honoured. The cases to which I particularly desire to refer are: *Fenner v Blake* [1900] 1 QB 426, *In re Wickham* (1917) 34 TLR 158, *Re William Porter & Co. Ltd* [1937] 2 All ER 361 and *Buttery v Pickard* [1946] WN 25. As I have said they are not cases of estoppel in the strict sense. They are really promises—promises intended to be binding, intended to be acted on, and in fact acted on. *Jorden v Money* can be distinguished, because there the promisor made it clear that she did not intend to be legally bound, whereas in the cases to which I refer the proper inference was that the promisor did intend to be bound. In each case the court held the promise to be binding on the party making it, even though under the old common law it might be difficult to find any consideration for it. The courts have not gone so far as to give a cause of action in damages for the breach of such a promise, but they have refused to allow the party making it to act inconsistently with it. It is in that sense, and that sense only, that such a promise gives rise to an estoppel. The decisions are a natural result of the fusion of law and equity: for the cases of *Hughes v Metropolitan Ry. Co.* (1877) 2 App Cas 439, *Birmingham and District Land Co. v London & North Western Ry. Co.* (1888) 40 Ch D 268 and *Salisbury (Marquess) v Gilmore* [1942] 2 KB 38, afford a sufficient basis for saying that a party would not be allowed in equity to go back on such a promise. In my opinion, the time has now come for the validity of such a promise to be recognised. The logical consequence, no doubt is that a promise to accept a smaller sum in discharge of a larger sum, if acted upon, is binding notwithstanding the absence of consideration: and if the fusion of law and equity leads to this result, so much the better. That aspect was not considered in *Foakes v Beer* (1884) 9 App Cas 605. At this time of day however, when law and equity have been joined together for over seventy years, principles must be reconsidered in the light of their combined effect. It is to be noticed that in the Sixth Interim Report of the Law Revision Committee, pars. 35, 40, it is recommended that such a promise as that to which I have referred, should be enforceable in law even though no consideration for it has been given by the promisee. It seems to me that, to the extent I have mentioned, that result has now been achieved by the decisions of the courts.

I am satisfied that a promise such as that to which I have referred is binding and the only question remaining for my consideration is the scope of the promise in the present case. I am satisfied on all the evidence that the promise here was that the ground rent should be reduced to 1,250*l.* a year as a temporary expedient while the block of flats was not fully, or substantially fully let, owing to the conditions prevailing. That means that the reduction in the rent applied throughout the years down to the end of 1944, but early in 1945 it is plain that the flats were fully let . . . I find that the conditions prevailing at the time when the reduction in rent was made, had completely passed away by the early months of 1945. I am satisfied that the promise was understood by all parties only to apply under the conditions prevailing at the time when it was made, namely, when the flats were only partially let, and that it did not extend any further than that. When the flats became fully let, early in 1945, the reduction ceased to apply.

If the case had been one of estoppel, it might be said that in any event the estoppel would cease when the conditions to which the representation applied came to an end, or it also might be said that it would only come to an end on notice. In either case it is only a way of ascertaining what is the scope of the representation. I prefer to apply the principle that a promise intended to be binding, intended to be acted on and in fact acted on, is binding so far as its terms properly apply. Here it was binding as covering the period down to the early part of 1945, and as from that time full rent is payable.

I therefore give judgment for the plaintiff company for the amount claimed.

? QUESTIONS

1. Although the claimant company did not make a retrospective claim for the full rent for the war years, Denning J indicated *obiter* that such a claim would fail because of promissory estoppel. Can this be reconciled with *Foakes v Beer*, in which it was held that it was possible to go back on such a promise and sue for the balance?

2. Could the defendants in *High Trees* have sued the claimants if the claimants had not complied with its promise to accept the reduced rent?

NOTE Denning J purported to rely in particular on the decision and statement of principle in *Hughes v Metropolitan Railway Co.* (1877) 2 App Cas 439 as jus-tifying his use of a doctrine of promissory estoppel. It is interesting, however, that this case was not seen as being relevant in *Foakes v Beer*.

Hughes v Metropolitan Railway Co.
(1877) 2 App Cas 439 (HL)

On 22 October 1874, the landlord gave the tenant company six months' notice to repair the premises. However, on 28 November, negotiations began between the parties for the sale of the remainder of the lease back to the landlord. The tenant stated that the company would defer commencing the repairs until it had heard whether its proposal was acceptable. After the six months had elapsed, the landlord claimed that the lease was forfeited for breach of covenant and sought to eject the tenant. The tenant sought a stay of execution.

Held: The tenant was entitled in equity to be relieved against forfeiture of the lease because the negotiations had the effect of suspending the notice and, while they continued, the six-month period did not run. It ran again only from the time that the negotiations ended.

LORD CAIRNS: It was not argued at your Lordships' Bar, and it could not be argued, that there was any right of a Court of Equity, or any practice of a Court of Equity, to give relief in cases of this kind, by way of mercy, or by way merely of saving property from forfeiture, but it is the first principle upon which all Courts of Equity proceed, that if parties who have entered into definite and distinct terms involving certain legal results—certain penalties or legal forfeiture—afterwards by their own act or with their own consent enter upon a course of negotiation which has the effect of leading one of the parties to suppose that the strict rights arising under the contract will not be enforced, or will be kept in suspense, or held in abeyance, the person who otherwise might have enforced those rights will not be allowed to enforce them where it would be inequitable having regard to the dealings which have thus taken place between the parties . . .

NOTES

1. While the negotiations continued, the landlord had *impliedly* promised not to enforce the notice and the tenant had relied on this in not carrying out the repairs.

2. The principle in *Hughes v Metropolitan Railway Co.* appears to be intended to cover a different situation from that which arose on the facts in *High Trees*. If a landlord tells the tenant that he does not have to perform an obligation under the contract and consequently the tenant does not do so, then the landlord cannot treat this as a breach of contract (and,

in *Hughes*, could not forfeit the lease). In *High Trees*, the landlord was not alleging that the tenant was in breach of contract by paying half the rent.

3. In *Foakes v Beer* (1884) 9 App Cas 605 (*page 111, 3.1.4*), the issue was the same as that in *High Trees*—namely, that if one party tells the other that the other does not have to perform a contractual obligation, can that party change his mind and insist on the performance if performance is still possible? In *High Trees*, the landlord was seeking to change its mind and insist on proper performance of the contract terms.

3.2.2 When will the doctrine operate and in what way?

3.2.2.1 Clear and unequivocal promise

There must be a clear and unequivocal promise or representation that existing legal rights will not be fully enforced. This representation can be implied, as in *Hughes v Metropolitan Railway Co.* (1877) 2 App Cas 439.

Woodhouse A. C. Israel Cocoa Ltd SA v Nigerian Produce Marketing Co. Ltd
[1972] AC 741 (HL)

A sale contract provided for payment in Nigerian pounds in Lagos. The buyer had asked if the seller would be prepared to accept sterling in Lagos; the seller had replied, on 30 September 1967, that 'payment can be made in sterling and in Lagos'. The pound sterling was devalued, so that it was worth 15 per cent less than the Nigerian pound. The buyer argued that the seller's letter amounted either to a variation (supported by consideration) or a representation that it could make payment in sterling in Lagos on the basis of one pound sterling for one Nigerian pound, so that the seller was estopped from going back on it.

Held: To found a promissory estoppel, a representation had to be clear and unequivocal (i.e. expressed so that it would be understood in the sense required). The seller's representation was not sufficiently precise either to amount to a variation of the contract terms (i.e. an alteration supported by consideration) or to found an estoppel.

LORD HAILSHAM LC: Counsel for the [buyers] was asked whether he knew of any case in which an ambiguous statement had ever formed the basis of a purely promissory estoppel, as contended for here, as distinct from estoppel of a more familiar type based on factual misrepresentation. He candidly replied that he did not. I do not find this surprising, since it would really be an astonishing thing if, in the case of a genuine misunderstanding as to the meaning of an offer, the offeree could obtain by means of the doctrine of promissory estoppel something that he must fail to obtain under the conventional law of contract. I share the feeling of incredulity expressed by Lord Denning MR in the course of his judgment in the instant case when he said [1971] 2 QB 23, 59–60:

> If the judge be right, it leads to this extraordinary consequence: A letter which is not sufficient to *vary* a contract is, nevertheless, sufficient to work an *estoppel*—which will have the same effect as a *variation*.

There seem to me to be so many and such conclusive reasons for dismissing this appeal that it may be thought a work of supererogation to add yet another. But basically I feel convinced that there was never here any real room for the doctrine or estoppel at all. If the exchange of letters was not variation, I believe it was nothing. The buyers asked for a variation in the mode of discharge of a contract of sale. If the proposal meant what they claimed, and was accepted and acted upon, I venture to think that the vendors would have been bound by their acceptance at least until they gave reasonable notice to terminate, and I imagine that a modern court would have found no difficulty in discovering consideration for such a promise. Business men know their own business best even when they appear to grant an indulgence, and in the present case I do not think that there would have been insuperable difficulty in spelling out consideration from the earlier correspondence. If, however, the two letters were insufficiently unambiguous and precise to form the basis, if accepted, for a variation in the contract I do not think their combined effect is sufficiently unambiguous or precise to form the basis of an estoppel which would produce the result of reducing the purchase price by no less than 14 per cent against a vendor who had never consciously agreed to the proposition . . .

NOTE In *Kim v Chasewood Park Residents Ltd* [2013] EWCA Civ 239, [2013] HLR 24, the Court of Appeal held that a reference to 'no ground rent to pay' in a letter concerning a possible purchase of the reversion sent to tenants by a residents' association was not a clear representation intended to induce the tenants to support the purchase of that reversion; rather, it highlighted only a potential benefit that might arise. Accordingly, the statement could not form the basis for any estoppel and, in particular, it could not operate to prevent the management company from subsequently recovering ground rent.

In *Baird Textile Holdings Ltd v Marks & Spencer plc* [2001] EWCA Civ 274, [2002] 1 All ER (Comm) 737 (*page 157*, 4.1.2.3 for the facts), one reason why the claim based on estoppel failed was that the alleged representation was not sufficiently certain for a court to be able to give effect to it. Baird attempted to sidestep this deficiency (and the formal requirements for a binding contract) by limiting the claim to the recovery of wasted expenditure (referred to as 'reliance loss', discussed at *page 695, 14.3.2*), as opposed to a claim for loss of expected profit. The Court of Appeal considered that there was no authority justifying such a radical conclusion:

MANCE LJ: 91 In the present case, what is submitted is that the law ought to attach legal consequences to a bare assurance or conventional understanding (falling short of contract) between two parties, without any actual contract or third party being involved or affected. The suggested justification is the limitation of the relief claimed to reliance loss. On this submission, the requirements of contract (consideration, certainty and an intention to create legal relations) are irrelevant because no contract is asserted. The requirements of estoppel (e.g. that is an unequivocal promise to found a promissory estoppel or conventional conduct of sufficient clarity to found an estoppel by convention and, secondly, the objective intention to affect some actual or apparent pre-existing legal relationship) are by-passed by the limitation of relief. But no authority in this jurisdiction supports the submission that estoppel can here achieve so expanded an application, simply by limiting recovery to reliance loss (assuming that reliance loss could anyway be distinguished satisfactorily from expectation loss—an apparent difficulty which I have already mentioned). Any development of English law in such a direction could and should, in my view, now take place in the highest court.

NOTE In *Omak Maritime Ltd v Mamola Challenger Shipping Co.* [2010] EWHC 2026 (Comm), [2011] Bus LR 212 *(page 692, 14.3.2)*, Teare J considered that wasted expenditure (here referred to as 'reliance loss') was, in fact, a claim for lost expectation and this would explain the difficulties, noted by Mance LJ in the *Baird* case, in making any distinction.

3.2.2.2 A Defence and not a cause of action

Combe v Combe
[1951] 2 KB 215 (CA)

An ex-husband promised to pay his ex-wife £100 per annum maintenance, free of income tax. However, he failed to pay and, six years later, the wife brought an action claiming the arrears. She had given no consideration for her husband's promise, since she had chosen not to apply to the Divorce Court for maintenance and had not refrained from doing so at her husband's request (her income in fact being greater than her husband's). Nevertheless, Byrne J gave judgment for the wife on the basis of the doctrine in *High Trees*. He held that the husband's promise was clear, it was intended to be binding and acted upon, and it was acted upon by the wife.

Held (by the Court of Appeal, allowing the appeal): The wife had provided no consideration for the husband's promise and could not rely on promissory estoppel, which did not give rise to a cause of action.

DENNING LJ: Much as I am inclined to favour the principle stated in the *High Trees* case [1947] KB 130, it is important that it should not be stretched too far, lest it should be endangered. That principle does not create new causes of action where none existed before. It only prevents a party from insisting upon his strict legal rights, when it would be unjust to allow him to enforce them, having regard to the dealings which have taken place between the parties. That is the way it was put in *Hughes v Metropolitan Railway* (1877) 2 App Cas 439, the case in the House of Lords in which the principle was first stated, and in *Birmingham, etc., Land Co. v London and North-Western Railway Co.* (1888) 40 Ch D 268, the case in the Court of Appeal where the principle was enlarged. It is also implicit in all the modern cases in which the principle has been developed. Sometimes it is a plaintiff who is not allowed to insist on his strict legal rights. Thus, a creditor is not allowed to enforce a debt which he has deliberately agreed to waive, if the debtor has carried on business or in some other way changed his position in reliance on the waiver . . . On other occasions it is a defendant who is not allowed to insist on his strict legal rights. His conduct may be such as to debar him from relying on some condition, denying some allegation, or taking some other point in answer to the claim . . .

The principle, as I understand it, is that, where one party has, by his words or conduct, made to the other a promise or assurance which was intended to affect the legal relations between them and to be acted on accordingly, then, once the other party has taken him at his word and acted on it, the one who gave the promise or assurance cannot afterwards be allowed to revert to the previous legal relations as if no such promise or assurance had been made by him, but he must accept their legal relations subject to the qualification which he himself has so introduced, even though it is not supported in point of law by any consideration but only by his word.

Seeing that the principle never stands alone as giving a cause of action in itself, it can never do away with the necessity of consideration when that is an essential part of the cause of action. The doctrine of consideration is too firmly fixed to be overthrown by a side-wind. Its ill-effects have been largely mitigated of late, but it still remains a cardinal necessity of the formation of a contract, though not of its modification or discharge. I fear that it was my failure to make this clear which misled Byrne J, in the present case. He held that the wife could sue on the husband's promise as a separate and independent cause of action by itself, although as he held, there was no consideration for it. That is not correct. The wife can only enforce it if there was consideration for it. That is, therefore, the real question in the case: was there sufficient consideration to support the promise? . . .

There was . . . clearly no promise by the wife, express or implied, to forbear from applying to the court. All that happened was that she did in fact forbear—that is, she did an act in return for a promise. Is that sufficient consideration? Unilateral promises of this kind have long been enforced, so long as the act or forbearance is done on the faith of the promise and at the request of the promisor, express or implied . . . my difficulty is to accept the finding of Byrne J, that the promise was 'intended to be acted upon'. I cannot find any evidence of any intention by the husband that the wife should forbear from applying to the court for maintenance, or, in other words, any request by the husband, express or implied, that the wife should so forbear. He left her to apply if she wished to do so. She did not do so, and I am not surprised, because it is very unlikely that the Divorce Court would have then made any order in her favour, seeing that she had a bigger income than her husband. Her forbearance was not intended by him, nor was it done at his request. It was therefore no consideration.

ASQUITH LJ: The judge has decided that, while the husband's promise was unsupported by any valid consideration, yet the principle in *Central London Property Trust Ltd v High Trees House Ltd* [1947] KB 130 entitles the wife to succeed. It is unnecessary to express any view as to the correctness of that decision, though I certainly must not be taken to be questioning it; and I would remark, in passing, that it seems to me a complete misconception to suppose that it struck at the roots of the doctrine of consideration. But assuming, without deciding, that it is good law, I do not think, however, that it helps the plaintiff at all. What that case decides is that when a promise is given which (1) is intended to create legal relations, (2) is intended to be acted upon by the promisee, and (3) is in fact so acted upon, the promisor cannot bring an action against the promisee which involves the repudiation of his promise or is inconsistent with it. It does not, as I read it, decide that a promisee can sue on the promise. On the contrary, Denning, J, expressly stated the contrary . . .

NOTES

1. Promissory estoppel is available only where there has been an alteration to an existing contract. It cannot be used to render unnecessary consideration on the formation of a contract.

2. Birkett LJ explicitly approved counsel for the husband's argument that promissory estoppel can be 'used as a shield and not a sword'. It cannot be used to force a party to comply with a promise in a direct way and can be used only to prevent a party from ignoring his promise that he would not insist on his strict legal rights. This explains why the tenants in *High Trees* could not have sued on the landlord's promise to enforce their claim to pay reduced rent and why the claimant carpenter in *Williams v Roffey Bros.* [1991] 1 QB 1 (*page 106, 3.1.3.7*) did not base the claim on promissory estoppel.

3. The future of this limitation on the doctrine of promissory estoppel in English law is the subject of debate in light of the approach adopted by the High Court of Australia in *Waltons Stores (Interstate) Ltd v Maher* (1988) 164 CLR 387 (*page 137, 3.2.3.1*) and comments made, particularly in the judgment of Russell LJ, in *Roffey* (*page 106, 3.1.3.7*). In *Baird Textile Holdings Ltd v Marks & Spencer plc* [2001] EWCA Civ 274, [2002] 1 All ER (Comm) 737 (*page 157, 4.1.2.3*), there was an unsuccessful attempt to rely on a general category of estoppel (based on *Waltons Stores*). However, the judgments disclose that, faced with an appropriate case, the House of Lords might well reconsider this limitation.

3.2.2.3 The representation or promise was intended to be binding and acted upon and was, in fact, acted upon

Lord Denning confirmed that detrimental reliance was not a necessary requirement to establish promissory estoppel, as opposed to other types of estoppel. The promisee merely needed to have acted differently from the way in which it would have acted absent the promise.

W. J. Alan & Co. Ltd v El Nasr Export and Import Co.
[1972] 2 QB 189 (CA)

The sellers in Kenya contracted to sell coffee to the buyers at 262 (Kenyan) shillings per cwt. Two shipments were to be made and payment was to be 'by confirmed irrevocable letter of credit to be opened one month prior to shipment'. The irrevocable letter of credit was opened in sterling rather than Kenyan shillings, but the sellers operated the credit by presenting invoices in sterling for payment in sterling. The second shipment was made on 16 November 1967 and the sellers made out an invoice in sterling. However, on 18 November, before the invoice could be presented for payment, sterling was devalued. Payment under the credit was made against the invoice and the sellers then claimed an additional sum to bring the price that they received up to 262 Kenyan shillings.

Held: By accepting payment under the sterling letter of credit, the sellers had irrevocably 'waived' their right to be paid in Kenyan currency. The majority (Megaw and Stephenson LJJ) considered that this was a variation of the sale contract (supported by consideration), whereas Lord Denning relied on the doctrine of promissory estoppel.

LORD DENNING MR: The principle of waiver is simply this: If one party, by his conduct, leads another to believe that the strict rights arising under the contract will not be insisted upon, intending that the other should act on that belief, and he does act on it, then the first party will not afterwards be allowed to insist on the strict legal rights when it would be inequitable for him to do so: see *Plasticmoda Societa per Azioni v Davidsons (Manchester) Ltd* [1952] 1 Lloyd's Rep 527, 539. There may be no consideration moving from him who benefits by the waiver. There may be no detriment to him by acting on it. There may be nothing in writing. Nevertheless, the one who waives his strict rights cannot afterwards insist on them. His strict rights are at any rate suspended so long as the waiver lasts. He may on occasion be able to revert to his strict legal rights for the future by giving reasonable notice in that behalf, or otherwise making it plain by his conduct that he will thereafter insist upon them: *Tool Metal Manufacturing Co. Ltd v Tungsten Electric Co. Ltd* [1955] 1 WLR 761. But there are cases where no withdrawal is possible. It may be too late to withdraw: or it cannot be done without injustice to the other party. In that event he is bound by his waiver. He will not be allowed to revert to his strict legal rights. He can only enforce them subject to the waiver he has made.

Instances of these principles are ready to hand in contracts for the sale of goods. A seller may, by his conduct, lead the buyer to believe that he is not insisting on the stipulated time for exercising an option: *Bruner v Moore* [1904] 1 Ch 305. A buyer may, by requesting delivery, lead the seller to believe that he is not insisting on the contractual time for delivery: *Charles Rickards Ltd v Oppenheim* [1950] 1 KB 616, 621. A seller may, by his conduct, lead the buyer to believe that he will not insist on a confirmed letter of credit: *Plasticmoda* [1952] 1 Lloyd's Rep. 527, but will accept an unconfirmed one instead: *Panoutsos v Raymond Hadley Corporation of New York* [1917] 2 KB 473; *Enrico Furst & Co v W.E. Fischer* [1960] 2 Lloyd's Rep 340. A seller may accept a less sum for his goods than the contracted price, thus inducing him to believe that he will not enforce payment of the balance: *Central London Property Trust Ltd v High Trees House Ltd* [1947] KB 130 and *D. & C. Builders Ltd v Rees* [1966] 2 QB 617, 624. In none of these cases does the party who acts on the belief suffer any detriment. It is not a detriment, but a benefit to him, to have an extension of time or to pay less, or as the case may be. Nevertheless, he has conducted his affairs on the basis that he has that benefit and it would not be equitable now to deprive him of it.

The judge rejected this doctrine because, he said, 'there is no evidence of the buyers having acted to their detriment.' I know that it has been suggested in some quarters that there must be detriment. But I can find no support for it in the authorities cited by the judge. The nearest approach to it is the statement of Viscount Simonds in the *Tool Metal* case [1955] 1 WLR 761, 764, that the other must have been led 'to alter his position,' which was adopted by Lord Hodson in *Ajayi v R.T. Briscoe (Nigeria) Ltd* [1964] 1 WLR 1326, 1330. But that only means that he must have been led to act differently from what he otherwise would have done. And if you study the cases in which the doctrine has been applied, you will see that all that is required is that the one should have '*acted* on the belief induced by the other party.' That is how Lord Cohen put it in the *Tool Metal* case [1955] 1 WLR 761, 799, and that is how I would put it myself . . .

MEGAW LJ: As I see it, the necessary consequence of that offer and acceptance of a sterling credit is that the original term of the contract of sale as to the money of account was varied from Kenyan currency to sterling. The payment, and the sole payment, stipulated by the contract of sale was by the letter of credit. The buyers, through the confirming bank, had opened a letter of credit which did not conform because it provided sterling as the money of account. The sellers accepted that offer by making use of the credit to receive payment for a part of the contractual goods. By that acceptance, as the sellers must be deemed to have known, not only did the confirming bank become irrevocably bound by the terms of the offer (and by no other terms), but so also did the buyers become bound. Not only did they incur legal obligations as a result of the sellers' acceptance—for example, an obligation to indemnify the bank—but also the buyers could not thereafter have turned round and said to the sellers (for example, if Kenyan currency had been devalued against sterling) that the bank would thereafter pay less for the contractual goods than the promised sterling payment of £262 per ton. If the buyers could not revert unilaterally to the original currency of account, once they had offered a variation which had been accepted by conduct, neither could the sellers so revert. The contract had been varied in that respect . . .

In my view, if there were no variation, the buyers would still be entitled to succeed on the ground of waiver. The relevant principle is, in my opinion, that which was stated by Lord Cairns LC in *Hughes v Metropolitan Railway Co.* (1877) 2 App Cas 439, 448 . . .

STEPHENSON LJ: By not objecting to the non-conforming letter of credit, by obtaining payment on it in sterling from the bank and by extending it the sellers clearly accepted and agreed to it and were treated as having done so not only by the bank but by the buyers, who may be presumed (although there was no evidence about it) to have paid charges and incurred liabilities such as a liability to indemnify the bank. The sellers never indicated any reservations about the change from Kenya shillings to pounds sterling or asked for any adjustment, probably for the simple reason that they considered sterling as good as Kenya shillings if not better. When after devaluation of sterling they invoiced the balance of the goods against part payment of the balance of the price and claimed the difference created by devaluation from the buyers, they were attempting to assert a liability which, whether by variation or waiver, they had allowed the buyers to alter.

. . . I would leave open the question whether the action of the other party induced by the party who 'waives' his contractual rights can be any alteration of his position, as Lord Denning MR has said, or must, as the judge thought, be an alteration to his detriment, or for the worse, in some sense. In this case the buyers did, I think, contrary to the judge's view, act to their detriment on the sellers' waiver, if that is what it was, and the contract was varied for good consideration, which may be another way of saying the same thing: so that I need not, and do not, express a concluded opinion on that controversial question . . .

Stephenson LJ considered that the buyers had acted to their detriment following the seller's representation. This detriment was the possibility that Kenyan shillings might have been devalued and they would have been bound to pay more under the sterling letter of credit. Was this the consideration for the seller's promise so that a binding variation had been made? Does this mean that if a promisee acts to his detriment, there will be a binding variation and therefore that promissory estoppel will be irrelevant?

NOTE Although detriment is essential (see e.g. *High Trees* as an example of no detriment), where the promisee *has* acted to his detriment, it is easier to establish that it is inequitable for the promisor to go back on that promise (*page 132, 3.2.2.4*).

Société Italo-Belge pour le Commerce et l'Industrie SA v Palm and Vegetable Oils (Malaysia) Sdn Bhd, The Post Chaser
[1982] 1 All ER 19

The sellers agreed to sell palm oil to the buyers, who contracted to sell it to sub-buyers. The sellers failed to advise the buyers of the ship's identity used for shipment until a month after it had sailed. This would have justified the buyers in refusing to accept the documents. However, the buyers did not protest, and instead requested the sellers to hand the documents relating to the consignment to the sub-buyers. Two days later, when the sub-buyers rejected the documents, the buyers also rejected them, and the sellers were forced to sell the palm oil elsewhere at a loss. The sellers claimed this loss from the buyers and the crucial question was whether the buyers had waived their right to reject the documents.

Held: The buyers had waived their right to reject the documents by requesting that the sellers hand the documents to the sub-buyers, since this was a representation that they were prepared to accept the documents. However, although the sellers had acted on this representation, by presenting the documents as requested, their position had not been prejudiced owing to the very short time between the date of the representation and reliance and the date of rejection. Therefore, it was not inequitable for the buyers to enforce their legal right to reject.

ROBERT GOFF J: I approach the matter as follows. The fundamental principle is that stated by Lord Cairns LC [in *Hughes v Metropolitan Railway Co.* (*page 122*, 3.2.1)], viz that the representor will not be allowed to enforce his rights 'where it would be inequitable having regard to the dealings which have thus taken place between the parties'. To establish such inequity, it is not necessary to show detriment; indeed, the representee may have benefited from the representation, and yet it may be inequitable, at least without reasonable notice, for the representor to enforce his legal rights. Take the facts of *Central London Property Trust Ltd v High Trees House Ltd (1946)* [1956] 1 All ER 256, [1947] KB 130, the case in which Denning J breathed new life into the doctrine of equitable estoppel. The representation was by a lessor to the effect that he would be content to accept a reduced rent. In such a case, although the lessee has benefited from the reduction in rent, it may well be inequitable for the lessor to insist on his legal right to the unpaid rent, because the lessee has conducted his affairs on the basis that he would only have to pay rent at the lower rate; and a court might well think it right to conclude that only after reasonable notice could the lessor return to charging rent at the higher rate specified in the lease. Furthermore it would be open to the court, in any particular case, to infer from the circumstances of the case that the representee must have conducted his affairs in such a way that it would be inequitable for the representor to enforce his rights, or to do so without reasonable notice. But it does not follow that in every case in which the representee has acted, or failed to act, in reliance on the representation, it will be inequitable for the representor to enforce his rights for the nature of the action, or inaction, may be insufficient to give rise to the equity, in which event a necessary requirement stated by Lord Cairns LC for the application of the doctrine would not have been fulfilled.

3.2.2.4 It must be inequitable to allow the promisor to go back on its promise

D. & C. Builders Ltd v Rees
[1966] 2 QB 617 (CA)

In July 1964, the defendant owed the claimant builders £482, a debt unpaid in November. The claimant was in desperate financial straits and it was alleged that the defendant's wife knew this when she offered to pay the claimant £300 in full settlement, indicating that if this were not accepted the claimant would get nothing. The claimant said that it had no choice but to accept and received a cheque for £300 'in completion of the account'. The claimant then claimed the balance.

Held: There was no binding settlement. Danckwerts and Winn LJJ concentrated on rejecting the argument that consideration had been provided because the payment of a smaller amount had been made by cheque (and a cheque was different from payment in cash). Lord Denning examined promissory estoppel, but held that it could not operate on these facts because, since the promise was not freely given, it was not inequitable for the claimant to go back on its promise.

LORD DENNING MR: [The] doctrine of the common law [relating to part payment of debts] has come under heavy fire. It was ridiculed by Sir George Jessel in *Couldery v Bartram* [(1881) 19 Ch D 394, 399]. It was said to be mistaken by Lord Blackburn in *Foakes v Beer*. It was condemned by the Law Revision Committee (1945 Cmd 5449), paras 20 and 21. But a remedy has been found. The harshness of the common law has been relieved. Equity has stretched out a merciful hand to help the debtor. The courts have invoked the broad principle stated by Lord Cairns in *Hughes v Metropolitan Railway Co*.

. . . It is worth noticing that the principle may be applied, not only so as to suspend strict legal rights, but also so as to preclude the enforcement of them.

This principle has been applied to cases where a creditor agrees to accept a lesser sum in discharge of a greater. So much so that we can now say that, when a creditor and a debtor enter upon a course of negotiation, which leads the debtor to suppose that, on payment of the lesser sum, the creditor will not enforce payment of the balance, and on the faith thereof the debtor pays the lesser sum and the creditor accepts it as satisfaction: then the creditor will not be allowed to enforce payment of the balance when it would be inequitable to do so. This was well illustrated during the last war. Tenants went away to escape the bombs and left their houses unoccupied. The landlords accepted a reduced rent for the time they were empty. It was held that the landlords could not afterwards turn round and sue for the balance, see *Central London Property Trust Ltd v High Trees House Ltd* [1947] KB 130. This caused at the time some eyebrows to be raised in high places. But they have been lowered since. The solution was so obviously just that no one could well gainsay it.

In applying this principle, however, we must note the qualification: The creditor is only barred from his legal rights when it would be *inequitable* for him to insist upon them. Where there has been a *true accord*, under which the creditor voluntarily agrees to accept a lesser sum in satisfaction, and the debtor *acts upon* that accord by paying the lesser sum and the creditor accepts it, then it is inequitable for the creditor afterwards to insist on the balance. But he is not bound unless there has been truly an accord between them.

In the present case, on the facts as found by the judge, it seems to me that there was no true accord. The debtor's wife held the creditor to ransom . . .

In my opinion there is no reason in law or equity why the creditor should not enforce the full amount of the debt due to him . . .

? QUESTION

The promise in *D. & C. Builders Ltd v Rees* would now be voidable under the doctrine of economic duress (*page 511*, 10.1.3). It is not clear, however, what the position will be if the pressure is not as explicit as it was in *D. & C. Builders v Rees*. It appears from *Williams v Roffey* (*page 106*, 3.1.3.7) to make a difference depending upon who initiates a compromise. Was any pressure exerted in *High Trees*?

3.2.2.5 Does promissory estoppel extinguish rights or merely suspend them?

This is a vital question, since if promissory estoppel can extinguish the right for all time, then it conflicts with *Foakes v Beer* (1884) 9 App Cas 605 (*page 111*, 3.1.4), which held that if a promisor represented that it would not insist on its strict contractual rights, in the absence of consideration provided by the promisee, the promisor was free to change its mind.

Tool Metal Manufacturing Co. Ltd v Tungsten Electric Co. Ltd
[1955] 1 WLR 761 (HL)

By a contract in 1938, Tool Metal (TMMC) granted Tungsten Electric (TECO) a licence to import, manufacture, use, and sell certain hard metal alloys covered by patents owned by TMMC. If TECO's sales exceeded a set quota in any given month, they were to pay 'compensation' of 30 per cent to TMMC. After the outbreak of war in 1939, TMMC agreed not to enforce its right to the 'compensation' and no compensation was paid after 31 December 1939. In 1945, TECO commenced an action against TMMC; in March 1946, TMMC counterclaimed for the compensation in respect of the material used from June 1945, but not for the period before this. The Court of Appeal held that the counterclaim failed, because this temporary arrangement to suspend compensation could be terminated only by giving reasonable notice and this had not been done. In this subsequent action in 1950, TMMC claimed the compensation from January 1947, and the issue was whether reasonable notice had been given by TMMC to resume its strict legal rights.

Held: TMMC was entitled to compensation, since the delivery of the counterclaim in March 1946 constituted notice by TMMC that it intended to resume its legal rights, and the period of nine months between the date of the counterclaim and the date from which the compensation was claimed was a sufficient period of notice.

LORD TUCKER: The sole question, therefore, before the courts on this issue in the present action has been throughout: Was the counterclaim in the first action a sufficient intimation to terminate the period of suspension which has been found to exist? . . . It is, of course, clear . . . that there are some cases where the period of suspension clearly terminates on the happening of a certain event or the cessation of a previously existing state of affairs or on the lapse of a reasonable period thereafter. In such cases no intimation or notice of any kind may be necessary. But in other cases where there is nothing to fix the end of the period which may be dependent on the will of the person who has given or made the concession, equity will no doubt require some notice or intimation together with a reasonable period for readjustment before the grantor is allowed to enforce his strict rights. No authority has been cited which binds your Lordships to hold that in all such cases the notice must take any particular form or specify a date for the termination of the suspensory period. This is not surprising having regard to the infinite variety of circumstances which may give rise to this principle which was stated in broad terms and must now be regarded as of general application. It should, I think, be applied with great caution to purely creditor and debtor relationships which involve no question of forfeiture or cancellation, and it would be unfortunate if the law were to introduce into this field technical requirements with regard to notice and the like which might tend to penalise or discourage the making of reasonable concessions.

NOTES

1. This case confirms the general view that promissory estoppel is merely suspensory and the promisor can resume its rights under the contract, where it is no longer inequitable to do so, after giving reasonable notice of this intention.

2. Both *High Trees* and *Tool Metal* concerned individual periodic payments (of rent and monthly compensation); in both cases, it seems that it would not have been possible to claim back the instalments before notice was given or the estoppel ceased. Thus, there is an important difference between the general right, which can be revived once the conditions under which the estoppel operated cease to exist or at the end of a period of reasonable notice, and individual periodic payments which are extinguished. There is therefore a practical difference between the operation of promissory estoppel in single debt obligations (where promissory estoppel operates only to allow more time to pay) and debt obligations taking the form of instalment payments (where, in the period covered by the estoppel, the balance on the individual instalments is extinguished). Lord Denning MR, in *D. & C. Builders Ltd v Rees* [1966] 2 QB 617, 624 (*page 132*, 3.2.2.4), stated: 'It is worth noticing that the principle may be applied, not only so as to suspend strict legal rights, but also so as to preclude the enforcement of them.' It is possible to reconcile this statement with the case law by arguing that Lord Denning was referring to the individual periodic payments, which could be extinguished by promissory estoppel.

However, in the next case, Arden LJ appeared to suggest that promissory estoppel would always operate to extinguish rights, which, if true, would put the doctrine in direct conflict with *Foakes v Beer*.

Collier v P. & M. J. Wright (Holdings) Ltd
[2007] EWCA Civ 1329, [2008] 1 WLR 643 (CA)

The Court of Appeal accepted that an alleged agreement to accept a smaller sum in full satisfaction did not constitute a binding agreement because of the absence of consideration (*Foakes v Beer*), but considered that there was an arguable defence of promissory estoppel.

However, Arden LJ suggested that it would automatically be inequitable for a creditor who accepts a smaller sum to sue for the balance later, even if the debtor's circumstances have changed. This also suggests that promissory estoppel can extinguish rights in a more general sense than has traditionally been supposed.

ARDEN LJ: 42. The facts of this case demonstrate that, if (1) a debtor offers to pay part only of the amount he owes; (2) the creditor voluntarily accepts that offer, and (3) in reliance on the creditor's acceptance the debtor pays that part of the amount he owes in full, the creditor will, by virtue of the doctrine of promissory estoppel, be bound to accept that sum in full and final satisfaction of the whole debt. For him to resile will of itself be inequitable. In addition, in these circumstances, the promissory estoppel has the effect of extinguishing the creditor's right to the balance of the debt. This part of our law originated in the brilliant obiter dictum of Denning J, as he then was, in the *High Trees* case. To a significant degree it achieves in practical terms the recommendation of the Law Revision Committee chaired by Lord Wright MR in 1937.

NOTES

1. This appears to be incorrect, as is recognized by Longmore LJ, since going back on such a promise cannot be necessarily inequitable unless the promise was *not* freely given. Equity does not operate in this way. Instead, it is important to assess each individual scenario to determine whether the claimant's conduct in going back on its voluntary promise can be assessed as inequitable in all of the circumstances. The circumstances will include the conduct of the debtor, in addition to that of the creditor, and should not automatically follow from mere acceptance of a smaller sum. For example, should a creditor be bound if he agrees to accept £10,000 in part payment for a debt of £100,000 when, the next day, the debtor wins a lottery prize of £1 million?

Arden LJ's approach would significantly elevate and alter the nature of promissory estoppel and its status, since it has traditionally been treated as not being equivalent in terms of effect to a finding that a promise is supported by consideration.

2. More recently, the requirement to evaluate each situation for inequity was accepted as correct by Stuart-Smith J in *Virulite LLC v Virulite Distribution Ltd*. The judge drew a distinction between a representation that was time-limited from the outset and what he termed 'an open-ended forbearance'.

Virulite LLC v Virulite Distribution Ltd
[2014] EWHC 366 (QB), [2015] 1 All ER (Comm) 2014

The promisor represented that a sum of £25,000 due in accordance with the contract terms did not need to be paid until clearance by a third party (the FDA—US Food & Drug Administration) had been received. This representation had been relied upon (with attempts being made to secure the third party clearance), and it was held to be inequitable to go back on it, and insist on the payment in accordance with the time limit set for payment, until that clearance had been obtained. It followed that non-payment could not be used as a ground to terminate the contract. (This is similar to the representation that gave rise to the effective waiver in *Hughes v Metropolitan Railway Co.* (1877) LR 2 App Cas 439, discussed at *page 122*, 3.2.1.) The judge discussed the components of promissory estoppel which had become the focus of judicial argument.

STUART-SMITH J: 121 It is not necessary for LLC to show that it has acted to its detriment. What is required is that a party's acts (or desisting from acting) should make it inequitable for the representor thereafter to enforce his legal rights inconsistently with his representation.

When does the doctrine suspend and when does it extinguish rights?

122 The effect of a representation is generally revocable: see *Chitty on Contracts* 3–082, 3–095 to 3–097. As *Chitty* makes clear, the determinative consideration is whether it is inequitable *in all the circumstances* for the representor to enforce his rights inconsistently with his representation. Those circumstances will include, but are not limited to, the precise terms of the representation, how the representee has responded to the representation, and whether it remains possible for the representee to comply with his original obligation.

123 Where, as in *Hughes v Metropolitan Railway* (1877) 2 App Cas 439 the representation has been in the nature of an open-ended forebearance, the effect will generally be to suspend the representor's ability to rely upon the underlying contractual obligation and any breach of it until reasonable notice is given that brings the period of suspension to an end. When the period of suspension is ended, the representor will be allowed to rely upon the underlying contractual obligation as from that date, but he is generally not entitled to enforce the obligations as if they had been in full force during the period of suspension. So in *Hughes*, the Appellant's representations in November and December 1874 had the effect of suspending the notice issued in October 1874 to the Respondents requiring them to repair premises within six months. That period of suspension did not come to an end until 31 December 1874, until which time the operation of the notice was waived. Time ran under the notice from the end of the period of suspension; but no time during the period of suspension could retrospectively be relied upon by the Appellant: see Lord Cairns LC at 447. It could therefore be said that the effect of the suspension was to extinguish the Appellant's right to rely upon the rights that would otherwise have accrued to him during the period of suspension.

124 In *Collier v P & MJ Wright Ltd* [2008] 1 WLR 643 at [37] Arden LJ cited the decision of Denning J in *Central London Property Trust Ltd v High Trees House Limited* [1947] KB 130 as a case where the effect of resiling would be sufficiently inequitable that the right to recover the original debt was not merely postponed but extinguished. At first sight, the representation in *High Trees* was a simple forebearance by a landlord agreeing to accept a reduced ground rent, which was duly paid. However, Denning J interpreted the landlord's promise as being 'that the ground rent should be reduced to £1,250 a year as a temporary expedient while the block of flats was not fully, or substantially fully let, owing to the conditions prevailing' as a result of the war. The landlord gave notice by letter dated 21 September 1945 requiring full payment of the rent going forward and arrears of over £7,000. Denning J allowed the claim going forward, because the war conditions no longer prevailed; but he refused the claim for the arrears. In reaching that conclusion he said:

> If the case had been one of estoppel, it might be said that in any event the estoppel would cease when the conditions to which the representation applied came to an end, or it also might be said that it would only come to an end on notice. In either case it is only a way of ascertaining what is the scope of the representation. I prefer to apply the principle that a promise intended to be binding, intended to be acted on and in fact acted on, is binding so far as its terms properly apply. Here it was binding as covering the period down to the early part of 1945, and as from that time full rent is payable.

125 *High Trees* would be a clearer factual example of the extinguishing effect of a representation if the landlord had given notice at a time when the war conditions still prevailed and had been held not to be entitled to recover the full ground rent until they ceased to prevail at some point in the future. It seems to me that there is scope for confusion in the use of the terms 'suspensory' and 'extinguishing' in this context, since a representation may be revocable, and in that sense suspensory, while effectively extinguishing the representor's right to rely upon his contractual rights during the period of suspension. However, the approach adopted by Denning J in the passage set out above, supports the proposition that the terms of the representation are highly material when deciding whether it is suspensory (i.e. revocable) or extinguishes the representor's right (i.e. irrevocable) to rely upon a breach of the established terms of the underlying contract going forward. While the law of waiver and estoppel has been extensively developed since *High Trees*, I consider that there may be a material difference between an open-ended forebearance and a promise not to enforce until a particular date is reached or a particular set of circumstances prevails when considering whether it is inequitable to allow the representor to rely upon the original rights and obligations arising under the contract.

NOTE It is therefore a matter of semantics for the period of the 'suspension' of legal rights. In some circumstances it can be argued that the effect will be to 'extinguish' the legal right, e.g. the right to foreclose *in accordance with the original six months' notice* in *Hughes*. Equally, the critical fact in *High Trees* seems to have been that the claim was for future full rent after the bombing had ceased. As the judge makes clear, the position on the nature of promissory estoppel would have been clearer had the claim been made when the bombing was continuing since the right to full rent would clearly have been suspended until the bombing ceased. The net effect of this is to extinguish that right during the period of the bombing and prevent recovery of the balance on the individual periodic payments of rent in that period. However, it is clear that there is an envisaged 'end point' for the general suspension, and this alone can determine whether it is inequitable to allow the general legal right (e.g. to full rent) to revive.

3.2.3 How far can the doctrine be extended?

The exact scope of promissory estoppel is unclear. In particular, questions have been raised as to whether it can be extended to give rise to a cause of action, whether it can be applied where there is no existing legal relationship between the parties, the exact scope and meaning of its suspensory effect, and the extent to which the concept of inequitable conduct will affect the estoppel.

3.2.3.1 A new flexibility?

Waltons Stores (Interstate) Ltd v Maher
(1988) 164 CLR 387 (High Court of Australia)

Waltons had negotiated with Maher, landowners, that Maher would demolish a building on the land, construct a new one in accordance with Waltons' specifications, and then lease the building to Waltons as retail premises. Maher did not wish to start until it was clear that there were no problems with the lease that Waltons was to take. Maher signed its part of the lease and forwarded it to Waltons' solicitors for execution 'by way of exchange', then began to demolish the building. Waltons had second thoughts about proceeding and told its solicitors to 'go slow'. Waltons knew that 40 per cent of the work had been completed when it informed Maher that it would not proceed. Maher sought specific performance and, on appeal, sought to argue that Waltons was estopped from going back on its implied promise to complete the lease contract. Waltons argued that even if it had made a representation as to its future conduct, there was no pre-existing legal relationship between the parties and Maher could not use the estoppel to create a cause of action.

Held: Waltons knew that Maher was exposed to a detriment in carrying out the demolition and building work in reliance on the representation, and, since it was unconscionable to adopt a course of inaction encouraging that detriment, Waltons was estopped from denying that it was bound. The majority (Mason CJ, Wilson J, and Brennan J) appeared to confirm that promissory estoppel could create a cause of action and that this could be reconciled with the doctrine of consideration on the ground that the object of the promissory estoppel doctrine was not to enforce promises but to avoid detriment to the promisee resulting from the unconscionable departure by the promisor from the terms of his promise. In addition, it was not necessary to establish a pre-existing relationship between the parties before this estoppel could be relied upon.

MASON CJ AND WILSON J: There has been for many years a reluctance to allow promissory estoppel to become the vehicle for the positive enforcement of a representation by a party that he would do something in the future. Promissory estoppel, it has been said, is a defensive equity: *Hughes v Metropolitan Railway Co.* (1877) 2 App Cas 439; *Combe v Combe* [1951] 2 KB 215 and the traditional notion has been that estoppel could only be relied upon defensively as a shield and not as a sword. *High Trees* [1947] KB 130 itself was an instance of the defensive use of promissory estoppel. But this does not mean that a plaintiff cannot rely on an estoppel. Even according to traditional orthodoxy, a plaintiff may rely on an estoppel if he has an independent cause of action, where in the words of Denning LJ in *Combe v Combe*, the estoppel 'may be part of a cause of action, but not a cause of action in itself'.

But the respondents ask us to drive promissory estoppel one step further by enforcing directly in the absence of a pre-existing relationship of any kind a non-contractual promise on which the representee has relied to his detriment. For the purposes of discussion, we shall assume that there was such a promise in the present case. The principal objection to the enforcement of such a promise is that it would outflank the principles of the law of contract. Denning LJ 'The doctrine of consideration is too firmly fixed to be overthrown by a side-wind', said that such a promise could only be enforced if it was supported by sufficient consideration.

There is force in these objections and it may not be a sufficient answer to repeat the words of Lord Denning MR in *Crabb v Arun District Council* [1976] 1 Ch 179: 'Equity comes in, true to form, to mitigate the rigours of strict law.' True it is that in the orthodox case of promissory estoppel, where the promisor promises that he will not exercise or enforce an existing right, the elements of reliance and detriment attract equitable intervention on the basis that it is unconscionable for the promisor to depart from his promise, if to do so will result in detriment to the promisee. And it can be argued that there is no justification for applying the doctrine of promissory estoppel in this situation, yet denying it in the case of a non-contractual promise in the absence of a pre-existing relationship. The promise, if enforced, works a change in the relationship of the parties, by altering an existing legal relationship in the first situation and by creating a new legal relationship in the second. The point has been made that it would be more logical to say that when the parties have agreed to pursue a course of action, an alteration of the relationship by non-contractual promise will not be countenanced, whereas the creation of a new relationship by a simple promise will be recognised: see D. Jackson, 'Estoppel as a Sword', *Law Quarterly Review*, vol. 81 (1965) 223, at p. 242.

[T]he doctrine [of promissory estoppel] extends to the enforcement of voluntary promises on the footing that a departure from the basic assumptions underlying the transaction between the parties must be unconscionable. As failure to fulfil a promise does not of itself amount to unconscionable conduct, mere reliance on an executory promise to do something, resulting in the promisee changing his position or suffering detriment, does not bring promissory estoppel into play. Something more would be required. *Humphreys Estate* [*AG (Hong Kong) v Humphreys Estate Ltd* [1987] 1 AC 114] suggests that this may be found, if at all, in the creation or encouragement by the party estopped in the other party of an assumption that a contract will come into existence or a promise will be performed and that the other party relied on that assumption to his detriment to the knowledge of the first party . . . [T]he crucial question remains: was the appellant entitled to stand by in silence when it must have known that the respondents were proceeding on the assumption that they had an agreement and that completion of the exchange was a formality? The mere exercise of its legal right not to exchange contracts could not be said to amount to unconscionable conduct on the part of the appellant. But there were two other factors present in the situation which require to be taken into consideration. The first was the element of urgency that pervaded the negotiation of the terms of the proposed lease . . . The respondents' solicitor had said to the appellant's solicitor on 7 November that it would be impossible for Maher to complete the building within the agreed time unless the agreement were concluded 'within the next day or two'. The outstanding details were agreed within a day or two thereafter, and the work of preparing the site commenced almost immediately.

The second factor of importance is that the respondents executed the counterpart deed and it was forwarded to the appellant's solicitor on 11 November. The assumption on which the respondents acted thereafter was that completion of the necessary exchange was a formality. The next their solicitor heard from the appellant was a letter from its solicitors dated 19 January, informing him that the appellant did not intend to proceed with the matter. It had known, at least since 10 December, that costly work was proceeding on the site.

It seems to us, in the light of these considerations, that the appellant was under an obligation to communicate with the respondents within a reasonable time after receiving the executed counterpart deed and certainly when it learnt on 10 December that demolition was proceeding . . .

. . . The appellant's inaction, in all the circumstances, constituted clear encouragement or inducement to the respondents to continue to act on the basis of the assumption which they had made. It was unconscionable for it, knowing that the respondents were exposing themselves to detriment by acting on the basis of a false assumption, to adopt a course of inaction which encouraged them in the course they had adopted. To express the point in the language of promissory estoppel the appellant is estopped in all the circumstances from retreating from its implied promise to complete the contract.

NOTES

1. It must be doubted whether *Waltons Stores* is, strictly speaking, a promissory estoppel case, since it appears to support a single general doctrine of estoppel preventing unconscionable conduct. This idea of a unifying estoppel is supported by the judgments in *Commonwealth of Australia v Verwayen* (1990) 170 CLR 394, which require that the doctrine should not be seen as a 'series of independent rules'.

2. Duthie (1988) 104 LQR 362 argued that the denial of a future right should be treated in the same way as insistence on an existing right, so that if the legal relationship would exist were it not for the unconscionable conduct, the lack of such a relationship should not prevent reliance on the doctrine of promissory estoppel.

3. The decision has not determined the type of conduct that will be unconscionable and prevent a promisor from going back on his promise in these circumstances (although see the judgment of Mason CJ and Wilson J for guidance). It appeared that 'detrimental reliance' was required in order for a promise to found a claim based on this estoppel. Significantly, however, in *Giumelli v Giumelli* (1999) 163 ALR 473, the High Court of Australia was of the opinion that this is not the only basis for the estoppel.

4. The advantage of this approach in *Waltons Stores* is that it allows the doctrine of consideration to be reconciled with more flexible requirements for the promissory estoppel doctrine. Thus, in theory, Maher was not seeking to enforce an implied promise, but to avoid the detriment that would be suffered if Waltons were to be permitted to continue in its unconscionable conduct of not complying with the promise.

5. In *Waltons Stores*, the High Court of Australia gave effect to the estoppel by awarding damages in lieu of specific performance. An interesting debate surrounds the remedy required to satisfy the 'minimum equity' and, in particular, it might appear that wasted expenditure damages would be the appropriate remedy in this context: see Robertson [1998] LS 360. However, in *Giumelli v Giumelli*—see Edelman (1999) 15 JCL 179—the High Court of Australia considered that, prima facie, the remedy should fulfil the promisee's expectation engendered by the promise so that the expectation measure of damages would be appropriate. The High Court considered that it was only in instances of detrimental reliance that a wasted expenditure-based remedy would be appropriate.

6. The American Restatement (2d) Contracts (1979), § 90(1), allows promissory estoppel to operate as a cause of action, but the courts are given a discretion to determine the appropriate remedy, so that there may not be full enforcement of the promise:

A promise which the promisor should reasonably expect to induce action or forbearance on the part of the promisee or a third person and which does induce such action or forbearance is binding if injustice can be avoided only by enforcement of the promise. The remedy granted for breach may be limited as justice requires.

7. This flexible estoppel has been advocated for use by the English courts (discussion at *page 111, 3.1.4*, note 5). A requirement of detrimental reliance would have seriously limited the usefulness of such an estoppel and it is important that it was rejected in *Giumelli v Giumelli*. However, it remains to be seen whether the English courts will be prepared to adopt such an estoppel. This argument proved unsuccessful before the Court of Appeal in *Baird Textile Holdings Ltd v Marks & Spencer plc*.

Baird Textile Holdings Ltd v Marks & Spencer plc
[2001] EWCA Civ 274, [2002] 1 All ER (Comm) 737 (CA)

Page 157, 4.1.2.3 for the facts and the argument based on an implied contract.

One aspect of the pleadings was the argument that the defendant was prevented by estoppel from determining the arrangements between the parties without giving reasonable notice and was prevented from denying the understanding that the relationship was long-term. The latter argument had been permitted to proceed to trial by the judge at first instance. However, the defendant claimed that, on the basis of established authority, such a claim had no prospect of success. The Court of Appeal agreed that the estoppel claim had no real prospect of success, since English law did not currently create or recognize the right contended for on these facts. Quite apart from the fact that the obligation alleged was insufficiently certain to found an estoppel (*page 125,* 3.2.2.1), the estoppel alleged did not create a cause of action.

MORRITT VC: 34 Counsel for M&S submits that the judge was wrong. He contends . . . that this court is, as the judge was, bound by three decisions of the Court of Appeal to conclude that the estoppel claim has no real prospect of success either. The three decisions and the propositions they respectively established are: (1) a common law or promissory estoppel cannot create a cause of action (*Combe v Combe* [1951] 1 All ER 767, [1951] 2 KB 215); (2) an estoppel by convention cannot create a cause of action either (*Amalgamated Investment and Property Co Ltd (in liq) v Texas Commerce International Bank Ltd* [1981] 3 All ER 577, [1982] QB 84); and (3) accepting that a proprietary or equitable estoppel may create a cause of action it is limited to cases involving property rights, whether or not confined to land (*Western Fish Products Ltd v Penwith DC* [1981] 2 All ER 204 at 217).

35 Counsel for Baird did not dispute that those cases established the propositions for which M&S contended. Rather, he submitted, it is wrong to categorise particular types of estoppel and then impose limitations in each category not applicable to one or more of the other categories. He suggested that English law permits some cross-fertilisation between one category and another. He contended that English law should follow where the High Court of Australia has led in *Waltons Stores (Interstate) Ltd v Maher* (1988) 164 CLR 387 and *Commonwealth of Australia v Verwayen* (1990) 170 CLR 394 and permit estoppel to create causes of action in non-proprietary cases. In reply counsel for M&S conceded that if the Australian cases, to the effect that promissory estoppel extends to the enforcement of voluntary promises, represent the law of England then the judge was right and the cross-appeal must fail.

36 Warnings against categorisation have been given by Robert Goff J and Lord Denning MR in the *Amalgamated Investment* case [1981] 1 All ER 923 at 935, 936 and 584 [*sic*], [1982] QB 84 at 103, 104 and 122, by Scarman LJ in *Crabb v Arun DC* [1975] 3 All ER 865 at 875, [1976] Ch 179 at 192, 193 and by Lord Bingham of Cornhill in *Johnson v Gore Wood & Co* [2001] 1 All ER 481, [2001] 2 WLR 72. But dicta to the contrary effect are to be found in *First National Bank plc v Thompson* [1996] 1 All ER 140 at 144, [1996] Ch 231 at 236 per Millett LJ, *McIlkenny v Chief Constable of West Midlands Police Force* [1980] 2 All ER 227 at 235, [1980] 1 QB 283 at 317 per Lord Denning MR and in *Johnson v Gore Wood & Co* [2001] 1 All ER 481 at 507, 508, [2001] 2 WLR 72 at 99 per Lord Goff of Chieveley.

37 As in the case of the contractual claim, it is important to appreciate exactly what is being alleged and why. The material allegation . . . is that M&S is estopped from denying that 'the relationship with BTH could only be determined by the giving of reasonable notice'. But by itself this claim, which has

undoubted echoes of *Hughes v Metropolitan Rly Co* (1877) 2 App Cas 439, [1874–80] All ER Rep 187 and *Central London Property Trust Ltd v High Trees House Ltd (1946)* [1956] 1 All ER 256, [1947] 1 KB 130, does not lead to the relief sought. For that purpose it is essential to establish an obligation by estoppel that, in the words of [Baird's claim], 'during the subsistence of the relationship Marks & Spencer would acquire garments from BTH in quantities and at prices which in all the circumstances were reasonable'. As counsel for Baird put it in their written argument, 'BTH contends that an equity generated by estoppel can be a cause of action' . . .

38 In my view English law, as presently understood, does not enable the creation or recognition by estoppel of an enforceable right of the type and in the circumstances relied on in this case. First, it would be necessary for such an obligation to be sufficiently certain to enable the court to give effect to it. That such certainty is required in the field of estoppels such as is claimed in this case as well as in contract was indicated by the House of Lords in *Woodhouse AC Israel Cocoa Ltd SA v Nigerian Produce Marketing Co Ltd* [1972] 2 All ER 271, [1972] AC 741 and by Ralph Gibson LJ in *Troop v Gibson* [1986] 1 EGLR 1 at 6. For the reasons I have already given I do not think that the alleged obligation is sufficiently certain. Second, in my view, the decisions in the three Court of Appeal decisions on which M&S rely do establish that such an enforceable obligation cannot be established by estoppel in the circumstances relied on in this case. This conclusion does not involve the categorisation of estoppels but is a simple application of the principles established by those cases to the obligation relied on in this . . .

JUDGE LJ: 50 Two specific aspects of the current principles of the law of estoppel which may be open for reconsideration need mention. First, it is possible to envisage that the different principles encapsulated under the heading 'Estoppel' should cease to be treated as if they were individually compartmentalised. The most illuminating analysis of the disadvantages of rigidity was summarised by Robert Goff J in *Amalgamated Investment and Property Co Ltd (in liq) v Texas Commerce International Bank Ltd* [1981] 1 All ER 923, [1982] QB 84, where he said:

> Of all doctrines, equitable estoppel is surely one of the most flexible . . . It is no doubt helpful to establish, in broad terms, the criteria which, in certain situations, must be fulfilled before an equitable estoppel can be established; but it cannot be right to restrict equitable estoppel to certain defined categories, and indeed some of the categories proposed are not easy to defend . . . Thus in Snell . . . the learned editors isolate two categories of equitable estoppel, promissory estoppel and proprietary estoppel. It may be possible nowadays to identify the former with some degree of precision; but the latter is much more difficult to accept as a separate category . . . As a separate category, proprietary estoppel may be regarded as an amalgam of doubtful utility . . . It is not therefore surprising to discover a tendency in the more recent authorities to reject any rigid classification of equitable estoppel into exclusive and defined categories . . . (See [1981] 1 All ER 923 at 935, 936, [1982] QB 84 at 103, 104.)

. . .

51 The less graphic, but equally trenchant comment by Millett LJ, as he then was, in *First National Bank plc v Thompson* [1996] 1 All ER 140 at 144, [1996] Ch 231 at 236, summarises the opposite contention:

> . . . (the) attempt . . . to demonstrate that all estoppels other than estoppel by record are now subsumed in the single and all-embracing estoppel by representation and that they are all governed by the same requirements has never won general acceptance.

52 The removal of formal classifications would represent the starting point from which to consider the second possible development, consigning to history the misleading aphorism that estoppel is a shield, not a sword. In reality that principle has no application to what is described as a proprietary estoppel. The cause of action founded on proprietary estoppel may, and should, so the argument runs, be extended

generally in this jurisdiction, both in accordance with the recent decisions in the High Court of Australia in *Waltons Stores (Interstate) Ltd v Maher* (1988) 164 CLR 387 and *Commonwealth of Australia v Verwayen* (1990) 170 CLR 394, . . . and also on the basis that if the compartmentalisation of 'estoppel' were broken down, the remedies provided for one form of estoppel (proprietary estoppel) would then be extended to the others.

53 These, very briefly summarised, were the considerations which led me to the preliminary view that although BTH's argument in contract was unsustainable, the possible development of the law in relation to estoppel might properly justify allowing the case to proceed to trial.

54 If it did, however, both the trial judge and this court would be bound to hold that the principles relating to proprietary estoppel are limited to 'rights and interests created in and over land' and, possibly, 'to other forms of property'. (*Western Fish Products v Penwith DC* [1981] 2 All ER 204 at 218, where, in this specific context, Megaw LJ observed: 'The question of new rights and remedies is a matter for Parliament, not the judges.') Moreover, assuming for present purposes only that this authority could be distinguished, the difficulties arising from the underlying uncertainties referred to in the judgment of the Vice-Chancellor extend to the estoppel as well as the contractual issue (*Woodhouse AC Israel Cocoa Ltd SA v Nigerian Produce Marketing Co Ltd* [1972] 2 All ER 271, [1972] AC 741). In reality, BTH's possible success in this litigation would depend on establishing liability against M&S in equity when it would not otherwise be liable in contract, and would represent a dramatic, if not indeed a revolutionary, development of the legal principles governing the enforcement of private obligations.

55 On reflection, I am persuaded by the judgments of the Vice-Chancellor and Mance LJ, and for the reasons given by them, that there is no real prospect of the claim succeeding unless and until the law is developed, or corrected, by the House of Lords . . .

NOTE The *Waltons Stores* argument was doomed to failure because of the deficiencies of the representation or promise relied upon. Leave to appeal to the House of Lords was refused. Thus, any reconsideration by the highest court of the scope of the estoppel, or categories of estoppel, is still awaited.

3.2.3.2 Binding variations in New Zealand

The Court of Appeal of New Zealand introduced a further alternative approach and suggested that consideration would not be required to enforce alteration promises where those promises had been acted upon.

Antons Trawling Co. Ltd v Smith
[2003] 2 NZLR 23 (Court of Appeal of New Zealand)

The claimant was employed as master of one of the defendants' fishing vessels. The defendants held a small fishing quota. The claimant claimed that he had been promised a 10 per cent share of any additional quota allocated to the defendants if the claimant was able to demonstrate that there were fish in sufficient commercial quantities to justify the government setting a larger quota. The government increased the quota for policy reasons without establishing any increase in commercial quantities and the defendants' catch increased by 80 tonnes. The defendants argued that the increased quota was not the result of any actions by the claimant and he had therefore supplied no consideration to support the promise of the 10 per cent share.

He was required to fish under the terms of his contract and had done no more than he was contractually bound to do.

Held: There was a binding variation. Where an alteration promise had been acted upon, in the absence of policy reasons to the contrary, the parties should be bound by such an alteration agreement.

BARAGWANATH J [giving the judgment of the Court]: [92] The reasoning in *Williams v Roffey Bros. & Nicholls (Contractors) Ltd*, accepted by this Court in *Attorney-General for England and Wales* ([2002] 2 NZLR 91), has been trenchantly criticised by Professor Coote in (1990) 3 JCL 23. He argues with force that mere performance of a duty already owed to the promisee under a contract cannot constitute consideration and that the only principled way to such a result is to decide that consideration should not be necessary for the variation of contract. That is the approach of the Uniform Commercial Code, s 2–209(1) and it is vigorously supported by Reiter in 'Courts, Consideration, and Commonsense' (1977) 27 University of Toronto Law Journal 439 especially at p 507, observing that a rigid requirement of consideration in modern commercial contract modifications fails to recognise:

> . . . the illogicality of equating modifying with originating promises or to see that, insofar as consideration serves to exclude gratuitous promise, it is of little assistance in the context of on-going, arms-length, commercial transactions where it is utterly fictional to describe what is being conceded as a gift, and in which there ought to be a strong presumption that good commercial 'considerations' underlie any seemingly detrimental modification . . .

[93] We are satisfied that *Stilk v Myrick* can no longer be taken to control such cases as *Roffey Bros*, *Attorney-General for England and Wales* and the present case where there is no element of duress or other policy factor suggesting that an agreement, duly performed, should not attract the legal consequences that each party must reasonably be taken to have expected. On the contrary, a result that deprived Mr Smith of the benefit of what Antons promised he should receive would be inconsistent with the essential principle underlying the law of contract, that the law will seek to give effect to freely accepted reciprocal undertakings. The importance of consideration is as a valuable signal that the parties intend to be bound by their agreement, rather than an end in itself. Where the parties who have already made such intention clear by entering legal relations have acted upon an agreement to a variation, in the absence of policy reasons to the contrary they should be bound by their agreement. Whichever option is adopted, whether that of *Roffey Bros.* or that suggested by Professor Coote and other authorities, the result is in this case the same.

NOTES

1. The Court of Appeal of New Zealand seems to be suggesting that such a radical approach is the net effect of the decision in *Williams v Roffey* (*page 106, 3.1.3.7*), since factual benefit amounts to invented consideration. However, it is clear that because *Roffey* and *Stilk v Myrick* are difficult to reconcile, the court considered the approach of Coote (1990) 3 JCL 23 to be preferable, i.e. to accept that a promise to pay more will not occur unless there are perceived subjective benefits to the promisor in making that promise. The factual benefit will therefore necessarily be present—and hence that consideration can be found where there is an alteration promise to pay more. The same should also be true of promises to accept less.

2. The result of *Antons Trawling* is that variations would be binding unless 'duress or other policy factors' were at work. However, it is unclear what would be included within 'other policy factors'. Given the importance of the issue of duress to the enforceability of promises (as is already clear from *Roffey*), it would be imperative to establish where the line will be drawn between threats and simple statements of fact (*page 516, 10.1.3.3.1*).

3. The *Antons Trawling* solution would eliminate many of the limitations on the enforceability of alteration promises under English law (such as whether promissory estoppel can create a cause of action) by removing the need to rely on this doctrine. However, since *Antons Trawling* is limited in its application to variations, there is still be scope for the development of an estoppel based on unconscionability in the formation context, as in *Waltons Stores v Maher*, and the debate on this issue is likely to continue.

4. This case is discussed by Professor Coote (2004) 120 LQR 19.

? QUESTION

The Court of Appeal of New Zealand appears to restrict the binding nature of variation promises where consideration need not be established to those promises that have been relied upon/performed. Is this tantamount to stating that reliance replaces consideration as the enforceability criterion in relation to alterations?

Chapter 4

Intention to be legally bound and capacity to contract

4.1 Intention to be legally bound

Intention to create legal relations (or to be legally bound) depends on the parties' intentions, objectively judged. Traditionally, the starting point for determining this intention is the use of different presumptions for domestic and commercial agreements.

4.1.1 Domestic and social agreements

For domestic and social agreements there is a presumption of no intention to create legal relations.

4.1.1.1 Husband and wife

Balfour v Balfour
[1919] 2 KB 571 (CA)

The defendant husband held a post in Ceylon. He and his wife, the claimant, returned to England on leave in 1915. When the defendant returned to Ceylon in 1916, the claimant remained temporarily in England on medical advice. The claimant alleged that, before the defendant returned to Ceylon, they had entered into an oral agreement by which the defendant agreed to pay her £30 a month in consideration for her agreeing not to call upon him for further maintenance. The parties later became estranged and the claimant sought to enforce the agreement.

Held: Since it was a domestic agreement between husband and wife, it was not an enforceable contract.

ATKIN LJ: The defence to this action on the alleged contract is that the defendant, the husband, entered into no contract with his wife, and for the determination of that it is necessary to remember that there are agreements between parties which do not result in contracts within the meaning of that term in our law. The ordinary example is where two parties agree to take a walk together, or where there is an offer and an acceptance of hospitality. Nobody would suggest in ordinary circumstances that those agreements result in what we know as a contract, and one of the most usual forms of agreement which does not constitute a contract appears to me to be the arrangements which are made between husband and wife. It is quite common, and it is the natural and inevitable result of the relationship of husband and wife, that the two spouses should make arrangements between themselves—agreements such as are in dispute in this action—agreements for allowances, by which the husband agrees that he will pay to his wife a certain sum of money, per week, or per month, or per year, to cover either her own expenses or the necessary expenses of the household and of the children of the marriage, and in which the wife promises either expressly or impliedly to apply the allowance for the purpose for which it is given. To my mind those agreements, or many of them, do not result in contracts at all, and they do not result in contracts even though there may be what as between other parties would constitute consideration for the agreement . . . [T]hey are not contracts because the parties did not intend that they should be attended by legal consequences. To my mind it would be of the worst possible example to hold that agreements such as this resulted in legal obligations which could be enforced in the Courts. It would mean this, that when the husband makes his wife a promise to give her an allowance of 30s. or 2/. a week, whatever he can afford to give her, for the maintenance of the household and children, and she promises so to apply it, not only could she sue him for his failure in any week to supply the allowance, but he could sue her for non-performance of the obligation, express or implied, which she had undertaken upon her part. All I can say is that the small Courts of this country would have to be multiplied one hundredfold if these arrangements were held to result in legal obligations. They are not sued upon, not because the parties are reluctant to enforce their legal rights when the agreement is broken, but because the parties, in the inception of the arrangement, never intended that they should be sued upon. Agreements such as these are outside the realm of contracts altogether. The common law does not regulate the form of agreements between spouses. Their promises are not sealed with seals and sealing wax. The consideration that really obtains for them is that natural love and affection which counts for so little in these cold Courts. The terms may be repudiated, varied or renewed as performance proceeds or as disagreements develop, and the principles of the common law as to exoneration and discharge and accord and satisfaction are such as find no place in the domestic code . . . [I]t appears to me to be plainly established that the promise here was not intended by either party to be attended by legal consequences. I think the onus was upon the plaintiff, and the plaintiff has not established any contract. The parties were living together, the wife intending to return. The suggestion is that the husband bound himself to pay 30/. a month under all circumstances, and she bound herself to be satisfied with that sum under all circumstances, and, although she was in ill-health and alone in this country, that out of that sum she undertook to defray the whole of the medical expenses that might fall upon her, whatever might be the development of her illness, and in whatever expenses it might involve her. To my mind neither party contemplated such a result . . .

NOTES

1. Although Atkin LJ states that, objectively, the parties did not intend legal consequences to follow, the decision appears to rest on the argument that such agreements should not be enforced for public policy reasons. Two policy factors are specifically referred to—namely, the 'floodgates' argument and the argument that because such agreements follow from 'natural love and affection which counts for so little in these cold courts', they are outside the jurisdiction of the courts.

2. As argued, given that a criterion to enforce an agreement is the presence of consideration (or a bargain), there is no additional necessity to require an intention to create legal relations: see Hepple [1970] CLJ 122. The decision in *Shadwell v Shadwell* (1860) 9 CB NS 159, 142 ER 62 (*page 99, 3.1.3.6*) supports the proposition that consideration should be sufficient. However, in *Balfour v Balfour*, Atkin LJ confirmed that both requirements are necessary. It is possible that an intention to be legally bound will replace consideration as the sole criterion for enforceability, since consideration is not a concept recognized in continental jurisdictions. See the comments of the Court of Appeal of New Zealand in *Antons Trawling Co. Ltd v Smith* [2003] 2 NZLR 23 (discussed at *page 142, 3.2.3.2*) suggesting that consideration is no more than evidence of the existence of an intention to create legal relations.

Merritt v Merritt
[1970] 1 WLR 1211 (CA)

After the husband left his wife, he stated that he would pay her £40 a month, from which she had to pay the outstanding mortgage payments on the house. He also signed a written note that provided that, when the mortgage payments had all been made, he would transfer the house to his wife in consideration for her paying all household charges. The wife paid off the mortgage, but the husband refused to transfer the house.

Held: The written agreement was intended to create legal relations between the parties. The presumption against such an intention did not apply when the husband and wife were not living in amity, but were separated or about to separate.

LORD DENNING MR: The first point taken on his behalf by [counsel for the husband] is that the agreement was not intended to create legal relations. It was, he says, a family arrangement such as was considered by the court in *Balfour v Balfour* [1919] 2 KB 571 and in *Jones v Padavatton* [1969] 1 WLR 328. So the wife could not sue upon it.

I do not think those cases have any application here. The parties there were living together in amity. In such cases their domestic arrangements are ordinarily not intended to create legal relations. It is altogether different when the parties are not living in amity but are separated, or about to separate. They then bargain keenly. They do not rely on honourable understandings. They want everything cut and dried. It may safely be presumed that they intend to create legal relations.

[Counsel for the husband] then relied on the recent case of *Gould v Gould* [1970] 1 QB 275, when the parties had separated, and the husband agreed to pay the wife £12 a week 'so long as he could manage it'. The majority of the court thought that those words introduced such an element of uncertainty that the agreement was not intended to create legal relations. But for that element of uncertainty, I am sure that the majority would have held the agreement to be binding. They did not differ from the general proposition which I stated [in *Gould v Gould*] at p. 280 that:

> when . . . husband and wife, at arm's length, decide to separate, and the husband promises to pay a sum as maintenance to the wife during the separation, the court does, as a rule, impute to them an intention to create legal relations.

NOTES

1. The Court of Appeal also stressed that the terms of the agreement in this case were sufficiently certain to enable it to be enforced, and it appears from *Gould v Gould* [1970] 1 QB 275 that if the terms are uncertain (a promise to pay 'for so long as I can manage it'), the language will indicate that the parties do not intend to be bound even if they are separated.

2. The fact that the wife in *Merritt v Merritt* relied on the agreement in paying the mortgage repayments is an additional reason why the Court of Appeal held there was an intention to create legal relations here.

3. *Merritt v Merritt* clearly demonstrates that agreements between husband and wife in a 'business context' that are sufficiently certain will rebut the presumption. This is well illustrated by the Supreme Court's approach in *Granatino v Radmacher* [2010] UKSC 42, [2011] 1 AC 534, to a prenuptial agreement between husband and wife concerning the ownership of matrimonial assets. Baroness Hale stated, at [142]:

> There is nothing to stop a husband and wife from making legally binding arrangements, whether by contract or settlement, to regulate their property and affairs while they are still together (type (a) agreements). These days, the commonest example of this is an agreement to share the ownership or tenancy of the matrimonial home, bank accounts, savings or other assets. Agreements for housekeeping or personal allowances, on the other hand, might run into difficulties.

The same is true of dealings between other relatives in a business context, e.g. *Snelling v John G. Snelling Ltd* [1973] 1 QB 87.

4.1.1.2 **Parent and child**

There is a presumption against an intention to create legal relations in agreements between parent and child. To rebut it, clear evidence of an intention to give rise to legal consequences, reliance on the agreement, and certainty of terms are required.

Jones v Padavatton
[1969] 1 WLR 328 (CA)

In August 1962, a daughter accepted her mother's offer to go to England and study for the Bar. The agreement, not put in writing, was that the mother would pay the fees and provide maintenance of $200 a month. The mother had intended this to be in West Indian dollars (£42 a month), whereas the daughter thought it was to be in US dollars (£70 a month). However, when the maintenance payments arrived, the daughter accepted them without objection. In 1964, the mother orally agreed to buy a house where the daughter could live and it was agreed that the rents from letting the other rooms would provide the maintenance in place of the £42 a month. In 1967, the mother claimed possession of the house. At the date of the hearing, the daughter had still not completed her studies for the Bar. The daughter relied upon the agreement as her defence to the possession action.

Held (Danckwerts and Fenton Atkinson LJJ): The mother was entitled to possession because the agreement was a family arrangement and not intended to be legally binding. Moreover, it was far too vague and uncertain to be enforceable as a contract.

FENTON ATKINSON LJ: The problem is, in my view, a difficult one, because though one would tend to regard a promise by a parent to pay an allowance to a child during a course of study as no more than a family arrangement, on the facts of this case this particular daughter undoubtedly gave up a great deal on the strength of the mother's promise.

In my judgment it is the subsequent history which gives the best guide to the parties' intention at the material time. There are three matters which seem to me important: (1) The daughter thought that her mother was promising her 200 United States dollars, or £70 a month, which she regarded as the minimum necessary for her support. The mother promised 200 dollars, but she had in mind 200 British West Indian dollars, £42 a month, and that was what she in fact paid from November 1962 to December 1964. Those payments were accepted by the daughter without any sort of suggestion at any stage that the mother had legally contracted for the larger sum. (2) When the arrangements for the purchase of No. 181, Highbury Quadrant were being discussed, and the new arrangement was made for maintenance to come out of the rents, many material matters were left open: how much accommodation was the daughter to occupy; how much money was she to have out of the rents; if the rents fell below expectation, was the mother to make up the difference below £42, or £42 less the sum saved by the daughter in rent; for how long was the arrangement to continue, and so on. The whole arrangement was, in my view, far too vague and uncertain to be itself enforceable as a contract; but at no stage did the daughter bring into the discussions her alleged legal right to £42 per month until her studies were completed, and how that right was to be affected by the new arrangement. (3) It is perhaps not without relevance to look at the daughter's evidence in cross examination. She was asked about the occasion when the mother visited the house, and she, knowing perfectly well that the mother was there, refused for some hours to open the door. She said: 'I didn't open the door because a normal mother doesn't sue her daughter in court. Anybody with normal feelings would feel upset by what was happening.' Those answers and the daughter's conduct on that occasion provide a strong indication that she had never for a moment contemplated the possibility of her mother or herself going to court to enforce legal obligations, and that she felt it quite intolerable that a purely family arrangement should become the subject of proceedings in a court of law.

At the time when the first arrangement was made, mother and daughter were, and always had been, to use the daughter's own words, 'very close'. I am satisfied that neither party at that time intended to enter into a legally binding contract, either then or later when the house was bought. The daughter was prepared to trust her mother to honour her promise of support, just as the mother no doubt trusted her daughter to study for the Bar with diligence, and to get through her examinations as early as she could.

NOTES

1. Salmon LJ agreed that the mother was entitled to possession but did so by a different route. Although he stressed the daughter's reliance in giving up her job and moving to England, and considered that the agreement originally made was intended by both parties to have contractual force, Salmon LJ implied a term that the agreement would last for a reasonable time to enable the daughter to complete her studies. The reasonable period was five years. This had elapsed at the time of the action and the daughter could therefore not rely on the agreement.

2. Although there was reliance in *Jones v Padavatton*, the presumption of no intention was not rebutted since the terms were uncertain. However, it was rebutted in *Parker v Clark* [1960] 1 WLR 286 for an agreement between relatives to share a home. Their agreement contained very detailed terms as to the payment of household expenses, and the claimants had relied upon it in selling their own home and lending the money to their daughter to buy a flat. The defendants had also made a will leaving the house to the female claimant, her sister, and daughter.

4.1.2 Commercial agreements

There is a presumption of an intention to create legal relations in commercial agreements.

A mere puff is not enforceable because it is not intended to be taken literally and is not promissory in nature. A counsel's argument for the Smoke Ball Company in *Carlill v Carbolic Smoke Ball Co.* [1893] 1 QB 256 that the advertisement was no more than an advertising gimmick was rejected by the Court of Appeal, because the Company had deposited £1,000 with its bank as proof of its intention to be bound (*Chapter 1*).

Bowerman v Association of British Travel Agents Ltd
[1996] CLC 451 (CA)

The claimants had booked a school skiing holiday through a tour operator, an ABTA member. Shortly before the date of the holiday, the tour operator became insolvent and had ceased to trade. ABTA reimbursed the cost of the holiday, but deducted £10 per head to represent the holiday insurance premium paid, stating that this sum was excluded from the ABTA protection scheme. The claimants sought the return of these insurance premiums, claiming a direct contractual relationship with ABTA entitling them to full reimbursement of the holiday cost, relying on an ABTA notice displayed by tour operators, para. 5 of which provided: 'Where holidays or other travel arrangements have not yet commenced at the time of failure, ABTA arranges for you to be reimbursed the money you have paid in respect of your holiday arrangements.' The trial judge had accepted—and it was common ground—that the correct approach was to read the notice as the public would understand it. However, he rejected the claimants' claim as there was no offer, no intention to create legal relations, and the terms of the notice were too vague and inconsistent to constitute a legally enforceable promise.

Held (Waite and Hobhouse LJJ; Hirst LJ dissenting): There was a direct contractual relationship between ABTA and members of the public who booked their holidays with ABTA members. The ABTA notice displayed on the premises of each member tour operator constituted a contractual offer on terms obliging ABTA to reimburse the cost of insurance, since it was intended to be read—and would reasonably be read—as an offer that a customer would accept by booking a holiday with an ABTA member.

HOBHOUSE LJ: Turning to the document itself, it is accepted that the words of Bowen LJ [in *Carlill v Carbolic Smoke Ball Co.*] are apt:

> It was intended to be issued to the public and to be read by the public. How would an ordinary person reading this document construe it?

The rival contentions, both of which can be persuasively argued for as is demonstrated by the difference of judicial opinion to which this case has given rise, are whether the document is simply telling the public about a scheme which ABTA has for its own members or whether it goes further than this and contains an offer which a member of the public can take up and hold ABTA to should the ABTA member with whom the member of the public is dealing fail financially.

I prefer the latter view. I recognise that the document is headed 'Notice describing ABTA's scheme of protection' and that in para. 4 and 5 the present tense is used—'ABTA seeks'—'ABTA ensures'—'ABTA arranges'—and not the future tense—'ABTA will ensure' or 'ABTA will arrange'. These points undoubtedly support the view of the judge and the defendants' argument. But the document has to be read as a whole. It is clearly intended to have an effect on the reader and to lead him to believe that he is getting something of value. The scheme is an ABTA scheme in relation to its members but it is a scheme of protection of the customers of ABTA members. It emphasises that it is 'to protect you their customers' and is 'for your benefit'. This is further underlined in para. 3 where the final sentence reads:

> If an ABTA member ceases to belong to ABTA and thereafter fails financially ABTA still protects you if you made the booking before the time when ABTA membership ceased.

ABTA is offering to protect the reader of the notice, the prospective customer. It is an inevitable inference that what ABTA is saying is that it, ABTA, will do something for the customer if the member should fail financially.

. . . In my judgment this document is intended to be read and would reasonably be read by a member of the public as containing an offer of a promise which the customer is entitled to accept by choosing to do business with an ABTA member. A member of the public would not analyse his situation in legal terms but he would clearly understand that this notice would only apply to him if he should choose to do business with an ABTA member and he would also understand that if he did do so he would be entitled to hold ABTA to what he understood ABTA to be promising in this document. In my judgment it satisfies the criteria for a unilateral contract and contains promises which are sufficiently clear to be capable of legal enforcement. The principles established in the *Carbolic Smoke Ball* case apply. The claimants are entitled to enforce the right of reimbursement given to them in para. 5.

This conclusion also covers ABTA's further argument that it had no intention to create legal relations. The document as reasonably read by a member of the public would be taken to be an offer of a legally enforceable promise. Given that this is the effect of the document which ABTA has chosen to publish, it does not advance ABTA's case to say that ABTA privately did not intend to expose itself to any legal liability to the public. It suffices that ABTA intentionally published a document which had that effect. A contracting party cannot escape liability by saying that he had his fingers crossed behind his back.

. . . Like in the *Carbolic Smoke Ball* case, we have had urged on us the potential size of the obligations which ABTA would be accepting should a number of its members fail and the difficulty of meeting all the claims which might be made on ABTA. This was a matter for the judgment of ABTA before it chose to issue the notice. It is the job of ABTA and no concern of the customer to see that its bonding and mutual and external insurance arrangements suffice. The argument has no more merit than the equivalent argument which was advanced in the *Carbolic Smoke Ball* case.

The existence of consideration to support the contractual obligation of ABTA is clear. A picture was presented to us, wholly unrealistically, of ABTA as some benevolent body which gained no benefit from and had no interest in travellers choosing to deal with ABTA members. The function of ABTA is to promote its members. It was also argued that as Mr Wallace was required by the local education authority and by the children's parents to buy only ABTA backed holidays that meant that Mr Wallace and those on whose behalf he was acting gave no consideration because, so it was argued, Mr Wallace was already under an obligation to buy an ABTA backed holiday. Mr Wallace was under no obligation to buy any holiday at all nor were the parents. No doubt there are other tour operators and travel agents, not members of ABTA, who are able to undercut ABTA prices. ABTA's members prominently market themselves as members of ABTA and anybody who chooses to do business with them is certainly giving consideration to ABTA for any contract or 'collateral' contract which may ensue. The analogy with such cases as *Shanklin Pier Ltd v Detel Products Ltd* [1951] 2 KB 854 [*page 325*, 7.4] is fully made out.

I therefore cannot agree with the [judge] and consider that this appeal should be allowed. The claimants were entitled to and did accept the offer contained in the document issued by ABTA and it fills one with disquiet that any organisation in the position of ABTA should after the event, when it finds that its liabilities are greater than it had anticipated, seek to contend otherwise. As counsel pointed out, if ABTA had wished to deny that it was accepting any legal obligation to the traveller or wished to say that it was not making any promises, nothing would have been simpler than for it to have said so in the document. For obvious commercial reasons ABTA did not choose this course. To have included such words would have destroyed the value of the document in the eyes of the public and nullified the very effect which ABTA intended it to, and which it did, achieve—to induce the public to book with and entrust their money to ABTA members.

I would allow the appeal.

NOTES

1. Hirst LJ (dissenting) considered that this was a non-promissory notice intended only to reassure:

In his argument [counsel for the plaintiffs] submit ted that on its proper construction the language of the notice was the language of contract. He drew particular attention to the two subsidiary headings 'Scheme of protection' and 'The protection is that . . . ', which he submitted were indicating a promise; he emphasised the repeated use of the personal pronoun or adjective 'you' and 'your', and submitted that it was a highly personal notice honing in on the individual customer; he contended that the reference in para. (1) to the provision by the tour operators of bonds guarantees and other securities to ABTA added legitimacy to the binding obligation which he submitted the document conveyed; he drew particular attention to the words 'ensures' and 'arranges' in para. (4) and (5) which he submitted were words of commitment; and he submitted that the final four paragraphs under the heading 'Limitations'

reinforced the contractual commitment in the earlier part of the document.

In support of his argument [counsel for the plaintiffs] placed strong reliance on the famous case of *Carlill v Carbolic Smoke Ball Co.* [1893] 1 QB 256 . . .

This advertisement, he submitted, was comparable with the ABTA notice in the present case, and I accept without reservation that, if the words of this notice are truly promissory in character, it would be capable of constituting a contractual offer to the public in general.

The crucial point is therefore to determine whether, on its proper construction, the notice is indeed promissory in character, and on this I am unable to accept [counsel for the plaintiffs'] arguments.

First, it is essential in my judgment to give full weight to the main heading, to which I attach great importance, viz.: 'Notice describing ABTA's scheme of protection against the financial failure of ABTA members'. This in my view is an accurate epitome of the terms of the notice as a whole, which is descriptive rather than contractual in character.

The headings 'Scheme of protection' and 'The protection is that . . . ' are no more than subheadings characterising the details of the scheme. Equally the language, in particular the verbs used in para. (3) to (5) ('protects', 'seeks to arrange' 'ensures' and 'arranges') are grammatically descriptive, rather than promissory phrases such as, for example, 'will insure', 'will arrange', etc. By the same token the statement in para. (1) that 'all ABTA tour operators are required to provide bonds guarantee or other securities to ABTA', is also essentially descriptive.

Indeed, nowhere in the first five paragraphs of the notice do I find any specific words of promise or any firm commitment, and nothing in the last four paragraphs headed 'Limitation' points in a different direction.

By contrast, the crisp wording of the advertisement in the *Carlill* case ('£100 reward *will be paid* . . . ') is essentially promissory in character, and indeed to my mind highlights the shortcomings from the appellant's point of view of the wording in the present notice.

My view as to the non-contractual nature of this document is reinforced by the vague and equivocal nature of several of the statements contained in the following numbered paragraphs:

(3) . . . other travel arrangements . . .

(4) . . . seeks to arrange . . .

(5) . . . other travel arrangements . . . your holidays arrangements . . . [and] . . . in some instances ABTA may however be able to arrange . . . or offer . . .

All these considerations to my mind strongly support the view that the ordinary member of the public would not interpret this document as constituting a contractual offer to him personally—and the use of the direct words 'you', and 'your', which carry no contractual commitment, do no more than focus the attention of the customer personally on the information contained in the notice, rather like Lord Kitchener's famous recruiting poster in the First World War.

I wish to make it clear that I do not doubt that the ordinary member of the public would interpret the notice as drawing his attention to something of value to him, but that does not seem to me to assist either way in determining whether its character is informative or contractual.

I also wish to make it clear that in reaching my conclusion I have, I believe correctly, confined my attention solely to the wording of the notice itself, and I have left out of account both the submissions from both sides as to surrounding circumstances, which were unknown to Mr Wallace [the second plaintiff, the teacher who had booked the trip] . . . On similar grounds, I would hold that there was no intention on ABTA's part to create a legal relationship with the individual customer.

In support of her argument on this first and main point [counsel for the defendant] relied on the case of *Kleinwort Benson v Malaysia Mining Corp Berhad* [1989] 1 WLR 379; (1989) 5 BCC 337 [*page 154*, 4.1.2.1] in which the Court of Appeal held that a paragraph in a letter of comfort did not have contractual status, but was no more than a representation as to the current policy adopted by the defendant company.

Although as [counsel for the plaintiffs] rightly pointed out that the facts of that case are very different from the present, seeing that the parties involved were two very large commercial enterprises, I think that the judge was right in concluding that the analogy between that case and the present one is sound, in that the essential function of the present notice is to reassure the customer by reference to the existence of the ABTA scheme of protection which it describes . . .

For these reasons, which are closely in accord with the judge's analysis, I would dismiss this appeal.

The different approaches may be explained by the fact that, whereas the majority considered all of the background circumstances and the position of the holiday consumer, Hirst LJ expressly limited himself to considering only the wording of the notice itself.

2. In *Dhanani v Crasnianski* [2011] EWHC 926 (Comm), [2011] 2 All ER (Comm) 799, in the commercial context, Teare J confirmed the more contextual approach:

[80] Whether the parties intended to enter a contract, that is to create legal relations, depends not upon a detailed textual analysis but upon 'how a reasonable man versed in business would have understood the exchanges between the parties' (per Andrew Smith J in *Maple Leaf Macro Volatility Master Fund v Rouvroy* [[2009] EWHC 257 (Comm)] [2009] 2 All ER (Comm) 287, [223]).

In this case, the signing of each page of a letter and term sheet indicated this intention.

3. The majority judgments also reinforce the need to use express words to exclude any intention to be legally bound if this is the desired objective. (See the discussion of honour clauses at *page 155*, *4.1.2.2*.)

Esso Petroleum Ltd v Commissioners of Customs and Excise
[1976] 1 WLR 1 (HL)

Esso had a sales promotion scheme by which garage owners offered a 'free' World Cup coin with every four gallons of petrol. The Customs and Excise Commissioners claimed that the coins were chargeable to purchase tax because they were 'produced in quantity for general sale'.

Held (Lord Fraser dissenting): The coins were not being sold, since if there was a contract (an issue on which there was some disagreement), the consideration for the transfer of the coin was not money, but the customer's undertaking to enter into a collateral contract to purchase four gallons of petrol.

The majority reasoning differed as to whether there was a contract relating to the coins. Viscount Dilhorne and Lord Russell considered the coins to be a gift (as opposed to a sale); the coins had little intrinsic value, there was therefore no intention to create legal relations in such an arrangement. Lords Simon and Wilberforce came to the opposite conclusion since the arrangement was set in the context of business relations.

LORD RUSSELL: . . . The first question . . . is whether, notwithstanding the liberal references in the documents attending the promotion scheme to 'giving', 'gifts', and 'free', that which would and did take place gave rise to a contract, enforceable by a motorist who bought four gallons from a participating proprietor, that he should receive one of these medals. It is to be borne in mind in this connection that the mere fact that Esso and the garage proprietors undoubtedly had a commercial aim in promoting the scheme does not deprive the delivery of a medal of the quality of a gift as distinct from a sale: for benevolence is not a necessary feature of a gift, which may well be motivated by self interest. On the other hand it is trite law that if on analysis a transaction has in law one character, the fact that the parties either accidentally or deliberately frame the transaction in language appropriate to a transaction of a different character will not deny to it its true character.

We have here, my Lords, a promotion scheme initiated by Esso, who procured the production of the medals. Each medal was of negligible intrinsic value, though the incentive to soccer enthusiasts to collect all 30 may have been strong. Plainly it was never in Esso's mind that this negligible intrinsic value should be reflected in an increase in the pump price of petrol, and it never was: indeed the price of a gallon could not be increased by 3/16 of a penny. In my opinion it would have been thought by Esso, and rightly, that there could have been no occasion, in order to ensure success of the scheme, for an outlet proprietor to subject himself to a contractual liability to deliver a coin to a motorist who had bought four gallons. The subject matter was trivial: the proprietor was directly interested in the success of the scheme and would be in the highest degree unlikely to renege on the free gift offer, and indeed there is no suggestion that a motorist who qualified and wanted a medal ever failed to get one: from the motorist's viewpoint, if this had ever happened, I cannot think that he would have considered that he had a legal grievance, though he might have said that he would not patronise that outlet again: similarly in my opinion if a garage advertised 'Free Air' and after buying petrol or oil the motorist was told that the machine was out of order that day. In my opinion, the incentive for the garage proprietor to carry out the scheme was such as to make it quite unnecessary to invest, or for Esso to intend to invest, the transaction with the additional compulsion of a contractual obligation, and in all the circumstances of the case I am unable to regard that which under the scheme was intended by Esso to take place in relation to the medals, and did take place, as something which would be intended to or regarded as creating a legal contractual relationship. In forming that opinion I regard the minimal intrinsic value of a medal as important. I would not wish it to be thought that my opinion, if correct, would, in other cases in which a sales promotion scheme involves substantial benefits, give carte blanche to participants to renege on 'free' offers. I am simply of opinion, in agreement with the Court of Appeal, though not I fear with the majority of your Lordships, that in the instant case, because of the absence of any contractual element, it should not be said that any medal was produced for general sale.

LORD SIMON: I am, however, my Lords, not prepared to accept that the promotion material put out by Esso was not envisaged by them as creating legal relations between the garage proprietors who adopted it and the motorists who yielded to its blandishments. In the first place, Esso and the garage proprietors put the material out for their commercial advantage, and designed it to attract the custom of motorists. The whole transaction took place in a setting of business relations. In the second place, it seems to me in general undesirable to allow a commercial promoter to claim that what he has done is a mere puff, not intended to create legal relations (cf *Carlill v Carbolic Smoke Ball Co.* [1893] 1 QB 256). The coins may have been themselves of little intrinsic value; but all the evidence suggests that Esso contemplated that they would be attractive to motorists and that there would be a large commercial advantage to themselves from the scheme, an advantage to which the garage proprietors also would share. Thirdly, I think that authority supports the view that legal relations were envisaged.

. . . I venture to add that it begs the question to assert that no motorist who bought petrol in consequence of seeing the promotion material prominently displayed in the garage forecourt would be likely to bring an action in the county court if he were refused a coin. He might be a suburb Hampden who was not prepared to forgo what he conceived to be his rights or to allow a tradesman to go back on his word.

Believing as I do that Esso envisaged a bargain of some sort between the garage proprietor and the motorist, I must try to analyse the transaction. The analysis that most appeals to me is one of the ways in which Lord Denning MR considered the case [1975] 1 WLR 406, 409B-D, namely a collateral contract of the sort described by Lord Moulton in *Heilbut, Symons & Co v Buckleton* [1913] AC 30, 47:

> . . . there may be a contract the consideration for which is the making of some other contract. 'If you will make such and such a contract I will give you £100', is in every sense of the word a complete legal contract. It is collateral to the main contract, . . .

So here. The law happily matches the reality. The garage proprietor is saying, 'If you will buy four gallons of my petrol, I will give you one of these coins'. None of the reasons which have caused the law to consider advertising or display material as an invitation to treat rather than an offer applies here. What the garage proprietor says by his placards is in fact and in law an offer of consideration to the motorist to enter into a contract of sale of petrol. Of course, not every motorist will notice the placard, but nor will every potential offeree of many offers be necessarily conscious that they have been made. However, the motorist who does notice the placard, and in reliance thereon drives in and orders the petrol, is in law doing two things at the same time. First, he is accepting the offer of a coin if he buys four gallons of petrol. Secondly, he is himself offering to buy four gallons of petrol: this offer is accepted by the filling of his tank.

. . . Here the coins were not transferred for a money consideration. They were transferred in consideration of the motorist entering into a contract for the sale of petrol. The coins were therefore not produced for sale, and do not fall within the schedule. They are exempt from purchase tax.

NOTES

1. For Lord Simon, the determining factor cannot be whether the parties would actually sue to enforce the agreement. Atiyah (1976) 39 MLR 335 very firmly argued that the triviality of the transaction and the unwillingness to litigate are not the tests of an intention to create legal relations.

2. For the majority, the coins were not produced for 'sale' because the consideration for the transfer of the coin was not money, but the entering of a contract to purchase the petrol. This is somewhat artificial since, to get the coin, the customer had to pay the price of the 4 gallons of petrol and the price would appear to be part of the consideration.

3. Lord Fraser (dissenting) considered that it was a single contract of sale to purchase 4 gallons of petrol and a coin.

4.1.2.1 Comfort letters

In *Kleinwort*, the Court of Appeal held that a comfort letter was not legally enforceable, since it did not constitute a promise.

Kleinwort Benson Ltd v Malaysia Mining Corporation Berhad
[1989] 1 WLR 379 (CA)

The parent company of MMC Metals Ltd gave the claimant merchant bank a comfort letter which stated that 'it is our policy to ensure that the business of Metals is at all times in a position to meet its liabilities to you under the above arrangements'. When the subsidiary company (MMC Metals) went into liquidation, the claimant merchant bank sought to recover from the parent company relying on the comfort letter.

Held: The correct test to determine the status of a comfort letter was to ask whether a promise was being made, rather than the test applied by Hirst J at first instance—[1988] 1 WLR 799— of whether there was an intention to create legal relations. The words of this comfort letter amounted to a policy statement only and did not constitute a promise.

> RALPH GIBSON LJ: [I]n this case it is clear, in my judgment, that the concept of a comfort letter, to which the parties had resort when the defendants refused to assume joint and several liability or to give a guarantee, was known by both sides at least to extend to or to include a document under which the defendants would give comfort to the plaintiffs by assuming, not a legal liability to ensure repayment of the liabilities of their subsidiary, but a moral responsibility only . . . The comfort letter was drafted in terms which in paragraph 3 do not express any contractual promise and which are consistent with being no more than a representation of fact. If they are treated as no more than a representation of fact, they are in that meaning consistent with the comfort letter containing no more than the assumption of moral responsibility by the defendants in respect of the debts of Metals. There is nothing in the evidence to show that, as a matter of commercial probability or common sense, the parties must have intended paragraph 3 to be a contractual promise, which is not expressly stated, rather than a mere representation of fact, which is so stated.

NOTES

1. Clearly, this was a commercial agreement. The presumption of an intention can therefore be rebutted in relation to comfort letters where the wording used does not amount to a promise. This can lead to fine distinctions dependent on the wording of the comfort letter. See Brown [1990] JBL 281.

2. This decision was relied upon by Hirst LJ (dissenting) in *Bowerman v ABTA Ltd* [1996] CLC 451 (*page 149, 4.1.2*) in reaching his conclusion that ABTA's notice was not promissory in nature, but merely a statement of policy or reassurance.

4.1.2.2 Honour clauses

The presumption of an intention to create legal relations can also be rebutted by the use of an 'honour clause', which excludes the courts and states that the agreement is binding in honour only.

Rose and Frank Co. v J. R. Crompton and Brothers Ltd

By agreement, the claimants had been appointed sole US agents of the defendants. The agreement contained the following clause:

> This arrangement is not entered into, nor is this memorandum written, as a formal or legal agreement, and shall not be subject to legal jurisdiction in the Law Courts either of the United States or England, but it is only a definite expression and record of the purpose and intention of the three parties concerned to which they each honourably pledge themselves with the fullest confidence, based on past business with each other, that it will be carried through by each of the three parties with mutual loyalty and friendly co-operation.

The defendants terminated the agency agreement without the required notice and refused to execute orders received before termination. The claimants brought an action for breach of contract and non-delivery of the goods for which orders had already been placed.

[1923] 2 KB 261 (CA)

The Court of Appeal held there was no binding contract and consequently there could be no action based upon it. A majority (Atkin LJ dissenting) also held that the orders and acceptances of those orders were not legally binding contracts to deliver.

ATKIN LJ: To create a contract there must be a common intention of the parties to enter into legal obligations, mutually communicated expressly or impliedly. Such an intention ordinarily will be inferred when parties enter into an agreement which in other respects conforms to the rules of law as to the formation of contracts. It may be negatived impliedly by the nature of the agreed promise or promises, as in the case of offer and acceptance of hospitality, or of some agreements made in the course of family life between members of a family as in *Balfour v Balfour* [1919] 2 KB 571. If the intention may be negatived impliedly it may be negatived expressly. In this document, construed as a whole, I find myself driven to the conclusion that the clause in question expresses in clear terms the mutual intention of the parties not to enter into legal obligations in respect to the matters upon which they are recording their agreement. I have never seen such a clause before, but I see nothing necessarily absurd in business men seeking to regulate their business relations by mutual promises which fall short of legal obligations, and rest on obligations of either honour or self-interest, or perhaps both. In this agreement I consider the clause a dominant clause, and not to be rejected, as the learned judge thought, on the ground of repugnancy.

[1925] AC 445 (HL)

The House of Lords agreed that there was no legally binding contract because of the honour clause, but considered (agreeing with Atkin LJ in the Court of Appeal) that the orders had been accepted and delivery was therefore legally required.

LORD PHILLIMORE: According to the course of business between the parties which is narrated in the unenforceable agreement, goods were ordered from time to time, shipped, received, and paid for, under an established system; but the agreement being unenforceable, there was no obligation on the American company to order goods or upon the English companies to accept an order. Any actual transaction between the parties, however, gave rise to the ordinary legal rights; for the fact that it was not of obligation to do the transaction did not divest the transaction when done of its ordinary legal significance. This, my Lords, will, I think, be plain if we begin at the latter end of each transaction.

Goods were ordered, shipped, and received. Was there no legal liability to pay for them? One stage further back. Goods were ordered, shipped, and invoiced. Was there no legal liability to take delivery? I apprehend that in each of these cases the American company would be bound. If the goods were short-shipped or inferior in quality, or if the nature of them was such as to be deleterious to other cargo on board or illegal for the American company to bring into their country, the American company would have its usual legal remedies against the English companies or one of them. Business usually begins in some mutual understanding without a previous bargain . . .

NOTE Clearly, the House of Lords was influenced by a desire to hold parties to their obligations under executed agreements, although there was technically no contractual obligation.

Jones v Vernon's Pools Ltd
[1938] 2 All ER 626

The claimant alleged to have sent in a pools coupon to the defendants; the defendants denied receiving it. The conditions on the coupon stated that:

[T]he sending in of the coupon or any transaction entered into in respect of the pool should not be attended by or give rise to any legal relationship, rights, duties or consequences whatsoever, or be legally enforceable or the subject of litigation, but that all such arrangements, agreements and transactions should be binding in honour only.

Held: This condition prevented any legal action relating to the pools coupon.

ATKINSON J: If it means what I think that they intend it to mean, and what certainly everybody who sent a coupon and who took the trouble to read it would understand, it means that they all trusted to the defendants' honour, and to the care they took, and that they fully understood that there should be no claim possible in respect of the transactions.

One can see at once the impossibility of any other basis. I am told that there are a million coupons received every week-end. Just imagine what it would mean if half the people in the country could come forward and suddenly claim that they had posted and sent in a coupon which they never had, bring actions against the pool alleging that, and calling evidence to prove that they had sent in a coupon containing the list of winning teams, and if Vernons had to fight case after case to decide whether or not those coupons had been sent in and received. The business could not be carried on for a day on terms of that kind. It could only be carried on on the basis that everybody is trusting them, and taking the risk themselves of things going wrong. It seems to me that, even if the plaintiff established that this coupon was received, it was received on the basis of these rules, and that he has agreed in the clearest way that, if anything does go wrong, he is to have no legal claim. In other words, he has agreed that the money which *prima facie* became due to him if that coupon reached them is not to be the subject of an action at law. There is to be no legal liability to pay. He has got to trust to them, and, if something goes wrong, as I say, it is his funeral, and not theirs. I am convinced that that is the position here, and, even if the coupon were received, he has failed to establish that he would have a claim which he could come to the courts to enforce . . .

4.1.2.3 Implied agreements in the commercial context

For commercial contracts, the presumption of intention to create legal relations does not apply where the allegation is that a contract should be implied from the parties' conduct, as opposed to a contract between them resulting from express agreement. The party asserting the existence of such a contract has the burden of establishing the necessity for implying it and this depends on the ability to establish the existence of an intention to be legally bound. This, in turn, is linked to certainty of the alleged terms.

Baird Textile Holdings Ltd v Marks & Spencer plc
[2001] EWCA Civ 274, [2001] 1 All ER (Comm) 737 (CA)

The claimant had been one of the principal suppliers for the defendant retailer for 30 years. In October 1999, the defendant cancelled the arrangement from the end of that season. The claimant sought damages on the basis that the arrangement could be terminated only on reasonable notice of three years. This was in part based on an allegation that there was an implied contractual obligation to that effect, there being no express contract between the parties (*page 137*, 3.2.3.1, for a discussion of the alternative argument based on estoppel).

Held: The argument based on the implied contract failed because there was no intention to create legal relations, since the alleged contract's terms lacked certainty (*page 21*, 2.1.1).

Clearly, the reason why there was no express contract was the deliberate decision by the defendants to maintain flexibility in the commercial relationship. Mance LJ explained the position and the burden of proof in such cases.

MANCE LJ: 59 . . . For a contract to come into existence, there must be both (a) an agreement on essentials with sufficient certainty to be enforceable and (b) an intention to create legal relations.

60 Both requirements are normally judged objectively. Absence of the former may involve or be explained by the latter. But this is not always so. A sufficiently certain agreement may be reached, but there may be either expressly (i.e. by express agreement) or impliedly (e.g. in some family situations) no intention to create legal relations.

61 An intention to create legal relations is normally presumed in the case of an express or apparent agreement satisfying the first requirement: see Chitty on Contracts (28th ed.) vol. 1 para. 2-146 It is otherwise, when the case is that an implied contract falls to be inferred from parties' conduct: Chitty, para. 2-147. It is then for the party asserting such a contract to show the necessity for implying it. As Morison J [the judge at first instance] said . . . , if the parties would or might have acted as they did without any such contract, there is no necessity to imply any contract. It is merely putting the same point another way to say that no intention to make any such contract will then be inferred.

62 That the test of any such implication is necessity is, in my view, clear, both on the authority of *The Aramis* [1989] I Lloyd's Rep 213, *Blackpool and Fylde Aero Club Ltd v Blackpool BC* [1990] 3 All ER 25, [1990] 1 WLR 1195, *Wilson & Co A/S v Partenreederei Hannah Blumenthal, The Hannah Blumenthal* [1983] 1 All ER 34, [1983] 1 AC 854 and *Mitsui & Co Ltd v Novorossiysk Shipping Co, The Gudermes* [1993] 1 Lloyd's Rep 311, cited by [Morritt VC] the Vice-Chancellor, and also a matter of consistency. It could not be right to adopt a test of necessity when implying terms into a contract and a more relaxed test when implying a contract—which must itself have terms.

63 Here it is sought by the claimant to argue in reverse. First, the issue of intention to create legal relations is addressed and it is suggested that the judge gave only one reason . . . for negativing any such intention. Then, having sought to show that reason as ill-founded, it is argued that the only barrier to an enforceable contract is 'essentially one of interpretation' and of giving effect to an intention on the part of the parties to contract.

64 It is, in my judgment, more appropriate to take the requirements in the order in which I have set them out, and to recognise their potential interrelationship. If there is no sufficient agreement on essentials, that is on any view fundamental, and it may well also reflect an absence of intention to create legal relations.

65 Here, Baird has pleaded in detail facts and matters showing and concerning an exceptionally close and interactive commercial relationship with M&S. The more I have heard and read about the closeness of the parties' commercial co-operation in the past, the less able I have felt to see how its effect could be expressed in terms having any contractual certainty. The parties were in constant contact, discussing, developing, adapting or altering their arrangements. Baird submits that the answer lies in recognising that there were on each side broad obligations (a) to continue the longstanding purchaser-supplier relationship (unless and until one or other gave reasonable notice to determine it, put at three years) and, in that context, (b) for M&S to purchase and for Baird to supply a 'reasonable' or 'appropriate' share of whatever were M&S's requirements from time to time, so as (c) to ensure, at least to that extent, that the production facilities that Baird had devoted to M&S's business to date were maintained, or (at all events) run down in a less abrupt and painful way than actually occurred.

66 The terms of the suggested contract are more particularly . . . :

. . . in exchange for BTH [Baird] agreeing (a) to supply [M&S] with garments year by year on a seasonal basis; (b) to allow [M&S] to be closely involved in the design and manufacture of the garments so supplied; (c) to establish and maintain a workforce and manufacturing capacity sufficient to meet and be highly responsive to [M&S] continuing requirements; (d) not to act in a manner which in the view of [M&S] was contrary to its interests; and (e) to deal with [M&S] in good faith and reasonably having regard to the objective of the relationship, the relationship would continue long term and would be terminable only upon the giving of reasonable notice; and that during the subsistence of the relationship [M&S] would acquire garments from BTH in quantities and at prices which in all the circumstances were reasonable and would deal with BTH in good faith and reasonably having regard to the objective of the relationship.

. . .

68 When the suggested long-term contract is put in these terms, it becomes clear that it would, in case of any dispute, involve the court writing a 'reasonable' contract for the parties, after making a complete review of their situations, needs, abilities and expectations. It could only become relevant to seek to identify the impact of such long-term obligations in a situation where actual co-operation had broken down or one or the other party wanted to reduce its commitment to the minimum. So the court would be expected to undertake the exercise in the very situation where the parties' actual behaviour could no longer serve as a guide to the answer. I agree with the Vice-Chancellor that this is not an exercise that the court can or should undertake, or, indeed, which the parties can objectively be taken to have intended. The presence in the suggested contractual formulation of implied duties of good faith is an additional barrier in the way of the conclusion for which Baird contends, in view of English law's general refusal to recognise any duty of this nature as an implied contractual term.

69 Objectively, the only sensible analysis of the present situation is in my judgment that the parties had an extremely good long-term commercial relationship, but not one which they ever sought to express, or which the court would ever seek to express, in terms of long-term contractual obligations. The upshot is that I agree with the judge's conclusion that there was never here any agreement on essentials.

70 In addition, I consider that the fact that there was never any agreement to reach or even to set out the essential principles which might govern any legally binding long-term relationship indicates that neither party can objectively be taken to have intended to make any legally binding commitment of a long-term nature. Their conduct in this regard contrasts with their conduct in entering into short-term commitments relating to each season . . .

4.1.3 A different approach?

It may be difficult to classify an agreement as either social/domestic or commercial. In *Edmonds v Lawson* [2000] QB 501, the Court of Appeal made no such determination, but focused on the specific context surrounding the making of an offer of pupillage in chambers.

Edmonds v Lawson
[2000] QB 501 (CA)

A pupil barrister claimed that her unpaid 12-month pupillage constituted a contract of employment, so that she was a 'worker' within the meaning of the National Minimum Wage Act 1998. Chambers argued that the offer of pupillage was not enforceable as a contract since there was no intention to create legal relations and Ms Edmonds had not provided any consideration. The allegation was that the provisions of the Bar Council's Code of Conduct regulated the relationship and that no further contract was therefore necessary. The judge at first instance held that this pupillage was a contract of apprenticeship, because it was a business arrangement and the presumption of intention to create legal relations applied. Accordingly, the claimant was a 'worker' within the Act.

Held (in the Court of Appeal, allowing the appeal): Although there was a binding contract because, in the context, there was the necessary intention to create legal relations and the agreement was supported by consideration, this was not a contract of apprenticeship and the claimant therefore did not qualify as a 'worker' within the meaning of the 1998 Act.

LORD BINGHAM CJ [giving the judgment of the court]:

The first issue: was there a contract?

. . . Whether the parties intended to enter into legally binding relations is an issue to be determined objectively and not by inquiring into their respective states of mind. The context is all-important. From the defendants' point of view the written offer of pupillage to the claimant came at the end of a long, time-consuming and expensive process. It was also a process of great long-term consequence to them since, although barristers in practice are independent self-employed practitioners, it is of benefit to all, at every level, that chambers as a whole consist of talented and hardworking members, and the defendants, like other chambers, recruit most of their tenants from the pool of those recruited as pupils. So, quite apart from considerations of professional duty and the public interest, it is of direct practical consequence to chambers to attract and select the ablest pupils. That is why, in part at least, many chambers including the defendants' fund pupillages for a proportion of their pupils, sometimes very generously. From the pupil's point of view, obtaining a pupillage in a flourishing set of chambers practising in the pupil's chosen field is a step with potentially immense consequences, both professional and financial, in both the short and the long term. Obtaining a pupillage does not of course guarantee a tenancy, but it guarantees the pupil an opportunity to show his quality and thereby seek a tenancy. When, as the culmination of a long process of application, shortlisting and interview an offer is formally made and formally accepted it would in our judgment be surprising to infer that the parties intended to bind themselves in honour only.

In arguing that there was no intent to create legal relations [counsel] for the defendants relied on the educational nature of the arrangement, suggesting that it lacked the characteristics of a commercial contract and involved no payment by the pupil. It was a voluntary and gratuitous offer by the chambers to provide education and training. He also relied on the doubt which, he said, existed as to who entered into the arrangement on the chambers' side. There was, he suggested, no need for a contract because the relationship was already regulated by the documents to which reference has been made above [Bar Council's Code of Conduct], and if chambers should resile from an undertaking to provide pupillage the pupil would have ample redress through the Bar disciplinary machinery, which would in practice preclude such dishonourable behaviour. The absence of written terms and conditions, he argued, pointed strongly against any intention to contract.

Neither singularly nor cumulatively do we find these points in any way persuasive on the question of intent. It is true that the content of the arrangement was educational, but as already pointed out the practical implications of the arrangement for both parties were potentially very significant and, subject to the point on consideration discussed below, there is no reason why a binding contract cannot be made for the provision of education and training. Whereas once the arrangement of pupillage was a one-to-one engagement between pupil and pupil master, that has ceased to be so, as evidenced by the responsibility imposed on and accepted by heads of chambers, by the procedure in practice adopted by chambers and by the management of pupillage as a chambers' responsibility. The claimant was not interviewed, nor was the offer of pupillage made, by either of those who became her successive pupil masters, and when the offer was made and accepted she did not know who they would be. The regulatory materials governing pupillage . . . were impliedly incorporated by reference into the arrangement made between the parties, and to that extent the terms of the arrangement were recorded in writing; but the functions and obligations of the parties were so clearly specified in these materials that any detailed negotiation of terms and conditions to be recorded in a written agreement between the parties was rendered unnecessary. It is of course unlikely that any chambers, certainly any reputable chambers, having made an offer of pupillage which has been accepted, would resile from that arrangement without very good reason, but the existence of a disciplinary sanction does not in our view point against the existence of a contract. To our mind this arrangement had all the characteristics of a binding contract. It makes no difference that, if the pupil defaulted, the chambers would be most unlikely to sue; the same is true if an employer engages a junior employee under an employment contract which is undoubtedly binding, and the employee fails to turn up on the appointed day.

The defendants' argument on consideration is, we think, much stronger, for while chambers undertake to provide a closely prescribed curriculum of education and training the pupil no longer pays any fee and does not in our view undertake to do anything beyond that which is conducive to his or her education and training. In working on the pupil master's papers (making factual summaries, or drafting chronologies, or writing advices or preparing pleadings) the pupil will be seeking to acquire, under the tutelage of the pupil master, the skills of a professional adviser, pleader and advocate, even though the pupil master will often benefit from the pupil's work and from discussion with him. If the pupil carries out legal research or keeps a note in court, he is again learning and applying professional skills necessary for practice. If the pupil produces any work of real value, whether to the pupil master or any other member of the Bar, the beneficiary is under a professional duty to remunerate the pupil. While any pupil of ordinary common sense would, if asked, carry out mundane tasks (such as photocopying authorities or making a cup of tea) which do not in any way promote his professional development, there is in our view no obligation or duty on the pupil to do anything for the pupil master which is not conducive to his own professional development.

This conclusion, if correct, would we think be fatal to any argument that there was a contract between the pupil and the individual pupil master, for the pupil would provide no consideration for the pupil master's educational services. But the claimant does not rely on any contract said to have been made with an individual pupil master and we think a broader view has to be taken of the relationship between chambers and pupil. For reasons on which we have already touched, members of chambers have a strong incentive to attract talented pupils, and their future prospects will to some extent depend on their success in doing so. The funding of awards is not an exercise in pure altruism but reflects an obvious (and wholly unobjectionable) element of self-interest. The agreement of the claimant and other pupils to undertake pupillage at chambers such as the defendants' provides a pool of selected candidates who can be expected to compete with each other for recruitment as tenants. We do not regard this argument as undermined by the fact that some pupils who are accepted as such may be regarded as unlikely candidates for tenancy. The process must be viewed in the round, and not on a pupil by pupil basis, and chambers may well see an advantage in developing close relationships with pupils who plan to practise as employed barristers or to practise overseas. On balance we take the view that pupils such as the claimant provide consideration for the offer made by chambers such as the defendants' by agreeing to enter into the close, important and potentially very productive relationship which pupillage involves.

We agree with the judge, although for somewhat different reasons, that the claimant did make a legally binding contract with the defendants.

Context—specifically, the context of an existing employment relationship—was also important to the Court of Appeal in determining the existence of an intention to create legal relations in relation to a 'promise' of a bonus in the next case.

Dresdner Kleinwort Ltd and another v Attrill and others
[2013] EWCA Civ 394, [2013] 3 All ER 607 (CA)

This case concerned the legal enforceability of an announcement concerning bonus awards under a contract of employment that provided for discretionary bonus awards. In August 2008, the Bank's chief executive officer had announced a guaranteed minimum bonus pool for distribution, which would be 'allocated in the usual way', and in December of that year the Bank's employees were notified of their individual provisional bonus awards. However, in February 2009, the Bank reduced the bonuses by 90 per cent. Employees claimed that this amounted to a breach of contractual entitlement, since the announcement constituted a legally binding promise. At first instance, the judge agreed.

Held (on appeal): The announcement had been made with the intention that it amounted to a legally binding promise (offer). The Bank's employees were under no obligation to communicate acceptance of the bonus offer. The Bank had dispensed with the need for any acceptance response, since the promise involved no disadvantage to the employees, and nobody hearing the announcement would expect that an employee could benefit only if he were positively to accept the offer (*page 46*, 2.4.4.1). The Bank was therefore under an obligation to pay the bonus sums claimed.

ELIAS LJ (with whose judgment Beatson and Maurice Kay LJJ agreed):

The intention to create legal relations.

61 I will first set out the analysis of the judge on this point. He started from the following three premises. The first was that the question whether there is an intention to create legal relations must be considered objectively. He referred to the following passage from the judgment of Lord Clarke in *RTS Flexible Systems Ltd v Molkerei Alois Mueller GmbH and Co KG (UK) Productions* [2010] UKSC 14, [2010] Bus LR 776, [2010] 1 WLR 753 (SC), para 45:

> Where there is a binding contract between the parties and, if so, upon what terms depends upon what they have agreed. It depends not upon their subjective state of mind, but upon a consideration of what was communicated between them by words or conduct, and whether that leads objectively to a conclusion that they intended to create legal relations and had agreed upon all the terms which they regarded or the law requires as essential for the formulation of legally binding relations.

62 To similar effect is the observation of Lord Bingham CJ as he then was in *Edmonds v Lawson* [2000] All ER 31, at para 21 when he said:

> Whether the parties intended to enter into legally binding relations is an issue to be determined objectively and not by enquiring into their respective states of mind. The context is all important.

63 Second, the judge held that the onus of proving that there was a lack of intention to create legal relations would be on the Bank since they were asserting that no legal effects were intended. He relied for this proposition on certain observations of Megaw J in *Edwards v Skyways* [1964] 1 WLR 349 at 355, and Aikens J in *Mamidoil Jetoil Greek Petroleum: SA v Okta Crude Oil Refinery AD* [2003] 1 Lloyd's Rep 554.

64 Third, he emphasised what Lord Bingham CJ had said in *Edmonds v Lawson*, namely that 'the context is all important.'

65 In considering context the judge noted the following features: that the guaranteed bonus pool was created to stabilise the work force; that it arose in part in response to FSA requests that a retention strategy should be put in place; that both the decision to establish the pool and the method of communicating it had been approved by the Compensation Committees of both DBAG and Allianz; that the reference to a 'guaranteed' minimum bonus pool was strongly indicative of an intention to undertake a binding legal obligation; and that subsequent statements which on numerous occasions reasserted the existence of the guaranteed bonus pool reinforced the conclusion that there was an intention to create legal relations . . .

89 . . . [I]n my view there was a very strong presumption that a promise of this nature would be intended to be legally enforceable, and there were a whole series of matters supporting that conclusion. Perhaps the critical one is that this was a promise made in the context of a pre-existing legal relationship. In my judgment, viewed objectively, the natural inference would be that any promises made to staff relating to the terms of their employment would take effect in the same way as other contractual terms. Other factors reinforcing that conclusion include the fact that the source of the promise was the Chief Executive Officer with the obvious implication that the creation of the bonus pool must have been approved by the highest levels in the Bank; that it was part of a vitally important strategy to retain staff and prevent the potential collapse of the investment banking division; that the nature of the promise assured staff that the fund was guaranteed come what may; and that it was related to pay, the most fundamental obligation under the employment contract. There was, in truth, overwhelming evidence justifying the conclusion that this promise was intended to be legally binding . . .

90 I should add that I have taken on board three further points addressed by [counsel for the Bank] which did not perhaps figure as significantly before the judge [at first instance]. First, he emphasised that his submission did not mean that the promise, even if non-contractual, would have no legal significance. Any failure to respect the promise could be challenged under the term not to undermine trust and confidence, which was indeed precisely what the claimants have done as an alternative to their main case. It was therefore wrong of the judge to say that 'if [the announcement] was not intended to have legal effect, it is difficult to see how it could have the intended effect'.

91 Second, it was submitted that to make the obligation legally binding would mean that the court would ultimately have to become embroiled in fixing the bonuses of staff, something which Lord Justice Mummery had said in *Keen v Commerzbank* [2007] ICR 623 the court would not do. His Lordship observed in that case that it was not for the courts to act as wage fixing bodies for the banking industry.

92 Third, it was said that the staff gave nothing in exchange for the promise.

93 None of these points, in my view, carries any significant weight, and certainly not enough to cast doubt on the judge's conclusion. As to the first, the fact that the promise may be subject to some legal controls even if not contractually enforceable does not justify a court starting from the premise that this tells against an inference that there was an intention to create a binding contractual term. An objective analysis of intention would not start from the assumption that because there are general legal controls over the exercise of discretions by the employer, this is a factor pointing away from an intention to create contractual relations. Moreover, the judge's observations to the effect that the purpose of introducing the promise would not have been achieved without the promise being legally binding were justified. It is fanciful to believe that the stability of staff would have been secured anything like as effectively had staff been told that the promise made to them was not contractually binding but that it might be indirectly secured by virtue of a general implied duty of trust and confidence.

94 As to the *Keen* point, I do not envisage that the court would have to fix the bonuses. It would simply require that when the Bank did so it distributed the full amount of the bonus pool. No doubt in the unlikely event that the Bank refused to do so the court may have to interfere *faute de mieux*, but as Maurice Kay LJ pointed out in the course of argument, this is something which courts exceptionally have to do from time to time when dealing with discretionary trusts. In any event, the Bank could not set up its own unwillingness to co-operate as a reason for inferring that there was no intention to create legal relations.

95 Finally, as regards the lack of anything in exchange, that is wrong as a matter of fact. The judge found in terms that each of these claimants had given good consideration in that the bonus pool was at least a factor, to a greater or lesser extent, in their decision to remain with the Bank. That was so notwithstanding that there may have been some reduction in job opportunities after the financial crash in September.

96 It follows that in my view there was an intention to enter into legal relations when this offer was made.

NOTE In *Blue v Ashley* [2017] EWHC 1928, the context as a setting was, amongst other factors, to assess the seriousness of an offer and the intention to create relation between commercial parties.

Leggatt J stated about the setting:

81. As described by Mr Tracey, it was 'five guys and a barman in a pub'. A fair amount of alcohol had been consumed. Those circumstances by themselves do not prevent a contract from being made – any more than did the fact that in *MacInnes v Gross* [2017] EWHC 46 (QB) the relevant discussion took place over dinner in a smart restaurant. As Coulson J said in that case (at para 81), a contract can be made anywhere in any circumstances. But an evening of drinking in a pub with three investment bankers is an unlikely setting in which to negotiate a contractual bonus arrangement with a consultant who was meeting them on behalf of the company.

82. It was argued on behalf of Mr Blue that, while this might be true in the case of an ordinary businessman, Mr Ashley is not an ordinary businessman but is someone who adopts an 'unorthodox approach to taking business decisions in informal settings while consuming substantial amounts of alcohol'. In particular, Mr Blue relied on the fact that, at Sports Direct's weekly senior management meetings he had witnessed Mr Ashley (and others) drinking alcohol, sometimes allegedly in copious quantities. When Mr Blue was working at Sports Direct such meetings were held at the Lion Hotel in Worksop. Between 10 and 20 members of Sports Direct's senior management would typically attend and Mr Blue attended these meetings regularly . . .

This is clearly to be appreciated objectively, on the particular circumstances of this case. Leggatt J therefore concluded:

82. Mr Blue said that he thought Mr Ashley made alcohol freely available at these meetings as a deliberate strategy to encourage his senior managers to speak more openly than might otherwise be the case in a more formal meeting environment . . . He may well be right about this but the evidence about these meetings does not seem to me to carry Mr Blue's case very far. The Sports Direct senior management meetings certainly show that Mr Ashley is happy to combine discussion of business matters with the consumption of alcohol. But there is no evidence to suggest that Mr Ashley has ever negotiated or concluded a contract at one of these meetings. The evening at the Horse & Groom was, in any event, a considerably less formal occasion than the senior management meetings, as there was no agenda or structure for the occasion and the conversation was largely social or general chat, rather than being specifically directed to any business subject.

On the facts, Leggatt J considered seven additional factors, such as the purpose of the meeting, the vagueness of the offer, and the incongruity of Mr Blue's role to reject the claim that a serious offer had been made, and concluded (at [142]):

In the course of a jocular conversation with three investment bankers in a pub on the evening of 24 January 2013, Mr Blue said that he would pay Mr Blue £15 million if Mr Blue could get the price of Sports Direct shares (then trading at around £4 per share) to £8. Mr Blue expressed his agreement to that proposal and everyone laughed . . . The fact that Mr Blue has since convinced himself that the offer was a serious one, and that a legally binding agreement was made, shows only that the human capacity for wishful thinking knows few bounds.

4.2 Capacity to contract: minors' contracts

With some exceptions, a contract between a minor (someone under the age of 18) and an adult is not binding on the minor unless, after attaining the age of 18, the minor ratifies the contract.

4.2.1 Contracts for necessaries

These contracts are binding on a minor to the extent that the minor must pay a reasonable price for necessaries sold and delivered to him.

Sale of Goods Act 1979

3. Capacity to buy and sell

(2) Where necessaries are sold and delivered to a minor or to a person who by reason of mental incapacity or drunkenness is incompetent to contract, he must pay a reasonable price for them.

(3) . . . 'necessaries' means goods suitable to the condition in life of the minor or other person concerned and to his actual requirements at the time of the sale and delivery.

Nash v Inman
[1908] 2 KB 1 (CA)

The claimant supplied clothing to the defendant, a Cambridge undergraduate, to the value of £145 10s. 3d. The clothing included 11 fancy waistcoats. The defendant argued that he was a minor at the time that the goods were supplied and that they were not 'necessaries'. The defendant's father gave evidence that his son was already amply supplied with clothes.

Held: The onus of proving that the goods supplied were suitable to the condition in life of the minor and that the defendant was not already adequately supplied with such goods was on the claimant. The claimant had failed to establish this.

? QUESTION

Why is the minor liable only for the reasonable price of necessaries and not their actual cost?

4.2.2 Beneficial contracts of service

A minor is bound by an employment contract if, on the whole, it is for his benefit.

Doyle v White City Stadium
[1935] 1 KB 110 (CA)

The claimant, a minor, applied to the British Boxing Board of Control for a licence as a boxer and agreed to be bound by the rules of the Board. He was issued with a boxer's licence. A few months later, the rules were altered. Instead of a rule providing that a boxer's money was to be stopped only if he was disqualified for a deliberate foul, the new rule was that, in any case of disqualification, the boxer was to receive only certain expenses. The claimant had arranged to box in return for £3,000 (win, lose, or draw), but he was disqualified for fouling. The Board withheld most of his £3,000. The claimant claimed the whole sum.

Held: The contract as a whole between the claimant and the Board was beneficial to the claimant and, therefore, was binding on him.

LORD HANWORTH MR: I turn to *De Francesco v Barnum* (1890) 45 Ch D 430, where Fry LJ says: 'I approach this subject with the observation that it appears to me that the question is this, Is the contract for the benefit of the infant? Not, Is any one particular stipulation for the benefit of the infant? Because it is obvious that the contract of apprenticeship or the contract of labour must, like any other contract, contain some stipulations for the benefit of the one contracting party, and some for the benefit of the other. It is not because you can lay your hand on a particular stipulation which you may say is against the infant's benefit, that therefore the whole contract is not for the benefit of the infant. The Court must look at the whole contract, having regard to the circumstances of the case, and determine, subject to any principles of law which may be ascertained by the cases, whether the contract is or is not beneficial. That appears to me to be in substance a question of fact' . . .

The learned judge on the question of fact has held that the terms of the agreement in this case are favourable and to the advantage of the infant, and it seems therefore that the application of the rules cannot be held to be prevented by reason of the plaintiff's infancy.

However, if the contract is not interpreted as an employment contract or as a contract for 'necessaries', it will be regarded as voidable.

166

Proform Sports Management Ltd v Proactive Sports Management Ltd
[2006] EWHC 2903 (Ch), [2007] Bus LR 93

At the age of 15 (i.e. when he was a minor), the footballer Wayne Rooney had entered into a player representation agreement with the claimant whereby the claimant company was to act as his executive agent and represent him. Under Football Association (FA) rules, Rooney could not become a professional footballer until he reached the age of 17 and, therefore, he was employed as a trainee. The claimant alleged that the defendant had also entered into a player representation agreement with Rooney whilst its contract was still operating. The claimant therefore brought an action against the defendant for unlawful interference with and/or procuring the breach of its contract with Rooney.

Held:

(a) The agreement with the claimant was not enforceable against Rooney because he was a minor and the general rule was that contracts were voidable at his option.

(b) It was not analogous to a contract for necessaries and could not be analogous to a contract of apprenticeship, education, or service (which would generally be enforceable against a minor), since Rooney was already with a football club and could not yet become a professional footballer; therefore, the contract with the agent did not enable him to earn a living or advance his skills.

It followed that the defendant could not be liable for the tort of inducing the breach of contract, since this contract was voidable at Rooney's option.

4.2.3 Contracts involving continuing obligations and the ability to repudiate during minority

This category includes tenancy agreements, partnership agreements, and agreements to take shares in a company that are only partly paid. The minor is at liberty to repudiate the obligations arising under these agreements as long as this is achieved during the period of minority or within a reasonable time of reaching majority: *Edwards v Carter* [1893] AC 360. However, in the absence of such repudiation, the contract will be binding on both parties.

If repudiation takes place, the minor can recover money paid or property transferred only if there has been a total failure of consideration.

Steinberg v Scala (Leeds) Ltd
[1923] 2 Ch 452 (CA)

The claimant, while a minor, applied for shares in a company and paid the amount due on allotment. She paid the amounts due on the first call, but received no dividends and attended no company meetings. Eighteen months later, while still a minor, she repudiated the contract and requested repayment of the money that she had paid to the company.

Held: Since she was a minor, she was entitled to repudiate the contract, but because there had been no failure of consideration, she could not recover the money paid to the company.

LORD STERNDALE MR: I think the argument for the respondent has rather proceeded upon the assumption that the question whether she can rescind and the question whether she can recover her money back are the same. They are two quite different questions, as is pointed out by Turner LJ in his judgment in *Ex parte Taylor* (1856) 8 DM & G 254. He there says: 'It is clear that an infant cannot be absolutely bound by a contract entered into during his minority. He must have a right upon his attaining his majority to elect whether he will adopt the contract or not.' Then he proceeds: 'It is, however, a different question whether, if an infant pays money on the footing of a contract, he can afterwards recover it back. If an infant buys an article which is not a necessary, he cannot be compelled to pay for it, but if he does pay for it during his minority he cannot on attaining his majority recover the money back.' That seems to me to be only stating in other words the principle which is laid down in a number of other cases that, although the contract may be rescinded the money paid cannot be recovered back unless there has been an entire failure of the consideration for which the money has been paid. Therefore it seems to me that the question to which we have to address ourselves is: Has there here been a total failure of the consideration for which the money was paid?

Now the plaintiff has had the shares allotted to her and there is evidence that they were of some value, that they had been dealt in from 9s. to 10s. a share . . .

In those circumstances is it possible to say that there was a total failure of consideration? If the plaintiff were a person of full age suing to recover the money back on the ground, and the sole ground, that there had been a failure of consideration it seems to me it would have been impossible for her to succeed, because she would have got the very thing for which the money was paid and would have got a thing of tangible value.

I cannot see any difference when you come to consider whether there has been consideration or not between the position of a person of full age and an infant. The question whether there has been consideration or not must, I think, be the same in the two cases . . .

4.2.4 Restitution by the minor

The court has a discretion to order the return of non-necessaries that the minor has obtained under an unenforceable contract.

Minors' Contracts Act 1987

3. Restitution

(1) Where—

    . . .

    (b) the contract is unenforceable against the defendant (or he repudiates it) because he was a minor when the contract was made, the court may, if it is just and equitable to do so, require the defendant to transfer to the plaintiff any property acquired by the defendant under the contract, or any property representing it.

Content, interpretation, performance, and privity

Chapter 5

Content of the contract and principles of interpretation

We need to consider what precisely the parties have undertaken to do, i.e. the contract terms, and to determine the meaning of those terms.

5.1 Pre-contractual statements: terms or mere representations?

If a mere representation is false, remedies will arise in misrepresentation (*Chapter 9*); if a term is broken, remedies are for breach of contract.

If there is a breach of contract, an automatic right to claim damages arises. However, damages for misrepresentation can be claimed only on proof of fault.

The damages recoverable for breach of contract aim to put the claimant into the position in which they would have been had the contract been properly performed; the tortious measure of damages for misrepresentation puts the claimant into the position in which they would have been had the misrepresentation not been made.

Under the traditional remoteness principle, a claimant in a claim for breach of contract can recover for all losses that were within both parties' reasonable contemplations when they made the contract as the probable result of the breach of it. This test is far more restrictive than the remoteness test for misrepresentation, which, for fraudulent misrepresentation and negligent misrepresentation under the Misrepresentation Act 1967, s. 2(1), allows the recovery of all direct loss regardless of whether it was foreseeable (*page 481*, 9.3.2.2.2).

The distinction between terms and representations rests upon the intentions of the parties objectively ascertained, i.e. did the parties intend that the statement maker was making a binding promise as to the truth of the statement? The courts have determined some guidelines to assist in ascertaining this intention. Lord Moulton, in *Heilbut, Symons & Co. v Buckleton* [1913] AC 30, pp. 50–1, warned that these guidelines are not decisive tests of intention:

[T]hey cannot be said to furnish decisive tests, because it cannot be said as a matter of law that the presence or absence of those features is conclusive of the intention of the parties. The intention of the parties can only be deduced from the totality of the evidence and no secondary principles of such a kind can be universally true.

5.1.1 Accepting responsibility or advising on verification

Schawel v Reade
[1913] 2 IR 81 (HL)

The claimant required a stallion for stud purposes and went to the defendant's stables where he began examining a horse. He was told by the defendant: 'You need not look for anything; the horse is perfectly sound. If there was anything the matter with the horse I would tell you.' Therefore, the claimant stopped the examination and purchased the horse, which was found to be totally unfit for stud purposes. To the question whether the defendant's statement amounted to a term or a representation, the jury had answered 'yes': did the defendant represent to the claimant, so that the claimant might purchase the horse, that the horse was fit for stud purposes?

Held: The jury found that the statement was a term.

LORD MOULTON: Now, it would be impossible, in my mind, to have a clearer example of an express warranty where the word 'warrant' was not used. The essence of such warranty is that it becomes plain by the words, and the action, of the parties that it is intended that in the purchase the responsibility of the soundness shall rest upon the vendor; and how in the world could a vendor more clearly indicate that he is prepared and intends to take upon himself the responsibility of the soundness than by saying, 'You need not look at that horse, because it is perfectly sound,' and sees that the purchaser thereupon desists from his immediate independent examination?

NOTES

1. The courts generally use the word 'warranty' to mean a contract term. A warranty is also a particular type of term (*page 635, 13.3*).

2. In *Hopkins v Tanqueray* (1854) 15 CB 130, 139 ER 369, the claimant purchased the defendant's horse at auction. The previous day, the defendant had found the claimant examining the horse's legs and had said: 'You need not examine his legs: you have nothing to look for. I assure you that he is perfectly sound in every respect.' The Court of Common Pleas held that the defendant's statement was not a warranty, but only a representation. How can these cases be reconciled? Arguably, the important fact was the evidence of the defendant in *Hopkins v Tanqueray* that horses that were sold at auction were never warranted unless this was expressly stated in the catalogue.

3. In *Harling v Eddy* [1951] 2 KB 739, Evershed MR distinguished these cases on the ground that, in *Hopkins v Tanqueray*, the statement was made the day before the contract, whereas in *Schawel v Reade* the statement was made the same day. If there is a delay between the time when the statement was made and the formation of the contract, then it is less likely to be intended as a term.

If the statement indicates that the recipient of the statement should check it, then the statement maker indicates that the statement is not intended to be a contractual term, since s/he is explicitly refusing to take responsibility for its truth.

Ecay v Godfrey
(1947) 80 Lloyd's Rep 286

The claimant orally agreed to buy the defendant's motor cruiser for £750. There was evidence of a conversation between the parties in which the claimant had asked questions relating to the condition of the cruiser. The defendant had asked whether the claimant was going to have a survey completed and the claimant had replied that he would not. The cruiser was, in fact, unsound and the claimant claimed damages for breach of warranty.

Held: It had to be shown that there was an undertaking by the defendant that the boat was a sound boat. Looking at the whole of the conversation, including the question about the survey, it amounted to no more than an innocent misrepresentation, so that the claimant's claim failed.

LORD GODDARD CJ: I think it is impossible to come to the conclusion that if these two parties had sat down and written out their contract, intending thereby to put down on paper exactly what they bargained about and all the terms of their bargain, Mr Godfrey would have said, 'And I promise you' (or 'And I undertake') 'that the vessel is in good condition.' It would be quite inconsistent, I think, with his statement to the plaintiff at the time, 'Aren't you going to have a survey?' or 'Are you intending to have a survey?', because if he was intending to warrant at the time that this boat was in good condition, there would be no point in having a survey. I will not go quite so far as that, because a man might say: 'Although you are willing to warrant, I am not going to be satisfied with that, because your warranty may turn out to be wrong and if I am going to part with £750 I should like to have your warranty confirmed by a survey'; but I think that the conversation with regard to the survey is material in coming to the conclusion whether there was a warranty or not.

Whatever was said here no doubt was said in the course of the negotiations leading up to the sale, but the sale did not in fact take place on that day. It did not take place until the next day, because after the meeting at the boat the plaintiff had not made up his mind and went away to think about it. Then, without any further communication with Mr Godfrey, he bought the boat. It may very likely be that the plaintiff does not understand, or did not understand—there are a great many buyers who do not understand—the difference between a representation and a warranty; but if he wanted a warranty, I think he should have got it and got it in very much more precise terms than anything that was said, or is alleged to have been said, here . . .

5.1.2 'Importance attached' test

Bannerman v White
(1861) 10 CB NS 844, 142 ER 685 (Court of Common Pleas)

A prospective buyer of hops asked the seller if any sulphur had been used in the growth or treatment of the hops, adding that he would not even ask the price if sulphur had been used. The seller replied that sulphur had not been used, when in fact it had.

Held: This statement was a term of the contract entitling the buyer to terminate for breach.

Couchman v Hill
[1947] KB 554 (CA)

The claimant bought the defendant's heifer at auction. The catalogue described the heifer as unserved and the claimant required an unserved heifer for service by his bull. The catalogue also stated that the auctioneers were not responsible for the correct description or for any fault or defect in any lot and were not giving any warranty. Before the sale, the claimant asked the defendant and the auctioneer to confirm that the heifer was unserved, which they did. Seven weeks later, the heifer suffered a miscarriage and died. The claimant brought an action for damages for breach of warranty.

Held: The statement amounted to a warranty by the defendant, which overrode the condition in the printed terms.

SCOTT LJ: There was no contract in existence until the hammer fell. The offer was defined, the auctioneer's authority was defined, but it was in law open to any would-be purchaser to intimate in advance before bidding for any particular heifer offered from the rostrum that he was not willing to bid for the lot unless the defendant modified the terms of sale contained in the two documents in some way specified by him. There is no doubt that the plaintiff did make some attempt of the kind in order to protect himself from the risk of buying an animal that was not of the kind described.

The real question is, what did the parties understand by the question addressed to and the answer received from both the defendant and the auctioneer. It is contended by the defendant that the question meant 'having regard to the onerous stipulations which I know I shall have to put up with if I bid and the lot is knocked down to me, can you give me your honourable assurance that the heifers have in fact not been served? If so, I will risk the penalties of the catalogue.' The alternative meaning is: 'I am frightened of contracting on your published terms, but I will bid if you will tell me by word of mouth that you accept full responsibility for the statement in the catalogue that the heifers have not been served, or, in other words, give me a clean warranty. That is the only condition on which I will bid.' If that was the meaning there was clearly an oral offer of a warranty which over-rode the stultifying condition in the printed terms, that offer was accepted by the plaintiff when he bid, and the contract was made on that basis when the lot was knocked down to him . . .

NOTES An oral assurance of this type (a collateral warranty) may override any conflicting written terms of the contract. For example, in *Thinc Group v Armstrong* [2012] EWCA Civ 1227, it was held that an oral assurance given to two financial advisers whom the financial services company was seeking to recruit, overrode subsequent express written terms in the employment contract. The assurance related to an upfront payment, which the company promised could be reclaimed *only* if the advisers were to leave within three years (and so not if their contracts were terminated by the company). However, the contract provided for this sum to be repayable on various repayment events, including termination by the company. To allow the written contract to prevail would be a wholly unreasonable construction and would undermine the basis on which the advisers had agreed to contract.

? QUESTIONS

1. Is it correct that one bidder at an auction should be able to negotiate for a warranty in advance where the auction is to be one without warranty?

In *Hopkins v Tanqueray* (1854) 15 CB 130, 139 ER 369, in such circumstances, it was held that a representation made the day before the auction was not a contractual term. There is an editorial note to the report of *Couchman v Hill* indicating that if this authority had been cited in *Couchman* then the result may have been different. However, the statement in *Couchman* was made on the same day as the auction, whereas in *Hopkins* it was made on the previous day.

2. Is *Couchman v Hill* a case of a collateral warranty—see *Esso Petroleum Co. Ltd v Mardon* [1976] QB 801 (*page 175, 5.1.3*)—since the warranty existed before the contract itself and was the consideration for entering into the main sale contract?

5.1.3 Special knowledge of the statement maker

Oscar Chess Ltd v Williams
[1957] 1 WLR 370 (CA)

In June 1955, the defendant sold a second-hand Morris car to the claimants, motor dealers, for £290. The registration book, which was examined by the claimants' representative, showed that the car was first registered in 1948, and the defendant honestly believed that it was a 1948 model. The purchase price was calculated on this basis. In January 1956, the claimants discovered from the manufacturers that the car was a 1939 model (so the true price was £175) and claimed damages for breach of warranty.

Held (Denning and Hodson LJJ; Morris LJ dissenting): The defendant was not liable to the claimants in damages for breach of warranty because, as the claimants knew, the defendant had no personal knowledge of the date of the manufacture of the car and the claimants were in at least as good a position to know this. The defendant had made an innocent, i.e. non-fraudulent, misrepresentation. (Damages were available at this time only if the misrepresentation was fraudulent.)

DENNING LJ: The crucial question is: was it a binding promise or only an innocent misrepresentation? The technical distinction between a 'condition' and a 'warranty' is quite immaterial in this case, because it is far too late for the buyer to reject the car. He can at best only claim damages. The material distinction here is between a statement which is a term of the contract and a statement which is only an innocent misrepresentation. This distinction is best expressed by the ruling of Lord Holt: Was it intended as a warranty or not? using the word warranty there in its ordinary English meaning: because it gives the exact shade of meaning that is required. It is something to which a man must be taken to bind himself.

In applying Lord Holt's test, however, some misunderstanding has arisen by the use of the word 'intended'. It is sometimes supposed that the tribunal must look into the minds of the parties to see what they themselves intended. That is a mistake. Lord Moulton made it quite clear [in *Heilbut, Symons & Co. v Buckleton* [1913] AC 51] that 'The intention of the parties can only be deduced from the totality of the evidence . . . ' The question whether a warranty was intended depends on the conduct of the parties, on their words and behaviour, rather than on their thoughts. If an intelligent bystander would reasonably infer that a warranty was intended, that will suffice. And this, when the facts are not in dispute, is a question of law . . .

It is instructive to take some recent instances to show how the courts have approached this question. When the seller states a fact which is or should be within his own knowledge and of which the buyer is ignorant, intending that the buyer should act on it and he does so, it is easy to infer a warranty; see *Couchman v Hill* ([1947] KB 554), where the farmer stated that the heifer was unserved, and *Harling v Eddy* ([1951] KB 739), where he stated that there was nothing wrong with her. So also if he makes a promise about something which is or should be within his own control: see *Birch v Paramount Estates Ltd* ((1956) 16 Estates Gazette 396), decided on October 2, 1956, in this court, where the seller stated that the house would be as good as the show house. But if the seller, when he states a fact, makes it clear that he has no knowledge of his own but has got his information elsewhere, and is merely passing it on, it is not so easy to imply a warranty. Such a case was *Routledge v McKay* ([1954] 1 WLR 615, 636), where the seller 'stated that a motor cycle combination was a 1942 model, and pointed to the corroboration of that statement to be found in the book', and it was held that there was no warranty.

Turning now to the present case, much depends on the precise words that were used. If the seller says 'I believe it is a 1948 Morris. Here is the registration book to prove it', there is clearly no warranty. It is a statement of belief, not a contractual promise. But if the seller says: 'I guarantee that it is a 1948 Morris. This is borne out by the registration book, but you need not rely solely on that. I give you my own guarantee that it is', there is clearly a warranty. The seller is making himself contractually responsible, even though the registration book is wrong.

. . . What is the proper inference from the known facts? It must have been obvious to both that the seller had himself no personal knowledge of the year when the car was made. He only became owner after a great number of changes. He must have been relying on the registration book. It is unlikely that such a person would warrant the year of manufacture. The most that he would do would be to state his belief, and then produce the registration book in verification of it. In these circumstances the intelligent bystander would, I suggest, say that the seller did not intend to bind himself so as to warrant that it was a 1948 model. If the seller was asked to pledge himself to it, he would at once have said 'I cannot do that. I have only the log-book to go by, the same as you'.

. . . It seems to me clear that the motor dealers who bought the car relied on the year stated in the log-book. If they had wished to make sure of it, they could have checked it then and there, by taking the engine number and chassis number and writing to the makers. They did not do so at the time, but only eight months later. They are experts, and, not having made that check at the time, I do not think that they should now be allowed to recover against the innocent seller who produced to them all the evidence he had, namely, the registration book. I agree that it is hard on the dealers to have paid more than the car is worth: but it would be equally hard on the seller to make him pay the difference. He would never have bought the Hillman at all unless he had got the allowance of £290 for the Morris. The best course in all these cases would be to 'shunt' the difference down the train of innocent sellers until one reached the rogue who perpetrated the fraud: but he can rarely be traced, or if he can, he rarely has the money to pay the damages. So one is left to decide between a number of innocent people who is to bear the loss. That can only be done by applying the law about representations and warranties as we know it: and that is what I have tried to do. If the rogue can be traced, he can be sued by whosoever has suffered the loss: but if he cannot be traced, the loss must lie where it falls. It should not be inflicted on innocent sellers, who sold the car many months, perhaps many years before, and have forgotten all about it and have conducted their affairs on the basis that the transaction was concluded. Such a seller would not be able to recollect after all this length of time the exact words he used, such as whether he said 'I believe it is a 1948 model', or 'I warrant it is a 1948 model'. The right course is to let the buyer set aside the transaction if he finds out the mistake quickly and comes promptly before other interests have irretrievably intervened, otherwise the loss must lie where it falls: and that is, I think, the course prescribed by law . . .

? QUESTION

In this case the question was which of two innocent parties should suffer for the loss caused by a third party (the person who altered the registration book). Was the loss correctly placed on the party who was better able to bear it (the motor dealers)?

NOTES

1. The majority decision seems to be the result of a desire to protect a layman who had acted in good faith on the basis of the registration book.

2. Applying the 'importance attached' test here, had the claimants known the true age of the car, they would probably still have offered to part exchange it at the 1939 valuation because they wanted the sale of the new car. This would indicate that their decision to contract did not turn on the age of manufacture

of the car, but only the price. This test was not mentioned by the Court of Appeal.

3. Denning LJ in *Oscar Chess* discussed the question of whether there had been any acceptance of responsibility for the statement by the defendant.

The important fact was that the registration book had been used as justifying the statement as to the age of the car. There was no independent guarantee of the truth of the statement.

Compare the following case.

Dick Bentley Productions Ltd v Harold Smith (Motors) Ltd
[1965] 1 WLR 623 (CA)

The claimant asked the defendants, who were car dealers, to find him a 'well vetted' Bentley car. A car was found. The defendants informed the claimant that the car had been fitted with a replacement engine and gear box, and had since travelled only 20,000 miles. The defendants relied on the odometer reading and had not checked the details. The claimant bought the car and discovered that the statement as to the mileage was untrue and sued for damages for breach of contract.

Held: The statement amounted to a warranty and therefore the claimant was entitled to damages.

LORD DENNING MR: The first point is whether this representation, namely, that it had done 20,000 miles only since it had been fitted with a replacement engine and gearbox, was an innocent misrepresentation (which does not give rise to damages), or whether it was a warranty. It was said by Holt CJ and repeated in *Heilbut, Symons & Co. v Buckleton* ([1913] AC 30, 49) that: 'An affirmation at the time of the sale is a warranty, provided it appear on evidence to be so intended.' But that word 'intended' has given rise to difficulties. I endeavoured to explain in *Oscar Chess Ltd v Williams* ([1957] 1 WLR 370, 375) that the question whether a warranty was intended depends on the conduct of the parties, on their words and behaviour, rather than on their thoughts. If an intelligent bystander would reasonably infer that a warranty was intended, that will suffice. What conduct, then? What words and behaviour lead to the inference of a warranty?

Looking at the cases once more, as we have done so often, it seems to me that if a representation is made in the course of dealings for a contract for the very purpose of inducing the other party to act upon it, and actually inducing him to act upon it by entering into the contract, that is prima facie ground for inferring that it was intended as a warranty. It is not necessary to speak of it as being collateral. Suffice it that it was intended to be acted upon and was in fact acted on. But the maker of the representation can rebut this inference if he can show that it really was an innocent misrepresentation, in that he was in fact innocent of fault in making it, and that it would not be reasonable in the circumstances for him to be bound by it. In the *Oscar Chess* case the inference was rebutted. There a man had bought a second-hand car and received with it a log-book, which stated the year of the car, 1948. He afterwards resold the car. When he resold it he simply repeated what was in the log-book and passed it on to the buyer. He honestly believed on reasonable grounds that it was true. He was completely innocent of any fault. There was no warranty by him, but only an innocent misrepresentation. Whereas in the present case it is very different. The inference is not rebutted. Here we have a dealer, Smith, who was in a position to know, or at least to find out, the history of the car. He could get it by writing to the makers. He did not do so. Indeed, it was done later. When the history of this car was examined, his statement turned out to be quite wrong. He ought to have known better. There was no reasonable foundation for it.

? QUESTION

Is this another example of protecting the consumer buyer, since had the statement not been held to be a term of the contract there would have been no remedy in damages? (The statement was made negligently and, prior to the Misrepresentation Act 1967, damages were available only for fraudulent misrepresentations.)

NOTE Applying the 'importance attached' test, the claimant made it clear that he wanted a car that was 'well vetted'; he was unlikely to have purchased the car had its actual mileage been disclosed.

Esso Petroleum Co. Ltd v Mardon
[1976] QB 801 (CA)

In 1961, the claimants' employee, with 40 years' experience, calculated that the potential throughput of a petrol station was likely to reach 200,000 gallons by the third year of operation of the station. The local planning authority refused permission for the pumps to front onto the street, so they had to be placed at the back of the site. In 1963, the defendant, a prospective tenant for the petrol station, was given the same estimate of throughput by the claimants' employee. The defendant suggested that 100,000 or 150,000 gallons was a more likely figure, but his doubts were quelled by his trust in the greater experience of the claimants' employee. The defendant entered into a three-year tenancy. In the first 15 months, the throughput was only 78,000 gallons. The losses continued and eventually the claimants cut off the defendant's supply of petrol because of non-payment. They sought possession of the station and sums that they were owed. The defendant claimed damages, inter alia, for breach of warranty as to the potential throughput of the station.

Held: The statement was a contractual warranty because it was a factual statement on a crucial matter by a party professing to have special knowledge to induce the defendant to enter into the contract. This warranty was not a promise that the station would, in fact, have this throughput, but a warranty that the forecast had been made with reasonable care and skill. The claimants were liable in damages for the amount that the defendant had lost by being induced to enter into the contract.

LORD DENNING MR:

Collateral warranty

Ever since *Heilbut, Symons & Co. v Buckleton* [1913] AC 30, we have had to contend with the law as laid down by the House of Lords that an innocent misrepresentation gives no right to damages. In order to escape from that rule, the pleader used to allege—I often did it myself—that the misrepresentation was fraudulent, or alternatively a collateral warranty. At the trial we nearly always succeeded on collateral warranty. We had to reckon, of course, with the dictum of Lord Moulton, at p. 47, that 'such collateral contracts must from their very nature be rare.' But more often than not the court elevated the innocent misrepresentation into a collateral warranty: and thereby did justice—in advance of the Misrepresentation Act 1967. I remember scores of cases of that kind, especially on the sale of a business. A representation as to the profits that had been made in the past was invariably held to be a warranty. Besides that experience, there have been many cases since I have sat in this court where we have readily held a representation—which induces a person to enter into a contract—to be a warranty sounding in damages . . . [This] was not a warranty—in this sense—that it did *not guarantee* that the throughput *would be* 200,000 gallons. But, nevertheless, it was a forecast made by a party—Esso—who had special knowledge and skill. It was the yardstick . . . by which they measured the worth of a filling station. They knew the facts. They knew the traffic in the town. They knew the throughput of comparable stations. They had much experience and expertise at their disposal. They were in a much better position than Mr Mardon to make a forecast. It seems to me that if such a person makes a forecast, intending that the other should act upon it—and he does act upon it, it can well be interpreted as a warranty that the forecast is sound and reliable in the sense that they made it with reasonable care and skill. It is just as if Esso said to Mr Mardon: 'Our forecast of throughput is 200,000 gallons. You can rely upon it as being a sound forecast of what the service station should do. The rent is calculated on that footing.' If the forecast turned out to be an unsound forecast such as no person of skill or experience should have made, there is a breach of warranty . . .

In the present case it seems to me that there was a warranty that the forecast was sound, that is, Esso made it with reasonable care and skill. That warranty was broken.

NOTES

1. Now that damages are available for negligent misrepresentation (on a very favourable basis) under the Misrepresentation Act 1967, it is unnecessary to resort to the collateral warranty to secure a damages award in such circumstances, although it is necessary to consider that the measures of damages in a breach of contract claim and under s. 2(1) of the Misrepresentation Act 1967 are very different (see discussion on measures in *page 479, 9.3.2.2.1*).

2. In *Howard Marine v Ogden & Sons* [1978] QB 574 (for the facts, see *page 479, 9.3.2.2.1*), the defendants had argued that the marine manager's statement amounted to a collateral oral warranty as to the carrying capacity of the barges, which had induced them to hire the barges. The Court of Appeal held that it was not a warranty because it was not given in circumstances indicating that a contractual promise was being made.

5.2 Written contracts

Contracts can be written or oral, or partly written and partly oral.

5.2.1 The parol evidence rule

The parol evidence rule applies to *written contracts* and prevents the parties from adducing extrinsic evidence to add to, vary, or contradict the writing. For an application of the parol evidence rule, see the speech of Lord Hobhouse in *Shogun Finance Ltd v Hudson* [2003] UKHL 62, [2004] 1 AC 919 (*page 368*, 8.3.2.1). However, a party cannot rely on a written contract when he has secured the other's consent only by means of an oral assurance.

5.2.1.1 Contracts partly written and partly oral

Construing a contract as partly written and partly oral will enable the courts to avoid the parol evidence rule. This is because the parol evidence rule applies only to those contracts in which *the writing was intended to contain the whole of the agreement*. Where the contract is construed as partly written and partly oral, this cannot be the intention.

J. Evans & Son (Portsmouth) Ltd v Andrea Merzario Ltd
[1976] 1 WLR 1078 (CA)

The claimants, importers of machines, contracted with the defendants for carriage of machines to England. The contract was on the standard conditions of the forwarding trade, giving the defendants complete freedom as to the method of transportation unless the claimants gave express written instructions. The conditions exempted the defendants from liability for loss or damage of the goods. Prior to 1967, because the machines were liable to rust if carried on deck, the defendants had arranged for the transportation of the machines in crates or trailers below deck. In 1967, the defendants proposed changing over to containers and, during discussions, the defendants gave the claimants an oral assurance that these containers would be shipped below deck. The claimants therefore agreed to containerized transportation of the machines. Owing to an oversight by the defendants, a container was shipped on deck and fell overboard. The claimants claimed damages from the defendants for loss of the machine, alleging that the carriage of the container on deck had been a breach of the carriage contract.

Held (Roskill and Geoffrey Lane LJJ): The oral assurance was an express term of the contract and, because the contract was partly oral and partly written, evidence of the oral term was admissible. The defendants were therefore liable for breach of this oral promise unless they could rely on the printed conditions (*page 261*, 6.3.4).

ROSKILL LJ: The real question, as I venture to think, is not whether one calls this an assurance or a guarantee, but whether that which was said amounted to an enforceable contractual promise by the defendants to the plaintiffs that any goods thereafter entrusted by the plaintiffs to the defendants for carriage from Milan to the United Kingdom via Rotterdam and thence by sea to England would be shipped under deck. The matter was apparently argued before the judge on behalf of the plaintiffs on the basis that the defendants' promise (if any) was what the lawyers sometimes call a collateral oral warranty . . . But that doctrine, as it seems to me, has little or no application where one is not concerned with a contract in writing (with respect I cannot accept [counsel for the defendants'] argument that there was here a contract in writing) but with a contract which, as I think, was partly oral, partly in writing and partly by conduct. In such a case the court does not require to have recourse to lawyers' devices such as collateral oral warranty in order to seek to adduce evidence which would not otherwise be admissible. The court is entitled to look at and should look at all the evidence from start to finish in order to see what the bargain was that was struck between the parties . . . When one does that, one finds first, as I have already mentioned, that these parties had been doing business in transporting goods from Milan to England for some time before; secondly, that transportation of goods from Milan to England was always done on trailers which were always under deck; thirdly, that the defendants wanted a change in the practice—they wanted containers used instead of trailers; fourthly, that the plaintiffs were only willing to agree to that change if they were promised by the defendants that those containers would be shipped under deck, and would not have agreed to the change but for that promise. The defendants gave such a promise, which to my mind against this background plainly amounted to an enforceable contractual promise. In those circumstances it seems to me that the contract was this: 'If we continue to give you our business, you will ensure that those goods in containers are shipped under deck'; and the defendants agreed that this would be so. Thus there was a breach of that contract by the defendants when this container was shipped on deck; and it seems to me to be plain that the damage which the plaintiffs suffered resulted from that breach . . .

NOTE Wedderburn [1959] CLJ 58 argued that this
device means that the parol evidence rule is no more
than a 'self-evident tautology'. It will always be cor-
rect because if there is a written contract, the rule applies and oral evidence cannot be admitted. If the
contract is not intended to be completely written,
then the rule does not apply and the oral evidence
is admissible.

5.2.1.2 **Collateral contract**

The court may hold that, in fact, there are two contracts: the written contract, to which the
parol evidence rule applies, and the oral collateral contract (without which the main written
contract would not have been made), to which the rule does not apply.

Lord Moulton's statement in *Heilbut, Symons & Co. v Buckleton* [1913] AC 30, p. 47, relating to
collateral contracts, is restrictive and confusing because the distinction between a collateral
warranty (*page 175, 5.1.3*) and a collateral contract is not preserved:

> [T]here may be a contract the consideration for which is the making of some other contract. 'If you
> will make such and such a contract I will give you one hundred pounds,' is in every sense of the word a
> complete legal contract. It is collateral to the main contract, but each has an independent existence,
> and they do not differ in respect of their possessing to the full the character and status of a contract. But
> such collateral contracts must from their very nature be rare. The effect of a collateral contract such as
> that which I have instanced would be to increase the consideration of the main contract by 100l., and
> the more natural and usual way of carrying this out would be by so modifying the main contract and not
> by executing a concurrent and collateral contract. Such collateral contracts, the sole effect of which is
> to vary or add to the terms of the principal contract, are therefore viewed with suspicion by the law. They
> must be proved strictly. Not only the terms of such contracts but the existence of an animus contrahendi
> on the part of all the parties to them must be clearly shewn. Any laxity on these points would enable
> parties to escape from the full performance of the obligations of contracts unquestionably entered into
> by them and more especially would have the effect of lessening the authority of written contracts by
> making it possible to vary them by suggesting the existence of verbal collateral agreements relating to
> the same subject-matter.

Lord Denning MR adopted the device of the collateral contract in *J. Evans v Andrea Merzario*
[1976] 1 WLR 1078, pp. 1081C–H (*page 187, 5.2.2*):

> [T]he forwarding agents said there was no contractual promise that the goods would be carried under
> deck. Alternatively, if there was, they relied on the printed terms and conditions. The judge held there
> was no contractual promise that these containers should be carried under deck. He thought that, in order
> to be binding, the initial conversation ought to be contemporaneous; and that here it was too remote in
> point of time from the actual transport. Furthermore that, viewed objectively, it should not be considered
> binding. The judge quoted largely from the well known case of *Heilbut, Symons & Co. v Buckleton* [1913]
> AC 30 in which it was held that a person is not liable in damages for an innocent misrepresentation; and
> that the courts should be slow to hold that there was a collateral contract. I must say that much of what
> was said in that case is entirely out of date. We now have the Misrepresentation Act 1967 under which
> damages can be obtained for innocent misrepresentation of fact. This Act does not apply here because
> we are concerned with an assurance as to the future. But even in respect of promises as to the future,
> we have a different approach nowadays to collateral contracts. When a person gives a promise or an
> assurance to another, intending that he should act on it by entering into a contract, and he does act on it
> by entering into the contract, we hold that it is binding: see *Dick Bentley Productions Ltd v Harold Smith*

(Motors) Ltd [1965] 1 WLR 623. That case was concerned with a representation of fact, but it applies also to promises as to the future. Following this approach, it seems to me plain that Mr Spano gave an oral promise or assurance that the goods in this new container traffic would be carried under deck. He made the promise in order to induce Mr Leonard to agree to the goods being carried in containers. On the faith of it, Mr Leonard accepted the quotations and gave orders for transport. In those circumstances the promise was binding. There was a breach of that promise and the forwarding agents are liable—unless they can rely on the printed conditions.

The terms of the collateral contract may even override conflicting terms in the main written contract.

City and Westminster Properties (1934) Ltd v Mudd
[1959] Ch 129

The defendant was a tenant of a lock-up shop and had slept in the office at the back of the shop. In 1947, during negotiations for a new lease, the defendant was sent a draft contract containing a covenant by the lessee 'not to permit or suffer the demised premises or any part thereof to be used as a place for lodging, dwelling or sleeping'. The claimants' agent told the defendant that if he were to sign the lease, the claimants would not object to his continuing to live in the shop. The lease was signed. In 1956, the claimants sought forfeiture of the lease on the ground of breach of this covenant. The defendant denied a breach, claiming that the claimants had waived the covenant or were estopped from relying on it (see the discussion of promissory estoppel, at *page 122*, 3.2).

Held: Because the defendant had signed the lease only on the basis of the promise by the claimants' agent, he was entitled to rely on that promise as long as he was in occupation of the shop.

HARMAN J: This is not a case of a representation made after contractual relations existed between the parties to the effect that one party to the contract would not rely on his rights. If the defendant's evidence is to be accepted, as I hold it is, it is a case of a promise made to him before the execution of the lease that, if he would execute it in the form put before him, the landlord would not seek to enforce against him personally the covenant about using the property as a shop only. The defendant says that it was in reliance on this promise that he executed the lease and entered on the onerous obligations contained in it. He says, moreover, that but for the promise made he would not have executed the lease, but would have moved to other premises available to him at the time. If these be the facts, there was a clear contract acted upon by the defendant to his detriment and from which the claimants cannot be allowed to resile . . . The promise was that so long as the defendant personally was tenant, so long would the landlords forbear to exercise the rights which they would have if he signed the lease. He did sign the lease on this promise and is therefore entitled to rely on it so long as he is personally in occupation of the shop.

NOTES

1. This was not a case based on the promissory estoppel doctrine because it was a promise to induce a contract rather than a promise to alter the terms of an existing contract.

2. The collateral contract device gave more effective protection than the doctrine of promissory estoppel, since it may be possible to go back on an estopped promise assuming that it is not inequitable to do so, after giving reasonable notice of such an intention (*page 133, 3.2.2.5*).

5.2.1.3 Entire agreement clauses

The presence of an entire agreement clause will deprive a collateral warranty of its legal effect. An entire agreement clause states that the written document is intended and agreed to contain the entirety of the contract between the parties, and that each party acknowledges that it has not relied upon any promise or undertaking in entering into the agreement that is not expressly contained in the written document.

Inntrepreneur Pub Co. v East Crown Ltd
[2000] 2 Lloyd's Rep 611

The claimant sought to enforce a covenant in a lease for a public house in which the defendant had agreed to purchase its supply of beer from the claimant. The defendant alleged a collateral warranty whereby the covenant had been released, but the claimant submitted that, because the lease contained an entire agreement clause, the defendant could not rely on this alleged collateral undertaking.

Held: Even if a collateral warranty could be established (and this had not been established on the facts), it would be deprived of legal effect by the entire agreement clause making it clear that the only agreed terms were those in the written agreement.

LIGHTMAN J:

Entire agreement clause

The purpose of an entire agreement clause is to preclude a party to a written agreement from threshing through the undergrowth and finding in the course of negotiations some (chance) remark or statement (often long forgotten or difficult to recall or explain) on which to found a claim such as the present to the existence of a collateral warranty. The entire agreement clause obviates the occasion for any such search and the peril to the contracting parties posed by the need which may arise in its absence to conduct such a search. For such a clause constitutes a binding agreement between the parties that the full contractual terms are to be found in the document containing the clause and not elsewhere, and that accordingly any promises or assurances made in the course of the negotiations (which in the absence of such a clause might have effect as a collateral warranty) shall have no contractual force, save insofar as they are reflected and given effect in that document. The operation of the clause is not to render evidence of the collateral warranty inadmissible in evidence as is suggested in *Chitty on Contract*, 28th ed., vol. 1, para. 12–102: it is to denude what would otherwise constitute a collateral warranty of legal effect.

Entire agreement clauses come in different forms. In the leading case of *Deepak v Imperial Chemical Industries plc* [1998] 2 Lloyd's Rep 139, affirmed [1999] 1 Lloyd's Rep 387 the clause read as follows:

> **10.16 Entirety of Agreement**
>
> This contract comprises the entire agreement between the PARTIES . . . and there are not any agreements, understandings, promises or conditions, oral or written, express or implied, concerning the subject matter which are not merged into this CONTRACT and superseded thereby . . .

Mr Justice Rix and the Court of Appeal held in that case (in particular focusing on the words 'promises or conditions') that this language was apt to exclude all liability for a collateral warranty. In *Alman & Benson v Associated Newspapers Group Ltd*, unreported, 20 June 1980 (cited by Mr Justice Rix at p. 168), Mr Justice Browne-Wilkinson reached the same conclusion where the clause provided that the written contract 'constituted the entire agreement and understanding between the parties with respect to all matters therein referred to' focusing on the word 'understanding'. In neither case was it necessary to decide whether the clause would have been sufficient if it had been worded merely to state that the agreement containing it comprised or constituted the entire agreement between the parties. That is the question raised in this case, where the formula of words used in the clause is abbreviated to an acknowledgement by the parties that the agreement constitutes the entire agreement between them. In my judgment that formula is sufficient, for it constitutes an agreement that the full contractual terms to which the parties agree to bind themselves are to be found in the agreement and nowhere else and that what might otherwise constitute a side agreement or collateral warranty shall be void of legal effect. That can be the only purpose of the provision. This view is entirely in accord with the judgment of Mr John Chadwick QC (as he then was) sitting as a deputy High Court Judge in *McGrath v Shah* (1987) 57 P & CR 452 . . .

It seems to me therefore that cl. 14.1 of the agreement provides in law a complete answer to any claim by Crown based on the alleged collateral warranty.

In *Axa Sun Life Services plc v Campbell Martin Ltd* [2011] EWCA Civ 133, [2012] Bus LR 203, [2011] 1 CLC 312, a question was whether clause 24 prevented the defendants from relying on alleged misrepresentations and/or breaches of warranty. Clause 24 was an entire agreement clause, which provided:

This Agreement and the Schedules and documents referred to herein constitute the entire agreement and understanding between you and us in relation to the subject matter thereof. Without prejudice to any variation as provided in clause 1.1, this Agreement shall supersede any prior promises, agreements, representations, undertakings or implications whether made orally or in writing between you and us relating to the subject matter of this Agreement but this will not affect any obligations in any such prior agreement which are expressed to continue after termination.

The Court of Appeal held that although clause 24 was not sufficiently clear to exclude misrepresentations relating to matters that were not the subject of the terms of the agreement, it did exclude collateral warranties.

STANLEY BURNTON LJ: 63 The purpose of entire agreement clauses such as clause 24 is obvious. It was accurately described by Lightman J in *Inntrepreneur Pub Co v East Crown Ltd* [2000] 2 Ll Rep 611 . . .

[Stanley Burnton LJ then referred to the passage from Lightman J's judgment that is extracted at page 183 earlier in this section and continued:]

64 A clause such as clause 24 gives both sides certainty as to the terms of their contract. In circumstances in which the sums involved in any dispute are likely to be relatively modest, if unchallenged it has the effect of limiting the costs involved in litigation; indeed, it may result in litigation being avoided. It is nonetheless more beneficial to AXA than to the Defendants, since it is AXA who decided on the terms of the Agreement.

65 The effect of clause 24 is limited to collateral warranties. I consider that sensible parties, faced with a written agreement of the length and detail of the Agreements, would not expect it to be attended by oral collateral agreements, and would expect their contract to be contained in the document they sign . . .

NOTE By comparison, in *Thinc Group v Armstrong* [2012] EWCA Civ 1227 (for facts, see *page 173, 5.1.2*), although the contract contained a 'no reliance clause' relating to prior representations, this did not extend to exclude the possibility of relying on a collateral warranty, i.e. there was no specific entire agreement clause or wording relating to contractual promises.

5.2.1.4 **No oral modification clause (NOM)**

NOMs are similar in their effect to entire agreement clauses in that they prevent the contract from being validly modified unless the variation is in writing. Although they are widely used in businesses, they have only just been formally accepted by the Supreme Court in *Rock Advertising Ltd v Business Exchange Centres Ltd* [2018] UKSC 24. Lord Sumption (with whom Lady Hale, Lord Wilson, and Lord Lloyd-Jones agree) gave the following judgment for the Supreme Court:

10. In my opinion the law should and does give effect to a contractual provision requiring specified formalities to be observed for a variation.

11. The starting point is that the effect of the rule applied by the Court of Appeal in the present case is to override the parties' intentions. They cannot validly bind themselves as to the manner in which future changes in their legal relations are to be achieved, however clearly they express their intention to do so. In the Court of Appeal, Kitchin LJ observed that the most powerful consideration in favour of this view is 'party autonomy': para 34. I think that this is a fallacy. Party autonomy operates up to the point when the contract is made, but thereafter only to the extent that the contract allows. Nearly all contracts bind the parties to some course of action, and to that extent restrict their autonomy. The real offence against party autonomy is the suggestion that they cannot bind themselves as to the form of any variation, even if that is what they have agreed. There are many cases in which a particular form of agreement is prescribed by statute: contracts for the sale of land, certain regulated consumer contracts, and so on. There is no principled reason why the parties should not adopt the same principle by agreement.

12. The advantages of the common law's flexibility about formal validity are that it enables agreements to be made quickly, informally and without the intervention of lawyers or legally drafted documents. Nevertheless, No Oral Modification clauses like clause 7.6 are very commonly included in written agreements. This suggests that the common law's flexibility has been found a mixed blessing by businessmen and is not always welcome. There are at least three reasons for including such clauses. The first is that it prevents attempts to undermine written agreements by informal means, a possibility which is open to abuse, for example in raising defences to summary judgment. Secondly, in circumstances where oral discussions can easily give rise to misunderstandings and crossed purposes, it avoids disputes not just about whether a variation was intended but also about its exact terms. Thirdly, a measure of formality in recording variations makes it easier for corporations to police internal rules restricting the authority to agree them. These are all legitimate commercial reasons for agreeing a clause like clause 7.6. I make these points because the law of contract does not normally obstruct the legitimate intentions of businessmen, except for overriding reasons of public policy. Yet there is no mischief in No Oral Modification clauses, nor do they frustrate or contravene any policy of the law.

13. The reasons advanced in the case law for disregarding them are entirely conceptual. The argument is that it is conceptually impossible for the parties to agree not to vary their contract by word of mouth because any such agreement would automatically be destroyed upon their doing so. The difficulty about this is that if it is conceptually impossible, then it cannot be done, short of an overriding rule of law (presumably statutory) requiring writing as a condition of formal validity. Yet it is plain that it can. There are legal systems which have squared this particular circle. They impose no formal requirements for the validity of a commercial contract, and yet give effect to No Oral Modification clauses. The Vienna Convention on Contracts for the International Sale of Goods (1980) has been ratified by 89 states, not including the United Kingdom. It provides by article 11 that a contract of

sale 'need not be concluded in or evidenced by writing and is not subject to any other requirement as to form.' Nonetheless, article 29(2) provides:

> A contract in writing which contains a provision requiring any modification or termination by agreement to be in writing may not be otherwise modified or terminated by agreement. However, a party may be precluded by his conduct from asserting such a provision to the extent that the other party has relied on that conduct.

Similarly, article 1.2 of the UNIDROIT Principles of International Commercial Contracts, 4th ed (2016), provides that 'nothing in these Principles requires a contract, statement or any other act to be made in or evidenced by a particular form.' Yet article 2.1.18 provides that

> A contract in writing which contains a clause requiring any modification or termination by agreement to be in a particular form may not be otherwise modified or terminated. However, a party may be precluded by its conduct from asserting such a clause to the extent that the other party has reasonably acted in reliance on that conduct.

These widely used codes suggest that there is no conceptual inconsistency between a general rule allowing contracts to be made informally and a specific rule that effect will be given to a contract requiring writing for a variation.

After drawing a parallel with entire agreement clause, at [14], Lord Sumption then concluded:

15. If, as I conclude, there is no conceptual inconsistency between a general rule allowing contracts to be made informally and a specific rule that effect will be given to a contract requiring writing for a variation, then what of the theory that parties who agree an oral variation in spite of a No Oral Modification clause must have intended to dispense with the clause? This does not seem to me to follow. What the parties to such a clause have agreed is not that oral variations are forbidden, but that they will be invalid. The mere fact of agreeing to an oral variation is not therefore a contravention of the clause. It is simply the situation to which the clause applies. It is not difficult to record a variation in writing, except perhaps in cases where the variation is so complex that no sensible businessman would do anything else. The natural inference from the parties' failure to observe the formal requirements of a No Oral Modification clause is not that they intended to dispense with it but that they overlooked it. If, on the other hand, they had it in mind, then they were courting invalidity with their eyes open.

16. The enforcement of No Oral Modification clauses carries with it the risk that a party may act on the contract as varied, for example by performing it, and then find itself unable to enforce it. It will be recalled that both the Vienna Convention and the UNIDROIT model code qualify the principle that effect is given to No Oral Modification clauses, by stating that a party may be precluded by his conduct from relying on such a provision to the extent that the other party has relied (or reasonably relied) on that conduct. In some legal systems this result would follow from the concepts of contractual good faith or abuse of rights. In England, the safeguard against injustice lies in the various doctrines of estoppel. This is not the place to explore the circumstances in which a person can be estopped from relying on a contractual provision laying down conditions for the formal validity of a variation. The courts below rightly held that the minimal steps taken by Rock Advertising were not enough to support any estoppel defences. I would merely point out that the scope of estoppel cannot be so broad as to destroy the whole advantage of certainty for which the parties stipulated when they agreed upon terms including the No Oral Modification clause. At the very least, (i) there would have to be some words or conduct unequivocally representing that the variation was valid notwithstanding its informality; and (ii) something more would be required

for this purpose than the informal promise itself: see *Actionstrength Ltd v International Glass Engineering In Gl En SpA* [2003] 2 AC 541, paras 9 (Lord Bingham), 51 (Lord Walker).

17. I conclude that the oral variation which Judge Moloney found to have been agreed in the present case was invalid for the reason that he gave, namely want of the writing and signatures prescribed by clause 7.6 of the licence agreement.

5.2.2 The effect of signature

Generally, if a person signs a contractual document, they will be bound by its terms even if they have not read the document.

L'Estrange v F. Graucob Ltd
[1934] 2 KB 394 (Divisional Court)

The claimant bought an automatic cigarette vending machine from the defendants. She signed an order form that contained the following term in small print: '[A]ny express or implied condition, statement or warranty, statutory or otherwise not stated herein is hereby excluded.' The defendants gave her a printed confirmation of this order. When the machine was delivered, it did not work satisfactorily, and the claimant sought damages for breach of the implied statutory term that the machine was fit for the purpose for which it was sold. The defendants sought to rely on the exemption clause, but the claimant argued that she had not read the order form and did not know what it contained.

Held: Because the claimant had signed the written contract and had not been induced to do so by any misrepresentation, she was bound by its terms. It was wholly immaterial that she had not read the document and did not know its contents.

SCRUTTON LJ: In cases in which the contract is contained in a railway ticket or other unsigned document, it is necessary to prove that an alleged party was aware, or ought to have been aware, of its terms and conditions. These cases have no application when the document has been signed. When a document containing contractual terms is signed, then, in the absence of fraud, or, I will add, misrepresentation, the party signing it is bound, and it is wholly immaterial whether he has read the document or not.

NOTES

1. Signature, for these purposes, includes electronic signature: Electronic Communications Act 2000, s. 7.

2. Contracts of guarantee must be evidenced in writing and signed by the guarantor: Statute of Frauds 1677, s. 4. Can an automatic email signature be a 'signature' for these purposes? In *J. Pereira Fernandes SA v Mehta* [2006] EWHC 813 (Ch), [2006] 1 WLR 1543, Mehta had sent an email offering a personal guarantee of £25,000 to cover debts owed by a company of which he was the director. The body of

the email did not mention Mehta's name and there was no signature at the bottom. However, the service provider automatically indicated the email address of the sender in the email header of all messages sent and received. Was there a binding guarantee? The court held that the email did not satisfy the s. 4 requirements, so that the guarantee was unenforceable, since it contained no signature. The name of the sender inserted at the end of the body of the text would constitute a signature if it were clear that it had been inserted to give authenticity to the guarantee commitment, but the automatic insertion of the email address in this instance was merely an 'incidental' inclusion.

JUDGE PELLING QC:

The signature issue

26 . . . [I]n *Caton v Caton* (1867) LR 2 HL 127, . . . the House was concerned with a document that started by referring to 'the under mentioned parties' and then referred to the parties in question by name in relation to various promises. Neither party signed the document and the question was whether the document constituted a sufficient note or memorandum signed by the parties to be bound within section 4. The House of Lords held that it was not. In arriving at this conclusion, Lord Chelmsford LC said, at p 139:

> The cases upon this point . . . establish that the mere circumstance of the name of a party being written by himself in the body of a memorandum of agreement will not of itself constitute a signature. It must be inserted in the writing in such a manner as to have the effect of 'authenticating the instrument', or 'so as to govern the whole agreement' . . .

The name of the party, and its application to the whole of the instrument, can alone satisfy the requisites of a signature. Lord Westbury said, at p 143, that what is alleged to constitute the signature must

> be so placed as to show that it was intended to relate and refer to, and that in fact it does relate and refer to, every part of the instrument . . . it must govern every part of the instrument. It must shew that every part of the instrument emanates from the individual so signing, and that the signature was intended to have that effect. *It follows, therefore, that if a signature be found in an instrument incidentally only*, or having relation and reference only to a portion of the instrument, *the signature cannot have that legal effect and force which it must have in order to comply with the statute, and to give authenticity to the whole of the memorandum.* [Emphasis added]

27 In the light of the dicta cited above, it seems to me that a party can sign a document for the purposes of section 4 by using his full name or his last name prefixed by some or all of his initials or using his initials, and possibly by using a pseudonym or a combination of letters and numbers (as can happen for example with a Lloyds slip scratch), providing always that whatever was used was inserted into the document in order to give, and with the intention of giving, authenticity to it. Its inclusion must have been intended as a signature for these purposes . . .

29 I have no doubt that if a party creates and sends an electronically created document then he will be treated as having signed it to the same extent that he would in law be treated as having signed a hard copy of the same document. The fact that the document is created electronically as opposed to as a hard copy can make no difference. However, that is not the issue in this case. Here the issue is whether the automatic insertion of a person's e-mail address after the document has been transmitted by either the sending and/or receiving internet service provider constitutes a signature for the purposes of section 4.

30 In my judgment the inclusion of an e-mail address in such circumstances is a clear example of the inclusion of a name which is incidental in the sense identified by Lord Westbury in the absence of evidence of a contrary intention. Its appearance divorced from the main body of the text of the message emphasises this to be so. Absent evidence to the contrary, in my view it is not possible to hold that the automatic insertion of an e-mail address is . . . 'intended for a signature'. To conclude that the automatic insertion of an e-mail address in the circumstances I have described constituted a signature for the purposes of section 4 would I think undermine, or potentially undermine, what I understand to be the Act's purpose, would be contrary to the underlying principle to be derived from the cases to which I have referred and would have widespread and wholly unintended legal and commercial effects. In those circumstances, I conclude that the e-mail . . . did not bear a signature sufficient to satisfy the requirements of section 4 . . .

3. Even if the document containing the terms has been signed, it may still be unenforceable as a result of the application of the Unfair Contract Terms Act (UCTA) 1977 (B2B—business to business—contracts) or Part 2, Consumer Rights Act (CRA) 2015 (B2C—trader and consumer—contracts) (see 6.4 and 6.5). For example, s. 6(1A) of UCTA 1977 would now govern the exemption clause in *L'Estrange v Graucob*. It is a B2B contract since the claimant is not a consumer given the business purpose underpinning the order of the vending machine (see s. 2(3) CRA 2015). The implied condition that goods are fit for purpose can be excluded if the exclusion satisfies the reasonableness requirement. Schedule 2(c) provides that a relevant factor in assessing reasonableness is 'whether the customer knew or ought reasonably to have known of the existence and extent of the term', which was interpreted in *AEG (UK) Ltd v Logic Resource Ltd* [1996] CLC 265 (*page 280*, 6.4.5), as being concerned with the realities of the consent to an incorporated term.

4. If a party signs a written document, the written terms that it contains will be incorporated and this includes any terms incorporated by reference, such as a set of standard terms, even if the person signing has not read those standard terms.

5. The decision in *Grogan v Robin Meredith Plant Hire* [1996] CLC 1127 (*page 192, 5.3.1.1*) makes it clear that terms in a document that is not a formation document, e.g. a timesheet, will not be incorporated by signature.

6. In *L'Estrange v Graucob*, Scrutton LJ was clear that a person will not be bound by a signed document if the other party misrepresented its effect.

Curtis v Chemical Cleaning & Dyeing Co.
[1951] 1 KB 805 (CA)

The claimant took a white satin wedding dress to the defendants' shop to be cleaned. The shop assistant asked her to sign a 'receipt', which in fact contained a condition excluding the defendants' liability for any damage however arising. When the claimant asked why she had to sign, the assistant told her that the defendants would not accept liability for damage to the beads and sequins with which the dress was trimmed. The claimant signed. When the dress was returned, it was stained. The defendants argued that the clause excluded their liability.

Held: The defendants could not rely on the exemption clause because of the assistant's innocent misrepresentation, which had misled the claimant as to the extent of the exemption and thereby induced her to sign the receipt.

DENNING LJ: In my opinion any behaviour, by words or conduct, is sufficient to be a misrepresentation if it is such as to mislead the other party about the existence or extent of the exemption. If it conveys a false impression, that is enough. If the false impression is created knowingly, it is a fraudulent misrepresentation; if it is created unwittingly, it is an innocent misrepresentation; but either is sufficient to disentitle the creator of it to the benefit of the exemption . . . When one party puts forward a printed form for signature, failure by him to draw attention to the existence or extent of the exemption clause may in some circumstances convey the impression that there is no exemption at all, or at any rate not so wide an exemption as that which is in fact contained in the document. The present case is a good illustration. The customer said in evidence: 'When I was asked to sign the document I asked 'why? The assistant said I was to accept any responsibility for damage to beads and sequins. I did not read it all before I signed it'. In those circumstances, by failing to draw attention to the width of the exemption clause, the assistant created the false impression that the exemption only related to the beads and sequins, and that it did not extend to the material of which the dress was made. It was done perfectly innocently, but nevertheless a false impression was created.

NOTES

1. *Interfoto Picture Library Ltd v Stiletto Visual Programmes Ltd* [1989] QB 433 (*page 196, 5.3.1.4*) indicates that onerous or unusual terms will need to be expressly disclosed to be incorporated. However, this principle is an aspect of the doctrine enabling written terms to be incorporated into *oral contracts by notice*. In *Do-Buy 925 Ltd v National Westminster Bank plc* [2010] All ER (D) 231 (Nov), the judge considered the scope of the *Interfoto* requirement and whether it applied to onerous or unusual terms in signed writings.

ANDREW POPPLEWELL QC [sitting as a deputy High Court judge]: 91. . . . [Counsel] rightly points out that it remains an undecided question whether the *Interfoto* principle can ever apply to a signed contract. In that case the Defendant was held not to be bound by a term in a printed set of conditions which had been provided to him in the form of a delivery note, but which he had neither signed nor read. In *Ocean Chemical Transport v Exnor Crags Ltd* [2000] 1 Lloyds 466, Evans LJ, with whom Henry and Waller LLJ agreed, was prepared to assume that the principle might

apply to onerous and unusual clauses in a signed contract 'in an extreme case where a signature was obtained under pressure of time or other circumstances'. In *HIH v New Hampshire* [2001] 2 Lloyds 161, Rix LJ doubted whether the principle was properly applicable outside the context of incorporation by notice (paragraph 209). In *Amiri Flight Authority v BAE Systems Plc* [2004] 1 All ER 385, 392, Mance LJ, with whom Rix and Potter LLJ agreed, noted the doubts of Rix LJ in *HIH v New Hampshire* and stated that it was unnecessary to decide whether the principle could ever apply to signed contracts. He envisaged that it might do so where for example a car owner was asked to sign a ticket on entering a car park or a holiday maker asked to sign a long small print document when hiring a car which in either case proved to have a provision of 'an extraneous or wholly unusual nature'; but that such cases might be ones where the application of the provision was precluded by an implied representation as to the nature of the document. He reiterated the normal rule that in the absence of any misrepresentation, the signature of a contractual document must operate as an incorporation and acceptance of all its terms. This is a reflection of the well known principle whose existence and importance was recently emphasised by Moore-Bick LJ in *Peekay v Australia and New Zealand Banking Group* [2006] 2 Lloyd's Reports 511, 520 at paragraph 43 [see extract below] . . .

92. This is not an extreme case, nor one in which there is any reason to depart from the principle that a party should be bound by a contract he has signed. The signature on the Application Form was immediately below an acknowledgement that the signatory had read the General Terms and Conditions which came at the end of a section headed 'Important—you should read this carefully'. Ms Searle accepted that she was provided with the General Terms and Conditions and had had an opportunity to read them; and that the Bank were entitled to assume that she had done so. I see no room for the application of the *Interfoto* principle in this case, even were it capable of applying to some signed contracts.

In any event, it would seem that there are other more appropriate contractual doctrines to call in aid in such a situation, such as duress and undue influence, or even the plea of *non est factum*. There is also the possible argument of misrepresentation as to the effect of the document or its terms.

2. In *Peekay Intermark Ltd v Australia and New Zealand Banking Group Ltd* [2006] EWCA Civ 386, [2006] 2 Lloyd's Rep 511, [2006] 1 CLC 582, there was an unsuccessful argument based on misrepresentation in an attempt to avoid being bound by the signed writing. An experienced customer had signed a written investment contract without reading it on the basis that he claimed to have relied on an informal description of the product given over the telephone. The question for the court related to whether there had been a misrepresentation that had induced the contract and whether that misrepresentation operated despite the existence of the signature to the conflicting terms describing the product in the written document. The Court of Appeal held that, since the true position appeared clearly on the face of the signed written document, by signing the claimant was taking the risk that the final contract terms would not be to his liking. Accordingly, the oral description over the telephone had not induced the contract and there was no actionable misrepresentation.

MOORE-BICK LJ [with whose judgment Chadwick LJ and Lawrence Collins J agreed]: 43 . . . [T]he true position appeared clearly from the terms of the very contract which the claimant says it was induced to enter into by the misrepresentation. Moreover, it was not buried in a mass of small print but appeared on the face of the documents as part of the description of the investment product to which the contract related. It was accepted that a person who signs a document knowing that it is intended to have legal effect is generally bound by its terms, whether he has actually read them or

not. The classic example of this is to be found in *L'Estrange v Graucob* [1934] 2 KB 394. It is an important principle of English law which underpins the whole of commercial life; any erosion of it would have serious repercussions far beyond the business community. Nonetheless, it is a rule which is concerned with the content of the agreement rather than its validity. Accordingly, as both Scrutton LJ and Maugham LJ recognised in that case, the contract may be rescinded if one party has been induced to enter into it by fraud or misrepresentation.

44 From time to time one party to a contract misrepresents to the other the content or effect of the document which is intended to embody their agreement. In such cases it has been held that the party making the misrepresentation is prevented from enforcing the contract in accordance with its terms. An example is to be found in the well-known case of *Curtis v The Chemical Cleaning and Dyeing Co Ltd* [1951] 1 KB 805 in which the defendant was prevented from relying on a general exemption clause on the back of the cleaning ticket after its shop assistant had induced the customer to sign it by telling her that it excluded liability only for damage to beads or sequins . . .

[Moore-Bick LJ accepted that there was a representation on the facts and then turned to whether the representation had induced the contract.]

52 . . . No doubt Mr Pawani had been led to expect documents relating to an investment of a certain kind, but he was aware that the FTCs contained the only formal description he would receive of the investment in which Peekay was being invited to participate. The description he had been given by Mrs Balasubramaniam was at best informal and, as the judge found, 'rough and ready'. The FTCs were the first and only opportunity he was given to satisfy himself that the nature of the investment and the terms relating to it were consistent with the broad description she had given him and that it was satisfactory to him in all other respects. He may not have been expecting the documents to contain any nasty surprises, but only by reading them could he satisfy himself that the product was what he had been led to expect. In those circumstances the only conclusion open to the judge in my view was that Mr Pawani was induced to sign the documents and enter into the contract not by what Mrs Balasubramaniam had told him, but by his own assumption that the investment product to which they related corresponded to the description he had previously been given.

In any event, there was an entire agreement clause (a risk disclosure statement) placing the burden on the investor to satisfy himself as to the nature of the transaction and the risk to which the investor would be exposed. This prevented him later seeking to deny this responsibility by raising allegations of misrepresentation (discussion *page 498*, 9.4.3.1).

3. For a recent application of the 'Interfoto principle' in a consumer context, see *Higgins & Co Lawyers Ltd v Evans* [2019] EWHC 2809 (QB) (discussed in *Poole's Textbook on Contract Law*, 15th edn (Oxford University Press, 2021), *page 268*, 6.6.4.4).

5.3 Oral contracts: incorporation of written terms

5.3.1 Reasonable notice

Parker v South Eastern Railway
(1877) 2 CPD 416 (CA)

The claimant deposited his bag in the defendants' cloakroom, paid 2d., and received a ticket. On the face of the ticket, the words 'see back' were printed; on the back, a notice stated that the company would not be responsible for the value of any package in excess of £10. A notice containing the same condition was displayed in the cloakroom. The claimant's bag was lost or stolen and he claimed its value, which was more than £10. He argued that he had taken the ticket without reading it and thought that it was only a receipt for 2d. or evidence that the company had possession of his bag. He had not seen the notice in the cloakroom.

Held: The trial judge had misdirected the jury, since he had not asked them to consider whether the defendants had taken reasonable steps to give the claimant notice of the condition.

MELLISH LJ: The question then is, whether the plaintiff was bound by the conditions contained in the ticket. In an ordinary case, where an action is brought on a written agreement which is signed by the defendant, the agreement is proved by proving his signature, and, in the absence of fraud, it is wholly immaterial that he has not read the agreement and does not know its contents. The parties may, however, reduce their agreement into writing, so that the writing constitutes the sole evidence of the agreement, without signing it; but in that case there must be evidence independently of the agreement itself to prove that the defendant has assented to it. In that case, also, if it is proved that the defendant has assented to the writing constituting the agreement between the parties, it is, in the absence of fraud, immaterial that the defendant had not read the agreement and did not know its contents. Now if in the course of making a contract one party delivers to another a paper containing writing, and the party receiving the paper knows that the paper contains conditions which the party delivering it intends to constitute the contract, I have no doubt that the party receiving the paper does, by receiving and keeping it, assent to the conditions contained in it, although he does not read them, and does not know what they are . . .

Now, I am of opinion that we cannot lay down, as a matter of law, either that the plaintiff was bound or that he was not bound by the conditions printed on the ticket, from the mere fact that he knew there was writing on the ticket, but did not know that the writing contained conditions. I think there may be cases in which a paper containing writing is delivered by one party to another in the course of a business transaction, where it would be quite reasonable that the party receiving it should assume that the writing contained in it no condition, and should put it in his pocket unread. For instance, if a person driving through a turnpike-gate received a ticket upon paying the toll, he might reasonably assume that the object of the ticket was that by producing it he might be free from paying toll at some other turnpike-gate, and might put it in his pocket unread. On the other hand, if a person who ships goods to be carried on a voyage by sea receives a bill of lading signed by the master, he would plainly be bound by it, although afterwards in an action against the shipowner for the loss of the goods, he might swear that he had never read the bill of lading, and that he did not know that it contained the terms of the contract of carriage, and that the shipowner was protected by the exceptions contained in it. Now the reason why the person receiving the bill of lading would be bound seems to me to be that in the great majority of cases persons shipping goods do know that the bill of lading contains the terms of the contract of carriage; and the shipowner, or the master delivering the bill of lading, is entitled to assume that the person shipping goods has that knowledge. It is, however, quite possible to suppose that a person who is neither a man of business nor a lawyer might on some particular occasion ship goods without the least knowledge of what a bill of lading was, but in my opinion such a person must bear the consequences of his own exceptional ignorance, it being plainly impossible that business could be carried on if every person who delivers a bill of lading had to stop to explain what a bill of lading was.

Now the question we have to consider is whether the railway company were entitled to assume that a person depositing luggage, and receiving a ticket in such a way that he could see that some writing was printed on it, would understand that the writing contained the conditions of contract, and this seems to me to depend upon whether people in general would in fact, and naturally, draw that inference. The railway company, as it seems to me, must be entitled to make some assumptions respecting the person who deposits luggage with them: I think they are entitled to assume that he can read, and that he understands the English language, and that he pays such attention to what he is about as may be reasonably expected from a person in such a transaction as that of depositing luggage in a cloak-room. The railway company must, however, take mankind as they find them, and if what they do is sufficient to inform people in general that the ticket contains conditions, I think that a particular plaintiff ought not to be in a better position than other persons on account of his exceptional ignorance or stupidity or carelessness. But if what the railway company do is not sufficient to convey to the minds of people in general that the ticket contains conditions, then they have received goods on deposit without obtaining the consent of the persons depositing them to the conditions limiting their liability. I am of opinion, therefore, that the proper direction to leave to the jury in these cases is, that if the person receiving the ticket did not see or know that there was any writing on the ticket, he is not bound by the conditions; that if he knew there was writing, and knew or believed that the writing contained conditions, then he is bound by the conditions; that if he knew there was writing on the ticket, but did not know or believe that the writing contained conditions, nevertheless he would be bound, if the delivering of the ticket to him in such a manner that he could see there was writing upon it, was, in the opinion of the jury, reasonable notice that the writing contained conditions.

NOTES

1. Clearly there is no requirement that the contracting party be fully aware of what the terms state. If the document is a 'mere receipt' for money paid, it will not be a contractual document.

2. Mellish LJ refers to the fact that *the terms must be contained in or referred to in a contractual document.*

5.3.1.1 The term must be contained in a contractual document

Chapelton v Barry Urban District Council
[1940] 1 KB 532 (CA)

The claimant wished to hire a deckchair to sit on the beach. The defendant council had left a pile of deckchairs with a notice giving the hire charge and stating that tickets were obtainable from the deckchair attendant. The notice itself contained no exempting conditions. The claimant obtained two chairs from the attendant and received two tickets. The claimant did not know that the tickets contained conditions, because he simply glanced at them and put them into his pocket. On the reverse side of the ticket were the words: 'The council will not be liable for any accident or damage arising from the hire of the chair.' Following the council's negligence, the canvas on the claimant's chair gave way when he sat on it. The council argued that the clause on the ticket exempted it from liability.

Held: The ticket was a mere voucher or receipt and not a contractual document. Only the notice was capable of containing conditions and that made no mention of an exemption. Slesser LJ stressed that there was no reason why a person taking a chair should obtain the ticket at that time. That person might sit on the chair for an hour or more before the attendant came for the money.

NOTES

1. In *Chapelton v Barry Urban District Council*, the pile of deckchairs was held to constitute a standing offer, a contract was thus formed when a deckchair was removed from the pile. The ticket might be obtained some time later and could not therefore be seen as a 'contractual document', because notice of any terms that it contained would be given too late.

2. The fact that a document is called a 'receipt' is not conclusive that it is non-contractual.

3. In *Grogan v Robin Meredith Plant Hire* [1996] CLC 1127, the Court of Appeal held that a condition on a timesheet was not incorporated into the hire contract. The hire contract had already been made before the timesheet was signed. In addition, the signed timesheet did not vary the original contract because it was not a document that a reasonable man would expect to contain relevant contractual conditions. Auld LJ stated that documents such as a timesheet, an invoice, or a statement of account do not normally have contractual purpose as documents making or varying a contract. They are normally intended to record the performance of an existing contractual obligation rather than to provide evidence of its terms.

By comparison, in *Photolibrary Group Ltd (trading as Garden Picture Library) v Burda Senator Verlag GmbH* [2008] EWHC 1343 (QB), [2008] 2 All ER (Comm) 881, terms on a delivery note supplied with various photographic transparencies were considered to be incorporated, since this delivery, accompanied by the delivery note, was analysed as an offer, which was accepted by taking receipt of the transparencies.

5.3.1.2 What constitutes reasonable notice?

As Mellish LJ made clear in *Parker v South Eastern Railway* (1877) 2 CPD 416, it is sufficient that reasonable steps have been taken to bring the clause to the notice of people in general.

Thompson v London, Midland & Scottish Railway
[1930] 1 KB 41 (CA)

The claimant's excursion ticket contained a notice on its reverse side stating that it was issued subject to the conditions in the defendant company's timetables. The timetables, which could be obtained for 6d., stated (on p. 552) that the ticket was issued subject to the condition that no action would lie against the company 'in respect of injury (fatal or otherwise) . . . however caused'. The claimant, who could not read, was injured when, owing to the defendant's negligence, she got off the train when it was unsafe to do so. She sought damages; the defendant company relied on the exemption clause.

Held: The fact that the claimant could not read did not alter the fact that she was bound by the condition on the ticket. An indication of where a condition could be found in another document was sufficient notice of the existence of the clause so that it was validly incorporated.

NOTES

1. This particular clause would now be unenforceable under s. 65(1) CRA 2015 which provides that terms in a consumer contract cannot operate to exclude or restrict death or personal injury resulting from the trader's negligence. In addition, Sch. 2, Part 1, para. 1 provides that terms that purport to exclude or limit the trader's liability for death or personal injury resulting from an act or omission—presumably falling short of negligence—may be regarded as unfair.

2. In *O'Brien v MGN Ltd* [2001] EWCA Civ 1279, [2002] CLC 33 (*page 26, 2.3.1*, note 3), one issue was whether the 'normal Mirror Group rules' as a whole had been incorporated into the scratch card contract, since the rules had not been published in full

in the newspaper on the relevant day (3 July 1995). It was held that reasonable steps had been taken to achieve incorporation of the rules in a general sense, since there was a reference to the rules on the face of the scratch card. The rules could be ascertained from back issues of the newspaper or on request from the offices of the newspaper. It is sufficient that the terms are contained in a separate document as long as there is sufficient reference to it. (The question of whether there had been sufficient incorporation of rule 5 is discussed at *page 196, 5.3.1.4*, note 3 and associated text.)

3. A blank page instead of terms and conditions may not, however, constitute sufficient incorporation by reasonable notice in the absence of a prior consistent course of dealing between the parties concerned. In *Sterling Hydraulics Ltd v Dichtomatik Ltd* [2006] EWHC 2004 (QB), [2007] 1 Lloyd's Rep 8, the seller's faxed acknowledgement of the buyer's purchase order contained a blank page 2 rather than the seller's terms and conditions. The faxed page stated only that delivery was 'based on our [the seller's] General Terms of Sale'. When the goods supplied proved defective, the seller claimed that the contract incorporated its standard terms and conditions containing exemption clauses. However, the judge held that these terms had not been incorporated.

JUDGE HAVELOCK-ALLAN QC: 19 . . . [T]he words 'Delivery based on our General Terms of Sale' at the foot of the first page of the acknowledgement of order were not sufficient, in my judgment, to convert the acknowledgement into a counter-offer. It is DL's case that its Sales and Delivery Conditions were printed on the reverse of the acknowledgement of order and on the reverse of the delivery orders. Whilst I am prepared to accept that that was the case (albeit that the original documents were not in evidence), the practice of DL was to send acknowledgements of orders by fax without faxing the reverse of the page. It follows that SHL did not receive a copy of DL's standard terms when it received the acknowledgement on this, or any previous, occasion. That is not in itself an end of the matter because the words of purported incorporation on the face of the acknowledgement did not refer to terms 'on the reverse' or 'overleaf'. They simply referred to DL's 'General Terms of Sale'. There can be no argument that in appropriate cases words of reference of this kind are capable of incorporating standard terms which are to be found elsewhere. It is also true that they are more likely to do so in a commercial or business context, where the parties to the transaction might be expected to have trading terms which they want to govern their transactions. Nevertheless, even in this context, adequate notice of the terms must be given if they are to prevent the acknowledgement of an offer made on different terms from resulting in a binding contract.

4. In *Transformers & Rectifiers Ltd v Needs Ltd* [2015] EWHC 269 (TCC), [2015] BLR 336, the judge imposed even more exacting standards for valid incorporation. The claimant's purchase order made

no mention of the existence of terms and conditions on the reverse and the defendant's counter-offer acknowledgement referred to its own terms and conditions and stated that copies were available on request, although no request had been made. The judge held that neither party's terms had been incorporated.

EDWARDS-STUART J: 44 In my judgment a buyer who wishes to incorporate his own standard terms and conditions when orders are sent by fax or e-mail must give the seller reasonable notice of the terms and conditions and must do so in circumstances that make it clear to the other party that he intends to rely on them.

[He then referred to *Sterling Hydraulics* and the need to send a separate fax of the terms and conditions on the back of the purchase order so that both the front-page purchase order and back-page terms and conditions were sent. This was all the more important where, as here, there was no front-page reference to terms on the reverse].

46 Viewed objectively, therefore, I consider that by not sending its terms and conditions when placing the purchase orders by fax or e-mail, even though they were printed on the reverse of purchase orders which from time to time were sent by post, the Claimant did not make it clear to a reasonable person in the position of the Defendant that it was seeking to rely on them. In my judgment if the Claimant did not follow a consistent practice of enclosing its terms and conditions with every purchase order, particularly in circumstances where the purchase order that was sent did not on its face refer to any terms and conditions, the Defendant was entitled to assume that the Claimant was not intending to rely on them.

47 I therefore agree with the Defendant's submission that the Claimant did not do what was necessary to incorporate its terms and conditions into the contract.

48 I now turn to the Defendant's terms and conditions. As I have already mentioned, the Defendant took no steps to provide the Claimant with a copy of these terms and conditions and at the time the Claimant did not ask for them. They were not standard terms and conditions of some trade association, but were the terms and conditions of the Defendant.

49 . . . [I]t seems to me that a seller who wishes to incorporate his terms and conditions by referring to them in his acknowledgement of order—thus making it a counter offer—must, at the very least, refer to those conditions on the face of the acknowledgement of order in terms that make it plain that they are to govern the contract. Having done that, if the conditions are not in a form that is in common use in the relevant industry, the seller must give the buyer reasonable notice of the conditions by printing them on the reverse of the acknowledgement of order accompanied by a statement on the face of the acknowledgement of order that it is subject to the conditions on the back.

50 An alternative way in which the same end may be achieved (if the terms and conditions are not printed on the back of the order) is for the seller to send the buyer a copy of his terms and conditions, making it clear that they are the only terms and conditions upon which the seller is prepared to do business.

. . .

53 I accept that the position may be different if the terms and conditions which the seller seeks to impose are those which are routinely applied to contracts of the type in question, because, for example, they are the terms and conditions of a particular trade association, as in the *Circle Freight* case [*Circle Freight International Ltd v Medeast Gulf Exports Ltd* [1988] 2 Lloyd's Rep 427]. In those circumstances it may be sufficient for the seller simply to refer to those conditions on the face of the acknowledgement of order stating that copies are available on request—but that is not this case.

54 Since the Defendant neither printed its terms and conditions on the reverse of the acknowledgement of order nor provided the Claimant with a copy of those terms and conditions, I consider that it did not do enough to bring those terms and conditions to the attention of the Claimant and thereby turn the acknowledgement of order into a counter offer.

The safest course of action therefore is to make an express reference on the face and ensure that the terms and conditions are provided on each occasion. Nevertheless, a reference to 'website conditions' and the relevant website address will be sufficient to achieve incorporation by reference. In *Impala Warehousing & Logistics (Shanghai) Co. Ltd v Wanxiang Resources (Singapore) Pte Ltd* [2015] EWHC 811 (Comm), [2015] 2 All ER (Comm) 234, the judge considered that since contractual terms are frequently found on websites, a front-page reference to terms and conditions, together with a reference on the reverse page of the contractual document to the latest applicable terms and conditions as being posted on the company's website, was sufficient to incorporate the website terms and conditions.

5.3.1.3 Before or at the time of contracting

In *Olley v Marlborough Court Ltd* [1949] 1 KB 532, a contract was made at a hotel reception desk. In the hotel room upstairs, there was a notice excluding the hotel's responsibility for articles lost or stolen unless they were deposited for safe custody. When the claimant's furs and jewellery were stolen, she brought an action for damages against the hotel. The Court of Appeal held that, since the contract was made at the reception desk, the terms of the notice in the bedroom came too late to be incorporated.

Thornton v Shoe Lane Parking Ltd
[1971] 2 QB 163 (CA)

The claimant went to park his car in the defendants' automatic car park. A notice at the entrance to the car park gave details of the charges and stated that all cars were 'parked at owner's risk'. When a car was driven up to it, a machine dispensed a ticket. The claimant took the ticket, which gave the car's time of arrival and stated in small print that it was 'issued subject to conditions displayed on the premises'. Inside the car park, there was a notice stating, inter alia, that the defendants would not be liable for any injury to customers that occurred when their cars were on the premises. The claimant was injured in the car park and, in a negligence action, the defendants relied on the exemption in the ticket.

Held: The ticket came too late, since the contract was concluded when the motorist drove up to the machine. The exemption in the ticket was the only one wide enough to exempt the defendants from liability for personal injury, but it could not be relied upon.

LORD DENNING MR: [T]he company seek by this condition to exempt themselves from liability, not only for damage to the car, but also for injury to the customer howsoever caused. The condition talks about insurance. It is well known that the customer is usually insured against damage to the car. But he is not insured against damage to himself. If the condition is incorporated into the contract of parking, it means that Mr Thornton will be unable to recover any damages for his personal injuries which were caused by the negligence of the company.

We have been referred to the ticket cases of former times from *Parker v South Eastern Railway Co.* (1877) 2 CPD 416 to *McCutcheon v David MacBrayne Ltd* [1964] 1 WLR 125. They were concerned with railways, steamships and cloakrooms where booking clerks issued tickets to customers who took them away without reading them. In those cases the issue of the ticket was regarded as an *offer* by the company. If the customer took it and retained it without objection, his act was regarded as an acceptance of the offer: see *Watkins v Rymill* (1833) 10 QBD 178, 188 and *Thompson v London, Midland and Scottish Railway Co.* [1930] 1 KB 41, 47. These cases were based on the theory that the customer, on being handed the ticket, could refuse it and decline to enter into a contract on those terms. He could ask for his money back. That theory was, of course, a fiction. No customer in a thousand ever read the conditions. If he had stopped to do so, he would have missed the train or the boat.

None of those cases has any application to a ticket which is issued by an automatic machine. The customer pays his money and gets a ticket. He cannot refuse it. He cannot get his money back. He may protest to the machine, even swear at it. But it will remain unmoved. He is committed beyond recall. He was committed at the very moment when he put his money into the machine. The contract was concluded at that time. It can be translated into offer and acceptance in this way: the offer is made when the proprietor of the machine holds it out as being ready to receive the money. The acceptance takes place when the customer puts his money into the slot. The terms of the offer are contained in the notice placed on or near the machine stating what is offered for the money. The customer is bound by those terms as long as they are sufficiently brought to his notice before-hand, but not otherwise. He is not bound by the terms printed on the ticket if they differ from the notice, because the ticket comes too late. The contract has already been made: see *Olley v Marlborough Court Ltd* [1949] 1 KB 532. The ticket is no more than a voucher or receipt for the money that has been paid (as in the deckchair case, *Chapelton v Barry Urban District Council* [1940] 1 KB 532) on terms which have been offered and accepted before the ticket is issued.

In the present case the offer was contained in the notice at the entrance giving the charges for garaging and saying 'at owner's risk,' i.e., at the risk of the owner so far as damage to the car was concerned. The offer was accepted when Mr Thornton drove up to the entrance and, by the movement of his car, turned the light from red to green, and the ticket was thrust at him. The contract was then concluded, and it could not be altered by any words printed on the ticket itself. In particular, it could not be altered so as to exempt the company from liability for personal injury due to their negligence.

NOTES

1. Lord Denning's judgment sets out the process of offer and acceptance in ticket cases (which is based on a fiction), and the process of offer and acceptance using automatic machines. Automatic machines have altered over the years and it is now possible to purchase a railway ticket from such a machine. If I buy a ticket at Euston station to travel to Birmingham, is the offer and acceptance position different depending on whether I buy my ticket from the automatic machine or the ticket office? Consider Newey LJ's assessment of a hypothetical scenario in pay and display machines in a car park in *National Car Parks Ltd v Revenue & Customs Commissioners* [2019] EWCA Civ 854 at [18]–[20]. The case is discussed in *Poole's Textbook on Contract Law*, 2.3.2.4.

2. In any event, Lord Denning considered that the clause exempting from personal injury was too wide and took away important rights. He suggested that, in such cases, the clause would need to be drawn explicitly to the car park user's attention.

5.3.1.4 **Higher standard of incorporation for onerous or unusual clauses**

Interfoto Picture Library Ltd v Stiletto Visual Programmes Ltd
[1989] QB 433 (CA)

The defendants ordered photographic transparencies from the claimants. The transparencies were sent packed in a bag with a delivery note. This delivery note stated that the transparencies had to be returned by 19 March and that a holding fee of £5 per day plus VAT would be charged for each day they were retained beyond that. The defendants did not use the transparencies and completely forgot about them. They were eventually returned on 2 April. The claimants sent an invoice for £3,783.50 (the holding charge per transparency per day from 19 March to 2 April). The defendants refused to pay.

Held: If the condition is a particularly onerous or unusual one that would not generally be known to the other party, then the party seeking to enforce it had to show that it had fairly and reasonably been brought to the other party's attention. Condition 2 was unreasonable and extortionate, and the claimants had not brought it to the attention of the defendants. Instead, the claimants were entitled to an award of £3.50 per transparency per week.

DILLON LJ: The question is therefore whether condition 2 was sufficiently brought to the defendants' attention to make it a term of the contract which was only concluded after the defendants had received, and must have known that they had received the transparencies *and* the delivery note.

This sort of question was posed, in relation to printed conditions, in the ticket cases, such *Parker v South Eastern Rly Co* (1877) 2 CPD 416, in the last century. At that stage the printed conditions were looked at as a whole and the question considered by the courts was whether the printed conditions as a whole had been sufficiently drawn to a customer's attention to make the whole set of conditions part of the contract; if so the customer was bound by the printed conditions even though he never read them.

More recently the question has been discussed whether it is enough to look at a set of printed conditions as a whole. When for instance one condition in a set is particularly onerous does something special need to be done to draw customers' attention to that particular condition? In an obiter dictum in *J. Spurling Ltd v Bradshaw* [1956] 1 WLR 461, 466 (cited in *Chitty on Contracts*, 25th ed. 1983) vol 1, (p. 408) Denning LJ stated:

> Some clauses which I have seen would need to be printed in red ink on the face of the document with a red hand pointing to it before the notice could be held to be sufficient.

Then in *Thornton v Shoe Lane Parking Ltd* [1971] 2 QB 163 both Lord Denning MR and Megaw LJ held as one of their grounds of decision, as I read their judgments, that where a condition is particularly onerous or unusual the party seeking to enforce it must show that that condition, or an unusual condition of that particular nature, was fairly brought to the notice of the other party. Lord Denning MR, at pp. 169H–170D, restated and applied what he had said in the *Spurling* case, and held that the court should not hold any man bound by such a condition unless it was drawn to his attention in the most explicit way . . .

At the time of the ticket cases in the last century it was notorious that people hardly ever troubled to read printed conditions on a ticket or delivery note or similar document. That remains the case now. In the intervening years the printed conditions have tended to become more and more complicated and more and more one-sided in favour of the party who is imposing them, but the other parties, if they notice that there are printed conditions at all, generally still tend to assume that such conditions are only concerned with ancillary matters of form and are not of importance. In the ticket cases the courts held that the common law required that reasonable steps be taken to draw the other parties' attention to the printed conditions or they would not be part of the contract. It is, in my judgment, a logical development of the common law into modern conditions that it should be held, as it was in *Thornton v Shoe Lane Parking Ltd* [1971] 2 QB 163, that, if one condition in a set of printed conditions is particularly onerous or unusual, the party seeking to enforce it must show that that particular condition was fairly brought to the attention of the other party.

In the present case, nothing whatever was done by the plaintiffs to draw the defendants' attention particularly to condition 2; it was merely one of four columns' width of conditions printed across the foot of the delivery note. Consequently condition 2 never, in my judgment, became part of the contract between the parties.

? QUESTION

Was this condition invalid as a penalty? (*page 753*, 14.10.1.)

NOTES

1. It is difficult to see why such a rule affecting incorporation is needed given the protection provided by the UCTA 1977 and, in the consumer context, by Part 2 of the CRA 2015.

2. The difficulty resulting from *Interfoto v Stiletto* is how to decide whether a clause is onerous or unreasonable.

AEG (UK) Ltd v Logic Resource Ltd
[1996] CLC 265 (CA)

In a sales contract, one of the terms required the purchaser to return defective goods at its own expense.

Held: The Court of Appeal majority (Hirst and Waite LJJ) considered that it was the particular clause relating to its use that needed to be onerous or unusual. Applying this test, the clause was onerous because it imposed the costs of returning the goods on the buyer. In addition, the majority did not regard it as a standard or common term and so concluded that it was unusual. Applying the test in *Interfoto*, the existence of the clause had not fairly and reasonably been brought to the defendant's attention and was therefore not incorporated.

However, Hobhouse LJ (dissenting) considered that the type of clause needed to be onerous or unusual. Since he considered that this type of clause was not unusual, he considered that the higher standard was not required. The approach adopted by Hobhouse LJ would have restricted the operation of the *Interfoto* principle.

? QUESTIONS

1. Is the approach of the majority tantamount to assessing whether this was a reasonable term to include? See Bradgate (1997) 60 MLR 582.

2. Is it sufficient that the clause in question should be onerous *or* unusual, or does the clause need to be both onerous *and* unusual for the higher standard of incorporation to apply? In *HIH Casualty & General Insurance Ltd v New Hampshire Insurance Co.* [2001] EWCA Civ 735, [2001] 2 Lloyd's Rep 161, [211], Rix LJ (with whose judgment Mummery and Peter Gibson LJJ agreed) stated that the requirement for a higher standard of incorporation was not satisfied simply because the term was unusual; the term in question would *also* need to be 'onerous, unreasonable and extortionate'. This issue appears to be linked to the question of whether the type of clause or the particular clause needs to be onerous or unusual. If it is the type of clause that is examined for these purposes, it is not unusual for certain types of clause to appear in contracts, although the particular clause in question might be a particularly onerous version of this type of term. On the other hand, if it is accepted that it is the particular clause that is assessed, then either requirement ought to be sufficient to attract the need for the higher standard of incorporation. (See the decision of the Court of Appeal in *Ocean Chemical Transport*, below.)

Part 2 — Content, interpretation, performance, and privity

In the next case, it was confirmed that it is the meaning and effect of the *particular clause* that must be onerous or unusual, rather than clauses of that general type.

Ocean Chemical Transport Inc. v Exnor Craggs Ltd
[2000] 1 All ER (Comm) 519, [2000] 1 Lloyd's Rep 446 (CA)

The case was concerned with a time limitation clause in a contract for the sale of bunkers. It provided that 'all liability whatsoever on [the seller's] part shall cease unless suit is brought within six months after delivery of the goods or the date when the goods should have been delivered'. Seventeen months after the bunkers had been supplied, it was alleged that the seller had not paid the original supplier for the bunkers and the vessel to which they had been supplied was arrested in Egypt. The buyer paid for the release of the vessel and then sought to claim damages for breach of contract against the seller. The judge applied clause 10 and held that the claim was time-barred. One of the issues on appeal was whether clause 10 was incorporated, i.e. whether the seller had taken sufficient steps to bring this clause to the attention of the buyer given that no prominence had been given to it. The judge had considered the clause in a general sense as a clause that sought to prevent claims being brought after a specified period and concluded that the clause in question was therefore neither onerous nor unusual. Counsel argued that the correct approach was to examine the particular clause and the specific circumstances of the case.

Held (on appeal, dismissing the appeal): Since the buyer had expressly acknowledged the existence of the terms, it could not allege that insufficient notice of this clause had been given.

EVANS LJ [with whose judgment Henry and Waller LJJ agreed]: 42. With regard to the judgments in the *AEG* case, [counsel] showed us that the majority held that, in applying the test of incorporation . . . , it was appropriate to consider what may be called, for short, the construction and effect of the particular clause. That appears specifically at page 273D in the judgment of Hirst LJ. On the other hand, Hobhouse LJ, who dissented, held that the proper approach was to consider what kind of clause was in issue, and then to decide whether sufficient steps had been taken to bring the existence of that kind of clause to the notice of the other party and also to decide whether the particular clause was onerous or unusual by reference to the kind of clause that it was. It was wrong, he said, to apply that test to the specific terms of the clause in question. As he pointed out at page 277B and following, that was a case where difficulties arose because the clauses, which were not of an unusual kind, were unreasonably drafted. He thought that to concentrate upon the precise meaning of the particular clause in question meant that:

> . . . one is completely distorting the contractual relationship between the parties and the ordinary mechanisms of making contracts. It will introduce uncertainty into the law of contract.

43. [Counsel] emphasised that diversity of view because in the present case the learned judge referred to the judgment of Hobhouse LJ with approval and it was that which had led him, Mr Charkham submitted, to consider not so much the effect of this particular clause as simply the kind of clause which it was.

. . .

47 . . . It seems to me that the question of incorporation must always depend upon the meaning and effect of the clause in question. It may be that the type of clause is relevant. It may mean that the effect of the particular clause in the particular case is relevant. That, of course, was the division of opinion in the *AEG* case. But whichever it is, applying that test in the present case, the first stage is to ask what type of

clause clause 10 is. It is a clause which has the effect of a time bar clause which excludes liability after a certain period has passed. Mr Charkham does not submit, as I understand it, that that type of clause could properly be regarded as either onerous or even unusual in a contract of this kind. But, assuming in his favour that it is necessary to apply the majority test in *AEG*, then the question arises whether this clause, which provides a six-month time limit, can justify either of those adjectives. Then the preliminary question, which was decided by the learned judge as his first ground of decision, was that the authorities are of doubtful application in a case such as the present where there was an express acknowledgement in the contractual documents that the terms and conditions in question were incorporated.

48. [Counsel] submits that the *Interfoto* test, as he called it, has to be applied, even in a case where the other party has signed an acknowledgement of the terms and conditions and their incorporation. It seems to me that Mr Charkham could be right in what might be regarded as an extreme case, where a signature was obtained under pressure of time or other circumstances, and where it was possible to satisfy the *Interfoto* test; that is to say, that the clause was one which was particularly onerous or unusual for incorporation in the contract in question. I would prefer to put the matter more broadly and to say that the question is whether the defendants have discharged the duty which lies upon them of bringing the existence of the clause upon which they rely (and, if Mr Charkham is right, of the effect of that particular clause) to the notice of the other party in the circumstances of the particular case.

49. As I have indicated, in some extreme circumstances, even a signature might not be enough. On the other hand, in the present case there was an express acknowledgement. It seems to me that, given the nature of this term and condition and its effect, as relied upon by the respondents, it cannot be said that the respondents failed in their duty to bring the existence of that term to the notice of the buyers, through, of course, their agents, to whom the term had been long available for their perusal. Mr Charkham does not hesitate to submit that the clause in question should have had, as he puts it, the red hand approach. I would doubt very much whether that is practical in the context of a commercial contract such as this. In my view, the respondents did, in this particular case, where there was an express acknowledgement of the existence of the terms, certainly discharge their duty of bringing it sufficiently to the notice of the buyers for the clause to form part of the contract. That makes it unnecessary to make any explicit findings, as the learned judge did, as to whether this clause was properly to be regarded as onerous or unusual; but, as I have already indicated, I have taken account of the effect of this clause in reaching the conclusion which I have already stated. It seems to me that there is in fact no evidence which supports the proposition that this clause is in any way extreme or totally unexpected to be found in a contract such as this.

NOTES

1. In *Kaye v Nu Skin UK Ltd* [2012] EWHC 958 (QB), [2012] CTLC 69, the question was whether a particular version of an arbitration clause in a distribution agreement between English parties was onerous or unusual so that it needed to be fairly and reasonably brought to the attention of the other party. Arbitration clauses are a common type of clause, although this one required disputes to be resolved by binding arbitration in the US state of Utah. The judge held that this was not so onerous that it should specifically have been brought to the other party's attention. Accordingly, it had been incorporated.

2. In *Shepherd Homes Ltd v Encia Remediation Ltd* [2007] EWHC 70 (TCC), [2007] BLR 135, it was held that a limitation of a construction contractor's liability to the contract price could not be said to be

onerous or unusual and that, in general terms, the scope of terms that are regarded as *usual terms in the trade* will tend to reduce the scope for argument that the term in question should be subject to the *Interfoto* test.

3. In *O'Brien v MGN Ltd* [2001] EWCA Civ 1279, [2002] CLC 33 (*page 193, 5.3.1.2*), the critical question was whether rule 5 of the newspaper's rules was an unusual or onerous term so that the *Interfoto* test of incorporation applied. Rule 5 provided that 'should more prizes be claimed than are available in any prize category . . . a simple draw will take place for the prize'. The claimant alleged that the effect of this term was to 'turn winners into losers'. The Court of Appeal considered that this rule was not onerous or unusual, whereas Evans LJ considered that it did require greater prominence, but was not prepared to

interfere with a finding of fact by the judge at first instance.

HALE LJ [with whose judgment Potter LJ agreed]: 19 In my view the judge was right to hold that the contract was made on 3 July. The offer was contained in the paper that day. In my view it was accepted when the claimant telephoned to claim his prize. The offer and therefore the contract clearly incorporated the term 'Normal Mirror Group rules apply'. The words were there to be read and it makes no difference whether or not the claimant actually read or paid attention to them.

20 The question, therefore, is whether those words, in the circumstances, were enough to incorporate the rules, including r. 5, into the contract. In the words of Bingham LJ in *Interfoto Library v Stiletto* [1989] QB 433 at p. 445E, can the defendant 'be said fairly and reasonably to have brought [those rules] to the notice of the claimant?' This is a question of fact. It is clear . . . that one has to look at the particular contract made on the particular day between the particular parties. But what is fair and reasonable notice will depend upon the nature of the transaction and upon the nature of the term. As Dillon LJ summed it up in *Interfoto* at pp. 438H–439A:

> In the ticket cases the courts held that the common law required that reasonable steps be taken to draw the other parties' attention to the printed conditions or they would not be part of the contract. It is, in my judgment, a logical development of the common law into modern conditions that it should be held, as it was in *Thornton v Shoe Lane Parking Ltd* [1971] 2 QB 163, that if one condition in a set of printed conditions is particularly onerous or unusual, the party seeking to enforce it must show that that particular condition was fairly brought to the attention of the other party.

Bingham LJ put the same point in this way at p. 443C:

> what would be good notice of one condition would not be good notice of another. The reason is that the more outlandish the clause the greater the notice which the other party, if he is to be bound, must in all fairness be given.

21 In my view, although r. 5 does turn an apparent winner into a loser, it cannot by any normal use of language be called 'onerous' or 'outlandish'. It does not impose any extra burden upon the claimant, unlike the clause in *Interfoto*. It does not seek to absolve the defendant from liability for personal injuries negligently caused, unlike the clause in *Thornton v Shoe Lane Parking*. It merely deprives the claimant of a windfall for which he has done very little in return. He bought two newspapers, although in fact he could have acquired a card and discovered the hotline number without doing either. He made a call to a premium rate number, which will have cost him some money and gained the newspaper some, but only a matter of pennies, not pounds.

22 The more difficult question is whether the rule is 'unusual' in this context. The judge found that the claimant knew that there was a limit on the number of prizes and that there were relevant rules. Miss Platell's evidence [for the defendant] was that these games and competitions always have rules. Indeed I would accept that this is common knowledge. This is not a situation in which players of the game would assume that the newspaper bore the risk of any mistake of any kind which might lead to more people making a claim than had

been intended. Some people might assume that the 'get out' rule would provide for the prize to be shared amongst the claimants. Some might assume that it would provide for the drawing of lots. In the case of a single prize some might think drawing lots more appropriate; but it seems to me impossible to say that either solution would be 'unusual'. There is simply no evidence to that effect. Such evidence as there is was to the effect that such rules are not unusual.

23 In any event, the words 'onerous or unusual' are not terms of art. They are simply one way of putting the general proposition that reasonable steps must be taken to draw the particular term in question to the notice of those who are to be bound by it and that more is required in relation to certain terms than to others depending on their effect. In the particular context of this particular game, I consider that the defendants did just enough to bring the rules to the claimant's attention. There was a clear reference to rules on the face of the card he used. There was a clear reference to rules in the paper containing the offer of a telephone prize. There was evidence that those rules could be discovered either from the newspaper offices or from back issues of the paper. The claimant had been able to discover them when the problem arose.

24 The judge had 'great sympathy for Mr O'Brien who struck me as a thoroughly decent young man who must have suffered a cruel disappointment when his hopes were raised only to be dashed'. There can be little sympathy for a newspaper which introduces such a game to attract publicity and readers, and then devotes space which could have been devoted to printing the rules to hyperbole about the prizes to be won and the people who have won them. But the fact of the matter is that there was nothing at all outlandish about the rules of this game and indeed it would have been surprising if there had been no protection on the lines of r. 5. I would dismiss this appeal.

SIR ANTHONY EVANS LJ: 25 I agree that the appeal should be dismissed, but I do so for one reason only. I feel constrained to accept [counsel for the respondents'] final submission, that this court should not interfere with the judge's finding on an issue of fact, unless the finding is clearly wrong. The issue is whether the respondents took reasonable steps to draw the particular term to the notice of those who are to be bound by it . . .

26 The words 'Normal Mirror Group rules apply' clearly formed part of the contract. Unless it was established that the claimant had actual knowledge of r. 5, which it was not, it is immaterial in my judgment that he had had the opportunity to read it on previous occasions, or was aware from the earlier editions of the newspapers that some rules did exist. If those matters were relevant, it would mean that whether he was bound by it would itself be a matter of chance in the individual case.

27 There was no obvious reason why the rules could not appear in every edition which offered tickets for the game, except as Hale LJ has said the editor's wish to use the space for publishing hyperbole about the prizes to be won and the people who had won them. The reference to the rules could have been accompanied by some indication of where they had been printed or could be found, for example 'last Friday's copy' or 'published on' a particular weekday. Instead,

on Monday 3 July the only publication in the Daily Mirror during the previous month had been on 10 June and 30 June. A person reading the offer on 3 July could not be expected to have ready access to back issues, even if he or she knew what date to look for. Whether the reader could discover what the rules were was left essentially as a matter of chance. The promise of significant riches, in my judgment, deserves more.

28 I would also have considered that a rule which gave the 'winner' no more than a further chance to obtain the prize was sufficiently onerous, if not unusual, to require greater prominence than was given to this one. This, in my judgment, was the strength of [Counsel's] main submission.

29 However, the judge concluded differently, and my colleagues agree with him. I cannot say that he was clearly wrong, and so reluctantly, I must agree that the appeal should be dismissed.

This case provides a further useful illustration of the divergence of opinion that can exist on this question of whether a term is onerous or unusual.

5.3.2 Course of dealing

Incorporation by this method is difficult to establish because of the requirement that it be a *consistent* course of dealing.

McCutcheon v David MacBrayne Ltd
[1964] 1 WLR 125 (HL)

The respondents carried goods by sea from the Western Isles of Scotland to the mainland. The appellant asked his brother-in-law, McSporran, to arrange for the appellant's car to be shipped to the mainland. The usual practice of the respondents was to ask customers to sign a risk note under which they agreed to be bound by the conditions printed on it. The conditions included a statement that the goods were shipped at the owner's risk. On this occasion, the risk note had been made out, but McSporran had not been asked to sign it. McSporran had shipped goods in a similar manner on previous occasions. He had sometimes signed risk notes, but had never read the conditions. The ship sank as a result of the negligence of the respondents and the car was lost. The respondents argued that the exclusion clause on the risk note was incorporated by reason of the previous dealings.

Held: There was no consistent course of dealing by which the clause could have been incorporated. Lords Pearce, Hodson, and Guest considered that the pattern of dealings was inconsistent: the past dealings had all involved written terms (incorporation via signing the risk note), whereas this contract was entirely oral. Lord Reid considered that there was no need for the present transaction to be consistent in this sense with the previous transactions. However, it was inconsistent because, on some occasions, McSporran had been asked to sign the risk note and, on others, he had not.

LORD REID: The only other ground on which it would seem possible to import these conditions is that based on a course of dealing. If two parties have made a series of similar contracts each containing certain conditions, and then they make another without expressly referring to those conditions it may be that those conditions ought to be implied. If the officious bystander had asked them whether they had intended to leave out the conditions this time, both must, as honest men, have said 'of course not'. But again the facts here will not support that ground. According to Mr McSporran, there had been no constant course of dealing; sometimes he was asked to sign and sometimes not. And, moreover, he did not know what the conditions were. This time he was offered an oral contract without any reference to conditions, and he accepted the offer in good faith . . .

The judicial task is not to discover the actual intentions of each party: it is to decide what each was reasonably entitled to conclude from the attitude of the other (*Gloag on Contract*, 2nd ed., p. 7). In this case I do not think that either party was reasonably bound or entitled to conclude from the attitude of the other, as known to him, that these conditions were intended by the other party to be part of this contract.

NOTES

1. Lord Reid's reasoning is accepted as correct. The approach taken by Lords Pearce, Hodson, and Guest has been criticized as taking 'consistency too far'.

2. In *Henry Kendall & Sons v William Lillico & Sons Ltd (on appeal from Hardwick Game Farm v Suffolk Agricultural Poultry Producers Association)* [1969] 2 AC 31, there was a consistent course of dealing since, although the 'sold note' had been sent after the conclusion of an oral contract, there had been three or four transactions a month between the parties over a three-year period using the same 'note'.

3. In *Petrotrade Inc. v Texaco Ltd* [2000] CLC 1341, the commercial contract had been concluded by telephone before the telex was sent that specified the terms and conditions. The Court of Appeal held that these terms were incorporated on the basis of the previous dealings between the parties since, over a 13-month period prior to this contract, there had been five other contracts between the parties for the sale of the same or similar products.

4. In *Frans Maas (UK) Ltd v Samsung Electronics (UK) Ltd* [2004] EWHC 1502 (Comm), [2004] 2 Lloyd's Rep 251, goods had been stored on a regular basis for a period of 14 years. This was held to constitute a course of dealing incorporating the British International Freight Association (BIFA) standard terms. However, in *Transformers & Rectifiers Ltd v Needs Ltd* [2015] EWHC 269 (TCC), [2015] BLR 336 (the facts are given at *page 193, 5.3.1.2, note 4*), the parties' relationship extended over 20 years and orders had been placed on an almost weekly basis. Sometimes the purchase orders were sent by post and in the case of these purchase orders the terms were printed on the back. However, the claimant had failed to use a consistent form of dealing because the majority of the purchase orders had been sent by fax or email and the terms and conditions had not been included with these orders. As a result of this inconsistency, it was not clear to a reasonable person that the claimant intended to rely on those terms.

5. It is very difficult to establish a consistent course of dealing where the terms in question are being relied upon as against a consumer. In *Hollier v Rambler Motors (AMC) Ltd* [1972] 2 QB 71 (*page 256, 6.3.2.2.2*), the claimant (consumer) had had his car repaired at the defendants' garage on three or four occasions over a five-year period. On at least two of these occasions, he had signed a form containing an exemption clause, which he had not read. The Court of Appeal held that this was not a sufficient course of dealing for the clause to be incorporated.

6. In *Hollier v Rambler Motors*, at pp. 77A–B, Salmon LJ distinguished *Kendall v Lillico* (see note 2 above) with the following comment:

> That case is obviously very different from the present case. The *Hardwick Game Farm* case seems to be a typical case where a consistent course of dealing between the parties makes it imperative for the court to read into the contract the condition for which the sellers were contending. Everything that the buyer had done, or failed to do, would have convinced any ordinary seller that the buyer was agreeing to the terms in question. The fact that the buyer had not read the term is beside the point. The seller could not be expected to know that the buyer had not troubled to acquaint himself with what was written in the form that had been sent to him so often, year in and year out during the previous three years, in transactions exactly the same as the transaction then in question.

5.3.3 Common understanding of the parties

British Crane Hire Corporation v Ipswich Plant Hire Ltd
[1975] QB 303 (CA)

Both the claimants and the defendants hired out heavy earth-moving equipment. The defendants hired a dragline crane by telephone from the claimants. After delivery, the claimants sent the defendants a printed form setting out the conditions of hire, which were similar to those used by all plant-hiring firms and stated that the defendants were liable to indemnify the claimants against all expenses in connection with the use of the crane. Before the defendants signed this form, the crane sank in marshy ground. The claimants sought to recover the cost of the crane, and the defendants claimed that the conditions had not been incorporated.

Held: The defendants knew that printed conditions in similar terms to the claimants' were in common use in the business, and the claimants were therefore entitled to conclude that the defendants were accepting the crane on the terms in their conditions.

LORD DENNING MR: In support of the course of dealing, the plaintiffs relied on two previous transactions in which the defendants had hired cranes from the plaintiffs. One was February 20, 1969; and the other October 6, 1969. Each was on a printed form which set out the hiring of a crane, the price, the site, and so forth; and also setting out the conditions the same as those here. There were thus only two transactions many months before and they were not known to the defendants' manager who ordered this crane. In the circumstances I doubt whether those two would be sufficient to show a course of dealing. In *Hollier v Rambler Motors (AMC) Ltd* [1972] 2 QB 71, 76, Salmon LJ said he knew of no case

> in which it has been decided or even argued that a term could be implied into an oral contract on the strength of a course of dealing (if it can be so called) which consisted at the most of three or four transactions over a period of five years.

That was a case of a private individual who had had his car repaired by the defendants and had signed forms with conditions on three or four occasions. The plaintiff there was not of equal bargaining power with the garage company which repaired the car. The conditions were not incorporated.

But here the parties were both in the trade and were of equal bargaining power. Each was a firm of plant hirers who hired out plant. The defendants themselves knew that firms in the plant-hiring trade always imposed conditions in regard to the hiring of plant: and that their conditions were on much the same lines. The defendants' manager, Mr Turner (who knew the crane), was asked about it. He agreed that he had seen these conditions or similar ones in regard to the hiring of plant. He said that most of them were, to one extent or another, variations of a form which he called 'the Contractors' Plant Association form'. The defendants themselves (when they let out cranes) used the conditions of that form. The conditions on the plaintiffs' form were in rather different words, but nevertheless to much the same effect . . .

From that evidence it is clear that both parties knew quite well that conditions were habitually imposed by the supplier of these machines: and both parties knew the substance of those conditions. In particular that if the crane sank in soft ground it was the hirer's job to recover it: and that there was an indemnity clause. In these circumstances, I think the conditions on the form should be regarded as incorporated into the contract. I would not put it so much on the course of dealing, but rather on the common understanding which is to be derived from the conduct of the parties, namely, that the hiring was to be on the terms of the plaintiffs' usual conditions . . .

? QUESTIONS

1. Considerable stress was put on the fact that this was not a case involving business reliance on a clause against a consumer. The knowledge of business practice required to establish common understanding is far more likely to be held by a business person than a consumer.

This case is said to turn on the fact that the parties were 'of equal bargaining power'. However, is the crucial point that they were both in the same business, since only on that basis could such common knowledge of terms used in the business be attributed?

»

2. In *Grogan v Robin Meredith Plant Hire* [1996] CLC 1127 (*page 192, 5.3.1.1,* note 3), the judge at first instance had disputed the conclusion that the Contractors' Plant Association conditions were common knowledge within the industry. Was it important that the parties in *Grogan* were not in exactly the same business? (Triact was a civil engineering company laying pipes and Meredith was in the plant hire business.)

British Crane Hire was also distinguished in the next case—partly, it seems, on the basis that the parties were not in exactly the same business.

Ofir Scheps v Fine Art Logistic Ltd
[2007] EWHC 541 (QB)

The claimant had purchased a sculpture at auction, which was being stored by the auction house. The claimant engaged the defendant to collect and store it. The sculpture went missing while being stored. The defendant alleged that the agreement with the claimant incorporated the defendant's standard terms and conditions, limiting its liability to a fixed figure. It alleged, relying on *British Crane Hire v Ipswich*, that this was common knowledge in the transport and storage business, so that the claimant, which had considerable experience of arranging for transport of such works of art, must have been aware of it.

Held (distinguishing *British Crane Hire*): The terms were not incorporated since: (i) the defendant had not provided the claimant with a copy of these terms or with a document referring to them; and (ii) there was no evidence that the claimant had any particular knowledge of them.

TEARE J [referred to the *British Crane Hire* case and Lord Denning's concluding remarks (see *page 204* above) and continued]:

25 It is readily understandable how the principle referred to by Lord Denning applied. By reason of the plaintiffs and the defendants being in the same business and of equal bargaining power, trading upon similar terms derived from the Contractors Plant Association and having in fact traded on two occasions in the immediate past upon on [*sic*] the plaintiffs' terms the plaintiffs could readily conclude that the defendants intended to trade on the plaintiffs' terms . . .

28 The present case is, in my judgment, very different . . . The Defendant at no stage provided the Claimant with a copy of its terms and conditions or with a document which referred to them. The Claimant was a private customer of the Defendant's. There was nothing about the status in which the Claimant dealt with the Defendant which might have led the Defendant to believe that the Claimant was dealing with the Defendant on the basis of the Defendant's terms and conditions. Nor was there anything done or said by the Claimant which might have led the Defendant to believe that the Claimant was contracting with the Defendant upon the basis of the Defendant's terms and conditions. Although it is more likely than not that the Claimant understood that the Defendant would probably supply its services pursuant to certain terms and conditions which might well include limits on the Defendant's liability, that does not, in my judgment, entitle the Defendant to rely upon its terms and conditions against the Claimant because the Defendant at no stage mentioned its terms and conditions and, objectively, there was no reason why the Defendant might reasonably conclude that the Claimant intended to contract with the Defendant on the basis of the Defendant's terms and conditions.

29 For these reasons I have concluded that the Defendant's terms and conditions were not incorporated into the agreement between the Claimant and the Defendant.

NOTE Such an argument for incorporation based on *British Crane Hire* was also rejected on similar grounds in *Balmoral Group Ltd v Borealis (UK) Ltd* [2006] EWHC 1900 (Comm), [2006] 2 Lloyd's Rep 629, [2006] 2 CLC 220, discussed at *page 286, 6.4.5.2*).

CHRISTOPHER CLARKE J: 357 I am not persuaded that when Balmoral first contracted to purchase polyethylene from Borealis in December 1994 the common understanding between them was that the purchase was on Borealis' terms and conditions. In *British Crane Hire* both parties were crane hirers. They each hired out cranes on similar conditions. The defendants had signed and sent back the plaintiff's conditions twice before; and would have done so again if the accident had not happened. In December 2004 Balmoral had not purchased material from Borealis before; nor had they ever signed or sent back Borealis' conditions; nor, so far as the evidence shows, had they received a copy of those conditions when they sent their purchase order or took delivery. In those circumstances I do not think that Borealis was entitled to conclude that Balmoral had agreed to their terms.

5.4 Implied terms

5.4.1 Terms implied at common law by the courts

Liverpool City Council v Irwin
[1977] AC 239 (HL)

A local authority owned the tower block in which the appellants lived. The tenancy agreement contained a list of obligations imposed on the tenants and made no mention of any obligations imposed on the landlords. The appellants withheld their rent as a protest against conditions in the block. The local authority sought possession and the appellants counterclaimed for nominal damages, alleging that the local authority was in breach of its duty to repair and maintain the common parts of the building. They alleged that the lifts did not work, that the lighting on the stairs was inadequate, and that the rubbish chutes were blocked. The question was whether there was any implied duty (term) to this effect in the absence of any express provision.

Held: The nature of the contract required a term to be implied that there was an obligation to take reasonable care to keep the common parts in reasonable repair and in use. However, on the facts, the local authority had taken reasonable care in the circumstances and there was no breach. The House of Lords expressly rejected the suggestion of Lord Denning in the Court of Appeal that a term could be implied if it was reasonable.

LORD WILBERFORCE: [T]here are varieties of implications which the courts think fit to make and they do not necessarily involve the same process. Where this is, on the face of it, a complete, bilateral contract, the courts are sometimes willing to add terms to it, as implied terms: this is very common in mercantile contracts where there is an established usage: in that case the courts are spelling out what both parties know and would, if asked, unhesitatingly agree to be part of the bargain. In other cases, where there is an apparently complete bargain, the courts are willing to add a term on the ground that without it the contract will not work—this is the case, if not of *The Moorcock* (1889) 14 PD 64 itself on its facts, at least of the doctrine of *The Moorcock* as usually applied. This is, as was pointed out by the majority in the Court of Appeal, a strict test—though the degree of strictness seems to vary with the current legal trend—and I think that they were right not to accept it as applicable here. There is a third variety of implication, that which I think Lord Denning MR favours, or at least did favour in this case, and that is the implication of reasonable terms. But though I agree with many of his instances, which in fact fall under one or other of the preceding heads, I cannot go so far as to endorse his principle; indeed, it seems to me, with respect, to extend a long, and undesirable, way beyond sound authority.

The present case, in my opinion, represents a fourth category, or I would rather say a fourth shade on a continuous spectrum. The court here is simply concerned to establish what the contract is, the parties not having themselves fully stated the terms. In this sense the court is searching for what must be implied.

What then should this contract be held to be? There must first be implied a letting, that is, a grant of the right of exclusive possession to the tenants. With this there must, I would suppose, be implied a covenant for quiet enjoyment, as a necessary incident of the letting. The difficulty begins when we consider the common parts. We start with the fact that the demise is useless unless access is obtained by the staircase; we can add that, having regard to the height of the block, and the family nature of the dwellings, the demise would be useless without a lift service; we can continue that, there being rubbish chutes built into the structures and no other means of disposing of light rubbish, there must be a right to use the chutes. The question to be answered—and it is the only question in this case—is what is to be the legal relationship between landlord and tenant as regards these matters.

There can be no doubt that there must be implied (i) an easement for the tenants and their licensees to use the stairs, (ii) a right in the nature of an easement to use the lifts, (iii) an easement to use the rubbish chutes.

But are these easements to be accompanied by any obligation upon the landlord, and what obligation? There seem to be two alternatives. The first, for which the council contends, is for an easement coupled with no legal obligation, except such as may arise under the Occupiers' Liability Act 1957 as regards the safety of those using the facilities, and possibly such other liability as might exist under the ordinary law of tort. The alternative is for easements coupled with some obligation on the part of the landlords as regards the maintenance of the subject of them, so that they are available for use.

My Lords, in order to be able to choose between these, it is necessary to define what test is to be applied, and I do not find this difficult. In my opinion such obligation should be read into the contract as the nature of the contract itself implicitly requires, no more, no less: a test, in other words, of necessity. The relationship accepted by the corporation is that of landlord and tenant: the tenant accepts obligations accordingly, in relation inter alia to the stairs, the lifts and the chutes. All these are not just facilities, or conveniences provided at discretion: they are essentials of the tenancy without which life in the dwellings, as a tenant, is not possible. To leave the landlord free of contractual obligation as regards these matters, and subject only to administrative or political pressure, is, in my opinion, inconsistent totally with the nature of this relationship. The subject matter of the lease (high rise blocks) and the relationship created by the tenancy demand of their nature some contractual obligation . . .

I do not think that this approach involves any innovation as regards the law of contract. The necessity to have regard to the inherent nature of a contract and of the relationship thereby established was stated in this House in *Lister v Romford Ice and Cold Storage Co. Ltd* [1957] AC 555. That was a case between master and servant and of a search for an 'implied term'. Viscount Simonds, at p. 579, makes a clear distinction between a search for an implied term such as might be necessary to give 'business efficacy' to the particular contract and a search, based on wider considerations, for such a term as the nature of the contract might call for, or as a legal incident of this kind of contract. If the search were for the former, he says, ' . . . I should lose myself in the attempt to formulate it with the necessary precision.' (p. 576.) We see an echo of this in the present case, when the majority in the Court of Appeal, considering a 'business efficacy term'—i.e., a '*Moorcock*' term (*The Moorcock*, 14 PD 64)—found themselves faced with five alternative terms and therefore rejected all of them. But that is not, in my opinion, the end, or indeed the object, of the search . . .

It remains to define the standard. My Lords, if, as I think, the test of the existence of the term is necessity the standard must surely not exceed what is necessary having regard to the circumstances. To imply an absolute obligation to repair would go beyond what is a necessary legal incident and would indeed be unreasonable. An obligation to take reasonable care to keep in reasonable repair and usability is what fits the requirements of the case. Such a definition involves—and I think rightly—recognition that the tenants themselves have their responsibilities. What it is reasonable to expect of a landlord has a clear relation to what a reasonable set of tenants should do for themselves.

. . . It has not been shown in this case that there was any breach of [the] obligation.

. . . My Lords, it will be seen that I have reached exactly the same conclusion as that of Lord Denning MR, with most of whose thinking I respectfully agree. I must only differ from the passage in which, more adventurously, he suggests that the courts have power to introduce into contracts any terms they think reasonable or to anticipate legislative recommendations of the Law Commission. A just result can be reached, if I am right, by a less dangerous route.

NOTE There are two types of term implied by the courts. First, a term can be implied if it is a necessary incident of this type of contract ('terms implied in law'), as in *Liverpool City Council v Irwin*. Such a term is implied into all contracts of a particular type as a matter of policy rather than because that is what the parties intended. In addition to being necessary, this type of term must also be a reasonable one to imply: see Peden (2001) 117 LQR 459.

Secondly, a term can be implied on a 'one-off' basis to give effect to the presumed intentions of the parties by filling the gaps to reflect what both parties would have considered to be 'so obvious it goes without saying' or 'necessary to give business efficacy' to the contract—and therefore must be taken to have intended (*page 211*, 5.4.1.2).

5.4.1.1 Terms implied in law

Lord Denning, in *Shell UK Ltd v Lostock Garage Ltd* [1976] 1 WLR 1187, at p. 1196C–G (*page 221*, 5.4.1.2.1) explained this category of implied terms.

LORD DENNING:

(i) The first category

The first category comprehends all those relationships which are of common occurrence. Such as the relationship of seller and buyer, owner and hirer, master and servant, landlord and tenant, carrier by land or by sea, contractor for building works, and so forth. In all those relationships the courts have imposed obligations on one party or the other, saying they are 'implied terms'. These obligations are not founded on the intention of the parties, actual or presumed, but on more general considerations: see *Luxor (Eastbourne) Ltd v Cooper* [1941] AC 108 per Lord Wright; *Lister v Romford Ice and Cold Storage Co* [1957] AC 555, 576 per Viscount Simonds, and at p. 594 by Lord Tucker (both of whom give interesting illustrations); and *Liverpool City Council v Irwin* [1976] 2 WLR 562, 571 per Lord Cross of Chelsea and at p. 579 by Lord Edmund-Davies. In such relationships the problem is not solved by asking what did the parties intend? Or, would they have unhesitatingly agreed to it, if asked? It is to be solved by asking: has the law already defined the obligation or the extent of it? If so, let it be followed. If not, look to see what would be reasonable in the general run of such cases: see by Lord Cross of Chelsea at p. 570H: and then say what the obligation shall be. The House in *Liverpool City Council v Irwin* went through that very process. They examined the existing law of landlord and tenant, in particular that relating to easements, to see if it contained the solution to the problem: and, having found that it did not, they imposed an obligation on the landlord to use reasonable care. In these relationships the parties can exclude or modify the obligation by express words; but unless they do so, the obligation is a legal incident of the relationship which is attached by the law itself and not by reason of any implied term . . .

As Lord Denning explained, *Liverpool City Council v Irwin* is an example of a term implied in law into all contracts of a particular type because it is necessary. Another example is *Scally v Southern Health and Social Services Board* [1992] 1 AC 294.

In this category of implication of a term, the term must be a reasonable one to imply as well as being necessary in this type of contract. However, a term cannot be implied simply on the basis that it is reasonable. As Lord Bridge stated in *Scally v Southern Health and Social Services Board*, at p. 307D: 'I fully appreciate that the criterion to justify an implication of this kind is necessity, not reasonableness.'

An example of a term implied in law into employment contracts is provided by the House of Lords in *Mahmud v Bank of Credit and Commerce International SA (in liquidation)* (also known as *Malik v BCCI*).

Mahmud v Bank of Credit and Commerce International SA (in liquidation)
[1998] AC 20 (HL)

This case is also discussed at *page 749, 14.8.2.*

BCCI's banking business had collapsed and the regulatory authorities had then discovered that the business had been carried on fraudulently over a number of years. The applicants were former employees, who found that they could not obtain employment in the financial services industry. They alleged that this was because of the stigma attached to the fact that they were former employees of BCCI and they sought compensation for the financial consequences of this alleged stigma.

Held: As an aspect of the implied obligation not to undermine the relationship of trust and confidence, an employer was under an implied obligation to its employees not to conduct a dishonest or corrupt business. Therefore, if it was reasonably foreseeable that a breach of this implied obligation would result in the serious possibility of damage to the employee's future employment prospects, that employee could recover damages for the financial loss resulting from that breach.

LORD STEYN:

The implied term of mutual trust and confidence

The applicants do not rely on a term implied in fact. They do not therefore rely on an individualised term to be implied from the particular provisions of their employment contracts considered against their specific contextual setting. Instead they rely on a standardised term implied by law, that is, on a term which is said to be an incident of all contracts of employment: *Scally v Southern Health and Social Services Board* [1992] 1 A.C. 294, 307B. Such implied terms operate as default rules. The parties are free to exclude or modify them.

NOTE In both *Mahmud v BCCI* and *Scally v Southern Health*, the implied terms are formulated and applied as narrow principles. An attempt to achieve a more general implied term failed in *Crossley v Faithful & Gould Holdings Ltd*.

Crossley v Faithful & Gould Holdings Ltd
[2004] EWCA Civ 293, [2004] 4 All ER 447 (CA), [2004] ICR 1615

The court held that, for terms implied in law, it was better to focus on questions of reasonableness, fairness, and the balancing of competing policy considerations, rather than the elusive concept of 'necessity'. The court rejected the argument for an implied term whereby an employer should take reasonable care of an employee's economic well-being (by advising him of the financial consequences of his early retirement). Such a term was considered to involve too large an extension of the law in this area, and to place an unfair and unreasonable burden upon employers.

DYSON LJ:

Implied term to take care for economic well-being of employee

33 In my view, the judge was right to reject the 'portmanteau obligation' contended for by Mr White ie an implied term of any contract of employment that the employer will take reasonable care for the economic well-being of his employee. This would be a standardised term to be implied by law, that is to say a term which, in the absence of any contrary intention, is an incident of all contracts of employment. It is not a term implied to give business efficacy to the particular contract in question which is dependent on an intention imputed to the parties from the express terms of the contract and the surrounding circumstances.

34 It is submitted by [counsel for the defendant] that it is a prerequisite of such an implied term that it is *necessary*. There is some support for this submission in the authorities. But the word 'necessary' is somewhat protean. In *Liverpool CC v Irwin* [1977] AC 239 the House of Lords held that there was a term to be implied in a council letting (as a legal incident of the relationship) that the landlord would keep the means of access in reasonable repair. Lord Wilberforce said (p 254F) that such an obligation should be read into the contract 'as the nature of the relationship implicitly requires, no more, no less: a test, in other words, of necessity'. Means of access is an essential of a tenancy without which life in the premises, as a tenant, is not possible. It is easy enough to see how in that context the implied term was necessary. As Lord Wilberforce put it: 'the subject-matter of the lease (high rise blocks) and the relationship created by the tenancy demand, of their nature, some contractual obligation on the landlord'.

35 . . . In *Scally*, the implied term was said to be necessary, because unless the employer informed the employee of the terms of the scheme, the employee would have no means of knowing what they were, and would therefore not be able to avail himself of one of the benefits of his contract of employment. But . . . it is difficult to see in what sense it is *necessary* to imply into a contract of employment the term that the employer will take reasonable care for the physical and mental health and safety of his employees. It obviously makes sense to imply such a term into a contract of employment on wider policy grounds. But that is different from saying that the nature of the employer/employee relationship implicitly requires such a term.

36 It seems to me that, rather than focus on the elusive concept of necessity, it is better to recognise that, to some extent at least, the existence and scope of standardised implied terms raise questions of reasonableness, fairness and the balancing of competing policy considerations: see *Peden* [2001] LQR 459, 467–475. Such considerations are, I believe, reflected in the recent significant developments in the field of the employer/employee.

NOTE Although this case may be limited factually to the employment context, Dyson LJ's negative comment concerning the 'necessity' requirement has wider significance for terms implied in law. Clearly the necessity test for terms implied in law is very different from the necessity test in the context of terms implied in fact, and different terminology should be employed to avoid any confusion. Unfortunately, although Dyson LJ hints at this, he fails to go further and to reformulate the test other than in vague terms of reasonableness, fairness, and policy.

5.4.1.2 Terms implied in fact

This involves the implication of terms into the individual contract as a one-off on the basis of necessity. Until *Attorney-General of Belize v Belize Telecom Ltd* [2009] UKPC 10, [2009] 1 WLR 1988, it was generally thought that the courts implied terms in some cases to fill gaps in the express terms, i.e. as a process of addition. Such terms were implied as a matter of necessity and on a 'one-off' basis to reflect what must have been the parties' objective intentions. These terms implied in fact were traditionally implied to give business efficacy to the contract (to render it workable) or on the basis that the term would be considered by reasonable people in the position of both parties to be 'so obvious' that it went without saying (the so-called 'officious bystander test' for the implication of terms in fact).

This was considered by legal academics and judges alike to have been altered by the decision in *Attorney-General of Belize v Belize Telecom Ltd* since Lord Hoffmann in *Belize* had considered that the implication of terms in fact was not a process of 'addition' but rather involved a process of construction of the whole contract to give effect to the objectively assessed intentions of the parties, i.e. the implied terms were not 'added' but existed all along as reflecting imputed party intention. Lord Hoffmann appeared to reject the use of the previous 'business efficacy' and 'obviousness' tests as the basis for implication of terms in fact, although subsequent case law appeared to reintroduce elements of business efficacy by stressing the need for the term to be necessary 'to make the contract work'. The Supreme Court in the *Marks & Spencer* case has now explained that the previously accepted requirements for terms implied in fact are still the applicable tests and that the law remains unchanged despite Lord Hoffmann's judgment in *Belize*.

Marks & Spencer plc v BNP Paribas Securities Services Trust Co. (Jersey) Ltd
[2015] UKSC 72, [2015] 3 WLR 1843 (SC)

Marks & Spencer served a valid break notice in relation to its lease so that the lease would end in January 2012, which was after it would pay the next quarter's rent in December 2011. It paid the December quarter's rent in full and on time and had also paid the break premium. Having validly exercised the break, the retailer then demanded repayment of the rent relating to the post-break period, i.e. from the effective date in January until the end of the quarter covered by the December rent payment which was March 2012. However, since there was no express term in the lease which entitled Marks & Spencer to this repayment, they needed to argue for such a term to be implied.

Held: A term would only be implied into a detailed commercial contract if it was necessary to give business efficacy to the contract or was so obvious that its implication went without saying. The Supreme Court therefore refused to imply such a term since it was well-established that rent paid in advance could not be apportioned on a time basis and a different intention was not clearly established on the facts.

LORD NEUBERGER OF ABBOTSBURY PSC (with whom LORD SUMPTION and LORD HODGE JJSC agreed):

Implied terms in contracts

14 It is rightly accepted on behalf of the claimant that there is no provision in the lease which expressly obliges the landlords to pay the apportioned sum to the tenant. Accordingly, it follows that in order to succeed the claimant has to establish that such an obligation must be implied into the lease.

15 As Baroness Hale of Richmond JSC pointed out in *Geys v Société Générale* . . . [2013] 1 AC 523, para 55, there are two types of contractual implied term. The first, with which this case is concerned, is a term which is implied into a particular contract, in the light of the express terms, commercial common sense, and the facts known to both parties at the time the contract was made. The second type of implied terms arises because, unless such a term is expressly excluded, the law (sometimes by statute, sometimes through the common law) effectively imposes certain terms into certain classes of relationship.

16 There have, of course, been many judicial observations as to the nature of the requirements which have to be satisfied before a term can be implied into a detailed commercial contract. They include three classic statements, which have been frequently quoted in law books and judgments. In *The Moorcock* (1889) 14 PD 64, 68, Bowen LJ observed that in all the cases where a term had been implied, 'it will be found that . . . the law is raising an implication from the presumed intention of the parties with the object of giving the transaction such efficacy as both parties must have intended that at all events it should have'. In *Reigate v Union Manufacturing Co (Ramsbottom) Ltd* [1918] 1 KB 592, 605, Scrutton LJ said that 'A term can only be implied if it is necessary in the business sense to give efficacy to the contract'. He added that a term would only be implied if 'it is such a term that it can confidently be said that if at the time the contract was being negotiated' the parties had been asked what would happen in a certain event, they would both have replied: 'Of course, so and so will happen; we did not trouble to say that; it is too clear.' And in *Shirlaw v Southern Foundries (1926) Ltd* [1939] 2 KB 206, 227, MacKinnon LJ observed that, 'Prima facie that which in any contract is left to be implied and need not be expressed is something so obvious that it goes without saying'. Reflecting what Scrutton LJ had said 20 years earlier, MacKinnon LJ also famously added that a term would only be implied 'if, while the parties were making their bargain, an officious bystander were to suggest some express provision for it in their agreement, they would testily suppress him with a common "Oh, of course!"'

17 Support for the notion that a term will only be implied if it satisfies the test of business necessity is to be found in a number of observations made in the House of Lords. Notable examples included Lord Pearson (with whom Lord Guest and Lord Diplock agreed) in *Trollope & Colls Ltd v North West Metropolitan Regional Hospital Board* [1973] 1 WLR 601, 609, and Lord Wilberforce, Lord Cross of Chelsea, Lord Salmon and Lord Edmund-Davies in *Liverpool City Council v Irwin* [1977] AC 239, 254, 258, 262 and 266 respectively. More recently, the test of 'necessary to give business efficacy' to the contract in issue was mentioned by Baroness Hale JSC in *Geys v Société Générale* [2013] 1 AC 523, para 55 and by Lord Carnwath JSC in *Arnold v Britton* [2015] AC 1619, para 112.

18 In the Privy Council case *BP Refinery (Westernport) Pty Ltd v Shire of Hastings* (1977) 180 CLR 266, 282–283, Lord Simon of Glaisdale (speaking for the majority, which included Viscount Dilhorne and Lord Keith of Kinkel) said that:

> for a term to be implied, the following conditions (which may overlap) must be satisfied: (1) it must be reasonable and equitable; (2) it must be necessary to give business efficacy to the contract, so that no term will be implied if the contract is effective without it; (3) it must be so obvious that 'it goes without saying'; (4) it must be capable of clear expression; (5) it must not contradict any express term of the contract.

19 In *Philips Electronique Grand Public SA v British Sky Broadcasting Ltd* [1995] EMLR 472, 481, Bingham MR set out Lord Simon's formulation, and described it as a summary which 'distil[led] the essence of much learning on implied terms' but whose 'simplicity could be almost misleading.' Bingham MR then explained, at pp 481–482, that it was 'difficult to infer with confidence what the parties must have intended when they have entered into a lengthy and carefully-drafted contract but have omitted to make provision for the matter in issue', because 'it may well be doubtful whether the omission was the result of the parties' oversight or of their deliberate decision', or indeed the parties might suspect that 'they are unlikely to agree on what is to happen in a certain . . . eventuality' and 'may well choose

to leave the matter uncovered in their contract in the hope that the eventuality will not occur.' Bingham MR went on to say, at p 482:

> The question of whether a term should be implied, and if so what, almost inevitably arises after a crisis has been reached in the performance of the contract. So the court comes to the task of implication with the benefit of hindsight, and it is tempting for the court then to fashion a term which will reflect the merits of the situation as they then appear. Tempting, but wrong. [He then quoted the observations of Scrutton LJ in the *Reigate* case, and continued] it is not enough to show that had the parties foreseen the eventuality which in fact occurred they would have wished to make provision for it, unless it can also be shown either that there was only one contractual solution or that one of several possible solutions would without doubt have been preferred . . .

20 Bingham MR's approach in the *Philips* case was consistent with his reasoning, as Bingham LJ in the earlier case *Atkins International HA v Islamic Republic of Iran Shipping Lines (The APJ Priti)* [1987] 2 Lloyd's Rep 37, 42, where he rejected the argument that a warranty, to the effect that the port declared was prospectively safe, could be implied into a voyage charterparty. His reasons for rejecting the implication were 'because the omission of an express warranty may well have been deliberate, because such an implied term is not necessary for the business efficacy of the charter and because such an implied term would at best lie uneasily beside the express terms of the charter.'

21 In my judgment, the judicial observations so far considered represent a clear, consistent and principled approach. It could be dangerous to reformulate the principles, but I would add six comments on the summary given by Lord Simon in the *BP Refinery* case 180 CLR 266 as extended by Bingham MR in the *Philips case* [1995] EMLR 472 and exemplified in *The APJ Priti* [1987] 2 Lloyd's Rep 37. First, in *Equitable Life Assurance Society v Hyman* [2002] 1 AC 408, 459, Lord Steyn rightly observed that the implication of a term was 'not critically dependent on proof of an actual intention of the parties' when negotiating the contract. If one approaches the question by reference to what the parties would have agreed, one is not strictly concerned with the hypothetical answer of the actual parties, but with that of notional reasonable people in the position of the parties at the time at which they were contracting. Secondly, a term should not be implied into a detailed commercial contract merely because it appears fair or merely because one considers that the parties would have agreed it if it had been suggested to them. Those are necessary but not sufficient grounds for including a term. However, and thirdly, it is questionable whether Lord Simon's first requirement, reasonableness and equitableness, will usually, if ever, add anything: if a term satisfies the other requirements, it is hard to think that it would not be reasonable and equitable. Fourthly, as Lord Hoffmann I think suggested in *Attorney General of Belize v Belize Telecom Ltd* [2009] 1 WLR 1988, para 27, although Lord Simon's requirements are otherwise cumulative, I would accept that business necessity and obviousness, his second and third requirements, can be alternatives in the sense that only one of them needs to be satisfied, although I suspect that in practice it would be a rare case where only one of those two requirements would be satisfied. Fifthly, if one approaches the issue by reference to the officious bystander, it is 'vital to formulate the question to be posed by [him] with the utmost care', to quote from *Lewison, The Interpretation of Contracts* 5th ed (2011), p 300, para 6.09. Sixthly, necessity for business efficacy involves a value judgment. It is rightly common ground on this appeal that the test is not one of 'absolute necessity', not least because the necessity is judged by reference to business efficacy. It may well be that a more helpful way of putting Lord Simon's second requirement is, as suggested by Lord Sumption JSC in argument, that a term can only be implied if, without the term, the contract would lack commercial or practical coherence.

NOTES

1. The fact that the Supreme Court has recognized the realities of the 'business necessity' test, which had been applied in practice despite *Belize*, is to be welcomed. The 'obviousness' or 'officious bystander test' is also explained in objective terms. There was no good reason to move away from the

practicality of these tests as indicating the parties' intentions.

2. However, this approach necessarily involves a conflict between the position adopted by Lord Hoffmann in *Attorney-General of Belize v Belize Telecom Ltd* [2009] UKPC 10, [2009] 1 WLR 1988, and the position of the majority of the Supreme Court Justices in *Marks & Spencer*. This required an expla-nation. The majority of the Supreme Court put clear water between the processes of contractual construc-tion (or interpretation) and the implication of terms which Lord Hoffmann, in jurisprudence extending over a number of critical decisions for the law of con-tract, had sought to combine as a single construction exercise.

It is now clear that the process of interpretation of the express terms needs to take place sepa-rately and ahead of any discussion of whether terms need to be implied.

Marks & Spencer plc v BNP Paribas Securities Services Trust Co. (Jersey) Ltd
[2015] UKSC 72, [2015] 3 WLR 1843 (SC)

LORD NEUBERGER OF ABBOTSBURY PSC (with whom LORD SUMPTION and LORD HODGE JJSC agreed): 22 Before leaving this issue of general principle, it is appropriate to refer a little further to the *Belize Telecom* case, where Lord Hoffmann suggested that the process of implying terms into a contract was part of the exercise of the construction, or interpretation, of the contract. In summary, he said at para 21 that 'There is only one question: is that what the instrument, read as a whole against the rel-evant background, would reasonably be understood to mean?' There are two points to be made about that observation.

23 First, the notion that a term will be implied if a reasonable reader of the contract, knowing all its provisions and the surrounding circumstances, would understand it to be implied is quite acceptable, provided that (i) the reasonable reader is treated as reading the contract at the time it was made and (ii) he would consider the term to be so obvious as to go without saying or to be necessary for business efficacy. (The difference between what the reasonable reader would understand and what the parties, acting reasonably, would agree, appears to me to be a notional distinction without a practical difference.) The first proviso emphasises that the question whether a term is implied is to be judged at the date the contract is made. The second proviso is important because otherwise Lord Hoffmann's formulation may be interpreted as suggesting that reasonableness is a sufficient ground for implying a term. (For the same reason, it would be wrong to treat Lord Steyn's statement in *Equitable Life Assurance Society v Hyman* [2002] 1 AC 408, 459 that a term will be implied if it is 'essential to give effect to the reasonable expec-tations of the parties' as diluting the test of necessity. That is clear from what Lord Steyn said earlier on the same page, namely that 'The legal test for the implication of . . . a term is . . . strict necessity', which he described as a 'stringent test'.)

24 It is necessary to emphasise that there has been no dilution of the requirements which have to be satisfied before a term will be implied, because it is apparent that the *Belize Telecom* case [2009] 1 WLR 1988 has been interpreted by both academic lawyers and judges as having changed the law. Examples of academic articles include Chris Peters, 'The Implication of Terms in Fact' [2009] CLJ 513, Paul S Davies, 'Recent Developments in the Law of Implied Terms' [2010] LMCLQ 140, John McCaughran, 'Implied Terms: The Journey of the Man on the Clapham Omnibus' [2011] CLJ 607 and JW Carter and Wayne Courtney, '*Belize Telecom*: a reply to Professor McLauchlan' [2015] LMCLQ 245. And in *Foo Jong Peng v Phua Kiah Mai* [2012] 4 SLR 1267, paras 34–36, the Singapore Court of Appeal refused to follow the reasoning in the *Belize Telecom* case at least in so far as 'it suggest[ed] that the traditional "business efficacy" and "officious bystander" tests are not central to the implication of terms' (reasoning which was followed in *Sembcorp Marine Ltd v PPL Holdings Pte Ltd* [2013] SGCA 43). The Singapore Court of

Appeal were in my view right to hold that the law governing the circumstances in which a term will be implied into a contract remains unchanged following the *Belize Telecom* case.

25 The second point to be made about what was said in the *Belize Telecom* case concerns the suggestion that the process of implying a term is part of the exercise of interpretation. Although some support may arguably be found for such a view in the *Trollope* case [*Trollope & Colls Ltd v NorthWest Metropolitan Regional Hospital Board*] [1973] 1 WLR 601, 609, the first clear expression of that view to which we were referred was in *Banque Bruxelles Lambert SA v Eagle Star Insurance Co Ltd* [1997] AC 191, 212, where Lord Hoffmann suggested that the issue of whether to imply a term into a contract was 'one of construction of the agreement as a whole in its commercial setting.' Lord Steyn quoted this passage with approval in the *Equitable Life* case [2002] 1 AC 408, 459, and, as just mentioned, Lord Hoffmann took this proposition further in the *Belize Telecom case* [2009] 1 WLR 1988, paras 17–27. Thus, at para 18, he said that 'the implication of the term is not an addition to the instrument. It only spells out what the instrument means'; and at para 23, he referred to 'The danger . . . in detaching the phrase "necessary to give business efficacy" from the basic process of construction'. Whether or not one agrees with that approach as a matter of principle must depend on what precisely one understands by the word 'construction'.

26 I accept that both (i) construing the words which the parties have used in their contract and (ii) implying terms into the contract, involve determining the scope and meaning of the contract. However, Lord Hoffmann's analysis in the *Belize Telecom* case could obscure the fact that construing the words used and implying additional words are different processes governed by different rules.

27 Of course, it is fair to say that the factors to be taken into account on an issue of construction, namely the words used in the contract, the surrounding circumstances known to both parties at the time of the contract, commercial common sense, and the reasonable reader or reasonable parties, are also taken into account on an issue of implication. However, that does not mean that the exercise of implication should be properly classified as part of the exercise of interpretation, let alone that it should be carried out at the same time as interpretation. When one is implying a term or a phrase, one is not construing words, as the words to be implied are ex hypothesi not there to be construed; and to speak of construing the contract as a whole, including the implied terms, is not helpful, not least because it begs the question as to what construction actually means in this context.

28 In most, possibly all, disputes about whether a term should be implied into a contract, it is only after the process of construing the express words is complete that the issue of an implied term falls to be considered. Until one has decided what the parties have expressly agreed, it is difficult to see how one can set about deciding whether a term should be implied and if so what term. This appeal is just such a case. Further, given that it is a cardinal rule that no term can be implied into a contract if it contradicts an express term, it would seem logically to follow that, until the express terms of a contract have been construed, it is, at least normally, not sensibly possible to decide whether a further term should be implied. Having said that, I accept Lord Carnwath JSC's point in para 71 to the extent that in some cases it could conceivably be appropriate to reconsider the interpretation of the express terms of a contract once one has decided whether to imply a term, but, even if that is right, it does not alter the fact that the express terms of a contract must be interpreted before one can consider any question of implication.

29 In any event, the process of implication involves a rather different exercise from that of construction. As Bingham MR trenchantly explained in the *Philips* case [1995] EMLR 472, 481:

> The courts' usual role in contractual interpretation is, by resolving ambiguities or reconciling apparent inconsistencies, to attribute the true meaning to the language in which the parties themselves have expressed their contract. The implication of contract terms involves a different and altogether more ambitious undertaking: the interpolation of terms to deal with matters for which, ex hypothesi, the parties themselves have made no provision. It is because the implication of terms is so potentially intrusive that the law imposes strict constraints on the exercise of this extraordinary power.

30 It is of some interest to see how implication was dealt with in the recent case in this court of *Aberdeen City Council v Stewart Milne Group Ltd* 2012 SLT 205. At para 20, Lord Hope of Craighead DPSC described the implication of a term into the contract in that case as 'the product of the way I would interpret this contract'. And at para 33, Lord Clarke of Stone-cum-Ebony JSC said that the point at issue should be resolved 'by holding that such a term should be implied rather than by a process of interpretation.' He added that 'The result is of course the same'.

31 It is true that the *Belize Telecom case* [2009] 1 WLR 1988 was a unanimous decision of the Judicial Committee of the Privy Council and that the judgment was given by Lord Hoffmann, whose contributions in so many areas of law have been outstanding. However, it is apparent that Lord Hoffmann's observations in the *Belize Telecom* case, paras 17–27 are open to more than one interpretation on the two points identified in paras 23–24 and 25–30 above, and that some of those interpretations are wrong in law. In those circumstances, the right course for us to take is to say that those observations should henceforth be treated as a characteristically inspired discussion rather than authoritative guidance on the law of implied terms.

NOTE Thus, the only relevant paragraph of Lord Hoffmann's judgment in *Attorney-General of Belize v Belize Telecom Ltd* [2009] UKPC 10, [2009] 1 WLR 1988, that remains is [16] and this relates essentially to the objective approach to interpretation:

The court has no power to improve upon the instrument which it is called upon to construe, whether it be a contract, a statute or articles of association. It cannot introduce terms to make it fairer or more reasonable. It is concerned only to discover what the instrument means. However, that meaning is not necessarily or always what the authors or parties to the document would have intended. is the meaning which the instrument would convey to a reasonable person having all the background knowledge which would reasonably be available to the audience to whom the instrument is addressed: see *Investors Compensation Scheme Ltd v West Bromwich Building Society* [1998] 1 WLR 896, 912–913. It is this objective meaning which is conventionally called the intention of the parties, or the intention of Parliament, or the intention of whatever person or body was or is deemed to have been the author of the instrument.

Prior to the decision in *Marks & Spencer*, the courts had found it necessary to explain and reinterpret *Belize* to make it a workable principle by suggesting that nothing had changed as a result of *Belize*, e.g. *Mediterranean Salvage and Towage Ltd v Seamar Trading and Commerce Inc., The Reborn* [2009] EWCA Civ 531, [2009] 1 CLC 909, [2010] 1 All ER (Comm) 1. The need to provide this explanation is probably attributable to the words of Lord Hoffmann in *Belize* at [27] (extracted in the judgment of Lord Carnwath at *page 220*, later in this section). Relying largely on the response of Lord Clarke in *The Reborn*, Lord Carnwath therefore considered that *Belize* underpinned the decision in *Marks & Spencer*, whereas an alternative question might be to ask whether, if this interpretation is correct, *Belize* is needed at all. Lord Clarke stated that he agreed with the approaches of both Lord Neuberger and Lord Carnwath, although Lord Carnwath denied that his approach is the same as that adopted by Lords Neuberger, Sumption, and Hodge.

Marks & Spencer plc v BNP Paribas Securities Services Trust Co. (Jersey) Ltd
[2015] UKSC 72, [2015] 3 WLR 1843 (SC)

LORD CARNWATH JSC: 57 I agree that the appeal should be dismissed for the reasons given by Lord Neuberger of Abbotsbury PSC so far as addressed to the issues between the parties. I add some brief comments only on the issue of implied terms, and in particular Lord Neuberger PSC's comments on the status of the Privy Council judgment in *Attorney General of Belize v Belize Telecom Ltd* [2009] 1 WLR 1988.

58 Unlike him, I would have been content to take my starting point not in the 19th century cases (such as *The Moorcock* (1889) 14 PD 64), but in the most modern treatment at the highest level. That

is undoubtedly to be found in the judgment of the Privy Council in the *Belize* case [2009] 1 WLR 1988. It is important to remember that this was not an expression of the views of Lord Hoffmann alone, as is implied in some commentaries, but was the considered and unanimous judgment of the Board as a whole (including Baroness Hale of Richmond, and Lord Rodger of Earlsferry, Lord Carswell, Lord Brown of Eaton-under-Heywood, none of them known for lack of independent thought). In the leading textbook on the subject (Lewison, *The Interpretation of Contracts*, 5th ed with the 2nd supplement), the judgment is realistically taken to 'represent the current state of the law of England and Wales': p 284, para 6.03. The rest of that chapter contains an illuminating discussion of the working out of the principles stated by Lord Hoffmann, as applied by the courts in different contractual contexts and different factual situations. We would need very good reasons for treating the judgment as less than authoritative, and we have not been asked by the parties to do so.

59 In the present case, there has been no dispute as to the authority of the *Belize* judgment, only as to its interpretation. The claimants seek to interpret it as supporting a more liberal approach than the traditional 'necessity' test (in the words of their printed case):

> those courts which purport to follow *Belize*, but in so doing apply the tests of business efficacy, absolute necessity and the officious bystander, are departing from the test decided by the Privy Council. The issue, therefore, is whether the type of necessity that is required for the implication of a term is what may be termed (a) absolute necessity (ie the contract simply will not operate without the term); or (b) reasonable necessity (ie the contract will not operate as it must reasonably have been intended by the parties to operate).

The defendants by contrast submit that, properly understood, the judgment should not be read as involving any watering down of the traditional tests.

60 To my mind there is no doubt that the defendants' interpretation is correct. This is so, whether one looks to the words of Lord Hoffmann alone, or to subsequent authority in the higher courts of this country. The claimants have sought to support their submission by a commendably thorough review of the many cases in which the *Belize* case has been cited, in this country and in other common law jurisdictions. In my view, with the possible exception of the Singapore case referred to by Lord Neuberger PSC to which I will come, such support is lacking.

61 Very soon after it was given, the *Belize* judgment was subject to detailed consideration by Lord Clarke of Stone-cum-Ebony MR in the Court of Appeal in *Mediterranean Salvage and Towage Ltd v Seamar Trading and Commerce Inc [The Reborn* [2009] EWCA Civ 531] [2010] 1 All ER (Comm) 1. The judgment was 'adopted' also by Rix LJ: para 48. As the third member of the court, I was more cautious at that early stage, deciding the appeal on the narrow basis that the implied term had not been shown by the owners to be 'necessary', and their case was not improved by substituting 'any of the other formulations of the test discussed in the cases': para 63.

62 Lord Clarke MR began by predicting (accurately as it has turned out) that Lord Hoffmann's analysis 'will soon be as much referred to as his approach to the construction of contracts in *Investors Compensation Scheme Ltd v West Bromwich Building Society* [1998] 1 WLR 896, 912–913': para 8. He observed that 'the implication of a term is an exercise in the construction of the contract as a whole': para 9, citing the two House of Lords authorities referred to by Lord Hoffmann. He then quoted extensively from the judgment, including its citation of Lord Simon of Glaisdale's summary of the tests for implication of a term: see Lord Neuberger PSC, para 18. He did not see the judgment as involving a loosening of the traditional tests, at para 15:

> It is thus clear that the various formulations of the test identified by Lord Simon are to be treated as different ways of saying much the same thing. Moreover, as I read Lord Hoffmann's analysis, although he is emphasising that the process of implication is part of the process of construction of the contract, he is not in any way resiling from the often stated proposition that it must be necessary to imply the proposed term. It is never sufficient that it should be reasonable.

In support he cited also the speech of Lord Wilberforce in *Liverpool City Council v Irwin* [1977] AC 239, 253–254, rejecting the more flexible approach proposed in the Court of Appeal by Lord Denning MR. Lord Clarke MR also noted (para 17) the contrast drawn by Bingham MR in *Philips Electronique* [1995] EMLR 472, 481 (a passage cited by Lord Neuberger PSC at para 29) between the court's 'usual role' in contractual interpretation of finding the 'true meaning' of the words actually used by the parties, and the 'more ambitious undertaking' involved in 'the interpolation of terms to deal with matters for which . . . [they] have made no provision.' Lord Clarke MR concluded this passage by noting the 'stress' laid by the authorities on 'the importance of the test of necessity. Is the proposed implied term necessary to make the contract work?': para 18.

63 The claimants cite a number of later cases in the Court of Appeal in which the *Belize* judgment has been discussed in some detail . . . None of these involves any material departure from Lord Clarke MR's analysis. More significantly it gains direct support from the succinct observation by Baroness Hale of Richmond JSC (herself a party to the *Belize* judgment) in *Geys v Société Générale* . . . [2013] 1 AC 523, para 55 (paraphrased by Lord Neuberger PSC, at para 15), where she referred to:

> those terms which are implied into a particular contract because, on its proper construction, the parties must have intended to include them: see *Attorney General of Belize v Belize Telecom Ltd* [2009] 1 WLR 1988. Such terms are only implied where it is necessary to give business efficacy to the particular contract in question.

64 The claimants refer also to the treatment of the *Belize* judgment in other common law countries, including Canada, Australia, New Zealand and Hong Kong. None of these citations raises any doubt as to the authority of the *Belize* judgment, nor any reason to question Lord Clarke MR's interpretation of it. The one exception appears to be the Singapore Court of Appeal, in which (as Lord Neuberger PSC points out: para 24) the judgment has been subject to detailed and critical analysis in *Foo Jong Peng v Phua Kiah Mai* [2012] 4 SLR 1267 (followed in *Sembcorp Marine Ltd v PPL Holdings Pte Ltd* [2013] SGCA 43). Their analysis draws, inter alia, on criticisms made by Paul S Davies, 'Recent Developments in the Law of Implied Terms' [2010] LMCLQ 140. I note that there is no criticism in that article of Lord Clarke MR's judgment as such. Rather it is cited as a supposed example of the less than 'wholly enthusiastic' reception which the *Belize* judgment is thought to have received in later cases.

65 That and other academic articles, as well as the judgment of the Singapore Court of Appeal, have themselves been subject to critical examination in a recent article by Professor Richard Hooley, 'Implied Terms after *Belize Telecom*' [2014] CLJ 315, in which he welcomes, at p 347, the 'doctrinal coherence to interpretation and implication' brought by the *Belize* judgment. Other academic views, before and since, are cited by Lord Neuberger PSC: para 24.

66 I see no purpose in reviewing the respective academic contributions in any detail, given the weight of judicial authority for the proposition (with which I understand we all agree) that the judgment is not to be read as involving any relaxation of the traditional, highly restrictive approach to implication of terms. Once that point is established, then I am not convinced with respect that the other points made by the Singapore court are sufficient to justify undermining the authority of the Board's reasoning . . .

[Lord Carnwath then discussed the position of the Singapore Court of Appeal accepting the relevance of the test of business efficacy and the officious bystander test. He considered that in relation to that judgment:]

67 . . . [T]he key points come down to three: (i) although the implication of terms is one aspect of 'the concept of interpretation', it should be treated as 'separate and distinct from the more general process of interpretation'; (ii) the court is concerned not with 'what it thinks ought to be the contractual relationship between the contracting parties', but rather with their 'presumed intention' as ascertained through 'objective evidence'; (iii) the central place of the 'business efficacy' and 'officious bystander' tests should be affirmed as 'an integral as well as indispensable part' of the law of Singapore.

68 The first point is an interesting debating point, but to my mind of little practical significance. It is not a point addressed by the parties before us—understandably, if they regarded it (as I would) as settled, if not by the *Belize* judgment itself, then by the authorities relied on by Lord Hoffmann (noted by Lord Neuberger PSC at para 25). Lord Neuberger PSC (para 28) prefers a sequential approach: first interpretation, then implication. However, as he accepts (para 26) both processes are parts of the exercise of 'determining the scope and meaning of the contract.'

69 On this point also I see no reason to depart from what was said in the *Belize* case. While I accept that more stringent rules apply to the process of implication, it can be a useful discipline to remind oneself that the object remains to discover what the parties have agreed or (in Baroness Hale JSC's words in the *Geys* case [2013] 1 AC 523, para 55) 'must have intended' to agree. In that respect it remains, and must be justified as, a process internal to the relationship between the parties, rather than one imposed from outside by statute or the common law (see the distinction noted by Lord Neuberger PSC: para 15).

70 Nor do I agree that support for such a division can be found in the judgments referred to by Lord Neuberger PSC: that is, the judgments of Bingham MR in the *Philips* case [1995] EMLR 472, and of this court in the *Aberdeen City Council* case 2012 SLT 205. The passage from the former is useful as emphasising the narrow constraints on implication. But I do not read Bingham MR as treating it as a notionally separate exercise from that of interpretation. (Nor did Lord Clarke MR when quoting the same passage in the *Mediterranean Salvage* case [2010] 1 All ER (Comm) 1: see above.) The contrast rather is between two aspects of the court's task in respect of 'contractual interpretation': the 'usual role' involving the resolution of ambiguities in the language used by the parties, and the 'extraordinary power' involving interpolation of terms that they have not used.

71 In the same way the passages cited from the *Aberdeen City Council* case do not appear to support a sharp distinction between interpretation and implication, still less for the necessity of a sequential approach. No one thought it necessary to refer to the *Belize* case [2009] 1 WLR 1988. Lord Clarke MR preferred implication, but acknowledged that the two processes achieved the same result. There is no indication that he had changed his view since the *Mediterranean Salvage* case. He seems to have treated them as two sides of the same coin. Lord Hope of Craighead DPSC who gave the lead speech (which also had majority support) clearly saw them as part of a single exercise: the implied term was the 'product' of interpretation. The case seems if anything to illustrate an 'iterative', rather than sequential, process: see Lord Grabiner QC, 'The Iterative Process of Contractual Interpretation' (2012) 128 LQR 41. The results of different interpretative techniques were considered and compared, in the light of the language used and its business context, to achieve a result which best represented the assumed intentions of the parties.

72 On the second point, in so far as there is a difference from the Singapore court, I prefer the approach of Lord Neuberger PSC which seems to me entirely consistent with the *Belize* case. As he says (para 21), one is concerned not with 'the hypothetical answer of the actual parties', but with that of 'notional reasonable people in the position of the parties at the time at which they were contracting', or in other words of Lord Hoffmann's 'reasonable addressee': the *Belize* case, para 18.

73 On the third point, there is no doubt as to the continuing significance of the traditional tests, as summarised by Lord Simon. If however the Singapore court intended thereby to prescribe a more rigid application of those tests, whether individually or cumulatively, I prefer the approach of the Board in the *Belize* case, para 27:

> The Board considers that this list is best regarded, not as [a] series of independent tests which must each be surmounted, but rather as a collection of different ways in which judges have tried to express the central idea that the proposed implied term must spell out what the contract actually means, or in which they have explained why they did not think that it did so.

This passage is also cited, albeit with only qualified approval, by Lord Neuberger PSC: para 21.

74 In conclusion, while I accept that Lord Hoffmann's judgment has stimulated more than usual academic controversy, I would not myself regard that as a sufficient reason to question its continuing authority. On the contrary, properly understood, I regard it as a valuable and illuminating synthesis of the factors which should guide the court. Applying that approach to the present case leaves me in no doubt that the appeal should be dismissed.

LORD CLARKE OF STONE-CUM-EBONY JSC: 75 I agree that the appeal should be dismissed for the reasons given by Lord Neuberger of Abbotsbury PSC. I only add a few words of my own because of the debate between Lord Neuberger PSC and Lord Carnwath JSC on Lord Hoffmann's view on the relationship between the approach to construction and the approach to the implication of a term which he expressed on behalf of the Judicial Committee of the Privy Council in *Attorney General of Belize v Belize Telecom Ltd* [2009] 1 WLR 1988. I do so in part in order to clarify what I said in the cases referred to by Lord Carnwath JSC, especially *Mediterranean Salvage and Towage Ltd v Seamar Trading and Commerce Inc (The Reborn)* [2009] EWCA Civ 531, [2010] 1 All ER (Comm) 1 and *Aberdeen City Council v Stewart Milne Group Ltd* 2012 SLT 205.

76 As Lord Carnwath JSC says, at para 62, I did not doubt Lord Hoffmann's observation that 'the implication of a term is an exercise in the construction of the contract as a whole'. I recognise, however, in the light of Lord Neuberger PSC's judgment, especially, at paras 22–31, that Lord Hoffmann's view involves giving a wide meaning to 'construction' because, as Lord Neuberger PSC says, at para 27, when one is implying a word or phrase, one is not construing words in the contract because the words to be implied are ex hypothesi and not there to be construed. However, like Lord Neuberger PSC (at para 26) I accept that both (i) construing the words which the parties have used in their contract and (ii) implying terms into the contract, involve determining the scope and meaning of the contract. On that basis it can properly be said that both processes are part of construction of the contract in a broad sense.

77 I agree with Lord Neuberger PSC and Lord Carnwath JSC that the critical point is that in the *Belize* case [2009] 1 WLR 1988 the Judicial Committee was not watering down the traditional test of necessity. I adhere to the view I expressed at para 15 of my judgment in the *Mediterranean Salvage and Towage case* [2010] 1 All ER (Comm) 1 (which is quoted by Lord Carnwath JSC, at para 62) that in the *Belize* case, although Lord Hoffmann emphasised that the process of implication was part of the process of construction of the contract, he was not resiling from the often stated proposition that it must be necessary to imply the term and that it is not sufficient that it would be reasonable to do so. Another way of putting the test of necessity is to ask whether it is necessary to do so in order to make the contract work: see the detailed discussion by Lord Wilberforce in *Liverpool City Council v Irwin* [1977] AC 239, 253–254.

NOTE It follows from the majority view at least that we are back to the position before the *Belize* case, involving two separate steps. As a first step the courts construe the express terms of the contract to identify party intentions through interpretation of the words they have used (see the discussion at 5.5 for these principles). This is very different from the separate exercise of attempting to fill the gaps in those words by implication of terms, albeit both are about 'determining the scope and meaning of the contract'. Yet, the Supreme Court in *Wells v Devani* [2019] UKSC 4, [2019] 2 WLR 617 was criticized for blurring that distinction (Davies (2019) 78(2) CLJ 267) when it held, unanimously, that in principle, a term can be implied so as to render an otherwise invalid contract valid. Lord Kitchin stated (at [33]) 'it is possible to imply something that is so obvious that it goes without saying into anything, including something the law regards as no more than an offer'. It must be stressed that on the facts there was no need to imply such a term. Yet, Lord Kitchin was clear that had it been necessary, he would have done so. The impact of the case is as yet unclear, but it is nevertheless approved, in part, by academics.

The Moorcock
(1889) 14 PD 64 (CA)

The defendants had contracted to allow the claimants to load and unload at the defendants' wharf on the River Thames. It was known to both parties that, at low tide, any vessel at the wharf would be grounded, but there was no express provision governing this in the contract. The claimants' ship moored alongside the wharf, settled on the ground, and was damaged because of the condition of the riverbed. The defendants had taken no steps to ascertain the condition of the riverbed. The claimants brought an action for damages in respect of the damage done to the ship.

Held: The contract contained an implied a term whereby the defendants warranted that they had taken reasonable care to see that the berth was safe and they were in breach of this term.

BOWEN LJ: The question which arises here is whether when a contract is made to let the use of this jetty to a ship which can only use it, as is known by both parties, by taking the ground, there is any implied warranty on the part of the owners of the jetty, and if so, what is the extent of the warranty. Now, an implied warranty, or, as it is called, a covenant in law, as distinguished from an express contract or express warranty, really is in all cases founded on the presumed intention of the parties, and upon reason. The implication which the law draws from what must obviously have been the intention of the parties, the law draws with the object of giving efficacy to the transaction and preventing such a failure of consideration as cannot have been within the contemplation of either side; and I believe if one were to take all the cases, and they are many, of implied warranties or covenants in law, it will be found that in all of them the law is raising an implication from the presumed intention of the parties with the object of giving to the transaction such efficacy as both parties must have intended that at all events it should have. In business transactions such as this, what the law desires to effect by the implication is to give such business efficacy to the transaction as must have been intended at all events by both parties who are business men; not to impose on one side all the perils of the transaction, or to emancipate one side from all the chances of failure, but to make each party promise in law as much, at all events, as it must have been in the contemplation of both parties that he should be responsible for in respect of those perils or chances.

Now what did each party in a case like this know? For if we are examining into their presumed intention we must examine into their minds as to what the transaction was. Both parties knew that this jetty was let out for hire, and knew that it could only be used under the contract by the ship taking the ground. They must have known that it was by grounding that she used the jetty; in fact, except so far as the transport to the jetty of the cargo in the ship was concerned, they must have known, both of them, that unless the ground was safe the ship would be simply buying an opportunity of danger, and that all consideration would fail unless some care had been taken to see that the ground was safe. In fact the business of the jetty could not be carried on except upon such a basis. The parties also knew that with regard to the safety of the ground outside the jetty the shipowner could know nothing at all, and the jetty owner might with reasonable care know everything. The owners of the jetty, or their servants, were there at high and low tide, and with little trouble they could satisfy themselves, in case of doubt, as to whether the berth was reasonably safe. The ship's owner, on the other hand, had not the means of verifying the state of the jetty, because the berth itself opposite the jetty might be occupied by another ship at any moment.

Now the question is how much of the peril of the safety of this berth is it necessary to assume that the shipowner and the jetty owner intended respectively to bear—in order that such a minimum of efficacy should be secured for the transaction, as both parties must have intended it to bear? . . . The berth outside the jetty was not under the actual control of the jetty owners. It is in the bed of the river, and it may be said that those who owned the jetty had no duty cast upon them by statute or common law to repair the bed of the river, and that they had no power to interfere with the bed of the river unless under the licence of the Conservators . . .

[I]t may well be said that the law will not imply that the persons who have not the control of the place have taken reasonable care to make it good, but it does not follow that they are relieved from all responsibility. They are on the spot. They must know that the jetty cannot be used unless reasonable care is taken, if not to make it safe, at all events to see whether it is safe. No one can tell whether reasonable safety has been secured except themselves, and I think if they let out their jetty for use they at all events imply that they have taken reasonable care to see whether the berth, which is the essential part of the use of the jetty, is safe, and if it is not safe, and if they have not taken such reasonable care, it is their duty to warn persons with whom they have dealings that they have not done so . . .

NOTES

1. The critical distinction between the application of the business efficacy test in *The Moorcock* and that applying in the light of the Supreme Court in *Marks & Spencer* is that the emphasis is not on giving effect to the presumed intentions of the parties on the basis of identifying the *actual* intentions of the parties. This was explained by Lord Neuberger in his first point in *Marks & Spencer* at [21]: 'If one approaches the question by reference to what the parties would have agreed, one is not strictly concerned with the hypothetical answer of the actual parties, but with that of notional reasonable people in the position of the parties at the time at which they were contracting.'

2. The references to 'reasonableness' also need to be understood in the light of the case law since *The Moorcock* and the fact that the Supreme Court in *Marks & Spencer* emphatically rejected this as the test for terms implied in fact. Such an implied term in fact needs to be reasonable but the test for implication is one of necessity; unless a term is a necessary term to imply, its reasonableness will be irrelevant. This is also explained in Lord Neuberger's second and third points at [21] in *Marks & Spencer*. This strict

approach can be seen in two Court of Appeal cases involving loans. In *Al Jaber v Al Ibrahim* [2018] EWCA Civ 1690, [2018] WLR(D) 46, the Court of Appeal held that in relation to the repayment of the loan, implying a term to include interest on the loan was not necessary or obvious (at [35]). In *Bou-Simon v BGC Brokers LP* [2018] EWCA Civ 1525, the Court of Appeal refused to imply a term that a loan, given in the context of an employment contract, be repaid if the employee failed to serve the full terms of the initial period. The fact that a term will be implied only if necessary was also confirmed by the Supreme Court in *Wells v Devani* [2019] UKSC 4 although on the facts, there was no need to imply a term.

3. In *Marks & Spencer* it was accepted 'that business necessity and obviousness can be alternatives in the sense that only one of them needs to be satisfied'. This is Lord Neuberger's fourth point in *Marks & Spencer* at [21], although he also considered that in most factual situations both tests would be satisfied. Some years ago, Phang ([1998] JBL 1) had argued that the officious bystander test was merely a general way of expressing the business efficacy test.

For terms to be implied in fact using the 'officious bystander' test, both parties must have considered the term to be strictly necessary.

Shell UK Ltd v Lostock Garage Ltd
[1976] 1 WLR 1187 (CA)

Lostock operated a 'tied' garage (it could sell only petrol supplied by Shell). In December 1975, a petrol price 'war' began, and in Lostock's neighbourhood two garages which were not tied to Shell reduced their petrol price. As a result, Shell introduced a support scheme, whereby it subsidized two Shell garages in that neighbourhood so that they could compete. Lostock's garage was excluded from the support scheme and was forced to trade at a loss. Lostock obtained petrol from another supplier. Shell brought an action seeking damages for breach of contract and an injunction against Lostock. Lostock argued, inter alia, that the agreement was subject to an implied obligation placed upon Shell not to discriminate abnormally against Lostock in favour of competing and neighbouring garages so as to render Lostock's petrol uneconomic, and that Shell were in breach of that term by operating the support scheme and excluding Lostock from it.

Held (Bridge LJ dissenting): the court refused to imply the term on the basis that (i) it was not necessary to give efficacy to the agreement and (ii) that such a term could not be formulated with sufficient precision. However, they held that no injunction could be issued to restrain a breach of the tie provision while the support scheme was in place.

LORD DENNING MR: . . . Into which of the two categories does the present case come? I am tempted to say that a solus agreement between supplier and buyer is of such common occurence [*sic*] nowadays that it could be put into the first category: so that the law could imply a term based on general considerations. But I do not think this would be found acceptable. Nor do I think the case can be brought within the second category. If the Shell company had been asked at the beginning: 'Will you agree not to discriminate abnormally against the buyer?' I think they would have declined. It might be a reasonable term, but it is not a necessary term. Nor can it be formulated with sufficient precision . . . In the circumstances, I do not think any term can be implied.

In *Equitable Life Assurance Society v Hyman*, the House of Lords accepted the implication of a term in fact based on a test of strict necessity.

Equitable Life Assurance Society v Hyman
[2002] 1 AC 408 (HL)

The Society had been issuing retirement 'with-profits' policies with a guaranteed annuity rate (GAR). However, the Society found this commitment to be too expensive to honour when the general annuity rate fell below this guaranteed rate. Therefore, in the mid-1990s, the Society adopted a policy of declaring a lower final bonus on such policies, citing a provision in its articles of association giving the directors an absolute discretion as to the amount of any bonus and stating that the directors' decision on the award of bonuses was final and conclusive. This action of declaring a lower final bonus was held to be lawful at first instance, but reversed by the Court of Appeal.

Held (on appeal to the House of Lords, affirming the Court of Appeal decision): It was necessary to imply a term to the effect that the directors were not to adopt a policy depriving the GAR policies of the value inherent in their original purpose. The whole purpose of such a policy had been to protect holders of such policies in the event of a fall in market rates by ensuring that they would be better off. Therefore, there was a reasonable expectation that the directors would not exercise any discretion so as to conflict with this. It was necessary to imply a term to give effect to these expectations.

LORD STEYN: If properly construed the powers of the directors under article 65 are wide enough to override the terms of the guaranteed annuity rates, the GAR policyholders can have no valid complaint. On the other hand, if article 65 expressly or impliedly contains a prohibition on directors exercising their discretion to override or undermine guaranteed annuity rates, the Society's practice is invalid. Beyond that there can be no liability on the Society . . . Everything hinges on the meaning of article 65.

The meaning of article 65

It is necessary to distinguish between the processes of interpretation and implication. The purpose of interpretation is to assign to the language of the text the most appropriate meaning which the words can legitimately bear. The language of article 65(1) contains no relevant express restriction on the powers of the directors. It is impossible to assign to the language of article 65(1) by construction a restriction precluding the directors from overriding GARs. To this extent I would uphold the submissions made on behalf of the Society. The critical question is whether a relevant restriction may be implied into article 65(1). It is certainly not a case in which a term can be implied by law in the sense of incidents impliedly annexed to particular forms of contracts. Such standardised implied terms operate as general default rules: see *Scally v Southern Health and Social Services Board* [1992] 1 AC 294. If a term is to be implied, it could only be a term implied from the language of article 65 read in its particular commercial setting. Such implied terms operate as ad hoc gap fillers. In *Luxor (Eastbourne) Ltd v Cooper* [1941] AC 108, 137 Lord Wright explained this distinction as follows:

> The expression 'implied term' is used in different senses. Sometimes it denotes some term which does not depend on the actual intention of the parties but on a rule of law, such as the terms, warranties or conditions which, if not expressly excluded, the law imports, as for instance under the Sale of Goods Act and the Marine Insurance Act . . . But a case like the present is different because what it is sought to imply is based on an intention imputed to the parties from their actual circumstances.

It is only an individualised term of the second kind which can arguably arise in the present case. Such a term may be imputed to parties: it is not critically dependent on proof of an actual intention of the parties. The process 'is one of construction of the agreement as a whole in its commercial setting': *Banque Bruxelles Lambert SA v Eagle Star Insurance Co Ltd* [1997] AC 191, 212e, per Lord Hoffmann. This principle is sparingly and cautiously used and may never be employed to imply a term in conflict with the express terms of the text. The legal test for the implication of such a term is a standard of strict necessity. This is how I must approach the question whether a term is to be implied into article 65(1) which precludes the directors from adopting a principle which has the effect of overriding or undermining the GARs.

The inquiry is entirely constructional in nature: proceeding from the express terms of article 65, viewed against its objective setting, the question is whether the implication is strictly necessary. My Lords, as counsel for the GAR policyholders observed, final bonuses are not bounty. They are a significant part of the consideration for the premiums paid. And the directors' discretions as to the amount and distribution of bonuses are conferred for the benefit of policyholders. In this context the self-evident commercial object of the inclusion of guaranteed rates in the policy is to protect the policyholder against a fall in market annuity rates by ensuring that if the fall occurs he will be better off than he would have been with market rates. The choice is given to the GAR policyholder and not to the Society. It cannot be seriously doubted that the provision for guaranteed annuity rates was a good selling point in the marketing by the Society of the sGAR policies. It is also obvious that it would have been a significant attraction for purchasers of GAR policies. The Society points out that no special charge was made for the inclusion in the policy of GAR provisions. So be it. This factor does not alter the reasonable expectations of the parties. The supposition of the parties must be presumed to have been that the directors would not exercise their discretion in conflict with contractual rights. These are the circumstances in which the directors of the Society resolved upon a differential policy which was designed to deprive the relevant guarantees of any substantial value. In my judgment an implication precluding the use of the directors' discretion in this way is strictly necessary. The implication is essential to give effect to the reasonable expectations of the parties. The stringent test applicable to the implication of terms is satisfied.

In substantial agreement with Lord Woolf MR, I would hold that the directors were not entitled to adopt a principle of making the final bonuses of GAR policyholders dependent on how they exercised their rights under the policy. In adopting the principle of a differential policy in respect of GAR policyholders the directors acted in breach of article 65(1).

? QUESTION

Would both parties have considered such a term to be essential at the time of making the contract? It is at least arguable that they would have done so. The Society had sold the GAR policies on the basis of this protective feature.

5.4.1.2.2 *The implied 'Braganza' duty to exercise a discretion rationally and in good faith*

In *Braganza v BP Shipping Ltd and another* [2015] UKSC 17, [2015] 1 WLR 1661, the claimant's husband, an engineer for the defendant, disappeared whilst working on a tanker. A term of his employment contract (clause 7.6.3) allowed BP to review the circumstances of his death to decide whether death duties were due. After careful consideration, BP concluded that the most likely explanation for his disappearance was suicide, triggering the employer's right not to pay death in service benefits under clause 7.6.3 which stated that 'compensation for death . . . shall not be payable, if, in the opinion of the company or its insurers, the death . . . resulted from among other things, the officer's wilful act, default or misconduct whether at sea or ashore'.

Lady Hale, for the majority (Lord Neuberger dissenting), started by highlighting the rule that when a party is given the power to exercise a discretion, such a power, so as not to be abused is therefore subject to the control of the courts:

18. Contractual terms in which one party to the contract is given the power to exercise a discretion, or to form an opinion as to relevant facts, are extremely common. It is not for the courts to rewrite the parties' bargain for them, still less to substitute themselves for the contractually agreed decision-maker. Nevertheless, the party who is charged with making decisions which affect the rights of both parties to the contract has a clear conflict of interest. That conflict is heightened where there is a significant imbalance of power between the contracting parties as there often will be in an employment contract. The courts have therefore sought to ensure that such contractual powers are not abused. They have done so by implying a term as to the manner in which such powers may be exercised, a term which may vary according to the terms of the contract and the context in which the decision-making power is given.

[Her Ladyship then asked whether the review by the courts in the private sphere should be the same as that of the process of judicial review (at [19]), which her Ladyship summarized as follows:]

24 . . . . the test of the reasonableness of an administrative decision which was adopted by Lord Greene MR in *Associated Provincial Picture Houses Ltd v Wednesbury Corpn* [1948] 1 KB 223, 233–234. His test has two limbs:

'The court is entitled to investigate the action of the local authority with a view to seeing whether they have taken into account matters which they ought not to take into account, or conversely, have refused to take into account or neglected to take into account matters which they ought to take into account. Once that question is answered in favour of the local authority, it may still be possible to say that, although the local authority have kept within the four corners of the matters which they ought to consider, they have nevertheless come to a conclusion so unreasonable that no reasonable authority could ever have come to it.'

The first limb focuses on the decision-making process—whether the right matters have been taken into account in reaching the decision. The second focuses on its outcome—whether, even though the right things have been taken into account, the result is so outrageous that no reasonable decision-maker could have reached it. The latter is often used as a shorthand for the Wednesbury principle, but without necessarily excluding the former.

[Her Ladyship held that the control is the same:]

25. The parties in this case disagree as to whether the term to be implied into this contract includes both limbs. Mrs Braganza argues that the employer must 'keep within the four corners of the matters which they ought to consider', while the employer argues that its decision may only be impugned if it is a decision which no reasonable employer could have reached.

26. Mrs Braganza can pray in aid the approach of Mocatta J in *The Vainqueur José*. He held that the common law principles applicable to the exercise of a contractual discretion include fairness, reasonableness, bona fides and absence of misdirection in law (p 574). He later quoted (p 575), without reservation, Lord Greene's summary of the public law concept of reasonableness. There is nothing on Mocatta J's judgment to suggest that only the second of those elements is applicable to the exercise of a contractual discretion. He did (at 574) contrast the contractual principles with the principles applicable to the exercise of a statutory discretion by Ministers of the Crown, but on the basis that, in addition, the Minister's decision had to be consistent with the objects and other provisions of the statute in question, citing *Laker Airways Ltd v Department of Trade* [1977] QB 643.

27. On that point, on the other hand, in *Hayes v Willoughby*, just before the passage quoted in para 23 above, Lord Sumption stated that rationality 'has ... in recent years played an increasingly significant role in the law relating to contractual discretions, where the law's object is also to limit the decision-maker to some relevant contractual purpose': [2013] 1 WLR 935, para 14. This is consistent with his earlier observations in *British Telecommunications Plc v Telefónica O2 UK Ltd* [2014] UKSC 42, [2014] Bus LR 765, at para 37:

> 'As a general rule, the scope of a contractual discretion will depend on the nature of the discretion and the construction of the language conferring it. But it is well established that in the absence of very clear language to the contrary, a contractual discretion must be exercised in good faith and not arbitrarily or capriciously [citing *Abu Dhabi*, Gan, and *Paragon*, above]. This will normally mean that it must be exercised consistently with its contractual purpose [citing *Ludgate Insurance*, above and *Equitable Life Assurance Society v Hyman* [2002] 1 AC 408, 459 (Lord Steyn), 461 (Lord Cooke of Thorndon)].'

28. There are signs, therefore, that the contractual implied term is drawing closer and closer to the principles applicable in judicial review. The contractual cases do not in terms discuss whether both limbs of the *Wednesbury* test apply. However, in *Gan Insurance*, where the issue was the limits, if any, to the reinsurers' power to withhold approval to the insured's agreement to settle a claim, Mance LJ first commented that 'what was proscribed was unreasonableness in the sense of conduct or a decision to which no reasonable person having the relevant discretion could have subscribed' (para 64); but he concluded that 'any withholding of approval by reinsurers should take place in good faith after consideration of and on the basis of the facts giving rise to the particular claim and not with reference to considerations wholly extraneous to the subject matter of the particular reinsurance ....' (para 67).

29. If it is part of a rational decision-making process to exclude extraneous considerations, it is in my view also part of a rational decision-making process to take into account those considerations which are obviously relevant to the decision in question. It is of the essence of '*Wednesbury* reasonableness' (or '*GCHQ* rationality') review to consider the rationality of the decision-making process rather than to concentrate upon the outcome. Concentrating on the outcome runs the risk that the court will substitute its own decision for that of the primary decision-maker.

30. It is clear, however, that unless the court can imply a term that the outcome be objectively reasonable—for example, a reasonable price or a reasonable term—the court will only imply a term that the decision-making process be lawful and rational in the public law sense, that the decision is made rationally (as well as in good faith) and consistently with its contractual purpose. For my part, I would include both limbs of the *Wednesbury* formulation in the rationality test. Indeed, I understand Lord Neuberger (at para 103 of his judgment) and I to be agreed as to the nature of the test.

31. But whatever term may be implied will depend upon the terms and the context of the particular contract involved. I would add to that Mocatta J's observation in *The Vainqueur José*, that 'it would be a mistake to expect [of a lay body] the same expert, professional and almost microscopic investigation of the problems, both factual and legal, that is demanded of a suit in a court of law' (577). Nor would 'some slight misdirection' matter, at least if it were clear that, had the legal position been properly appreciated, the decision would have been the same. It may very well be that the same high standards of decision-making ought not to be expected of most contractual decision-makers as are expected of the modern state.

32. However, it is unnecessary to reach a final conclusion on the precise extent to which an implied contractual term may differ from the principles applicable to judicial review of administrative action. Given that the question may arise in so many different contractual contexts, it may well be that no precise answer can be given. The particular context of this case is an employment contract, which, as Lord Hodge explains, is of a different character from an ordinary commercial contract. Any decision-making function entrusted to the employer has to be exercised in accordance with the implied obligation of trust and confidence. This must be borne in mind in considering how the contractual decision-maker should approach the question of whether a person has committed suicide.

33. Teare J directed himself, in relation to his own decision as to the cause of Mr Braganza's disappearance, that 'before a finding of suicide is made there must be evidence of sufficient cogency commensurate with or proportionate to the seriousness of the finding' (para 46), citing the observation of Watkins LJ in *R v West London Coroner, Ex p Gray* [1988] QB 467, 477–478, that suicide is 'still a drastic action which often leaves in its wake serious social, economic and other consequences'. He also directed himself, following the House of Lords' decision in *The Popi M* [1985] 1 WLR 948, 955–956, that, where two improbable causes are suggested, he was not bound to make a finding one way or another. I agree with Lord Neuberger, at para 100 of his judgment, that it is also perfectly proper for the employer to conclude that he or she is unable to form an opinion as to the cause of death. But the question is how he or she should go about making a positive finding of suicide.

. . .

36. However, Longmore LJ also took the view that the employer did not have to approach the matter in this way. I respectfully disagree. The employer is entrusted with making a decision which has serious consequences for the family of a deceased employee. It deprives them of what would otherwise be a contractual right. There is no reason why the employer should not approach that decision in the same way that any other decision-maker should do. On the contrary, in view of the special nature of the employment relationship, there is every reason why they should do so. Employers can reasonably be expected to inform themselves of the principles which are relevant to the decisions which they have to make. Employment law is complicated and demanding in many legal systems, but employers are expected to know it. They can also reasonably be expected to know how they should approach making the important decisions which they are required or empowered to make under the terms of the employment contract. In my view, a decision that an employee has committed suicide is not a rational or reasonable decision, in the terms discussed above, unless the employer has had it clearly in mind that suicide is such an improbability that cogent evidence is required to form the positive opinion that it has taken place.

37. The employer now accepts that it is for him to show that the decision which it reached was a reasonable decision in the sense which is required by the contract.

[Applying it to the facts, her Ladyship allowed the appeal on the ground that:]

42 . . . . the investigation team's report and conclusion could not be regarded as sufficiently cogent evidence to justify Mr Sullivan, and hence BP, in forming the positive opinion that he had committed suicide. No-one suggests that his decision was "arbitrary, capricious or perverse", but in my view it was unreasonable in the *Wednesbury* sense, having been formed without taking relevant matters into account.

NOTE The decision is clearly important since it gives considerable power to the court to use, in the private sphere of contracts, 'public-law inspired' powers. Yet, aside the fact that the decision appears to have gone almost unnoticed for years, its impact is further limited by the fact that it only applies to a contractual discretion and not an 'absolute right' as held in *Mid Essex Hospital Services NHS Trust v Compass Group UK and Ireland Ltd (t/a Medirest)* [2013] EWCA Civ 200. A right to terminate a contract is an absolute right (*TAQA Bratani Ltd and others v Rockrose* [2020] EWHC 58 (Comm)). This is however not the end of the discission. As highlighted by *Pacific Airways Ltd v Lufthansa Technik AG* [2020] EWHC 1789 (Ch), this area is 'in a state of development'.

5.4.1.2.3 *Alleged implied term of good faith in performance*

In *Yam Seng Pte Ltd v International Trade Corporation Ltd* [2013] EWHC 111 (QB), [2013] 1 CLC 662, [2013] 1 All ER (Comm) 1321, Leggatt J considered, *obiter*, that a contract for a licence to distribute and supply branded goods contained an implied term of good faith in its performance. This implied term manifested itself so as to impose an obligation whereby one party was not *knowingly* to provide false information on which the other party was likely to rely. However, the judge also went further in appearing to advocate a general implied term in fact to perform in good faith in all commercial contracts on the basis of giving effect to the reasonable expectations of the parties, although accepting that the content of the duty would always depend on its context.

LEGGATT J: 131 Under English law a duty of good faith is implied by law as an incident of certain categories of contract, for example contracts of employment and contracts between partners or others whose relationship is characterised as a fiduciary one. I doubt that English law has reached the stage, however, where it is ready to recognise a requirement of good faith as a duty implied by law, even as a default rule, into all commercial contracts. Nevertheless, there seems to me to be no difficulty, following the established methodology of English law for the implication of terms in fact, in implying such a duty in any ordinary commercial contract based on the presumed intention of the parties.

132 Traditionally, the two principal criteria used to identify terms implied in fact are that the term is so obvious that it goes without saying and that the term is necessary to give business efficacy to the contract. More recently, in *Attorney General of Belize v Belize Telecom Ltd* [2009] 1 WLR 1988 at 1993–5, the process of implication has been analysed as an exercise in the construction of the contract as a whole . . .

133 The modern case law on the construction of contracts has emphasised that contracts, like all human communications, are made against a background of unstated shared understandings which inform their meaning. The breadth of the relevant background and the fact that it has no conceptual limits have also been stressed, particularly in the famous speech of Lord Hoffmann in *Investors Compensation Scheme Ltd v West Bromwich Building Society* [1997] CLC 1243 at pp. 1257–8; [1998] 1 WLR 896 at pp. 912–3, as further explained in *BCCI v Ali* [2002] 1 AC 251 at p. 269.

134 Importantly for present purposes, the relevant background against which contracts are made includes not only matters of fact known to the parties but also shared values and norms of behaviour. Some of these are norms that command general social acceptance; others may be specific to a particular trade or commercial activity; others may be more specific still, arising from features of the particular

contractual relationship. Many such norms are naturally taken for granted by the parties when making any contract without being spelt out in the document recording their agreement.

[The judge referred to expectations of honesty and trust in commercial agreements and continued:]

137 As a matter of construction, it is hard to envisage any contract which would not reasonably be understood as requiring honesty in its performance. The same conclusion is reached if the traditional tests for the implication of a term are used. In particular the requirement that parties will behave honestly is so obvious that it goes without saying. Such a requirement is also necessary to give business efficacy to commercial transactions.

138 In addition to honesty, there are other standards of commercial dealing which are so generally accepted that the contracting parties would reasonably be understood to take them as read without explicitly stating them in their contractual document. A key aspect of good faith, as I see it, is the observance of such standards. Put the other way round, not all bad faith conduct would necessarily be described as dishonest. Other epithets which might be used to describe such conduct include 'improper', 'commercially unacceptable' or 'unconscionable'.

139 Another aspect of good faith which overlaps with the first is what may be described as fidelity to the parties' bargain. The central idea here is that contracts can never be complete in the sense of expressly providing for every event that may happen. To apply a contract to circumstances not specifically provided for, the language must accordingly be given a reasonable construction which promotes the values and purposes expressed or implicit in the contract . . .

141 What good faith requires is sensitive to context. That includes the core value of honesty . . .

144 Although its requirements are sensitive to context, the test of good faith is objective in the sense that it depends not on either party's perception of whether particular conduct is improper but on whether in the particular context the conduct would be regarded as commercially unacceptable by reasonable and honest people . . . This follows from the fact that the content of the duty of good faith is established by a process of construction which in English law is based on an objective principle. The court is concerned not with the subjective intentions of the parties but with their presumed intention, which is ascertained by attributing to them the purposes and values which reasonable people in their situation would have had.

145 Understood in the way I have described, there is in my view nothing novel or foreign to English law in recognising an implied duty of good faith in the performance of contracts.

NOTES

1. This approach must now be interpreted in the light of a much tighter general approach to implication of terms and to construction by the Supreme Court in *Marks & Spencer* and in *Arnold v Britton* [2015] UKSC 36, [2015] AC 1619 (*page 240*, 5.5.3). In particular, the Supreme Court in *Marks & Spencer* (e.g. Lord Neuberger at [21]) was clear that a court has no power to introduce a term by implication merely to make the contract fairer where the contract was detailed and negotiated at arm's length by commercial parties.

2. Subsequent case law has also rejected any such implied duty of good faith as a matter of routine: see *Mid Essex Hospital Services NHS Trust v Compass Group UK and Ireland Ltd (t/a Medirest)* [2013] EWCA Civ 200, [2013] BLR 265; *TSG Building Services plc v South Anglia Housing Ltd* [2013] EWHC 1151 (TCC); *Hamsard 3147 Ltd (t/a Mini Mode Childrenswear) v Boots UK Ltd* [2013] EWHC 3251 (Pat); and *Greenclose Ltd*

v National Westminster Bank plc [2014] EWHC 1156 (Ch), [2014] 2 Lloyd's Rep 169, [2014] 1 CLC 562. In *Greenclose* Andrews J confirmed that *Yam Seng* had very restricted application:

150 So far as the 'good faith condition' is concerned, there is no general doctrine of good faith in English contract law and such a term is unlikely to arise by way of necessary implication in a contract between two sophisticated commercial parties negotiating at arms' length. Leggatt J's judgment in *Yam Seng Pte Ltd v International Trade Corp Ltd* [2011] EWHC 111 (QB); [2013] 1 CLC 662, on which Greenclose heavily relies, is not to be regarded as laying down any general principle applicable to all commercial contracts. As Leggatt J expressly recognized at [147] of that judgment, the implication of an obligation of good faith is heavily dependent on the context. Thus in some situations where a contracting party is given a discretion, the court will more readily imply an obligation that the discretion should not be exercised in bad faith or in an arbitrary or capricious manner, but the

context is vital. A discretion given to the board of directors of a company to award bonuses to its employees may be more readily susceptible to such implied restrictions on its exercise than a discretion given to a commercial party to act in its own commercial interests.

3. *Yam Seng* has been approved in some instances, such as in *Bristol Groundschool Ltd v Intelligent Data Capture Ltd* [2014] EWHC 2145 (Ch), where Richard Spearman QC (sitting as Deputy Judge of the Chancery Division) implied a general duty of good faith into a 'relational contract' which he described as according with the type described by Leggatt J in *Yam Seng*. Nevertheless, it is important not to overstate the significance of this decision because the judge appeared to consider that the Court of Appeal

in *Mid Essex* had not disapproved of *Yam Seng* and had not focused on the general issue of the implied duty of good faith outside the categories explicitly mentioned by Leggatt J as accepted instances for such implication (i.e. as terms implied in law, such as duties of good faith implied by law into contracts of employment). Furthermore, the Court of Appeal in *Mid Essex*, particularly in the judgment of Jackson LJ, appeared to state that outside of these accepted instances of terms implied in law, any duty of good faith would need to be included as an express term of the parties' agreement. For a discussion over the English approach to good faith, see *Poole's Textbook on Contract Law*, chapter 1.

5.4.1.2.4 *Implied good faith: a special case for relational contracts?*

From the above, it is undeniable that good faith has a restricted application. Yet, in more recent years, the courts appear to have heard the lament of Leggatt J (as he then was) in *Yam Seng* about the dichotomy between commercial contracts and fiduciary contracts as too simplistic and appear to be ready to imply such a notion in the emerging category of what is referred to in judgments as 'relational contracts'. We have mentioned earlier *Bristol Groundschool Ltd v Intelligent Data Capture Ltd* where Richard Spearman QC implied a general duty of good faith in the performance of a contract which he described as a 'relational contract'. In this case, the parties had agreed to collaborate to produce training manuals for pilots. Before the end of the joint venture which had badly deteriorated, the claimant downloaded the material which they used to sell as electronic training manuals. Although the downloading was not prohibited under the contract, the judge found that such behaviour, which he said would be characterized as 'unacceptable by reasonable and honest people' (at [196]) amounted to a breach of the implied duty of good faith. In *D&G Cars Ltd v Essex Police Authority* [2015] EWHC 226 (QB), D&G Cars contracted with the defendant to dispose of the defendant's vehicles. The contract was also defined as 'a relational contract par excellence'. Dove J implied a term of 'honesty and integrity' rather than an obligation of good faith in order 'to capture the requirements of fair dealing and transparency' (at [175]). By their conduct, D&G—who, against express instructions by the defendant to destroy a car had instead reconditioned it and used it in their own fleet—were found to be in breach of the implied term. Perhaps sensing the limitations of the lack of contours of this emerging notion of relational contracts (on this, Collins in Degeling, Edelman, and Goudkamp (eds.), *Contract in Commercial Law* (2016), 37–59) and why such relations are more deserving of an implied duty of good faith (Saintier [2017] JBL 441), Leggatt J returned to it in one of his last cases on the bench, *Al Nehayan v Ioannis Kent* [2018] EWHC 333. In this case, Leggatt J addresses some of the judicial concerns that requiring good faith from a party would automatically entail that party to subordinate its own interests to those of the other party:

167 It does not follow from the conclusion that he did not owe any fiduciary duties to Mr Kent that the Sheikh's entitlement to pursue his own self-interest was untrammelled. I have previously suggested in *Yam Seng Pte Ltd v International Trade Corp* [2013] EWHC 111 (QB), at para 142, that it is a mistake to draw a simple dichotomy between relationships which give rise to fiduciary duties and other contractual

relationships and to treat the latter as all alike. In particular, I drew attention to a category of contract in which the parties are committed to collaborating with each other, typically on a long term basis, in ways which respect the spirit and objectives of their venture but which they have not tried to specify, and which it may be impossible to specify, exhaustively in a written contract. Such 'relational' contracts involve trust and confidence but of a different kind from that involved in fiduciary relationships. The trust is not in the loyal subordination by one party of its own interests to those of another. It is trust that the other party will act with integrity and in a spirit of cooperation. The legitimate expectations which the law should protect in relationships of this kind are embodied in the normative standard of good faith.

Leggatt J also explained why, in this particular case, the relationship was such that it was more than a pure commercial agreement, even though it did give rise to fiduciary duties.

173 I have held that Sheikh Tahnoon did not agree to provide funding on an open-ended basis and did not owe any fiduciary duties to Mr Kent. *But I think it clear that the nature of their relationship was one in which they naturally and legitimately expected of each other greater candour and cooperation and greater regard for each other's interests than ordinary commercial parties dealing with each other at arm's length.* When Sheikh Tahnoon agreed to become an equal owner of the Aquis business with Mr Kent, the two men entered into a joint venture agreement which was intended to be a long-term collaboration, in which their interests were inter-linked and which they saw, commercially albeit not in law, as a partnership. Their collaboration was formed and conducted on the basis of a personal friendship and involved much greater mutual trust than is inherent in an ordinary contractual bargain between shareholders in a company. Although day to day management of the businesses was left to Mr Kent, strategic decisions which would involve further capital investment, such as whether to purchase a hotel or the decision to acquire the majority stake in YouTravel, were (of necessity) taken jointly and could only be reached by consensus between them. The pursuit of the venture therefore required a high degree of co-operation between the two participants. *They did not attempt to formalise the basis of their cooperation in any written contract but were content to deal with each other entirely informally on the basis of their mutual trust and confidence that they would each pursue their common project in good faith.* [Emphasis added.]

Leggatt J also reconciled his position in the light of more recent developments with implied terms:

174 In the circumstances the contract made between these parties seems to me to be a classic instance of a relational contract. In my view, the implication of a duty of good faith in the contract is essential to give effect to the parties' reasonable expectations and satisfies the business necessity test which Lord Neuberger in *Marks & Spencer Plc v BNP Paribas Securities Services Trust Co (Jersey) Ltd* [2016] AC 742, [2015] UKSC 72 at paras 16 to 31 reiterated as the relevant standard for the implication of a term into a contract. I would also reach the same conclusion by applying the test adumbrated by Lord Wilberforce in *Liverpool City Council v Irwin* [1976] AC 239 at 254 for the implication of a term in law, on the basis that the nature of the contract as a relational contract implicitly requires (in the absence of a contrary indication) treating it as involving an obligation of good faith.

NOTE The position on relational contracts appears as divisive as that on good faith. The matter is discussed in *Poole's Textbook on Contract Law,* chapter 1.

5.4.2 Terms implied by statute: B2B (business to business contracts) which are outside the CRA 2015

5.4.2.1 Terms implied into a B2B contract for the sale of goods

Sale of Goods Act 1979

12. Implied terms about title, etc.

(1) In a contract of sale, . . . there is an implied term on the part of the seller that in the case of a sale he has a right to sell the goods, and in the case of an agreement to sell he will have such a right at the time when the property is to pass.

(2) In a contract of sale . . . there is also an implied term that—

(a) the goods are free, and will remain free until the time when the property is to pass, from any charge or encumbrance not disclosed or known to the buyer before the contract is made, and

(b) the buyer will enjoy quiet possession of the goods except so far as it may be disturbed by the owner or other person entitled to the benefit of any charge or encumbrance so disclosed or known.

. . .

(5A) As regards England and Wales and Northern Ireland, the term implied by subsection (1) above is a condition and the terms implied by subsections (2) . . . above are warranties.

. . .

(7) This section does not apply to a contract to which Chapter 2 of Part 1 of the Consumer Rights Act 2015 applies (but see the provision made about such contracts in section 17 of that Act).

13. Sale by description

(1) Where there is a contract for the sale of goods by description, there is an implied term that the goods will correspond with the description.

(1A) As regards England and Wales and Northern Ireland, the term implied by subsection (1) above is a condition.

. . .

(5) This section does not apply to a contract to which Chapter 2 of Part 1 of the Consumer Rights Act 2015 applies (but see the provision made about such contracts in section 11 of that Act).

14. Implied terms about quality or fitness

(1) Except as provided by this section and section 15 below and subject to any other enactment, there is no implied term about the quality or fitness for any particular purpose of goods supplied under a contract of sale.

(2) Where the seller sells goods in the course of a business, there is an implied term that the goods supplied under the contract are of satisfactory quality.

. . .

(3) Where the seller sells goods in the course of a business and the buyer, expressly or by implication, makes known—

(a) to the seller, or

(b) where the purchase price or part of it is payable by instalments and the goods were previously sold by a credit-broker to the seller, to that credit-broker, any particular purpose for which the goods are being bought, there is an implied term that the goods supplied under the contract are reasonably fit for that purpose, whether or not that is a purpose for which such goods are commonly supplied, except where the circumstances show that the buyer does not rely, or that it is unreasonable for him to rely, on the skill or judgment of the seller or credit-broker. . . .

(6) As regards England and Wales and Northern Ireland, the terms implied by subsections (2) and (3) above are conditions.

. . .

(9) This section does not apply to a contract to which Chapter 2 of Part 1 of the Consumer Rights Act 2015 applies (but see the provision made about such contracts in sections 9, 10 and 18 of that Act).

15. *Sale by sample*

(1) A contract of sale is a contract for sale by sample where there is an express or implied term to that effect in the contract.

(2) In the case of a contract for sale by sample there is an implied term—

   (a) that the bulk will correspond with the sample in quality;

   (b) that the goods will be free from any defect, making their quality unsatisfactory, which would not be apparent on reasonable examination of the sample.

(3) As regards England and Wales and Northern Ireland, the term implied by subsection (2) above is a condition.

. . .

(5) This section does not apply to a contract to which Chapter 2 of Part 1 of the Consumer Rights Act 2015 applies (but see the provision made about such contracts in sections 13 and 18 of that Act).

5.4.2.2 Terms implied into B2B contracts of hire purchase

A contract of hire purchase is defined at *page 69*, 2.6.1. See the Supply of Goods (Implied Terms) Act 1973, ss. 8–11.

5.4.2.3 Terms implied into B2B contracts for work and materials in relation to the materials supplied

These are contracts that primarily relate to the provision of work, but under which goods are also supplied, e.g. car repairs and building contracts.

The Supply of Goods and Services Act (SGSA) 1982, ss. 2–5, relating to the materials supplied are set out in similar terms to the above provisions.

5.4.2.4 Terms implied into B2B hire contracts

These are contracts under which the hirer gains possession, but not ownership. See the Supply of Goods and Services Act 1982, ss. 7–10.

5.4.2.5 Terms implied into B2B contracts for the supply of a service

These are contracts whereby a supplier agrees to carry out a service. In a contract for work and materials, the service element will be combined with a transfer of property in goods (5.4.2.3 for implied obligations in relation to the materials supplied). For implied obligations relating to contracts for the supply of a service, see the SGSA 1982, ss. 13–15 (s. 13 appears at *page 628*, 13.1, and s. 15 at *page 76*, 2.6.3.4).

TABLE 5.1 Comparison of provisions in the Sale of Goods Act (SGA) 1979 and SGSA 1982 with the B2C provisions in the CRA 2015

SGA 1979 (sale of goods) and SGSA 1982 (transfer of goods, hire and supply of service)	CRA 2015 provisions
s. 12 SGA: Seller's right to sell (title) sale of goods s. 2 SGSA (transfer of goods) s. 7 SGSA (hire)	s. 17 CRA: Trader to have the right to supply goods
s. 13 SGA: Sale by description s. 3 SGSA (transfer of goods) s. 8 SGSA (hire)	s. 11 CRA: Goods to be as described
s. 14(2) SGA: Satisfactory quality where sale in the course of a business s. 4(2) SGSA (transfer of goods) s. 9(2) SGSA (hire)	s. 9 CRA: Goods to be of satisfactory quality—(1) Every contract to supply goods is to be treated as including a term that the quality of the goods is satisfactory.
s. 14(3) SGA: Fitness for purpose where sale in the course of a business s. 4(4)(5) SGSA (transfer of goods) s. 9(4)(5) SGSA (hire)	s. 10 CRA: Goods to be fit for a particular purpose
s. 15 SGA: Sale by sample s. 5 SGSA (transfer of goods) s. 10 SGSA (hire)	s. 13 CRA: Goods to match a sample
	s. 14 CRA: Goods to match a model seen or examined

TABLE 5.2 Comparison of the terms implied into a contract for the supply of a service by the SGSA 1982 and the CRA 2015

SGSA (B2B)	CRA (B2C)
s. 13 SGSA: Supply of service with reasonable care and skill	s. 49 CRA: Supply of a service with reasonable care and skill

5.4.3 Terms implied by statute: B2C (trader and consumer) contracts within the CRA 2015

5.4.3.1 Terms implied into a B2C contract for the supply of goods

Sales, hire, and work and materials contracts all involve the 'supply of goods, digital content or services' for the purposes of the relevant legislation, namely the Consumer Rights Act (CRA) 2015 (s. 3(4)) and the Act applies only where this contract is between a 'trader' and a 'consumer' (as defined by s. 2(2) and (3), *page 293*, 6.5.2).

5.4.3.2 Terms implied into a B2C contract for the supply of a service

For detailed discussion of these terms, see *Poole's Textbook on Contract Law*, 6.6.

5.5 Interpretation

In practice, many contract cases involve questions of interpretation (or construction) of contract terms, i.e. to determine meaning and to determine whether a particular term or clause covers the events that have occurred.

The process of interpreting the express words contained in the contract is the first step identified by the Supreme Court in *Marks & Spencer plc v BNP Paribas Securities Services Trust Co. (Jersey) Ltd* [2015] UKSC 72, [2015] 3 WLR 1843. The basic rule is that when seeking to identify the meaning of a contract the court must find the intention of the parties. This intention is determined objectively and is therefore based on notional rather than actual intentions of the parties. It is not necessary to be limited by the 'four corners of the contract' and instead interpretation involves focusing on the words chosen and their natural meaning in the context for their use (*Arnold v Britton* [2015] UKSC 36, [2015] AC 1619). This context includes the other terms, the purpose underpinning this term and this contract, as well as 'commercial common sense'. The critical tension is between the natural meaning of the words that the parties chose to use and a more purposive interpretation which would make commercial common sense but can be accused of rewriting the contract to account for imprudence in bargaining. The principles in *West Bromwich* are applicable as part of the interpretation of the words in their context but, it seems, the starting point is the words chosen by the parties rather than 'commercial common sense'. Where the words used are ambiguous, commercial common sense should prevail (*Rainy Sky SA v Kookmin Bank*).

5.5.1 *West Bromwich*: contextual interpretation in accordance with principles of commercial common sense

In *Investors Compensation Scheme Ltd v West Bromwich Building Society* [1998] 1 WLR 896, Lord Hoffmann referred to the fundamental change in the approach to interpretation in English contract law from a literal (four corners) approach to a more contextual approach examining 'the matrix of fact' in a way that reflected commercial common sense.

Investors Compensation Scheme Ltd v West Bromwich Building Society (No. 1)
[1998] 1 WLR 896 (HL)

LORD HOFFMANN: I do not think that the fundamental change which has overtaken this branch of the law, particularly as a result of the speeches of Lord Wilberforce in *Prenn v Simmonds* [1971] 1 WLR 1381, 1384–1386 and *Reardon Smith Line Ltd v Yngvar Hansen-Tangen* [1976] 1 WLR 989, is always sufficiently appreciated. The result has been, subject to one important exception, to assimilate the way in which such documents are interpreted by judges to the common sense principles by which any serious utterance would be interpreted in ordinary life. Almost all the old intellectual baggage of 'legal' interpretation has been discarded. The principles may be summarised as follows.

(1) Interpretation is the ascertainment of the meaning which the document would convey to a reasonable person having all the background knowledge which would reasonably have been available to the parties in the situation in which they were at the time of the contract.

(2) The background was famously referred to by Lord Wilberforce [in *Prenn v Simmonds* [1971] 1 WLR 1381, 1383–4] as the 'matrix of fact' but this phrase is, if anything, an understated description of what the background may include. Subject to the requirement that it should have been reasonably available to the parties and to the exception to be mentioned next, it includes absolutely anything which would have affected the way in which the language of the document would have been understood by a reasonable man.

(3) The law excludes from the admissible background the previous negotiations of the parties and their declarations of subjective intent. They are admissible only in an action for rectification. The law makes this distinction for reasons of practical policy and, in this respect only, legal interpretation differs from the way we would interpret utterances in ordinary life. The boundaries of this exception are in some respects unclear. But this is not the occasion on which to explore them.

(4) The meaning which a document (or any other utterance) would convey to a reasonable man is not the same thing as the meaning of its words. The meaning of words is a matter of dictionaries and grammars; the meaning of the document is what the parties using those words against the relevant background would reasonably have been understood to mean. The background may not merely enable the reasonable man to choose between the possible meanings of words which are ambiguous but even (as occasionally happens in ordinary life) to conclude that the parties must, for whatever reason, have used the wrong words or syntax: see *Mannai Investments Co Ltd v Eagle Star Life Assurance Co Ltd* [1997] AC 749.

(5) The 'rule' that words should be given their 'natural and ordinary meaning' reflects the common-sense proposition that we do not easily accept that people have made linguistic mistakes, particularly in formal documents. On the other hand, if one would nevertheless conclude from the background that something must have gone wrong with the language, the law does not require judges to attribute to the parties an intention which they plainly could not have had. Lord Diplock made this point more vigorously when he said in *Antaios Compania Naviera S.A. v Salen Rederierna A.B.* [1985] AC 191, 201:

if detailed semantic and syntactical analysis of words in a commercial contract is going to lead to a conclusion that flouts business commonsense, it must be made to yield to business commonsense.

? QUESTION

Principles 4 and 5 refer to the need to give the words a meaning that reflects 'business common sense'. In *Mannai Investments Co. Ltd v Eagle Star Life Assurance* [1997] AC 749, 771, Lord Steyn commented that 'words are . . . interpreted in the way in which a reasonable commercial person would construe them. And the standard of the reasonable commercial person is hostile to technical interpretations and undue emphasis on niceties of language.'

Is there any generally accepted understanding of what is meant by 'business common sense'? Can this approach be criticized as giving rise to uncertainty? See Staughton [1999] CLJ 303.

NOTE In *Bank of Credit and Commerce International SA (in liquidation) v Ali (No. 1)* [2001] UKHL 8, [2001] 2 WLR 735, a BCCI employee had signed a release when being made redundant by the bank. However, subsequent case law permitted a particular form of claim that had not previously been thought to exist. This claim meant that former employees were able to bring claims for financial loss resulting from the stigma attached to having worked for the bank, which was found to have acted in breach of a duty of trust and confidence: *Mahmud v BCCI SA* [1998] AC 20 (*page 749*, 14.8.2). The question was whether the former employee was barred from bringing such an action by the terms of the release. The majority of the House of Lords construed the terms of the release and concluded that, by examining all of the surrounding circumstances, the parties could not have intended to provide for the release of rights and the surrender of claims that had never been within their contemplations, i.e. future possible claims that were not related to the termination of the employee's contract, such as future stigma losses. Lord Hoffmann (dissenting on the construction of the release) took the opportunity to clarify his principles in *West Bromwich*.

LORD HOFFMANN: 39 . . . I should in passing say that when, in *Investors Compensation Scheme Ltd v West Bromwich Building Society* [1998] 1 WLR 896, 913, I said that the admissible background included 'absolutely anything which would have affected the way in which the language of the document would have been understood by a reasonable man', I did not think it necessary to emphasise that I meant anything which a reasonable man would have regarded as *relevant*. I was merely saying that there is no conceptual limit to what can be regarded as background. It is not, for example, confined to the factual background but can include the state of the law (as in cases in which one takes into account that the parties are unlikely to have intended to agree to something unlawful or legally ineffective) or proved common assumptions which were in fact quite mistaken. But the primary source for understanding what the parties meant is their language interpreted in accordance with conventional usage: 'we do not easily accept that people have made linguistic mistakes, particularly in formal documents'. I was certainly not encouraging a trawl through 'background' which could not have made a reasonable person think that the parties must have departed from conventional usage.

5.5.2 Linguistic mistakes and language having more than one potential meaning

Rainy Sky SA v Kookmin Bank
[2011] UKSC 50, [2011] 1 WLR 2900 (SC)

This case concerned the interpretation of the terms of refund guarantees issued by the bank to guarantee the instalments of the price being paid to the shipbuilders in the event of various default events specified in a number of shipbuilding contracts. The terms of the guarantees involved a promise (para. 3) to pay the buyer 'all such sums due to you under the Contract', and was expressed to be 'in consideration of your agreement to make the pre-delivery instalments under the contract'. The shipbuilder became insolvent after instalments had been paid and the claimants (buyers) sought to enforce the advance payment bonds. The bank rejected these claims on the basis that it had not undertaken to guarantee payment of refunds if the default event was the builder's insolvency. The judge at first instance considered that the bank's construction of para. 3 would have an uncommercial result and gave judgment for the claimants. The Court of Appeal, allowing the bank's appeal, held, by a majority, that the construction contended for by the bank would not produce an absurd or irrational result and that it was not for the court to substitute its own judgment of the commerciality of the transaction for that of the parties.

Held (on appeal to the Supreme Court, allowing the appeal): When construing a commercial contract and where there were two possible constructions, as here, the court was entitled to prefer the construction that was consistent with business common sense and to reject the other. It was not necessary, as the Court of Appeal had done, to conclude that a particular construction would have an absurd or irrational result before having regard to the commercial purpose of the agreement. Since the two possible interpretations of para. 3 contended for by the claimants and by the bank were both arguable, it was appropriate for the court to have regard to considerations of commercial common sense in resolving the question as to what a reasonable person would have understood the parties to have meant. The claimant's construction was to be preferred, since it was consistent with the commercial purpose of the advance payment bonds in a way that the bank's construction was not. The builder's insolvency was the situation for which the bonds were most likely to be needed.

LORD CLARKE OF STONE-CUM-EBONY JSC [with whom the other Supreme Court Justices agreed]:

The correct approach to construction

21 The language used by the parties will often have more than one potential meaning. I would accept the submission made on behalf of the appellants that the exercise of construction is essentially one unitary exercise in which the court must consider the language used and ascertain what a reasonable person,

that is a person who has all the background knowledge which would reasonably have been available to the parties in the situation in which they were at the time of the contract, would have understood the parties to have meant. In doing so, the court must have regard to all the relevant surrounding circumstances. If there are two possible constructions, the court is entitled to prefer the construction which is consistent with business common sense and to reject the other . . .

23 Where the parties have used unambiguous language, the court must apply it. This can be seen from the decision of the Court of Appeal in *Co-operative Wholesale Society Ltd v National Westminster Bank plc* [1995] 1 EGLR 97. The court was considering the true construction of rent review clauses in a number of different cases. The underlying result which the landlords sought in each case was the same. The court regarded it as a most improbable commercial result. Where the result, though improbable, flowed from the unambiguous language of the clause, the landlords succeeded, whereas where it did not, they failed. The court held that ordinary principles of construction applied to rent review clauses and applied the principles in *Antaios Cia Naviera SA v Salen Rederierna AB (The Antaios)* [1985] AC 191 . . . Hoffmann LJ said, at p 99:

> This . . . does not, however, mean that one can rewrite the language which the parties have used in order to make the contract conform to business common sense. But language is a very flexible instrument and, if it is capable of more than one construction, one chooses that which seems most likely to give effect to the commercial purpose of the agreement.

24 . . . Simon Brown LJ, at p 101, said that, having regard to the improbable result for which the land-lords contended, only the most unambiguous of such clauses could properly be found to bear the landlords' construction and that in the case of only one of the leases did the clause 'unambiguously . . . achieve the improbable result for which the landlords contend'. The case is of interest because Simon Brown LJ considered that, of the other three cases, one unambiguously failed to achieve the result sought by the landlords, whereas, of the other two, he said this, at p 102:

> For my part, I would accept that the more obvious reading of both favours the landlord's construction. I am persuaded, however, that they are capable of being, and therefore, for the reasons already given, should be, construed differently.

That case is therefore an example of the adoption and application of the principle endorsed by the judge and by Sir Simon Tuckey [in the minority in the Court of Appeal] . . .

25 In 1997, writing extra-judicially in 'Contract law: Fulfilling the reasonable expectations of honest men' 113 LQR 433, 441, Lord Steyn expressed the principle thus:

> Often there is no obvious or ordinary meaning of the language under consideration. There are competing interpretations to be considered. In choosing between alternatives a court should primarily be guided by the contextual scene in which the stipulation in question appears. And speaking generally commercially minded judges would regard the commercial purpose of the contract as more important than niceties of language. And, in the event of doubt, the working assumption will be that a fair construction best matches the reasonable expectations of the parties.

I agree. He said much the same judicially in *Society of Lloyd's v Robinson* [1999] WLR 756, 763:

> Loyalty to the text of a commercial contract, instrument, or document read in its contextual setting is the paramount principle of interpretation. But in the process of interpreting the meaning of the language of a commercial document the court ought generally to favour a commercially sensible construction. The reason for this approach is that a commercial construction is likely to give effect to the intention of the parties. Words ought therefore to be interpreted in the way in which a reasonable commercial person would construe them. And the reasonable commercial person can safely be assumed to be unimpressed with technical interpretations and undue emphasis on niceties of language.

. . .

29 Finally, it is worth setting out two extracts from the judgment of Longmore LJ in *Barclays Bank plc v HHY Luxembourg SARL* [2010] EWCA Civ 1248, [2011] 1 BCLC 336, paras 25 and 26:

25. The matter does not of course rest there because when alternative constructions are available one has to consider which is the more commercially sensible. On this aspect of the matter [counsel for the first appellant] has all the cards . . .

26. The judge said that it did not flout common sense to say that the clause provided for a very limited level of release, but that, with respect, is not quite the way to look at the matter. If a clause is capable of two meanings, as on any view this clause is, it is quite possible that neither meaning will flout common sense. In such circumstances, it is much more appropriate to adopt the more, rather than the less, commercial construction.

30 In my opinion Longmore LJ has there neatly summarised the correct approach to the problem. That approach is now supported by a significant body of authority. As stated in a little more detail in para 21 above, it is in essence that, where a term of a contract is open to more than one interpretation, it is generally appropriate to adopt the interpretation which is most consistent with business common sense. For these reasons I prefer the approach of the judge and Sir Simon Tuckey . . .

40 . . . Since the language of paragraph 3 is capable of two meanings it is appropriate for the court to have regard to considerations of commercial common sense in resolving the question what a reasonable person would have understood the parties to have meant.

41 . . . [T]he judge described the bank's construction of the bonds as having what he called the surprising and uncommercial result that the buyers would not be able to call on the bonds on the happening of the event, namely insolvency of the builder, which would be most likely to require the first class security. I agree with Sir Simon Tuckey that an appellate court is entitled to take account of the fact that an experienced judge of the Commercial Court reached that conclusion. In any event, Sir Simon Tuckey expressed essentially the same view in strong terms, at para 30:

> . . . On the bank's construction the bonds covered each of the situations in which the buyers were entitled to a return or refund of the advance payments which they had made under the contracts apart from the insolvency of the builder. No credible commercial reason has been advanced as to why the parties (or the buyers' financiers) should have agreed to this. On the contrary, it makes no commercial sense. As the judge said, insolvency of the builder was the situation for which the security of an advance payment bond was most likely to be needed. The importance attached in these contracts to the obligation to refund in the event of insolvency can be seen from the fact that they required the refund to be made immediately. It defies commercial common sense to think that this, among all other such obligations, was the only one which the parties intended should not be secured. Had the parties intended this surprising result I would have expected the contracts and the bonds to have spelt this out clearly but they do not do so.

I agree . . .

45 . . . I agree with the judge and Sir Simon Tuckey that, of the two arguable constructions of paragraph 3 of the bonds, the buyers' construction is to be preferred because it is consistent with the commercial purpose of the bonds in a way in which the bank's construction is not . . .

47 For these reasons I would allow the appeal and restore the order of the judge.

NOTE There are some dangers in adopting a process of construction that seeks to give the contract the meaning that makes commercial sense, since the court may move too far away from the actual words used by the parties and replace them with the meaning that the court believes would be 'reasonable' in the circumstances. The courts have shown that they are aware of this danger: see e.g. *BMA Special Opportunity Hub Fund Ltd v African Minerals Finance Ltd* [2013] EWCA Civ 416, [24], per Aikens LJ, and the Court of Appeal in *Dear v Jackson* [2013] EWCA Civ 89. As Moore-Bick LJ explained in *Procter & Gamble Co. v Svenska Cellulosa Aktiebolaget SCA* [2012] EWCA Civ 1413:

22 [Counsel] submitted on the authority of *Rainy Sky S.A. and others v Kookmin Bank* [2011] UKSC 50, [2011] 1 WLR 2900 that the Agreement was open to two possible constructions and that the construction for which he contended should be preferred because it made better commercial sense. I entirely agree that if a clause is reasonably capable of bearing two possible meanings (and is therefore ambiguous),

the court should prefer that which better accords with the overall objective of the contract or with good commercial sense, but the starting point must be the words the parties have used to express their intention and in the case of a carefully drafted agreement of the present kind the court must take care not to fall into the trap of re-writing the contract in order to produce what it considers to be a more reasonable meaning. In my view the Agreement, considered as a whole, is not reasonably capable of being given two possible meanings.

5.5.3 The primacy of the natural meaning of the words used: *Arnold v Britton*

While the *West Bromwich* principles were generally applied without fail, it was acknowledged (see the above note) that there could be dangers when interpreting contracts in giving predominance to 'commercial common sense'. The statement of Moore-Bick LJ in *Procter & Gamble Co. v Svenska Cellulosa Aktiebolaget SCA* [2012] EWCA Civ 1413, at [22] seems particularly astute in terms of the later decision of the Supreme Court in *Arnold v Britton*.

Arnold v Britton
[2015] UKSC 36, [2015] AC 1619 (SC)

This case was concerned with the interpretation of service charge provisions in leases of chalets at a caravan park on the Gower Peninsula which had been granted at a time of high inflation in the late 1970s and 80s. Each lease contained a clause requiring the lessee to pay a fixed service charge and provided for this to increase at a compound rate. A typical clause required the lessee:

> To pay to the lessors without any deductions in addition to the said rent a proportionate part of the expenses and outgoings incurred by the lessors in the repair maintenance renewal and the provision of services hereafter set out the yearly sum of £90 and VAT (if any) for the first three years of the term hereby granted increasing thereafter by ten pounds per hundred for every subsequent three year period or part thereof.

The compounding of the amount of the annual increase would have resulted in a charge of over £500,000 per annum by the end of the 99-year term. The lessees therefore argued that this could not have been the intention of the provision and that the clause should be read as limiting their contribution to paying a proportionate part of the reasonable expenses incurred by the lessors subject to a cap of the fixed amount increasing after the first year on a compound basis. The lessors argued that the clause required payment as it was drafted. The lessors succeeded in securing a declaration to this effect from the High Court on the basis that the lessees' interpretation involved rewriting the clause. The Court of Appeal upheld this decision.

Held (on appeal to the Supreme Court; Lord Carnwath JSC dissenting): the appeal by the lessees was rejected. Interpretation required an identification of the meaning given by the parties to the provision assessed from the perspective of the reasonable reader. The starting point for this determination would usually be the words used in the provision. Although the less clear the words were, the more the court could properly depart from their natural meaning, the court was not to embark on an exercise of searching for drafting infelicities in order to facilitate a departure from the natural meaning. Commercial common sense was relevant only to the extent of how matters would or could have been perceived by reasonable people in the parties' position at the date the contract was made. It was not the role of the court to interpret in a way which gave the language a meaning corresponding with what the court thought the parties should have agreed in order to protect a party from an imprudent contract as matters had developed.

The majority considered that nothing had gone wrong with the drafting of the clause and it was not ambiguous. In addition, they were able to find commercial justifications for it in the form of the certainty provided to both parties through a fixed rate charge. Inflation had been rampant at the time when the majority of the leases had been granted in the late 1970s, and often at a rate over 10 per cent, so that fixing a 10 per cent compound escalation was not absurd at the time when the leases were granted on these terms. It had merely proved to be imprudent over time.

LORD NEUBERGER OF ABBOTSBURY PSC (with whom LORD SUMPTION and LORD HUGHES JJSC agreed):

Interpretation of contractual provisions

14 Over the past 45 years, the House of Lords and Supreme Court have discussed the correct approach to be adopted to the interpretation, or construction, of contracts in a number of cases starting with *Prenn v Simmonds* [1971] 1 WLR 1381 and culminating in *Rainy Sky SA v Kookmin Bank* [2011] 1 WLR 2900.

15 When interpreting a written contract, the court is concerned to identify the intention of the parties by reference to 'what a reasonable person having all the background knowledge which would have been available to the parties would have understood them to be using the language in the contract to mean', to quote Lord Hoffmann in *Chartbrook Ltd v Persimmon Homes Ltd* [2009] AC 1101, para 14. And it does so by focussing on the meaning of the relevant words, in this case clause 3(2) of each of the 25 leases, in their documentary, factual and commercial context. That meaning has to be assessed in the light of (i) the natural and ordinary meaning of the clause, (ii) any other relevant provisions of the lease, (iii) the overall purpose of the clause and the lease, (iv) the facts and circumstances known or assumed by the parties at the time that the document was executed, and (v) commercial common sense, but (vi) disregarding subjective evidence of any party's intentions. In this connection, see *Prenn* [1971] 1 WLR 1381, 1384–1386; *Reardon Smith Line Ltd v Yngvar Hansen-Tangen (trading as HE Hansen-Tangen)* [1976] 1 WLR 989 995–997, per Lord Wilberforce; *Bank of Credit and Commerce International SA v Ali* [2002] 1 AC 251, para 8, per Lord Bingham of Cornhill; and the survey of more recent authorities in *Rainy Sky* [2011] 1 WLR 2900, paras 21–30, per Lord Clarke of Stone-cum-Ebony JSC.

16 For present purposes, I think it is important to emphasise seven factors.

17 First, the reliance placed in some cases on commercial common sense and surrounding circumstances (eg in *Chartbrook* [2009] AC 1101, paras 16–26) should not be invoked to undervalue the importance of the language of the provision which is to be construed. The exercise of interpreting a provision involves identifying what the parties meant through the eyes of a reasonable reader, and, save perhaps in a very unusual case, that meaning is most obviously to be gleaned from the language of the provision. Unlike commercial common sense and the surrounding circumstances, the parties have control over the language they use in a contract. And, again save perhaps in a very unusual case, the parties must have been specifically focussing on the issue covered by the provision when agreeing the wording of that provision.

18 Secondly, when it comes to considering the centrally relevant words to be interpreted, I accept that the less clear they are, or, to put it another way, the worse their drafting, the more ready the court can properly be to depart from their natural meaning. That is simply the obverse of the sensible proposition

that the clearer the natural meaning the more difficult it is to justify departing from it. However, that does not justify the court embarking on an exercise of searching for, let alone constructing, drafting infelicities in order to facilitate a departure from the natural meaning. If there is a specific error in the drafting, it may often have no relevance to the issue of interpretation which the court has to resolve.

19 The third point I should mention is that commercial common sense is not to be invoked retrospectively. The mere fact that a contractual arrangement, if interpreted according to its natural language, has worked out badly, or even disastrously, for one of the parties is not a reason for departing from the natural language. Commercial common sense is only relevant to the extent of how matters would or could have been perceived by the parties, or by reasonable people in the position of the parties, as at the date that the contract was made. Judicial observations such as those of Lord Reid in *Wickman Machine Tools Sales Ltd v L Schuler AG* [1974] AC 235, 251 and Lord Diplock in *Antaios Cia Naviera SA v Salen Rederierna AB (The Antaios)* [1985] AC 191, 201, quoted by Lord Carnwath JSC at para 110, have to be read and applied bearing that important point in mind.

20 Fourthly, while commercial common sense is a very important factor to take into account when interpreting a contract, a court should be very slow to reject the natural meaning of a provision as correct simply because it appears to be a very imprudent term for one of the parties to have agreed, even ignoring the benefit of wisdom of hindsight. The purpose of interpretation is to identify what the parties have agreed, not what the court thinks that they should have agreed. Experience shows that it is by no means unknown for people to enter into arrangements which are ill-advised, even ignoring the benefit of wisdom of hindsight, and it is not the function of a court when interpreting an agreement to relieve a party from the consequences of his imprudence or poor advice. Accordingly, when interpreting a contract a judge should avoid re-writing it in an attempt to assist an unwise party or to penalise an astute party.

21 The fifth point concerns the facts known to the parties. When interpreting a contractual provision, one can only take into account facts or circumstances which existed at the time that the contract was made, and which were known or reasonably available to both parties. Given that a contract is a bilateral, or synallagmatic, arrangement involving both parties, it cannot be right, when interpreting a contractual provision, to take into account a fact or circumstance known only to one of the parties.

22 Sixthly, in some cases, an event subsequently occurs which was plainly not intended or contemplated by the parties, judging from the language of their contract. In such a case, if it is clear what the parties would have intended, the court will give effect to that intention. An example of such a case is *Aberdeen City Council v Stewart Milne Group Ltd* 2012 SC (UKSC) 240, where the court concluded that 'any . . . approach' other than that which was adopted 'would defeat the parties' clear objectives', but the conclusion was based on what the parties 'had in mind when they entered into' the contract: see paras 21 and 22.

23 Seventhly, reference was made in argument to service charge clauses being construed 'restrictively'. I am unconvinced by the notion that service charge clauses are to be subject to any special rule of interpretation. Even if (which it is unnecessary to decide) a landlord may have simpler remedies than a tenant to enforce service charge provisions, that is not relevant to the issue of how one interprets the contractual machinery for assessing the tenant's contribution.

NOTE This decision clearly emphasizes that the starting point for interpretation is the language the parties have chosen. If this language is clear and unambiguous, the courts will not interfere with the words chosen in the parties' bargain. The clause should therefore be interpreted in accordance with 'commercial common sense' only in instances of ambiguity or clear drafting problems—and not simply because one of the parties objects to the outcome of its natural meaning.

5.5.4 Interpretation as a 'unitary exercise': *Wood v Capita*

In *Wood v Capita Insurance Services Ltd*, the Supreme Court put some order into apparently different approaches and emphases between individual judges towards contract interpretation.

Wood v Capita Insurance Services Ltd
[2017] UKSC 24, [2017] 2 WLR 1095, [2017] AC 765

This case was concerned with the interpretation of an indemnity clause (clause 7.11) in a contract for the sale and purchase of shares in a specialist insurance broking company. The clause in question covered 'all actions, proceedings, losses, claims, damages, expenses and liability suffered or incurred' but only when such losses were sustained 'following and arising out of claims or complaints registered with the FSA'. Shortly after the company was bought, following some misleading practices by telephone operators, the company referred itself to the FSA and the customers in question were compensated. Capita therefore sought to rely on the indemnity clauses to recoup the losses incurred. Lord Hodge, speaking for the Supreme Court as a whole, upheld the court of appeal's decision that the losses were not covered.

Contractual interpretation

8. In his written case counsel for Capita argued that the Court of Appeal had fallen into error because it had been influenced by a submission by Mr Wood's counsel that the decision of this court in *Arnold v Britton* [2015] AC 1619 had 'rowed back' from the guidance on contractual interpretation which this court gave in *Rainy Sky SA v Kookmin Bank* [2011] 1 WLR 2900. This, he submitted, had caused the Court of Appeal to place too much emphasis on the words of the SPA and to give insufficient weight to the factual matrix. He did not have the opportunity to develop this argument as the court stated that it did not accept the proposition that *Arnold* had altered the guidance given in *Rainy Sky*. The court invited him to present his case without having to refer to the well-known authorities on contractual interpretation, with which it was and is familiar.

9. It is not appropriate in this case to reformulate the guidance given in *Rainy Sky* and *Arnold*; the legal profession has sufficient judicial statements of this nature. But it may assist if I explain briefly why I do not accept the proposition that *Arnold* involved a recalibration of the approach summarised in *Rainy Sky*.

10. The court's task is to ascertain the objective meaning of the language which the parties have chosen to express their agreement. It has long been accepted that this is not a literalist exercise focused solely on a parsing of the wording of the particular clause but that the court must consider the contract as a whole and, depending on the nature, formality and quality of drafting of the contract, give more or less weight to elements of the wider context in reaching its view as to that objective meaning. In *Prenn v Simmonds* [1971] 1 WLR 1381 (1383H–1385D) and in *Reardon Smith Line Ltd v Yngvar Hansen-Tangen* [1976] 1 WLR 989 (997), Lord Wilberforce affirmed the potential relevance to the task of interpreting the parties' contract of the factual background known to the parties at or before the date of the contract, excluding evidence of the prior negotiations. When in his celebrated judgment in *Investors Compensation Scheme Ltd v West Bromwich Building Society* [1998] 1 WLR 896 Lord Hoffmann (pp 912–913) reformulated the principles of contractual interpretation, some saw his second principle, which allowed consideration of the whole relevant factual background available to the parties at the time of the contract, as signalling a break with the past. But Lord Bingham in an extra-judicial writing, *A new thing under the sun? The interpretation of contracts and the ICS decision* Edin LR Vol 12, 374–390, persuasively demonstrated that the idea of the court putting itself in the shoes of the contracting parties had a long pedigree.

11. Lord Clarke elegantly summarised the approach to construction in *Rainy Sky* at para 21f. In *Arnold* all of the judgments confirmed the approach in *Rainy Sky* (Lord Neuberger paras 13–14; Lord Hodge para 76; and Lord Carnwath para 108). Interpretation is, as Lord Clarke stated in *Rainy Sky* (para 21), a unitary exercise; where there are rival meanings, the court can give weight to the implications of rival constructions by reaching a view as to which construction is more consistent with business common sense. But, in striking a balance between the indications given by the language and the implications of the competing constructions the court must consider the quality of drafting of the clause (*Rainy Sky* para 26, citing Mance LJ in *Gan Insurance Co Ltd v Tai Ping Insurance Co Ltd (No. 2)* [2001] 2 All ER (Comm) 299 paras 13 and 16); and it must also be alive to the possibility that one side may have agreed to something which with hindsight did not serve his interest: *Arnold* (paras 20 and 77). Similarly, the court must not lose sight of the possibility that a provision may be a negotiated compromise or that the negotiators were not able to agree more precise terms.

12. This unitary exercise involves an iterative process by which each suggested interpretation is checked against the provisions of the contract and its commercial consequences are investigated: *Arnold* para 77 citing *In re Sigma Finance Corpn* [2010] 1 All ER 571, para 10 per Lord Mance. To my mind once one has read the language in dispute and the relevant parts of the contract that provide its context, it does not matter whether the more detailed analysis commences with the factual background and the implications of rival constructions or a close examination of the relevant language in the contract, so long as the court balances the indications given by each.

13. Textualism and contextualism are not conflicting paradigms in a battle for exclusive occupation of the field of contractual interpretation. Rather, the lawyer and the judge, when interpreting any contract, can use them as tools to ascertain the objective meaning of the language which the parties have chosen to express their agreement. The extent to which each tool will assist the court in its task will vary according to the circumstances of the particular agreement or agreements. Some agreements may be successfully interpreted principally by textual analysis, for example because of their sophistication and complexity and because they have been negotiated and prepared with the assistance of skilled professionals. The correct interpretation of other contracts may be achieved by a greater emphasis on the factual matrix, for example because of their informality, brevity or the absence of skilled professional assistance. But negotiators of complex formal contracts may often not achieve a logical and coherent text because of, for example, the conflicting aims of the parties, failures of communication, differing drafting practices, or deadlines which require the parties to compromise in order to reach agreement. There may often therefore be provisions in a detailed professionally drawn contract which lack clarity and the lawyer or judge in interpreting such provisions may be particularly helped by considering the factual matrix and the purpose of similar provisions in contracts of the same type. The iterative process, of which Lord Mance spoke in *Sigma Finance Corpn* (above), assists the lawyer or judge to ascertain the objective meaning of disputed provisions.

14. On the approach to contractual interpretation, *Rainy Sky* and *Arnold* were saying the same thing.

15. The recent history of the common law of contractual interpretation is one of continuity rather than change. One of the attractions of English law as a legal system of choice in commercial matters is its stability and continuity, particularly in contractual interpretation.

NOTES

1. The order brought by *Wood v Capita* to this fraught area has clearly been embraced by the courts. The latest iteration being that of *First National Trustco (UK) Ltd v McQuitty* [2020] EWCA Civ 107 (at [33] per Jackson LJ).

2. Although the crucial role that the courts play in interpreting contracts clearly applies to 'written words' it is clearly not limited to them as it can also apply to a conversation as held by the Supreme Court, in *Wells v Devani* [2019] UKSC 4, [2019] 2 WLR 617 (*page 211, 5.4.1.2*). Overturning the Court of

Appeal's position, the Supreme Court held that it was possible to find that there was a contract by interpreting what was communicated between the parties and that this communication could be interpreted by words as well as conduct (at [18]). Lord Kitchin added that 'the only sensible interpretation of what they said to each other in the course of their telephone conversation on 29 January 2008 and the circumstances in which that conversation took place' was that payment would become due on completion and made from the proceeds of sale (at [19]). In doing so, the Supreme Court has been approved in part (Davies (2019) 78(2) CLJ 267; Pilkington and Eldridge (2019) 135 LQR 526).

5.5.5 Admissibility of pre-contractual negotiations

The wider circumstances surrounding the conclusion of the contract do not generally include the pre-contract negotiations. In *Prenn v Simmonds* [1971] 1 WLR 1381, Lord Wilberforce said that 'such evidence is unhelpful' because only when the contract is finally made is there a consensus and, until that time, the parties' respective intentions may change or be refined. There can be no guarantee, therefore, that an intention appearing during negotiations has remained constant until the time of contracting. This position receives further support in Lord Hoffmann's third principle of interpretation in *West Bromwich* and was considered afresh in the next case.

Chartbrook Ltd v Persimmon contains the authoritative discussion of the admissibility of pre-contractual negotiations. However, the decision involves a classic case post-*West Bromwich* of the application of 'commercial common sense' being preferred over the parties' language. This application may be different in the light of *Arnold v Britton* [2015] UKSC 36, [2015] AC 1619 (*page 240, 5.5.3*).

Chartbrook Ltd v Persimmon Homes Ltd
[2009] UKHL 38, [2009] 3 WLR 267 (HL)

Under the terms of an agreement for the development of land, Persimmon would receive the proceeds of sale of the constructed units and use those proceeds to pay Chartbrook a price for the land, based on the total land value and an additional residential payment (ARP), which was defined in the contract. The parties' dispute arose because they gave different interpretations to the ARP and its calculation. Chartbrook claimed that it had been underpaid. At first instance and in the Court of Appeal, the APR definition was interpreted on the basis of ordinary rules of syntax, since 'the words made sense on their own'.

Held (on appeal to the House of Lords): An interpretation based on the ordinary rules of syntax made no commercial sense and would not accord with what a reasonable person, having all of the background knowledge that would have been available to the parties, would have understood the parties to have meant.

The House of Lords, having found in favour of Persimmon on the construction issue, made *obiter* observations as a response to an argument that account should be taken of the pre-contractual negotiations, particularly two letters that Persimmon claimed supported its interpretation of the agreement. The main ground discussed for permitting such evidence to be admissible was that, in some cases, such evidence would clearly be 'helpful' and 'relevant'.

LORD HOFFMANN: 27. If your Lordships agree with this conclusion about the construction of the contract, the appeal must be allowed. There is no need to say anything more. But Persimmon advanced two alternative arguments of very considerable general importance and I think it is appropriate that your Lordships should deal with them. The first was that (contrary to the unanimous opinion of the judge and the Court of Appeal) the House should take into account the pre-contractual negotiations, which in the opinion of Lawrence Collins LJ (at paragraph 132), were determinative confirmation of Persimmon's argument on construction. The second was that the judge and the Court of Appeal had misunderstood the principles upon which rectification may be decreed and that if Persimmon had failed on construction, the agreement should have been rectified.

28 . . . . The rule that pre-contractual negotiations are inadmissible was clearly reaffirmed by this House in *Prenn v Simmonds* [1971] 1 WLR 1381, where Lord Wilberforce said (at p. 1384) that earlier authorities 'contain little to encourage, and much to discourage, evidence of negotiation or of the parties' subjective intentions.' It is clear that the rule of inadmissibility has been established for a very long time . . .

30. To allow evidence of pre-contractual negotiations to be used in aid of construction would therefore require the House to depart from a long and consistent line of authority, the binding force of which has frequently been acknowledged: . . . The House is nevertheless invited to do so, on the ground that the rule is illogical and prevents a court from, as the Lord Justice Clerk in *Inglis v John Buttery & Co* (1878) 3 App Cas 552 said, putting itself in the position of the parties and ascertaining their true intent.

31. In *Prenn v Simmonds* [1971] 1 WLR 1381, 1384 Lord Wilberforce said by way of justification of the rule: 'The reason for not admitting evidence of these exchanges is not a technical one or even mainly one of convenience, (though the attempt to admit it did greatly prolong the case and add to its expense). It is simply that such evidence is unhelpful. By the nature of things, where negotiations are difficult, the parties' positions, with each passing letter, are changing and until the final agreement, though converging, still divergent. It is only the final document which records a consensus' . . .

32. Critics of the rule, such as Thomas J in New Zealand (*Yoshimoto v Canterbury Golf International Ltd* [2001] 1 NZLR 523, 538–549) Professor David McLauchlan ('Contract Interpretation: What is it About?' (2009) 31:5 Sydney Law Review 5–51) and Lord Nicholls of Birkenhead ('My Kingdom for a Horse: The Meaning of Words' (2005) 121 LQR 577–591) point out that although all this may usually be true, in some cases it will not. Among the dirt of aspirations, proposals and counter-proposals there may gleam the gold of a genuine consensus on some aspect of the transaction expressed in terms which would influence an objective observer in construing the language used by the parties in their final agreement. Why should court deny itself the assistance of this material in deciding what the parties must be taken to have meant? [Counsel for Persimmon], went so far as to say that in saying that such evidence was unhelpful, Lord Wilberforce was not only providing a justification for the rule but delimiting its extent. It should apply only in cases in which the pre-contractual negotiations are actually irrelevant. If they do assist a court in deciding what an objective observer would have construed the contract to mean, they should be admitted. I cannot accept this submission. It is clear from what Lord Wilberforce said and the authorities upon which he relied that the exclusionary rule is not qualified in this way. There is no need for a special rule to exclude irrelevant evidence.

33. I do however accept that it would not be inconsistent with the English objective theory of contractual interpretation to admit evidence of previous communications between the parties as part of the background which may throw light upon what they meant by the language they used. The general rule, as I said in *Bank of Credit and Commerce International SA v Ali* [2002] 1 AC 251, 269, is that there are no conceptual limits to what can properly be regarded as background. Prima facie, therefore, the negotiations are potentially relevant background. They may be inadmissible simply because they are irrelevant to the question which the court has to decide, namely, what the parties would reasonably be taken to have meant by the language which they finally adopted to express their agreement. For the reasons given by Lord Wilberforce, that will usually be the case. But not always. In exceptional cases, as Lord Nicholls has forcibly argued, a rule that prior negotiations are always inadmissible will prevent the court from giving effect to what a reasonable man in the position of the parties would have taken them

to have meant. Of course judges may disagree over whether in a particular case such evidence is helpful or not. In *Yoshimoto v Canterbury Golf International Ltd* [2001] 1 NZLR 523. Thomas J thought he had found gold in the negotiations but the Privy Council said it was only dirt. As I have said, there is nothing unusual or surprising about such differences of opinion. In principle, however, I would accept that previous negotiations may be relevant.

34. It therefore follows that while it is true that, as Lord Wilberforce said, inadmissibility is normally based in irrelevance, there will be cases in which it can be justified only on pragmatic grounds. I must consider these grounds, which have been explored in detail in the literature and on the whole rejected by academic writers but supported by some practitioners.

35. The first is that the admission of pre-contractual negotiations would create greater uncertainty of outcome in disputes over interpretation and add to the cost of advice, litigation or arbitration. Everyone engaged in the exercise would have to read the correspondence and statements would have to be taken from those who took part in oral negotiations. Not only would this be time-consuming and expensive but the scope for disagreement over whether the material affected the construction of the agreement (as in the *Yoshimoto* case) would be considerably increased. As against this, it is said that when a dispute over construction is litigated, evidence of the pre-contractual negotiations is almost invariably tendered in support of an alternative claim for rectification (as in *Prenn v Simmonds* and in this case) or an argument based on estoppel by convention or some alleged exception to the exclusionary rule. Even if such an alternative claim does not succeed, the judge will have read and possibly been influenced by the evidence. The rule therefore achieves little in saving costs and its abolition would restore some intellectual honesty to the judicial approach to interpretation.

36 . . . . There is certainly a view in the profession that the less one has to resort to any form of background in aid of interpretation, the better. The document should so far as possible speak for itself . . .

38 . . . . I rather doubt whether the *ICS* case produced a dramatic increase in the amount of material produced by way of background for the purposes of contractual interpretation. But pre-contractual negotiations seem to me capable of raising practical questions different from those created by other forms of background. Whereas the surrounding circumstances are, by definition, objective facts, which will usually be uncontroversial, statements in the course of pre-contractual negotiations will be drenched in subjectivity and may, if oral, be very much in dispute. It is often not easy to distinguish between those statements which (if they were made at all) merely reflect the aspirations of one or other of the parties and those which embody at least a provisional consensus which may throw light on the meaning of the contract which was eventually concluded. But the imprecision of the line between negotiation and provisional agreement is the very reason why in every case of dispute over interpretation, one or other of the parties is likely to require a court or arbitrator to take the course of negotiations into account. Your Lordships' experience in the analogous case of resort to statements in Hansard under the rule in *Pepper v Hart* [1993] AC 593 suggests that such evidence will be produced in any case in which there is the remotest chance that it may be accepted and that even these cases will be only the tip of a mountain of discarded but expensive investigation. *Pepper v Hart* has also encouraged ministers and others to make statements in the hope of influencing the construction which the courts will give to a statute and it is possible that negotiating parties will be encouraged to improve the bundle of correspondence with similar statements.

39. Supporters of the admissibility of pre-contractual negotiations draw attention to the fact that Continental legal systems seem to have little difficulty in taking them into account. Both the *Unidroit Principles of International Commercial Contracts* (1994 and 2004 revision) and the *Principles of European Contract Law* (1999) provide that in ascertaining the 'common intention of the parties', regard shall be had to prior negotiations: articles 4.3 and 5.102 respectively. The same is true of the United Nations Convention on Contracts for the International Sale of Goods (1980). But these instruments reflect the French philosophy of contractual interpretation, which is altogether different from that of English law. As

Professor Catherine Valcke explains in an illuminating article ('On Comparing French and English Contract Law: Insights from Social Contract Theory') (16 January 2009), French law regards the intentions of the parties as a pure question of subjective fact, their *volonté psychologique*, uninfluenced by any rules of law. It follows that any evidence of what they said or did, whether to each other or to third parties, may be relevant to establishing what their intentions actually were. There is in French law a sharp distinction between the ascertainment of their intentions and the application of legal rules which may, in the interests of fairness to other parties or otherwise, limit the extent to which those intentions are given effect. English law, on the other hand, mixes up the ascertainment of intention with the rules of law by depersonalising the contracting parties and asking, not what their intentions actually were, but what a reasonable outside observer would have taken them to be. One cannot in my opinion simply transpose rules based on one philosophy of contractual interpretation to another, or assume that the practical effect of admitting such evidence under the English system of civil procedure will be the same as that under a Continental system.

40. In his judgment in the present case, Briggs J thought that the most powerful argument against admitting evidence of pre-contractual negotiations was that it would be unfair to a third party who took an assignment of the contract or advanced money on its security. Such a person would not have been privy to the negotiations and may have taken the terms of the contract at face value. There is clearly strength in this argument, but it is fair to say that the same point can be made (and has been made, notably by Saville LJ in *National Bank of Sharjah v Dellborg* [1997] EWCA Civ 2070, which is unreported, but the relevant passage is cited in Lord Bingham's paper in the Edinburgh Law Review) in respect of the admissibility of any form of background. The law sometimes deals with the problem by restricting the admissible background to that which would be available not merely to the contracting parties but also to others to whom the document is treated as having been addressed. Thus in *Bratton Seymour Service Co Ltd v Oxborough* [1992] BCLC 693 the Court of Appeal decided that in construing the articles of association of the management company of a building divided into flats, background facts which would have been known to all the signatories were inadmissible because the articles should be regarded as addressed to anyone who read the register of companies, including persons who would have known nothing of the facts in question. In *The Starsin* (*Homburg Houtimport BV v Agrosin Private Ltd* [2004] 1 AC 715) the House of Lords construed words which identified the carrier on the front of a bill of lading without reference to what it said on the back, on the ground that the bankers to whom the bill would be tendered could not be expected to read the small print. Ordinarily, however, a contract is treated as addressed to the parties alone and an assignee must either inquire as to any relevant background or take his chance on how that might affect the meaning a court will give to the document. The law has sometimes to compromise between protecting the interests of the contracting parties and those of third parties. But an extension of the admissible background will, at any rate in theory, increase the risk that a third party will find that the contract does not mean what he thought. How often this is likely to be a practical problem is hard to say. In the present case, the construction of the agreement does not involve reliance upon any background which would not have been equally available to any prospective assignee or lender.

41. The conclusion I would reach is that there is no clearly established case for departing from the exclusionary rule. The rule may well mean, as Lord Nicholls has argued, that parties are sometimes held bound by a contract in terms which, upon a full investigation of the course of negotiations, a reasonable observer would not have taken them to have intended. But a system which sometimes allows this to happen may be justified in the more general interest of economy and predictability in obtaining advice and adjudicating disputes. It is, after all, usually possible to avoid surprises by carefully reading the documents before signing them and there are the safety nets of rectification and estoppel by convention. Your Lordships do not have the material on which to form a view. It is possible that empirical study (for example, by the Law Commission) may show that the alleged disadvantages of admissibility are not in practice very significant or that they are outweighed by the advantages of

doing more precise justice in exceptional cases or falling into line with international conventions. But the determination of where the balance of advantage lies is not in my opinion suitable for judicial decision. Your Lordships are being asked to depart from a rule which has been in existence for many years and several times affirmed by the House. There is power to do so under the *Practice Statement (Judicial Precedent)* [1966] 1 WLR 1234. But that power was intended, as Lord Reid said in *R v National Insurance Comrs, Ex p Hudson* [1972] AC 944, 966, to be applied only in a small number of cases in which previous decisions of the House were 'thought to be impeding the proper development of the law or to have led to results which were unjust or contrary to public policy'. I do not think that anyone can be confident that this is true of the exclusionary rule.

42. The rule excludes evidence of what was said or done during the course of negotiating the agreement for the purpose of drawing inferences about what the contract meant. It does not exclude the use of such evidence for other purposes: for example, to establish that a fact which may be relevant as background was known to the parties, or to support a claim for rectification or estoppel. These are not exceptions to the rule. They operate outside it . . .

47 . . . There are two legitimate safety devices which will in most cases prevent the exclusionary rule from causing injustice. But they have to be specifically pleaded and clearly established. One is rectification. The other is estoppel by convention, which has been developed since the decision in the *Karen Oltmann*: see *Amalgamated Investment & Property Co. Ltd v. Texas Commerce International Bank Ltd* [1982] QB 84. If the parties have negotiated an agreement upon some common assumption, which may include an assumption that certain words will bear a certain meaning, they may be estopped from contending that the words should be given a different meaning. Both of these remedies lie outside the exclusionary rule, since they start from the premise that, as a matter of construction, the agreement does not have the meaning for which the party seeking rectification or raising an estoppel contends.

NOTES

1. Lord Hoffmann was clear that although the exclusionary rule excluded evidence of pre-contractual negotiations for the purpose of interpreting the parties' intended meaning, such evidence was not thereby excluded if sought to be introduced for other purposes, e.g. to establish that a fact that might be relevant as background was known to the parties—see *Estor Ltd v Multifit (UK) Ltd* [2009] EWHC 2565 (TCC), [2010] CILL 2800, in which the court used pre-contract information to identify the parties to the contract on this basis—and clearly such evidence was admissible to support a claim for rectification (*page 26, 2.3.1*) or estoppel. Indeed, this was frequently used by parties to bring the excluded pre-contractual evidence before the court. This evidence was not an exception to the rule, but rather it operated outside the rule.

2. This position was also confirmed by the Supreme Court in *Oceanbulk Shipping and Trading SA v TMT Asia Ltd* [2010] UKSC 44, [2011] 1 AC 662, in which Lord Clarke noted:

39. Trial judges frequently have to distinguish between material which forms part of the pre-contractual negotiations which is part of the factual matrix and therefore admissible as an aid to interpretation and material which forms part of the pre-contractual negotiations but which is not part of the factual matrix and is not therefore admissible. This is often a straightforward task but sometimes it is not. In my opinion this problem is not relevant to the question whether, where the pre-contractual negotiations that form part of the factual matrix are without prejudice, evidence of those negotiations is admissible as an aid to construction of the settlement agreement.

Thus, whereas objective facts communicated in pre-contractual negotiations are part of the factual matrix and are therefore admissible, anything subjective in those same pre-contractual negotiations is inadmissible.

3. Baroness Hale in *Chartbrook Ltd v Persimmon Homes Ltd*, whilst purporting to agree with Lord Hoffmann and Lord Walker, conceded:

99. But I have to confess that I would not have found it quite so easy to reach this conclusion [as to the meaning of ARP] had we not been made aware of the agreement which the parties had reached on this aspect of their bargain during the negotiations which led up to the formal contract. On any objective view, that made the matter crystal clear. This, to me, increased the attractions of accepting counsel's eloquent invitation to reconsider the rule in *Prenn v Simmonds* [1971] 1 WLR 1381, the pot so gently but effectively stirred by Lord Nicholls of Birkenhead in his Chancery Bar Association lecture of 2005 ('My Kingdom for a Horse: The Meaning of Words' (2005) 121 LQR 577). My experience at the Law Commission has shown me how difficult

it is to achieve flexible and nuanced reform to a rule of the common law by way of legislation. In the end abolition may be the only workable legislative solution . . . The courts, on the other hand, are able to achieve step-by-step changes which can distinguish cases in which such evidence is helpful from cases in which it is not.

These negotiations had been introduced quite legitimately in relation to the rectification claim, but it is worrying that, whilst purporting to support the exclusionary rule, her Ladyship also conceded that she had taken account of this evidence in reaching her conclusion on the interpretation of the meaning of the disputed words and that the courts could determine in which cases such evidence is 'helpful', possibly by looking at whether, in terms of the law of rectification, a 'consensus' had been reached in the negotiations. If there were no consensus, then the evidence of the negotiations would necessarily be 'unhelpful'.

4. The position is helpfully summarized in *Merthyr (South Wales) Ltd v Merthyr Tydfil County Borough Council* [2019] EWCA Civ 526 by Leggatt LJ (with Longmore and David Richard LJJ agreeing). Leggatt LJ used Lord Wilberforce's phrase 'genesis and aim of the transaction' in *Prenn v Simmonds* to summarize the application of the 'exclusionary rule' by stating that pre-contractual negotiations could be used as evidence to identify 'the genesis and aim of the transaction' but not 'for the purpose of drawing inferences about what the contract should be understood to mean' (at [53]–[54]). For Leggatt LJ, that distinction was also in line with the position in *Chartbrook Ltd v Persimmon Homes Ltd* [2009] UKHL 38, [2009] 1 AC 1101 (at [54]).

Chapter 6

Exemption clauses and unfair contract terms

Generally, an exemption clause is defined as a term in a contract or notice that either seeks to exclude liability or remedies for breach of contract and/or negligence (referred to as 'exclusion clauses' in this casebook), or seeks to limit that liability to a specified sum (referred to as 'limitation clauses').

6.1 The general approach to exemption clauses

There are distinct advantages in using exemption clauses to allocate risk, e.g. the avoidance of duplicate insurance and lower pricing. However, at common law, the courts were very concerned to protect a party against an exemption clause imposed without negotiation by a party who had superior bargaining power. The courts could achieve this by finding that the clause had not been incorporated as a term of the contract, e.g. *Thornton v Shoe Lane Parking Ltd* [1971] 2 QB 163 (page 195, 5.3.1.3), although this option was not available if the weaker party had signed a standard form contract without reading it: *L'Estrange v Graucob Ltd* [1934] 2 KB 394 (*page 187*, 5.2.2). More frequently, they resorted to construing the clause so that it did not provide protection for the stronger party in the circumstances that had occurred. To achieve this, the courts often construed the clause artificially: *Hollier v Rambler Motors (AMC) Ltd* [1972] 2 QB 71 (*page 256*, 6.3.2.2.2).

Since the Unfair Contract Terms Act (UCTA) 1977, the Unfair Terms in Consumer Contracts Regulations (UTCCR) 1999, SI 1999/2083 (now revoked) and their subsequent replacement legislative protection contained in Part 2 of the Consumer Rights Act (CRA) 2015, it is no longer necessary for such judicial restrictive approaches to incorporation and construction. Lord Diplock stated in *Photo Production Ltd v Securicor Transport Ltd* [1980] AC 827, 851:

> My Lords, the reports are full of cases in which what would appear to be very strained constructions have been placed upon exclusion clauses, mainly in what today would be called consumer contracts and contracts of adhesion. As Lord Wilberforce has pointed out, any need for this kind of judicial distortion of the English language has been banished by Parliament's having made these kinds of contracts subject to the Unfair Contract Terms Act 1977. In commercial contracts negotiated between businessmen capable of looking after their own interests and of deciding how risks inherent in the performance of various kinds

of contract can be most economically borne (generally by insurance), it is, in my view, wrong to place a strained construction upon words in an exclusion clause which are clear and fairly susceptible of one meaning only.

6.2 Requirements that must be satisfied before an exemption clause can be relied upon

To rely on an exemption clause as a defence to liability that would otherwise exist, a party must show that:

(a) it has been incorporated as a term of the contract (see the discussion of incorporation of terms at *5.2.2–5.4*);

(b) on its natural and ordinary meaning, it covers the event(s) that has/have occurred (*6.3*); and

(c) it is not rendered unenforceable by the applicable legislation, i.e. UCTA 1977 (B2B—business to business—contracts) or the CRA 2015 (B2C—trader and consumer—contracts) (*6.4* and *6.5*).

6.3 Construction: on its natural and ordinary meaning, the clause covered what happened

Before UCTA 1977, the courts adopted a restrictive and often artificial approach to construction to protect the weaker party. Lord Denning admitted this in the Court of Appeal in *George Mitchell (Chester Hall) Ltd v Finney Lock Seeds Ltd* [1983] QB 284, at p. 297:

The heyday of freedom of contract

None of you nowadays will remember the trouble we had—when I was called to the Bar—with exemption clauses. They were printed in small print on the back of tickets and order forms and invoices. They were contained in catalogues or timetables. They were held to be binding on any person who took them without objection. No one ever did object. He never read them or knew what was in them. No matter how unreasonable they were, he was bound. All this was done in the name of 'freedom of contract.' But the freedom was all on the side of the big concern which had the use of the printing press. No freedom for the little man who took the ticket or order form or invoice. The big concern said, 'Take it or leave it.' The little man had no option but to take it. The big concern could and did exempt itself from liability in its own interest without regard to the little man. It got away with it time after time. When the courts said to the big concern, 'You must put it in clear words,' the big concern had no hesitation in doing so. It knew well that the little man would never read the exemption clauses or understand them.

It was a bleak winter for our law of contract. It is illustrated by two cases, *Thompson v London, Midland and Scottish Railway Co.* [1930] 1 KB 41 (in which there was exemption from liability, not on the ticket, but only in small print at the back of the timetable, and the company were held not liable) and *L'Estrange v F. Graucob Ltd* [1934] 2 KB 394 (in which there was complete exemption in small print at the bottom of the order form, and the company were held not liable).

The secret weapon

Faced with this abuse of power—by the strong against the weak—by the use of the small print of the conditions—the judges did what they could to put a curb upon it. They still had before them the idol, 'freedom of contract.' They still knelt down and worshipped it, but they concealed under their cloaks a secret weapon. They used it to stab the idol in the back. This weapon was called 'the true construction of the contract.' They used it with great skill and ingenuity. They used it so as to depart from the natural meaning of the words of the exemption clause and to put upon them a strained and unnatural construction. In case after case, they said that the words were not strong enough to give the big concern exemption from liability; or that in the circumstances the big concern was not entitled to rely on the exemption clause . . .

When examining many of the cases that follow, remember that the courts are unlikely to adopt such a restrictive approach to the question of construction when legislative regulation is available.

6.3.1 **Contra proferentem**

Any ambiguity in an exemption clause will be resolved against the party seeking to rely upon it.

Houghton v Trafalgar Insurance Co. Ltd
[1954] 1 QB 247 (CA)

A car insurance policy excluded liability for damage 'caused or arising whilst the car is conveying any load in excess of that for which it was constructed'. At the time of the accident, six people were in a car with seating accommodation for five; the insurers denied liability, claiming that this was a load in excess of that for which the car was constructed.

Held: The word 'load' covered only cases in which there was a specified weight that must not be exceeded, as in the case of lorries or vans.

ROMER LJ: I think that it would be most regrettable if a provision of this kind were held to have the force for which the defendants contend. It would be a serious thing for a motorist involved in a collision if he were told that the particular circumstances of the accident excluded him from the benefit of the policy. I think that any clause or provision that purports to have that effect ought to be clear and unambiguous so that the motorist knows exactly where he stands. This provision is neither clear nor unambiguous. If applied to a private motor-car I have not the least idea what it means . . .

NOTES

1. As Romer LJ appears to be suggesting, policy reasons may also have caused the Court of Appeal to reject the insurers' suggested interpretation, which would have had a devastating effect on the ability of innocent third parties to recover on car insurance policies in those circumstances.

2. In *Andrews Brothers (Bournemouth) Ltd v Singer & Co. Ltd* [1934] 1 KB 17, the exemption covered all implied obligations, but the Court of Appeal held that the defendants could not rely on this as exempting them from liability for breach of the express obligation that the car be 'new'.

3. The *contra proferentem* rule is expressly incorporated in the Consumer Rights Act (CRA) 2015, s. 69.

---

69 Contract terms that may have different meanings

(1) If a term in a consumer contract, or a consumer notice, could have different meanings, the meaning that is most favourable to the consumer is to prevail.

6.3.2 Liability for negligence

It can be difficult to grasp the concept that, in an action in negligence, the defendant may seek to rely on an exemption clause in a contract to which he is a party to protect himself (as to the position where a third party seeks to do this, *Chapter 7*).

Traditionally, the courts' approach has been to limit the scope of exclusion clauses and construe them so that they cover only contractual liability unless the clause expressly extends to negligence.

In *Canada Steamship Lines Ltd v R* [1952] AC 192, 208, Lord Morton of Henryton laid down a construction test to ascertain whether the clause covers negligence liability:

Their Lordships think that the duty of a court in approaching the consideration of such clauses may be summarised as follows:—

(1) If the clause contains language which expressly exempts the person in whose favour it is made (hereafter called 'the proferens') from the consequence of the negligence of his own servants, effect must be given to that provision . . .

(2) If there is no express reference to negligence, the court must consider whether the words used are wide enough, in their ordinary meaning, to cover negligence on the part of the servants of the proferens. If a doubt arises at this point, it must be resolved against the proferens . . .

(3) If the words used are wide enough for the above purpose, the court must then consider whether 'the head of damage may be based on some ground other than that of negligence,' to quote again Lord Greene, in the *Alderslade* case [1945] KB 189. The 'other ground' must not be so fanciful or remote that the proferens cannot be supposed to have desired protection against it; but subject to this qualification, which is no doubt to be implied from Lord Greene's words, the existence of a possible head of damage other than that of negligence is fatal to the proferens even if the words used are prima facie wide enough to cover negligence on the part of his servants . . .

6.3.2.1 The first possibility is that the clause expressly refers to negligence or a synonym of negligence

Most clauses will use more general words, but the following case concerned a clause that covered negligence liability, because the words 'neglect or default' were synonymous with negligence.

If the clause expressly refers to negligence, it will cover negligence liability *and* any other liability that may arise on the facts, e.g. breach of statutory duty or strict contractual liability.

Monarch Airlines Ltd v London Luton Airport Ltd
[1997] CLC 698

Loose paving blocks had damaged one of the claimant airline's aircraft as it was preparing to take off from the airport. When the claimant sued to recover damages for negligence and/or breach of duty under s. 2 of the Occupiers' Liability Act 1957, the defendant sought to rely on clause 10 of its standard conditions, which excluded the liability of the airport, its servants, and agents for any damage to aircraft 'arising or resulting directly or indirectly from any act, omission, neglect or default . . . unless done with intent to cause damage or recklessly and with knowledge that damage would probably result'. The claimant submitted that this clause did not cover the liability that had occurred since, applying the test in *Canada Steamship v R*, clause 10 did not cover negligence liability.

Held (Clarke J): The clause excluded liability for negligence and any breach of statutory duty unless the negligence or breach was caused either with intent to cause damage or recklessly and with knowledge that damage would probably result. The words 'neglect or default' were synonymous with negligence. The clause therefore passed Lord Morton's first test.

6.3.2.2 The second possibility requires that the words be wide enough to cover negligence

In *Lamport & Holt Lines Ltd v Coubro & Scrutton (M & I) Ltd, The Raphael* [1982] 2 Lloyd's Rep 42, the words 'any act or omission' were held to be words that were wide enough to cover negligence.

6.3.2.2.1 *Is there any other liability arising on these facts?*

Provided the words are wide enough to cover negligence, we can then ask *whether there is any other liability that exists on these facts*, e.g. breach of a strict (or absolute) contractual obligation. If so, the clause is confined to this alternative liability and cannot apply to cover the liability in negligence.

White v John Warwick & Co. Ltd
[1953] 1 WLR 1285 (CA)

The claimant contracted with the defendants for the hire of a tradesman's tricycle. The tricycle supplied under the agreement had a defective saddle. The claimant was thrown off the tricycle when the saddle tipped up, and was injured. Clause 11 of their agreement provided that the defendants would not be liable 'for any personal injuries to the riders of the machines hired'. The claimant sought damages, alleging that: (i) the defendants were strictly liable in contract in supplying a tricycle that was not reasonably fit for the purpose for which it was required; and (ii) the defendants were negligent as they had failed to take care to ensure that the tricycle supplied was in a proper state of repair and in working condition. Counsel for the claimant argued that although clause 11 might apply to the breach of contract claim, it did not—and could not—apply to the negligence. The Court of Appeal agreed.

Held: The clause applied only to exempt the defendants from contractual liability.

DENNING LJ: In this type of case two principles are well settled. The first is that if a person desires to exempt himself from a liability which the common law imposes on him, he can only do so by a contract freely and deliberately entered into by the injured party in words that are clear beyond the possibility of misunderstanding. The second is: if there are two possible heads of liability on the part of defendant, one for negligence, and the other a strict liability, an exemption clause will be construed, so far as possible, as exempting the defendant only from his strict liability and not as relieving him from his liability for negligence.

In the present case, there are two possible heads of liability on the defendants, one for negligence, the other for breach of contract. The liability for breach of contract is more strict than the liability for negligence. The defendants may be liable in contract for supplying a defective machine even though they were not negligent. (See *Hyman v Nye* (1881) 6 QBD 685). In these circumstances, the exemption clause must, I think, be construed as exempting the defendants only from their liability in contract, and not from their liability for negligence.

NOTE Thus the clause could not operate in a claim based on negligence. This decision pre-dates the legislative regulation. Nowadays, even if the clause is wide enough to cover negligence, it will still need to satisfy either s. 2 UCTA 1977 (*page 275, 6.4.3*) in the B2B context or ss. 62 and 65 CRA 2015 (*pages 295–297,* 6.5.3). Given the scope of this protection, e.g. not permitting reliance on any clause that excludes or restricts liability for death or personal injury resulting from negligence, it may no longer be necessary to adopt such a restrictive approach to construction and negligence liability to protect the weak.

6.3.2.2.2 *Is negligence the only liability arising on the facts?*

Where the only basis of liability is negligence, the courts are more willing to construe the clause to cover that negligence.

Alderslade v Hendon Laundry Ltd
[1945] 1 KB 189 (CA)

The claimant left ten large Irish linen handkerchiefs with the defendants to be washed. The laundry lost the handkerchiefs, but in an action by the claimant for damages for £2 1s. 5½d. (the cost of replacement handkerchiefs), the defendants sought to rely on condition 3 of the terms on which the handkerchiefs had been accepted. This provided that '[t]he maximum amount allowed for lost or damaged articles is 20 times the charge made for laundering' (calculated as 11s. 5d. here).

Held: The only liability that could arise from the loss of the handkerchiefs by the defendants was by establishing that the defendants were negligent. They owed only *a duty to take reasonable care* of the handkerchiefs, so that there could be no strict liability for such loss. The condition could therefore be applied to limit that negligence liability and the damages payable to the claimant.

LORD GREENE MR: It was argued before us for the defendants that the clause did apply and was effective to limit liability for lost articles; and reliance was placed on a well-known line of authority dealing with clauses of this description. The effect of those authorities can I think be stated as follows: where the head of damage in respect of which limitation of liability is sought to be imposed by such a clause is one which rests on negligence and nothing else, the clause must be construed as extending to that head of damage, because it would otherwise lack subject-matter. Where, on the other hand, the head of damage may be based on some other ground than that of negligence, the general principle is that the clause must be confined in its application to loss occurring through that other cause, to the exclusion of loss arising through negligence. The reason is that if a contracting party wishes in such a case to limit his liability in respect of negligence, he must do so in clear terms in the absence of which the clause is construed as relating to a liability not based on negligence. A common illustration of the principle is to be found in the case of common carriers. A common carrier is frequently described, though perhaps not quite accurately, as an insurer, and his liability in respect of articles entrusted to him is not necessarily based on negligence. Accordingly if a common carrier wishes to limit his liability for lost articles and does not make it quite clear that he is desiring to limit it in respect of his liability for negligence, then the clause will be construed as extending only to his liability on grounds other than negligence. If, on the other hand, a carrier not being a common carrier, makes use of such a clause, then unless it is construed so as to cover the case of negligence there would be no content for it at all seeing that his only obligation is to take reasonable care. That, broadly speaking, is the principle which falls to be applied in this case.

It was argued by counsel for the plaintiff that the clause must be construed in the present case so as to exclude loss by negligence . . . It was said that the loss of a customer's property might take place for one of two reasons, namely, negligence and mere breach of contract, and that in the absence of clear words referring to negligence, loss through negligence cannot be taken to be covered by the clause. In my opinion that argument fails. It is necessary to analyse the legal relationship between the customer and the defendants. What I may call the hard core of the contract, the real thing to which the contract is directed, is the obligation of the defendants to launder. That is the primary obligation. It is the contractual obligation which must be performed according to its terms, and no question of taking due care enters into it. The defendants undertake, not to exercise due care in laundering the customer's goods, but to launder them, and if they fail to launder them it is no use their saying, 'We did our best, we exercised due care and took reasonable precautions, and we are very sorry if as a result the linen is not properly laundered.' That is the essence of the contract, and in addition there are certain ancillary obligations into which the defendants enter if they accept goods from a customer to be laundered. The first relates to the safe custody of the goods while they are in the possession of the defendants. The customer's goods may have to wait for a time in the laundry premises to be washed, and while they are so waiting there is an obligation to take care of them, but it is in my opinion not the obligation of an insurer but the obligation to take reasonable care for the protection of the goods. If while they are waiting to be washed in the laundry a thief, through no fault of the defendants, steals them, the defendants are not liable. The only way in which the defendants could be made liable for the loss of articles awaiting their turn to be washed would, I think, quite clearly be if it could be shown that they had been guilty of negligence in performing their duty to take care of the goods. That is one ancillary obligation which is inherent in a contract of this kind. Another relates to the delivery of the goods. The laundry company in most cases, and indeed in this case, make a practice of delivering the goods to the customer, and in the ordinary way the customer expects to receive that service. But what is the precise obligation of the laundry in respect of the return of the goods after the laundering has been completed? In my opinion it stands on the same footing as the other ancillary obligation that I have mentioned, namely, the obligation to take reasonable care in looking after and safeguarding the goods. It cannot I think be suggested that the obligation of the laundry company in the matter of returning the goods after they have been laundered is the obligation of an insurer. To say that they have undertaken by contract an absolute obligation to see that they are returned seems to me to go against common sense. Supposing the defendants are returning the goods by van to their customer and while the van is on its way a negligent driver of a lorry drives into it and overturns it with the result that it is set on fire and the goods destroyed. No action would lie by the customer for damages for the loss of those goods any more than it would lie against any ordinary transport undertaking which was not a common carrier. To hold otherwise would mean that in respect of that clearly ancillary service the defendants were undertaking an absolute obligation that the goods would, whatever happened, be returned to the customer. It seems to me that the only obligation on the defendants in the matter of returning the goods is to take reasonable care.

In the present case all that we know about the goods is that they are lost. There seems to me to be no case of lost goods in respect of which it would be necessary to limit liability, unless it be a case where the goods are lost by negligence. Goods sent to the laundry will not be lost in the act of washing them. On the other hand, they may be lost while they are in the custody of the defendants before washing or after washing has been completed. They may be lost in the process of returning them to the customer after they have been washed, but in each of those two cases, if my view is right, the obligation of the defendants is an obligation to take reasonable care and nothing else. Therefore, the claim of a customer that the defendants are liable to him in respect of articles that have been lost must, I think, depend on the issue of due care on their part. If that be right, to construe this clause, so far as it relates to loss, in such a way as to exclude loss occasioned by lack of proper care, would be to leave the clause so far as loss is concerned—I say nothing about damage—without any content at all. The result is in my opinion is that the clause must be construed as applying to the case of loss through negligence . . .

NOTES

1. The laundry company supplies a service in the course of a business it impliedly undertakes (or includes a term) whereby the service must be performed 'with reasonable care and skill' (Supply of Goods and Services Act 1982, s. 13 (B2B), or CRA 2015, s. 49 (B2C)). Therefore, it seems that Lord Greene's identification of a strict obligation to launder properly might need to be amended in the light of this provision. However, in the B2B context which is still based on the implication of terms (as opposed to entrenched terms in the CRA 2015), s. 16 of the 1982 Act leaves open the possibility that a court may imply terms that are stricter than the qualified standard in s. 13. Other obligations, such as not losing the handkerchiefs, are clearly qualified (i.e. the duty owed is one of reasonable care and skill), and the laundry company is negligent if it fails to exercise reasonable care and skill to prevent loss.

2. Lord Greene indicated that it was an *automatic* conclusion that, where negligence is the only liability that can arise, the exemption clause *must* be construed as applying to it. However, this was not accepted by the Court of Appeal in the next case.

Hollier v Rambler Motors (AMC) Ltd
[1972] 2 QB 71 (CA)

The claimant's car was being repaired at the defendants' garage when it was damaged by a fire caused by the defendants' negligence. The claimant claimed damages for breach of the implied term that the defendants would take reasonable care of his car. The defendants sought to rely on a clause in their standard form for repair, which provided that: 'The Company is not responsible for damage caused by fire to customers' cars on the premises.'

Held: The clause had not been incorporated because there was not a consistent course of dealing (*page 202*, 5.3.2). It was also held that, in any event, the language of this clause did not exclude liability for the defendants' negligence, but was merely a 'warning' that the defendants would not be liable for fire damage that was not attributable to their own negligence.

SALMON LJ: It is well settled that a clause excluding liability for negligence should make its meaning plain on its face to any ordinarily literate and sensible person. The easiest way of doing that, of course, is to state expressly that the garage, tradesman or merchant, as the case may be, will not be responsible for any damage caused by his own negligence. No doubt merchants, tradesmen, garage proprietors and the like are a little shy of writing in an exclusion clause quite so bluntly as that. Clearly it would not tend to attract customers, and might even put many off. I am not saying that an exclusion clause cannot be effective to exclude negligence unless it does so expressly, but in order for the clause to be effective the language should be so plain that it clearly bears that meaning. I do not think that defendants should be allowed to shelter behind language which might lull the customer into a false sense of security by letting him think—unless perhaps he happens to be a lawyer—that he would have redress against the man with whom he was dealing for any damage which he, the customer, might suffer by the negligence of that person.

The principles are stated by Scrutton L.J. with his usual clarity in *Rutter v. Palmer* [1922] 2 K.B. 87, 92:

> For the present purposes a rougher test will serve. In construing an exemption clause certain general rules may be applied: First the defendant is not exempted from liability for the negligence of his servants unless adequate words are used; secondly, the liability of the defendant apart from the exempting words must be ascertained; then the particular clause in question must be considered; and if the only liability of the party pleading the exemption is a liability for negligence, the clause will more readily operate to exempt him.

Scrutton LJ was far too great a lawyer, and had far too much robust common sense, if I may be permitted to say so, to put it higher than that 'if the only liability of the party pleading the exemption is a liability for negligence, the clause will more readily operate to exempt him.' He does not say that 'if the only liability of the party pleading the exemption is a liability for negligence, the clause will necessarily exempt him.' . . .

Alderslade v Hendon Laundry Ltd [1945] 1 KB 189 . . . was a case where negligence was not expressly excluded. The question was: what do the words mean? I have no doubt that they would mean to the ordinary housewife who was sending her washing to the laundry that, if the goods were lost or damaged in the course of being washed through the negligence of the laundry, the laundry would not be liable for more than 20 times the charge made for the laundering. I say that for this reason. It is, I think, obvious that when a laundry loses or damages goods it is almost invariably because there has been some neglect or default on the part of the laundry. I think that the ordinary sensible housewife, or indeed anyone else who sends washing to the laundry, who saw that clause must have appreciated that almost always goods are lost or damaged because of the laundry's negligence, and therefore this clause could apply only to limit the liability of the laundry, when they were in fault or negligent.

But [counsel for the defendants] has drawn our attention to the way in which the matter was put by Lord Greene MR in delivering the leading judgment in this court, and he contends that Lord Greene MR was in fact making a considerable extension to the law . . .

I do not think that Lord Greene MR was intending to extend the law in the sense for which [counsel for the defendants] contends. If it were so extended, it would make the law entirely artificial by ignoring that rules of construction are merely our guides and not our masters; in the end you are driven back to construing the clause in question to see what it means . . . The words are: 'The company is not responsible for damage caused by fire to customers' cars on the premises.' What would that mean to any ordinarily literate and sensible car owner? I do not suppose that any such, unless he is a trained lawyer, has an intimate or indeed any knowledge of the liability of bailees in law. If you asked the ordinary man or woman: 'Supposing you send your car to the garage to be repaired, and there is a fire, would you suppose that the garage would be liable?' I should be surprised if many of them did not answer, quite wrongly: 'Of course they are liable if there is a fire.' Others might be more cautious and say: 'Well, I had better ask my solicitor,' or, 'I do not know. I suppose they may well be liable.' That is the crucial difference, to my mind, between the present case and *Alderslade v Hendon Laundry Ltd* . . . [H]ere I think the ordinary man or woman would be . . . surprised and horrified to learn that if the garage was so negligent that a fire was caused which damaged their car, they would be without remedy because of the words in the condition. I can quite understand that the ordinary man or woman would consider that, because of these words, the mere fact that there was a fire would not make the garage liable. Fires can occur from a large variety of causes, only one of which is negligence on the part of the occupier of the premises, and that is by no means the most frequent cause. The ordinary man would I think say to himself: 'Well, what they are telling me is that if there is a fire due to any cause other than their own negligence they are not responsible for it.' To my mind, if the defendants were seeking to exclude their responsibility for a fire caused by their own negligence, they ought to have done so in far plainer language than the language here used . . .

? QUESTION

This case was severely criticized for its artificial approach to construction of the clause. Do you think that this case would be decided in the same way today? If the clause is held to cover negligence, it would be subject to the unfairness test in s. 62 CRA 2015. Section 62(4) CRA 2015 provides that 'a term is unfair if, contrary to the requirement of good faith, it causes a significant imbalance in the parties' rights and obligations under the contract to the detriment of the consumer'. Do you think that the clause in this case would satisfy this s. 62(4) test (*pages 295–297*, 6.5.3)?

NOTE The *Canada Steamship* principles need to be understood in the light of general construction principles. In the speeches of the House of Lords in *HIH Casualty & General Insurance Ltd v Chase Manhattan Bank* [2003] UKHL 6, [2003] 1 All ER (Comm) 349, their Lordships had confirmed that Lord Morton's guidelines would need to be read in light of the more contextual approach to contractual interpretation consequent on the principles developed in *Investors Compensation Scheme Ltd v West Bromwich Building Society* [1998] 1 WLR 896 (*page 235*, 5.5.1). In *HIH Casualty* Lord Bingham stated, at [111], that Lord Morton:

> was giving helpful guidance on the proper approach to interpretation and not laying down a code. The passage does not provide a litmus test which, applied to the terms of the contract, yields a certain and predictable result. The courts' task of ascertaining what the particular parties intended in their particular commercial context, remains.

Following the clarification of the interpretation process as an 'unitary exercise' in *Wood v Capita Insurance Services Ltd* [2017] UKSC 24, [2017] AC 117 (*page 243*, 5.5.4), the words used by the parties are still the starting point of interpretation but those words nevertheless have to be assessed in the commercial context of the contract.

Although important, Lord Morton's guidelines are no more than guidelines and are not to be applied mechanically (*Lictor Anstalt v MIR Steel UK Ltd* [2012] EWCA Civ 1397, [2013] 2 All ER (Comm) 54, [2013] CP Rep 7). Specifically, they are not to be applied in a way that would produce a result at odds with the parties' intentions in the context of the relevant background. Nevertheless, clear words are still required to exclude a person's liability for the consequences of their own negligence and the starting point to determine this must be the words the parties have used. Furthermore, doubts as to their continuing application continue to accrue. Most recently, in *Persimmon Homes Ltd v Ove Arup & Partners Ltd* [2017] EWCA Civ 373, [2017] BLR 417, Jackson LJ stated that those guidelines are now confined to indemnity clauses (at [56]).

6.3.3 Limitation clauses

Ailsa Craig Fishing Co. Ltd v Malvern Fishing Co. Ltd
[1983] 1 WLR 964 (HL)

Securicor had agreed to provide a security service in Aberdeen harbour for the fishing boats of the members of an association that were berthed there. Ailsa Craig's vessel fouled another boat in the harbour and sank. Clause 2(f) purported to limit Securicor's liability to £1,000. Ailsa Craig claimed damages against Securicor, alleging that the loss was caused by breach of contract and/or negligence. The trial judge awarded damages of £55,000. Securicor appealed, alleging that condition 2(f) applied.

Held: The limitation clause operated to limit liability to £1,000. Limitation clauses were not to be construed by the exacting standards applicable to exclusion clauses. This clause was clear and unambiguous; it was therefore wide enough to cover liability in negligence.

> LORD WILBERFORCE: Whether a clause limiting liability is effective or not is a question of construction of that clause in the context of the contract as a whole. If it is to exclude liability for negligence, it must be most clearly and unambiguously expressed, and in such a contract as this, must be construed *contra proferentem*. I do not think that there is any doubt so far. But I venture to add one further qualification, or at least clarification: one must not strive to create ambiguities by strained construction, as I think that the appellants have striven to do. The relevant words must be given, if possible, their natural, plain meaning. Clauses of limitation are not regarded by the courts with the same hostility as clauses of exclusion: this is because they must be related to other contractual terms, in particular to the risks to which the defending party may be exposed, the remuneration which he receives, and possibly also the opportunity of the other party to insure.
>
> LORD FRASER: In my opinion these principles [per Lord Morton of Henryton in *Canada Steamship Lines Ltd v R* [1952] AC 192] are not applicable in their full rigour when considering the effect of clauses merely limiting liability. Such clauses will of course be read *contra proferentem* and must be clearly expressed, but there is no reason why they should be judged by the specially exacting standards which are applied to exclusion and indemnity clauses. The reason for imposing such standards on these clauses is the inherent improbability that the other party to a contract including such a clause intended to release the proferens from a liability that would otherwise fall upon him. But there is no such high degree of improbability that he would agree to a limitation of the liability of the proferens, especially when . . . the potential losses that might be caused by the negligence of the proferens or its servants are so great in proportion to the sums that can reasonably be charged for the services contracted for. It is enough in the present case that the clause must be clear and unambiguous.

? QUESTION

Is this special construction of limitation clauses justifiable?

The legislation applies equally to limitation and exclusion clauses, and it may simply be that many limitation clauses are more likely to satisfy the reasonableness requirement in s. 11 UCTA 1977 or the test of fairness in s. 62 CRA 2015. The High Court of Australia, in *Darlington Futures Ltd v Delco Australia Pty Ltd* (1986) 161 CLR 500, (1986) 61 ALJR 76, considered this distinction in construction to be unsupportable, since if the limitation clause were to set the figure for recovery at a very low level, its effects would be much the same as those applicable to total exclusion clauses.

6.3.4 Inconsistent terms

If an exemption clause is inconsistent with another express term of the contract or an oral undertaking given at or before the time of contracting, then the exemption clause is overridden by that term or undertaking.

Mendelssohn v Normand Ltd
[1970] 1 QB 177 (CA)

The claimant was told by the parking attendant that the rules required the car to be left unlocked. The claimant explained that he had a suitcase in the car containing valuables, and the attendant agreed to lock the car as soon as he had moved it. The claimant was then given a ticket exempting the garage from responsibility for loss or damage to vehicles or their contents, however caused. On his return, the claimant found the car unlocked and later discovered that his suitcase was missing. Were the defendants liable for the loss of the suitcase?

Held: The defendants were liable, since the attendant's promise (to lock up the car, which implied that he would see that the contents were safe) took priority over the printed condition, because the printed condition was repugnant to that express promise.

LORD DENNING MR: Such a statement is binding on the company. It takes priority over any printed condition. There are many cases in the books when a man has made, by word of mouth, a promise or a representation of fact, on which the other party acts by entering into the contract. In all such cases the man is not allowed to repudiate his representation by reference to a printed condition, see *Couchman v Hill* [1947] KB 554; *Curtis v Chemical Cleaning & Dyeing Co.* [1951] 1 KB 805; and *Harling v Eddy* [1951] 2 KB 739; nor is he allowed to go back on his promise by reliance on a written clause, see *City and Westminster Properties (1934) Ltd v Mudd* [1959] Ch 129, 145 by Harman J. The reason is because the oral promise or representation has a decisive influence on the transaction—it is the very thing which induces the other to contract—and it would be most unjust to allow the maker to go back on it. The printed condition is rejected because it is repugnant to the express oral promise or representation. As Devlin J said in *Firestone Tyre and Rubber Co. Ltd v Vokins & Co. Ltd* [1951] 1 Lloyd's Rep 32, 39: 'It is illusory to say: "We promise to do a thing, but we are not liable if we do not do it".' To avoid this illusion, the law gives the oral promise priority over the printed clause.

NOTE *J. Evans & Son (Portsmouth) v Andrea Merzario Ltd* [1976] 1 WLR 1078 (*page 179*, 5.2.1.1) provides another example. The printed conditions gave the defendants complete freedom to decide the method of transportation of goods and exempted the defendants from liability for loss of or damage to the goods. However, the claimants had been given an oral assurance that the containers would be stored below deck. The defendants were not entitled to rely upon the printed conditions to exempt them from liability for this breach, because this would render the oral promise illusory.

6.3.5 Fundamental breach

A 'fundamental' breach is a serious breach that goes to the root of the contract. It may include so-called 'breach of a fundamental term', e.g. a breach of condition. A fundamental breach would be considered to be repudiatory. In the 1950s and early 1960s, as part of their restrictive approach to construction, the courts took particular exception to the use of an exemption clause to protect against liability where the breach in question was 'fundamental' and held, in a series of cases, that exemption clauses could not operate to exclude liability for such breaches. The courts used to consider that a repudiatory breach destroyed the contract and its terms, including any exemption clauses. However, this is clearly incorrect, since repudiatory breach offers only the option to terminate the contract, i.e. to discharge future obligations. In *Suisse Atlantique Société d'Armement Maritime SA v NV Rotterdamsche Kolen Centrale* [1967] 1 AC 361, the House of Lords held, *obiter*, that there was no such rule of law applicable to fundamental breaches. The House of Lords also considered that it was a question of construction whether an exemption clause covered a fundamental breach, or any breach, of contract.

The House of Lords confirmed the construction approach in the next case.

Photo Production Ltd v Securicor Transport Ltd
[1980] AC 827 (HL)

The claimants, factory owners, entered into a contract with the defendants whereby the defendants would patrol the factory at a cost of £8 15s. per week. The contract, on the defendants' standard form, included the following clause:

> Under no circumstances shall the company [Securicor] be responsible for any injurious act or default by any employee of the company unless such act or default could have been foreseen and avoided by the exercise of due diligence on the part of the company as his employer; nor, in any event, shall the company be held responsible for (a) any loss suffered by the customer through burglary, theft, fire or any other cause, except insofar as such loss is solely attributable to the negligence of the company's employees acting within the course of their employment . . .

A defendants' employee patrolling the factory started a fire by discarding a lighted match. The flames spread, destroying the factory and causing a loss of £615,000. The claimants claimed damages from the defendants. Applying the 'fundamental breach rule' the Court of Appeal held that the contract had been brought to an end, so that the defendants were not able to rely on this clause as excluding their liability. The House of Lords allowed the defendants' appeal.
Held:

(a) It was not good law to say that, on termination of a contract for a fundamental breach, the contract terms (including any exemption clauses) came to an end.

(b) The question of whether and to what extent an exemption clause was to be applied to any breach of contract was a question of construction of the contract.

(c) Normally, when the parties were bargaining on equal terms, they should be free to apportion the risks as they saw fit.

(d) On their true construction, the words of the exclusion clause covered deliberate acts, and therefore the defendants were relieved from responsibility for breach of their implied duty to operate with due regard to the safety of the premises.

> LORD WILBERFORCE: It is first necessary to decide upon the correct approach to a case such as this where it is sought to invoke an exception or limitation clause in the contract. The approach of Lord Denning MR in the Court of Appeal was to consider first whether the breach was 'fundamental.' If so, he said, the court itself deprives the party of the benefit of an exemption or limitation clause ([1978] 1 WLR 856, 863). Shaw and Waller LJJ substantially followed him in this argument . . .
>
> My Lords, whatever the intrinsic merit of this doctrine, as to which I shall have something to say later, it is clear to me that so far from following this House's decision in the *Suisse Atlantique* it is directly opposed to it and that the whole purpose and tenor of the *Suisse Atlantique* was to repudiate it. The lengthy, and perhaps I may say sometimes indigestible speeches of their Lordships, are correctly summarised in the headnote—holding No. 3 [1967] 1 AC 361, 362—'That the question whether an exceptions clause

was applicable where there was a fundamental breach of contract was one of the true construction of the contract.' That there was any rule of law by which exceptions clauses are eliminated, or deprived of effect, regardless of their terms, was clearly not the view of Viscount Dilhorne, Lord Hodson, or of myself. The passages invoked for the contrary view of a rule of law consist only of short extracts from two of the speeches—on any view a minority. But the case for the doctrine does not even go so far as that. Lord Reid, in my respectful opinion, and I recognise that I may not be the best judge of this matter, in his speech read as a whole, cannot be claimed as a supporter of a rule of law . . . I am convinced that, with the possible exception of Lord Upjohn whose critical passage, when read in full, is somewhat ambiguous, their Lordships, fairly read, can only be taken to have rejected those suggestions for a rule of law which had appeared in the Court of Appeal and to have firmly stated that the question is one of construction, not merely of course of the exclusion clause alone, but of the whole contract.

Much has been written about the *Suisse Atlantique* case. Each speech has been subjected to various degrees of analysis and criticism, much of it constructive. Speaking for myself I am conscious of imperfections of terminology, though sometimes in good company. But I do not think that I should be conducing to the clarity of the law by adding to what was already too ample a discussion a further analysis which in turn would have to be interpreted. I have no second thoughts as to the main proposition that the question whether, and to what extent, an exclusion clause is to be applied to a fundamental breach, or a breach of a fundamental term, or indeed to any breach of contract, is a matter of construction of the contract. Many difficult questions arise and will continue to arise in the infinitely varied situations in which contracts come to be breached—by repudiatory breaches, accepted or not, by anticipatory breaches, by breaches of conditions or of various terms and whether by negligent, or deliberate action or otherwise. But there are ample resources in the normal rules of contract law for dealing with these without the superimposition of a judicially invented rule of law. I am content to leave the matter there with some supplementary observations.

1. The doctrine of 'fundamental breach' in spite of its imperfections and doubtful parentage has served a useful purpose. There was a large number of problems, productive of injustice, in which it was worse than unsatisfactory to leave exception clauses to operate. Lord Reid referred to these in the *Suisse Atlantique* case [1967] 1 AC 361, 406, pointing out at the same time that the doctrine of fundamental breach was a dubious specific. But since then Parliament has taken a hand: it has passed the Unfair Contract Terms Act 1977. This Act applies to consumer contracts and those based on standard terms and enables exception clauses to be applied with regard to what is just and reasonable. It is significant that Parliament refrained from legislating over the whole field of contract. After this Act, in commercial matters generally, when the parties are not of unequal bargaining power, and when risks are normally borne by insurance, not only is the case for judicial intervention undemonstrated, but there is everything to be said, and this seems to have been Parliament's intention, for leaving the parties free to apportion the risks as they think fit and for respecting their decisions.

At the stage of negotiation as to the consequences of a breach, there is everything to be said for allowing the parties to estimate their respective claims according to the contractual provisions they have themselves made, rather than for facing them with a legal complex so uncertain as the doctrine of fundamental breach must be. What, for example, would have been the position of the respondents' factory if instead of being destroyed it had been damaged, slightly or moderately or severely? At what point does the doctrine (with what logical justification I have not understood) decide, ex post facto, that the breach was (factually) fundamental before going on to ask whether legally it is to be regarded as fundamental? How is the date of 'termination' to be fixed? Is it the date of the incident causing the damage, or the date of the innocent party's election, or some other date? All these difficulties arise from the doctrine and are left unsolved by it.

At the judicial stage there is still more to be said for leaving cases to be decided straightforwardly on what the parties have bargained for rather than upon analysis, which becomes progressively more refined, of decisions in other cases leading to inevitable appeals. The learned judge was able to decide this case on normal principles of contractual law with minimal citation of authority. I am sure that most commercial judges have wished to be able to do the same . . . In my opinion they can and should.

2. . . . I have . . . been unable to understand how the doctrine can be reconciled with the well accepted principle of law, stated by the highest modern authority, that when in the context of a breach of contract one speaks of 'termination,' what is meant is no more than that the innocent party or, in some cases, both parties, are excused from further performance. Damages, in such cases, are then claimed under the contract, so what reason in principle can there be for disregarding what the contract itself says about damages—whether it 'liquidates' them, or limits them, or excludes them? These difficulties arise in part from uncertain or inconsistent terminology. A vast number of expressions are used to describe situations where a breach has been committed by one party of such a character as to entitle the other party to refuse further performance: discharge, rescission, termination, the contract is at an end, or dead, or displaced; clauses cannot survive, or simply go. I have come to think that some of these difficulties can be avoided; in particular the use of 'rescission,' even if distinguished from rescission ab initio, as an equivalent for discharge, though justifiable in some contexts (see *Johnson v Agnew* [1980] AC 367) may lead to confusion in others. To plead for complete uniformity may be to cry for the moon. But what can and ought to be avoided is to make use of these confusions in order to produce a concealed and unreasoned legal innovation: to pass, for example, from saying that a party, victim of a breach of contract, is entitled to refuse further performance, to saying that he may treat the contract as at an end, or as rescinded, and to draw from this the proposition, which is not analytical but one of policy, that all or (arbitrarily) some of the clauses of the contract lose, automatically, their force, regardless of intention . . .

In this situation the present case has to be decided. As a preliminary, the nature of the contract has to be understood. Securicor undertook to provide a service of periodical visits for a very modest charge which works out at 26p per visit. It did not agree to provide equipment. It would have no knowledge of the value of the plaintiffs' factory: that, and the efficacy of their fire precautions, would be known to the respondents. In these circumstances nobody could consider it unreasonable, that as between these two equal parties the risk assumed by Securicor should be a modest one, and that the respondents should carry the substantial risk of damage or destruction.

The duty of Securicor was, as stated, to provide a service. There must be implied an obligation to use due care in selecting their patrolmen, to take care of the keys and, I would think, to operate the service with due and proper regard to the safety and security of the premises. The breach of duty committed by Securicor lay in a failure to discharge this latter obligation. Alternatively it could be put upon a vicarious responsibility for the wrongful act of Musgrove—viz., starting a fire on the premises: Securicor would be responsible for this upon the principle stated in *Morris v C.W. Martin & Sons Ltd* [1966] 1 QB 716, 739. This being the breach, does condition 1 apply? It is drafted in strong terms, 'Under no circumstances' . . . 'any injurious act or default by any employee.' These words have to be approached with the aid of the cardinal rules of construction that they must be read *contra proferentem* and that in order to escape from the consequences of one's own wrongdoing, or that of one's servant, clear words are necessary. I think that these words are clear. The respondents in facts [*sic*] relied upon them for an argument that since they exempted from negligence they must be taken as not exempting from the consequence of deliberate acts. But this is a perversion of the rule that if a clause can cover something other than negligence, it will not be applied to negligence. Whether, in addition to negligence, it covers other, e.g., deliberate, acts, remains a matter of construction requiring, of course, clear words. I am of opinion that it does, and being free to construe and apply the clause, I must hold that liability is excluded . . .

NOTES

1. Following a general construction test, it is unnecessary to distinguish a fundamental breach. It appears that the only relevance of a fundamental breach is that clearer words will be required for the clause to cover it.

2. However, in *AstraZeneca UK Ltd v Albermarle International Corporation* [2011] EWHC 1574 (Comm), [2011] 2 CLC 252, [2012] Bus LR D1, speaking *obiter*, Flaux J rejected the approach that had earlier been taken by the judge in *Internet Broadcasting Corporation Ltd (t/a NETTV) v Mar LLC (t/a MARHedge)* [2009] EWHC 844 (Ch), [2010] 1 All ER (Comm) 112, [2009] 2 Lloyd's Rep 295, as 'heterodox and regressive'. The judge in *MARHedge* had stated that there was a strong presumption against an exemption clause being construed to cover a deliberate repudiatory breach. Flaux J considered that this risked a return to the doctrine of fundamental breach that had been rejected in *Suisse Atlantique* and in the *Photo Production* case. Instead, the correct test 'was one of construing the clause, albeit strictly, but without any presumption'. The clause in *AstraZeneca* provided that '[n]o claims by [AZ] of any kind, whether as to the products delivered or for non-delivery of the products' would be permitted. The judge considered that this was 'sufficiently clearly worded to cover any breach of the delivery obligations, deliberate or otherwise'.

3. In *Regus (UK) Ltd v Epcot Solutions Ltd* [2008] EWCA Civ 361, [2009] 1 All ER (Comm) 586, the Court of Appeal rejected an argument that the words 'in any circumstances' were wide enough to exclude recovery of losses for fraudulent or malicious damage.

4. In *Photo Production* the House of Lords also explicitly rejected the previous misconception that the effect of termination for fundamental breach was to bring the contract to an end so that the contractual terms no longer applied. On the contrary, although future performance is no longer required, the contract is *not* treated as being void *ab initio*. The terms are still relevant, e.g. for the purposes of assessing the measure `of damages, and any exemption clause is still relevant for the purposes of assessing if liability has been excluded or limited.

5. The House of Lords in *Photo Production* seems to have been greatly influenced by the fact that the parties were 'of equal bargaining power', and so must be taken to have allocated the risk and, consequently, the burden of securing insurance cover. The other relevant factor was that the House viewed the cost of the service provided by Securicor as being very modest.

? QUESTION

Is it true to say that the parties were of equal bargaining power when the claimants contracted on the defendants' standard terms?

George Mitchell (Chesterhall) Ltd v Finney Lock Seeds Ltd
[1983] 2 AC 803 (HL)

The claimants purchased 30 lbs of Finney's Late Dutch special cabbage seed, at a price of £201.60, from the defendant seed merchants with whom they had contracted for many years. The conditions of sale on the back of the invoice limited liability to replacement of the goods or a refund of the purchase price. The seed supplied was not late cabbage seed, but autumn cabbage seed of inferior variety. The claimants had planted the seed in 63 acres, but it did not grow into cabbage plants and had to be ploughed in. The claimants' loss was more than £61,000. They claimed damages. Parker J, at first instance, held that since what was delivered was wholly different in kind from what had been ordered and agreed to be supplied, there was a fundamental breach and the clause could not operate. The majority of the Court of Appeal (Oliver and Kerr LJJ)—[1983] 1 QB 284—agreed, although they also found that the clause was unenforceable by virtue of the Sale of Goods Act 1979, s. 55, since it was not 'fair and reasonable' to allow reliance on it.

Held: The House of Lords agreed with Lord Denning MR, in the minority in the Court of Appeal, that the task of the judge was to give the clause its natural meaning and that, on their true construction, the conditions did cover the loss that had occurred. However, the House agreed with the Court of Appeal that it would not be 'fair and reasonable' to allow reliance on them. (On the question of the reasonableness of the clause, *page 282*, 6.4.5.1.)

LORD BRIDGE: My Lords, it seems to me, with all due deference, that the judgments of the learned trial judge and of Oliver LJ on the common law issue come dangerously near to re-introducing by the back door the doctrine of 'fundamental breach' which this House in *Securicor 1 [Photo Production]* [1980] AC 827, had so forcibly evicted by the front. The learned judge discusses what I may call the 'peas and beans' or 'chalk and cheese' cases, sc. those in which it has been held that exemption clauses do not apply where there has been a contract to sell one thing, e.g. a motor car, and the seller has supplied quite another thing, e.g. a bicycle . . .

In my opinion, this is not a 'peas and beans' case at all. The relevant condition applies to 'seeds' . . . The relevant condition, read as a whole, unambiguously limits the appellants' liability to replacement of the seeds or refund of the price. It is only possible to read an ambiguity into it by the process of strained construction which was deprecated by Lord Diplock [1980] AC 827, 851C in *Securicor 1* and by Lord Wilberforce in *Securicor 2 [Ailsa Craig]* [1983] 1 WLR 964, 966G.

In holding that the relevant condition was ineffective to limit the appellants' liability for a breach of contract caused by their negligence, Kerr LJ applied the principles stated by Lord Morton of Henryton giving the judgment of the Privy Council in *Canada Steamship Lines Ltd v The King* [1952] AC 192, 208. The learned Lord Justice stated correctly that this case was also referred to by Lord Fraser of Tullybelton in *Securicor 2* [1983] 1 WLR 964, 970. He omitted, however, to notice that . . . the whole point of Lord Fraser's reference was to express his opinion that the very strict principles laid down in the *Canada Steamship Lines* case as applicable to exclusion and indemnity clauses cannot be applied in their full rigour to limitation clauses. Lord Wilberforce's speech contains a passage to the like effect, and Lord Elwyn-Jones, Lord Salmon and Lord Lowry agreed with both speeches. Having once reached a conclusion in the instant case that the relevant condition unambiguously limited the appellants' liability, I know of no principle of construction which can properly be applied to confine the effect of the limitation to breaches of contract arising without negligence on the part of the appellants. In agreement with Lord Denning MR, I would decide the common law issue in the appellants' favour.

NOTES

1. See Adams (1983) 46 MLR 771.

2. It is clear that any argument based upon the 'peas and beans' cases is unlikely to succeed in future as a method of preventing reliance on an exemption clause, since, given that there are to be no strained constructions, a court may not construe what has been delivered as being wholly different from what was ordered. The House of Lords construed this contract as a contract to deliver seed and seed had been delivered.

6.4 Clause in a B2B contract must not be rendered unenforceable by the Unfair Contract Terms Act 1977

6.4.1 Scope of UCTA 1977

UCTA 1977 places statutory restrictions on the extent to which liability or remedies can be 'excluded or restricted' by means of exemption clauses in B2B (business to business) contracts.

Since UCTA 1977 broadly reflects a policy of non-intervention in such B2B cases, the scope of application of the Act is reduced now that, following the CRA 2015, it no longer applies to B2C (trader to consumer) contracts.

6.4.1.1 Section 13(1)

Section 13(1) of UCTA 1977 extends the definition of exemption clauses that may be regulated under the Act.

Unfair Contract Terms Act 1977

13. Varieties of exemption clause

(1) To the extent that this Part of this Act prevents the exclusion or restriction of any liability it also prevents—

  (a) making the liability or its enforcement subject to restrictive or onerous conditions;

  (b) excluding or restricting any right or remedy in respect of the liability, or subjecting a person to any prejudice in consequence of his pursuing any such right or remedy;

  (c) excluding or restricting rules of evidence or procedure;

  and (to that extent) sections 2, 6 and 7 also prevent excluding or restricting liability by reference to terms and notices which exclude or restrict the relevant obligation or duty.

6.4.1.1.1 *'No set-off' clauses*

Stewart Gill Ltd v Horatio Myer & Co. Ltd
[1992] 1 QB 600 (CA)

The claimants were to supply the defendants with an overhead conveyor system. Payment was in stages, with the final 10 per cent payable in the form of 5 per cent on completion and 5 per cent 30 days thereafter. The claimants' general conditions of sale provided that the defendants could not withhold payment of any amount due on grounds of set-off or counterclaim in respect of incorrect or defective goods. The defendants withheld the final 10 per cent. They argued that the claimants had committed various breaches of contract and that these losses could be set off against the amount claimed.

Held: The clause prohibiting set-off was unenforceable. Section 13(1)(b) extended the meaning of ss. 3 and 7 to cover this clause, since it excluded a right that would otherwise be available. Therefore, the clause had to be shown to be reasonable. A term preventing an overpayment being set off against a claim for the price was prima facie unreasonable and, since the offending parts could not be severed, the whole clause was unenforceable.

LORD DONALDSON MR: Section 3 of the 1977 Act applies where, as here, one party to a contract deals with the other on that other's written standard terms of business. However, it is limited to terms excluding or restricting liability or entitling the party concerned to render no contractual performance or a performance which is substantially different from that which was reasonably expected of him. Clause 12.4 is not such a clause, but the section is relevant to a consideration of section 13, although it is not there referred to in express terms.

Section 7 applies where, as here, the contract transfers the ownership of goods otherwise than under a contract for the sale or hire-purchase of goods. Unlike section 3, it is referred to in section 13 but, like section 3, it is concerned with exclusion or restriction of liability.

[Lord Donaldson then referred to section 13:]

It is a trite fact (as contrasted with being trite law) that there are more ways than one of killing a cat. Section 13 addresses this problem. On behalf of the plaintiffs it was submitted that it only did so to the extent of rendering ineffective any unreasonable term which by for example introducing restrictive or onerous conditions, indirectly achieved the exclusion or restriction of liability which, if achieved directly, would fall within the scope of other sections. The plaintiffs rightly say that clause 12.4 does not have this effect. On behalf of the defendants it was submitted that it had a wider scope.

The answer is, of course, to be found in the wording of the section, but it does not exactly leap out of the print and hit one between the eyes. Analysing the section and disregarding words which are irrelevant, it seems to deal with the matter as follows: 'To the extent that this Part of this Act prevents the exclusion or restriction of any liability it also prevents . . .' This seems to me to do no more than give expression to the 'cat' approach. Both sections 3 and 7 would render ineffective any clause in the plaintiffs' written standard terms of business which excluded or restricted liability in respects which are here material and section 13 extends this in some way. In order to find out in what way, one must read on:

> it also prevents—(a) making the liability or its enforcement subject to restrictive or onerous conditions; (b) excluding or restricting any right or remedy in respect of the liability . . . (c) excluding or restricting rules of . . . procedure . . .

Now clause 12.4 can perhaps be said to make the enforcement of the plaintiffs' liability subject to a condition that the defendants shall not have sought to set off their own claims against their liability to pay the price and this might well be said to be onerous. However, I do not think it necessary to pursue this, because it is quite clear that clause 12.4 excludes the defendants' 'right' to set off their claims against the plaintiffs' claim for the price and further excludes the remedy which they would otherwise have of being able to enforce their claims against the plaintiffs by means of a set-off: see paragraph (b). It also excludes or restricts the procedural rules as to set off: see paragraph (c). Thus far, therefore, the defendants can bring themselves within the section.

We then get to the words:

> and (to that extent) sections 2 and 5 to 7 also prevent excluding or restricting liability by reference to terms and notices which exclude or restrict the relevant obligation or duty.

Although I find this obscure, I do not think that these words restrict the ambit of the preceding words. I think that they constitute an extension and that what is intended to be covered is an exclusion or restriction of liability not by contract but by reference to notices or terms of business which are not incorporated in a contract. If this is correct, it is irrelevant to the present case.

NOTES

1. Compare this decision with *Schenkers Ltd v Overland Shoes Ltd* [1998] 1 Lloyd's Rep 498 (*page 286, 6.4.5.2*).

2. Since s. 5 UCTA 1977 was repealed by the CRA 2015, the final words of s. 13 now apply only to ss. 2, 6, and 7 UCTA 1977.

Section 13(1) provides that clauses are subject to ss. 2, 6, or 7 of UCTA 1977 if they are worded as clauses that exclude or restrict the obligation or duty.

Smith v Eric S. Bush
[1990] 1 AC 831 (HL)

A prospective purchaser applied for a mortgage and the building society instructed the defendants to value the property. The applicant signed a form containing a disclaimer, which stated that neither the building society nor its surveyor warranted that the report and valuation would be accurate, and that the report and valuation were supplied without any acceptance of responsibility. The report also contained a similar disclaimer. The valuation stated that no essential repairs were required. It was negligently prepared and the purchaser claimed damages in tort from the defendants. The defendants argued that the disclaimer was effective to protect them and was not subject to UCTA 1977, s. 2(2) (*page 275*, 6.4.3), because it was not a clause that excluded liability.

Held: A duty of care was owed by the valuers to the prospective purchaser. The disclaimer was subject to UCTA 1977, s. 2, in that the last part of s. 13(1) stated that s. 2 applied to clauses that purported to prevent the duty ever arising.

LORD TEMPLEMAN: In *Harris v Wyre Forest DC* [1988] QB 835 the Court of Appeal . . . accepted an argument that the 1977 Act did not apply because the council by their express disclaimer refused to obtain a valuation save on terms that the valuer would not be under any obligation to Mr and Mrs Harris to take reasonable care or exercise reasonable skill. The council did not exclude liability for negligence but excluded negligence so that the valuer and the council never came under a duty of care to Mr and Mrs Harris and could not be guilty of negligence. This construction would not give effect to the manifest intention of the Act but would emasculate the Act. The construction would provide no control over standard form exclusion clauses which individual members of the public are obliged to accept. A party to a contract or a tortfeasor could opt out of the Act of 1977 by declining in the words of Nourse LJ, at p. 845, to recognise 'their own answerability to the plaintiff'. Caulfield J said, at p. 850, that the Act 'can only be relevant where there is on the facts a potential liability'. But no one intends to commit a tort and therefore any notice which excludes liability is a notice which excludes a potential liability. Kerr LJ, at p. 853, sought to confine the Act to 'situations where the existence of a duty of care is not open to doubt' or where there is 'an inescapable duty of care'. I can find nothing in the Act of 1977 or in the general law to identify or support this distinction. In the result the Court of Appeal held that the Act does not apply to 'negligent misstatements where a disclaimer has prevented a duty of care from coming into existence'; per Nourse LJ, at p. 848. My Lords, this confuses the valuer's report with the work which the valuer carries out in order to make his report. The valuer owed a duty to exercise reasonable skill and care in his inspection and valuation. If he had been careful in his work, he would not have made a 'negligent misstatement' in his report.

. . . Section 13(1) of the Act prevents the exclusion of any right or remedy and (to that extent) section 2 also prevents the exclusion of liability: 'by reference to . . . notices which exclude . . . the relevant obligation or duty.'

. . .

The answer to the second question involved in these appeals is that the disclaimer of liability made by the council on its own behalf in the *Harris* case and by the Abbey National on behalf of the appellant surveyors in the *Smith* case constitute notices which fall within the Unfair Contract Terms Act 1977 and must satisfy the requirement of reasonableness.

NOTE This scenario would now fall within Part 2 of the CRA 2015. However, it provides useful continuing authority for the fact that a disclaimer of duty or responsibility in a B2B contract can be subjected to UCTA 1977 regulation as falling within the definition of an exemption clause.

6.4.1.2 Clauses transferring liability from the tortfeasor to a third party are not subject to UCTA 1977

Thompson v T. Lohan (Plant Hire) Ltd & J. W. Hurdiss Ltd
[1987] 1 WLR 649 (CA)

The defendants, a plant hire company, hired an excavator and driver to Hurdiss for use by Hurdiss at its quarry. The hire was on the terms and conditions of the Contractors' Plant Association, clause 8 of which provided:

> When a driver or operator is supplied by the owner with the plant, the owner shall supply a person competent in operating the plant and such person shall be under the direction and control of the hirer. Such drivers or operators shall for all purposes in connection with their employment in the working of the plant be regarded as the servants or agents of the hirer . . . who alone shall be responsible for all claims arising in connection with the operation of the plant by the said drivers or operators. The hirer shall not allow any other person to operate such plant without the owner's previous consent to be confirmed in writing.

Clause 13 provided that the hirer was to 'fully and completely indemnify the owner in respect of all claims by any person whatsoever for injury to person or property caused by or in connection with or arising out of the use of the plant'. The claimant's husband was killed in an accident caused by the negligence of the driver in operating the excavator at the quarry. The claimant succeeded in her claim for damages in tort from the defendants, and the defendants sought to rely on clauses 8 and 13 to recover the damages from Hurdiss. Hurdiss argued, inter alia, that the conditions were contrary to s. 2(1) of UCTA 1977 (*page 275*, 6.4.3) and could not be relied upon.

Held: Clause 8 transferred liability for the driver's negligence to the third party, Hurdiss, who therefore had to indemnify the defendants under clause 13. Section 2 of the 1977 Act was intended to prevent the *exclusion* of liability in negligence to the victim of the negligence (the claimant) and was not concerned with arrangements, such as those made in clause 8, for sharing or transferring the burden of compensating the victim. It therefore had no application on the facts.

The Court of Appeal distinguished *Phillips Products Ltd v Hyland* [1987] 1 WLR 659. In *Phillips*, the claimants hired an excavator and a driver from the defendants to carry out building work at the claimants' factory. The contract of hire incorporated clause 8 of the Contractors' Plant Association conditions. The driver negligently drove the excavator into a wall and caused considerable damage to the claimants' property. The claimants claimed damages from the defendants, who sought to rely on clause 8. The claimants alleged that clause 8 was subject to s. 2(2) of UCTA 1977, since it purported to 'exclude or restrict' liability in negligence. The Court of Appeal agreed. The court considered that, in deciding whether a clause had excluded or restricted liability, the court had to look at the substance and effect of the term rather than its form. In the circumstances, the effect of clause 8 was to negative the common law duty in tort, which otherwise would have been owed by the defendants. Therefore clause 8 had the *effect* of excluding liability and fell within s. 2(2) of the 1977 Act.

The position was very different on the facts in *Thompson,* as Fox LJ explained.

FOX LJ: In the *Phillips* case there was a tortfeasor, Hamstead, who were vicariously liable to Phillips for the damage done by their servant, Hyland. Thus Hamstead were liable to Phillips for negligence, but were seeking to exclude that liability by relying on clause 8. If that reliance had been successful, the result in the *Phillips* case would be that the victim would be left with no remedy by virtue of the operation of clause 8. Prima facie the victim was entitled to damages for negligence against Hamstead, because Hamstead were vicariously liable in negligence for the acts of their own servant. So one starts from that point. There was a plain liability of Hamstead to Phillips. That was, as Slade LJ said, a case of a plant owner excluding his liability for negligence in the relevant sense by reference to the contract term, clause 8 . . .

If one then turns to the present case, the sharp distinction between it and the *Phillips* case is this, that whereas in the *Phillips* case there was a liability in negligence of Hamstead to Phillips (and that was sought to be excluded), in the present case there is no exclusion or restriction of the liability sought to be achieved by reliance upon the provisions of clause 8. The plaintiff has her judgment against Lohan and can enforce it. The plaintiff is not prejudiced in any way by the operation sought to be established of clause 8. All that has happened is that Lohan and the third party have agreed between themselves who is to bear the consequences of Mr Hill's negligent acts. I can see nothing in section 2(1) of the Act of 1977 to prevent that. In my opinion, section 2(1) is concerned with protecting the victim of negligence, and of course those who claim under him. It is not concerned with arrangements made by the wrongdoer with other persons as to the sharing or bearing of the burden of compensating the victim. In such a case it seems to me there is no exclusion or restriction of the liability at all. The liability has been established by Hodgson J. It is not in dispute and is now unalterable. The circumstance that the defendants have between themselves chosen to bear the liability in a particular way does not affect that liability; it does not exclude it, and it does not restrict it. The liability to the plaintiff is the only relevant liability in the case, as it seems to me, and that liability is still in existence and will continue until discharge by payment to the plaintiff. Nothing is excluded in relation to the liability, and the liability is not restricted in any way whatever. The liability of Lohan to the plaintiff remains intact. The liability of Hamstead to Phillips was sought to be excluded.

NOTE The loss in *Phillips Products v Hyland* was incurred by the hirer, so that the clause could easily be seen as excluding liability, whereas in *Thompson* it was the loss of a third party. They are consistent in that in both it is the position of the victim that is important.

6.4.1.3 Evasion by means of secondary contract

Unfair Contract Terms Act 1977

10. Evasion by means of secondary contract

A person is not bound by any contract term prejudicing or taking away rights of his which arise under, or in connection with the performance of, another contract, so far as those rights extend to the enforcement of another's liability which this Part of this Act prevents that other from excluding or restricting.

Tudor Grange Holdings Ltd v Citibank NA
[1992] Ch 53

Tudor Grange brought an action against Citibank. Citibank sought to have it struck out on the ground that Tudor Grange had agreed a deed of release that prevented the action. This deed of release released the bank from 'all claims, demands and causes of action whether or not presently known or suspected', but Tudor Grange claimed that it was unenforceable under

s. 10 of UCTA 1977. The company argued that the release took away its rights under the banking contract with Citibank, including its right to complain of breaches of the duty of care owed in the banking contract, which the bank was precluded by UCTA 1977 from excluding or restricting unless the release was shown to be reasonable.

Held: Section 10 did not apply to a contract to settle disputes that had arisen concerning the performance of an earlier contract. In addition, it could not apply where the parties to both contracts were the same. The release was therefore binding on Tudor Grange.

BROWNE-WILKINSON V-C: This argument that s. 10 of the Act may apply to compromises or settlement of existing disputes has been foreseen by a number of textbook writers as an unfortunate possibility. They are unanimous in their hope that the courts will be robust in resisting it. If [counsel for the plaintiffs'] construction is correct, the impact will be very considerable. The Act of 1977 is normally regarded as being aimed at exemption clauses in the strict sense, that is to say, clauses in a contract which aim to cut down prospective liability arising in the course of the performance of the contract in which the exemption clause is contained. If [counsel for the plaintiffs'] argument is correct, the Act will apply to all compromises or waivers of existing claims arising from past actions. Any subsequent agreement to compromise contractual disputes falling within sections 2 or 3 of the Act will itself be capable of being put in question on the grounds that the compromise or waiver is not reasonable. Even an action settled at the door of the court on the advice of solicitors and counsel could be reopened on the grounds that the settlement was not reasonable within the meaning of the Act. If I am forced to that conclusion by the words of section 10 properly construed, so be it. But, in my judgment, it is improbable that Parliament intended that result: it would be an end to finality in seeking to resolve disputes.

The starting point in construing section 10 is, in my judgment, to determine the mischief aimed at by the Act itself. For this purpose, it is legitimate to look at the second report on exemption clauses of the Law Commission on *Exemption Clauses* (1975) (Law Com No. 69): (see *Smith v Eric S Bush* [1990] AC 831, 857E, per Lord Griffiths). This report was the genesis of the Act of 1977. The report is wholly concerned with remedying injustices which are caused by exemption clauses in the strict sense. So far as I can see, the report makes no reference of any kind to any mischief relating to agreements to settle disputes.

Next, the marginal note to section 10 reads: 'Evasion by means of secondary contract.' . . . This side-note clearly indicates that it is aimed at devices intended to evade the provisions of Pt 1 of the Act of 1977 by the use of another contract. In my judgment, a contract to settle disputes which have arisen concerning the performance of an earlier contract cannot be described as an evasion of the provisions in the Act regulating exemption clauses in the earlier contract. Nor is the compromise contract 'secondary' to the earlier contract.

The textbooks, to my mind correctly, identify at least one case which section 10 is designed to cover. Under contract 1, the supplier (S) contracts to supply a customer (C) with a product. Contract 1 contains no exemption clause. However, C enters into a servicing contract, contract 2, with another party (X). Under contract 2, C is precluded from exercising certain of his rights against S under contract 1. In such a case section 10 operates to preclude X from enforcing contract 2 against C so as to prevent C enforcing his rights against S under contract 1. The extent of the operation of section 10 in such circumstances may be doubtful: see Treitel on *The Law of Contract*, 7th edn, (1987), p. 206. But there is no doubt that such a case falls squarely within the terms of section 10.

In the case that I have just postulated, the references in section 10 to 'another's liability' and 'that other' are references to someone other than X, i.e. to the original supplier, S. On [counsel for the plaintiffs'] construction the words 'another' and 'that other' are taken as referring to someone other than C, the customer whose rights are restricted, so as to make the section apply to a case such as the present where there is no third party, X. Although as a matter of language the words of the section are capable of referring to anyone other than C, in my judgment, read in context and having regard to the purpose both of the Act and of the section itself, the reference to 'another' plainly means someone other than X, that is to say someone other than the party to the secondary contract. In my judgment, section 10 does not apply where the parties to both contracts are the same.

This view is reinforced by a further factor. If the Act were intended to apply to terms in subsequent compromise agreements between the same parties as the original contract, section 10 would be quite unnecessary. Under sections 2 and 3 there is no express requirement that the contract term excluding or restricting S's liability to C has to be contained in the same contract as that giving rise to S's liability to C. If S and C enter into two contracts, it makes no difference if the exemption clause is contained in a different contract from that under which the goods are supplied. Sections 2 and 3 by themselves will impose the test of reasonableness. Why then should Parliament have thought that in section 10 there was some possibility of evasion in such circumstances?

In my judgment, the Act of 1977 is dealing solely with exemption clauses in the strict sense (i.e. clauses in a contract modifying prospective liability) and does not affect retrospective compromises of existing claims. Section 10 is dealing only with attempts to evade the Act's provisions by the introduction of such an exemption clause into a contract with a third party . . . Accordingly, for those reasons, section 10 cannot apply to the release . . .

NOTE Section 10 is limited to attempts to avoid the operation of the provisions of UCTA 1977 by the use of an exemption clause in a secondary contract with a third party.

By comparison, s. 72 CRA 2015 contains a provision addressing so-called 'evasion by secondary contract' in the B2C context and, whereas this provision is clear that it does not apply to bring the secondary contract clause in question within Part 2 CRA 2015, if it is a settlement agreement in relation to the main contract liabilities, it will apply to other secondary contracts—whether between the parties to the main contract or with a third party.

6.4.1.4 Business liability

The main provisions of the 1977 Act (ss. 2–7) apply only to 'business liability'.

Unfair Contract Terms Act 1977

1. *Scope of Part I*

(3) In the case of both contract and tort, sections 2 to 7 apply (except where the contrary is stated in section 6(4)) only to business liability, that is liability for breach of obligations or duties arising—

(a) from things done or to be done by a person in the course of a business (whether his own business or another's); or

(b) from the occupation of premises used for business purposes of the occupier; and references to liability are to be read accordingly but liability of an occupier of premises for breach of an obligation or duty towards a person obtaining access to the premises for recreational or educational purposes, being liability for loss or damage suffered by reason of the dangerous state of the premises, is not a business liability of the occupier unless granting that person such access for the purposes concerned falls within the business purposes of the occupier.

NOTE 'Business' is defined by s. 14 as including 'a profession and the activities of any government department or local or public authority'. Section 6(4) extends the liabilities in s. 6 beyond business liability.

6.4.2 Basic scheme of UCTA 1977

UCTA 1977 deals with exemption clauses as follows: either the clause is rendered totally unenforceable in the circumstances; or the clause is unenforceable unless it is established that it is reasonable (thus not every clause is subject to the reasonableness requirement).

The first step is to find the section applicable to the liability sought to be excluded. This will then tell us whether the clause is totally unenforceable or subject to the reasonableness requirement.

6.4.3 Negligence liability (s. 2)

Unfair Contract Terms Act 1977

1. Scope of Part I

For the purposes of this Part of this Act, 'negligence' means the breach—
(a) of any obligation, arising from the express or implied terms of a contract, to take reasonable care or exercise reasonable skill in the performance of the contract;
(b) of any common law duty to take reasonable care or exercise reasonable skill (but not any stricter duty);
(c) of the common duty of care imposed by the Occupiers' Liability Act 1957 or the Occupiers' Liability Act (Northern Ireland) 1957.

For the purposes of the Act, certain breaches of contract are treated as negligence (i.e. breaches of qualified contractual obligations to take reasonable care or to exercise reasonable skill).

Unfair Contract Terms Act 1977

2. Negligence liability

(1) A person cannot by reference to any contract term or to a notice given to persons generally or to particular persons exclude or restrict his liability for death or personal injury resulting from negligence.
(2) In the case of other loss or damage, a person cannot so exclude or restrict his liability for negligence except in so far as the term or notice satisfies the requirement of reasonableness.

NOTE Clauses that purport to exclude or restrict negligence liability for death or personal injury are rendered totally unenforceable. 'Other loss or damage' means loss or damage other than death or personal injury, and would include property damage and economic loss. Clauses falling within s. 2(2) are enforceable only if shown to be reasonable. When a clause aims to exclude liability for death or personal injury as well as other grounds, *Goodlife Foods Ltd v Hall Fire Protection Ltd* [2017] EWHC 767 (TCC), [2017] BLR 389 highlights that the part pertaining to excluding death and personal injury is severed. The clause is then assessed solely on the permitted exclusion.

Section 2 does not apply to consumer contracts (UCTA 1977, s. 2(4)), but s. 65 CRA 2015 is an equivalent provision.

6.4.4 Contractual liability

Contractual liability is dealt with in two places in the 1977 Act. Special rules in ss. 6–7 cover certain implied obligations (e.g. as to title, description, fitness for purpose, satisfactory quality, and correspondence with sample) in sale of goods and hire purchase contracts, contracts for work and materials, and hire contracts (for details of these contracts and terms, *page 232*, 5.4.2). Secondly, a general provision covers contractual liability where one party deals on the other's written standard terms of business (s. 3). If this is not the position, then s. 3 regulation cannot apply.

6.4.4.1 Contractual liability covered by ss. 6–7

Unfair Contract Terms Act 1977

6. Sale and hire purchase

(1A) Liability for breach of the obligations arising from—

(a) section 13, 14 or 15 of the 1979 Act (seller's implied undertakings as to conformity of goods with description or sample, or as to their quality or fitness for a particular purpose);

(b) section 9, 10 or 11 of the 1973 Act (the corresponding things in relation to hire purchase), cannot be excluded or restricted by reference to a contract term except in so far as the term satisfies the requirement of reasonableness.

NOTES

1. Under s. 6(1) of UCTA 1977 the implied obligations as to title cannot be excluded or restricted. Under s. 7(3A) liability for breach of s. 2 of the Supply of Goods and Services Act 1982 (relating to the transfer of goods in a work and materials contract) cannot be excluded or restricted. However, liability for breach of s. 7 of the 1982 Act (implied obligation concerning the right to transfer possession of goods in a hire contract) can be excluded or restricted if the clause satisfies the reasonableness test (UCTA 1977, s. 7(4)).

2. Similarly, under ss. 6(1A) and 7(1A) liability for breach of these implied goods obligations can be excluded provided the clause is reasonable. Of note, s. 6(1A) applies to sale of goods and hire purchase contracts; s. 7(1A) applies to work and materials contracts or hire contracts.

6.4.4.2 Section 3 (general contractual liability)

Any clause that attempts to exclude or restrict liability for *strict (absolute) obligations* arising under a contract, other than those covered by ss. 6–7 of UCTA 1977, may be covered by s. 3, if it applies.

Unfair Contract Terms Act 1977

3. Liability arising in contract

(1) This section applies as between contracting parties where one of them deals on the other's written standard terms of business.

(2) As against that party, the other cannot by reference to any contract term—

(a) when himself in breach of contract, exclude or restrict any liability of his in respect of the breach; or

(b) claim to be entitled—

    (i) to render a contractual performance substantially different from that which was reasonably expected of him, or

    (ii) in respect of the whole or any part of his contractual obligation, to render no performance at all,

except in so far as (in any of the cases mentioned above in this subsection) the contract term satisfies the requirement of reasonableness.

(3) This section does not apply to a term in a consumer contract (but see the provision made about such contracts in section 62 of the Consumer Rights Act 2015).

NOTE Section 3, when applicable, is subject to the reasonableness requirement (see next paragraph). Two particular issues arise before that requirement can come into play. First, s. 3 does not apply to general contractual liability between two businesses unless one of the parties is dealing 'on the other's written standard terms of business', as per s. 3(1). The expression is however not defined by the Act. Secondly, precisely what s. 3(2)(b) is meant to cover must also be assessed.

6.4.4.2.1 *Dealing 'on the other's written standard terms'*

Yuanda (UK) Co. Ltd v WW Gear Construction Ltd
[2010] EWHC 720 (TCC), [2011] Bus LR 360, [2011] 1 All ER (Comm) 550

EDWARDS-STUART J: 21 . . . The conditions have to be standard in that they are terms which the company in question uses for all, or nearly all, of its contracts of a particular type without alteration (apart from blanks which have to be completed showing the price, name of the other contracting party and so on). One encounters such terms on a regular basis—whether when buying goods over the internet or by mail order or when buying a ticket for travel by air or rail.

22 In my view, it is the essence of such terms that they are not varied from transaction to transaction. If they were, they would no longer be 'standard.' However, there is a class of transactions where the standard terms are incorporated by reference as one part of a larger package of terms. For example, the standard terms so incorporated may relate only to delivery and acceptance of goods and have nothing to do with other aspects of the contract, such as the fitness for purpose of the goods or their suitability for a particular purpose. In such cases it is probably a matter of degree whether one contracting party is or is not dealing on its written standard terms . . .

24 [The defendant, Gear, seeking to deny the application of s.3 UCTA on the facts] . . . relied on a decision of Judge Thayne Forbes QC in *Salvage Association v CAP Financial Services Ltd* [1995] FSR 654, in which he listed a number of facts that it might be appropriate to take into account when deciding whether or not one party dealt with the other on the latter's 'written standard terms of business'. He said, at p 672:

> The terms of the second contract were based on and closely followed CAP's standard conditions of business and the use of those standard conditions as the starting point for negotiating and agreeing the precise terms of the second contract was an obvious and sensible way to approach the matter. In my opinion, the fact that a set of CAP's standard conditions of business was used for this purpose does not necessarily mean that SA 'dealt' on CAP's 'written standard terms of business'. In such circumstances, whether it continues to be correct to describe the terms of the contract

eventually agreed by the parties as the standard terms of business of the party who originally put them forward will be a question of fact and degree to be decided in all the circumstances of the particular case. Without attempting to give an exhaustive list of the type of facts which I think would be appropriate to take into account in arriving at such a decision, I consider that the following would be included: (i) the degree to which the 'standard terms' are considered by the other party as part of the process of agreeing the terms of the contract; (ii) the degree to which the 'standard terms' are imposed on the other party by the party putting them forward; (iii) the relative bargaining power of the parties; (iv) the degree to which the party putting forward the 'standard terms' is prepared to entertain negotiations with regard to the terms of the contract generally and the 'standard terms' in particular; (v) the extent and nature of any agreed alterations to the 'standard terms' made as a result of the negotiations between the parties; (vi) the extent and duration of the negotiations.

25 In *St Albans City and District Council v International Computers Ltd* [1996] 4 All ER 481, 490–491 Nourse LJ said:

. . . Did the plaintiffs 'deal' on the defendant's written standard terms of business? [Counsel] submitted that the question must be answered in the negative, on the ground that you cannot be said to deal on another's standard terms of business if, as was here the case, you negotiate with him over those terms before you enter into the contract. In my view that is an impossible construction for two reasons: first, because as a matter of plain English 'deals' means 'makes a deal', irrespective of any negotiations that may have preceded it; secondly, because section 12(1) (a) equates the expression 'deals as consumer' with 'makes the contract'. Thus it is clear that in order that one of the contracting parties may deal on the other's written standard terms of business within section 3(1) it is only necessary for him to enter into the contract on those terms. [Counsel] sought to derive support for his submission from observations of Judge Thayne Forbes QC in *Salvage Association v CAP Financial Services Ltd* [1995] FSR 654, 671–672. In my view, those observations do not assist the defendant. In that case the judge had to consider, in relation to two contracts, whether certain terms satisfied the description 'written standard terms of business' and also whether there had been a 'dealing' on those terms. In relation to the first contract he said, at p 671: 'I am satisfied that the terms in question were ones which had been written and produced in advance by CAP as a suitable set of contract terms for use in many of its future contracts of which the first contract with [the Salvage Association] happened to be one. It is true that Mr Jones felt free to and did negotiate and agree certain important matters and details relating to the first contract at the meeting of 27 February 1987. However, although he had read and briefly considered CAP's conditions of business, he did not attempt any negotiation with regard to those conditions, nor did he or Mr Ellis consider that it was appropriate or necessary to do so. The CAP standard conditions were terms that he and Mr Ellis willingly accepted as incorporated into the first contract in their predetermined form. In those circumstances, it seems to me that those terms still satisfy the description "written standard terms of business" and, so far as concerns the first contract, the actions of Mr Jones and Mr Ellis constituted "dealing" on the part of [the Salvage Association] with CAP on its written standard terms of business within the meaning of section 3 of the [Unfair Contract Terms Act 1977].' It is true that the judge found that the Salvage Association did not negotiate with CAP over the latter's standard terms and that he held that, in entering into the contract, the Salvage Association dealt with CAP on those terms within section 3. I do not, however, read his observations as indicating a view that the 'dealing' depended on the absence of negotiations. I think that even if there had been negotiations over the standard conditions his view would have been the same. Scott Baker J dealt with this question as one of fact, finding that the defendant's general conditions remained effectively untouched in the negotiations and that the plaintiffs accordingly dealt on the defendant's written standard terms for the purposes of section 3(1): see [1995] FSR 686, 706. I respectfully agree with him.

26 I agree that factors (i), (ii) and (iv) of those identified in the *Salvage Association* case may be relevant in deciding whether or not a particular set of terms may constitute a party's standard terms of business, at least when they are proffered, but I do not consider that the existence of negotiations is itself a relevant consideration: the *St Albans* case held that it was not. In my view, the only important factor of those listed in the *Salvage Association* case is (v). If there is any significant difference between the terms proffered

and the terms of the contract actually made, then the contract will not have been made on one party's written standard terms of business.

27 Whilst I would be prepared to accept in principle that some alterations to the proffered standard terms may be so insignificant as to make it possible to hold that the party has dealt on the others written standard terms of business (as was the case in *Horace Holman Group Ltd v Sherwood International Group Ltd* (unreported) 12 April 2000), I am quite satisfied that that is not the case here. The alterations negotiated by Yuanda were material, from a contractual point of view, and cannot be dismissed as de minimis.

28 In my judgment, therefore, this is plainly not a case where Yuanda dealt on Gear's written standard terms of business. There are at least two reasons for this, both of which are fatal to Yuanda's case. First, Yuanda itself negotiated some material alterations to the proffered 'standard' terms and this means that it did not deal on the 'standard' terms. As the decision in the *St Albans* case [1996] 4 All ER 481 makes clear, the reference to dealing in section 3 of the 1977 Act is to the making of the contract, not to its negotiation.

29 Second, the evidence shows that few, if any, of the 30-odd trade contractors entered into contracts which were on the same terms. Nearly all of them, during the pre-contract negotiations, appear to have secured alterations to the schedule of amendments originally put forward by Gear. This in itself shows that Gear did not have standard terms on which it dealt. The court is concerned with the terms on which the contract is actually made, not the terms that were proffered by one party to the other as the basis for the proposed contract. Whilst the latter may have been standard, so far as Gear was concerned, the former were not.

30 For these reasons I conclude that Yuanda did not deal on Gear's written standard terms of business for the purposes of section 3 of the 1977 Act.

NOTE *Yuanda*, and other first instance decisions dealing with the issue, were approved by the Court of Appeal in *African Export-Import Bank v Shebah Exploration and Production Co Ltd* [2017] EWCA Civ 854, [2018] 1 WLR 487. Summarizing the issues, Longmore LJ stated, at [18], that the most important elements are whether the term is part of the other party's standard terms of business and whether the party is dealing on those written standard term of business. On the latter one and whether *on the facts* this is indeed the case, Longmore LJ specifically agreed with the regularity element highlighted by Edwards-Stuart J in *Yuanda* (at [21]). He therefore concluded at [25] that 'it is relevant to inquire whether there have been more insubstantial variations to *the terms which may have otherwise been habitually used by the other party to the transaction'* (emphasis added).

6.4.4.2.2 *The meaning of s 3(2)(b)*

Clauses covered by s. 3(2)(b) are those that define the obligation in a more limited way, so that a breach is less likely. This is necessary because the last part of s. 13 does not apply to s. 3 (*page 268, 6.4.1.1*).

Section 3(2)(b)(i) is seemingly designed to cover the possibility that the clause may allow the contractual performance to be altered in some way. In *AXA Sun Life Services plc v Campbell Martin* [2011] EWCA Civ 133, [2012] Bus LR 2013, [2011] 1 CLC 312, Stanley Burnton LJ noted that it was not clear how s. 3(2)(b)(i) should operate.

50 . . . Quite how that 'paragraph' should operate is not entirely clear, as is demonstrated by the somewhat tentative discussion in *Chitty on Contracts*, 30th ed (2008), vol 1, para 14–073. I have no doubt that it is principally aimed at the small print that entitles a party to a contract to provide something other than that defined by the principal terms of the contract, as where a holiday company reserves the right to substitute a hotel or resort for that specified in the main part of the contract. In most cases, as *Chitty* suggests, the

Exemption clauses and unfair contract terms

6

> performance reasonably expected of a party is that which is defined by the written contract between the parties. But this 'paragraph' of section 3 refers not to the performance specified in the contract but to the performance 'which was reasonably expected' of that party.

The issue will therefore be whether the clause is unreasonable in allowing changes to be made unilaterally from what had apparently been agreed under the main provisions of the contract and what was 'reasonably expected'. However, this raises the question of how these reasonable expectations are to be established.

Once it is clear that s. 3 applies, the clause in question must satisfy the reasonableness requirement in s. 11 to be enforceable.

6.4.5 The reasonableness requirement

NOTE Apply this test only if the applicable section requires this, e.g. ss. 2(2), 3, 6(1A), and 7(1A).

Unfair Contract Terms Act 1977

11. The 'reasonableness' test

(1) In relation to a contract term, the requirement of reasonableness for the purposes of this Part of this Act . . . is that the term shall have been a fair and reasonable one to be included having regard to the circumstances which were, or ought reasonably to have been, known to or in the contemplation of the parties when the contract was made.

(2) In determining for the purposes of section 6 or 7 above whether a contract term satisfies the requirement of reasonableness, regard shall be had in particular to the matters specified in Schedule 2 to this Act; but this subsection does not prevent the court or arbitrator from holding, in accordance with any rule of law, that a term which purports to exclude or restrict any relevant liability is not a term of the contract.

(3) In relation to a notice (not being a notice having contractual effect), the requirement of reasonableness under this Act is that it should be fair and reasonable to allow reliance on it, having regard to all the circumstances obtaining when the liability arose or (but for the notice) would have arisen.

(4) Where by reference to a contract term or notice a person seeks to restrict liability to a specified sum of money, and the question arises (under this or any other Act) whether the term or notice satisfies the requirement of reasonableness, regard shall be had in particular (but without prejudice to subsection (2) above in the case of contract terms) to—

(a) the resources which he could expect to be available to him for the purpose of meeting the liability should it arise; and

(b) how far it was open to him to cover himself by insurance.

(5) It is for those claiming that a contract term or notice satisfies the requirement of reasonableness to show that it does.

NOTES

1. The reasonableness of the clause is to be judged at the time the contract was made. Some of the case law on reasonableness was actually decided on the basis of the test used in the Supply of Goods (Implied Terms) Act 1973 (Sale of Goods Act 1979, s. 55), i.e. whether it is fair and reasonable to allow reliance on the term. In these cases, reasonableness was judged after the breach had occurred. The Sale of Goods Act (SGA) 1979, s. 55 (set out in SGA 1979, Sch. 1, para. 11) applied to contracts made between the date on which the 1973 Act came into force and the date on which UCTA 1977 came into force.

2. What factors are relevant in determining reasonableness? Under section 11(4) two factors are particularly relevant to reasonableness. The availability and cost of insurance is one of these factors, but it has been used more generally by the courts: see e.g. *Photo Production Ltd v Securicor Transport Ltd* [1980] AC 827 and again in *Goodlife Foods Ltd v Hall Fire Protection Ltd* [2018] EWCA Civ 1371.

3. Section 11(2) refers to guidelines in Sch. 2, which are stated to be relevant to reasonableness in ss. 6 and 7. Owing to their factual relevancy, however, they have been used more widely: see Stuart Smith LJ in *Stewart Gill Ltd v Horatio Myer & Co. Ltd* [1992] 1 QB 600, 608.

Unfair Contract Terms Act 1977

Schedule 2 'Guidelines' for application of reasonableness test

The matters to which regard is to be had in particular for the purposes of sections 6(1A), 7(1A) and

(4) . . . are any of the following which appear to be relevant—

(a) the strength of the bargaining positions of the parties relative to each other, taking into account (among other things) alternative means by which the customer's requirements could have been met;

(b) whether the customer received an inducement to agree to the term, or in accepting it had an opportunity of entering into a similar contract with other persons, but without having to accept a similar term;

(c) whether the customer knew or ought reasonably to have known of the existence and extent of the term (having regard, among other things, to any custom of the trade and any previous course of dealing between the parties);

(d) where the term excludes or restricts any relevant liability if some condition is not complied with, whether it was reasonable at the time of the contract to expect that compliance with that condition would be practicable;

(e) whether the goods were manufactured, processed or adapted to the special order of the customer.

NOTES

1. The most fundamental factor in practice has been the question of the parties' bargaining positions. It is clearly more reasonable to use such a clause where the parties' bargaining position is equal.

2. As regards condition (c), the Court of Appeal in *AEG (UK) Ltd v Logic Resource Ltd* [1996] CLC 265 (*page 196, 5.3.1.4*) made it clear that the fact that a clause had been incorporated as a term did not necessarily mean that the clause would satisfy the reasonableness test. Schedule 2(c) requires an examination of the reality of the consent to the term. It presupposes that the term has already been incorporated as a term of the contract, but assesses the extent to which the party has *actually consented* to it.

3. The presentation of the clause can be significant when assessing its reasonableness. In *Stag Line Ltd v Tyne Ship Repair Group Ltd, The Zinnia* [1984] 2 Lloyd's Rep 211, the most important factor affecting reasonableness was that the parties were of equal bargaining power, but Staughton J stated *obiter*, at p. 222:

I would have been tempted to hold that all the conditions are unfair and unreasonable for two reasons: first, they are in such small print that one can barely read them; secondly, the draughtsmanship is so convoluted and prolix that one almost needs an LL.B. to understand them. However, neither of those arguments was advanced before me, so I say no more about them.

Exemption clauses and unfair contract terms

6

6.4.5.1 **How should the courts approach this reasonableness requirement and what factors have been relevant in the B2B context?**

George Mitchell (Chester Hall) Ltd v Finney Lock Seeds Ltd
[1983] 2 AC 803 (HL)

The facts of this case appear at *page 262, 6.3.5*.

Held: Although, on its true construction, the clause applied to what had happened, it was not fair and reasonable to allow reliance on the clause (within s. 55 of the SGA 1979). A number of factors were stressed, as follows.

(a) It had been the defendants' practice to settle claims in excess of the limitation if they considered them to be justified. It therefore appeared that the defendants did not always consider the clause to be fair and reasonable.

(b) The defendants could have insured against crop failure without materially increasing the price of the seed.

(c) The supply of incorrect seed was the result of negligence and this was important in relation to the 'reasonableness' of the clause.

LORD BRIDGE: My Lords, at long last I turn to the application of the statutory language to the circumstances of the case. Of the particular matters to which attention is directed by paragraphs (a) to (e) of section 55(5), only those in (a) to (c) are relevant. As to paragraph (c), the respondents admittedly knew of the relevant condition (they had dealt with the appellants for many years) and, if they had read it, particularly clause 2, they would, I think, as laymen rather than lawyers, have had no difficulty in understanding what it said. This and the magnitude of the damages claimed in proportion to the price of the seeds sold are factors which weigh in the scales in the appellants' favour.

The question of relative bargaining strength under paragraph (a) and of the opportunity to buy seeds without a limitation of the seedsman's liability under paragraph (b) were inter-related. The evidence was that a similar limitation of liability was universally embodied in the terms of trade between seedsmen and farmers and had been so for very many years. The limitation had never been negotiated between representative bodies but, on the other hand, had not been the subject of any protest by the National Farmers' Union. These factors, if considered in isolation, might have been equivocal. The decisive factor, however, appears from the evidence of four witnesses called for the appellants, two independent seedsmen, the chairman of the appellant company, and a director of a sister company (both being wholly-owned subsidiaries of the same parent). They said that it had always been their practice, unsuccessfully attempted in the instant case, to negotiate settlements of farmers' claims for damages in excess of the price of the seeds, if they thought that the claims were 'genuine' and 'justified.' This evidence indicated a clear recognition by seedsmen in general, and the appellants in particular, that reliance on the limitation of liability imposed by the relevant condition would not be fair or reasonable.

Two further factors, if more were needed, weight the scales in favour of the respondents. The supply of autumn, instead of winter, cabbage seeds was due to the negligence of the appellants' sister company. Irrespective of its quality, the autumn variety supplied could not, according to the appellants' own evidence be grown commercially in East Lothian. Finally, as the trial judge found, seedsmen could insure against the risk of crop failure caused by supplying the wrong variety of seeds without materially increasing the price of seeds.

My Lords, even if I felt doubts about the statutory issue, I should not, for the reasons explained earlier, think it right to interfere with the unanimous original decision of that issue by the Court of Appeal.

As it is, I feel no such doubts. If I were making the original decision, I should conclude without hesitation that it would not be fair or reasonable to allow the appellants to rely on the contractual limitation of their liability.

NOTES

1. At pp. 815F–816B, Lord Bridge gave guidance on how the reasonableness question should be approached:

> This is the first time your Lordships' House has had to consider a modern statutory provision giving the court power to override contractual terms excluding or restricting liability, which depends on the court's view of what is 'fair and reasonable.' The particular provision of the modified section 55 of the Act of 1979 which applies in the instant case is of limited and diminishing importance. But the several provisions of the Unfair Contract Terms Act 1977 which depend on 'the requirement of reasonableness', defined in section 11 by reference to what is 'fair and reasonable,' albeit in a different context, are likely to come before the courts with increasing frequency. It may, therefore, be appropriate to consider how an original decision as to what is 'fair and reasonable' made in the application of any of these provisions should be approached by an appellate court. It would not be accurate to describe such a decision as an exercise of discretion. But a decision under any of the provisions referred to will have this in common with the exercise of a discretion, that, in having regard to the various matters to which the modified section 55(5) of the Act of 1979, or section 11 of the Act of 1977 direct attention, the court must entertain a whole range of considerations, put them in the scales on one side or the other, and decide at the end of the day on which side the balance comes down. There will sometimes be room for a legitimate difference of judicial opinion as to what the answer should be, where it will be impossible to say that one view is demonstrably wrong and the other demonstrably right. It must follow, in my view, that, when asked to review such a decision on appeal, the appellate court should treat the original decision with the utmost respect and refrain from interference with it unless satisfied that it proceeded upon some erroneous principle or was plainly and obviously wrong.

2. For examples of cases in which an appellate court has overturned a first instance finding on reasonableness, see *Watford Electronics Ltd v Sanderson CFL Ltd* [2001] EWCA Civ 317, [2001] 1 All ER (Comm) 696 (*page 286, 6.4.5.2*), and *Regus (UK) Ltd v Epcot Solutions Ltd* [2008] EWCA Civ 361, [2009] 1 All ER (Comm) 586 (*page 286, 6.4.5.2*).

3. In *Cleaver v Schyde Investments* [2011] EWCA Civ 929, [2011] 2 P & CR 21, Longmore LJ explained that the assessment of reasonableness in any case is limited to the facts of that case.

> 55 But the question is not whether the clause is, in general, a reasonable clause. The question is whether it was a reasonable clause in the contract made between *this* vendor and *this* purchaser at the time when the contract was made.

It is therefore very difficult to give advice on whether a clause is likely to satisfy the reasonableness requirement in s. 11. However, reviewing the case law highlights recurring factors.

R. W. Green Ltd v Cade Brothers Farms
[1978] 1 Lloyd's Rep 602

The sellers, seed potato merchants, sold to the buyers, who were farmers, 20 tons of uncertified King Edward potatoes at a price of £28 per ton. The sale was made on the standard terms of the National Association of Seed Potato Merchants, clause 5 of which provided that:

> Time being the essence of this Contract . . . notification of rejection, claim or complaint must be made to the Seller giving a statement of the grounds for such rejection claim or complaint within three days after the arrival of the seed at its destination . . . It is specifically provided and agreed that compensation and damages payable under any claim or claims arising out of this Contract under whatsoever pretext shall not under any circumstances amount in aggregate to more than the Contract price of the potatoes forming the subject of the claim or claims.

In fact, it was later discovered that the potatoes were infected with a potato virus, which was not discoverable by inspecting the seeds. The sellers brought an action to recover monies owed for seed supplied and the buyers counterclaimed to set off against this their loss of profit on the crop (£6,000). The sellers argued that they were protected from such a claim by their conditions of sale and that the buyers could recover only the price of the potatoes (£634).

Held: It was not fair and reasonable (within s. 55 of the SGA 1979) to allow reliance on that part of the clause imposing a three-day time limit for complaints, since it was not possible to discover the defect within that time. However, the part of the clause limiting liability to the cost of the potato seeds was reasonable because the parties were of equal bargaining power, the clause had been in use for many years, and it had evolved following trade practice and discussion between the Seed Potato Merchants Association and the National Farmers' Union. In addition, the buyers could have purchased certified seed at a higher price and would have been guaranteed against the virus.

GRIFFITHS J: This contract, like any commercial contract, must be considered and construed against the background of the trade in which it operates. The plaintiffs' conditions are based upon a standard form of conditions produced by the National Association of Seed Potato Merchants. They are used by a large majority of seed potato merchants and they have been in use in their present form for over 20 years. They have evolved over a much longer period as the result both of trade practice and discussions between the Association and the National Farmers' Union. They are therefore not conditions imposed by the strong upon the weak; but are rather a set of trading terms upon which both sides are apparently content to do business . . .

On my findings no complaint was made about the potatoes until 13 days after delivery. The plaintiffs therefore say that the claim is out of time and barred by the condition that it must be made within three days of delivery. The plaintiffs' directors, in their evidence, explained that such a term was necessary in the trade because potatoes are a very perishable commodity and may deteriorate badly after delivery, particularly if they are not properly stored. So it was thought reasonable to give the farmer three days to inspect and make his complaint. This appears to me to be a very reasonable requirement in the case of damage that is discoverable by reasonable inspection. But the presence of virus Y in the potatoes was not discoverable by inspection, and the complaint that was made did not relate to this defect, which neither the farmer nor the potato merchant suspected.

At the time this contract was made no one would expect it to have been practicable for the farmer to complain of virus Y in the potatoes within three days of delivery, for the simple reason that he would not know of its presence. It would therefore, in my judgment, not be fair or reasonable that this claim should be defeated because no complaint was made within three days of delivery. I therefore declare that that part of cl. 5 is unenforceable in this action and provides no defence to the plaintiffs.

Is the claim to be limited to the contract price of the potatoes? . . . The parties were of equal bargaining strength; the buyer received no inducement to accept the term. True, it appears that he could not easily have bought potatoes without this term in the contract, but he had had the protection of the National Farmers' Union to look after his interests as the contract evolved and he knew that he was trading on these conditions.

No moral blame attaches to either party; neither of them knew, nor could be expected to know, that the potatoes were infected. There was of course a risk; it was a risk that the farmer could largely have avoided by buying certified seed, but he chose not to do so. To my mind the contract in clear language places the risk in so far as damage may exceed the contract price, on the farmer. The contract has been in use for many years with the approval of the negotiating bodies acting on behalf of both seed potato merchants and farmers, and I can see no grounds upon which it would be right for the Court to say in the circumstances of this case that such a term is not fair or reasonable.

NOTES

1. A number of the Sch. 2 guidelines were applicable in this case, as follows:

(a) The parties were of equal bargaining power since, although they contracted on the sellers' standard terms, these terms had been negotiated by the relevant trade bodies. It was also possible to purchase certified seed and the buyers had chosen not to do so.

(b) It was not possible to contract for the purchase of uncertified seeds and thus avoid this clause, but this was offset by the factors in (a) above.

(c) The parties had dealt on these terms for five or six years, and the buyers ought to have been aware of them.

(d) The first part of the clause requiring defects to be notified within three days of delivery is a condition affecting liability, and the test in Sch. 2 condition (d) is whether compliance with this was reasonably practicable. Griffiths J held that it was not.

2. In *Stewart Gill Ltd v Horatio Myer & Co. Ltd* [1992] 1 QB 600 (*page 268, 6.4.1.1.1*), the Court of Appeal refused to sever unreasonable words in a clause when assessing reasonableness. The clause in *R. W. Green v Cade Brothers Farms* does, however, appear to be separable into two distinct issues and is therefore distinguishable. Equally, in *Regus (UK) Ltd v Epcot Solutions Ltd* [2008] EWCA Civ 361, [2009] 1 All ER (Comm) 586, the Court of Appeal commented (*obiter*) that if clauses are seen as independent, i.e. serving different purposes, they can be severed and enforced. As seen earlier in *Goodlife Foods Ltd v Hall Fire Protection Ltd* [2017] EWHC 767 (TCC), [2017] BLR 389 (*page 275, 6.4.3*), this too is the case for a clause purporting to exclude liability for death and personal injury for negligence as well as other risks.

St Albans City and District Council v International Computers Ltd
[1995] FSR 686, [1996] 4 All ER 481 (CA)

The claimant, a local authority, had contracted with the defendants for the provision and installation of software to enable the local authority to create a database of eligible payers of the Poll Tax. The software contained an error, so that the figure submitted to central government was overstated and the local authority therefore suffered loss. The local authority brought an action for damages and the defendants sought to rely on a limitation clause in the contract limiting their liability to £100,000. Scott Baker J, at first instance, held that the limitation clause was unreasonable and could not be relied upon.

The following factors were identified as leading to the conclusion that the limitation was unreasonable.

(a) The defendant company was very substantial and, as a wholly owned subsidiary of a multinational, had ample resources to meet any liability.

(b) The defendant company had product liability insurance cover of £50 million and could not justify the limit of liability to £100,000, which was small compared to the potential risk and the actual loss.

(c) The defendant company was in a very strong bargaining position relative to the claimant, since it was one of a limited number of companies capable of fulfilling the local authority's requirements. The alternative companies also dealt on similar standard conditions.

(d) The practical consequence of a contrary finding of reasonableness would be that the loss would be borne by the local authority's population, either through increased taxation or reduced services, whereas the defendants were covered by insurance and should carry the risk, since they were the party that stood to make the profit on the contract.

On appeal, the Court of Appeal was mainly concerned with the measure of the damages award and, in part, allowed the appeal on that issue.

NOTES

1. These factors outweighed those on the other side of the balance—namely, that this contract was between two 'businesses' that should be free to contract on whatever terms they chose, that the local authority was aware of the limitation when it contracted, and that limitations of this kind were commonplace in the industry.

2. Prior to *St Albans*, it was thought likely that a limitation clause in a contract between two 'businesses' would be reasonable in the vast majority

of cases. However, the judge in *St Albans* adopted a protectionist attitude towards the local authority, which, although a 'business' within UCTA 1977, was in a distinct position and arguably in greater need of protection than a large public limited company. Clearly, inequality of bargaining power can exist in a B2B contract.

This case can be compared with *Southwark London Borough Council v IBM UK Ltd* [2011] EWHC 549 (TCC), 135 Con LR 136, in which Akenhead J concluded, *obiter*, that the exclusion of any statutory implied terms would be reasonable given the equal bargaining power of the parties, the fact that a protracted negotiation had taken place, and that the local authority had achieved some enhancements of the software to suit its requirements.

6.4.5.2 The recent approach to reasonableness in commercial contracts

In *Monarch Airlines Ltd v London Luton Airport Ltd* [1997] CLC 698 (*page 255, 6.3.2.1*), Clarke J also had to consider whether clause 10 was unenforceable under UCTA 1977. On the facts, s. 2(2) applied, hence the defendant had to establish that the clause satisfied the reasonableness requirement in s. 11. The judge held, at p. 712, that the clause was reasonable at the time that the contract was made:

> [The clause] was generally accepted in the market, including the insurance market. Indeed, so far as I am aware, there has been no suggestion in the market (whether it be from the airlines, the airports or the insurers) that the clause be amended in any way. It was accepted by the plaintiff without demur. It has a clear meaning and the insurance arrangements of both parties could be made on the basis that the contract was governed by standard terms which had already been held to be reasonable in principle.

NOTE For a commercial contract, it should be much easier to establish the reasonableness of the clause, especially if the clause in question is contained in a standard form generally accepted in the industry. This accords with the approach adopted in *Photo Production v Securicor* [1980] AC 827 (*page 262, 6.3.5*) of non-interventionism, and leaving it to the parties to allocate the risks and responsibility for insurance cover. More recently, in *Regus (UK) Ltd v Epcot Solutions Ltd* [2008] EWCA Civ 361, [2009] 1 All ER (Comm) 586, it was held that there was nothing unreasonable in a clause limiting liability for loss of profits and consequential losses in a commercial contract, since the parties were of equal bargaining power, had negotiated their contract, and the evidence was that the customer used a similar clause in its own business. Customers were advised to take out insurance to cover their business losses, and it was generally more appropriate for the customer to take out this insurance than the service supplier. Insurance was again an important factor in assessing the reasonableness of the clause in *Goodlife Foods Ltd v Hall Fire Protection Ltd* [2018] EWCA Civ 1371. Two particular factors underlie the importance of insurance: first the identity of the party best placed to take out insurance and, secondly, the manner in which the clause was drafted (at [76]–[77]).

In *Granville Oil & Chemicals Ltd v Davies Turner & Co. Ltd* [2003] EWCA Civ 570, [2003] 1 All ER (Comm) 819, Tuckey LJ (with whose judgment Potter LJ and Hart J agreed) made the following comment on the s. 11 discretion in commercial contracts:

> [31] . . . I am less enthusiastic about its [the 1977 Act's] intrusion into contracts between commercial parties of equal bargaining strength, who should generally be considered capable of being able to make contracts of their choosing and expect to be bound by their terms.

This statement is now cited with approval as a matter of course in the context of commercial contracts involving an assessment of reasonableness. This non-interventionist approach was recently reasserted in *Goodlife Foods Ltd v Hall Fire Protection Ltd* [2018] EWCA Civ 1371 where the Court of Appeal reiterated its support for party autonomy and freedom of contract, especially where the parties are of equal bargaining power (at [103]). This non-interventionist approach highlights the judicial view that exclusion clauses are, on a construction basis, used as tools to allocate risk.

Schenkers Ltd v Overland Shoes Ltd
[1998] 1 Lloyd's Rep 498 (CA)

The claimants, freight forwarders, had contracted with the defendants, shoe importers, on the British International Freight Association (BIFA) standard trading conditions. Clause 23(A) of these conditions was a 'no set-off clause' in the following terms:

> The Customer shall pay to the Company in cash . . . all sums immediately when due, without reduction or deferment on account of any claim, counterclaim or set-off.

The defendants sought to set off a sum for value added tax (VAT), which they claimed that the claimants should have reclaimed for the benefit of the defendants. The claimants sought to rely on clause 23(A). The defendants claimed that it was unreasonable to exclude the right of set-off, that the clause had not been relied upon in practice in their long course of previous dealings, and that they were in a position of unequal bargaining power.

Held: The claimants had proved the clause was reasonable within s. 3 of UCTA 1977.

PILL LJ: In my judgment the plaintiffs have satisfied the burden upon them of establishing that cl. 23(A) in the circumstances satisfies the requirement of reasonableness. The clause was in common use and well known in the trade following comprehensive discussions between reputable and representative bodies mindful of the considerations involved. It reflects a general view as to what is reasonable in the trade concerned. It was sufficiently well known that any failure by the defendant's officers, in the course of long and substantial dealings, to put their minds to the clause cannot be relied on to establish that it was unfair or unreasonable to include it in the contracts . . . In a situation in which there was no significant inequality of bargaining position, the customs of the trade were an important factor. The parties were well aware of the circumstances in which business was conducted, the heads of expenditure to be incurred and the risks involved.

In present circumstances, I see little merit in the defendants' argument that the clause had not in practice been relied upon. The give and take practised by the parties in the course of substantial dealings upon the running account was admirable and conducive to a good business relationship but did not in my judgment prevent the plaintiffs, when the dispute arose, relying upon the term agreed. In *George Mitchell*, there was evidence that neither party expected the limitation of liability clause to [be] applied literally and a recognition that reliance on the clause was unreasonable. While there was evidence in the present case that there was no ready or frequent resort to the clause, there was no such recognition. I cannot find conduct which permits the defendants to claim that reliance on the clause would be unfair or unreasonable.

NOTES

1. Significantly, having regard to the scale of the defendants' operation and the fact that the freight forwarding market in Far East trade was very competitive, the Court of Appeal rejected the defendants' argument that it was in a position of unequal bargaining power.

2. It is highly relevant that the Court of Appeal chose to distinguish *George Mitchell* regarding the lack of previous reliance on the clause. This, and the trends in recent case law, indicates that the court's approach to reasonableness in the context of commercial contracts is nearer to the *Photo Production* approach than that in *George Mitchell*. See further the assessment by Adams and Brownsword (1988) 104 LQR 94.

The central case cited in support of the non-interventionist approach to exemption clauses in commercial contracts is the following decision of the Court of Appeal.

Watford Electronics Ltd v Sanderson CFL Ltd
[2001] EWCA Civ 317, [2001] 1 All ER (Comm) 696 (CA)

A contract for the supply of a bespoke integrated software system included (i) a clause purporting to exclude any liability for indirect or consequential losses and (ii) a clause limiting liability in a general sense to the price paid under the contract (£104,600). The system was faulty and the claimant sought damages for breach of contract amounting to £5.5 million, for loss of profits, the increased costs of working, and reimbursement of the cost of a replacement software system. At first instance, the judge held that the exemption clauses were unreasonable in their entirety.

Held (on appeal): The clauses were reasonable having been negotiated by two experienced business people who represented substantial companies of equal bargaining power.

CHADWICK LJ [with whom Peter Gibson LJ and Buckley J agreed]: Was the term a fair and reasonable one to be included?

49 . . . I am satisfied that this is a case in which, if this court takes a different view from that of the judge on the question whether the inclusion of the limit of liability clause in Sanderson's standard terms and conditions was fair and reasonable having regard to the circumstances which were, or ought reasonably to have been, known to or in the contemplation of the parties when the contract was made, it is entitled to give effect to its own view. That is because I am satisfied that the judge reached his conclusion on the wrong basis.

50 . . . [O]n a true analysis of the limit of liability clause, it comprises two distinct contract terms in relation to which it is necessary to consider whether the requirement of reasonableness is satisfied. One (to which I shall refer for convenience as 'the term excluding indirect loss') is that contained in the first sentence of the clause. The other ('the term limiting direct loss') is contained in the second sentence. It is, I think, appropriate to consider, separately in relation to each term, whether the requirement of reasonableness is satisfied; although, of course, in considering whether that requirement is satisfied in relation to each term, the existence of the other term in the contract is relevant.

51 I turn, therefore, to consider whether the requirement of reasonableness is satisfied in relation to the term excluding indirect loss. It is important to keep in mind (i) that, as a matter of construction, the term does not seek to exclude loss resulting from pre-contractual statements in relation to which a claim lies (if at all) in tort or under the 1967 Act and (ii) that the term is qualified by the addenda so that it does not exclude indirect or consequential loss resulting from breach of warranty unless Sanderson has used its best endeavours to ensure that the equipment and the software does comply with the warranty.

52 I accept that the court is required to have regard, in the present case, to the 'guideline' matters set out in Schedule 2 to the 1977 Act. There are factors, identified by the guidelines, which point to a conclusion that the term excluding indirect loss was a fair and reasonable one to include in this contract. The parties were of equal bargaining strength; the inclusion of the term was, plainly, likely to affect Sanderson's decision as to the price at which was [sic] prepared to sell its product; Watford must be

taken to have appreciated that; Watford knew of the term, and must be taken to have understood what effect it was intended to have; the product was, to some extent, modified to meet the special needs of the customer. Other factors point in the opposite direction. The judge found that, although there were other mail order packages on the market, Mailbrain was the only one which appeared to fulfil Watford's needs . . .; and, further, that Watford could not reasonably have expected to have been able to have acquired a similar software package, if available, on better terms as to performance and as to the supplier's potential liability for non-performance.

53 I do not, for my part, accept that the term excluding indirect loss is a term to which s. 11(4) of the 1977 Act applies. It is not, I think, properly to be regarded as a term by which a person (Sanderson) seeks to restrict liability to a specified sum of money; rather the term seeks to exclude liability for indirect or consequential loss altogether, in those circumstances in which it is intended to have effect. Nevertheless, it seems to me right to have regard, as part of the circumstances which were, or ought reasonably to have been, known to or in the contemplation of the parties when the contract was made, both to the resources which could be expected to be available to each party for the purpose of meeting indirect or consequential loss resulting from the failure of the equipment or software to perform in accordance with specification, and to the possibility that such loss could be covered by insurance.

54 It seems to me that the starting point in an enquiry whether, in the present case, the term excluding indirect loss was a fair and reasonable one to include in the contract which these parties made is to recognise (i) that there is a significant risk that a non-standard software product, 'customised' to meet the particular marketing, accounting or record-keeping needs of a substantial and relatively complex business (such as that carried on by Watford), may not perform to the customer's satisfaction, (ii) that, if it does not do so, there is a significant risk that the customer may not make the profits or savings which it had hoped to make (and may incur consequential losses arising from the product's failure to perform), (iii) that those risks were, or ought reasonably to have been, known to or in the contemplation of both Sanderson and Watford at the time when the contract was made, (iv) that Sanderson was in the better position to assess the risk that the product would fail to perform but (v) that Watford was in the better position to assess the amount of the potential loss if the product failed to perform, (vi) that the risk of loss was likely to be capable of being covered by insurance, but at a cost, and (vii) that both Sanderson and Watford would have known, or ought reasonably to have known, at the time when the contract was made, that the identity of the party who was to bear the risk of loss (or to bear the cost of insurance) was a factor which would be taken into account in determining the price at which the supplier was willing to supply the product and the price at which the customer was willing to purchase. With those considerations in mind, it is reasonable to expect that the contract will make provision for the risk of indirect or consequential loss to fall on one party or the other. In circumstances in which parties of equal bargaining power negotiate a price for the supply of product under an agreement which provides for the person on whom the risk of loss will fall, it seems to me that the court should be very cautious before reaching the conclusion that the agreement which they have reached is not a fair and reasonable one.

55 Where experienced businessmen representing substantial companies of equal bargaining power negotiate an agreement, they may be taken to have had regard to the matters known to them. They should, in my view, be taken to be the best judge of the commercial fairness of the agreement which they have made; including the fairness of each of the terms in that agreement. They should be taken to be the best judge on the question whether the terms of the agreement are reasonable. The court should not assume that either is likely to commit his company to an agreement which he thinks is unfair, or which he thinks includes unreasonable terms. Unless satisfied that one party has, in effect, taken unfair advantage of the other—or that a term is so unreasonable that it cannot properly have been understood or considered—the court should not interfere.

NOTES

1. In *AXA Sun Life Services plc v Campbell Martin* [2011] EWCA Civ 133, [2012] Bus LR 203, [2011] 1 CLC 312, Stanley Burnton LJ made the following opening comment in his assessment of reasonableness:

> 59 In my judgment, the starting point in the consideration of the question of reasonableness is that the Agreements were made between commercial organisations and in a commercial context. Admittedly, AXA was an immeasurably larger organisation than the companies with which it contracted, and the guarantors of the companies' liabilities were, I assume, persons of modest means. However, as financial advisors, they were accustomed to deal with written agreements, such as insurance and pension policies, and I think it fair to assume that they would generally, if not always, advise their clients to ensure that they were content with the written terms of their policies. I would therefore have expected the Defendants to have read the Agreements, and in the case of the individual Defendants the guarantees that they signed.
>
> 60 . . . The contractual provisions in issue are not unusual in the insurance industry: the evidence before the judge was that they are standard terms. Two of the company Defendants . . . had entered into previous agreements with AXA on materially identical terms.

2. Although the Court of Appeal in *Watford Electronics* had emphasized that commercial men 'should be taken to be the best judge of the commercial fairness of each of the terms of the agreement', it does not follow that an exemption clause in such a contract can *never* be unreasonable. For example, in *Overseas Medical Supplies Ltd v Orient Transport Services Ltd* [1999] CLC 1243, the defendant was protected by a limitation clause if it lost the equipment it was transporting. However, it was also a term of the contract that the defendant was to insure this equipment and the defendant had failed to do this. It was held that, although the limitation of liability was reasonable in relation to loss of the goods, it was unreasonable in respect of the loss arising through the failure to insure. It is therefore necessary to evaluate the overall purpose and effect of the clauses.

3. It would appear that, in the context of the supply of computer software, an exclusion of consequential loss will be reasonable if the contract permits some recovery for direct loss, such as a money-back guarantee.

The underlying explanation for the finding of reasonableness of the exemption covering consequential losses in computer software contracts is disclosed in the 'soft drinks' cases—namely, the nature of the risk and the scope of the potential liability.

The 'soft drinks' cases concerned the supply of carbon dioxide to manufacturers of soft drinks, where that supply was found to be contaminated with traces of benzene. In *Britvic Soft Drinks v Messer UK Ltd* [2002] EWCA Civ 548, [2002] 2 Lloyd's Rep 368, and *Bacardi-Martini Beverages Ltd v Thomas Hardy Packaging* [2002] EWCA Civ 549, [2002] 2 Lloyd's Rep 379, the exclusion clause relied upon purported to exclude implied warranties and conditions as to quality, description, and fitness for purpose. The Court of Appeal in each case held that the clause was unreasonable.

In *Britvic*, Mance LJ criticized the approach of the judge at first instance on the assessment of reasonableness and distinguished *Watford Electronics*.

MANCE LJ: 21 The Judge accepted that the parties were to be regarded as having been of equal bargaining power—see par. (a) in Sch 2 to the Act. There were other suppliers (Hydrogas and BOC) to which THP and Brothers could have gone. The Judge also treated it as axiomatic for the purposes of par. (c) that 'on the footing that the terms are applicable at all' the buyers 'must be regarded as cognizant of their existence and effect'. I am not satisfied that par. (c) can be quite so easily disposed of. Contractual incorporation may in some circumstances occur without a party either knowing, or being realistically in a position where he or it can be blamed for not knowing, of the extent of certain terms. Take someone contracting for the carriage of a parcel by rail or air on the carriers' standard conditions. No-one really expects him to obtain or read the terms. Nor do I think that par. (c) is to be necessary even to be read as equating the positions of someone who actually knows and someone who 'ought reasonably to have known' of the existence and extent of a term. It seems to me legitimate to consider and take into account the actual extent and quality of the knowledge of a party, however much he or it may, under ordinary contractual principles, have become contractually bound by the particular term(s).

22 Thus, in the case of *Watford Electronics Ltd v Sanderson CFL Ltd* [2001] EWCA Civ 317, [2001] 1 All ER (Comm) 696, cited to the Judge and to us, the Judge found as a relevant factor under par. (c) that the buyer of the relevant software was—

> . . . aware of the existence of the term, only first learned of its existence towards the end of the pre-contract discussions, attempted unsuccessfully to have it substantially amended, only succeeded in achieving a make-weight amendment and learnt from Sanderson [the supplier] that a term excluding liability was standard software industry practice.

23 The Court of Appeal in *Watford*, in upholding the validity of an exclusion of liability for any 'claims for indirect or consequential losses whether arising from negligence or otherwise', regarded that as a most material factor, as appears from the judgment given by Lord Justice Chadwick (with which Mr Justice Buckley agreed) at pars. 54(vii) and 56 and that of Lord Justice Peter Gibson at par. 62(4). In the present case, the commercial and contractual background were significantly different. The manufacture of carbon dioxide so as to exclude benzene does not compare with the provision of software (an exercise notoriously liable to give rise to problems). No-one would have contemplated that the manufacturing process would allow benzene in, or (despite cl 11.2) that the buyers (THP and Brothers) would test for benzene, or indeed for compliance with BS 4105, which Messer anyway warranted. The parties did not discuss or negotiate with regard to the specific provisions of the contract, cll 11.1 and 11.2 in particular. Clauses 11.1 and 11.2 were simply incorporated as part of Messer's standard provisions. Although this is not a consideration specifically identified in Schedule 2 [to the 1977 Act], it seems to me that it can be relevant under par. (c) and anyway as a general consideration under s. 11(2) (cf also by analogy s. 3(1)).

Thus, the fact that the contamination of the carbon dioxide would not have been contemplated was a reason favouring acceptance of liability rather than a reason favouring the reasonableness of exclusion of that liability.

It was also considered important in *Bacardi-Martini* that the contamination was the result of a manufacturing error and it was considered that the supplier ought not to be able to transfer responsibility for that risk to the buyer. The same might be said of defective computer software, but it appears to be accepted that such defects are considerably more likely, and therefore it is appropriate and reasonable at least to limit liability.

The question of the appropriateness of the risk allocation can be seen in *Balmoral Group Ltd v Borealis (UK) Ltd* [2006] EWHC 1900 (Comm), [2006] 2 Lloyd's Rep 629, [2006] 2 CLC 220, which held that, since the clause required Balmoral to bear the entire risk of latent defects in Borealis's product, it was unreasonable and an inappropriate allocation of the risk. Balmoral had no choice other than to accept Borealis's terms and Borealis could have covered the risk in relation to its own products with insurance.

CHRISTOPHER CLARKE J: 421 When the contracts were made Borealis knew that Balmoral was buying borecene for the purpose of making oil tanks and that it was relying on Borealis to supply a polymer capable of being used to make consistently satisfactory tanks. It was the assumption of both sides that it was so capable. The supply of a product which, because of a latent defect . . . made the manufacture of consistently satisfactory tanks impossible would confound those assumptions. In those circumstances a blanket exclusion of any liability whatever is *prima facie* unreasonable (as was the exclusion of any liability for the supply of carbon dioxide with an excessive benzene content in *Britvic Soft Drinks Ltd v Messer UK* [2002] 2 Lloyd's Rep 368; and *Bacardi-Martini Beverages v Thomas Hardy Packaging Ltd* [2002] 2 Lloyd's Rep 379). I do not regard the supply of product with a latent defect as so remote a contingency that it ought to play no weight in determining the reasonableness of the exclusion. Nor were these contracts in respect of which there were notorious difficulties in successful performance or a high risk of failure.

Exemption clauses and unfair contract terms

6

422 A determination of the reasonableness of a contractual exclusion requires consideration of whether the allocation of risk effected by the exclusion is appropriate. I have not been persuaded that requiring Balmoral to bear the entire risk of a latent defect in Borealis' product is an appropriate allocation of risk. The Sale of Goods Act itself recognises that, all other things being equal, it should be the seller who bears the responsibility. Borealis has extensive insurance against just such a risk. Whilst product recall insurance would probably have been available to Balmoral, albeit expensively, Balmoral did not have such insurance. The evidence does not establish that product recall insurance would have been normal for someone in Balmoral's position.

423 But commercial parties habitually make agreements amongst themselves that allocate risk; and the court should not lightly treat such agreements as unreasonable. The present case is not, however, one in which the contracts made were the result of a serious negotiation as to the incidence of risk: cf the *Watford* case where that was exactly what took place. Borealis' terms were presented on a take-it-or-leave-it basis and Balmoral's scope for going elsewhere on any better terms was very limited . . . Whilst Borealis UK's terms were standard in the trade they are not the product of any agreed process of negotiation between representatives of sellers and buyers.

424 I take into account the submissions made by Borealis . . . as to the extent of their potential liability and the cost implications of their being potentially liable for claims in respect of unfitness for any of the many purposes for which borecene might be bought. In respect of these submissions two matters strike me as of particular relevance. First, whilst liability for fitness for purpose can be onerous it is not unqualified. It only arises when the buyer reasonably relies on the seller and the goods are not reasonably fit for what the seller knows is their intended purpose. The defect must be one that lies within the seller's sphere of expertise. The seller can, of course, still be liable for a latent defect of which he is himself unaware. But, as between seller and buyer, it is more appropriate that loss from such a defect should be borne by the seller. As Scott Baker, J, as he then was, said in *St Alban's City and District Council v International Computers Ltd* [1995] FSR 686 it is not unreasonable that he who stands to make the profit should carry the loss. Borealis is a very large organisation, much larger than Balmoral both in term of assets and technical expertise, and has insurance against liabilities such as these. It can spread the cost of that insurance, and of any exposure not covered by insurance, over a very wide range of purchasers. Balmoral might be able to pass on the cost of product recall insurance but whether that is so is, on the present evidence, an open question.

425 It is material also to look at the consequences. If borecene was, contrary to my findings, not suitable for making oil tanks because of a latent defect, Balmoral will have suffered a huge loss (a foreseeable consequence of such a defect) which they had no real opportunity to avoid at the manufacturing stage. It is not reasonable that they should be without any redress from the manufacturer at all.

426 Lastly, it is not without significance that Borealis settled some of Balmoral's claims, without reference to Borealis' conditions. That cannot automatically mean that reliance on the impugned terms would have been unreasonable, or that the terms themselves were unreasonable. But, especially when the settlement is as high as £170,000, it is an indication to that effect.

6.5 Clause in a B2C contract must not be rendered unenforceable by Part 2 of the Consumer Rights Act 2015

6.5.1 Background to, and the general scope of, the Act

Directive 93/13/EEC on Unfair Terms in Consumer Contracts was originally implemented in English law by the Unfair Terms in Consumer Contracts Regulations 1994, SI 1994/3159, which substantially reproduced the wording, if not the order of presentation, of the Directive itself. The 1994 Regulations were repealed and replaced by the Unfair Terms in Consumer Contracts Regulations (UTCCR) 1999, SI 1999/2083. There is now a unified regime for consumer regulations under Part 2 of the CRA 2015. Although the UTCCR 1999 have been repealed in their entirety, as the language of Directive 93/13 is largely preserved in the 2015 Act, case law based on the UTCCR will have continuing relevance for the interpretation of many of the provisions contained in Part 2 CRA 2015 and must therefore be considered.

Whereas the UCTA 1977 regulation in the B2B context is limited to exemption clauses, i.e. clauses which purport to exclude or limit liability or remedies (as further extended by s. 13 UCTA 1977), the regulation in the consumer sphere is far more extensive since it applies to 'unfair terms' which are not regarded by the legislation as 'core terms'.

6.5.2 When does the Act apply?

Consumer Rights Act 2015

61 Contracts and notices covered by this Part

(1) This Part applies to a contract between a trader and a consumer.

(2) This does not include a contract of employment or apprenticeship.

(3) A contract to which this Part applies is referred to in this Part as a *'consumer contract'*.

The section also states that in addition to 'terms' in consumer contracts, this Part also covers 'consumer notices'.

2 Key definitions

. . .

(2) *'Trader'* means a person acting for purposes relating to that person's trade, business, craft or profession, whether acting personally or through another person acting in the trader's name or on the trader's behalf.

(3) *'Consumer'* means an individual acting for purposes that are wholly or mainly outside that individual's trade, business, craft or profession.

(4) A trader claiming that an individual was not acting for purposes wholly or mainly outside the individual's trade, business, craft or profession must prove it.

Technically, a sole trader is an individual and it might be necessary to determine whether they are 'acting for purposes that are wholly or mainly outside' their trade, business, craft, or profession.

The 'purpose' (or intention) is important and a decision under the UTCCR 1999 may be of assistance in making the distinction where the contract is made by an individual sole trader, albeit that the definition of a 'consumer' in the CRA 2015 does not require that the consumer be acting wholly for non-business purposes whereas the UTCCR 1999 definition did require this.

Overy v Paypal (Europe) Ltd
[2012] EWHC 2659 (QB), [2013] Bus LR D1

An individual had applied to use Paypal's electronic payment services to collect competition entry fees (the competition prize being his house). He had indicated that the payment service was required for business purposes, because this enabled payments to be made to him directly, but had supplied a mixture of personal details and details of his photography business on the application form. Could he seek the protection of the UTCCR 1999 when the defendant cancelled his access to the services? Did he qualify as a 'consumer' within reg. 3 UTCCR 1999 which required him to act 'for purposes which were outside his trade, business or profession'?

Held: A contract would be treated as having been concluded for a purpose outside the person's business, trade, or profession only if this business purpose were insignificant or negligible and the focus was on satisfying the consumer's needs in terms of private consumption. Although the claimant's purpose in opening the account was outside his business or profession, he also intended to use the account for payments relating to his photography business and so could not be a consumer. The judge also stressed the nature of the representations made when opening the account. The claimant was therefore acting for business purposes.

JUDGE HEGARTY QC (sitting as a High Court judge): 172 I turn, therefore, to consider the preliminary question itself as to whether the 1999 Regulations apply to the agreement made on 22 January 2007 between Mr Overy and Paypal. As I have previously held, a major purpose for which he opened the account with Paypal was to facilitate the disposal of the property which was his home by means of the competition which he was in the process of organising. It was submitted by [counsel] on behalf of Paypal that this was not in itself a purpose which was outside his trade, business or profession. [Counsel] contended that it should be categorised as a business venture, even though it was limited to the disposal of a single asset by means of a single transaction or linked series of transactions. It was intended, he submitted, to obtain for Mr Overy what would, in effect, be a trading profit over and above the price that he could have expected to receive on a sale in the open market by conventional means. Mr Overy, on the other hand, contended that he was a photographer by profession, and not an estate agent, so that his competition could not properly be regarded as an activity which fell within the activities of his trade, business or profession.

173 For reasons which I have already stated, I do not consider that this question can be answered simply by seeking to categorise Mr Overy's normal business activities and then asking whether this particular venture fell within the scope of such activities. An individual may be involved in more than one, perhaps many different, trading activities at the same time, some or all of which may overlap. Furthermore, I can see no reason why a single business venture cannot be taken into account in determining whether a particular contract is one to which the 1999 Regulations apply. So it is no answer, certainly no definitive answer, for Mr Overy simply to assert that he was a photographer and not an estate agent.

174 In the end, the question is a matter of fact and degree which has to be resolved by an application of the wording adopted by the 1999 Regulations and of the underlying Directive, assisted by the gloss placed upon that test by the Court of Justice in the *Benincasa v Dentalkit Srl* (Case C-269/95) [1997] ECR I-3767; [1998] All ER (EC) 135. I have come to the conclusion that the competition was not an adventure in the nature of trade. It involved the sale or realisation of a property which he and his wife occupied as their personal residence, albeit by wholly unorthodox means which he designed in order to maximise the amount which he was likely to realise on the disposal of the property. In principle, it seems to me to be little different from a disposal of the same asset by public auction, which itself differs from a private sale

through an estate agent only in the means chosen to achieve the sale. I take the view, therefore, that, if this had been the sole purpose for which Mr Overy had opened the Paypal account, it would have been a purpose outside any trade, business or profession in which he was involved.

175 But, as I have previously found, that was not the only purpose for which Mr Overy opened his Paypal account. I am satisfied that it was also intended to facilitate the receipt of payments for goods and services which he provided in connection with his photography and videography business. To that extent, therefore, when he entered into the contract with Paypal on 22 January 2007, he was not acting for purposes which were outside his trade, business or profession. Furthermore, in my judgment, that purpose could not reasonably be regarded as one which was insignificant or negligible. Accordingly, in view of the principles which I have attempted to summarise earlier in this judgment, he was not entitled to the protection of the 1999 Regulations.

176 But, even if I were wrong in the foregoing conclusion, I am quite satisfied that this is a case in which he would be disentitled from relying upon the 1999 Regulations, even if his purpose had in fact been wholly outside his trade, business or profession. In my judgment, by the nature of the application which he made to Paypal online and the information which he provided in so doing, he clearly conducted himself in such a way as to lead to the obvious conclusion that he was acting in his trade or professional capacity.

6.5.3 The assessment for fairness and terms and notices which are excluded from that assessment

Consumer Rights Act 2015

62 Requirement for contract terms and notices to be fair

(1) An unfair term of a consumer contract is not binding on the consumer.

(2) An unfair consumer notice is not binding on the consumer.

(3) This does not prevent the consumer from relying on the term or notice if the consumer chooses to do so.

(4) A term is unfair if, contrary to the requirement of good faith, it causes a significant imbalance in the parties' rights and obligations under the contract to the detriment of the consumer.

(5) Whether a term is fair is to be determined—

    (a) taking into account the nature of the subject matter of the contract, and

    (b) by reference to all the circumstances existing when the term was agreed and to all of the other terms of the contract or of any other contract on which it depends.

. . .

(8) This section does not affect the operation of—

    (a) section 31 (exclusion of liability: goods contracts),

    (b) section 47 (exclusion of liability: digital content contracts),

    (c) section 57 (exclusion of liability: services contracts), or

    (d) section 65 (exclusion of negligence liability).

63 Contract terms which may or must be regarded as unfair

(1) Part 1 of Schedule 2 contains an indicative and non-exhaustive list of terms of consumer contracts that may be regarded as unfair for the purposes of this Part.

NOTES

1. Section 62 is the key to the control mechanism adopted by Directive 93/13—unfair terms—which introduced the concept of good faith into English law. The key notion is a 'significant imbalance in the parties' rights and obligations arising under the contract' that is in some way contrary to the 'requirement of good faith'. These are vague and ill-defined criteria, and the CRA 2015 fails to make clear the relationship between them. In particular, following the drafting of s. 62(4), it is unclear whether the requirement of lack of good faith is additional to the condition of imbalance between the parties, or whether imbalance is to be regarded in itself as evidence of a lack of good faith. The general principles contained in s. 62(5) are limited. Consequently, identification of the criteria for compliance with the terms of the Act is a process of deduction from what is termed, in s. 63(1), an 'indicative and non-exhaustive list of terms . . . that may be regarded as unfair' and which is contained in Sch. 2, Part 1 of the CRA 2015. Twenty 'items' are listed.

There is also a small, but significant, body of case law under the UTCCR which may assist in terms of application (*page 297, 6.5.4*).

2. An unfair term is not binding on the consumer at the consumer's option. However, by s. 67 'the contract continues, so far as practicable, to have effect in every other respect', i.e. the unfair term may be severable.

3. Under s. 62(8) it is impossible to exclude liability for breach of the entrenched rights in a consumer contract. Thus, the terms providing for the goods in a consumer sale of goods to be of satisfactory quality, fit for purpose, and corresponding to description and sample etc., cannot be excluded or restricted (s. 31 CRA 2015). This clarifies one area of uncertainty that used to exist under the UTCCR 1999 (i.e. although the old s. 6(2) SGA 1979 stated that it was not possible to exclude or restrict the satisfactory quality term in a consumer contract, the term would still have needed to be shown to be unfair under the UTCCR 1999). This is no longer the case.

Consumer Rights Act 2015

65 Bar on exclusion or restriction of negligence liability

(1) A trader cannot by a term of a consumer contract or by a consumer notice exclude or restrict liability for death or personal injury resulting from negligence.

NOTE Section 65 mirrors s. 2(1) UCTA 1977 and provides that (with some exceptions such as an insurance contract and certain liability of occupiers, s. 66) a term or notice cannot exclude or restrict liability for death or personal injury resulting from negligence. This is crucial because under the UTCCR 1999, terms which sought to exclude or restrict liability in negligence for death or personal injury were not barred automatically but subjected to the fairness test. Where the term seeks to exclude or restrict other loss or damage, e.g. death or personal injury which does not result from negligence, or financial loss resulting from negligence, it is subject to the fairness test.

Consumer Rights Act 2015

71 Duty of court to consider fairness of term

(1) Subsection (2) applies to proceedings before a court which relate to a term of a consumer contract.

(2) The court must consider whether the term is fair even if none of the parties to the proceedings has raised that issue or indicated that it intends to raise it.

(3) But subsection (2) does not apply unless the court considers that it has before it sufficient legal and factual material to enable it to consider the fairness of the term.

NOTE The critical issue pertaining to the s. 62 fairness test relates to where the burden of proof on this matter lies. Under the UTCCR 1999, the burden of proving unfairness was on the consumer. The Law Commission had proposed the reversal of this burden of proof. However, nothing is stated explicitly in the Act to indicate a reversal of this burden. Section 71 CRA 2015 may provide the explanation in the new statutory acceptance that the court has a duty to consider whether a term is fair. This might imply that the 'fairness test' would now be determined by the court rather than relying specifically on the consumer to establish it, i.e. the court would look at all the evidence to determine whether the term was fair and permitted.

Consumer Rights Act 2015

64 Exclusion from assessment of fairness

(1) A term of a consumer contract may not be assessed for fairness under section 62 to the extent that—

   (a) it specifies the main subject matter of the contract, or

   (b) the assessment is of the appropriateness of the price payable under the contract by comparison with the goods, digital content or services supplied under it.

(2) Subsection (1) excludes a term from an assessment under section 62 only if it is transparent and prominent.

(3) A term is transparent for the purposes of this Part if it is expressed in plain and intelligible language and (in the case of a written term) is legible.

(4) A term is prominent for the purposes of this section if it is brought to the consumer's attention in such a way that an average consumer would be aware of the term.

(5) In subsection (4) '*average consumer*' means a consumer who is reasonably well-informed, observant and circumspect.

(6) This section does not apply to a term of a contract listed in Part 1 of Schedule 2.

NOTES

1. The CRA 2015 excludes certain (so-called 'core') terms, potentially within the scope of the Act, from any assessment of their fairness under s. 62. Yet, the terms listed in Part 1 of Sch. 2 will always be subject to such an assessment since 'they *may be* regarded as unfair' (s. 63(1), emphasis added).

2. This apart, s. 64 excludes from this assessment any term which is transparent and prominent (i.e. not hidden in the small print) and which 'specifies the main subject matter of the contract'. It is also not possible to assess the price term where the assessment for fairness would involve assessing 'the appropriateness of the price payable . . . by comparison with the goods, digital content or services supplied under it'. However, when assessing price terms under the UTCCR 1999, reg. 6(2), the courts had drawn a not altogether convincing distinction between 'core' terms relating to the price (which could not be assessed) and 'ancillary' price terms, which could be assessed for fairness because they fell outside the exclusion from assessment in reg. 6(2). The intention behind the slightly adapted wording in s. 64(1) CRA 2015 is to distinguish between 'the price' and 'aspects of the price other than the amount', e.g. such as provisions concerned with the timing of the payment or cancellation rights for non-payment, and to eliminate the concept of ancillary terms relating to the price amount or any aspect of calculating the price.

6.5.4 Case law explaining the operation of the Unfair Terms in Consumer Contracts Regulations

6.5.4.1 Director General of Fair Trading v First National Bank plc

Director General of Fair Trading v First National Bank plc
[2001] UKHL 52, [2002] 1 AC 481 (HL)

A term in a consumer loan agreement provided for interest to be paid at the contractual rate on sums owing both before and after any judgment. Thus, if judgment on the debt were obtained, interest at the contractual rate would remain payable until the judgment was discharged, despite the fact that all of the instalments due under the judgment had been paid. A debtor might budget for, and pay, judgment instalments only to discover that he owed a further sum in interest. The Director General of Fair Trading considered that this term was 'unfair' and sought an injunction to prevent its continued use. The case concerned the 1994 version of the Regulations.

The bank claimed that: (i) the Regulations had no application to the term in question, because it was a 'core term' defining the main subject matter of the contract, or concerning the adequacy of the price or remuneration (reg. 3(2) UTCCR 1994, later reg. 6(2) of the UTCCR 1999 and the equivalent provision can be found in CRA 2015, s. 64(1) and (2)—*pages 295–297, 6.5.3*); and (ii), in any event, the term was not unfair.

The judge at first instance had considered that the term was not a 'core term' and that it was not unfair. Although the Court of Appeal agreed that it was not a 'core term', it overturned that decision because it considered the term to be unfair in view of the element of unfair surprise for the debtor.

Held (on appeal to the House of Lords):

(a) The term did not fall within reg. 3(2)(b), because it was an incidental term setting out the consequences of a borrower's default. The term did not concern the adequacy of the interest earned by the bank as remuneration for the loan and so did not express the substance of the parties' bargain. Accordingly, the Regulations applied to the term.

(b) The term was not unfair within the test prescribed in the Regulations and contained nothing detrimental to the consumer.

LOR D BINGHAM [with whose reasons the other members of the House of Lords agreed]:

(1) The applicability of the Regulations

. . .

10 In reliance on regulation 3(2)(b) Lord Goodhart QC, on behalf of the bank, submitted that no assessment might be made of the fairness of the term because it concerns the adequacy of the bank's remuneration as against the services supplied, namely the loan of money. A bank's remuneration under a credit agreement is the receipt of interest. The term, by entitling the bank to post-judgment interest, concerns the quantum and thus the adequacy of that remuneration . . .

12 In agreement with the judge and the Court of Appeal, I do not accept the bank's submission on this issue. The regulations, as Professor Sir Guenter Treitel QC has aptly observed (*The Law of Contract*, 10th ed, 1999, p 248) 'are not intended to operate as a mechanism of quality or price control' and regulation 3(2) is of 'crucial importance in recognising the parties' freedom of contract with respect to the essential features of their bargain' (*ibid*, at p 249). But there is an important 'distinction between the term or terms which express the substance of the bargain and "incidental" (if important) terms which surround them' (*Chitty on Contracts*, 28th ed, 1999, 'Unfair Terms in Consumer Contracts', p 747, para 15-025). The object of the regulations and the directive is to protect consumers against the inclusion of unfair and prejudicial terms in standard-form contracts into which they enter, and that object would plainly be frustrated if regulation 3(2)(b) were so broadly interpreted as to cover any terms other than those falling squarely within it. In my opinion the term, as part of a provision prescribing the consequences of default, plainly does not fall within it. It does not concern the adequacy of the interest earned by the bank as its remuneration but is designed to ensure that the bank's entitlement to interest does not come to an end

on the entry of judgment. I do not think the bank's argument on merger advances its case. It appears that some judges in the past have been readier than I would be to infer that a borrower's covenant to pay interest was not intended to extend beyond the entry of judgment. But even if a borrower's obligation were ordinarily understood to extend beyond judgment even in the absence of an independent covenant, it would not alter my view of the term as an ancillary provision and not one concerned with the adequacy of the bank's remuneration as against the services supplied. It is therefore necessary to address the second question.

(2) Unfairness

[Lord Bingham set out the test of unfairness in the then reg. 4 of the 1994 Regulations, later regs. 5 and 6 and Sch. 2 of the 1999 Regulations and now s. 62(4) and (5), s. 63(1), and Sch. 2, Part 1 CRA 2015, set out at *pages 295–297*, 6.5.3.]

17 The test laid down by regulation 4(1), deriving as it does from article 3(1) of the directive, has understandably attracted much discussion in academic and professional circles and helpful submissions were made to the House on it. It is plain from the recitals to the directive that one of its objectives was partially to harmonise the law in this important field among all member states of the European Union. The member states have no common concept of fairness or good faith, and the directive does not purport to state the law of any single member state. It lays down a test to be applied, whatever their pre-existing law, by all member states. If the meaning of the test were doubtful, or vulnerable to the possibility of differing interpretations in differing member states, it might be desirable or necessary to seek a ruling from the European Court of Justice on its interpretation. But the language used in expressing the test, so far as applicable in this case, is in my opinion clear and not reasonably capable of differing interpretations. A term falling within the scope of the regulations is unfair if it causes a significant imbalance in the parties' rights and obligations under the contract to the detriment of the consumer in a manner or to an extent which is contrary to the requirement of good faith. The requirement of significant imbalance is met if a term is so weighted in favour of the supplier as to tilt the parties' rights and obligations under the contract significantly in his favour. This may be by the granting to the supplier of a beneficial option or discretion or power, or by the imposing on the consumer of a disadvantageous burden or risk or duty. The illustrative terms set out in Schedule 3 to the regulations provide very good examples of terms which may be regarded as unfair; whether a given term is or is not to be so regarded depends on whether it causes a significant imbalance in the parties' rights and obligations under the contract. This involves looking at the contract as a whole. But the imbalance must be to the detriment of the consumer; a significant imbalance to the detriment of the supplier, assumed to be the stronger party, is not a mischief which the regulations seek to address. The requirement of good faith in this context is one of fair and open dealing. Openness requires that the terms should be expressed fully, clearly and legibly, containing no concealed pitfalls or traps. Appropriate prominence should be given to terms which might operate disadvantageously to the customer. Fair dealing requires that a supplier should not, whether deliberately or unconsciously, take advantage of the consumer's necessity, indigence, lack of experience, unfamiliarity with the subject matter of the contract, weak bargaining position or any other factor listed in or analogous to those listed in Schedule 2 of the regulations. Good faith in this context is not an artificial or technical concept; nor, since Lord Mansfield was its champion, is it a concept wholly unfamiliar to British lawyers. It looks to good standards of commercial morality and practice. Regulation 4(1) lays down a composite test, covering both the making and the substance of the contract, and must be applied bearing clearly in mind the objective which the regulations are designed to promote . . .

20 In judging the fairness of the term it is necessary to consider the position of typical parties when the contract is made. The borrower wants to borrow a sum of money, often quite a modest sum, often for

purposes of improving his home. He discloses an income sufficient to finance repayment by instalments over the contract term. If he cannot do that, the bank will be unwilling to lend. The essential bargain is that the bank will make funds available to the borrower which the borrower will repay, over a period, with interest. Neither party could suppose that the bank would willingly forgo any part of its principal or interest. If the bank thought that outcome at all likely, it would not lend. If there were any room for doubt about the borrower's obligation to repay the principal in full with interest, that obligation is very clearly and unambiguously expressed in the conditions of contract. There is nothing unbalanced or detrimental to the consumer in that obligation; the absence of such a term would unbalance the contract to the detriment of the lender . . .

LORD STEYN: 36 . . . It is now necessary to refer to the provisions which prescribe how it should be determined whether a term is unfair. Implementing article 3(1) of the directive regulation 4(1) provides:

> 'unfair term' means any term which contrary to the requirement of good faith causes a significant imbalance in the parties' rights and obligations under the contract to the detriment of the consumer.

There are three independent requirements. But the element of detriment to the consumer may not add much. But it serves to make clear that the directive is aimed at significant imbalance against the consumer, rather than the seller or supplier. The twin requirements of good faith and significant imbalance will in practice be determinative. Schedule 2 to the Regulations, which explains the concept of good faith, provides that regard must be had, amongst other things, to the extent to which the seller or supplier has dealt fairly and equitably with the consumer. It is an objective criterion. Good faith imports, as Lord Bingham has observed in his opinion, the notion of open and fair dealing: see also *Interfoto Picture Library Ltd v Stiletto Visual Programmes Ltd* [1989] QB 433. And helpfully the commentary to the 2000 edition of Principles of European Contract Law, prepared by the Commission of European Contract Law, explains that the purpose of the provision of good faith and fair dealing is 'to enforce community standards of fairness and reasonableness in commercial transactions': at 113; *A fortiori* that is true of consumer transactions. Schedule 3 to the Regulations (which corresponds to the Annex to the directive) is best regarded as a check list of terms which must be regarded as potentially vulnerable. The examples given in Schedule 3 convincingly demonstrate that the argument of the bank that good faith is predominantly concerned with procedural defects in negotiating procedures cannot be sustained. Any purely procedural or even predominantly procedural interpretation of the requirement of good faith must be rejected.

37. That brings me to the element of significant imbalance. It has been pointed out by Hugh Collins that the test 'of a significant imbalance of the obligations obviously directs attention to the substantive unfairness of the contract': 'Good Faith in European Contract Law,' (1994), 14 Oxford Journal of Legal Studies 229, 249. It is however, also right to say that there is a large area of overlap between the concepts of good faith and significant imbalance.

38. It is now necessary to turn to the application of these requirements to the facts of the present case. The point is a relatively narrow one. I agree that the starting point is that a lender ought to be able to recover interest at the contractual rate until the date of payment, and this applies both before and after judgment. On the other hand, counsel for the Director advanced a contrary argument. Adopting the test of asking what the position of a consumer is in the contract under consideration with or without clause 8, he said that the consumer is in a significantly worse position than he would have been if there had been no such provision. Certainly, the consumer is worse off. The difficulty facing counsel, however, is that this disadvantage to the consumer appears to be the consequence not of clause 8 but of the County Courts (Interest on Judgment Debts) Order 1991. Under this Order no statutory interest is payable on a county court judgment given in proceedings to recover money due under a regulated agreement: see

regulation 2. Counsel said that for policy reasons it was decided that in such a case no interest may be recovered after judgment. He said that it is not open to the House to criticise directly or indirectly this legal context. In these circumstances he submitted that it is not legitimate for a court to conclude that fairness requires that a lender must be able to insist on a stipulation designed to avoid the statutory regime under the 1991 Order. Initially I was inclined to uphold this policy argument. On reflection, however, I have been persuaded that this argument cannot prevail in circumstances where the legislature has neither expressly nor by necessary implication barred a stipulation that interest may continue to accrue after judgment until payment in full.

39. For these reasons as well as the reasons given by Lord Bingham I agree that clause 8 is not unfair . . .

NOTES

1. 'Significant imbalance' imports considerations of the substantive fairness of the term judged in the context of the contract terms as a whole.

2. Professor Beale, 'Legislative control of fairness: The Directive on Unfair Terms in Consumer Contracts', in Beatson and Friedmann (eds.), *Good Faith and Fault in Contract Law* (Oxford University Press, 1995), p. 245, regarded good faith as having a dual operation—namely, the procedural aspects of good faith (preventing unfair surprise) and the substantive aspect concerning any imbalance in the content of the clause to the detriment of the consumer. Their Lordships clearly accepted that 'significant imbalance' is substantive, but appeared to consider that 'good faith' refers to both procedural and substantive unfairness. Lord Bingham identified 'good faith' as a requirement of 'fair and open dealing'. Whereas 'openness' clearly refers to procedural matters, 'fairness' can encompass both substantive and procedural matters, and Lord Bingham's examples refer to issues of unconscionability such as taking advantage of a weakness in bargaining position. Lord Steyn commented, at [37], that 'there is a large area of overlap between the concepts of good faith and significant imbalance', which also suggests that he saw good faith as involving substantive fairness.

3. The House of Lords was prepared to accept on these facts that the position for consumers was unsatisfactory. However, any unfairness did not result from the term in question, but from the inability of the county court to take account of contractual interest when giving judgment on a debt. This has since been amended via the Consumer Credit Act 2006.

4. This decision relates to the 1994 Regulations, but the language of the provisions was also largely reflected in the 1999 Regulations and also, as regards the test of fairness, in Part 2 of the CRA 2015. The exception is the reference in Lord Bingham's speech to Sch. 2 to the 1994 Regulations, which resembled Sch. 2 to UCTA 1977. There was no equivalent provision in the 1999 Regulations and no such provision is included in the CRA 2015.

5. The statutory provision covering 'core terms' is rather different to its predecessors (s. 64 CRA 2015, *pages 295–297, 6.5.3*) in that it is made clear that the Sch. 2 terms can never be 'core terms'. Neither can any term which specifies the main subject matter of the contract or if the assessment would involve assessing the appropriateness of the price amount, assuming that the term is transparent and prominent. If it is not, then even these terms are subject to the s. 62 fairness test.

6. The leading European case on the assessment of unfairness is *Aziz v Caixa d'Estalvis de Catalunya, Tarragona i Manresa (Catalunyacaixa)* (Case C-415/11) [2013] All ER (EC) 770. The Court of Justice of the European Union (CJEU) held (at [68]) that whether there is a 'significant imbalance in the parties' rights' is evaluated as a comparative exercise with national law to consider whether the consumer is 'in a legal situation less favourable than that provided for by the national law in force'. An imbalance alone is not enough for the term to be unfair, the imbalance must be 'contrary to the requirement of good faith', which requires courts to assess 'whether the seller or supplier, dealing fairly and equitably with the consumer, could reasonably assume that the consumer would have agreed to such a term in individual contract negotiations' (at [69]). The CJEU then added that in the light of Art. 4 of the Directive (reg. 6(1) in our case), this requires the court to determine whether the term in question 'is appropriate for securing the attainment of the objectives pursued by it in the Member State concerned and does not go beyond what is necessary to achieve them' (at [74]).

7. The Supreme Court in *ParkingEye Ltd v Beavis* [2015] UKSC 67, [2016] AC 1172 (discussed at *page 765*, and for penalty ruling at *page 765, 14.10.1.2.*) followed this approach and found a charge of £85 for overstaying in a free car park not to be unfair.

6.5.4.2 **Terms excluded from the assessment of fairness: so-called 'core terms'**

Under the UTCCR 1999 if the terms were excluded from the scope of the Regulations as 'core terms' by reg. 6(2) they could not be assessed for unfairness. The courts sometimes sought to avoid this conclusion as part of a protectionist approach by holding that reg. 6(2) ('core terms') was to be interpreted restrictively, so allowing more terms to be assessed for unfairness.

Bairstow Eves London Central Ltd v Smith
[2004] EWHC 263 (QB), [2004] 2 EGLR 25

A term in an estate agency contract provided for commission at the rate of 1.5 per cent if paid in full within ten days of completion or agreed alternative payment date; otherwise, commission was payable at 3 per cent on the sale price with interest at 3 per cent above base. The judge had concluded that this was not a 'core term' (i.e. did not concern the adequacy of the price or remuneration), and that the 3 per cent term was unfair and so not binding on the vendors. The estate agents appealed on the applicability of the Regulations.

Held: The issue here was whether the core rate was 3 per cent with an option to pay 1.5 per cent (in which case, reg. 6(2) was applicable) or whether the core rate was 1.5 per cent with a 'default' provision of 3 per cent. The judge concluded that the 1.5 per cent was contemplated as the price, with a default position of 3 per cent if the vendors failed to pay within ten days. Accordingly, reg. 6(2) did not apply and the Regulations as a whole were applicable. The issue of unfairness was not appealed.

Relying on the guidance in *Director General of Fair Trading v First National Bank*, the judge concluded as follows.

GROSS J: 25 . . . Guided by this authority, the landscape becomes clear. The object of the Regulations is *not* price control nor are the Regulations intended to interfere with the parties' freedom of contract as to the essential features of their bargain. But, that said, regulation 6(2) must be given a restrictive interpretation; otherwise a coach and horses could be driven through the Regulations. So, while it is not for the Court to re-write the parties' bargain as to the fairness or adequacy of the price itself, regulation 6(2) may be unlikely to shield terms as to price escalation or default provisions from scrutiny under the fairness requirement contained in regulation 5(1). I say 'may be unlikely' because, of course, much depends on the individual contract under consideration. When, however, regulation 6(2) is inapplicable so that regulation 5(1) is engaged, it does not follow that a term will be adjudged unfair; whether or not a term is unfair involves a separate inquiry but one which cannot be undertaken at all insofar as regulation 6(2) is applicable and bars the way.

NOTES

1. Although the judge is clear that 'much depends on the individual contract under consideration', the approach to assessing whether a term fell within reg. 6(2) must now be read in the light of the approach taken by the Supreme Court in *Office of Fair Trading v Abbey National plc* [2009] UKSC 6, [2010] 1 AC 696. On the facts, terms relating to bank charges were held to fall within reg. 6(2) on the plain meaning of the words in that regulation, so construction may be more important than policy.

2. In *Baybut v Eccle Riggs Country Park Ltd* (2006) The Times, 13 November, an express term providing for a yearly licence to use a static caravan park was held to be 'a core term' within reg. 6(2) as defining the main subject matter of the contract.

Moreover, although the UTCCR 1999 are not expressly limited to express terms, the judge considered it 'highly unlikely' that they were intended to have any application to implied terms. Terms implied by the courts at common law can be implied only if reasonable, so that the judge considered they could not then be found to be 'unfair'.

6.5.4.2.1 *The bank charges litigation*

The scope of reg. 6(2) UTCCR 1999 was at issue in the 'bank charges' litigation, in which the banks alleged that the terms imposing such charges could not be assessed for unfairness since they were 'core terms' within the then reg. 6(2)(b), i.e. the terms imposing charges related to 'the adequacy of the price or remuneration, as against the goods or services supplied in exchange'. (Banking is generally free for those customers who stay in credit, but fixed fees and interest are payable by customers with overdrafts—particularly customers who have unauthorized overdrafts.) The Court of Appeal concluded that the bank charges were 'ancillary' and so not part of 'the core terms' of the contract to which reg. 6(2)(b) applied. However, the Supreme Court reversed this, accepting the argument of the banks that the bank charges were part of the 'core bargain' and fell within reg. 6(2)(b) as being 'the price or remuneration, as against the service supplied in exchange'.

Office of Fair Trading v Abbey National plc
[2009] UKSC 6, [2010] 1 AC 696 (SC)

LORD WALKER OF GESTINGTHORPE JSC: 40 . . . [A] supply of services may be simple (an entertainer booked to perform for an hour at a children's party) or composite (a week's stay at a five-star hotel offering a wide variety of services) . . . [T]here is no principled basis on which the court could decide that some services are more essential to the contract than others and . . . the main subject matter must be described in general terms—hotel services. The services that banks offer to their current account customers are a comparable package of services. These include the collection and payment of cheques, other money transmission services, facilities for cash distribution (mainly by ATM machines either at manned branches or elsewhere) and the provision of statements in printed or electronic form.

41 When one turns to the other part of the quid pro quo of a consumer contract, the price or remuneration, the difficulty of deciding which prices are essential is just the same, and regulation 6(2)(b) contains no indication that only an 'essential' price or remuneration is relevant. Any monetary price or remuneration payable under the contract would naturally fall within the language of paragraph (b) (I discount the absence of a reference to part of the price or remuneration . . .).

42 In the case of banking services supplied to a current account customer under the 'free-if-in-credit' regime, the principal monetary consideration received by the bank consists of interest and charges on authorised and unauthorised overdrafts, and specific charges for particular non-routine services (such as expedited or foreign money transmission services). The most important element of the consideration, however, consists of the interest foregone by customers whose current accounts are in credit, since whether their credit balance is large or small, they will be receiving a relatively low rate of interest on it (sometimes a very low rate or no interest at all) . . . [Counsel] was wary about committing himself as to whether interest foregone constituted part of the bank's price or remuneration for the purposes of regulation 6(2)(b). Whatever view is taken as to that, it is clear that just as banking services to current account customers can aptly be described as a package, so can the consideration that moves from the customer to the bank. Interest foregone is an important part of that package for customers whose accounts are in credit, and overdraft interest and charges are the most important element for those customers who are not in credit. Lawyers are very used to speaking of a package (or bundle) of rights and obligations, and in that sense every obligation which a consumer undertakes by a consumer contract could be seen as part of the price or remuneration received by the supplier. But non-monetary obligations undertaken by a consumer contract (for instance, to take proper care of goods on hire-purchase, or to treat material supplied for a distance-learning course as available only to the customer personally) are not part of the

'price or remuneration' within the regulation. That is the point of Lord Steyn's observation in the *First National Bank* case [2002] 1 AC 481, para 34, that 'in a broad sense all terms of the contract are in some way related to the price or remuneration'.

43 The House of Lords' decision in the *First National Bank* case shows that not every term that is in some way linked to monetary consideration falls within regulation 6(2)(b). Paragraphs (d), (e), (f) and (l) of the 'greylist' in Schedule 2 to the 1999 Regulations are an illustration of that. But the relevant term in the *First National Bank* case was a default provision. Traders ought not to be able to outflank consumers by 'drafting themselves' into a position where they can take advantage of a default provision. But *Bairstow Eves London Central Ltd v Smith* [2004] 2 EGLR 25 shows that the court can and will be astute to prevent that. In the *First National Bank* case Lord Steyn, at para 34, indicated that what is now regulation 6(2) should be construed restrictively, and Lord Bingham said, at para 12, that it should be limited to terms 'falling squarely within it'. I respectfully agree. But in my opinion the relevant terms and the relevant charges do fall squarely within regulation 6(2)(b) . . .

The application of regulation 6(2)

47 . . . Charges for unauthorised overdrafts are monetary consideration for the package of banking services supplied to personal current account customers. They are an important part of the banks' charging structure, amounting to over 30% of their revenue stream from all personal current account customers. The facts that the charges are contingent, and that the majority of customers do not incur them, are irrelevant. On the view that I take of the construction of regulation 6(2), the fairness of the charges would be exempt from review in point of appropriateness under regulation 6(2)(b) even if fewer customers paid them, and they formed a smaller part of the banks' revenue stream. Even if the Court of Appeal's interpretation had been correct, I do not see how it could have come to the conclusion [2009] 2 WLR 1286, para 111 that charges amounting to over 30% of the revenue stream were 'not part of the core or essential bargain' . . .

Conclusion

51 For these reasons I would allow the appeal . . . I would declare that the bank charges levied on personal current account customers in respect of unauthorised overdrafts (including unpaid item charges and other related charges) constitute part of the price or remuneration for the banking services provided and, in so far as the terms giving rise to the charges are in plain intelligible language, no assessment under the Unfair Terms in Consumer Contracts Regulations 1999 of the fairness of those terms may relate to their adequacy as against the services supplied.

NOTES

1. The Supreme Court rejected the distinction between sums that represented the core bargain and ancillary sums. There was no principled basis for treating some terms as more essential than others in this context. The Court of Appeal in the 'bank charges' case—*Office of Fair Trading v Abbey National plc* [2009] EWCA Civ 116, [2009] 2 WLR 1286—and Mann J in *Office of Fair Trading v Foxtons Ltd* [2009] EWHC 1681(Ch), [2009] EGLR 133, [2009] EG 98 (CS), had placed great reliance on this distinction and on the perceptions of customers concerning the nature of the respective charges. In the *Foxtons* case, the issue was whether renewal commissions were part of a single category of 'commission payment' and so part of the 'price' for the service.

2. In *Abbey National* the question was only whether the charges represented the monetary price for the service provided in exchange under the contract. Not all terms would fall within this definition—*First National Bank* and *Bairstow Eves* were cited as examples—but these charges clearly did. They were part of the customer's package and the price paid for banking services.

3. Although it was expressly rejected by the Court of Appeal and by Mann J in the *Foxtons* case, the Supreme Court settled on a construction approach to whether terms fell within reg. 6(2), rather than an approach that tried to assess how the term was perceived by customers, including reasonable expectations, and whether it was seen as an essential or ancillary part of the core bargain.

4. In *Office of Fair Trading v Ashbourne Management Services Ltd* [2011] EWHC 1237 (Ch), [2011] ECC 31, the court had to consider whether terms setting minimum membership periods of between 12 and 36 months in contracts for gym membership were core terms within reg. 6(2), or ancillary and so capable of being assessed under the Regulations. Although it might be thought that the main subject of such an agreement is the membership and right to use the club, and that the period of time for which this applied would be ancillary to this, the judge held that the period of membership was a core term. However, since reg. 6(2)(b) precluded the assessment of fairness only by reference to the adequacy of the price or remuneration as against the services supplied, the judge thought that reg. 6(2)(a) should also preclude an assessment for fairness only by reference to the definition of the main subject matter. It was therefore possible to assess this clause for fairness pertaining to the consequences for members of early termination of their memberships.

Some of the minimum periods were weighted to cause a significant imbalance in the parties' respective positions, which was contrary to good faith. These periods were designed to exploit consumer's overestimation of their use of their gym membership.

KITCHIN J:

Does the term imposing a minimum membership period fall within the scope of regulation 6(2)(a) UTCCR?

152 Turning now to the application of these principles in the context of this case, I believe that the main subject matter of each of Ashbourne's standard form agreements involves, on the one hand, the agreement by the gym club that a consumer may become a member of the club and use and access its facilities for the minimum period and, on other hand, the payment by the member of a monthly subscription of a certain sum, again for that minimum period. I do not accept that a term providing for the minimum period is not a 'core term' but is merely a 'subsidiary provision', as the OFT urged upon me. There is a danger in using these expressions as shorthand for the words of reg. 6(2) as the Supreme Court explained in the *Abbey National* case. However, in so far as it is helpful to use them, I believe that cl. 2 of each of the agreements is a core term rather than a subsidiary provision because it defines the period during which the member is entitled to use the facilities of the gym club and, in return, must pay a particular monthly subscription. Nor do I believe the OFT gains any assistance from paras 1(b), (e) or (o) of the indicative list of terms. These all concern terms dealing in one way or another with default or non-performance. I therefore believe that cl. 2 of each of the agreements does fall within the scope of reg. 6(2).

153 That is not the end of the analysis, however, because the question then arises as to whether reg. 6(2)(a) precludes any assessment of the fairness of cl. 2 of each of the agreements or whether the regulation only precludes an assessment relating to the definition of the main subject matter of the contract, that is to say its meaning, description and clarity. In the *Abbey National* case the Supreme Court was, of course, only concerned with the scope of para. (b) of reg. 6(2). Nevertheless, it seems to me that there is no basis for drawing a distinction between the two paragraphs in this regard. If reg. 6(2)(b) only precludes the assessment of the fairness of a term by reference to the adequacy of the price or remuneration as against the goods or services supplied then, in my judgment, it follows that reg. 6(2)(a) also precludes the assessment of the fairness of a term by reference to the definition of the main subject matter of the contract. This is not only the natural meaning of the words used in reg. 6(2) but also gives effect to the purpose of its two paragraphs as explained by Lord Walker JSC. Moreover, as the House of Lords explained in the *First National Bank* case, this regulation should be given no wider an interpretation than necessary . . .

Fairness

173 In all these circumstances I believe that the defendants' business model is designed and calculated to take advantage of the naivety and inexperience of the average consumer using gym clubs at the lower end of the market. As the many complaints received by the OFT show, the defendants' standard form agreements contain a trap into which the average consumer is likely to fall.

174 I must of course give weight to the requirement that there must be a *significant* imbalance. Taking this and all the other matters to which I have referred into account I have reached the conclusion that the terms of agreements 1–10 setting minimum membership periods of 12, 24 or 36 months are so weighted as to cause a significant imbalance in the parties' rights and obligations in a manner and to an extent which is contrary to good faith. The position in relation to agreements 11–13 is, I believe, different because they do extend the circumstances in which members may terminate before the end of the minimum period. In the case of these agreements I have come to the conclusion that the threshold is higher and that a significant imbalance in the parties' rights and obligations in a manner or to an extent which is contrary to good faith only arises in those cases in which the minimum term exceeds 12 months, that is to say those which provide for a minimum membership period of 24 or 36 months. My conclusion in relation to these later agreements might well have been different had they permitted the member to terminate after 12 months on, say, 30 days' notice, perhaps with a provision requiring the member to pay the difference between the agreed subscription and

that for a rolling monthly membership for the period prior to the date of termination.

175 This brings me to the final part of the analysis, namely whether this assessment of fairness relates to the definition of the main subject matter of the agreements. In my judgment it does not. The assessment does not relate to the meaning or description of the length of the minimum period, the facilities to which the member gains access or the monthly subscription which he has to pay; nor does it relate to the adequacy of the price as against the facilities provided. Instead it relates to the obligation upon members to pay monthly subscriptions for the minimum period when they have overestimated the use they will make of their memberships and failed to appreciate that unforeseen circumstances may make their continued use of a gym impractical or their memberships unaffordable. Put another way, it relates to the consequences to members of early termination in light of the minimum membership period. Accordingly I believe the assessment is not precluded by reg. 6(2).

5. The wording of s. 64 CRA 2015 (*pages 295–297, 6.5.3*) is seemingly designed to eliminate any need for 'ancillary' terms by clearly indicating that the only 'core terms' are those that 'specify the main subject matter of the contract' or relate to the amount of the price paid for the goods or services. Even these core terms must be transparent and prominent or they will fall within the scope of the test for fairness.

Chapter 7

Privity of contract and third party rights

7.1 Origins of the privity doctrine and its relationship with consideration

The doctrine of privity of contract provides that only the parties to a contract can enjoy the benefits of that contract or suffer the burdens of it.

Consideration must move from the promisee. Traditionally, this was interpreted to mean that a person could not sue on a contract if the consideration was provided by another, even where the contract was made for his benefit.

Tweddle v Atkinson
(1861) 1 B&S 393, 121 ER 762 (QB)

John Tweddle and William Guy each agreed to pay a sum of money to the claimant (Tweddle's son) in consideration of his marrying Guy's daughter. Guy failed to pay and the claimant sought to enforce his promise against Guy's executor.

Held: The son could not enforce the promise despite the fact that the contract was for his benefit, since he had given no consideration for it.

CROMPTON J: [T]he consideration must move from the party entitled to sue upon the contract. It would be a monstrous proposition to say that a person was a party to the contract for the purpose of suing upon it for his own advantage, and not a party to it for the purpose of being sued. It is said that the father in the present case was agent for the son in making the contract, but that argument ought also to make the son liable upon it. . .

WIGHTMAN J: [I]t is now established that no stranger to the consideration can take advantage of a contract, although made for his benefit.

NOTES

1. The judgments concentrate on the fact that the consideration for Guy's promise was not provided by the claimant, but by John Tweddle. However, the claimant was also not a party to the contract.

2. Crompton J justified not allowing the claimant to enforce a contract expressly made for his benefit on the ground that it would be unfair if a person could enforce a contract under which he could not

be sued. (This problem has been addressed as part of the debate concerning reform of the third party beneficiary rule: see e.g. Iacobucci J in *London Drugs* *Ltd v Kuehne and Nagel International Ltd* (1992), 1992 CarswellBC 913, 1992 CarswellBC 315, 97 DLR (4th) 261 (SCC) (*page 320, 7.3.2*).)

Dunlop Pneumatic Tyre Co. Ltd v Selfridge & Co. Ltd
[1915] AC 847 (HL)

Dew & Co. agreed with the claimants, Dunlop, to buy a specific quantity of the claimants' tyres in consideration for obtaining discounts on the list price. Dew & Co. also agreed not to sell these tyres to trade buyers for less than list price unless a similar undertaking was given by those trade buyers that they would observe the claimants' list price. The defendants ordered Dunlop tyres from Dew & Co. and agreed with Dew & Co., in return for receiving a discount from that company, that they would not sell or offer these tyres to any private customers at less than list price. However, the defendants did sell tyres at below list price and the claimants sued them for breach of their undertaking.

Held: There was no consideration moving from the claimants to the defendants and therefore the contract was not enforceable by the claimants. Viscount Haldane LC also recognized the doctrine of privity (i.e. that no stranger to the contract can enforce it).

VISCOUNT HALDANE LC: My Lords, in the law of England certain principles are fundamental. One is that only a person who is a party to a contract can sue on it. Our law knows nothing of a jus quaesitum tertio arising by way of contract. Such a right may be conferred by way of property, as, for example, under a trust, but it cannot be conferred on a stranger to a contract as a right to enforce the contract in personam. A second principle is that if a person with whom a contract not under seal has been made is to be able to enforce it consideration must have been given by him to the promisor or to some other person at the promisor's request. . . A third proposition is that a principal not named in the contract may sue upon it if the promisee really contracted as his agent. But again, in order to entitle him so to sue, he must have given consideration either personally or through the promisee, acting as his agent in giving it.

My Lords, in the case before us, I am of opinion that the consideration, the allowance of what was in reality part of the discount to which Messrs Dew, the promisees, were entitled as between themselves and the appellants, was to be given by Messrs Dew on their own account, and was not in substance, any more than in form, an allowance made by the appellants. . .

LORD DUNEDIN: My Lords, I confess that this case is to my mind apt to nip any budding affection which one might have had for the doctrine of consideration. For the effect of that doctrine in the present case is to make it possible for a person to snap his fingers at a bargain deliberately made, a bargain not in itself unfair, and which the person seeking to enforce it has a legitimate interest to enforce. . .

Now the agreement sued on is an agreement which on the face of it is an agreement between Dew and Selfridge. But speaking for myself, I should have no difficulty in the circumstances of this case in holding it proved that the agreement was truly made by Dew as agent for Dunlop, or in other words that Dunlop was the undisclosed principal, and as such can sue on the agreement. None the less, in order to enforce it he must show consideration, moving from Dunlop to Selfridge.

In the circumstances, how can he do so? The agreement in question is not an agreement for sale. It is only collateral to an agreement for sale; but that agreement for sale is an agreement entirely between Dew and Selfridge. The tyres, the property in which upon the bargain is transferred to Selfridge, were the property of Dew, not of Dunlop, for Dew under his agreement with Dunlop held these tyres as proprietor, and not as agent. What then did Dunlop do, or forbear to do, in a question with Selfridge? The answer must be, nothing. He did not do anything, for Dew, having the right of property in the tyres, could give a good title to any one he liked, subject, it might be, to an action of damages at the instance of Dunlop for breach of contract, which action, however, could never create a vitium reale in the property of the tyres. He did not forbear in anything, for he had no action against Dew which he gave up, because Dew had fulfilled his contract with Dunlop in obtaining, on the occasion of the sale, a contract from Selfridge in the terms prescribed.

To my mind, this ends the case. That there are methods of framing a contract which will cause persons in the position of Selfridge to become bound, I do not doubt. But that has not been done in this instance; and as Dunlop's advisers must have known of the law of consideration, it is their affair that they have not so drawn the contract.

NOTE Viscount Haldane treated the privity doctrine and the rule that consideration must move from the promisee as two separate principles. Although these principles may produce the same result in a *Tweddle v Atkinson* situation in which the promise is made to one person, they may not do so where the promise is made to more than one person, but the consideration is provided by only one of these promisees.

In its Consultation Paper No. 121, *Privity of Contract: Contracts for the benefit of third parties* (1991), the Law Commission considered that the two principles were separate, since the issue of the promises that are enforceable (consideration) is distinct from the issue of who may enforce a promise (privity). In its subsequent Report No. 242, *Privity of Contract: Contracts for the benefit of third parties* (Cm. 3329, 1996), Part VI, paras. 6.1–6.8, the Law Commission accepted that because the requirement that 'consideration must move from the promisee' can be interpreted to mean 'consideration must move from the claimant', its proposals for reform of the privity rule in the context of third party beneficiaries would be ineffectual if the third party could be prevented from enforcing the contract on the basis that he had not provided consideration. However, the Law Commission considered that this was covered by the central provision of the proposed reform allowing third party enforcement, which necessarily also reformed the consideration rule where this was interpreted to mean consideration moving from the claimant. In other words, although consideration had to be provided, it would suffice that it 'move from the promisee' (contracting party) and need not be provided by the third party. Although the Contracts (Rights of Third Parties) Act 1999 gives third parties the right to enforce contractual terms in certain circumstances, there is no provision addressing the issue of consideration. Therefore, although consideration is required, it will no longer need to be provided by a third party.

? QUESTION

Does this mean that a third party is being placed in a more advantageous position than a promisee who must supply consideration for the promise?

7.2 Reform of the privity doctrine and the Contracts (Rights of Third Parties) Act 1999

It has been argued that, where a third party is the intended beneficiary, he should be able to enforce the contract. To deny this would defeat the parties' intentions, which are normally paramount in contract law.

In *Darlington Borough Council v Wiltshier Northern Ltd* [1995] 1 WLR 68, 76–8, (*page 338, 7.6.2.1*), Steyn LJ commented:

The case for recognising a contract for the benefit of a third party is simple and straightforward. The autonomy of the will of the parties should be respected. The law of contract should give effect to the reasonable expectations of contracting parties. Principle certainly requires that a burden should not be imposed on a third party without his consent. But there is no doctrinal, logical or policy reason why the law should deny effectiveness to a contract for the benefit of a third party where that is the expressed intention of the parties. Moreover, often the parties, and particularly third parties, organise their affairs on the faith of the contract. They rely on the contract. It is therefore unjust to deny effectiveness to such a contract. I will not struggle further with the point since nobody seriously asserts the contrary; but see a valuable article by Jack Beatson, . . . 'Reforming the Law of Contracts for the Benefit of Third Parties: a Second Bite at the Cherry' (1992) 45 CLP 1.

The genesis of the privity rule is suspect. It is attributed to *Tweddle v Atkinson* (1861) B&S 393. It is more realistic to say that the rule originated in the misunderstanding of *Tweddle v Atkinson*: see Atiyah, *The Rise and Fall of Freedom of Contract* (1979) p. 414 and Simpson, *A History of the Law of Contract: the Rise of the Action of Assumpsit* (1975) p. 475. While the privity rule was barely tolerable in Victorian England, it has been recognised for half a century that it has no place in our more complex commercial world. Indeed, as early as *Dunlop Pneumatic Tyre Co. Ltd v Selfridge & Co. Ltd* [1915] AC 847, 855, when the House of Lords restated the privity rule, Lord Dunedin observed in a dissenting speech that the rule made it possible for a person to snap his fingers at a bargain deliberately made, a bargain not in itself unfair, and which the person seeking to enforce it has a legitimate interest to enforce.

Among the majority, Viscount Haldane LC asserted as a self-evident truth at p. 853, that 'only a person who is a party to a contract can sue on it'. Today the doctrinal objection to the recognition of a *stipulatio alteri* continues to hold sway. While the rigidity of the doctrine of consideration has been greatly reduced in modern times, the doctrine of privity of contract persists in all its artificial technicality.

In 1937 the Law Revision Committee in its Sixth Report [*Statute of Frauds and the Doctrine of Consideration*] (Cmd 5449, paras 41–8) proposed the recognition of a right of a third party to enforce the contract which by its express terms purports to confer a benefit directly on him. In 1967 *Beswick v Beswick* [1968] AC 58, 72, Lord Reid observed that if there was a long period of delay in passing legislation on the point the House of Lords might have to deal with the matter. Twelve years later Lord Scarman, who as a former chairman of the Law Commission usually favoured legislative rather than judicial reform where radical change was involved, reminded the House that it might be necessary to review all the cases which 'stand guard over this unjust rule': *Woodar Investment Development Ltd v Wimpey Construction UK Ltd* [1980] 1 WLR 277, 300G. See also Lord Keith of Kinkel, at pp. 297H–298A. In 1981 Dillon J described the rule as 'a blot on our law and most unjust': *Forster v Silvermere Golf and Equestrian Centre Ltd* (1981) 125 Sol Jo 397. In 1983 Lord Diplock described the rule as 'an anachronistic shortcoming that has for many years been regarded as a reproach to English private law': *Swain v Law Society* [1983] 1 AC 598, 611D.

. . . And we do well to remember that the civil law legal systems of other members of the European Union recognise such contracts. That our legal system lacks such flexibility is a disadvantage in the single market. Indeed it is a historical curiosity that the legal system of a mercantile country such as England, which in other areas of the law of contract (such as, for example, the objective theory of the interpretation of contracts) takes great account of the interests of third parties, has not been able to rid itself of this unjust rule deriving from a technical conception of a contract as a purely bilateral *vinculum juris*.

In 1991 the Law Commission revisited this corner of the law. In cautious language appropriate to a consultation paper the Law Commission has expressed the provisional recommendation that 'there should be a (statutory) reform of the law to allow third parties to enforce contractual provisions made in their favour': 'Privity of Contract: Contracts for the Benefit of Third Parties', Consultation Paper No. 121, p. 132. The principal value of the consultation paper lies in its clear analysis of the practical need for the recognition of a contract for the benefit of third parties, and the explanation of the unedifying spectacle of judges trying to invent exceptions to the rule to prevent demonstrable unfairness. No doubt there will be a report by the Law Commission in the not too distant future recommending the abolition of the privity of contract rule by statute. What will then happen in regard to the proposal for legislation? The answer is really quite simple: probably nothing will happen.

But on this occasion I can understand the inaction of Parliament. There is a respectable argument that it is the type of reform which is best achieved by the courts working out sensible solutions on a case by case basis, e.g., in regard to the exact point of time when the third party is vested with enforceable contractual rights: see Consultation Paper, No. 121, para. 5.8. But that requires the door to be opened by the House of Lords reviewing the major cases which are thought to have entrenched the rule of privity of contract. Unfortunately, there will be few opportunities for the House of Lords to do so. After all, by and large, courts of law in our system are the hostages of the arguments deployed by counsel. And [counsel] for the council, the third party, made it clear to us that he will not directly challenge the privity rule if this matter should go to the House of Lords. He said that he is content to try to bring his case within exceptions to the privity rule or what Lord Diplock in *Swain v The Law Society* [1983] 1 AC 598, 611D, described as 'juristic subterfuges . . . to mitigate the effect of the lacuna resulting from the non-recognition of a jus quaesitum tertio . . .'

NOTES

1. In its Report No. 242, *Privity of Contract: Contracts for the benefit of third parties* (Cm. 3329, 1996), the Law Commission proposed a detailed legislative scheme for reform of the third party rule in preference to judicial reform. The report recommended that third parties should have the right to enforce contractual provisions if they could satisfy the test of enforceability.

2. Steyn LJ was unduly pessimistic about the prospects of legislation, because in December 1998, the government introduced the Contracts (Rights of Third Parties) Bill into the House of Lords. The Contracts (Rights of Third Parties) Act 1999 received royal assent on 11 November 1999. For a discussion of the Act, see MacMillan (2000) 63 MLR 721 and Andrews [2001] CLJ 353.

3. The 1999 Act provides that a third party may enforce a contractual term if either the contract expressly gives him the right to enforce it (s. 1(1)(a)), or the term purports to confer a benefit on him and there is nothing in the contract to indicate that the parties did not intend that the third party should be able to enforce the term (s. 1(1)(b) and s. 1(2)). In addition, 'the third party must be expressly identified in the contract by name, as a member of a class or as answering a particular description, but need not be in existence when the contract is entered into' (s. 1(3)). It is important to bear in mind that this test is not as generous as it may appear. Practice since the Act has largely involved drafting to avoid its application rather than, as might have been anticipated, drafting to ensure the application of the test of enforceability.

4. Section 4 of the 1999 Act makes it clear that the promisee retains the right to enforce the contract, and there is a provision to protect the promisor from double liability in the event of an action by both the third party and the promisee (s. 5).

5. Section 7(1) provides that the right of enforcement given by s. 1 does 'not affect any right or remedy of a third party that exists or is available' apart from this legislation. This means that it will still be necessary to consider the various devices that have been employed by the courts in an effort to avoid the application of the privity rule to third party beneficiaries. It is also necessary to consider to what extent, if at all, these devices are rendered redundant by the Act.

7.2.1 Case Law Interpretation of the Contracts (Rights of Third Parties) Act 1999, s. 1(1)(b) and (2)

7.2.1.1 Section 1(1)(b): the contract must 'purport to confer a benefit' on the 'third party'

Dolphin & Maritime & Aviation Services Ltd v Sveriges Angfartygs Assurans Forening, The Swedish Club
[2009] EWHC 716 (Comm), [2009] 1 CLC 460, [2009] 2 Lloyd's Rep 123

The claimant, Dolphin, was a recovery agent acting on behalf of the insurers in relation to a vessel entered with the Swedish Club, which had been involved in a collision. Acting on behalf of the insurers, Dolphin had entered into an agreement with the Club whereby sums recoverable from the owner of the vessel that had caused the collision were to be paid to Dolphin. However, the insurers had settled directly with the Club and the underwriters refused to pay Dolphin's commission. Dolphin had therefore sought to enforce the terms of its agreement with the Club.

Held: The agreement with the Club related only to the means by which payment was to be made to the insurers. The intended beneficiaries were the insurers on whose behalf the payment was to be received and not Dolphin, albeit that Dolphin's position would be improved if the Club had paid Dolphin (since the commission could have been deducted from this sum). It followed that the agreement with the Club did not 'purport to confer a benefit' on Dolphin.

CHRISTOPHER CLARKE J:

Discussion

72 In *Prudential Assurance Co Ltd v Ayres* ([2007] EWHC 775 (Ch)) [2007] 3 All ER 946 Lindsay J held that section 1(1)(b) of the Act was satisfied if, on a true construction of the term in question, its sense had the effect of conferring a benefit on the third party in question, and that there was within section 1(1)(b) no requirement that the benefit on the third party should be the predominant purpose or intent behind the term. In that case the term in question was a provision in a deed between a landlord and the assignee of a lease, which was a firm, that the liability of the assignee for future rent should not extend to the personal assets of the partners and that any recovery by the landlord against the assignee or 'any previous tenant' for default under the lease was limited to the assets of the partnership. The previous tenant sought to enforce this provision when sued by the landlord for arrears of rent (the assignee having failed to pay). Lindsay J held that the previous tenant was entitled to enforce this provision against the landlord (itself a lessee of a superior landlord).

73 The Court of Appeal [2008] 1 All ER 1266 reversed this decision holding that the relevant provision, properly interpreted, did not purport to confer a benefit on the previous tenant but to restrict the rights of the landlord and the previous tenant against the assignee. In those circumstances no question of the application of the 1999 Act arose.

Section 1(1)(b)

74 A contract does not purport to confer a benefit on a third party simply because the position of that third party will be improved if the contract is performed. The reference in the section to the term purporting to 'confer' a benefit seems to me to connote that the language used by the parties shows that one of the purposes of their bargain (rather than one of its incidental effects if performed) was to benefit the third party.

75 In my judgment the term in question does not purport to confer a benefit on Dolphin in the sense meant by section 1(1)(b) of the 1999 Act. The provision in the LOU that payment should be made to Dolphin or underwriters' solicitors was an agreement as to the means by which the Club's obligation to underwriters was to be discharged. It was not an indication that the agent payee was an intended beneficiary of the promise. The intended beneficiaries were the underwriters on whose behalf the payment was to be received.

76 A provision for payment of a sum to an agent on his principal's behalf is to be contrasted with an agreement by A and B that A will pay C (C not being A's agent or trustee). Further, the fact that payment is to be made either to one company (Dolphin) or any firm or company in a specified category (underwriters' solicitors) seems to me to indicate that it is not the purpose of the provision to benefit Dolphin or the solicitors rather than to specify the appropriate mode of payment.

77 Even if it be established that recovery agents usually deduct their commission from the recovery and agree with their clients that the recovery should be paid to them that would not in my judgment transform this agreement into one whose purpose was to confer a benefit on Dolphin. There are, no doubt, many agents who habitually deduct their fees or commission from the recovery that they make. That is not, in my judgment, sufficient to make an agreement to pay an agent on behalf of his principal an agreement which purports, so far as the contracting parties are concerned, to confer a benefit on the agent for the purposes of section 1(1)(b) of the 1999 Act.

7.2.1.2 **The effect of the s. 1(2) Proviso to s. 1(1)(b)**

Nisshin Shipping Co. Ltd v Cleaves & Co. Ltd
[2003] EWHC 2602 (Comm), [2004] 1 Lloyd's Rep 38

The shipbrokers (Cleaves) had negotiated nine time charters on behalf of the applicant owners (Nisshin). Each contract provided for the payment of commission to the brokers, Cleaves. There was also an arbitration clause in each contract. Cleaves sought payment of the commission, but the owners challenged the entitlement, alleging that the brokers were in repudiatory breach of the agency relationship. Cleaves purported to refer the commission issue to arbitration, although the brokers were not a party to any of the nine arbitration agreements. The arbitrator's decision that it had jurisdiction was challenged by Nisshin on the grounds that Cleaves could not rely on the 1999 Act as giving them the right to rely on the arbitration clauses. It was accepted by Cleaves that the clauses did not expressly provide that they could enforce the commission clauses directly against the owners and the central question therefore was whether they fell within s. 1(1)(b) of the Contracts (Rights of Third Parties) Act 1999, i.e. (i) whether the clause purported to confer a benefit on the brokers, and (ii) whether, on the true construction of the clause, the parties did not intend the term to be enforceable by the third party brokers.

Held: Cleaves was entitled to rely on the 1999 Act for the following reasons.

(a) The commission clauses did purport to confer a benefit on the brokers within s. 1(1)(b).

(b) Section 1(2) did not require that, for s. 1(1)(b) to apply, it had to be positively shown that the parties intended that the benefit of the term should be enforceable by the third party; rather, it merely stated that s. 1(1)(b) could not apply if, on the proper construction, it appeared that the parties *did not intend* the third party to have a right to enforcement. It was for Nisshin to allege that the parties had no such intention, so that s. 1(1)(b) should not apply. Where, as here, the contract did not express an intention to deny enforceability to the third party, but was neutral on this question, s. 1(1)(b) would apply.

(c) The charters created a trust of the promise to pay commission to the brokers, which was enforceable by the charterers as trustees (i.e. an express trust), but it did not follow from the existence of this trust that Cleaves was denied a direct right of enforcement under the 1999 Act. (In other words, the common law exceptions continue to apply and do not detract from the s. 1 direct right of enforcement. Of course, as Colman J recognized, direct enforceability will be far simpler.)

(d) The brokers (Cleaves) were therefore entitled to enforce the commission clauses in their own right under s. 1 of the Act.

COLMAN J:

Do Cleaves fall within s. 1 of the 1999 Act?

10. It is accepted on behalf of Cleaves that in none of the charters did the commission clauses expressly provide that Cleaves could enforce such clauses directly against the owners. However the real issues are (i) whether those clauses purported to confer a benefit on Cleaves within sub-s. (1)(b) of s. 1 and (ii) whether sub-s. 1(b) is disapplied by sub-s. (2) because 'on a proper construction of the contract it appears that the parties did not intend the term to be enforceable by the third party'.

[Colman J then considered an argument relating to whether the clauses conferred a benefit on Cleaves in its own right. He held that they did confer a benefit relating to the commission.]

15. It is then further argued by [counsel], on behalf of Nisshin, that on the proper construction of the charter-parties the parties to them did not intend the commission clause to be enforceable by Cleaves and accordingly s. 1(1)(b) of the 1999 Act is disapplied by s. 1(2).

16. In support of this argument Nisshin relies on three distinct points. . .

[The first argument related to the arbitration clause.]

22. Secondly, it is argued by [counsel] on behalf of Nisshin that there is no positive indication in the charter-parties that the parties did intend the brokers to have enforceable rights. There is no suggestion in those contracts that the owners and charterers were mutually in agreement that the brokers should be entitled to claim against the owners as if they were parties to the contract.

23. It is to be noted that s. 1(2) of the 1999 Act does not provide that sub-s. 1(b) is disapplied unless on a proper construction of the contract it appears that the parties intended that the benefit term should be enforceable by the third party. Rather it provides that sub-s. 1(b) is disapplied if, on a proper construction, it appears that the parties did not intend third party enforcement. In other words, if the contract is neutral on this question, sub-s. (2) does not disapply sub-s. 1(b). Whether the contract does express a mutual intention that the third party should not be entitled to enforce the benefit conferred on him or is merely neutral is a matter of construction having regard to all relevant circumstances. The purpose and background of the Law Commission's recommendations in relation to sub-s. (2) are explained in a paper by Professor Andrew Burrows who, as a member of the Law Commission, made a major contribution to the drafting of the bill as enacted. He wrote at [2000] LMCLQ 540 at p. 544:

The second test therefore uses a rebuttable presumption of intention. In doing so, it copies the New Zealand Contracts (Privity) Act, 1982, s. 4, which has used the same approach. It is this rebuttable presumption that provides the essential balance between sufficient certainty for contracting parties and the flexibility required for the reform to deal fairly with a huge range of different situations. The presumption is based on the idea that, if you ask yourself, 'When is it that parties are likely to have intended to confer rights on a third party to enforce a term, albeit that they have not expressly conferred that right', the answer will be: 'Where the term purports to confer a benefit on an expressly identified third party'. That then sets up the presumption. But the presumption can be rebutted if, as a matter of ordinary contractual interpretation, there is something else indicating that the parties did not intend such a right to be given.

24. In the present case,. . . the charter-parties are indeed neutral in the sense that they do not express any intention contrary to the entitlement of the brokers to enforce the commission term.

25. Thirdly, [counsel] submits that the parties' mutual intention on the proper construction of the contracts was to create a trust of a promise in favour of the brokers—a trust enforceable against the owners at the suit of the charterers as trustees. That being the proper construction of the contracts by reference to the state of the law at the time when the 1999 Act came into force, the very same contract wording did not, subsequently to that, evidence a different mutual intention. Accordingly, the mutual intention evidenced by the contracts was that the enforcement of the promise to pay commission would be at the suit of the charterers who must be joined by the brokers as co-claimants.

[The judge examined case law on the creation of a trust of brokers' commission, including *Les Affréteurs Réunis SA v Leopold Walford (London) Ltd* [1919] AC 801 (see *page 326, 7.5*), and concluded:]

28. Accordingly, the position in 1853 and 1919 was that when a charter-party was entered into and incorporated a term that the owners would pay commission to the brokers, the only means of enforcement of that promise was an action by the charterers and the brokers as co-plaintiff because, the charterer having contracted for commission on behalf of the broker, once the contract had been signed, the charterer became trustee of the broker's right to recover that commission, the broker being unable to enforce the promise direct and without the charterer's intervention because he was not a party to the contract and therefore had no cause of action available to him against the owner. With regard to this trustee relationship it could then be said that when the charter-party was entered into neither owners nor charterers contemplated that the brokers could sue the owners direct.

29. What is the position arising from the contract itself following the coming into force of the 1999 Act? As a matter of analysis of the underlying relationship between the parties, it must be precisely the same. Thus, the charterer is no less the trustee of the owners' promise to pay the commission, having regard to the fact that the charterer contracts for payment of the commission on behalf of a non-contracting party. Indeed, the only thing that has changed is the coming into force of the 1999 Act and the introduction of the statutory facility of a direct right of action for a non-contracting party on whom a contract purports to confer a benefit.

30. Accordingly, the argument advanced by the owners can only succeed if it is to be inferred from the existence of the underlying trustee relationship that it was the mutual intention of owners and charterers that the broker beneficiary should not be entitled to avail himself of the facility of direct action by the 1999 Act.

31. This proposition is, in my judgment, entirely unsustainable. The fact that prior to the 1999 Act it would be the mutual intention that the only available facility for enforcement would be deployed by the broker does not lead to the conclusion that, once an additional statutory facility for enforcement had been introduced, the broker would not be entitled to use it, but would instead be confined to the use of the pre-existing procedure. Indeed, quite apart from the complete lack of any logical basis for such an inference, the very cumbersome and inconvenient nature of the procedure based on the trustee relationship (described by Lord Wright as a 'cumbrous fiction') would point naturally to the preferred use by the broker of the right to sue directly provided by the 1999 Act. Not only would that original procedure be inconvenient, but it might involve risk that the broker would be prevented from recovering his commission, for example, in a case where the charterer had been dissolved in its place of incorporation or where, in the absence of cooperation by the charterer, proceedings had to be served on it outside the jurisdiction and service could not be effected. There are therefore very strong

grounds pointing against any mutual intention to confine the brokers to the old procedure and to deny them the right to rely on the 1999 Act.

32. I therefore reject the third ground relied upon by Nisshin. In so doing I reach the same conclusion as the arbitrators.

33. It follows that Cleaves are entitled to enforce the commission clauses in their own right by reason of s. 1 of the 1999 Act.

NOTE This interpretation was subsequently confirmed by the Court of Appeal in *Laemthong International Lines Co. Ltd v Artis, The Laemthong Glory (No. 2)* [2005] EWCA Civ 519, [2005] 1 CLC 739, [2005] 2 All ER (Comm) 167.

Laemthong International Lines Co. Ltd v Artis, The Laemthong Glory (No. 2)
[2005] EWCA Civ 519, [2005] 1 CLC 739, [2005] 2 All ER (Comm) 167 (CA)

The case concerned a letter of indemnity between the charterers and receivers of goods whereby the receivers would indemnify the charterers, its servants, or its agents in respect of any liability resulting from delivery of the goods at the receivers' request that was made without presentation of the bill of lading. (Under the terms of the charter, delivery was to be on presentation of the bills of lading.) The question arose of whether the shipowners, who had delivered the cargo to the receivers, were covered by this indemnity.

Held (on appeal): The shipowners were covered by the indemnity promise and entitled to enforce it in their own name. The Court of Appeal considered that the shipowners were agents of the charterers for the purposes of delivery of the goods and therefore the indemnity purported to confer a benefit on them. The receivers had failed to discharge the burden imposed by s. 1(2) of proving that this indemnity was not intended by the parties (receivers and charterers) to be enforceable by the shipowners.

7.2.2 Section 1(3)

The s. 1(3) requirement applies to both limbs of s. 1(1) (i.e. (a) and (b)) and requires that the third party be '*expressly* identified in the contract by name, as a member of a class or as answering a particular description', although the third party need not be in existence at the time the contract is made.

Avraamides v Colwill
[2006] EWCA Civ 1533, [2007] BLR 76 (CA)

A had employed C to refurbish A's bathroom. C's performance was defective and C was therefore liable to A. However, C then sold his business to B on terms whereby B assumed C's liabilities 'to pay in the normal course of time any liabilities properly incurred by C as at 31 March 2003'. Could A rely on this, as a third party beneficiary, in order to enforce this provision against B?

Held: Since A, as a third party, was not *expressly* identified in the contract B/C by name, it could not be said that the intention and effect of the agreement was that persons with rights against C could enforce those rights directly against B.

WALLER LJ: 18 The temptation in the circumstances of a case such as this, to find a route which renders the appellants liable, is great. They have taken over the assets of the company and agreed with the company to meet liabilities. The remedy of the respondents if the 1999 Act does not apply seems to be to pursue the company which, according to the evidence, now has no assets, with the possibility of persuading the liquidator of the company to then pursue the appellants for failing to discharge the liabilities which under the transfer agreement they have agreed to do. Why not save the appellants that exercise by use of the 1999 Act?

19 The answer I am afraid is that section 1(3), by use of the word 'express', simply does not allow a process of construction or implication. I considered whether it would be possible for [counsel] to rely on the fact that 'customers' are identified in the contract as beneficiaries of the first part of paragraph 3, even if liabilities in the second part includes persons other than customers. Could he submit that even though others are included within the liabilities under the second part, 'customers' as a class are identified and that is sufficient. The difficulty is that the section is concerned with the benefit conferred on a third party, and with the identification of that person. The benefit from the obligation to pay liabilities properly incurred would benefit third parties but of a large number of unidentified classes.

20 I should add that, although both parties have fought the appeal on the basis that the written agreement evidences an agreement between the company and the appellants, the fact is that the written contract is between the appellants and the shareholders, and when one adds that point to the failure to identify, I am actually doubtful whether it can be said that this agreement, on its true construction, was one under which it was intended that any persons with rights against the company were to be able to enforce them directly against the appellants. . .

Privity of contract and third party rights

7

NOTES

1. This decision illustrates that the s. 1(3) requirement is the pivotal provision in relation to the scope of the legislation.

2. In *Avraamides v Colwill*, there was also a potential problem with the s. 1(2) proviso (discussed at [20]), since the contract may well have been construed to mean that it was not the intention that any such 'liabilities' were to have direct rights of enforcement.

3. To enable A to recover, the agreement would have needed to involve an agreement to pay the current creditors of the company, since A would then have fallen within that description (subject again to there being nothing in s. 1(2) to deny the intention to allow enforcement by those creditors).

4. In *Laemthong International Lines Co. Ltd v Artis, The Laemthong Glory (No. 2)* [2005] EWCA Civ 519, [2005] 1 CLC 739, [2005] 2 All ER (Comm) 167 (*page 313, 7.2.1.2*), it was argued that the indemnity did not expressly identify the shipowners by name, but the Court of Appeal held that they must fall within the expression 'agents' of the charterer in the light of the rest of the wording of the indemnity and the fact that they were instructed to deliver the cargo on behalf of the charterers.

5. Although such an approach had been rejected by Waller LJ in *Avraamides*, the decision of Flaux J in *Starlight Shipping Co. v Allianz Marine & Aviation Versicherungs AG* [2014] EWHC 3068 (Comm), [2014] 2 CLC 503, [2014] 2 Lloyd's Rep 579, has the potential to extend the interpretation of s. 1(3) since it permits a more contextual interpretation of any words used in the clause relied upon as giving the direct right of enforcement. The judge construed 'underwriters' to include their servants and agents, specifically lawyers who had acted for the insurers and the adjuster which had investigated the insurance claim. It followed that they were third parties who were expressly identified (within s. 1(3)) as intended to be protected by the settlement terms.

FLAUX J: 88 . . . [Counsel's] primary position is that, on the basis of my decision that on the true construction of the CMI and LMI settlement agreements, 'Underwriters' in the settlement provisions encompasses the servants or agents of the insurers, then the HD parties are expressly identified by the use of that word in those clauses. Although my initial reaction was that this was not sufficient for express identification, having considered the matter further I have concluded that because 'Underwriters' in clause 2 of the CMI settlement agreement and clause 3 of the LMI settlement agreement encompasses servants or agents, that word expressly identifies a class of third party intended to have a benefit conferred on them by the settlement agreements. Accordingly, I consider that the HD parties do have a claim to damages for breach of those settlement agreements under the 1999 Act.

7.3 Agency

In *Dunlop Pneumatic Tyre Co. Ltd v Selfridge & Co. Ltd* [1915] AC 847 (*page 754, 14.10.1.1*), it was argued that Dew & Co. acted as Dunlop's agent for the purposes of extracting this undertaking from Selfridge. An agency relationship occurs where one party, the agent, is authorized by another, the principal, to negotiate and enter into contracts on its behalf. In this example, Dunlop would be the principal, so that technically the contract would be between Dunlop and Selfridge, thereby enabling Dunlop to enforce the contract. However, the agent must have the authority to act as agent for the principal and consideration must be supplied by the principal itself. On these facts, Dunlop had to have provided consideration for Selfridge's promise and the House of Lords held that none had been provided.

7.3.1 Can a third party rely on the protection of an exemption clause?

The agency argument often arose in case law in the context of whether a third party could enforce a provision (such as an exemption clause) in a contract to which he was not a party when he was sued in tort by one of the contractual parties or their assignees.

Scruttons Ltd v Midland Silicones Ltd
[1962] AC 446 (HL)

The shippers contracted with US Lines, the carrier, for the carriage from the United States to London of a drum containing chemicals. This contract of carriage contained an exemption clause limiting the liability of the carrier in the event of loss, damage, or delay to $500 (£179) per package. Scruttons was the stevedore, employed by a contract with the carrier, who negligently dropped and damaged the drum when delivering it to the consignees (Midland Silicones). Midland Silicones sued Scruttons in tort claiming the value of the drum's contents that had been lost—namely, £593. Scruttons sought to rely on the clause in the bill of lading between the shippers and US Lines, which limited their liability to £179.

Held (Lord Denning dissenting): The stevedores could not rely on the clause in a contract to which they were not parties because:

(a) there was nothing in that clause that expressly or impliedly indicated that the clause was to extend to the stevedores; and

(b) the carrier did not contract as agent for the stevedores for the benefit of the clause.

> LORD REID: I think it is necessary to have in mind certain established principles of the English law of contract. Although I may regret it, I find it impossible to deny the existence of the general rule that a stranger to a contract cannot in a question with either of the contracting parties take advantage of provisions of the contract, even where it is clear from the contract that some provision in it was intended to benefit him. That rule appears to have been crystallised a century ago in *Tweddle v Atkinson* (1861) 1 B &S 393 and finally established in this House in *Dunlop Pneumatic Tyre Co. Ltd v Selfridge & Co. Ltd* [1915] AC 847.

. . . The appellants in this case seek to get round this rule. . . they say that through the agency of the carrier they were brought into contractual relation with the shipper and that they can now found on that against the consignees, the respondents. And. . ., they say that there should be inferred from the facts an implied contract, independent of the bill of lading, between them and the respondents. . .

I can see a possibility of success of the agency argument if (first) the bill of lading makes it clear that the stevedore is intended to be protected by the provisions in it which limit liability, (secondly) the bill of lading makes it clear that the carrier, in addition to contracting for these provisions on his own behalf, is also contracting as agent for the stevedore that these provisions should apply to the stevedore, (thirdly) the carrier has authority from the stevedore to do that, or perhaps later ratification by the stevedore would suffice, and (fourthly) that any difficulties about consideration moving from the stevedore were overcome. . .

But again there is nothing of that kind in the present case. I agree with your Lordships that 'carrier' in the bill of lading does not include stevedore, and if that is so I can find nothing in the bill of lading which states or even implies that the parties to it intended the limitation of liability to extend to stevedores. Even if it could be said that reasonable men in the shoes of these parties would have agreed that the stevedores should have this benefit, that would not be enough to make this an implied term of the contract. And even if one could spell out of the bill of lading an intention to benefit the stevedore, there is certainly nothing to indicate that the carrier was contracting as agent for the stevedore in addition to contracting on his own behalf. So it appears to me that the agency argument must fail.

NOTE The House of Lords rejected the agency argument on these facts, but left the way open for a suitably drafted clause to succeed. This may be because their Lordships were recognizing the reality that such clauses are commercially efficient by allocating the risks and the burden of insurance in contracts. This is clearly recognized by Lord Goff in *The Mahkutai* [1996] AC 650, at p. 661.

New Zealand Shipping Co. Ltd v A. M. Satterthwaite & Co. Ltd, The Eurymedon
[1975] AC 154 (PC)

The facts of this case appear at *page 99, 3.1.3.6.*

Held (Viscount Dilhorne and Lord Simon of Glaisdale dissenting): The clause in question protected the third party stevedore.

LORD WILBERFORCE: The question in the appeal is whether the stevedore can take the benefit of the time limitation provision. The starting point, in discussion of this question, is provided by the House of Lords decision in *Midland Silicones Ltd v Scruttons Ltd* [1962] AC 446. There is no need to question or even to qualify that case in so far as it affirms the general proposition that a contract between two parties cannot be sued on by a third person even though the contract is expressed to be for his benefit. . . But *Midland Silicones* left open the case where one of the parties contracts as agent for the third person: in particular Lord Reid's speech spelt out, in four propositions, the prerequisites for the validity of such an agency contract.

[Lord Wilberforce referred to the four requirements stipulated by Lord Reid in *Scruttons Ltd v Midland Silicones Ltd.*]

The question in this appeal is whether the contract satisfies these propositions. Clause 1 of the bill of lading, whatever the defects in its drafting, is clear in its relevant terms. The carrier, on his own account, stipulates for certain exemptions and immunities: among these is that conferred by article III, rule 6, of the Hague Rules which discharges the carrier from all liability for loss or damage unless suit is brought within one year after delivery. In addition to these stipulations on his own account, the carrier as agent for, inter alios, independent contractors stipulates for the same exemptions.

Much was made of the fact that the carrier also contracts as agent for numerous other persons; the relevance of this argument is not apparent. It cannot be disputed that among such independent contractors, for whom, as agent, the carrier contracted, is the appellant company which habitually acts as stevedore in New Zealand by arrangement with the carrier and which is, moreover, the parent company of the carrier. The carrier was, indisputably, authorised by the appellant to contract as its agent for the purposes of clause 1. All of this is quite straightforward and was accepted by all the judges in New Zealand. The only question was, and is, the fourth question presented by Lord Reid, namely that of consideration.

See the extract from this judgment set out at *page 99, 3.1.3.6,* where Lord Wilberforce analysed this transaction as a unilateral offer of exemption made by the shipper to the stevedores through the carrier as agent. This unilateral offer was accepted when the stevedores performed services for the benefit of the shipper, i.e. unloading the goods. Since this is a unilateral contract, the act of acceptance is also the consideration. Lord Wilberforce continued:

A clause very similar to the present was given effect by a United States District Court in *Carle & Montanari Inc. v American Export Isbrandtsen Lines Inc.* [1968] 1 Lloyd's Rep 260. The carrier in that case contracted, in an exemption clause, as agent, for, inter alios, all stevedores and other independent contractors, and although it is no doubt true that the law in the United States is more liberal than ours as regards third party contracts, their Lordships see no reason why the law of the Commonwealth should be more restrictive and technical as regards agency contracts. Commercial considerations should have the same force on both sides of the Pacific.

In the opinion of their Lordships, to give the appellant the benefit of the exemptions and limitations contained in the bill of lading is to give effect to the clear intentions of a commercial document, and can be given within existing principles. They see no reason to strain the law or the facts in order to defeat these intentions. It should not be overlooked that the effect of denying validity to the clause would be to encourage actions against servants, agents and independent contractors in order to get round exemptions (which are almost invariable and often compulsory) accepted by shippers against carriers, the existence, and presumed efficacy, of which is reflected in the rates of freight. They see no attraction in this consequence.

NOTES

1. The type of clause used here is often referred to as a 'Himalaya clause'.

2. Viscount Dilhorne and Lord Simon (dissenting) considered that the contract with the stevedores would have to be bilateral and that such a contract was not supported by consideration, since the stevedores had not promised the shipper/consignee that they would unload the goods.

3. It is not possible to accept an offer about which you do not know, since the response must be in exchange for the promise: *R v Clarke* (1927) 40 CLR 227. Will the stevedores (third party) know of the terms of the bill of lading (contract of carriage) when they start to unload? This appears not to have been a problem in *The Eurymedon* because the stevedore company and the carrier company were companies in the same group, and therefore the stevedores probably did know of the carriage terms.

7.3.2 The technicalities

In general, the courts have shown themselves unwilling to make 'fine distinctions' in order to limit the applicability of the doctrine in *The Eurymedon*.

Lord Wilberforce in *Port Jackson Stevedoring Pty Ltd v Salmond & Spraggon (Australia) Pty Ltd, The New York Star* [1981] 1 WLR 138, at p. 144A–B, had stated that the Privy Council 'would not encourage a search for fine distinctions which would diminish the general applicability, in the light of established commercial practice, of the principle'. Accordingly, the Privy Council rejected an argument that it had not been shown that the carrier had authority to act on the stevedores' behalf for the benefit of the exemption clause. On the facts, the stevedores and carriers were companies in the same group, so that authority to act could be assumed.

However, problems existed in the context of building contracts resulting from the difficulty of showing that the main contractor had been authorized to act as agent for the subcontractor at the time when the main contract was made.

Southern Water Authority v Carey
[1985] 2 All ER 1077

The predecessor of the claimant water authority had entered into a contract with the main contractors for the construction of sewage works. This contract provided that, 12 months after completion, the main contractors, or their subcontractors, servants, or agents, were not to be liable for defects in the works or loss attributable to such defects. It also provided that the main contractors were to be deemed to have contracted on their own behalf and on behalf of their subcontractors, servants, and agents. The main contractor employed the defendant subcontractors. The claimant brought an action against those subcontractors alleging negligence, and the subcontractors sought to rely on the clause in the main contract.

Held: The subcontractors were not entitled to the benefit of a clause in a contract to which they were not party. They could not claim that the main contractor acted as their agent in contracting with the claimants, since, at the time the main contract was made, the subcontractors had not given the main contractor this authority. However, the defendants were not liable in tort because the clause in the main contract negatived the duty of care that they would normally have owed as subcontractors.

JUDGE DAVID SMOUT QC: I must be cautious before extending into a wider field those decisions in so far as they apply the principle of unilateral contract to the specialised practice of carriers and stevedores in mercantile law. To my mind the principle of the unilateral contract does not, taken by itself, fit easily onto the accepted facts in the instant case and it strikes me as uncomfortably artificial. It is, however, the agency element in *Satterthwaite's* case that is much to the point.

[The judge then referred to Lord Reid's four requirements mentioned in *Scruttons v Midland Silicones* (*page 318*, *7.3.1*) and continued:]

Let us then consider the four propositions in the context of the instant case. First, does the main contract make it clear that the sub-contractors are intended to be protected by the provisions in it which limit liability? To my mind the answer must be Yes. Second, does it make it clear that the main contractor in addition to contracting for these provisions on his own behalf is also contracting as agent for the subcontractors that the provisions should also apply to the sub-contractors? Again, I answer Yes: cl 30(vi) so states. The fourth proposition as to consideration poses no difficulty, for this is a contract under seal. It is the third proposition that is debatable in the instance case: had the main contractor authority from the sub-contractor, at the time of making the contract, and, if not, was there any later ratification that would suffice? Unlike *Satterthwaite's* case, there is no evidence here on which I could conclude that the main contractors had prior authority. What as to ratification? Counsel for the plaintiffs contends that there can be no ratification unless the principal was capable of being ascertained at the time when the act was done, i.e. when the deed was signed. Herein lies the defendants' difficulty. . . The fact that the fourth defendants were in the contemplation of the second defendants at the material time, as the documents show, and that it may be that the third defendants were also in contemplation, does not in my view suffice. . . I turn now away from contract to the argument as it has been put in tort. . .

No one would doubt that in an ordinary building case as between the subcontractors and the building owner who has suffered damage there is a sufficient relationship of proximity that in the reasonable contemplation of the sub-contractor carelessness on his part may be likely to cause damage to the building owner. Thus a prima facie duty of care lies on the sub-contractor. So also in this case. But one has to go on to consider whether there are any considerations which ought to negative or to reduce or limit the scope of that duty. And merely to ask the question in the context of this case seems to me to foretell the answer. Did not the plaintiffs' predecessor as building owner, as it were, itself stipulate that the sub-contractors should have a measure of protection following on the issue of appropriate taking-over certificates? We must look to see the nature of such limitation clause to consider whether or not it is relevant in defining the scope of the duty in tort. The contractual setting may not necessarily be overriding, but it is relevant in the consideration of the scope of the duty in tort for it indicates the extent of the liability which the plaintiffs' predecessor wished to impose. . . [T]he contractual setting defines the area of risk which the plaintiffs' predecessor chose to accept and for which it may or may not have sought commercial insurance. . .

. . . [T]he intent is clear, namely that the sub-contractor whose works have been so completed as to be the subject of a valid taking-over certificate should be protected in respect of those works from any liability in tort to the plaintiffs. As the plaintiffs' predecessor did so choose to limit the scope of the sub-contractors' liability, I see no reason why such limitation should not be honoured. . .

NOTES

1. Lord Reid in *Scruttons v Midland Silicones* (*page 318, 7.3.1*), had indicated that either the agent had to be authorized to act or the contract might be subsequently ratified. Ratification was not possible here, since the subcontractor was selected after the main contract was signed, whereas agency requires that the principal be capable of being ascertained at the time of the contract. This represented an important limitation on the usefulness of *The Eurymedon* since it was interpreted to mean that the subcontract had to exist at the time of the main contract. (By comparison, see now s. 1(3) of the Contracts (Rights of Third Parties) Act 1999.)

2. The practical effect of the decision on the duty of care in tort is that, although they were not a party to the main contract, the subcontractors were able to rely on its terms to protect them in relation to a claim in tort.

? QUESTIONS

1. Under the provisions of the Contracts (Rights of Third Parties) Act 1999, do you think that the stevedore in The Eurymedon and the subcontractor in Southern Water Authority v Carey could enforce the contractual provisions directly? In other words, would they satisfy the test of enforceability (see s. 1(1)–(3) at *pages 312–316, 7.2.1–7.2.2*)? If so, it will eliminate the technicality and artificiality of *The Eurymedon* analysis.

2. Would the provisions of the Act enable employees in the same position as those in the next case to enforce the contractual limitation directly? Does the clause 'purport to confer a benefit' on the employees and are they 'expressly identified in the contract by name, as members of a class or as answering a particular description'?

London Drugs Ltd v Kuehne and Nagel International Ltd
(1992), 1992 CarswellBC 913, 1992 CarswellBC315, 97 DLR (4th) 261 (SCC)

The claimants delivered a transformer to Kuehne and Nagel (the corporation) for storage upon the terms of their contract, which limited 'the warehouseman's liability' to $40. The transformer was damaged during lifting as a result of the negligence of two of the corporation's employees, and the claimants brought an action against them in tort claiming their full loss of $34,000. The question was whether the employees, who were not parties to the contract containing the limitation clause, could rely upon it. The Court of Appeal had reached a conclusion favourable to the employees by using two different approaches: (i) *The Eurymedon* analysis, although on the facts it was necessary to imply a term that the protection extended beyond the 'warehouseman' to 'employees', since it did not do so expressly; and (ii) the 'tort analysis', whereby the 'contractual matrix' including the limitation clause qualified the employees' duty of care and ensuing liability to $40.

Held (on appeal): The majority considered that the employees could rely on the limitation clause. Since they were acting in the course of their employment and performing the very services contracted for by the claimants, they were implicit third party beneficiaries of the clause.

IACOBUCCI J [L'HEUREUX-DUBE, SOPINKA, and CORY JJ concurring]: None of the traditional exceptions to privity is applicable in the case at bar. As noted by the appellant, there is no evidence to support a finding of agency or trust, and these matters were not fully argued before the courts below. While the respondents rely to a certain extent on the approach taken by Lambert J.A. in the Court of Appeal, I must say that I have much difficulty in supporting a conclusion that the approach described in *The Eurymedon*,. . . and *ITO-International Terminal Operators* [(1986) 28 DLR (4th) 641] is applicable to the facts of this case. Rather than artificially extending recognised exceptions beyond their accepted limits, I prefer approaching this matter on the basis that privity of contract would otherwise apply so as to preclude the respondents from obtaining the benefit of the limitation of liability clause. The questions I now need to address are whether this doctrine should be relaxed in the circumstances of this case and, if so, on what basis.

Should the doctrine of privity be relaxed?

. . . As noted by the appellant, the common law recognises certain exceptions to the doctrine, such as agency and trust, which enable courts, in appropriate circumstances, to arrive at results which conform with the true intentions of the contracting parties and commercial reality. However, as many have observed, the availability of these exceptions does not always correspond with their need. Accordingly, this court should not be precluded from developing the common law so as to recognise a further exception to privity of contract merely on the ground that some exceptions already exist. . .

There are few principled reasons for upholding the doctrine of privity in the circumstances of this case. . . most of the traditional reasons or justifications behind the doctrine are of little application in cases such as this one, when a third party beneficiary is relying on a contractual provision as a defence in an action brought by one of the contracting parties. There are no concerns about double recovery or flood gates of litigation brought by third party beneficiaries. The fact that a contract is a very personal affair, affecting only the parties to it, is simply a restatement of the doctrine of privity rather than a reason for its maintenance. Nor is there any concern about 'reciprocity', that is, there is no concern that it would be unjust to allow a party to sue on a contract when he cannot be sued on it.

Moreover, recognizing a right for a third party beneficiary to rely on a limitation of liability clause should have relatively little impact on the rights of contracting parties to rescind or vary their contracts, in comparison with the recognition of a third party right to sue on a contract. In the end, the most that can be said against the extension of exceptions to the doctrine of privity in this case is that the respondent employees are mere donees and have provided no consideration for the contractual limitation of liability.

The doctrine of privity fails to appreciate the special considerations which arise from the relationships of employer-employee and employer-customer. . . I am in no way suggesting that employees are a party to their employer's contracts in the traditional sense so that they can bring an action on the contract or be sued for breach of contract. However, when an employer and a customer enter into a contract for services and include a clause limiting the liability of the employer for damages arising from what will normally be conduct contemplated by the contracting parties to be performed by the employer's employees, and in fact so performed, there is simply no valid reason for denying the benefit of the clause to employees who perform the contractual obligations. The nature and scope of the limitation of liability clause in such a case coincides essentially with the nature and scope of the contractual obligations performed by the third party beneficiaries (employees).

Upholding a strict application of the doctrine of privity in the circumstances of this case would also have the effect of allowing the appellant to circumvent or escape the limitation of liability clause to which it had expressly consented. . .

. . . Holding the employees liable in these circumstances could lead to serious injustice especially when one considers that the financial position of the affected employees could vary considerably such that, for example, more well-off employees would be sued and left to look for contribution from the less well-off employees. Such a result creates also uncertainty and requires excessive expenditures on insurance in that it defeats the allocations of risk specifically made by the contracting parties and the reasonable expectations of everyone involved, including the employees. When parties enter into commercial agreements and decide that one of them *and* its employees will benefit from limited liability, or when these parties choose language such as 'warehouseman' which implies that employees will also benefit from a protection, the doctrine of privity should not stand in the way of commercial reality and justice.

How should the doctrine of privity be relaxed?

. . . In the end, the narrow question before this court is: in what circumstances should employees be entitled to benefit from a limitation of liability clause found in a contract between their employer and the plaintiff (customer)? Keeping in mind the comments made earlier and the circumstances of this appeal, I am of the view that employees may obtain such a benefit if the following requirements are satisfied:

(1) the limitation of liability clause must, either expressly or impliedly, extend its benefit to the employees (or employee) seeking to rely on it; and

(2) the employees (or employee) seeking the benefit of the limitation of liability clause must have been acting in the course of their employment *and* must have been performing the very services provided for in the contract between their employer and the plaintiff (customer) when the loss occurred. . .

It is clear that the parties did not choose express language in order to extend the benefit of the clause to employees. For example, there is no mention of words such as 'servants' or 'employees' in s. 11 (b) of the contract. As such, it cannot be said that the respondents are express third party beneficiaries with respect to the limitation of liability clause. However, this does not preclude a finding that they are *implied* third party beneficiaries. . .

When all the circumstances of this case are taken into account, including the nature of the relationship between employees and their employer, the identity of interest with respect to contractual obligations, the fact that the appellant knew that employees would be involved in performing the contractual obligations, and the absence of a clear indication in the contract to the contrary, the term 'warehouseman' in

s. 11 (b) of the contract must be interpreted as meaning 'warehousemen'. As such, the respondents are not complete strangers to the limitation of liability clause. Rather, they are unexpressed or implicit third party beneficiaries with respect to this clause. Accordingly, the first requirement of this new exception to the doctrine of privity is also met.

. . . While neither trust nor agency is applicable, the respondents are entitled to benefit directly from the limitation of liability clause in the contract between their employer and the appellant. This is so because they are third party beneficiaries with respect to that clause and because they were acting in the course of their employment and performing the very services contracted for by the appellant when the damages occurred. I acknowledge that this, in effect, relaxes the doctrine of privity and creates a limited *jus tertii*. However, when viewed in its proper context, it merely represents an incremental change to the law, necessary to see that the common law develops in a manner that is consistent with modern notions of commercial reality and justice.

? QUESTIONS

1. Would the employees satisfy the s. 1(3) requirement in the Contracts (Rights of Third Parties) Act 1999? In other words, are employees 'expressly identified in the contract by name, as a member of a class or as answering a particular description'?

2. The Law Commission's Report No. 242, *Privity of Contract: Contracts for the benefit of third parties* (Cm. 3329, 1996), Part V, rejected judicial reform of the third party beneficiary rule in favour of a detailed legislative scheme. Why was this?

7.4 The collateral contract

If a court can find the existence of a separate (collateral) contract between the promisor and the third party, it can avoid the difficulties of privity.

Shanklin Pier Ltd v Detel Products Ltd
[1951] 2 KB 854

Contractors were employed by the claimants, owners of a pier, to paint the pier. The contract permitted the claimants to specify the paint that the contractors were to use. The defendant company told the claimants that the paint they manufactured, known as 'DMU', would be suitable for the work and that two coats would have a life of at least seven years. On the faith of these statements, the claimants instructed the contractors to use two coats of DMU, and the contractors purchased the paint from the defendants. In fact, the paint lasted only three months. The claimants brought an action alleging breach of contract by the defendants. The problem was that the claimants were not party to the purchase contract between the contractors and the defendants.

Held: The claimants could succeed because there was a collateral contract between the defendants and the claimants based on the promise that the paint would last at least seven years. The consideration for this contract was the claimants' action in instructing the contractors to buy DMU from the defendants.

NOTES

1. This device has proved to be of particular use in combating the privity difficulties arising from finance agreements to enable the purchase of goods, e.g. cars. The dealer may make statements about the car, but the actual finance contract is made between the finance company and the customer. There is no contract between the dealer and the customer. If the dealer makes a promise to induce the contract with the finance company, a collateral contract will allow the customer to enforce that warranty against the dealer: *Andrews v Hopkinson* [1957] 1 QB 229.

2. In *Wells (Merstham) Ltd v Buckland Sand & Silica Ltd* [1964] 1 All ER 41, the claimants, chrysanthemum growers, asked the defendants, who were sand merchants, whether their sand would be suitable for growing chrysanthemums. The defendants confirmed that it was suitable. The claimants then bought this sand from a third party. Edmund Davies J held that the defendants were liable in contract

(following *Shanklin Pier v Detel*) when the sand did not conform to the warranty, since they had given a 'collateral undertaking' and the claimants had acquired the sand in reliance on it.

3. A further example of the application of this principle is provided by the decision of the majority of the Court of Appeal in *Bowerman v Association of British Travel Agents (ABTA) Ltd* [1996] CLC 451 (*page 149, 4.1.2*).

4. It must be doubtful whether parties in the same position as the claimants in *Shanklin Pier v Detel* would be able to satisfy the test of enforceability in the Contracts (Rights of Third Parties) Act 1999, thereby enabling them to enforce directly a contract to which they were not parties (such as the sale contract for the paint). This is because such a sale contract is unlikely to identify them expressly as being intended beneficiaries.

7.5 Trusts of contractual obligations

A trust is an equitable obligation placed on one person, the trustee, to hold property on behalf of another, the beneficiary. Is it possible to avoid the privity doctrine by showing that the contractual party holds the benefit of the promise on trust for the third party?

At one time, this device was frequently used to evade privity where a third party was intended to have the benefit of a contract. There was no requirement that the third party beneficiary had to provide any consideration for the promise.

Les Affréteurs Réunis SA v Leopold Walford (London) Ltd
[1919] AC 801 (HL)

In a charterparty contract, the shipowners promised the charterers that they would pay the broker 3 per cent commission. They later refused to pay this to the broker. The broker's action was treated as if the charterers had been added as claimants.

Held: The broker was entitled to the commission, since the charterers, as trustees for the broker, could enforce the clause against the shipowners.

NOTE However, there must now be a clear expression of intent to create a trust; a trust will not be implied. This is undoubtedly more realistic, since the difficulty with using a trust is that it is irrevocable and the parties cannot vary the terms of their agreement in the future. It must be doubtful whether the contracting parties would intend this, and if they do, they must make that intention clear.

Re Schebsman
[1944] Ch 83 (CA)

When Mr Schebsman's employment ended, his former employer agreed to pay him £5,500, in six annual instalments, as compensation for loss of his employment. If Mr Schebsman died, the payments were to be made to his widow and daughter. During the period of the agreement, Schebsman was adjudicated bankrupt and then died. His trustee in bankruptcy claimed that the amounts to be paid under the agreement were part of Mr Schebsman's estate and available to pay his creditors.

Held: The manifest intention of the agreement was that the widow should benefit and therefore the company was bound to make the payments to her. However, it was also held that the contract did not create a trust in favour of the widow and daughter.

LORD GREENE MR: The first question which arises is whether or not the debtor was a trustee for his wife and daughter of the benefit of the undertaking given by the English company in their favour. An examination of the decided cases does, it is true, show that the courts have on occasions adopted what may be called a liberal view on questions of this character, but in the present case I cannot find in the contract anything to justify the conclusion that a trust was intended. It is not legitimate to import into the contract the idea of a trust when the parties have given no indication that such was their intention. To interpret this contract as creating a trust would, in my judgment, be to disregard the dividing line between the case of a trust and the simple case of a contract made between two persons for the benefit of a third. That dividing line exists, although it may not always be easy to determine where it is to be drawn. In the present case I find no difficulty. . .

DU PARCQ LJ: It is true that, by the use possibly of unguarded language, a person may create a trust. . . without knowing it, but unless an intention to create a trust is clearly to be collected from the language used and the circumstances of the case, I think that the court ought not to be astute to discover indications of such an intention. I have little doubt that in the present case both parties (and certainly the debtor) intended to keep alive their common law right to vary consensually the terms of the obligation undertaken by the company, and if circumstances had changed in the debtor's lifetime injustice might have been done by holding that a trust had been created and that those terms were accordingly unalterable. . .

NOTES

1. Thus, there must be an express intention to create a trust of the promise: *Vandepitte v Preferred Accident Insurance Corporation of New York* [1933] AC 70. This occurred in *Nisshin Shipping Co. Ltd v Cleaves & Co. Ltd* [2003] EWHC 2602 (Comm), [2004] 1 Lloyd's Rep 38 (*page 313, 7.2.1.2*), although the judge also confirmed that it did not follow that there could therefore be no reliance on the direct enforceability rights contained in the 1999 Act.

2. In *Rolls-Royce Power Engineering plc v Ricardo Consulting Engineers Ltd* [2003] EWHC 2871 (TCC),

[2004] 2 All ER (Comm) 129, it was held that B (a contracting party) could not recover damages as trustee for C (a third party) unless, at the time of the contract, A (the other contracting party) knew, or had reason to know, that B was contracting as trustee. On the facts, there was no such knowledge of the interest of the parent company (the third party, C) in the contract, since it was only subsequently that the subsidiary company's (B's) business was transferred to the parent.

7.6 Action by the contracting party as a means of avoiding privity

Section 4 of the Contracts (Rights of Third Parties) Act 1999 makes it clear that the promisee can maintain a claim to enforce a contractual term even where a third party has enforcement rights under s. 1. In addition, where the third party is outside the scope of s. 1 and is not able to utilize a common law device (such as agency) to avoid the privity rule, its only hope of securing relief may be by means of a claim brought by the promisee.

What remedies can the contracting party secure?

7.6.1 Specific performance

Specific performance is a court order compelling the promisor to carry out his promise. However, it is a discretionary remedy and is available only if damages would be an inadequate remedy.

Beswick v Beswick
[1968] AC 58 (HL)

Peter Beswick agreed in writing with his nephew, the defendant, that he would transfer his coal-round business to the nephew. It was further agreed that the nephew would employ him as a consultant at £6 10s. a week for the rest of his life and, on his death, would pay his widow an annuity of £5 a week for life. The nephew took over the business, but, when Peter Beswick died, the nephew paid only one sum of £5 to his widow and refused to pay any more. The widow brought an action to compel the nephew to continue making the payments. She did so in two capacities:

(a) as administratrix of her late husband's estate; and

(b) in her personal capacity.

Held: She was entitled to an order of specific performance of the promise in her capacity as administratrix. There was no problem of privity or consideration, since it was as if Peter Beswick himself had been suing. However, she could not enforce the promise in her personal capacity because she was not a party to the contract.

In terms of the remedy on behalf of the estate: if damages were awarded, they would be nominal (but see Lord Pearce), since Peter Beswick's estate had not suffered any loss. To avoid this injustice to the widow, the House of Lords exercised its discretion and ordered specific performance. The overall effect was that she received the benefit of a promise in a contract to which, in her individual capacity, she was not a party.

LORD REID: For clarity I think it best to begin by considering a simple case where, in consideration of a sale by A to B, B agrees to pay the price of £1,000 to a third party X. . . what is the nature of B's obligation and who is entitled to enforce it?. . .

Lord Denning's view, expressed in this case not for the first time, is that X could enforce this obligation. But the view more commonly held in recent times has been that such a contract confers no right on X and that X could not sue for the £1,000. Leading counsel for the respondent based his case on other grounds, and as I agree that the respondent succeeds on other grounds, this would not be an appropriate case in which to solve this question. It is true that a strong Law Revision Committee recommended so long ago as 1937 (Cmd. 5449):

> That where a contract by its express terms purports to confer a benefit directly on a third party it shall be enforceable by the third party in his own name . . . (p. 31).

And, if one had to contemplate a further long period of Parliamentary procrastination, this House might find it necessary to deal with this matter. But if legislation is probable at any early date I would not deal with it in a case where that is not essential. So for the purposes of this case I shall proceed on the footing that the commonly accepted view is right.

What then is A's position?. . . The argument for the appellant is that A's only remedy is to sue B for damages for B's breach of contract in failing to pay the £1,000 to X. Then the appellant says that A can only recover nominal damages of 40s. because the fact that X has not received the money will generally cause no loss to A: he admits that there may be cases where A would suffer damage if X did not receive the money but says that the present is not such a case.

Applying what I have said to the circumstances of the present case, the respondent in her personal capacity has no right to sue, but she has a right as administratrix of her husband's estate to require the appellant to perform his obligation under the agreement. He has refused to do so and he maintains that the respondent's only right is to sue him for damages for breach of his contract. If that were so, I shall assume that he is right in maintaining that the administratrix could then only recover nominal damages because his breach of contract has caused no loss to the estate of her deceased husband.

If that were the only remedy available the result would be grossly unjust. It would mean that the appellant keeps the business which he bought and for which he has only paid a small part of the price which he agreed to pay. He would avoid paying the rest of the price, the annuity to the respondent, by paying a mere 40s. damages. . .

The respondent's second argument is that she is entitled in her capacity of administratrix of her deceased husband's estate to enforce the provision of the agreement for the benefit of herself in her personal capacity, and that a proper way of enforcing that provision is to order specific performance. That would produce a just result, and, unless there is some technical objection, I am of opinion that specific performance ought to be ordered. For the reasons given by your Lordships I would reject the arguments submitted for the appellant that specific performance is not a possible remedy in this case.

LORD PEARCE: My Lords, if the annuity had been payable to a third party in the lifetime of Beswick senior and there had been default, he could have sued in respect of the breach. His administratrix is now entitled to stand in his shoes and to sue in respect of the breach which has occured [*sic*] since his death.

It is argued that the estate can only recover nominal damages and that no other remedy is open, either to the estate or to the personal plaintiff. Such a result would be wholly repugnant to justice and commonsense. And if the argument were right it would show a very serious defect in the law.

In the first place, I do not accept the view that damages must be nominal. Lush LJ in *Lloyd's v Harper* (1880) 16 Ch D 290 said:

> Then the next question which, no doubt, is a very important and substantial one, is, that Lloyd's, having sustained no damage themselves, could not recover for the losses sustained by third parties by reason of the default of Robert Henry Harper as an underwriter. That, to my mind, is a startling and alarming doctrine, and a novelty, because I consider it to be an established rule of law that where a contract is made with A for the benefit of B, A can sue on the contract for the benefit of B, and recover all that B could have recovered if the contract had been made with B himself.

I agree with the comment of Windeyer J in the case of *Coulls v Bagot's Executor and Trustee Co. Ltd* (1967) 119 CLR 460 in the High Court of Australia that the words of Lush LJ cannot be accepted without qualification and regardless of context and also with his statement:

> I can see no reason why in such cases the damages which A would suffer upon B's breach of his contract to pay C $500 would be merely nominal: I think that in accordance with the ordinary rules for the assessment of damages for breach of contract they could be substantial. They would not necessarily be $500; they could I think be less or more.

In the present case I think that the damages, if assessed, must be substantial. It is not necessary, however, to consider the amount of damages more closely since this is a case in which, as the Court of Appeal rightly decided, the more appropriate remedy is that of specific performance.

The administratrix is entitled, if she so prefers, to enforce the agreement rather than accept its repudiation, and specific performance is more convenient than an action for arrears of payment followed by separate actions as each sum falls due. Moreover, damages for breach would be a less appropriate remedy since the parties to the agreement were intending an annuity for a widow; and a lump sum of damages does not accord with this. And if (contrary to my view) the argument that a derisory sum of damages is all that can be obtained be right, the remedy of damages in this case is manifestly useless.

The present case presents all the features which led the equity courts to apply their remedy of specific performance. The contract was for the sale of a business. The defendant could on his part clearly have obtained specific performance of it if Beswick senior or his administratrix had defaulted. Mutuality is a ground in favour of specific performance.

Moreover, the defendant on his side has received the whole benefit of the contract and it is a matter of conscience for the court to see that he now performs his part of it, Kay J said in *Hart v Hart* (1881) 18 Ch D 670:

> . . . when an agreement for valuable consideration . . . has been partially performed, the court ought to do its utmost to carry out that agreement by a decree for specific performance.

What, then, is the obstacle to granting specific performance?

It is argued that since the widow personally had no rights which she personally could enforce the court will not make an order which will have the effect of enforcing those rights. I can find no principle to this effect. The condition as to payment of an annuity to the widow personally was valid. The estate (though not the widow personally) can enforce it. Why should the estate be barred from exercising its full contractual rights merely because in doing so it secures justice for the widow who, by a mechanical defect of our law, is unable to assert her own rights? Such a principle would be repugnant to justice and fulfil no other object than that of aiding the wrongdoer. I can find no ground on which such a principle should exist.

? QUESTIONS

1. What do you think Lord Reid had in mind when he stated that 'there may be cases where A would suffer damage if X did not receive the money'? What if A, as the promisee, were contractually bound to pay the sum that B is to pay to X (the third party) if B does not do so? Could A then recover substantial damages in A's own right?

2. Would Mrs Beswick be able to enforce the nephew's promise directly under the provisions of the Contracts (Rights of Third Parties) Act 1999 (*pages 312–313, 7.2.1*)?

NOTES

1. Lord Reid referred in his judgment to 'Lord Denning's view'. Lord Denning, in *Smith and Snipes Hall Farm Ltd v River Douglas Catchment Board* [1949] 2 KB 500, had expressed the view that a promise deliberately made was enforceable by the person intended to be benefited by the promise, even though that person was not a party to the contract.

2. Lord Pearce was of the opinion that substantial, rather than nominal, damages should be recoverable by the contracting party in this situation.

3. Specific performance will not be granted if a contract has already been performed fully, but in a defective manner.

7.6.2 Promisee's action for damages

Can the promisee recover substantial damages for the loss suffered by the third party?

Jackson v Horizon Holidays Ltd
[1975] 1 WLR 1468 (CA)

The claimant booked a holiday with the defendants for himself, his wife, and his two small children at a price of £1,200. The claimant made it quite clear that he wished the holiday to be of the highest standard and specifically requested that the meals comprise four courses, with a choice of three or four dishes per course. The brochure issued by the defendants described the hotel as having excellent facilities. However, there were various breaches of these contractual terms. The claimant sought damages for the loss of the holiday, and for disappointment and distress, for himself, his wife, and children. The defendants did not contest liability, but appealed against the judge's award of £1,100 damages.

Held: Since the claimant had contracted for the benefit of himself and his family, as well as recovering for his own loss, he could also recover for that suffered by his family as a result of the breach of contract. Therefore, the damages award was not excessive.

LORD DENNING MR: We have had an interesting discussion as to the legal position when one person makes a contract for the benefit of a party. In this case it was a husband making a contract for the benefit of himself, his wife and children. Other cases readily come to mind. A host makes a contract with a restaurant for a dinner for himself and his friends. The vicar makes a contract for a coach trip for the choir. In all these cases there is only one person who makes the contract. It is the husband, the host or the vicar, as the case may be. Sometimes he pays the whole price himself. Occasionally he may get a contribution from the others. But in any case it is he who makes the contract. It would be a fiction to say that the contract was made by all the family, or all the guests, or all the choir, and that he was only an agent for them. Take this very case. It would be absurd to say that the twins of three years old were parties to the contract or that the father was making the contract on their behalf as if they were principals. It would equally be a mistake to say that in any of these instances there was a trust. The transaction bears no resemblance to a trust. There was no trust fund and no trust property. No, the real truth is that in each instance, the father, the host or the vicar, was making a contract himself for the benefit of the whole party. In short, a contract by one for the benefit of third persons.

What is the position when such a contract is broken? At present the law says that the only one who can sue is the one who made the contract. None of the rest of the party can sue, even though the contract was made for their benefit. But when that one does sue, what damages can he recover? Is he limited to his own loss? Or can he recover for the others? Suppose the holiday firm puts the family into a hotel which is only half built and the visitors have to sleep on the floor? Or suppose the restaurant is fully booked and the guests have to go away, hungry and angry, having spent so much on fares to get there? Or suppose the coach leaves the choir stranded half-way and they have to hire cars to get home? None of them individually can sue. Only the father, the host or the vicar can sue. He can, of course, recover his own damages. But can he not recover for the others? I think he can. The case comes within the principle stated by Lush LJ in *Lloyd's v Harper* (1880) 16 Ch D 290, 321:

> I consider it to be an established rule of law that where a contract is made with A for the benefit of B, A can sue on the contract for the benefit of B, and recover all that B could have recovered if the contract had been made with B himself.

It has been suggested that Lush LJ was thinking of a contract in which A was trustee for B. But I do not think so. He was a common lawyer speaking of the common law. His words were quoted with considerable approval by Lord Pearce in *Beswick v Beswick* [1968] AC 58, 88. I have myself often quoted them. I think they should be accepted as correct, at any rate so long as the law forbids the third persons themselves from suing for damages. It is the only way in which a just result can be achieved. Take the instance I have put. The guests ought to recover from the restaurant their wasted fares. The choir ought to recover the cost of hiring the taxis home. There is no one to recover for them except the one who made the contract for their benefit. He should be able to recover the expense to which they have been put, and pay it over to them. Once recovered, it will be money had and received to their use. (They might even, if desired, be joined as plaintiffs.) If he can recover for the expense, he should also be able to recover for the discomfort, vexation and upset which the whole party have suffered by reason of the breach of contract, recompensing them accordingly out of what he recovers.

Applying the principles to this case, I think that the figure of £1,100 was about right. It would, I think, have been excessive if it had been awarded only for the damage suffered by Mr Jackson himself. But when extended to his wife and children, I do not think it is excessive. People look forward to a holiday. They expect the promises to be fulfilled. When it fails, they are greatly disappointed and upset. It is difficult to assess in terms of money; but it is the task of the judges to do the best they can. I see no reason to interfere with the total award of £1,100. . .

NOTES

1. Orr LJ agreed with Lord Denning's judgment, and James LJ delivered a brief judgment indicating that this was a contract for a family holiday and that the claimant had not received this.

2. The Package Travel, Package Holidays and Package Tours Regulations 1992, SI 1992/3288, specifically now provide that 'the consumers' who are parties to the package holiday contract include 'the principal Contractor' and 'the other beneficiaries', so that members of the party have direct contractual rights (reg. 2(2)).

3. Section 5 of the Contracts (Rights of Third Parties) Act 1999 is designed to protect the promisor from double recovery, so that where a promisee has already recovered from a promisor in respect of a third party's loss and the third party then brings an action based on rights acquired under s. 1, the court has to reduce the award to the third party 'to such extent as it thinks appropriate to take account of the sum recovered by the promisee'. The section makes no express provision imposing liability on the promisee to account to the third party.

Woodar Investment Development Ltd v Wimpey Construction UK Ltd
[1980] 1 WLR 277 (HL)

Wimpey contracted to buy land for £850,000 and agreed to pay £150,000 on completion to a third party, Transworld Trade Ltd. The contract allowed the purchaser to repudiate the contract if, before completion, a statutory authority 'shall have commenced' to acquire the property by compulsory purchase. At the date of the contract, both parties knew that a draft compulsory purchase order had been made. Wimpey purported to terminate relying on this provision and Woodar sought damages, alleging that this amounted to a wrongful repudiation. Their damages claim included the loss suffered by the third party.

Held: There was no wrongful repudiation where a party was relying on a contract term to repudiate. The majority considered it necessary to examine the damages question in the light of *Jackson v Horizon Holidays*. (These remarks are necessarily *obiter*.)

LORD WILBERFORCE (*obiter*): The second issue in this appeal is one of damages. Both courts below have allowed Woodar to recover substantial damages in respect of condition I under which £150,000 was payable by Wimpey to Transworld Trade Ltd on completion. On the view which I take of the repudiation issue, this question does not require decision, but in view of the unsatisfactory state in which the law would be if the Court of Appeal's decision were to stand I must add three observations:

1. The majority of the Court of Appeal followed, in the case of Goff LJ with expressed reluctance, its previous decision in *Jackson v Horizon Holidays Ltd* [1975] 1 WLR 1468. I am not prepared to

dissent from the actual decision in that case. It may be supported either as a broad decision on the measure of damages (per James LJ) or possibly as an example of a type of contract—examples of which are persons contracting for family holidays, ordering meals in restaurants for a party, hiring a taxi for a group—calling for special treatment. As I suggested in *New Zealand Shipping Co. Ltd v A.M. Satterthwaite & Co. Ltd* [1975] AC 154, 167, there are many situations of daily life which do not fit neatly into conceptual analysis, but which require some flexibility in the law of contract. *Jackson's* case may well be one.

I cannot however agree with the basis on which Lord Denning MR put his decision in that case. The extract on which he relied from the judgment of Lush LJ in *Lloyd's v Harper* (1880) 16 Ch D 290, 321 was part of a passage in which the Lord Justice was stating as an 'established rule of law' that an agent (sc. an insurance broker) may sue on a contract made by him on behalf of the principal (sc. the assured) if the contract gives him such a right, and is no authority for the proposition required in *Jackson's* case, still less for the proposition, required here that, if Woodar made a contract for a sum of money to be paid to Transworld, Woodar can, without showing that it has itself suffered loss or that Woodar was agent or trustee for Transworld, sue for damages for non-payment of that sum. That would certainly not be an established rule of law, nor was it quoted as such authority by Lord Pearce in *Beswick v Beswick* [1968] AC 58.

2. Assuming that *Jackson's* case was correctly decided (as above), it does not carry the present case, where the factual situation is quite different. I respectfully think therefore that the Court of Appeal need not, and should not have followed it.

3. Whether in a situation such as the present—viz. where it is not shown that Woodar was agent or trustee for Transworld, or that Woodar itself sustained any loss, Woodar can recover any damages at all, or any but nominal damages, against Wimpey, and on what principle, is, in my opinion, a question of great doubt and difficulty—no doubt open in this House—but one on which I prefer to reserve my opinion.

LORD KEITH: That case [*Jackson v Horizon Holidays*] is capable of being regarded as rightly decided upon a reasonable view of the measure of damages due to the plaintiff as the original contracting party, and not as laying down any rule of law regarding the recovery of damages for the benefit of third parties. There may be a certain class of cases where third parties stand to gain indirectly by virtue of a contract, and where their deprivation of that gain can properly be regarded as no more than a consequence of the loss suffered by one of the contracting parties. In that situation there may be no question of the third parties having any claim to damages in their own right, but yet it may be proper to take into account in assessing the damages recoverable by the contracting party an element in respect of expense incurred by him in replacing by other means benefits of which the third parties have been deprived or in mitigating the consequences of that deprivation. The decision in *Jackson v Horizon Holidays Ltd* is not, however, in my opinion, capable of being supported upon the basis of the true ratio decidendi in *Lloyd's v Harper*, 16 Ch D 290, which rested entirely on the principles of agency.

I would also associate myself with the observations of my noble and learned friend, Lord Scarman, as to the desirability of this House having an opportunity of reviewing, in some appropriate future case, the general attitude of English law towards the topic of jus quaesitum tertio.

LORD SCARMAN: [B]ecause of its importance, I propose to say a few words on the question of damages.

The plaintiff company agreed to sell the land to the defendants for £850,000. They also required the defendants to pay £150,000 to a third party. The covenant for this payment was in the following terms:

1. Upon completion of the purchase of the whole or any part of the land the purchaser shall pay to Transworld Trade Ltd of 25 Jermyn Street, London, SW1 a sum of £150,000.

No relationship of trust or agency was proved to exist between the plaintiff company and Transworld Trade Ltd. No doubt, it suited Mr Cornwell to split up the moneys payable under the contract between the two companies: but it is not known, let alone established by evidence (though an intelligent guess is possible) why he did so, or why the plaintiffs desired this money to be paid to Transworld Trade. It is simply a case of B agreeing with A to pay a sum of money to C.

B, in breach of his contract with A, has failed to pay C. C, it is said, has no remedy, because the English law of contract recognises no 'jus quaesitum tertio': *Tweddle v Atkinson* (1861) 1 B&S 393. No doubt, it was for this reason that Transworld Trade is not a party to the suit. A, it is acknowledged, could in certain circumstances obtain specific performance of the promise to pay C: *Beswick v Beswick* [1968] AC 58. But, since the contract in the present case is admitted (for reasons which do not fall to be considered by the House) to be no longer in existence, specific performance is not available. A's remedy lies only in an award of damages to himself. It is submitted that, in the absence of any evidence that A has suffered loss by reason of B's failure to pay C, A is only entitled to nominal damages.

I wish to add nothing to what your Lordships have already said about the authorities which the Court of Appeal cited as leading to the conclusion that the plaintiff company is entitled to substantial damages for the defendants' failure to pay Transworld Trade. I agree that they do not support the conclusion. But I regret that this House has not yet found the opportunity to reconsider the two rules which effectually prevent A or C recovering that which B, for value, has agreed to provide.

First, the 'jus quaesitum tertio.' I respectfully agree with Lord Reid that the denial by English law of a 'jus quaesitum tertio' calls for reconsideration. In *Beswick v Beswick* [1968] AC 58, 72 Lord Reid, after referring to the Law Revision Committee's recommendation in 1937 (Cmnd. 5449) p. 31 that the third party should be able to enforce a contractual promise taken by another for his benefit, observed:

> And, if one had to contemplate a further long period of Parliamentary procrastination, this House might find it necessary to deal with this matter.

The committee reported in 1937: *Beswick v Beswick* was decided in 1967. It is now 1979: but nothing has been done. If the opportunity arises, I hope the House will reconsider *Tweddle v Atkinson* and the other cases which stand guard over this unjust rule.

Likewise, I believe it open to the House to declare that, in the absence of evidence to show that he has suffered no loss, A, who has contracted for a payment to be made to C, may rely on the fact that he required the payment to be made as prima facie evidence that the promise for which he contracted was a benefit to him and that the measure of his loss in the event of non-payment is the benefit which he intended for C but which has not been received. Whatever the reason, he must have desired the payment to be made to C and he must have been relying on B to make it. If B fails to make the payment, A must find the money from other funds if he is to confer the benefit which he sought by his contract to confer upon C. Without expressing a final opinion on a question which is clearly difficult, I think the point is one which does require consideration by your Lordships' House.

Certainly the crude proposition for which the defendants contend, namely that the state of English law is such that neither C for whom the benefit was intended nor A who contracted for it can recover it, if the contract is terminated by B's refusal to perform, calls for review: and now, not forty years on.

NOTES

1. The facts in *Woodar v Wimpey* did not fall within the categories of contracts made by one person for the benefit of a group of people. There was also no evidence that Woodar had suffered any loss as a result of the non-payment to Transworld Trade Ltd, whereas in *Jackson v Horizon Holidays*, Mr Jackson had also suffered loss. Lord Scarman appeared to indicate that there might be ways of

including the loss of the payment to the third party within the loss suffered by Woodar. This would presumably be the case if Woodar would otherwise have to satisfy that debt.

2. While the result in *Jackson v Horizon Holidays* has been confirmed, the principle has been restricted to limited circumstances—namely, contracts calling for 'special treatment' (see the extract from the speech given by Lord Wilberforce, at *pages 332–333*, earlier in this section).

Linden Gardens Trust Ltd v Lenesta Sludge Disposals Ltd (also known as the St Martin's Property appeal)
[1994] 1 AC 85 (HL)

In this case, there had been a transfer of property and an assignment of the benefit of a building contract regarding that property.

Held: The House of Lords found that the assignment of the benefit of the building contract was invalid, since it was in breach of a valid prohibition on assignment. As owner of the property, it was the assignee who suffered damage as a result of breach of the building contract, but, technically, contractual rights remained with the assignor, who no longer owned the property and therefore suffered no loss. Nevertheless, it was held that the assignor could recover substantial damages on the basis that it had been contemplated all along that the property development would be sold or leased, and therefore the building contract had been entered into on the basis that the assignor (first claimant) could enforce the contractual rights for the benefit of those suffering from defective performance (the second claimant, assignee) ('the narrow ground'). This had to be the position to prevent a 'black hole' when it came to recovery for breach since the terms of the contract (prohibiting assignment without written consent) meant that the acquirer of the property would not be able to acquire rights to hold the defendant (McAlpines) liable for breach.

Counsel for the defendant (McAlpines) had argued that only nominal damages could be recovered by the first claimant (who held contractual rights, but had suffered no loss), and he relied on case law concerning breaches of contracts for the carriage of goods such as *The Albazero* [1977] AC 774. The House of Lords concentrated on an exception to this.

LORD BROWNE-WILKINSON: Notwithstanding the apparent logic of [this] submission, I have considerable doubts whether it is correct. A contract for the supply of goods or of work, labour and materials (a supply contract) is not the same as a contract for the carriage of goods. A breach of a supply contract involves a failure to provide the very goods or services which the defendant had contracted to supply and for which the plaintiff has paid or agreed to pay. If the breach is discovered before payment of the contract price, the price is abated by the cost of making good the defects. . . [Counsel] accepted that this right to abatement of the price does not depend on ownership by the plaintiff of the goods and it would be odd if the plaintiff's rights arising from breach varied according to whether the breach was discovered before or after the payment of the price. . .

In contracts for the sale of goods, the purchaser is entitled to damages for delivery of defective goods assessed by reference to the difference between the contract price and the market price of the defective goods, irrespective of whether he has managed to sell on the goods to a third party without loss: *Slater v Hoyle & Smith Ltd* [1920] 2 KB 11; see also as to non-delivery *Williams Bros v E T Agius Ltd* [1914] AC 510. In those cases the judgments contained no consideration of the person in whom the property in the goods was vested although it appears that some of the subcontracts had been made prior to the breach of contract.

If the law were to be established that damages for breach of a supply contract were not quantifiable by reference to the beneficial ownership of goods or enjoyment of the services contracted for but by reference to the difference in value between that which was contracted for and that which is in fact supplied, it might also provide a satisfactory answer to the problems raised where a man contracts and pays for a supply to others, e.g. a man contracts with a restaurant for a meal for himself and his guests or with a travel company for a holiday for his family. It is apparently established that, if a defective meal or holiday is supplied, the contracting party can recover damages not only for his own bad meal or unhappy holiday but also for that of his guests or family: see *Jackson v Horizon Holidays Ltd* [1975] 1 WLR 1468 as explained in *Woodar Investment Development Ltd v Wimpey Construction UK Ltd* [1980] 1 WLR 277, 283–284, 293–294, 297, 300–301.

There is therefore much to be said for drawing a distinction between cases where the ownership of goods or property is relevant to prove that the plaintiff has suffered loss through the breach of a contract other than a contract to supply those goods or property and the measure of damages in a supply contract where the contractual obligation itself requires the provision of those goods or services. I am reluctant to express a concluded view on this point since it may have profound effects on commercial contracts which effects were not fully explored in argument. In my view the point merits exposure to academic consideration before it is decided by this House. Nor do I find it necessary to decide the point since, on any view, the facts of this case bring it within the class of exceptions to the general rule to which Lord Diplock referred in *The Albazero*.

In *The Albazero* Lord Diplock said [1977] A.C. 774, 846:

> Nevertheless, although it is exceptional at common law that a plaintiff in an action for breach of contract, although he himself has not suffered any loss, should be entitled to recover damages on behalf of some third person who is not a party to the action for a loss which that third person has sustained, the notion that there may be circumstances in which he is entitled to do so was not entirely unfamiliar to the common law and particularly to that part of it which, under the influence of Lord Mansfield and his successors, Lord Ellenborough and Lord Tenterden, had been appropriated from the law merchant.

[His Lordship considered recognized exceptions in which damages could be recovered on behalf of a third party.]

. . . [T]he decision in *The Albazero* itself established a further exception. This House was concerned with the status of a long-established principle based on the decision in *Dunlop v Lambert* (1839) 6 Cl & F 600 that a consignor of goods who had parted with the property in the goods before the date of breach could even so recover substantial damages for the failure to deliver the goods. Lord Diplock identified, at p. 847, the rationale of that rule as being:

> The only way in which I find it possible to rationalise the rule in *Dunlop v Lambert* so that it may fit into the pattern of the English law is to treat it as an application of the principle, accepted also in relation to policies of insurance on goods, that in a commercial contract concerning goods where it is in the contemplation of the parties that the proprietary interests in the goods may be transferred from one owner to another after the contract has been entered into and before the breach which causes loss or damage to the goods, an original party to the contract, if such be the intention of them both, is to be treated in law as having entered into the contract for the benefit of all persons who have or may acquire an interest in the goods before they are lost or damaged, and is entitled to recover by way of damages for breach of contract the actual loss sustained by those for whose benefit the contract is entered into . . .

In *The Albazero* it was held that the principle in *Dunlop v. Lambert* no longer applied to goods consigned under a bill of lading because both the property in the goods and the cause of action for breach of the contract of carriage passes to the consignee or endorsee by reason of the consignment or endorsement; therefore, since the consignee or endorsee will in any event be entitled to enforce the contract direct there is no ground on which one can impute to the parties an intention that the consignor is entering into the contract for the benefit of others who will acquire the property in the goods but no right of action for breach of contract.

However, this House was careful to limit its decision to cases of carriage by sea under a bill of lading, leaving in force the principle in *Dunlop v. Lambert* in relation to other contracts for the carriage of goods where such automatic assignment of the rights of action for breach does not take place. Lord Diplock, after the passage referring to the exceptions which I have already quoted, said, at pp. 846–847:

> My Lords, in the light of these other exceptions, particularly in the field of mercantile law, to the general rule of English law that apart from nominal damages the plaintiff can only recover in an action for breach of contract the actual loss he has himself sustained, I do not think that the fact that the rule which it is generally accepted was laid down by this House in *Dunlop v. Lambert*, 6 Cl. & F. 600 would add one more exception would justify your Lordships in declaring the rule to be no longer law. Nor do I think that the almost complete absence of reliance on the rule by litigants in actions between 1839 and 1962 provides a sufficient reason for abolishing it entirely. The development of the law of negligence since 1839 does not provide a complete substituted remedy for some types of loss caused by breach of a contract of carriage. Late delivery is the most obvious example of these. The Bills of Lading Act 1855 and the subsequent development of the doctrine laid down in *Brandt v. Liverpool, Brazil and River Plate Steam Navigation Co. Ltd.* [1924] 1 K.B. 575, have reduced the scope and utility of the rule in *Dunlop v. Lambert* . . . where goods are carried under a bill of lading. But the rule extends to all forms of carriage including carriage by sea itself where no bill of lading has been issued, and there may still be occasional cases in which the rule would provide a remedy where no other would be available to a person sustaining loss which under a rational legal system ought to be compensated by the person who has caused it. For my part, I am not persuaded that your Lordships ought to go out of your way to jettison the rule.

In my judgment the present case falls within the rationale of the exceptions to the general rule that a plaintiff can only recover damages for his own loss. The contract was for a large development of property which, to the knowledge of both Corporation and McAlpine, was going to be occupied, and possibly purchased, by third parties and not by Corporation itself. Therefore it could be foreseen that damage caused by a breach would cause loss to a later owner and not merely to the original contracting party, Corporation. As in contracts for the carriage of goods by land, there would be no automatic vesting in the occupier or owners of the property for the time being who sustained the loss of any right of suit against McAlpine. On the contrary, McAlpine had specifically contracted that the rights of action under the building contract could *not* without McAlpine's consent be transferred to third parties who became owners or occupiers and might suffer loss. In such a case, it seems to me proper, as in the case of the carriage of goods by land, to treat the parties as having entered into the contract on the footing that Corporation would be entitled to enforce contractual rights for the benefit of those who suffered from defective performance but who, under the terms of the contract, could not acquire any right to hold McAlpine liable for breach. It is truly a case in which the rule provides 'a remedy where no other would be available to a person sustaining loss which under a rational legal system ought to be compensated by the person who has caused it'.

. . . I would therefore hold that Corporation is entitled to substantial damages for any breach by McAlpine of the building contract.

? QUESTION

Would the new property owner be able to enforce the building contract directly under the provisions of the Contracts (Rights of Third Parties) Act 1999? See the test of enforceability, s. 1.

There were two possible grounds for entitling the assignor (first claimant) to recover substantial damages—namely, the 'narrow ground', for which there was majority support (Lords Browne-Wilkinson, Ackner, Bridge, and Keith) and the 'broad ground' advocated by Lord Griffiths (which Lord Browne-Wilkinson discussed but considered required further academic consideration). Lord Bridge was 'much attracted' by the broad ground and Lord Keith also stated that he had sympathy with this analysis.

7.6.2.1 The narrow ground

The *St Martin's Property* exception (the 'narrow ground') was applied in the following case.

Darlington Borough Council v Wiltshier Northern Ltd
[1995] 1 WLR 68 (CA)

The building contractor, Wiltshier, had entered into a contract with Morgan Grenfell (Local Authority Services) (MG) to construct a recreation centre for the benefit of the council who owned the land on which it was to be built. It was necessary to employ MG because of restrictions on local authority expenditure, but MG validly assigned its contractual rights to the council. The council sought to bring a breach of contract claim against the contractor, alleging that there were serious defects that would cost £2 million to remedy. The council faced a problem in that a person cannot assign greater rights than he actually has. It was successfully argued at first instance that MG had a right to recover only nominal damages, since it had no property interest in the recreation centre, so that the council was also restricted to nominal damages.

Held (on appeal): Applying the *St Martin's Property* exception, the assignor (MG) had the right to recover substantial damages, since it was clear to the contractor from the outset that the centre was being constructed for the benefit of the council and that the contractual rights were to be assigned to the council. Since these contractual rights (including the ability to recover substantial damages) had been validly assigned to the council, it followed that the council could recover substantial damages.

STEYN LJ: The council, as the assignees of Morgan Grenfell, is seeking to recover substantial damages for breach of the building contract against Wiltshier, namely the cost of the remedial works to the Darlington Centre. The council accepts that, as assignees, they can recover no more in damages than Morgan Grenfell could have recovered. In other words, the question is what the assignor (Morgan Grenfell) could have recovered against the builder (Wiltshier) had the assignment not taken place: *Dawson v Great Northern and City Railway Co.* [1905] 1 KB 260. The council invokes in the first place the narrower principle relied on by Lord Browne-Wilkinson in *Linden Gardens Trust Ltd v Lenesta Sludge Disposals Ltd* [1994] 1 AC 85 and, in particular, that part of his speech, at pp. 112E–115G, which dealt with the *McAlpine* appeal. In the alternative the council invokes the wider principle enunciated by Lord Griffiths in his speech, at pp. 96D–98F, which dealt mainly with the *McAlpine* appeal.

. . . [Counsel for Wiltshier] submits that Morgan Grenfell, the party in contractual relationship with Wiltshier, suffered no loss and could transfer no claim for substantial damages; and the council, which suffered the loss, is precluded by the privity rule from claiming the damages which it suffered. He submits that established doctrine deprives the council of a remedy and allows the contract-breaker to go scot-free. Recognising that this is hardly an attractive result, he reminds us of our duty to apply the law as it stands.

That brings me to the speech of Lord Browne-Wilkinson in the *Linden Gardens* case [1994] AC 85. In his speech Lord Browne-Wilkinson rested his decision on the exception to the rule that a plaintiff can only recover damages for his own loss which was enunciated in *The Albazero* [1977] AC 774 in the context of carriage of goods by sea, bills of lading and bailment.

[Steyn LJ quoted the passage cited in Lord Browne-Wilkinson's judgment in *Linden Gardens* from the judgment of Lord Diplock in *The Albazero*, and continued:]

Clearly, this passage did not exactly fit the material facts in the *Linden Gardens* case. But Lord Browne-Wilkinson extracted the rationale of the decision and by analogy applied it to the purely contractual situation in *Linden Gardens*. He particularly justified this extension of the exception in *The Albazero* by invoking Lord Diplock's words in *The Albazero*:

> there may still be occasional cases in which the rule would provide a remedy where no other would be available to a person sustaining loss which under a rational legal system ought to be compensated by the person who has caused it.

Lord Browne-Wilkinson's conclusion was supported by all members of the House of Lords although, it is right to say, Lord Griffiths wished to go further. Relying on the exception recognised in the *Linden Gardens* case, as well as on the need to avoid a demonstrable unfairness which no rational legal system should tolerate, I would rule that the present case is within the rationale of Lord Browne-Wilkinson's speech. I do not say that the relevant passages in his speech precisely fit the material facts of the present case. But it involves only a very conservative and limited extension to apply it by analogy to the present case. For these reasons I would hold that the present case is covered by an exception to the general rule that a plaintiff can only recover damages for his own loss.

NOTES

1. The decision of the Court of Appeal extends the application of the narrow ground to instances in which the promisee has never had any ownership interest in the property affected by the breach.

2. Steyn LJ pointed to the need, recognized previously by Lord Diplock and Lord Browne-Wilkinson in *Linden Gardens*, 'to provide a remedy where no other would be available to a person sustaining loss which under a rational legal system ought to be compensated by the person who has caused it'.

3. Dillon and Waite LJJ considered that, on these facts—which included a provision obliging MG to transfer all 'rights' that it had against the contractor—if, before the assignment, MG had itself brought an action for breach, it could have succeeded in recovering damages for the losses of the council and would have held such damages as constructive trustee for the council.

4. While the Contracts (Rights of Third Parties) Act 1999 preserves the promisee's right to enforce the contract despite the fact that the third party may also have that right, it does not deal with the question of reform of the remedies available to a promisee. The Law Commission Report No. 242, *Privity of Contract: Contracts for the benefit of third parties* (Cm. 3329, 1996), para. 5.17 recommended that this be left to the courts. See also Cartwright (1996) 10 JCL 244.

5. A 'black hole' problem arises where the loss takes place after the assignment. The courts have sought to avoid this possibility by holding that if work is carried out on property which to the knowledge of the supplier is intended to be sold to a third party, and damage occurs after the sale, the purchaser is entitled to bring a claim in respect of the damage. In *Technotrade Ltd v Larkstore Ltd* [2006] EWCA Civ 1079, [2006] 1 WLR 2926 the question was whether a soil investigation consultant, employed by the original owner of the site, was liable for a property developer's losses caused by a landslip; the obvious difficulty was that, since it did not own the property at the time of the landslip, the original site owner had suffered no loss and could not assign more than it had. The Court of Appeal avoided this difficulty by concluding that the owner's cause of action was complete when the consultant carried out the investigation, and it was that cause of action that had been assigned to the purchaser.

MUMMERY LJ:

Assignment point: general principles

30 The perceived problem of the effect of the assignment on the assignee's right to recover substantial damages is temporal in origin. It arises from the particular order in which the following events occurred: the breach of contract by Technotrade, the transfer of ownership of the site by Starglade to Larkstore, the damage caused by the landslip after the transfer, and the assignment of the cause of action by Starglade to Larkstore, which occurred years after the transfer of the site.

31 Here are three relevant points of time.

(1) The time of the breach of contract by Technotrade. The contractual cause of action against Technotrade arose when Starglade was the owner of the site. Starglade was only entitled to recover nominal damages at that time. No substantial damage

could be established until the occurrence of the landslip in October 2001.

(2) The time of the landslip. Larkstore was the owner of the site at the time when the landslip occurred and substantial damage was suffered. Starglade was still entitled to the chose in action, but it was not entitled to recover substantial damages, as it had ceased to own the site. Larkstore owned the site and suffered substantial damage, but was not entitled to recover damages form [sic] Technotrade for breach of contract, because it had no contract with Technotrade and, at that time, had no assignment from Starglade of the benefit of its contract, rights of action and remedies for breach of contract.

(3) The time of the assignment. Starglade could not, it was submitted, assign to Larkstore more than it had. It did not have a claim for substantial damages against Technotrade in contract, as it had ceased to own the site before the assignment and before the landslip.

32 The answer to the perceived problem of a limit on the damages which Larkstore, as assignee, is entitled to recover from Technotrade is to be found, in my judgment, in an analysis of the cause of action itself. In this case the cause of action was the right to sue Technotrade for breach of contract in respect of the preparation of the soil inspection report on the site. The cause of action was complete in December 1998 when Technotrade produced the soil report for Starglade.

33 It is accepted that the report and the rights of action and remedies in respect of it were assignable and were not personal to Starglade. It is also accepted that, although the damages which Starglade could have recovered at the date when the cause of action was complete would have been no more than nominal damages, Starglade, if it had remained the owner of the site, would have been entitled to claim and, if able to prove, recover substantial damages for the landslip which occurred in October 2001.

34 The remedy in damages for breach of contract is not limited to the loss that could have been proved at the date when the breach occurred and the cause of action first arose. Subject to factual and legal issues of causation, remoteness, quantum and limitation of actions, there is a remedy in damages against the contract-breaker for loss which occurs after the cause of action has accrued. A cause of action may arise years before any substantial -damage occurs, as, for example, in the case of negligent advice on title. There is no legal principle which protects the contract-breaker by excluding his liability for substantial damage that occurs after the initial breach of contract.

The general approach in *Offer-Hoar* was applied in *Saga Cruises BDF Ltd v Fincantieri SPA* [2016] EHWC 1875 (Comm). The defendant shipyard refitted a cruise vessel for the owners, and the owners then chartered the vessel to charterers. Defects became apparent at that stage. It was held that the charterers, as assignees, could recover damages. The reality of the situation was that the vessel had been refitted for the benefit of the charterers and that they were entitled to sue for their own losses.

7.6.2.1.1 *A limitation on the applicability of the narrow ground*

Alfred McAlpine Construction Ltd v Panatown Ltd
[2001] 1 AC 518 (HL)

A contract between Panatown and McAlpine provided that McAlpine was to construct an office building in Cambridge. The actual owner of the site on which the building was constructed was UIPL, but UIPL was not a party to the construction contract. A separate 'duty of care deed' was entered into between McAlpine and UIPL, giving UIPL a direct remedy against the contractor for breaches of qualified contractual terms.

Panatown alleged that the construction work was defective and sought damages. McAlpine argued that Panatown had suffered no financial loss because it did not own the site, and, in any event, the existence of the 'duty of care deed' giving UIPL a direct right of action (which UIPL had chosen not to enforce) prevented recovery of substantial damages by Panatown. The Court of Appeal—[1998] CLC 636—had applied the narrow ground in *St Martin's Property* to allow recovery of substantial damages, which would be held on constructive trust for the building owner, and had considered that this exception was 'contract-based'. The Court of Appeal had also considered that the existence of the 'duty of care deed' was not intended to deprive Panatown of this remedy.

Held (on appeal, Lords Goff and Millett dissenting): Under the *St Martin's Property* exception, an employer could recover substantial damages for a third party building owner in the event of the contractor's breach of contract only where that third party had no direct remedy against the contractor. Since there was a direct right to claim substantial damages under the duty of care deed, Panatown had no right to recover such damages for loss suffered by UIPL. Panatown was entitled to nominal damages only, because it had suffered no loss.

LORD CLYDE: [referred to the passage in Lord Diplock's speech in *The Albazero* [1977] AC 774 at 847 and continued:] It is particularly this passage in Lord Diplock's speech which has given rise to a question discussed in the present appeal whether *The Albazero* exception is a rule of law or is based upon the intention of the parties. The issue was identified by my noble and learned friend, Lord Goff of Chieveley, in his speech in *White v Jones* [1995] 2 AC 207, 267. The problem arises from two phrases in the speech of Lord Diplock the mutual relationship between which may not be immediately obvious. The two phrases, in the reverse order than that in which they appear, are 'is to be treated in law as having entered into the contract' and 'if such be the intention of the parties'. In my view it is preferable to regard it as a solution imposed by the law and not as arising from the supposed intention of the parties, who may in reality not have applied their minds to the point. On the other hand if they deliberately provided for a remedy for a third party it can readily be concluded that they have intended to exclude the operation of the solution which would otherwise have been imposed by law, the terms and provisions of the contract will then require to be studied to see if the parties have excluded the operation of the exception.

That appears to have been the conclusion adopted in *Linden Gardens Trust Ltd v Lenesta Sludge Disposals Ltd; St. Martins Property Corporation Ltd v Sir Robert McAlpine Ltd* [1994] 1 AC 85 (the *St. Martins* case), where my noble and learned friend, Lord Browne-Wilkinson, observed, at p. 115:

> In such a case, it seems to me proper, as in the case of the carriage of goods by land, to treat the parties as having entered into the contract on the footing that Corporation would be entitled to enforce contractual rights for the benefit of those who suffered from defective performance but who, under the terms of the contract, could not acquire any right to hold McAlpine liable for breach.

In that case the point was made that the contractor and the employer were both aware that the property was going to be occupied and possibly purchased by third parties so that it could be foreseen that a breach of the contract might cause loss to others than the employer. But such foresight may be an unnecessary factor in the applicability of the exception. So also an intention of the parties to benefit a third person may be unnecessary. Foreseeability may be relevant to the question of damages under the rule in *Hadley v Baxendale* (1854) 9 Exch 341, but in the context of liability it is a concept which is more at home in the law of tort than in the law of contract. If the exception is founded primarily upon a principle of law, and not upon the particular knowledge of the parties to the contract, then it is not easy to see why the necessity for the contemplation of the parties that there will be potential losses by third parties is essential. It appears that in the *St. Martins* case [1994] 1 AC 85 the damages claimed were in respect of the cost of remedial work which had been carried out. I see no reason why consequential losses should not also be recoverable under this exception where such loss occurs and the third party should have a right to recover for himself all the damages won by the original party on his behalf.

The Albazero exception will plainly not apply where the parties contemplate that the carrier will enter into separate contracts of carriage with the later owners of the goods, identical to the contract with the consignor. Even more clearly, as Lord Diplock explained [1977] AC 774, 848, will the exception be excluded if other contracts of carriage are made in terms different from those in the original contract. In *The Albazero* the separate contracts which were mentioned were contracts of carriage. That is understandable in the context of carriage by sea involving a charterparty and bills of lading, but the counterpart in a building contract to a right of suit under a bill of lading should be the provision of a direct entitlement in a third party to sue the contractor in the event of a failure in the contractor's performance. In the context of a building contract one does not require to look for a second building contract to exclude the exception. It would be sufficient to find the provision of a right to sue. Thus as my noble and learned friend, Lord Browne-Wilkinson, observed in the *St. Martins* case [1994] 1 AC 85, 115:

> If, pursuant to the terms of the original building contract, the contractors have undertaken liability to the ultimate purchasers to remedy defects appearing after they acquired the property, it is manifest the case will not fall within the rationale of *Dunlop v Lambert* 6 Cl & F 600. If the ultimate purchaser is given a direct cause of action against the contractor (as is the consignee or endorsee under a bill of lading) the case falls outside the rationale of the rule.

In the *St. Martins* case the employer started off as the owner of the property and subsequently conveyed it to another company. In the present case the employer never was the owner. But that has not featured as a critical consideration in the present appeal and I do not see that that factor affects the application of the exception. In the *St. Martins* case there was a contractual bar on the assignment of rights of action without the consent of the contractor. In the present case the extra qualification was added that the consent should not be unreasonably withheld. But again I do not see that difference as of significance. It does not follow that the presence of a provision enabling assignment without the consent of the contractor excludes the exception. As was held in *Darlington Borough Council v Wiltshier Northern Ltd* [1995] 1 WLR 68 where there is a right to have an assignment of any cause of action accruing to the employer against the contractor, the exception may still apply so as to enable the assignee to recover substantial damages. It may be that the exception could be excluded through some contractual arrangement between the employer and the third party who sustained the actual loss, but the law would probably be slow to find such an intention established where it would leave the black hole. At least an express provision for assignment of the employer's rights will not suffice.

I have no difficulty in holding in the present case that the exception cannot apply. As part of the contractual arrangements entered into between Panatown and McAlpine there was a clear contemplation that separate contracts would be entered into by McAlpine, the contracts of the deed of duty of care and the collateral warranties. The duty of care deed and the collateral warranties were of course not in themselves building contracts. But they did form an integral part of the package of arrangements which the employer and the contractor agreed upon and in that respect should be viewed as reflecting the intentions of all the parties engaged in the arrangements that the third party should have a direct cause of action to the exclusion of any substantial claim by the employer, and accordingly that the exception should not apply. There was some dispute upon the difference in substance between the remedies available under the contract and those available under the duty of care deed. Even if it is accepted that in the circumstances of the present case where the eventual issue may relate particularly to matters of reasonable skill and care, the remedies do not absolutely coincide, the express provision of the direct remedy for the third party is fatal to the application of *The Albazero* exception. On a more general approach the difference between a strict contractual basis of claim and a basis of reasonable care makes the express remedy more clearly a substitution for the operation of the exception. Panatown cannot then in the light of these deeds be treated as having contracted with McAlpine for the benefit of the owner or later owners of the land and the exception is plainly excluded.

NOTES

1. This is a significant decision because the judgments embark on an analysis of the essential nature of contractual performance and the identification of loss. See Coote (2001) 117 LQR 81. It is likely that this debate will continue for some time.

2. Although the 'narrow ground' in *St Martin's Property* was held to be excluded by the existence of

a right of direct action for the third party, in the absence of such a direct route for redress, the exception will remain applicable, and this is important in the light of s. 7 of the Contracts (Rights of Third Parties) Act 1999.

3. The House of Lords in *Panatown* regarded the narrow ground exception as being imposed by law, rather than being based on contractual intention and contemplations. Although this requires further theoretical justification, it does represent a practical acceptance of the realities of the situation and will avoid technical difficulties surrounding determining that intention. In future, the exception ought to apply where the third party suffers loss as the building owner and the employer's loss is purely nominal, either because he no longer owns the property in question or because he never owned it. It will only be in instances in which there is direct redress that this operation of law will be necessarily excluded.

It is unclear whether this interpretation of the 'narrow ground', as imposed by operation of law and not linked to the parties' intentions, has universal acceptance. In *Rolls-Royce Power Engineering plc v Ricardo Consulting Engineers Ltd* [2003] EWHC 2871 (TCC), [2004] 2 All ER (Comm) 129, for example, the judge applied the previous 'contractual' basis for the 'narrow ground' exception.

JUDGE RICHARD SEYMOUR QC: [124] In the existing state of the law it seems to me that a fundamental condition to be met if the rule in *Dunlop v. Lambert* is to be applied in any case is that it should at the time the relevant contract was made have been in the actual contemplation of the parties that an identified third party or a third party who was a member of an identified class would or might suffer damage in the event of a breach of the contract. In no case to which my attention was drawn was that condition not satisfied. Moreover, if the general rule, as everyone seems to accept, is that a party to a contract may not recover in respect of a breach of it substantial damages if he himself has not suffered such loss, any exception is an exception to that rule, not a wholesale replacement of it, and there must be special circumstances which take a particular case out of the ambit of the general rule. If the special circumstances which take a case out of the general are knowledge that an identified third party or a third party who is a member of an identified class will or might suffer damage if there is a breach of contract, that is something which ought to be capable of being readily demonstrated, it involves no obvious injustice, as the possibility of loss will have been known at the time the contract was made, and seems to do justice because it gives effect to the contemplation of the contracting parties and provides a means of compensating the third party for whose benefit, at least in part, the relevant contractual obligation was undertaken. If knowledge at the date of the contract of the interest of the third party as such or as a member of an identified class were unnecessary, the result would be that a claim for substantial damages could be advanced on behalf of anyone whomsoever who contended that they had suffered loss as a result of a breach of contract, however remote their apparent connection to the performance of the contract. Such a possibility would destroy the general rule.

The judge recognized that his approach was out of line with the 'rule of law' approach adopted by the House of Lords in *Panatown*.

By comparison, in *DRC Distribution Ltd v Ulva Ltd* [2007] EWHC 1716 (QB), Flaux J relied heavily on the analysis in *Panatown* that 'the narrow ground' was a rule of law that imputed to the parties the intention to enter into the contract for the benefit of the third party. However, it could apply only where it was clear from the surrounding circumstances that such an intention existed.

FLAUX J: 76 . . . What matters as I see it, for the purpose of the issues I have to decide, is what is the correct legal analysis of the *Albazero* exception as applied and refined by the later cases. I agree with [counsel's] submission that the exception involves a rule of law that imputes to the parties to the contract the intention to enter into the contract for the benefit of a third party . . .

77 However, whether this is a rule of law or simply a principle based upon the supposed intention of the parties, what is clear from the cases is that the court will examine the terms of the contract and the surrounding circumstances to see if the parties have excluded the operation of the exception. One scenario where the operation of the exclusion will be excluded is where it is clear that the parties cannot be treated as having contracted for the benefit of the third party. The existence of the duty of care deed in *Panatown* had that effect: see per Lord Clyde at 532C.

7.6.2.2 **The broad ground**

Lord Griffiths, in the *Linden Gardens* case, considered that, in the context of a contract for the supply of work and materials, the promisee did not need to show a proprietary interest in the subject matter of the contract in order to be able to recover damages for its breach.

Linden Gardens Trust Ltd v Lenesta Sludge Disposals Ltd
[1994] 1 AC 85 (HL)

For facts and 'narrow ground' discussion, *page 330, 7.6.2.*

LORD GRIFFITHS: I cannot accept that in a contract of this nature, namely for work, labour and the supply of materials, the recovery of more than nominal damages for breach of contract is dependent upon the plaintiff having a proprietary interest in the subject matter of the contract at the date of breach. In everyday life contracts for work and labour are constantly being placed by those who have no proprietary interest in the subject matter of the contract. To take a common example, the matrimonial home is owned by the wife and the couple's remaining assets are owned by the husband and he is the sole earner. The house requires a new roof and the husband places a contract with a builder to carry out the work. The husband is not acting as agent for his wife, he makes the contract as principal because only he can pay for it. The builder fails to replace the roof properly and the husband has to call in and pay another builder to complete the work. Is it to be said that the husband has suffered no damage because he does not own the property? Such a result would in my view be absurd and the answer is that the husband has suffered loss because he did not receive the bargain for which he had contracted with the first builder and the measure of damages is the cost of securing the performance of that bargain by completing the roof repairs properly by the second builder. To put this simple example closer to the facts of this appeal—at the time the husband employs the builder he owns the house but just after the builder starts work the couple are advised to divide their assets so the husband transfers the house to his wife. This is no concern of the builder whose bargain is with the husband. If the roof turns out to be defective the husband can recover from the builder the cost of putting it right and thus obtain the benefit of the bargain that the builder had promised to deliver. It was suggested in argument that the answer to the example I have given is that the husband could assign the benefit of the contract to the wife. But what if, as in this case, the builder has a clause in the contract forbidding assignment without his consent and refuses to give consent as McAlpine has done. It is then said that neither husband nor wife can recover damages; this seems to me to be so unjust a result that the law cannot tolerate it.

The principal authority relied upon by McAlpine in support of the proposition that the contracting party suffers no loss if they did not have a proprietary interest in the property at the time of the breach was *The Albazero* [1977] AC 774. The situation in that case was however wholly different from the present. *The Albazero* was not concerned with money being paid to enable the bargain, i.e. the contract of carriage, to be fulfilled. The damages sought in *The Albazero* were claimed for the loss of the cargo, and as at the date of the breach the property in the cargo was vested in another with a right to sue it is readily understandable that the law should deny to the original party to the contract a right to recover damages for a loss of the cargo which had caused him no financial loss. In cases such as the present the person who places the contract has suffered financial loss because he has to spend money to give him the benefit of the bargain which the defendant had promised but failed to deliver. I therefore cannot accept that it is a condition of recovery in such cases that the plaintiff has a proprietary right in the subject matter of the contract at the date of breach.

There is some support for the 'broad ground' in the judgment of Steyn LJ in the next case.

Darlington Borough Council v Wiltshier Northern Ltd
[1995] 1 WLR 68 (CA)

For facts and 'narrow ground' discussion, *page 338, 7.6.2.1.*

STEYN LJ:

The exception contained in Lord Griffiths's speech

The rationale of Lord Griffiths's wider principle is essentially that, if a party engages a builder to perform specified work and the builder fails to render the contractual service, the employer suffers a loss. He suffers a loss of bargain or of expectation interest. And that loss can be recovered on the basis of what it would cost to put right the defects. While other members of the House of Lords expressed sympathy with this view, they did not decide the point. The point has now been argued in some depth before us. We have also had the benefit of some academic comment on the point: John Cartwright 'Remedies in Respect of Defective Buildings after Linden Gardens' (1993) 9 Con LJ 281 and I N Duncan Wallace 'Assignment of Rights to Sue: Half a Loaf' (1994) 110 LQR 42. Subject to one qualification, it will be clear from what I said earlier that I am in respectful agreement with the wider principle. It seems to me that Lord Griffiths has based his principle on classic contractual theory. The qualification is, however, important. Lord Griffiths observed at p. 97:

> The court will of course wish to be satisfied that the repairs have been or are likely to be carried out but if they are carried out the cost of doing them must fall upon the defendant who broke his contract.

There was apparently no argument on this point in the House of Lords. For my part I would hold that in the field of building contracts, like sale of goods, it is no concern of the law what the plaintiff proposes to do with his damages. It is also no precondition to the recovery of substantial damages that the plaintiff does propose to undertake the necessary repairs. In this field English law adopts an objective approach to the ascertainment of damages for breach of contract. On this point I am in agreement with the observations of Kerr LJ in *Dean v Ainley* [1987] 1 WLR 1729, 1737H–1738A and Staughton LJ in *Ruxley Electronics and Construction Ltd v Forsyth* [1994] 1 WLR 650, 656A–657D. Subject to this qualification, I am in respectful agreement with Lord Griffiths's wider principle. And I gratefully adopt it as part of my reasoning.

NOTES

1. Steyn LJ's observations on the relevance of establishing what a claimant intends to do with his damages are discussed in the context of the decision in *Ruxley Electronics and Construction Ltd v Forsyth* [1996] 1 AC 344 (*page 681, 14.2.2*).

2. Dillon LJ found that it was not necessary to consider the broad ground and stated that he preferred not to do so.

7.6.2.2.1 *The future for the broad ground*

The dissenting members of the House of Lords in *Panatown* (Lords Goff and Millett) relied on the broad ground and considered that, on this basis, Panatown had suffered a loss as a result of the defective performance of the obligations for which it had contracted. The duty of care deed was irrelevant to this because it dealt not with a loss suffered by the employer, but with the ability of the third party to enforce the construction contract.

Alfred McAlpine Construction Ltd v Panatown Ltd
[2001] 1 AC 518 (HL)

For facts and earlier discussion, *page 338, 7.6.2.1*.

Privity of contract and third party rights

7

LORD GOFF [dissenting]: I wish to state that I find persuasive the reasoning and conclusion expressed by Lord Griffiths in his opinion in the *St. Martins* case [1994] 1 AC 85 that the employer under a building contract may in principle recover substantial damages from the building contractor, because he has not received the performance which he was entitled to receive from the contractor under the contract, notwithstanding that the property in the building site was vested in a third party. The example given by Lord Griffiths of a husband contracting for repairs to the matrimonial home which is owned by his wife is most telling. It is not difficult to imagine other examples, not only within the family, but also, for example, where work is done for charitable purposes—as where a wealthy man who lives in a village decides to carry out at his own expense major repairs to, or renovation or even reconstruction of, the village hall, and himself enters into a contract with a local builder to carry out the work to the existing building which belongs to another, for example to trustees, or to the parish council. Nobody in such circumstances would imagine that there could be any legal obstacle in the way of the charitable donor enforcing the contract against the builder by recovering damages from him if he failed to perform his obligations under the building contract, for example because his work failed to comply with the contract specification.

[Lord Goff noted that, in *Linden Gardens*, Lord Griffiths had also expressed the view that, in his example, if the work on the roof to the matrimonial home were to prove defective, it would be absurd to conclude that the husband who had contracted and paid for the roof had no remedy because he did not own the property. Lord Goff continued:]

I wish now to draw attention to the fact that, in his statement of the facts of his example, Lord Griffiths included the fact that the husband had to call in and pay another builder to complete the work. It might perhaps be thought that Lord Griffiths regarded that fact as critical to the husband's cause of action against the builder, on the basis that the husband only has such a cause of action in respect of defective work on another person's property if he himself has actually sustained financial loss, in this example by having paid the second builder. In my opinion, however, such a conclusion is not justified on a fair reading of Lord Griffiths's opinion. This is because he stated the answer to be that the husband has suffered loss because he did not receive the bargain for which he had contracted with the first builder and the measure of damages is the cost of securing the performance of that bargain by completing the roof repairs properly by the second builder.

It is plain, therefore, that the payment to the second builder was not regarded by Lord Griffiths as essential to the husband's cause of action.

The point can perhaps be made more clearly by taking a different example, of the wealthy philanthropist who contracts for work to be done to the village hall. The work is defective; and the trustees who own the hall suggest that he should recover damages from the builder and hand the damages over to them, and they will then instruct another builder, well known to them, who, they are confident, will do the work well. The philanthropist agrees, and starts an action against the first builder. Is it really to be suggested that his action will fail, because he does not own the hall, and because he has not incurred the expense of himself employing another builder to do the remedial work? Echoing the words of Lord Griffiths, I regard such a conclusion as absurd. The philanthropist's cause of action does not depend on his having actually incurred financial expense; as Lord Griffiths said of the husband in his example, he 'has suffered loss because he did not receive the bargain for which he had contracted with the first builder'.

There has been a substantial amount of academic discussion about the difference of opinion in the Appellate Committee in the *St. Martins* case and in particular about the merits of Lord Griffiths's opinion in that case. The Appellate Committee in the present case was supplied with copies of a number of relevant articles, which I have studied with interest and respect. I have not detected any substantial criticism of Lord Griffiths's broader ground, whereas there has been some criticism of the narrower ground adopted by the majority of the Appellate Committee in the *St. Martins* case [1994] 1 AC 85—see in particular the articles by Professor Treitel 'Damages in Respect of a Third Party's Loss' (1998) 114 LQR 527 and by Mr Duncan Wallace QC (the editor of *Hudson on Building Contracts*) 'Assignment of Right to Sue: Half a Loaf' (1994) 110 LQR 42 and 'Third Party Damage: No Legal Black Hole?' (1999) 115 LQR 394 (in which the writer supports Lord Griffiths's broader ground). I have found nothing in the academic material with which we were supplied which should deter those who are attracted to the broader ground from giving effect to it in an appropriate case. . .

It follows, in my opinion, that the principal argument advanced on behalf of McAlpine is inconsistent with authority and established principle. This conclusion may involve a fuller recognition of the importance of the protection of a contracting party's interest in the performance of his contract than has occurred in the past. But not only is it justified by authority, but the principle on which it is based is supported by a number of distinguished writers, notably Professor Brian Coote and Mr Duncan Wallace QC.

In truth, no question of a *jus quaesitum tertio* arises in this case at all. Lord Griffiths's broader ground is not concerned with privity of contract as such. It is concerned with the damages recoverable by one party to a contract (the employer) against another (the contractor) for breach of a contract for labour and materials, viz, a building contract. It does not seek to establish an exception to the old privity rule, though it may provide a principled basis for the recovery of damages (by a contracting party, not by a third party) in some cases, such as *Jackson v Horizon Holidays Ltd* [1975] 1 WLR 1468, in which the privity rule has been seen as a barrier to recovery (not by a contracting party but by a third party).

Furthermore, as Professor Hugh Beale stated some years ago in 'Privity of Contract: Judicial and Legislative Reforms' (1995) 9 JCL 103, 108:

> Even if the basic doctrine of privity were to be reformed along the lines suggested by the Law Commission, I think it is vital that the promisee should have adequate remedies to take care of those cases in which the third party does not acquire rights.

I would however go further. I do not regard Lord Griffiths's broader ground as a departure from existing authority, but as a reaffirmation of existing legal principle. Indeed, I know of no authority which stands in its way. On the contrary, there have been statements in the cases which provide support for his view. Thus in *Darlington Borough Council v Wiltshier Northern Ltd* [1995] 1 WLR 68, 80, Steyn LJ described Lord Griffiths's broader ground as based on classic contractual theory, a statement with which I respectfully agree. Moreover, Lord Griffiths's reasoning was foreshadowed in the opinions of members of the Appellate Committee in *Woodar Investment Development Ltd v Wimpey Construction UK Ltd* [1980] 1 WLR 277; see especially the opinion of Lord Keith of Kinkel, at pp. 297–298, and in addition the more tentative statements of Lord Salmon, at p. 291, and Lord Scarman, at pp. 300–301. Furthermore, as I have just indicated, full recognition of the importance of the performance interest will open the way to principled solution of other well-known problems in the law of contract, notably those relating to package holidays which are booked by one person for the benefit not only of himself but of others, normally members of his family (as to which see *Jackson v Horizon Holidays Ltd* [1975] 1 WLR 1468), and other cases of a similar kind referred to by Lord Wilberforce in his opinion in the *Woodar Investment* case [1980] 1 WLR 277, 283—cases of an everyday kind which are calling out for a sensible solution on a principled basis. Even if it is not thought, as I think, that the solution which I prefer is in accordance with existing principle, nevertheless it is surely within the scope of the type of development of the common law which, especially in the law of obligations, is habitually undertaken by appellate judges as part of their ordinary judicial function. That such developments in the law may be better left to the judges, rather than be the subject of legislation, is now recognised by the Law Commission itself, because legislation within a developing part of the common law can lead to ossification and a rigid segregation of legal principle which disfigures the law and impedes future development of legal principle on a coherent basis. It comes as no surprise therefore that, in its Report on Privity of Contract: Contracts for the Benefit of Third Parties (1996) (Law

Com. No. 242) para. 5.15, the Law Commission declined to make specific recommendations in relation to *the promisee's* remedies in a contract for the benefit of a third party (here referring to *The Albazero* [1977] AC 774 and *Linden Gardens Trust Ltd v Lenesta Sludge Disposals Ltd* (the *St. Martins* case) [1994] 1 AC 85 as cases in which 'the courts have gone a considerable way towards developing rules which in many appropriate cases do allow the promisee to recover damages on behalf of the third party'), and stated that the Commission 'certainly . . . would not wish to forestall further judicial development of this area of the law of damages'. This certainly does not sound like a warning to judicial trespassers to keep out of forbidden territory. . .

The present case provides, in my opinion, a classic example of a case which falls properly within the judicial province. I, for my part, have therefore no doubt that it is desirable, indeed essential, that the problem in the present case should be the subject of judicial solution by providing proper recognition of the plaintiff's interest in the performance of the contractual obligations which are owed to him. I cannot see why the proposed statutory reform of the old doctrine of privity of contract should inhibit the ordinary judicial function, and so prevent your Lordships' House from doing justice between the parties in the present case. . .

Lord Browne-Wilkinson, who was in the majority, attempted to link the two approaches by stating that, because of the duty of care deed, UIPL had a remedy against the contractor and it was for this reason that Panatown had not suffered any damage to its performance interest under the construction contract.

Lord Clyde (in the majority) argued against the application of the 'broad ground' (at least where the promisee (employer) had not spent any money in carrying out relevant repairs) for the following reasons.

LORD CLYDE: I turn accordingly to what was referred to in the argument as the broader ground. But the label requires more careful definition. The approach under *The Albazero* exception has been one of recognising an entitlement to sue by the innocent party to a contract which has been breached, where the innocent party is treated as suing on behalf of or for the benefit of some other person or persons, not parties to the contract, who have sustained loss as a result of the breach. In such a case the innocent party to the contract is bound to account to the person suffering the loss for the damages which the former has recovered for the benefit of the latter. But the so-called broader ground involves a significantly different approach. What it proposes is that the innocent party to the contract should recover damages for himself as a compensation for what is seen to be his own loss. In this context no question of accounting to anyone else arises. This approach however seems to me to have been developed into two formulations.

The first formulation, and the seeds of the second, are found in the speech of Lord Griffiths in the *St. Martins* case [1994] 1 AC 85, 96. At the outset his Lordship expressed the opinion that Corporation, faced with a breach by McAlpine of their contractual duty to perform the contract with sound materials and with all reasonable skill and care, would be entitled to recover from McAlpine the cost of remedying the defect in the work as the normal measure of damages. He then dealt with two possible objections. First, it should not matter that the work was not being done on property owned by Corporation. Where a husband instructs repairs to the roof of the matrimonial home it cannot be said that he has not suffered damage because he did not own the property. He suffers the damage measured by the cost of a proper completion of the repair:

In cases such as the present the person who places the contract has suffered financial loss because he has to spend money to give him the benefit of the bargain which the defendant had promised but failed to deliver. (See p. 97.)

The second objection, that Corporation had in fact been reimbursed for the cost of the repairs was answered by the consideration that the person who actually pays for the repairs is of no concern to the party who broke the contract. But Lord Griffiths added, at p. 97:

> The court will of course wish to be satisfied that the repairs have been or are likely to be carried out but if they are carried out the cost of doing them must fall upon the defendant who broke his contract.

In the first formulation this approach can be seen as identifying a loss upon the innocent party who requires to instruct the remedial work. That loss is, or may be measured by, the cost of the repair. The essential for this formulation appears to be that the repair work is to be, or at least is likely to be, carried out. This consideration does not appear to be simply relevant to the reasonableness of allowing the damages to be measured by the cost of repair. It is an essential condition for the application of the approach, so as to establish a loss on the part of the plaintiff. Thus far the approach appears to be consistent with principle, and in particular with the principle of privity. It can cover the case where A contracts with B to pay a sum of money to C and B fails to do so. The loss to A is in the necessity to find other funds to pay to C and provided that he is going to pay C, or indeed has done so, he should be able to recover the sum by way of damages for breach of contract from B. If it was evident that A had no intention to pay C, having perhaps changed his mind, then he would not be able to recover the amount from B because he would have sustained no loss, and his damages would at best be nominal.

But there can also be found in Lord Griffiths's speech the idea that the loss is not just constituted by the failure in performance but indeed consists in that failure. This is the 'second formulation'. In relation to the suggestion that the husband who instructs repair work to the roof of his wife's house and has to pay for another builder to make good the faulty repair work has sustained no damage Lord Griffiths observed, at p. 97:

> Such a result would in my view be absurd and the answer is that the husband has suffered loss because he did not receive the bargain for which he had contracted with the first builder and the measure of damages is the cost of securing the performance of that bargain by completing the roof repairs properly by the second builder.

That is to say that the fact that the innocent party did not receive the bargain for which he contracted is itself a loss. As Steyn LJ put it in *Darlington Borough Council v Wiltshier Northern Ltd* [1995] 1 WLR 68, 80: 'He suffers a loss of bargain or of expectation interest.' In this more radical formulation it does not matter whether the repairs are or are not carried out, and indeed in the *Darlington* case that qualification is seen as unnecessary. In that respect the disposal of the damages is treated as res inter alios acta. Nevertheless on this approach the intention to repair may cast light on the reasonableness of the measure of damages adopted. In order to follow through this aspect of the second formulation in Lord Griffiths's speech it would be necessary to understand his references to the carrying out of the repairs to be relevant only to that consideration.

I find some difficulty in adopting the second formulation as a sound way forward. First, if the loss is the disappointment at there not being provided what was contracted for, it seems to me difficult to measure that loss by consideration of the cost of repair. A more apt assessment of the compensation for the loss of what was expected should rather be the difference in value between what was contracted for and what was supplied. Secondly, the loss constituted by the supposed disappointment may well not include all the loss which the breach of contract has caused. It may not be able to embrace consequential losses, or losses falling within the second head of *Hadley v Baxendale* 9 Exch. 341. The inability of the wife to let one of the rooms in the house caused by the inadequacy of the repair, does not seem readily to be something for which the husband could claim as his loss. Thirdly, there is no obligation on the successful plaintiff to account to anyone who may have sustained actual loss as a result of the faulty performance. Some further mechanism would then be required for the court to achieve the proper disposal of the monies awarded to avoid a double jeopardy. Alternatively, in order to achieve an effective solution, it would seem to be necessary to add an obligation to account on the part of the person recovering the damages. But once that step is taken the approach begins to approximate to *The Albazero* exception. Fourthly, the 'loss' constituted by a breach of contract has usually been recognised as calling for an award of nominal damages, not substantial damages.

The loss of an expectation which is here referred to seems to me to be coming very close to a way of describing a breach of contract. A breach of contract may cause a loss, but is not in itself a loss in any meaningful sense. When one refers to a loss in the context of a breach of contract, one is in my view referring to the incidence of some personal or patrimonial damage. A loss of expectation might be a loss in the proper sense if damages were awarded for the distress or inconvenience caused by the disappointment. Professor Coote ('Contract Damages, *Ruxley* and the Performance Interest' [1997] CLJ 537) draws a distinction between benefits in law, that is bargained-for contractual rights, and benefits in fact, that is the enjoyment of the fruits of performance. Certainly the former may constitute an asset with a commercial value. But while frustration may destroy the rights altogether so that the contract is no longer enforceable, a failure in the obligation to perform does not destroy the asset. On the contrary it remains as the necessary legal basis for a remedy. A failure in performance of a contractual obligation does not entail a loss of the bargained-for contractual rights. Those rights remain so as to enable performance of the contract to be enforced, as by an order for specific performance. If one party to a contract repudiates it and that repudiation is accepted, then, to quote Lord Porter in *Heyman v Darwins Ltd* [1942] AC 356, 399, 'By that acceptance he is discharged from further performance and may bring an action for damages, but the contract itself is not rescinded'. The primary obligations under the contract may come to an end, but secondary obligations then arise, among them being the obligation to compensate the innocent party. The original rights may not then be enforced. But a consequential right arises in the innocent party to obtain a remedy from the party who repudiated the contract for his failure in performance. . .

It seems to me that a more realistic and practical solution is to permit the contracting party to recover damages for the loss which he and a third party has suffered, being duly accountable to them in respect of their actual loss, than to construct a theoretical loss in law on the part of the contracting party, for which he may be under no duty to account to anyone since it is to be seen as his own loss. The solution is required where the law will not tolerate a loss caused by a breach of contract to go uncompensated through an absence of privity between the party suffering the loss and the party causing it. In such a case, to avoid the legal black hole, the law will deem the innocent party to be claiming on behalf of himself and any others who have suffered loss. It does not matter that he is not the owner of the property affected, nor that he has not himself suffered any economic loss. He sues for all the loss which has been sustained and is accountable to the others to the extent of their particular losses. While it may be that there is no necessary right in the third party to compel the innocent employer to sue the contractor, in the many cases of the domestic or familial situation that consideration should not be a realistic problem. In the commercial field, in relation to the interests of such persons as remoter future proprietors who are not related to the original employer, it may be that a solution by way of collateral warranty would still be required. If there is an anxiety lest the exception would permit an employer to receive excessive damages, that should be set at rest by the recognition of the basic requirement for reasonableness which underlies the quantification of an award of damages. . .

NOTES

1. In *Rolls-Royce Power Engineering plc v Ricardo Consulting Engineers Ltd* [2003] EWHC 2871 (TCC), [2004] 2 All ER (Comm) 129, Judge Seymour QC made the following observation concerning Lord Griffiths' broad ground:

[128] Lord Griffiths' approach has not so far been adopted as a matter of decision in any case in England and Wales which counsel had been able to discover. It seems on its face to divorce the assessment of damages for breach of contract in a case in which it is adopted from proof of any particular loss sustained by the claimant, substituting some more or less notional quantification of damages for loss of bargain. As it is a notional loss of the actual claimant, if the person who has actually sustained the loss has some independent ground of claim, for example in tort, it would seem that the wrongdoer could find himself having to pay compensation for one wrong twice over. Settlement of the claim of the other contracting party would not obviously be a defence to the claim of the person who in fact sustained loss. Again, leaving aside that difficulty, it does not seem at all easy just as a practical matter to apply Lord Griffiths' approach in any case other than one in which the alleged damage is damage to, or failure to repair, property and there is no suggestion of any consequential loss. If may be that the cost of repairing damage to a house or a car or some other type of corporeal property is likely to be similar no matter who sustains it. It may be that the diminution in the value of an item of corporeal property is likely to be similar no matter who owns it. However, the nature and extent of any consequential loss—for example, loss of income from inability for a period to turn property to account—may well depend critically upon the particular circumstances of the owner and what he or she does with the property. A simple example is that an owner of a flat may live in it as his main residence, or he may keep it empty for occasional use by himself, or he may let it and derive an income from it. Inability to use the flat because it has been damaged in some way may cause no loss beyond the cost of repair in the second case—the owner can live in his main residence—and the measure of the loss in the other two cases may well be different, either the cost of renting alternative accommodation or loss of rental income. In a case such as the present, in which there has been no damage to corporeal property as a result of the defendant's alleged breach of contract, it is impossible to see how any assessment of damages could be made other than by reference to what actually happened to the other contracting party.

[129] In the *Lenesta Sludge* case itself, Lord Keith of Kinkel and Lord Bridge of Harwich expressly did not decide the appeals on the basis of the suggested principle of Lord Griffiths, whilst indicating some sympathy with his comments. Lord Ackner expressly agreed only with Lord Browne-Wilkinson and did not comment at all upon what Lord Griffiths said. In the *Darlington BC* case Dillon LJ, with whom Waite LJ agreed, expressly did not consider the principle suggested by Lord Griffiths, but the third member of the Court of Appeal, Steyn LJ, expressly adopted it as a ground for his decision concurring with the majority in the result. In the *Panatown* case [2000] 4 All ER 97 at 109–112, 143–148,

[2001] 1 AC 518 at 532–535, 568–574 Lord Clyde and Lord Jauncey of Tullichettle considered Lord Griffiths' suggested approach and identified difficulties with it. Lord Goff of Chieveley ([2000] 4 All ER 97 at 122, [2001] 1 AC 518 at 546) expressed his agreement with it. Lord Browne-Wilkinson ([2000] 4 All ER 97 at 151, [2001] 1 AC 518 at 577) assumed that it was sound. Lord Millett ([2000] 4 All ER 97 at 164, [2001] 1 AC 518 at 591) approved it, but limited its application to 'building contracts and other contracts for the supply of work and materials where the claim is in respect of defective or incomplete work or delay in completing it'.

[130] In the result there is a lack of unanimity of judicial utterance as to the appropriateness of the approach of Lord Griffiths to any class of case, and a respectable body of opinion that in some or all classes of case it is contrary to principle and/or difficult of practical application. In these treacherous waters I prefer to navigate by already published charts and to seek to apply the law as it has already clearly developed, rather than to speculate as to how it may develop in future.

2. In *DRC Distribution Ltd v Ulva Ltd* [2007] EWHC 1716 (QB), Flaux J discussed the 'broad ground' argument in the context of a sale of goods:

69 I rather doubt whether that broader ground can be said to represent the law in the light of the criticisms of it by the majority of the House of Lords in *Alfred McAlpine Construction v Panatown* [2001] 1 AC 518. I agree in particular with Lord Clyde's criticism of the concept of substantial damages for loss of expectation at 534D–E.

70 However, I do not need to decide whether the Lord Griffiths broader ground can stand after *Panatown*, since even the minority in that case (Lord Goff of Chieveley and Lord Millett) with whom it found favour, limited its scope to contracts for the supply of services, such as the building contract under consideration in that case: see per Lord Goff at 552E–G and Lord Millett at 591B–C. The present contract is for the sale of goods and does not fall into the same category. I cannot see any justification for extending the broader ground to a contract such as the present, even if, in the context of contracts such as building contracts, that broader ground represented good law.

3. In *BV Nederlandse Industrie Van Eiprodukten v Rembrandt Entreprises Inc.* [2019] EWCA Civ 596, NIVE agreed in May to supply egg products to Rembrandt. In September 2015 NIVE informed Rembrandt that around half the egg white powder would be supplied by an associated company, Henningsen. Rembrandt terminated the agreement. In the absence of a contract between Rembrandt and Henningsen, NIVE claimed damages from Rembrandt on behalf of Henningsen using the broad rule in *Linden Gardens Trust*. The Court of Appeal dismissed the claim. Longmore LJ said:

73. I have no hesitation in concluding that, as a matter of law, for a successful claim for transferred loss that seeks to rely on the so-called broader ground, as explained in Linden Gardens and Panatown, the claimant must show that, at the time that the underlying contract was made, there was a

common intention and/or a known object to benefit the third party or a class of persons to which the third party belonged.

74. On that basis, NIVE's claim for transferred loss must fail. At the time of the making of the contract, Rembrandt was not even aware of the existence of Henningsen, let alone the possibility that Henningsen might be providing some of the egg white powder on behalf of NIVE. NIVE therefore cannot bring itself within Lord Griffiths' broader ground. Of all the authorities noted above, the present claim for transferred loss is perhaps closest to the claim for loss of profits in *And So To Bed*. It must fail for the same underlying reasons.

75. It is perhaps worth pausing a moment to reflect on the consequences if Mr Morpuss was right, that this component was not required for a claim for transferred loss. As I have already pointed out, Henningsen was a domestic subcontractor to NIVE, being used to fulfil some of NIVE's own contractual obligations to Rembrandt. Its involvement was entirely a matter for NIVE: Rembrandt had no knowledge of Henningsen. So, if Mr Morpuss was right and the known third party benefit was irrelevant, it would mean that a main contractor would always be able to claim against the employer the losses suffered by his sub-contractor, even if the employer had no knowledge of the sub-contractor, or even that a sub-contractor was going to be used at all. That would not only be contrary to the general rule. . . that a party can only recover the losses that it has itself suffered, but it would also turn transferred loss, which is supposed to be a narrow exception to that rule, into a commonplace route of recovery. In my view, that would go far beyond even what Lord Griffiths had in mind in St Martins, and I do not consider that it is a correct analysis of the law.

7.7 Privity and burdens

The privity doctrine provides that a third party cannot be made subject to a burden by a contract to which he is not a party.

Law Commission Report No. 242, *Privity of Contract: Contracts for the benefit of third parties* (Cm. 3329, 1996), made recommendations in relation to benefits; the question of burdens imposed on third parties was outside its scope. Similarly, the Contracts (Rights of Third Parties) Act 1999 relates only to benefits.

7.7.1 Exemption clauses and bailment

Can a third party be bound by an exemption clause in a contract to which he is not a party?

Morris v C. W. Martin & Sons Ltd
[1966] 1 QB 716 (CA)

The claimant sent a mink stole to a furrier for cleaning and agreed that it should be passed to the defendants for cleaning. The furrier contracted with the defendants for the cleaning on current trade conditions, which provided that 'goods belonging to customers were held at the customer's risk' and that the defendants were not to be responsible for loss or damage during processing. M, the defendants' employee, was given the cleaning task and stole the fur while it was in his custody. The claimant sued the defendants for damages.

Held (Diplock and Salmon LJJ): The defendants were bailees for reward and therefore they owed a duty to the claimant to take care of the fur. However, the exemption clauses in the defendants' contract of cleaning with the furrier did not extend on their wording to cover liability to the claimant. (They were therefore able to avoid the more difficult privity question.) Lord Denning found that the clauses on their wording did not extend to cover the claimant, but considered that the claimant had impliedly consented to the furrier contracting for the cleaning on usual terms, so that, in principle, the defendants might rely on the exemptions in the bailment contract.

LORD DENNING MR: [C]an the plaintiff sue the cleaners direct for the misappropriation by their servant? And if she does, can she ignore the exempting conditions?

. . . [I]f the sub-bailment is for reward, the sub-bailee owes to the owner all the duties of a bailee for reward: and the owner can sue the sub-bailee direct for loss of or damage to the goods; and the sub-bailee (unless he is protected by any exempting conditions) is liable unless he can prove that the loss or damage occurred without his fault or that of his servants. So the plaintiff can sue the defendants direct for the loss of the goods by the misappropriation by their servant, and the cleaners are liable unless they are protected by the exempting conditions.

Now comes the question: Can the defendants rely, as against the plaintiff, on the exempting conditions although there was no contract directly between them and her? There is much to be said on each side. On the one hand, it is hard on the plaintiff if her just claim is defeated by exempting conditions of which she knew nothing and to which she was not a party. On the other hand, it is hard on the defendants if they are held liable to a greater responsibility than they agreed to undertake. As long ago as 1601 Lord Coke advised a bailee to stipulate specially that he would not be responsible for theft, see *Southcote's case* (1601) 4 Co Rep 83b, a case of theft by a servant. It would be strange if his stipulation was of no avail to him. The answer to the problem lies, I think, in this: the owner is bound by the conditions if he expressly or impliedly consented to the bailee making a sub-bailment containing those conditions, but not otherwise. Suppose the owner of goods lets them out on hire, and the hirer sends them for repair, and the repairer holds them for a lien. The owner is bound by the lien because he impliedly consented to the repairs being done, since they were reasonably incidental to the use of the car: see *Tappenden v Artus* [1964] 2 QB 185. So also if the owner of a ship accepts goods for carriage on a bill of lading containing exempting conditions (i.e. a 'bailment upon terms') the owner of the goods (although not a party to the contract) is bound by those conditions if he impliedly consented to them as being in 'the known and contemplated form,'. . .

In this case the plaintiff agreed that Beder should send the fur to the defendants, and by so doing I think she impliedly consented to his making a contract for cleaning on the terms usually current in the trade. But when I come to study the conditions I do not think that they are sufficient to protect the cleaners. We always construe such conditions strictly. Clause 9 applies only to 'goods belonging to customers', that is, goods belonging to Beder, and not to goods belonging to his customers such as the plaintiff. The conditions themselves draw a distinction between 'customer' and 'his own customer,' see clause 16. Clause 14 only applies to 'the loss of or damage to the goods during processing'. The loss here was not during processing. It was before or after processing. Seeing that the conditions do not protect the defendants, I am of opinion that they are liable for the loss due to the theft by their servant.

NOTE Bailment involves the delivery of goods under a contract by a bailor to the bailee for some purpose and, after that purpose has been fulfilled, their return to the bailor.

In the following case, the Privy Council applied and clarified Lord Denning's *obiter* principle in *Morris v Martin*.

K. H. Enterprise v Pioneer Container, The Pioneer Container

[1994] 2 AC 324 (PC)

The claimant cargo owners had contracted with carriers (Hanjin and Scandutch) for the carriage of their goods, but the contract had entitled the carriers to subcontract the carriage on any terms and carriage had been subcontracted to the defendants. Were the claimants bound by a clause in the subcontract between their carriers and the defendants, which stated that all disputes were to be determined in Taiwan?

Held: The claimants were bound by the exclusive jurisdiction clause in the contract between their carriers and the defendants because the claimants had consented to their cargo being sub-bailed on terms including the jurisdiction clause, and because the defendants had known that the cargo belonged to the claimants and not to Hanjin and Scandutch, the carriers.

LORD GOFF: In order to decide whether, like Steyn J [in *Singer Co. (UK) Ltd v Tees and Hartlepool Port Authority* [1988] 2 Lloyd's Rep 164] to accept the principle so stated by Lord Denning MR [in *Morris v Martin*], it is necessary to consider the relevance of the concept of 'consent' in this context. It must be assumed that, on the facts of the case, no direct contractual relationship has been created between the owner and the sub-bailee, the only contract created by the sub-bailment being that between the bailee and the sub-bailee. Even so, if the effect of the sub-bailment is that the sub-bailee voluntarily receives into his custody the goods of the owner and so assumes towards the owner the responsibility of a bailee, then to the extent that the terms of the sub-bailment are consented to by the owner, it can properly be said that the owner has authorised the bailee so to regulate the duties of the sub-bailee in respect of the goods entrusted to him, not only towards the bailee but also towards the owner. . .

Such a conclusion, finding its origin in the law of bailment rather than the law of contract, does not depend for its efficacy either on the doctrine of privity of contract or on the doctrine of consideration. . . [I]f the owner seeks to hold a sub-bailee responsible to him as bailee, he has to accept all the terms of the sub-bailment, warts and all; for either he will have consented to the sub-bailment on those terms or, if not, he will (by holding the sub-bailee liable to him as bailee) be held to have ratified all the terms of the sub-bailment. A negative answer to the question is however supported by other writers, notably by *Palmer's Bailment* pp. 31 et seq., where Professor Palmer cites a number of examples of bailment without the consent of the owner, and by Professor Tay in her article 'The essence of bailment' (1966) 5 Syd LR 239. On this approach, a person who voluntarily takes another person's goods into his custody holds them as bailee of that person (the owner); and he can only invoke, for example, terms of a sub-bailment under which he received the goods from an intermediate bailee as qualifying or otherwise affecting his responsibility to the owner if the owner consented to them. It is the latter approach which, as their Lordships have explained, has been adopted by English Law and, with English law, the law of Hong Kong.

Their Lordships wish to add that this conclusion, which flows from the decisions in *Morris v C W Martin & Sons Ltd* [1996] 1 QB 716 and the *Gilchrist Watt* case [*Gilchrist Watt and Sanderson Pty Ltd v York Products Pty Ltd*] [1970] 1 WLR 1262, produces a result which in their opinion is both principled and just. They incline to the opinion that a sub-bailee can only be said for these purposes to have voluntarily taken into his possession the goods of another if he has sufficient notice that a person other than the bailee is interested in the goods so that it can properly be said that (in addition to his duties to the bailee) he has, by taking the goods into his custody, assumed towards that other person the responsibility for the goods which is characteristic of a bailee. This they believe to be the underlying principle. Moreover, their Lordships do not consider this principle to impose obligations on the sub-bailee which are onerous or unfair, once it is recognised that he can invoke against the owner terms of the sub-bailment which the owner has actually (expressly or impliedly) or even ostensibly authorised. . .

NOTE The Court of Appeal in *Sandeman Coprimar SA v Transitos y Transportes Integrales SL* [2003] EWCA Civ 113, [2003] QB 1270 applied the principle in *The Pioneer Container*, since the importer had implicitly authorized the conclusion of a chain of contracts on certain terms and had therefore authorized sub-bailment on terms. An important development was that Lord Phillips MR held that this was the position on the basis of bailment or, alternatively, that there were collateral contracts between the importer and sub-bailees.

7.7.2 Restrictions on the use of chattels

If there is a restriction on a chattel in a contract between A and B, and C purchases the chattel with notice of the restriction, is C bound by the restriction?

Lord Strathcona Steamship Co. Ltd v Dominion Coal Co. Ltd
[1926] AC 108 (PC)

The owners of a steamship chartered her to the claimants for ten successive seasons commencing in 1916. When the defendants purchased the steamship, they had notice of the terms of the charterparty, and covenanted with the sellers to perform and accept all responsibilities under it. However, they then refused to perform the charterparty for the 1920 season. The claimants sought a declaration that the defendants were bound to carry out the charterparty and an injunction to restrain them from using the vessel in any way inconsistent with the charterparty. The defendants argued that they were not privy to the contract containing the restriction, so that it was not binding on them.

Held: Applying an *obiter dictum* of Knight Bruce LJ in *De Mattos v Gibson* (1858) 4 De G & J 276, since the defendants had purchased *with notice* of the terms of the charterparty relating to the use of the ship, the charterers could obtain an injunction to restrain them from employing the ship in any way inconsistent with the charterparty.

LORD SHAW: The position of the case is that the appellants are possessed of a ship with regard to which a long running charterparty is current, the existence of which was fully disclosed, together, indeed, with an obligation which the appellants appear to have accepted to respect and carry out that charterparty. The proposal of the appellants and the argument submitted by them is to the effect that they are not bound to respect and carry forward this charterparty either in law or in equity, but that, upon the contrary, they can, in defiance of its terms, of which they had knowledge, use the vessel at their will in any other way. It is accordingly, when the true facts are shown, a very simple case raising the question of whether an obligation affecting the user of the subject of sale, namely, a ship, can be ignored by the purchaser so as to enable that purchaser, who has bought a ship notified to be not a free ship but under charter, to wipe out the condition of purchase and use the ship as a free ship. It was not bought or paid for as a free ship, but it is maintained that the buyer can thus extinguish the charterer's rights in the vessel, of which he had notice, and that the charterer has no means, legal or equitable, of preventing this in law. In the opinion of the Board the case is ruled by *De Mattos v Gibson* (1858) 4 De G & J 276. . . Their Lordships think that the judgment of Knight Bruce LJ plainly applies to the present case:

> Reason and justice seem to prescribe that, at least as a general rule, where a man, by gift or purchase, acquires property from another, with knowledge of a previous contract, lawfully and for valuable consideration made by him with a third person, to use and employ the property for a particular purpose in a specified manner, the acquirer shall not to the material damage of the third person, in opposition to the contract and inconsistently with it, use and employ the property in a manner not allowable to the giver or seller.

. . . The general character of the principle on which a Court of equity acts was explained in *Tulk v Moxhay* (1848) 2 Ph 774, 41 ER 1143. . . [*Tulk v Moxhay*] analyses the true situation of a purchaser who having bought upon the terms of the restriction upon free contract existing, thereafter when vested in the lands, attempts to divest himself of the condition under which he had bought: 'it is said that the covenant being one which does not run with the land, this Court cannot enforce it; but the question is, not whether the covenant runs with the land, but whether a party shall be permitted to use the land in a manner inconsistent with the contract entered into by his vendor, and with notice of which he purchased. Of course, the price would be affected by the covenant, and nothing could be more inequitable than that the original purchaser should be able to sell the property the next day for a greater price, in consideration of the assignee being allowed to escape from the liability which he had himself undertaken.'

In the opinion of the Board these views, much expressive of the justice and good faith of the situation, are still part of English equity jurisprudence, and an injunction can still be granted thereunder to compel, as in a court of conscience, one who obtains a conveyance or grant sub conditione from violating the condition of his purchase to the prejudice of the original contractor. Honesty forbids this; and a Court of equity will grant an injunction against it.

. . . [T]he person seeking to enforce such a restriction must, of course, have, and continue to have, an interest in the subject matter of the contract. For instance, in the case of land he must continue to hold the land in whose favour the restrictive covenant was meant to apply. That was clearly the state of matters in the case of *Tulk v Moxhay* applicable to the possession of real estate in Leicester Square. It was also clearly the case in *De Mattos v Gibson*, in which the person seeking to enforce the injunction had an interest in the user of the ship. In short, in regard to the user of land or of any chattel, an interest must remain in the subject matter of the covenant before a right can be conceded to an injunction against the violation by another of the covenant in question. . . [T]he present is, as has been seen, a case as to the user of a ship, with regard to the subject matter of which, namely, the vessel, the respondent has, and will have during the continuance of the period covered by the charterparty, a plain interest so long as she is fit to go to sea. Again, to adopt the language of Knight Bruce LJ in the *De Mattos v Gibson* case:

> Why should it (the Court) not prevent the commission or continuance of a breach of such a contract, when, its subject being valuable, as for instance, a trading ship or some costly machine, the original owner and possessor, or a person claiming under him, with notice and standing in his right, having the physical control of the chattel, is diverting it from the agreed object, that object being of importance to the other? A system of laws in which such a power does not exist must surely be very defective. I repeat that, in my opinion, the power does exist here.

NOTES

1. A person who takes with notice of the restriction, and who probably pays a lower price in consequence, should not then be able to disregard that restriction.

2. The difficulty with this decision is its reliance on *Tulk v Moxhay* as establishing the principle, since the charterers in *Strathcona* lacked the independent proprietary interest that would be necessary to enforce a restrictive covenant under *Tulk v Moxhay*.

It is not the case, despite what Lord Shaw suggested, that the charterparty itself could give that right because a contract of hire gives only a personal right. In addition, because the interest is conferred by the very contract that it is sought to enforce, it could hardly be described as 'independent'. The decision has therefore been heavily criticized as contrary to principle: see Tettenborn [1982] CLJ 58.

3. In *Port Line Ltd v Ben Line Steamers Ltd* [1958] 2 QB 146, pp. 168–9, Diplock J refused to follow *Strathcona* because he considered that it was wrongly decided.

DIPLOCK J: It seems, therefore, that it is in this case for the first time after more than 30 years that an English court has to grapple with the problem of what principle was really laid down in the *Strathcona* case, and whether that case was rightly decided. The difficulty I have found in ascertaining its ratio decidendi, the impossibility which I find of reconciling the actual decision with well-established principles of law, the unsolved and, to me, insoluble problems which that decision raises combine to satisfy me that it was wrongly decided. I do not propose to follow it, I naturally express this opinion with great diffidence, but having reached a clear conclusion it is my duty to express it.

If I am wrong in my view that the case was wrongly decided, I am certainly averse from extending it one iota beyond that which, as I understand it, it purported to decide. In particular, I do not think that it purported to decide (1) that anything short of actual knowledge by the subsequent purchaser at the time of the purchase of the charterer's rights, the violation of which it is sought to restrain, is sufficient to give rise to the equity; (2) that the charterer has any remedy against the subsequent purchaser with notice except a right to restrain the use of the vessel by such purchaser in a manner inconsistent with the terms of the charter; (3) that the charterer has any positive right against the subsequent purchaser to have the vessel used in accordance with the terms of his charter. The third proposition follows from the second; ubi jus, ibi remedium. For failure by the subsequent purchaser to use the vessel in accordance with the terms of the charter entered into by his seller there is no remedy by specific performance as was held in the *Strathcona* case itself. There is equally no remedy in damages, a consideration which distinguishes the *Strathcona* case from such cases as *Lumley v Wagner* (1852) 1 De GM & G 604 and *Lumley v Gye* (1853) 2 E & B 216. The charterer's only right is coterminous with his remedy, namely, not to have the ship used by the purchaser in violation of his charter.

There must be actual, and not constructive, knowledge.

Swiss Bank Corporation v Lloyds Bank Ltd
[1979] Ch 548

The claimant agreed to lend money to IFT to enable IFT to acquire shares in FIBI. One of the terms of the loan agreement was that IFT should comply with the Bank of England's conditions attached to exchange control consents, including the conditions that the loan had to be used to acquire the FIBI securities, and that interest and repayment of the loan should be made out of the proceeds of sale of those securities. Without exchange control consent, IFT purported to grant a charge over those securities to Lloyds Bank, which, at the time, did not have actual notice of the terms of the exchange control consents. The securities were later sold without the knowledge of the claimant, and the claimant claimed damages and repayment of the loan out of the proceeds of sale.

Held: If a person took a charge on property with *actual knowledge* of a contractual obligation in favour of another person, that person could be restrained by injunction from exercising its rights so as to interfere with the performance of that contractual obligation. Lloyds Bank had only constructive knowledge, which was not sufficient.

> BROWNE-WILKINSON J: [I]n my judgment the authorities establish the following propositions. (1) The principle stated by Knight Bruce LJ in *De Mattos v Gibson*, 4 De G & J 276, is good law and represents the counterpart in equity of the tort of knowing interference with contractual rights. (2) A person proposing to deal with property in such a way as to cause a breach of a contract affecting that property will be restrained by injunction from so doing if when he acquired that property he had actual knowledge of that contract. (3) A plaintiff is entitled to such an injunction even if he has no proprietary interest in the property: his right to have his contract performed is a sufficient interest. (4) There is no case in which such an injunction has been granted against a defendant who acquired the property with only constructive, as opposed to actual, notice of the contract. In my judgment constructive notice is not sufficient, since actual knowledge of the contract is a requisite element in the tort.

NOTES

1. The equitable counterpart of the tort of knowing interference with contractual rights is the principle in *Lumley v Gye* (1853) 2 E & B 216. The claimant, a theatre owner, entered into a contract with Johanna Wagner whereby she was to sing at his theatre for a season and was not to sing elsewhere during that period without his written consent. The defendant, the owner of a rival theatre, persuaded Wagner to break this contract with the claimant by promising to pay her more. The claimant brought an action for damages against the defendant, alleging that the defendant had induced Wagner to break her contract with him. It was held that the claimant was entitled to damages, since the defendant had committed the tort of intentionally procuring a breach of contract.

Strathcona may well be based on this principle and not on *Tulk v Moxhay*. This is because the tort of knowing interference with another's contractual rights requires the person who interferes to have actual knowledge of the contract, whereas constructive notice is all that is required in *Tulk v Moxhay*. This would also remove the difficulties of establishing an independent proprietary interest as required by *Tulk v Moxhay*. However, the *Strathcona* principle is not as wide as *Lumley v Gye*, since it is limited to protection in the form of an injunction.

2. Hoffmann J in *Law Debenture Trust Corporation plc v Ural Caspian Oil Corporation Ltd* [1993] 1 WLR 138 was faced with these alternative arguments. The case concerned a covenant to pay compensation to the original shareholders in companies, the assets of which had been confiscated as a consequence of the Russian Revolution. The shares had subsequently been sold without securing a similar covenant from the new purchasers, as was required by the terms of the original covenant. It was alleged that the new purchasers had acquired the shares with knowledge of the covenant. The original shareholders sought the compensation in accordance with the covenant on the basis that the new purchasers had purchased with actual knowledge of the covenant (i.e. the principle in *Lumley v Gye*) and so had knowingly interfered with contractual rights. Alternatively, the new purchasers had taken the shares with knowledge of the covenant; they were therefore under an obligation to perform the covenant and a positive injunction should issue (i.e. the principle in *De Mattos v Gibson*). Although Hoffmann J considered it arguable that there had been an interference with a remedy that would otherwise have been available and that the way in which to address this was to order the retransfer of the shares so that the covenant would bite, the Court of Appeal—[1994] 3 WLR 1221—disagreed and concluded that there had been no interference.

Hoffmann J specifically rejected a claim based on the principle in *Strathcona* on the ground that the claimants were seeking to use that principle to obtain compliance with a positive covenant (to pay the compensation) when the principle could only ever permit the issue of an injunction to ensure compliance with a negative covenant. Hoffmann J stated specifically, at p.144:

> One thing is beyond doubt: [the principle] does not provide a panacea for outflanking the doctrine of privity of contract.

Although the decisions failed to resolve the uncertainties surrounding the relationship between the *Strathcona* principle and the tort of knowing interference with contractual rights, it is clear that they cannot be identical, in view of the restrictive scope and remedy of the *Strathcona* principle and the fact that they had been pleaded as alternatives.

Vitiating factors

Part

3

Chapter 8

Mistake

8.1 Classes of mistake

A mistake may occur that will 'negative consent' and prevent agreement. In *Great Peace Shipping Ltd v Tsavliris Salvage (International) Ltd* [2002] EWCA Civ 1407, [2003] QB 679, Lord Phillips MR stated:

> 28 A mistake can be simply defined as an erroneous belief. Mistakes have relevance in the law of contract in a number of different circumstances. They may prevent the mutuality of agreement that is necessary for the formation of a contract. In order for two parties to conclude a contract binding in law each must agree with the other the terms of the contract. Whether two parties have entered into a contract in this way must be judged objectively, having regard to all the material facts . . .

Traditionally, two categories of agreement mistakes relating to contractual formation exist:

(a) mutual mistakes (where the parties are at cross-purposes); and

(b) unilateral mistake (where one party is mistaken and the other knows or ought to know this).

There is a third category of mistake, non-agreement mistake, where the parties have entered into a contract under the same mistaken assumption. In such a case the contract may be void for 'common mistake' if the mistake is so fundamental that it 'nullifies' consent. This is often referred to as 'initial impossibility' because the impossibility already exists when the contract is made. The existence of express contractual provisions enables the parties to allocate the risks in the way that they wish, meaning that the use of such provisions reduces the potential scope of application of the doctrine of common mistake. Although determining the existence of either initial or subsequent impossibility (the doctrine of frustration discussed in *Chapter 12*) may turn on fine distinctions of timing, the legal consequences are quite different.

8

8.2 Mutual mistake

Raffles v Wichelhaus
(1864) 2 H & C 906, 159 ER 375 (Ex D)

The claimant agreed to sell the defendants 125 bales of Surat cotton to arrive ex *Peerless* from Bombay. However, two ships called *Peerless* were sailing from Bombay; one sailed in October and the other in December. The claimant brought an action against the defendants for refusing to take delivery of the goods that were shipped on the *Peerless* leaving in December. The defendants argued that there was a latent ambiguity in the contract (i.e. one that does not appear on the face of the contract), they should therefore be allowed to adduce evidence of their intention. The defendants alleged that they understood the ship in the agreement to be the ship sailing in October. The court found for the defendants. However, as no detailed judgment was given, the only indications of the reasoning underlying this decision must be sought in the questions put to counsel.

> Milward, in support of the demurrer [for the plaintiff]: The words 'to arrive ex *Peerless*,' only mean that if the vessel is lost on the voyage, the contract is to be at an end. [Pollock CB: It would be a question for the jury whether both parties meant the same ship called the *Peerless*.] That would be so if the contract was for the sale of a ship called the *Peerless*; but it is for the sale of cotton on board a ship of that name. [Pollock CB: The defendant only bought that cotton which was to arrive by a particular ship. It may as well be said, that if there is a contract for the purchase of certain goods in warehouse A, that is satisfied by the delivery of goods of the same description in warehouse B.] In that case there would be goods in both warehouses; here it does not appear that the plaintiff had any goods on board the other *Peerless*. [Martin B: It is imposing on the defendant a contract different from that which he entered into. Pollock CB: It is like a contract for the purchase of wine coming from a particular estate in France or Spain, where there are two estates of that name.] The defendant has no right to contradict by parol evidence a written contract good upon the face of it. He does not impute misrepresentation or fraud, but only says that he fancied the ship was a different one. Intention is of no avail, unless stated at the time of the contract. [Pollock CB: One vessel sailed in October and the other in December.] The time of sailing is no part of the contract.
>
> Mellish (Cohen with him), in support of the plea [for the defendants]: There is nothing on the face of the contract to shew that any particular ship called the *Peerless* was meant; but the moment it appears that two ships called the *Peerless* were about to sail from Bombay there is a latent ambiguity, and parol evidence may be given for the purpose of shewing that the defendant meant one *Peerless*, and the plaintiff another. That being so, there was no consensus ad idem, and therefore no binding contract. He was then stopped by the Court.

NOTES

1. The decision may be limited to the fact that the defendants were allowed to adduce evidence of their intentions owing to the latent ambiguity (as an exception to the parol evidence rule—*page 179, 5.2.1*). It is not clear whether the court accepted the argument that there was no agreement because of the mistake. *Raffles v Wichelhaus* was treated as a case of latent ambiguity by Lord Phillips MR in *Great Peace Shipping v Tsavliris Salvage*.

2. Although reference is made to the subjective approach to contract formation, the facts of the case can be used to illustrate an objective approach. Having allowed the introduction of evidence of each party's intentions, it would be for the jury to decide which party's interpretation was the more reasonable. If this could not be resolved because the agreement was totally ambiguous, then the mistake would prevent the existence of a contract.

3. This case is discussed by Grant Gilmore, *The Death of Contract* (Ohio State University Press, 1974), ch. II, and see also Simpson (1989) 11 Cardozo L Rev 287.

It appears that the court treated the ship to be used as a term of the contract and that performance could not be achieved by shipment on a different vessel. Is it correct to argue that this was part of the agreed means of performance?

Scriven Brothers & Co. v Hindley
[1913] 3 KB 564

The claimants instructed an auctioneer to sell a number of bales of hemp and tow. The goods were described in the auctioneer's catalogue as a number of bales in different lots with the same shipping marks. The catalogue did not indicate that some were hemp and some were tow, although it was extremely rare for different commodities to bear the same shipping marks. The defendants' manager examined only a sample, which was hemp. When the lots of tow were put up for sale, the defendants successfully bid for them at a price that was extravagant for tow. The claimants sued for the price of the tow and the defendants alleged a mistake as to the subject matter of the proposed contract. The jury found as facts that the auctioneer intended to sell tow and the defendants intended to bid for hemp.

Held: The parties were never *ad idem* as to the subject matter of the proposed sale, so that there was no contract and the defendants did not have to pay the price. The judge (A. T. Lawrence J) appears to have been influenced by the fact that the auctioneers had contributed to the mistake by not identifying the individual lots and considered that therefore the claimants should not benefit from their agent's mistake. The defendant buyer owed no duty to inspect lots that he did not wish to purchase.

Tamplin v James
(1880) 15 Ch D 215

Property was sold as: 'All that inn with the brewhouse, outbuildings and premises known as *The Ship* together with the saddler's shop and premises adjoining thereto, situated at N., Nos 454 and 455 on the tithe map.' Plans of Nos 454 and 455 were available for inspection in the sale room. At the back of the property, there were two pieces of garden occupied with the inn and saddler's shop, which were not owned by the vendor and not included in the plans as part of the land for sale. The defendant purchased the property, without checking the plan, in the belief that the property purchased included the two pieces of garden.

Held (Baggallay LJ and, on appeal, the Court of Appeal): The defendant could not resist an order of specific performance of the sale on the ground of mistake.

BAGGALLAY LJ: It is doubtless well established that a Court of Equity will refuse specific performance of an agreement when the Defendant has entered into it under a mistake, and where injustice would be done to him were performance to be enforced. The most common instances of such refusal on the ground of mistake are cases in which there has been some unintentional misrepresentation on the part of the Plaintiff (I am not now referring to cases of intentional misrepresentation which would fall rather under the category of fraud), or where from the ambiguity of the agreement different meanings have been given to it by the different parties . . . But where there has been no misrepresentation, and where there is no ambiguity in the terms of the contract, the Defendant cannot be allowed to evade the performance of it by the simple statement that he has made a mistake. Were such to be the law the performance of a contract could rarely be enforced upon an unwilling party who was also unscrupulous . . .

JAMES LJ: If a man will not take reasonable care to ascertain what he is buying, he must take the consequences. The defence on the ground of mistake cannot be sustained. It is not enough for a purchaser to swear, 'I thought the farm sold contained twelve fields which I knew, and I find it does not include them all,' or, 'I thought it contained 100 acres and it only contains eighty.' It would open the door to fraud if such a defence was to be allowed. Perhaps some of the cases on this subject go too far, but for the most part the cases where a Defendant has escaped on the ground of a mistake not contributed to by the Plaintiff, have been cases where a hardship amounting to injustice would have been inflicted upon him by holding him to his bargain, and it was unreasonable to hold him to it. *Webster v Cecil* (1861) 30 Beav 62 is a good instance of that. It is said that it is hard to hold a man to a bargain entered into under a mistake, but we must consider the hardship on the other side. Here are trustees realizing their testator's estate, and the reckless conduct of the Defendant may have prevented their selling to somebody else. If a man makes a mistake of this kind without any reasonable excuse he ought to be held to his bargain.

NOTE The argument that the parties were at cross-purposes so that no agreement resulted cannot be used by a party whose own interpretation is not a reasonable one. The defendant here had been reckless and could not be allowed to avoid the contract based upon his subjective intention.

8.3 Unilateral mistake

8.3.1 Nature of unilateral mistake

When one party is mistaken as to a *term* of the contract and the other party knew or ought to have realized this, no binding contract will ensue. See *Hartog v Colin & Shields* [1939] 3 All ER 566 (at *page 21*, 2.1.2), in which Singleton J held that the claimant (offeree) must have realized that a mistake was made in the offer and so could not be allowed to 'snap up' the offeror's mistake.

The nature of the knowledge required for the purposes of establishing a unilateral mistake was discussed by the Singapore Court of Appeal in *Chwee Kin Keong v Digilandmall.com Pte Ltd* [2004] 1 SLR(R) 594 (*page 57*, 2.4.4.6). If a party 'ought to have realized' the mistake in the light of the surrounding circumstances, that will be classified as actual knowledge within the extended definition of wilfully shutting one's eyes to the obvious. This is particularly relevant in relation to pricing mistakes on websites: see the discussion in *Poole's Textbook on Contract Law*, 15th edn (Oxford University Press, 2021), 2.3.2.3.1.

If it is not a mistake relating to a *term* of the contract, but concerns a 'collateral' matter—Adams and Brownsword, *Understanding Contract Law*, 5th edn (Sweet & Maxwell, 2007), pp. 64–6—or a matter relating to a quality of the subject matter, then it will not prevent agreement and there is no requirement that the offeror corrects the offeree's mistake where he knows it has been made.

The claimant offered to sell oats to the defendant and showed the defendant a sample. The defendant agreed to buy but later refused to accept the oats on the ground that they were new and he thought he was buying old oats. The claimant only intended to offer to sell 'green' oats and had no old oats to sell. The claimant brought an action for non-acceptance and the defendant alleged that the claimant knew he required old oats. The appeal concerned the correctness of the judge's direction to the jury. The judge had left two questions to the jury.

(a) Had the word 'old' been used by the claimant or the defendant in making the contract? If so, they had to return a verdict for the defendant. However, if they thought it had not been so used, then the second question had to be considered.

(b) Was the evidence that the claimant believed the defendant to believe that he was contracting for old oats? If yes, then the verdict had to be for the defendant, but if the evidence was that the claimant did not have such a belief, then the jury would need to find for the claimant.

Held: The court found that there had been a misdirection on the second question and ordered a new trial.

COCKBURN CJ: [W]e must assume that nothing was said on the subject of the defendant's manager desiring to buy *old* oats, nor of the oats having been said to be old; while, on the other hand, we must assume that the defendant's manager believed the oats to be old oats and that the plaintiff was conscious of the existence of such belief, but did nothing, directly or indirectly, to bring it about, simply offering his oats and exhibiting his sample, remaining perfectly passive as to what was passing in the mind of the other party. The question is whether, under such circumstances, the passive acquiescence of the seller in the self-deception of the buyer will entitle the latter to avoid the contract. I am of opinion that it will not . . .

I take the true rule to be, that where a specific article is offered for sale, without express warranty, or without circumstances from which the law will imply a warranty—as where, for instance, an article is ordered for a specific purpose—and the buyer has full opportunity of inspecting and forming his own judgment, if he chooses to act on his own judgment, the rule caveat emptor applies. If he gets the article he contracted to buy, and that article corresponds with what it was sold as, he gets all he is entitled to, and is bound by the contract. Here the defendant agreed to buy a specific parcel of oats. The oats were what they were sold as, namely, good oats according to the sample. The buyer persuaded himself they were old oats, when they were not so; but the seller neither said nor did anything to contribute to his deception. He has himself to blame . . .

Now, in this case, there was plainly no legal obligation in the plaintiff in the first instance to state whether the oats were new or old. He offered them for sale according to the sample, as he had a perfect right to do, and gave the buyer the fullest opportunity of inspecting the sample, which, practically, was equivalent to an inspection of the oats themselves. What, then, was there to create any trust or confidence between the parties, so as to make it incumbent on the plaintiff to communicate the fact that the oats were not, as the defendant assumed them to be, old oats? If, indeed, the buyer, instead of acting on his own opinion, had asked the question whether the oats were old or new, or had said anything which intimated his understanding that the seller was selling the oats as old oats, the case would have been wholly different; or even if he had said anything which shewed that he was not acting on his own inspection and judgment, but assumed as the foundation of the contract that the oats were old, the silence of the seller, as a means of misleading him, might have amounted to a fraudulent concealment, such as would have entitled the buyer to avoid the contract. Here, however, nothing of the sort occurs. The buyer in no way refers to the seller, but acts entirely on his own judgment.

It only remains to deal with an argument which was pressed upon us, that the defendant in the present case intended to buy old oats, and the plaintiff to sell new, so the two minds were not *ad idem*; and that consequently there was no contract. This argument proceeds on the fallacy of confounding what was merely a motive operating on the buyer to induce him to buy with one of the essential conditions of the contract. Both parties were agreed as to the sale and purchase of this particular parcel of oats. The defendant believed the oats to be old, and was thus induced to agree to buy them, but he omitted to make their age a condition of the contract. All that can be said is, that the two minds were not *ad idem* as to the age of the oats; they certainly were *ad idem* as to the sale and purchase of them. Suppose a person to buy a horse without a warranty, believing him to be sound; and the horse turns out unsound, could it be contended that it would be open to him to say that, as he had intended to buy a sound horse, and the seller to sell an unsound one, the contract was void, because the seller must have known from the price the buyer was willing to give, or from his general habits as a buyer of horses, that he thought the horse was sound? The cases are exactly parallel.

The result is that, in my opinion, the learned judge of the county court was wrong in leaving the second question to the jury, and that, consequently, the case must go down to a new trial.

NOTE The parties had agreed the terms for the sale and purchase of the oats; the question of the age had not been mentioned and, as such, was a 'collateral' matter. Consequently, unlike the mistake in *Hartog v Colin & Shields*, this was not a true agreement mistake, since it did not relate to offer and acceptance, and did not prevent agreement. If the buyer wanted old oats, he should have ensured that he bought old oats. Any other conclusion would encourage imprudent conduct by buyers.

Statoil ASA v Louis Dreyfus Energy Services LP, The Harriette N
[2008] EWHC 2257 (Comm), [2008] 2 Lloyd's Rep 685

The claimant, the seller of a cargo of oil and gas, sought the balance of demurrage (sum payable in accordance with the contract terms where the charterer has delayed) that it been required to pay to the shipowners from the defendant buyer. The claimant's calculation of the demurrage due was wrong because the wrong date had been used as the date for completion of discharge of the cargo (13 October, when it had not occurred until 24 October). The defendant realized the mistake, but decided to say nothing. The parties agreed (via the compromise agreement) the amount of demurrage on the basis of this mistaken calculation. The claimant then discovered the error and sought to argue that this agreement was void or voidable for unilateral mistake.

Held: The mistake was not a mistake as to a term of the agreement, but only as to the basis on which the decision to contract on those terms had been made. That was not sufficient to render the contract void even if the other party knew of the mistake. There was also no equitable jurisdiction to render the agreement voidable: *Great Peace Shipping Ltd v Tsavliris Salvage (International) Ltd* [2002] EWCA Civ 1407, [2003] QB 679 (*page 396, 8.4.5*). If there was no equitable jurisdiction to set aside contracts for common mistake, no such jurisdiction existed in the case of a unilateral mistake. In any event, the judge would not have exercised such a jurisdiction on these facts since the mistake was entirely the result of carelessness on the claimant's part.

AIKENS J:

Issue two: is the agreement of 26 January 2007 as to demurrage payable not binding on Statoil because of its unilateral mistake

87 . . . The general rule at common law is that if one party has made a mistake *as to the terms of the contract* and that mistake is known to the other party, then the contract is not binding. The reasoning is that although the parties appear, objectively, to have agreed terms, it is clear that they are not in agreement. Therefore the normal rule of looking only at the objective agreement of the parties is displaced and the court admits evidence to show what each side subjectively intended to agree by way of terms. If

it is clear from such evidence that there was not consensus, then there can be no contract, because the parties have not truly agreed on the terms

. . .

88 However, if one party has made a mistake about a fact on which he bases his decision to enter into the contract, but that fact does not form a term of the contract itself then, even if the other party knows that the first is mistaken as to this fact, the contract will be binding. That was the effect of the decision of the Court of Queen's Bench . . . in *Smith v Hughes* (1871) LR 6 QB 597, see particularly at page 603 per Cockburn CJ, and page 607 per Blackburn J. The correctness of that decision and the analysis in it has never been doubted.

89 . . . It seems to me that I have to ask, first of all, what, objectively, are the terms of the parties' agreement of 26 January 2007? Secondly, what was the state of mind of the two parties at that time? Thirdly, does that mean that the parties have not, in fact, reached consensus on the terms of the contract?

[Aikens J considered that the date for completion of discharge was not a term of the compromise, and that the claimant had wrongly believed the date of discharge was 13 October 2006 and the defendant had been aware of the claimant's mistake, but had said nothing. He continued:]

93 On this analysis, the facts fall outside the classic circumstances in which the courts have admitted evidence of subjective states of mind of the parties to see whether the unilateral mistake of one, which was known to the other, has created a situation where there was not, in fact, agreement. So the unilateral mistake does not affect the objective agreement of the parties.

94 However, [counsel] referred me to a report of a decision of the Singapore Court of Appeal in *Chwee Kin Keong v Digilandmall.com Pte Ltd* . . . In that case the unilateral mistake of the sellers was in accidentally putting on its website a much lower price for laser printers than was correct. The wrong price was the result of an error by one of the seller's employees, whose work on the seller's website accidentally altered the price of the printers from S $3,854 to S $66 per printer. The finding of the trial judge was that buyers had actual knowledge that the price was a mistake, but went ahead and ordered large quantities at the advertised low price. (See para 38 of the judgment of Chao Hick Tin JA on appeal.) The sellers refused to deliver the printers at that price. The judge declared the contracts void under the common law doctrine of unilateral mistake. The Court of Appeal, after an exhaustive judgment which examined both the common law and equitable doctrine on mistake, upheld the judgment.

95 To my mind this decision falls squarely within the classic rule. There was a unilateral mistake by the seller about the price of the printers. The buyers knew that the mistake had been made, but went ahead and 'snapped up the offer' (*Tamplin v James* (1880) 15 Ch D 215 at page 221 per James LJ). Plainly, when the subjective evidence was examined, the parties were not agreed as to the most fundamental term of the contract: the price.

96 So this case does not assist [counsel for the claimant] on her first submission. The common law rule on the circumstances when a unilateral mistake will mean a *prima facie* agreement is not binding is well settled. It only applies when there is a unilateral mistake as to a contract term. There was no such mistake by Mr Rostrup [the claimant] in this case.

8.3.2 Unilateral mistake as to identity

One party (commonly termed 'the rogue') may misrepresent his or her identity to persuade the other contracting party to contract or allow the rogue to take away goods on credit. In most situations, the rogue will sell the goods to an innocent third party. The mistaken party will then have to seek to recover the goods and damages for conversion from the innocent third party. This is possible only if the contract is void for mistake as to identity, so that the rogue did not acquire any title (ownership in the goods or property) to pass on.

Before the decision of the House of Lords in *Shogun Finance Ltd v Hudson* [2003] UKHL 62, [2004] 1 AC 919, the law as to mistaken identity was generally recognized to be in an unsatisfactory state.

8.3.2.1 Background to the Decision of the House of Lords in *Shogun v Hudson*

The courts have been faced with the difficult task of deciding which of two innocent parties should suffer because of the fraud of a third. Since the consequences for the innocent third party are regarded as harsh, the usual approach had been to protect that party by concluding that the contract was voidable for fraudulent misrepresentation relating to identity, rather than void for mistake as to identity. If the contract is merely voidable, since the right to rescind is lost when an innocent third party purchases the goods, the goods could not then be recovered from that innocent third party (SGA 1979, s. 23) and the innocent third party would not be liable in damages for their conversion.

However, this policy objective was furthered by an unfortunate distinction, which was difficult to explain and justify, between mistake as to identity and mistake as to attributes such as creditworthiness (attribute mistakes being insufficiently fundamental to render the contract void). More significantly, there could be a true mistake as to identity only where identity was regarded as crucial to the decision to contract, and that would be presumed not to be the case in face-to-face contracts, the presumption being that there was an intention to contract with the person physically present. Even in this context, there were apparently irreconcilable decisions: compare *Phillips v Brooks Ltd* and *Lewis v Averay* (voidable for fraudulent misrepresentation) with *Ingram v Little* (treated as void by the majority of the Court of Appeal on the basis that the offer was intended for the real P. G. M. Hutchinson and, therefore, only he could accept it, despite the fact that this was a face-to-face dealing).

Years earlier, the House of Lords in *Cundy v Lindsay* had concluded, in the context of a contract by written correspondence, that identity was crucially important to the decision to contract and had therefore held the contract to be void for mistake as to identity. Both *Cundy v Lindsay* and the majority of the Court of Appeal in *Ingram v Little* focused on an offer and acceptance analysis of the question of the identity of the parties to the contract and regarded identity as a term of the contract.

8.3.2.2 The key cases prior to the decision in *Shogun v Hudson*: face-to-face case law

In a face-to-face situation, the actual decision to sell does not normally rest on the question of the identity of the buyer, although the decision to allow the goods to be taken on credit will often be influenced by the attributes of the buyer.

Phillips v Brooks Ltd
[1919] 2 KB 243

A rogue, North, had entered the claimant's jewellery shop, and asked to see some pearls and a ring. He selected pearls at a price of £2,550 and a ring at the price of £450. He wrote out a cheque for £3,000, saying, 'You see who I am, I am Sir George Bullough', and he gave an address in St James's Square. The claimant knew that there was such a person and, having checked the address in a directory, asked the man in the shop if he would like to take the articles with him. The man took the ring. The cheque was dishonoured, but in the meantime the rogue had pledged the ring with the defendants—pawnbrokers, who acted without notice. The claimant sued the defendants for the return of the ring (or its value) and damages for its detention.

Held: The claimant intended to contract, and did contract, with the person in the shop. The mistake was allowing the goods to be taken away on credit which was not an identity mistake.

HORRIDGE J: I have carefully considered the evidence of the plaintiff, and have come to the conclusion that, although he believed the person to whom he was handing the ring was Sir George Bullough, he in fact contracted to sell and deliver it to the person who came into his shop, and who was not Sir George Bullough, but a man of the name of North, who obtained the sale and delivery by means of the false pretence that he was Sir George Bullough . . . The following expressions seem to me to fit the facts in this case: 'The minds of the parties met and agreed upon all the terms of the sale, the thing sold, the price and time of payment, the person selling and the person buying. The fact that the seller was induced to sell by fraud of the buyer made the sale voidable, but not void. He could not have supposed that he was selling to any other person; his intention was to sell to the person present, and identified by sight and hearing; it does not defeat the sale because the buyer assumed a false name or practised any other deceit to induce the vendor to sell.'

NOTES

1. *Hardman v Booth* (1863) 1 H & C 803, 158 ER 1107 established an exception to the usual position in face-to-face dealings. (For the facts, see the speech of Lord Phillips in *Shogun v Hudson* [2003] UKHL 62, [2004] 1 AC 919, [128]–[130], extracted at *page 368, 8.3.2.1*.) The contract will be void where the intention is to contract with a company and the contract purports to be made by a person on behalf of that company who, in fact, has no such authority to act.

2. *Ingram v Little* [1961] 1 QB 31, a decision of the Court of Appeal, is difficult to reconcile with *Phillips v Brooks Ltd*. The claimants, three elderly women, the joint owners of a car, advertised it for sale. A rogue, introducing himself as Hutchinson, offered to buy it. When he produced his chequebook to pay, the claimant told him that they expected cash and were not prepared to accept payment by cheque. The rogue then said he was P. G. M. Hutchinson, a reputable businessman who lived at Stanstead House, Stanstead Road, Caterham, and that he had business interests in Caterham. The claimants had never heard of this person, but one of them slipped out, went to the Post Office, and, on checking the telephone directory, ascertained that there was a P. G. M. Hutchinson living at that address. The claimant, believing the rogue to indeed be this P. G. M. Hutchinson, let him have the car in exchange for the cheque. He was not the real P. G. M. Hutchinson. The rogue's cheque was not met. Meanwhile, the rogue had sold the car to the defendant, who had bought it in good faith. The claimants sought the return of the car from the defendant, or alternatively damages for its conversion. It was held (Devlin LJ dissenting) that, since

the claimants had made an offer to the real P. G. M. Hutchinson, the rogue could therefore not accept it.

SELLERS LJ: It [*Phillips v Brooks Ltd* [1919] 2 KB 243] is not an authority to establish that where an offer or acceptance is addressed to a person (although under a mistake as to his identity) who is present in person, then it must in all circumstances be treated as if actually addressed to him. I would regard the issue as a question of fact in each case depending on what was said and done and applying the elementary principles of offer and acceptance . . .

The question in each case should be solved, in my opinion, by applying the test, which Slade J applied, 'How ought the promisee to have interpreted the promise' in order to find whether a contract has been entered into . . .

Cundy v Lindsay (1878) 3 App Cas 459 . . . was to the same effect as the present case. The plaintiffs intended to sell to Blenkiron & Co. but Blenkarn fraudulently assumed the position of the buyer. Therefore, an offer to sell to Blenkiron & Co. was knowingly 'accepted' by Blenkarn and there was no contract.

. . . There is a difference between the case where A makes an offer to B in the belief that B is not B but is someone else, and the case where A makes an offer to B in the belief that B is X. In the first case B does in fact receive an offer, even though the offeror does not know that it is to B he is making it, since he believes B to be someone else. In the second case, A does not in truth make any offer to B at all; he thinks B is X, for whom alone the offer is meant. There was an offer intended for and available only to X. B cannot accept it if he knew or ought to have known that it was not addressed to him.

PEARCE LJ: I agree. The question here is whether there was any contract, whether offer and acceptance met . . .

The real problem in the present case is whether the plaintiffs were in fact intending to deal with the person physically present, who had fraudulently endowed himself with the attributes of some other identity, or whether they were intending only to deal with that other identity. If the former, there was a valid but voidable contract and the property passed. If the latter, there was no contract and the property did not pass . . .

An apparent contract made orally *inter praesentes* raises particular difficulties. The offer is apparently addressed to the physical person present. Prima facie, he, by whatever name he is called, is the person to whom the offer is made. His physical presence identified by sight and hearing preponderates over vagaries of nomenclature. 'Praesentia corporistolli terrorem nominis' said Lord Bacon (*Law Tracts* (1737), p. 102). Yet clearly, though difficult, it is not impossible to rebut the prima facie presumption that the offer can be accepted by the person to whom it is physically addressed. To take two extreme instances. If a man orally commissions a portrait from some unknown artist who had deliberately passed himself off, whether by disguise or merely by verbal cosmetics, as a famous painter, the impostor could not accept the offer. For though the offer is made to him physically, it is obviously, as he knows, addressed to the famous painter. The mistake in identity on such facts is clear and the nature of the contract makes it obvious that identity was of vital importance to the offeror. At the other end of the scale, if a shopkeeper sells goods in a normal cash transaction to a man who misrepresents himself as being some well-known figure, the transaction will normally be valid. For the shopkeeper was ready to sell goods for cash to the world at large and the particular identity of the purchaser in such a contract was not of sufficient importance to override the physical presence identified by sight and hearing. Thus the nature of the proposed contract must have a strong bearing on the question of whether the intention of the offeror (as understood by his offeree) was to make his offer to some other particular identity rather than to the physical person to whom it was orally offered.

In our case, the facts lie in the debatable area between the two extremes. At the beginning of the negotiations, always an important consideration, the name or personality of the false Hutchinson were of no importance and there was no other identity competing with his physical presence. The plaintiffs were content to sell the car for cash to any purchaser. The contractual conversation was orally addressed to the physical identity of the false Hutchinson. The identity was the man present, and his name was merely one of his attributes. Had matters continued thus, there would clearly have been a valid but voidable contract.

I accept the judge's view that there was no contract at the stage when the man pulled out his cheque book. From a practical point of view negotiations reached an impasse at that stage. For the vendor refused to discuss the question of selling on credit . . . Payment and delivery still needed to be discussed and the parties would be expecting to discuss them. Immediately they did discuss them it became plain that they were not *ad idem* and that no contract had yet been created. But, even if there had been a concluded agreement before discussion of a cheque, it was rescinded. The man tried to make Miss Ingram take a cheque. She declined and said that the deal was off. He did not demur but set himself to reconstruct the negotiations. For the moment had come, which he must all along have anticipated, as the crux of the negotiations, the vital crisis of the swindle. He wanted to take away the car on credit against his worthless cheque, but she refused. Thereafter, the negotiations were of a different kind from what the vendor had mistakenly believed them to be hitherto. The parties were no longer concerned with a cash sale of goods where the identity of the purchaser was prima facie unimportant. They were concerned with a credit sale in which both parties knew that the identity of the purchaser was of the utmost importance . . .

The decision may be explained on policy grounds. Normally, the court is concerned to protect the innocent third party purchaser, but in *Ingram v Little* this third party was a car dealer and the Court of Appeal may have felt that the old ladies were more in need of protection.

Devlin LJ (dissenting) considered that the presumption in face-to-face contracts had not been rebutted and that this contract was voidable, rather than void. He went on to discuss the policy issues behind the distinction between void and voidable contracts where identity is in issue.

DEVLIN LJ [dissenting]: There can be no doubt, as all this difference of opinion shows, that the dividing line between voidness and voidability, between fundamental mistake and incidental deceit, is a very fine one. That a fine and difficult distinction has to be drawn is not necessarily any reproach to the law. But need the rights of the parties in a case like this depend on such a distinction? . . . Why should the question whether the defendant should or should not pay the plaintiff damages for conversion depend upon voidness or voidability, and upon inferences to be drawn from a conversation in which the defendant took no part? The true spirit of the common law is to override theoretical distinctions when they stand in the way of doing practical justice. For the doing of justice, the relevant question in this sort of case is not whether the contract was void or voidable, but which of two innocent parties shall suffer for the fraud of a third. The plain answer is that the loss should be divided between them in such proportion as is just in all the circumstances. If it be pure misfortune, the loss should be borne equally; if the fault or imprudence of either party has caused or contributed to the loss, it should be borne by that party in the whole or in the greater part. In saying this, I am suggesting nothing novel, for this sort of observation has often been made. But it is only in comparatively recent times that the idea of giving to a court power to apportion loss has found a place in our law. I have in mind particularly the Law Reform Acts of 1935, 1943 and 1945, that dealt respectively with joint tortfeasors, frustrated contracts and contributory negligence. These statutes, which I believe to have worked satisfactorily, show a modern inclination towards a decision based on a just apportionment rather than one given in black or in white according to the logic of the law. I believe it would be useful if Parliament were now to consider whether or not it is practicable by means of a similar act of law reform to provide for the victims of a fraud a better way of adjusting their mutual loss than that which has grown out of the common law.

The Twelfth Report of the Law Reform Committee, *Transfer of Title to Chattels* (Cmnd 2958, 1966), had considered the possibility of apportionment in instances of mistake as to identity, but decided that it would be impractical. However, the Committee did conclude that fine distinctions had developed that were a reproach to the law and recommended that a contract entered into as a result of a mistake as to identity should be voidable rather than void, thus protecting the innocent purchaser. This recommendation was not implemented, although it was clearly supported by Lord Denning in *Lewis v Averay*.

Lewis v Averay
[1972] 1 QB 198 (CA)

The claimant advertised his car for sale. A rogue came to see the car, introduced himself as 'Richard Green', and made the claimant believe that he was the well-known film actor Richard Greene (of *Robin Hood* fame). The rogue said that he would like to buy the car and take it away that night. He wrote out a cheque, signing it 'R. A. Green'. The claimant asked for proof that the buyer was Richard Greene, and the rogue showed him a pass to Pinewood Studios in the name of 'Richard A. Green' bearing a photograph of the rogue and an official stamp. The claimant was satisfied, and let the rogue have the logbook and the car. The cheque had come from a stolen chequebook and was dishonoured. Meanwhile, the rogue sold the car to Averay, who bought it in good faith. The claimant brought an action against Averay for the return of the car or its value and damages for conversion.

Held: Approving *Phillips v Brooks Ltd*, the presumption that the claimant had concluded a contract with the person physically present had not been rebutted. It was a mistake as to creditworthiness, rather than identity, which did not render the contract void. Averay had good title to the car.

LORD DENNING MR: The real question in the case is whether on May 8, 1969, there was a contract of sale under which the property in the car passed from Mr Lewis to the rogue. If there was such a contract, then, even though it was voidable for fraud, nevertheless Mr Averay would get a good title to the car. But if there was no contract of sale by Mr Lewis to the rogue—either because there was, on the face of it, no agreement between the parties, or because any apparent agreement was a nullity and void ab initio for mistake, then no property would pass from Mr Lewis to the rogue. Mr Averay would not get a good title because the rogue had no property to pass to him.

. . . Who is entitled to the goods? The original seller? Or the ultimate buyer? The courts have given different answers. In *Phillips v Brooks*, the ultimate buyer was held to be entitled to the ring. In *Ingram v Little* the original seller was held to be entitled to the car . . .

It seems to me that the material facts in each case are quite indistinguishable the one from the other. In each case there was, to all outward appearance, a contract: but there was a mistake by the seller as to the identity of the buyer. This mistake was fundamental. In each case it led to the handing over of the goods. Without it the seller would not have parted with them.

. . . [I]t has been suggested that a mistake as to the identity of a person is one thing: and a mistake as to his attributes is another. A mistake as to identity, it is said, avoids a contract: whereas a mistake as to attributes does not. But this is a distinction without a difference. A man's very name is one of his attributes. It is also a key to his identity. If then, he gives a false name, is it a mistake as to his identity? or a mistake as to his attributes? These fine distinctions do no good to the law.

As I listened to the argument in this case, I felt it wrong that an innocent purchaser (who knew nothing of what passed between the seller and the rogue) should have his title depend on such refinements.

After all, he has acted with complete circumspection and in entire good faith: whereas it was the seller who let the rogue have the goods and thus enabled him to commit the fraud. I do not, therefore, accept the theory that a mistake as to identity renders a contract void. I think the true principle is that which underlies the decision of this court in *King's Norton Metal Co. Ltd v Edridge Merrett & Co. Ltd* (1897) 14 TLR 98 and of Horridge J in *Phillips v Brooks* [1919] 2 KB 243, which has stood for these last 50 years. It is this: When two parties have come to a contract—or rather what appears, on the face of it, to be a contract—the fact that one party is mistaken as to the identity of the other does not mean that there is no contract, or that the contract is a nullity and void from the beginning. It only means that the contract is voidable, that is, liable to be set aside at the instance of the mistaken person, so long as he does so before third parties have in good faith acquired rights under it.

Applied to the cases such as the present, this principle is in full accord with the presumption stated by Pearce LJ and also Devlin LJ in *Ingram v Little* [1961] 1 QB 31, 61, 66. When a dealing is had between a seller like Mr Lewis and a person who is actually there present before him, then the presumption in law is that there is a contract, even though there is a fraudulent impersonation by the buyer representing himself as a different man than he is. There is a contract made with the very person there, who is present in person. It is liable no doubt to be avoided for fraud, but it is still a good contract under which title will pass unless and until it is avoided. In support of that presumption, Devlin LJ quoted, at p. 66, not only the English case of *Phillips v Brooks*, but other cases in the United States where 'the courts hold that if A appeared in person before B, impersonating C, an innocent purchaser from A gets the property in the goods against B.' That seems to me to be right in principle in this country also.

In this case Mr Lewis made a contract of sale with the very man, the rogue, who came to the flat. I say that he 'made a contract' because in this regard we do not look into his intentions, or into his mind to know what he was thinking or into the mind of the rogue. We look to the outward appearances. On the face of the dealing, Mr Lewis made a contract under which he sold the car to the rogue, delivered the car and the logbook to him, and took a cheque in return . . . It was, of course, induced by fraud. The rogue made false representations as to his identity. But it was still a contract, though voidable for fraud. It was a contract under which this property passed to the rogue, and in due course passed from the rogue to Mr Averay, before the contract was avoided.

Though I very much regret that either of these good and reliable gentlemen should suffer, in my judgment it is Mr Lewis who should do so.

MEGAW LJ: For myself, with very great respect, I find it difficult to understand the basis, either in logic or in practical considerations, of the test laid down by the majority of the court in *Ingram v Little* [1961] 1 QB 31. That test is, I think, accurately recorded in the headnote, as follows:

> where a person physically present and negotiating to buy a chattel fraudulently assumed the identity of an existing third person, the test to determine to whom the offer was addressed was how ought the promisee to have interpreted the promise.

The promisee, be it noted, is the rogue. The question of the existence of a contract and therefore the passing of property, and therefore the right of third parties, if this test is correct, is made to depend upon the view which some rogue should have formed, presumably knowing that he is a rogue, as to the state of mind of the opposite party to the negotiation, who does not know that he is dealing with a rogue.

. . . [I]n my view this appeal can be decided on a short and simple point . . . [I]t must be established that at the time of offering to sell his car to the rogue, Mr Lewis regarded the identity of the rogue as a matter of vital importance . . . [T]he mistake of Mr Lewis went no further than a mistake as to the attributes of the rogue. It was simply a mistake as to the creditworthiness of the man who was there present and who described himself as Mr Green . . .

NOTE Lord Denning stressed the need to protect the innocent third party. He saw the third party as being more innocent than the seller, whom he said had allowed the rogue to have the goods in the first place and had thus enabled the rogue to commit the fraud.

8.3.2.3 Contracts made by written correspondence

There is nineteenth-century House of Lords' authority that where a contract is made at a distance, identity will be vital, so that a mistaken party will intend to deal with the person named in the correspondence.

Cundy v Lindsay
(1878) 3 App Cas 459 (HL)

The claimants, linen manufacturers in Belfast, received a written order for handkerchiefs from a rogue, Blenkarn, who gave his address as 37 Wood Street, Cheapside. The name was written to appear as 'Blenkiron & Co.', a highly respected firm carrying on business at 123 Wood Street, Cheapside. The claimants had heard of Blenkiron & Co.'s reputation, although they did not know the number in Wood Street from which Blenkiron & Co. carried on business. The claimants sent the goods on credit to 'Messrs Blenkiron & Co., 37 Wood Street'. They were never paid. Blenkarn sold the goods to bona fide purchasers, who included the defendants. The claimants brought an action against the defendants for unlawful conversion of the handkerchiefs, which meant that they had to establish that the defendants had not obtained title to them.

Held: The contract was void for mistake as to identity.

LORD CAIRNS LC: Was there any contract which, with regard to the goods in question in this case, had passed the property in the goods from the Messrs. Lindsay to Alfred Blenkarn? If there was any contract passing that property, even although, as I have said, that contract might afterwards be open to a process of reduction, upon the ground of fraud, still, in the meantime, Blenkarn might have conveyed a good title for valuable consideration to the present Appellants.

. . . The principal parties concerned, the Respondents and Blenkarn, never came in contact personally—everything that was done was done by writing. What has to be judged of, and what the jury in the present case had to judge of, was merely the conclusion to be derived from that writing, as applied to the admitted facts of the case.

Now, my Lords, discharging that duty and answering that inquiry, what the jurors have found is in substance this . . . They have found that by the form of the signatures to the letters which were written by Blenkarn, by the mode in which his letters and his applications to the Respondents were made out, and by the way in which he left uncorrected the mode and form in which, in turn, he was addressed by the Respondents; that by all those means he led, and intended to lead, the Respondents to believe, and they did believe, that the person with whom they were communicating was not Blenkarn, the dishonest and irresponsible man, but was a well known and solvent house of Blenkiron & Co., doing business in the same street . . .

If that is so, what is the consequence? It is that Blenkarn—the dishonest man, as I call him—was acting here just in the same way as if he had forged the signature of Blenkiron & Co., the respectable firm, to the applications for goods, and as if, when, in return, the goods were forwarded and letters were sent, accompanying them, he had intercepted the goods and intercepted the letters, and had taken possession of the goods, and of the letters which were addressed to, and intended for, not himself but, the firm of Blenkiron & Co. Now, my Lords, stating the matter shortly in that way, I ask the question, how is it possible to imagine that in that state of things any contract could have arisen between the Respondents and Blenkarn, the dishonest man? Of him they knew nothing, and of him they never thought. With him they never intended to deal. Their minds never, even for an instant of time rested upon him, and as between him and them there was no *consensus* of mind which could lead to any agreement or any contract whatever. As between him and them there was merely the one side to a contract, where, in order to produce a contract, two sides would be required. With the firm of Blenkiron & Co. of course there was no contract, for as to them the matter was entirely unknown, and therefore the pretence of a contract was a failure.

The result, therefore, my Lords, is this, that your Lordships have not here to deal with one of those cases in which there is *de facto* a contract made which may afterwards be impeached and set aside, on the ground of fraud; but you have to deal with a case which ranges itself under a completely different chapter of law, the case namely in which the contract never comes into existence. My Lords, that being so, it is idle to talk of the property passing. The property remained, as it originally had been, the property of the Respondents, and the title which was attempted to be given to the Appellants was a title which could not be given to them.

NOTES

1. Since the contract was held to be void, the innocent party was the loser.

2. It appears important, on the facts, that the claimants knew of the existence of Blenkiron & Co., so that they were able to show they had mistaken one existing entity for another.

? QUESTION

Did the claimants send the goods because they thought that the buyer was a highly respected firm and would pay for the goods?

8.3.2.4 The opportunity presented by *Shogun Finance v Hudson*

The Court of Appeal in *Shogun Finance* criticized the law governing mistake as to identity. Brooke LJ referred to the law as 'still in the sorry condition' that it had been in when it was considered by the Law Reform Committee in 1966, and Sedley LJ noted 'the illogical and sometimes barely perceptible distinctions made in earlier decisions' that he acknowledged, in some cases, represented 'an unarticulated judicial policy on the incidence of loss as between innocent parties'. *Cundy v Lindsay*, as a decision of the House of Lords, was recognized by Sedley LJ as preventing comprehensive adjustment and he noted that Lord Denning had not referred to it in his analysis in *Lewis v Averay*. The legal principles were in desperate need of clarification and simplification by the House of Lords. However, whilst their Lordships provided *some* clarification, the principles they settled on are far from simple, and an arbitrary distinction between written contracts and face-to-face dealings has been put on a formal footing.

Shogun Finance Ltd v Hudson
[2004] 1 AC 919 (HL), [2003] UKHL 62

A rogue had expressed an interest in purchasing a Mitsubishi Shogun car from a motor dealer when visiting that dealer's premises. The rogue had pretended to be a Mr Durlabh Patel, had given Mr Patel's address, and had produced Mr Patel's stolen driving licence as proof of his identity. The dealer agreed the price for the car (£22,250) and had then faxed a draft hire purchase agreement to the claimant finance company with a copy of the driving licence. This hire purchase agreement had named Mr Patel as the customer, but had been signed by the rogue, forging the signature present on Mr Patel's driving licence on the agreement. The finance company checked Mr Patel's credit rating and approved the finance. The dealer therefore allowed the rogue to take possession of the vehicle, whereupon the rogue sold the car to Hudson, a purchaser in good faith, for £17,000. (Note that the dealer sells the car to the finance company, which then 'hires' it to the purchaser.)

The finance company brought a claim against the defendant for damages in the tort of conversion and the defendant counterclaimed that he had acquired good title in accordance with s. 27 of the Hire Purchase Act 1964. This counterclaim turned on the question of whether the rogue was a 'debtor' under the hire purchase agreement; if so, the defendant would have acquired good title.

The judge at first instance held that the defendant was not a 'debtor' and the majority of the Court of Appeal agreed on the basis that the hire purchase agreement had not been made with the rogue, but with Mr Patel. The real Mr Patel could not be liable on such an agreement because his signature had been forged. The majority of the Court of Appeal rejected the defendant's alternative argument that this was a face-to-face contract made between the rogue and the finance company via the dealer as agent, thereby raising the presumption that the finance company intended to deal with the rogue, as the person present. The majority considered that the dealer was not the agent for the finance company.

Held (on appeal to the House of Lords, by a majority of three to two, Lords Nicholls and Millett dissenting): The written agreement was made between the finance company and the real Mr Patel. However, this agreement was a nullity because it had been made without Mr Patel's authority. There was no valid contract between the rogue and the finance company, and the defendant was not protected by s. 27 because he was not the 'debtor'.

The speeches of the majority in the House of Lords reveal some differences in reasoning, if not in outcome, although all five Law Lords treated the basic issue as involving offer and acceptance, objectively ascertained.

Lord Hobhouse considered that the case was concerned only with the construction of the written hire purchase agreement. The written contract explicitly named Mr Patel and was described as an offer by Mr Patel to the finance company. Therefore, the finance company's acceptance related to that offer. Only the finance company and Mr Patel could be parties to the agreement. In accordance with the parol evidence rule, extrinsic oral evidence was not admissible to contradict the terms of the writing, e.g. to demonstrate that, in accordance with the face-to-face presumption, the rogue was the true 'debtor'.

Lord Walker stated that he was dismissing the appeal for the reasons given by Lord Hobhouse, but, unlike Lord Hobhouse, his speech deals with the broader issues arising in the mistake as to identity cases.

Lord Phillips (also in the majority) considered that the effect of mistake as to identity depended on whether there could be said to be an offer and acceptance. Lords Phillips and Walker drew a distinction between contracts made face-to-face (which might include telephone dealings, *per* Lord Walker) and contracts made through correspondence. In face-to-face situations, there is said to be a presumption that the offer is intended to be made to the person physically present and therefore that that person can accept. It followed that *Ingram v Little* was wrongly decided. However, this presumption could not apply to contracts made by means of written documents, including contracts made by post, email, and the present situation. In these cases, the offer and acceptance issue turned on the written documents.

Lords Nicholls and Millett (dissenting) focused on the arbitrary distinction between contracts made by post and face-to-face dealings. Lords Nicholls and Millett objected to a distinction that turns on the mode by which a transaction is completed. They therefore favoured a more general 'dealing' principle to replace the presumption (although this can be seen more clearly in the speech delivered by Lord Millett). Lord Millett distinguished formation of contract (a question of fact to be determined objectively) and the effect of the mistake or fraud, treating them as two separate stages in the analysis.

Mistake

LORD PHILLIPS OF WORTH MATRAVERS: 119 The critical issue in this case is whether a hire-purchase agreement was ever concluded between Shogun and the rogue. If an agreement was concluded, then the rogue was the 'debtor' under section 27 of the 1964 Act and passed good title in the vehicle to Mr Hudson. If no agreement was concluded, then the rogue stole the vehicle by deception and passed no title to Mr Hudson . . .

Formation of contract

123 A contract is normally concluded when an offer made by one party ('the offeror') is accepted by the party to whom the offer has been made ('the offeree'). Normally the contract is only concluded when the acceptance is communicated by the offeree to the offeror. A contract will not be concluded unless the parties are agreed as to its material terms. There must be *'consensus ad idem'*. Whether the parties have reached agreement on the terms is not determined by evidence of the subjective intention of each party. It is, in large measure, determined by making an objective appraisal of the exchanges between the parties. If an offeree understands an offer in accordance with its natural meaning and accepts it, the offeror cannot be heard to say that he intended the words of his offer to have a different meaning. The contract stands according to the natural meaning of the words used. There is one important exception to this principle. If the offeree knows that the offeror does not intend the terms of the offer to be those that the natural meaning of the words would suggest, he cannot, by purporting to accept the offer, bind the offeror to a contract: *Hartog v Colin and Shields* [1939] 3 All ER 566; *Smith v Hughes* (1871) LR 6 QB 597. Thus the task of ascertaining whether the parties have reached agreement as to the terms of a contract can involve quite a complex amalgam of the objective and the subjective and involve the application of a principle that bears close comparison with the doctrine of estoppel. Normally, however, the task involves no more than an objective analysis of the words used by the parties. The object of the exercise is to determine what each party *intended,* or must be deemed to have *intended.*

124 The task of ascertaining whether the parties have reached agreement as to the terms of a contract largely overlaps with the task of ascertaining what it is that the parties have agreed. The approach is the same. It requires the construction of the words used by the parties in order to deduce the *intention* of the parties—see *Chitty on Contracts*, 28th edn, vol. 1, paragraphs 12-042, 12-043 and the cases there cited. This is true, whether the contract is oral or in writing. The words used fall to be construed having regard to the relevant background facts and extrinsic evidence may be admitted to explain or interpret the words used. Equally, extrinsic evidence may be necessary to identify the subject matter of the contract to which the words refer.

125 Just as the parties must be shown to have agreed on the terms of the contract, so they must also be shown to have agreed the one with the other. If A makes an offer to B, but C purports to accept it, there will be no contract. Equally, if A makes an offer to B and B addresses his acceptance to C there will be no contract. Where there is an issue as to whether two persons have reached an agreement, the one with the other, the courts have tended to adopt the same approach to resolving that issue as they adopt when considering whether there has been agreement as to the terms of the contract. The court asks the question whether each *intended*, or must be deemed to have *intended,* to contract with the other. That approach gives rise to a problem where one person is mistaken as to the identity of the person with whom he is dealing, as the cases demonstrate . . .

The decided cases

126 In *Boulton v Jones* (1857) 27 LJ Ex 117 the owner of a shop named Brockenhurst sold his stock-in-trade and assigned his business to the plaintiff. The same day the plaintiff received an order in writing, addressed to Brockenhurst, from the defendant. The defendant had had previous dealings with Brockenhurst and proposed to set off against the price a debt owed by Brockenhurst. The plaintiff supplied

the goods and the defendant consumed them. When the plaintiff sent an invoice the defendant denied that he had concluded any contract with him. The Court ruled that there was no contract. Pollock CB said:

> Now the rule of law is clear, that if you propose to make a contract with A, then B cannot substitute himself for A without your consent and to your disadvantage, securing to himself all the benefit of the contract.

Martin B agreed, without the qualification '*to your disadvantage*':

> Where the facts prove that the defendant never meant to contract with A alone, B can never force a contract upon him; he has dealt with A, and a contract with no one else can be set up against him.

Bramwell B explained his reasons in this way:

> I do not lay it down that because a contract was made in one person's name another person cannot sue upon it, except in cases of agency. But when any one makes a contract in which the personality, so to speak, of the particular party contracted with is important, for any reason, whether because it is to write a book or paint a picture, or do any work of personal skill, or whether because there is a set-off due from that party, no one else is at liberty to step in and maintain that he is the party contracted with, that he has written the book or painted the picture, or supplied the goods; and that he is entitled to sue, although, had the party really contracted with sued, the defendant would have had the benefit of his personal skill, or of a set-off due from him.

Channell B also seemed to consider that it was material that the defendant had a set-off:

> The plaintiff is clearly not in a situation to sustain this action, for there was no contract between himself and the defendant. The case is not one of principal and agent; it was a contract made with B, who had transactions with the defendant and owed him money, and upon which A seeks to sue.

127 This early case does not demonstrate the full application of the principles that I have set out in relation to formation of contract, although the result accords with them. The focus was, however, on the intention of the defendant.

128 In *Hardman v Booth* (1863) 1 H & C 803 a fraud was perpetrated by one Edward Gandell who, it seems, carried on business in two capacities: (1) as clerk of a well known firm, Gandell & Co, of which his father was sole proprietor. There he had neither authority to contract nor was held out as having such authority. (2) He had formed a partnership with a man called Todd, which carried on business as Gandell & Todd. He purported to conclude a contract to purchase cloth from the plaintiffs, holding himself out as a member of Gandell & Co. The first instalment of the cloth was delivered to the premises of Gandell & Co and the second instalment was collected by Edward Gandell in a cart owned by Gandell & Co. Edward Gandell took the cloth to the defendant and purported to pledge it to secure a loan to Gandell & Todd. The issue was whether in these circumstances any contract was concluded between the plaintiffs and Gandell & Todd, under which the property in the cloth passed to them. The court held that no contract had been concluded.

129 Once again the Court attached critical importance to the intention of the vendors. Pollock C.B. summarised the position as follows at p. 806:

> . . . in this case I think it clear that there was no contract. Mr Hawkins contended that there was a contract personally with Edward Gandell, the individual with whom the conversations took place. It is true that the words were uttered by and to him, but the plaintiffs supposed that they were dealing with Gandell & Co., the packers, to whom they sent the goods; the fact being that Edward Gandell was not a member of that firm and had no authority to act as their agent. Therefore at no period of time were there two consenting minds to the same agreement.

130 Martin B emphasised that he had no doubt that the plaintiffs believed 'that they were dealing with Gandell & Co'. Channell B remarked 'I do not think there was a sale to Gandell and Todd . . . for it is evident that the plaintiffs believed that they were dealing with Gandell & Co'. Wilde B's judgment was to similar

Mistake

effect. Thus the Court proceeded on the simple premise that there could not be a contract between A and B if A did not intend to contract with B. The courts had not at this time begun to apply an objective test to the question of whether an agreement had been concluded between the parties.

. . .

[Lord Phillips then examined *Cundy v Lindsay* (1878) 3 App Cas 459 (for the facts and decision, *page 373*, *8.3.2.3*), and concluded:]

133 Here, once again, the focus was on the intention of the offeree. In deciding that his intention was to contract with Blenkiron & Co, the House had regard to the fact that the order was apparently signed 'Blenkiron & Co' and to the fact that the plaintiffs knew of a firm of that name and intended to deal with that firm. Thus extrinsic evidence was admitted in addition to the wording of the order in order to ascertain the intention of the plaintiffs.

. . .

[His Lordship then discussed *King's Norton Metal Co. Ltd v Edridge, Merrett & Co. Ltd* (1897) 14 TLR 98 (*page 379*, *later in this section*), and concluded:]

135 This case demonstrates that, if a person describes himself by a false name in contractual dealings, this will not, of itself, prevent the conclusion of a contract by a person who deals with him in that name. A L Smith LJ did not refer to 'intention' in his reported judgment. The result is, however, consistent with the approach to which I have referred in relation to formation of contract. The plaintiffs intended to deal with whoever was using the name of Hallam & Co. Extrinsic evidence was needed to identify who that was but, once Wallis was identified as the user of that name, the party with whom the plaintiffs had contracted was established. They could not demonstrate that their acceptance of the offer was intended for anyone other than Wallis.

136 *Phillips v Brooks Ltd* [1919] 2 KB 243 is the first case that involved a face-to-face transaction.

[Lord Phillips set out the facts and noted the passage from the judgment of Horridge J, extracted at *page 368*, *8.3.2.2*.]

138 *Phillips v Brooks Ltd* well illustrates the conundrum that the application of the test of *intention* raises when terms are negotiated between two persons who are face to face. It arises where the two persons, A and B, are not known to each other and where A gives a name which is not his own. If B is unaware of the existence of a third person who bears that name, there will be no problem. B will clearly intend to contract with A, treating the name given by A simply as the label by which A identifies himself. Equally A will know that B intends to contract with him. The problem arises where B is aware of a third person, C, who bears the name falsely adopted by A. In that situation it is B's intention to contract both with A and with C, for he does not distinguish between the two. No sensible answer can be given to the question: does B intend to contract with A or C? Nor can any sensible answer be given to the question: does A believe that B intends to contract with him or with C?

139 Horridge J solved the conundrum by drawing an 'inference' that the plaintiff intended to contract with the rogue, who was present, and not with the individual whose identity the rogue had assumed.

. . .

[Lord Phillips considered the other face-to-face cases, *Ingram v Little* and *Lewis v Averay*, and continued:]

153 The difficulty in applying a test of *intention* to the identification of the parties to a contract arises, so it seems to me, only where the parties conduct their dealings in some form of interpersonal contact, and where one purports to have the identity of a third party. There the innocent party will have in mind, when considering with whom he is contracting, both the person with whom he is in contact and the third party whom he imagines that person to be.

154 The same problem will not normally arise where the dealings are carried out exclusively in writing. The process of construction of the written instruments, making appropriate use of extrinsic evidence, will normally enable the court to reach a firm conclusion as to the person with whom a party intends to contract. This was the position in *Boulton v Jones* 27 LJ Ex 117, *Cundy v Lindsay* 3 App Cas 459 and

King's Norton Metal Co Ltd v Edridge, Merrett & Co Ltd 14 TLR 98. There is a substantial body of authority that demonstrates that the identity of a party to a contract in writing falls to be determined by a process of construction of the putative contract itself.

. . .

[Lord Phillips then referred to a number of authorities on the construction of written documents and concluded:]

161 The effect of these authorities is that a person carrying on negotiations in writing can, by describing as one of the parties to the putative agreement an individual who is unequivocally identifiable from that description, preclude any finding that the party to the putative agreement is other than the person so described. The process of construction will lead inexorably to the conclusion that the person with whom the other party intended to contract was the person thus described.

162 That the identification of the parties to a written contract involves construing the contract was the basis of the decision in *Hector v Lyons* (1988) 58 P & CR 156. The majority of the Court of Appeal in the present case considered that this decision weighed conclusively in favour of Shogun. *Hector v Lyons* involved a claim for specific performance of a contract to buy a house. The plaintiff ('the father') rejoiced in the name Martin Aloysius Handel Hector. He had a son, aged less than 18, more modestly christened Martin Aloysius Hector. The father negotiated the purchase of the house face to face with the defendant, who at all times understood that she was contracting with the father. The father instructed solicitors to draw up the formal contract for exchange. For reasons not apparent he led them to understand that the purchaser was to be his son, and they described the purchaser in the contract as 'Martin Aloysius Hector', understanding that they were thereby identifying the son. The father signed the purchaser's copy of the contract with a signature that differed from his normal signature . . .

163 The father sought to enforce the contract on the footing that he was the purchaser. The defendant argued that he was not a party to the written contract; the purchaser under that contract was the son. The trial judge found in her favour. The basis upon which he did so was that the solicitors handed over the purchaser's part of the contract as being the document of the son and the signature that it bore purported to be that of the son.

164 In the Court of Appeal counsel for the father argued that the contract had been concluded between the father and the defendant, relying on the line of cases ending with *Lewis v Averay* [1972] 1 QB 198. Sir Nicolas Browne-Wilkinson V-C dismissed this argument . . .:

> In my judgment the principle there enunciated has no application to a case such as the present where there is a contract and wholly in writing. There the identity of the vendor and the purchaser is established by the names of the parties included in the written contract. Once those names are there in the contract, the only question for the court is to identify who they are. In the present case the deputy judge has found as a fact that the party named in the written contract was Mr Hector junior. It follows, in my judgment, that in the absence of rectification, which has not been claimed, or [counsel's] alternative argument [for the father] based on agency, the only person who can enforce that contract is the party to it, namely Mr Hector junior. He has never at any stage sought to do so. It is for these purposes in my judgment irrelevant whom [the defendant] Mrs Lyons thought she was contracting with: she is entitled to say 'I entered into a contract with the person named in the contract, and nobody else.' . . .

166 . . . While the facts of this decision are not easy to follow, it supports the proposition that the identity of the parties to a contract in writing fall to be determined by a process of construction of the contract.

The result in the present case

167 I have had the advantage of reading in draft the opinions of my noble and learned friends who have sat with me on this appeal. Lord Hobhouse of Woodborough and Lord Walker of Gestingthorpe have concluded that, as the contract was a written document, the identity of the hirer falls to be ascertained by construing that document. Adopting that approach, the hirer was, or more accurately purported to be, Mr Patel. As he had not authorised the conclusion of the contract, it was void.

168 Lord Nicholls of Birkenhead and Lord Millett have adopted a different approach. They point out the illogicality of applying a special approach to face-to-face dealings. What of dealings on the telephone, or by videolink? There also it could be said that each of the parties to the dealings is seeking to make a contract with the other party to the dealings. And this can even be said when the dealings are conducted by correspondence. If A writes to B making an offer and B writes back responding to that offer, B is intending to contract with the person who made that offer. If a contract is concluded in face-to-face dealings, notwithstanding that one party is masquerading as a third party, why should the result be different when the dealings are by letter?

169 Lord Nicholls of Birkenhead and Lord Millett propose an elegant solution to this illogicality. Where two individuals *deal with each other*, by whatever medium, and agree terms of a contract, then a contract will be concluded between them, notwithstanding that one has deceived the other into thinking that he has the identity of a third party. In such a situation the contract will be voidable but not void. While they accept that this approach cannot be reconciled with *Cundy v Lindsay* 3 App Cas 459, they conclude that *Cundy v Lindsay* was wrongly decided and should no longer be followed.

170 While I was strongly attracted to this solution, I have found myself unable to adopt it. *Cundy v Lindsay* exemplifies the application by English law of the same approach to identifying the parties as is applied to identifying the terms of the contract. In essence this focuses on deducing the intention of the parties from their words and conduct. Where there is some form of personal contact between individuals who are conducting negotiations, this approach gives rise to problems. In such a situation I would favour the application of a strong presumption that each intends to contract with the other, with whom he is dealing. Where, however, the dealings are exclusively conducted in writing, there is no scope or need for such a presumption . . .

176 . . . I have not found the assessment of the law easy, but nor is the application of the law to the facts. Shogun's representatives were aware of the presence of the prospective hirer in the dealer's showrooms in Leicester. To an extent the dealings were interpersonal through the medium of the dealer. Should one treat them as comparable to face-to-face dealings and conclude that there was a presumption that Shogun intended to contract with the man with whom they were dealing? Should one treat the written agreement as no more than peripheral to the dealings and conclude that it does not override that presumption? I have concluded that the answer to these questions is 'no' . . .

178 . . . [T]he correct approach in the present case is to treat the agreement as one concluded in writing and to approach the identification of the parties to that agreement as turning upon its construction. The particulars given in the agreement are only capable of applying to Mr Patel. It was the intention of the rogue that they should identify Mr Patel as the hirer. The hirer was so identified by Shogun. Before deciding to enter into the agreement they checked that Mr Patel existed and that he was worthy of credit. On that basis they decided to contract with him and with no one else. Mr Patel was the hirer under the agreement. As the agreement was concluded without his authority, it was a nullity. The rogue took no title under it and was in no position to convey any title to Mr Hudson.

179 For these reasons I would dismiss this appeal.

LORD MILLETT [dissenting]: 56 My Lords, A makes an offer to B. B accepts it, believing that he is dealing with C. A knows of B's mistake, and may even have deliberately caused it. What is the result of the transaction? Is there a contract at all? There is obviously no contract with C, who is not a party to the transaction and knows nothing of it. But is there a contract with A? And if so is it void or merely voidable?

57 Generations of law students have struggled with this problem. They may be forgiven for thinking that it is contrived by their tutors to test their mettle. After all, the situation seems artificial and is one which

is seldom likely to arise in practice, at least in the absence of fraud. Unfortunately fraudulent impersonation is not at all uncommon today. The growth in the number of credit transactions, often entered into electronically between persons unknown to each other, has led to a surge in what has been called 'theft of identity', that is the fraudulent assumption of another's identity by a customer in order to have the wrong account debited or to misdirect inquiries into his own creditworthiness. In the classic case A, fraudulently masquerading as C, buys goods on credit from B; B, having conducted appropriate checks to satisfy himself that C is worthy of credit and believing A to be C, lets A have possession of the goods; and A thereupon sells the goods to D, an unsuspecting purchaser, before disappearing without paying for them. Who is to bear the loss? That depends on whether D, who has paid for the goods, has obtained title to them, for if not then B can reclaim them. But D will have obtained title only if A was able to transfer title to him, and this turns on whether the transaction between A and B resulted in a voidable contract for the purchase of the goods by A (which B will have been unable to avoid in time) or no contract at all.

58 The problem is sometimes mentioned in the textbooks in the section which deals with the formation of contract, where the question is whether a contract has been concluded; but it is more usually dealt with in the section which is concerned with the effect of mistake and in particular 'mistaken identity', where the question is said to turn on whether A's identity is (i) 'fundamental' (in which case the contract is completely void) or (ii) 'material' but not 'fundamental' (in which case the contract is merely voidable). In his dissenting judgment in *Ingram v Little* [1961] 1 QB 31, 64 Devlin LJ distinguished between the two questions and observed that it was easy to fall into error if one did not begin with the first question, whether there is sufficient correlation between offer and acceptance to bring a contract into existence. But if there is, I question whether the contract should be held to be void for mistake rather than merely voidable.

59 As I have said, the situation is seldom likely to arise in practice in the absence of fraud, and where the fraud is not directed to the identity of the offeror the contract is only voidable, not void, for the victim of deception ought to be able to elect to affirm the contract if he chooses to do so. It seems anomalous that a mistake which is induced by fraud should have a less vitiating effect than one which is not; and it is difficult to see why a mistake induced by fraud should make a contract altogether void if it is a mistake as to the offeror's identity (whatever that may mean) and not if it is a mistake as to some other attribute of his such as his creditworthiness which may be equally or more material.

60 As Treitel observes (*The Law of Contract*, 10th ed (1999), p 277) it is often difficult to say precisely what mistake has been made and, even when this is clear, it is often difficult to say whether it should be classified as a mistake of identity or of attribute. As between A and B themselves, of course, it does not normally matter whether the contract is void or merely voidable; it obviously cannot be enforced by A against B's wishes in either case. The question usually assumes importance only where an innocent third party is involved, and then it is critical. Under the law as it stands at present, his title depends on whether the fraudster obtained the goods in his own name by means of a false or forged credit reference or in the name of another by means of a genuine reference relating to that other. This is indefensible. I take the view that the law should if at all possible favour a solution which protects innocent third parties by treating the contract as voidable rather than void, whether for fraud or for mistake.

61 My Lords, I think that the time has come to follow the lead given by Lord Denning MR more than 30 years ago in *Lewis v Averay* [1972] 1 QB 198. He roundly rejected the theory that if a party is *mistaken* as to the identity of the person with whom he is contracting there is no contract, or that if there is a contract it is null and void so that no property can pass under it: see pp 206–7. He thought that the doctrine, derived from the writings of Pothier, should not be admitted as part of English law but should be 'dead and buried'. As he observed, it gives rise to fine distinctions which do no good to the law, and

it is unjust that an innocent third party, who knows nothing of what passed between the rogue and his vendor, should have his title depend on such refinements.

62 But it is still necessary to answer the logically anterior and more difficult question: does the transaction result in the formation of a contract between A and B? There is clearly a transaction between them, for B has let A have possession of the goods and take them away, usually with the intention that he should be free to deal with them as owner. But is the transaction contractual?

63 It is trite law, as Devlin LJ explained in the passage immediately following that cited above, that before a contract can come into existence there must be offer and acceptance, and these must correspond . . . It is not possible in law for a person to accept an offer made to someone else; or to intercept an acceptance of someone else's offer and treat it as an acceptance of his own.

64 This is usually straightforward enough, at least in the absence of fraud. As my noble and learned friend, Lord Phillips of Worth Matravers, observes, there is normally no difference between the identity of the person to whom the offer or acceptance is directed and the person for whom it is intended. But what if, by reason of fraud, the two are not the same? What if A, posing as C, makes an offer to B which B purports to accept? B *directs* his acceptance to A, but *intends* it for C. It does not help to substitute the question: 'To whom was B's acceptance made?' This merely raises the question: 'What do you mean by "made"?'

65 The outcome is said to depend on B's intention objectively ascertained, and this is usually treated as if it were a straightforward question of fact to be determined on the evidence. In *Ingram v Little* [1961] 1 QB 31 Pearce LJ said, at p 61, that 'Each case must be decided on its own facts.' This is singularly unhelpful, since it involves asking: did B intend to contract with A believing him to be C? Or with C believing him to be A? The question is meaningless. As Devlin LJ pointed out in *Ingram v Little*, at p 65:

> If Miss Ingram had been asked whether she intended to contract with the man in the room or with PGM Hutchinson, the question could have no meaning for her, since she believed them both to be one and the same . . .

66 In this situation the courts have distinguished between transactions entered into in writing and transactions entered into orally between parties who are in the presence of each other. In the former case B's intention is ascertained by construing the description of the counterparty in the contract. This naturally identifies C, the person whose identity A has fraudulently assumed, and (provided that C actually exists) invariably leads to the conclusion that there is no counterparty and therefore no contract. In the latter case, the courts have adopted a different approach. They have introduced a rebuttable presumption that, where parties deal with each other face-to-face, each of them intends to contract with the physical person to whom he addresses the words of contract. Unless the presumption is rebutted, this must lead to the conclusion that there is a contract with the impostor.

67 I do not find this satisfactory. What evidence is sufficient to rebut the presumption? As Devlin LJ stressed, it cannot be rebutted by piling up evidence that B would never have accepted the offer if he had not thought that it had been made by C. Such evidence merely shows that the deception was material; it does not establish the identity of B's counterparty. There might perhaps be something to be said for making the presumption conclusive . . .

68 But the real objection to the present state of the law, in my view, is that the distinction between the face-to-face contract and other contracts is unrealistic . . . My difficulty is that I cannot see that there is any difference in principle between the two situations when it comes to identifying B's counterparty. In both cases B's acceptance is directed to the impostor but intended for the person whose identity he has assumed . . .

69 In *Ingram v Little* [1961] 1 QB 31 Devlin LJ said, at p 66, that 'the presumption that a person is intending to contract with the person to whom he is actually addressing the words of contract seems to me to be a simple and sensible one . . .' I respectfully agree. But why should it be adopted only in the case of a contract entered into between persons who deal in the physical presence of each other? If the offeree's

words of acceptance are taken to be addressed to the physical person standing in his presence who made the offer, what is the position where they deal with each other by telephone? Is the disembodied voice to be equated with physical presence? Is it sufficient that the parties are in the hearing of each other? Does it make a difference if the dealing is by televisual link, so that the parties are in the hearing and sight but not the presence of each other? New means of communication make the distinction untenable.

70 But in truth the distinction was always unsound. If the offeree's words of acceptance are taken to be addressed to the physical person standing in his presence who made the offer, why is the contract entered into by correspondence different? Why is the offeree's letter of acceptance not taken to be addressed to the physical person who made the written offer which he is accepting? The offeree addresses the offeror by his assumed name in both cases. Why should this be treated as decisive in the one case and disregarded in the other? Indeed, the correlation between offer and acceptance is likely to be greater in the case of a contract entered into by correspondence, since the offeree's letter of acceptance will either be sent to the impostor at his own address or be delivered to him personally and it will almost certainly contain internal references to his offer.

71 In my opinion there are only two principled solutions to the problem. The law must give preference, either to the person for whom the offer or acceptance is intended, or to the person to whom it is directed, and must do so in all cases as a matter of law. The difficulty is in deciding which solution should be adopted, for there is much to commend each of them.

72 The first solution, which gives preference to the person for whom the offer or acceptance is intended, possibly accords more closely to the existing authorities, which treat the face-to-face transaction as an exception to the general rule, and with the decision in *Cundy v Lindsay* 3 App Cas 459, the only case on the subject which has come before the House. It also accords more closely with the parties' subjective intentions, for B intends to deal with C, especially if he has checked his creditworthiness, and not with A, of whom he has never heard; while A has no intention of being bound by contract at all. From his point of view the supposed contract is merely a pretence to enable him to get hold of goods without paying for them. He does not need a contract, for he is content with possession without title . . .

73 The strongest argument in favour of this solution, I suppose, is that it could be said to be based on the parties' own assessment of what they mean by the counterparty's 'identity'. Ultimately this must refer to a physical person, but a physical person can only be identified by describing his or her attributes. For this purpose it is customary to refer to a person's name and address, which are usually though not always unique to one person. But names are merely identifying labels and can be assumed without any intention to deceive. A person is free to adopt whatever name suits his fancy, and may validly contract under an alias. Even if he has assumed a false name for the sole purpose of deceiving the counterparty, there is a contract so long, at least, as there is no real person of that name: see *King's Norton Metal Co Ltd v Edridge, Merrett & Co Ltd* 14 TLR 98.

74 But as Treitel observes (*The Law of Contract*, 10th ed, p 277) a person may be identified by reference to any one of his attributes. He may be identified as 'the person in the room', 'the person who spoke on the telephone', 'the person who appended the illegible signature', 'the writer of the letter under reply', or 'the person who made the offer'; but he may also be identified, and sometimes more relevantly, as 'the person whose creditworthiness has been checked and found to be satisfactory'. Any of these may be the means of identifying a unique person. An automated telling machine is programmed to identify a customer by a combination of a PIN number and a number encrypted on the card which is inserted into the machine. In an increasingly electronic age we are accustomed to identifying ourselves by PIN numbers and passwords; the need to eliminate fraud may in time cause us to identify ourselves by retinal imagery, which at least has the advantage of being a feature of the physical body. But even in the case of a credit card transaction there is an ambiguity. Is the customer to be identified as the person who produces the card? Or as the person whose card is produced? The whole point of a credit card fraud is that the goods

should be supplied to the person who produces the card while the cost is debited to the account of the person whose card is produced.

75 Given the equivocal nature of a person's 'identity', there is something to be said for selecting those aspects of the offeror's identity which are material in causing the other party to accept the offer. In the present case, for example, Mr Patel's name, address and date of birth had no intrinsic relevance in themselves. The claimant would have entered into the transaction with anyone, whatever his name and address or date of birth, so long as it was satisfied that he was worthy of credit. Mr Patel's personal details were merely the information which enabled it to conduct inquiries into the credit of the person it assumed to be its customer. It makes commercial sense to treat a contract made in these circumstances as purporting to be made between the finance company and the subject of its inquiries rather than with the person who merely produced the information necessary to enable it to make them.

76 Nevertheless I have come to the conclusion that it is the second solution which ought to be adopted. All the considerations which I have mentioned, and which seem to favour the first solution, when properly analysed go to the mechanics of the deception and its materiality rather than to the identity of the offeror. They ought to come into play when consideration is given to the second question, whether the contract is voidable, rather than to the first, whether there is sufficient correlation between offer and acceptance ('consensus ad idem') to bring a contract into existence. Until the fraud is exposed and it is discovered that A is *not* C, the existence of a contract is not in doubt. The fraud is relevant to the question whether the contract is enforceable against B rather than its existence . . .

81 In my opinion, once one accepts that there are two questions involved: (i) did a contract come into existence at all? and (ii) if so was the contract vitiated by fraud or mistake? there is only one principled conclusion. Whatever the medium of communication, a contract comes into existence if, on an objective appraisal of the facts, there is sufficient correlation between offer and acceptance to make it possible to say that the impostor's offer has been accepted by the person to whom it was addressed. While a person cannot intercept and accept an offer made to some one else, he should normally be treated as intending to contract with the person with whom he is dealing. Provided that the offer is made to him, then whether his acceptance of the offer is obtained by deception or mistake and whether his mistake is as to the identity of the offeror or some material attribute of his, the transaction should result in a contract, albeit one which is voidable.

82 This rule is easy to apply and accords with principle by distinguishing between the formation of a contract as a question of fact to be determined objectively and the consequences of mistake or fraud which depend on its effect on the mind of the person affected. It avoids undesirable refinements and gives a measure of protection to innocent third parties. Of course, someone has to bear the loss where there is fraud, but it is surely fairer that the party who was actually swindled and who had an opportunity to uncover the fraud should bear the loss rather than a party who entered the picture only after the swindle had been carried out and who had none. In the present case, the claimant could easily have exposed the fraud by writing to Mr Patel, whose address it had been given, and asking him to confirm his intention to proceed with the proposed transaction. If it had been one for which statute required a cooling-off period, it no doubt would have done.

83 In the Court of Appeal [2002] QB 834 both Sedley LJ (who dissented) and Brooke LJ, at p 855, para 51, expressed disquiet at 'the sorry condition' of the law. In the former's view, with which I agree, the decision in *Cundy v Lindsay* 3 App Cas 459 stands in the way of a coherent development of this branch of the law. We have the opportunity to restate the law, and cannot shirk the duty of putting it on a basis which is both just and principled, even if it means deciding that we should no longer follow a previous decision of the House.

84 We cannot leave the law as it is. It is neither fair nor principled, and not all the authorities from which it is derived can be reconciled; some, at least, must be overruled if it is to be extricated from the present quagmire. If the law is to be rationalised and placed on a proper footing, the formulation which I have proposed has the merit of according with the recommendations made in the Twelth [*sic*] Report of the Law Reform Committee on the Transfer of Title to Chattels (Cmnd 2958) and in *Anson's Law of Contract*, 28th ed, p 332. It would also bring English law into line with the law both in the United States and in Germany . . .

87 Where does this leave the authorities? Most of those which are concerned with face-to-face transactions can stand with the exception of the decision of the majority of the Court of Appeal in *Ingram v Little* [1961] 1 QB 31, which is inconsistent with *Lewis v Averay* [1972] 1 QB 198 and should be overruled. I would confirm the decision in *Phillips v Brooks Ltd* [1919] 2 KB 243243, 246–247 where Horridge J held that the shopkeeper had

> contracted to sell and deliver [the ring] to the person who came into his shop . . . who obtained the sale and delivery by means of the false pretence that he was Sir George Bullough . . . [The shopkeeper's] intention was to sell to the person present, and identified by sight and hearing . . .

In my opinion the judge's reasoning cannot be faulted. He distinguished between the two questions, and treated the identity of the purchaser as a question of fact to be determined objectively and without regard to the evidence that the shopkeeper had no intention of selling the goods to anyone other than Sir George Bullough . . .

104 How should the question be answered in the present case? The case is not unlike *Hector v Lyons* 58 P & CR 156 [discussed in the judgment of Lord Phillips at [162]–[164]] with the important difference that in the present case the deception was material and induced the making of the contract. If there was a contract with the rogue, it was voidable for fraud . . .

106 The object of the deception was to misdirect the claimant's credit inquiries. In this it succeeded. Having satisfied itself that Mr Durlabh Patel, whom it believed to be its customer, was worthy of credit, it accepted the offer which the impostor had made, signed its part of the agreement, and authorised the dealer to deliver possession of the car to his customer as hirer under the agreement.

107 But who was his customer? It was not Mr Durlabh Patel. In my opinion it was plainly the impostor. Any other conclusion would mean that the dealer parted with the vehicle to the impostor without authority and would, presumably, be liable in conversion if the vehicle proved to be irrecoverable. This is far removed from reality. The claimant and the dealer both believed that the customer who was hiring the car and Mr Durlabh Patel were one and the same; but the claimant did not make that a condition of the dealer's authority to part with the car. From first to last it believed that the impostor who attended the dealer's showroom, gave his name as Mr Durlabh Patel, and signed the agreement in that name, was indeed Mr Durlabh Patel; in that belief it entered into a hiring agreement and authorised the dealer to deliver possession of the car to the customer who had so identified himself. In my opinion, the claimant not only took a credit risk, but also took the risk that the customer who was hiring the car was not Mr Durlabh Patel and that its credit inquiries had been fraudulently misdirected. I would hold that there was a hiring, and the impostor was the hirer.

108 This conclusion involves a departure from *Cundy v Lindsay* 3 App Cas 459, a decision of this House which has stood for more than 120 years. But its reasoning is unsound. It is vitiated by its subjective approach to the formation of contract and the necessary correlation between offer and acceptance; which may be why textbook writers treat it as an example of unilateral mistake even though this was not the basis on which it was decided. For the same reason it cannot be regarded as authoritative on the question whether a contract otherwise properly entered into is void for mistake rather than voidable. It has had

an unfortunate influence on the development of the law, leading to an unprincipled distinction between face-to-face transactions and others and the indefensible conclusion that an innocent purchaser's position depends on the nature of the mistake of a third party or the precise mechanics of the fraud which had been perpetrated on him. In my view it should now be discarded and the law put on a simpler and more principled and defensible basis.

109 In my opinion only the decision in *Cundy v Lindsay* stands in the way of a rational and coherent restatement of the law. My noble and learned friend, Lord Phillips of Worth Matravers, has expressed the view that the conclusion to which Lord Nicholls and I have come conflicts not only with that case but with the approach in almost all the numerous cases which he has cited. If they had preceded *Cundy v Lindsay*, that would be a strong reason for not adopting it. But they were merely following a decision of this House by which they were bound. Far from applying it generally, they attempted to distinguish it by carving out an unprincipled exception from it which Lord Nicholls has shown cannot be supported. While departing from *Cundy v Lindsay* would make obsolete the reasoning in those cases, dictated as it was by that decision, it would undermine the actual decision in very few cases. There is no long line of authority to be overruled. Indeed, only two cases need to be overruled; and neither of them can be supported even on the view that *Cundy v Lindsay* was rightly decided.

110 In my opinion *Cundy v Lindsay* 3 App Cas 459 should no longer be followed and *Ingram v Little* [1961] 1 QB 31 and *Hector v Lyons* 58 P & CR 156 should be overruled. I would allow the appeal.

NOTES

1. Despite the fundamental difference in approach between the majority and minority speeches, there is a degree of unanimity on the application of the presumption in face-to-face dealings that there is an intention to deal with the person physically present. Consequently, *Ingram v Little* should not be followed.

2. The minority approach involves two steps (or questions). The first is to determine the existence of a contract. The second is then to assess the effect of the fraud; this relates to the enforceability of the contract, because fraud negatives the rights that would normally follow from a contract. Thus, on the minority view, there was a contract between the finance company and the rogue because the car was being sold to the person physically present, i.e. the mistaken party is treated as possessing an intention to sell to that person and consents to the contract. The fact that this contract was the result of a fraud could not affect the formation of the contract itself, although it would render the contract voidable. By comparison, the approach of Lords Phillips and Walker focuses only on the question of agreement, and this is determined by asking whether the parties intended to deal with one another, as judged by their words and conduct. It is arguable that the majority view fails to place sufficient emphasis on the fraud.

3. Although Lord Hobhouse clearly takes the view that extrinsic evidence is not generally admissible (absent ambiguity or agency), it is far from clear that Lord Phillips felt himself to be similarly restricted by the written document. However, the evidence of subsequent case law is that a strict interpretation will be taken on construction and extrinsic evidence: see the decision of the Court of Appeal in *Dumford Trading AG v OAO Atlantrybflot* [2005] EWCA Civ 24, [2005] 1 Lloyd's Rep 289, and especially comments of Rix LJ, at [37], that the decision in *Shogun Finance* 'appears to emphasise the importance of construction of the written document even in matters of the identity of the parties, and also to underline the danger of using extrinsic material in what is fundamentally the role of construction'.

4. The result of the majority speeches is that finance companies granting hire purchase facilities to car buyers are given protection against the consequences of fraud. If it were conceivable that they might end up in a position of losing both the car and the finance despite having carried out credit checks, it might prove to be a disincentive to lending in such circumstances, especially given the rise in cases of identity fraud. Thus, the primacy of the written document ensures that this possibility is avoided. This position contrasts with the view taken by Sedley LJ in the Court of Appeal, who considered that the finance company had agreed to extend credit of over £20,000 'in a matter of minutes', i.e. that it was a question of business judgement.

There will always be policy considerations when deciding which of two innocent parties should be responsible for the fraud of a third and, whereas Lord Denning—and the minority in *Shogun*—clearly felt that the 'degrees of innocence' position favours the innocent third party purchaser, the majority position results in a distinction based on whether there is a written contract or whether the parties are dealing in a face-to-face situation. However, in many situations (outside the context of regulated credit agreements), it may be a matter of chance whether there is a written document or oral contract. This must be considered as the most unsatisfactory aspect of the decision in *Shogun Finance*.

5. See Macmillan [2005] CLJ 711.

? QUESTIONS

1. What would the position be if there were written documents, but the contract were the result of face-to-face dealing?

2. What would the position be in face-to-face dealings were the rogue to impersonate a person who is known to the mistaken party?

3. How can the decision in *King's Norton Metal Co. Ltd v Edridge, Merrett & Co. Ltd* (1897) 14 TLR 98 be explained?

King's Norton Metal Co. Ltd v Edridge, Merrett & Co. Ltd
(1897) 14 TLR 98 (CA)

The claimants received a letter purporting to come from Hallam & Co. in Sheffield. The letter heading depicted a large factory, and included a statement that the company had depots and agencies at Belfast, Lille, and Ghent. Hallam & Co. sent a written order for brass rivet wire. The goods were dispatched to Hallam & Co., but never paid for. A rogue named Wallis had, in fact, fraudulently used the name Hallam & Co. to obtain the goods and had then sold the goods to the defendants, who were innocent purchasers. The claimants brought a damages action for conversion of the wire, alleging that they intended to deal only with Hallam & Co. and had never heard of Wallis.

Held: This was not a case of mistaking one person for another, because there was only one person, and the claimants intended to deal with the writer of the letters, whoever it was. (This fact enabled the court to distinguish the facts of this case from the position in *Cundy v Lindsay*, in which there was another known entity with a similar name.) Accordingly, a contract had come into existence between the claimants and Wallis, although it was voidable for fraud.

NOTES

1. This case concerned a contract contained in written documents rather than a face-to-face contract and was bound to cause difficulties for the majority approach. Lord Phillips, at [135], concluded that:

[T]he plaintiff intended to deal with whoever was using the name Hallam & Co. Extrinsic evidence was needed to identify who that was but, once Wallis was identified as the user of that name, the party with whom the plaintiffs had contracted was established.

2. The party named must actually exist if the name in the written document is to be conclusive. However, as Lord Millett stated in his dissent in *Shogun Finance v Hudson*, the non-existence of another entity seems relevant to the fraud rather than to the formation of the contract, so that the result in the case (voidable for fraud) would be correct on the minority analysis.

LORD MILLETT: 78 It is unclear whether it would have made a difference if, unknown to the plaintiffs, there had been an entity called Hallam and Co; or if to the know-ledge of both parties there were many such entities, as in the cases where a man used to book a hotel room for himself and a girl-friend under a common but fictitious name in order to give the impression (when such things mattered) that they were married. The case is different where the impostor assumes the name and address of a real person of substance when entering into a credit transaction. In such a case his purpose is to direct inquiries to that person's credit rather than his own. A better explanation of *King's Norton Metal Co Ltd v Edridge, Merrett & Co Ltd* is that the rogue merely assumed a false name and did not go further and assume another person's identity. But the distinction is a fine one which it may not always be possible to draw, and in any case depends on the nature and purpose of the deception and is accordingly relevant to its effect on the mind of the offeree and not to the correlation between offer and acceptance.

8

Mistake

3. The fact that this may not be a formation issue at all may also be accepted by Lord Walker in *Shogun Finance* since he refers to the case as involving a deceit as to the standing and creditworthiness of Wallis. In essence, this 'mistake' involved an error of judgement on the part of the claimants in that they intended to send goods on credit to the company only because they thought that the company was creditworthy. Such an error should not affect the question of offer and acceptance.

8.4 Common mistake

8.4.1 Express allocation of the risk

If the contract places the burden of the risk of the event in question or of the risk of the existence of the subject matter on one party, that party will be responsible in the event that the risk materializes, and he cannot rely on the legal doctrine of mistake.

William Sindall plc v Cambridgeshire County Council
[1994] 1 WLR 1016 (CA)

Builders agreed to purchase land from the county council subject to easements, liabilities, and public rights affecting the land, but without prejudice to the vendor's duty to disclose all latent easements and incumbrances that it knew to affect the land. The council had stated that, as far as it was aware, there were no such incumbrances, and the sale contract was concluded in March 1989 at a price of £5 million. By the time that the builders had obtained planning permission for a residential development 18 months later, the land was worth less than half of that purchase price because of a fall in land values. In October 1990, the builders discovered that, unknown to either party, a foul sewer was buried under the land. The builders claimed that, since they had to leave a 6-ft wide maintenance strip, this affected their plans for a residential development on the land, and they sought to rescind the contract for misrepresentation and common mistake, and to recover the purchase price. The judge at first instance held that they were entitled to rescind (exercising his discretion not to award damages in lieu of rescission under s. 2(2) of the Misrepresentation Act 1967), so that the purchase price plus interest was recoverable.

Held (on appeal): It was not possible for the builders to rescind because: (i) the contract terms allocated the risk of incumbrances not known to the vendor to the purchaser, so that the law of mistake could not apply; and (ii) there could be no claim based on misrepresentation, since the council's representation was that it had no actual knowledge of the existence of the sewer (and this was true) and that it had made reasonable investigations. It was held that the council had made reasonable investigations and therefore it could not be liable.

HOFFMANN LJ: The judge found that in the absence of any actionable misrepresentation, Sindall was entitled to rescind the contract for a common mistake as to the existence of a sewer. This is at first sight a startling result. As Steyn J said in *Associated Japanese Bank (International) Ltd v Crédit du Nord SA* [1989] 1 WLR 255, 268:

Logically, before one can turn to the rules as to mistake, whether at common law or in equity, one must first determine whether the contract itself, by express or implied condition precedent or otherwise, provides who bears the risk of the relevant mistake. It is at this hurdle that many pleas of mistake will either fail or prove to have been unnecessary. Only if the contract is silent on the point is there scope for invoking mistake.

When the judge speaks of the contract allocating risk 'by express or implied condition precedent or otherwise' I think he includes rules of general law applicable to the contract and which, for example, provide that, in the absence of express warranty, the law is caveat emptor. This would, in my view, allocate the risk of an unknown defect in goods to the buyer, even though it is not mentioned in the contract. Similarly, the rule in *Hill v Harris* [1965] 2 QB 601 that a lessor or vendor does not impliedly warrant that the premises are fit for any particular purpose means that the contract allocates the risk of the premises being unfit for such a purpose. I should say that neither in *Grist v Bailey* [1967] Ch 532 nor in *Laurence v Lexcourt Holdings Ltd* [1978] 1 WLR 1128 did the judges who decided those cases at first instance advert to the question of contractual allocation of risk. I am not sure that the decisions would have been the same if they had.

In this case the contract says in express terms that it is subject to all easements other than those of which the vendor knows or has the means of knowledge. This allocates the risk of such incumbrances to the buyer and leaves no room for rescission on the grounds of mistake.

EVANS LJ: [O]n any view of the matter . . . the first question is whether the contract on its true construction covers the new situation which has arisen by reason of a change of circumstances (frustration) or the emergence of a factual situation different from that which was assumed (mutual mistake). If the scope of the contract is wide enough to cover the new, or newly discovered, situation, then there is no room either for discharge by frustration or for rescission in equity on the grounds of mistake. Put another way, if the agreed terms provide for this situation, then the parties have 'allocated the risk' as between themselves, as [counsel for the council] submits that they did in the present case.

[Evans LJ construed the terms so that they allocated the risk and continued:]

Subject, therefore, to the claims for rescission based on actionable misrepresentation, the contract for sale as a matter of construction requires the builders to accept the property notwithstanding the presence of the pipeline and the city council's easement . . .

Dana Gas PJSC v Dana Gas Sukuk Ltd
[2017] EWHC 2982 (Comm), [2018] 1 Lloyd's Rep 177

The defendant was the trustee of certificates issued by an Abu Dhabi company to raise finance from the capital markets. In order to overcome the prohibition by sharia law on the payment of interest, the Transaction Documents took the form of a sharing agreement (Mudarabah) under which the claimant invested skill and labour and the defendant invested capital, with the profits to be shared with investors. To protect investors against any shortfall in payments, the claimant entered into a Purchase Undertaking, effectively a guarantee under which the defendant was empowered to call upon the claimant to purchase the entirety of the defendant's interest in the event of default. One of the grounds of default was where 'at any time it is or will become unlawful . . . to perform or comply with any . . . obligations under the Transaction Documents . . . or any of the obligations . . . under the Transaction Documents are not, or cease to be legal, valid, binding and enforceable'. The claimant sought a declaration that the Purchase Undertaking was void for mistake on the ground that it was predicated on the validity of the Mudarabah Agreement and the surrounding agreements under sharia law.

Held: There was no mistake. Even if the Mudarabah Agreement was illegal (which had not yet been established) the parties had expressly agreed that if that was the case then the defendant could rely upon the Purchase Agreement. The risk had been contractually allocated and there was no room for the doctrine of mistake.

LEGGATT J: 57 When the parties to a contract enter into it on the basis of an assumption about its subject-matter which turns out to have been mistaken, English law will in certain circumstances treat the contract as void. But those circumstances are wholly exceptional and contracts which have been found to be void for mistake are few and far between.

. . .

[Leggatt J discussed *Bell v Lever Bros.* [1932] AC 161 and *Great Peace Shipping Ltd v Tsavliris Salvage (International) Ltd* [2003] QB 679, and continued:]

61 Where this leaves the common law doctrine of mistake, as it seems to me, is as follows. First, the doctrine is not based on an inquiry into the subjective beliefs of the parties but on an objective analysis of what they agreed. Second, the doctrine does not rest on the notion that the parties have impliedly agreed what is to happen in the event that an assumption underlying the contract proves to be false. It does, however, involve a question of construction of the contract. It is only where it is to be inferred from the terms of the contract or the surrounding circumstances that the contract was never intended to apply in the situation which in reality existed when the contract was made that the doctrine will apply. Such an inference will be drawn only if the difference between the state of affairs on which the contract was premised and the actual state of affairs is sufficiently fundamental.

62 Thus, the doctrine of mistake can only apply if there is a gap in the contract. If the parties have expressly or impliedly agreed what is to happen if they turn out to have been mistaken about the matter in question—in other words, if the risk of the mistake has been allocated by their contract—there is no scope for the doctrine . . .

64 The main reason why pleas of mistake seldom succeed is that the risk of a mistake is usually allocated by the contract to one of the parties. Plainly, there is no room for the doctrine to operate if the contract states expressly what is to happen if the relevant assumption proves to be false. It may be harder to determine whether the contract impliedly allocates the risk. To take one of the examples given by Lord Atkin in *Bell v Lever Bros* [1932] AC 161 at 224: 'A buys a picture from B; both A and B believe it to be the work of an old master, and a high price is paid. It turns out to be a modern copy.' In practice in such a case the answer is likely to be found through construction of the contract. If the authorship of the picture is part of the description of the goods so that the seller has impliedly warranted its attribution, the risk will lie with the seller. If on the other hand there is no such warranty, the ordinary inference based on the principle of *caveat emptor* would be that the buyer is taking the risk.

NOTE Although the judgments refer to the possibility of rescission for mutual mistake, it is important to appreciate that the term 'mutual' is often used in the case law to refer to a common mistake, and should not be confused with true mutual (or cross-purpose) mistake (*page 362*, 8.2). In addition, at the time of this decision, there was thought to be an equitable jurisdiction to rescind in equity (often on terms) for common mistake, in circumstances in which the mistake was not sufficiently fundamental at common law to render the contract void. The existence of such an equitable jurisdiction has now been denied by the Court of Appeal in *Great Peace Shipping Ltd v Tsavliris (International) Ltd* [2002] EWCA Civ 1407, [2003] QB 679. This aspect of the decision is discussed at *page 397, 8.4.5.2*.

8.4.2 Implied allocation of risk

McRae v Commonwealth Disposals Commission
(1951) 84 CLR 377 (High Court of Australia)

The Commission invited tenders for an oil tanker lying on Journaund Reef and said to contain oil. The claimants' tender was accepted and a sales advice note described what was sold as 'one oil tanker including contents'. In fact, there was no such tanker at that location. The claimants sought damages for breach of contract. The Commission alleged that, because the subject matter of the contract did not exist, the alleged contract was void.

Held: The claimants were entitled to damages for breach of contract because the Commission was in breach of its 'promise' that there was an oil tanker at the location.

DIXON AND FULLAGAR JJ: The position so far, then, may be summed up as follows. It was not decided in *Couturier v Hastie* (1856) 5 HL Cas 673 that the contract in that case was void. The question whether it was void or not did not arise. If it had arisen, as in an action by the purchaser for damages, it would have turned on the ulterior question whether the contract was subject to an implied condition precedent. Whatever might then have been held on the facts of *Couturier v Hastie*, it is impossible in this case to imply any such term. The terms of the contract and the surrounding circumstances clearly exclude any such implication. The buyers relied upon, and acted upon, the assertion of the seller that there was a tanker in existence. It is not a case in which the parties can be seen to have proceeded on the basis of a common assumption of fact so as to justify the conclusion that the correctness of the assumption was intended by both parties to be a condition precedent to the creation of contractual obligations. The officers of the Commission made an assumption, but the plaintiffs did not make an assumption in the same sense. They knew nothing except what the Commission had told them. If they had been asked, they would certainly not have said: 'Of course, if there is no tanker, there is no contract'. They would have said: 'We shall have to go and take possession of the tanker. We simply accept the Commission's assurance that there is a tanker and the Commission's promise to give us that tanker.' The only proper construction of the contract is that it included a promise by the Commission that there was a tanker in the position specified. The Commission contracted that there was a tanker there. If, on the other hand, the case of *Couturier v Hastie* and this case ought to be treated as cases raising a question of 'mistake', then the Commission cannot in this case rely on any mistake as avoiding the contract, because any mistake was induced by the serious fault of their own servants, who asserted the existence of a tanker recklessly and without any reasonable ground. There *was* a contract, and the Commission contracted that a tanker existed in the position specified. Since there was no such tanker, there has been a breach of contract, and the plaintiffs are entitled to damages for that breach.

NOTES

1. *Couturier v Hastie* (1856) 5 HL Cas 673, a mistake case, is discussed at *page 396, 8.4.5.1*.

2. From a practical perspective, if the High Court had dealt with this case on the basis that it was a common mistake, the contract would have been void, and although the claimants could have recovered the purchase price of the wreck, they could not have recovered the cost of the salvage expedition as damages.

3. In *Associated Japanese Bank (International) Ltd v Crédit du Nord SA* [1989] 1 WLR 255 (*page 393, 8.4.4.1*), Steyn J considered that a party seeking to rely on common mistake must have reasonable grounds for his belief. He cited *McRae* in support of this principle, i.e. that the Commission had no reasonable ground for asserting that there was a tanker in the position specified and was therefore at fault in inducing any mistake. The events giving rise to a claim based on mistake or frustration must not be attributable to the fault of one of the parties or that party will be taken to have accepted responsibility for them. (In the context of frustration, the situation in which the event occurs as a result of the fault of one of the parties is discussed at *page 599, 12.2.2*.)

8.4.3 Event occurs as a result of the fault of one of the parties

It is therefore clear that if there is an express or implied allocation of the risk, one party will be taking responsibility for the risk and there is no room for the doctrine of mistake.

Great Peace Shipping Ltd v Tsavliris Salvage (International) Ltd
[2002] EWCA Civ 1407, [2003] QB 679 (CA)

For the facts and a further discussion of this case, see pages 394 and 395, *8.4.4.2.*

LORD PHILLIPS MR [giving the judgment of the Court of Appeal]: 75 Just as the doctrine of frustration only applies if the contract contains no provision that covers the situation, the same should be true of common mistake. If, on true construction of the contract, a party warrants that the subject matter of the contract exists, or that it will be possible to perform the contract, there will be no scope to hold the contract void on the ground of common mistake.

76 If one applies the passage from the judgment of Lord Alverstone CJ in *Hobson v Pattenden* (1903) 19 TLR 186 to a case of common mistake, it suggests that the following elements must be present if common mistake is to avoid a contract: (i) there must be a common assumption as to the existence of a state of affairs; (ii) there must be no warranty by either party that that state of affairs exists; (iii) the non-existence of the state of affairs must not be attributable to the fault of either party; (iv) the non-existence of the state of affairs must render performance of the contract impossible; (v) the state of affairs may be the existence, or a vital attribute, of the consideration to be provided or circumstances which must subsist if performance of the contractual adventure is to be possible.

77 The second and third of these elements are well exemplified by the decision of the High Court of Australia in *McRae v Commonwealth Disposals Commission* (1951) 84 CLR 377.

. . .

[Lord Phillips then discussed the facts and leading judgment of Dixon and Fullagar JJ in *McRae* (extracted at *page 390, 8.4.2*), and continued:]

80 [The English doctrine of mistake] fills a gap in the contract where it transpires that it is impossible of performance without the fault of either party and the parties have not, expressly or by implication, dealt with their rights and obligations in that eventuality. In *Associated Japanese Bank (International) Ltd v Crédit du Nord SA* [1989] 1 WLR 255, 268 Steyn J observed:

> Logically, before one can turn to the rules as to mistake, whether at common law or in equity, one must first determine whether the contract itself, by express or implied condition precedent or otherwise, provides who bears the risk of the relevant mistake. It is at this hurdle that many pleas of mistake will either fail or prove to have been unnecessary. Only if the contract is silent on the point, is there scope for invoking mistake . . .

81 In *William Sindall plc v Cambridgeshire County Council* [1994] 1 WLR 1016, 1035 Hoffmann LJ commented that such allocation of risk can come about by rules of general law applicable to contract, such as 'caveat emptor' in the law of sale of goods or the rule that a lessor or vendor of land does not impliedly warrant that the premises are fit for any particular purpose, so that this risk is allocated by the contract to the lessee or purchaser . . .

84 Once the court determines that unforeseen circumstances have, indeed, resulted in the contract being impossible of performance, it is next necessary to determine whether, on true construction of the contract, one or other party has undertaken responsibility for the subsistence of the assumed state of affairs. This is another way of asking whether one or other party has undertaken the risk that it may not prove possible to perform the contract, and the answer to this question may well be the same as the answer to the question of whether the impossibility of performance is attributable to the fault of one or other of the parties.

85 Circumstances where a contract is void as a result of common mistake are likely to be less common than instances of frustration. Supervening events which defeat the contractual adventure will frequently not be the responsibility of either party. Where, however, the parties agree that something shall be done

which is impossible at the time of making the agreement, it is much more likely that, on true construction of the agreement, one or other will have undertaken responsibility for the mistaken state of affairs. This may well explain why cases where contracts have been found to be void in consequence of common mistake are few and far between.

NOTES

1. In *Dany Lions Ltd v Bristol Cars Ltd* [2013] EWHC 2997 (QB), [2014] 1 Lloyd's Rep 281, the terms of the contract were clear that the defendant garage had accepted the risk of performance of the contract to renovate a rare vintage car, including supplying and fitting an automatic gearbox. It was alleged that it had not been appreciated that fitting the automatic gearbox would impact adversely on the car's performance so that the contract should be void for common mistake. However, the judge considered that the contract contained a warranty by the garage that it would be possible to perform the contract so that it was not possible to attempt to rely on the doctrine of common mistake. In any event, there was no impossibility since the judge concluded (at [27]), that 'the greater part of the contract was wholly unaffected by whether the automatic gearbox could be supplied and fitted or not. The supply and fitting of the automatic gearbox was but one element in a much more extensive range of works which the Defendant agreed to undertake.'

2. Lord Phillips in *The Great Peace* made a very important practical point—namely, that, by its very nature, initial impossibility is likely to be less common than supervening impossibility (frustration, discussed in *Chapter 12*). It also follows from the nature of impossibility existing at the time of contracting that it is more likely that the contract will in fact have allocated that risk to one of the contractual parties.

In *An Introduction to the Law of Contract*, 5th edn (Clarendon, 1995), p. 226, Atiyah stated that 'as a rule pre-existing facts could have been discovered by the parties': see also the discussion in Smith, *Atiyah's Introduction to the Law of Contract*, 6th edn (Oxford University Press, 2006), pp. 178–80, assessing the reasons why relief for mistake is so rare. This may imply a degree of fault on the part of parties who have entered into a contract on the basis of a common mistake. It may well explain the fact that the doctrine of mistake is of limited scope and that the courts will not easily grant relief in such cases.

8.4.4 The theoretical basis for the doctrine of common mistake

8.4.4.1 The implied term theory

In the context of common mistake, there was alleged to be an implied condition precedent that the goods forming the subject matter of the contract should exist at the time that the contract was entered into. This implied term (implied condition precedent) argument has often been confused with contractual allocations of risk by implication, such as that in *McRae v Commonwealth Disposals Commission* (see *page 390, 8.4.2*).

The implied term (condition precedent) theory rests primarily on the decision of Steyn J in the next case.

Associated Japanese Bank (International) Ltd v Crédit du Nord
[1989] 1 WLR 255

Funds were raised against the security of certain non-existent machines on a 'sale and lease-back', i.e. the non-existent machines were sold to the claimant bank for more than £1 million and then immediately leased back. The defendant bank had guaranteed the payments due under this lease. When the perpetrator of the fraud defaulted on the lease payments and disappeared with the £1 million, the claimant bank sought to enforce the guarantee given by the defendant.

Held: The guarantee was subject to either an express or an implied condition precedent that the machines existed. Since the machines did not exist, the guarantee did not become effective and the defendant could not be liable under it.

> STEYN J: [I]t remains to be considered whether there was an *implied* condition precedent that the lease related to four existing machines. In the present contract such a condition may only be held to be implied if one of two applicable tests is satisfied. The first is that such an implication is necessary to give business efficacy to the relevant contract, i.e. the guarantee. In other words, the criterion is whether the implication is necessary to render the contract (the guarantee) workable . . .
>
> For both parties the guarantee of obligations under a lease with non-existent machines was essentially different from a guarantee of a lease with four machines which both parties at the time of the contract believed to exist. The guarantee is an accessory contract. The non-existence of the subject matter of the principal contract is therefore of fundamental importance. Indeed the analogy of the classic *res extincta* cases, so much discussed in the authorities, is fairly close. In my judgment the stringent test of common law mistake is satisfied: the guarantee is void ab initio.

NOTES

1. The recognition of an implied condition precedent was regarded by Steyn J as a first step involving an allocation of risk (i.e. that the machines had to exist for the guarantee to be valid) and as separate from the doctrine of mistake, whilst recognizing that there were close similarities with *res extincta* (*page 394*, 8.4.4.2). The implied condition precedent argument may have been thought to be necessary because of the nature of the guarantee as an accessory contract.

2. The implied condition precedent argument, based on the decision in *Associated Japanese Bank*, was relied upon in *Graves v Graves* [2007] EWCA Civ 660, [2007] 3 FCR 26, [2008] HLR 10 (discussed further at *page 415*, 8.4.5.6).

The Court of Appeal first implied a condition precedent into a tenancy agreement whereby the tenancy would end if housing benefit were not payable to the tenant (albeit by mistakenly employing a mistake-based test rather than the test for the implication of a term), and then concluded that the tenancy was 'determined' for the future from the time when it became clear that no housing benefit was, in fact, payable (suggesting a 'condition subsequent'). If the existence of housing benefit were a true condition precedent, then it should prevent the contract coming into existence, i.e. the contract would be void. However, that can have unfortunate consequences for the parties' positions and obligations, i.e. no rent is payable under a void contract.

3. An argument based on failure of an implied condition precedent was pleaded in the alternative to an argument that a contract was void for a fundamental mistake in *Golden Ocean Group Ltd v Humpuss Intermoda Transportasi Tbk Ltd* [2013] EWHC 1240 (Comm), [2013] 1 CLC 929 (discussed further at *page 395*, 8.4.4.2). It is clear from the judgment that the judge faced difficulties in reconciling principle since Lord Phillips in Great Peace made comments suggesting that the correct approach was based on the doctrine of mistake and a construction process to determine whether the mistake was sufficiently fundamental to render the contract void. As can be seen in *Graves v Graves*, there are practical advantages in avoiding the drastic doctrine of mistake, and this may explain the recent tendency to plead the failure of an implied condition precedent in the alternative where there is a clear instance of *res extincta* (in this case, a mistake as to the correct parties to an addendum).

8.4.4.2 The construction theory

Great Peace Shipping Ltd v Tsavliris Salvage (International) Ltd
[2002] EWCA Civ 1407, [2003] QB 679 (CA)

Lord Phillips first referred to the fact that Lord Atkin, in *Bell v Lever Bros. Ltd* [1932] AC 161 (*page 397*, 8.4.5.2), had adopted the implication of a term as the alternative basis for his test to determine the existence of a fundamental common mistake.

LORD PHILLIPS MR: 61 . . . It seems to us that this was a more solid jurisprudential basis for the test of common mistake that Lord Atkin was proposing. At the time of *Bell v Lever Bros Ltd* [1932] AC 161 the law of frustration and common mistake had advanced hand in hand on the foundation of a common principle. Thereafter frustration proved a more fertile ground for the development of this principle than common mistake, and consideration of the development of the law of frustration assists with the analysis of the law of common mistake.

. . .

[Lord Phillips then traced the development of frustration case law—especially the recognition that a contract would be frustrated if performance as originally envisaged would be radically different—and continued:]

73 What do these developments in the law of frustration have to tell us about the law of common mistake? First that the theory of the implied term is as unrealistic when considering common mistake as when considering frustration. Where a fundamental assumption upon which an agreement is founded proves to be mistaken, it is not realistic to ask whether the parties impliedly agreed that in those circumstances the contract would not be binding. The avoidance of a contract on the ground of common mistake results from a rule of law under which, if it transpires that one or both of the parties have agreed to do something which it is impossible to perform, no obligation arises out of that agreement.

74 In considering whether performance of the contract is impossible, it is necessary to identify what it is that the parties agreed would be performed. This involves looking not only at the express terms, but at any implications that may arise out of the surrounding circumstances. In some cases it will be possible to identify details of the 'contractual adventure' which go beyond the terms that are expressly spelt out, in others it will not . . .

82 Thus, while we do not consider that the doctrine of common mistake can be satisfactorily explained by an implied term, an allegation that a contract is void for common mistake will often raise important issues of construction. Where it is possible to perform the letter of the contract, but it is alleged that there was a common mistake in relation to a fundamental assumption which renders performance of the essence of the obligation impossible, it will be necessary, by construing the contract in the light of all the material circumstances, to decide whether this is indeed the case.

NOTE There can be little doubt therefore that Lord Phillips was advocating a construction test based on impossibility for both frustration and common mistake. It is clear, however, that this process of construction needs to be based on both the express and implied terms of the contract. It must be doubtful therefore whether it is necessary to plead implied condition precedent *and* mistake when there is a clear case of subject matter mistake, although it appears that it is acceptable to do so.

Golden Ocean Group Ltd v Humpuss Intermoda Transportasi Tbk Ltd
[2013] EWHC 1240 (Comm), [2013] 1 CLC 929

This case concerned a dispute relating to an addendum to a charterparty entered into between Genuine Maritime and Golden Ocean. Clause 1 of this addendum referred all disputes to arbitration in Singapore. However, the original charterparty to which this addendum related was alleged to be made between another company in the Genuine Maritime group, HIT, and Golden Ocean. Golden Ocean therefore claimed that clause 1 was ineffective as an agreement to submit disputes to arbitration in Singapore because, relying on *Associated Japanese Bank* and *Graves v Graves*, it was an implied condition of clause 1 of the addendum that the charterparty to which it related had been entered into between Golden Ocean and Genuine (parties to the addendum). This condition failed because HIT was party to the existing charterparty and its arbitration clause. The alternative argument was that clause 1 was void for mistake, since both parties to the addendum mistakenly believed the charterparty had been entered into between Genuine and Golden Ocean, and that this amounted to a fundamental mistake as to the subject matter of the addendum. The judge recognized that these arguments were 'closely related', but had difficulty in determining which was to be preferred.

POPPLEWELL J: 45 . . . [Counsel for Genuine] further submitted that there was no room for the application of any implied condition argument in the light of Lord Phillips' statement at [81] of *The Great Peace* that the doctrine of mistake can not satisfactorily be explained by an implied term. But, as *Graves v Graves* and *Associated Japanese Bank* illustrate, an implied condition may arise independently of the operation of the doctrine of mistake.

46 It is not possible on the current application to reach concluded views on these issues . . .

8.4.5 Categories of fundamental common mistake

The crucial characteristic of common mistake is that both parties make a mistake and it is the same mistake. In order for the contract to be void for common mistake, thereby excusing the parties from all performance, that mistake must be 'fundamental'. A mistake will be sufficiently fundamental if it involves a mistaken assumption of fact that would render performance in accordance with the contract terms essentially different from the performance originally contemplated by the parties. However, this test was described as 'narrow' by the Court of Appeal in *Great Peace Shipping Ltd v Tsavliris Salvage (International) Ltd* [2002] EWCA Civ 1407, [2003] QB 679, and will not be easily satisfied in the context of mistakes other than those relating to the existence of the subject matter of the contract.

8.4.5.1 The subject matter does not exist

Both parties are mistaken as to the existence of the subject matter of the contract.

Couturier v Hastie
(1856) 5 HL Cas 673, 10 ER 1065 (HL)

In May 1848, the parties entered into a contract for the sale of corn, which was believed to be in transit from Salonica to the UK. Shipment had occurred in February 1848 and, unknown to both parties, before the contract was made in May, the corn had deteriorated to such an extent that the master of the ship had sold it at Tunis. When he discovered this fact, the English buyer repudiated the contract, but the seller argued that the buyer was still liable for the price.

Held: The contract contemplated that there was an existing commodity to be sold and bought. Since this was not the case at the time of the sale to the buyer, he was not liable to pay the price.

NOTES

1. *Couturier v Hastie* is often cited as authority for the fact that a mistake by both parties as to the existence of the subject matter of the contract renders the contract void. This interpretation was placed on *Couturier v Hastie* by the drafters of the Sale of Goods Act 1893. Section 6 of the Sale of Goods Act (SGA) 1979 provides:

Where there is a contract for the sale of specific goods, and the goods without the knowledge of the seller have perished at the time when the contract is made, the contract is void.

However, the only issue that the House of Lords had to decide was whether the buyer was liable to pay the price. The House of Lords held that he was not so bound, but this could have been because there was a contract that the goods existed and there was a total failure of consideration destroying the basis of the contract. The word 'mistake' is not even mentioned in the case and the Lord Chancellor expressly stated that the whole question turned upon the construction of the contract.

2. Since s. 6 SGA 1979 seems to accept that the goods did once exist, it does not apply where the subject matter never existed.

The problem with this interpretation is that it both limits the application of s. 6 (to goods that have at one time existed) and it restricts the principle in *McRae v Commonwealth Disposals Commission* (*page 390*, 8.4.2) to situations in which one party accepts the risk that the goods do not exist at all.

3. Atiyah (1957) 73 LQR 340 argued that s. 6 is only a rule of construction, which can be ousted by a contrary intention. However, it is not likely that this was intended, since, although other sections of the 1979 Act state that their application is subject to contrary agreement, s. 6 does not.

8.4.5.2 Mistakes as to quality

A mistake as to quality made by both parties does not render performance as originally agreed impossible.

Bell v Lever Bros. Ltd
[1932] AC 161 (HL)

Bell and Snelling entered into a contract with the claimant company under which they agreed to serve for five years as chairman and vice-chairman of the claimant's subsidiary company. While acting in these capacities and in breach of duty, they entered into secret speculations in cocoa for their own benefit. Subsequently, their services were no longer required. The claimant company negotiated with them both to give up their appointments in return for monetary compensation. Being unaware of the breaches of duty and that these breaches would have justified terminating the agreements without compensation, the claimant company agreed to compensation of £30,000 and £20,000, respectively. The money was paid to the defendants, but on discovering the breaches of duty, the claimant company sought to recover it. (The jury found that, when they had agreed to the compensation, the defendants had forgotten about their breaches of duty. Therefore, it was a question of common mistake, because both parties had made the same mistake.)

Held: A majority (3:2) rejected the argument that the compensation agreement was void for the common mistake, since this was a mistake as to a quality of the service contracts. (The speeches refer to mutual mistake as meaning common mistake.)

LORD ATKIN [referred to *res extincta* and continued]: Mistake as to quality of the thing contracted for raises more difficult questions. In such a case a mistake will not affect assent unless it is the mistake of both parties, and is as to the existence of some quality which makes the thing without the quality essentially different from the thing as it was believed to be. Of course it may appear that the parties contracted that the article should possess the quality which one or other or both mistakenly believed it to possess. But in such a case there is a contract and the inquiry is a different one, being whether the contract as to quality amounts to a condition or a warranty, a different branch of the law . . .

Is an agreement to terminate a broken contract different in kind from an agreement to terminate an unbroken contract, assuming that the breach has given the one party the right to declare the contract at an end? . . . [O]n the whole, I have come to the conclusion that it would be wrong to decide that an agreement to terminate a definite specified contract is void if it turns out that the agreement had already been broken and could have been terminated otherwise. The contract released is the identical contract in both cases, and the party paying for release gets exactly what he bargains for. It seems immaterial that he could have got the same result in another way, or that if he had known the true facts he would not have entered into the bargain. A buys B's horse; he thinks the horse is sound and he pays the price of a sound horse; he would certainly not have bought the horse if he had known as the fact is that the horse is unsound. If B has made no representation as to soundness and has not contracted that the horse is sound, A is bound and cannot recover back the price. A buys a picture from B; both A and B believe it to be the work of an old master, and a high price is paid. It turns out to be a modern copy. A has no remedy in the absence of representation or warranty. A agrees to take on lease or to buy from B an unfurnished dwelling-house. The house is in fact uninhabitable. A would never have entered into the bargain if he had known the fact. A has no remedy, and the position is the same whether B knew the facts or not, so long as he made no representation or gave no warranty. A buys a roadside garage business from B abutting on a public thoroughfare: unknown to A, but known to B, it has already been decided to construct a bypass road which will divert substantially the whole of the traffic from passing A's garage. Again A has no remedy. All these cases involve hardship on A and benefit B, as most people would say, unjustly. They can be supported on the ground that it is of paramount importance that contracts should be observed, and that if parties honestly comply with the essentials of the formation of contracts—i.e., agree in the same terms on the same subject-matter—they are bound, and must rely on the stipulations of the contract for protection from the effect of facts unknown to them.

. . . [I]f the contract expressly or impliedly contains a term that a particular assumption is a condition of the contract, the contract is avoided if the assumption is not true. But we have not advanced far on the inquiry how to ascertain whether the contract does contain such a condition. Various words are to be found to define the state of things which make a condition. 'In the contemplation of both parties fundamental to the continued validity of the contract,' 'a foundation essential to its existence,' 'a fundamental reason for making it,' are phrases found in the important judgment of Scrutton LJ in the present case. The first two phrases appear to me to be unexceptionable. They cover the case of a contract to serve in a particular place, the existence of which is fundamental to the service, or to procure the services of a professional vocalist, whose continued health is essential to performance. But 'a fundamental reason for making a contract' may, with respect, be misleading. The reason of one party only is presumably not intended, but in the cases I have suggested above, of the sale of a horse or of a picture, it might be said that the fundamental reason for making the contract was the belief of both parties that the horse was sound or the picture an old master, yet in neither case would the condition as I think exist. Nothing is more dangerous than to allow oneself liberty to construct for the parties contracts which they have not in terms made by importing implications which would appear to make the contract more businesslike or more just. The implications to be made are to be no more than are 'necessary' for giving business efficacy to the transaction, and it appears to me that, both as to existing facts and future facts, a condition would not be implied unless the new state of facts makes the contract something different in kind from the contract in the original state of facts . . . We therefore get a common standard for mutual mistake, and implied conditions whether as to existing or as to future facts. Does the state of the new facts destroy the identity of the subject-matter as it was in the original state of facts? To apply the principle to the infinite combinations of facts that arise in actual experience will continue to be difficult, but if this case results in establishing order into what has been a somewhat confused and difficult branch of the law it will have served a useful purpose.

Associated Japanese Bank (International) Ltd v Crédit du Nord
[1989] 1 WLR 255

STEYN J: The first imperative must be that the law ought to uphold rather than destroy apparent contracts. Secondly, the common law rules as to a mistake regarding the quality of the subject matter, like the common law rules regarding commercial frustration, are designed to cope with the impact of unexpected and wholly exceptional circumstances on apparent contracts. Thirdly, such a mistake in order to attract legal consequences must substantially be shared by both parties, and must relate to facts as they existed at the time the contract was made. Fourthly, and this is the point established by *Bell v Lever Bros Ltd* [1932] AC 161, the mistake must render the subject matter of the contract essentially and radically different from the subject matter which the parties believed to exist. While the civilian distinction between the substance and attributes of the subject matter of a contract has played a role in the development of our law (and was cited in speeches in *Bell v Lever Bros Ltd*), the principle enunciated in *Bell v Lever Bros Ltd* is markedly narrower in scope than the civilian doctrine. It is therefore no longer useful to invoke the civilian distinction. The principles enunciated by Lord Atkin and Lord Thankerton represent the ratio decidendi of *Bell v Lever Bros Ltd*. Fifthly, there is a requirement which was not specifically discussed in *Bell v Lever Bros Ltd*. What happens if the party, who is seeking to rely on the mistake, had no reasonable grounds for his belief? An extreme example is that of the man who makes a contract with minimal knowledge of the facts to which the mistake relates but is content that it is a good speculative risk. In my judgment a party cannot be allowed to rely on a common mistake where the mistake consists of a belief which is entertained by him without any reasonable grounds for such belief: cf *McRae v Commonwealth Disposals Commission* 84 CLR 377, 408. That is not because principles such as estoppel or negligence require it, but simply because policy and good sense dictate that the positive rules regarding common mistake should be so qualified.

NOTES

1. The principle underlying the decision in *Bell v Lever Bros.* is that a mistake as to quality should not enable a completed contract to be undone since the parties have agreed in the same terms on the same subject matter. The net effect of *Bell v Lever Bros.* is that it promotes certainty, but at the expense of fairness and flexibility.

2. In *Associated Japanese Bank (International) Ltd v Crédit du Nord SA* [1989] 1 WLR 255, Steyn J considered that the *ratio* of *Bell v Lever Bros.* was that, for the contract to be void, the mistake as to quality had 'to make the thing without the quality essentially different from the thing as it was believed to be' (*per* Lord Atkin, at p. 218). However, Lord Atkin's examples of mistakes that will not be sufficiently fundamental to render the contract void indicate that this principle is very restrictive indeed.

Lord Thankerton stated, at p. 235, that the mistake must 'relate to something which both [parties] must necessarily have accepted in their minds as an essential element of the subject matter'. The evidence was that only the claimant company regarded the validity of the service contracts as essential.

3. The minority in *Bell v Lever Bros.* (Viscount Hailsham and Lord Warrington of Clyffe) considered that this mistake was sufficiently fundamental to the bargain. This may be because of the value involved in the mistake.

Sherwood v Walker
66 Mich 568 (1887), 33 NW 919 (Supreme Court of Michigan)

The claimants agreed to buy a cow from the defendants for $80. Both parties believed the cow to be barren, but the defendants then discovered that the cow was in calf at the time that the contract had been entered into (as a breeding cow, the value soared to between $750 and $1,000). The defendants refused to deliver the cow, arguing that a common mistake had been made that went to 'the very nature of the thing'.

Held (in the Supreme Court): The contract was void for mistake. The majority considered that this mistake went to the whole substance of the agreement, stressing the difference in the price of the cow. It was so fundamental a mistake that it went beyond a mere mistake as to quality and affected the very character of the animal for all time.

By comparison, a difference in value is not seen as determinative in English law: see *Leaf v International Galleries* [1950] 2 KB 86 (*page 452, 9.2.1.2*); *Kyle Bay Ltd (T/A Astons Nightclub) v Underwriters Subscribing Under Policy Number 019057/08/01* [2007] EWCA Civ 57, [2007] 1

CLC 164 (*page 412*, 8.4.5.5); and Lord Atkin's example in *Bell v Lever Bros.* of 'the old master'. A contractual promise as to subject matter (a term) is required.

Nicholson & Venn v Smith-Marriott
(1947) 177 LT 189

A set of linen napkins and tablecloths bearing a royal coat of arms was described as 'all with the crest and arms of Charles I and . . . the authentic property of that monarch'. The claimants, antique dealers, paid £787 for the linen on the faith of this description in the catalogue. In fact, it was Georgian and worth only £105.

Held: This was a sale by description within s. 13 of the Sale of Goods Act 1893 (now s. 13 SGA 1979), and since the linen did not correspond with the description there had been a breach of contract.

HALLETT J [*obiter*]: Clearly, in this case, as it seems to me, what the defendants were intending to sell and the plaintiffs intending to buy was not two fine table cloths and twelve fine table napkins as such, but something which I will describe as a Carolean relic. Using the language of Lord Atkin, I am disposed to the view that a Georgian relic, if there be such a thing—which I have no reason to suppose there is—is an 'essentially different' thing from a Carolean relic. I think that the absence of the crest and arms of Charles I—the absence of anything attesting or appearing to attest a connection between this table linen and that monarch, who at one time, after all, appeared in the English Prayer Book, if I am not mistaken, as a martyr, which none of the four Georgian kings did—did make the goods obtained different things in substance from those which the plaintiffs sought to buy and believed that they had bought. I should be disposed therefore, though recognising the great difficulties of the point and without any undue confidence in the correctness of my judgment, to hold if necessary that here there was a mutual mistake of the kind or category calculated to vitiate the assent of the parties and therefore to enable the plaintiffs to treat themselves as not bound by the contract.

NOTES

1. Applying the suggested solution in Peel, *Treitel's The Law of Contract*, 14th edn (Sweet & Maxwell, 2015), [8-019], if the parties had been asked what they were contracting about and had replied that it was 'Charles I napkins', then the contract would be void, but if they had merely replied 'antique table linen', it would be valid.

2. In *Solle v Butcher* [1950] 1 KB 671, Denning LJ disagreed with the *obiter* view in *Nicholson & Venn v Smith-Marriott* that the contract was void. This has thrown serious doubts on its application as an example of a sufficiently fundamental mistake.

As in *Nicholson & Venn v Smith-Marriott*, it may be possible to argue that a particular quality is a term of the contract. Section 13(1) SGA 1979 (applicable to B2B—business to business—contracts) provides:

Where there is a contract for the sale of goods by description, there is an implied term that the goods will correspond with the description.

However, in *Harlingdon & Leinster Enterprises Ltd v Christopher Hull Fine Art Ltd* [1991] 1 QB 564, the Court of Appeal held that, for the sale of goods to be a sale 'by description' within s. 13(1), the description had to be influential in the sale. The court had to be able to impute a common intention to the parties that the description should be a term of the contract, and this depended on whether it was within the contemplation of the parties that the buyer would rely on the description.

Section 13(1) SGA 1979 is now restricted in its application to B2B contracts but an equivalent provision for contracts of sale between a trader and a consumer can be found in s. 11 Consumer Rights Act (CRA) 2015 ('goods to be as described'). The consumer rights legislation implementing the European Consumer Rights Directive (CRD) 2011/83/EU also requires certain information concerning the goods to be provided to the consumer by the trader: see the Consumer Contracts (Information, Cancellation and Additional Charges) Regulations, SI 2013/3134. This information is to be treated as forming part of the description, i.e. as contractual terms (s. 12 CRA 2015).

There may be a misrepresentation as to quality. In *Leaf v International Galleries* [1950] 2 KB 86 (*page 452*, 9.2.1.2), both parties entered into the contract mistakenly thinking that the painting was by Constable. On the facts, there was a misrepresentation by the seller, but the only available remedy of rescission had been lost because of lapse of time. Evershed MR explained, at pp. 93–4, why such a mistake as to quality did not render the contract void:

> The plaintiff's case rested fundamentally upon this statement which he made: 'I contracted to buy a Constable. I have not had, and never had, a Constable.' Though that is, as a matter of language, perfectly intelligible, it nevertheless needs a little expansion if it is to be quite accurate. What he contracted to buy and what he bought was a specific chattel, namely, an oil painting of Salisbury Cathedral; but he bought it on the faith of a representation, innocently made, that it had been painted by John Constable. It turns out, as the evidence now stands and as the county court judge has found, that it was not so painted. Nevertheless it remains true to say that the plaintiff still has the article which he contracted to buy. The difference is no doubt considerable, but it is, as Denning LJ has observed, a difference in quality and in value rather than in the substance of the thing itself.

Great Peace Shipping Ltd v Tsavliris Salvage (International) Ltd
[2002] EWCA Civ 1407, [2003] QB 679 (CA)

A ship, *Cape Providence*, had suffered serious structural damage in the south Indian Ocean. Because there were concerns that the vessel might sink and thereby endanger the safety of the crew before a tug arrived, the appellants, a salvage company, sought a merchant vessel in the vicinity to assist with the evacuation of the crew. *The Great Peace* was identified as the nearest vessel. It was believed to be about 35 miles away from *Cape Providence* and able to rendezvous within a few hours. The appellants and the respondents therefore entered into a contract whereby *The Great Peace* was hired for a minimum of five days to deviate towards *Cape Providence*, and then escort and stand by *Cape Providence* for the purposes of saving life. The contract contained a cancellation clause giving the appellants the right to cancel on payment of five days' hire. In fact, the vessels were 410 miles apart (so that it would take about 39 hours for *The Great Peace* to arrive) and, after securing the services of an alternative vessel, the appellants cancelled the contract with the respondents. The respondents sought the five days' hire (US$82,500) under the terms of the contract, but the appellants alleged that the contract was either void at law or voidable in equity, since both parties had proceeded on the basis of the fundamental mistake of fact—namely, that the two vessels were in 'close proximity' at the time of contracting. Toulson J, at first instance, had given judgment for the respondents and, in particular, had denied any equitable jurisdiction to grant relief in these circumstances.

Held (on appeal): The critical issue in determining the existence of a fundamental common mistake as to quality was whether the common mistaken assumption of fact underpinning the contract meant that the performance of the contract in accordance with its terms would be essentially different from the performance contemplated by the parties. In this context, that was interpreted to mean whether the distance between the two vessels was such that the service that *The Great Peace* was in a position to provide was essentially different from what the parties had agreed. The fact that the appellants did not cancel the contract until they had secured the services of another vessel and the fact that *The Great Peace* would have arrived in time to provide several days' escort service indicated that performance of the contractual adventure had not been impossible. The contract was therefore not void for common mistake. In addition, there was no equitable jurisdiction to grant rescission for a common mistake that was not sufficiently fundamental at common law (*Bell v Lever Bros.* applied). Accordingly, the appellants were liable to pay the charge under the cancellation clause.

LORD PHILLIPS MR [giving the judgment of the court, first explained the issues]: 31 In the present case the parties were agreed as to the express terms of the contract. The defendants agreed that the *Great Peace* would deviate towards the *Cape Providence* and, on reaching her, escort her so as to be on hand to save the lives of her crew, should she founder. The contractual services would terminate when the salvage tug came up with the casualty. The mistake relied upon by the defendants is as to an assumption that they claim underlay the terms expressly agreed. This was that the *Great Peace* was within a few hours sailing of the *Cape Providence*. They contend that this mistake was fundamental in that it would take the *Great Peace* about 39 hours to reach a position where she could render the services which were the object of the contractual adventure.

32 Thus what we are here concerned with is an allegation of a common mistaken assumption of fact which renders the service that will be provided if the contract is performed in accordance with its terms something different from the performance that the parties contemplated. This is the type of mistake which fell to be considered in *Bell v Lever Bros Ltd* [1932] AC 161. We shall describe it as 'common mistake', although it is often alternatively described as 'mutual mistake'.

33 [Counsel] for the defendants puts his case in two alternative ways. First he submits that performance of the contract in the circumstances as they turned out to be would have been fundamentally different from the performance contemplated by the parties, so much so that the effect of the mistake was to deprive the agreement of the consideration underlying it. Under common law, so he submits, the effect of such a mistake is to render the contract void. [Counsel] draws a close analogy with the test to be applied when deciding whether a contract has been frustrated or whether there has been a fundamental breach. The foundation for this submission is *Bell v Lever Bros Ltd*.

34 If the facts of this case do not meet that test, [counsel] submits that they none the less give rise to a right of rescission in equity. He submits that such a right arises whenever the parties contract under a common mistake as to a matter that can properly be described as 'fundamental' or 'material' to the agreement in question. Here he draws an analogy with the test for rescission where one party, by innocent misrepresentation, induces the other to enter into a contract—indeed that is one situation where the parties contract under a common mistake. The foundation for this submission is *Solle v Butcher* [1950] 1 KB 671 . . .

8.4.5.3 Mistake as to quality at common law in *The Great Peace*

LORD PHILLIPS MR: 50 It is generally accepted that the principles of the law of common mistake expounded by Lord Atkin in *Bell v Lever Bros Ltd* [1932] AC 161 were based on the common law. The issue raised by [counsel's] submissions is whether there subsists a separate doctrine of common mistake founded in equity which enables the court to intervene in circumstances where the mistake does not render the contract void under the common law principles. The first step is to identify the nature of the common law doctrine of mistake that was identified, or established, by *Bell v Lever Bros Ltd*.

51 Lord Atkin and Lord Thankerton were breaking no new ground in holding void a contract where, unknown to the parties, the subject matter of the contract no longer existed at the time that the contract was concluded. The Sale of Goods Act 1893 . . . was a statute which set out to codify the common law. Section 6, to which Lord Atkin referred, provided: 'When there is a contract for the sale of specific goods, and the goods without the knowledge of the seller have perished at the time when the contract is made, the contract is void.'

52 Judge Chalmers, the draftsman of the Act, commented in the first edition of his book on the Act, *The Sale of Goods Act 1893* (1894), p 17: 'The rule may be based either on the ground of mutual mistake, or on the ground of impossibility of performance.'

53 He put at the forefront of the authorities that he cited in support *Couturier v Hastie* (1856) 5 HL Cas 673. That case involved the sale of a cargo of corn which, unknown to the parties, no longer existed at the time that the contract was concluded. Other decisions where agreements were held not to be binding were *Strickland v Turner* (1852) 7 Exch 208—the sale of an annuity upon the life of a person who, unknown

to the parties, had died—and *Pritchard v Merchant's and Tradesman's Mutual Life Assurance Society* (1858) 3 CBNS 622—an insurance policy renewed in ignorance of the fact that the assured had died . . .

55 Where that which is expressly identified as the subject of a contract does not exist, the contract will necessarily be one which cannot be performed. Such a situation can readily be identified. The position is very different where there is 'a mistake as to the existence of some quality of the subject matter which makes the thing without the quality essentially different from the thing as it was believed to be'. In such a situation it may be possible to perform the letter of the contract . . .

[Lord Phillips then considered the basis for the decision in *Bell* to have been the implied term. This mirrored the development of the theoretical basis of frustration at that time. He traced the subsequent development of the doctrine of frustration and continued:]

73 What do these developments in the law of frustration have to tell us about the law of common mistake? First that the theory of the implied term is as unrealistic when considering common mistake as when considering frustration. Where a fundamental assumption upon which an agreement is founded proves to be mistaken, it is not realistic to ask whether the parties impliedly agreed that in those circumstances the contract would not be binding. The avoidance of a contract on the ground of common mistake results from a rule of law under which, if it transpires that one or both of the parties have agreed to do something which it is impossible to perform, no obligation arises out of that agreement.

74 In considering whether performance of the contract is impossible, it is necessary to identify what it is that the parties agreed would be performed. This involves looking not only at the express terms, but at any implications that may arise out of the surrounding circumstances. In some cases it will be possible to identify details of the 'contractual adventure' which go beyond the terms that are expressly spelt out, in others it will not . . .

82 Thus, while we do not consider that the doctrine of common mistake can be satisfactorily explained by an implied term, an allegation that a contract is void for common mistake will often raise important issues of construction. Where it is possible to perform the letter of the contract, but it is alleged that there was a common mistake in relation to a fundamental assumption which renders performance of the essence of the obligation impossible, it will be necessary, by construing the contract in the light of all the material circumstances, to decide whether this is indeed the case . . .

86 Lord Atkin himself [in *Bell v Lever Bros*] gave no examples of cases where a contract was rendered void because of a mistake as to quality which made 'the thing without the quality essentially different from the thing as it was believed to be'. He gave a number of examples of mistakes which did not satisfy this test, which served to demonstrate just how narrow he considered the test to be. Indeed this is further demonstrated by the result reached on the facts of *Bell v Lever Bros Ltd* [1932] AC 161 itself.

[Lord Phillips considered *Associated Japanese Bank* and Steyn LJ's summary of the law extracted at page 393, *8.4.4.1*, and continued:]

91 The detailed analysis that we have carried out leads us to concur in this summary, subject to the proviso that the result in *McRae's* case can, we believe, be explained on the basis of construction . . .

94 Our conclusions have marched in parallel with those of Toulson J. We admire the clarity with which he has set out his conclusions, which emphasise the importance of a careful analysis of the contract and of the rights and obligations created by it as an essential precursor to consideration of the effect of an alleged mistake. We agree with him that, on the facts of the present case, the issue in relation to common mistake turns on the question of whether the mistake as to the distance apart of the two vessels had the effect that the services that the *Great Peace* was in a position to provide were something essentially different from that to which the parties had agreed . . .

[Lord Phillips concluded on the question of mistake at common law.]

The result in this case

162 We revert to the question that we left unanswered at paragraph 94. It was unquestionably a common assumption of both parties when the contract was concluded that the two vessels were in sufficiently close proximity to enable the *Great Peace* to carry out the service that she was engaged to perform. Was the distance between the two vessels so great as to confound that assumption and to render the contractual adventure impossible of performance? If so, the defendants would have an arguable case that the contract was void under the principle in *Bell v Lever Bros Ltd* [1932] AC 161 . . .

165 . . . [T]he fact that the vessels were considerably further apart than the defendants had believed did not mean that the services that the *Great Peace* was in a position to provide were essentially different from those which the parties had envisaged when the contract was concluded. The *Great Peace* would arrive in time to provide several days of escort service. The defendants would have wished the contract to be performed but for the adventitious arrival on the scene of a vessel prepared to perform the same services. The fact that the vessels were further apart than both parties had appreciated did not mean that it was impossible to perform the contractual adventure.

166 The parties entered into a binding contract for the hire of the *Great Peace*. That contract gave the defendants an express right to cancel the contract subject to the obligation to pay the 'cancellation fee' of five days' hire. When they engaged the *Nordfarer* they cancelled the *Great Peace*. They became liable in consequence to pay the cancellation fee. There is no injustice in this result.

167 For the reasons that we have given, we would dismiss this appeal.

8.4.5.4 Mistake as to quality in equity and *The Great Peace*

LORD PHILLIPS MR: 95 In *Solle v Butcher* [1950] 1 KB 671 Denning LJ held that a court has an equitable power to set aside a contract that is binding in law on the ground of common mistake. Subsequently, as Lord Denning MR, in *Magee v Pennine Insurance Co Ltd* [1969] 2 QB 507, 514 he said of *Bell v Lever Bros Ltd* [1932] AC 161:

> I do not propose today to go through the speeches in that case. They have given enough trouble to commentators already. I would say simply this: a common mistake, even on a most fundamental matter, does not make a contract void at law: but it makes it voidable in equity. I analysed the cases in *Solle v Butcher* [1950] 1 KB 671, and I would repeat what I said there, at p 693: 'A contract is also liable in equity to be set aside if the parties were under a common misapprehension either as to facts or as to their relative and respective rights, provided that the misapprehension was fundamental and that the party seeking to set it aside was not himself at fault.'

96 Neither of the other two members of the court in *Magee v Pennine Insurance Co Ltd* cast doubt on *Bell v Lever Bros Ltd*. Each purported to follow it, although reaching different conclusions on the facts. It is axiomatic that there is no room for rescission in equity of a contract which is void. Either Lord Denning MR was purporting to usurp the common law principle in *Bell v Lever Bros Ltd* and replace it with a more flexible principle of equity, or the equitable remedy of rescission that he identified is one that operates in a situation where the mistake is not of such a nature as to avoid the contract. Decisions have, hitherto, proceeded on the basis that the latter is the true position. Thus, in *Associated Japanese Bank (International) Ltd v Crédit du Nord SA* [1989] 1 WLR 255, 266 Steyn J remarked that it was clear that mistake in equity was not circumscribed by common law definitions. He went on to say, at pp 267–268:

> No one could fairly suggest that in this difficult area of the law there is only one correct approach or solution. But a narrow doctrine of common law mistake (as enunciated in *Bell v Lever Bros Ltd* [1932] AC 161), supplemented by the more flexible doctrine of mistake in equity (as developed in *Solle v Butcher* [1950] 1 KB 671 and later cases), seems to me

to be an entirely sensible and satisfactory state of the law: see *Sheikh Bros Ltd v Ochsner* [1957] AC 136. And there ought to be no reason to struggle to avoid its application by artificial interpretations of *Bell v Lever Bros Ltd* . . .

Common mistake in equity prior to *Bell v Lever Bros Ltd*

99 The doctrine of common mistake at common law which we have identified cannot be said to have been firmly established prior to *Bell v Lever Bros Ltd*: see the comments of the High Court of Australia in *McRae v Commonwealth Disposals Commission* 84 CLR 377 and of the authors of *Meagher, Gummow & Lehane, Equity: Doctrines and Remedies*, 3rd ed (1992), p. 372. Little wonder if litigants, confronted with what appeared to them to be agreements binding in law, should invoke the equitable jurisdiction of the court of Chancery in an attempt to be released from their obligations, when they considered justice so demanded. Nor is it surprising if the Chancery court granted the relief sought on the basis upon which it was claimed. It is not realistic to infer that when such relief was granted the court implicitly determined that the contract was binding in law.

100 The precise circumstances in which the court of Chancery would permit rescission of a contract were not clearly established in the latter half of the 19th century . . . While a number of 18th and 19th century cases prior to the decision in *Cooper v Phibbs* LR 2 HL 149 lend some support to the thesis that equity had taken that step, 'No coherent equitable doctrine of mistake can be spelt from them': see the discussion in *Goff & Jones, The Law of Restitution*, 5th ed (1998), pp 288–289 and *Meagher, Gummow & Lehane, Equity: Doctrines and Remedies*, pp 375–376. *Cooper v Phibbs* was however the decision primarily relied upon by Denning LJ in *Solle v Butcher* [1950] 1 KB 671 . . .

101 At the heart of the case was a dispute as to title to a fishery in Ireland. The fishery, together with a cottage, was the subject of an agreement for a three-year lease entered into by Phibbs, the respondent, with Cooper, the appellant. Phibbs was acting as agent for five sisters, who believed that they had inherited the fishery from their father. He, in the belief that he was the owner of the fishery in fee simple, had expended much money in improving it. Cooper contended that, after entering into the lease, he had discovered that the fishery had at all material times been trust property and that, in consequence of a series of events of very great complexity, he was entitled to an equitable life interest. It was ultimately not disputed, however, that the head lease of the cottage was vested in the sisters.

102 Cooper . . . [contended] that the agreement ought to be set aside as made under mistake of fact and that he should be declared to have title to the fishery.

103 The House of Lords resolved the issue of title in favour of Cooper. Lord Cranworth dealt with the legal consequences of this . . .

> It appears to me, therefore, that it is impossible to say that he is not entitled to the relief which he asks, namely, to have the agreement delivered up and the rent repaid. That being so, he would be entitled to relief, but he is only entitled to this relief on certain terms, to which I will presently advert.

. . .

113 In the House of Lords [in *Bell v Lever Bros*] [1932] AC 161 the report shows that the appellants relied on both common law authorities and *Cooper v Phibbs* LR 2 HL 149 in support of the submission that a common mistake had to be as to the existence of the subject matter of the contract if it was to render it void. The respondents do not appear to have suggested that equity might provide relief where common law would not. They relied upon frustration cases in support of the proposition that a mistake would render a contract void if it was based on a mistaken assumption that was contractual and was as to the essence of the contract . . .

118 . . . The House of Lords in *Bell v Lever Bros Ltd* [1932] AC 161 considered that the intervention of equity, as demonstrated in *Cooper v Phibbs* LR 2 HL 149, took place in circumstances where the common law would have ruled the contract void for mistake. We do not find it conceivable that the House of Lords

overlooked an equitable right in *Lever Bros* to rescind the agreement, notwithstanding that the agreement was not void for mistake at common law. The jurisprudence established no such right. Lord Atkin's test for common mistake that avoided a contract, while narrow, broadly reflected the circumstances where equity had intervened to excuse performance of a contract assumed to be binding in law.

The effect of *Solle v Butcher*

119 The material facts of *Solle v Butcher* [1950] 1 KB 671 can shortly be summarised as follows. The defendant agreed to let a flat to the plaintiff for £250 a year. The flat had previously been let at a rent of £140. Substantial work had been done on the flat and both parties believed that this so altered the nature of the premises as to free them from relevant rent control. In this they were mistaken. The defendant would have been able to charge the plaintiff an increased rent of £250 to reflect the work done on the flat had he complied with the requisite formalities but, under the influence of the mistake, he failed to do so. In the result he could not lawfully charge a rent higher than £140. The plaintiff obtained a declaration in the county court that the rent was restricted to £140 and an order for repayment of rent overpaid. The judge rejected the contention that the contract had been concluded under a common mistake of fact, holding that the mistake was one of law.

120 The Court of Appeal, by a majority, reversed this decision. Bucknill LJ held, at p 685, that the parties had concluded the agreement under a common mistake of fact, namely that the alterations had turned the premises into 'in effect, a different flat'. He held that this common mistake was on a matter of fundamental importance and that the defendant was entitled to rescind the agreement under the principle in *Cooper v Phibbs* LR 2 HL 149. He remarked that he had read the judgment of Denning LJ and agreed with the terms proposed by him on which the lease should be set aside . . .

122 Denning LJ first identified the effect of common mistake under principles of common law . . .

123 Applying those principles he held that it was clear that there was a contract. The parties had agreed in the same terms on the same subject matter. True it was that there was a fundamental mistake as to the rent which could be charged, but that did not render the lease a nullity. Turning to equity, he observed that the court could set aside a contract when it was unconscientious for the other party to take advantage of it. As to what was considered unconscientious, equity had shown a progressive development. A material misrepresentation would suffice, even if not fraudulent or fundamental. He continued, at p 693:

> A contract is also liable in equity to be set aside if the parties were under a common misapprehension either as to facts or as to their relative and respective rights, provided that the misapprehension was fundamental and that the party seeking to set it aside was not himself at fault.

124 . . . He added [1950] 1 KB 671, 695: '*Cooper v Phibbs* affords ample authority for saying that, by reason of the common misapprehension, this lease can be set aside on such terms as the court thinks fit.'

125 Denning LJ held, at p 695, that the lease should be set aside because there had been 'a common misapprehension, which was fundamental'. The terms on which the lease was set aside were such as, in effect, to give the tenant the option of substituting the lease for one at the full rent which the law permitted.

126 Toulson J described this decision by Denning LJ as one which 'sought to outflank *Bell v Lever Bros Ltd* [1932] AC 161'. We think that this was fair comment. It was not realistic to treat the House of Lords in *Bell v Lever Bros Ltd* as oblivious to principles of equity, nor to suggest that 'if it had been considered on equitable grounds the result might have been different'. For the reasons that we have given, we do not consider that *Cooper v Phibbs* LR 2 HL 149 demonstrated or established an equitable jurisdiction to grant rescission for common mistake in circumstances that fell short of those in which the common law held a contract void. In so far as this was in doubt, the House of Lords in *Bell v Lever Bros Ltd* delimited the ambit of operation of *Cooper v Phibbs* by holding, rightly or wrongly, that on the facts of that case the agreement in question was void at law and by holding that, on the facts in *Bell v Lever Bros Ltd*, the mistake had not had the effect of rendering the contract void . . .

127 It was not correct to state that *Cooper v Phibbs*, as interpreted by Denning LJ, was 'in no way impaired by *Bell v Lever Bros Ltd*', nor to make the inconsistent statement that the principle of *Cooper v Phibbs*, as interpreted by Denning LJ, had been 'fully restored' by *Norwich Union Fire Insurance Society Ltd v Wm H Price Ltd* [1934] AC 455. That was a decision of the Privy Council, on appeal from the Supreme Court of New South Wales. Insurers had paid the insured value on a cargo of lemons under a mistake, shared by the assured, that they had been destroyed by a peril insured against. In fact they had been sold in transit because they were ripening. The Privy Council allowed the insurers' appeal against the refusal of the Supreme Court to allow them to recover the insurance moneys on the ground that they had been paid under a mistake of fact. In their advice they observed, at pp 462–463:

> The mistake was as vital as that in *Cooper v Phibbs* LR 2 HL 149, 170 in respect of which Lord Westbury used these words: 'If parties contract under a mutual mistake and misapprehension as to their relative and respective rights, the result is, that that agreement is liable to be set aside as having proceeded upon a common mistake.' At common law such a contract (or simulacrum of a contract) is more correctly described as void, there being in truth no intention to contract. Their Lordships find nothing tending to contradict or overrule these established principles in *Bell v Lever Bros Ltd* [1932] AC 161.

128 This passage reinforces the approach of the House of Lords in *Bell v Lever Bros Ltd* of equating the test of common mistake in *Cooper v Phibbs* with one that renders a contract void at common law.

129 Nor was it accurate to state that *Cooper v Phibbs* afforded ample authority for saying that the lease could be set aside 'on such terms as the court thinks fit'. As we have demonstrated, the terms imposed by the House of Lords in *Cooper v Phibbs* were no more than necessary to give effect to the rights and interests of those involved.

130 In *Bell v Lever Bros Ltd* the House of Lords equated the circumstances which rendered a contract void for common mistake with those which discharged the obligations of the parties under the doctrine of frustration. Denning LJ rightly concluded that the facts of *Solle v Butcher* [1950] 1 KB 671 did not amount to such circumstances. The equitable jurisdiction that he then asserted was a significant extension of any jurisdiction exercised up to that point and one that was not readily reconcilable with the result in *Bell v Lever Bros Ltd*.

131 If the result in *Solle v Butcher* [1950] 1 KB 671 extended beyond any previous decision the scope of the equitable jurisdiction to rescind a contract for common mistake, the terms of Denning LJ's judgment left unclear the precise parameters of the jurisdiction. The mistake had to be 'fundamental', but how far did this extend beyond Lord Atkin's test [1932] AC 161, 218 of a mistake 'as to the existence of some quality which makes the thing without the quality essentially different from the thing as it was believed to be'? The difficulty in answering this question was one of the factors that led Toulson J to conclude that there was no equitable jurisdiction to rescind on the ground of common mistake a contract that was valid in law. Was it open to him after half a century and is it open to this court to find that the equitable jurisdiction that Denning LJ identified in *Solle v Butcher* was a chimera? . . .

Summary

153 A number of cases, albeit a small number, in the course of the last 50 years have purported to follow *Solle v Butcher* [1950] 1 KB 671, yet none of them defines the test of mistake that gives rise to the equitable jurisdiction to rescind in a manner that distinguishes this from the test of a mistake that renders a contract void in law, as identified in *Bell v Lever Bros Ltd* [1932] AC 161. This is, perhaps, not surprising, for Denning LJ, the author of the test in *Solle v Butcher*, set *Bell v Lever Bros Ltd* at nought. It is possible to reconcile *Solle v Butcher* and *Magee v Pennine Insurance Co Ltd* [1969] 2 QB 507 with *Bell v Lever Bros Ltd* only by postulating that there are two categories of mistake, one that renders a contract void at law and one that renders it voidable in equity. Although later cases have proceeded on this basis, it is not possible to identify that proposition in the judgment of any of the three Lords Justices, Denning,

8

Mistake

Bucknill and Fenton Atkinson, who participated in the majority decisions in the former two cases. Nor, over 50 years, has it proved possible to define satisfactorily two different qualities of mistake, one operating in law and one in equity.

154 In *Solle v Butcher* Denning LJ identified the requirement of a common misapprehension that was 'fundamental', and that adjective has been used to describe the mistake in those cases which have followed *Solle v Butcher*. We do not find it possible to distinguish, by a process of definition, a mistake which is 'fundamental' from Lord Atkin's mistake as to quality which 'makes the thing [contracted for] essentially different from the thing [that] it was believed to be': [1932] AC 161, 218.

155 A common factor in *Solle v Butcher* and the cases which have followed it can be identified. The effect of the mistake has been to make the contract a particularly bad bargain for one of the parties. Is there a principle of equity which justifies the court in rescinding a contract where a common mistake has produced this result?

> Equity is . . . a body of rules or principles which form an appendage to the general rules of law, or a gloss upon them. In origin at least, it represents the attempt of the English legal system to meet a problem which confronts all legal systems reaching a certain stage of development. In order to ensure the smooth running of society it is necessary to formulate general rules which work well enough in the majority of cases. Sooner or later, however, cases arise in which, in some unforeseen set of facts, the general rules produce substantial unfairness. (*Snell's Equity*, 30th ed (2000), para 1–03.)

156 Thus the premise of equity's intrusion into the effects of the common law is that the common law rule in question is seen in the particular case to work injustice, and for some reason the common law cannot cure itself. But it is difficult to see how that can apply here. Cases of fraud and misrepresentation, and undue influence, are all catered for under other existing and uncontentious equitable rules. We are *only* concerned with the question whether relief might be given for common mistake in circumstances wider than those stipulated in *Bell v Lever Bros Ltd* [1932] AC 161. But that, surely, is a question as to where the common law should draw the line; not whether, given the common law rule, it needs to be mitigated by application of some other doctrine. The common law has drawn the line in *Bell v Lever Bros Ltd*. The effect of *Solle v Butcher* [1950] 1 KB 671 is not to supplement or mitigate the common law: it is to say that *Bell v Lever Bros Ltd* was wrongly decided.

157 Our conclusion is that it is impossible to reconcile *Solle v Butcher* with *Bell v Lever Bros Ltd*. The jurisdiction asserted in the former case has not developed. It has been a fertile source of academic debate, but in practice it has given rise to a handful of cases that have merely emphasised the confusion of this area of our jurisprudence. In paras 110 to 121 of his judgment, Toulson J has demonstrated the extent of that confusion. If coherence is to be restored to this area of our law, it can only be by declaring that there is no jurisdiction to grant rescission of a contract on the ground of common mistake where that contract is valid and enforceable on ordinary principles of contract law. That is the conclusion of Toulson J.

. . .

160 . . . In this case we have heard full argument, which has provided what we believe has been the first opportunity in this court for a full and mature consideration of the relation between *Bell v Lever Bros Ltd* [1932] AC 161 and *Solle v Butcher*. In the light of that consideration we can see no way that *Solle v Butcher* can stand with *Bell v Lever Bros Ltd*. In these circumstances we can see no option but so to hold.

161 We can understand why the decision in *Bell v Lever Bros Ltd* did not find favour with Lord Denning MR. An equitable jurisdiction to grant rescission on terms where a common fundamental mistake has induced a contract gives greater flexibility than a doctrine of common law which holds the contract void in such circumstances. Just as the Law Reform (Frustrated Contracts) Act 1943 was needed to temper the effect of the common law doctrine of frustration, so there is scope for legislation to give greater flexibility to our law of mistake than the common law allows.

NOTES

1. See Chandler, Devenney, and Poole, 'Common mistake: Theoretical justification and remedial inflexibility' [2004] JBL 34.

2. The decision of the Court of Appeal has resolved one of the areas of academic debate—namely, the question of why the House of Lords in *Bell v Lever Bros.*, having first determined that the contract was valid at common law, did not then consider the application of an equitable jurisdiction to set aside the contract on terms. There is no such equitable jurisdiction in such circumstances, and *Solle v Butcher* and other Court of Appeal and first instance decisions applying such a jurisdiction are plainly incorrect. It also resolves what had become something of a judicial dilemma in trying to distinguish a mistake that was not sufficiently fundamental to render the contract void at common law from a mistake that was sufficiently fundamental for the contract to be set aside on terms in equity.

3. It now appears that there is Supreme Court acceptance (albeit *obiter*) of the fact that *Great Peace* has overruled *Solle v Butcher* (and hence the equitable jurisdiction): *Pitt v Holt* [2013] UKSC 26, [2013] 2 AC 108, [115] (Lord Walker of Gestinghope giving a single agreed judgment of the Supreme Court).

4. However, in *Chwee Kin Keong v Digilandmall.com Pte Ltd* [2004] 1 SLR(R) 594, albeit in the context of a unilateral mistake, the Singapore Court of Appeal criticized this aspect of the decision in *Great Peace Shipping* denying the existence of the equitable jurisdiction.

CHAO HICK TIN JA [delivering the judgment of the court]: 68 It seems to us that the principal reason the Court of Appeal in *Great Peace Shipping* re-examined the foundation of Denning LJ's judgment in *Solle v Butcher* was the absence of any test to determine how the equitable jurisdiction should be applied to rescind a contract which was distinct from that which rendered a contract void in law. It noted (at [153]) that since the decision in *Solle v Butcher*, it had not 'proved possible to define satisfactorily two different qualities of mistake, one operating in law and one in equity'. It said at [156] that *Bell v Lever Bros* had set out the perimeters of the common law rule and the effect of *Solle v Butcher* was 'not to supplement or mitigate the common law: it is to say that *Bell v Lever Bros Ltd* was wrongly decided'. The court was therefore constrained to declare that there was no jurisdiction in equity to grant rescission of a contract on the ground of common mistake where that contract was valid and enforceable on ordinary principles of contract law . . .

74 . . . [W]e would be loath to hold that there is no equitable jurisdiction in the courts with regard to . . . mistake just because it may be difficult to delineate the scope or extent of that jurisdiction. By its very nature, the manner in which equity should be applied must depend on the facts of each case and the dictates of justice. Equity has intervened in many aspects of human dealings in the contractual setting . . .

5. Whilst the ability to set aside the contract on terms for common mistake as to quality may be difficult to reconcile with *Bell v Lever Bros.*, it did have the advantage of allowing some remedial flexibility. This point is noted by Lord Phillips at [161]. It will be difficult in instances other than common mistake as to the existence of the subject matter to obtain relief, absent other possible forms of relief such as misrepresentation, since the test in *Bell v Lever Bros.* to determine whether a contract is void is notoriously narrow. In any event, if the contract is void, it will be an 'all or nothing' remedy. There are two points that can be made relating to this.

(a) Instances of initial impossibility are limited and it is likely that the risk of the event will have been allocated by the contract. It might therefore be suggested that there are likely to be few claims based only on common mistake (although a review of recent contract case law does not lend much support to such a conclusion).

(b) As Lord Phillips suggests, legislation may be necessary to provide for some adjustment to the parties' positions (bearing in mind that initial impossibility should be discovered reasonably quickly and that any adjustment to the parties' positions may not be significant) and/or the courts are likely to seek other avenues to achieve the desired remedial relief.

6. *Great Peace* confirms that, in determining whether a contract is void for common mistake as to quality at common law, the test is that expounded by Lord Atkin in *Bell v Lever Bros.* of essential difference and that this is a matter of contractual construction. However, this assessment is inevitably one of fact and it will be difficult to advise in individual cases whether performance will be 'essentially different'. In addition, the Court of Appeal in *Great Peace* appeared to have reformulated the 'essential difference' test in terms similar to the test for identification of a frustratory event—namely, whether performance as originally agreed is impossible. If this were limited to performance in accordance with the contract terms, it would effectively deny the possibility that the contract might ever be void for common mistake as to quality. However, the test does extend to a consideration of whether the contractual adventure is still possible.

7. In *Champion Investments Ltd v Ahmed* [2004] EWHC 1956 (QB), Blair QC concluded that the mistake in the parties' understanding as to the applicable rate of interest (i) was not essentially different from the position as the parties believed it to be, *and* (ii) did not render performance of the contract impossible. This suggests that the applicable test may require further clarification, if these are indeed cumulative hurdles.

8. The decision of the Court of Appeal in *EIC Services Ltd v Phipps* [2004] EWCA Civ 1069, [2005] 1 WLR 1377, suggested that the effect of the *Great Peace* 'impossibility test' for common mistakes had, in a practical sense, limited the doctrine's application to cases of total failure of consideration, such as *res extincta* or *res sua*.

The test has been expressed in a number of different ways. Leggatt J in *Dana Gas PJSC v Dana Gas Sukuk Ltd* [2017] EWHC 2982 (Comm), [2018] 1 Lloyd's Rep 177, put the matter in this way:

> 65 The second reason why most arguments of mistake fail is that the doctrine only applies if the mistake is sufficiently fundamental. Two different formulations of this requirement have been approved. One is that the mistake in question has rendered the contract 'impossible of performance'. The other is that the mistake 'must render the subject-matter of the contract essentially and radically different from the subject-matter which the parties believed to exist'. The two approaches may essentially amount to the same thing: see *Kyle Bay Ltd (t/a Astons Nightclub) v Underwriters subscribing under Policy No 019057/08/01* [2007] EWCA Civ 57, paras 24–25.

The following cases demonstrate that there are different ways of formulating the test, but that ultimately the outcome is fact-sensitive.

Triple Seven MSN 27251 Ltd v Azman Air Services Ltd
[2018] EWHC 1348 (Comm)

The claimants leased two aircraft to the defendant by an agreement dated 20 June 2016, it being understood that the aircraft were to be used to transport passengers from West Africa to Saudi Arabia for the Hajj and Umrah pilgrimages. On 15 June 2016 the National Hajj Commission of Nigeria (NAHCON) wrote to the defendant informing it that the General Authority of Civil Aviation of Saudi Arabia (GACA) had excluded Amzan from the 2016 airlift. The defendant received the letter some hours after signing the lease agreements. The defendant refused to pay hire and argued that the leases were void for common mistake.

Held: Applying the reasoning in *Dana Gas*, the leases were valid.

> PETER MACDONALD EGGERS QC:
> 76 Drawing these considerations together, the elements of a common mistake which has the effect of rendering the contract based on that common mistake void are as follows:
> (1) There must have been, at the time of the conclusion of the contract, an assumption as to the existence of a state of affairs substantially shared between the parties.
> (2) The assumption itself must have been fundamental to the contract.
> (3) That assumption must have been wrong at the time of the conclusion of the contract.
> (4) By reason of the assumption being wrong, the contract or its performance would be essentially and radically different from what the parties believed to be the case at the time of the conclusion of the contract; alternatively, the contract must be impossible to perform having regard to or in accordance with the common assumption. In other words, there must be a fundamental difference between the assumed and actual states of affairs.
> (5) The parties, or at least the party relying on the common mistake, would not have entered into the contract had the parties been aware that the common assumption was wrong.
> (6) The contract must not have made provision in the event that the common assumption was mistaken.
> . . .

86 The parties entered into the lease agreements on the assumptions that (1) NAHCON had provided its approval for Azman's participation in the 2016 Hajj airlift, (2) GACA might or might not provide its approval, (3) Azman expected to obtain GACA's approval, and (4) GACA had not yet made its decision whether to provide its approval.

87 In fact, at the time when the lease agreements were concluded, GACA had made its decision to exclude Azman from the 2016 Hajj airlift. In those circumstances, the third and fourth of the assumptions referred to above, namely Azman's expectation that it would obtain GACA's approval and that GACA had not yet made its decision, were wrong. In those circumstances, in my judgment, there was a mistake as to an existing state of affairs. I do not accept Mr Midwinter QC's submission that this amounted to no more than a misprediction. If GACA had made its decision after the lease agreements had been concluded, I would have acceded to the submission that there was no mistaken assumption as to an existing state of affairs, but in circumstances where GACA had already made its decision some five days before the lease agreements were concluded, the position is otherwise.

88 Further, I also reject the Claimants' submission that the mistake was attributable to Azman's fault. Based on the evidence, prior to the lease agreements being executed, Azman had been candid with the Claimants as to the then current status of the approvals obtained and not obtained for Azman's participation in the 2016 Hajj airlift . . .

89 However, I consider that the mistaken assumption shared by the parties was not sufficiently fundamental to the lease agreements and did not render the lease agreements essentially and radically different from what the parties understood or impossible to perform, so as to render the lease agreements void at common law . . .

91 Even if I had concluded that the shared mistaken assumption was sufficiently fundamental and/or rendered the lease agreements essentially and radically different from what the parties understood or impossible to perform, I would nevertheless also have concluded that the lease agreements allocated the risk of not obtaining GACA's approval to be borne by Azman, not the Claimants, with the result that the lease agreements are not void.

Apvodedo NV v Collins
[2008] EWHC 775 (Ch)

This case involved an application for summary judgment for money alleged to be owed under a contract with the defendant for the release of £1 million. The defendant (Collins) required this sum in order to secure the release of documentation relating to a purported sale of the Ritz Hotel from parties claiming to act for the hotel's owners. The terms of the agreement with the claimant required that, on completion of the purchase, the defendant would resell the hotel to the claimant. In addition, if the documentation had not been received by a specified date, the agreement required the defendant to repay the £1 million. The £1 million was paid, but it later transpired that there was no planned sale of the hotel, and that the intention had been to defraud the claimant and defendant. The defendant claimed that it should not be liable under the terms of its agreement with the claimant, since the agreement was void for common mistake, i.e. that, contrary to the parties' assumptions, there was no sale documentation for the hotel, and the agreement was subject to an implied condition precedent that there was such documentation and that the parties acting had authority to negotiate the sale of the hotel. The claimant alleged that this argument must fail since there was a provision for the express allocation of this risk in the agreement, i.e. the defendant would have to repay the £1 million.

Held: The application for summary judgment was refused because there was a need for a proper trial of the issues in the context of the factual matrix.

Henderson J made some interesting comments concerning the impossibility test in *Great Peace* and the re-emergence to prominence of the principle in *Associated Japanese Bank*.

> HENDERSON J: 43. Taking the elements of common mistake identified in paragraph 76 of *Great Peace* [extracted at *p. 619*], element (i) would clearly be satisfied because there would have been a common assumption as to the existence of a state of affairs. Element (ii) would raise the question whether the parties intended the allocation of the risk of non-production of the documents in clause 10.2 to be unqualified, or whether it was predicated upon the truth of the common assumption. As to element (iii), nobody suggests that the non-existence of the state of affairs was attributable to the fault of any party to the Exclusivity Agreement. Element (iv), if read literally, would still not be satisfied, because it would still be possible for Mr Collins to pay the £1 million. However, *Associated Japanese* shows that there are cases where a defence of common mistake can succeed even though performance of the relevant contractual obligation is possible (in that case payment by a bank under a guarantee). This suggests that the true test may rather be whether the non-existence of the state of affairs renders performance of the contract *in accordance with the common assumption* impossible. Finally, the state of affairs (namely the existence of a genuine vendor and of the Documentation) would arguably be circumstances which had to subsist if performance of the contractual adventure was to be possible. Again, much would depend on precisely how the 'contractual adventure' was identified, and here too *Associated Japanese* might help Mr Collins to surmount this hurdle.

NOTES

1. There is no reported evidence that the case went to trial.

2. These comments suggest that the 'contractual adventure' or purpose of the contract (i.e. a construction question) may be one method of increasing the possibility for a finding of impossibility, i.e. the 'contractual adventure' may include an assumption about the existence of a state of affairs (albeit that this encourages evidence of how important this matter is to the parties, e.g. the evidence in *Great Peace* that the purpose was not immediately considered lost since the charter was not cancelled as soon as the true position was known). Alternatively, reliance on *Associated Japanese Bank* so that the existence of a particular fact or subject matter is considered to be an implied (or even an express) condition precedent to performance, rather than being considered merely a quality of that subject matter, will permit a conclusion that the contract is void where that fact or subject matter does not exist in accordance with the parties' common assumptions. This blurs the distinction between subject matter and the identification of qualities or attributes associated with the subject matter, and seems to move the distinction to an assessment of the importance attached by the parties to a factor or state of affairs. It is also not at all clear that Lord Phillips in *Great Peace* envisaged such an argument in these circumstances: see the discussion of the implied condition precedent argument at page 393, *8.4.4.1*.

8.4.5.5 The *Great Peace* test in the context of compromise agreements

By comparison, the evidence is that the courts will be less accommodating to an argument based on a common mistaken assumption concerning contract A that would have the effect of upsetting an agreement to compromise a claim based on that contract (contract B).

Brennan v Bolt Burdon
[2004] EWCA Civ 1017, [2005] QB 303 (CA)

The claimant's claim for damages for personal injury was issued on 7 June 2001, four months before the limitation period expired, and purportedly served on the defendants on 6 October. A judge held that it was served outside the limitation period on 8 October. Accordingly, the claimant agreed to compromise the claim. However, the case in which the decision on service had been made was subsequently overruled and the claimant successfully appealed the judge's decision that the claim form had been served out of time. The defendants applied to stay the proceedings, alleging that there was a binding contractual compromise. The claimant alleged that the compromise agreement was void for a common mistake of law.

The Court of Appeal accepted that a mistake of law is capable of rendering a contract void—*Kleinwort Benson Ltd v Lincoln City Council* [1999] 2 AC 359 applied in this context—but said that there would not be a mistake as to law if the law were merely in doubt, and, on these facts, the parties could have discovered that the relevant decision was being appealed. When entering into compromise agreements, each party accepted the risk that its own view of the law might turn out to be mistaken. Sedley LJ considered, at [64], that 'this shift [in the law] cannot be allowed to undo a compromise of litigation entered into in the knowledge both of how the law now stood and of the fact—for it is always a fact—that it might not remain so'. (Thus, there is a considerable policy influence in this decision.)

It was a question of construction as to whether a mistake rendered the contract void and, in any event, it was doubtful that a mistake of law would be capable of passing the applicable test in *Great Peace*—namely, whether the mistake rendered the agreed performance (or contractual adventure) impossible. This was not a case of impossibility of performance, since the compromise was at all times performable.

Sedley LJ expressed some difficulty with this test in the context of mistakes of law and considered that 'a different test may be necessary'. He considered, at [60], that: 'The equivalent question needs to be whether, had the parties appreciated that the law was what it is now known to be, there would still have been an intelligible basis for their agreement.'
In the next case, however, the Court of Appeal considered that, in the context of compromise agreements, the preferable test was one of 'essential difference' rather than strict contractual impossibility, albeit that it was recognized that the Court of Appeal in *Great Peace* had equated these tests.

Kyle Bay Ltd (T/A Astons Nightclub) v Underwriters Subscribing Under Policy Number 019057/08/01
[2007] EWCA Civ 57, [2007] 1 CLC 164 (CA)

When a nightclub was destroyed by fire, it became clear to the appellants (nightclub owners) that a different type of insurance cover was in place from that requested by them and they were advised to agree to compromise the claim for £205,000—about a third less than the figure to which they would have been entitled had the cover applied for in fact been in place. They therefore entered into a compromise agreement with the respondent underwriters on this basis. However, it later transpired that the nightclub's policy had been of the type requested, so that a larger sum should have been payable under the claim, and that the settlement had been entered into on the basis of a mistake. Thus, as in *Brennan v Bolt Burdon*, this case also concerned the validity of a compromise agreement.

Held: The mistake was not sufficient to render the compromise agreement void. This was because, since the settlement compromise remained capable of performance at all times, the subject matter was not rendered 'essentially and radically different' by the mistake.

NEUBERGER LJ [Wilson and Ward LJJ agreeing]:

The case on mistake

20 On this issue, the facts are simple and were not in dispute before the Judge. The settlement for the claimant's business interruption claim against the defendant underwriters was settled at about £205,000

on the common assumption that the Policy was not declaration-linked, whereas it was so linked, and, had the parties been aware of this, they would (I assume for present purposes) have settled at a figure about 50% higher.

21 As the Judge said, the leading modern case in which the circumstances in which a common mistake can vitiate a contract were considered was the decision of this court in *Great Peace Shipping Ltd v Tsavliris Salvage (International) Ltd* [2002] EWCA Civ 1407; [2003] 2 CLC 16. Relying on what Lord Phillips of Worth Matravers MR (giving the judgment of the court) said at paragraphs [73] to [76], the Judge held that the proper test to apply in this case was whether the mistake in question rendered the contract in issue 'impossible of performance' (the expression also used by Lord Phillips when ultimately formulating the critical question in the *Great Peace* case itself at paragraph [162]). At least on the face of it, it seems difficult to quarrel with the Judge's view that, if that is the right test, it was self-evidently not satisfied here.

22 [Counsel] for the claimant runs as his main argument the contention that this test was inappropriate in a case such as this; his alternative argument is that the test, if properly applied, was in any event satisfied here. I should in this context refer to the decision of this court in *Brennan v Bolt Burdon* [2004] EWCA Civ 1017; [2005] QB 303. In that case, a personal injuries action was settled on the common assumption that the claim form had been served out of time, and a subsequent decision of this court showed that that assumption was wrong. The claimant unsuccessfully sought to impeach the settlement.

23 In paragraph [22] of his judgment, Maurice Kay LJ gave three reasons why the *Great Peace* decision gave rise to difficulties for the claimant, the first of which was that it was 'quite simply not a case of impossibility of performance. The compromise has at all times remained performable . . .' Sedley LJ, however, was more concerned about the application of the 'impossibility of performance' test in cases of common mistake of law—see at paragraphs [60] to [61]. At the end of paragraph [59], he had identified the 'difficulty . . . in seeing how the effect of [a common mistake of law . . . on an agreement by which litigation is compromised] can be equiparated with the impossibility of a contractual venture'. The third member of the court, Bodey J, did not discuss this aspect.

24 In my opinion, it is unnecessary for us on this appeal to decide which view is preferable. Indeed, I suspect that ultimately, the two approaches may essentially amount to the same thing. If the doubts of Sedley LJ are justified, then, as [counsel] argues, the right test is that propounded by Steyn J in *Associated Japanese Bank (International) Ltd v Credit du Nord SA* [1989] 1 WLR 255. In a passage at p. 268F, cited and expressly approved in the *Great Peace* case at paragraphs [90] and [91], Steyn J said that, in order to vitiate a contract, 'the mistake must render the subject matter of the contract essentially and radically different from the subject matter which the parties believed to exist'. He justified this at p. 268E on the basis that 'the law ought to uphold rather than destroy apparent contracts'.

25 It appears to me that, by approving Steyn J's observations and by applying the 'impossible to perform' test, this court in the *Great Peace* case must have considered that the two approaches amounted to much the same thing. In practice, the concept of impossibility of performance, at least in a case such as this, can be said to raise an issue of definition: if one defines the contract as the assessment of compensation under a declaration-linked policy, then it is, at least in a sense, impossible to perform if both parties negotiate on the basis that the policy is not declaration-linked. It seems to me, therefore, that there is much to be said for applying, as [counsel] argues we should, Steyn J's test in the *Associated Japanese Bank* case in the instant case.

26 In my judgment, applying that approach, the mistake in this case did not render what the parties believed to be the 'subject matter of the [Settlement agreement] essentially and radically different' from what it actually was . . .

NOTE Although the amount recovered under the terms of the compromise was significantly different from the amount that should have been payable, this did not result in the compromise being 'essentially and radically different'. It is interesting to compare the approach of the American courts, where a difference in monetary value can be a relevant consideration: *Sherwood v Walker*, 66 Mich 568 (1887), 33 NW 919 (Supreme Court of Michigan) (*page 397, 8.4.5.2*).

8.4.5.6 A case of confused principles

Graves v Graves
[2007] EWCA Civ 660, [2007] 3 FCR 26, [2008] HLR 10 (CA)

An ex-husband had agreed to let his ex-wife live as a tenant in a house that he owned on the basis that 90 per cent of the rent would be paid through housing benefit. Both parties had reasonably assumed that the ex-wife was entitled to this benefit. However, she was not and, because she was unable to pay the rent, the ex-husband brought proceedings for possession.

Held: To conclude that there was an implied condition that the tenancy contract would end if housing benefit were not payable, it needed to be shown that the tenancy was impossible to perform (obviously not the case) or 'essentially and radically different' in kind. The court concluded that, since the tenancy was made on the basis that 90 per cent of the rent would be covered by housing benefit and that basis did not in fact exist, the agreement was different in kind from that originally contemplated, so that the condition could be implied. The court then went on to adjust the parties' positions in relation to the deposit and the rent paid for occupation in the interim.

NOTES

1. The Court of Appeal therefore considered that, although the impossibility test was not satisfied, the essential difference test was. This suggests that the tests may not be equated in some contexts.

2. This is a very strange decision and must be unreliable. The decision, on the facts, appears to be motivated by policy considerations, but the choice of principle is remarkable. It would have been far easier to have applied the principles determining implication of a contractual term (as applied by Steyn J in Associated Japanese Bank to identify an implied condition precedent) than to seek to show either impossibility or essential difference (as traditionally understood), which are tests applicable when alleging that a contract is void for common mistake as to quality.

3. In addition, mistake is a strange argument to attempt where the court wishes to make an adjustment to the parties' positions, i.e. to ensure that the wife could not recover her deposit and rent paid, since a finding that the contract is void would rule out such adjustments. This curious approach demonstrates some confusion of principle. The court ought to have approached this as an argument based on implication of a term that the agreement would be determined if it were to transpire that housing benefit was not payable, i.e. a condition subsequent. This would have resulted in the contract being determined for the future, so that past rent could not have been recovered.

8.4.6 The relationship between common mistake and frustration

Although common mistake relates to the formation of a contract and renders it void *ab initio*, and frustration (*Chapter 12*) relates to its discharge, the same issue is raised—namely, the allocation of the risk of an extraneous event between two parties.

Amalgamated Investment & Property Co. Ltd v John Walker & Sons Ltd
[1977] 1 WLR 164 (CA)

In July 1973, the claimants agreed to purchase some commercial property belonging to the defendants, which had been advertised as suitable for redevelopment at a price of £1,710,000. The defendants were aware that the claimants wished to redevelop the property. In the pre-contractual inquiries, the claimants specifically asked the defendants whether the property was designated as a building of special architectural or historic interest. On 14 August, the defendants replied that it was not, but, unknown to both parties, the Department of the Environment had included the property in a list of buildings proposed to be designated as being of special architectural or historical interest. The parties signed the contract of sale on 25 September; the next day, the Department of the Environment informed the defendant that the property was to be listed. The listing in fact took place on 27 September and resulted in the property being worth £1,500,000 less than the contract price. The claimants sought to have the contract set aside on the basis of mistake, or alternatively argued that the listing had frustrated the contract.

Held: This was not a case to which common mistake could apply, since that mistake had to exist at the date of the contract. The property was not listed at the date of the contract (25 September). Rejecting the frustration argument, the Court of Appeal held, applying *Davis Contractors v Fareham Urban District Council* [1956] UKHL 3 (*page 636, 13.3.1*), that performance of the contract following the listing was not radically different from the performance contemplated by the parties; it was merely economically disadvantageous. The risk of a property becoming listed was an inherent risk that was to be borne by the purchaser. The claimants had even asked about this possibility.

SIR JOHN PENNYCUICK: 1. *Mistake.* At the date of the contract, namely September 25, 1973, the property had not in fact been listed. The parties were therefore under no mistake in believing that the property was not subject to any existing fetter in this respect. [Counsel for the plaintiffs] accepts that, but contends that there was a common mistake, that mistake arising from the belief of the parties that the property was ripe for development, i.e. (as he puts it) suitable for and capable of development, whereas in truth it was not ripe for development because the listing of the property was then pending and would prevent development. It is certainly true that knowledge that the listing of the property was under consideration in the office concerned would vitally affect the minds of the parties negotiating the purchase of the property . . . The mere possibility that the property would be listed would certainly affect the mind of anybody contemplating a purchase of the property and considering what price he was prepared to pay. I think, however, that the mere possibility or probability, be it small or great, of some future event occurring is too uncertain to be taken into account in considering whether the belief of the parties as to ripeness for development should be treated as mistaken. The purchaser of property takes subject to the risk of future events, and it is for him to evaluate these risks in considering whether to buy and at what price. The possibility of listing is inherent in any building today and represents to my mind precisely such a risk . . .

2. *Frustration.* The contract dated September 25, 1973, is a contract for the sale and purchase of a specified property at a specified price. Certainly the purpose of the plaintiffs was to develop the property, and the plaintiffs would not have paid a fraction of the price which they contracted to pay if they had known that the property would not be available for development. Again certainly, the defendants knew the plaintiffs' purpose and knew that the price would have been much less if the plaintiffs had known that the property would not be available for development, even if the plaintiffs had been willing to purchase at all. But, on the other hand, it was not a term or condition of the contract that the property should continue to be available for development at the date of completion; nor, I think, can such a condition be implied into the contract. The subject matter of the contract is simply a specified piece of land described in the contract and nothing more. Can it then be said that listing before completion frustrated the contract?

We were referred to *Davis Contractors Ltd v Fareham Urban District Council* [1956] AC 696, in the House of Lords, in particular to the speech of Lord Radcliffe [see an extract from the judgment at *page 636,*

13.3.1] . . . The listing struck down the value of the property as might a fire or a compulsory purchase order or a number of other events. It seems to me, however, that the listing did not in any respect prevent the contract from being carried to completion according to its terms; that is to say, by payment of the balance of the purchase price and by conveyance of the property. The property is none the less the same property by reason that listing imposed a fetter on its use. It seems to me impossible to bring the circumstances of the present case within the test enunciated by Lord Radcliffe. One cannot say that the circumstances in which performance, i.e. completion, will be called for would render that performance a thing radically different from that which was undertaken by the contract. On the contrary, completion, according to the terms of the contract, would be exactly what the purchaser promised to do, and of course the vendors.

? **QUESTION**

Why did the listing not take place when the decision to list was made? In *Griffith v Brymer* (1903) 19 TLR 434 (see page *616*), the relevant time was taken to be the point at which the decision to cancel the procession was made.

NOTE The date of the listing determined the applicable legal treatment. If it had been accepted as a common mistake as to quality, at the time of this decision the contract could have been set aside in equity on terms: *Solle v Butcher* [1950] 1 KB 671. This might have permitted greater flexibility than a finding that the contract was frustrated, followed by statutory adjustment of the parties' positions under the Law Reform (Frustrated Contracts) Act 1943. As a result of the decision in *Great Peace Shipping Ltd v Tsavliris Salvage (International) Ltd* [2002] EWCA Civ 1407, [2003] QB 679 (see *page 397, 8.4.5.2*), in which *Solle v Butcher* was not followed, there is no such flexibility in terms of the legal effect of such a mistake. At common law, such a mistake would render the contract void. Therefore, greater remedial flexibility is permitted under the rules applicable to frustration.

8.5 Document mistakes

8.5.1 Rectification

The court may be asked to rectify a written document to reflect accurately what the parties in fact agreed. (This is an exception to the parol evidence rule—*page 179*, 5.2.1—since oral evidence is admissible to show the error in the written document.) Denning LJ, as he then was, explained in the next case that '[i]n order to get rectification it is necessary to show that the parties were in complete agreement on the terms of their contract, but by an error wrote them down wrongly'.

Frederick E. Rose (London) Ltd v William H. Pim Junior & Co. Ltd
[1953] 2 QB 450 (CA)

Buyers asked the claimants to supply them with 'Moroccan horsebeans described as feveroles'. The claimants did not know what feveroles were, but were informed by the defendants that feveroles and horsebeans were the same thing. The claimants contracted with the defendants for the supply of 'horsebeans', which the claimants would then sell to the buyers, both parties believing that feveroles were just horsebeans. In fact, 'feveroles' were a superior type of horsebean, and the buyers had claimed damages from the claimants for not supplying 'feveroles'. The claimants wanted to have their written contract with the defendants rectified to read 'feveroles' (so that the defendants would have been in breach in supplying the wrong goods).

Held: The Court of Appeal refused to rectify the agreement, since the parties had agreed on the sale of horsebeans and the agreement correctly reflected this. The problem was that both parties mistakenly thought that horsebeans were feveroles.

DENNING LJ: Rectification is concerned with contracts and documents, not with intentions. In order to get rectification it is necessary to show that the parties were in complete agreement on the terms of their contract, but by an error wrote them down wrongly; and in this regard, in order to ascertain the terms of their contract, you do not look into the inner minds of the parties—into their intentions—any more than you do in the formation of any other contract. You look at their outward acts, that is, at what they said or wrote to one another in coming to their agreement, and then compare it with the document which they have signed. If you can predicate with certainty what their contract was, and that it is, by a common mistake, wrongly expressed in the document, then you rectify the document; but nothing less will suffice . . . There is a passage in *Crane v Hegeman-Harris Co. Inc.* ([1939] 1 All ER 662, 664), which suggests that a continuing common intention alone will suffice; but I am clearly of opinion that a continuing common intention is not sufficient unless it has found expression in outward agreement. There could be no certainty at all in business transactions if a party who had entered into a firm contract could afterwards turn round and claim to have it rectified on the ground that the parties intended something different. He is allowed to prove, if he can, that they *agreed something different*: see *Lovell & Christmas v Wall* ([1911] 104 LT 85, 88), per Lord Cozens-Hardy, MR, and per Buckley LJ (93) but not that they *intended* something different.

The present case is a good illustration of the distinction. The parties no doubt intended that the goods should satisfy the inquiry of the Egyptian buyers, namely, 'horsebeans described in Egypt as feveroles'. They assumed that they would do so, but they made no contract to that effect. Their agreement, as outwardly expressed, both orally and in writing, was for 'horsebeans'. That is all that the defendants ever committed themselves to supply, and all they should be bound to. There was, no doubt, an erroneous assumption underlying the contract—an assumption for which it might have been set aside on the ground of misrepresentation or mistake—but that is very different from an erroneous expression of the contract, such as to give rise to rectification.

NOTES

1. On the facts, there was a mistake as to quality and, at the time, it was recognized that a contract could be set aside on terms in equity for such a mistake. The Court of Appeal in *Great Peace Shipping Ltd v Tsavliris Salvage (International) Ltd* [2002] EWCA Civ 1407, [2003] QB 679, has since denied the existence of such an equitable jurisdiction. However, on the facts in *Rose v Pim*, the remedy of rescission for mistake in equity was barred, since the buyers and sub-buyers had accepted the goods.

2. The Court of Appeal in *Joscelyne v Nissen* [1970] 2 QB 86 made it clear that *Rose v Pim* was not authority for the fact that an antecedent complete concluded contract is required for rectification. Russell LJ stated, at p. 97B, that *Rose v Pim* 'only shows that prior accord on a term or the meaning of a phrase to be used must have been outwardly expressed or communicated between the parties'.

3. In *FSHC Group Holdings Ltd v GLAS Trust Corp. Ltd* [2019] EWCA Civ 1361, [2020] 2 WLR 429 the Court of Appeal was of the view that the law had moved on since *Rose v Pim*, and that it has now been recognized that rectification is available where the words of the document were purposely used but it was mistakenly considered that they bore a different meaning from their correct meaning as a matter of true construction. *Rose v Pim* was to be explained on the basis that the contract of which rectification was sought was part of a chain of contracts involving third parties but that it was impossible to rectify the others and so it would be unfair to rectify this contract.

Joscelyne v Nissen
[1970] 2 QB 86 (CA)

The claimant father and his daughter, the defendant, shared a house owned by the daughter. They agreed that the father was to transfer his car hire business to his daughter; in return, the daughter was to pay him a weekly pension and pay certain household expenses, such as gas, electricity, and coal bills. However, the contract specified that she was to 'discharge all expenses in connection with the whole premise . . . and shall indemnify [the claimant] from and against any claim arising in respect of the same'. The claimant sought rectification of this contract to provide for the payment of gas, electricity, and coal bills on the basis that this reflected what had been orally agreed between the parties during negotiations. At first instance, the judge had found that, although there was no complete concluded antecedent agreement, the agreement should be rectified.

Held (in the Court of Appeal): Dismissing the appeal, it was not necessary to find a concluded contract antecedent to the agreement. Rectification could be ordered as long as there was a common continuing intention (objectively ascertained) regarding a particular provision.

RUSSELL LJ: [Russell LJ referred to the following statement by Simonds J in *Crane v Hegeman-Harris Co. Inc.* [1939] 1 All ER 662, 664:]

. . . [I]in order that this court may exercise its jurisdiction to rectify a written instrument, it is not necessary to find a concluded and binding contract between the parties antecedent to the agreement which it is sought to rectify . . . [I]t is sufficient to find a common continuing intention in regard to a particular provision or aspect of the agreement. If one finds that, in regard to a particular point, the parties were in agreement up to the moment when they executed their formal instrument, and the formal instrument does not conform with that common agreement, then this court has jurisdiction to rectify, although it may be that there was, until the formal instrument was executed, no concluded and binding contract between the parties . . .

Secondly, I want to say this upon the principle of the jurisdiction. It is a jurisdiction which is to be exercised only upon convincing proof that the concluded instrument does not represent the common intention of the parties. That is particularly the case where one finds prolonged negotiations between the parties eventually assuming the shape of a formal instrument in which they have been advised by their respective skilled legal advisers. The assumption is very strong in such a case that the instrument does represent their real intention, and it must be only upon proof which Lord Eldon, I think, in a somewhat picturesque phrase described as 'irrefragable' that the court can act. I would rather, I think, say that the court can only act if it is satisfied beyond all reasonable doubt that the instrument does not represent their common intention, and is further satisfied as to what their common intention was. For let it be clear that it is not sufficient to show that the written instrument does not represent their common intention unless positively also one can show what their common intention was. It is in the light of those principles that I must examine the facts of this somewhat complicated case.

In our judgment the law is as expounded by Simonds J in *Crane's* case with the qualification that some outward expression of accord is required.

NOTE In *Chartbrook v Persimmon Homes Ltd* [2009] UKHL 38, [2009] 1 AC 1101 (*page 245, 5.5.5*) Lord Hoffmann considered that it would be sufficient if the parties had a common continuing intention, objectively assessed, in respect of which rectification was sought. In order to get rectification, it had to be shown that the parties were in complete agreement on the terms of their contract, but by an error wrote them down wrongly. This could be demonstrated on the facts in this case by reliance on pre-contractual letters as an outward expression of the continuing common intention. Had it been necessary, Persimmon would have been entitled to rectification on this basis. The objective test was applied with some reluctance in *Daventry District Council v Daventry and District Housing Ltd* [2011] EWCA Civ 1153, [2012] 1 WLR 1333, [2012] Bus LR 485, but was rejected by the Court of Appeal in *FSHC Group Holdings Ltd v GLAS Trust Corp. Ltd* [2019] EWCA Civ 1361, [2020] 2 WLR 429.

Mistake

FSHC Group Holdings Ltd v GLAS Trust Corp. Ltd
[2019] EWCA Civ 1361, [2020] 2 WLR 429

The claimant sought rectification of two deeds executed on 18 November 2016. The purpose of the deeds was to provide security which the claimant had previously agreed to provide in connection with a corporate acquisition which took place in 2012. The security had been omitted by oversight and was spotted on a review of the documentation in 2016. By mistake, the deeds did not merely provide the missing security, but also led to the claimant acceding to two pre-existing security agreements imposing additional and onerous obligations. The judge found that the common intention of the parties had been merely to fill the gap. The defendant argued that the test for rectification was objective; namely, to identify the intention of the parties as an objective observer would have thought it to be. The claimant argued that the test was subjective, so that the judge's finding was one of fact against which there could be no appeal rather than a point of law against which there could be an appeal.

Held: The test was subjective and not objective, so the judge's decision was on a point of fact and not law so that there was no basis for an appeal to the Court of Appeal.

LEGGATT LJ:

The traditional approach of courts of equity

51. The jurisdiction of the Court of Chancery to correct mistakes in written instruments by rectification can be traced back to its roots in canon and Roman law. Cases in which the remedy was recognised can be found in the sixteenth and seventeenth centuries. In the middle of the eighteenth century, in *Henkle v Royal Exchange Assurance Co* (1749) 1 Ves S 317, 318, Lord Hardwicke LC sitting in the Court of Chancery was in 'no doubt, that this court has jurisdiction to relieve in respect of a plain mistake in contracts in writing as well as against frauds in contracts: so that if reduced into writing contrary to intent of the parties, on proper proof that would be rectified.' In *Shelburne v Inchiquin* (1784) 1 Bro CC 336, 341, on a claim to rectify a written agreement made in contemplation of marriage, Lord Thurlow LC considered it 'impossible to refuse, as incompetent, parol evidence, which goes to prove, that the words taken down in writing were contrary to the current intention of all parties.' These statements of principle were approved by Lord Eldon LC in *Townshend v Stangroom* (1801) 6 Ves 328, 333. Half a century later in *Fowler v Fowler* (1859) 4 De G & J 250, 264, Lord Chelmsford LC said:

> The power which the court possesses of reforming written agreements where there has been an omission or insertion of stipulations contrary to the intention of the parties and under a mutual mistake is one which has been frequently and most usefully exercised.

52. There can be no doubt that where, in these and other cases in which rectification was claimed, judges referred to the 'intention' of the parties, they were referring to what the parties actually intended. Indeed, the use of the term 'intention' to refer to what an 'objective' observer would reasonably have understood the parties' intention to be from their communications (irrespective of their actual states of mind) is, we believe, a comparatively recent legal artefact. That the court was concerned on a claim for rectification of a written contract (or other instrument) to identify what the parties actually intended its terms to be is confirmed by the fact that they were allowed, and indeed expected, to give evidence of what was in their minds when they executed the document.

. . .

The antecedent contract theory

56. Notwithstanding this long line of authority, there developed in the second part of the nineteenth century and early twentieth century what eventually became a 'formidable array of judicial opinion' (per

Buckley LJ in *Joscelyne v Nissen* [1970] 2 QB 86, 93) in support of the view that a contractual document could only be rectified in order to bring it into conformity with a contract that already existed before the document was executed and which the document failed accurately to record as a result of a mutual mistake. This view seems to have originated in the following statement of James V-C in *Mackenzie v Coulson* (1869) LR 8 Eq 368, 375:

> Courts of Equity do not rectify contracts; they may and do rectify instruments purporting to have been made in pursuance of the terms of contracts. But it is always necessary for a plaintiff to show that there was an actual concluded contract antecedent to the instrument which is sought to be rectified; and that such contract is inaccurately represented in the instrument.

. . .

Rose v Pim: the 'horsebeans' case

63. The 'lost cause' (per Buckley LJ in *Joscelyne v Nissen* [1970] 2 QB 86, 91) of *Lovell & Christmas Ltd v Wall* was re-discovered in *Frederick E Rose (London) Ltd v William H Pim Jnr & Co Ltd* [1953] 2 QB 450. This was the 'horsebeans' case, which 'has amused generations of law students' (per Tadgell JA in *Club Cape Schanck Resort Co Ltd v Cape Country Club Pty Ltd* (2001) 3 VR 526, para 5). The plaintiffs, who were London merchants, had been asked by Egyptian buyers to supply 'feveroles'. Not knowing what this term meant, they asked the defendants' representative, who responded that 'feveroles' meant horsebeans. Relying on this information, the plaintiffs contracted to buy a quantity of horsebeans from the defendants, which they then sold on as 'feveroles' to the Egyptian buyers. To fulfil the contract, the defendants purchased 'horsebeans' from an Algerian supplier. There are in fact different varieties of horsebeans and those supplied were 'feves', which were less valuable than 'feveroles'. The Egyptian buyers claimed the difference in value as damages from the plaintiffs, who then sought to rectify their contract with the defendants by adding the word 'feveroles' after the references to 'horsebeans'. The judge granted rectification, but that decision was reversed by the Court of Appeal on the ground that the written contract correctly recorded what the parties had agreed.

64. A passage in the judgment of Denning LJ (at 461) has since been relied on, most importantly in the *Chartbrook* case, as expounding an objective approach to rectification:

> Rectification is concerned with contracts and documents, not with intentions. In order to get rectification it is necessary to show that the parties were in complete agreement on the terms of their contract, but by an error wrote them down wrongly; and in this regard, in order to ascertain the terms of their contract, you do not look into the inner minds of the parties – into their intentions – any more than you do in the formation of any other contract. You look at their outward acts, that is, at what they said or wrote to one another in coming to their agreement, and then compare it with the document which they have signed. If you can predicate with certainty what their contract was, and that it is, by a common mistake, wrongly expressed in the document, then you rectify the document; but nothing less will suffice.

The need for an 'outward expression of accord'

72. *Joscelyne v Nissen* clearly and authoritatively established that a prior concluded contract is not necessary for rectification and that a common intention continuing at the time when a contract is made is sufficient, subject only to the qualification that some 'outward expression of accord' is required. That qualification did no more than spell out the sense in which, as discussed earlier, Simonds J in *Crane's* case used the phrase 'common intention' to refer to what he also called the 'common agreement' of the parties or the 'true consensus of their minds'—in other words, an intention which the parties not only each held but understood each other to share as a result of communication between them. The same principle was stated by Buckley LJ in *Lovell & Christmas Ltd v Wall* (1911) 104 LT 85, 93, . . . when he said:

> For rectification it is not enough to set about to find what one or even both of the parties to the contract intended. What you have to find out is what intention was communicated by one side to the other, and with what common intention and common agreement they made their bargain.

By insisting on the requirement of an outward expression of accord, the Court of Appeal was thus making clear that it is not sufficient for rectification to prove that each party privately and independently had the same intention as the other with regard to a particular provision of their contract. There can be no common intention of a kind with which the written contract can justifiably be made to conform if the relevant intentions remained 'locked separately in the breast of each party' without being communicated by each party to the other. At the same time, the judgment in *Joscelyne v Nissen* makes it equally clear that the insistence on an outward expression of accord does not supplant or detract from the need to establish what the parties actually intended the relevant term of the contract (or its effect) to be. The Court of Appeal was not suggesting that only outward appearances are relevant for rectification and that, provided they appear outwardly to be in agreement, the actual intentions of the parties do not matter. On the contrary, the unequivocal holding in *Joscelyne v Nissen* that the law was correctly stated by Simonds J in *Crane's* case leaves no room for doubt that, in order to find a common intention, it is necessary to establish what was in the minds of the parties. As we have outlined and as was considered in detail in the *Shipley* case, which was then approved in *Crane's* case, that has always been the basis of the equitable remedy of rectification. The essence of the remedy is that, in a proper case where there is shown to have been a real mistake, the terms of a written contract (or other document) should be reformed in order to give effect to the parties' real intention.

. . .

Uncommunicated intentions

75. The decision in *Joscelyne v Nissen* was not received with universal approval. Shortly after it was decided, Mr Leonard Bromley QC in an article published in the Law Quarterly Review argued that the Court of Appeal was wrong to require an 'outward expression of accord' and that all that is required for rectification is:

> the establishment of the subjective intention of the party or of the parties to the instrument (in the latter case an identical intention). Intercommunication, however necessary in the common law of contract, properly plays no part either in the theory or in the practice of this equitable doctrine . . .

See L Bromley, 'Rectification in Equity' (1971) 87 LQR 532. Mr Bromley submitted that the presence or absence of an outward expression of accord 'may well go to whether the burden of proof can be discharged' but is not '*per se* a requirement of rectification'.

76. The suggestion that an outward expression of accord is not an absolute requirement for rectification but only of evidential value in proving the parties' intentions has also from time to time been made by others. It is endorsed in *Chitty on Contracts* (33rd Edn, 2018), vol 1, para 3-064, and was advanced by counsel for the Parent in their skeleton argument for this appeal. Apart from pension cases which we will consider shortly, the authority relied on in *Chitty* is *Munt v Beasley* [2006] EWCA Civ 370, para 36, where Mummery LJ expressed the view that an outward expression of accord, although established on the facts of that case, was not a strict legal requirement for rectification where the party resisting rectification had in fact admitted that his true state of belief when he entered into the transaction was the same as that of the other party. Mummery LJ saw the trend in recent cases as being 'to treat the expression "outward expression of accord" more as an evidential factor rather than a strict legal requirement in all cases of rectification.' The cases cited by Mummery LJ for this proposition, however, do not in our view support it. The only English authority cited which might at first blush appear to do so is *Gallaher v Gallaher Pensions Ltd* [2005] Pens LR 103, para 117. But that was a case involving a pension scheme where, as we are about to discuss, proof of a consensus established through communication between the parties is not required because the relevant transaction is not a contract. In any case, *Joscelyne v Nissen* clearly held

that it is essential for rectification of a written contract to show an agreement, not in the sense of a prior concluded contract but 'in the more general sense of an outwardly expressed accord of minds', and this requirement has been affirmed by the Court of Appeal on many subsequent occasions, as we will see.

77. We also consider that the requirement is sound in principle. As has often been observed, the power of the court to rectify a contractual document is not a power to make an agreement for the parties; it is a power to correct mistakes in recording what the parties have actually agreed. Moreover, the effect of rectification is not merely to prevent a party from enforcing the written terms of a contract: it is to alter those terms so as to establish legal rights and obligations which differ from those recorded in the original contractual document. Leaving aside for the time being cases of rectification for unilateral mistake, establishing new contractual rights and obligations in this way is only justified if they are founded on mutual agreement. Whether the test applied is subjective or objective, it is fundamental that contractual rights and obligations should be based on mutual assent which the parties have manifested to each other and not on uncommunicated intentions which happen, without the parties knowing it, to coincide. Thus, as noted in *Tartsinis v Navona Management Co* [2015] EWHC 57 (Comm), para 88, it would be capricious if a document which the parties have agreed as the formal record of their contract could be altered to make it conform to the private intention of a party just because, although unknown to that party at the time, it turns out that the other party had a similar intention. We agree with the answer implied to the following question posed by Campbell JA in the Australian case of *Ryledar Pty Ltd v Euphoric Pty Ltd* [2007] NSWCA 65; [2007] NSWLR 603 at para 315:

> If two negotiating parties each had a particular intention about the agreement they would enter, and their intentions were identical, but that intention was disclosed by neither of them, and they later entered [into] a document that did not accord with that intention, what would be the injustice or unconscientiousness in either of them enforcing the document according to its terms?

. . .

From *Joscelyne* to *Chartbrook*

98. In the 40 years after *Joscelyne v Nissen* was decided the requirements for rectification for common mistake laid down in that case were applied and re-affirmed by the Court of Appeal on several occasions in addition to the *Britoil* case. For example, in *Co-operative Insurance Society Ltd v Centremoor Ltd* [1983] 2 EGLR 52 at 53, Dillon LJ said:

> In view of the decision in *Joscelyne v Nissen* [1970] 2 QB 86, we can take it in this court . . . that a claimant for rectification has to show a common continuing intention of the parties, outwardly expressed or communicated between them, which is not reflected in the concluded instrument which they have executed, but does not have to show that that common continuing intention amounted to a complete concluded contract antecedent to the instrument which it is sought to have rectified. Such a common continuing intention is conveniently referred to as an 'agreement' in inverted commas.

99. In *Agip SpA v Navigazione Alta Italia SpA (The 'Nai Genova')* [1984] 1 Lloyd's Rep 353 at 359, Slade LJ (with whom Oliver and Robert Goff LJJ agreed) summarised the requirements in this way:

> First, there must be a common intention in regard to the particular provisions of the agreement in question, together with some outward expression of accord. Secondly, this common intention must continue up to the time of execution of the instrument. Thirdly, there must be clear evidence that the instrument as executed does not accurately represent the true agreement of the parties at the time of its execution. Fourthly, it must be shown that the instrument, if rectified as claimed, would accurately represent the true agreement of the parties at that time . . .

100. To similar effect, in *Swainland Builders Ltd v Freehold Properties Ltd* [2002] EWCA Civ 560; [2002] 2 EGLR 71, para 33, Peter Gibson LJ said that the party seeking rectification must show that:

(1) the parties had a common continuing intention, whether or not amounting to an agreement, in respect of a particular matter in the instrument to be rectified;
(2) there was an outward expression of accord;
(3) the intention continued at the time of the execution of the instrument sought to be rectified;
(4) by mistake, the instrument did not reflect that common intention.

101. This last summary of the requirements for rectification has often been cited. It was quoted with approval by Lord Hoffmann in the *Chartbrook* case (at para 48), though as we will shortly discuss the approach taken by Lord Hoffmann differs from that established by *Joscelyne v Nissen* and summarised in the *Swainland* case, which requires an actual common intention to be proved together with an outward expression of accord.

102. A yet further decision of the Court of Appeal which treated it as necessary to establish that both parties actually intended their written contract to contain a particular term as well as giving outward expression to that common intent is *The Demetra K* [2002] EWCA Civ 1070; [2002] 2 Lloyd's Rep 581, para 22. Lord Phillips MR (who gave the judgment of the court) cited in support of these requirements, in addition to *Joscelyne v Nissen*, the following statement of Lord Diplock in *American Airlines Inc v Hope* [1974] 2 Lloyds Rep 301, 307:

> Rectification is a remedy which is available where parties to a contract, intending to reproduce in a more formal document the terms of an agreement upon which they are already *ad idem*, use in that document words which are inapt to record the true agreement reached between them. The formal document may then be rectified so as to conform with the true agreement which it was intended to reproduce and enforced in its rectified form.

We think it clear that in this passage the expression 'true agreement' is being used to refer, not to a mere appearance of agreement, but to an actual '*consensus ad idem*' or what in *Joscelyne v Nissen* [1970] 2 QB 86, 97, the Court of Appeal described as an 'outwardly expressed accord of minds'.

Unilateral mistake

103. It has come to be accepted that the jurisdiction to rectify a written contract is not limited to cases where there was a common mistake and that in certain circumstances rectification may be granted even though at the time of execution of the contract only one of the parties was mistaken about its terms or effect. The development of the modern doctrine stems from the approval in *A Roberts & Co Ltd v Leicestershire County Council* [1961] Ch 555 of the following statement of principle in *Snell's Equity* (25th Edn, 1960) at 570:

> . . . a party is entitled to rectification of a contract upon proof that he believed a particular term to be included in the contract, and that the other party concluded the contract with the omission or a variation of that term in the knowledge that the first party believed the term to be included.

104. The precise scope of this principle remains controversial. But there is no doubt that it covers at least a case, such as the facts found in *Thomas Bates & Son Ltd v Wyndham's (Lingerie) Ltd* [1981] 1 WLR 505, where the parties had a common intention that each had communicated to the other but one party before executing the contract realised that the document did not give effect to that intention and changed their mind without telling the other party.

105. The recognition of this principle is consistent with the traditional rationale of rectification for common mistake and gives effect to the same underlying equity. In the case of common mistake it is

inequitable for a party to the contract to seek to apply the contract inconsistently with what that party knew to be the common intention of the parties when the written contract was executed. The doctrine of unilateral mistake extends this principle to the situation where a party seeks to apply the contract inconsistently with what that party knew the other party believed to be the common intention of the parties when the written contract was executed.

The *Chartbrook* case

107. This apparently settled state of the law was thrown into doubt by the observations of Lord Hoffmann on the question of rectification in *Chartbrook Ltd v Persimmon Homes Ltd* [2009] UKHL 38; [2009] AC 1101.

108. In summary, the facts were that owners of land (Chartbrook) made a contract with a developer (Persimmon) granting Persimmon a licence to develop the land for commercial and residential use. Planning permission was granted and the development was built. The sums payable to Chartbrook under the contract included an 'additional residential payment' (or 'ARP') which was to be calculated according to a defined formula. On what Chartbrook contended—and the trial judge (Briggs J) and the Court of Appeal held—was the correct interpretation of the contractual formula, the amount payable to Chartbrook was some £4.4m, whereas on Persimmon's case it was only some £900,000. On Persimmon's alternative claim to rectify the contract, Briggs J found that there had been no common mistake, as the two directors of Chartbrook had understood both the relevant clause in the contract and a pre-contractual exchange of letters describing the ARP as having the effect for which Chartbrook contended. The Court of Appeal declined to interfere with that finding.

109. The House of Lords allowed Persimmon's appeal on the issue of interpretation holding that, objectively construed, it was clear that something had gone wrong with the language used to define the ARP in the contract and that a reasonable person would have understood the contractual definition to bear the meaning for which Persimmon contended—essentially because Chartbrook's interpretation, although consistent with ordinary rules of syntax, made no commercial sense. The House of Lords reached that conclusion without taking account of what was said in the pre-contractual correspondence, having declined to depart from the established rule that what is said in the course of negotiating a contract is not admissible for the purpose of drawing inferences about what the contract means.

110. In these circumstances the question whether Persimmon was entitled to have the wording of the contract rectified did not arise. Nevertheless, while acknowledging that the question was 'academic', Lord Hoffmann expressed the opinion that, had it not succeeded on the issue of interpretation, Persimmon would have been entitled to an order for rectification. The basis for this opinion was an argument advanced for the first time on behalf of Persimmon in the House of Lords, encouraged in particular by an article in the Law Quarterly Review by Marcus Smith (now Mr Justice Marcus Smith): 'Rectification of Contracts for Common Mistake, *Joscelyne v Nissen* and Subjective States of Mind' (2007) 123 LQR 116. The argument was that the prior consensus or 'continuing common intention' which must be shown in order to found a claim for rectification need not involve any concurrence of the parties' actual subjective intentions. Its existence must be ascertained objectively by asking what a reasonable observer would have understood the intentions of the parties to be. This was the same argument as had previously been advanced by the defendants in the *Britoil* case, and Lord Hoffmann once again agreed with it.

111. The starting point for his legal analysis was the observation of Lord Cozens-Hardy MR in *Lovell & Christmas Ltd v Wall* (1911) 104 LT 85, 88 (quoted at paragraph 57 above) that rectification 'may be regarded as a branch of the doctrine of specific performance'. As Lord Hoffmann explained (at para

59), what Lord Cozens-Hardy clearly meant by this was that, if parties contractually agree to execute a document containing particular terms but instead execute a document containing different terms, the court can specifically perform the contract by rectifying the document. For this purpose, Lord Hoffmann reasoned, the terms of the contract to which the subsequent document must conform must be objectively determined in the same way as any other contract.

112. Lord Hoffmann then extended this reasoning to cases where there is no prior contract in the following key sentence (at para 60):

> Now that it has been established that rectification is also available when there was no binding antecedent agreement but the parties had a common continuing intention in respect of a particular matter in the instrument to be rectified, it would be anomalous if the 'common continuing intention' were to be an objective fact if it amounted to an enforceable contract but a subjective belief if it did not.

Lord Hoffmann also relied on the same three authorities on which he had relied in expressing a similar opinion in the *Britoil* case. He distinguished the *Britoil* case (at para 63) on the ground that the difference between himself and the majority of the Court of Appeal in that case had merely been about whether the language of the heads of agreement was sufficiently certain to establish a prior common agreement or intention, ascertained objectively, and that the judgment of Hobhouse LJ lent no support to the view that, in order for rectification to be granted, a party must be mistaken as to whether the document reflects what that party subjectively understood to have been agreed.

113. Applying this approach to the facts of the *Chartbrook* case, Lord Hoffmann considered that a reasonable observer would have understood from the pre-contractual exchange of letters between the parties that they intended the ARP formula to operate in the way for which Persimmon contended. There was no suggestion that the contract was intended to depart from what had previously been discussed. In these circumstances, if the wording of the contract had, on its proper interpretation, borne the meaning for which Chartbrook contended, Persimmon would have been entitled to have the contract rectified to make it accord with the prior consensus expressed in correspondence. That would have been so, even though (on the undisturbed factual findings of the trial judge) Chartbrook's directors had understood the formula agreed in correspondence as well as the wording of the contract to mean something different.

114. Each of the other members of the appellate committee either agreed or saw no reason to differ from Lord Hoffmann's observations on what Lord Walker and Baroness Hale respectively referred to as 'the important questions that we do not have to decide' (para 97) and 'the issues which we do not have to decide' (para 101).

The *Daventry* case

115. The first case following the *Chartbrook* case in which the Court of Appeal had to analyse a claim for rectification was *Daventry District Council v Daventry & District Housing Ltd* [2011] EWCA Civ 1153; [2012] 1 WLR 1333. In somewhat simplified summary, the claimant council sought rectification of a contract by which it transferred its housing stock and the staff employed in its housing department to the defendant company. There was a deficit of £2.4m in the staff pension scheme referable to the transferred employees and the contract provided for the council to fund this deficit. An earlier non-binding document which was agreed in principle and signed during the negotiations, objectively interpreted, provided that the cost of funding the deficit would be shared equally between the parties. This was how the council's agent understood it (as the company's negotiator knew) but the company's negotiator thought that a different interpretation of the document was tenable and told the company's board of directors that the deal was for the council to fund the deficit.

116. When the formal contract was prepared, the company's funders proposed the inclusion of a clause which had the clear effect that the council was to fund the pension scheme deficit. The council's agent approved the inclusion of this clause, and the council executed the contract, without realising its effect. When the error was discovered, the council brought a claim to rectify the contract. Although the claim failed before the judge (Vos J), the Court of Appeal by a majority (Lord Neuberger MR and Toulson LJ, with Etherton LJ dissenting) held that the council was entitled to rectification.

117. The judgments of the Court of Appeal are long and have been described by Professor Burrows in his *Casebook on Contract* (6th Edn, 2018) at 739 as 'mind-bogglingly difficult'. Their preparation evidently involved what in current jargon was an 'iterative process' by which, as Lord Neuberger explained at para 187, 'we have effectively been conducting a dialogue through the exchange and consequent refining of successive drafts of our respective judgments.' The following general points may, however, be extracted.

118. First, the case was argued, both before the judge and on the appeal, on the basis that Lord Hoffmann's observations about the law of rectification in the *Chartbrook* case were correct, and the Court of Appeal—while recognising that those observations were *obiter dicta*—thought it right to proceed on that basis.

119. Second, although Etherton LJ thought that Lord Hoffmann's observations in the *Chartbrook* case had 'set out established principles rather than seeking to change them' and that both parties had 'rightly' proceeded on the basis that those observations correctly stated the existing law (see para 78), the other two members of the court expressed considerable reservations about the correctness of Lord Hoffmann's analysis. Toulson LJ pointed out at some length objections to it, stating at para 176:

> Notwithstanding the immense respect due to Lord Hoffmann and the other members of the House of Lords, I have difficulty in accepting it as a general principle that a mistake by both the parties as to whether a written contract conformed with a prior non-binding agreement, objectively construed, gives rise to a claim for rectification.

Lord Neuberger agreed (at para 195) that 'the analysis is not without its difficulties and has not met with universal approval in learned articles, and may have to be reconsidered or at least refined.'

120. Third, all the members of the court were in agreement that, proceeding on the basis of the approach outlined in the *Chartbrook* case, the question whether there was a common mistake was to be judged 'objectively' by reference to what a hypothetical reasonable observer would have concluded; but they had different opinions about exactly what this test required. Etherton LJ regarded Lord Hoffmann's 'clarification' as being that the required 'common continuing intention' was what an objective observer would have thought the intention to be. He suggested that the requirements for rectification for common mistake could be rephrased so that, instead of treating a 'common continuing intention' and 'an outward expression of accord' as separate conditions, what is required is a common continuing intention which is 'to be established objectively, that is to say by reference to what an objective observer would have thought the intentions of the parties to be' (para 80).

121. Lord Neuberger also proceeded on the basis that the issue as to whether there was a common mistake must be judged objectively and said that he agreed with Etherton LJ's analysis of the law (paras 225 and 227). However, in identifying differences between rectification and contractual interpretation, Lord Neuberger said (para 198):

> Even in relation to written contracts, some subjective evidence of intention or understanding is not merely admissible, but is normally required in a rectification claim: the party seeking rectification must show that he indeed made the relevant mistake when he entered into the contract.

Etherton LJ may have been saying the same thing when he stated at para 82:

> . . . a party can always give evidence that the wording of the document was the result of a mistake. That is an essential part of the cause of action.

122. This is at odds with the assumption that the question whether there was a mistake should be judged wholly objectively by reference to what a hypothetical reasonable observer would have concluded and suggests that, to succeed in a claim to rectify a contract, the claimant must show that he or she was actually (i.e. subjectively) mistaken about what the contract provided. Such a requirement is consistent with the law as it was understood before the *Chartbrook* case. But once it is accepted that an actual mistake by the claimant is an essential part of the cause of action, it seems to us logically to follow that it is also necessary to show such a mistake on the part of the defendant. The principle under consideration is not that of rectification based on a unilateral mistake by the claimant: it is rectification for common mistake. Whatever the appropriate test of a mistake, the very idea of a 'common mistake' requires that the same test must apply to both parties.

123. Applying his understanding of the *Chartbrook* test to the facts of the *Daventry* case, Etherton LJ thought that the critical question was whether objectively, prior to the execution of the contract, the company communicated to the council that it intended to contract in relation to the pension deficit on a different basis from the accord reflected in the earlier non-binding document (para 91). In Etherton LJ's view, the objective observer would have thought that, when the company put forward the clause which made different provision for the pension deficit from that contained in the earlier non-binding agreement, the company no longer adhered to that earlier agreement.

124. As well as questioning whether the principle adopted in the *Chartbrook* case on the rectification issue was right, Toulson LJ differed from Etherton LJ about how the principle operated. Toulson LJ considered that where on an objective analysis the form of the written contract differs from the effect of a previous non-binding agreement, the relevant question to ask is 'whether on a fair view there was a renegotiation or a mistake in the drafting of the contract'. To answer that question, it is necessary to ask whether the parties 'behaved in such a way that they would reasonably understand one another to be involved in a process of seeking to negotiate a different deal from the one originally agreed or as involved in a process of drafting an agreement intended to accord with the deal originally agreed' (para 160). Applying that test, Toulson LJ concluded that the new clause put forward would not reasonably have been understood as an attempt by the company to renegotiate or vary the earlier non-binding agreement (paras 167–170).

125. Lord Neuberger agreed with Etherton LJ's approach of looking solely at whether the company had indicated an intention to resile from the prior accord, rather than also looking at the council's reaction and asking whether the reasonable observer would have thought that the council was agreeing to what the company proposed, as Toulson LJ's approach required (paras 205–207). However, on the facts of the case, Lord Neuberger reached the same result as Toulson LJ. In Lord Neuberger's view (para 213):

> Despite the clear terms of the proffered clause . . . the hypothetical observer would not have concluded that [the company] was signalling a departure from the prior accord: the observer would have believed that [the company] was making a mistake.

In these circumstances Lord Neuberger agreed with Toulson LJ that the council was entitled to have the contract rectified on the ground of common mistake.

. . .

Commentary

129. In his judgment in the *Daventry* case at paras 173–176, Toulson LJ quoted from a case comment by Professor David McLauchlan which criticised the approach taken to rectification in the *Chartbrook* case:

'*Chartbrook Ltd v Persimmon Homes Ltd*: Common-sense Principles of Interpretation and Rectification?' (2010) 126 LQR 8. This comment made the point that, on the undisturbed findings of fact:

> . . . it is difficult to accept that Chartbrook was mistaken, at least in any usual sense of that word. The company intended the contract to provide the benefits that (we assume) it did provide for.

Toulson LJ saw 'much force' in the criticism made (para 174). Since the *Daventry* case, the criticism has become something of a chorus. At our request, we were provided with a full bundle of relevant academic and extra-judicial commentary. Journal articles which we have found particularly helpful are one by James Ruddell, 'Common Intention and Rectification for Common Mistake' [2014] LMCLQ 48, and two articles by Professor Paul Davies, 'Rectifying the Course of Rectification' (2012) 75 MLR 412 and 'Rectification versus Interpretation: The Nature and Scope of the Equitable Jurisdiction' (2016) 75 CLJ 62.

130. The controversial nature of the issues raised by the *Chartbrook* and *Daventry* cases is also reflected in the number of lectures—unprecedented in our experience—in which judges or retired judges have commented on those issues. In addition to the two lectures mentioned earlier given by Sir Kim Lewison and Sir Nicholas Patten, we have had the benefit of reading nine other such lectures, comprising two given by each of Lord Hoffmann and Sir Terence Etherton and one by each of Sir Christopher Nugee, Sir Paul Morgan, Lord Toulson, Lord Neuberger and Lord Briggs, as well as an article in the Cambridge Law Journal by Sir Richard Buxton: '"Construction" and rectification after *Chartbrook*' (2010) 69 CLJ 253.

131. Much of this academic and extra-judicial commentary has been reviewed in detail by David Hodge QC in his comprehensive treatise on *Rectification* (2nd Edn, 2016). He concludes (at para 3-81) that:

> . . . there is general acceptance that the present state of the law of rectification is unsatisfactory. It is over-complicated, unpredictable in its outcome, capable of producing unacceptable consequences, and creates confusion between cases of common and unilateral mistake.

132. In *A Restatement of the English Law of Contract* (2016), prepared by Professor Andrew Burrows assisted by an advisory group of academics, judges and practitioners, there were two 'issues of topical dispute' which it was decided, 'after considerable debate', that the *Restatement* would have to leave open. One (the approach to illegality) has since been resolved. The other is 'whether Lord Hoffmann was correct in *obiter dicta* in *Chartbrook Ltd v Persimmon Homes Ltd* to regard the common continuing intention needed for rectification as objective rather than subjective' (see xi–xii).

The need for reconsideration

133. Like the Court of Appeal in the *Daventry* case, we recognise the immense respect due to an opinion expressed by Lord Hoffmann on a point of law which commanded the unanimous agreement of the House of Lords. Nevertheless, Lord Hoffmann's observations in the *Chartbrook* case were expressly acknowledged to be *obiter dicta* and are therefore not binding authority. In circumstances where Lord Hoffmann's opinion that a purely objective approach should be adopted in determining whether the parties had a 'common continuing intention' has been disputed by the Parent on this appeal, we think it necessary to decide whether it is correct in law.

134. We are satisfied that we are not prevented from doing so by this court's decision in the *Daventry* case because in that case the Court of Appeal proceeded on the basis that Lord Hoffmann's analysis was correct in circumstances where the parties argued the case on that assumption. Moreover, two members of the court expressed concerns about the reasoning in the *Chartbrook* case, suggesting that it may have to be reconsidered in a future case.

135. A similar question potentially arose in *Joscelyne v Nissen* [1970] 2 QB 86, 98–99, as to whether the Court of Appeal was bound by its previous decision in *Crane v Hegeman-Harris Co Inc* [1939] 4 All ER 68 which approved the analysis of Simonds J, but did so in circumstances where the correctness of that

analysis had not been disputed. On the question whether a binding precedent had nevertheless been created, the members of the Court of Appeal in *Joscelyne* expressed themselves 'attracted by a suggestion that the conceded point of law should be open to argument in another case,' provided it was made plain that this would not apply where 'an argument, though put forward, had been only weakly or inexpertly put forward'.

136. Subsequent authorities have clearly established that the suggestion which attracted the Court of Appeal in *Joscelyne v Nissen* is a correct approach and that a court is not bound by a proposition of law which was not the subject of argument because it was not disputed in an earlier case (even if that proposition formed part of the *ratio decidendi* of the case). In *Re Hetherington, deceased* [1990] Ch 1 at 10, Sir Nicolas Browne-Wilkinson V-C held that, as a first instance judge, he was entitled to decline to follow even a decision of the House of Lords in which a proposition of law necessary for the decision was not disputed. After a review of the authorities, he concluded that:

> . . . the authorities therefore clearly establish that even where a decision of a point of law in a particular sense was essential to an earlier decision of a superior court, but that superior court merely assumed the correctness of the law on a particular issue, a judge in a later case is not bound to hold that the law is decided in that sense.

See also *R (Kadhim) v Brent London Borough Council* [2001] QB 955, para 33; *Rawlinson & Hunter Trustees SA v SFO (No2)* [2014] EWCA Civ 1129; [2015] 1 WLR 797, para 43.

137. Furthermore, because of the assumption on which the case was conducted, the Court of Appeal in the *Daventry* case was not referred to and did not consider the substantial body of case law which we have reviewed establishing the need to show an actual (and not merely objectively inferred) common intention and mistake in order to obtain rectification of a contract. In particular, the important decisions of this court in *Joscelyne v Nissen* [1970] 2 QB 86 and *Britoil plc v Hunt Overseas Oil Inc* [1994] CLC 561 were not cited in the *Daventry* case. In a lecture given to TECBAR on 31 October 2013, 'Does Rectification Require Rectifying?', Lord Toulson (as he by then was) drew attention to the *Britoil* case and observed:

> When a similar problem arises, as no doubt it will, it will be a matter for argument whether a court should follow the reasoning in *Britoil* or in *Chartbrook*. In principle, a court should follow a binding decision of the Court of Appeal rather than a later opinion expressed *obiter* by the House of Lords.

138. In addition, the differences of view which emerged between the members of the Court of Appeal in the *Daventry* case, and the difficulties encountered in that case in attempting to analyse and apply a purely 'objective' test, together with the controversy and uncertainty that currently afflicts the test of rectification for common mistake, make it all the more imperative, in our view, to identify the true principle of law that underpins the doctrine.

139. In considering whether the approach approved in the *Chartbrook* case is correct, we will examine it from the point of view of (i) principle, (ii) precedent and (iii) policy considerations.

Principle

140. In later lectures in which he has sought to explain and further justify his opinion in the *Chartbrook* case, Lord Hoffmann has drawn a distinction between two forms of rectification, based on different principles. As described in his recent TECBAR Lecture, 21 November 2018, 'Rectifying Rectification':

> . . . we have two forms of rectification, based on altogether different principles. The first is rectification of a document because it does not reflect what the parties agreed. . . . Whether there was an agreement is an objective fact. The underlying moral principle is that parties should keep their promises to each other; they should be bound by what they agreed to record in the document and not by a document which does not give effect to that agreement. The second, more recent form of rectification is entirely concerned with the parties' intentions, their subjective states of mind. A party who subjectively

knows that the other party is mistaken about the terms of the contract . . . cannot enforce those terms and the mistaken party may be entitled to rectification. . . . The underlying moral principle is that persons negotiating a contract have to observe certain standards of good faith.

See also Lord Hoffmann, Lecture to the Commercial Bar Association, 3 November 2015, 'Rectification and other Mistakes', paras 27–29.

141. We find this analysis illuminating. Applying the distinction between the two forms of rectification, it can be seen that the judges who at one time espoused the view that it was necessary to find a prior concluded contract before an order for rectification could be made were treating the only permissible form of rectification for common mistake as the first form of rectification described by Lord Hoffmann, based on the principle that the court should give effect to what the parties have contractually agreed to record in their document. This explains the *dictum* of James V-C in *Mackenzie v Coulson* (1869) LR 8 Eq 368, 375, that:

Courts of Equity do not rectify contracts; they may and do rectify instruments purporting to have been made in pursuance of the terms of contracts.

It also explains, as Lord Hoffmann pointed out in the *Chartbrook* case at para 59, the observation of Lord Cozens-Hardy MR in *Lovell & Christmas Ltd v Wall* (1911) 104 LT 85, 88, that rectification 'may be regarded as a branch of the doctrine of specific performance'. We agree with the reasoning (as did the majority of the Court of Appeal in the *Britoil* case) that, if parties make a binding agreement to execute a document containing particular terms but instead execute a document containing different terms, the court may specifically enforce the agreement by rectifying the document; and that, in such a case, the terms of the contract to which the subsequent document is made to conform must be objectively determined in the same way as any other contract.

142. We do not, however, accept that the same reasoning can be applied to a situation in which parties have not made any prior contract but had a common continuing intention in respect of a particular matter in the document sought to be rectified. Where, as we see it, the analysis in the *Chartbrook* case went awry was in regarding rectification to reflect a common intention where there was no prior contract as also based on the principle that agreements must be kept. As we have seen, that was not historically the principle on which equity interfered with written contracts which mistakenly failed to reflect the common intention of the parties; nor in our view does it provide a proper basis for such interference. Rather, rectification to give effect to a 'common continuing intention' not amounting to a legally enforceable contract is justified, and is only capable of being justified, as an instance of the second form of rectification, based on an equitable principle of good faith.

143. The principle that a contractual document should be reformed so as to enforce what the parties have (objectively) agreed has no validity where the prior 'agreement' is not a legally binding contract but a non-binding expression of intent. There is no principle which requires or justifies a court in holding the parties to the terms of an objective consensus reached during negotiations but never intended to be binding: it is in the very nature of such a consensus—even where, as in the *Britoil* and *Daventry* cases, it is embodied in a document which the parties have signed—that it should not have any legal effect and represents only a stage in negotiations from which either party is free to walk away. Still less does the principle that parties should keep their promises to each other justify giving such a consensus priority over the terms of a formal written contract by which (objectively) the parties did intend to be bound. To adopt this course is to impose on the parties a contract they never made in place of one which they did make. It is to do exactly what on the reasoning of cases like *Lovell & Christmas Ltd v Wall* and Denning

LJ's judgment in *Rose v Pim* courts should not do: it is to rectify the contract made by the parties and not simply a document which fails to give effect to the terms of a contract.

144. It is in the very nature of a formal written contract that it is objectively intended to have priority over any earlier informal non-binding record of the parties' intention, as objectively assessed. In so far as there is a difference between them, it is therefore the contractual document which must prevail. As Professor Paul Davies has aptly put it:

> The objective approach to rectification involves too much objectivity: objectively, a binding written contract with a particular meaning, ascertained through the process of interpretation, has been concluded.

See 'Construing commercial contracts: no need for violence' in M Freeman and F Smith (eds), *Law and Language: Current Legal Issues Volume 15* (2013), 444.

145. Nor is it an answer to argue that rectifying a written contract to accord with a prior objective consensus is legitimate as, on a rectification claim, more facts can be taken into account by the hypothetical observer than can be taken into account in interpreting the final contract because evidence of the parties' negotiations is admissible. Rectification does not simply involve deciding whether the parties have made a contract and, if so, what effect it has, applying the same objective test as where the question is one of interpretation but having recourse to a wider range of material. It involves altering the terms of the written contract and doing so in some cases even where those terms cannot reasonably be read, however much material (including evidence of antecedent negotiations) is admitted as background, as having the effect which rectification seeks to achieve. The present case is a good example.

146. The justification for rectifying a contractual document to conform to a 'continuing common intention' is therefore not to be found in the principle that agreements (as objectively determined) must be kept. It lies elsewhere. It rests on the equitable doctrine that a party will not be allowed to enforce the terms of a written contract, objectively ascertained, when to do so is against conscience because it is inconsistent with what both parties in fact intended (and mutually understood each other to intend) those terms to be when the document was executed. This basis for rectification is entirely concerned with the parties' subjective states of mind. The underlying moral principle can be characterised, to adopt Lord Hoffmann's analysis, as being that persons who make a contract have to observe certain standards of good faith.

147. It is not, however, a new principle, as suggested by Lord Hoffmann in the passage we have quoted from his recent lecture. Nor is it limited, as also there suggested, to cases of unilateral mistake. We have seen that the principle is of ancient origin and was, historically, the rationale for granting rectification in cases of common mistake. Moreover, it is just as contrary to good faith—if not more obviously so—for a party to take advantage of a mistake about the content or effect of a written contract in a case where both parties were mistaken in believing when the contract was executed that it faithfully recorded their common intention than it is to do so in a case where only one party made such a mistake (to the other's knowledge). Rectification for unilateral mistake can, as we noted earlier (at paragraph 105 above), be understood as an extension of the same basic equitable principle. It is fundamental to the doctrine, in either aspect, that an actual mistake was made by one or more real people in believing that the written contract gave effect to what either was or was understood by one party to be the parties' actual common intention. As it was put in the passage from Story's *Commentaries*, quoted earlier, to allow the terms of the written contract to prevail where such a mistake was made:

> would be to allow an act, originating in innocence, to operate ultimately as a fraud, by enabling the party, who receives the benefit of the mistake, to resist the claims of justice, under the shelter of a rule framed to promote it.

The objective test and its limits

148. To elucidate this further, it is useful to consider why English law applies an objective test in interpreting contracts at all and asks, as stated earlier in Lord Hoffmann's judgment in the *Chartbrook* case at para 14, 'what a reasonable person having all the background knowledge which would have been available to the parties would have understood them to be using the language in the contract to mean.' The reasons lie in the greater predictability and consistency of decision-making that such an approach is considered to bring.

149. In many, if not most, cases in which parties to a contract disagree about how it should be interpreted, it is likely, if not certain, that they had no relevant intention when they entered into the contract that the particular clause should have the particular effect for which they later contend—let alone a common intention in that regard which they had communicated to each other. One reason for this is that contracts often contain standard terms, the meaning of which will often (for good practical reasons) have been given little thought by the parties or their agents when entering into the contract, if indeed they read them at all. Another reason is that it is impossible to foresee when a contract is made all the future eventualities to which its terms will fall to be applied. Nevertheless, English law proceeds on the assumption that the words used have a single specific meaning (the 'proper interpretation' or 'true construction' of the contract) which is established objectively by asking what the language should reasonably be understood to mean rather than by enquiring into what, if anything, the parties subjectively meant.

150. This approach has many practical advantages. It enables a party to predict with a reasonable degree of certainty when entering into a contract how its provisions will be interpreted, without having to probe or be concerned about whether the other party shares this understanding. It also allows third parties to ascertain the meaning of contractual provisions without requiring them to have been privy to the actual intentions of the parties to the contract. In addition, this approach facilitates contractual ventures by giving content to contractual obligations even in circumstances which the parties did not specifically envisage. In all these ways the objective approach enhances the ability of parties to plan and act in reliance on contracts.

151. The reasons for enforcing a contract in accordance with its objective meaning lose their force, however, in a situation where the parties did have an agreed understanding or common intention about what a particular provision in their contract required but the contract as objectively interpreted does not reflect that common intention. In such a situation, provided the common intention is clearly demonstrated, there is no sound justification for giving effect to the meaning that a hypothetical reasonable observer would have attributed to the words used in preference to what the parties actually intended the effect of their contract to be. Indeed, to do so will result in injustice.

152. Lord Wright explained the position very clearly in *Inland Revenue Commissioners v Raphael* [1935] AC 96, 143, when he said that:

> ... the principle of the common law has been to adopt an objective standard of construction and to exclude general evidence of actual intention of the parties; the reason for this has been that otherwise all certainty would be taken from the words in which the parties have recorded their agreement or their dispositions of property. If in some cases hardship or injustice may be effected by this rule of law, such hardship or injustice can generally be obviated by the power in equity to reform the contract, in proper cases and on proper evidence that there has been a real intention and a real mistake in expressing that intention: these matters may be established, as they generally are, by extrinsic evidence. The Court will thus reform or re-write the clauses in order to give effect to the real intention. But that is not construction, but rectification.

153. For these reasons, there is in our view no anomaly in applying an objective test where rectification is based on a prior concluded contract and a subjective test where it is based on a common continuing intention. Different principles are in play.

. . .

Comparison with unilateral documents

164. To apply an objective test of intention where the claim is to rectify a written contract is also inconsistent with the law that applies to the rectification of unilateral documents—where it remains well settled that it is a party's actual intention that matters. For example, as mentioned earlier, in *Day v Day* [2013] EWCA Civ 280; [2014] Ch 114 the Court of Appeal confirmed that, on a claim to rectify a voluntary settlement, what is relevant is the subjective intention of the settlor.

165. Such a difference of approach cannot be justified on the ground that the objective principle of interpretation does not apply to unilateral documents, since it is clearly established that it does. English law takes the same approach to the interpretation of unilateral documents such as wills, contractual notices and patents as it does to the interpretation of contracts: see e.g. *Mannai Ltd Investment Co Ltd v Eagle Star Life Assurance Co Ltd* [1997] AC 749; and *Marley v Rawlings* [2014] UKSC 2; [2015] AC 129, paras 20–23. The test in each case is what a reasonable person would have understood the words used, in their context, to mean. However, where in the case of a unilateral document it is demonstrated that the words used, as objectively interpreted, do not correctly express the maker's subjective intention, a court may order rectification. The fact that a contract is agreed between two or more parties provides a reason for requiring proof of a common intention communicated between them before rectification may be granted. But it does not provide a reason for dispensing with the need to show any actual mistake and for ignoring the parties' actual intentions in favour of what a hypothetical objective observer would have thought. We cannot see any difference of principle between a one party and a two party case which is capable of justifying such a radical difference of approach.

166. The illogicality of such a distinction is highlighted in the present case by the fact that the Parent could, as Mr Masefield accepted, have satisfied its contractual obligation to assign its interest in the shareholder loan as security by executing a unilateral document and giving notice of the assignment. As Flaux LJ pointed out in the course of argument, if the Parent had done that, it is clear that the court would be interested only in the Parent's subjective intention. As it happens, the Parent chose instead to invite Barclays to countersign deeds which, although the difference was of little, if any, practical importance, were bilateral documents because Barclays as security agent undertook obligations pursuant to the IRSAs to apply any proceeds of the shareholder loan in specified ways. Because the transaction was structured in this way, with consideration given by Barclays, the alternative case advanced by the Parent in a respondent's notice on this appeal that the deeds were unilateral documents cannot be accepted. But it is hard to see why the difference should be material to the test of intention such that, just because a bilateral structure was chosen, a purely objective test should be adopted and the court ignore the Parent's actual intention (unless for some reason it sheds light on what an objective observer would have thought).

. . .

Injustice

175. Finally, what we see as the potential unfairness of the objective approach approved in the *Chartbrook* case can be illustrated by reference to the facts of that case itself. As noted earlier, on the facts found, the directors of Chartbrook honestly believed that there was no mistake in the final contractual document and that the ARP formula as expressed both in that document and in the pre-contractual correspondence

meant what Chartbrook contended in the proceedings that it meant. The House of Lords was considering Persimmon's claim for rectification on the assumption that the Chartbrook directors were wrong about the objective meaning of the pre-contractual correspondence but right about the objective meaning of the final contract. We cannot in these circumstances see any equity in treating Chartbrook as bound by the objective meaning of communications which were not intended by either party to be binding rather than the objective meaning of the final document by which the parties intended to be bound. As Christopher Nugee QC (now Mr Justice Nugee), who argued the case successfully for Persimmon, subsequently observed:

> [Chartbrook] admittedly agreed to the letter but they also agreed to the draft contract. Why are they stuck with the consensus objectively shown in the letter and not the consensus objectively shown in the draft contract?

A conclusion that Chartbrook was bound to the earlier, informal objective consensus in priority to the objective meaning of the contract would, in his view, have been 'rather unfair': see C Nugee, 'Rectification after *Chartbrook v Persimmon*: where are we now?' (2012) 26 Trust Law International 76. We agree.

Conclusion on the law

176. For all these reasons, we are unable to accept that the objective test of rectification for common mistake articulated in Lord Hoffmann's *obiter* remarks in the *Chartbrook* case correctly states the law. We consider that we are bound by authority, which also accords with sound legal principle and policy, to hold that, before a written contract may be rectified on the basis of a common mistake, it is necessary to show either (1) that the document fails to give effect to a prior concluded contract or (2) that, when they executed the document, the parties had a common intention in respect of a particular matter which, by mistake, the document did not accurately record. In the latter case it is necessary to show not only that each party to the contract had the same actual intention with regard to the relevant matter, but also that there was an 'outward expression of accord'—meaning that, as a result of communication between them, the parties understood each other to share that intention.

Conclusion on the facts

177. As mentioned earlier, the judge in this case made findings of fact that, when they executed the accession deeds, the Parent and Barclays each intended to execute a document which satisfied the Parent's obligation to grant security over the shareholder loan and did no more than this. The judge also found that the relevant individuals acting for and advising Barclays (Mr Branwhite and Mr Kandola) derived their understanding of the purpose of executing the accession deeds from communications, including telephone conversations, with Mr Baker who was acting for the Parent. Although the judge did not say so in terms, it is implicit in his findings about the effect of these telephone conversations that Mr Baker must have understood that he had successfully communicated to Mr Branwhite and Mr Kandola his own (and the Parent's) understanding of the purpose of executing the accession deeds, such that they shared a common intention.

178. Given these findings, to which no challenge is made on this appeal, it follows from our analysis of the law that the appeal must fail

8.5.2 The plea of *non est factum*

Generally, this means that a person will be bound by a written document that he has signed, whether or not he has read or understood it: see *L'Estrange v F. Graucob Ltd* [1934] 2 KB 394 (*page 187*, 5.2.2).

Where it is not possible to rely on misrepresentation or mistake, the plea of *non est factum* ('this is not my deed') may be a last resort. A successful plea renders the contract void, so that a third party cannot acquire a good title under it. However, because innocent third parties may have relied to their detriment upon this signature as being binding, the plea has been very narrowly construed.

Saunders v Anglia Building Society (sub nom Gallie v Lee)
[1971] AC 1004 (HL)

An elderly widow aged 78 had a leasehold interest in a house. She knew that her nephew wished to raise money on the house and that his business associate, Lee, was to assist him in obtaining this. The widow wanted to be sure that she could live in the house for the rest of her life. Lee asked her to sign a document, but she had broken her spectacles and could not read it. She asked what the document was and signed it when Lee told her that it was a deed of gift of the house to her nephew. In fact, it was an assignment of the house to Lee for £3,000. Lee mortgaged the house for £2,000 to the building society (the innocent third party). When Lee defaulted on the mortgage instalments, the building society sought possession of the house. The widow pleaded *non est factum* and asked for a declaration against the building society that the transfer was void.

Held: The plea failed because the transaction into which the widow had entered was not fundamentally different in substance from that which she had intended to enable the nephew to raise money on the security of the house. She had also been careless in signing the document.

LORD REID: The plea of *non est factum* obviously applies when the person sought to be held liable did not in fact sign the document. But at least since the sixteenth century it has also been held to apply in certain cases so as to enable a person who in fact signed a document to say that it is not his deed. Obviously any such extension must be kept within narrow limits if it is not to shake the confidence of those who habitually and rightly rely on signatures when there is no obvious reason to doubt their validity. Originally this extension appears to have been made in favour of those who were unable to read owing to blindness or illiteracy and who therefore had to trust someone to tell them what they were signing. I think it must also apply in favour of those who are permanently or temporarily unable through no fault of their own to have without explanation any real understanding of the purport of a particular document, whether that be from defective education, illness or innate incapacity.

But that does not excuse them from taking such precautions as they reasonably can. The matter generally arises where an innocent third party has relied on a signed document in ignorance of the circumstances in which it was signed, and where he will suffer loss if the maker of the document is allowed to have it declared a nullity. So there must be a heavy burden of proof on the person who seeks to invoke this remedy. He must prove all the circumstances necessary to justify its being granted to him, and that necessarily involves his proving that he took all reasonable precautions in the circumstances. I do not say that the remedy can never be available to a man of full capacity. But that could only be in very exceptional circumstances: certainly not where his reason for not scrutinising the document before signing it was that he was too busy or too lazy. In general I do not think he can be heard to say that he signed in reliance on someone he trusted. But, particularly when he was led to believe that the document which he signed was not one which affected his legal rights, there may be cases where this plea can properly be applied in favour of a man of full capacity.

The plea cannot be available to anyone who was content to sign without taking the trouble to try to find out at least the general effect of the document. Many people do frequently sign documents put before them for signature by their solicitor or other trusted advisers without making any inquiry as to their purpose or effect. But the essence of the plea *non est factum* is that the person signing believed that the document he signed had one character or one effect whereas in fact its character or effect was quite different. He could not have such a belief unless he had taken steps or been given information which gave him some grounds for his belief. The amount of information he must have and the sufficiency of the particularity of his belief must depend on the circumstances of each case . . .

Finally, there is the question as to what extent or in what way must there be a difference between that which in fact he signed and that which he believed he was signing. In an endeavour to keep the plea within bounds there have been many attempts to lay down a dividing line . . .

There must, I think, be a radical difference between what he signed and what he thought he was signing—or one could use the words 'fundamental' or 'serious' or 'very substantial.' But what amounts to a radical difference will depend on all the circumstances. If he thinks he is giving property to A whereas the document gives it to B, the difference may often be of vital importance, but in the circumstances of the present case I do not think that it is. I think that it must be left to the courts to determine in each case in light of all the facts whether there was or was not a sufficiently great difference. The plea *non est factum* is in a sense illogical when applied to a case where the man in fact signed the deed. But it is none the worse for that if applied in a reasonable way.

Norwich & Peterborough Building Society v Steed (No. 2)
[1993] Ch 116 (CA)

The appellant, Steed, sought to rely on the plea of *non est factum* on the basis that he had executed a power of attorney in favour of his mother, but, as a result of trickery, his mother had then transferred his house to his sister and her husband, who had used the house as security for a loan on which they had defaulted. Steed alleged that his mother thought that she was signing a document concerning her own affairs and did not know that she was signing a transfer of the property. She was therefore mistaken as to the essential character of the document signed.

Held: The plea could not succeed.

SCOTT LJ: Submissions on these lines . . . place Mr Steed on a species of Morton's fork. Let it be supposed that Mrs Steed was a lady of sufficient general understanding and capability to be a suitable donee of the power of appointment. Why then did she not inform herself of the purport and effect of the transfer before signing it? . . . On the other hand, let it be supposed that she lacked ordinary competence and capacity. Lord Wilberforce [in *Saunders v Anglia Building Society*] referred to persons 'illiterate, or blind, or lacking in understanding'. If Mrs Steed falls into this category, what was Mr Steed about when he appointed her his attorney? The donor of a power of attorney who appoints as his attorney a person incapable of understanding the import of a simple transfer can hardly be allowed, if the donee signs a transfer without any understanding of what he or she is doing, to repudiate the transfer on the ground of a lack of understanding on the part of the donee.

As to Mrs Steed's ignorance of the power of attorney, if she was ignorant of it, the ignorance was attributable to Mr Steed's incomprehensible failure to tell her either that he was about to or that he had made the appointment. It is known that he and she spoke on the telephone at about the time the power of attorney was executed. If it was really the case that he did not mention the power of attorney when speaking to her on that occasion and left her in ignorance of her responsibilities and status, his failure shows, in my opinion, such a want of care as to preclude him from relying, in support of his *non est factum* plea, on her ignorance of the power. As between an innocent third party purchaser such as the building society on the one hand, and Mr Steed on the other hand, his failure to take the ordinary precautionary and prudent step of informing his mother of her appointment as his attorney requires, in my judgment, that the building society be preferred . . .

NOTE There is a rare recent instance (described by the judge as 'exceptional facts') in which the doctrine was invoked successfully in the context of a fraud perpetrated against the employee defendant who was led to believe that he was merely witnessing the signatures of others, rather than signing as the guarantor of the lease of the company that employed him: *Trustees of Beardsley Theobalds Retirement Benefit Scheme v Yardley* [2011] EWHC 1380 (QB). There were, however, also successful defences to enforcement based on undue influence and fraudulent misrepresentation on these facts.

Chapter 9

Misrepresentation

A statement made during contractual negotiations may be a mere puff, a representation, or a contractual term. The essence of a representation is that the maker asserts the truth of certain facts and this operates to induce the contract. A term, on the other hand, is essentially a *promise*, so that there is an obligation to fulfil it (*page 171*, *5.1*, for a discussion of the distinction between representations and terms).

Since a representor does not make a promise, the most appropriate remedy in misrepresentation is for the party induced to be put into the position in which he would have been had he not been induced to contract. An actionable misrepresentation therefore renders the contract voidable, i.e. liable to be set aside (rescinded). Damages may also be available with the aim of restoring the parties to their original positions.

(This area of contract law tends to overlap with tort. Factual situations that give rise to a claim in misrepresentation may also give rise to a claim in tort for negligent misstatement.)

The law governing misrepresentations in B2C (trader and consumer) contracts has undergone a radical transformation with the introduction of the Consumer Protection (Amendment) Regulations 2014, SI 2014/870. These Regulations added new civil remedies for misleading actions and aggressive commercial practices that induced the making of a consumer contract to the existing CPR regime (Consumer Protection from Unfair Trading Regulations (CPRs) 2008, SI 2008/1277). This has the potential to create largely separate misrepresentation regimes for commercial and consumer contracts if consumers choose to adopt the CPRs when seeking relief. They are encouraged to do so since s. 2(4) Misrepresentation Act (MA) 1967 now provides that s. 2 'does not entitle a person to be paid damages in respect of a misrepresentation if the person has a right to redress under Part 4A of the Consumer Protection from Unfair Trading Regulations 2008 (SI 2008/1277) in respect of the conduct constituting the misrepresentation'. Thus, whereas a consumer can seemingly choose to seek a remedy using the existing principles of common law and equity (reg. 27L CPRs 2008), it would appear that if they had 'a right to redress' under the CPRs any such claim would be seriously limited in relation to damages by the unavailability of the s. 2 remedy. This may be too literal an interpretation since the expression 'right to redress' may not be intended to preclude s. 2 damages where the consumer has chosen not to seek recovery under the CPRs and there is therefore no double recovery. However, that is not what s. 2(4) states. As a final point on this relationship, there appears to be no 'right to redress' for a consumer who complains of 'misleading omissions' (as opposed to 'misleading actions') so that such a consumer should retain the ability to recover damages under s. 2. There are therefore a number of issues that have the potential to cause confusion unless they are rapidly addressed through interpretation by the courts.

9.1 Actionable misrepresentation

An actionable misrepresentation is an unambiguous false statement of fact that induces the other party to enter into the contract.

9.1.1 Unambiguous false statement

9.1.1.1 Conduct

A 'statement' can include conduct.

Gordon v Selico Co. Ltd
(1986) 278 EG 53 (CA)

On behalf of the owners, the estate agents of a flat instructed an independent contractor to do work to the flat 'to bring it up to a very good standard for the purpose of selling'. The contractor deliberately covered up patches of dry rot without attempting to eradicate it. The claimants saw the flat with a view to purchasing it and later went ahead with the purchase.

Held: The Court of Appeal agreed with Goulding J at first instance that this concealment amounted to a fraudulent misrepresentation to the claimants that the flat did not suffer from dry rot.

> **? QUESTION**
>
> I wish to sell my house. I put up wood panelling in the dining room, partly because the room needs decorating and partly to hide serious cracks in a wall. You buy my house and subsequently discover that the wall is defective. Would you have a remedy in misrepresentation or under the CPRs 2008 in these circumstances?

NOTES

1. It had been argued that the claimants had inspected the flat and that this meant that they were precluded by *Horsfall v Thomas* (1862) 1 H & C 90 from complaining of misrepresentation. In *Horsfall v Thomas*, a defect in a gun was concealed, but it was held that there was no actionable misrepresentation. However, this was because the defect in the gun was discoverable on inspection, but no inspection had taken place. Therefore, the claimant in *Horsfall v Thomas* could not argue that he had relied upon (and been induced by) the misrepresentation. However, in *Gordon v Selico*, not only was the defect deliberately concealed, but also it was not discovered on routine inspection. It was intended to deceive and did deceive, so there was no question of the claimant not having relied upon the misrepresentation.

2. In *Spice Girls Ltd v Aprilia World Service BV* [2002] EWCA Civ 15, [2002] EMLR 27, it was held that when the pop group Spice Girls took part in a photo shoot and promotions for the defendant, a motor scooter manufacturer, prior to the signing of a sponsorship agreement for their tour, this amounted to a misrepresentation by conduct. The misrepresentation was that the group did not know, and had no reasonable grounds to believe, that any member of the group had an intention to leave before the sponsorship agreement ended. This was false because, as the judge found on the evidence, one member of the group (Geri Halliwell) had already declared an intention to leave the group.

9.1.1.2 **Implied representations as to a present intention**

Crystal Palace Football Club (2000) Ltd v Dowie
[2007] EWHC 1392 (QB), [2007] IRLR 682

The defendant football manager's contract contained a provision requiring compensation of £1 million to be paid if he left Crystal Palace Football Club to take up employment at a premiership club before the end of his contract term.

The defendant had agreed a compromise agreement with the Club whereby it had agreed to release him without compensation, since he had falsely stated that he wanted to leave to move north for family reasons and had had no contact with the premiership club Charlton Athletic. Eight days after this agreement had been entered into, the defendant had been appointed as the manager of Charlton Athletic. The claimant Club alleged that it had been deceived. The defendant claimed that he had no contract with the premiership club when he made the compromise agreement.

Held: When the defendant represented that he had received no contact from Charlton at the relevant time, he was impliedly representing that he had no present intention to join Charlton, whereas he did have such an intention. He therefore knew the representations to be false and these misrepresentations had induced the making of the compromise agreement to forego the compensation payment.

9.1.1.3 **Silence**

9.1.1.3.1 *Does silence amount to misrepresentation? Is there a duty of disclosure?*

Keates v The Earl of Cadogan
(1851) 10 CB 591, 138 ER 234 (Common Pleas)

The defendant let a house to the claimant knowing that the claimant wanted it for immediate occupation, but did not tell the claimant that the house was in fact uninhabitable.

Held: In the absence of fraud, the defendant was under no implied duty to disclose the state of the house.

> JERVIS CJ: It is not pretended that there was any warranty, express or implied, that the house was fit for immediate occupation: but it is said, that, because the defendant knew that the plaintiff wanted it for immediate occupation, and knew that it was in an unfit and dangerous state, and did not disclose that fact to the plaintiff, an action of deceit will lie. The declaration does not allege that the defendant made any misrepresentation, or that he had reason to suppose that the plaintiff would not do what any man in his senses would do, viz. make proper investigation, and satisfy himself as to the condition of the house before he entered upon the occupation of it. There is nothing amounting to deceit: it was a mere ordinary transaction of letting and hiring . . .

NOTE This case is based on the principle of *caveat emptor*. Contracting parties should not be expected to share every piece of information with one another where they deal at 'arm's length' unless the non-disclosure is fraudulent (*Gordon v Selico, page 440, 9.1.1.1*). *Caveat emptor* does not apply to claims based on deceit.

9.1.1.3.2 *Exceptions to non-disclosure*

(a) Misleading statements: half-truths

Dimmock v Hallett
(1866) LR 2 Ch App 21 (CA)

Land for sale was described as 'let to Hickson at £130 p.a.' and another farm was described as 'let to Wigglesworth at £160 p.a.'. In fact, both tenants had given notice to quit, but this was not mentioned, although there were statements that some of the other tenants had given notice to quit.

Held: It was a fair inference that these tenants had not given notice to quit, so that the statement that the farms were let was misleading and amounted to a misrepresentation.

(b) Change of circumstances

What is the position regarding statements that are true when made, but which become false before the contract is entered into?

With v O'Flanagan
[1936] Ch 575 (CA)

In January 1934, negotiations were entered into for the sale of a medical practice, which the vendor represented as having an income of £2,000 per annum. However, by the time the contract was signed in May, the practice had declined as a result of the vendor's illness, but this was not disclosed. The purchasers sought rescission.

Held: The representation was made to induce purchasers to enter into the contract and had to be treated as continuing until the contract was signed. Once it became false, to the knowledge of the representor, there was a misrepresentation if he failed to correct it.

NOTES

1. The misrepresentation occurs when the change of circumstances is not disclosed.

2. It is more difficult to establish that such a misrepresentation is fraudulent. Lord Wright MR stated in this case, at p. 584:

> [T]he failure to disclose, though wrong and a breach of duty, may be due to inadvertence or a failure to realise that the duty rests upon the party who has made the representation not to leave the other party under an error when the representation has become falsified by a change of circumstances . . .

In *Thomas Witter Ltd v TBP Industries Ltd* [1996] 2 All ER 573 (*page 458, 9.3.1*), Jacob J held that a company selling a business had not been fraudulent in failing to disclose a change in accounting method affecting the profit estimates, since there was no evidence of dishonesty on the part of the officers concerned. (the definition of fraudulent misrepresentation at *page 458, 9.3.1*.)

Nevertheless, there are examples of fraudulent misrepresentation being established in these circumstances. In *Erlson Precision Holdings Ltd (formerly GG132 Ltd) v Hampson Industries Ltd* [2011] EWHC 1137 (Comm), in negotiations over a ten-month period, various income and customer forecasts had been supplied to the potential buyer of the shares in a company. These forecasts included details of the contracts with the company's second biggest customer, although that customer had terminated its supply arrangement a few months after the initial forecasts had been made available to the buyer. This information would have made the business unsaleable. The chief executive officer was aware that these forecasts were being made available to the potential buyer, but decided not to correct them. The buyer relied on these forecasts in purchasing the business. It was held that the CEO ought to have corrected the details about the customer and that the failure to do so constituted a fraudulent misrepresentation.

3. A further example of change of circumstances and failure to disclose is provided by the decision in *Spice Girls Ltd v Aprilia World Service BV* [2002] EWCA Civ 15, [2002] EMLR 27.

4. It has traditionally been an accepted principle that the duty to disclose does not apply to statements of intention, so that if the contracting party changed

its declared intention before the conclusion of the contract, there was no obligation to communicate that change of intention. The authority for this principle is *Wales v Wadham*.

Wales v Wadham
[1977] 1 WLR 199

In February 1973, during divorce negotiations, the husband promised to pay the wife £13,000 to settle finally the wife's claim for financial provision. The wife remarried shortly after the divorce decree was made absolute in September 1973, so that, but for the agreement, the ex-husband would have been under no obligation to make financial provision for her. The ex-husband claimed that the agreement should be rescinded for fraudulent misrepresentation, in that the ex-wife had stated on numerous occasions that she would not remarry.

Held: The wife had made an honest representation of her intention, which was not a statement of fact or an intention that she did not actually hold at the time. As a result, she was under no duty to inform her husband that she had changed her mind.

TUDOR EVANS J: It is submitted that even if the wife's statement that she would never remarry was honestly held, she was under a duty to tell the husband of her changed circumstances, but that she failed to do so. Counsel has referred me to *With v O'Flanagan* [1936] Ch 575, in the Court of Appeal . . . Lord Wright MR, at p. 582, quoted, with approval, observations of Fry J in *Davies v London & Provincial Marine Insurance Co.* (1878) 8 Ch D 469, 475, where he said:

> So, again, if a statement has been made which is true at the time, but which during the course of negotiations becomes untrue, then the person who knows that it has become untrue is under an obligation to disclose to the other the changed circumstances.

The representations in both of these cases related to existing fact and not to a statement of intention in relation to future conduct. A statement of intention is not a representation of existing fact, unless the person making it does not honestly hold the intention he is expressing, in which case there is a misrepresentation of fact in relation to the state of that person's mind. That does not arise on the facts as I have found them. On the facts of this case, the wife made an honest statement of her intention which was not a representation of fact, and I can find no basis for holding that she was under a duty in the law of contract to tell the husband of her change of mind.

NOTE   *page 445, 9.1.2.2*, on the distinction between a statement of fact and a statement of intention.

However, in *Inclusive Technology v Williamson* [2009] EWCA Civ 718, [2010] 1 P & CR 2, it was explained that this principle will depend on the context and nature of the statement of intention, i.e. whether it is a continuing statement of intention into the future.

The landlord had issued a statutory termination notice of a tenancy, which indicated an intention to refurbish. However, having given the tenant notice to quit, the landlord then changed his mind about the refurbishment, but did not inform the tenant. The Court of Appeal distinguished *Wales v Wadham* and treated this statement as a representation that had meaning only if it was a continuing representation into the future given the purpose of the notice and the statutory time frame. As such, it carried with it a duty to speak to correct it if there were a change in the previously declared intention to refurbish. It followed that there was a misrepresentation in order to secure possession.

9.1.2 Of fact

9.1.2.1 Statements of belief or opinion

If the maker of the statement is in no better a position to know the truth of the statement than the recipient of it, and the recipient is aware of this, then the maker's statement is likely to be construed as a statement of opinion and, if false, will not amount to an actionable misrepresentation.

Bisset v Wilkinson
[1927] AC 177 (PC)

The owner of a farm told a prospective purchaser that he believed that it would support 2,000 sheep.

Held: On the evidence, the statement was merely a statement of opinion that the owner honestly held. The evidence was that the owner was not in any better position than the purchaser to know the farm's true capacity, since the land had not been used as a sheep farm before. Therefore, the purchaser was aware that the vendor could do no more than state his belief.

LORD MERRIVALE: [I]t is . . . essential to ascertain whether that which is relied upon is a representation of a specific fact, or a statement of opinion, since an erroneous opinion stated by the party affirming the contract, though it may have been relied upon and have induced the contract on the part of the party who seeks rescission, gives no title to relief unless fraud is established. The application of this rule, however, is not always easy, as is illustrated in a good many reported cases, as well as in this. A representation of fact may be inherent in a statement of opinion and, at any rate, the existence of the opinion in the person stating it is a question of fact.

In ascertaining what meaning was conveyed to the minds of the now respondents by the appellant's statement as to the two thousand sheep, the most material fact to be remembered is that, as both parties were aware, the appellant had not and, so far as appears, no other person had at any time carried on sheep-farming upon the unit of land in question. That land as a distinct holding had never constituted a sheep-farm . . . In these circumstances . . . the defendants were not justified in regarding anything said by the plaintiff as to the carrying capacity as being anything more than an expression of his opinion on the subject . . .

If, however, the statement maker is in a better position to know the facts, then his statement contains an implied assertion that he knows of facts justifying his opinion.

Smith v Land and House Property Corporation
(1884) 28 Ch D 7 (CA)

The claimants advertised a hotel for sale, stating in the particulars that it was let to 'Mr Frederick Fleck (a most desirable tenant)'. In fact, Fleck was in arrears with his rent at the time and distress had been threatened (i.e. the taking of goods by the landlord to cover the non-payment of rent). The defendant agreed to purchase the hotel, but then refused to complete. The claimants sued for specific performance.

Held: This description was not a mere expression of opinion, but contained an implied assertion that the vendors knew of no facts leading to the conclusion that Fleck was not a most desirable tenant.

> BOWEN LJ: It is material to observe that it is often fallaciously assumed that a statement of opinion cannot involve the statement of a fact. In a case where the facts are equally well known to both parties, what one of them says to the other is frequently nothing but an expression of opinion. The statement of such opinion is in a sense a statement of a fact, about the condition of the man's own mind, but only of an irrelevant fact, for it is of no consequence what the opinion is. But if the facts are not equally known to both sides, then a statement of opinion by the one who knows the facts best involves very often a statement of a material fact, for he impliedly states that he knows facts which justify his opinion.

NOTES

1. In *Springwell Navigation Corporation v JP Morgan Chase Bank (formerly Chase Manhattan Bank)* [2010] EWCA Civ 1221, [2010] 2 CLC 705 (also discussed at *page 498, 9.4.3.1*), the Court of Appeal held that there had been no misrepresentation when a bank employee had allegedly stated that certain investments were 'a conservative and liquid investment and without currency risk'. These statements were not made in absolute terms and had to be seen in context; in particular, the word 'conservative' could not 'be lifted like a fish out of water'. The statements were no more than statements of opinion without any implied representation by the employee that the statements were based on objectively reasonable grounds.

2. The *Smith v Land & House* principle was further extended in *Esso Petroleum Co. Ltd v Mardon* [1976] QB 801 (for the full discussion, *page 175, 5.1.3*). The Court of Appeal stated that where a forecast is made by a person with greater skill and expertise in relation to the subject matter, that person is impliedly stating that reasonable care and skill has been used in preparing the forecast. Lord Denning MR said, at p. 818:

> [I]t was a forecast made by a party—Esso—who had special knowledge and skill. It was the yardstick . . . by which they measured the worth of a filling station. They knew the facts. They knew the traffic in the town. They knew the through-put of comparable stations. They had much experience and expertise at their disposal. They were in a much better position than Mr Mardon to make a forecast. It seems to me that if such a person makes a forecast, intending that the other should act upon it—and he does act upon it, it can

> well be interpreted as a warranty that the forecast is sound and reliable in the sense that they made it with reasonable care and skill. It is just as if Esso said to Mr Mardon: 'Our forecast of throughput is 200,000 gallons. You can rely upon it as being a sound forecast of what the service station should do. The rent is calculated on that footing.' If the forecast turned out to be an unsound forecast such as no person of skill or experience should have made, there is a breach of warranty . . . It is very different from the New Zealand case where the land had never been used as a sheep farm and both parties were equally able to form an opinion as to its carrying capacity: see particularly *Bisset v Wilkinson* [1927] AC 177, 183–184.

Although this comment relates to establishing a collateral warranty (term), a statement by an expert will be a statement of fact, since the expert is impliedly stating that there are facts to support his forecast.

3. According to Adams and Brownsword, *Understanding Contract Law*, 5th edn (Sweet & Maxwell, 2007), the overall effect of *Esso v Mardon* is that people with 'special informational advantages' are held to their representations. It is interesting to compare this with the general discussion of the duty of disclosure and *Keates v Cadogan*. It appears that a person with special information cannot be compelled, as a general rule, to disclose that information, but if he does disclose it, then he will be responsible for that disclosure.

4. If the maker of the statement has no special skill or knowledge relating to the statement, his statements of opinion will not amount to misrepresentations even if his belief is unreasonable: *Hummingbird Motors Ltd v Hobbs* [1986] RTR 276.

9.1.2.2 Statements as to future conduct and intention

Edgington v Fitzmaurice
(1885) 29 Ch D 459 (CA)

The directors of a company issued a prospectus inviting subscriptions for debentures (loans to the company), stating that the money raised would be used to complete alterations in the buildings of the company, to purchase horses and vans, and to develop the trade of the company. However, the real object of the loan was to enable the directors to pay off pressing liabilities. The claimant advanced money on some of the debentures under the mistaken belief that the prospectus offered a charge upon the property of the company, and stated in his evidence that he would not have advanced his money but for such belief, but that he also relied upon the statements contained in the prospectus.

Held: The misstatement of the company's intentions amounted to a misstatement of fact.

> BOWEN LJ: There must be a misstatement of an existing fact: but the state of a man's mind is as much a fact as the state of his digestion. It is true that it is very difficult to prove what the state of a man's mind at a particular time is, but if it can be ascertained it is as much a fact as anything else. A misrepresentation as to the state of a man's mind is, therefore, a misstatement of fact . . .

NOTES

1. The difficulty resulting from *Edgington v Fitzmaurice* is an evidential one—namely, to prove what the maker's true intention was at the time of making the statement.

2. In *Inntrepreneur Pub Co. (CPC) Ltd v Sweeney* [2002] EWHC 1060 (Ch), [2003] ECC 17, [2002] 2 EGLR 132, the tenant of a public house alleged that he had been induced to take a new lease from the defendant landlord as a result of a statement predicting that the tenant would be released from an associated beer tie by the end of March 1998. This statement was no more than a statement of intention. It was honestly held, since it was the defendant's policy at that time to release all pubs from the tie (the defendant having given undertakings to this effect to the Secretary of State for Trade and Industry). As a result, the statement could not constitute an actionable misrepresentation. In addition, although the statement might constitute a statement of fact on the basis that it was an opinion or prediction that impliedly stated that the defendant had good grounds for making it—*Smith v Land & House; Esso v Mardon*—it was not a *false* statement of fact precisely because there were *good grounds* to justify the statement at the time it was made.

However, even if a statement of intention is true when made, depending on the circumstances and whether the statement of intention is a continuing one, the statement maker may come under a duty to correct a statement of intention where the intention changes before the contract is made: see *Inclusive Technology v Williamson* [2009] EWCA Civ 718, [2010] 1 P & CR 2 (*page 442, 9.1.1.3.2*).

9.1.2.3 Statements of law can give rise to a claim based on actionable misrepresentation

Pankhania v Hackney London Borough Council
[2002] EWHC 2441 (Ch), [2002] NPC 123

The claimant had bid for commercial property, part of which was occupied by National Car Parks Ltd (NCP) and used as a car park. The claimant alleged that he had been induced to purchase the properties as a result of misrepresentations in the auction brochure to the effect that NCP was a contractual licensee whose occupation could be terminated by giving three months' notice, when in fact NCP was a business tenant and protected under the Landlord and Tenant Act 1954. The claimant sought damages for misrepresentation to cover the payment made to NCP to secure its departure from the car park. The defendants claimed that any misrepresentations were misrepresentations as to law and there was a long-standing rule that statements of law were not actionable.

Held: Since the decision of the House of Lords in *Kleinwort Benson Ltd v Lincoln City Council* [1999] 2 AC 349 to the effect that it was not the case that there was no remedy available for a mistake of law, a misrepresentation of law could be an actionable misrepresentation.

The judge awarded damages under s. 2(1) MA 1967 (*page 481, 9.3.2.2*), on the basis that the defendant could not show that it reasonably believed its statements relating to NCP to be true: see *Pankhania v Hackney London Borough Council* [2004] EWHC 323 (Ch), [2004] 1 EGLR 135, *page 460, 9.3.1.1*, for the damages award.

This was a statement of the application of law to particular facts, which has traditionally been actionable. Therefore, it must remain unclear whether there can be an actionable misrepresentation in relation to an abstract statement of law.

9.1.3 Induces the other party to contract

The defendant must prove that they were induced to enter into the contract by the false statement. The inducement requirement is less strict in fraud cases.

BV Nederlandse Industrie Van Eiprodukten v Rembrandt Entreprises Inc
[2019] EWCA Civ 596

In May 2015 the defendant agreed to purchase 4,200 metric tons of egg products from the claimant on condition that the claimant obtained regulatory approval. In June 2015 a new contract was made with increased prices for the products, based on a representation by the claimant that there had been unanticipated regulatory costs. The representation was fraudulently made in that a part of the increased price was purely for the claimant's profit. At first instance, [2018] EWHC 1857 (Comm), Teare J held that the misrepresentation had induced the second contract and accordingly that it could be rescinded. The Court of Appeal saw no reason to overturn that factual finding, and laid down the relevant principles applicable to inducement.

LONGMORE LJ:

14. It is also important to know what has to be proved by the party who has the onus of proof. Is it that the representee would/would not have acted differently but for the misrepresentation? Or is it that the representation played a part (or influenced) the decision of the representee? Or is it sufficient that the representee might/might not have acted differently?

15. It is surprising that these are still controversial questions in English law especially since the test for inducement in cases of innocent or negligent representation appears to be settled in the form that the representee has the burden of showing inducement in the sense that he has to show he would not have entered into the relevant contract had the representation not been made see: *Assicurazioni Generali SpA v Arab Insurance Group* [2003] 1 All ER (Comm) 140, *Pan Atlantic Insurance Co Ltd v Pine Top Insurance Co Ltd* [1995] 1 A.C. 501, Chitty, *Contracts*, 33rd edition, para 7-039 . . .

32. [T]he law at the end of the nineteenth century had assimilated the requirement of inducement in the tort of deceit and in actions for rescission for fraudulent misrepresentation and could be stated as being that the representee had to prove he had been materially 'influenced' by the representations in the sense that it was 'actively present to his mind' to use Bowen LJ's phrase [in *Edgington v Fitzmaurice* (1885) 29 Ch. D. 459]: that, whereas there is a presumption that a statement, likely to induce a representee to enter into a contract, did so induce him, that is merely a presumption of fact which is to be taken into account along with all the evidence. There was no requirement as a matter of law, that the representee should state in terms that he would not have made the contract but for the misrepresentation but the absence of such a statement was part of the overall evidential picture from which the judge had to ascertain whether there was inducement or not. The fact that there were other reasons (besides the representation) for the claimant to have made the contract did not mean that he was not induced by the representation made. Insofar as *Reynell v Sprye* (1852) 1 De G. M.&G. 660 had said that there was no need for evidence from the claimant or that it was sufficient if the claimant 'might' have made the contract, if there had been

no representation, that did not represent the law at any rate if 'might' meant something different from 'influencing' his decision in deciding whether to make the contract . . .

43. It seems to me, therefore, that overall the modern authorities do not add much to the conclusions that I drew from the Victorian authorities in para [32] above. I do not think that Barton v Armstrong [1976] AC 104 intended to reverse the legal burden of proof but, if it did, this court must prefer the later analysis of the House of Lords and the Supreme Court that there is an evidential presumption of fact (not law) that a representee will have been induced by a fraudulent representation intended to cause him to enter the contract and that the inference will be 'very difficult to rebut' to use the words of Lord Clarke.

44. There remains the question whether, if it be the case that the burden of proof is on the representee to show that he was induced (albeit with the help of the presumption which is very difficult to rebut), it is sufficient for him to show that he might have acted differently. Both Christopher Clarke J in *Raiffeisen Zentralbank Osterreich AG v Royal Bank of Scotland plc* [2010] EWHC 1392 (Comm) and Hamblen J in *Cassa di Risparmio della Republica di San Marino SpA v Barclays Bank Ltd* [2011] EWHC 484 (Comm) have *obiter* given some support for this being an appropriate test in cases of fraudulent misrepresentation, see paras 196–199 and 232–233 respectively.

45. I have already pointed out the ambiguity in the word 'might' which was in fact used in *Barton v Armstrong*. If it means no more than being actively present in the mind of the representee to repeat the phrase of Bowen LJ, it is perhaps a convenient shorthand. But if it means that the court cannot make up its mind on inducement and therefore decides as a matter of law to give the representee the benefit of the doubt, it is not a helpful concept because that would be contrary to the law as I conceive it to be, see para 32 above, which requires the representee to prove inducement albeit with the assistance of a presumption that 'will be very difficult to rebut'. To some extent this is a matter of terminology but terminology can be important in some cases.

Redgrave v Hurd
(1881) 20 Ch D 1 (CA)

The claimant, a solicitor who was shortly to retire, placed an advertisement offering to take a partner in the practice who would also agree to purchase the claimant's house. The defendant replied to the advertisement and was told by the claimant that the practice brought in about £300 a year. The claimant had shown the defendant summaries for three years, showing a business of just less than £200 a year, and had stated that the rest of the income was made up of business not included in the summaries, which was detailed in a bundle of papers shown to the defendant. The defendant did not examine these papers, which in fact showed that there was next to no additional business, so that income from the business was only £200 a year. The defendant signed an agreement to purchase the house for £1,600 and paid a deposit of £100. Subsequently, the defendant discovered the true facts about the business and refused to complete. The claimant brought an action for specific performance, and the defendant counterclaimed for rescission of the contract and damages alleging misrepresentation.

Held: If a material misrepresentation is made to a party, then he must be taken to have relied on it in entering into the contract, unless it can be shown that the representee knew of the facts showing the representation to be untrue, or that he either expressly stated or showed by his conduct that he did not rely on the representation. The defendant was therefore entitled to have the contract rescinded and his deposit returned. (However, he was not entitled to damages because, at the time of this case, damages were available only where the misrepresentation was fraudulent, and fraud had not been pleaded by the defendant in his counterclaim.)

JESSEL MR: If a man is induced to enter into a contract by a false representation it is not a sufficient answer to him to say, 'If you had used due diligence you would have found out that the statement was untrue. You had the means afforded you of discovering its falsity, and did not choose to avail yourself of them.' I take it to be a settled doctrine of equity, not only as regards specific performance but also as regards rescission, that this is not an answer.

NOTES

1. The *Redgrave v Hurd* principle was applied in the analysis of the Court of Appeal in *Peekay Intermark Ltd v Australia and New Zealand Banking Group Ltd* [2006] EWCA Civ 386, [2006] 2 Lloyd's Rep 511, [2006] 1 CLC 582 (*page 187, 5.2.2*). The question was whether the claimant had been induced to sign an investment contract by relying on the informal (and incorrect) description of the product given over the telephone rather than the formal written terms and conditions in the signed writing. Although the Court of Appeal held that there had been no inducement, it was stressed that the defendant bank could not argue that the claimant was bound because he *should* have read the final terms and conditions before signing. Constructive notice will not suffice to prevent inducement; the knowledge of the true position must be actual.

2. It might be argued that the buyer is negligent in failing to make inquiries where the opportunity is available to him, and his damages should consequently be reduced for contributory negligence. The argument in favour of apportionment is, however, incompatible with the tone of the judgment of Jessel MR in *Redgrave v Hurd* that the buyer has no obligation to investigate, a view recently endorsed by the Supreme Court in *Hayward v Zurich Insurance Co. plc* [2016] UKSC 48, set out below. See also the discussion of contributory negligence, at *page 487, 9.3.2.4.*

3. It is clear from *Horsfall v Thomas* (1862) 1 H & C 90, that a representation cannot induce a contract unless the representee knew of it. In that case, the defect might have been discovered by the buyer if he had inspected the gun, but he did not, and the representation could not therefore have induced the contract.

Attwood v Small
(1838) 6 Cl & F 232, [1835–42] All ER Rep 258 (HL)

The vendor made statements about the earning capacity of mines that he was selling. The prospective buyers arranged for their co-directors and experienced agents to examine the property and accounts. They reported (incorrectly) that the vendor's statements were true. The buyers purchased the mine, but later claimed to rescind, alleging fraudulent misrepresentation by the vendor.

Held: First, there was no fraud, and secondly, the buyers had not relied on the vendor's statements, because they had tested their accuracy and relied on the results of their own investigations.

NOTES

1. *Attwood v Small* is often cited as authority for the fact that if the representee carries out his own investigations, then he does not rely on the representation. However, it was stated *obiter* in *S. Pearson & Son Ltd v Dublin Corporation* [1907] AC 351 that even if a representee carries out his own investigations, the representor will be liable for misrepresentation if the misrepresentation is made fraudulently.

2. In addition, for *Attwood v Small* to preclude a claim based on a representation, the claimant must have relied *only* on the results of his investigations and not at all on the representation itself, since a representation need not be the only reason inducing a contract as long as it is one of the reasons: *Edgington v Fitzmaurice* (1885) 29 Ch D 459 (*page 445, 9.1.2.2*).

This point is aptly illustrated by *Morris v Jones* [2002] EWCA Civ 1790. The claimant had been negotiating to purchase a leasehold interest in a basement flat and the defendant had represented that it had been 'tanked'. However, the claimant had received three survey reports identifying problems of dampness in the basement. The defendant therefore alleged that the misrepresentation had not induced the making of the contract. The Court of Appeal held, relying on *Edgington v Fitzmaurice*, that the claimant could still rely on the misrepresentation as a factor inducing the making of the contract. (The judge had found that the representation was fraudulent and this point was not contested on appeal, which may explain why the fraud point in *S. Pearson & Son Ltd v Dublin Corporation* was not argued.)

The claimant was in June 1998 injured at work due to the negligence of his employer. The claimant brought proceedings against the employer and sought damages of £419,316.59. Investigations by the employer's liability insurers demonstrated that the injuries had been overstated, and the claimant was ultimately awarded £14,720. By a settlement contract given effect by a court order (a Tomlin order) in October 2003 the insurers agreed to pay a total of £134,973.11 including costs and interest. Information was subsequently provided to the employer by the claimant's neighbours, indicating that he had fully recovered a year before the settlement. The insurers commenced the present proceedings to recover their payment. The Court of Appeal, overturning the judgment of the trial judge, rejected the insurers' action, holding that the insurers had been aware at the time of the settlement of the real possibility of fraud but had chosen to settle nonetheless. The Supreme Court allowed the appeal and set out in detail the principles applicable to inducement.

LORD CLARKE: 18. It must be shown that the defendant made a materially false representation which was intended to, and did, induce the representee to act to its detriment. To my mind it is not necessary, as a matter of law, to prove that the representee believed that the representation was true. In my opinion there is no clear authority to the contrary. However, that is not to say that the representee's state of mind may not be relevant to the issue of inducement. Indeed, it may be very relevant. For example, if the representee does not believe that the representation is true, he may have serious difficulty in establishing that he was induced to enter into the contract or that he has suffered loss as a result. The judge makes this point clearly and accurately in the third sentence of para 2.5 of his admirable judgment.

19. He makes a further point in the same paragraph which is of importance in the context of this somewhat unusual case. It is this. A person in the position of the employer or its insurer may have suspicions as to whether the representation is true. It may even be strongly of the view that it is not true. However, the question in a case like this is not what view the employer or its insurer takes but what view the court may take in due course. This is just such a case, as the judge correctly perceived. As he put it, the employer and its advisers must take into account the possibility that Mr Hayward would be believed by the judge at the trial. That is because the views of the judge will determine the amount of damages awarded.

20. In any event this is not a case in which Zurich or the employer knew that Mr Hayward was deliberately exaggerating the seriousness and long term effects of his injuries. We now know that he was thoroughly dishonest from October 1999 and that he continued to make false claims in the witness box at the trial even when the evidence against him was overwhelming.

22. [The] pleas show that Zurich was suspicious of Mr Hayward but no very clear allegations were, or could be, made. However, it is not in dispute that Zurich did as much as it reasonably could to investigate the position before the settlement. The evidence was not as good from its point of view as it might have hoped but the fact is that Zurich did not know the extent of Mr Hayward's misrepresentations. The case was settled at a time when the only difference between the experts was the likely duration of future loss. The figure agreed was about half way between the respective opinions of the experts. It was not until the advent of Mr and Mrs Cox that Zurich realised the true position. Hence, as the judge expressly found, the amount of the settlement was very much greater than it would have been but for the fraudulent misrepresentations made by Mr Hayward. The small amount ultimately awarded by the judge, which is not challenged, shows the extent of the dishonest nature of the claim. I am not persuaded that the importance of encouraging settlement, which I entirely agree is considerable, is sufficient to allow Mr Hayward to retain moneys which he only obtained by fraud.

9.2 The remedy of rescission

As misrepresentation renders the contract voidable at the option of the misrepresentee, the main remedy will be rescission, which *in principle* is available for fraudulent, negligent, and innocent misrepresentation, and which involves the return from each party of anything that has passed under the contract.

Note, however, that, as part of the new consumer regime of remedies for misleading actions, the Consumer Protection (Amendment) Regulations 2014, SI 2014/870, provide for a right to unwind or a right to a discount in misrepresentation claims falling within the CPRs. The right to unwind will exist only within the relevant time period (90 days) and only if the product is capable of being rejected at that time, e.g. is not fully consumed (CPRs 2008, reg. 27E). The consumer will then become entitled to a refund (CPRs 2008, reg. 27F). Alternatively, the consumer could exercise his right to receive a discount (CPRs 2008, reg. 27I). The level of the discount turns on matters such as the seriousness of the trader's conduct, the impact that it had on the consumer, and the time that has elapsed. There are separate discount provisions if the value of the product exceeds £5,000. Where the consumer has a right to a discount, either party may also elect to terminate the contract (in the sense of discharging obligations relating to future performance) but cannot also unwind the pre-existing contractual obligations.

The consumer will have the burden of establishing causation, i.e. that the prohibited practice was a significant factor in his decision to contract or make payment.

9.2.1 Limits to the right to rescind

Rescission is an equitable remedy and is subject to a number of bars preventing its exercise. These bars to rescission (with the exception of s. 2(2) MA 1967) apply to all instances in which the remedy of rescission is available, e.g. duress or undue influence: *Halpern and others v Halpern and another* [2007] EWCA Civ 291, [2007] 3 WLR 849.

9.2.1.1 Affirmation

Long v Lloyd
[1958] 1 WLR 753 (CA)

The defendant advertised a lorry for sale in a newspaper and described it as being in 'exceptional condition'. The claimant saw the vehicle at the defendant's premises and the defendant stated that it was capable of a speed of 40 miles per hour. On 22 October, the claimant, accompanied by the defendant, took the lorry for a trial run and the defendant represented that the lorry's fuel consumption was 11 miles to the gallon. The claimant then bought the lorry for £750. Two days later, on 24 October, the claimant attempted a journey in the lorry, but the dynamo ceased to function and the claimant was advised to fit a reconstructed dynamo. He also noticed that an oil seal was defective, that there was a crack in one of the wheels, and that the vehicle had consumed 8 gallons of fuel when it had travelled only 40 miles. When the defendant was advised of these defects, he offered to pay half the cost of the reconstructed dynamo and the claimant accepted this offer. The repair having taken place, the claimant's brother took the vehicle on a journey (on 25 October); on 26 October, the claimant learned that the lorry had broken down on this journey. The claimant brought an action for rescission of the contract on the ground of non-fraudulent misrepresentation. (Note that there was no right to damages for such a misrepresentation at this time.)

Held: Certainly, by the time that the claimant sent the lorry on a journey on 25 October, he had affirmed the misrepresentations and accepted the lorry, in full knowledge of the condition and performance of the vehicle. (Thus, the claimant was left with no remedy at all.)

PEARCE LJ: [A] strict application to the facts of the present case of Denning LJ's view to the effect that the right (if any) to rescind after completion on the ground of innocent misrepresentation is barred by acceptance of the goods must necessarily prove fatal to the plaintiff's case. Apart from special circumstances, the place of delivery is the proper place for examination and for acceptance. It was open to the plaintiff to have the lorry examined by an expert before driving it away, but he chose not to do so. It is true, however, that the truth of certain of the representations, for example, that the lorry would do 11 miles to the gallon—could not be ascertained except by user and, therefore—the plaintiff should have a reasonable time to test it. Until he had had such an opportunity it might well be said that he had not accepted the lorry, always assuming, of course that he did nothing inconsistent with the ownership of the seller. An examination of the facts, however, shows that on any view he must have accepted the lorry before he purported to reject it.

NOTES

1. Pearce LJ also suggested that rescission might well have been lost much earlier. He appears to have relied upon Denning LJ's comments in *Leaf v International Galleries* (9.2.1.2), seeking to equate this area of law with the principles in the Sale of Goods Act (SGA) 1979 on the right to reject for breach of condition. At this time, there was also no available remedy in damages for such a misrepresentation, although damages were clearly available for breach of contract even where the right to reject had been lost.

2. In *Harsten Developments Ltd v Bleaken* [2012] EWHC 2704 (Ch), it was alleged that the vendor of a plot with planning permission had misrepre-

sented the boundary with neighbouring land. The developer sought rescission of the contract, but had reapplied for the planning permission since the date of the contract. The judge considered that rescission was nevertheless available in principle because the developer had not been aware of the ability to rescind. The judge then considered the exercise of the discretion in s. 2(2) MA 1967 to award damages in lieu of that rescission (discussed at *page 489, 9.3.3*), a discretion which would arguably not have been available to the court but for the decision that rescission had not been lost by the developer's action in reapplying for the planning permission.

9.2.1.2 Lapse of time

Leaf v International Galleries
[1950] 2 KB 86 (CA)

In 1944, the defendants sold the claimant a picture, which they represented to have been painted by Constable. In 1949, the claimant tried to sell it and discovered that it was not by Constable. He sought rescission and repayment of the purchase price.

Held: This remedy had been lost because it had not been exercised within a reasonable time.

DENNING LJ: The question is whether the plaintiff is entitled to rescind the contract on the ground that the picture in question was not painted by Constable. I emphasise that it is a claim to rescind only: there is no claim in this action for damages for breach of condition or breach of warranty. The claim is simply one for rescission. At a very late stage before the county court judge counsel did ask for leave to amend by claiming damages for breach of warranty, but it was not allowed. No claim for damages is before us at all. The only question is whether the plaintiff is entitled to rescind . . .

In my opinion, this case is to be decided according to the well known principles applicable to the sale of goods. This was a contract for the sale of goods. There was a mistake about the quality of the subject-matter, because both parties believed the picture to be a Constable; and that mistake was in one sense essential or fundamental. But such a mistake does not avoid the contract: there was no mistake at all about the subject-matter of the sale. It was a specific picture, 'Salisbury Cathedral.' The parties were agreed in the same terms on the same subject-matter, and that is sufficient to make a contract: see *Solle v Butcher* [1950] 1 KB 671.

There was a term in the contract as to the quality of the subject-matter: namely, as to the person by whom the picture was painted—that it was by Constable. That term of the contract was, according to our terminology, either a condition or a warranty. If it was a condition, the buyer could reject the picture for breach of the condition at any time before he accepted it, or is deemed to have accepted it; whereas, if it was only a warranty, he could not reject it at all but was confined to a claim for damages.

I think it right to assume in the buyer's favour that this term was a condition, and that, if he had come in proper time he could have rejected the picture; but the right to reject for breach of condition has always been limited by the rule that, once the buyer has accepted, or is deemed to have accepted, the goods in performance of the contract, then he cannot thereafter reject, but is relegated to his claim for damages: see s. 11, sub-s. 1 (c), of the Sale of Goods Act, 1893, and *Wallis, Son & Wells v Pratt & Haynes* [1911] AC 394.

The circumstances in which a buyer is deemed to have accepted goods in performance of the contract are set out in s. 35 of the Act, which says that the buyer is deemed to have accepted the goods, amongst other things, 'when, after the lapse of a reasonable time, he retains the goods without intimating to the seller that he has rejected them.' In this case the buyer took the picture into his house and, apparently, hung it there, and five years passed before he intimated any rejection at all. That, I need hardly say, is much more than a reasonable time. It is far too late for him at the end of five years to reject this picture for breach of any condition. His remedy after that length of time is for damages only, a claim which he has not brought before the court.

Is it to be said that the buyer is in any better position by relying on the representation, not as a condition, but as an innocent misrepresentation? . . .

Although rescission may in some cases be a proper remedy, it is to be remembered that an innocent misrepresentation is much less potent than a breach of condition; and a claim to rescission for innocent misrepresentation must at any rate be barred when a right to reject for breach of condition is barred. A condition is a term of the contract of a most material character, and if a claim to reject on that account is barred, it seems to me a fortiori that a claim to rescission on the ground of innocent misrepresentation is also barred.

So, assuming that a contract for the sale of goods may be rescinded in a proper case for innocent misrepresentation, the claim is barred in this case for the self-same reason as a right to reject is barred. The buyer has accepted the picture. He had ample opportunity for examination in the first few days after he had bought it. Then was the time to see if the condition or representation was fulfilled. Yet he has kept it all this time. Five years have elapsed without any notice of rejection. In my judgment he cannot now claim to rescind. His only claim, if any, as the county court judge said, was one for damages, which he has not made in this action . . .

NOTES

1. The damages claim to which Denning LJ was referring was that for breach of contract. Nowadays, there is a right to *claim* damages in misrepresentation, but only if the misrepresentation was at least negligent.

2. Since *Leaf v International Galleries* was a case of non-fraudulent misrepresentation, time ran from the date of the contract. One of the advantages in alleging fraudulent misrepresentation is that time runs from the date on which the fraud was—or could, with reasonable diligence, have been—discovered.

3. In *Salt v Stratstone Specialist Ltd (t/a Stratstone Cadillac Newcastle)* [2015] EWCA Civ 745, [2015] CTLC 206, the claimant had purchased a luxury car from the defendant car dealer in 2007 on the basis that it was a new car. In 2008 he sought to return the car on the basis that it had many defects and then learnt that the car was in fact two years old and had been involved in a collision. He therefore sought rescission for the misrepresentation that the car was new. The county court judge had refused rescission on the basis that the car had been registered after the sale so that *restitutio in integrum* was impossible

and that too much time had elapsed since the sale. (The county court instead awarded damages in lieu of rescission under s. 2(2) MA 1967 but this explanation of s. 2(2) was overturned on appeal by the Court of Appeal, see the discussion at *page 489, 9.3.3*). The High Court overturned the county court decision on rescission and this was upheld on appeal so that rescission was permitted. The claimant had brought his claim a reasonable time after learning of the misrepresentation and that was sufficient.

Of course, this is at odds with the principle that, in the absence of fraud, time runs from the date of the contract. However, it was open to the Court of Appeal seeking to preserve the ability to rescind to hold that the delay was not unreasonable on the facts, particularly given the absence of any fault attributable to the claimant for the delay in achieving rescission for the misrepresentation.

9.2.1.3 Restitution is impossible

Clarke v Dickson
(1858) EB & E 148, 120 ER 463 (Queen's Bench)

In 1853, the claimant purchased shares in a mining company as a result of representations made by the defendants, who were directors of this company. The company was later wound up. The claimant then discovered that the representations made to him had been fraudulent. He wanted to give up the shares and recover the purchase price.

Held: He could not because he could not restore the shares in the same state as he took them.

ERLE J: In 1853 the plaintiff accepted the shares; and from that time he was, in point of law, in possession of the mine, and worked it by his agent . . . After three years working of the mine, and trying to make a profit, he cannot restore the shares as they were before this was done. But, further, he not only had the chance of profit, but dividends were declared, and received by him. They were not received in money, it is true; but the receipt of money's worth has the same effect in law. Then he has also changed the nature of the article: the shares he received were shares in a company on the cost book principle; the plaintiff offers to restore them after he has converted them into shares in a joint stock corporation. Lastly, the offer to restore these shares is not made till after the Company is in the course of being wound up, when all chance of profit is over, and the shares can only be a source of loss . . .

Halpern and others v Halpern and another
[2007] EWCA Civ 291, [2007] 3 WLR 849 (CA)

This case concerned a compromise agreement alleged to have been reached between a number of the deceased's sons and daughter (the appellants) and another son and grandson (the respondents) relating to inheritance issues and an arbitration before a Beth Din. One term of the compromise was that all documents produced during the arbitration had to be destroyed or handed over. The appellants raised the issue of duress in relation to this compromise agreement when sued for damages for its breach and the respondents claimed that, since the relevant documents had been destroyed, the compromise could not be rescinded, because it would not be possible to make restitution and thereby put the parties back into the position in which they were before the compromise. The appellants contended that an inability to give counter-restitution should not be a bar to a claim based on rescission for duress.

Held: Rescission for duress was no different in principle from rescission for other vitiating factors, such as misrepresentation.

CARNWATH LJ [with whose judgment on this issue both Waller and Sedley LJJ agreed]: 60 Before the deputy judge [Nigel Teare QC, [2006] EWHC 1728 (Comm), [2007] QB 88], the argument turned specific-ally on the requirements of rescission for duress at common law. This was contrasted, on the one hand, with common law rescission for fraud, for which counter-restitution was a well-established requirement: see eg *Western Bank of Scotland v Addie* (1867) LR 1 Sc & Div 145; and, on the other, with equitable rescission for undue influence, for which again a form of counter-restitution was required, albeit subject to a more flexible criterion of 'practical justice'. The classic statement of the latter approach is in *Erlanger v New Sombrero Phosphate Co* (1878) 3 App Cas 1218, 1278–1279, per Lord Blackburn: 'a court of equity could not give damages, and, unless it can rescind the contract, can give no relief. And, on the other hand, it can take accounts of profits, and make allowance for deterioration. And I think the practice has always been for a court of equity to give this relief whenever, by the exercise of its powers, it can do *what is practically just*, though it cannot restore the parties precisely to the state they were in before the contract.' (Emphasis added.) In more modern times, the same approach was adopted and applied by this court in *O'Sullivan v Management Agency and Music Ltd* [1985] QB 428, 458 per Dunn LJ.

61 Before the deputy judge, [counsel] for the defendants had submitted that duress at common law was to be distinguished, in that there was no necessary requirement for the party seeking rescission to offer counter-restitution. He relied on the lack of any reported cases in which such a requirement had been imposed, and on the following passage by *Burrows, The Law of Restitution*, p 218:

> Most importantly, it appears that the bar that restitutio in integrum is impossible generally does not apply to rescission for duress. The explanation for that is that it would generally contradict the basis for the claimant's restitution to recognise a counter-claim by the defendant: if it was illegitimate for the defendant to demand a sum of money for a particular consideration, for example, carrying out work, it would be inconsistent then to award the defendant counter-restitution for that work.

62 The judge rejected this argument. He could see no sensible reason for distinguishing between fraud and duress in this respect. He cited Lord Cross of Chelsea in *Barton v Armstrong* [1976] AC 104, 118:

> There is an obvious analogy between setting aside a disposition for duress or undue influence and setting it aside for fraud. In each case—and to quote the words of Holmes J in *Fairbanks v Snow* (1887) 13 NE 596, 598—'the party has been subjected to an improper motive for action.'

He also referred to a passage in Enonchong, *Duress, Undue Influence and Unconscionable Dealing* (2006), para 28–012:

> The issue of restitutio in integrum has not presented itself in cases of rescission for common law duress. This is probably because in most cases of duress the complainant has simply paid money or agreed to pay money without receiving any benefit that he needs to return upon rescission. Since in such cases the question is only about the repayment of the money by the defendant, there is no issue in restitutio in integrum. The lack of discussion on this issue in case of rescission for duress should not be taken to mean that restitutio in integrum is not a requirement for rescission on the grounds of duress. If A is induced by B's duress to enter into a contract to buy B's car, it is unlikely that the court will allow rescission of the contract so that A can recover the price paid to B without insisting that A should return B's car. It would not be inconsistent with the basis of A's restitution for the court to insist on counter-restitution by A. In any event, restitutio in integrum is clearly a requirement in the case of rescission for other common law vitiating factors such as fraudulent misrepresentation.

Misrepresentation

9

63 . . . [In his original skeleton argument (August 2006), counsel] had sought to justify a special rule for common law duress:

> Whereas fraudulent misrepresentation or indeed any misrepresentation is reliant upon a wrong that is extrinsic to the contract itself, as it merely induces a contract, duress by contrast is directly and intimately bound up with the contract formation, that is to say, the improper conduct operates at the point of entry into the contract itself. Effectively the victim's autonomy is threatened. Since mutuality is at the heart of contract an avoided contract cannot be enforced in either direction and no benefits including counter-restitution can be sought. Effectively, once the contract is avoided for duress and the victim as an act of self-help takes back that which he parted with and/or is relieved from unperformed obligations, the loss lies where it falls in a manner analogous to illegality.

64 However, in his supplementary skeleton (February 2007 . . .) he seems to have moved towards an argument based, not on the distinction between law and equity, but on their assimilation:

> the modern statement of the law is that, impossibility of restitutio in integrum is no longer a bar to relief when a claimant seeks to avoid/rescind a contract on the grounds of duress or under influence. Instead the court's approach is to do practical justice between the parties by making orders for counter-restitution, even if they cannot restore them to the precise position they were in prior to the contract being rescinded . . . (ii) The correct approach is that counter-restitution is never in fact impossible: it should always be possible for the party seeking to rescind to pay a defendant a sum of money to reflect counter-restitution of the value of benefits received by him. There can be no rational reason in a system of fused administration of law and equity why the liberal approach taken in equity cannot also be taken at common law . . .

Just as in *Erlanger v New Sombrero Phosphate Co* the value of depreciation of a phosphate mine could be measured in order to make counter-restitution in equity, so, it is argued, the court can in the present case put an appropriate monetary value on the loss of the documents, even if this is represented by a reduction in the claimant's prospects of success in the arbitration (cf *Kitchen v Royal Air Force Association* [1958] 1 WLR 563) . . .

68 Thus, it seems, the defendants have abandoned the stance that common law duress was to be distinguished from undue influence at equity. Instead they have embraced the *Erlanger* practical justice criterion as applicable to both. But they have taken it a stage further, by arguing that by this test counter-restitution is never impossible. Counsel for the claimants do not dispute the practical justice approach, but submit that the extension is wrong in principle, and contrary to authority . . .

75 Returning to the question posed by the preliminary issue in this case, a definitive response is not possible or appropriate, until the facts have been found. I would be inclined to agree with the deputy judge that rescission for duress should be no different in principle from rescission for other 'vitiating factors'. However, the practical effect of counter-restitution, in the terms explained by Lord Blackburn in the *Erlanger* case 3 App Cas 1218, will depend on the circumstances of the particular case. In the present case, if (contrary to Christopher Clarke J's expectations) the defendants are able to establish that their consent to the compromise agreement was procured by improper pressure (whether that is characterised as duress or undue influence), it would be surprising if the law could not provide a suitable remedy. The form of the remedy, whether equitable or tortious, is a matter which cannot sensibly be decided until the facts are known, not only as to the nature and effect of the improper pressure, but also as to the identity and significance of the documents destroyed.

NOTES

1. On the facts, the inability to make counter-restitution was directly attributable to a condition of the agreement said to be affected by the duress, which surely calls for some different outcome on the facts, if not in terms of legal principle.

2. The Court of Appeal noted that, given this situation, 'it would be surprising if the law could not provide a suitable remedy', although did not specify at this stage (before the full facts were known) what this remedy would be or its basis in law other than securing 'practical justice'. However, it is conceded

by the Court of Appeal that 'the primary objective may not always need to be to restore *both* parties to their previous positions' and the envisaged means appears to be the principle in *Erlanger v New Sombrero Phosphate Co.* (1878) 3 App Cas 1218, i.e. in cases of substantial restitution, the court may exercise an equitable discretion to order rescission whilst allowing for a financial adjustment in order to take account of the inability to make total restitution.

3. Regrettably, as a result of the amendment of the pleadings, the Court of Appeal did not discuss the nature of rescission as a 'self-help' remedy (below).

In *Thomas Witter v TBP Industries Ltd* [1996] 2 All ER 573, 588F–H (for the facts, see *page 458*, *9.3.1*), Jacob J held that rescission for misrepresentation was not available because of the inability to make restitution:

> [Counsel for the plaintiff] tied his claim to rescission to the claim in fraud. I never was quite sure why, since rescission is available also for innocent misrepresentation. Even if I had found fraud, however, I would not have granted rescission. This remedy is not available where it is not possible to restore the parties to their position before the contract. Although Melton Medes kept the Witter business separate, it is unrealistic to regard it as the same as the business conveyed. There have been numerous changes to staff and personnel (including the departure of Mr Francis who had exceptional sales skills). Those personnel who have stayed have been in different pension schemes, there are mortgagees of the business and so on. Time has moved on and third parties would, I think, be affected. [Counsel's] actual submission was that it was not shown that third parties would be affected. So he was suggesting that the onus was on the defendants to avoid rescission by showing innocent third parties would be affected. I cannot think that is right. The Thomas Witter business has been in the hands of Melton Medes for four years. It is they who would know who or what might be affected by a transfer back to Tarmac.

This suggests that rescission of a contract to purchase a business can be lost by the vendor contesting the right to rescind, so that the misrepresentee has to seek a remedy of rescission via court action. It is generally assumed that rescission is a self-help remedy, i.e. the innocent party's election to rescind is determinative rather than court action. The problem in practice is that the guilty party may not accept rescission and a court has to determine the innocent party's ability to rescind. In *Thomas Witter*, Jacob J assessed the availability of rescission at the date of the hearing when, if rescission is achieved by the party's action, he should have considered the position at the date of that action to rescind. However, it is unrealistic for a court to evaluate the ability to achieve *restitutio in integrum* at that date, since time and events will not have stood still in the interim: see O'Sullivan [2000] CLJ 509.

9.2.1.4 Where third party rights have intervened or a bona fide third party purchaser has acquired the goods before rescission

In *Crystal Palace Football Club (2000) Ltd v Dowie* [2007] EWHC 1392 (QB), [2007] IRLR 682 (for the facts, see *page 441*, *9.1.1.2*), rescission was unavailable because of third party interests, since it would have the effect of retrospectively reviving the defendant's employment with the Club when both had moved on, i.e. the defendant had since been employed elsewhere (Coventry City) and Crystal Palace had a new manager. The defendant could not work for two clubs at the same time and the rights of his new club needed to be taken into account. Instead, it was appropriate to order damages or other financial relief as compensation.

See also the discussion of mistake as to identity, at *page 367*, *8.3.2*, where an innocent third party acquires goods from a rogue before the party making the mistake about the purchaser's identity has discovered the mistake and taken action.

9.2.1.5 **Where the court exercises its discretion under s. 2(2) to award damages instead of rescission**

See *page 489, 9.3.3*.

9.3 Types of misrepresentation and damages

The nature of the damages available for misrepresentation turns on the type of misrepresentation, but it is no longer the case that damages can be claimed only in relation to fraudulent misrepresentation.

Rescission alone may have the effect of restoring the parties to their original positions, but may not do so where, for example, the representee has incurred consequential expenses. In such cases, damages may be available *in addition* to rescission for fraudulent and negligent misrepresentations. Where rescission is not available, the only remedy will be damages for misrepresentation, although damages cannot be *claimed* for innocent misrepresentation.

The Consumer Protection (Amendment) Regulations 2014, SI 2014/870, have introduced a right to damages in consumer contracts falling within the scope of the CPRs, as amended, for certain identified losses which would not have been incurred had the misrepresentation not taken place (CPRs 2008, reg. 27J). The identified losses must be financial loss or non-pecuniary loss, such as distress, discomfort, or inconvenience where a significant purpose of the contract was to provide pleasure, relaxation, or peace of mind to the consumer. However, this is a limited ability to recover damages since there is no right to be paid financial loss damages covering the difference between the market price of the product and the amount paid or payable for it under the contract (i.e. it is possible to recover consequential financial losses and these must also have been reasonably foreseeable at the time of the misrepresentation). This compares unfavourably with the measure of recovery permitted for fraudulent misrepresentation and damages under s. 2(1) MA 1967. In addition, under the CPRs 2008 the trader is provided with a due diligence defence (reg. 27J(5)). The 2014 Amendment Regulations make it clear that the statutory damages claims and discretions contained in s. 2 MA 1967 are no longer available to consumers who have a 'right to redress' under the CPRs (MA 1967, s. 2(4)). Outside s. 2 (e.g. claims for damages in the tort of deceit), these new consumer rights are additional to any common law claims available to the consumer in respect of the prohibited practice, although there can be no double recovery. The overall effect therefore is to reduce considerably the potential damages available to a consumer misrepresentee when compared to the damages available in the B2B (business to business) context for the same misrepresentation.

9.3.1 Fraudulent misrepresentation: the tort of deceit

Derry v Peek
(1889) 14 App Cas 337 (HL)

LORD HERSCHELL: I think the authorities establish the following propositions: First, in order to sustain an action of deceit, there must be proof of fraud, and nothing short of that will suffice. Secondly, fraud is proved when it is shewn that a false representation has been made (1) knowingly, or (2) without belief in its truth, or (3) recklessly, careless whether it be true or false. Although I have treated the second and third as distinct cases, I think the third is but an instance of the second, for one who makes a statement under such circumstances can have no real belief in the truth of what he states. To prevent a false statement being fraudulent, there must, I think, always be an honest belief in its truth. And this probably covers the whole ground, for one who knowingly alleges that which is false, has obviously no such honest belief. Thirdly, if fraud be proved, the motive of the person guilty of it is immaterial. It matters not that there was no intention to cheat or injure the person to whom the statement was made.

Thomas Witter Ltd v TBP Industries Ltd
[1996] 2 All ER 573

The defendants owned a carpet manufacturing business, which the claimant wished to purchase. During the negotiations, the defendants provided the claimant with audited accounts and management accounts for 1988, and estimated profit figures for 1989. They also allowed the claimant to see the October 1989 management accounts, which included a special one-off expense of £120,000 in respect of problems with carpets supplied to one customer. However, the defendants did not indicate that these accounts were prepared on a different basis from the audited accounts and contained deferred pattern book expenditure. The parties concluded the contract for the sale of the business.

Within six months, the claimant claimed that it had been induced by representations made in the accounts—namely, (i) the statement that they included the special one-off expense of £120,000 (thereby implying that general profits would otherwise be higher), when the actual amount of this expense would be no more than £50,000, and (ii) by not disclosing the change in accounting basis.

The allegation was that these representations had been made recklessly (and so were fraudulent). Alternatively, it was alleged that they were negligent.

Held: These misrepresentations were not made fraudulently. Recklessness for the purposes of fraudulent misrepresentation required the statements to have been made dishonestly. Although there was no evidence of dishonesty since there was a belief that these statements were true, the misrepresentations were made negligently.

JACOB J:

Findings of fact in relation to fraudulent misrepresentation

So what I have to decide is whether Mr Simpson or Mr Lloyd deliberately set out to mislead Mr Puri, not by a deliberate untruth (for that is not alleged) but by its equivalent, such recklessness as to amount to a disregard for the truth. I have no difficulty in acquitting these witnesses of any such intent. I must explain why.

So far as pattern book expenditure deferrals in the October management accounts are concerned, I accept Mr Simpson's evidence that he did not know of these right up until the time of the contract. Nor did Mr Lloyd. By the time of the contract both thought that until November pattern book expenditure was written off as it was incurred. No one had ever suggested that the management accounts sometimes had ad hoc deferrals for 'smoothing' purposes.

In relation to the Allied problem . . . it is clear that by the time of the contract the representation had been defined as set out in the disclosure letter, namely £120,000 charged to the September and October accounts.

Misrepresentation

9

What does matter is whether Mr Simpson was so reckless in the estimate that he should be regarded as fraudulent. He says he was given the figure of £120,000 by Mr Hogarth as a 'fag packet' calculation at a Witter board meeting on 21 November. Mr Hogarth has no recollection whatever of the cost of the Allied problem being discussed. There appears never to have been a detailed estimate of the figure being worked out. Now I accept Mr Simpson's evidence that he got a rough estimate from Mr Hogarth. It was obviously important. So I think he was negligent not to get a proper estimate, or to tell Mr Puri that he had not got a proper estimate. But it was not dishonest of him to give that rough estimate to Mr Puri. He believed it, but knowing there was no proper check, his belief was not reasonable.

NOTES

1. This case clarified the distinction between recklessness and negligence. In order to be reckless, the statement maker would need to be in a position in which he does not know whether a statement is true or false, but takes the risk and asserts that it is true. There is no such dishonesty involved in a statement that is negligent, since the statement maker honestly believes that his statement is true, even if he ought to have known that it was false and was careless in not checking first.

2. Since an action based on fraudulent misrepresentation is in the tort of deceit, the measure of damages is tortious.

3. The standard of proof in relation to an allegation of fraud is demanding, i.e. proof that at the time of the representation the representor had no belief in its truth. In *Smith New Court v Scrimgeour Vickers* [1997] AC 254, at p. 274, Lord Steyn explained that:

while as a matter of law fraud only has to be proved to the civil standard, proof to that standard must necessarily take into account the consideration that the more serious the allegation is, the greater the proof is needed to persuade a court that it can be satisfied that the allegation is established. In other words, the very gravity of an allegation of fraud is a circumstance which has to be weighed in the scale in deciding as to the balance of probabilities.

4. It may be necessary to plead fraud in order, for example, to seek to increase a damages award which would otherwise be affected by a limitation of liability applying to non-fraudulent misrepresentations, e.g. *Ticket2final OU v Wigan Athletic AFC Ltd* [2015] EWHC 61b (Ch).

9.3.1.1 Measure of damages for fraudulent misrepresentation

9.3.1.1.1 *All direct loss flowing from the transaction*

The proper measure of damages for deceit was held by the Court of Appeal in *Doyle v Olby (Ironmongers) Ltd* [1969] 2 QB 158 to be 'all the damage directly flowing from the tortious act of fraudulent inducement which was not rendered too remote by the plaintiff's own conduct, whether or not the defendant could have foreseen the loss'.

Doyle v Olby was approved and applied in the following case.

Smith New Court Securities Ltd v Scrimgeour Vickers (Asset Management) Ltd
[1997] AC 254 (HL)

In July 1989, the claimant company had purchased a parcel of shares in FIS Inc., at the price of 82.25p per share, as a result of representations by the vendors of the shares that there were two other bidders involved. In fact, this was not the case. However, before this was discovered, it was announced in the September that FIS Inc. had been the victim of a major fraud by a third party. This resulted in a considerable fall in the share price and the claimant was eventually able to sell the shares for only 30–40p per share. The claimant sought damages for fraudulent misrepresentation. The trial judge assessed the damages as being the difference between the price paid and the real value of the shares at the date of the sale, taking into account the then undiscovered fraud, i.e. the difference between 82.25p and 44p. This resulted in a damages award of £10.7 million. On appeal, the Court of Appeal reversed this award, and held that the correct measure was the difference between the price paid and the market value at the date of the sale, i.e. the difference between 82.25p and 78p. The damages award was therefore reduced to just under £1.2 million.

Held (allowing the appeal): The victim of fraud was entitled to compensation for all actual loss, including consequential loss, which flowed directly from the transaction irrespective of whether it was foreseeable loss. Although the normal method of calculating such loss would be the difference between the price paid and the real value of the shares as at the date of the share purchase, on these facts that would not compensate the claimant for loss suffered. The fraudulent misrepresentation had led the claimant to pay too high a price for the shares and, given that the shares had been purchased with a view to retaining them and selling later, the claimant was locked into the transaction. Therefore, the damages award was the difference between 82.25p and 44p.

LORD BROWNE-WILKINSON: *Doyle v Olby (Ironmongers) Ltd* establishes four points. First, that the measure of damages where a contract has been induced by fraudulent misrepresentation is reparation for all the actual damage directly flowing from (i.e. caused by) entering into the transaction. Second, that in assessing such damages it is not an inflexible rule that the plaintiff must bring into account the value as at the transaction date of the asset acquired: although the point is not adverted to in the judgments, the basis on which the damages were computed shows that there can be circumstances in which it is proper to require a defendant only to bring into account the actual proceeds of the asset provided that he has acted reasonably in retaining it. Third, damages for deceit are not limited to those which were reasonably foreseeable. Fourth, the damages recoverable can include consequential loss suffered by reason of having acquired the asset.

In my judgment *Doyle v Olby (Ironmongers) Ltd* was rightly decided on all these points . . .

In sum, in my judgment the following principles apply in assessing the damages payable where the plaintiff has been induced by a fraudulent misrepresentation to buy property: (1) the defendant is bound to make reparation for all the damage directly flowing from the transaction; (2) although such damage need not have been foreseeable, it must have been directly caused by the transaction; (3) in assessing such damage, the plaintiff is entitled to recover by way of damages the full price paid by him, but he must give credit for any benefits which he has received as a result of the transaction; (4) as a general rule, the benefits received by him include the market value of the property acquired as at the date of acquisition; but such general rule is not to be inflexibly applied where to do so would prevent him obtaining full compensation for the wrong suffered; (5) although the circumstances in which the general rule should not apply cannot be comprehensively stated, it will normally not apply where either (a) the misrepresentation has continued to operate after the date of the acquisition of the asset so as to induce the plaintiff to retain the asset or (b) the circumstances of the case are such that the plaintiff is, by reason of the fraud, locked into the property. (6) In addition, the plaintiff is entitled to recover consequential losses caused by the transaction; (7) the plaintiff must take all reasonable steps to mitigate his loss once he has discovered the fraud . . .

How then do those principles apply in the present case? First, there is no doubt that the total loss incurred by Smith was caused by the Roberts fraud, unless it can be said that Smith's own decision to retain the shares until after the revelation of the Guerin fraud was a causative factor. The Guerin fraud had been committed before Smith acquired the shares on 21 July 1989. Unknown to everybody, on that date the shares were already pregnant with disaster. Accordingly when, pursuant to the Roberts fraud, Smith acquired the Ferranti shares they were induced to purchase a flawed asset. This is not a case of the difficult kind that can arise where the depreciation in the asset acquired between the date of acquisition and the date of realisation may be due to factors affecting the market which have occurred after the date of the defendant's fraud. In the present case the loss was incurred by reason of the purchasing of the shares which were pregnant with the loss and that purchase was caused by the Roberts fraud.

Can it then be said that the loss flowed not from Smith's acquisition but from Smith's decision to retain the shares? In my judgment it cannot. The judge found that the shares were acquired as a market-making risk and at a price which Smith would only have paid for an acquisition as a market-making risk. As such, Smith could not dispose of them on 21 July 1989 otherwise than at a loss. Smith were in a special sense locked into the shares having bought them for a purpose and at a price which precluded them from sensibly disposing of them. It was not alleged or found that Smith acted unreasonably in retaining the shares for as long as they did or in realising them in the manner in which they did.

In the circumstances, it would not in my judgment compensate Smith for the actual loss they have suffered (i.e. the difference between the contract price and the resale price eventually realised) if Smith were required to give credit for the shares having a value of 78p on 21 July 1989. Having acquired the shares at 82¼p for stock Smith could not commercially have sold on that date at 78p. It is not realistic to treat Smith as having received shares worth 78p each when in fact, in real life, they could not commercially have sold or realised the shares at that price on that date. In my judgment, this is one of those cases where to give full reparation to Smith, the benefit which Smith ought to bring into account to be set against its loss for the total purchase price paid should be the actual resale price achieved by Smith when eventually the shares were sold.

NOTES

1. Lord Mustill suggested, at p. 269F–G, that, 'in the future when faced with situations such as the present, courts would do well to be guided by the seven propositions set out by . . . Lord Browne-Wilkinson'.

2. Lord Steyn explained the policy rationale underlying the principles determining remedies for fraudulent misrepresentation (deceit), at pp. 279G–280C:

Such a policy of imposing more stringent remedies on an intentional wrongdoer serves two purposes. First it serves a deterrent purpose in discouraging fraud . . . And in the battle against fraud civil remedies can play a useful and beneficial role. Secondly, as between the fraudster and the innocent party, moral considerations militate in favour of requiring the fraudster to bear the risk of misfortunes directly caused by his fraud. I make no apology for referring to moral considerations. The law and morality are inextricably interwoven. To a large extent the law is simply formulated and declared morality. And, as *Oliver Wendell Holmes, The Common Law* (1968) p. 106 observed, the very notion of deceit with its overtones of wickedness is drawn from the moral world.

3. Although the remoteness rules in a claim for deceit and negligent misrepresentation under s. 2(1) MA 1967 allow recovery of all direct losses—see e.g. *Naughton v O'Callaghan* [1990] 3 All ER 191 (*page 481, 9.3.2.2.2*), in which Waller J allowed recovery under s. 2(1) of the difference between the price paid and the value of the horse at the time that the misrepresentation was discovered, on the basis that retaining the horse in order to train it was precisely the action to be expected in the circumstances—in *Smith New Court*, Lord Steyn made one distinction clear by stating, at p. 283C, that:

[I]n an action for deceit the claimant is entitled to recover all his loss directly flowing from the fraudulently induced *transaction*. In the case of a negligent misrepresentation the rule is narrower: the recoverable loss does not extend beyond the consequences flowing from the negligent *misrepresentation* (see *Banque Bruxelles Lambert SA v Eagle Star Insurance Co. Ltd* [1995] 2 All ER 769, [1995] QB 375). [Emphasis added]

This may prove significant where there are a number of misrepresentations inducing the making of the contract.

This distinction was also discussed at first instance in *Man Nutfahrzeuge AG v Freightliner* [2005] EWHC 2347 (Comm).

MOORE-BICK LJ: 193 . . . Since the agreement expressly recognises that MN relied on the representations in connection with the purchase of ERF, I think it must be accepted that they played some part in inducing it to enter into the Share Purchase Agreement. It does not necessarily follow, however, that the indemnity provided by section 12 extends to losses of every kind flowing from entering into the agreement. In *South Australia Asset Management Corporation v York Montague Ltd* [1997] A.C. 191 at page 214 Lord Hoffmann suggested that, if a person who is under a duty to take care in providing information on which he knows that another will decide upon a course of action is negligent and as a result provides inaccurate information, he is not generally regarded as responsible for all the consequences of that course of action, but only for those consequences attributable to the fact that the information he provided was wrong. The reason, he suggested, is because it is necessary to find a sufficient causal connection between the breach of duty and the loss in question before it is possible to regard the maker of the statement as responsible for it. Although these comments were made in the context of determining the scope of a duty of care at common law, they do in my view reflect the response of a reasonable person to the provision of inaccurate information under a contract of this kind and are therefore factors that are properly to be taken into account when construing the indemnity provided by section 12.1. The critical distinction for this purpose is, as Lord Steyn later described it in *Smith New Court Securities Ltd v Citibank N.A.* [1997] A.C. 254 at page 283C, between losses flowing from the *misrepresentation* and losses flowing from the *transaction*.

194 This distinction was emphasised by [counsel] when he submitted that it would be very odd if a minor, albeit material, misrepresentation made honestly and without any want of due care were to expose Western Star to liability for any losses suffered by MN as a result of entering into the Share Purchase Agreement. I agree and I find it difficult to accept that that is what the parties really intended . . .

196 . . . In my view the parties clearly did intend to impose on Western Star an obligation to indemnify MN against all the costs and expenses arising out of the inaccuracy of any of the representations, including losses incurred as a result of taking steps in reliance on their accuracy, but not against the entire consequences of entering into the agreement insofar as they could not be said to flow from the inaccuracy of the particular representation.

197 Accordingly, I am unable to accept [counsel's] submission that MN is entitled to recover . . . the whole of the losses it has suffered as a result of having entered into the Share Purchase Agreement. The indemnity available under section 12.1 is limited to the losses that flow from the inaccuracy of that particular representation, namely, the amounts that ERF is liable to pay by way of arrears of VAT, penalty and expenses incurred in connection with the proceedings that have since been brought by Customs & Excise.

See also the discussion of the significance of this distinction in Poole and Devenney [2007] JBL 269.

4. In *Pankhania v Hackney London Borough Council* [2004] EWHC 323 (Ch), [2004] 1 EGLR 135 (for the facts, see *page 446, 9.1.2.3*), Geoffrey Vos QC appeared to accept that, in principle, *Smith New Court* could be applied to a s. 2(1) claim for damages because of the fiction of fraud (*page 481, 9.3.2.2.2*). However, on the facts, there was no continuing misrepresentation or lock-in, and the property could have been sold at any time subject to the NCP tenancy of the car park. Thus, the *Smith New Court* measure was inapplicable on the facts. The judge therefore applied 'the normal measure' of damages (i.e. the difference between the

sum paid and the actual value of the property—a figure of £500,000). He accepted that mitigation applied to claims for fraudulent misrepresentation and to damages claims under s. 2(1), but considered that the claimant had not acted unreasonably in seeking to obtain possession, so that the damages would not be reduced to take account of what had happened to the property in the meantime.

5. In assessing the measure of damages, it is normally appropriate to take account of the difference between the amount paid by the claimant and the actual value of the subject matter at the date the contract was made. In *OMV Petroleum SA v Glencore International* [2016] EWCA Civ 778 the defendant delivered substandard crude oil, and the claimant sought damages for fraudulent misrepresentation based on the difference between the price paid and the actual value of what had been delivered, amounting to some US$40 million. The Court of Appeal rejected the defendant's alternative method of calculation which focused on the fact that the crude oil was to be refined and looked at the difference between the yield from contractual standard crude oil and from the crude oil actually delivered. The Court of Appeal held that there was no basis for varying the date of assessment of loss, and that what might have happened thereafter was immaterial to the assessment of damages. In the same way, it was held in *Quilter v Hodson Developments Ltd* [2016] EWCA Civ 1125, confirming the earlier decision in *Hussey v Eels* [1990] 2 QB 227, that if the claimant is induced by misrepresentation to purchase property, the defendant is liable for the difference between actual value and contract value at the date of the contract, so that if the property subsequently appreciates then any profits made by the claimant on resale are to be left out of account. As was said by Floyd LJ (at para. 36): 'Many people buying property with a defect will not want to move for a while and, if any subsequent sale is not undertaken as part of their obligation to mitigate their loss, should be able to recover loss calculated on the traditional basis of the difference in value between the value of the property as represented and the property's true value at the date of purchase.'

9.3.1.2 Can loss of profits be recovered if fraudulent misrepresentation induced the purchase of a business? If so, how will those lost profits be calculated?

East v Maurer
[1991] 1 WLR 461 (CA)

In 1979, the claimants bought one of the two hair salon businesses in Bournemouth, which belonged to the defendant for £20,000, and were induced to do so in part by a representation

Misrepresentation

9

by the defendant that he did not intend to work in the other salon except in emergencies. In fact, he continued to work full-time at the other salon, and this had such an effect on the claimants' business that it was never profitable. They eventually sold it in 1989 for £7,500 and brought an action alleging fraudulent misrepresentation. The trial judge assessed damages so as to include an award of £15,000 for loss of profits, which was based on the profit that the defendant would have made in the salon if he had not sold it, less a deduction of 25 per cent for the fact that the claimants were not as experienced. The defendant appealed against this assessment of loss of profits.

Held: Relying on *Doyle v Olby*, loss of profits, although normally claimed in contract as part of lost expectation, could be recovered in an action for deceit on the basis that it was actual damage directly flowing from the misrepresentation. However, this loss of profits had to be calculated using tortious principles so as to compensate the claimants for the profit that they might have made had the misrepresentation not been made (i.e. the profit that they might have expected to make in another hairdressing business bought for a similar sum), rather than on the contractual basis of the profits that this business might have made had the representation been true and had the defendant not worked in the other salon. Consequently, the award for loss of profits was reduced to £10,000.

BELDAM LJ: [Counsel] for the defendants, submits that there is a difference in the manner in which damages are assessed for breach of contract and for the tort of deceit. He says that the authorities show that no damages at all are recoverable for loss of profits in an action of deceit. Although there is no express decision which states that to be the case, in no case which has dealt with the proper measure of damage in an action of deceit has there been an award for loss of profits, although one would have expected to see one . . . Finally, he submits that even if damages for loss of profit are recoverable the judge assessed the figure at too high a level, and on an incorrect basis.

That the measure of damages for the tort of deceit and for breach of contract are different no longer needs support from authority. Damages for deceit are not awarded on the basis that the plaintiff is to be put in as good a position as if the statement had been true; they are to be assessed on a basis which would compensate the plaintiff for all the loss he has suffered, so far as money can do it.

This was confirmed in *Doyle v Olby (Ironmongers) Ltd* [1969] 2 QB 158, to which both the judge and this court were referred and was a case in which the facts were similar to those of the present case.

. . . [I]t seems to me clear that there is no basis upon which one could say that loss of profits incurred whilst waiting for an opportunity to realise to its best advantage a business which has been purchased, are irrecoverable. It is conceded that losses made in the course of running the business of a company, are recoverable. If in fact the plaintiffs lost the profit which they could reasonably have expected from running a business in the area of a kind similar to the business in this case, I can see no reason why those do not fall within the words of Lord Atkin in *Clark v Urquhart* [1930] AC 28, 'actual damage directly flowing from the fraudulent inducement.'

So I consider that on the facts found by the judge in the present case, the plaintiffs did establish that they had suffered a loss due to the defendants' misrepresentation which arose from their inability to earn the profits in the business which they hoped to buy in the Bournemouth area . . .

However, I am not satisfied that in arriving at the figure of £15,000 the judge approached the quantification of those damages on the correct basis. It seems to me that he was inclined to base his award on an assessment of the profits which the business actually bought by the plaintiffs might have made if the statement made by the first defendant had amounted to a warranty that customers would continue to patronise the salon in Exeter Road; further that he left out of account a number of significant factors. What he did was to found his award on an evaluation which he made of the profits of the business at Exeter Road made by the first defendant in the year preceding the purchase of the business by the plaintiffs. Basing himself on figures which had been given to him by an accountant, and making an allowance for inflation he arrived at a figure for the profits which might have been made if the first defendant had continued to run the business at Exeter Road during the 3¼ years. He then made an allowance only for the fact that the second plaintiff's experience in hair styling and hairdressing was not as extensive or as cosmopolitan as that of the first defendant. Thus he based his award on an assessment of what the profits would have been, less a deduction of 25 per cent for the second plaintiff's lack of experience.

It seems to me that he should have begun by considering the kind of profit which the second plaintiff might have made if the representation which induced her to buy the business at Exeter Road had not been made, and that involved considering the kind of profits which *she* might have expected to make in another hairdressing business bought for a similar sum . . .

The judge . . . had two clear starting points. First, that any person investing £20,000 in a business would expect a greater return than if the sum was left safely in the bank or in a building society earning interest, and a reasonable figure for that at the rates then prevailing would have been at least £6,000. Secondly, that the salary of a hairdresser's assistant in the usual kind of establishment was at this time £40 per week and that the assistant could expect tips in addition. That would produce a figure of over £7,000, but the proprietor of a salon would clearly expect to earn more, having risked his money in the business. It seems to me that those are valid points from which to start to consider what would be a reasonable sum to award for loss of profits of a business of this kind. As was pointed out by Winn LJ in *Doyle v Olby (Ironmongers) Ltd* [1969] 2 QB 158, 169, this is not a question which can be considered on a mathematical basis. It has to be considered essentially in the round, making what he described as a 'jury assessment'.

Taking all the factors into account, I think that the judge's figure was too high; for my part I would have awarded a figure of £10,000 for that head of damage, and to this extent I would allow the appeal.

NOTES

1. This is an example of a statement of intention amounting to a statement of fact because it was found as a fact that the defendant did not actually have the expressed intention when he made his statement. See *Edgington v Fitzmaurice* (1885) 29 Ch D 459 (*page 445, 9.1.2.2*).

2. See Marks (1992) 108 LQR 386.

3. Although, in *East v Maurer*, the Court of Appeal was prepared to assess profits based upon a hypothetical identical salon without evidence that any such salon existed, in *Davis v Churchward* (unreported, 6 May 1993)—noted by Chandler (1994) 110 LQR 35—the Court of Appeal looked at actual similar public houses that could have been purchased for the same amount and held that, because the weekly turnover on these public houses would have been the same as the actual weekly turnover on the public house purchased (£1,500), there could be no recovery for lost profits. In particular, unlike Beldam LJ in *East v Maurer*, Nourse LJ refused to take account of the profit that would have been made had the purchase money instead been invested in a building society, on the basis that this was hypothetical, since it had been found as a fact that another public house would have been purchased.

Nevertheless, this is an example of a contract induced by a fraudulent misrepresentation of weekly turnover, and it must be asked whether it is likely that the claimant would indeed have purchased a similar public house knowing that the actual turnover of that public house was only £1,500.

In *Dadourian Group International Inc. v Simms (Damages)* [2006] EWHC 2973 (Ch), the judge refused to accept a claim for loss of profits resulting from being deprived from entering into a sale agreement with 'some other purchaser', considering that there had to be evidence of another purchaser in the market. Even if this evidence were to exist, the claim for loss of profits following a fraudulent misrepresentation would also need to take account of the duty to mitigate that loss. (The decision was affirmed by the Court of Appeal—[2009] EWCA Civ 169, [2009] 1 Lloyd's Rep 601—although on other grounds, since this point was not appealed.)

4. By comparison, in both *4 Eng Ltd v Harper* [2008] EWHC 915 (Ch), [2009] Ch 91, and *Parabola*

Investments Ltd v Browallia Cal Ltd [2010] EWCA Civ 486, [2011] QB 477, lost profits were held to be recoverable in a claim in deceit despite an inability to identify a specific alternative (and profitable) contract that would have been entered into had it not been for the fraudulent misrepresentation.

5. Loss of profits can be recovered on the *Smith New Court* basis, down to the date of judgment.

In *Parabola Investments*, the Court of Appeal agreed with the trial judge that a claim could be made in deceit by an investment company not only for loss of the capital investment induced by the fraudulent misrepresentation and the profits that could have been made in relation to this lost investment, but also for the lost profits that could have been made had the fraud not occurred and had the investment

company made an alternative investment. There was no principled reason why the discovery of the fraud should be the cut-off point for such losses, so that the company could recover for the profits lost on investments right down to the date of the trial. The Court of Appeal accepted that it was conducting an entirely hypothetical exercise and that it could only make its best attempt to evaluate the chances of particular alternative investments being made or being profitable given that the losses are entirely speculative.

However, if this is applied by analogy in the context of damages under s. 2(1) MA 1967 (fiction of fraud—*page 481, 9.3.2.2.2*), it would be a startling conclusion.

In *4 Eng Ltd v Harper* [2008] EWHC 915 (Ch), [2009] Ch 91, damages were awarded in a claim in deceit on a loss of a chance basis for the lost opportunity of entering into another transaction that would have been profitable. The company purchased was worthless and there was another identified company that it was found the claimant would have sought to purchase. The acceptance of the fact that this is a lost chance is welcome, since the requirements of proof for loss of a chance should apply and hypothetical evaluations are a necessary part of determining recovery. It should follow that the 'chance' is fixed as a percentage. The judge considered that there was a good chance on these facts, assessed at 80 per cent, that the owners of the actual alternative company would have agreed to sell to the claimant, and thus awarded damages as 80 per cent of the income and capital gain arising from this alternative investment.

DAVID RICHARDS J: 43 The defendants accept that in principle damages for the loss of an alternative purchase, if caused by the defendants' fraudulent misrepresentation and the claimant's reliance on it, are recoverable in an action for deceit. The Court of Appeal so held in *East v Maurer* [1991] 1 WLR 461 . . .

In the *Smith New Court* case [1997] AC 254, 282, Lord Steyn observed that *East v Maurer*:

shows that an award based on the hypothetical profitable business in which the plaintiff would have engaged but for deceit is permissible: it is classic consequential loss.

44 The defendants make a number of submissions. First, they say that 4 Eng's claim in this case involves an impermissible attempt to rely on two distinct strands of authority: damages for loss directly caused to the claimant and damages for a loss of chance. In my judgment, a combination of such claims involves no error of principle. If the loss of the chance is damage directly caused by the defendants' deceit, it is as much within the scope of damages for deceit as payments or liabilities in fact made or incurred by the claimant or as damages for the loss of profits in a hypothetical alternative business established on the balance of probabilities as in *East v Maurer* [1991] 1 WLR 461. That decision predated the decision of the Court of Appeal in *Allied Maples Group Ltd v Simmons & Simmons* [1995] 1 WLR 1602 by over four years. It does not seem to me to be an objection that the loss is assessed as a loss of chance, not as a loss established on the balance of probabilities. It is true that it does not previously appear to have been decided that damages for loss of a chance are recoverable for deceit, but there is in my judgment no objection in principle. If damages for loss of a chance are recoverable in negligence, why should they not also be recoverable in deceit?

45 Secondly, while accepting that damages for the profits that would have been earned in an alternative business are recoverable, the defendants submit that damages for a loss of capital profits, ie the

increase in the value of the alternative business between the date of assumed acquisition and the date of its presumed disposal, which will be the date of trial if not earlier, are too remote and are not recoverable.

46 The foreseeability of a head of loss is irrelevant in the award of damages for deceit, as the House of Lords established in *Smith New Court Securities Ltd v Scrimgeour Vickers (Asset Management) Ltd* [1997] AC 254. A loss is too remote only if it is not in the eyes of the law directly caused by a defendant's deceit. Once it is accepted that the claimant would have purchased an alternative business, and is entitled to recover damages for the loss of profits which would have been earned during the period of ownership, why should the claimant not also recover for the loss of the capital profit in the rise of the value of the business? If the claimant had not been induced by the defendants' deceit to purchase their business, the claimant would have purchased an alternative business from which it would have benefited in two ways: first, it would have received profits from it while owning it and, secondly, it would have been able to sell the business at a profit over the price it had paid for it. Both are losses suffered by it as a direct result of the defendants' deceit.

9.3.1.3 Can the misrepresentee recover damages in deceit on the basis that he would otherwise have entered into a more profitable contract on better terms?

Clef Aquitaine SARL v Laporte Materials (Barrow) Ltd
[2001] QB 488 (CA)

The claimant company had agreed to purchase quotas of goods from the defendant and to distribute them in France. The defendant had fraudulently stated that the price list applicable represented the lowest prices at which the defendant's salesmen could sell the goods to trade customers. In fact, other price lists were used for trade customers, and the evidence was that certain trade customers had obtained big discounts on these prices. The claimant managed to resell the goods purchased at a profit, but sought damages in the tort of deceit representing the difference between the price paid for the goods and the price that probably could have been negotiated but for the misrepresentation. The judge awarded such damages and the defendant appealed, arguing that damages for deceit were limited to instances of loss-making transactions.

Held (upholding the judge's assessment of damages): There was no absolute rule that the transaction had to be loss making before damages for deceit could be recovered. If the claimant *could prove* that a more favourable transaction would have been entered into with the defendant but for the deceit, its loss of opportunity could be recovered on that basis.

SIMON BROWN LJ:

Damages for deceit

[Counsel] for the defendants challenges the whole basis of this second head of claim. He argues that it is an attempt to obtain by another route damages for loss of a bargain which are not recoverable for the tort of deceit. Damages for deceit are only to compensate the person deceived for loss suffered. Here the plaintiffs failed to prove any such loss . . . They can prove no more than that they would have made a still greater profit had they entered into yet more favourable agreements, and that, submits [counsel] is insufficient to sustain the claim . . .

[T]he judge [at first instance] concluded on the balance of probabilities that, but for Mr Dent's deceit, the plaintiffs could and would have entered into the same distribution agreements but on more favourable terms as to price, and that their loss was therefore the difference between the lower prices which in those

Misrepresentation

9

circumstances they would have paid and the prices actually paid . . . Having been referred to a number of authorities, most notably *Smith New Court Securities Ltd v Scrimgeour Vickers (Asset Management) Ltd* [1997] AC 254; *East v Maurer* [1991] 1 WLR 461 and *Downs v Chappell* [1997] 1 WLR 426, the judge said:

> . . . The result may be the same as a loss of bargain claim, but, as [counsel for the plaintiff] argued, that does not mean that it is a loss of bargain claim. It is the best way of judging the loss, if any, which was caused directly to the plaintiffs by being induced by the deceit to enter the agreements which they did . . . It establishes the loss, if any, which the plaintiffs have suffered with a view to putting them in the position they would have been in if no representations had been made . . .

[Counsel for the defendant] criticises the judge's reasoning throughout that section of the judgment. It is, he submits, contrary to principle to seek to reconstruct the deal which would have been reached but for the deceit.

. . . This whole case, the defendants argue, is an attempt to create for the plaintiffs a contractual claim to which they were never entitled. These to my mind are powerful arguments and I do not pretend to have found the point an easy one.

In the *Smith New Court* case [1997] AC 254, 267 Lord Browne-Wilkinson, summarising the principles applicable in assessing damages payable where the plaintiff has been induced by a fraudulent misrepresentation to buy property, stated the first three as follows:

> (1) the defendant is bound to make reparation for all the damage directly flowing from the transaction; (2) although such damage need not have been foreseeable, it must have been directly caused by the transaction; (3) in assessing such damage, the plaintiff is entitled to recover by way of damages the full price paid by him, but he must give credit for any benefits which he has received as a result of the transaction . . .

The difficulty in the present case, as it seems to me, is in deciding whether 'all the damage (actual loss) directly flowing from the transaction' (Lord Browne-Wilkinson's first principle . . .) can encompass, in a case like the present where the actual transaction entered into has been profitable rather than loss-making, the loss occasioned through the party deceived having entered into that particular transaction rather than a different transaction which would have been yet more profitable. In submitting that it cannot, [counsel] not surprisingly places considerable reliance on Lord Steyn's statement [in *Smith New Court*] [1997] AC 254, 283 that:

> it is not necessary . . . after . . . ascertain[ing] the loss directly flowing from the victim having entered into the transaction, to embark on a hypothetical reconstruction of what the parties would have agreed had the deceit not occurred.

Indeed this very statement, he submits, usefully contrasts 'the loss directly flowing from . . . the transaction' with any idea of comparing one profitable transaction with another in order to find a loss in this way. To do that, he submits, is also to offend against Lord Steyn's first three propositions: it is to protect the plaintiffs in respect of their positive interest rather than compensate them in respect of their negative interest, in this bargain; to create for them a contractual measure of damages. It comes to this: unless and until the plaintiffs can show (which they cannot) that these distributorship agreements caused them loss, they have no claim in tort. It is not sufficient for their purpose to show only that other distributorship agreements would have given them greater profit.

It is helpful at this point to consider *East v Maurer* [1991] 1 WLR 461, the authority principally relied upon by the judge below in carrying out the exercise he did . . .

Mustill LJ, at p. 468:

> the best course in a case of this kind is to begin by comparing the position of the plaintiff as it would have been if the act complained of had not taken place with the position of the plaintiff as it actually became. This establishes the actual loss which the plaintiff has suffered and often helps to avoid the pitfalls of double counting, omissions and impermissible

awards of both a capital and an income element in respect of the same loss . . . In the present case the act complained of is the making of the fraudulent representation, coupled with the reliance placed upon it by the plaintiffs in concluding the bargain. If this had not happened the plaintiffs would, on the judge's findings, have . . . bought a new business in Bournemouth, albeit not the one in Exeter Road . . . It is objected that the loss of profits is not properly recoverable because it is appropriate not to a claim in fraud but to a claim based on a contractual warranty of profits, for in such a case the loss of profits does not stem from the making of the contract but from the fact that the profit made was not what was anticipated. I should have thought this argument sound if the judge had included an item for loss of the Exeter Road profits; but he has not done so. The loss of profits awarded relates to the hypothetical profitable business in which the plaintiffs would have engaged but for buying the Exeter Road business, and the profits of the latter are treated by the judge solely as some evidence of what the profits of the other business might have been . . .

[Counsel for the defendant] submits that *East v Maurer* [1991] 1 WLR 461 was a very different case from the present and that the point established there and approved in the *Smith New Court* case [1997] AC 254 cannot avail the plaintiffs here. It is one thing to say that, in quantifying the undoubted losses resulting from the plaintiffs' tortiously induced purchase of the salon in Exeter Road, they could properly include as consequential loss the profits they might reasonably have expected to make in another business which they would, but for the defendant's fraud, have purchased; quite another to say that, even had Exeter Road proved profitable, they could have claimed in tort on the basis that, but for the fraud, it would have been more profitable still.

The novelty of the present case lies in the plaintiffs having suffered no loss from the transaction save only from having entered into that transaction rather than a still more profitable one. That distinguishes this case from all the others we were shown. Is it, however, a distinction fatal to the plaintiffs' success? [Counsel for the plaintiff] submits not. His starting point is Lord Steyn's sixth proposition in the *Smith New Court* case [1997] AC 254, 282 with regard to 'the overriding compensatory principle':

> The legal measure is to compare the position of the plaintiff as it was before the fraudulent statement was made to him with his position as it became as a result of his reliance on the fraudulent statement.

The plaintiffs' argument is quite straightforward. Before Mr Dent's fraudulent statement, the plaintiffs were anxious to become Sovereign's exclusive distributors in France and were negotiating agreements, and in particular prices and a price increase formula, to that end. In reliance on the fraudulent statement they became locked into these long-term agreements and a commitment to pay prices and price increases larger than would otherwise have been the case. The judge below did no more and no less than compensate them for having thereby worsened their position. This accorded with the overriding principle.

In my judgment this argument is correct. The judge did not, be it noted, make the mistake of awarding damages by reference to the contractual measure . . .

As for Lord Steyn's statement [1997] AC 254, 283 that it is unnecessary 'to embark on a hypothetical reconstruction of what the parties would have agreed had the deceit not occurred,' this has to be understood in the context of Hobhouse LJ's 'qualification' in *Downs v Chappell* [1997] 1 WLR 426, 444, which Lord Steyn was criticising. What Hobhouse LJ had done, by way of a 'check' on the conventional measure, was 'to compare the loss consequent upon entering into the transaction with what would have been the position had the represented, or supposed, state of affairs actually existed.' To reject that exercise (a different exercise, be it noted, from that undertaken by the judge in the present case) was not to reject the possibility that the ascertainment of loss in the first place might itself require a 'hypothetical reconstruction of what the parties would have agreed had the deceit not occurred.' If, as was held in *East v Maurer* [1991] 1 WLR 461 (a holding expressly approved by Lord Steyn [1997] AC 254, 282), consequential loss can be established and awarded by reference to 'the hypothetical profitable business in which the plaintiff would have engaged but for [the] deceit,' why should that loss, to be recoverable, have to be parasitic on some other, more direct, loss, and why should the alternative 'hypothetical profit-able business' have to be a business (or, as here, contract) notionally acquired from some third party?

True it is that in *Downs v Chappell* [1997] 1 WLR 426, 433 Hobhouse LJ, in a part of the judgment not criticised in the *Smith New Court* case [1997] AC 254, said:

> It was wrong both factually and legally for the judge to create the hypothesis that the second defendants could and would have given the plaintiffs accurate figures so as to give them an accurate basis upon which to decide whether to make a contract with Mr Chappell.

But that was in the context of establishing liability, not quantifying damage. True it is too that later in his judgment, having referred to *East v Maurer* [1991] 1 WLR 461, Hobhouse LJ said [1997] 1 WLR 426, 441:

> In general, it is irrelevant to inquire what the representee would have done if some different representation had been made to him or what other transactions he might have entered into if he had not entered onto the transaction in question. Such matters are irrelevant speculations . . .

That, however, was expressed to be 'in general' and, as I conclude, there will be particular cases, of which this is one, where to give effect to the overriding compensatory rule it will be both possible on the facts, and appropriate in law, to hypothesise. Not every hypothesis involves irrelevant speculation.

I have, in short, reached the conclusion that there is no absolute rule requiring the person deceived to prove that the actual transaction into which he was induced to enter was itself loss making . . .

It will sometimes be possible, as it was here, to prove instead that a different and more favourable transaction (either with the defendant or with some third party) would have been entered into but for the fraud, and to measure and recover the plaintiffs' loss on that basis . . .

NOTES

1. This decision is criticized in Poole and Devenney [2007] JBL 269.

2. There is a clear emphasis in the judgments on the need to achieve justice and some redress for the claimant, which had been 'overcharged'. However, the effect of this decision is to include this loss (assuming that it can be proved) as a direct loss flowing from the fraudulent misrepresentation under what Simon Brown LJ refers to as 'the overriding compensatory rule'. The tension arises because, at first sight, it appears to be a loss of bargain (or contractual) claim, just as the loss of profits claim appeared to be contractual in *East v Maurer* and similar difficulties arise in trying to assess damages based on hypotheticals. There is a fine line between putting a person in the position in which he would have been had the misrepresentation not been made and putting the person into the position in which he would have been had a true statement been made. This dilemma is referred to in the judgment of Ward LJ, at pp. 512G–513C:

> WARD LJ: I confess to have been worrying whether there is any meaningful difference between, on the one hand, being put in the position one would have been in had one not been told a lie and, on the other hand, being put in the position one would have been in had one been told the truth. I think the answer is to follow Lord Steyn's approach to its logical

conclusion because if one is truly to compare the position of the plaintiff as it was before the fraudulent statement was made to him with his position as it became as a result of his reliance on the fraudulent statement, then just before the fraudulent statement was made the plaintiff was battling in what he believed to be honest negotiations to ascertain the defendant's bottom line and he was denied finding it because of the lies that were told to him. My other concern, reflecting [counsel's] argument, was why, if one cannot get damages for the loss of one's bargain, should one be allowed to get damages for the loss of the bargain one might have made. On reflection, I think the answer to this argument is that the loss of the bargain contemplated in breach of warranty cases is the bargain to be made with third parties when selling on the goods whereas the bargain one might have made if told the truth is the different bargain which might have been struck with the defendant. I am now satisfied that so long as the hypothetical questions are asked and answered as the means of establishing value in the absence of a market or of any other precise means of establishing that value, then the hypothetical approach, which is essentially what [the judge] was adopting, is well justified by the authorities. On this basis I would uphold [the judge's] assessment of damages.

3. In *Yam Seng Pte Ltd v International Trade Corporation Ltd* [2013] EWHC 111 (QB), [2013] 1 CLC 662, [2013] 1 All ER (Comm) 1321 (*page 211, 5.4.1.2*), Leggatt J considered that any losses that might have been made on an alternative transaction ought also to be brought into account in this process.

LEGGATT J:

Relevance of alternative transactions

209 This argument raises a question of principle: in assessing damages for fraudulent misrepresentation or under s. 2(1), is it relevant to consider what, if any, other transaction the claimant would have entered into if the misrepresentation had not been made? One approach would be to say that it is not. It might be said that where the claimant has been induced to enter into a contract by misrepresentation the object of an award of damages is simply to restore the claimant to the position before the contract was made: there is no warrant for going further and examining what the claimant would or would not have done if it had not made the contract and then bringing into account in assessing damages the financial consequences of such hypothetical alternative transactions. This approach finds support in a dictum of Hobhouse LJ in *Downs v Chappell* [1996] CLC 1492 at 1504; [1997] 1 WLR 426 at 441:

In general, it is irrelevant to inquire what the representee would have done if some different representation had been made to him or what other transactions he might have entered into if he had not entered into the transaction in question. Such matters are irrelevant speculations.

. . .

212 . . . [T]here is a line of cases in which courts have inquired and taken account in assessing damages of what other transaction the claimant would have entered into if no misrepresentation had been made.

[The judge then explained the decisions in *East v Maurer, Clef Aquitaine SARL v Laporte Materials (Barrow) Ltd*, and *4 Eng Ltd v Harper*, and continued:]

216 In all these cases the hypothetical alternative transaction which the claimant would otherwise have entered into was one which would have been profitable. Should account also be taken of a transaction which would probably have resulted in a loss? *Chitty on Contracts* (31st edn) at para. 6–064 suggests not, citing an observation of Lord Steyn in *Smith New Court* [1996] CLC 1958 at 1979; [1997] AC 254 at 283 that:

. . . it is not necessary for the judge to embark on a hypothetical reconstruction of what the parties would have agreed had the deceit not occurred.

Similarly, *Clerk & Lindsell on Torts* (20th edn) at para. 18–45 states that:

where a defendant deceives the claimant into entering a business transaction, the claimant is entitled to recover the loss he suffers as a result, without reference to the fact that he might otherwise have invested his money in some other unprofitable way and lost it anyway.

The editors add in a footnote, however, that such an attitude is difficult to defend and that:

if the claimant can increase his recovery by showing he would have invested his money profitably, by parity of reasoning the defendant ought to be able to reduce his exposure by showing that, but for his deceit, the claimant would have lost it in any case.

217 In my view such an attitude would be not merely difficult but impossible to defend. In circumstances where it is established that the claimant can recover a profit that would have been obtained from entering into some other transac-tion, it must in principle be equally relevant to take account of any loss. Nor in my view does the case law justify any different conclusion. In particular:

(1) The dictum of Hobhouse LJ in *Downs v Chappell* quoted above begins with the words 'in general'. It cannot therefore have been intended to state a rule of law—all the more so since it immediately follows a reference to *East v Maurer* where the plaintiffs were awarded profits which they would have been made if they had entered into a different transaction.

(2) The observation of Lord Steyn in *Smith New Court* quoted in *Chitty* is taken out of context. The hypo-thetical reconstruction which Lord Steyn was disap-proving was a reconstruction of the kind suggested separately by Hobhouse LJ in *Downs v Chappell* of what the claimant would have done if the representa-tion had been true; Lord Steyn's observation should not be interpreted as a statement that it is never relevant to consider what alternative transaction would have been entered into if the representation had not been made—not least since Lord Steyn (at 1978; 282) specifically approved *East v Maurer* as showing that 'an award based on the hypothetical profitable business in which the plaintiff would have engaged but for deceit is permissible: it is classic consequential loss.'

(3) The statements of Hobhouse LJ in *Downs v Chappell* and of Lord Steyn in *Smith New Court* were both considered by the Court of Appeal in *Clef Aquitaine* and explained by Simon Brown LJ in the way I have indicated above.

(4) There is no difference in principle between an alter-native transaction which would have been more prof-itable and one which would have been less profitable than the actual transaction such that it can be rel-evant to take account of the former but not the latter.

(5) The evidential burden will be on the defendant, how-ever, to show that if the misrepresentation had not been made the claimant would have incurred a loss. In seeking to discharge this burden, the defendant (unlike the claimant) does not have the benefit of the principle that if the financial outcome of the alter-native transaction is uncertain the court will make reasonable assumptions in its favour (for example by allowing damages to be calculated on a loss of a chance basis) to assist in the proof of loss.

(6) Unless the defendant can demonstrate with a rea-sonable degree of certainty, therefore, both the fact that the claimant would probably have suffered a loss from entering into an alternative transaction and the amount of that loss, the damages will not be reduced on that account. In this respect there is a disparity, but a principled one, between hypothetical transac-tions which would have made the claimant worse off and those which would have made the claimant better off.

(7) *Slough Estates* [*Slough Estates plc v Welwyn Hatfield District Council* [1996] 2 PLR 50] and *Naughton v O'Callaghan* [[1990] 3 All ER 191] are both con-sistent with this analysis. In those cases there was evidence which justified a very general inference that

the claimant would quite likely have suffered some loss if it had not entered into the contract in question (by investing in another property development or buying another horse). But there was no way of estimating with any certainty or precision what loss, if any, the claimant would have incurred from any such transaction. As it was the defendant rather than the claimant who wished to rely on such a loss, that difficulty was insuperable and meant that there was no quantifiable loss which could be taken into account.

Conclusions on right to damages for misrepresentation

218 I therefore consider that in this case it would in principle be open to ITC to show that, if the misrepresentations regarding ITC's legal right to manufacture and sell the Manchester United products had not been made and the agreement had not been concluded, Yam Seng would nevertheless have entered into a similar contract at a later date and lost money. However, in order to reduce the damages recoverable by Yam Seng on this basis, it would be necessary for ITC to quantify a sum of money which the court can conclude with reasonable confidence that Yam Seng would have lost. That is not

an exercise which ITC has attempted to undertake, nor which I would be able to undertake.

Since it will be for the fraudulent misrepresentor to prove that 'if the misrepresentation had not been made, the claimant would have incurred a loss' and the actual measure of that loss, this may make little practical, as opposed to theoretical, difference. For example, in *Naughton v O'Callaghan* [1990] 3 All ER 191 (*page 481, 9.3.2.2.2*), the claimant might well have suffered some loss had he not entered into the contract in question, but purchased another horse, but this was impossible to establish without the use of hypothetical assumptions and that will not suffice in this context. Equally, it is possible to envisage an argument that a claimant might well have made a loss through the purchase of an alternative investment, but without knowing which one, or entering into speculation, that would be equally impossible to establish.

9.3.1.4 Mitigation of loss in a claim based on fraudulent misrepresentation

Downs v Chappell
[1997] 1 WLR 426 (CA)

In 1988, the claimants were interested in purchasing a bookshop business owned by Chappell, the first defendant. The sale particulars represented that, in 1987, the business had a turnover of approximately £109,000 and a gross profit of £33,500. The claimants asked the first defendant for independent verification and, at the first defendant's request, the second defendant, accountants, wrote to the claimants broadly confirming these figures. The claimants therefore purchased the business for £120,000 considering that, on the basis of these figures and with a mortgage of £60,000, they could still generate an adequate income. However, they later discovered that the figures had been overstated and that the business would not generate sufficient income to cover their costs. They therefore sought to sell it. Up until March 1990, the business was making a profit, although it did not accord with the profit level that had been represented. In March 1990, the claimants refused two offers of £76,000 for the business, in the belief that they could get more if they held out. However, they eventually sold the business for less than £60,000, and claimed damages in the tort of deceit against the first defendant and damages in negligence against the second defendant. They also claimed an annual alleged loss of £5,000 profit by comparing the actual profitability of the business with that represented.

Held: Since the claimants had been induced by fraudulent and negligent misrepresentations relating to profitability to purchase a business, the damages recoverable were their income and capital losses to the date on which they discovered the misrepresentations and had the opportunity to avoid further losses. However, they could not recover for income losses because they were still trading at a profit up to March 1990. In addition, as far as the capital loss was concerned, they could not recover the difference between the £120,000 price paid and the price at which they eventually sold the business. The capital loss was £44,000 (£120,000 less £76,000).

HOBHOUSE LJ [with whose judgment Butler-Sloss and Roch LJJ agreed]: It is not in dispute that it was possible for the plaintiffs to sell out in the first quarter of 1990. If necessary they would have had to abandon the business. Indeed, one or more of those expressing an interest in buying the shop and the flat in the early part of 1990 were not doing so for the purpose of running a bookshop. Since the business was unlikely to be capable of covering the cost of servicing its capital, it is not suggested that its goodwill had then a significant market value. It follows that any losses which the plaintiffs suffered after the spring of 1990 were not caused by the defendants' torts but by the plaintiffs' decision not to sell out at that date for a figure of about £75,000. The only basis upon which the plaintiffs might have been able to recover any later loss would have been that they had been reasonably but unsuccessfully attempting to mitigate their loss further and had unhappily increased their loss: see *McGregor on Damages* 15th ed. (1988), pp. 197–199, paras. 323–324. On the facts of this case the plaintiffs are unable to make such a claim and have not sought to do so. They have argued that they did not act unreasonably in rejecting the offers of £76,000 in March 1990. Even accepting that they acted reasonably, the fact remains that it was their choice, freely made, and they cannot hold the defendants responsible if the choice has turned out to have been commercially unwise. They were no longer acting under the influence of the defendants' representations. The causative effect of the defendants' faults was exhausted; the plaintiffs' right to claim damages from them in respect of those faults had likewise crystallised. It is a matter of causation.

The correct finding of fact is that the plaintiffs suffered a loss of £44,000 as a result of entering into the contract with Mr Chappell.

NOTES

1. This demonstrates the dangers of such voluntary action in trying to avoid the consequences of a purchase induced by misrepresentation. The causal link with the defendants' misrepresentations had ended. It would therefore appear sensible to accept the first reasonable offer to purchase after discovering the misrepresentation or, in preference, seek to rescind (assuming this to be possible). In both *Downs v Chappell* and *Smith New Court* [1997] AC 254, there appears to have been no attempt to rescind. (In *Smith New Court*, an argument to rescind after the sale of the shares was not pursued at the trial and, it is submitted, would not have succeeded because it would not have been possible to return the shares.)

2. The trial judge had held that, although there were false statements made by the defendants, the claimants had not established on the balance of probabilities that they would not have purchased the business had the true figures been quoted. However, not surprisingly, the Court of Appeal rejected this and held that an actionable misrepresentation required only that the claimants establish that the figures induced the transaction.

3. Hobhouse LJ stated that damages for fraudulent misrepresentation should not be greater than the loss that would have been suffered 'had the represented, or supposed, state of affair actually existed'. In other words, the defendant should not be liable for loss that would have been suffered by the purchaser of the business even if the representation had been true, e.g. a general fall in market price. It was therefore necessary to compare the loss suffered with the hypothetical position had the representation, in fact, been true. However, *Downs v Chappell* was overruled on this point by the House of Lords in *Smith New Court*. No such check is necessary.

4. In *Standard Chartered Bank v Pakistan National Shipping Corporation* [1999] 1 Lloyd's Rep 747, Toulson J held that the test of whether the claimant had acted reasonably in mitigation of loss in a claim based on fraud was the same as in any tort or breach of contract action. The judge considered that if the loss could reasonably have been avoided, it could not be regarded as having been caused by the misrepresentation. See also the comment of Potter LJ, on appeal to the Court of Appeal—[2001] EWCA Civ 55, [2001] 1 All ER (Comm) 822, [41]—that, in the tort of deceit, the concepts of causation and mitigation are 'two sides of the same coin'.

9.3.1.5 There is no defence of contributory negligence where the defendant's misrepresentation is fraudulent

Standard Chartered Bank v Pakistan National Shipping Corporation (No. 2)
[2002] UKHL 43, [2003] 1 AC 959 (HL)

The seller, an English company, had contracted to ship a cargo to a Vietnamese buyer, with payment to be made by a letter of credit issued by a Vietnamese bank (the issuing bank) and confirmed by Standard Chartered Bank (SCB). This letter of credit required shipment to be made before 25 October and required the documents to be presented before 10 November 1993. The cargo was not shipped on time and, on 8 November, the shipowners and the managing director of the sellers had agreed that documents with a false shipping date would be issued. SCB accepted these documents on 15 November and authorized payment, although it knew that the documents were presented after the expiry of the credit. SCB then sought reimbursement from the issuing bank, falsely stating that the documents had been presented before the expiry date of the credit. The issuing bank refused payment because of other discrepancies in the documents. SCB claimed damages for deceit against the shipowners and managing director of the sellers based on the falsely dated documents. However, they claimed that SCB had suffered loss partly as a result of its own deceit on the issuing bank. They alleged that this constituted 'fault' within s. 4 of the Law Reform (Contributory Negligence) Act 1945, so that damages were to be apportioned to take account of SCB's 'contributory negligence'.

Held: The defendants could not rely on the claimant's contributory negligence as a defence to a claim based on fraudulent misrepresentation. There had been no such defence available at common law and, since the 1945 Act had not been intended to alter the position on absolute defences at common law, there was no such defence under that Act.

LORD HOFFMANN [with whose speech the other members of the House agreed]: 10. My Lords, I shall consider first the defence of contributory negligence. The relevant provisions of the 1945 Act are sections 1(1) and the definition of 'fault' in section 4:

> 1(1) Where any person suffers damage as the result partly of his own fault and partly of the fault of any other person or persons, a claim in respect of that damage shall not be defeated by reason of the fault of the person suffering the damage, but the damages recoverable in respect thereof shall be reduced to such extent as the court thinks just and equitable having regard to the claimant's share in the responsibility for the damage . . .

> 4. . . . 'fault' means negligence, breach of statutory duty or other act or omission which gives rise to a liability in tort or would, apart from this Act, give rise to a defence of contributory negligence.

11. In my opinion, the definition of 'fault' is divided into two limbs, one of which is applicable to defendants and the other to plaintiffs. In the case of a defendant, fault means 'negligence, breach of statutory duty or other act or omission' which gives rise to a liability in tort. In the case of a plaintiff, it means 'negligence, breach of statutory duty or other act or omission' which gives rise (at common law) to a defence of contributory negligence. The authorities in support of this construction are discussed by Lord Hope of Craighead in *Reeves v Commissioner of Police of the Metropolis* [2000] 1 AC 360, 382. It was also the view of Professor Glanville Williams in *Joint Torts and Contributory Negligence* (1951) at p 318.

12. It follows that conduct by a plaintiff cannot be 'fault' within the meaning of the Act unless it gives rise to a defence of contributory negligence at common law. This appears to me in accordance with the purpose of the Act, which was to relieve plaintiffs whose actions would previously have failed and not to reduce the damages which previously would have been awarded against defendants. Section 1(1) makes this clear when it says that 'a claim in respect of that damage shall not be defeated by reason of the fault

of the person suffering the damage, but [instead] the damages recoverable in respect thereof shall be reduced . . . '

13. The question is therefore whether at common law SCB's conduct would be a defence to its claim for deceit. Sir Anthony Evans thought that it would. He said that although the conduct of SCB in making a false statement about when the documents had been presented was intentional or reckless, the House of Lords had decided in *Reeves*'s case [2000] 1 AC 360 that an intentional act could give rise to a defence of 'contributory negligence' at common law and therefore count as 'fault' for the purpose of the Act. I am not sure that it was necessary to rely upon *Reeves* for this purpose, because the Act requires fault in relation to the damage which has been suffered. That damage was SCB's loss of the money it paid Oakprime. In *Reeves*, the plaintiff's husband had intended to cause the damage he suffered. He intended to kill himself. But SCB did not intend to lose its money. It would be more accurate to say that it was careless in making payment against documents which, as it knew or ought to have known, did not comply with the terms of the credit, on the assumption that it could successfully conceal these matters from Incombank. In respect of the loss suffered, SCB was in my opinion negligent.

14. Be that as it may, the real question is whether the conduct of SCB would at common law be a defence to a claim in deceit. Sir Anthony Evans said that the only rule supported by the authorities was that if someone makes a false representation which was intended to be relied upon and the other party relies upon it, it is no answer to a claim for rescission or damages that the claimant could with reasonable diligence have discovered that the representation was untrue. *Redgrave v Hurd* (1881) 20 Ch D 1 is a well known illustration. That was not the case here. SCB should not have paid even if they could not have discovered that the representation about the bill of lading was untrue. But in my opinion there are other cases which can be explained only on the basis of a wider rule. In *Edgington v Fitzmaurice* (1885) 29 Ch D 459 the plaintiff invested £1,500 in debentures issued by a company formed to run a provision market in Regent Street. Five months later the company was wound up and he lost nearly all his money. He sued the directors who had issued the prospectus, alleging that they had fraudulently or recklessly represented that the debenture issue was to raise money for the expansion of the company's business ('develop the arrangements . . . for the direct supply of cheap fish from the coast') when in fact it was to pay off pressing liabilities. The judge found the allegation proved and that the representation played a part in inducing the plaintiff to take the debentures. But another reason for his taking the debentures was that he thought, without any reasonable grounds, that the debentures were secured upon the company's land. Cotton LJ said, at p 481, that this did not matter:

> It is true that if he had not supposed he would have a charge he would not have taken the debentures; but if he also relied on the misstatement in the prospectus, his loss nonetheless resulted from that misstatement. It is not necessary to shew that the misstatement was the sole cause of his acting as he did. If he acted on that misstatement, though he was also influenced by an erroneous supposition, the defendants will still be liable.

Bowen and Fry LJJ gave judgments to the same effect.

15. This case seems to me to show that if a fraudulent representation is relied upon, in the sense that the claimant would not have parted with his money if he had known it was false, it does not matter that he also held some other negligent or irrational belief about another matter and, but for that belief, would not have parted with his money either. The law simply ignores the other reasons why he paid. As Lord Cross of Chelsea said in *Barton v Armstrong* [1976] AC 104, 118:

> If . . . Barton relied on the [fraudulent] misrepresentation Armstrong could not have defeated his claim to relief by showing that there were other more weighty causes which contributed to his decision to execute the deed, for in this field the court does not allow an examination into the relative importance of contributory causes. 'Once make out that there has been anything like deception and no contract resting in any degree on that foundation can stand': per Lord Cranworth LJ in *Reynell v Sprye* (1852) 1 De G M & G 660, 708.

Misrepresentation

9

16. In *Edgington v Fitzmaurice* 29 Ch D 459 the defence was not that the plaintiff could have discovered that the representation was false. It was that he was also induced by mistaken beliefs of his own, but for which he would not have subscribed for the debentures. That is very like the present case. It is said here that although SCB would not have paid if they had known the bill of lading to be falsely dated, they would also not have paid if they had not mistakenly and negligently thought that they could obtain reimbursement. In my opinion, the law takes no account of these other reasons for payment. This rule seems to me based upon sound policy. It would not seem just that a fraudulent defendant's liability should be reduced on the grounds that, for whatever reason, the victim should not have made the payment which the defendant successfully induced him to make.

17. As Sir Anthony Evans correctly pointed out, the rule in *Redgrave v Hurd* 20 Ch D 1 applies to both innocent and fraudulent misrepresentations. The wider rule in *Edgington v Fitzmaurice* probably applies only to fraudulent misrepresentations. In *Gran Gelato Ltd v Richcliff (Group) Ltd* [1992] Ch 560 Sir Donald Nicholls V-C said that, in principle, a defence of contributory negligence should be available in a claim for damages under section 2(1) MA 1967. But since the alleged contributory negligence was that the plaintiff could with reasonable care have discovered that the representation was untrue, the rule in *Redgrave v Hurd* prevented the conduct of the plaintiff from being treated as partly responsible for the loss. This left open the possibility that, in a case of innocent representation, some other kind of negligent causative conduct might be taken into account.

18. In the case of fraudulent misrepresentation, however, I agree with Mummery J in *Alliance & Leicester Building Society v Edgestop Ltd* [1993] 1 WLR 1462 that there is no common law defence of contributory negligence. (See also Carnwath J in *Corporacion Nacional del Cobre de Chile v Sogemin Metals Ltd* [1997] 1 WLR 1396 and Blackburn J in *Nationwide Building Society v Thimbleby & Co* [1999] Lloyd's Rep PN 359). It follows that, in agreement with the majority in the Court of Appeal, I think that no apportionment under the 1945 Act is possible.

9.3.2 Negligent misrepresentation

Negligent misrepresentation involves a statement made honestly, but without reasonable grounds for the belief.

9.3.2.1 At common law

Hedley Byrne & Co. Ltd v Heller & Partners Ltd
[1964] AC 465 (HL)

Hedley Byrne, who were advertising agents, asked their bank to inquire as to the financial standing of Easipower Ltd. Heller & Partners, who were Easipower's bankers, replied 'without responsibility' that Easipower was 'considered good for its ordinary business engagements'. Relying on this reference, Hedley Byrne booked advertising time for Easipower on terms under which they were personally responsible for payment. Easipower went into liquidation and Hedley Byrne lost £17,000 on these contracts. They brought an action against Heller & Partners for damages for negligence.

Held: Such a statement could give rise to an action for damages for financial loss in tort (there being no contractual relationship between the parties concerned). This was because a duty of care would be owed where there was a special relationship between the parties. However, on these facts, that duty had been expressly excluded by the disclaimer of responsibility.

LORD MORRIS OF BORTH-Y-GEST: [I]rrespective of any contractual or fiduciary relationship and irrespective of any direct dealing, a duty may be owed by one person to another. It is said, however, that where careless (but not fraudulent) misstatements are in question there can be no liability in the maker of them unless there is either some contractual or fiduciary relationship with a person adversely affected by the making of them or unless, through the making of them, something is created or circulated or some situation is created which is dangerous to life, limb or property. In logic I can see no essential reason for distinguishing injury which is caused by a reliance upon words from injury which is caused by a reliance upon the safety of the staging to a ship or by a reliance upon the safety for use of the contents of a bottle of hair wash or a bottle of some consumable liquid. It seems to me, therefore, that if A claims that he has suffered injury or loss as a result of acting upon some misstatement made by B who is not in any contractual or fiduciary relationship with him, the inquiry that is first raised is whether B owed any duty to A: if he did the further inquiry is raised as to the nature of the duty. There may be circumstances under which the only duty owed by B to A is the duty of being honest: there may be circumstances under which B owes to A the duty not only of being honest but also a duty of taking reasonable care. The issue in the present case is whether the bank owed any duty to Hedleys and if so what the duty was . . .

My Lords, I consider that it follows and that it should now be regarded as settled that if someone possessed of a special skill undertakes, quite irrespective of contract, to apply that skill for the assistance of another person who relies upon such skill, a duty of care will arise. The fact that the service is to be given by means of or by the instrumentality of words can make no difference. Furthermore, if in a sphere in which a person is so placed that others could reasonably rely upon his judgment or his skill or upon his ability to make careful inquiry, a person takes it upon himself to give information or advice to, or allows his information or advice to be passed on to, another person who, as he knows or should know, will place reliance upon it, then a duty of care will arise.

NOTE Liability under *Hedley Byrne v Heller* turns on whether there was a special relationship between the claimant and the defendant, and an 'assumption of responsibility' for a statement: *Henderson v Merrett Syndicates Ltd* [1995] 2 AC 145. To establish the special relationship, first, the defendant must arguably either have or profess to have some special skill in relation to the subject matter or, at the very least, must have taken it upon himself to make representations and, secondly, it must have been reasonable for the claimant to rely upon the defendant's statement. As a third requirement, the defendant must either know that the claimant will rely on the statement or it must be reasonably foreseeable that he will rely on it. Finally, the defendant must have some knowledge of the type of transaction for which the information is required: *Caparo Industries plc v Dickman* [1990] 2 AC 605.

Hedley Byrne v Heller can apply to pre-contractual statements where a contract finally resulted between the parties.

Esso Petroleum Co. Ltd v Mardon
[1976] QB 801 (CA)

The facts of this case appear at *page 175, 5.1.3*.

LORD DENNING MR:

Negligent misrepresentation

. . . [T]he question arises whether Esso are liable for negligent misstatement under the doctrine of *Hedley Byrne & Co. Ltd v Heller & Partners Ltd* [1964] AC 465. It has been suggested that *Hedley Byrne* cannot be used so as to impose liability for negligent pre-contractual statements: and that, in a pre-contract situation the remedy (at any rate before the Act of 1967) was only in warranty or nothing . . .

In arguing this point, [counsel for Esso] . . . submitted that when the negotiations between two parties resulted in a contract between them, their rights and duties were governed by the law of contract and not by the law of tort. There was, therefore, no place in their relationship for *Hedley Byrne* [1964] AC 465, which was solely on liability in tort . . . [D]ecisions show that, in the case of a professional man, the duty to use reasonable care arises not only in contract, but is also imposed by the law apart from contract, and is therefore actionable in tort . . . A professional man may give advice under a contract for reward; or without a contract, in pursuance of a voluntary assumption of responsibility, gratuitously without reward. In either case he is under one and the same duty to use reasonable care: see *Cassidy v Ministry of Health* [1951] 2 KB 343, 359–360. In the one case it is by reason of a term implied by law. In the other, it is by reason of a duty imposed by law. For a breach of that duty he is liable in damages: and those damages should be, and are, the same, whether he is sued in contract or in tort.

It follows that I cannot accept [counsel for Esso's] proposition. It seems to me that *Hedley Byrne & Co. Ltd v Heller & Partners Ltd* [1964] AC 465, properly understood, covers this particular proposition: if a man, who has or professes to have special knowledge or skill, makes a representation by virtue thereof to another—be it advice, information or opinion—with the intention of inducing him to enter into a contract with him, he is under a duty to use reasonable care to see that the representation is correct, and that the advice, information or opinion is reliable. If he negligently gives unsound advice or misleading information or expresses an erroneous opinion, and thereby induces the other side to enter into a contract with him, he is liable in damages . . .

Applying this principle, it is plain that Esso professed to have—and did in fact have—special knowledge or skill in estimating the throughput of a filling station. They made the representation—they forecast a throughput of 200,000 gallons—intending to induce Mr Mardon to enter into a tenancy on the faith of it. They made it negligently. It was a 'fatal error.' And thereby induced Mr Mardon to enter into a contract of tenancy that was disastrous to him. For this misrepresentation they are liable in damages.

NOTES

1. In a claim based on negligent misstatement, the claimant has the burden of proving the existence of the duty of care.

2. It will be the only available claim where, as in *Hedley Byrne v Heller* itself, the misrepresentor is not a party to the contract, or where no contract results following the negotiations in which the statement was made.

3. Damages for negligent misstatement are tortious, in that the aim is to put the claimant into the position in which he would have been had the misrepresentation not been made. In *Esso v Mardon* at pp. 820–1, Lord Denning explained it as follows.

The measure of damages

Mr Mardon is not to be compensated here for 'loss of a bargain.' He was given no bargain that the throughput *would* amount to 200,000 gallons a year. He is only to be compensated for having been induced to enter into a contract which turned out to be disastrous for him. Whether it be called breach of warranty or negligent misrepresentation, its effect was *not* to warrant the throughput, but only to induce him to enter the contract. So the damages in either case are to be measured by the loss he suffered. Just as in *Doyle v Olby (Ironmongers) Ltd* [1969] 2 QB 158, 167 he can say: ' . . . I would not have entered into this contract at all but for your representation. Owing to it, I have lost all the capital I put into it. I also incurred a large overdraft. I have spent four years of my life in wasted endeavour without reward: and it will take me some time to re-establish myself.'

For all such loss he is entitled to recover damages.

4. Recovery is not as wide in the tort of negligent misstatement when compared with the position for fraudulent misrepresentation, since the claimant can recover only for loss that was reasonably foreseeable at the time of the statement.

9.3.2.2 Under statute

Misrepresentation Act 1967, s. 2

2. Damages for misrepresentation

(1) Where a person has entered into a contract after a misrepresentation has been made to him by another party thereto and as a result thereof he has suffered loss, then, if the person making the

misrepresentation would be liable to damages in respect thereof had the misrepresentation been made fraudulently, that person shall be so liable notwithstanding that the misrepresentation was not made fraudulently, unless he proves that he had reasonable ground to believe and did believe up to the time the contract was made that the facts represented were true.

NOTE Section 2(4) MA 1967 provides that s. 2 'does not entitle a person to be paid damages in respect of a misrepresentation if the person has a right to redress under Part 4A of the Consumer Protection from Unfair Trading Regulations 2008 (SI 2008/1277) in respect of the conduct constituting the misrepresentation'. Therefore, if the consumer has a remedy within the CPRs, s. 2(1) damages will not be available to her.

9.3.2.2.1 *The burden of proof*

The normal burden of proof is reversed in a s. 2(1) damages claim, so that the representor has to disprove negligence.

Howard Marine and Dredging Co. Ltd v A. Ogden & Sons (Excavations) Ltd
[1978] QB 574 (CA)

During negotiations between the defendants (civil engineering contractors) and the claimants (owners of two sea barges) for the hire of barges, the claimants' marine manager stated that the capacity of each barge was '850 cubic metres' and that this was equivalent to about 1,600 tonnes deadweight carrying capacity. He based this figure on his recollection of an entry in Lloyd's Register, which gave the capacity of the barges as 1,800 tonnes. The register was, in fact, incorrect and the correct figure was 1,055 tonnes. This correct figure could have been ascertained from the ship's documents, which were in the claimants' possession. The defendants agreed to take the barges. Six months after taking delivery, the defendants discovered the correct capacity and refused to pay the full hire. The claimants claimed the outstanding hire charges and the defendants counterclaimed, inter alia, for damages under s. 2(1) MA 1967 on the basis of the misrepresentation as to the barges' capacity.

Held (Bridge and Shaw LJJ): The claimants had failed to prove that their marine manager had had reasonable grounds to believe, and did believe up to the time at which the contract was made, that the facts he represented were true, since the correct figure was contained in the ships' documents and they had failed to show any 'objectively reasonable ground' for relying instead on the figure in Lloyd's Register.

BRIDGE LJ: The first question then is whether Howards would be liable in damages in respect of Mr O'Loughlin's misrepresentation if it had been made fraudulently, that is to say, if he had known that it was untrue. An affirmative answer to that question is inescapable. The judge found in terms that what Mr O'Loughlin said about the capacity of the barges was said with the object of getting the hire contract for Howards, in other words, with the intention that it should be acted on. This was clearly right. Equally clearly the misrepresentation was in fact acted on by Ogdens. It follows, therefore, on the plain language of the statute that, although there was no allegation of fraud, Howards must be liable unless they proved that Mr O'Loughlin had reasonable ground to believe what he said about the barges' capacity.

. . . If the representee proves a misrepresentation which, if fraudulent, would have sounded in damages, the onus passes immediately to the representor to prove that he had reasonable ground to believe the facts represented. In other words the liability of the representor does not depend upon his being under a duty of care the extent of which may vary according to the circumstances in which the representation is made. In the course of negotiations leading to a contract the statute imposes an absolute obligation not to state facts which the representor cannot prove he had reasonable ground to believe.

. . . [I]t is to be assumed that Mr O'Loughlin was perfectly honest throughout. But the question remains whether his evidence, however benevolently viewed, is sufficient to show that he had an objectively reasonable ground to disregard the figure in the ship's documents and to prefer the Lloyd's Register figure. I think it is not. Accordingly I conclude that Howards failed to prove that Mr O'Loughlin had reasonable ground to believe the truth of his misrepresentation to Mr Redpath.

Lord Denning MR (dissenting) thought that the burden of disproving negligence had been discharged.

LORD DENNING MR [dissenting]: This enactment imposes a new and serious liability on anyone who makes a representation of fact in the course of negotiations for a contract. If that representation turns out to be mistaken—then however innocent he may be—he is just as liable as if he made it fraudulently. But how different from times past! For years he was not liable in damages at all for innocent misrepresentation: see *Heilbut, Symons & Co. v Buckleton* [1913] AC 30. Quite recently he was made liable if he was proved to have made it negligently: see *Esso Petroleum Co. Ltd v Mardon* [1976] QB 801. But now with this Act he is made liable—unless he proves—and the burden is on him to prove—that he had reasonable ground to believe and did in fact believe that it was true.

Section 2(1) certainly applies to the representation made by Mr O'Loughlin on July 11, 1974, when he told Ogdens that each barge could carry 1,600 tonnes. The judge found that it was a misrepresentation: that he said it with the object of getting the hire contract for Howards. They got it: and, as a result, Ogdens suffered loss. But the judge found that Mr O'Loughlin was not negligent: and so Howards were not liable for it.

The judge's finding was criticised before us: because he asked himself the question: was Mr O'Loughlin negligent? Whereas he should have asked himself: did Mr O'Loughlin have reasonable ground to believe that the representation was true? I think that criticism is not fair to the judge. By the word 'negligent' he was only using shorthand for the longer phrase contained in s. 2(1) which he had before him. And the judge, I am sure, had the burden of proof in mind: for he had come to the conclusion that Mr O'Loughlin was not negligent. The judge said in effect: 'I am satisfied that Mr O'Loughlin was not negligent': and being so satisfied, the burden need not be further considered.

It seems to me that when one examines the details, the judge's view was entirely justified. He found that Mr O'Loughlin's state of mind was this: Mr O'Loughlin had examined Lloyd's Register and had seen there that the deadweight capacity of each barge was 1,800 tonnes. That figure stuck in his mind. The judge found that 'the 1,600 tonnes was arrived at by knocking off what he considered a reasonable margin for fuel, and so on, from the 1,800 tonnes summer deadweight figure in Lloyd's Register, which was in the back of his mind.' The judge said that Mr O'Loughlin had seen at some time the German shipping documents and had seen the deadweight figure of 1,055.135 tonnes: but it did not register. All that was in his mind was the 1,800 tonnes in Lloyd's Register which was regarded in shipping circles as the Bible. That afforded reasonable ground for him to believe that the barges could each carry 1,600 tonnes pay load: and that is what Mr O'Loughlin believed.

So on this point, too, I do not think we should fault the judge. It is not right to pick his judgment to pieces—by subjecting it—or the shorthand note—to literal analysis. Viewing it fairly, the judge (who had s. 2(1) in front of him) must have been of opinion that the burden of proof was discharged.

NOTES

1. The decision of the majority is that, to escape liability under s. 2(1) MA 1967, the representor must positively prove reasonable grounds for his belief in addition to disproving negligence. Bridge LJ went as

far as stating that s. 2(1) imposed an absolute obligation on the representor not to state facts that he could
not prove he had reasonable grounds to believe.

Inevitably, this means that liability to pay damages for negligent misrepresentation will more easily
be established under s. 2(1) than at common law.

2. In *Spice Girls Ltd v Aprilia World Service BV*
[2002] EWCA Civ 15, [2002] EMLR 27 (for the facts,
see *page 440, 9.1.1.1*), Aprilia recovered damages
under s. 2(1) because the onus was on the Spice Girls

to show that they had reasonable grounds to believe,
and did believe at the date of the agreement, that the
representation was true. Since it had been established
that they knew that one member intended to leave,
they were unable to discharge this burden.

3. Section 2(1) only applies where the misrepresentation induces the representee to enter into a
contract with the representor, and this is the most
important limitation on its application.

9.3.2.2.2 *The measure of damages under s. 2(1)*

Much emphasis has been placed on the fact that the section itself does not make clear how
damages are to be assessed. The drafting of the section rests upon the 'fiction of fraud', in
that *liability* in damages is said to exist where it would exist had the misrepresentation been
fraudulent even though it is not fraudulent. This has been interpreted to mean that the *damages* are determined in accordance with the principles applicable to damages for fraudulent
misrepresentation.

Royscot Trust Ltd v Rogerson
[1991] 2 QB 297 (CA)

A customer agreed to buy a car for £7,600 from a dealer. The deposit was £1,200, with the balance
of £6,400 on hire purchase terms. In order to satisfy a 20 per cent deposit requirement, the dealer
represented to the finance company that the purchase price was £8,000 and that a deposit of
£1,600 had been paid (leaving the same balance of £6,400). The hire purchase contract was made
on this basis. When £2,775 of instalments had been paid, the customer dishonestly sold the car for
£7,200 to an innocent purchaser. The company recovered damages of £1,600 against the dealer, i.e.
the extra amount that the company had been induced to pay as a result of the misrepresentation.
(If the deposit actually paid—£1,200—had been correctly stated, the true price of the car would
have been £6,000 and the company would have paid the dealer £4,800, not £6,400.) The finance
company claimed that the damages against the dealer should be £3,625 (the difference between
the amount paid to the dealer and the amount received from the customer). Therefore, the first
issue was whether damages under s. 2(1) were tortious, so as to put the representee into the position in which he would have been had he never entered into the contract. The dealer contended
that he should pay no damages because the customer's sale of the car during the continuance of
the hire purchase agreement was not a reasonably foreseeable loss.

Held: The measure of damages under s. 2(1) was tortious, in that the measure had to be the
same as for fraudulent misrepresentation because of the fiction of fraud. It followed that the
finance company could recover for all losses directly flowing from the misrepresentation, even
if that loss was unforeseeable (although on the facts, it was considered foreseeable). The finance
company was therefore entitled to recover the £3,625, being the tortious measure of damages.

BALCOMBE LJ: The finance company's cause of action against the dealer is based on s. 2(1) of the
Misrepresentation Act 1967 . . .

As a result of some dicta by Lord Denning MR in two cases in the Court of Appeal—*Gosling v Anderson*
[1972] EGD 709 and *Jarvis v Swans Tours Ltd* [1973] QB 233, 237—and the decision at first instance in
Watts v Spence [1976] Ch 165, there was some doubt whether the measure of damages for an innocent
misrepresentation giving rise to a cause of action under the Act of 1967 was the tortious measure, so

as to put the representee in the position in which he would have been if he had never entered into the contract, or the contractual measure, so as to put the representee in the position in which he would have been if the misrepresentation had been true, and thus in some cases give rise to a claim for damages for loss of bargain. Lord Denning MR's remarks in *Gosling v Anderson* were concerned with an amendment to a pleading, while his remarks in *Jarvis v Swans Tours Ltd* were clearly obiter. *Watts v Spence* was disapproved by this court in *Sharneyford Supplies Ltd v Edge* [1987] Ch 305, 323. However, there is now a number of decisions which make it clear that the tortious measure of damages is the true one. Most of these decisions are at first instance and will be found in *Chitty on Contract*, 26th ed. (1989), vol 1, p. 293, para 439, note 63 and in *McGregor on Damages*, 15th ed. (1988) pp 1107–1108, para 1745. One at least, *Chesneau v Interhome Ltd* (1983) 134 NLJ 341 . . . is a decision of this court. The claim was one under s. 2(1) of the 1967 Act and the appeal concerned the assessment of damages. In the course of his judgment Eveleigh LJ said:

> [Damages] should be assessed in a case like the present one on the same principles as damages are assessed in tort. The subsection itself says: '. . . if the person making the misrepresentation would be liable to damages in respect thereof had the misrepresentation been made fraudulently, that person shall be so liable . . .' By 'so liable' I take it to mean liable as he would be if the misrepresentation had been made fraudulently.

In view of the wording of the subsection it is difficult to see how the measure of damages under it could be other than the tortious measure and, despite the initial aberrations referred to above, that is now generally accepted. Indeed counsel before us did not seek to argue the contrary.

The first main issue before us was: accepting that the tortious measure is the right measure, is it the measure where the tort is that of fraudulent misrepresentation, or is it the measure where the tort is negligence at common law? The difference is that in cases of fraud a plaintiff is entitled to any loss which flowed from the defendant's fraud, even if the loss could not have been foreseen: see *Doyle v Olby (Ironmongers) Ltd* [1969] 2 QB 158. In my judgement the wording of the subsection is clear: the person making the innocent misrepresentation shall be 'so liable', i.e. liable to damages as if the representation had been made fraudulently. This was the conclusion to which Walton J came in *F & B Entertainments Ltd v Leisure Enterprises Ltd* (1976) 240 EG 455, 461. See also the decision of Sir Douglas Franks QC sitting as a High Court judge in *McNally v Welltrade International Ltd* [1978] IRLR 497. In each of these cases the judge held that the basis for the assessment of damages under s. 2(1) of the Act of 1967 is that established in *Doyle v Olby (Ironmongers) Ltd*. This is also the effect of the judgment of Eveleigh LJ in *Chesneau v Interhome Ltd* already cited: 'By so liable I take it to mean liable as he would be if the misrepresentation had been made fraudulently.'

This was also the original view of the academic writers. In an article, 'The Misrepresentation Act 1967' (1967) 30 MLR 369 by P. S. Atiyah and G. H. Treitel, the authors say, at pp. 373–4:

> The measure of damages in the statutory action will apparently be that in an action of deceit . . . But more probably the damages recoverable in the new action are the same as those recoverable in an action of deceit . . .

Professor Treitel has since changed his view. In *Treitel, The Law of Contract*, 7th ed. (1987), p. 278, he says:

> Where the action is brought under section 2(1) of the Misrepresentation Act, one possible view is that the deceit rule will be applied by virtue of the fiction of fraud. But the preferable view is that the severity of the deceit rule can only be justified in cases of actual fraud and that remoteness under section 2(1) should depend, as in actions based on negligence, on the test of foreseeability.

The only authority cited in support of the 'preferable' view is *Shepheard v Broome* [1904] AC 342, a case under s. 38 of the Companies Act 1867, which provided that in certain circumstances a company director, although not in fact fraudulent, should be 'deemed to be fraudulent'. As Lord Lindley said, at

p. 346: 'To be compelled by Act of Parliament to treat an honest man as if he were fraudulent is at all times painful', but he went on to say: 'but the repugnance which is naturally felt against being compelled to do so will not justify your Lordships in refusing to hold the appellant responsible for acts for which an Act of Parliament clearly declares he is to be held liable . . . '

The House of Lords so held.

It seems to me that that case, far from supporting Professor Treitel's view, is authority for the proposition that we must follow the literal wording of s. 2(1), even though that has the effect of treating, so far as the measure of damages is concerned, an innocent person as if he were fraudulent. *Chitty on Contracts*, 26th ed. (1989), vol. 1, p. 293, para 439, says: it is doubtful whether the rule that the plaintiff may recover even unforeseeable losses suffered as the result of fraud would be applied; it is an exceptional rule which is probably justified only in cases of actual fraud.

No authority is cited in support of that proposition save a reference to the passage in Professor Treitel's book cited above.

Professor Furmston in *Cheshire Fifoot, and Furmston's Law of Contract*, 11th ed. (1986) p. 286, says: 'It has been suggested—and the reference is to the passage in Atiyah and Treitel's article cited above— that damages under s. 2(1) should be calculated on the same principles as govern the tort of deceit. This suggestion is based on a theory that s. 2(1) is based on a "fiction of fraud". We have already suggested that this theory is misconceived. On the other hand the action created by s. 2(1) does look much more like an action in tort than one in contract and it is suggested that the rules for negligence are the natural ones to apply.'

The suggestion that the 'fiction of fraud' theory is misconceived occurs at p. 271, in a passage which includes:

> Though it would be quixotic to defend the drafting of the section, it is suggested that there is no such 'fiction of fraud' since the section does not say that a negligent misrepresentor shall be treated for all purposes as if he were fraudulent. No doubt the wording seeks to incorporate by reference some of the rules relating to fraud but, for instance, nothing in the wording of the subsection requires the measure of damages for deceit to be applied to the statutory action.

With all respect to the various learned authors whose works I have cited above, it seems to me that to suggest that a different measure of damage applies to an action for innocent misrepresentation under the section than that which applies to an action for fraudulent misrepresentation (deceit) at common law is to ignore the plain words of the subsection and is inconsistent with the cases to which I have referred. In my judgment, therefore, the finance company is entitled to recover from the dealer all the losses which it suffered as a result of its entering into the agreements with the dealer and the customer, even if those losses were unforeseeable, provided that they were not otherwise too remote.

NOTES

1. See Wadsley (1992) 55 MLR 698 and Hooley (1991) 107 LQR 547.

2. The application of the fiction of fraud has drawn a clear distinction between fraudulent and negligent misrepresentation under s. 2(1), and negligent misstatement at common law. It is difficult to see why there should be a more generous measure of damages under s. 2(1) than that available for negligent misstatement in tort when both claims could arise on the same facts. Not only does the burden of proof favour the representee under s. 2(1), but the representee can also recover for a much wider category of loss.

Royscot Trust v Rogerson is likely to result in infrequent reliance on *Hedley Byrne v Heller* where s. 2(1) is available—namely, where there is a contract between the representor and representee. It may also mean that there is little point in a representee seeking to establish fraudulent misrepresentation when the same measure of damages can be obtained under s. 2(1) with the advantage of the reversal of the burden of proof.

However, see Lord Steyn's comment in *Smith New Court Securities Ltd v Scrimgeour Vickers (Asset Management) Ltd* [1997] AC 254 (extracted at *page 460, 9.3.1.1.1,* note 3), noting a distinction between losses flowing from the transaction and the specific misrepresentation.

3. It is difficult to justify a decision that will result in an honest, but negligent, representor being held liable as if he were fraudulent. In principle, some distinction should persist.

4. In *Smith New Court,* at p. 282 (*page 460, 9.3.1.1.1*), Lord Steyn raised the question of whether 'the rather loose wording of the statute compels the court to treat a person who was morally innocent as if he was guilty of fraud when it comes to the measure of damages'. However, since the issue did not arise directly on the facts of that case, Lord Steyn did not express any concluded view on this matter. Lord Browne-Wilkinson also stated that he was not expressing any view on the correctness of the decision in *Royscot Trust.*

5. In *Spice Girls Ltd v Aprilia World Service BV* [2001] EMLR 8, Arden J held that she was bound to follow *Royscot Trust* and calculate damages under s. 2(1) on the basis of compensating Aprilia for all direct losses (i.e. the fraud measure), which included consequential loss. See also the acceptance of this position in *Pankhania v Hackney London Borough Council* [2004] EWHC 323 (Ch), [2004] 1 EGLR 135 (*page 446, 9.1.2.3*).

6. Remarkably, in *Avon Insurance plc v Swire Fraser Ltd* [2000] 1 All ER (Comm) 573, Rix J considered that, because of the application of the fraud principles of damages to negligent misrepresentation under s. 2(1), a court should not be too willing to find there to be an actionable misrepresentation where that court had some room for the exercise of judgment. He stated:

> 201. If, on the other hand, the rule in the *Royscot Trust Ltd* case were one day to be found to be a misunderstanding of the 1967 Act, and the way were to become open to treat an innocent misrepresentation under s. 2(1) as though it was a case of negligence in *Hedley Byrne*, so that in the typical case of the provision of negligent information it would be possible to tailor the damages to the risk undertaken by the negligent representor, as in the *Banque Bruxelles* case, then there would be nothing to be said against adopting a more closely focused approach to the proof of misrepresentation.

This may be a sign of the deep misgivings over *Royscot Trust,* but seems a wholly inappropriate solution.

Following *Royscot Trust,* the crucial question will now be: does the loss flow directly from the misrepresentation, i.e. did the misrepresentation *cause* this loss?

Naughton v O'Callaghan
[1990] 3 All ER 191

The claimants bought a thoroughbred yearling colt for 26,000 guineas and trained the colt for two seasons. The colt was unplaced in all of its six races and its value fell to £1,500. The claimants then discovered that the pedigree had not been correctly described, and sought to recover the purchase price and training fees. If the colt had originally been correctly described, it could have sold for 23,500 guineas. There was a breach of contract, but the contractual measure of damages was only the difference in value at the date of the contract. The claimants therefore formulated their claim in misrepresentation, and sought the difference between the price paid and the fall in value at the time that the misrepresentation was discovered, on the basis that the fall in value was a direct loss.

Held: Waller J awarded damages of the difference between 26,000 guineas and £1,500. The judge accepted that the aim of damages under s. 2(1) was tortious and based on the fiction of fraud, so that all direct loss flowing from the misrepresentation was recoverable. Training and racing were exactly the types of conduct to be expected and was reasonable conduct in the circumstances.

WALLER J [quoting Winn LJ in *Doyle v Olby* [1969] 2 QB 158]: It appears to me that in a case where there has been a breach of warranty of authority, and still more clearly where there has been a tortious wrong consisting of a fraudulent inducement, the proper starting point for any court called on to consider what damages are recoverable by the defrauded person is to compare his position before the representation was made to him with his position after it, brought about by that representation, always bearing in mind that no element in the consequential position can be regarded as attributable loss and damage if it be too remote a consequence: it will be too remote not necessarily because it was not contemplated by the representor but in any case where the person deceived has not himself behaved with reasonable prudence, reasonable common sense or can in any true sense be said to have been the author of his own misfortune. The damage that he seeks to recover must have flowed directly from the fraud perpetrated on him.

Winn LJ then assessed the damages in that case by reference to precisely what the plaintiff had done after acquiring the business including selling the business at some later time and giving credit for that sale price. (I should perhaps make clear that *Doyle v Olby (Ironmongers) Ltd* was concerned with fraud, but in relation to a claim for damages under the Misrepresentation Act 1967 the approach is the same . . .).

What, as it seems to me, makes this case different from the norm is, first, that what the plaintiffs in fact purchased in reliance on the representation in the catalogue was a different animal altogether; second, if they had known of the misrepresentation within a day or so they could, and as I have found would, have sold Fondu for its then value; third, their decision to keep Fondu and race it was precisely what the sellers would have expected: Fondu was not a commodity like, for example, rupee paper, which it would be expected that the defendants would go out and sell; fourth, the fall in Fondu's value if it did not win races was not due to a general fall in the market in racehorses, but was special to Fondu and to be expected if Fondu did not win. It might well not have happened if Fondu had been the different animal as it had been originally described.

Accordingly, in my judgment it would be unjust if the plaintiffs were not entitled to recover the difference between 26,000 guineas and £1,500, and on that aspect of the case accordingly I award that sum.

[Waller J also awarded the training fees and costs of upkeep of the horse up to the date on which the misrepresentation was discovered.]

. . . It seems to me that in relation to this particular horse, applying Winn LJ's test in *Doyle v Olby (Ironmongers) Ltd* [1969] 2 All ER 119 at 123–124, [1969] 2 QB 158 at 168, the cost of training and keeping Fondu should be recoverable. But is it right to apply blinkers and consider the purchase of this particular animal and the expenditure on him? The defendant says that expenditure would have been incurred anyway on some yearling purchased at those September sales. To which the plaintiffs retort that that may be so, but if they bought the horse described by the defendant it *might* have paid for its keep and reaped for them rich rewards.

I have concluded that the plaintiffs are entitled to ask the court to look simply at the contract they made in reliance on the representation which induced them to enter into that bargain. They are entitled to say that there must be no speculation one way or the other about what would have happened if they had not purchased this horse and if no misrepresentation had been made to them. They are entitled to say (putting it in broad terms) we bought one horse and we spent money training it and entering it for races. We discovered two years after the purchase that it was not the horse we thought we had bought; it is not the horse on which we would have spent any money training or keeping, and therefore that is money only spent in reliance on the representation made.

NOTES

1. This case illustrates that many misrepresentation cases will turn on proving the direct loss, i.e. that the loss was caused by the misrepresentation. The representee's acts must be reasonable in the circumstances or the chain of causation may be broken.

2. In *Butler-Creagh v Hersham* [2011] EWHC 2525 (QB), in a deceit claim concerning the purchase of a property as a result of a fraudulent misrepresentation concerning its value, the cost of development, and the need for urgency in completing, Eady J stressed the importance of causation. The judge noted, at [113]:

One cannot simply spend money in a situation of this kind and express it as a loss flowing from the actionable misrepresentations . . . It needs . . . to be demonstrated that it was necessary or reasonable to spend the money, not merely as a matter of choice, but as a result of being placed wrongfully in a particular predicament as a result of the misrepresentation(s) comprising the cause of action.

Therefore, the stamp duty on the purchase and the borrowing costs flowed directly from the deci-sion to purchase, as did reasonable maintenance costs to ensure that the property did not deteriorate before it could be sold.

9.3.2.3 Can damages be awarded for losses arising out of a contract entered into with a third party?

In *Taberna Europe CDO II plc v Selskabet AF 1.September 2008* [2016] EWCA Civ 1262 the Court of Appeal considered, *obiter*, the measure of damages under s. 2(1) where a false statement made by A to B leads B to enter into a contract with C. Taberna, an Irish investment vehicle, purchased securities in Roskilde Bank from Deutsche Bank for €27 million, relying on a statement by Roskilde that the amount of its non-performing loans was DKK57 million whereas the true figure was DKK3.5 billion. The claim was dismissed by reason of a disclaimer issued by Roskilde, but the Court of Appeal considered whether in principle damages could be awarded against Roskilde for a representation causing Taberna to enter into a contract with Deutsche Bank.

> MOORE-BICK LJ: 37 Section 2(1) of the Misrepresentation Act 1967 provides as follows:
>
> > Where a person has entered into a contract after a misrepresentation has been made to him by another party thereto and as a result thereof he has suffered loss, then, if the person making the misrepresentation would be liable to damages in respect thereof had the misrepresentation been made fraudulently, that person shall be so liable notwithstanding that the misrepresentation was not made fraudulently, unless he proves that he had reasonable ground to believe and did believe up to the time the contract was made that the facts represented were true.
>
> 38 It is generally recognised that the Act was passed principally to remedy two perceived defects in the existing law: the inability of a person who had been induced to enter into a contract by a misrepresentation that was not fraudulent to recover damages, and the inadequate nature of the remedy of rescission in the case of innocent misrepresentation. That would suggest that the draftsman was setting out to modify the law relating to the relationship between the two parties to the contract, rather than the law relating to negligent misstatement in general. In my view, the opening words of the subsection . . . are consistent with that interpretation, which involves reading the word 'thereof' as referring to the entering into a contract. Mr Lord, however, submitted that it refers simply to the misrepresentation and that the representee is entitled to recover for all the consequences of the misrepresentation.
>
> 39 In order to understand the scope of section 2(1) it is helpful to consider it in the context of the other provisions of the Act, in particular section 2(2), which gives the court the power to award damages in lieu of rescission. Rescission is a remedy available to a party to a contract in cases where he has been induced to enter into it by an innocent misrepresentation on the part of the other party to it. Moreover, by section 2(3) any damages awarded under section 2(2) are to be taken into account when assessing damages under section 2(1). All that supports the conclusion that the Act is dealing only with the relationship between the two contracting parties arising out of or in relation to a contract which has been induced by misrepresentation on the part of one of them. This was a point made by Mustill J. in *Resolute Maritime Inc v Nippon Kaiji Kyokai (The 'Skopas')* [1983] 1 W.L.R. 857 . . .
>
> 44 In my view, the background to the legislation and the language of section 2(1) itself read in the context of section 2(2) point to the conclusion that it is concerned only with representations made by a person who enters into a contract with the representee and with losses arising as a result of entering into that contract. That conclusion is reinforced by certain observations of Hoffmann L.J. in *William Sindall Plc v Cambridgeshire County Council* [1994] 1 WLR 1016. The case concerned a misrepresentation by the vendor of development land that it was not subject to any undisclosed encumbrances. Some time after the sale had been completed it was discovered that the site was subject to an easement of drainage.

The buyer sought to rescind the contract and a question arose whether the court should award damages in lieu of rescission under the Misrepresentation Act and, if so, what the measure of damages should be.

. . .

47 For all these reasons I have reached the clear conclusion that section 2(1) of the Act entitles the representee to recover only such damages as flow from his having entered into a contract with the representor.

9.3.2.4 Contributory negligence

Can the damages awarded to the representee under s. 2(1) be reduced for contributory negligence?

Gran Gelato Ltd v Richcliff (Group) Ltd
[1992] Ch 560

In 1984, Gran Gelato had been granted a ten-year underlease by Richcliff. The headlease contained a redevelopment break clause, which was exercisable by 12 months' notice expiring on or after June 1989. Gran Gelato and their solicitors had no notice of this restriction, and, in reply to an inquiry, Richcliff's solicitors had stated that 'to the lessor's knowledge' there were no such rights affecting the headlease that would inhibit the tenant's enjoyment of the property. In November 1988, the head lessor exercised the break clause, and Gran Gelato brought an action claiming damages for negligent misstatement at common law and damages under s. 2(1) MA 1967 for negligent misrepresentation. In answer to Richcliff's claim that Gran Gelato was contributorily negligent in proceeding without first seeing the headlease, Gran Gelato argued that s. 1 of the Law Reform (Contributory Negligence) Act 1945 did not apply to a damages claim under the MA 1967.

Held: Since there were concurrent claims for damages for negligence at common law and under the 1967 Act, apportionment for contributory negligence under the 1945 Act applied to both claims. On the facts, however, it was not just and equitable to make a reduction in the damages.

SIR DONALD NICHOLLS VC: Richcliff has advanced a defence of contributory negligence. Clearly, this is available as a defence to the claim against Richcliff for damages for breach of the common law duty of care; but is it available to the claim against Richcliff under s. 2(1) of the Misrepresentation Act 1967? In other words, does s. 1 of the Law Reform (Contributory Negligence) Act 1945 apply to a claim by a plaintiff for damages under the Misrepresentation Act 1967?

[The judge cited ss. 1(1) and 4 of the Law Reform (Contributory Negligence) Act 1945 (extracted at *page 709, 14.5.2*). He also referred to s. 2(1) MA 1967 and continued:]

Thus, in short, liability under the Misrepresentation Act 1967 is essentially founded on negligence, in the sense that the defendant, the representor, did not have reasonable grounds to believe that the facts represented were true. (Of course, if he did not believe the facts represented were true he will be liable for fraud.) This being so, it would be very odd if the defence of contributory negligence were not available to a claim under that Act. It would be very odd if contributory negligence were available as a defence to a claim for damages based on a breach of a duty to take care in and about the making of a particular representation, but not available to a claim for damages under the Act in respect of the same representation.

In my view, the answer to this point is provided by the decision of the Court of Appeal in *Forsikringsaktieselskapet Vesta v Butcher* [1989] AC 852. There the court held that the Act of 1945 applies to a case where there is a claim for damages for negligence at common law even if, in addition, there is a claim in contract to the same effect. O'Connor LJ, at p. 866, adopted the view expressed by Prichard J in *Rowe v Turner Hopkins & Partners* [1980] 2 NZLR 550, 556, regarding the equivalent section of the New Zealand legislation:

> I therefore conclude, in the absence of any clear authority to the contrary, that the first limb of the definition of s. 2 determines the meaning of the word 'fault' as it relates to the plaintiff's cause of action: that accordingly, the Contributory Negligence Act cannot apply unless the cause of action is founded on some act or omission on the part of the defendant which gives rise to liability in tort: that if the defendant's conduct meets that criterion, the Act can apply—whether or not the same conduct is also actionable in contract.

Neill LJ, at p. 875, agreed with this approach, and I do not read Sir Roger Ormrod's judgment as differing on this point.

In the present case the conduct of which Gran Gelato complains founds a cause of action both in negligence at common law and under the Act of 1967. As already noted, under the Act of 1967 liability is essentially founded on negligence. By parity of reasoning with the conclusion in *Forsikringsaktieselskapet Vesta v Butcher* [1989] AC 852 regarding concurrent claims in negligence in tort and contract, the Act of 1945 applies in the present case where there are concurrent claims against Richcliff in negligence in tort and under the Act of 1967 . . .

NOTES

1. This should also be the case where only a s. 2(1) claim is made, otherwise it would be possible to avoid apportionment by framing the claim only under the Misrepresentation Act 1967. Given that the 1945 Act applies to 'fault' on the part of the innocent party, it is wide enough to cover s. 2(1).

However, in *Alliance & Leicester Building Society v Edgestop Ltd* [1994] 2 All ER 38, Mummery J held that contributory negligence could not apply to apportion damages in an action in the tort of deceit. The House of Lords in *Standard Chartered Bank v Pakistan National Shipping Corporation (No. 2)* [2002] UKHL 43, [2003] 1 AC 959 (*page 474, 9.3.1.5*), has also confirmed that there is no defence of contributory negligence where the misrepresentation is fraudulent.

In this respect, it appears that if the fiction of fraud were applied to assessing damages in an action under s. 2(1) MA 1967—*Royscot Trust v Rogerson* (*page 481, 9.3.2.2.2*)—then contributory negligence should not apply, since it would not be applicable in an action for fraudulent misrepresentation. This would be highly unsatisfactory, given that negligent misstatement in tort is clearly covered by the 1945 Act. Some clarification and reform in this area is urgently required: see Chandler and Higgins [1994] LMCLQ 326 and Oakley [1994] CLJ 218.

2. The issue arose for direct decision in *Taberna Europe CDO II plc v Selskabet (formerly Roskilde Bank A/S in Bankruptcy)* [2015] EWHC 871 (Comm) (facts, *9.3.2.3*). Could the damages awarded under a s. 2(1) claim be reduced on account of the other party's contributory negligence in failing to take specialist market advice, relying on out-of-date advice and information, and failing to make a proper assessment of capital adequacy prior to making the investment? The argument for the investor was that damages could not be reduced under s. 2(1) where the claim was limited to s. 2(1) and there was no alternative claim based on negligent misstatement at common law. At first instance, Eder J rejected this conclusion.

> EDER J: 109 . . . [I]t does not seem to me that the question as to whether a defendant can rely upon the 1945 Act should depend on the happenstance as to whether the claimant advances a claim based on a breach of a concurrent duty of care. Rather, the question should, in my judgment, depend on whether or not there is or would be concurrent liability. That seems a more principled approach which also derives at least some support from what Lord Hoffmann stated in *Standard Chartered Bank v Pakistan Shipping Corporation* [2003] 1 AC 959 at p 967F where he referred with apparent approval to what Sir Donald Nicholls V-C said in *Gran Gelato* viz that, in principle, a defence of contributory negligence should be available in a claim for damages under s 2(1) of the 1967 Act.
>
> 110 Here, [counsel] submitted that insofar as any representations are found to have been made to Taberna (made with the necessary intent), the circumstances giving rise to that conclusion would also be likely to generate a common law duty of care. I agree. It follows that if Roskilde is guilty of any misrepresentation giving rise to a liability under s 2(1) of the 1967 Act, it is my conclusion that it would in principle be entitled to rely on a defence of contributory negligence under the 1945 Act.

Nevertheless, Eder J concluded that on the facts it was not 'just and equitable' under the 1945 Act to reduce the damages based on the alleged instances of contributory negligence relied upon. The case was appealed to the Court of Appeal, [2016] EWCA Civ 1262, and the ruling of Eder J in favour of the claimant was reversed on the ground that the defendant was entitled to rely upon an exclusion clause. However, Moore-Bick LJ agreed with Eder J's ruling on this point.

52 Section 2(1) of the Misrepresentation Act creates a form of statutory liability sounding in negligence. In principle, therefore, contributory negligence ought to be available as a defence and in *Standard Chartered Bank v Pakistan National Shipping Corpn and Others (Nos 2 and 4)* [2002] UKHL 43 [2003] 1 AC 959, to which Mr. Béar drew our attention, Lord Hoffmann in paragraphs 16 and 17 appears to have accepted that that was so. However, whether it is equitable to apportion part of the responsibility for the loss to the claimant will depend on the facts of the case. Mr. Béar submitted that in this case Taberna had failed to make the sort of enquiries into Roskilde's financial position that would have been expected of any prudent investor and must thus bear part of the blame for its loss. The judge was not persuaded of that, but more importantly, he was not persuaded that, even if Taberna had been negligent, this was a case in which it would be equitable to reduce its damages. That involved an assessment by the judge of the particular circumstances of the case, with which, in my view, this court ought to be slow to interfere. I am not persuaded that there are grounds for interfering with the judge's decision on this issue.

9.3.3 Section 2(2) of the Misrepresentation Act 1967: damages in lieu of rescission

Misrepresentation Act 1967

2. Damages for misrepresentation

. . .

(2) Where a person has entered into a contract after a misrepresentation has been made to him otherwise than fraudulently, and he would be entitled, by reason of the misrepresentation, to rescind the contract, then, if it is claimed, in any proceedings arising out of the contract, that the contract ought to be or has been rescinded, the court or arbitrator may declare the contract subsisting and award damages in lieu of rescission, if of opinion that it would be equitable to do so, having regard to the nature of the misrepresentation and the loss that would be caused by it if the contract were upheld, as well as to the loss that rescission would cause to the other party.

NOTES

1. In the context of negligent or wholly innocent misrepresentation (i.e. honest and based on reasonable grounds), it is for the court in its discretion to decide to award damages instead of rescission if it feels that, in the circumstances, it would be fair to do so. In particular, if the misrepresentation were wholly innocent, then rescission may be an overreaction where damages would adequately compensate the misrepresentee, especially if the misrepresentation relates to a trivial matter.

2. In *Thomas Witter Ltd v TBP Industries Ltd* [1996] 2 All ER 573, p. 591a–d, Jacob J sought (*obiter*) to identify the differences between damages under s. 2(1) and (2):

[W]hat is the difference between s. 2(2) and s. 2(1)? In particular, since s. 2(1) has a defence of 'innocence' is that in practical terms useless because damages can be had under s. 2(2)? There is, of course, overlap between the two subsections on any construction and s. 2(3) explicitly recognises this. But if my construction covered all the cases covered by s. 2(1) then the latter would be pointless and my construction would probably be wrong. However, I do not think there is complete overlap. First, under s. 2(1) damages can be awarded in addition to rescission. So if there is 'innocence' the representor cannot have both remedies and never could, whatever the date of the decision. Secondly, the question of an award of damages under s. 2(2) is discretionary and the court must take into account the matters referred to in the concluding words of the subsection. Thirdly, the measure of damages under the two subsections may be different—s. 2(3) certainly contemplates that this may be so and moreover contemplates that s. 2(1) damages may be more than s. 2(2) damages and not the other way round . . .

3. Although there is some assistance in the Act identifying the factors relevant to the decision to award damages in lieu of rescission, the section does not identify the measure of damages under s. 2(2).

4. Section 2 MA 1967, including s. 2(2), does not apply where a consumer has a right to redress under the CPRs 2008 (MA 1967, s. 2(4)).

For the facts, see *page 388, 8.4.1.*

Held: There was no misrepresentation so that rescission was not available and therefore no question of damages in lieu of rescission arose.

HOFFMANN LJ [*obiter*]: My conclusion that there are no grounds for rescission . . . means that it is unnecessary to consider whether the judge correctly exercised his discretion under s. 2(2) of the Misrepresentation Act 1967 not to award damages in lieu of rescission. But in case this case goes further, I should say that in my judgment the judge approached this question on a false basis, arising from his mistake about the seriousness of the defect . . .

The discretion conferred by s. 2(2) is a broad one, to do what is equitable. But there are three matters to which the court must in particular have regard.

The first is the nature of the misrepresentation. It is clear from the Law Reform Committee's Report that the court was meant to consider the importance of the representation in relation to the subject matter of the transaction. I have already said that in my view, in the context of a £5m sale of land, a misrepresentation which would have cost £18,000 to put right and was unlikely seriously to have interfered with the development or resale of the property was a matter of relatively minor importance.

The second matter to which the court must have regard is 'the loss that would be caused by it [the misrepresentation] if the contract were upheld'. The section speaks in terms of loss suffered rather than damages recoverable but clearly contemplates that if the contract is upheld, such loss will be compensated by an award of damages. Section 2(2) therefore gives a power to award damages in circumstances in which no damages would previously have been recoverable. Furthermore, such damages will be compensation for loss caused by the misrepresentation, whether it was negligent or not. This is made clear by s. 2(3), which provides:

> Damages may be awarded under subsection (2) of this section whether or not he is liable to damages under subsection (1) thereof, but where he is so liable any award under subsection (2) shall be taken into account in assessing his liability under the said subsection (1).

Damages under s. 2(2) are therefore damages for the misrepresentation as such. What would be the measure of such damages? This court is not directly concerned with quantum, which would be determined at an inquiry. But since the court, in the exercise of its discretion, needs to know whether damages under s. 2(2) would be an adequate remedy and to be able to compare such damages with the loss which rescission would cause to Cambridgeshire, it is necessary to decide in principle how the damages would be calculated . . .

Under s. 2(1), the measure of damages is the same as for fraudulent misrepresentation i.e. all loss caused by the plaintiff having been induced to enter into the contract: *Cemp Properties (UK) Ltd v Dentsply Research and Development Corp* [1991] 2 EGLR 197. This means that the misrepresentor is invariably deprived of the benefit of the bargain (e.g. any difference between the price paid and the value of the thing sold) and may have to pay additional damages for consequential loss suffered by the representee on account of having entered into the contract. In my judgment, however, it is clear that this will not necessarily be the measure of damages under s. 2(2).

First, s. 2(1) provides for damages to be awarded to a person who 'has entered into a contract after a misrepresentation has been made to him by another party and as a result thereof—sc. of having entered into the contract—he has suffered loss'. In contrast s. 2(2) speaks of 'the loss which would be caused by it—sc. the misrepresentation—if the contract were upheld'. In my view, s. 2(1) is concerned with the damage flowing from having entered into the contract, while s. 2(2) is concerned with damage caused by the property not being what it was represented to be.

Secondly, s. 2(3) contemplates that damages under s. 2(2) may be less than damages under s. 2(1) and should be taken into account when assessing damages under the latter subsection. This only makes sense if the measure of damages may be different.

Thirdly, the Law Reform Committee Report makes it clear that s. 2(2) was enacted because it was thought that it might be a hardship to the representor to be deprived of the whole benefit of the bargain on account of a minor misrepresentation. It could not possibly have intended the damages in lieu to be assessed on a principle which would invariably have the same effect.

The Law Reform Committee drew attention to the anomaly which already existed by which a minor misrepresentation gave rise to a right of rescission whereas a warranty in the same terms would have grounded no more than a claim for modest damages. It said that this anomaly would be exaggerated if its recommendation for abolition of the bar on rescission after completion were to be implemented. I think that s. 2(2) was intended to give the court a power to eliminate this anomaly by upholding the contract and compensating the plaintiff for the loss he has suffered on account of the property not having been what it was represented to be. In other words, damages under s. 2(2) should never exceed the sum which would have been awarded if the representation had been a warranty. It is not necessary for present purposes to discuss the circumstances in which they may be less.

If one looks at the matter when Sindall purported to rescind, the loss which would be caused if the contract were upheld was relatively small: the £18,000 it would have cost to divert the sewer, the loss of a plot and interest charges on any consequent delay at the rate of £2,000 a day. If one looks at the matter at the date of trial, the loss would have been nil because the sewer had been diverted.

The third matter to be taken into account under s. 2(2) is the loss which would be caused to Cambridgeshire by rescission. This is the loss of the bargain at the top of the market (cf *The Lucy* [1983] 1 Lloyd's Rep 188) having to return about £8m in purchase price and interest in exchange for land worth less than £2m.

Having regard to these matters, and in particular the gross disparity between the loss which would be caused to Sindall by the misrepresentation and the loss which would be caused to Cambridgeshire by rescission, I would have exercised my discretion to award damages in lieu of rescission.

EVANS LJ [*obiter*]: Section 2(3) makes it clear that the statutory power to award damages under s. 2(2) is distinct from the plaintiff's right to recover damages under s. 2(1). Quoting from s. 2(2) itself, such damages are awarded 'in lieu of rescission' and the court has to have regard to three factors in particular, namely, the nature of the misrepresentation, the loss that would be caused by it (sc the misrepresentation) if the contract was upheld, and the loss that rescission would cause to the other party (sc the non-fraudulent author of the misrepresentation). It has not been suggested that these three are the only factors which the court may take into account. The discretion is expressed in broad terms 'if of opinion that it would be equitable to do so'. The three factors, however, in all but an exceptional case, are likely to be the ones to which most weight would be given, even if the subsection were silent in this respect.

No real difficulty arises in the present case as regards the nature of the misrepresentation, if any was made, nor as regards the loss which would be caused to the council, if rescission were upheld. There was no blameworthiness, on the judge's findings, so far as the council's officers in 1988–89 were concerned . . . The consequences of the misrepresentation were not negligible, but they were small in relation to the purchase and the project as a whole. The loss caused to the council by rescission would be very great. They would repay in excess of £5m, together with interest, and would have restored to them land worth only a fraction of that amount. In other words, they would suffer the decline in market values which has occurred since 1988. And, even if the easement had been discovered immediately and the contract had been rescinded then, the council would have suffered significant loss, simply by reason of the need to repeat the tendering process and find another buyer.

There is, however, much room for debate as to the 'loss that would be caused if the contract were upheld'. The subsection assumes, as I read it, that this loss will be compensated by the damages awarded, if the contract is upheld. But if the measure is the same as those awarded in respect of a fraudulent misrepresentation (*Doyle v Olby (Ironmongers) Ltd* [1969] 2 QB 158), or under s. 2(1) (*Cemp Properties (UK) Ltd v Dentsply Research and Development Corp* [1991] 2 EGLR 197; cf *Royscot Trust Ltd v Rogerson* [1991] 2 QB 297), in cases where the contract continues in force, then two consequences seem to follow. First, damages under s. 2(2) are co-extensive with those under s. 2(1), whereas s. 2(3) suggests that they are or may be different. Secondly, an innocent and non-negligent defendant will be liable under s. 2(2) for damages which he is specifically excused under s. 2(1). Furthermore, if the plaintiff recovers full compensation under s. 2(2), if the contract is upheld, then he will not suffer any net loss, assuming that the damages are paid.

The cost of remedying the defect in the land was almost insignificant, and any delay and inconvenience suffered by Sindall can be compensated by a relatively small additional sum. The real issue is whether account should be taken of the decline in market values which affects Sindall if the contract stands, just as it would affect Cambridgeshire if rescission was upheld . . .

[Counsel for Sindall's] argument is that Sindall are entitled to recover the whole of the loss which they have suffered as a result of entering into the transaction, including the fall in market values from 1988 until at least the time of purported rescission in December 1990 . . .

In my judgment, it is not correct that the measure of damages under s. 2(2) for the loss that would be caused by the misrepresentation if the contract were upheld is the same measure as under s. 2(1). The latter is established by the common law, and it is the amount required to compensate the party to whom the misrepresentation was made for all the losses which he has sustained by reason of his acting upon it at the time when he did. But the damages contemplated by s. 2(2) are damages in lieu of rescission. The starting point for the application of the subsection is the situation where a plaintiff has established a right to rescind the contract on grounds of innocent misrepresentation; its object is to ameliorate for the innocent misrepresentor the harsh consequences of rescission for a wholly innocent (meaning, non-negligent as well as non-fraudulent) misrepresentor, in a case where it is fairer to uphold the contract and award damages against him. Such an award of damages was not permitted in law or equity before 1967. The court, therefore, exercises a statutory jurisdiction and it does so having regard to the circumstances at the date of the hearing, when otherwise rescission would be ordered . . . When there has been a decline in market values since the date of the contract, then one party or the other will suffer that loss, depending on whether rescission is ordered or not. But that loss is not caused by the misrepresentation, except in the sense that the decline has occurred since the representation was made, and it does not measure the loss caused by the misrepresentation either when the representation was acted upon or when the court decides whether to order rescission or not. The 'loss caused by it', in my judgment, can be measured by the cost of remedying the defect, or alternatively by the reduced market value attributable to the defect, together with additional compensation, if appropriate . . .

When the court is required to form its own view of what is equitable between the parties at the date of the hearing, it is dangerous to lay down any hard-and-fast rule to the effect that no account can be taken of changed market values . . . Moreover, if it is right to take account of the current market value in assessing the loss which would be sustained by the council, if rescission was ordered, then it would be 'inequitable' not to have regard to this factor in the case of the builders also. But the effect of doing so is merely to re-state the issue which the court has to decide: in the circumstances of the case, should the loss of market remain where it presently lies?

Viewed in this way, it would be substantially unjust, in my judgment, to deprive Cambridgeshire of the bargain which it made in 1988, albeit that the bargain was induced by a misrepresentation innocently made, but which was of little importance in relation to the contract as a whole. That misrepresentation apart, Sindall made what has proved to be so far an unfortunate bargain for them (although they remain owners of an important potential development site in what is a notoriously cyclical market). To permit them to transfer the financial consequences to Cambridgeshire, in the circumstances of this case, could properly be described as a windfall for them.

For the above reasons, and taking into account the nature of the alleged representation and the history of the matter generally, including Sindall's deliberate failure to make any serious attempt to find a solution to the difficulty which arose when the sewer was discovered, the equitable balance, in my judgment, lies in favour of upholding the contract and awarding damages in lieu of rescission in this case. If there were a live issue under s. 2(2), I would award damages in lieu of rescission and order the amount of such damages to be assessed.

There remains the question of whether these damages should include the decline in the market value of the land since the contract was made. As indicated above, in my judgment they should not. This conclusion may be inconsistent with the view expressed in *McGregor on Damages* 15th ed. (1988), para 1752, and in deference to the distinguished author I should explain my reasons briefly. He suggests that the measure to be adopted is:

> the same as the normal measure of damages in tort where the plaintiff has been induced to contract by fraudulent or negligent misrepresentation . . . The overall result, therefore, is that the damages will be held to be the difference between the value transferred and the value received . . . no recovery being possible for consequential losses.

If the 'value transferred' (meaning the price paid by the plaintiff, to whom the representation was made) was the market value of the property, then there is no difference between this formula and what *McGregor* calls the contract measure, that is to say, the difference between the actual value received and the value which the property would have had, if the representation was true: . . . By adopting the tort measure, therefore, . . . the author impliedly rejects the contract measure, whereas in my judgment that becomes the correct measure in circumstances where the plaintiff is entitled to an order for rescission, but rescission is refused under s. 2(2) of the Act. This is because the difference in value between what the plaintiff was misled into believing that he was acquiring, and the value of what he in fact received seems to me to be the measure of the loss caused to him by the misrepresentation in a case where he cannot rescind the contract and therefore retains the property which he received.

As *McGregor on Damages* points out, the tortious measure benefits a plaintiff who made a bad bargain, that is to say, who agreed to pay more than the market value of the property in the state in which he believed it to be, more so than the contract measure would do. Conversely, it disbenefits one who paid less than the market value, because it disentitles him from recovering the whole of the difference which the contract measure would otherwise produce. Likewise, the right to rescind benefits a plaintiff who has paid, or agreed to pay more than, with hindsight, he should have done. The period of hindsight may be short or long; where it is long, and the value has fallen in line with the market and therefore for reasons unconnected with the misrepresentation, there is no justification, in my view, for holding that the author of the misrepresentation is liable to compensate the plaintiff for that loss, in a case where rescission is refused.

It is unnecessary to explore the wider questions whether a tortious measure should ever include damages for a fall in market values, and whether this measure, as described by Lord Denning MR in *Doyle v Olby (Ironmongers) Ltd* [1969] 2 QB 158, 166, is necessarily exclusive of, or inconsistent with, the contractual measure to the extent which has been suggested. The recovery of such damages in the present case, even if the tortious measure under s. 2(2) applies, appears to be barred by the following three obstacles: (1) such damage was caused, not by the misrepresentation, but by the subsequent fall in market values, an extraneous cause; (2) the authorities suggest that the plaintiff's loss has to be assessed at the date when the property was transferred: *McGregor on Damages* 15th ed., para. 1727, citing *Waddell v Blockey* (1879) 4 QBD 678; and (3) if a subsequent rise, or fall, in market values is relevant at the date of trial, then a chance element enters into the calculation, whether the contract is rescinded or not. I should add, however, that the reported authorities are sparse, as *McGregor* emphasises, and as I read them they do not purport to decide the question whether a decline in value until the time of discovery of the true facts is necessarily excluded.

It is sufficient for present purposes to say that an award of damages in lieu of rescission under s. 2(2) should in my view be calculated as I have described above.

NOTES

1. Hoffmann LJ discusses the three factors identified in the subsection as relevant to the exercise of the court's discretion to award damages in lieu of rescission—namely, the nature of the misrepresentation, the loss caused by the misrepresentation if the contract is upheld (i.e. damages to award to the representee instead of rescission), and the loss that would be caused to the non-fraudulent representor by rescission. The discussion of the measure of damages under s. 2(2) is relevant to the second of these factors. Significantly, unlike s. 2(1) damages, which are concerned with damages resulting from the misrepresentation leading to the making of the contract, s. 2(2) damages are to be assessed on the basis of losses caused by the misrepresentation if the contract is upheld, i.e. losses arising because the subject matter of the contract is not what it was represented to be (difference in value). It follows that, whereas consequential loss can be recovered under s. 2(1), such loss cannot be recovered under s. 2(2): see Jacob J (*obiter*) in *Thomas Witter v TBP Industries Ltd* [1996] 2 All ER 573. However, the measure of loss in this context cannot be contractual, which is the result of the difference in value measure. It may be that this measure would have to be limited to contracts that turn out to be bad bargains, as was the case in *Sindall*.

2. The difficulty on the facts with the measure of damages concerned whether the builders could recover for the fall in the value of the land. However, as the Court of Appeal pointed out, that loss was not actually caused by the misrepresentation, but by the general fall in land values. Evans LJ argued that the loss caused by the misrepresentation is 'measured by the cost of remedying the defect, or alternatively by the reduced market value attributable to the defect', judged at the date of the contract.

3. In *UCB Corporate Services Ltd v Thomason* [2005] EWCA Civ 225, [2005] 1 All ER (Comm) 601, a husband and wife had given two guarantees to the bank. There had been a compromise with the husband's credi-

tors to avoid bankruptcy and the bank agreed, on the basis that there had been full disclosure of the couple's assets, to release the liability under the guarantees (a waiver agreement). The bank later sought to enforce the guarantees or to rescind the waiver agreement for misrepresentation on the basis that there had not been full disclosure. The Court of Appeal considered the discretion to award damages in lieu under s. 2(2) and held that the judge at first instance had been correct in that, given the financial position of the couple, the loss caused by the misrepresentation was the lost chance of recovering more money had the bank known the truth (and therefore not agreed to the waiver), rather than the amount of the guaranteed debt (i.e. the difference in value). If rescission of the waiver agreement were permitted, in theory at least, it would have exposed the couple to a considerable liability by comparison with the loss caused by the misrepresentation, which would need to be compensated by the damages amount. Accordingly, in exercising its discretion under s. 2(2), the Court of Appeal considered damages in lieu to be the appropriate remedy. (There is inevitable distortion here, since the reality of the couple's ability to pay seems to be treated as irrelevant when assessing the consequences of ordering rescission, but is relevant to the loss caused by the misrepresentation, i.e. it is clearly necessary to look at the actual chance of recovering more money.)

4. In *Thomas Witter v TBP Industries*, at p. 591f, Jacob J concluded that: 'The constant and justified academic criticism of the [Misrepresentation] Act indicates a subject well worth the attention of the Law Commission.'

5. In *Harsten Developments Ltd v Bleaken* [2012] EWHC 2704 (Ch) (*page 451, 9.2.1.1*), the judge considered the exercise of the s. 2(2) discretion, but rejected its application on the facts. This appears to be because the misrepresentation was more serious than the alleged misrepresentation in the *Sindall* case in that the property transferred was substantially different from the property that the developer

had been led to expect. If rescission were refused, the developer would retain the land, which it did not want because of the fall in property values since the sale, and would claim damages from the vendors in accordance with s. 2(2). However, if rescission were allowed, the land would be retransferred to the vendors, and they would have to return the price plus interest and any damages under s. 2(1) (covering the sale expenses, etc.). It was recognized that lapse of time might be a factor in the exercise of the s. 2(2) discretion in future, but it had not been argued that this had any effect on the vendors despite the fall in property values. It is possibly more surprising that there was no argument that the lapse of time constituted affirmation (*page 451*, *9.2.1.1*), since time would have started to run from the date of the sale contract in 2007.

9.3.3.1 Must the ability to rescind exist at the date when the discretion under s. 2(2) is exercised?

It had traditionally been considered that if the right to the remedy of rescission had been lost (see bars to rescission, at *page 451*, *9.2.1*), then the court had no discretion to award damages in lieu of it under s. 2(2). In such cases, there would be no remedy at all for innocent misrepresentation and it may be doubtful that this is what Parliament intended. In *Thomas Witter Ltd v TBP Industries Ltd* [1996] 2 All ER 573 (*page 458*, *9.3.1*), Jacob J (*obiter*, because, on the facts, negligence was established) considered that it was sufficient if the right to rescind had at some time existed. However, in more recent cases, the traditional interpretation has been followed on the basis that the wording of the section ('the injured party would otherwise be entitled to rescind') requires that the remedy of rescission should exist at the date of the hearing if damages are to be awarded in lieu of that remedy: see *Floods of Queensferry v Shand Construction Ltd (No. 3)* [2000] BLR 81, p. 93 (Humphrey Lloyd QC) and *Government of Zanzibar v British Aerospace (Lancaster House) Ltd* [2000] 1 WLR 2333 (Raymond Jack QC).

Judge Raymond Jack QC, in *Government of Zanzibar v British Aerospace (Lancaster House) Ltd*, assessed the position as follows:

To my mind the wording of s. 2(2) shows clearly enough that the effect of the subsection is to give the court an alternative to rescission where a right to rescission has been established but the court considers that damages would be a more equitable solution. I refer in particular to 'and he would be entitled,' 'if it is claimed . . . that the contract ought to be or has been rescinded,' 'the court . . . may declare the contract subsisting and award damages in lieu of rescission' and 'as well as to the loss that rescission would cause to the other party.' The last part of the section contemplates a balancing exercise between the situation if damages are awarded and that if rescission were granted: this supposes that rescission is an option open to the court. So I would disagree with the editors of *Chitty on Contracts*, 28th ed. (1999), vol. 1, pp. 383–384, para. 6–097 where it is stated that the words are far from clear.

The scheme of the section is thus in my view that s. 2(1) gives a right to damages for non-fraudulent misrepresentation subject to the defence that the representor had reasonable grounds to believe his representation true, whereas s. 2(2) gives the court power to award damages where this would be more equitable than making an order for rescission or upholding a previous rescission by act of party. Because it is no defence to a claim for rescission that the representor had reasonable grounds to believe the representation true, that is not a defence where the court is considering damages under s. 2(2). In this way, where rescission remains an option, a claimant may do better under s. 2(2) because that defence is not available against him. That is no doubt why Zanzibar seeks to rely on it in addition to s. 2(1). It is also stated in *Chitty*, pp. 383–4, para. 6–097 that, if the power to award damages under s. 2(2) is restricted to situations in which rescission remains possible, then it would be strange because there would be no power to award damages in situations where the right has been lost, for example, because a car which has been misrepresented has been resold. The answer to that point is the claim to damages under s. 2(1), though here as a matter of policy it has been enacted that there should be the reasonable-grounds-of-belief defence . . .

The issue was considered and decided by Jacob J in *Thomas Witter Ltd. v. T.B.P. Industries Ltd.* [1996] 2 All ER 573. He had held that rescission was no longer available because it was not possible to restore the parties to their positions before the contract. He held that the wording of section 2(2) was sufficiently ambiguous to justify reference to the proceedings in Parliament at the Act's passing. He referred to a reply given by the Solicitor-General (Hansard (H.C. Debates), 20 February 1967, cols. 1388–1389). He held that this showed that it was the Solicitor-General's view that damages could be awarded under section 2(2) where rescission was no longer possible. He accordingly held, at p. 590, that the power to award damages under section 2(2) did not depend on an extant right to rescission—it only depended on a right having existed in the past. I accept that the reply taken by itself does suggest that that was the Solicitor-General's view, though it may not be absolutely clear. But, given that this was an extempore answer given a little after 3 o'clock in the morning, I question how much weight should be given to it where it does not accord with other statements . . .

I conclude that both the report of the Law Reform Committee (Tenth Report, 'Innocent Misrepresentation' (1962) Cmnd 1782) and the manner in which cl. 2(2) of the Bill was introduced in the House of Lords make clear that s. 2(2) gives the court a discretionary power to hold the contract to be subsisting and to award damages where it would otherwise be obliged to grant rescission or to hold that the contract had been rescinded by the representee. The court does not have that power, and does not need to have that power, where rescission is no longer available. In short, the power to award damages is an alternative to an order for rescission or the upholding of a prior rescission by the representee if that has occurred.

In *Pankhania v Hackney London Borough Council* [2002] EWHC 2441 (Ch), [2002] NPC 123, [74] (*page 446, 9.1.2.3*), the judge stated *obiter* that 'the introduction of s. 2(2) was to mitigate the effect on the vendor of rescission, which would otherwise be available to the purchaser, and in certain circumstances was an over-harsh remedy, rather than to provide a remedy where there was none'. In other words, the intention was to provide an alternative remedy in a particular situation in which there was an existing remedy, but not to create a remedy where none existed before. This reasoning appears compelling.

Support for this interpretation is growing and this first instance approach has now been endorsed as correct by the Court of Appeal in *Salt v Stratstone Specialist Ltd (t/a Stratstone Cadillac Newcastle)* [2015] EWCA Civ 745, [2015] CTLC 206.

LONGMORE LJ: 17 The point appears to be open at the level of the Court of Appeal. The words of the statute are 'if it is claimed . . . that the contract ought to be or has been rescinded the court . . . may declare the contract subsisting and award damages in lieu of rescission'. No doubt a claimant can be said to make a claim even if he is subsequently held not to be entitled to do so. But the words 'in lieu of rescission' must, in my view, carry with them the implication that rescission is available (or was available at the time the contract was rescinded). If it is not (or was not available in law) because e.g. the contract has been affirmed, third party rights have intervened, an excessive time has elapsed or restitution has become impossible, rescission is not available and damages cannot be said to be awarded 'in lieu of rescission'.

18 On the hypothesis, therefore, that [the judge] was correct to say that restitutio in integrum was not possible, the discretion under section 2(2) to award damages was not available to him. Any discretion he may have had was exercised on a wrong basis.

9.4 Excluding or limiting liability for misrepresentation

9.4.1 Distinguish B2B (business to business) and B2C (trader to consumer) contracts

Misrepresentation Act 1967 (as amended)

3. *Avoidance of provision excluding liability for misrepresentation*

(1) If a contract contains a term which would exclude or restrict—

   (a) any liability to which a party to a contract may be subject by reason of any misrepresentation made by him before the contract was made; or

   (b) any remedy available to another party to the contract by reason of such a misrepresentation,

   that term shall be of no effect except in so far as it satisfies the requirement of reasonableness as stated in section 11(1) of the Unfair Contract Terms Act 1977; and it is for those claiming that the term satisfies that requirement to show that it does.

(2) This section does not apply to a term in a consumer contract within the meaning of Part 2 of the Consumer Rights Act 2015 (but see the provision made about such contracts in section 62 of that Act).

NOTES

1. Since the Consumer Rights Act 2015, s. 3 applies only to B2B (business to business) contracts and provides that any term of such a contract which purports to exclude or limit liability or remedies in misrepresentation will need to be shown to satisfy the reasonableness test in s. 11 of the Unfair Contract Terms Act (UCTA) 1977 before it can be relied upon.

2. Under the original version of s. 3 MA 1967, before it was amended by s. 8 UCTA 1977 and again by the Consumer Rights Act (CRA) 2015 (Sch. 4 para. 1), reasonableness was judged at the time of the judgment; it is now judged, according to s. 11 UCTA 1977, at the time that the contract was made. Much of the case law, such as there is, is based on the unamended version of s. 3, and therefore it is important to be aware of this difference.

3. In the B2C context, s. 3 MA 1967 no longer applies (MA 1967, s. 3(2)) and a term excluding or restricting liability or remedies for misrepresentation is made subject to the general test for unfairness in s. 62 CRA 2015 (discussion at *page 292, 6.5*). The ability of the trader to avoid certain 'commitments' made by others on the trader's behalf may be regarded as an unfair term on the basis that it is contained in the list in Sch. 2, Part 1, para. 17.

9.4.2 Clauses that purport to exclude liability for fraud

A party cannot exclude liability for his own fraud: *S. Pearson & Sons Ltd v Dublin Corporation* [1907] AC 351.

In *HIH Casualty and General Insurance Co. Ltd v Chase Manhattan Bank* [2003] UKHL 6, [2003] 1 All ER (Comm) 349, [2003] 2 Lloyd's Rep 61, the House of Lords confirmed that a party cannot exclude liability for his own fraud and held that, to exclude liability for the fraud of agents, a contractor would need to use clear and unambiguous words. This was the position despite the fact that the inclusion of such explicit language might deter the other party from contracting on this basis.

In *BSkyB Ltd v HP Enterprise Services UK Ltd (formerly Electronic Data Systems Ltd)* [2010] EWHC 86 (TCC), [2010] BLR 267, 129 Con LR 147, EDS had successfully tendered for the design and implementation of a new customer relationship management (CRM) system for BSkyB. BSkyB later sought damages for fraudulent misrepresentations, which it alleged had led to EDS being selected in the first place, and also for negligent misrepresentation and breach of contract. However, there was a contractual limitation of liability (capped at £30 million) and only if the misrepresentation could be established to be fraudulent would it have been possible to avoid this. Ramsey J held that BSkyB succeeded in the claim for fraudulent misrepresentation based on the time estimates that had been submitted by EDS to secure the contract. These were considered to be 'dishonest'.

In *Thomas Witter v TBP Industries* [1996] 2 All ER 573 (*page 458, 9.3.1*), Jacob J had considered that a clause that had the potential to apply to fraud would be unreasonable within s. 3 MA 1967. This would be the case where the clause in question referred to all types of liability such as 'any liability' or 'any misrepresentation'. He noted, at p. 598D: 'If it excludes liability for one kind of misrepresentation it does so for all. I cannot think it reasonable to exclude liability for fraudulent misrepresentation.'

However, in *Government of Zanzibar v British Aerospace (Lancaster House) Ltd* [2000] 1 WLR 2333, Judge Raymond Jack QC rejected this argument and limited the non-applicability of the clause to where there was an allegation of fraud. Further, in *Six Continent Hotels Inc. v Event Hotels GmbH* [2006] EWHC 2317 (QB), (2006) 150 SJLB 1251, the term in question provided that: 'Each of the parties agree that it shall not commence any lawsuit or assert any claim . . . against the other party . . . based on actions, discussions or agreements . . . which occurred prior to the signing of this Agreement.' Counsel argued, relying on *Thomas Witter*, that this clause could not be relied upon because it was drafted so widely as to be capable of covering fraudulent misrepresentation, in addition to negligent and wholly innocent misrepresentation, and the coverage of fraud could not be severed. However, Gloster J (*obiter*, since there was no misrepresentation) preferred the approach in *Government of Zanzibar v British Aerospace Ltd* [2000] 1 WLR 2333 and considered that the clause would not necessarily fail.

9.4.3 The scope of s. 3

The clause in question must be purporting to exclude or limit liability or remedies for misrepresentation. Section 3 will not apply if this conclusion can be avoided.

9.4.3.1 Entire agreement clauses purporting to cover misrepresentation

The decision in *Inntrepreneur Pub Co. v East Crown Ltd* [2000] 2 Lloyd's Rep 611 (for the facts, see *page 181, 5.2.1.2*) makes it clear that the existence of an entire agreement clause relating to contractual terms does not affect the status of a statement as a misrepresentation. Of course, there may be both a provision stating that the contract contains all of the terms of the parties' agreement and a provision designed to exclude liability for misrepresentation, i.e. a provision stating that there has been no reliance on any other statements or representations. Where this is the case, it was held in *Inntrepreneur* that in principle s. 3 MA 1967 would apply to the clause excluding the liability for misrepresentation, but not the other part of the entire agreement clause dealing with the terms.

However, the critical question is whether the non-reliance clause operates as an exclusion of liability for misrepresentation on the particular facts.

Watford Electronics Ltd v Sanderson CFL Ltd
[2001] EWCA Civ 317, [2001] 1 All ER (Comm) 696 (CA)

For the facts, see *page 286, 6.4.5.2.*

The contract contained a clause stating that the terms and conditions represented the entire agreement between the parties, and that 'no statement or representations by either party have been relied upon'. The judge had considered that the non-reliance clause fell within s. 3, because in substance it was excluding liability for misrepresentation, since a clause could exclude reliance only on the basis that there was a statement that was capable of being relied upon. He held the non-reliance clause to be unreasonable in the context of the agreement as a whole.

However, the Court of Appeal adopted a very different approach. Chadwick LJ, relying on his own judgment in *E. A. Grimstead & Son Ltd v McGarrigan* (unreported, 27 October 1999) considered (*obiter*) that a non-reliance clause in a commercial contract meant that the innocent party was estopped from asserting reliance on any misrepresentation, so that s. 3 was inapplicable. He considered that, for reasons of commercial certainty, it was important for commercial parties to be able to make clear what matters had been relied upon in entering into any agreement.

CHADWICK LJ: 39 The effect of an acknowledgement of non-reliance, in terms which were sufficiently similar to those in the second part of the entire agreement clause in the present case as to be indistinguishable, was considered in this court in *Grimstead (EA) & Son Ltd v McGarrigan* [1999] CA Transcript 1733. In a passage which was obiter dicta—but which followed full argument on the point—I said this (at p 32A–C of the transcript):

> In my view an acknowledgement of non-reliance . . . is capable of operating as an evidential estoppel. It is apt to prevent the party who has given the acknowledgement from asserting in subsequent litigation against the party to whom it has been given that it is not true. That seems to me to be a proper use of an acknowledgement of this nature . . .

I went on, at p 35A–C, to say this:

> There are, as it seems to me, at least two good reasons why the courts should not refuse to give effect to an acknowledgement of non-reliance in a commercial contract between experienced parties of equal bargaining power—a fortiori, where those parties have the benefit of professional advice. First, it is reasonable to assume that the parties desire commercial certainty. They want to order their affairs on the basis that the bargain between them can be found within the document which they have signed. They want to avoid the uncertainty of litigation based on allegations as to the content of oral discussions at pre-contractual meetings. Second, it is reasonable to assume that the price to be paid reflects the commercial risk which each party—or, more usually, the purchaser—is willing to accept. The risk is determined, in part at least, by the warranties which the vendor is prepared to give. The tighter the warranties, the less the risk and (in principle, at least) the greater the price the vendor will require and which the purchaser will be prepared to pay. It is legitimate, and commercially desirable, that both parties should be able to measure the risk, and agree the price, on the basis of the warranties which have been given and accepted.

40 Those passages were not cited to the judge. He held that Sanderson could not rely on the acknowledgement of non-reliance contained in the second part of the entire agreement clause. He said this, at paragraph 107 of his judgment:

> . . . the clause is, in substance, one that excludes liability rather than precludes liability from ever occurring. The clause states that no statement or representation has been relied on. It follows that the clause can only first bite once a statement or representation has been made that is capable of being relied on. The clause bites, therefore, on a potential misrepresentation that has been made. It is not preventing words that have been uttered from being a misrepresentation at all. Furthermore, the words that were used did, as a matter of fact, as I have found, induce the contract. Thus, this clause is one which is in substance an exclusion clause to which s 3 of the 1967 Act is applicable.

I confess to some difficulty in following the reasoning in that passage. It is true that an acknowledgement of non-reliance does not purport to prevent a party from proving that a representation was made, nor that it was false. What the acknowledgement seeks to do is to prevent the person to whom the representation was made from asserting that he relied upon it. If it is to have that effect, it will be necessary—as I sought to point out in the *Grimstead* case—for the party who seeks to set up the acknowledgement as an evidential estoppel to plead and prove that the three requirements identified by this court in *Lowe v Lombank Ltd* [1960] 1 WLR 196 are satisfied. That may present insuperable difficulties; not least because it may be impossible for a party who has made representations which he intended should be relied upon to satisfy the court that he entered into the contract in the belief that a statement by the other party that he had not relied upon those representations was true. But the fact that, on particular facts, the acknowledgement of non-reliance may not achieve its purpose does not lead to the conclusion that the acknowledgement is 'in substance an exclusion clause to which s 3 of the 1967 Act is applicable'. Nor does it lead to the conclusion that the entire agreement clause can be disregarded when construing the earlier limit of liability clause—cl 7.3 in the Terms and Conditions of sale and cl.10.6 in the Terms and Conditions of Software Licence.

41 The importance of the entire agreement clause in the present context—and, in particular, the importance of the acknowledgement of non-reliance which constitutes the second part of that clause—is that the first sentence in cl 7.3 (or cl 10.6, as the case may be) has to be construed on the basis that the parties intend that their whole agreement is to be contained or incorporated in the document which they have signed and on the basis that neither party has relied on any pre-contract representation when signing that document. On that basis, there is no reason why the parties should have intended, by the words which they have used in the first sentence of the limit of liability clause, to exclude liability for negligent pre-contract misrepresentation. Liability in damages under the 1967 Act can arise only where the party who has suffered the damage has relied upon the representation. Where both parties to the contract have acknowledged, in the document itself, that they have not relied upon any pre-contract representation, it would be bizarre (unless compelled to do so by the words which they have used) to attribute to them an intention to exclude a liability which they must have thought could never arise.

NOTES

1. Chadwick LJ considered that, in the context of commercial negotiations conducted by parties of equal bargaining power who had the benefit of professional advisers, a court should be reluctant to refuse recognition to a non-reliance clause. However, the clause cannot fulfil its objective where there is a fraudulent misrepresentation, since it cannot be claimed that there was no reliance on such a statement. Therefore, an acknowledgement of non-reliance will not operate to exclude liability for fraudulent misrepresentation and such clauses should be drafted to exclude their application to fraud.

2. Chadwick LJ notes the difficulties presented by the requirements to establish evidential estoppel, i.e. that, for a defendant to be estopped from denying that the claimant had relied on the defendant's misrepresentation, the claimant would need to show that the claimant believed the declaration of non-reliance to be true and had intended the defendant to act upon it.

3. This aspect of the decision in *Watford Electronics* was refined and explained in *Peekay Intermark Ltd v Australia and New Zealand Banking Group Ltd*, so that the estoppel can be contractual rather than evidential. Where the estoppel is a contractual estoppel, it means that it can be invoked merely on the basis of the statement in the contract and without the necessity for the party relying on it to establish that it believed the statement to be true.

Peekay Intermark Ltd v Australia and New Zealand Banking Group Ltd
[2006] EWCA Civ 386, [2006] 2 Lloyd's Rep 511, [2006] 1 CLC 582 (CA)

For the facts, see *page 187, 5.2.2.*

When signing the written contract, the claimant had also signed a risk disclosure statement stating that he understood the transaction and its terms and conditions and had 'independently satisfied' himself. It followed that the effect of such a clause 'in principle' was to give up any right to assert that the claimant had been induced to contract by misrepresentation and the clause therefore operated as a *contractual estoppel* (*Watford Electronics*).

MOORE-BICK LJ: 56. There is no reason in principle why parties to a contract should not agree that a certain state of affairs should form the basis for the transaction, whether it be the case or not. For example, it may be desirable to settle a disagreement as to an existing state of affairs in order to establish a clear basis for the contract itself and its subsequent performance. Where parties express an agreement of that kind in a contractual document neither can subsequently deny the existence of the facts and matters upon which they have agreed, at least so far as concerns those aspects of their relationship to which the agreement was directed. The contract itself gives rise to an estoppel: see *Colchester Borough Council v Smith* [1991] Ch 448, affirmed on appeal [1992] Ch 421.

57. It is common to include in certain kinds of contracts an express acknowledgment by each of the parties that they have not been induced to enter the contract by any representations other than those contained in the contract itself. The effectiveness of a clause of that kind may be challenged on the grounds that the contract as a whole, including the clause in question, can be avoided if in fact one or other party was induced to enter into it by misrepresentation. However, I can see no reason in principle why it should not be possible for parties to an agreement to give up any right to assert that they were induced to enter into it by misrepresentation, provided that they make their intention clear, or why a clause of that kind, if properly drafted, should not give rise to a contractual estoppel of the kind recognised in *Colchester Borough Council v Smith*. However, that particular question does not arise in this case. A clause of that kind may (depending on its terms) also be capable of giving rise to an estoppel by representation if the necessary elements can be established: see *E A Grimstead & Son Ltd v McGarrigan* (CA) 27 October 1999, unreported.

NOTES

1. In *Springwell Navigation Corporation v JP Morgan Chase Bank (formerly Chase Manhattan Bank)* [2010] EWCA Civ 1221, [2010] 2 CLC 705, the Court of Appeal held that a purchaser of securities was bound on the basis of a contractual estoppel by the statement in these securities and in dealing letters that no representation or warranty had been made by Chase Manhattan.

AIKENS LJ: 144 So, in principle and always depending on the precise construction of the contractual wording, I would say that A and B can agree that A has made no pre-contract representations to B about the quality or nature of a financial instrument that A is selling to B. Should it make any difference that both A and B know at and before making the contract, that A did, in fact, make representations, so that the statement that A had not is contrary to what each side knows is the case? Apart from the remarks of Diplock J in *Lowe v Lombank*, [counsel] did not show us any case that might support the proposition that parties cannot agree that X is the case even if both know that is not so. I am unaware of any legal principle to that effect. The only possible exception might be if the particular agreement between A and B on the certain state of affairs concerned contradicts some other specific or more general rule of English public policy. Like Moore-Bick LJ in *Peekay* I see commercial utility in such clauses being enforceable, so that parties know precisely the basis on which they are entering into their contractual relationship.

2. Thus s. 3 is applicable only if there has been an actionable misrepresentation and attempt to exclude or limit liability for it. Where there is no actionable misrepresentation because the parties have agreed that there is no reliance and are estopped from denying that position, the statutory control is irrelevant and conflicts with the party agreement.

Where a contractual estoppel arises in the commercial context, the parties cannot deny the effect of the words in the clause so that there will be no misrepresentation where there has been 'no reliance'. However, it is clear that the position depends on the precise wording of the clause in question. The Court of Appeal in *Axa Sun Life Services plc v Campbell Martin Ltd* [2011] EWCA Civ 133, [2012] Bus LR 203, [2011] 1 CLC 312 had to assess a different type of clause in order to determine whether it was excluding liability for misrepresentation. It came to a different conclusion on the question of whether a contractual estoppel applied.

The clause in question provided that 'this agreement shall supersede any prior promises, agreements, representations, undertakings or implications whether orally or in writing' between the parties relating to the subject matter. The Court of Appeal held that this clause did not prevent the defendants from relying on misrepresentations on the basis of a contractual estoppel. No such estoppel applied, despite the reference to 'representations' in the clause. Rix LJ noted that 'representations' in this context referred to representations that, but for the wording of the clause, might have become terms. All of the other words in the clause were contractual in nature. The entire agreement clause therefore did not apply to other false statements that had been relied upon in concluding the contract.

This difference in position emphasizes the necessity for very careful drafting of such clauses, and knowledge of the current interpretation, in order to achieve the intentions of the parties. To determine the applicability or otherwise of s. 3, an assessment will therefore need to be made relating to the 'substance and not the form' of the clause in question: *IFE Fund SA v Goldman Sachs International* [2006] EWHC 2887 (Comm), [2006] CLC 1043, [2007] 1 Lloyd's Rep 264, *per* Toulson J.

Raiffeisen Zentralbank Osterreich AG v Royal Bank of Scotland plc
[2010] EWHC 1392 (Comm), [2011] 1 Lloyd's Rep 123, [2011] Bus LR D65

Christopher Clarke J referred to examples of clauses given by Toulson J in *IFE Fund SA v Goldman Sachs International* [2006] EWHC 2887 (Comm), [2006] CLC 1043, [2007] 1 Lloyd's Rep 264.

CHRISTOPHER CLARKE J: 292 . . . . [T]he seller of a car . . . says to a buyer '*I have serviced the car since it was new, it has had only one owner and the clock reading is accurate.*' Such statements would be representations and would remain so even if the seller had added the words '*but those statements are not statements on which you can rely.*'

293. By contrast, if the seller of the car said '*The clock reading is 20,000 miles, but I have no knowledge whether the reading is true or false*' the position would be different because the qualifying words could not fairly be regarded as an attempt to exclude liability for a false representation arising from the first half of the sentence.

 . . .

304 . . . . [T]he effect of any clause must depend on its wording, which usually takes one or other of the following forms:

(a) X agrees with Y that Y is not giving, or has not given, or is deemed not to have given, any representations of any kind (or is only giving certain specified representations); or that he does not intend anything he has said to be relied on;

(b) X agrees with Y that he is not entering into the contract as a result of any representations by Y; or that he has not relied and does not rely upon any representations and/or that he has exercised an independent judgment and/or has sought independent advice;

(c) X agrees with Y that Y is not acting as an adviser or assuming any responsibility.

In the drafting the word '*representations*' is often followed by one or more of '*warranties, assurances, statements, undertakings etc*'. In some cases X may acknowledge rather than agree.

305. Although contractual estoppel clauses are increasingly common, particularly in the case of complex financial instruments or investments, their use is not restricted to that field. They may also be used in everyday contracts made with consumers or between businesses great and small. Any interpretation of section 3 must accommodate the car dealer as well as the bond dealer.

306. Suppose, to take a version of Toulson J's example, a car is sold. The dealer says '*I have serviced the car since it was new, it has had only one owner and the clock reading is accurate*'. He is not fraudulent but mistaken, carelessly confusing one car for another, in relation to which the statement is true. Relying on his statement the buyer purchases the car. Without it he would not have done so. The car has had

several owners, no known service history, and the clock reading is substantially inaccurate. The contract of sale provides (in one of many paragraphs on the back of the form which the buyer does not read and to which his attention is not directed) that the buyer is entering into the contract on the basis that no representations have been made to, or relied on by, the purchaser.

307. In that example there has been a clear statement of fact, on a matter said to be within the representor's personal knowledge, which was in fact intended to induce the contract, upon which the purchaser in fact relied, which is false. If section 3 has no application in respect of a contractual estoppel there is no further control mechanism on its operation, which does not require detrimental reliance. The seller (and any other similar seller) may, subject to any applicable consumer protection laws, make non-fraudulent misrepresentations of that type with impunity.

308. In such a situation section 3 is, as it seems to me, applicable because, on those facts, there has been what the person to whom the statement was made would reasonably understand to be a representation, which was intended to be and was in fact relied on. The clause seeks to avoid liability for what, absent the clause, would be a clear liability in misrepresentation. The situation might be different in the unlikely scenario that before he contracts the buyer sees the clause and, eyes wide open, agrees that he is not relying on what he may have been told . . .

. . .

310. As has already been said, the essential question is whether the clause in question goes to whether the alleged representation was made (or, I would add, was intended to be understood and acted on as a representation), or whether it excludes or restricts liability in respect of representations made, intended to be acted on and in fact acted on; and that question is one of substance not form.

311. Everything must depend on the facts. In some cases the effect of the clause will be to show that what might otherwise have been a representation of fact to be relied on is no more than a statement of belief, or of opinion, or a statement of what the maker has been told, or a statement of a very limited character ('*the clock says 20,000 but I do not know whether that is true*'). Thus in *IFE Fund* Goldman Sachs supplied information from others in an information memorandum. The representations alleged were said to be implicit in what was said in that memorandum. Goldman Sachs' non acceptance of responsibility was apt to make it plain that it was not itself making any representations about the accuracy of the information.

312. Similarly the clause in question may show that no representation is in fact being made, or rebut any suggestion of an implicit statement of fact contained within an express statement, particularly one of opinion (where the existence of an implied statement of fact and the nature of that statement is debatable . . .).

. . .

314 . . . . [T]he key question, as it seems to me, is whether the clause attempts to rewrite history or parts company with reality. If sophisticated commercial parties agree, in terms of which they are both aware, to regulate their future relationship by prescribing the basis on which they will be dealing with each other and what representations they are or are not making, a suitably drafted clause may properly be regarded as establishing that no representations (or none other than honest belief) are being made or are intended to be relied on. Such parties are capable of distinguishing between statements which are to be treated as representations on which the recipient is entitled to rely, and statements which do not have that character, and should be allowed to agree among themselves into which category any given statement may fall.

315. Per contra, to tell the man in the street that the car you are selling him is perfect and then agree that the basis of your contract is that no representations have been made or relied on, may be nothing more than an attempt retrospectively to alter the character and effect of what has gone before, and in substance an attempt to exclude or restrict liability.

NOTE Comments relating to the application of s. 3 MA 1967 in the B2C examples given must now be read in the light of the changes made by the CRA 2015 and the non-applicability of s. 3 to B2C contracts (MA 1967, s. 3(2)).

9.4.3.2 Terms excluding or limiting an agent's authority to bind by misrepresentation

If a misrepresentation is made by an agent on behalf of a party, then any term excluding or limiting that agent's authority operates to protect the principal and is outside the scope of s. 3.

Overbrooke Estates Ltd v Glencombe Properties Ltd
[1974] 1 WLR 1355

The conditions of sale at an auction stated that: 'The vendors do not make or give and neither the Auctioneers nor any person in the employment of the Auctioneers has any authority to make or give any representation or warranty in relation to [the property].' On 5 November, in response to an inquiry from the defendants, the auctioneers, who were agents for the claimants, informed the defendants that no local authorities had schemes or plans for the property or were interested in it for compulsory purchase. At the auction on 8 November, the defendants successfully bid for the property and paid a deposit, and the auctioneers signed a memorandum of contract. The defendants later learned that the property might well be included in a slum clearance programme, so they stopped payment on the deposit cheque and informed the claimants that they would not now be proceeding. The claimants claimed specific performance, relying on the clause excluding any warranty or representation, and the defendants alleged in their defence that the clause relied on had to be fair and reasonable within s. 3.

Held: This was not a clause that excluded or restricted liability for misrepresentation. It amounted only to a public limitation on the ostensible authority of this agent. The claimants knew about this limitation before they bid, since it was contained in the conditions of sale that they received in advance. As a result, s. 3 did not apply.

NOTES

1. This limitation on the ostensible authority of the agent was defining the contractual duty itself rather than excluding or restricting liability for its breach. Section 3 MA 1967, it appears, has not therefore been extended by UCTA 1977, s. 13 (*6.1*), to cover provisions that exclude or restrict the duty or obligation itself.

2. Ostensible authority occurs where an agent's usual authority to bind the principal has been restricted, but the third party has no notice of this restriction and deals with the agent on the basis that there is no restriction. The principal will be bound to the third party. (Here, the third party had notice of the restriction, so that the principal could not be liable.)

3. In the context of consumer contracts to which Part 2 of the Consumer Rights Act (CRA) 2015 applies, it may be that a clause 'limiting the trader's obligation to respect commitments undertaken by the trader's agents or making the trader's commitments subject to compliance with a particular formality', such as approval of the principal, may be an unfair term and, as such, not binding on the consumer as an unfair term (CRA 2015, s. 62 and Sch. 2, Part 1, para. 17). Of course, this leaves open the interpretation of the expression 'commitment' and whether this covers a representation or is limited to a contractual promise. If the former, clauses such as that in *Overbrooke Estates* may be unfair in a consumer contract.

9.4.3.3 Allegation that the statement is merely a statement of opinion so as to deny the existence of misrepresentation

It is not possible to avoid the application of s. 3 where the clause purports to deny the existence of any representation by treating the statement as opinion.

Cremdean Properties Ltd v Nash
(1977) 244 EG 547 (CA)

The claimants claimed rescission of contracts for the sale of two properties, alleging misrepresentation in the particulars of the invitation to tender as to the area of lettable office space, which was within the planning permission with which the property was sold. The defendant relied in its defence on a footnote clause in the conditions of sale by tender, which provided:

a) These particulars are prepared for the convenience of an intending purchaser or tenant and although they are believed to be correct their accuracy is not guaranteed and any error, omission or misdescription shall not annul the sale or be grounds on which compensation may be claimed and neither do they constitute any part of an offer of a contract.
b) Any intending purchaser or tenant must satisfy himself by inspection or otherwise as to the correctness of each of the statements contained in these particulars.

Held (on a preliminary issue): The defendant was refused a declaration that the footnote clause operated to exclude any liability imposed by the 1967 Act. However, the question of whether there was a misrepresentation, and if so, what effect the clause had upon it, could be decided only at the trial when all of the facts were known.

BRIDGE LJ: In effect what [counsel for the defendant] says is this. The terms of the footnote are not simply, if contractual at all, a contractual exclusion either of any liability to which the defendant would otherwise be subject for any misrepresentation in the document, or of any remedy otherwise available on that ground to the plaintiff. The footnote is effective, so the argument runs, to nullify any representation in the document altogether; it is effective, so it is said, to bring about a situation in law as if no representation at all had ever been made. For my part, I am quite unable to accept that argument. I reject it primarily on the simple basis that on no reading of the language of the footnote could it have the remarkable effect contended for . . .

[After referring to *Overbrooke Estates Ltd v Glencombe Properties Ltd* [1974] 3 All ER 511, Bridge LJ continued:]

It is one thing to say that s. 3 does not inhibit a principal from publicly giving notice limiting the ostensible authority of his agents; it is quite another thing to say that a principal can circumvent the plainly intended effect of s. 3 by a clause excluding his own liability for a representation which he has undoubtedly made.

I am quite content to found my judgment in this case on the proposition that the language of the footnote relied upon . . . simply does not, on its true interpretation, have the effect contended for. But I would go further and say that if the ingenuity of a draftsman could devise language which would have that effect, I am extremely doubtful whether the court would allow it to operate so as to defeat s. 3. Supposing the vendor included a clause which the purchaser was required to, and did, agree to in some such terms as 'notwithstanding any statement of fact included in these particulars the vendor shall be conclusively deemed to have made no representation within the meaning of the Misrepresentation Act 1967,' I should have thought that that was only a form of words the intended and actual effect of which was to exclude or restrict liability, and I should not have thought that the courts would have been ready to allow such ingenuity in forms of language to defeat the plain purpose at which s. 3 is aimed.

I should add that on this part of the case we heard a further argument . . . purporting to draw a distinction between giving information or making a statement of opinion or belief on the one hand, and making a representation on the other. For my part, the distinction seems to be one without a difference. The word

Misrepresentation

9

'representation' is an extremely wide term; I cannot see why one should not be making a representation when giving information or when stating one's opinion or belief. To my mind it would be a retrograde step if the court were to give the word 'representation,' when it appears in the Misrepresentation Act 1967, any narrow or limited construction, less wide than the perfectly natural meaning of the word.

SCARMAN LJ: . . . [T]he case for the [defendant] does have an audacity and a simple logic which I confess I find attractive. It runs thus: a statement is not a representation unless it is also a statement that what is stated is true. If in context a statement contains no assertion, express or implied, that its content is accurate, there is no representation. *Ergo*, there can be no misrepresentation; *ergo*, the Misrepresentation Act 1967 cannot apply to it. Humpty Dumpty would have fallen for this argument. If we were to fall for it, the Misrepresentation Act would be dashed to pieces which not all the King's lawyers could put together again.

Chapter 10

Duress, undue influence, and unconscionable bargains

Although English law is not generally concerned with the fairness of the bargain reached by the parties and does not recognize any general duty of contractual fairness, there are recognized instances in which it will intervene owing to the circumstances surrounding the way in which the contract was made, or if its content infringes the statutory and common law rules designed to prevent onerous or unfair terms, e.g. the Consumer Credit Act 1974, including ss. 140A–D enabling the courts to interfere in 'unfair credit agreements', Part 2 of the Consumer Rights Act (CRA) 2015 enabling interference to control 'unfair terms' in contracts between traders and consumers (*page 292*, 6.5), the penalty rule (*page 754*, 14.10.1.1), and the Consumer Protection from Unfair Trading Regulations 2008 (CPRs), SI 2008/1277, implementing the European Unfair Commercial Practices Directive 2005/29/EC. The CPRs prohibit unfair commercial practices (reg. 3), and this includes aggressive commercial practices (reg. 7) that cause, or are likely to cause, the making of a contract under which these practices significantly impair or are likely to impair consumer freedom of choice as a result of 'harassment, coercion or undue influence'. 'Undue influence' in this context is defined as 'exploiting a position of power in relation to the consumer so as to apply pressure, even without using or threatening to use physical force, in a way which significantly limits the consumer's ability to make an informed choice' (reg. 7(3)). The amending regulations, the Consumer Protection (Amendment) Regulations 2014/870, introduced statutory civil rights of redress in relation to activities falling within the CPRs, following the recommendations in Law Commission Report No. 332, *Consumer Redress for Misrepresentation and Aggressive Practices* (Cm. 8323, 2012), which advocated this reform in order to implement Art. 27 of the Consumer Rights Directive (CRD) 2011/83/EU. These statutory civil rights are discussed at *page 292*, *6.5.1*.

The CRD enhances and clarifies cancellation rights of consumers, and is implemented into domestic law by means of the Consumer Contracts (Information, Cancellation and Additional Payments) Regulations 2013, SI 2013/3134. These consumer rights are also embodied in the Common European Sales Law (CESL).

In *Interfoto Picture Library Ltd v Stiletto Visual Programmes Ltd* [1989] 1 QB 433, 439 (for the facts, see *page 196*, *5.3.1.4*), Bingham LJ commented:

> In many civil law systems, and perhaps in most legal systems outside the common law world, the law of obligations recognises and enforces an overriding principle that in making and carrying out contracts parties should act in good faith. This does not simply mean that they should not deceive each other,

a principle which any legal system must recognise; its effect is perhaps most aptly conveyed by such metaphorical colloquialisms as 'playing fair,' 'coming clean' or 'putting one's cards face upwards on the table.' It is in essence a principle of fair and open dealing. In such a forum it might, I think, be held on the facts of this case that the claimants were under a duty in all fairness to draw the defendants' attention specifically to the high price payable if the transparencies were not returned in time and, when the 14 days had expired, to point out to the defendants the high cost of continued failure to return them.

English law has, characteristically, committed itself to no such overriding principle but has developed piecemeal solutions in response to demonstrated problems of unfairness. Many examples could be given. Thus equity has intervened to strike down unconscionable bargains. Parliament has stepped in to regulate the imposition of exemption clauses and the form of certain hire-purchase agreements. The common law also has made its contribution, by holding that certain classes of contract require the utmost good faith, by treating as irrecoverable what purport to be agreed estimates of damage but are in truth a disguised penalty for breach, and in many other ways.

The well known cases on sufficiency of notice are in my view properly to be read in this context. At one level they are concerned with a question of pure contractual analysis, whether one party has done enough to give the other notice of the incorporation of a term in the contract. At another level they are concerned with a somewhat different question, whether it would in all the circumstances be fair (or reasonable) to hold a party bound by any conditions or by a particular condition of an unusual and stringent nature.

At common law and in equity, the doctrines of duress and undue influence allow a contract to be set aside if one party has put unfair and improper pressure on the other in the negotiations leading up to the contract.

In *Royal Bank of Scotland plc v Etridge (No. 2)* [2001] UKHL 44, [2002] 2 AC 773, Lord Nicholls explained that such situations are difficult to identify with any precision:

6 . . . Undue influence is one of the grounds of relief developed by the courts of equity as a court of conscience. The objective is to ensure that the influence of one person over another is not abused. In everyday life people constantly seek to influence the decisions of others. They seek to persuade those with whom they are dealing to enter into transactions, whether great or small. The law has set limits to the means properly employable for this purpose. To this end the common law developed a principle of duress. Originally this was narrow in its scope, restricted to the more blatant forms of physical coercion, such as personal violence.

7 Here, as elsewhere in the law, equity supplemented the common law. Equity extended the reach of the law to other unacceptable forms of persuasion. The law will investigate the manner in which the intention to enter into the transaction was secured: 'how the intention was produced', in the oft repeated words of Lord Eldon LC, from as long ago as 1807 (*Huguenin v Baseley* 14 Ves 273, 300). If the intention was produced by an unacceptable means, the law will not permit the transaction to stand. The means used is regarded as an exercise of improper or 'undue' influence, and hence unacceptable, whenever the consent thus procured ought not fairly to be treated as the expression of a person's free will. It is impossible to be more precise or definitive. The circumstances in which one person acquires influence over another, and the manner in which influence may be exercised, vary too widely to permit of any more specific criterion.

10.1 Duress

10.1.1 Duress to the person

Barton v Armstrong
[1976] AC 104 (PC)

B, the managing director of a public company, had executed a deed in favour of the company's former chairman whereby the company agreed to pay $140,000 in cash to A and to purchase A's shares in the company for $180,000. B had been informed by the company's principal lender that it would not advance further money following the departure of the chairman, and B believed that if the deed were executed and A paid off, the lender would agree to provide further finance. It was established that A had threatened to kill B and had made threatening telephone calls to B. B also genuinely believed that A had hired a criminal to kill him. Despite the deed, the company's principal lender still refused to advance any money to the company, which was soon in financial difficulties. B claimed that the deed was void because it had been executed under duress. The trial judge, Street J, had considered that the sole reason why B had executed the deed was commercial necessity. The Court of Appeal of the Supreme Court of New South Wales held that the onus was on B to show that, but for the threats, he would not have signed the agreement, and B had failed to discharge that onus. The Privy Council by a majority of three to two (Lord Wilberforce and Lord Simon of Glaisdale dissenting) overturned this decision.

Held: Duress to the person had to be treated in the same way as fraudulent misrepresentation, so that as long as A's threats were *one* of the reasons why B executed the deed, B was entitled to relief: see *Edgington v Fitzmaurice* (1885) 29 Ch D 459 (*page 445*, 9.1.2.2). Once unlawful pressure was established, it was for A to establish that the threats and unlawful pressure exerted on B had in no way affected B's decision to enter the agreement. The majority of the Privy Council held that A had not established this, and therefore the deed was 'void' for duress.

LORD CROSS OF CHELSEA: It is hardly surprising that there is no direct authority on the point, for if A threatens B with death if he does not execute some document and B, who takes A's threats seriously, executes the document it can be only in the most unusual circumstances that there can be any doubt whether the threats operated to induce him to execute the document. But this is a most unusual case and the findings of fact made below do undoubtedly raise the question whether it was necessary for Barton in order to obtain relief to establish that he would not have executed the deed in question but for the threats . . . There is an obvious analogy between setting aside a disposition for duress or undue influence and setting it aside for fraud . . . Had Armstrong made a fraudulent misrepresentation to Barton for the purpose of inducing him to execute the deed of January 17, 1967 the answer to the problem which has arisen would have been clear. If it were established that Barton did not allow the representation to affect his judgment then, he could not make it a ground for relief even though the representation was designed and known by Barton to be designed to affect his judgment. If on the other hand Barton relied on the misrepresentation Armstrong could not have defeated his claim to relief by showing that there were other more weighty causes which contributed to his decision to execute the deed, for in this field the court does not allow an examination into the relative importance of contributory causes.

'Once make out that there has been anything like deception, and no contract resting in any degree on that foundation can stand': per Lord Cranworth LJ in *Reynell v Sprye* (1852) 1 De GM & G 660, 708 . . . Their Lordships think that the same rule should apply in cases of duress and that if Armstrong's threats were 'a' reason for Barton's executing the deed he is entitled to relief even though he might well have entered into the contract if Armstrong had uttered no threats to induce him to do so . . . If Barton had to establish that he would not have made the agreement but for Armstrong's threats, then their Lordships would not dissent from the view that he had not made out his case. But no such onus lay on him. On the contrary it was for Armstrong to establish, if he could, that the threats which he was making and the unlawful pressure which he was exerting for the purpose of inducing Barton to sign the agreement and which Barton knew were being made and exerted for this purpose in fact contributed nothing to Barton's decision to sign. The judge has found that during the 10 days or so before the documents were executed Barton was in genuine fear that Armstrong was planning to have him killed if the agreement was not signed. His state of mind was described by the judge as one of 'very real mental torment' and he believed that his fears would be at an end when once the documents were executed . . . The proper inference to be drawn from the facts found is, their Lordships think, that though it may be that Barton would have executed the documents even if Armstrong had made no threats and exerted no unlawful pressure to induce him to do so the threats and unlawful pressure in fact contributed to his decision to sign the documents and to recommend their execution by Landmark and the other parties to them.

In the result therefore the appeal should be allowed and a declaration made that the deeds in question were executed by Barton under duress and are void so far as concerns him . . .

The dissenting judgment of Lord Wilberforce and Lord Simon of Glaisdale does not differ from the majority on the law applicable to duress to the person. However, the minority considered that they could not overturn Street J's findings of fact and found the contract to be valid. In addition, they took account of the fact that Barton had taken nearly a year to seek to set aside the agreement.

NOTES

1. Although Lord Cross refers to duress as rendering a contract void *ab initio*, it is only voidable. If Lord Cross were stating the consequence *after* avoidance, his statement could be reconciled with accepted principle. (Because duress renders a contract voidable, the bars to rescission apply so that the remedy can, for example, be lost by affirmation.)

2. The Privy Council held that absence of choice is not sufficient on its own to negate consent, since the pressure must be illegitimate, and *Barton v Armstrong* has clearly confirmed that threats to life are illegitimate. In other categories of duress, the definition of 'illegitimate threats' is not as obvious.

3. In the case of this type of duress, the burden of proof is placed upon the party exerting the pressure to establish that the threats in no way influenced the contract. This will be very difficult to establish.

10.1.2 Duress to property

Duress to property occurs when there is a threat to seize the owner's property or to damage it. In *Occidental Worldwide Investment Corporation v Skibs A/S Avanti, The Siboen and The Sibotre* [1976] 1 Lloyd's Rep 293, 335, Kerr J considered that a contract could be avoided in such cases:

[Counsel] submitted that although money paid under duress to goods is recoverable, a contract can only be set aside for duress to the person but not in any other case of duress. He said that in every case in which a party enters into a contract otherwise than under duress to the person, any payment or forbearance pursuant to such contract is regarded as voluntary, whatever may have been the nature or degree of compulsion, short of violence to the person, which may have caused him to enter into the contract. He relied mainly on a line of authority in which *Skeate v Beale*, (1841) 11 Ad. & E. 983 is the leading case.

I do not think that English law is as limited . . . For instance, if I should be compelled to sign a lease or some other contract for a nominal but legally sufficient consideration under an imminent threat of having my house burnt down or a valuable picture slashed, though without any threat of physical violence to anyone, I do not think that the law would uphold the agreement. I think that a plea of coercion or compulsion would be available in such cases . . .

10.1.3 Economic duress

It is only comparatively recently that the courts have accepted that a contract can be set aside where illegitimate commercial pressure is exerted by one party on another. The previous mechanism to prevent such promises from being enforceable was the doctrine of consideration: *Stilk v Myrick* (1809) 2 Camp 317, 6 Esp 129 (*page 107, 3.1.3.7*) and *Atlas Express v Kafco Ltd* [1989] 1 All ER 641.

Following the Court of Appeal's decision in *Williams v Roffey Bros. & Nicholls (Contractors) Ltd* [1991] 1 QB 1 (*page 106, 3.1.3.7*), the emphasis is considered to have shifted, so that economic duress will be vitally important in preventing extortion in the future. The limits of the doctrine therefore need to be clearly defined and, in the view of academic commentators, it needs to be given a sounder conceptual basis.

10.1.3.1 Coercion of the will that vitiates consent

Occidental Worldwide Investment Corporation v Skibs A/S Avanti, The Siboen and The Sibotre
[1976] 1 Lloyd's Rep 293

In 1970, the defendants agreed to let two tankers for three years to Concord, a subsidiary company of Occidental Petroleum, at a rate of hire of $4.40 per ton per month. In the autumn of 1971, Occidental had financial problems and sought to renegotiate the charter to reduce the rates of hire. The impression given was that Concord, the charterer, did not have any substantial assets and that it required the continuing support of its parent company. If the hire was not reduced, the charterer threatened cancellation of the charter and alleged that the parent company would allow the charterer to go bankrupt, so that the owners would not even be able to seek a remedy for breach of the charter. This was a gross distortion of the truth. The defendants agreed to reduce the hire to $4.10, but later withdrew both vessels. The charterer sought damages for wrongful repudiation and the defendants counterclaimed, arguing that they had agreed to the alteration only under duress.

Held: The duress argument failed, because although the defendants had acted under great pressure in agreeing to the altered rate, it could not be regarded in law as a coercion of their will so as to vitiate their consent.

KERR J: But even assuming, as I think, that our law is open to further development in relation to contracts concluded under some form of compulsion not amounting to duress to the person, the Court must in every case at least be satisfied that the consent of the other party was overborne by compulsion so as to deprive him of any animus contrahendi. This would depend on the facts of each case. One relevant factor would be whether the party relying on duress made any protest at the time or shortly thereafter. Another would be to consider whether or not he treated the settlement as closing the transaction in question and as binding upon him, or whether he made it clear that he regarded the position as still open. The question whether or not there was any intention to close the transaction is referred to in the judgments of Lord Reading, CJ, and Lord Justice Buckley in *Maskell v Horner*, [1915] 3 KB 106. But the facts of the present case fall a long way short of the test which would in law be required to make good a defence of compulsion or duress. Believing the statements about the charterers' financial state to be true, as must for this purpose be assumed, Captain Tschudi made no protest about having to conclude the addenda, either at the Paris meeting on Mar. 26, 1972, or at any time before the telex of Apr. 28, 1973. He repeatedly said in his evidence that he regarded the agreement then reached as binding and sought to uphold it in the subsequent arbitration. He was acting under great pressure, but only commercial pressure, and not under anything which could in law be regarded as a coercion of his will so as to vitiate his consent. I therefore hold that the plea of duress fails.

Pao On v Lau Yiu Long
[1980] AC 614 (PC)

The full facts of this case appear at *page 95, 3.1.3.3.1.*

The claimants threatened not to perform their promise that they would not sell 60 per cent of their shares in the Fu Chip Company for one year unless the defendants, the majority shareholders in the company, agreed to indemnify them against a loss in the value of their shares in that period. The defendants agreed to this demand and signed a written indemnity to compensate the claimants if the market price fell below $2.50 a share. The share price dropped and the claimants sought to rely on the indemnity, but the defendants refused to comply with its terms. One of the questions related to whether the defendants' consent to the indemnity was vitiated by duress.

Held: Although the defendants had been subjected to commercial pressure, their will had not been coerced because they had taken a commercial decision. They had considered that the risk of a loss of public confidence in the company if the sale of the shares by the claimants to the company did not take place was greater than the risk that the share price would fall and that they would have to pay under the indemnity.

LORD SCARMAN: Duress, whatever form it takes, is a coercion of the will so as to vitiate consent. Their Lordships agree with the observation of Kerr J in *Occidental Worldwide Investment Corporation v Skibs A/S Avanti* [1976] 1 Lloyd's Rep 293, 336 that in a contractual situation commercial pressure is not enough. There must be present some factor 'which could in law be regarded as a coercion of his will so as to vitiate his consent.' This conception is in line with what was said in this Board's decision in *Barton v Armstrong* [1976] AC 104, 121 by Lord Wilberforse [*sic*] and Lord Simon of Glaisdale—observations with which the majority judgment appears to be in agreement. In determining whether there was a coercion of will such that there was no true consent, it is material to inquire whether the person alleged to have been coerced did or did not protest; whether, at the time he was allegedly coerced into making the contract, he did or did not have an alternative course open to him such as an adequate legal remedy; whether he was independently advised; and whether after entering the contract he took steps to avoid it. All these matters are, as was recognised in *Maskell v Horner* [1915] 3 KB 106, relevant in determining whether he acted voluntarily or not.

In the present case there is unanimity amongst the judges below that there was no coercion of the first defendant's will. In the Court of Appeal the trial judge's finding . . . that the first defendant considered the matter thoroughly, chose to avoid litigation, and formed the opinion that the risk in giving the guarantee was more apparent than real was upheld. In short, there was commercial pressure, but no coercion. Even if this Board was disposed, which it is not, to take a different view, it would not substitute its opinion for that of the judges below on this question of fact.

It is, therefore, unnecessary for the Board to embark upon an inquiry into the question whether English law recognises a category of duress known as 'economic duress.' But, since the question has been fully argued in this appeal, their Lordships will indicate very briefly the view which they have formed. At common law money paid under economic compulsion could be recovered in an action for money had and received: *Astley v Reynolds* (1731) 2 Str 915. The compulsion had to be such that the party was deprived of 'his freedom of exercising his will' (p. 916). It is doubtful, however, whether at common law any duress other than duress to the person sufficed to render a contract voidable: see *Blackstone's Commentaries*, Book 1, 12th ed. pp. 130–131 and *Skeate v Beale* (1841) 11 Ad & E 983. American law (*Williston on Contracts*, 3rd ed.) now recognises that a contract may be avoided on the ground of economic duress. The commercial pressure alleged to constitute such duress must, however, be such that the victim must have entered the contract against his will, must have had no alternative course open to him, and must have been confronted with coercive acts by the party exerting the pressure: *Williston on Contracts*, 3rd ed., vol. 13 (1970), section 1603. American judges pay great attention to such evidential matters as the effectiveness of the alternative remedy available, the fact or absence of protest, the availability of independent advice, the benefit received, and the speed with which the victim has sought to avoid the contract. Recently two English judges have recognised that commercial pressure may constitute duress the pressure of which can render a contract voidable: Kerr J in *Occidental Worldwide Investment Corporation v Skibs A/S Avanti* [1976] 1 Lloyd's Rep 293 and Mocatta J in *North Ocean Shipping Co. Ltd v Hyundai Construction Co. Ltd* [1979] QB 705. Both stressed that the pressure must be such that the victim's consent to the contract was not a voluntary act on his part. In their Lordship's view, there is nothing contrary to principle in recognising economic duress as a factor which may render a contract voidable provided always that the basis of such recognition is that it must amount to a coercion of will, which vitiates consent. It must be shown that the payment made or the contract entered into was not a voluntary act . . .

North Ocean Shipping Co. Ltd v Hyundai Construction Co. Ltd, The Atlantic Baron
[1979] QB 705

The claimants entered into a contract with the defendant shipbuilding company to build a tanker for a fixed price, payable in five instalments. The defendant agreed to open a letter of credit to provide security for the repayment of the instalments if there were any default in performance of the contract. After the claimants had paid the first instalment, the US dollar was devalued by 10 per cent and the defendant claimed an increase of 10 per cent in the remaining instalments, threatening not to complete the contract if this increase were not paid. Since the claimants were negotiating a very lucrative contract for the charter of the tanker, in June 1973, they agreed to make the additional payments 'without prejudice' to their rights and asked the company to make a corresponding increase in the letter of credit, which the company did. The tanker was delivered in November 1974 without protest, but in July 1975 the claimants sought the return of the extra 10 per cent paid on the last four instalments. There were two issues in the case: first, had the defendant provided consideration for the claimants' promise to pay more (case discussed at *page 103*, 3.1.3.7); and secondly, if it had, was it nevertheless an agreement entered into under duress and so voidable?

Held: This threat to breach the contract without any legal justification amounted to duress by means of economic pressure and therefore the agreement was voidable. However, as a result of the delay between November 1974 and July 1975, the claimants must be taken to have affirmed the contract so that the claim failed.

MOCATTA J: First, I do not take the view that the recovery of money paid under duress other than to the person is necessarily limited to duress to goods falling within one of the categories hitherto established by the English cases . . . Secondly, from this it follows that the compulsion may take the form of 'economic duress' if the necessary facts are proved. A threat to break a contract may amount to such 'economic duress.' Thirdly, if there has been such a form of duress leading to a contract for consideration, I think that contract is a voidable one which can be avoided and the excess money paid under it recovered.

I think the facts found in this case do establish that the agreement to increase the price by 10 per cent reached at the end of June 1973 was caused by what may be called 'economic duress.' The Yard were adamant in insisting on the increased price without having any legal justification for so doing and the owners realised that the Yard would not accept anything other than an unqualified agreement to the increase. The owners might have claimed damages in arbitration against the Yard with all the inherent unavoidable uncertainties of litigation, but in view of the position of the Yard vis-à-vis their relations with Shell it would be unreasonable to hold that this is the course they should have taken: see *Astley v Reynolds* (1731) 2 Str. 915. The owners made a very reasonable offer of arbitration coupled with security for any award in the Yard's favour that might be made, but this was refused. They then made their agreement, which can truly I think be said to have been made under compulsion, by the telex of June 28 without prejudice to their rights . . .

If I am right in the conclusion reached with some doubt earlier that there was consideration for the 10 per cent increase agreement reached at the end of June 1973, and it be right to regard this as having been reached under a kind of duress in the form of economic pressure, then what is said in *Chitty on Contracts*, 24th ed. (1977), vol. 1, para. 442, p. 207, to which both counsel referred me, is relevant, namely, that a contract entered into under duress is voidable and not void:

> . . . consequently a person who has entered into a contract under duress, may either affirm or avoid such contract after the duress has ceased; and if he has so voluntarily acted under it with a full knowledge of all the circumstances he may be held bound on the ground of ratification, or if, after escaping from the duress, he takes no steps to set aside the transaction, he may be found to have affirmed it.

. . . There was . . . a delay between November 27, 1974, when the *Atlantic Baron* was delivered and July 30, 1975, before the owners put forward their claim.

. . . I have come to the conclusion that the important points here are that since there was no danger at this time in registering a protest, the final payments were made without any qualification and were followed by a delay until July 31, 1975, before the owners put forward their claim, the correct inference to draw, taking an objective view of the facts, is that the action and inaction of the owners can only be regarded as an affirmation of the variation in June 1973 of the terms of the original contract by the agreement to pay the additional 10 per cent . . . I do not think that an intention on the part of the owners not to affirm the agreement for the extra payments not indicated to the Yard can avail them in the view of their overt acts. As was said in *Deacon v Transport Regulation Board* [1958] VR 458, 460 in considering whether a payment was made voluntarily or not: 'No secret mental reservation of the doer is material. The question is—what would his conduct indicate to a reasonable man as his mental state.' I think this test is equally applicable to the decision this court has to make whether a voidable contract has been affirmed or not, and I have applied this test in reaching the conclusion I have just expressed.

10.1.3.2 The reality of the 'voluntary' consent

It is incorrect to argue that duress is based upon consent being vitiated so that the act is not voluntary, since the victim of duress undoubtedly submits intentionally and knows what he is doing. Duress, it is argued, does not deprive a person of all choice; rather, it presents him with a choice between evils. Professor Atiyah (1982) 98 LQR 197 severely criticized the concept of consent being vitiated by duress on this basis. Lord Scarman clearly accepted this point in *The Universe Sentinel* [1983] 1 AC 366 (*page 516, 10.1.3.3.2*) when he stressed that duress is intentional submission by a victim of duress because the victim realizes that there is no other practical choice available. Similarly, in *The Evia Luck* [1991] 4 All ER 871, Lord Goff doubted whether it was helpful to speak of the claimant's will having been coerced. In reality, it is not any absence of consent that determines duress, but the nature of the threat that has been made and the choices available to the victim in consequence.

In *DSND Subsea Ltd v Petroleum Geo-Services ASA* [2000] BLR 530, Dyson J formulated the criteria for economic duress as requiring that the pressure or threat being applied should have the effect of producing a feeling of compulsion or lack of practical choice:

131. The ingredients of actionable duress are that there must be pressure, (a) whose practical effect is that there is compulsion on, or a lack of practical choice for, the victim, (b) which is illegitimate, and (c) which is a significant cause inducing the claimant to enter into the contract: see *Universal Tankships of Monrovia v ITWF* [1983] AC 336, 400B–E, and *The Evia Luck* [1992] 2 AC 152, 165G.

It was held that there was no realistic choice in the next case despite the theoretical ability to sue when the threatened breach occurred.

B & S Contracts & Design Ltd v Victor Green Publications Ltd
[1984] ICR 419 (CA)

The claimants had agreed to erect exhibition stands for the defendants at Olympia for an exhibition that was to begin on 23 April 1979. A week before this date, the claimants' workers refused to work until a demand for £9,000 severance pay had been met. They rejected an offer by the claimants of £4,500, and the claimants informed the defendants that the contract would be cancelled unless the defendants paid the other £4,500 to meet this demand. The defendants paid this sum to avoid serious losses and claims from exhibitors to whom they had let stands. However, the defendants then deducted £4,500 from the contract price that they paid to the claimants.

Held: The cancellation of the contract would have caused such serious damage to the defendants' economic interests that they had no choice but to pay. Although they could have refused to pay this figure and sued the claimants for breach of contract, it was felt that this action would be too damaging.

KERR LJ: [T]he plaintiffs were clearly saying in effect, 'This contract will not be performed by us unless you pay an additional sum of £4,500.' This faced the defendants with a disastrous situation in which there was no way out for them, and in the face of this threat—which is what it was—they paid the £4,500. In the light of the authorities it is perhaps important to emphasise that there is no question in this case of the defendants having subsequently approbated this payment or failed to seek to avoid it, which in some cases (such as the *North Ocean Shipping Co. Ltd v Hyundai Construction Co. Ltd* [1979]

QB 705) . . . would be fatal. In the present case the defendants took immediate action by deducting that £4,500 from the invoice price.

I also bear in mind that a threat to break a contract unless money is paid by the other party can, but by no means always will, constitute duress. It appears from the authorities that it will only constitute duress if the consequences of a refusal would be serious and immediate so that there is no reasonable alternative open, such as by legal redress, obtaining an injunction, etc . . .

NOTE In *Adam Opel GmbH v Mitras Automotive (UK) Ltd* [2007] EWHC 3205 (QB), [2008] CILL 2561, [2008] Bus LR D55 (*page 103*, 3.1.3.7), Mitras had been the sole supplier of a particular type of van bumper mounts for car manufacturers, Opel. Following a redesign of the van, Opel had given Mitras six months' notice of termination, at which point Mitras sought payment of 'compensation' and an increase in the price paid for the supply of the bumper mounts or it threatened to suspend supplies. Since Opel had only 24 hours' worth of supplies left and would suffer large losses if the supply were to stop, including knock-on effects for suppliers of other van parts, it had initially sought an injunction to compel Mitras to supply. Since Mitras had then responded by refusing to allow collection of the mounts, Opel had agreed to enter into a compromise agreement for the payment of additional sums in order to ensure continued supply. However, Opel later sought repayment on the basis that this compromise agreement had been entered into under duress, whereas Mitras claimed there was a realistic alternative course of action by seeking an injunction. The judge had no difficulty in concluding that there had been duress and that there had been no realistic alternative given the serious consequences if supply ceased. Although it might have been possible to secure an injunction, the possible delay before it was obtained could not be countenanced in the circumstances given that Mitras was refusing to allow collection of supplies and Opel was entitled to consider that the injunction might not have been granted.

10.1.3.3 **There must be pressure that is illegitimate**

10.1.3.3.1 *Pressure*

In *Alec Lobb (Garages) Ltd v Total Oil GB Ltd* [1985] 1 WLR 173, the Court of Appeal held that it was not sufficient that, on the facts, the claimants were in serious financial difficulties and had no realistic alternative but to make the leaseback agreement with the defendant containing a 'tie' covenant. The defendant had exerted no pressure on them and was reluctant to enter into the transaction, and it was the claimants who had sought the defendant's assistance to avert financial collapse.

In *Williams v Roffey Bros. & Nicholls (Contractors) Ltd* [1991] 1 QB 1 (*page 106*, 3.1.3.7), it was the main contractor who had initiated the new arrangement rather than the subcontractor, and the Court of Appeal therefore proceeded on the assumption that there was no economic duress. This is likely to lead to fine distinctions between 'advising' a main contractor of factors likely to result in an impending breach and applying pressure by threatening breach, i.e. the difference between an implicit and an explicit threat—and see *Occidental Worldwide Investment Corporation v Skibs A/S Avanti, The Siboen and The Sibotre* [1976] 1 Lloyd's Rep 293 (for the facts, see *page 511*, 10.1.3.1). Such a distinction will be impossible to operate in practice—or, at least, to explain.

10.1.3.3.2 *Illegitimate*

Universe Tankships Inc. of Monrovia v International Transport Workers Federation, The Universe Sentinel
[1983] 1 AC 366 (HL)

A ship had docked at Milford Haven on 17 July 1978 and had discharged its cargo, but had been 'blacked' by ITF (a trade union) so that it was unable to leave port. The owners agreed to comply with ITF's demands, which included a contribution of $6,480 to a general welfare fund for sailors, because they feared disastrous economic consequences if they refused, since the ship was off-hire under a time charter while the blacking continued. The ship was able to sail on 29 July; on 10 August, the owners claimed the return of the $6,480 paid under duress. However, s. 13 of the Trade Union and Labour Relations Act 1974 granted immunity in tort to the trade union in relation to actions, which included blacking vessels, if its actions had been taken in furtherance of a 'trade dispute' within s. 29 of that Act (i.e. this would have technically legitimated the trade union's acts).

Held (by a majority, Lord Scarman and Lord Brandon of Oakbrook dissenting): The payment to the welfare fund was recoverable. The money had been paid under economic duress and, since s. 29(1)(a) required the trade dispute to relate to 'terms and conditions of employment' of the crew members, s. 13 did not protect the trade union in respect of this payment to a general welfare fund. It followed that there was no protection or immunity provided by the legislation.

LORD DIPLOCK: [I]t is conceded that the financial consequences to the shipowners of the *Universe Sentinel* continuing to be rendered off-hire under her time charter to Texaco, while the blacking continued, were so catastrophic as to amount to a coercion of the shipowners' will which vitiated their consent to those agreements and to the payments made by them to ITF . . .

It is . . . in my view crucial to the decision of the instant appeal to identify the rationale of this development of the common law. It is not that the party seeking to avoid the contract which he has entered into with another party, or to recover money that he has paid to another party in response to a demand, did not know the nature or the precise terms of the contract at the time when he entered into it or did not understand the purpose for which the payment was demanded. The rationale is that his apparent consent was induced by pressure exercised upon him by that other party which the law does not regard as legitimate, with the consequence that the consent is treated in law as revocable unless approbated either expressly or by implication after the illegitimate pressure has ceased to operate on his mind. It is a rationale similar to that which underlies the avoidability of contracts entered into and the recovery of money exacted under colour of office, or under undue influence or in consequence of threats of physical duress.

Commercial pressure, in some degree, exists wherever one party to a commercial transaction is in a stronger bargaining position than the other party. It is not, however, in my view, necessary, nor would it be appropriate in the instant appeal, to enter into the general question of the kinds of circumstances, if any, in which commercial pressure, even though it amounts to a coercion of the will of a party in the weaker bargaining position, may be treated as legitimate and, accordingly, as not giving rise to any legal right of redress. In the instant appeal the economic duress complained of was exercised in the field of industrial relations to which very special considerations apply . . .

Lord Scarman disagreed with the majority view of s. 29(1)(a). He considered that this was a legitimate exercise of pressure and did not constitute duress.

LORD SCARMAN: It is, I think, already established law that economic pressure can in law amount to duress; and that duress, if proved, not only renders voidable a transaction into which a person has entered under its compulsion but is actionable as a tort, if it causes damage or loss: *Barton v Armstrong* [1976] AC 104 and *Pao On v Lau Yiu Long* [1980] AC 614. The authorities upon which these two cases were based reveal two elements in the wrong of duress: (1) pressure amounting to compulsion of the will of the victim; and (2) the illegitimacy of the pressure exerted. There must be pressure, the practical effect of which is compulsion or the absence of choice. Compulsion is variously described in the authorities as coercion or the vitiation of consent. The classic case of duress is, however, not the lack of will to submit but the victim's intentional submission arising from the realisation that there is no other practical choice open to him. This is the thread of principle which links the early law of duress (threat to life or limb) with later developments when the law came also to recognise as duress first the threat to property and now the threat to a man's business or trade . . .

The absence of choice can be proved in various ways, e.g. by protest, by the absence of independent advice, or by a declaration of intention to go to law to recover the money paid or the property transferred: see *Maskell v Horner* [1915] 3 KB 106. But none of these evidential matters goes to the essence of duress. The victim's silence will not assist the bully, if the lack of any practicable choice but to submit is proved. The present case is an excellent illustration. There was no protest at the time, but only a determination to do whatever was needed as rapidly as possible to release the ship. Yet nobody challenges the judge's finding that the owner acted under compulsion. He put it thus [1981] ICR 129, 143:

> It was a matter of the most urgent commercial necessity that the plaintiffs should regain the use of their vessel. They were advised that their prospects of obtaining an injunction were minimal, the vessel would not have been released unless the payment was made, and they sought recovery of the money with sufficient speed once the duress had terminated.

The real issue in the appeal is, therefore, as to the second element in the wrong duress: was the pressure applied by the ITF in the circumstances of this case one which the law recognises as legitimate? For, as Lord Wilberforce and Lord Simon of Glaisdale said in *Barton v Armstrong* [1976] AC 104, 121D: 'the pressure must be one of a kind which the law does not regard as legitimate.'

As the two noble and learned Lords remarked at p. 121D, in life, including the life of commerce and finance, many acts are done 'under pressure, sometimes overwhelming pressure': but they are not necessarily done under duress. That depends on whether the circumstances are such that the law regards the pressure as legitimate.

In determining what is legitimate two matters may have to be considered. The first is as to the nature of the pressure. In many cases this will be decisive, though not in every case. And so the second question may have to be considered, namely, the nature of the demand which the pressure is applied to support.

The origin of the doctrine of duress in threats to life or limb, or to property, suggests strongly that the law regards the threat of unlawful action as illegitimate, whatever the demand. Duress can, of course, exist even if the threat is one of lawful action: whether it does so depends upon the nature of the demand. Blackmail is often a demand supported by a threat to do what is lawful, e.g. to report criminal conduct to the police. In many cases, therefore, 'What [one] has to justify is not the threat, but the demand . . . ': see *per* Lord Atkin in *Thorne v Motor Trade Association* [1937] AC 797, 806.

The present is a case in which the nature of the demand determines whether the pressure threatened or applied, i.e. the blacking, was lawful or unlawful. If it was unlawful, it is conceded that the owner acted under duress and can recover. If it was lawful, it is conceded that there was no duress and the sum sought by the owner is irrecoverable. The lawfulness or otherwise of the demand depends upon whether it was an act done in contemplation or furtherance of a trade dispute. If it was, it would not be actionable in tort: section 13(1) of the Act. Although no question of tortious liability arises in this case and section 13(1) is not, therefore, directly in point, it is not possible, in my view, to say of acts which are protected by statute from suit in tort that they nevertheless can amount to duress. Parliament having enacted that such acts are not actionable in tort, it would be inconsistent with legislative policy to say that, when the remedy sought is not damages for tort but recovery of money paid, they become unlawful.

NOTES

1. Lord Diplock avoids defining what is acceptable commercial pressure and what is illegitimate. Lord Scarman does provide some assistance by stating that pressure *may* be illegitimate if what is threatened is in itself unlawful, e.g. to injure the victim or to breach a contract. Pressure may also be illegitimate even though what is threatened is lawful if the way in which that pressure is exerted is illegitimate, e.g. if the advantage that the party is seeking to obtain is illegitimate. Lord Scarman used blackmail to illustrate this. A threat to disclose a particular fact about a person may be perfectly lawful and yet the demand of money is unlawful.

2. In *Vantage Navigation Corporation v Suhail and Saud Bahwan Building Materials LLC, The Alev* [1989] 1 Lloyd's Rep 138, the claimants had time-chartered the vessel to the charterers, who had loaded a cargo. The charterers defaulted in the payment of hire, but the claimants were contractually obliged to carry the cargo to its destination. They advised the defendants, cargo owners, that unless the defendants agreed to pay what the claimants demanded, they would not get their cargo. The defendants agreed to pay port expenses and discharging costs, and the claimants agreed to refrain from arresting or detaining the vessel. The defendants pleaded duress. Hobhouse J held that the defendants' promise had clearly been made under duress. The pressure exerted by the claimants was illegitimate, since the claimants had no rights over the goods and could not refuse to deliver the cargo. Similarly, in *Borrelli v Ting* [2010] UKPC 21, [2010] Bus LR 1718, the defendant's behaviour, consisting of delays, forgery, and false evidence with the aim of seeking to prevent the company's liquidators from investigating the defendant's conduct, had led those liquidators to agree a settlement with the defendant. This settlement agreement was set aside for duress because the agreement had been obtained 'by illegitimate means'.

3. However, in *Huyton SA v Peter Cremer GmbH & Co.* [1999] 1 Lloyd's Rep 620, Mance J concluded that there was no illegitimate pressure, so that the agreement was enforceable.

Huyton had agreed to buy wheat from Cremer on terms whereby Huyton was to arrange freight, which was to be paid for by Cremer, and payment for the goods was to be made against documents. The vessel engaged by Huyton had incurred considerable port demurrage (payable for delay under the charter). Although the vessel had discharged its cargo and the goods were in the possession of sub-buyers, as a result of various discrepancies on the documents, Huyton had withheld payment for the goods. Cremer claimed that, because the cargo had been accepted, Huyton had waived any right to reject the documents, whereas Huyton claimed that Cremer was in repudiatory breach by not presenting conforming documents.

During the negotiations aimed at settling the dispute, it had been agreed that Huyton would pay against re-tendered conforming documents if Cremer were to agree to pay the demurrage and not to submit the dispute to arbitration. Cremer had reluctantly agreed to do this, but, having been paid, had then claimed that it was not bound by this agreement, alleging economic duress—namely, that Huyton's threat not to pay the purchase price properly due amounted to illegitimate pressure. It was held that there was no illegitimate pressure on Cremer because its presentation of non-conforming documents constituted a repudiatory breach, which had been accepted by Huyton, so that it was not possible thereafter to re-tender conforming documents or to claim the contractual price. In any event, even if the pressure had been illegitimate, it had not been shown to be a significant cause in Cremer's decision to enter into the agreement.

4. In *R v Attorney-General of England and Wales* [2003] UKPC 22, [2003] EMLR 24, the Privy Council (with Lord Scott dissenting) held that a threat to return an SAS member to his ordinary unit if he did not sign a confidentiality agreement to cover the period during which he left the service, although considered a disgrace and a severe penalty by SAS members, was a lawful act because the Ministry of Defence had the ability to make such a transfer. It followed that the agreement had not been signed under duress. The Privy Council cited the approach of Lord Scarman in *Universe Tankship*—namely, that the legitimacy of pressure must be examined in two respects: (i) 'the nature of the pressure'; and (ii) 'the nature of the demand which the pressure is applied to support'. Whereas, generally speaking, the threat of any form of unlawful action would be regarded as illegitimate, the fact that the threat was lawful would not necessarily render the pressure legitimate, e.g. instances of blackmail using a lawful threat. On these facts, it was held that the demand supported by the lawful threat could be justified, since the Ministry was reasonably entitled to regard anyone unwilling to accept the confidentiality agreement as unsuitable for the SAS.

? QUESTION

Is a threat to breach a contract automatically illegitimate? It is not automatic, but is certainly likely, since the threat will often consist of a threat to withhold performance under the contract motivated by a desire to secure a higher price for that performance, e.g. *Kolmar Group AG v Traxpo Enterprises Pvt Ltd* [2010] EWHC 113 (Comm), [2010] 2 Lloyd's Rep 653, [2011] 1 All ER (Comm) 46, which involved a threat to withhold performance on a 'take it or leave it' basis that required the buyer to accept less and pay more, when the goods were required urgently to supply a very important client and were not readily available in the market. In addition, the buyer was bound to pay hire on the vessel that it had chartered to transport the goods and could not risk any delay in loading.

Whereas, in *Carillion Construction Ltd v Felix (UK) Ltd* [2001] BLR 1, a threat by a subcontractor to withhold deliveries until settlement of its final account was considered as an illegitimate threat to breach the contract, the same judge (Dyson J) in *DSND Subsea Ltd v Petroleum Geo-Services ASA* [2000] BLR 530 held that a threat to breach the contract by ceasing part of the work was not an illegitimate threat. It seems that the distinguishing feature in *DSND* was that the threat was made in an attempt to get the insurance arrangements clarified, so that DSND was 'entirely justified in wanting to resolve this' and the threat was no more than a reasonable attempt to resolve the position.

Does it follow that there is a distinction in terms of whether the threat was made in good or bad faith? See the judgment of Mance J in *Huyton SA v Peter Cremer GmbH & Co.* [1999] 1 Lloyd's Rep 620 (*page 519*, earlier in this section) on the question of the effect of bad faith.

10.1.3.4 Lawful act duress

CTN Cash and Carry Ltd v Gallaher Ltd
[1994] 4 All ER 714 (CA)

The claimants purchased consignments of cigarettes from the defendants on the defendants' standard terms. The defendants had also arranged credit facilities for the claimants, which they could withdraw for any reason at any time. One consignment had been incorrectly delivered to the wrong warehouse, but before the defendants could deliver it to the correct warehouse, it had been stolen from the claimants' premises. The defendants genuinely believed that the goods were at the claimants' risk at the time of the theft and accordingly invoiced them for the goods. The claimants refused to pay and did so only after the defendants threatened to withdraw their credit facilities. The claimants then claimed the return of the money paid, on the basis that it had been obtained as a result of economic duress and that the pressure was illegitimate because the defendants had demanded money to which they were not entitled.

Held: The defendants' conduct did not constitute duress.

STEYN LJ: The present dispute . . . does not arise in the context of dealings between a supplier and a consumer. The dispute arises out of arm's length commercial dealings between two trading companies. It is true that the defendants were the sole distributors of the popular brands of cigarettes. In a sense the defendants were in a monopoly position. The control of monopolies is, however, a matter for Parliament. Moreover, the common law does not recognise the doctrine of inequality of bargaining power in commercial dealings (see *National Westminster Bank plc v Morgan* [1985] 1 All ER 821, [1985] AC 686).

The fact that the defendants were in a monopoly position cannot therefore by itself convert what is not otherwise duress into duress.

A second characteristic of the case is that the defendants were in law entitled to refuse to enter into any future contracts with the plaintiffs for any reason whatever or for no reason at all. Such a decision not to deal with the plaintiffs would have been financially damaging to the defendants, but it would have been lawful. *A fortiori*, it was lawful for the defendants, for any reason or for no reason, to insist that they would no longer grant credit to the plaintiffs. The defendants' demand for payment of the invoice, coupled with the threat to withdraw credit, was neither a breach of contract nor a tort.

A third, and critically important, characteristic of the case is the fact that the defendants *bona fide* thought that the goods were at the risk of the plaintiffs and that the plaintiffs owed the defendants the sum in question. The defendants exerted commercial pressure on the plaintiffs in order to obtain payment of a sum which they *bona fide* considered due to them. The defendants' motive in threatening withdrawal of credit facilities was commercial self-interest in obtaining a sum that they considered due to them . . .

I . . . readily accept that the fact that the defendants have used lawful means does not by itself remove the case from the scope of the doctrine of economic duress. Professor Birks, in *An Introduction to the Law of Restitution* (1989) p. 177, lucidly explains:

> Can lawful pressures also count? This is a difficult question, because, if the answer is that they can, the only viable basis for discriminating between acceptable and unacceptable pressures is not positive law but social morality. In other words, the judges must say what pressures (though lawful outside the restitutionary context) are improper as contrary to prevailing standards. That makes the judges, not the law or the legislature, the arbiters of social evaluation. On the other hand, if the answer is that lawful pressures are always exempt, those who devise outrageous but technically lawful means of compulsion must always escape restitution until the legislature declares the abuse unlawful. It is tolerably clear that, at least where they can be confident of a general consensus in favour of their evaluation, the courts are willing to apply a standard of impropriety rather than technical unlawfulness.

And there are a number of cases where English courts have accepted that a threat may be illegitimate when coupled with a demand for payment even if the threat is one of lawful action (see *Thorne v Motor Trade Association* [1937] 3 All ER 157 at 160–161, [1937] AC 797 at 806–807, *Mutual Finance Ltd v John Wetton & Sons Ltd* [1937] 2 All ER 657, [1937] 2 KB 389 and *Universe Tankships Inc of Monrovia v International Transport Workers' Federation* [1982] 2 All ER 67 at 76, 89, [1983] 1 AC 366 at 384, 401). On the other hand, Goff and Jones *Law of Restitution* (3rd edn, 1986) p. 240 observed that English courts have wisely not accepted any general principle that a threat not to contract with another, except on certain terms, may amount to duress.

We are being asked to extend the categories of duress of which the law will take cognisance. That is not necessarily objectionable, but it seems to me that an extension capable of covering the present case, involving 'lawful-act duress' in a commercial context in pursuit of a *bona fide* claim, would be a radical one with far-reaching implications. It would introduce a substantial and undesirable element of uncertainty in the commercial bargaining process. Moreover, it will often enable *bona fide* settled accounts to be reopened when parties to commercial dealings fall out. The aim of our commercial law ought to be to encourage fair dealing between parties. But it is a mistake for the law to set its sights too highly when the critical inquiry is not whether the conduct is lawful but whether it is morally or socially unacceptable. That is the inquiry in which we are engaged. In my view there are policy considerations which militate against ruling that the defendants obtained payment of the disputed invoice by duress.

Outside the field of protected relationships, and in a purely commercial context, it might be a relatively rare case in which 'lawful-act duress' can be established. And it might be particularly difficult to establish duress if the defendant *bona fide* considered that his demand was valid. In this complex and changing branch of the law I deliberately refrain from saying 'never'. But as the law stands, I am satisfied that the defendants' conduct in this case did not amount to duress.

The claimants were small family-owned travel agents selling airline tickets to the local Pakistani community. The rules of the International Air Transport Association required them to enter into agency agreements with airlines, one of which was the defendant, Pakistan's national airline. The relevant agreements were entered into in 2008 and entitled the claimants to 9 per cent commission. In September 2012, when the commission remained unpaid, the defendant gave lawful notice terminating the agency agreements. New agreements were entered into in October 2012, but those agreements required the claimants not to participate in proceedings to recover unpaid commission.

Held: There was no duress.

DAVID RICHARDS LJ:

43. Historically, the avoidance of contracts on grounds of duress was confined to acts or threats of personal violence or imprisonment and, more recently, unlawful threats to property.

44. The scope of duress was significantly broadened with the acknowledgement that a contract might be avoided on grounds of economic duress. This was recognised for the first time in English law in two first instance commercial cases: *Occidental Worldwide Investment Corp v Skibbs A/S Avanti* [1976] 1 Lloyd's Rep 293 and *North Ocean Shipping Co Ltd v Hyundai Construction Co Ltd* [1979] QB 705. In the first of these cases, a charterer of vessels alleged that it had no substantial assets and threatened that if the hire rates were not reduced it would go into bankruptcy. These statements were fraudulently made and the owners were held entitled to avoid the contract containing the lower hire rates on that ground. Kerr J rejected a case of duress on the facts but said that English law was open to development in relation to contracts concluded under some form of compulsion not amounting to duress to the person or to property. In the latter case, Mocatta J held that the plaintiff would have been entitled to avoid for duress a contract whereby it agreed to pay an increased price for the construction of a ship as a result of threats by the shipyard to terminate the shipbuilding contract in breach of its terms, if it had not subsequently affirmed the revised contract. He held at p. 719 that a contract made under the coercion of economic duress was voidable and that a threat to break a contract could amount to economic duress.

45. In both these early cases, the pressure amounting to economic duress comprised unlawful threats: fraudulent statements in one case and a threatened breach of contract in the other. The legality or otherwise of the relevant threats was also at the heart of the two decisions of the House of Lords which authoritatively established the existence in English law of a principle of economic duress. Both cases involved the 'blacking' of vessels, whereby trade unions instructed their members not to provide tug services to the vessels and thereby prevent them leaving port. This involved the unions in inducing their members to break their contracts of employment.

46. In the first of these cases, *Universe Tankships Inc of Monrovia v International Transport Workers Federation* [1983] AC 366, the instructions constituted a tort, unless they were issued in furtherance of a trade dispute in which event the union enjoyed immunity under the Trade Union and Labour Relations Act 1974. The demand for one of the payments which the plaintiff shipowner was required to make in order to secure the release of its vessel docked at Milford Haven was held to be outside the statutory immunity. The blacking of the vessel in order to obtain that payment was therefore tortious and constituted economic duress, entitling the shipowner to recover it. In the second case, *Dimskal Shipping Co SA v International Transport Workers Federation* [1992] 2 AC 152, the facts were similar, except that the vessel was docked in Sweden. Under Swedish law, the union enjoyed immunity but did not do so under English law. The House of Lords held that the legality of the blacking of the vessel was to be judged by the governing law

of the contract whereby the shipowner agreed with the union to make payments to secure its release. As this was English law, the blacking was tortious and was held to amount to economic duress, entitling the shipowner to avoid the contract.

. . .

56. The first clear discussion of the possibility of lawful act duress in the authorities was in the judgments of this court in *CTN Cash and Carry Ltd v Gallagher Ltd* [1994] 4 All ER 714. The defendant supplied cigarettes to the plaintiff company on a regular basis and arranged credit facilities. Each supply was under a separate contract and the defendant was not obliged either to make further supplies or to provide credit facilities. It invoiced the plaintiff for a consignment that had been stolen before it reached the correct delivery address. Gallagher did so in good faith, wrongly believing that it was entitled to payment. When the plaintiff refused to pay the invoice, the defendant terminated its credit facilities and refused to reinstate them unless the invoice was paid. Against this pressure, the plaintiff paid the invoice but subsequently brought proceedings to recover the payment on the grounds that it had been procured by means of economic duress.

57. In rejecting the claim of economic duress, Steyn LJ, giving the leading judgment, stressed three characteristics of the case. First, it did not involve either a protected relationship, thus engaging the equitable doctrine of undue influence, or dealings between a supplier and a consumer, thus engaging the legislation that gives protection to consumers. Nor could the defendant's monopoly of supply of particular brands of popular cigarettes convert what was not duress into duress. Second, the defendant was lawfully entitled to refuse to enter into further supply contracts with the plaintiff and to withdraw credit facilities. The third characteristic was stated by Steyn LJ at p. 718 as follows:

> A third, and critically important, characteristic of the case is the fact that the defendants bona fide thought that the goods were at the risk of the plaintiffs and that the plaintiffs owed the defendants the sum in question. The defendants exerted commercial pressure on the plaintiffs in order to obtain payment of a sum which they bona fide considered due to them. The defendants' motive in threatening withdrawal of credit facilities was commercial self-interest in obtaining a sum that they considered due to them.

. . .

62. In my view, *CTN Cash and Carry v Gallagher* can be taken to establish that where A uses lawful pressure to induce B to concede a demand to which A does not bona fide believe itself to be entitled, B's agreement is voidable on grounds of economic duress. It cannot be taken to establish that if A genuinely but unreasonably believes the demand to be well-founded, the same result follows.

. . .

105. My conclusion on the central legal issue is that the doctrine of lawful act duress does not extend to the use of lawful pressure to achieve a result to which the person exercising pressure believes in good faith it is entitled, and that is so whether or not, objectively speaking, it has reasonable grounds for that belief. The common law and equity set tight limits to setting aside otherwise valid contracts. In this way undesirable uncertainty in a commercial context is reduced. I appreciate that in the context of the present case, which concerns the reasonableness of the grounds for resisting a claim, it can be said that a test of unreasonableness is not uncertain, because it can be tested and decided according to conventional legal standards. But that will not be the case in the much more common situation of a party using lawful commercial pressure in support of a purely commercial demand. There is no yardstick by which to judge such demands, save those that can be set out in legislation such as that applying to consumer contracts. Such demands are a matter of negotiation against the background of the pressures operating on both parties.

106. The relevant considerations go beyond uncertainty. In judging the use of lawful acts or threats of lawful acts as commercial pressure, there is a sharp distinction between such use to pursue demands made in good faith and those made in bad faith. As I earlier mentioned, a lack of good faith on the part of

a contracting party is a feature in a number of the grounds on which contracts may be avoided. Rescission on grounds of fraudulent misrepresentation or unconscionable transaction are examples. It is a clear criterion involving conduct which all can agree is unacceptable and which is a fact capable of proof, often as it happens by reference to the lack of any reasonable grounds for the belief. By contrast, not only is reasonableness in this context a standard of very uncertain content but it is also very unclear why or on what basis the common law should hold that a party with a private law right, whose exercise is not subject to any overriding duty, cannot use it to achieve a purpose which is both lawful and advanced in good faith.

107. Moreover, it is relevant to note that the economic pressure that PIAC was able to apply in this case resulted from its position at that time as a monopoly supplier of tickets for direct flights between the UK and Pakistan. As I have earlier mentioned, the common law has always rejected the use, or abuse, of a monopoly position as a ground for setting aside a contract, leaving it to be regulated by statute. In my judgment, it would be unprincipled to develop the doctrine of economic duress as a means of controlling the lawful use of monopoly power. As Steyn LJ said in *CTN Cash and Carry*, 'In a sense the defendants were in a monopoly position. The control of monopolies is, however, a matter for Parliament. Moreover, the common law does not recognise the doctrine of inequality of bargaining power in commercial dealings . . . The fact that the defendants were in a monopoly position cannot therefore by itself convert what is not otherwise duress into duress'.

NOTE See also *Flying Music Co. v Theater Entertainment SA* [2017] EWHC 3192 (QB), where the claimant was held to be entitled to enforce guarantee given by the second defendant failing which a contract under which the first defendant had agreed to stage performances of Michael Jackson's *Thriller* in Greece would be cancelled: there had been default by the first defendant in making payment for performances that had taken place so that the threat of cancellation was lawful; and the second defendant was a lawyer able to look after his own interests.

10.2 Undue influence

The doctrine of undue influence is an equitable doctrine allowing a contract to be set aside where there has been a wrongful (undue) exercise of influence by one party over the other. What sort of influence will the courts view as being wrongful?

10.2.1 Types of undue influence

The traditional classification of cases of undue influence was summarized by Lord Browne-Wilkinson in *Barclays Bank plc v O'Brien* [1994] 1 AC 180, pp. 189B–190A and 190C–E:

A person who has been induced to enter into a transaction by the undue influence of another (the wrongdoer) is entitled to set that transaction aside as against the wrongdoer. Such undue influence is either actual or presumed. In *Bank of Credit and Commerce International SA v Aboody* [1990] 1 QB 923, 953, the Court of Appeal helpfully adopted the following classification.

Class 1: Actual undue influence. In these cases it is necessary for the claimant to prove affirmatively that the wrongdoer exerted undue influence on the complainant to enter into the particular transaction which is impugned.

Class 2: Presumed undue influence. In these cases the complainant only has to show, in the first instance, that there was a relationship of trust and confidence between the complainant and the wrongdoer of such a nature that it is fair to presume that the wrongdoer abused that relationship in procuring the complainant to enter into the impugned transaction. In Class 2 cases therefore there is no need to produce evidence that actual undue influence was exerted in relation to the particular transaction impugned: once a confidential relationship has been proved, the burden then shifts to the wrongdoer to prove that the complainant entered into the impugned transaction freely, for example by showing that the complainant had independent advice. Such a confidential relationship can be established in two ways, viz:

Class 2(A). Certain relationships (for example solicitor and client, medical advisor and patient) as a matter of law raise the presumption that undue influence has been exercised.

Class 2(B). Even if there is no relationship falling within Class 2(A), if the complainant proves the de facto existence of a relationship under which the complainant generally reposed trust and confidence in the wrongdoer, the existence of such relationship raises the presumption of undue influence. In a Class 2(B) case therefore, in the absence of evidence disproving undue influence, the complainant will succeed in setting aside the impugned transaction merely by proof that the complainant reposed trust and confidence in the wrongdoer without having to prove that the wrongdoer exerted actual undue influence or otherwise abused such trust and confidence in relation to the particular transaction impugned . . .

Although there is no Class 2(A) presumption of undue influence as between husband and wife, it should be emphasised that in any particular case a wife may well be able to demonstrate that de facto she did leave decisions on financial affairs to her husband thereby bringing herself within Class 2(B), i.e. that the relationship between husband and wife in the particular case was such that the wife reposed confidence and trust in her husband in relation to their financial affairs and therefore undue influence is to be presumed. Thus, in those cases which still occur where the wife relies in all financial matters on her husband and simply does what he suggests, a presumption of undue influence within Class 2(B) can be established solely from the proof of such trust and confidence without proof of actual undue influence . . .

This classification distinguished cases in which the undue influence was proved affirmatively and those in which it is presumed, either because the parties' relationship falls within a class of protected relationships (Class 2A) or because, on the facts, the particular relationship between these parties was of such a nature that undue influence could be presumed.

Whereas it remains important to distinguish these three factual scenarios, the House of Lords in *Royal Bank of Scotland plc v Etridge (No. 2)* [2001] UKHL 44, [2002] 2 AC 773 confirmed that the law on so-called 'presumed undue influence' had not been accurately stated, since the 'presumption' is no more than an evidential presumption that influence has been exercised and does not become an evidential presumption of *undue* influence unless there is something suspicious, or something that calls for an explanation, on the facts, e.g. resulting from the size or nature of the transfers.

Royal Bank of Scotland plc v Etridge (No. 2)
[2001] UKHL 44, [2002] 2 AC 773 (HL)

LORD NICHOLLS [whose speech was supported by the other members of the House of Lords]: 8 Equity identified broadly two forms of unacceptable conduct. The first comprises overt acts of improper pressure or coercion such as unlawful threats. Today there is much overlap with the principle of duress as this principle has subsequently developed. The second form arises out of a relationship between two persons where one has acquired over another a measure of influence, or ascendancy, of which the ascendant person then takes unfair advantage. An example from the 19th century, when much of this law developed, is a case where an impoverished father prevailed upon his inexperienced children to charge their reversionary interests under their parents' marriage settlement with payment of his mortgage debts: see *Bainbrigge v Browne* (1881) 18 Ch D 188.

9 In cases of this latter nature the influence one person has over another provides scope for misuse without any specific overt acts of persuasion. The relationship between two individuals may be such that, without more, one of them is disposed to agree a course of action proposed by the other. Typically this occurs when one person places trust in another to look after his affairs and interests, and the latter betrays this trust by preferring his own interests. He abuses the influence he has acquired. In *Allcard v Skinner* (1887) 36 Ch D 145, a case well known to every law student, Lindley LJ, at p 181, described this class of cases as those in which it was the duty of one party to advise the other or to manage his property for him. In *Zamet v Hyman* [1961] 1 WLR 1442, 1444–1445 Lord Evershed MR referred to relationships where one party owed the other an obligation of candour and protection.

10 The law has long recognised the need to prevent abuse of influence in these 'relationship' cases despite the absence of evidence of overt acts of persuasive conduct. The types of relationship, such as parent and child, in which this principle falls to be applied cannot be listed exhaustively. Relationships are infinitely various. Sir Guenter Treitel QC has rightly noted that the question is whether one party has reposed sufficient trust and confidence in the other, rather than whether the relationship between the parties belongs to a particular type: see Treitel, *The Law of Contract*, 10th ed (1999), pp 380–381. For example, the relation of banker and customer will not normally meet this criterion, but exceptionally it may: see *National Westminster Bank plc v Morgan* [1985] AC 686, 707–709.

11 Even this test is not comprehensive. The principle is not confined to cases of abuse of trust and confidence. It also includes, for instance, cases where a vulnerable person has been exploited. Indeed, there is no single touchstone for determining whether the principle is applicable. Several expressions have been used in an endeavour to encapsulate the essence: trust and confidence, reliance, dependence or vulnerability on the one hand and ascendancy, domination or control on the other. None of these descriptions is perfect. None is all embracing. Each has its proper place . . .

Burden of proof and presumptions

13 Whether a transaction was brought about by the exercise of undue influence is a question of fact. Here, as elsewhere, the general principle is that he who asserts a wrong has been committed must prove it. The burden of proving an allegation of undue influence rests upon the person who claims to have been wronged. This is the general rule. The evidence required to discharge the burden of proof depends on the nature of the alleged undue influence, the personality of the parties, their relationship, the extent to which the transaction cannot readily be accounted for by the ordinary motives of ordinary persons in that relationship, and all the circumstances of the case.

14 Proof that the complainant placed trust and confidence in the other party in relation to the management of the complainant's financial affairs, coupled with a transaction which calls for explanation, will normally be sufficient, failing satisfactory evidence to the contrary, to discharge the burden of proof. On proof of these two matters the stage is set for the court to infer that, in the absence of a satisfactory explanation, the transaction can only have been procured by undue influence. In other words, proof of these two facts is prima facie evidence that the defendant abused the influence he acquired in the parties' relationship. He preferred his own interests. He did not behave fairly to the other. So the evidential burden then shifts to him. It is for him to produce evidence to counter the inference which otherwise should be drawn.

15 *Bainbrigge v Browne* 18 Ch D 188, already mentioned, provides a good illustration of this commonplace type of forensic exercise. Fry J held, at p 196, that there was no direct evidence upon which

he could rely as proving undue pressure by the father. But there existed circumstances 'from which the court will infer pressure and undue influence'. None of the children were entirely emancipated from their father's control. None seemed conversant with business. These circumstances were such as to cast the burden of proof upon the father. He had made no attempt to discharge that burden. He did not appear in court at all. So the children's claim succeeded. Again, more recently, in *National Westminster Bank plc v Morgan* [1985] AC 686, 707. Lord Scarman noted that a relationship of banker and customer may become one in which a banker acquires a dominating influence. If he does, and a manifestly disadvantageous transaction is proved, 'there would then be room' for a court to presume that it resulted from the exercise of undue influence.

16 Generations of equity lawyers have conventionally described this situation as one in which a presumption of undue influence arises. This use of the term 'presumption' is descriptive of a shift in the evidential onus on a question of fact. When a plaintiff succeeds by this route he does so because he has succeeded in establishing a case of undue influence. The court has drawn appropriate inferences of fact upon a balanced consideration of the whole of the evidence at the end of a trial in which the burden of proof rested upon the plaintiff. The use, in the course of the trial, of the forensic tool of a shift in the evidential burden of proof should not be permitted to obscure the overall position. These cases are the equitable counterpart of common law cases where the principle of res ipsa loquitur is invoked. There is a rebuttable evidential presumption of undue influence.

17 The availability of this forensic tool in cases founded on abuse of influence arising from the parties' relationship has led to this type of case sometimes being labelled 'presumed undue influence'. This is by way of contrast with cases involving actual pressure or the like, which are labelled 'actual undue influence': see *Bank of Credit and Commerce International SA v Aboody* [1990] 1 QB 923, 953, and *Royal Bank of Scotland plc v Etridge (No. 2)* [1998] 4 All ER 705, 711–712, paras 5–7. This usage can be a little confusing. In many cases where a plaintiff has claimed that the defendant abused the influence he acquired in a relationship of trust and confidence the plaintiff has succeeded by recourse to the rebuttable evidential presumption. But this need not be so. Such a plaintiff may succeed even where this presumption is not available to him; for instance, where the impugned transaction was not one which called for an explanation.

18 The evidential presumption discussed above is to be distinguished sharply from a different form of presumption which arises in some cases. The law has adopted a sternly protective attitude towards certain types of relationship in which one party acquires influence over another who is vulnerable and dependent and where, moreover, substantial gifts by the influenced or vulnerable person are not normally to be expected. Examples of relationships within this special class are parent and child, guardian and ward, trustee and beneficiary, solicitor and client, and medical adviser and patient. In these cases the law presumes, irrebuttably, that one party had influence over the other. The complainant need not prove he actually reposed trust and confidence in the other party. It is sufficient for him to prove the existence of the type of relationship.

19 It is now well established that husband and wife is not one of the relationships to which this latter principle applies. In *Yerkey v Jones* (1939) 63 CLR 649, 675 Dixon J explained the reason. The Court of Chancery was not blind to the opportunities of obtaining and unfairly using influence over a wife which a husband often possesses. But there is nothing unusual or strange in a wife, from motives of affection or for other reasons, conferring substantial financial benefits on her husband. Although there is no presumption, the court will nevertheless note, as a matter of fact, the opportunities for abuse which flow from a wife's confidence in her husband. The court will take this into account with all the other evidence in the case. Where there is evidence that a husband has taken unfair advantage of his influence over his wife, or her confidence in him, 'it is not difficult for the wife to establish her title to relief': see *In re Lloyds Bank Ltd; Bomze and Lederman v Bomze* [1931] 1 Ch 289, 302, per Maugham J.

Independent advice

20 Proof that the complainant received advice from a third party before entering into the impugned transaction is one of the matters a court takes into account when weighing all the evidence. The weight, or importance, to be attached to such advice depends on all the circumstances. In the normal course, advice from a solicitor or other outside adviser can be expected to bring home to a complainant a proper understanding of what he or she is about to do. But a person may understand fully the implications of a proposed transaction, for instance, a substantial gift, and yet still be acting under the undue influence of another. Proof of outside advice does not, of itself, necessarily show that the subsequent completion of the transaction was free from the exercise of undue influence. Whether it will be proper to infer that outside advice had an emancipating effect, so that the transaction was not brought about by the exercise of undue influence, is a question of fact to be decided having regard to all the evidence in the case.

NOTE Lord Nicholls therefore accepted that the classification of types of undue influence depends upon how that undue influence is proved. Thus, in some cases (actual undue influence: Class 1), both the influence and the fact that it is undue will be affirmatively proven, since there is clear evidence to support this. In other cases, the influence will be presumed (in the absence of actual evidence of undue influence), either because of the existence of a protected relationship or because, on the facts, there is a relationship of trust and confidence between these individual parties.

Thus, cases of presumed undue influence are of two types. The distinction is that, in the first category of 'protected' relationships, the influence is automatically (and irrebuttably) presumed, whereas in those cases falling outside these 'protected relationships', such as husband and wife, and banker and customer, the party alleging undue influence needs to establish that trust and confidence was placed in the other party in order for the presumption of influence to arise. Such influence is not automatically assumed. In the case of both types of presumed undue influence, the presumption of *undue* influence can then arise only if there is something suspicious about the transaction that calls for an explanation.

However, once this presumption of undue influence has arisen, the burden of proof shifts, so that it is for the other party to seek to show that no undue influence was in fact exercised and that the transaction was the product of a 'free and informed consent'. One possible way in which to do this would be by showing that independent legal advice had been received. However, there is some residual uncertainty concerning the role and effect of independent legal advice in this context (see the comment of Lord Nicholls at [20]). It may not be as significant as had been thought pre-*Etridge*.

10.2.1.1 Is there a requirement of manifest disadvantage?

In *National Westminster Bank plc v Morgan* [1985] AC 686 (*page 535*, 10.2.4), the House of Lords considered that the party claiming undue influence needed to establish that the transaction was manifestly disadvantageous to him. The existence of such a requirement has proven controversial.

10.2.1.1.1 *Actual undue influence*

Although the Court of Appeal in *Bank of Credit and Commerce International SA v Aboody* [1990] 1 QB 923 had held that a transaction could not be set aside for actual undue influence unless the transaction in question were manifestly disadvantageous to the party affected, the House of Lords in *CIBC Mortgages plc v Pitt* [1994] 1 AC 200 emphatically rejected this requirement in the context of actual undue influence.

LORD BROWNE-WILKINSON: My Lords, I am unable to agree with the Court of Appeal's decision in *Aboody*. I have no doubt that the decision in *Morgan* does not extend to cases of actual undue influence. Despite two references in Lord Scarman's speech to cases of actual undue influence, as I read his speech he was primarily concerned to establish that disadvantage had to be shown, not as a constituent element of the cause of action for undue influence, but in order to raise a presumption of undue influence within class 2. That was the only subject matter before the House of Lords in *Morgan* . . . With the exception of a passing reference to *Ormes v Beadel* (1860) 2 Gif 166, all the cases referred to by Lord Scarman were cases of presumed undue influence. In the circumstances, I do not think that this House can have been intending to lay down any general principle applicable to all claims of undue influence, whether actual or presumed.

Whatever the merits of requiring a complainant to show manifest disadvantage in order to raise a Class 2 presumption of undue influence, in my judgment there is no logic in imposing such a requirement where actual undue influence has been exercised and proved. Actual undue influence is a species of fraud. Like any other victim of fraud, a person who has been induced by undue influence to carry out a transaction which he did not freely and knowingly enter into is entitled to have that transaction set aside as of right. No case decided before *Morgan* was cited (nor am I aware of any) in which a transaction proved to have been obtained by actual undue influence has been upheld nor is there any case in which a court has even considered whether the transaction was, or was not, advantageous. A man guilty of fraud is no more entitled to argue that the transaction was beneficial to the person defrauded than is a man who has procured a transaction by misrepresentation. The effect of the wrongdoer's conduct is to prevent the wronged party from bringing a free will and properly informed mind to bear on the proposed transaction which accordingly must be set aside in equity as a matter of justice.

I therefore hold that a claimant who proves actual undue influence is not under the further burden of proving that the transaction induced by undue influence was manifestly disadvantageous: he is entitled as of right to have it set aside.

10.2.1.1.2 *Presumed undue influence*

In both cases of presumed undue influence, the fact that the influence was 'undue', i.e. that advantage was taken of a protected relationship position or of a relationship based on trust and confidence, needs to be established, and Lord Nicholls in *Royal Bank of Scotland plc v Etridge (No. 2)* [2001] UKHL 44, [2002] 2 AC 773, indicated that there is a link between the existence of 'disadvantage' in the transaction and the ability to establish that the influence was 'undue' in this context.

LORD NICHOLLS: 12 In *CIBC Mortgages plc v Pitt* [1994] 1 AC 200 your Lordships' House decided that in cases of undue influence disadvantage is not a necessary ingredient of the cause of action. It is not essential that the transaction should be disadvantageous to the pressurised or influenced person, either in financial terms or in any other way. However, in the nature of things, questions of undue influence will not usually arise, and the exercise of undue influence is unlikely to occur, where the transaction is innocuous. The issue is likely to arise only when, in some respect, the transaction was disadvantageous either from the outset or as matters turned out.

Of course, the non-existence of manifest disadvantage would not eliminate the possibility of undue influence and other evidence may establish that, despite the apparent fairness of the transaction, advantage was taken of the party influenced to contract. In addition, in purely theoretical terms, it is difficult to see that the position of the claimant should be relevant to an assessment of the undue nature of the influence exercised by the defendant, so that it clearly cannot be the *only* factor.

Lord Nicholls therefore went on to reformulate the manifest disadvantage requirement in the context of presumed undue influence (or Class 2 situations) as a test of whether the transaction is readily explicable by the relationship of the parties, i.e. a small gift between relatives might be readily explicable, whereas a very large transfer might raise the suspicion that undue influence may have been exercised and so shift the burden of proof to the other party.

Royal Bank of Scotland plc v Etridge (No. 2)
[2001] UKHL 44, [2002] 2 AC 773

LORD NICHOLLS: 21 As already noted, there are two prerequisites to the evidential shift in the burden of proof from the complainant to the other party. First, that the complainant reposed trust and confidence in the other party, or the other party acquired ascendancy over the complainant. Second, that the transaction is not readily explicable by the relationship of the parties.

22 Lindley LJ summarised this second prerequisite in the leading authority of *Allcard v Skinner* 36 Ch D 145, where the donor parted with almost all her property. Lindley LJ pointed out that where a gift of a small amount is made to a person standing in a confidential relationship to the donor, some proof of the exercise of the influence of the donee must be given. The mere existence of the influence is not enough. He continued, at p 185 'But if the gift is so large as not to be reasonably accounted for on the ground of friendship, relationship, charity, or other ordinary motives on which ordinary men act, the burden is upon the donee to support the gift.' In *Bank of Montreal v Stuart* [1911] AC 120, 137 Lord Macnaghten used the phrase 'immoderate and irrational' to describe this concept.

23 The need for this second prerequisite has recently been questioned: see Nourse LJ in *Barclays Bank plc v Coleman* [2001] QB, 20, 30–32, one of the cases under appeal before your Lordships' House. [Counsel] invited your Lordships to depart from the decision of the House on this point in *National Westminster Bank plc v Morgan* [1985] AC 686.

24 My Lords, this is not an invitation I would accept. The second prerequisite, as expressed by Lindley LJ, is good sense. It is a necessary limitation upon the width of the first prerequisite. It would be absurd for the law to presume that every gift by a child to a parent, or every transaction between a client and his solicitor or between a patient and his doctor, was brought about by undue influence unless the contrary is affirmatively proved. Such a presumption would be too far-reaching. The law would be out of touch with everyday life if the presumption were to apply to every Christmas or birthday gift by a child to a parent, or to an agreement whereby a client or patient agrees to be responsible for the reasonable fees of his legal or medical adviser. The law would be rightly open to ridicule, for transactions such as these are unexceptionable. They do not suggest that something may be amiss. So something more is needed before the law reverses the burden of proof, something which calls for an explanation. When that something more is present, the greater the disadvantage to the vulnerable person, the more cogent must be the explanation before the presumption will be regarded as rebutted.

25 This was the approach adopted by Lord Scarman in *National Westminster Bank plc v Morgan* [1985] AC 686, 703–707. He cited Lindley LJ's observations in *Allcard v Skinner* 36 Ch D 145, 185, which I have set out above. He noted that whatever the legal character of the transaction, it must constitute a disadvantage sufficiently serious to require evidence to rebut the presumption that in the circumstances of the parties' relationship, it was procured by the exercise of undue influence. Lord Scarman concluded, at p 704:

> the Court of Appeal erred in law in holding that the presumption of undue influence can arise from the evidence of the relationship of the parties without also evidence that the transaction itself was wrongful in that it constituted *an advantage taken of the person subjected to the influence which, failing proof to the contrary, was explicable only on the basis that undue influence had been exercised to procure it.* (Emphasis added)

26 Lord Scarman attached the label 'manifest disadvantage' to this second ingredient necessary to raise the presumption. This label has been causing difficulty. It may be apt enough when applied to straightforward transactions such as a substantial gift or a sale at an undervalue. But experience has now

shown that this expression can give rise to misunderstanding. The label is being understood and applied in a way which does not accord with the meaning intended by Lord Scarman, its originator.

27 The problem has arisen in the context of wives guaranteeing payment of their husband's business debts. In recent years judge after judge has grappled with the baffling question whether a wife's guarantee of her husband's bank overdraft, together with a charge on her share of the matrimonial home, was a transaction manifestly to her disadvantage.

28 In a narrow sense, such a transaction plainly ('manifestly') is disadvantageous to the wife. She undertakes a serious financial obligation, and in return she personally receives nothing. But that would be to take an unrealistically blinkered view of such a transaction. Unlike the relationship of solicitor and client or medical adviser and patient, in the case of husband and wife there are inherent reasons why such a transaction may well be for her benefit. Ordinarily, the fortunes of husband and wife are bound up together. If the husband's business is the source of the family income, the wife has a lively interest in doing what she can to support the business. A wife's affection and self-interest run hand-in-hand in inclining her to join with her husband in charging the matrimonial home, usually a jointly owned asset, to obtain the financial facilities needed by the business. The finance may be needed to start a new business, or expand a promising business, or rescue an ailing business.

29 Which, then, is the correct approach to adopt in deciding whether a transaction is disadvantageous to the wife: the narrow approach, or the wider approach? The answer is neither. The answer lies in discarding a label which gives rise to this sort of ambiguity. The better approach is to adhere more directly to the test outlined by Lindley LJ in *Allcard v Skinner* 36 Ch D 145, and adopted by Lord Scarman in *National Westminster Bank plc v Morgan* [1985] AC 686, in the passages I have cited.

30 I return to husband and wife cases. I do not think that, in the ordinary course, a guarantee of the character I have mentioned is to be regarded as a transaction which, failing proof to the contrary, is explicable only on the basis that it has been procured by the exercise of undue influence by the husband. Wives frequently enter into such transactions. There are good and sufficient reasons why they are willing to do so, despite the risks involved for them and their families. They may be enthusiastic. They may not. They may be less optimistic than their husbands about the prospects of the husbands' businesses. They may be anxious, perhaps exceedingly so. But this is a far cry from saying that such transactions as a class are to be regarded as prima facie evidence of the exercise of undue influence by husbands.

31 I have emphasised the phrase 'in the ordinary course'. There will be cases where a wife's signature of a guarantee or a charge of her share in the matrimonial home does call for explanation. Nothing I have said above is directed at such a case.

NOTE This is a helpful explanation, since much confusion had been generated in the case law concerning the meaning of 'manifestly disadvantageous' and, in particular, the relationship between this requirement and the requirement in *Barclays Bank plc v O'Brien* (*page 524*, 10.2.1) for a third party surety to be put on inquiry (that the transaction on its face was not to the financial advantage of the party alleging undue influence).

However, it follows that there is no longer a distinct 'manifest disadvantage' requirement for undue influence. Instead, in the context of presumed undue influence only, it is one aspect of the circumstances determining whether the transaction is suspicious, so that it calls for an explanation, thereby raising the presumption that the influence is 'undue'. In *Thompson v Foy* [2009] EWHC 1076 (Ch), [2009] 22 EG 119 (CS), Lewison J put the matter clearly:

99 . . . Disadvantage to the donor is not a necessary ingredient of undue influence. However, it may have an evidential value, because it is relevant to the questions whether any allegation of abuse of confidence can properly be made, and whether any abuse actually occurred.

A wife may struggle to establish both the presumption of influence and that any influence is 'undue' on the facts.

Dailey v Dailey
[2003] UKPC 65, [2003] 3 FCR 369 (PC)

Property previously held jointly had been transferred to the husband in ancillary relief proceedings. It was alleged that the transfer had occurred as a result of undue influence.

Held:

(a) Because the relationship was that of husband and wife, the wife needed to establish that an evidential presumption should arise because of the particular features of their relationship, and she had failed to do so.

(b) In any event, since the case involved a transfer by the wife of her interest in land to her husband as part of proceedings for ancillary relief and in return for a fair value, this was not a transaction in which the presumption of *undue* influence arose.

Accordingly, the wife could not succeed in setting aside the transaction unless she established actual undue influence and she had failed to do this.

LORD HOPE: 24. Care needs to be taken to distinguish between cases where the wife has entered into a transaction with her husband which is gratuitous and those where the agreement is for her to receive full value for the property or interest which she is to transfer to him. In the former case, as Lindley LJ explained in *Allcard v Skinner* (1887) 36 Ch D 145, 185, the burden is on the donee to support the gift if it is so large as not to be reasonably accounted for on the ground of the relationship. A transaction which is entered into for full value needs no such explanation. There is no presumption to rebut. That is not to say that a transaction of this type is immune from the exercise of undue influence. But if it is to be set aside on this ground it is for the party who makes the allegation to prove that undue influence was in fact exercised.

This can be contrasted with the facts and decision of the Court of Appeal in the next case where there was clear evidence of suspicion.

Goodchild v Bradbury
[2006] EWCA Civ 1868, [2007] WTLR 463 (CA)

The case was concerned with alleged undue influence affecting the gift of land by a frail and elderly gentleman (while in hospital suffering from a stroke) to his great-nephew and the subsequent sale of that land by the great-nephew to a property developer for only £1,800. The evidence was that the property developer had arranged for the solicitor, who acted for the great-nephew in the transfer of the land from his great-uncle.

Held: A presumption of influence had arisen. The great-uncle placed trust and confidence in the great-nephew, so that the great-uncle was vulnerable. The gift was not in the interests of the great-uncle, since the evidence was that the sale of adjacent land for development would devalue the great-uncle's remaining property. Accordingly, the gift was not one that could be explained by reference to the ordinary motives by which people are accustomed to act, and the presumption of 'undue' influence was raised on the facts. It was therefore for the great-nephew to show that his great-uncle was fully aware of what he was doing and that he had intended to make this gift. However, the great-uncle had not received any advice on this gift from his solicitor. Both transfers were therefore set aside for undue influence.

CHADWICK LJ: 27 The circumstances that the donor is vulnerable—in the sense that the relationship between the donor and the donee has potential for abuse—and that the gift is one which is not to be explained by the ordinary considerations by which men act lead, as a matter of public policy, as Sir Martin Nourse pointed out in *Hammond v Osborne* [*sic*], to the need for the donee to show that the donor really did understand and intend what he was doing. That is why it is necessary to show that the gift was made after full free and informed consideration. A gift which is made without informed consideration by a person vulnerable to influence, and which he could not have been expected to make if he had been acting in accordance with the ordinary motives which lead men's actions, needs to be justified on the basis that the donor knew and understood what he was doing. In this case, that requirement was not met.

NOTE Interestingly, Chadwick LJ considered the fact that the great-uncle had given evidence to the effect that the great-nephew had not asked for the transfer of this land to be no answer, based on observations in *Hammond v Osborn* [2002] EWCA Civ 885, [2002] WTLR 1125, to a claim based on undue influence. In *Hammond v Osborn*, the Court of Appeal considered that a defendant could not avoid a finding of undue influence by establishing an absence of any intention to commit a wrong, i.e. that her conduct had been unimpeachable.

10.2.2 Actual undue influence

Slade LJ in *Bank of Credit and Commerce International SA v Aboody* [1990] 1 QB 923, 967E, stated:

[W]e think that a person relying on a plea of actual undue influence must show that (a) the other party to the transaction (or someone who induced the transaction for his own benefit) had the capacity to influence the complainant; (b) the influence was exercised; (c) its exercise was undue; (d) its exercise brought about the transaction . . .

As a result of the 'cautionary note' introduced by Lord Nicholls in *Royal Bank of Scotland plc v Etridge (No. 2)* [2001] UKHL 44, [2002] 2 AC 773, it will be more difficult than had previously been thought to establish actual undue influence in the context of husband–wife relationships. However, it is clear that misrepresentations of fact will suffice for this purpose: see *UCB Corporate Services Ltd v Williams* [2002] EWCA Civ 555, [2003] 1 P & CR 12 (*page 534, later in this section*).

Royal Bank of Scotland plc v Etridge (No. 2)
[2001] UKHL 44, [2002] 2 AC 773

LORD NICHOLLS:

A cautionary note

32 I add a cautionary note, prompted by some of the first instance judgments in the cases currently being considered by the House. It concerns the general approach to be adopted by a court when considering whether a wife's guarantee of her husband's bank overdraft was procured by her husband's undue influence. Undue influence has a connotation of impropriety. In the eye of the law, undue influence means that influence has been misused. Statements or conduct by a husband which do not pass beyond the bounds of what may be expected of a reasonable husband in the circumstances should not, without more, be castigated as undue influence. Similarly, when a husband is forecasting the future of his business, and

expressing his hopes or fears, a degree of hyperbole may be only natural. Courts should not too readily treat such exaggerations as misstatements.

33 Inaccurate explanations of a proposed transaction are a different matter. So are cases where a husband, in whom a wife has reposed trust and confidence for the management of their financial affairs, prefers his interests to hers and makes a choice for both of them on that footing. Such a husband abuses the influence he has. He fails to discharge the obligation of candour and fairness he owes a wife who is looking to him to make the major financial decisions.

Since actual undue influence is akin to fraud—see *CIBC Mortgages plc v Pitt* [1994] 1 AC 200—it follows that it is not a defence, where actual undue influence has been proved, to claim that the person influenced would have entered into the transaction anyway.

UCB Corporate Services Ltd v Williams
[2002] EWCA Civ 555, [2003] 1 P & CR 12 (CA)

The defendant's husband had been a partner in a business to which the claimant had lent money, secured in part on the home jointly owned by the defendant. She alleged that she had executed this charge in favour of the claimant lender because of the undue influence of her husband. It was found as a fact that the defendant had been the victim of fraudulent misrepresentation and actual undue influence. However, the judge considered that the defendant would have signed the charge of her own free will even if she had known of the full facts and the risks involved.

Held (allowing the appeal): The fraud had deprived the defendant of the opportunity to make a free and informed choice to contract, and it was not relevant to ask whether she would have entered into the transaction in any event. The only relevant factor was that the actual undue influence was *a* factor inducing her to execute the charge. The claimant was fixed with constructive notice of the defendant's right to have the transaction set aside for undue influence and fraudulent misrepresentation.

JONATHAN PARKER LJ [with whom Peter Gibson and Kay LJJ agreed]: 86 Undue influence is exerted when improper means of persuasion are used to procure the complainant's consent to participate in a transaction, such that 'the consent thus procured ought not fairly to be treated as the expression of [the complainant's] free will' (see *Etridge* at para 7 per Lord Nicholls). In such a case, equity proceeds on the basis that the complainant did not consent to the transaction. Is that enough to give rise to an equity in the complainant to set aside the transaction as against the wrongdoer? In my judgment, it is. That conclusion seems to me to follow clearly from what Lord Browne-Wilkinson said in *CIBC v Pitt* . . . 'Actual undue influence is a species of fraud.' That being so, I cannot see any reason in principle why (for example) a husband who has fraudulently procured the consent of his wife to participate in a transaction should be able, in effect, to escape the consequences of his wrongdoing by establishing that had he not acted fraudulently, and had his wife had the opportunity to make a free and informed choice, she would have acted in the same way. The fact is that the husband's fraud deprived the wife of the opportunity to make such a choice, and, as I see it, it is that fact which founds the wife's equity (as against her husband) to set aside the transaction.

NOTE This question might equally well have been decided by reliance on the principle in *Edgington v Fitzmaurice* (1885) 29 Ch D 459 (*page 445, 9.1.2.2*) that a fraudulent misrepresentation need be *only one* of the reasons inducing the misrepresentee to contract. It need not be *the only* reason.

10.2.3 Presumed (or evidential) undue influence: protected relationships

There are two categories of presumed undue influence. Slade LJ defined them in *BCCI v Aboody* [1990] 1 QB 923, p. 953D–F:

> There are well established categories of relationship, such as a religious superior and inferior and doctor and patient where the relationship as such will give rise to the presumption (frequently referred to in argument before us as 'class 2A' cases). The relationship of husband and wife does not as such give rise to the presumption: see *National Westminster Bank Plc v Morgan* [1985] AC 686, 703b, and *Bank of Montreal v Stuart* [1911] AC 120. Nor does the normal relationship of banker and customer as such give rise to it. Nevertheless, on particular facts (frequently referred to in argument as 'class 2B' cases) relationships not falling within the class 2A category may be shown to have become such as to justify the court in applying the same presumption.

NOTES

1. The language used in *Aboody* (classes 2A and 2B) has been abandoned as a result of the *Etridge* reformulation. In addition, the presumption to which Slade LJ refers has since been interpreted to mean an evidential presumption of influence and not a presumption that the influence was undue: Lord Nicholls in *Royal Bank of Scotland plc v Etridge* (No. 2) [2001] UKHL 44, [2002] 2 AC 773 (*page 524*, 10.2.1).

2. The law recognizes that there are certain 'protected relationships' that raise an irrebuttable presumption of influence. These relationships include religious adviser and disciple: *Allcard v Skinner* (1887) 36 Ch D 145; parent and child: *Bainbrigge v Browne* (1881) Ch D 188; and solicitor and client: *Wright v Carter* [1903] 1 Ch 27. The relationship between husband and wife is not a protected relationship: *Bank of Montreal v Stuart* [1911] AC 120.

3. However, it is still necessary to prove that the influence was wrongful. The fact that the transaction is not readily explicable in view of the relationship between the parties is evidence of the existence of *undue* influence: see Lord Nicholls in *Etridge (No. 2)*, [22] and [24] (pages 529–533, 10.2.1.1.2).

10.2.4 Presumed (or evidential) undue influence: other cases established on the facts

In instances in which it is not possible to prove affirmatively the existence of actual undue influence and in which the relationship between the parties is not within one of the categories of protected relationships, it may nevertheless be possible to establish undue influence on the facts. There are two steps involved, which were explained by the Court of Appeal in *Turkey v Awadh* [2005] EWCA Civ 382, [2005] 2 FCR 7, as follows:

(a) Facts must be established that would persuade the court that the party in question was in a position to influence the will of the other in relation to the transaction, i.e. establishing a relationship of trust and confidence on the facts.

(b) The transaction must then be shown to be one that cannot be explained by reference to the ordinary motives by which people are accustomed to act, i.e. suggesting that it is unlikely that the other would have entered into it unless 'his will was overborne'.

Both steps are necessary to establish the existence of an evidential presumption of undue influence. This presumption is then capable of being rebutted by evidence to establish that there was no abuse of trust, which might include evidence that the party received independent advice from another.

Much of the pre-*Etridge* case law remains relevant in terms of identifying relationships where it has been established that the necessary trust and confidence was placed in the other party and this trust was abused.

Lloyds Bank Ltd v Bundy
[1975] QB 326 (CA)

The defendant, an elderly farmer, and his son had been customers of the claimant bank for many years. The son's company account was held at the same branch. Previously, the defendant had given a guarantee and a charge for £7,500 over his farmhouse (his only asset) to secure this company's overdraft. On that occasion, he had been advised by a solicitor that this was the most that he could afford to put into his son's business. In December 1969, the son and the assistant bank manager visited the defendant, and the assistant manager told the defendant that the bank could allow the company's overdraft to increase only if the defendant would guarantee the account up to £11,000 and give a further charge on the farmhouse to bring the total charge up to that amount. The defendant signed that charge documentation. The evidence was that the assistant manager knew that the defendant relied on him as his bank manager for advice on the transaction and that he knew that the house was the defendant's only asset. Subsequently, the bank enforced the charge and sought possession of the house.

Held: The charge should be set aside for undue influence. The bank had a conflict of interest and the defendant had received no independent advice as to the wisdom of the transaction.

SIR ERIC SACHS [with whose judgment Cairns LJ concurred]: The first and most troublesome issue which here falls for consideration is as to whether on the particular and somewhat unusual facts of the case, the bank was, when obtaining his signatures on December 17, 1969, in a relationship with Mr Bundy that entailed a duty on their part of what can for convenience be called fiduciary care . . .

Everything depends on the particular facts, and such a relationship has been held to exist in unusual circumstances as between purchaser and vendor, as between great uncle and adult nephew, and in other widely differing sets of circumstances. Moreover, it is neither feasible nor desirable to attempt closely to define the relationship, or its characteristics, or the demarcation line showing the exact transition point where a relationship that does not entail that duty passes into one that does.

On the other hand, whilst disclaiming any intention of seeking to catalogue the elements of such a special relationship, it is perhaps of a little assistance to note some of those which have in the past frequently been found to exist where the court has been led to decide that this relationship existed as between adults of sound mind. Such cases tend to arise where someone relies on the guidance or advice of another, where the other is aware of that reliance and where the person upon whom reliance is placed obtains, or may well obtain, a benefit from the transaction or has some other interest in it being concluded. In addition, there must, of course, be shown to exist a vital element which in this judgment will for convenience be referred to as confidentiality. It is this element which is so impossible to define and which is a matter for the judgment of the court on the facts of any particular case.

Confidentiality, a relatively little used word, is being here adopted, albeit with some hesitation, to avoid the possible confusion that can arise through referring to 'confidence.' Reliance on advice can in many circumstances be said to import that type of confidence which only results in a common law duty to take care—a duty which may co-exist with but is not coterminous with that of fiduciary care. 'Confidentiality' is intended to convey that extra quality in the relevant confidence that is implicit in the phrase 'confidential relationship', and may perhaps have something in common with 'confiding' and also 'confidant' when, for instance, referring to someone's 'man of affairs.' It imports some quality beyond that inherent in the confidence that can well exist between trustworthy persons who in business affairs deal with each other at arm's length. It is one of the features of this element that once it exists, influence naturally grows out of it (cf. Sir Raymond Evershed MR, *Tufton's case* [*Tufton v Sperni*] [1952] 2 TLR 516, 523) . . .

It was inevitably conceded on behalf of the bank that the relevant relationship can arise as between banker and customer. Equally, it was inevitably conceded on behalf of Mr Bundy that in the normal course of transactions by which a customer guarantees a third party's obligations, the relationship does not arise. The onus of proof lies on the customer who alleges that in any individual case the line has been crossed and the relationship has arisen.

Before proceeding to examine the position further, it is as well to dispose of some points on which confusion is apt to arise. Undue influence is a phrase which is commonly regarded—even in the eyes of a number of lawyers—as relating solely to occasions when the will of one person has become so dominated by that of another that, to use the county court judge's words, 'the person acts as the mere puppet of the dominator.' Such occasions, of course, fall within what Cotton LJ in *Allcard v Skinner*, 36 Ch D 145, 171 described as the first class of cases to which the doctrine on undue influence applies. There is, however, a second class of such cases. This is referred to by Cotton LJ as follows:

> In the second class of cases the court interferes, not on the ground that any wrongful act has in fact been committed by the donee, but on the ground of public policy, and to prevent the relations which existed between the parties and the influence arising there from being abused.

It is thus to be emphasised that as regards the second class the exercise of the court's jurisdiction to set aside the relevant transaction does *not* depend on proof of one party being 'able to dominate the other as though a puppet' nor any wrongful intention on the part of the person who gains a benefit from it; but on the concept that once the special relationship has been shown to exist, no benefit can be retained from the transaction unless it has been positively established that the duty of fiduciary care has been entirely fulfilled . . .

It is also to be noted that what constitutes fulfilment of that duty (the second issue in the case now under consideration) depends again on the facts before the court . . .

Having discussed the nature of the issues to which the county court judge should have directed his mind, it is now convenient to turn to the evidence relating to the first of them—whether the special relationship has here been shown to exist at the material time.

. . . [W]hat happened on December 17, 1969, has to be assessed in the light of the general background of the existence of the long-standing relations between the Bundy family and the bank. It not infrequently occurs in provincial and country branches of great banks that a relationship is built up over the years, and in due course the senior officials may become trusted counsellors of customers of whose affairs they have an intimate knowledge. Confidential trust is placed in them because of a combination of status, goodwill and knowledge . . .

It is, of course, plain that when Mr Head was asking Mr Bundy to sign the documents, the bank would derive benefit from the signature, that there was a conflict of interest as between the bank and Mr Bundy, that the bank gave him advice, that he relied on that advice, and that the bank knew of the reliance. The further question is whether on the evidence concerning the matters already recited there was also established that element of confidentiality which has been discussed. In my judgment it is thus established . . .

What was required to be done on the bank's behalf once the existence of that duty is shown to have been established? . . .

The documents Mr Bundy was being asked to sign could result, if the company's troubles continued, in Mr Bundy's sole asset being sold, the proceeds all going to the bank, and his being left penniless in his old age. That he could thus be rendered penniless was known to the bank—and in particular to Mr Head. That the company might come to a bad end quite soon with these results was not exactly difficult to deduce (less than four months later, on April 3, 1970, the bank were insisting that Yew Tree Farm be sold).

The situation was thus one which to any reasonably sensible person, who gave it but a moment's thought, cried aloud Mr Bundy's need for careful independent advice. Over and above the need any man has for counsel when asked to risk his last penny on even an apparently reasonable project, was the need here for informed advice as to whether there was any real chance of the company's affairs becoming viable if the documents were signed . . . without which Mr Bundy could not come to an informed judgment as to the wisdom of what he was doing.

No such advice to get an independent opinion was given; on the contrary, Mr Head chose to give his own views on the company's affairs and to take this course, though he had at trial to admit: 'I did not explain the company's affairs very fully as I had only just taken over' . . .

There remains to mention that [counsel for the Bank], whilst conceding that the relevant special relationship could arise as between banker and customer, urged in somewhat doom-laden terms that a decision taken against the bank on the facts of this particular case would seriously affect banking practice. With all respect to that submission, it seems necessary to point out that nothing in this judgment affects the duties of a bank in the normal case where it is obtaining a guarantee, and in accordance with standard practice explains to the person about to sign its legal effect and the sums involved. When, however, a bank, as in the present case, goes further and advises on more general matters germane to the wisdom of the transaction, that indicates that it may—not necessarily must—be crossing the line into the area of confidentiality so that the court may then have to examine all the facts including, of course, the history leading up to the transaction, to ascertain whether or not that line has, as here, been crossed. It would indeed be rather odd if a bank which vis-à-vis a customer attained a special relationship in some ways akin to that of a 'man of affairs'—something which can be a matter of pride and enhance its local reputation—should not, where a conflict of interest has arisen as between itself and the person advised, be under the resulting duty now under discussion. Once, as was inevitably conceded, it is possible for a bank to be under that duty, it is, as in the present case, simply a question for 'meticulous examination' of the particular facts to see whether that duty has arisen. On the special facts here it did arise and it has been broken.

NOTE In the light of *Etridge*, this case can be interpreted as turning on the proof of the trust and confidence placed by Mr Bundy in the advice of the bank manager in relation to his financial affairs. This would raise a presumption of influence, and the nature of the transaction and the circumstances (including the benefit to the bank in securing the transaction) would provide evidence to support the fact that 'undue' influence had been exercised. The bank manager was not able to show that Mr Bundy had received independent advice in order to counter the inference of undue influence and that he had known that Mr Bundy was relying solely on him for financial advice.

National Westminster Bank plc v Morgan
[1985] AC 686 (HL)

A husband and wife had a building society mortgage, but in 1977 the building society had begun proceedings for repossession. The husband's business was also in difficulty. The claimant bank agreed to refinance the building society loan on the normal condition that they obtained a charge over the property. The husband signed the charge instrument and the bank manager visited the wife to obtain her signature. The wife was concerned about the effect of the charge. She did not possess much confidence in her husband's business and did not want any security to extend to borrowing by the business. The bank manager innocently misled her into thinking that the charge was only to cover the home debt, when in fact it also covered lending to the husband's business. Later, the bank brought proceedings for possession. The wife claimed undue influence by the bank in obtaining her signature to the charge.

Held: The relationship between the wife and the bank had never gone beyond the normal business relationship of banker and customer, and therefore no presumption of undue influence arose on the facts. At this time, the transaction had to be to the manifest disadvantage of the person seeking to avoid it and the wife had benefited from the transaction because, if the bank had not given the mortgage, her home would have been repossessed by the building society. Therefore, the bank was not under any duty to ensure that she received independent advice.

LORD SCARMAN: As to the facts, I am far from being persuaded that the trial judge fell into error when he concluded that the relationship between the bank and Mrs Morgan never went beyond the normal business relationship of banker and customer. Both Lords Justices saw the relationship between the bank and Mrs Morgan as one of confidence in which she was relying on the bank manager's advice. Each took the view that the confidentiality of the relationship was such as to impose upon him a 'fiduciary duty of care.' It was his duty, in their view, to ensure that Mrs Morgan had the opportunity to make an independent and informed decision: but he failed to give her any such opportunity. They, therefore, concluded that it was a case for the presumption of undue influence.

My Lords, I believe that the Lords Justices were led into a misinterpretation of the facts by their use, as is all too frequent in this branch of the law, of words and phrases such as 'confidence,' 'confidentiality,' 'fiduciary duty.' There are plenty of confidential relationships which do not give rise to the presumption of undue influence (a notable example is that of husband and wife, *Bank of Montreal v Stuart* [1911] AC 120); and there are plenty of non-confidential relationships in which one person relies upon the advice of another, e.g. many contracts for the sale of goods . . .

The principle justifying the court in setting aside a transaction for undue influence can now be seen to have been established by Lindley LJ in *Allcard v Skinner*, 36 Ch D 145. It is not vague 'public policy' but specifically the victimisation of one party by the other. It was stated by Lindley LJ in a famous passage, at pp. 182–183:

> The principle must be examined. What then is the principle? Is it that it is right and expedient to save persons from the consequences of their own folly? or is it that it is right and expedient to save them from being victimised by other people? In my opinion the doctrine of undue influence is founded upon the second of these two principles. Courts of equity have never set aside gifts on the ground of the folly, imprudence, or want of foresight on the part of donors. The courts have always repudiated any such jurisdiction. It would obviously be to encourage folly, recklessness, extravagance and vice if persons could get back property which they foolishly made away with, whether by giving it to charitable institutions or by bestowing it on less worthy objects. On the other hand, to protect people from being forced, tricked or misled in any way by others into parting with their property is one of the most legitimate objects of all laws; and the equitable doctrine of undue influence has grown out of and been developed by the necessity of grappling with insidious forms of spiritual tyranny and with the infinite varieties of fraud.

The wrongfulness of the transaction must, therefore, be shown: it must be one in which an unfair advantage has been taken of another . . .

This brings me to *Lloyds Bank Ltd v Bundy* [1975] QB 326. It was, as one would expect, conceded by counsel for the respondent that the relationship between banker and customer is not one which ordinarily gives rise to a presumption of undue influence: and that in the ordinary course of banking business a banker can explain the nature of the proposed transaction without laying himself open to a charge of undue influence. This proposition has never been in doubt, though some, it would appear, have thought that the Court of Appeal held otherwise in *Lloyds Bank Ltd v Bundy*. If any such view has gained currency, let it be destroyed now once and for all time . . . I would prefer to avoid the term 'confidentiality' as a description of the relationship which has to be proved. In truth, as Sir Eric recognised, the relationships which may develop a dominating influence of one over another are infinitely various. There is no substitute in this branch of the law for a 'meticulous examination of the facts.'

A meticulous examination of the facts of the present case reveals that Mr Barrow never 'crossed the line.' Nor was the transaction unfair to Mrs Morgan. The bank was, therefore, under no duty to ensure that she had independent advice. It was an ordinary banking transaction whereby Mrs Morgan sought to save her home.

NOTE Both *Lloyds Bank v Bundy* and *National Westminster Bank v Morgan* are cases involving alleged undue influence by the other contracting party, i.e. the bank.

? QUESTION

Would it have helped Mrs Morgan in *National Westminster Bank v Morgan* if the transaction had been set aside for undue influence or misrepresentation?

R v Attorney-General of England and Wales
[2003] UKPC 22, [2003] EMLR 24 (PC)

It was argued, in the alternative, that the confidentiality agreement was the product of undue influence. However, the Privy Council applied *Etridge* and concluded (Lord Scott dissenting) that there was no undue influence.

LORD HOFFMANN: 21 . . . Like duress at common law, undue influence is based upon the principle that a transaction to which consent has been obtained by unacceptable means should not be allowed to stand. Undue influence has concentrated in particular upon the unfair exploitation by one party of a relationship which gives him ascendancy or influence over the other.

22 The burden of proving that consent was obtained by unacceptable means is upon the party who alleges it. Certain relationships—parent and child, trustee and beneficiary, etc.—give rise to a presumption that one party had influence over the other. That does not of course in itself involve a presumption that he unfairly exploited his influence. But if the transaction is one which cannot reasonably be explained by the relationship, that will be prima facie evidence of undue influence. Even if the relationship does not fall into one of the established categories, the evidence may show that one party did in fact have influence over the other. In such a case, the nature of the transaction may likewise give rise to a prima facie inference that it was obtained by undue influence. In the absence of contrary evidence, the court will be entitled to find that the burden of proving unfair exploitation of the relationship has been discharged.

23 The absence of independent legal advice may or may not be a relevant matter according to the circumstances. It is not necessarily an unfair exploitation of a relationship for one party to enter into a transaction with the other without ensuring that he has obtained independent legal advice. On the other hand, the transaction may be such as to give rise to an inference of undue influence even if the induced party was advised by an independent lawyer and understood the legal implications of what he was doing.

24 In the present case it is said that the military hierarchy, the strong regimental pride which R shared and his personal admiration for his commanding officer created a relationship in which the Army as an institution or the commanding officer as an individual were able to exercise influence over him. Their Lordships are content to assume that this was the case. But the question is whether the nature of the transaction was such as to give rise to an inference that it was obtained by an unfair

exploitation of that relationship. Like the Court of Appeal, their Lordships do not think that the confidentiality agreement can be so described. As in the case of duress, their Lordships think that the finding that it was an agreement which anyone who wished to serve or continue serving in the SAS could reasonably have been required to sign is fatal to such a conclusion. The reason why R signed the agreement was because, at the time, he wished to continue to be a member of the SAS. If facing him with such a choice was not illegitimate for the purposes of duress, their Lordships do not think that it could have been an unfair exploitation of a relationship which consisted in his being a member of the SAS. There seems to their Lordships to be some degree of contradiction between R's claim, in the context of duress, that he signed only because he was threatened with return to his unit and his claim, for the purposes of undue influence, that he signed because of the trust and confidence which he reposed in the Army or his commanding officer . . .

27 The legal question, however, is whether failing to provide an opportunity for obtaining legal advice made the transaction one in which the MOD had unfairly exploited its influence over R. Here it is important to note that R does not allege that he did not understand the implications of what he was being asked to do. The contract was in simple terms and the explanatory memorandum even plainer. He does say that he had originally thought that it would only prevent publication of matter which remained confidential. However, a moment's thought would have told him that this would not have prevented the publications to which he and other members of the SAS most objected, namely *The One That Got Away* and the film which followed. In any case, when he saw the actual contract he knew what it meant.

28 In these circumstances, their Lordships do not think that the absence of legal advice affected the fairness of the transaction. The most that R can say is that a lawyer might have advised him to reflect upon the matter and, as in fact he changed his mind within a fairly short time after signing, that might have led to his not signing at all. But that is a decision which he could have made without a lawyer's advice.

10.2.4.1 Rebutting the presumption of undue influence

Absence of bad faith will not be sufficient to rebut the presumption of undue influence. It is not the case that the party in the position of influence has to set out to deceive the other: *Lloyds Bank v Bundy* [1975] QB 326 and *Hammond v Osborn* [2002] EWCA Civ 885, [2002] WTLR 1125.

The case law establishes that consent needs to be 'full, free, and informed', and therefore the obvious way in which to rebut the presumption might be to point to the fact that independent legal advice has been given. However, in *R v Attorney-General of England and Wales*, the Privy Council indicated that the existence of independent legal advice may or may not be a factor, and this also appears to be the position accepted by Lord Nicholls in *Etridge*. Despite this position, it was treated as the pivotal factor in *Hammond v Osborn*, in which an elderly donor had made a number of sizeable gifts (nearly £300,000) to the defendant who was his neighbour and had been taking care of him when his health began to decline. These gifts represented more than 90 per cent of the donor's liquid assets and exposed him to a considerable tax liability. A relationship of trust and confidence was shown to exist on the facts and there was clearly something suspicious about gifts of this size in these circumstances. The defendant had not been able to rebut this presumption, since the donor had received no advice concerning the wisdom of his actions and the implications. Therefore, the gifts could not be the result of full, free, and informed thought.

It seems that any such advice would need to be quite detailed, and would need to include advice concerning the nature of the transaction and its potential implications. Thus, it will be extremely difficult to rebut the evidential presumption of undue influence, although this may be no bad thing, since a rigorous requirement to rebut the presumption will not only protect donors after the event, but also, hopefully, improve the nature and quality of the advice given, so that imprudent transactions might be avoided.

Other factors may also indicate that the presumption has been rebutted. In *De Wind (administratrix of Mrs Elsie Wedge deceased) v Wedge* [2008] EWHC 514 (Ch), the presumption of undue influence arose because there had been a sizeable gift of the proceeds of the sale of a property to a sibling who had been given a power of attorney in relation to that sale. The other sibling objected and alleged undue influence. The circumstances of the 'gift' clearly called for an explanation. However, the sibling who had received the 'gift' could rebut the presumption of undue influence, since he was able to establish that his mother had transferred the proceeds to him on discovering that his sister had borrowed large sums of money from her brother and other family members. The mother had been acting on her own initiative in an attempt to redress the balance. The judge therefore took account of a number of factors in rebutting the presumption, including the history of the relationship between the parties.

10.2.5 Undue influence exercised by a third party

Can a transaction be set aside on the ground that undue influence was exercised by a third party, e.g. if a wife gives a guarantee and charge over the matrimonial home to a bank, but later wishes to have that contract with the bank set aside on the basis that she entered into the contract only because of her husband's undue influence?

10.2.5.1 Pre-*Etridge* law

The courts traditionally laid down very limited circumstances in which such a transaction could be set aside. It first needed to be established that there was either actual undue influence by the husband, or that the presumption could be shown to arise on the facts (Class 2B). Note that husband and wife is not a Class 2A case: *Bank of Montreal v Stuart* [1911] AC 120.

In *Bank of Credit and Commerce International SA v Aboody* [1990] 1 QB 923, Slade LJ (*obiter*) explained the additional requirements before the bank could be affected by Mr Aboody's undue influence over his wife and the transaction set aside as against the bank:

> There are two distinct grounds on which the bank could be affected by Mr Aboody's action: (i) agency; and (ii) notice; although in some of the authorities cited to us these two grounds appear to have become mixed.
>
> **(i) Agency**
>
> Some confusion may have been caused by the use of the word 'agent'. We are not concerned here with the question as to whether or not the bank is vicariously responsible for the acts of Mr Aboody. The issue is whether the bank can be in any better position than Mr Aboody if, when Mr Aboody was acting on its behalf, Mr Aboody exerted (or, if this had been a class 2 case, was presumed to have exerted) undue influence. As we have made clear . . . , the undue influence is required to have brought about the transaction, and it would be inconsistent with the equitable nature of the relief for the bank not to be affected by the undue influence exerted by its agent when the transaction would not exist but for the wrongful acts of its agent. As a matter of principle, the bank in such circumstances should not be entitled to rely on the transaction and this is the view which has been taken by a series of authorities going back to the beginning of this century. The clearest statement of the principle, which we would adopt, is to be found in the judgment of Dillon LJ in *Kings North Trust Ltd v Bell* [1986] 1 WLR 119, 123:

if a creditor, or potential creditor, of a husband desires to obtain, by way of security for the husband's indebtedness, a guarantee from his wife or a charge on property of his wife and if the creditor entrusts to the husband himself the task of obtaining the execution of the relevant document by the wife, then the creditor can be in no better position than the husband himself, and the creditor cannot enforce the guarantee or the security against the wife if it is established that the execution of the document by the wife was procured by undue influence by the husband and the wife had no independent advice . . .

(ii) Notice

If a creditor has actual or constructive notice, at the time of the execution of the charge or guarantee in question, that the guarantee or charge on which it relies has been procured by the exercise of undue influence, it cannot enforce the transaction; an equity is raised against the creditor irrespective of any question of agency. Examples of the application of this principle are to be found in *Kempson v Ashbee* (1874) LR 10 Ch App 15 and *Bainbrigge v Browne* (1881) 18 Ch D 188. In the former case James LJ said, at p. 21:

> The first question, therefore, is, whether the bond of 1859 was obtained by the undue exercise of influence of the stepfather, and was it obtained under such exercise as that the knowledge of it can be imputed to [the creditor]?

What notice will be requisite will depend on the nature of the undue influence alleged. Thus, in a class 1 case (actual undue influence), the creditor must have notice of the circumstances alleged to constitute the actual exercise of the undue influence; in a class 2 case it must have notice of the circumstances from which the presumption of undue influence is alleged to arise.

NOTE On the facts in *Aboody*, there was no evidence that the bank had entrusted Mr Aboody with obtaining his wife's signature so as to have appointed him agent for the bank. However, the solicitor appointed and paid by the bank to give Mrs Aboody advice had witnessed the actual undue influence by the husband, and the Court of Appeal therefore considered that the solicitor's knowledge was to be imputed to his client, the bank.

Barclays Bank plc v O'Brien
[1994] 1 AC 180 (HL)

Mr O'Brien was a shareholder in a company and arranged an overdraft for the company with the company's bank on the basis that he would guarantee the company's indebtedness and that it would be secured by a second charge over the matrimonial home, which he jointly owned with his wife. Although the bank manager gave instructions that both husband and wife should be made aware of the nature and effect of the documents that they were signing and should be advised to take independent advice, the bank staff had not followed those instructions. Mrs O'Brien had signed the charge document at the bank without reading it. When the company's indebtedness exceeded the agreed overdraft, the bank brought proceedings to enforce the guarantee. Mrs O'Brien claimed that she had signed because of her husband's undue influence and that he had misrepresented the nature of the document, so that she thought she was signing a charge up to only £60,000 to last only three weeks, when in fact the charge covered £135,000. The Court of Appeal—[1993] QB 109—held that the husband had not exercised undue influence, but that, as a matter of policy married women providing security for their husband's debts were to be treated as a specially protected class of surety, so that the transaction could be set aside as against the bank even if it had no knowledge of any undue influence or misrepresentation and had not appointed the husband as its agent. Since the relationship giving rise to a likelihood of influence was known to the bank, the bank had a duty to take reasonable steps to ensure that the married woman understood the nature and effect of the transaction, and that the consent given was true and informed. The bank had failed in that duty, so that the charge was not enforceable beyond £60,000.

Held (on appeal to the House of Lords): Rejecting the case for special treatment, in the circumstances the bank was fixed with constructive notice of the wrongful misrepresentation made by the husband to his wife. She was therefore entitled as against the bank to set aside the legal charge on the matrimonial home.

LORD BROWNE-WILKINSON:

Undue influence, misrepresentation and third parties

Up to this point I have been considering the right of a claimant wife to set aside a transaction as against the wrongdoing husband when the transaction has been procured by his undue influence. But in surety cases the decisive question is whether the claimant wife can set aside the transaction, not against the wrongdoing husband, but against the creditor bank. Of course, if the wrongdoing husband is acting as agent for the creditor bank in obtaining the surety from the wife, the creditor will be fixed with the wrong-doing of its own agent and the surety contract can be set aside as against the creditor. Apart from this, if the creditor bank has notice, actual or constructive, of the undue influence exercised by the husband (and consequentially of the wife's equity to set aside the transaction) the creditor will take subject to that equity and the wife can set aside the transaction against the creditor (albeit a purchaser for value) as well as against the husband: see *Bainbrigge v Browne* (1881) 18 Ch D 188 and *BCCI v Aboody* [1990] 1 QB 923, 973. Similarly, in cases such as the present where the wife has been induced to enter into the transaction by the husband's misrepresentation, her equity to set aside the transaction will be enforceable against the creditor if either the husband was acting as the creditor's agent or the creditor had actual or constructive notice.

. . . In my judgment your Lordships should seek to restate the law in a form which is principled, reflects the current requirements of society and provides as much certainty as possible.

Conclusions

(a) Wives

My starting point is to clarify the basis of the law. Should wives (and perhaps others) be accorded special rights in relation to surety transactions by the recognition of a special equity applicable only to such persons engaged in such transactions? Or should they enjoy only the same protection as they would enjoy in relation to their other dealings? In my judgment, the special equity theory should be rejected. First, I can find no basis in principle for affording special protection to a limited class in relation to one type of transaction only. Second, to require the creditor to prove knowledge and understanding by the wife in all cases is to reintroduce by the back door . . . a presumption of undue influence of Class 2(A) (which has been decisively rejected) . . . Third, although Scott LJ found that there were two lines of cases one of which supported the special equity theory, on analysis although many decisions are not inconsistent with that theory the only two cases which support it are *Yerkey v Jones* (1940) 63 CLR 649 and the decision of the Court of Appeal in the present case. Finally, it is not necessary to have recourse to a special equity theory for the proper protection of the legitimate interests of wives as I will seek to show.

In my judgment, if the doctrine of notice is properly applied, there is no need for the introduction of a special equity in these types of cases. A wife who has been induced to stand as a surety for her husband's debts by his undue influence, misrepresentation or some other legal wrong has an equity as against him to set aside that transaction. Under the ordinary principles of equity, her right to set aside that transaction will be enforceable against third parties (e.g. against a creditor) if either the husband was acting as the third party's agent or the third party had actual or constructive notice of the facts giving rise to her equity. Although there may be cases where, without artificiality, it can properly be held that the husband was acting as the agent of the creditor in procuring the wife to stand as surety, such cases will be of very rare occurrence. The key to the problem is to identify the circumstances in which the creditor will be taken to have had notice of the wife's equity to set aside the transaction.

The doctrine of notice lies at the heart of equity. Given that there are two innocent parties, each enjoying rights, the earlier right prevails against the later right if the acquirer of the later right knows of the earlier right (actual notice) or would have discovered it had he taken proper steps (constructive notice). In particular, if the party asserting that he takes free of the earlier rights of another knows of certain facts which put him on inquiry as to the possible existence of the rights of that other and he fails to make such inquiry or take such other steps as are reasonable to verify whether such earlier right does or does not exist, he will have constructive notice of the earlier right and take subject to it. Therefore where a wife has agreed to stand surety for her husband's debts as a result of undue influence or misrepresentation, the creditor will take subject to the wife's equity to set aside the transaction if the circumstances are such as to put the creditor on inquiry as to the circumstances in which she agreed to stand surety.

It is at this stage that, in my view, the 'invalidating tendency' or the law's 'tender treatment' of married women, becomes relevant. As I have said above in dealing with undue influence, this tenderness of the law towards married women is due to the fact that, even today, many wives repose confidence and trust in their husbands in relation to their financial affairs. This tenderness of the law is reflected by the fact that voluntary dispositions by the wife in favour of her husband are more likely to be set aside than other dispositions by her: a wife is more likely to establish presumed undue influence of Class 2(B) by her husband than by others because, in practice, many wives do repose in their husbands trust and confidence in relation to their financial affairs. Moreover the informality of business dealings between spouses raises a substantial risk that the husband has not accurately stated to the wife the nature of the liability she is undertaking, i.e. he has misrepresented the position, albeit negligently.

Therefore, in my judgment a creditor is put on inquiry when a wife offers to stand surety for her husband's debts by the combination of two factors: (a) the transaction is on its face not to the financial advantage of the wife; and (b) there is a substantial risk in transactions of that kind that, in procuring the wife to act as surety, the husband has committed a legal or equitable wrong that entitles the wife to set aside the transaction.

It follows that, unless the creditor who is put on inquiry takes reasonable steps to satisfy himself that the wife's agreement to stand surety has been properly obtained, the creditor will have constructive notice of the wife's rights.

What, then are the reasonable steps which the creditor should take to ensure that it does not have constructive notice of the wife's rights, if any? Normally the reasonable steps necessary to avoid being fixed with constructive notice consist of making inquiry of the person who may have the earlier right (i.e. the wife) to see whether such right is asserted. It is plainly impossible to require of banks and other financial institutions that they should inquire of one spouse whether he or she has been unduly influenced or misled by the other. But in my judgment the creditor, in order to avoid being fixed with constructive notice, can reasonably be expected to take steps to bring home to the wife the risk she is running by standing as surety and to advise her to take independent advice. As to past transactions, it will depend on the facts of each case whether the steps taken by the creditor satisfy this test. However for the future in my judgment a creditor will have satisfied these requirements if it insists that the wife attend a private meeting (in the absence of the husband) with a representative of the creditor at which she is told of the extent of her liability as surety, warned of the risk she is running and urged to take independent legal advice. If these steps are taken in my judgment the creditor will have taken such reasonable steps as are necessary to preclude a subsequent claim that it had constructive notice of the wife's rights. I should make it clear that I have been considering the ordinary case where the creditor knows only that the wife is to stand surety for her husband's debts. I would not exclude exceptional cases where a creditor has knowledge of further facts which render the presence of undue influence not only possible but probable. In such cases, the creditor to be safe will have to insist that the wife is separately advised.

I am conscious that in treating the creditor as having constructive notice because of the risk of Class 2(B) undue influence or misrepresentation by the husband I may be extending the law as stated by Fry J in *Bainbrigge v Browne* (1881) 18 Ch D 188 at 197 and the Court of Appeal in the *Aboody* case [1990] 1 QB 923, 973. Those cases suggest that for a third party to be affected by constructive notice of presumed undue influence the third party must actually know of the circumstances which give rise to a presumption of undue influence. In contrast, my view is that the risk of Class 2(B) undue influence or misrepresentation is sufficient to put the creditor on inquiry. But my statement accords with the principles of notice: if the known facts are such as to indicate the possibility of an adverse claim that is sufficient to put a third party on inquiry.

If the law is established as I have suggested, it will hold the balance fairly between on the one hand the vulnerability of the wife who relies implicitly on her husband and, on the other hand, the practical problems of financial institutions asked to accept a secured or unsecured surety obligation from the wife for her husband's debts. In the context of suretyship, the wife will not have any right to disown her obligations just because subsequently she proves that she did not fully understand the transaction: she will, as in all other areas of her affairs, be bound by her obligations unless her husband has, by misrepresentation, undue influence or other wrong, committed an actionable wrong against her. In the normal case, a financial institution will be able to lend with confidence in reliance on the wife's surety obligation provided that it warns her (in the absence of the husband) of the amount of her potential liability and of the risk of standing surety and advises her to take independent advice . . .

(b) Other persons

I have hitherto dealt only with the position where a wife stands surety for her husband's debts. But in my judgment the same principles are applicable to all other cases where there is an emotional relationship between cohabitees. The 'tenderness' shown by the law to married women is not based on the marriage ceremony but reflects the underlying risk of one cohabitee exploiting the emotional involvement and trust of the other. Now that unmarried cohabitation, whether heterosexual or homosexual, is widespread in our society, the law should recognise this. Legal wives are not the only group which are now exposed to the emotional pressure of cohabitation. Therefore if, but only if, the creditor is aware that the surety is cohabiting with the principal debtor, in my judgment the same principles should apply to them as apply to husband and wife.

In addition to the cases of cohabitees, the decision of the Court of Appeal in *Avon Finance Co. Ltd v Bridger* [1985] 2 All ER 281 shows (rightly in my view) that other relationships can give rise to a similar result. In that case a son, by means of misrepresentation, persuaded his elderly parents to stand surety for his debts. The surety obligation was held to be unenforceable by the creditor inter alia because to the bank's knowledge the parents trusted the son in their financial dealings. In my judgment that case was rightly decided: in a case where the creditor is aware that the surety reposes trust and confidence in the principal debtor in relation to his financial affairs, the creditor is put on inquiry in just the same way as it is in relation to husband and wife.

Summary

I can therefore summarise my views as follows. Where one cohabitee has entered into an obligation to stand as surety for the debts of the other cohabitee and the creditor is aware that they are cohabitees: (1) the surety obligation will be valid and enforceable by the creditor unless the suretyship was procured by the undue influence, misrepresentation or other legal wrong of the principal debtor; (2) if there has been undue influence, misrepresentation or other legal wrong by the principal debtor, unless the creditor has taken reasonable steps to satisfy himself that the surety entered into the obligation freely and in knowledge of the true facts, the creditor will be unable to enforce the surety obligation because he will be fixed with constructive notice of the surety's right to set aside the transaction; (3) unless there are special exceptional circumstances, a creditor will have taken such reasonable steps to avoid being fixed with constructive notice if the creditor warns the surety (at a meeting not attended by the principal debtor) of the amount of her potential liability and of the risks involved and advises the surety to take independent legal advice.

I should make it clear that in referring to the husband's debts I include the debts of a company in which the husband (but not the wife) has a direct financial interest.

The decision of this case

Applying those principles to this case, to the knowledge of the bank Mr and Mrs O'Brien were man and wife. The bank took a surety obligation from Mrs O'Brien, secured on the matrimonial home, to secure the debts of a company in which Mr O'Brien was interested but in which Mrs O'Brien had no direct pecuniary interest. The bank should therefore have been put on inquiry as to the circumstances in which Mrs O'Brien had agreed to stand as surety for the debt of her husband . . . [T]o the knowledge of the bank (through the clerk at the Burnham branch) Mrs O'Brien signed the documents without any warning of the risks or any recommendation to take legal advice. In the circumstances the bank (having failed to take reasonable steps) is fixed with constructive notice of the wrongful misrepresentation made by Mr O'Brien to Mrs O'Brien. Mrs O'Brien is therefore entitled as against the bank to set aside the legal charge on the matrimonial home securing her husband's liability to the bank.

NOTES

1. The decision of the Court of Appeal in this case had been interpreted as suggesting that a married woman could avoid such a contract as against the bank simply by stating that she did not understand the nature and effect of what she had signed and that the bank had failed in its duty to advise her.

2. Lord Browne-Wilkinson stressed the policy considerations and the need to balance the desire to protect married women against losing their homes with the need to ensure that banks would be prepared to lend money on the security of a jointly owned home. The banks required some guidance on the steps that they needed to take in order to protect themselves against the risk of losing their security because of the undue influence of a third party. This guidance was provided first by the House of Lords in

O'Brien and was subsequently revised by the House of Lords in *Etridge* (page 549, 10.2.5.2).

3. The House of Lords made it clear that there must first be a legal wrong, i.e. undue influence (actual or presumed) or misrepresentation by the third party. The question of whether the bank would be affected by that wrong would, in practice, turn on the bank's notice of that influence, actual or constructive. The bank dealing with a wife or other cohabitee would be put on inquiry because of the likelihood of undue influence resulting from the relationship of trust and confidence where the transaction was not of obvious financial advantage to that party. The bank would then come under a duty to take the reasonable steps specified, and if it were to fail to do so, it would be affected by constructive notice of the third party's undue influence.

CIBC Mortgages plc v Pitt
[1994] 1 AC 200 (HL)

The House of Lords applied these principles, but concluded that the lender was not affected by constructive notice of the third party's undue influence.

The husband had influenced his wife into agreeing to let him borrow money on the security of the matrimonial home. This was for the purpose of enabling him to buy shares on the stock market. However, on the joint application form for the loan, they had both expressed the loan to be for the purpose of paying off the outstanding mortgage and using the balance to purchase a holiday home. The wife did not read the relevant documents, did not know the amount being borrowed, and did not receive any advice about the transaction. The husband used the money to speculate, but when he became unable to repay the mortgage payments, the lender sought possession of the matrimonial home.

Held: The lender was not fixed with constructive notice, since there was nothing in the loan agreement to put the lender on inquiry.

LORD BROWNE-WILKINSON: Applying the decision of this House in *O'Brien*, Mrs Pitt has established actual undue influence by Mr Pitt. The plaintiff will not however be affected by such undue influence unless Mr Pitt was, in a real sense, acting as agent of the plaintiff in procuring Mrs Pitt's agreement or the plaintiff had actual or constructive notice of the undue influence. The judge has correctly held that Mr Pitt was not acting as agent for the plaintiff. The plaintiff had no actual notice of the undue influence. What, then, was known to the plaintiff that could put it on inquiry so as to fix it with constructive notice?

So far as the plaintiff was aware, the transaction consisted of a joint loan to husband and wife to finance the discharge of an existing mortgage on 26 Alexander Avenue and, as to the balance, to be applied in buying a holiday home. The loan was advanced to both husband and wife jointly. There was nothing to indicate to the plaintiff that this was anything other than a normal advance to husband and wife for their joint benefit.

[Counsel] for Mrs Pitt argued that the invalidating tendency which reflects the risk of there being class 2B undue influence was, in itself, sufficient to put the plaintiff on inquiry. I reject this submission without hesitation. It accords neither with justice nor with practical common sense. If third parties were to be fixed with constructive notice of undue influence in relation to every transaction between husband and wife, such transactions would become almost impossible. On every purchase of a home in joint names, the building society or bank financing the purchase would have to insist on meeting the wife separately from her husband, advise her as to the nature of the transaction and recommend her to take legal advice separate from that of her husband. If that were not done, the financial institution would have to run the risk of a subsequent attempt by the wife to avoid her liabilities under the mortgage on the grounds of undue influence or misrepresentation. To establish the law in that sense would not benefit the average married couple and would discourage financial institutions from making the advance.

What distinguishes the case of the joint advance from the surety case is that, in the latter, there is not only the possibility of undue influence having been exercised but also the increased risk of it having in fact been exercised because, at least on its face, the guarantee by a wife of her husband's debts is not for her financial benefit. It is the combination of these two factors that puts the creditor on inquiry.

NOTES

1. The husband had clearly exercised undue influence over the wife in relation to completion of the mortgage application form, but the decision in *O'Brien* makes it clear that, where the bank has no actual knowledge, it need not specifically inquire of the wife whether she was the victim of undue influence and can rely on what is stated in an application form.

The same position will apply post-*Etridge*: *Chater v Mortgage Agency Services Number Two Ltd* [2003] EWCA Civ 490, [2004] 1 P & CR 4, in which the application form referred to the loan as being for joint purposes (home improvements) and the proceeds were issued in the form of a joint cheque to son and mother. In reality, the loan was needed for the purposes of the son's business, but the lender had no way of knowing the true position.

2. In *Royal Bank of Scotland plc v Etridge (No. 2)* [2001] UKHL 44, [2002] 2 AC 773, [19] and [30]–[31] (*page 549, 10.2.5.2*), Lord Nicholl recognized that a wife might have a variety of motives for 'conferring substantial financial benefits' on her husband and entering into guarantee transactions that might not appear to be wholly or even partly for her benefit. Whilst it might be relatively easy to establish trust and confidence in the context of a relationship between husband and wife, there could be no blanket assumption of undue influence in such cases. It was still necessary to establish that a wrong had occurred, i.e. that the husband had abused his position and

taken advantage of the trust placed in him. Thus, the notice question will be irrelevant if the husband's undue influence cannot in fact be presumed.

3. In *O'Brien*, Lord Browne-Wilkinson referred to other relationships (falling short of cohabitation) in which the lender is put on inquiry because of its knowledge of the circumstances. In *Credit Lyonnais Bank Nederland BV v Burch* [1997] 1 All ER 144, the surety was a junior employee in a company, who had done some babysitting for and was a family friend of the claimant, the main shareholder in that company. The defendant had agreed to the claimant's request that she should give a second charge over her flat to secure the unlimited liabilities of the claimant's company, although she had no financial interest in the company. The Court of Appeal held that the bank had notice of facts from which a relationship of trust and confidence could be inferred (i.e. notice of the relationship of employer and employee), and should have realized that there was a real risk that undue influence had occurred. Despite this, the bank had failed to follow the necessary steps and was therefore fixed with constructive notice of the claimant's undue influence. Millett LJ described it as 'an extreme case' and one that 'shocks the conscience of the court'. If anything, the absence of cohabitation or a sexual relationship between the parties made the transaction more inexplicable, since there were no obvious indirect benefits to the junior employee in entering into the surety transaction, whereas a wife or partner might consider that the family's livelihood required that the family home be put at risk.

4. The wife (or other surety) has the burden of pleading and proving that the lender had the necessary constructive notice of the undue influence: *Barclays Bank plc v Boulter* [1999] 1 WLR 1919.

10.2.5.2 The position post-*Etridge*

In *Royal Bank of Scotland plc v Etridge (No. 2)* [2001] UKHL 44, [2002] 2 AC 773, the House of Lords reformulated the principles applicable to surety transactions, i.e. the situation in which the party alleging undue influence is seeking to have the transaction set aside against a third party. In so doing, their Lordships explained the context for the development of legal principles and the need to balance the interests of the lenders and those giving security.

LORD BINGHAM: 2 The transactions which give rise to these appeals are commonplace but of great social and economic importance. It is important that a wife (or anyone in a like position) should not charge her interest in the matrimonial home to secure the borrowing of her husband (or anyone in a like position) without fully understanding the nature and effect of the proposed transaction and that the decision is hers, to agree or not to agree. It is important that lenders should feel able to advance money, in run-of-the-mill cases with no abnormal features, on the security of the wife's interest in the matrimonial home in reasonable confidence that, if appropriate procedures have been followed in obtaining the security, it will be enforceable if the need for enforcement arises. The law must afford both parties a measure of protection. It cannot prescribe a code which will be proof against error, misunderstanding or mishap. But it can indicate minimum requirements which, if met, will reduce the risk of error, misunderstanding or mishap to an acceptable level. The paramount need in this important field is that these minimum requirements should be clear, simple and practically operable.

LORD NICHOLLS:

The complainant and third parties: suretyship transactions

34 The problem considered in *O'Brien's* case and raised by the present appeals is of comparatively recent origin. It arises out of the substantial growth in home ownership over the last 30 or 40 years and, as part of that development, the great increase in the number of homes owned jointly by husbands and wives. More than two-thirds of householders in the United Kingdom now own their own homes. For most home-owning couples, their homes are their most valuable asset. They must surely be free, if they so wish, to use this asset as a means of raising money, whether for the purpose of the husband's business or for any other purpose. Their home is their property. The law should not restrict them in the use they may make

of it. Bank finance is in fact by far the most important source of external capital for small businesses with fewer than ten employees. These businesses comprise about 95% of all businesses in the country, responsible for nearly one-third of all employment. Finance raised by second mortgages on the principal's home is a significant source of capital for the start-up of small businesses.

35 If the freedom of home-owners to make economic use of their homes is not to be frustrated, a bank must be able to have confidence that a wife's signature of the necessary guarantee and charge will be as binding upon her as is the signature of anyone else on documents which he or she may sign. Otherwise banks will not be willing to lend money on the security of a jointly owned house or flat.

36 At the same time, the high degree of trust and confidence and emotional interdependence which normally characterises a marriage relationship provides scope for abuse. One party may take advantage of the other's vulnerability. Unhappily, such abuse does occur. Further, it is all too easy for a husband, anxious or even desperate for bank finance, to misstate the position in some particular or to mislead the wife, wittingly or unwittingly, in some other way. The law would be seriously defective if it did not recognise these realities.

37 In *O'Brien's* case this House decided where the balance should be held between these competing interests. On the one side, there is the need to protect a wife against a husband's undue influence. On the other side, there is the need for the bank to be able to have reasonable confidence in the strength of its security. Otherwise it would not provide the required money. The problem lies in finding the course best designed to protect wives in a minority of cases without unreasonably hampering the giving and taking of security. The House produced a practical solution. The House decided what are the steps a bank should take to ensure it is not affected by any claim the wife may have that her signature of the documents was procured by the undue influence or other wrong of her husband. Like every compromise, the outcome falls short of achieving in full the objectives of either of the two competing interests. In particular, the steps required of banks will not guarantee that, in future, wives will not be subjected to undue influence or misled when standing as sureties. Short of prohibiting this type of suretyship transaction altogether, there is no way of achieving that result, desirable although it is. What passes between a husband and wife in this regard in the privacy of their own home is not capable of regulation or investigation as a prelude to the wife entering into a suretyship transaction.

38 The jurisprudential route by which the House reached its conclusion in *O'Brien's* case has attracted criticism from some commentators. It has been said to involve artificiality and thereby create uncertainty in the law. I must first consider this criticism. In the ordinary course a bank which takes a guarantee security from the wife of its customer will be altogether ignorant of any undue influence the customer may have exercised in order to secure the wife's concurrence. In *O'Brien* Lord Browne-Wilkinson prayed in aid the doctrine of constructive notice. In circumstances he identified, a creditor is put on inquiry. When that is so, the creditor 'will have constructive notice of the wife's rights' unless the creditor takes reasonable steps to satisfy himself that the wife's agreement to stand surety has been properly obtained: see [1994] 1 AC 180, 196.

39 Lord Browne-Wilkinson would be the first to recognise this is not a conventional use of the equitable concept of constructive notice. The traditional use of this concept concerns the circumstances in which a transferee of property who acquires a legal estate from a transferor with a defective title may nonetheless obtain a good title, that is, a better title than the transferor had. That is not the present case. The bank acquires its charge from the wife, and there is nothing wrong with her title to her share of the matrimonial home. The transferor wife is seeking to resile from the very transaction she entered into with the bank, on the ground that her apparent consent was procured by the undue influence or other misconduct, such as misrepresentation, of a third party (her husband). She is seeking to set aside her contract of guarantee and, with it, the charge she gave to the bank.

40 The traditional view of equity in this tripartite situation seems to be that a person in the position of the wife will only be relieved of her bargain if the other party to the transaction (the bank, in the present instance) was privy to the conduct which led to the wife's entry into the transaction. Knowledge is required: see *Cobbett v Brock* (1855) 20 Beav 524, 528, 531, per Sir John Romilly MR, *Kempson v Ashbee* (1874) LR 10 Ch App 15, 21, per James LJ, and *Bainbrigge v Browne* 18 Ch D 188, 197, per Fry J. The law imposes no obligation on one party to a transaction to check whether the other party's concurrence was obtained by undue influence. But *O'Brien* has introduced into the law the concept that, in certain circumstances, a party to a contract may lose the benefit of his contract, entered into in good faith, if he ought to have known that the other's concurrence had been procured by the misconduct of a third party.

41 There is a further respect in which *O'Brien* departed from conventional concepts. Traditionally, a person is deemed to have notice (that is, he has 'constructive' notice) of a prior right when he does not actually know of it but would have learned of it had he made the requisite inquiries. A purchaser will be treated as having constructive notice of all that a reasonably prudent purchaser would have discovered. In the present type of case, the steps a bank is required to take, lest it have constructive notice that the wife's concurrence was procured improperly by her husband, do not consist of making inquiries. Rather, *O'Brien* envisages that the steps taken by the bank will reduce, or even eliminate, the risk of the wife entering into the transaction under any misapprehension or as a result of undue influence by her husband. The steps are not concerned to discover whether the wife has been wronged by her husband in this way. The steps are concerned to minimise the risk that such a wrong may be committed.

42 These novelties do not point to the conclusion that the decision of this House in *O'Brien* is leading the law astray. Lord Browne-Wilkinson acknowledged he might be extending the law: see [1994] 1 AC 180, 197. Some development was sorely needed. The law had to find a way of giving wives a reasonable measure of protection, without adding unreasonably to the expense involved in entering into guarantee transactions of the type under consideration. The protection had to extend also to any misrepresentations made by a husband to his wife. In a situation where there is a substantial risk the husband may exercise his influence improperly regarding the provision of security for his business debts, there is an increased risk that explanations of the transaction given by him to his wife may be misleadingly incomplete or even inaccurate.

43 The route selected in *O'Brien* ought not to have an unsettling effect on established principles of contract. *O'Brien* concerned suretyship transactions. These are tripartite transactions. They involve the debtor as well as the creditor and the guarantor. The guarantor enters into the transaction at the request of the debtor. The guarantor assumes obligations. On the face of the transaction the guarantor usually receives no benefit in return, unless the guarantee is being given on a commercial basis. Leaving aside cases where the relationship between the surety and the debtor is commercial, a guarantee transaction is one-sided so far as the guarantor is concerned. The creditor knows this. Thus the decision in *O'Brien* is directed at a class of contracts which has special features of its own. That said, I must at a later stage in this speech return to the question of the wider implications of the *O'Brien* decision.

The threshold: when the bank is put on inquiry

44 In *O'Brien* the House considered the circumstances in which a bank, or other creditor, is 'put on inquiry'. Strictly this is a misnomer. As already noted, a bank is not required to make inquiries. But it will be convenient to use the terminology which has now become accepted in this context. The House set a low level for the threshold which must be crossed before a bank is put on inquiry. For practical reasons the level is set much lower than is required to satisfy a court that, failing contrary evidence, the court may infer that the transaction was procured by undue influence. Lord Browne-Wilkinson said [1994] 1 AC 180, 196:

> Therefore in my judgment a creditor is put on inquiry when a wife offers to stand surety for her husband's debts by the combination of two factors: (a) the transaction is on its face not to the financial advantage of the wife; and (b) there is a substantial risk in transactions of that kind that, in procuring the wife to act as surety, the husband has committed a legal or equitable wrong that entitles the wife to set aside the transaction.

In my view, this passage, read in context, is to be taken to mean, quite simply, that a bank is put on inquiry whenever a wife offers to stand surety for her husband's debts.

45 The Court of Appeal, comprising Stuart-Smith, Millett and Morritt LJJ, interpreted this passage more restrictively. The threshold, the court said, is somewhat higher. Where condition (a) is satisfied, the bank is put on inquiry if, but only if, the bank is aware that the parties are cohabiting or that the particular surety places implicit trust and confidence in the principal debtor in relation to her financial affairs: see *Royal Bank of Scotland plc v Etridge (No. 2)* [1998] 4 All ER 705, 719.

46 I respectfully disagree. I do not read (a) and (b) as factual conditions which must be proved in each case before a bank is put on inquiry. I do not understand Lord Browne-Wilkinson to have been saying that, in husband and wife cases, whether the bank is put on inquiry depends on its state of knowledge of the parties' marriage, or of the degree of trust and confidence the particular wife places in her husband in relation to her financial affairs. That would leave banks in a state of considerable uncertainty in a situation where it is important they should know clearly where they stand. The test should be simple and clear and easy to apply in a wide range of circumstances. I read (a) and (b) as Lord Browne-Wilkinson's broad explanation of the reason why a creditor is put on inquiry when a wife offers to stand surety for her husband's debts. These are the two factors which, taken together, constitute the underlying rationale.

47 The position is likewise if the husband stands surety for his wife's debts. Similarly, in the case of unmarried couples, whether heterosexual or homosexual, where the bank is aware of the relationship: see Lord Browne-Wilkinson in *O'Brien's* case, at p 198. Cohabitation is not essential. The Court of Appeal rightly so decided in *Massey v Midland Bank plc* [1995] 1 All ER 929: see Steyn LJ, at p 933.

48 As to the type of transactions where a bank is put on inquiry, the case where a wife becomes surety for her husband's debts is, in this context, a straightforward case. The bank is put on inquiry. On the other side of the line is the case where money is being advanced, or has been advanced, to husband and wife jointly. In such a case the bank is not put on inquiry, unless the bank is aware the loan is being made for the husband's purposes, as distinct from their joint purposes. That was decided in *CIBC Mortgages plc v Pitt* [1994] 1 AC 200.

49 Less clear cut is the case where the wife becomes surety for the debts of a company whose shares are held by her and her husband. Her shareholding may be nominal, or she may have a minority shareholding or an equal shareholding with her husband. In my view the bank is put on inquiry in such cases, even when the wife is a director or secretary of the company. Such cases cannot be equated with joint loans. The shareholding interests, and the identity of the directors, are not a reliable guide to the identity of the persons who actually have the conduct of the company's business.

NOTES

1. Lord Nicholls confirms that, once undue influence by the husband has been affirmatively established, or been established on the evidential presumption in circumstances in which the wife placed trust and confidence in her husband, the bank will be put on inquiry whenever a wife (and other persons falling within the scope of this principle) stands as surety for her husband's debts or those of a company in which her husband is involved. This is clear and important in terms of certainty, because lenders will know that, in all such situations, they will need to follow the appropriate steps in order to avoid being fixed with constructive notice of the husband's undue influence.

2. However, the surety contract will not be set aside without proof of a 'wrong' by a third party, and it appears that the evaluation of indirect benefits to a wife giving a charge over the matrimonial home in order to secure the liabilities of her husband's company is now relevant to the wife's burden

of establishing that the evidential presumption of undue influence has arisen (i.e. that there is something in the transaction that calls for an explanation): see comments of Lord Nicholls in *Etridge*, [27]–[33] (*page 549*, 10.2.5.2). For example, what weight should be given to the indirect benefits that a wife receives from the husband's company and the fact that the family may be financially dependent on its success? Does it follow that, where the wife has given a second charge on the matrimonial home to secure the company debts, she will struggle to establish that the charge is a transaction calling for an explanation? Technically, only if there is something suspicious in the transaction will the husband's undue influence be established and will there be any question of implications for the lender and whatever steps it may or may not have taken. In practice, the lender may not wish to take the risk in relation to matters of which it may have little knowledge, and so may assume that it is put on inquiry in any non-

commercial relationship and take the appropriate steps to avoid the loss of its security.

To this extent, at least in practical terms, *Etridge* may alter the protection granted to sureties, since *O'Brien* required a transaction that was financially disadvantageous (in order to establish the presumption of the wrong) *and* had also considered the question of whether the transaction was in the financial interests of the wife to be relevant to the steps the bank needed to take. *Etridge* requires that the lender's steps be taken anyway and provides that questions such as joint benefit—*CIBC v Pitt*—or indirect benefits relate only to whether there can be presumed undue influence in the first place. It would follow that there is no such restriction if the claim is based on actual undue influence or misrepresentation by the husband. In such instances, the lender will always be put on enquiry in non-commercial surety transactions.

10.2.5.3 The steps that the lender needs to take once it has been put on inquiry

In *Royal Bank of Scotland plc v Etridge (No. 2)* [2001] UKHL 44, [2002] 2 AC 773, the House of Lords explained, in precise terms, the steps required by a lender to avoid being fixed with constructive notice of the husband's undue influence. The balance between the competing interests has moved towards bank protection. In general terms, the bank needs to take only reasonable steps to satisfy itself that the practical implications of the proposed transaction have been explained to the wife and can rely on confirmation from the bank's solicitor that this advice has been given, unless the bank knows or ought to realize that the appropriate advice was not received.

LORD NICHOLLS:

The steps a bank should take

50 The principal area of controversy on these appeals concerns the steps a bank should take when it has been put on inquiry. In *O'Brien* [1994] 1 AC 180, 196–197 Lord Browne-Wilkinson said that a bank can reasonably be expected to take steps to bring home to the wife the risk she is running by standing as surety and to advise her to take independent advice . . . For the future a bank satisfies these requirements if it insists that the wife attend a private meeting with a representative of the bank at which she is told of the extent of her liability as surety, warned of the risk she is running and urged to take independent legal advice. In exceptional cases the bank, to be safe, has to insist that the wife is separately advised.

51 The practice of the banks involved in the present cases, and it seems reasonable to assume this is the practice of banks generally, is not to have a private meeting with the wife. Nor do the banks themselves take any other steps to bring home to the wife the risk she is running. This has continued to be the practice since the decision in *O'Brien's* case. Banks consider they would stand to lose more than they would gain by holding a private meeting with the wife. They are, apparently, unwilling to assume the responsibility of advising the wife at such a meeting. Instead, the banking practice remains, as before, that in general the bank requires a wife to seek legal advice. The bank seeks written confirmation from a solicitor that he has explained the nature and effect of the documents to the wife.

52 Many of the difficulties which have arisen in the present cases stem from serious deficiencies, or alleged deficiencies, in the quality of the legal advice given to the wives . . . On behalf of the wives it has

been submitted that under the current practice the legal advice is often perfunctory in the extreme and, further, that everyone, including the banks, knows this. Independent legal advice is a fiction. The system is a charade. In practice it provides little or no protection for a wife who is under a misapprehension about the risks involved or who is being coerced into signing. She may not even know the present state of her husband's indebtedness.

53 My Lords, it is plainly neither desirable nor practicable that banks should be required to attempt to discover for themselves whether a wife's consent is being procured by the exercise of undue influence of her husband. This is not a step the banks should be expected to take. Nor, further, is it desirable or practicable that banks should be expected to insist on confirmation from a solicitor that the solicitor has satisfied himself that the wife's consent has not been procured by undue influence. As already noted, the circumstances in which banks are put on inquiry are extremely wide. They embrace every case where a wife is entering into a suretyship transaction in respect of her husband's debts. Many, if not most, wives would be understandably outraged by having to respond to the sort of questioning which would be appropriate before a responsible solicitor could give such a confirmation. In any event, solicitors are not equipped to carry out such an exercise in any really worthwhile way, and they will usually lack the necessary materials. Moreover, the legal costs involved, which would inevitably fall on the husband who is seeking financial assistance from the bank, would be substantial. To require such an intrusive, inconclusive and expensive exercise in every case would be an altogether disproportionate response to the need to protect those cases, presumably a small minority, where a wife is being wronged.

54 The furthest a bank can be expected to go is to take reasonable steps to satisfy itself that the wife has had brought home to her, in a meaningful way, the practical implications of the proposed transaction. This does not wholly eliminate the risk of undue influence or misrepresentation. But it does mean that a wife enters into a transaction with her eyes open so far as the basic elements of the transaction are concerned.

55 This is the point at which, in the *O'Brien* case, the House decided that the balance between the competing interests should be held. A bank may itself provide the necessary information directly to the wife. Indeed, it is best equipped to do so. But banks are not following that course. Ought they to be obliged to do so in every case? I do not think Lord Browne-Wilkinson so stated in *O'Brien*. I do not understand him to have said that a personal meeting was the only way a bank could discharge its obligation to bring home to the wife the risks she is running. It seems to me that, provided a suitable alternative is available, banks ought not to be compelled to take this course. Their reasons for not wishing to hold a personal meeting are understandable. Commonly, when a bank seeks to enforce a security provided by a customer, it is met with a defence based on assurances alleged to have been given orally by a branch manager at an earlier stage: that the bank would continue to support the business, that the bank would not call in its loan, and so forth. Lengthy litigation ensues. Sometimes the allegations prove to be well founded, sometimes not. Banks are concerned to avoid the prospect of similar litigation which would arise in guarantee cases if they were to adopt a practice of holding a meeting with a wife at which the bank's representative would explain the proposed guarantee transaction. It is not unreasonable for the banks to prefer that this task should be undertaken by an independent legal adviser.

56 I shall return later to the steps a bank should take when it follows this course. Suffice to say, these steps, together with advice from a solicitor acting for the wife, ought to provide the substance of the protection which *O'Brien* intended a wife should have. Ordinarily it will be reasonable that a bank should be able to rely upon confirmation from a solicitor, acting for the wife, that he has advised the wife appropriately.

57 The position will be otherwise if the bank knows that the solicitor has not duly advised the wife or, I would add, if the bank knows facts from which it ought to have realised that the wife has not received the appropriate advice. In such circumstances the bank will proceed at its own risk . . .

The content of the legal advice

61 . . . [I]n the present type of case it is not for the solicitor to veto the transaction by declining to confirm to the bank that he has explained the documents to the wife and the risks she is taking upon herself. If the solicitor considers the transaction is not in the wife's best interests, he will give reasoned advice to the wife to that effect. But at the end of the day the decision on whether to proceed is the decision of the client, not the solicitor. A wife is not to be precluded from entering into a financially unwise transaction if, for her own reasons, she wishes to do so.

62 That is the general rule. There may, of course, be exceptional circumstances where it is glaringly obvious that the wife is being grievously wronged. In such a case the solicitor should decline to act further. In *Wright v Carter* [1903] 1 Ch 27, 57–58. Stirling LJ approved Farwell J's observations in *Powell v Powell* [1900] 1 Ch 243, 247. But he did so by reference to the extreme example of a poor man divesting himself of all his property in favour of his solicitor.

63 In *Royal Bank of Scotland plc v Etridge (No. 2)* [1998] 4 All ER 705, 722, para 49, the Court of Appeal said that if the transaction is 'one into which no competent solicitor could properly advise the wife to enter', the availability of legal advice is insufficient to avoid the bank being fixed with constructive notice. It follows from the views expressed above that I am unable to agree with the Court of Appeal on this point.

[Lord Nicholls set out the advice a solicitor can be expected to give and continued:]

Independent advice

69 I turn next to the much-vexed question whether the solicitor advising the wife must act for the wife alone . . .

71 . . . [A] simple and clear rule is needed, preferably of well nigh universal application.

. . .

74 In my view . . . , [t]he advantages attendant upon the employment of a solicitor acting solely for the wife do not justify the additional expense this would involve for the husband. When accepting instructions to advise the wife the solicitor assumes responsibilities directly to her, both at law and professionally. These duties, and this is central to the reasoning on this point, are owed to the wife alone. In advising the wife the solicitor is acting for the wife alone. He is concerned only with her interests. I emphasise, therefore, that in every case the solicitor must consider carefully whether there is any conflict of duty or interest and, more widely, whether it would be in the best interests of the wife for him to accept instructions from her. If he decides to accept instructions, his assumption of legal and professional responsibilities to her ought, in the ordinary course of things, to provide sufficient assurance that he will give the requisite advice fully, carefully and conscientiously. Especially so, now that the nature of the advice called for has been clarified. If at any stage the solicitor becomes concerned that there is a real risk that other interests or duties may inhibit his advice to the wife he must cease to act for her.

Agency

. . .

77 . . . Confirmation from the solicitor that he has advised the wife is one of the bank's preconditions for completion of the transaction. But it is central to this arrangement that in advising the wife the solicitor is acting for the wife and no one else. The bank does not have, and is intended not to have, any knowledge of or control over the advice the solicitor gives the wife. The solicitor is not accountable to the bank for the advice he gives to the wife. To impute to the bank knowledge of what passed between the solicitor and the wife would contradict this essential feature of the arrangement. The mere fact that, for its own purposes, the bank asked the solicitor to advise the wife does not make the solicitor the bank's agent in giving that advice.

78 In the ordinary case, therefore, deficiencies in the advice given are a matter between the wife and her solicitor. The bank is entitled to proceed on the assumption that a solicitor advising the wife has done his job properly. I have already mentioned what is the bank's position if it knows this is not so, or if it knows facts from which it ought to have realised this is not so.

79 I now return to the steps a bank should take when it has been put on inquiry and for its protection is looking to the fact that the wife has been advised independently by a solicitor.

(1) One of the unsatisfactory features in some of the cases is the late stage at which the wife first became involved in the transaction. In practice she had no opportunity to express a view on the identity of the solicitor who advised her. She did not even know that the purpose for which the solicitor was giving her advice was to enable him to send, on her behalf, the protective confirmation sought by the bank. Usually the solicitor acted for both husband and wife.

Since the bank is looking for its protection to legal advice given to the wife by a solicitor who, in this respect, is acting solely for her, I consider the bank should take steps to check directly with the wife the name of the solicitor she wishes to act for her. To this end, in future the bank should communicate directly with the wife, informing her that for its own protection it will require written confirmation from a solicitor, acting for her, to the effect that the solicitor has fully explained to her the nature of the documents and the practical implications they will have for her. She should be told that the purpose of this requirement is that thereafter she should not be able to dispute she is legally bound by the documents once she has signed them. She should be asked to nominate a solicitor whom she is willing to instruct to advise her, separately from her husband, and act for her in giving the necessary confirmation to the bank. She should be told that, if she wishes, the solicitor may be the same solicitor as is acting for her husband in the transaction. If a solicitor is already acting for the husband and the wife, she should be asked whether she would prefer that a different solicitor should act for her regarding the bank's requirement for confirmation from a solicitor.

The bank should not proceed with the transaction until it has received an appropriate response directly from the wife.

(2) Representatives of the bank are likely to have a much better picture of the husband's financial affairs than the solicitor. If the bank is not willing to undertake the task of explanation itself, the bank must provide the solicitor with the financial information he needs for this purpose. Accordingly it should become routine practice for banks, if relying on confirmation from a solicitor for their protection, to send to the solicitor the necessary financial information. What is required must depend on the facts of the case. Ordinarily this will include information on the purpose for which the proposed new facility has been requested, the current amount of the husband's indebtedness, the amount of his current overdraft facility, and the amount and terms of any new facility. If the bank's request for security arose from a written application by the husband for a facility, a copy of the application should be sent to the solicitor. The bank will, of course, need first to obtain the consent of its customer to this circulation of confidential information. If this consent is not forthcoming the transaction will not be able to proceed.

(3) Exceptionally there may be a case where the bank believes or suspects that the wife has been misled by her husband or is not entering into the transaction of her own free will. If such a case occurs the bank must inform the wife's solicitors of the facts giving rise to its belief or suspicion.

(4) The bank should in every case obtain from the wife's solicitor a written confirmation to the effect mentioned above.

NOTES

1. Prior to this decision, solicitors had been placed in the unenviable position of having to decide whether, having explained the position to the wife, they should decline to act and veto the transaction on the basis that the transaction was seriously disadvantageous to the wife. In particular, if it was a transaction that 'no competent solicitor could properly advise the wife to enter', the accepted view was that the solicitor should decline to act: *per* Stuart-Smith LJ in the Court of Appeal in *Royal Bank of Scotland v Etridge (No. 2)* [1998] 4 All ER 705. This statement was seized upon by counsel in subsequent cases to support an argument that the lender had failed to take the necessary steps. For example, in *Credit Lyonnais Bank Nederland BV v Burch* [1997] 1 All ER 144, the Court of Appeal held that the transaction was of such a nature that the solicitor should have refused to act for the employee when she persisted with it after being advised not to do so. The difficulty was that the vast majority of these surety cases appear to be unwise with hindsight and, arguably, the balance had swung too far against the solicitor, who can be sued for negligent advice where there is a causal link between the advice and the giving of the security. The House of Lords has redressed this in *Etridge*, at [62], by accepting that, in the absence of a 'glaringly obvious' 'grievous wrong' and on the assumption that appropriate advice has been received, the onus is on the wife to decide whether to proceed with the transaction. It would be far too paternalistic to place a more onerous policing responsibility on solicitors.

2. Whilst the wife cannot be wholly protected from undue influence and its consequences, she will at least have received a warning and have received appropriate advice. If there are deficiencies in the advice given, she will have a claim against the solicitor, although the solicitor is protected by the clear guidance of the House of Lords concerning the nature of the advice to be given and the circumstances in which that advice can be given, e.g. where there is a potential conflict of interest. The decision has therefore resolved many of the issues examined in the case law since *O'Brien*. One obvious negative is that what is required of solicitors is more demanding, which means that it will clearly take more time and therefore lead to increased costs.

On the other hand, the lender is entitled to rely on the fact that the solicitor has properly advised the wife unless it is aware, or ought to be aware, that this is not the case.

Overall, this would appear to be a more satisfactory attempt to strike the right balance. The only 'loser' would appear to be the wife, who, as a result of the decision of the House of Lords in *Etridge*, has lost the benefit of the presumption of undue influence and must prove on the evidence that the husband has committed a wrong, albeit that this may not prove too problematical where the transaction is wholly in favour of the husband.

10.2.6 The effect of undue influence

The effect of undue influence is to render the contract voidable, so that both parties are to be restored to their original positions.

However, in exceptional circumstances, it may be possible to sever the objectionable parts of an instrument. In *Barclays Bank v Caplan* [1998] FLR 532, in relation to the original charge covering a home loan and guaranteeing a loan to one of Mr Caplan's companies, the bank had taken reasonable steps and accordingly was not fixed with constructive notice of any undue influence exercised by Mr Caplan over his wife. Nevertheless, the bank had later obtained Mrs Caplan's signature to a side-letter extending that charge to cover guarantees of Mr Caplan's debts in respect of a further three companies for an unlimited amount. In relation to the side-letter, the bank had failed to ensure that the necessary steps were taken. The judge confirmed that only rarely would it be possible to sever objectionable parts of an instrument following a finding of undue influence, since such a finding vitiated consent. On these facts, although it was clear that Mrs Caplan had freely consented to the first guarantee, she had not been properly advised in relation to the other guarantees. In addition, it was possible to sever these objectionable parts of the instrument without effectively rewriting it. Accordingly, the first loan was validly secured.

It is clear from *Dunbar Bank plc v Nadeem* [1998] 3 All ER 876 that, if undue influence is established, the victim needs to make restitution of all that he has obtained from the transaction. The judge at first instance interpreted this to mean that Mrs Nadeem had to make restitution to the bank for the benefit that she had received from the use of the money advanced for the purchase of a longer lease of the matrimonial home—namely, one half of the money advanced with interest. However, the Court of Appeal held *obiter* (since there was a finding that there had been no undue influence) that, if the wife had been entitled to have half the charge set aside, then it was her beneficial interest in the lease for which she needed to make restitution. That would involve restoring her beneficial interest to her husband, which would have resulted in the bank enjoying the beneficial interest in the whole of the lease.

10.2.6.1 What is the position if restoration to the original positions cannot be achieved?

Cheese v Thomas
[1994] 1 WLR 129 (CA)

In 1990, the 86-year-old claimant and the defendant, his great-nephew, had agreed to purchase a house. The purchase price was £83,000. The house was purchased in the sole name of the defendant, with the claimant contributing £43,000 and the defendant £40,000, by means of a building society mortgage on the property. It was agreed that the claimant would live in the property until his death and then the defendant would be solely entitled. The defendant failed to keep up the mortgage payments. The claimant claimed that the transaction should be set aside for undue influence and wanted the return of his £43,000. The house was sold for only £55,000.

Held: Where it was not possible to restore the parties to their exact original positions, the court would look at the circumstances, and do what was fair and just in practical terms. Since the purpose of the transaction had been to benefit both parties, it would not be just for the defendant to suffer the entire loss of market value. Each party should receive a proportionate share of the net proceeds (i.e. 43:40).

10.3 Unconscionability

10.3.1 Protection for the 'poor and ignorant'

Outside the statutory context—see further *Poole's Textbook on Contract Law*, 15th edn (Oxford University Press, 2021), 10.3.4—and the doctrines of duress and undue influence, English law intervenes in contracts on grounds of unconscionability only in very limited circumstances based on characteristics possessed by a victim that necessarily mean that he requires protection, coupled with a taking advantage of the position by the other party.

Earl of Aylesford v Morris
(1873) 8 Ch App 484

As soon as he reached majority, Aylesford borrowed from Morris at a rate of over 60 per cent interest in order to pay off the large debts that he had incurred in his minority. He had an allowance of less than £500 a year at that time, but would have been entitled on his father's death to a large inheritance. Lord Selborne LC referred to a presumption of fraud arising from the circumstances or conditions of the parties, with weakness on one side and extortion or advantage taken of that weakness on the other side.

LORD SELBORNE LC: Fraud does not here mean deceit or circumvention; it means an unconscientious use of the power arising out of these circumstances and conditions; and when the relative position of the parties is such as *prima facie* to raise this presumption, the transaction cannot stand unless the person claiming the benefit of it is able to repel the presumption by contrary evidence, proving it to have been in point of fact fair, just, and reasonable.

NOTES

1. *Fry v Lane* (1888) 40 Ch D 312 involved sales by 'poor and ignorant' persons at considerable undervalues without independent advice. Kay J held that, in those circumstances, a court of equity could set aside the sales. He said, at p. 322:

The result of the decisions is that where a purchase is made from a poor and ignorant man at a considerable undervalue, the vendor having no independent advice, a Court of Equity will set aside the transaction . . .

The circumstances of poverty and ignorance of the vendor, and absence of independent advice, throw upon the purchaser, when the transaction is impeached, the onus of proving, in Lord Selborne's words, that the purchase was 'fair, just, and reasonable.'

2. In *Cresswell v Potter* [1978] 1 WLR 255, Megarry J extended the scope of the principle in *Fry v Lane* by holding that a lady who was a Post Office telephonist and who sought to avoid a conveyance of her rights in the matrimonial home to her husband was 'poor and ignorant'. He said, at pp. 257–9:

The judge [Kay J in *Fry v Lane*] thus laid down three requirements. What has to be considered is, first, whether the plaintiff is poor and ignorant; second, whether the sale was at a considerable undervalue; and third, whether the vendor had independent advice. I am not, of course, suggesting that these are the only circumstances which will suffice; thus there may be circumstances of oppression or abuse of confidence which will invoke the aid of equity. But in the present case only these three requirements are in point . . . I must therefore consider whether the three requirements laid down in *Fry v Lane* are satisfied.

I think that the plaintiff may fairly be described as falling within whatever is the modern equivalent of 'poor and ignorant.' Eighty years ago, when *Fry v Lane* was decided, social conditions were very different from those which exist today. I do not, however, think that the principle has changed, even though the euphemisms of the 20th century may require the word 'poor' to be replaced by 'a member of the lower income group' or the like, and the word 'ignorant' by 'less highly educated.' The plaintiff has been a van driver for a tobacconist, and is a Post Office telephonist. The evidence of her means is slender. The defendant told me that the plaintiff probably had a little saved, but not much; and there was evidence that her earnings were about the same as the defendant's, and

that these were those of a carpenter. The plaintiff also has a legal aid certificate.

In those circumstances I think the plaintiff may properly be described as 'poor' in the sense used in *Fry v Lane*, where it was applied to a laundryman who, in 1888, was earning £1 a week. In this context, as in others, I do not think that 'poverty' is confined to destitution. Further, although no doubt it requires considerable alertness and skill to be a good telephonist. I think that a telephonist can properly be described as 'ignorant' in the context of property transactions in general and the execution of conveyancing documents in particular. I have seen and heard the plaintiff giving evidence, and I have reached the conclusion that she satisfies the requirements of the first head . . . [The second question was whether the sale was at a 'considerable undervalue'. Megarry J found that it was.]

As for independent advice, from first to last there is no suggestion that the plaintiff had any. The defendant, his solicitor and the inquiry agent stood on one side: on the other the plaintiff stood alone. This was, of course, a conveyancing transaction, and English land law is notoriously complex. I am certainly not saying that other transactions, such as hire-purchase agreements, are free from all difficulty. But the authorities put before me on setting aside dealings at an undervalue all seem to relate to conveyancing transactions, and one may wonder whether the principle is confined to such transactions, and, if so, why. I doubt whether the principle is restricted in this way; and it may be that the explanation is that it is in conveyancing matters that, by long usage, it is regarded as usual, and, indeed, virtually essential, for the parties to have the services of a solicitor. The absence of the aid of a solicitor is thus, as it seems to me, of especial significance if a conveyancing matter is involved. The more usual it is to have a solicitor, the more striking will be his absence, and the more closely will the courts scrutinise what was done.

. . . [Counsel for the defendant] points out that the plaintiff was not bereft of possible legal assistance; for on or before July 28, 1959, when she was having difficulty in getting some furniture and effects from Slate Hall, she consulted a Colchester firm of solicitors . . . If she wanted legal advice, he said, this shows that she knew how to get it. However, what matters, I think, is not whether she could have obtained proper advice but whether in fact she had it; and she did not. Nobody, of course, can be compelled to obtain independent advice: but I do not think that someone who seeks to uphold what is, to him, an advantageous conveyancing transaction can do so merely by saying that the other party could have obtained independent advice, unless something has been done to bring to the notice of that other party the true nature of the transaction and the need for advice . . .

At the end of the day, my conclusion is that this transaction cannot stand. In my judgment the plaintiff has made out her case, and so it is for the defendant to prove that the transaction was 'fair, just, and reasonable.' This he has not done . . .

Is the crucial factor in this case 'ignorance' rather than poverty, since considerable emphasis was placed on the fact that a conveyancing document is not easy for the layman to understand without legal advice?

3. Since there is no precise definition of 'poor and ignorant', situations covered by this principle are unclear.

4. In *Watkin v Watson-Smith* (1986) The Times, 3 July, Hirst J held *obiter* (because the contract was vitiated for mistake) that an old man aged 80 who signed a contract to sell his bungalow for £2,950 instead of £29,500 could have relied on the principle in *Fry v Lane* even though he was not 'poor and ignorant'. The judge held that the desire for a quick sale and the old man's age, together with the accompanying diminution of his mental capacity and judgement, could suffice in place of 'poor and ignorant'.

Thus, *Fry v Lane* appears not to be restricted to the traditional three requirements and it may be that, if this were desired, it could be extended to cover a general concept of 'unconscionability'. However, an imbalance in bargaining position will not be sufficient on its own. In *Alec Lobb v Total Oil GB Ltd* [1985] 1 WLR 173, Dillon LJ held that it had to be shown that the conduct of the stronger party was oppressive or unconscionable. This was confirmed in *Hart v O'Connor* [1985] AC 1000, in which it was stressed that there must be victimization, i.e. the stronger party must take advantage of the weaker party. A more general doctrine of unconscionability is recognized in other jurisdictions, e.g. see the decision of the High Court of Australia in *Commercial Bank of Australia Ltd v Amadio* (1983) 151 CLR 447.

5. In *Boustany v Pigot* (1993) 69 P & CR 298—noted by Cartwright (1993) 109 LQR 530—the Privy Council set aside a transaction entered into by an ageing lady whose affairs were normally conducted by her cousin, and stressed that it is not sufficient that the transaction is unreasonable or unfair. What is required is unconscionable conduct in the sense of an 'abuse' of position. Unconscionability cannot simply be inferred from the existence of the *Fry v Lane* requirements.

6. *Greenwood Forest Products (UK) Ltd v Roberts*, QBD (Leeds), 12 March 2010, concerned a claim to set aside a transaction as an unconscionable bargain.

STEPHEN MORRIS QC [sitting as a deputy High Court judge]: 269. A transaction may be set aside as an unconscionable bargain, where three conditions are established.

270. First, one party suffers from a disability or serious disadvantage. Whilst originally the categories of disability were established as illiteracy, lack of education, age and poverty, more recently this condition has been stated more widely as arising where 'one party has been at a serious disadvantage to the other, whether through poverty, or ignorance, or lack of advice or otherwise, so that circumstances existed of which unfair advantage could be taken' (per Peter Millett QC in *Alec Lobb Ltd v Total Oil (Great Britain) Ltd* [1983] 1 WLR 87 at 94–95, subsequently approved by the Court of Appeal in *Credit Lyonnais Bank Nederland NV . . .* and *Jones v Morgan* [2001] EWCA Civ 995)

271. Secondly, the transaction is 'overreaching and oppressive', such that it shocks the conscience of the court, and not merely hard or improvident: see *Alec Lobb*, supra at 95.

272. Thirdly, the other, stronger, party must have acted unconscionably, in the sense that he acted in a morally reprehensible manner. This will be shown where the stronger party knowingly took advantage of the weaker party's disabling condition or circumstances: see *Boustany v Pigott* (1995) 69 P & CR 298 and *Irvani v Irvani* [2000] 1 Lloyd's Rep 412.

273. Once these three conditions are established, the burden then shifts to the stronger party to show that the transaction is fair, just and reasonable.

274. As regards the effect of independent legal advice, this may well defeat an allegation of unconscionable bargain, either because the receipt of such advice means that there is no relevant disability or disadvantage (as in *Jones v Morgan* [2001] EWCA Civ 995 at [40]) or because it cannot be said that the stronger party 'took advantage' of the weaker party or because the transaction was fair, just and reasonable, as the weaker party was fully aware of what he was doing . . .

The allegation of unconscionable bargain failed on the facts of the case, because the party alleged to be suffering the disability was an experienced businessman who received advice and the transactions were not at an undervalue or oppressive. In addition, the other party had not 'knowingly taken advantage'.

Such claims are often included as a final submission in addition to claims based on misrepresentation, duress, or undue influence, and these may be more easily established, because their ingredients are conceptually more certain.

7. In *Evans v Lloyd* [2013] EWHC 1725 (Ch), [2013] WTLR 1137, [2013] 2 P & CR DG21, Wynne Evans, had lived with the Lloyds from the age of 14 and worked for them on the farm. A close relationship had been established and he was regarded as a member of the family. Wynne had left school at an early age and it was accepted that he had little worldly experience. He made a gift of all of his property to the Lloyds without the benefit of legal advice. It was alleged that since the Lloyds had knowingly taken advantage of Wynne's position, the gifts should be set aside on the

basis of unconscionability. While the judge accepted that the gifts were disadvantageous to Wynne in a practical sense and that he could be classed as 'poor' and 'ignorant', he rejected the unconscionability claim on the basis that it was not possible to say that Mr and Mrs Lloyd were morally culpable.

8. In *Alec Lobb (Garages) Ltd v Total Oil GB Ltd*, the conduct of the defendants was not unconscionable. Mr Lobb's bargaining position was weak because of his financial difficulties, but he did have clear legal advice throughout and rejected it in favour of entering into an unfavourable leaseback arrangement, which included a tie to purchase the defendants' petrol for 21 years. The price and rent charged were either at or below market price, the defendants had been reluctant, and the initiative for financial assistance from them had come from Mr Lobb.

10.3.2 The relationship between undue influence and unconscionability

In *Credit Lyonnais Bank Nederland BV v Burch* [1997] 1 All ER 144, Nourse LJ considered that the principle in *Fry v Lane* was capable of being adapted 'to different transactions entered into in changing circumstances', and he considered it to be arguable that, applying this principle, Miss Burch could have had the legal charge set aside on the ground of unconscionability. However, he did not decide the case on this basis because there had been no argument on this ground in the court below.

It is interesting, however, that Nourse LJ considered that unconscionability was directly material to the undue influence issue, but see Birks and Chin, 'On the nature of undue influence', in Beatson and Friedmann (eds.) *Good Faith and Fault in Contract Law* (Clarendon Press, 1995).

Millett LJ appeared to consider that, in both cases, the impropriety by one party, e.g. taking advantage of the situation, could be inferred from the harshness of the terms of the transaction. He stated, at 152j–153d, that:

> Miss Burch did not seek to have the transaction set aside as a harsh and unconscionable bargain. To do so she would have had to show not only that the terms of the transaction were harsh or oppressive, but that 'one of the parties to it has imposed the objectionable terms in a morally reprehensible manner, that is to say, in a way which affects his conscience' (see *Multiservice Bookbinding Ltd v Marden* [1978] 2 All ER 489 at 502, [1979] Ch 84 at 110 per Browne-Wilkinson J and *Alec Lobb (Garages) Ltd v Total Oil GB Ltd* [1983] 1 All ER 944 at 961, [1983] 1 WLR 87 at 95, where I pointed out that there must be some impropriety, both in the conduct of the stronger party and in the terms of the transaction itself, but added that 'the former may often be inferred from the latter in the absence of an innocent explanation').
>
> In the present case, the bank did not obtain the guarantee directly from Miss Burch. It was provided to the bank by Mr Pelosi, who obtained it from Miss Burch by the exercise of undue influence. In such a context, the two equitable jurisdictions to set aside harsh and unconscionable bargains and to set aside transactions obtained by undue influence have many similarities. In either case it is necessary to show that the conscience of the party who seeks to uphold the transaction was affected by notice, actual or constructive, of the impropriety by which it was obtained by the intermediary, and in either case the court may in a proper case infer the presence of the impropriety from the terms of the transaction itself.

In *Dunbar Bank plc v Nadeem* [1998] 3 All ER 876, Millett LJ again appeared to recognize a link between unconscionability and undue influence. He stated, at 884:

> The court of equity is a court of conscience. It sets aside transactions obtained by the exercise of undue influence because such conduct is unconscionable. But however the present case is analysed, whether

as a case of actual or presumed influence, the influence was not undue. It is impossible, in my judgment, to criticise Mr Nadeem's conduct as unconscionable.

Chen-Wishart [1997] CLJ 60, 62–3, argued that 'unconscionability should be recognised as the informing principle at the root of the *O'Brien* formulation' and that unconscionability would give *O'Brien* 'a sound theoretical basis'.

Portman Building Society v Dusangh
[2000] 2 All ER (Comm) 221 (CA)

The defendant, then aged 72 and regarded as poor and illiterate, had been granted a 25-year mortgage on his property. The advance was to be used by the defendant's son in order to purchase a supermarket business. The son was the guarantor of the mortgage and had agreed to pay it off. The son defaulted and the building society sought possession. The defendant alleged, inter alia, that the transaction had been entered into as a result of undue influence and it was an unconscionable bargain (relying on *Credit Lyonnais v Burch*). These defences were rejected and the defendant appealed.

Held (on appeal): The requirements to establish undue influence and unconscionability were similar, but none had been established in this case.

WARD LJ:

Does *Barclays Bank v O'Brien* apply?

That was a case concerned with undue influence. A person who has been induced to enter into a transaction by undue influence of another (the wrongdoer) is entitled to set that transaction aside as against the wrongdoer. Where a person is unconscionably prevailed upon by the wrongdoer to enter into a transaction, then equity again allows rescission. There is some interesting argument for merging the two doctrines: see the article by David Capper 'Undue Influence and Unconscionability: A Rationalisation' (1998) 114 LQR 479, from which I gratefully acknowledge having drawn some of these ideas. Professors Birks and Chin in their article 'On the Nature of Undue Influence', in J Beatson and D Friedmann (eds) *Good Faith and Fault in Contract Law* (1995) would preserve the distinction. They see undue influence as being 'plaintiff-sided' and concerned with the weakness of the claimant's consent owing to an excessive dependence upon the defendant, and unconscionability as being 'defendant-sided' and concerned with the defendant's exploitation of the claimant's vulnerability. I do not find it necessary to resolve this debate. I am content to accept for present purposes the judgment of Mason J in the *Commercial Bank of Australia Ltd* case (1983) 151 CLR 447 at 461:

> Historically, courts have exercised jurisdiction to set aside contracts and other dealings on a variety of equitable grounds. They include fraud, misrepresentation, breach of fiduciary duty, undue influence and unconscionable conduct. In one sense they all constitute species of unconscionable conduct on the part of a party who stands to receive a benefit under a transaction which, in the eye of equity, cannot be enforced because to do so would be inconsistent with equity and good conscience. But relief on the ground of 'unconscionable conduct' is usually taken to refer to the class of case in which a party makes unconscientious use of his superior position or bargaining power to the detriment of a party who suffers from some special disability or is placed in some special situation of disadvantage, e.g . . . . an unfair contract made by taking advantage of a person who is seriously affected by intoxicating drink. Although unconscionable conduct in this narrow sense bears some resemblance to the doctrine of undue influence, there is a difference between the two. In the latter the will of the innocent party is not independent and voluntary because it is overborne. In the former the will of the innocent party, even if independent and voluntary, is the result of the disadvantageous position in which he is placed and of the other party unconscientiously taking advantage of that position.

In *Barclays Bank plc v O'Brien* [1993] 4 All ER 417 at 428, [1994] 1 AC 180 at 195 Lord Browne Wilkinson said:

> A wife who has been induced to stand as a surety for her husband's debts by his undue influence, misrepresentation *or some other legal wrong* has an equity as against him to set aside that transaction. Under the ordinary principles of equity, her right to set aside her transaction will be enforceable against third parties (e.g. against a creditor) if . . . the third party had actual or constructive notice of the facts giving rise to her equity. (My emphasis)

Unconscionable conduct is 'some other legal wrong'

In *Burch's* case [1997] 1 All ER 144 at 153 Millett LJ said:

> . . . the two equitable jurisdictions to set aside harsh and unconscionable bargains and to set aside transactions obtained by undue influence have many similarities. In either case it is necessary to show that the conscience of the party who seeks to uphold the transaction was affected by notice, actual or constructive, of the impropriety by which it was obtained by the intermediary, and in either case the court may in a proper case infer the presence of the impropriety from the terms of the transaction itself . . .

Unconscionable conduct by the building society itself

This became the primary basis of the appeal. The case was that the father was entitled to set aside the charge directly against the building society as an unconscionable bargain. It was submitted that the transaction was unconscionable in the light of knowledge possessed by the building society that the borrower was a retired man of 72 years who might well be dead before the expiry of the 25-year term of the borrowing, whose existing mortgage was only £4,000 and whose ability to repay the £33,750 lent on this occasion could not be supported by his income even when supplemented by his son. It was an improvident transaction which put the borrower's home at risk. Furthermore, had the society's own policies been followed, then the society would have learnt that the borrower was illiterate with a poor understanding of English, had no need to mortgage his own home and did so solely for his son's benefit. The case put was:

> In summary the advance was unconscionable in that [the father] by reason of his age, illiteracy, lack of education and poverty was under some serious disadvantage affecting his ability to protect himself . . .

The first defendant's argument derives from an application of the judgment of Kay J in *Fry v Lane* . . . (1888) 40 Ch D 312 at 322, as modernised by Megarry J in *Cresswell v Potter* [1978] 1 WLR 255n. The first defendant concentrates on the three elements there referred to: first, the 'poor and ignorant man'; second, the considerable undervalue/manifest disadvantage; and, third, the lack of independent advice.

It may be that the absence of legal advice is not so much an essential free-standing requirement, but rather a powerful factor confirming the suspicion of nefarious dealing which the presence of advice would serve to dispel. As Megarry J pointed out in *Cresswell's* case [1978] 1 WLR 255 at 258, the authorities seem to have related to conveyancing transactions where, by long usage, it was regarded as usual, and, indeed, virtually essential, for the parties to have the services of a solicitor. He added, and I agree: 'The more usual it is to have a solicitor, the more striking will be his absence, and the more closely will the courts scrutinise what was done.' Assuming, however, that all three elements are required and that they are all established then, as Millett LJ put it in *Burch's* case [1997] 1 All ER 144 at 152: 'The transaction gives rise to grave suspicion. It cries out for an explanation.' The burden then falls on the beneficiary of the transaction to show, in Lord Selborne LC's words, that it was 'fair, just and reasonable'.

I venture to think, however, that when Kay J cast the onus on the purchaser, he had in mind no more than that the facts would give rise to an evidential presumption of wrongdoing. I tend to agree with Capper (p. 496) that that means that:

> ... where a sufficiently bad case of relational inequality and transactional imbalance exists, one which almost speaks for itself that there has been unconscionability, then unconscionable conduct can be inferred unless the defendant can offer an explanation to displace it. To hold that a presumption arising upon the mere coincidence of the first two elements of the doctrine of unconscionability would be to deny the effect of high authority clearly stating that unconscionable conduct is an essential part of this doctrine.

> That is the weakness of the first defendant's case. What the first defendant's approach on the facts of this case appears to me to miss is this: for the lending by the building society to be unconscionable, it must, as is implicit in the very word, be against the conscience of the lender—he must act with no conscience, with no moral sense that he is doing wrong. Making all the assumptions in the first defendant's favour of the frailties of the father, the lack of wisdom in taking on this large commitment with limited income, the real risk of foreclosure, the failure by the building society to follow its own rules, even an assumption that the building society in those heady days of rising property prices was lending money almost irresponsibly, none of that, in my judgment, gets near to establishing morally reprehensible conduct on its part. The family wanted to raise money: the building society was prepared to lend it. One shakes one's head, but with sadness and with incredulity at the folly of it all, alas not with moral outrage. I am afraid the moral conscience of the court has not been shocked. That is an end of the matter.

> Accordingly the appeal should be dismissed.

NOTE Unfortunately, the Court of Appeal does not give an in-depth assessment of the relationship between undue influence and unconscionability, but does accept that they are very similar in their requirements. Ward LJ was prepared to rely on the statement of Mason J in *Commercial Bank of Australia Ltd v Amadio* (1983) 151 CLR 447, although this also identifies a fundamental distinction between the doctrines without resolving its effect, if any, in terms of outcome.

Chapter 11

Illegality

Contracts may be illegal or void on grounds of public policy.

11.1 Illegal contracts

In *Patel v Mirza* [2016] UKSC 42 Lord Toulson summarized the principles governing illegality in English law.

> LORD TOULSON: 1. 'No court will lend its aid to a man who founds his cause of action upon an immoral or an illegal act.' So spoke Lord Mansfield in *Holman v Johnson* (1775) 1 Cowp 341, 343, ushering in two centuries and more of case law about the extent and effect of this maxim. He stated that the reason was one of public policy:
>
> > If, from the plaintiff's own stating or otherwise, the cause of action appears to arise ex turpi causa, or the transgression of a positive law of this country, there the court says he has no right to be assisted. It is upon that ground the court goes; not for the sake of the defendant, but because they will not lend their aid to such a plaintiff. So if the plaintiff and defendant were to change sides, and the defendant was to bring his action against the plaintiff, the latter would then have the advantage of it; for where both are equally in fault, potior est conditio defendentis.
>
> 2. Illegality has the potential to provide a defence to civil claims of all sorts, whether relating to contract, property, tort or unjust enrichment, and in a wide variety of circumstances.
>
> 3. Take the law of contract. A contract may be prohibited by a statute; or it may be entered into for an illegal or immoral purpose, which may be that of one or both parties; or performance according to its terms may involve the commission of an offence; or it may be intended by one or both parties to be performed in a way which will involve the commission of an offence; or an unlawful act may be committed in the course of its performance. The application of the doctrine of illegality to each of these different situations has caused a good deal of uncertainty, complexity and sometimes inconsistency.
>
> 4. *Holman v Johnson* involved a claim for the price of goods which the plaintiff sold to the defendant in Dunkirk, knowing that the defendant's purpose was to smuggle the goods into England. The plaintiff was met with a defence of illegality. The defence failed. Lord Mansfield held that knowledge on the part of the plaintiff that the defendant intended to smuggle the goods did not affect the plaintiff's entitlement to recover the price of the goods, since he was not himself involved in the smuggling. By contrast, in *Pearce v Brooks* (1866) LR 1 Ex 213 a claim by a coachbuilder against a prostitute for the hire of what was described in the law report as an 'ornamental brougham' was held to be unenforceable for illegality after the jury found that the defendant hired it for the purpose of prostitution and that the plaintiff knew

that this was her purpose. It would seem that the difference between *Holman v Johnson* and *Pearce v Brooks* had to do with the type of goods supplied, because in both cases the plaintiff knew that the defendant was entering into the contract for an illegal or immoral purpose. In *JM Allan (Merchandising) Ltd v Cloke* [1963] 2 QB 340, 348, Lord Denning MR endeavoured to rationalise the authorities by saying that 'active participation debars, but knowledge by itself does not'. However, the Law Commission commented in its discussion of the subject in its Consultation Paper on *Illegal Transactions: the Effect of Illegality on Contracts and Trusts*, LCCP 154 (1999) that the case law lacks clear guidance on what amounts to 'participation' in this context.

5. It is unclear to what extent the doctrine of illegality applies to a contract whose object includes something which is in some respect unlawful, or the performance of which will involve some form of illegality, but not in a way which is central to the contract. In *St John Shipping Corpn v Joseph Rank Ltd* [1957] 1 QB 267, 288, Devlin J said:

> If a contract has as its whole object the doing of the very act which the statute prohibits, it can be argued that you can hardly make sense of a statute which forbids an act and yet permits to be made a contract to do it; that is a clear implication. But unless you get a clear implication of that sort, I think that a court ought to be very slow to hold that a statute intends to interfere with the rights and remedies given by the ordinary law of contract. Caution in this respect is, I think, especially necessary in these times when so much of commercial life is governed by regulations of one sort or another, which may easily be broken without wicked intent.

6. As to illegality in the manner of performance of a contract, Mance LJ observed in *Hall v Woolston Hall Leisure Ltd* [2001] 1 WLR 225, 246, that the conceptual basis on which a contract not illegal nor prohibited at the time of its formation may become unenforceable due to the manner of its performance is open to debate. In *Anderson Ltd v Daniel* [1924] 1 KB 138 a claim for the price of goods was held to be unenforceable because the seller had failed to give the buyer an invoice containing details which the seller was required to give him by statute. In the *St John Shipping* case Devlin J rejected the interpretation that the claim in *Anderson Ltd v Daniel* failed because in the course of performing a legal contract the plaintiff had done something illegal. The correct interpretation, he said, was that 'the way in which the contract was performed turned it into the sort of contract that was prohibited by the statute': [1957] 1 QB 267, 284. In the *St John Shipping* case the claim was for freight under a charter party. In the course of taking on bunkers the vessel was overloaded and the master thereby committed an offence, for which he was prosecuted and fined £1,200. The extra freight earned by the overloading was £2,295 and to that extent the ship owners stood to profit from their wrong. The cargo owners refused to pay that part of the freight. Devlin J rejected their defence. He held that since the goods had been delivered safely, the ship owners had proved all that they needed. He was not prepared to construe the statute as having the effect of making the contract prohibited. If it had been otherwise, the ship owners would not have been entitled to any freight and would therefore have suffered an additional penalty, much greater than that provided for by Parliament, for conduct which might have been unintentional.

7. In *Ashmore, Benson, Pease and Co Ltd v Dawson* [1973] 1 WLR 828 the Court of Appeal adopted a different approach. Manufacturers of heavy engineering equipment entered into a contract of carriage with road hauliers. There was nothing illegal in the formation of the contract, but the hauliers overloaded the vehicles which were to transport the load, in breach of road traffic regulations, and one of the lorries toppled over during the journey as a result of the driver's negligence. The manufacturers' transport manager was present when the goods were loaded and was aware of the overloading. A claim by the manufacturers for the cost of repair of the damaged load was rejected on grounds of illegality. The Court of Appeal did not perform the same analysis as had Devlin J in the *St John Shipping* case. They held simply that the manufacturers participated in the illegal performance of the contract and were therefore barred from suing on it.

NOTES

1. This extract identifies the different ways in which illegality can affect a contract.

(a) A statute or the common law may render the making of a contract unlawful, in which case the contract is illegal in its formation.

(b) In performing the contract, one of the parties may commit an act which is unlawful. The questions here are whether illegal performance renders the entire contract illegal, whether illegal performance does not affect the contract as a whole but prevents the illegal performer from enforcing rights under the contract, or whether the illegal performance is purely peripheral and leaves rights unaffected.

(c) Where benefits have been conferred under a contract which is illegal or cannot be enforced, there is a further question of whether the innocent party has the right to recover benefits transferred under the contract.

2. *Patel v Mirza* was a decision of a specially constituted nine-member Supreme Court, to resolve irreconcilable statements of principle in a series of earlier Supreme Court decisions, *Hounga v Allan* [2014] UKSC 47, *Les Laboratories Servier v Apotex Inc.* [2014] UKSC 55 and *Bilta (UK) Ltd (in liquidation) v Nazir* [2015] UKSC 23. The key question was whether, as regards point (b) and (c) above, the fact that the claimant had to rely upon illegality to make a claim should automatically bar the claim (as seemingly held by the House of Lords in *Tinsley v Milligan* [1994] 1 AC 340) or whether wider principles should be applicable. By a 6:3 majority the Supreme Court ruled in favour of the latter flexible approach.

11.1.1 Contracts prohibited by statute

11.1.1.1 Express prohibition

Re Mahmoud & Ispahani
[1921] 2 KB 716 (CA)

In 1919, under regulations issued under the Defence of the Realm Act 1914, an Order was made prohibiting the purchase or sale of linseed oil without a licence. The claimant, who had a licence, sold linseed oil to the defendant, having been incorrectly assured by the defendant that the defendant also had the required licence. The defendant subsequently refused to accept delivery of the linseed oil, pleading that, owing to his own absence of a licence, the contract was illegal.

Held: Since the defendant had no licence, the contract of sale was prohibited under the Order. It was therefore illegal and unenforceable by the claimant.

ATKIN LJ: When the Court has to deal with the question whether a particular contract or class of contract is prohibited by statute, it may find an express prohibition in the statute, or it may have to infer the prohibition from the fact that the statute imposes a penalty upon the person entering into that class of contract. In the latter case one has to examine very carefully the precise terms of the statute imposing the penalty upon the individual. One may find that the statute imposes a penalty upon an individual, and yet does not prohibit the contract if it is made with a party who is innocent of the offence which is created by the statute . . . [H]ere it appears to me to be plain that this particular contract was expressly prohibited by the terms of the Order which imposes the necessity of a compliance with the licence . . . When one looks at the licence one finds an express prohibition against the plaintiff selling to the defendant as the latter had not a licence.

Illegality

11

NOTE If a contract is illegal by statute, neither party can enforce it. The innocence of the claimant in *Re Mahmoud & Ispahani* did not allow him to recover damages under the illegal contract.

Mohamed v Alaga & Co. (a firm)
[2000] 1 WLR 1815 (CA)

The claimant, a leading member of the Somali community in the UK, had sought payment under an alleged oral contract that he claimed he had made with the defendant firm of solicitors. The claimant alleged that, in return for his assistance in introducing Somali refugees whom the defendant would seek to represent, the defendant was to pay him half of the fees that it received from the Legal Aid Board in connection with the refugees' applications for asylum. However, the Solicitors' Practice Rules, made under s. 31 of the Solicitors Act 1974, expressly prohibited solicitors from entering into such contracts and from making such payments. The defendant therefore claimed that even if there were any such agreement, it was illegal and unenforceable.

    Held: The contract was illegal because it was expressly prohibited by legislation. It made no difference that the claimant did not know of the prohibition.

    The Court rejected a claim for recovery on a *quantum meruit* for the value of the services in introducing clients because this would be tainted with the same illegality affecting the alleged contract. However, the Court of Appeal did grant leave for the claim to be amended to allow recovery on a *quantum meruit* for the translation services provided by the claimant, since he was blameless and, since this service could be separated from the illegal introduction fee, no public policy would be infringed by allowing him to recover for translation services.

An innocent party may have some remedy if he can establish the existence of a collateral undertaking by the other party to ensure that the contract is not illegal. However, this will be of use only in exceptional cases.

Strongman (1945) Ltd v Sincock
[1955] 2 QB 525 (CA)

Builders entered into a contract with the architect owner whereby they were to supply materials and carry out work at his premises. The architect owner orally promised to obtain all of the licences required under the Defence (General) Regulations 1939, SI 1939/927. Licences were obtained for £2,150 of authorized costs, but the total value of the work carried out was £6,905. The architect had paid £2,900 and sought to avoid paying the balance by arguing that performance of the contract was illegal. The builders sought the unpaid sum or damages for breach of the warranty that the architect would obtain any necessary licences.

    Held: Although the builders could not recover the contract price, since the contract was prohibited by the Regulations, the assurance amounted to a warranty or collateral promise by the architect that he would obtain any necessary licences, and they were entitled to damages for breach of that promise.

? QUESTION

Can this case be distinguished from *Re Mahmoud & Ispahani* (earlier in this section)?

11.1.1.2 Contracts impliedly illegal in formation

The courts are reluctant to hold that a statute impliedly prohibits the making of a contract.

Archbolds (Freightage) Ltd v S. Spanglett Ltd
[1961] 1 QB 374 (CA)

The defendants owned a number of vans with 'C' licences, enabling them, under the Road and Rail Traffic Act 1933, to carry their own goods, but not the goods of others, for payment. The claimants, believing that the defendants had 'A' licences enabling them to carry goods for others for reward, employed the defendants to carry whisky from Leeds to London. The whisky was stolen en route owing to the driver's negligence and the claimants claimed damages for the loss. The defendants pleaded illegality, in that their van did not have an 'A' licence as required by statute.

Held: This contract was not prohibited either expressly or impliedly by statute, and therefore was not illegal at its inception; rather, it was performed by the defendants in an illegal manner. Since the claimants were unaware of the true facts and were innocent parties, they could recover damages for breach of contract.

PEARCE LJ: If a contract is expressly or by necessary implication forbidden by statute, or if it is ex facie illegal, or if both parties know that though ex facie legal it can only be performed by illegality or is intended to be performed illegally, the law will not help the plaintiffs in any way that is a direct or indirect enforcement of rights under the contract. And for this purpose both parties are presumed to know the law.

The first question, therefore, is whether this contract of carriage was forbidden by statute. The two cases on which the defendants mainly rely are *In re an Arbitration between Mahmoud and Ispahani* [1921] 2 KB 716 and *J. Dennis & Co. Ltd v Munn* [1949] 2 KB 327. In both those cases the plaintiffs were unable to enforce their rights under contracts forbidden by statute . . . In neither case could the plaintiff bring his contract within the exception that alone would have made its subject-matter lawful, namely, by showing the existence of a licence. Therefore, the core of both contracts was the mischief expressly forbidden by the statutory order and the statutory regulation respectively.

In *Mahmoud's* case the object of the order was to prevent (except under licence) a person buying and a person selling, and both parties were liable to penalties. A contract of sale between those persons was therefore expressly forbidden. In *Dennis's* case the object of the regulation was to prevent (except under licence) owners from performing building operations, and builders from carrying out the work for them. Both parties were liable to penalties and a contract between these persons for carrying out an unlawful operation would be forbidden by implication.

The case before us is somewhat different. The carriage of the plaintiffs' whisky was not as such prohibited; the statute merely regulated the means by which carriers should carry goods. Therefore this contract was not expressly forbidden by the statute.

Was it then forbidden by implication? The Road and Rail Traffic Act, 1933, section 1, says: 'no person shall use a goods vehicle on a road for the carriage of goods . . . except under licence,' and provides that such use shall be an offence. Did the statute thereby intend to forbid by implication all contracts whose performance must on all the facts (whether known or not) result in a contravention of that section? . . .

The object of the Road and Rail Traffic Act, 1933, was not (in this connection) to interfere with the owner of goods or his facilities for transport, but to control those who provided the transport with a view to promoting its efficiency. Transport of goods was not made illegal but the various licence holders were prohibited from encroaching on one another's territory, the intention of the Act being to provide an orderly and comprehensive service. Penalties were provided for those licence holders who went outside the bounds of their allotted spheres. These penalties apply to those using the vehicle but not to the goods owner. Though the latter could be convicted of aiding and abetting any breach, the restrictions were not aimed at him. Thus a contract of carriage was not impliedly forbidden by the statute.

This view is supported by common sense and convenience. If the other view were held it would have far-reaching effects. For instance, if a carrier induces me (who am in fact ignorant of any illegality) to entrust goods to him and negligently destroys them, he would only have to show that (though unknown to me) his licence had expired, or did not properly cover the transportation, or that he was uninsured, and I should then be without a remedy against him. Or, again, if I ride in a taxicab and the driver leaves me stranded in some deserted spot, he would only have to show that he was (though unknown to me) unlicensed or uninsured, and I should be without remedy. This appears to me an undesirable extension of the implications of a statute.

? QUESTION

What would the position have been in *Archbolds v Spanglett* if the claimants had known that there was no 'A' licence?

NOTE *Re Mahmoud & Ispahani* (*page 567, 11.1.1.1*) was distinguished because the statute in that case expressly prohibited the sale to an unlicensed person. In *Archbolds v Spanglett*, the carriage of the whisky was not prohibited, but the statute did regulate the manner of the transportation. This contract was not illegal from the beginning, but was performed by the defendants in an illegal way.

11.1.2 Contracts that are illegal in their performance

Anderson Ltd v Daniel
[1924] 1 KB 138 (CA)

It was an offence to sell artificial fertilizers without giving the buyer an invoice stating the percentages of certain chemicals in the fertilizers. No invoice was issued by the seller and, since the object of the statute in requiring the invoice was to protect purchasers, this could be achieved only by rendering the sale without an invoice illegal.

SCRUTTON LJ: When the policy of the Act in question is to protect the general public or a class of persons by requiring that a contract shall be accompanied by certain formalities or conditions, and a penalty is imposed on the person omitting those formalities or conditions, the contract and its performance without those formalities or conditions is illegal, and cannot be sued upon by the person liable to the penalties . . . Now here the provision as to the invoice is clearly to protect a particular class of the public—namely, the people who buy artificial manures. The seller is required to give on or before or as soon as possible after delivery of the article an invoice stating the percentages of its ingredients. The vendors did not do so. It follows from the principle that I have stated that when they come to sue for the price they can be met with the defence that the way in which they performed the contract was illegal . . . [T]he giving of the invoice is part of the performance of the contract . . . [T]he vendors have committed an illegality in the performance of their contract, and that as the statutory provision was enacted for the protection of a class, including the purchaser who is now being sued, the vendors cannot recover the price.

NOTE The illegal performer of a contract that has become illegal because of the way in which it has been performed cannot enforce that contract. Thus, in *Anderson Ltd v Daniel*, the seller could not claim the price of the fertilizers because his failure to present the invoice had rendered the contract illegal.

However, it is important to consider the prohibition that was, in fact, intended by the statute and whether this renders performance of the contract illegal.

St John Shipping Corporation v Joseph Rank Ltd
[1957] 1 QB 267

It was an offence under the Merchant Shipping (Safety and Load Line Conventions) Act 1932 to load a ship to such an extent that the load line was below water. The claimant charterers overloaded the ship and caused the load line to be submerged. The master was prosecuted and fined £1,200 for this offence. The defendants, who were the consignees of part of the cargo, withheld some of the freight due (equivalent to the amount due on the overloaded cargo) and argued that the claimants had performed the charter in an illegal manner.

Held: The claimants could recover the freight due. Illegal performance of a contract did not render the contract illegal unless the contract as performed was one that the statute meant to prohibit. This Act merely punished infringements of the load line rules and did not prohibit the contract of carriage, which was performed in breach of the rules.

DEVLIN J: There are two general principles. The first is that a contract which is entered into with the object of committing an illegal act is unenforceable. The application of this principle depends upon proof of the intent, at the time the contract was made, to break the law; if the intent is mutual the contract is not enforceable at all, and, if unilateral, it is unenforceable at the suit of the party who is proved to have it. This principle is not involved here. Whether or not the overloading was deliberate when it was done, there is no proof that it was contemplated when the contract of carriage was made. The second principle is that the court will not enforce a contract which is expressly or impliedly prohibited by statute. If the contract is of this class it does not matter what the intent of the parties is; if the statute prohibits the contract, it is unenforceable whether the parties meant to break the law or not. A significant distinction between the two classes is this. In the former class you have only to look and see what acts the statute prohibits; it does not matter whether or not it prohibits a contract; if a contract is deliberately made to do a prohibited act, that contract will be unenforceable. In the latter class, you have to consider not what acts the statute prohibits, but what contracts it prohibits; but you are not concerned at all with the intent of the parties; if the parties enter into a prohibited contract, that contract is unenforceable.

Two questions are involved. The first—and the one which hitherto has usually settled the matter—is: does the statute mean to prohibit contracts at all? But if this be answered in the affirmative, then one must ask: does this contract belong to the class which the statute intends to prohibit? For example, a person is forbidden by statute from using an unlicensed vehicle on the highway. If one asks oneself whether there is in such an enactment an implied prohibition of all contracts for the use of unlicensed vehicles, the answer may well be that there is, and that contracts of hire would be unenforceable. But if one asks oneself whether there is an implied prohibition of contracts for the carriage of goods by unlicensed vehicles or for the repairing of unlicensed vehicles or for the garaging of unlicensed vehicles, the answer may well be different. The answer might be that collateral contracts of this sort are not within the ambit of the statute

. . . [A]n implied prohibition of contracts of loading does not necessarily extend to contracts for the carriage of goods by improperly loaded vessels. Of course, if the parties knowingly agree to ship goods by an overloaded vessel, such a contract would be illegal; but its illegality does not depend on whether it is impliedly prohibited by the statute, since it falls within the first of the two general heads of illegality I noted above where there is an intent to break the law. The way to test the question whether a particular class of contract is prohibited by the statute is to test it in relation to a contract made in ignorance of its effect.

In my judgment, contracts for the carriage of goods are not within the ambit of this statute at all. A court should not hold that any contract or class of contracts is prohibited by statute unless there is a clear implication, or 'necessary inference,' that the statute so intended. If a contract has as its whole object the doing of the very act which the statute prohibits, it can be argued that you can hardly make sense of a statute which forbids an act and yet permits to be made a contract to do it; that is a clear implication. But unless you get a clear implication of that sort, I think that a court ought to be very slow to hold that a statute intends to interfere with the rights and remedies given by the ordinary law of contract. Caution in this respect is, I think, especially necessary in these times when so much of commercial life is governed by regulations of one sort or another, which may easily be broken without wicked intent. Persons who deliberately set out to break the law cannot expect to be aided in a court of justice, but it is a different matter when the law is unwittingly broken. To nullify a bargain in such circumstances frequently means that in a case—perhaps of such triviality that no authority would have felt it worth while to prosecute—a seller, because he cannot enforce his civil rights, may forfeit a sum vastly in excess of any penalty that a criminal court would impose; and the sum forfeited will not go into the public purse but into the pockets of someone who is lucky enough to pick up the windfall or astute enough to have contrived to get it. It is questionable how far this contributes to public morality . . . [T]he courts should be slow to imply the statutory prohibition of contracts, and should do so only when the implication is quite clear. The Act of 1932 imposes a penalty which is itself designed to deprive the offender of the benefits of his crime. It would be a curious thing if the operation could be performed twice—once by the criminal law and then again by the civil. It would be curious, too, if in a case in which the magistrates had thought fit to impose only a nominal fine, their decision could, in effect, be overridden in a civil action.

NOTES

1. In *Shaw v Groom* [1970] 2 QB 504, a rent book did not contain all of the information required by statute, which was an offence punishable with a maximum fine of £50. When the claimant landlord claimed arrears of rent, the tenant relied on the failure to provide a proper rent book as prohibiting the claimant from recovering any rent. The Court of Appeal held that the contract was not illegal, since this provision was not intended to prevent the recovery of rent.

2. The contract in *Archbolds v Spanglett* (*page 569, 11.1.1.2*) had become illegal because of the way in which it was performed, but the innocent party, who was ignorant of the unlawful performance, could have sued upon it.

Thus an innocent party can sue on a contract performed in an illegal manner unless that party 'participated' in the illegality.

Ashmore, Benson, Pease & Co. Ltd v A. V. Dawson Ltd
[1973] 1 WLR 828 (CA)

The claimant company had manufactured two 25-ton tube banks and had agreed with the defendants, a small road haulage firm, for the carriage of these tube banks to the port of shipment. The claimant company's transport manager was present when one of the tube banks was loaded onto the defendants' lorry in contravention of the Road Traffic Act 1960, s. 64(2), which specified that the maximum weight laden of the lorry was not to exceed 30 tons. The weight of the lorry with the tube bank was 35 tons, but the claimant company's transport manager raised no objection and did not insist on the use of a low loader, although he knew that this was the appropriate vehicle for such a load. On the journey, one of the lorries toppled over, damaging the tube bank. The defendants claimed that the contract was void for illegality because the claimants' servants knew that carriage of such loads on these lorries was in breach of the statute.

Held (Phillimore LJ dissenting): Although this contract was lawful in its inception, it had been performed in an unlawful manner to the knowledge of, and with the participation of, the claimants' servants. Therefore, the claimant company could not recover in damages.

NOTE Whereas, in *Archbolds v Spanglett* (*page 569, 11.1.1.2*), the claimants did not need to rely on the illegality to support the claim for damages for theft of the whisky, in *Ashmore* the claimant company would have to plead the illegal act of overloading the lorry in order to establish how the loss occurred.

Marles v Philip Trant & Sons Ltd
[1954] 1 QB 29 (CA)

The defendants, seed merchants, bought wheat, described as spring wheat known as 'Fylgia', from a third party. The defendants resold it under the same description to the claimant farmers. In fact, it was not spring wheat and was known as 'Vilmorin'. The claimants recovered damages against the defendants. The defendants then claimed an indemnity and damages from the third party supplier. The third party alleged that the defendants had not delivered a statement to the claimants as they should have done under s. 1 of the Seeds Act 1920, specifying particulars of the variety, purity, and germination of the seeds, so that the contract between the claimants and the defendants was illegal.

   Held: The contract was not illegal in itself, although it was illegal in the manner of its performance. This meant that the contract between the claimants and the defendants was unenforceable by the defendants (they could not have sued for the price), but (Hodson LJ dissenting) the contract between the third party supplier and the defendants was not unlawful, and the defendants could recover from the supplier for their loss on the contract with the claimants.

DENNING LJ: There can be no doubt that the contract between the seed merchants and the farmer was not unlawful when it was made. If the farmer had repudiated it before the time for delivery arrived, the seed merchants could certainly have sued him for damages. Nor was the contract rendered unlawful simply because the seed was delivered without the prescribed particulars. If it were unlawful, the farmer himself could not have sued upon it as he has done. The truth is that it was not the contract itself which was unlawful, but only the performance of it. The seed merchants performed it in an illegal way in that they omitted to furnish the prescribed particulars. That renders the contract unenforceable by them, but it does not render the contract illegal . . .

   Once rid of the notion that the contract with the farmer was itself illegal, the question becomes: what is the effect of the admitted illegality in performance? It certainly prevents the seed merchants from suing the farmer for the price, but does it prevent them suing their supplier for damages? I think not. There was nothing unlawful in the contract between the seed merchants and their supplier, neither in the formation of it, nor in the performance of it. The seed merchants must therefore be entitled to damages for the breach of it. So far so good, but the difficulty comes when they seek to prove their damages. They want to be indemnified for the damages which they have been ordered to pay to the farmer. To prove those damages, they have to prove the contract with the farmer, and the circumstances under which the damages were awarded. It is said that once they begin to rely on their deliveries to the farmer, they seek aid from their own illegality; and that that is a thing which they are not allowed to do. The maxim is invoked: *Ex turpi causa non oritur actio.* That maxim must not, however, be carried too far. Lord Wright gave a warning about it 15 years ago in *Beresford v Royal Insurance Co. Ltd* [1938] AC 586 when he said: 'The maxim itself, notwithstanding the dignity of a learned language, is, like most maxims, lacking in precise definition. In these days there are many statutory offences which are the subject of the criminal law, and in that sense are crimes, but which would, it seems afford no moral justification for a court to apply the maxim. There are likewise some crimes of inadvertence which, it is true, involve mens rea in the legal sense but are not deliberate or, as people would say, intentional.' Those observations apply with especial force in this case. The omission by the seed merchants to deliver the prescribed particulars was an act of inadvertence. It was not a deliberate breach of the law. I venture to assert that there is no moral justification for the court to apply the maxim in this case. But is there any legal justification? A distinction must be drawn, I think, between an illegality which destroys the cause of action and an illegality which affects only the damages recoverable.

? QUESTION

Can this case be distinguished from *Anderson Ltd v Daniel* (*page 570, 11.1.2*)?

In *Anderson Ltd v Daniel*, statute punished sellers who failed to issue the required invoice. As a result, the seller could not sue on such a contract because it was illegal in performance. However, the other party to the contract is not deprived of his civil remedies.

The Supreme Court in *Patel v Mirza* has now confirmed a more complex analysis involving greater flexibility. This case was about the restitution of benefits paid over under an illegal contract. The Supreme Court unanimously allowed the claimant to recover. The majority did so on the basis of a flexible, policy-based approach to the recovery of benefits, whereas the minority—Lords Mance, Clarke, and Sumption—rejected that approach and permitted recovery on the narrow ground that there was an established exception to recovery of benefits in a case where the contract had not been performed. Those issues are considered below. What is important about *Patel v Mirza* is that it sets out principles governing the enforceability of contracts where one of the parties has committed an unlawful act in the course of performance and is required to rely upon that illegality to justify the claim.

Patel v Mirza
[2016] UKSC 42

LORD TOULSON: 11. Mr Patel transferred sums totalling £620,000 to Mr Mirza for the purpose of betting on the price of RBS shares, using advance insider information which Mr Mirza expected to obtain from RBS contacts regarding an anticipated government announcement which would affect the price of the shares. Mr Mirza's expectation of a government announcement proved to be mistaken, and so the intended betting did not take place, but Mr Mirza failed to repay the money to Mr Patel despite promises to do so. Mr Patel thereupon brought this claim for the recovery of the sums which he had paid . . .

12. The agreement between Mr Patel and Mr Mirza amounted to a conspiracy to commit an offence of insider dealing under section 52 of the Criminal Justice Act 1993. In order to establish his claim to the return of his money, it was necessary for Mr Patel to explain the nature of the agreement . . .

The reliance principle and *Tinsley v Milligan*

17. The facts of *Tinsley v Milligan* are well known. Miss Tinsley and Miss Milligan each contributed to the purchase of a home. It was vested in Miss Tinsley's sole name, but on the mutual understanding that they were joint beneficial owners. It was put in her sole name so as to assist Miss Milligan to make false

benefit claims from the Department of Social Security (DSS), which she did over a number of years with Miss Tinsley's connivance. The money obtained from the DSS helped them to pay their bills, but it played only a small part in the acquisition of the equity in the house. Eventually Miss Milligan confessed to the DSS what she had done and made terms with it, but the parties fell out. Miss Tinsley gave Miss Milligan notice to quit and brought a claim against her for possession. Miss Milligan counterclaimed for a declaration that the property was held by Miss Tinsley on trust for the parties in equal shares.

18. The Court of Appeal by a majority decided in favour of Miss Milligan by applying the test whether it would be 'an affront to the public conscience' to grant the relief claimed by her. The House of Lords unanimously rejected the 'public conscience' test, but by a three to two majority upheld the Court of Appeal's decision. The leading speech was given by Lord Browne-Wilkinson. His starting point was that title to property can pass under an unlawful transaction; but he held that the court would not assist an owner to recover the property if he had to rely on his own illegality to prove his title. The Court of Appeal had recognised that distinction in *Bowmakers Ltd v Barnet Instruments Ltd* [1945] KB 65 in a case concerning personal property, referred to in more detail at para 111 below, and Lord Browne-Wilkinson held that the same applied to real property in which the claimant had a beneficial interest. Lord Browne-Wilkinson held that it was enough for Miss Milligan to show that she had contributed to the purchase of the property and that there was a common understanding that the parties were joint owners. She did not have to explain why the property had been put into Miss Tinsley's sole name. If the relationship between them had been that of daughter and mother, and each had contributed to the purchase of a property in the daughter's name, the result would have been different, because there would then have been a presumption of advancement in the daughter's favour. The mother would in those circumstances have had to rely on the illegal nature of the transaction to rebut the presumption, and her claim would therefore have been defeated by the doctrine of illegality. Lord Browne-Wilkinson acknowledged the procedural nature of this approach at [1994] 1 AC 340, 374:

> The effect of illegality is not substantive but procedural. The question therefore is, 'In what circumstances will equity refuse to enforce equitable rights which undoubtedly exist.'

19. Lord Goff, in the minority, held at p 356 that if A puts property in the name of B intending to conceal A's interest for a fraudulent or illegal purpose, neither law nor equity will allow A to recover the property, and equity will not assist him in asserting an equitable interest in it. It made no difference whether A's case could be advanced without reference to the underlying purpose. He recognised, at p 363, the resulting hardship and said that he did not disguise his unhappiness at the result, but he did not regard it as appropriate for the courts to introduce a discretion. He considered, at p 364, that reform should be instituted only by the legislature, after a full inquiry by the Law Commission, which would embrace not only the advantages and disadvantages of the present system, but also the likely advantages and disadvantages of a discretionary system. He added that he would be more than happy if a new system could be evolved which was both satisfactory in its effect and capable of avoiding the kind of result which in his judgment flowed from the established rules in cases such as *Tinsley v Milligan*.

20. *Tinsley v Milligan* has been the subject of much criticism in this and other jurisdictions, for its reasoning rather than its result, but this is the first time in this jurisdiction that its reasoning has been directly called into question . . .

72. [T]here have been three decisions by the Supreme Court involving the doctrine of illegality. The first was *Hounga v Allen* [2014] 1 WLR 2889 . . . Miss Hounga was a 14-year old Nigerian. Mr and Mrs Allen offered to employ her as a home help in the UK in return for schooling and £50 per month. With their help she entered the UK on false identity documents and obtained a six months' visitor's visa. The plan was masterminded by Mrs Allen's brother who lived in Lagos. He drafted an affidavit for Miss Hounga

to swear, giving her surname as that of Mrs Allen's mother and a false date of birth. The affidavit led to the issue of a passport in that name. Mrs Allen's family then arranged for Miss Hounga to be taken to the British High Commission in Lagos, where she produced a document purporting to be an invitation from Mrs Allen's mother pretending to invite her granddaughter to visit her in the United Kingdom. The High Commission was duped into issuing her with entry clearance. Mrs Allen's brother then bought a ticket for Miss Hounga to travel to England. On arrival at Heathrow Miss Hounga confirmed to an immigration officer that the purpose of her visit was to stay with her grandmother. Subsequently a psychologist reported that Miss Hounga, who was illiterate, had low cognitive functioning, a learning disability and a developmental age much lower than her chronological age. Nevertheless she knew that she had entered the UK on false pretences, that it was illegal for her to remain beyond six months and that it was illegal for her to take employment in the UK.

73. After her arrival Miss Hounga lived at the Allens' home, looking after their children and doing housework. She was not enrolled in a school or paid any wages. She was told by Mrs Allen that if she were found by the police she would be sent to prison. This caused her extreme concern. Mrs Allen also subjected her to serious physical abuse. After 18 months an incident occurred in which Mrs Allen beat Miss Hounga, threw her out of the house and poured water over her. Miss Hounga slept that night in the Allens' garden in wet clothes. Next day they refused to let her back in, and she made her way to a supermarket car park, where she was found and taken to the social services department of the local authority.

74. Miss Hounga brought claims against the Allens in the employment tribunal for unfair dismissal, breach of contract and unpaid wages. They were dismissed on the ground that her contract of employment was unlawful. She appealed unsuccessfully to the appeal tribunal and she did not seek to appeal further . . .

75. Miss Hounga also claimed to have been the victim of the statutory tort of unlawful discrimination under the Race Relations Act 1976, section 4(2)(c), in relation to her dismissal. The tribunal found that she had been dismissed because of her vulnerability consequent upon her immigration status. She was therefore the victim of unlawful discrimination and she was awarded compensation for her resulting injury to feelings. The tribunal's order was set aside by the Court of Appeal, which held that the claim was tainted by the illegal nature of her employment and that for the court to uphold it would be to condone the illegality, but it was restored by the Supreme Court. The leading judgment was given by Lord Wilson, with whom Lady Hale and Lord Kerr agreed.

76. Lord Wilson did not consider that the solution of the case lay either in asking whether Miss Allen needed to rely on an illegal contract or in asking whether there was an inextricable link between the illegality to which she was a party and her claim. At the heart of the judgment Lord Wilson set out his approach in para 42:

> The defence of illegality rests on the foundation of public policy. 'The principle of public policy is this . . .' said Lord Mansfield by way of preface to his classic exposition of the defence in *Holman v Johnson* (1775) 1 Cowp 341, 343. 'Rules which rest on the foundation of public policy, not being rules which belong to the fixed or customary law, are capable, on proper occasion, of expansion or modification': *Maxim Nordenfelt Guns and Ammunition Co v Nordenfelt* [1893] 1 Ch 630, 661 (Bowen LJ). So it is necessary, first, to ask 'What is the aspect of public policy which founds the defence?' and, second, to ask 'But is there another aspect of public policy to which the application of the defence would run counter?'

80. After *Hounga v Allen* came the decision of the Supreme Court in *Les Laboratoires Servier v Apotex Inc* [2015] AC 430. The issue of illegality arose in the context of a claim to enforce a cross-undertaking in damages given as a condition of an interlocutory injunction in proceedings which ultimately failed.

The claim was therefore akin to a claim in contract. The facts were somewhat complicated but do not matter for present purposes. The court held unanimously that the Court of Appeal had reached the right result, but the majority of this court expressed the view, at para 21, that the Court of Appeal's decision could not possibly be justified by the considerations put forward by that court, which had in broad terms followed the approach commended by the Law Commission. I expressed a different view, at para 62, observing that the Court of Appeal had adopted a similar approach to that taken by this court in *Hounga v Allen*.

81. After *Les Laboratoires Servier v Apotex Inc* came *Bilta (UK) Ltd v Nazir (No. 2)* [2016] AC 1. There was a sharp division of opinion about the proper approach to the defence illegality between, on the one hand, a strictly rule-based approach and, on the other hand, a more flexible approach by which the court would look at the policies underlying the doctrine and decide whether they militated in favour of the defence, taking into account a range of potentially relevant factors. The majority did not consider it necessary to resolve the difference in that case, since it did not affect the result, but Lord Neuberger said at para 15 that it needed to be addressed as soon as appropriately possible.

The law at a crossroads

82. In his *Restatement of the English Law of Contract* (Oxford University Press, 2016), pp 221–222, Professor Andrew Burrows explained the difficulty of attempting to state the law in relation to illegality . . .

83. Since the law was at a crossroads, Professor Burrows set out alternative possible formulations of a 'rule-based approach' and a 'range of factors approach'.

84. One possible version of a rule-based approach, at p 224, which *Tinsley v Milligan* and *Les Laboratoires Servier v Apotex Inc* could be interpreted as supporting, would be a single master rule based on reliance:

> If the formation, purpose or performance of a contract involves conduct that is illegal (such as a crime) or contrary to public policy (such as a restraint of trade), a party cannot enforce the contract if it has to rely on that conduct to establish its claim.

85. An alternative rule-based formulation, at p 225, saw the reliance rule as only one of a number of rules and essentially confined to the creation of property rights. On this approach a formulation of the rules might be:

> Rule 1. A contract which has as its purpose, or is intended to be performed in a manner that involves, conduct that is illegal (such as a crime) or contrary to public policy (such as a restraint of trade) is unenforceable (a) by either party if both parties knew of that purpose or intention; or (b) by one party if only that party knew of that purpose or intention.
>
> Rule 2. If rule 1 is inapplicable because it is only the performance of a contract that involves conduct that is illegal or contrary to public policy, the contract is unenforceable by the party who performed in that objectionable way but is enforceable by the other party unless that party knew of, and participated in, that objectionable performance.
>
> Rule 3. Proprietary rights created by a contract that involves conduct that is illegal or contrary to public policy will not be recognised unless the claimant can establish the proprietary rights without reliance on that conduct.

86. Professor Burrows identified six criticisms of those rules and, more generally, of a 'rule-based' approach to illegality.

87. First, the difficulty with the *Tinsley v Milligan* reliance rule, whether as a master rule or as a rule restricted to cases involving the assertion of proprietary rights, was that it could produce different results according to procedural technicality which had nothing to do with the underlying policies. The decision of the Court of Appeal in *Collier v Collier* [2002] EWCA 1095; [2002] BPIR 1057 provides a good illustration. A father granted a lease of property to his daughter to hold on trust for him in order to deceive creditors. His claim to beneficial title was rejected on the ground of illegality, because it was held that he needed

to rely on the illegal purpose in order to rebut the presumption of illegality which arose in favour of the daughter. Mance LJ considered at paras 105–106 what appeared to be the distinction introduced by *Tinsley v Milligan* between a beneficial interest which could be established by 'some objectively provable and apparently neutral fact' and a beneficial interest arising only from an agreement made for an unlawful purpose. He described the effect as 'little more than cosmetic' where the court was perfectly well aware of the close involvement of both parties in the illegality. Tempted as he was to adopt a severely limited view of the meaning of reliance (encouraged by the judgment of Dawson J in *Nelson v Nelson*), he rightly did not consider that it was open to the Court of Appeal on the authorities to do so. He expressed strong sympathy with the criticisms of the law expressed by the Law Commission, and he concluded at para 113 that he had no liking for the result which the court was compelled to reach.

88. Second, the difficulties with rule 1 were illustrated by the *ParkingEye* case. The illegality in that case went to the contract as formed, because from the outset it was intended to send out to customers a form of letter of demand which contained some deliberate inaccuracies. The rule as stated did not permit differentiation between minor and serious illegality or between peripheral and central illegality. To have deprived ParkingEye of what would otherwise have been a contractual entitlement to damages of £350,000 would have been disproportionate. Moreover, as Sir Robin Jacob pointed out in that case, at paras 33–34, there was something odd about a rule which differentiated according to whether the intention was formed before or after the contract was made.

89. Third, as with the criticism of rule 1, the reference in rule 2 to performance that involved illegal conduct drew no distinction between serious criminality and relatively minor breach of a statutory regulation.

90. Fourth, although a purported advantage of firm rules is greater certainty, the cases do not always fit the rules because courts have often sought ways around them when they do not like the consequence. The flexible approach would not only produce more acceptable results, but would in practice be no less certain than the rule-based approach.

91. Fifth, although Lord Mansfield made it clear in *Holman v Johnson* that the illegality defence operates as a rule of public policy and is not designed to achieve justice between the parties, that does not mean that any result, however arbitrary, is acceptable. The law should strive for the most desirable policy outcome, and it may be that it is best achieved by taking into account a range of factors.

92. Sixth, although it may be argued that if there are deficiencies in the traditional rules, the way forward is to refine the rules to remove the deficiencies by appropriate exceptions, that task is one which has never been satisfactorily accomplished. The reason is that there are so many variables, for example, in seriousness of the illegality, the knowledge and intentions of the parties, the centrality of the illegality, the effect of denying the defence and the sanctions which the law already imposes. To reach the best result in terms of policy, the judges need to have the flexibility to consider and weigh a range of factors in the light of the facts of the particular case before them.

93. If a 'range of factors' approach were preferred, Professor Burrows suggested, at pp 229–230, that a possible formulation would read as follows:

> If the formation, purpose or performance of a contract involves conduct that is illegal (such as a crime) or contrary to public policy (such as a restraint of trade), the contract is unenforceable by one or either party if to deny enforcement would be an appropriate response to that conduct, taking into account where relevant—
>
> (a) how seriously illegal or contrary to public policy the conduct was;
>
> (b) whether the party seeking enforcement knew of, or intended, the conduct;
>
> (c) how central to the contract or its performance the conduct was;
>
> (d) how serious a sanction the denial of enforcement is for the party seeking enforcement;

(e)   whether denying enforcement will further the purpose of the rule which the conduct has infringed;

(f)   whether denying enforcement will act as a deterrent to conduct that is illegal or contrary to public policy;

(g)   whether denying enforcement will ensure that the party seeking enforcement does not profit from the conduct;

(h)   whether denying enforcement will avoid inconsistency in the law thereby maintaining the integrity of the legal system.

Professor Burrows noted that the final factor is capable of a wider or narrower approach, depending on what one understands by inconsistency.

94. The reference to what is an 'appropriate response' brings to the surface the moral dimension underlying the doctrine of illegality, which inevitably influences the minds of judges and peeps out in their judgments from time to time. *Tinsley v Milligan* caused disquiet to Lord Goff and others precisely because its reasoning jarred with their sense of what was just and appropriate . . .

The way forward

99. [T]here are two broad discernible policy reasons for the common law doctrine of illegality as a defence to a civil claim. One is that a person should not be allowed to profit from his own wrongdoing. The other, linked, consideration is that the law should be coherent and not self-defeating, condoning illegality by giving with the left hand what it takes with the right hand . . .

101. So how is the court to determine the matter if not by some mechanistic process? In answer to that question I would say that one cannot judge whether allowing a claim which is in some way tainted by illegality would be contrary to the public interest, because it would be harmful to the integrity of the legal system, without a) considering the underlying purpose of the prohibition which has been transgressed, b) considering conversely any other relevant public policies which may be rendered ineffective or less effective by denial of the claim, and c) keeping in mind the possibility of overkill unless the law is applied with a due sense of proportionality. We are, after all, in the area of public policy. That trio of necessary considerations can be found in the case law.

102. The relevance of taking into account the purpose of the relevant prohibition is self-evident. The importance of taking account of the relevant statutory context is illustrated by *Hardy v Motor Insurers' Bureau* [1964] 2 QB 745. The Road Traffic Act 1960 required a motorist to be insured against the risk of causing death or personal injury through the use of a vehicle on a road, but a line of authorities established that a contract to indemnify a person against the consequences of a deliberate criminal act is unenforceable. The plaintiff, a security officer at a factory, was injured when he was trying to question the driver of a van, who drove off at speed and dragged him along the road. The driver was convicted of unlawfully causing grievous bodily harm. The driver being uninsured, the plaintiff sued the defendant under an agreement between the defendant and the Minister of Transport, by which the defendant agreed to satisfy any judgment against a motorist for a liability required to be covered under a motor insurance policy. The defendant relied on the maxim *ex turpi causa*, arguing that a contract purporting to insure the driver against his own deliberate criminal conduct would have been unlawful.

103. *Hounga v Allen* and *R (Best) v Chief Land Registrar* are illustrations of cases in which there were countervailing public interest considerations, which needed to be balanced . . .

107. In considering whether it would be disproportionate to refuse relief to which the claimant would otherwise be entitled, as a matter of public policy, various factors may be relevant. Professor Burrows' list is helpful but I would not attempt to lay down a prescriptive or definitive list because of the infinite possible variety of cases. Potentially relevant factors include the seriousness of the conduct, its centrality to the contract, whether it was intentional and whether there was marked disparity in the parties' respective culpability.

108. The integrity and harmony of the law permit—and I would say require—such flexibility. Part of the harmony of the law is its division of responsibility between the criminal and civil courts and tribunals.

Illegality

11

Punishment for wrongdoing is the responsibility of the criminal courts and, in some instances, statutory regulators. It should also be noted that under the Proceeds of Crime Act 2002 the state has wide powers to confiscate proceeds of crime, whether on a conviction or without a conviction. Punishment is not generally the function of the civil courts, which are concerned with determining private rights and obligations. The broad principle is not in doubt that the public interest requires that the civil courts should not undermine the effectiveness of the criminal law; but nor should they impose what would amount in substance to an additional penalty disproportionate to the nature and seriousness of any wrongdoing. *ParkingEye* is a good example of a case where denial of claim would have been disproportionate. The claimant did not set out to break the law. If it had realised that the letters which it was proposing to send were legally objectionable, the text would have been changed. The illegality did not affect the main performance of the contract. Denial of the claim would have given the defendant a very substantial unjust reward. Respect for the integrity of the justice system is not enhanced if it appears to produce results which are arbitrary, unjust or disproportionate.

109. The courts must obviously abide by the terms of any statute, but I conclude that it is right for a court which is considering the application of the common law doctrine of illegality to have regard to the policy factors involved and to the nature and circumstances of the illegal conduct in determining whether the public interest in preserving the integrity of the justice system should result in denial of the relief claimed. I put it in that way rather than whether the contract should be regarded as tainted by illegality, because the question is whether the relief claimed should be granted . . .

113. Critics of the 'range of factors' approach say that it would create unacceptable uncertainty. I would make three points in reply. First, one of the principal criticisms of the law has been its uncertainty and unpredictability. Doctrinally it is riven with uncertainties: see, for example, paras 4–8 above. There is also uncertainty how a court will in practice steer its way in order to reach what appears to be a just and reasonable result. Second, I am not aware of evidence that uncertainty has been a source of serious problems in those jurisdictions which have taken a relatively flexible approach. Third, there are areas in which certainty is particularly important. Ordinary citizens and businesses enter into all sorts of everyday lawful activities which are governed by well understood rules of law . . .

115. In the present case I would endorse the approach and conclusion of Gloster LJ. She correctly asked herself whether the policy underlying the rule which made the contract between Mr Patel and Mr Mirza illegal would be stultified if Mr Patel's claim in unjust enrichment were allowed. After examining the policy underlying the statutory provisions about insider dealing, she concluded that there was no logical basis why considerations of public policy should require Mr Patel to forfeit the moneys which he paid into Mr Mirza's account, and which were never used for the purpose for which they were paid. She said that such a result would not be a just and proportionate response to the illegality. I agree. It seems likely that Lord Mansfield would also have agreed: see *Walker v Chapman*. Mr Patel is seeking to unwind the arrangement, not to profit from it . . .

LORD NEUBERGER: 174. I have come to the conclusion that the approach suggested by Lord Toulson in para 101 above provides as reliable and helpful guidance as it is possible to give in this difficult field. When faced with a claim based on a contract which involves illegal activity (whether or not the illegal activity has been wholly, partly or not at all undertaken), the court should, when deciding how to take into account the impact of the illegality on the claim, bear in mind the need for integrity and consistency in the justice system, and in particular (a) the policy behind the illegality, (b) any other public policy issues, and (c) the need for proportionality . . .

LORD MANCE (dissenting): 206. What is apparent is that this [new] approach, would introduce not only a new era but entirely novel dimensions into any issue of illegality. Courts would be required to make a value judgment, by reference to a widely spread mélange of ingredients, about the overall 'merits' or strengths, in a highly unspecific non-legal sense, of the respective claims of the public interest and of each of the parties. But courts could only do so, by either allowing or disallowing enforcement of the contract as between the two parties to it, unless they were able (if and when this was possible) to adopt the yet further novelty, pioneered by the majority of the Australian court in *Nelson v Nelson* [1995] HCA 25, (1995) 184 CLR 538, of requiring the account to the public for any profit unjustifiably made at the public expense, as a condition of obtaining relief.

LORD CLARKE (dissenting): . . . 214. I have always thought that the power of the court to deny recovery on the ground of illegality should be limited to well defined circumstances. I agree with Lord Mance . . . that, in the absence of such circumstances, claimants should not be deprived of the opportunity to obtain damages for wrongs or to put themselves in the position in which they should have been. As I see it, there is no need to replace that approach with what he calls an open and unsettled range of factors . . .

LORD SUMPTION (dissenting): 265. I regret that I cannot agree with the conclusion of Lord Toulson that that the application of the illegality principle should depend on

> the policy factors involved and . . . the nature and circumstances of the illegal conduct, in determining whether the public interest in preserving the integrity of the justice system should result in the denial of the relief claimed.

In my opinion, this is far too vague and potentially far too wide to serve as the basis on which a person may be denied his legal rights. It converts a legal principle into an exercise of judicial discretion, in the process exhibiting all the vices of 'complexity, uncertainty, arbitrariness and lack of transparency' which Lord Toulson attributes to the present law. I would not deny that in the past the law of illegality has been a mess. The proper response of this court is not to leave the problem to case by case evaluation by the lower courts by reference to a potentially unlimited range of factors, but to address the problem by supplying a framework of principle which accommodates legitimate concerns about the present law. We would be doing no service to the coherent development of the law if we simply substituted a new mess for the old one.

11.2 Contracts void on grounds of public policy: contracts in restraint of trade

A restraint of trade is a contractual undertaking whereby one party agrees to restrict its freedom to trade or to conduct its business in a particular area for a specified period of time.

11.2.1 Basic principles

Nordenfelt v Maxim Nordenfelt Guns & Ammunition Co. Ltd
[1894] AC 535 (HL)

The defendant, who owned patents and operated a business of manufacturing quick-firing guns and ammunition, sold the business and its goodwill to a company. The agreement contained a covenant on the part of the defendant that, for 25 years, the defendant would not, directly or indirectly, engage in the business of a manufacturer of guns or ammunition except on behalf of the company, and would not engage in any business competing or liable to compete in any way with the business being carried on by the company. The House of Lords was asked to consider only the first part of the covenant (relating to engaging in a gun manufacturing business).

Held: This first part of the covenant was valid because, even though it was a worldwide restriction, there were only a limited number of customers (governments of this and other countries), so that the restriction was not wider than was necessary to protect the company and it was not injurious to the public interest. (The Court of Appeal had held that the second part was void because it went further than was necessary to protect the business acquired.)

LORD MACNAGHTEN: In the age of Queen Elizabeth all restraints of trade, whatever they were, general or partial, were thought to be contrary to public policy, and therefore void. In time, however, it was found that a rule so rigid and far-reaching must seriously interfere with transactions of every-day occurrence. Traders could hardly venture to let their shops out of their own hands; the purchaser of a business was at the mercy of the seller; every apprentice was a possible rival. So the rule was relaxed . . .

. . . The public have an interest in every person's carrying on his trade freely: so has the individual. All interference with individual liberty of action in trading, and all restraints of trade of themselves, if there is nothing more, are contrary to public policy, and therefore void. That is the general rule. But there are exceptions: restraints of trade and interference with individual liberty of action may be justified by the special circumstances of a particular case. It is a sufficient justification, and indeed it is the only justification, if the restriction is reasonable—reasonable, that is, in reference to the interests of the parties concerned and reasonable in reference to the interests of the public, so framed and so guarded as to afford adequate protection to the party in whose favour it is imposed, while at the same time it is in no way injurious to the public.

NOTES

1. The presumption that contracts in restraint of trade are void can be rebutted by a party seeking to rely on the restraint showing that the restraint is reasonable as between the parties. Once this is established, the restraint can be relied upon, unless the party seeking to prevent its enforcement shows that it is contrary to the public interest.

2. *Nordenfelt v Maxim Nordenfelt* concerned a covenant on the sale of a business, i.e. that the vendor would not carry on a business competing with the business purchased. These covenants are more likely to be held to be reasonable and enforceable because a price will be paid for the goodwill of the business, and therefore the purchaser has a legitimate interest in protecting that goodwill and the business connections. It would be unfair to the purchaser if the vendor could then set up a competing business.

11.2.2 Covenants between employer and employee

The restriction must seek to protect a *legitimate interest* of the employer (i.e. influence over customers or trade secrets) as opposed to protection against skills acquired by the employee that might render him a potential competitor. The restriction must be reasonable as between the parties and no wider than reasonably necessary to protect the business connections or confidential information of the employer. There are three factors: subject matter, area, and duration.

Herbert Morris Ltd v Saxelby
[1916] 1 AC 688 (HL)

The claimant company, leading manufacturers of hoisting machinery in the UK, employed the defendant as a draftsman and then as an engineer on a two-year contract. The terms of this contract contained a covenant by the defendant that he would not:

> during a period of seven years from ceasing to be employed by the company, either in the United Kingdom of Great Britain or Ireland, carry on either as principal, agent, servant or otherwise, alone or jointly or in connection with any other person, firm or company, or be concerned or assist, directly or indirectly, whether for reward or otherwise, in the sale or manufacture of pulley blocks, hand overhead runways, electric overhead runways, or hand overhead travelling cranes.

The claimant company sought to enforce this covenant.

Held: The covenant was wider than was required for the protection of the claimant company and was not enforceable.

LORD PARKER OF WADDINGTON: It will be observed that in Lord Macnaghten's opinion [in *Nordenfelt*] two conditions must be fulfilled if the restraint is to be held valid. First, it must be reasonable in the interests of the contracting parties, and, secondly, it must be reasonable in the interests of the public. In the case of each condition he lays down a test of reasonableness. To be reasonable in the interests of the parties the restraint must afford adequate protection to the party in whose favour it is imposed; to be reasonable in the interests of the public it must be in no way injurious to the public.

With regard to the former test, I think it clear that what is meant is that for a restraint to be reasonable in the interests of the parties it must afford *no more than* adequate protection to the party in whose favour it is imposed. So conceived the test appears to me to be valid both as regards the covenantor and covenantee, for though in one sense no doubt it is contrary to the interests of the covenantor to subject himself to any restraint, still it may be for his advantage to be able so to subject himself in cases where, if he could not do so, he would lose other advantages, such as the possibility of obtaining the best terms on the sale of an existing business or the possibility of obtaining employment or training under competent employers. As long as the restraint to which he subjects himself is no wider than is required for the adequate protection of the person in whose favour it is created, it is in his interest to be able to bind himself for the sake of the indirect advantages he may obtain by so doing. It was at one time thought that, in order to ascertain whether a restraint were reasonable in the interests of the covenantor, the Court ought to weigh the advantages accruing to the covenantor under the contract against the disadvantages imposed upon him by the restraint, but any such process has long since been rejected as impracticable. The Court no longer considers the adequacy of the consideration in any particular case. If it be reasonable that a covenantee should, for his own protection, ask for a restraint, it is in my opinion equally reasonable that the covenantor should be able to subject himself to this restraint. The test of reasonableness is the same in both cases.

It was suggested in argument that the interests of the public ought to be considered and weighed in determining whether a restraint is reasonable in the interests of the parties. I dissent from this view. It would, indeed, entirely destroy the value of Lord Macnaghten's tests of reasonableness. The first question in every case is whether the restraint is reasonable in the interests of the parties. If it is not, the restraint is bad. If it is, it may still be shown that it is injurious to the public, though . . . the onus of so showing would lie on the party alleging it.

My Lords, it appears to me that Lord Macnaghten's statement of the law requires amplification in another respect. If the restraint is to secure no more than 'adequate protection' to the party in whose favour it is imposed, it becomes necessary to consider in each particular case what it is for which and what it is against which protection is required. Otherwise it would be impossible to pass any opinion on the adequacy of the protection

. . . It was argued before your Lordships that no distinction can be drawn between the position of the purchaser of the goodwill of a business taking a covenant from his vendor and the case of the owner of a business taking a covenant from his servant or apprentice. In both cases it was said that the property to be protected was the same and the dangers to be guarded against the same. I am of opinion that this argument cannot be accepted. The distinction between the two cases is, I think, quite clear, and is recognised both by Lord Macnaghten and Lord Herschell in the *Nordenfelt Case* [1894] AC 535. The goodwill of a business is immune from the danger of the owner exercising his personal knowledge and skill to its detriment, and if the purchaser is to take over such goodwill with all its advantages it must, in his hands, remain similarly immune. Without, therefore, a covenant on the part of the vendor against competition, a purchaser would not get what he is contracting to buy, nor could the vendor give what he is intending to sell. The covenant against competition is, therefore, reasonable if confined to the area within which it would in all probability enure to the injury of the purchaser.

It is quite different in the case of an employer taking such a covenant from his employee or apprentice. The goodwill of his business is, under the conditions in which we live, necessarily subject to the competition of all persons (including the servant or apprentice) who choose to engage in a similar trade. The employer in such a case is not endeavouring to protect what he has, but to gain a special advantage which he could not otherwise secure. I cannot find any case in which a covenant against competition by a servant or apprentice has, as such, ever been upheld by the Court. Wherever such covenants have been upheld it had been on the ground, not that the servant or apprentice would, by reason of his employment or training, obtain the skill and knowledge necessary to equip him as a possible competitor in the trade, but that he might obtain such personal knowledge of and influence over the customers of his employer, or such an acquaintance with his employer's trade secrets as would enable him, if competition were allowed, to take advantage of his employer's trade connection or utilise information confidentially obtained.

In *Mason v Provident Clothing and Supply Co.* [1913] AC 724 it was argued . . . that an employer might reasonably say 'I will not have the skill and knowledge acquired in my employment imparted to my trade rivals,' and that the validity of the restraint did not depend upon personal contact with the employer's customers, but upon the fact that the employee gained that general knowledge which put him into a position to compete with his master and made him a source of danger, against which the master was entitled to protect himself.

This argument was rejected by your Lordships' House, and the restraint in question was held bad, as being wider than was necessary to protect the employer from injury by misuse of the employee's acquaintance with customers or knowledge of trade secrets. In fact the reason, and the only reason, for upholding such a restraint on the part of an employee is that the employer has some proprietary right, whether in the nature of trade connection or in the nature of trade secrets, for the protection of which such a restraint is—having regard to the duties of the employee—reasonably necessary. Such a restraint has, so far as I know, never been upheld, if directed only to the prevention of competition or against the use of the personal skill and knowledge acquired by the employee in his employer's business.

My Lords, it remains to apply what I have said to the particular circumstances of the present case. Mr Herbert Morris, the managing director of the plaintiff company, very candidly admitted that the real object of the plaintiff company in imposing the restraint was to preclude competition on the part of the defendant after he had left the company's employment. The company objected, he said, to skill and knowledge acquired in its service being put at the disposition of any trade rival, and the skill and knowledge he referred to was the general skill and knowledge which an employee of any ability must necessarily obtain as opposed to knowledge of any matter and skill in any process in which the company could be said to have any property at all . . . As directed against competition or against the use of this skill and knowledge, I am clearly of opinion that the restraint was in no way required for the plaintiffs' protection, and therefore unreasonable and bad in law.

An attempt was, however, made in argument to justify the restraint on the ground that it was no more than adequate for the protection of the plaintiffs' trade connection and trade secrets. I am of opinion that this attempt completely failed. With regard to the plaintiffs' connection, there is little or no evidence that the defendant ever came into personal contact with the plaintiffs' customers. For a period, it is true, he was manager of the London branch of the plaintiffs' business, and for another period sales manager at Loughborough. With the exception of these periods he was employed entirely in the engineering department. Had the restraint been confined to London and Loughborough and a reasonable area round each of these centres, it might possibly have been supported as reasonably necessary to protect the plaintiffs' connection, but a restraint extending over the United Kingdom was obviously too wide in this respect.

With regard to trade secrets, I am not satisfied that the defendant was entrusted with any trade secret in the proper sense of the word at all . . .

Mason v Provident Clothing & Supply Co. Ltd
[1913] AC 724 (HL)

The defendant was employed as a canvasser by the claimants for the district of Islington in London. The defendant covenanted not to work in any similar business for three years within 25 miles of London.

Held: Because the defendant's duties were confined to the district of Islington, the clause was wider than was reasonably necessary to protect the claimants' interests.

LORD MOULTON: Are the restrictions which the covenant imposes upon the freedom of action of the servant after he has left the service of the master greater than are reasonably necessary for the protection of the master in his business?

The first task of the Court, therefore, is to ascertain with due particularity the nature of the master's business and of the servant's employment therein . . . The nature of the employment of the appellant in this business was solely to obtain members and collect their instalments. A small district in London was assigned to him, which he canvassed and in which he collected the payments due, and outside that small district he had no duties. His employment was therefore that of a local canvasser and debt collector, and nothing more.

Such being the nature of the employment, it would be reasonable for the employer to protect himself against the danger of his former servant canvassing or collecting for a rival firm in the district in which he had been employed. If he were permitted to do so before the expiry of a reasonably long interval he would be in a position to give to his new employer all the advantages of that personal knowledge of the inhabitants of the locality, and more especially of his former customers, which he had acquired in the service of the respondents and at their expense. Against such a contingency the master might reasonably protect himself, but I can see no further or other protection which he could reasonably demand. If the servant is employed by a rival firm in some district which neither includes that in which he formerly worked for the respondents, nor is immediately adjoining thereto, there is no personal knowledge which he has acquired in his former master's service which can be used to that master's prejudice. The respondents would be in no different position from that in which they would be if the appellant had acquired his experience in the service of some other company carrying on a like business.

Considering the strictly local character of the employment, I have no hesitation in saying that I should be prepared to hold that [the] area [here] is very far greater than could be reasonably required for the protection of his former employers.

11.2.3 Exclusive dealing agreements

Esso Petroleum Co. Ltd v Harper's Garage (Stourport) Ltd
[1968] AC 269 (HL)

The parties entered into agreements relating to the supply of Esso petrol to two garages belonging to Harper. Under these agreements, Harper agreed to purchase petrol only from Esso, in return for which Harper obtained a small discount on the price. For the first garage, the tie was to last for four years and five months, but for the second garage, a loan of £7,000 was made and the tie was to last for 21 years while the mortgage repayments were made on this loan. An injunction was sought to prevent Harper from buying petrol from another supplier.

Held: These exclusive dealing agreements were within the restraint of trade doctrine because Harper had given up a right to sell other petrol. Although the restraint that operated for four-and-a-half years was not longer than was necessary to afford adequate protection to Esso's legitimate interests in maintaining a stable system of distribution, the tie of 21 years went beyond a reasonable period and therefore that restraint agreement was void.

LORD REID: In my view this agreement is within the scope of the doctrine of restraint of trade as it had been developed in English law. Not only have the respondents agreed negatively not to sell other petrol but they have agreed positively to keep this garage open for the sale of the appellants' petrol at all reasonable hours throughout the period of the tie. It was argued that this was merely regulating the respondent's trading and rather promoting than restraining his trade. But regulating a person's existing trade may be a greater restraint than prohibiting him from engaging in a new trade. And a contract to take one's whole supply from one source may be much more hampering than a contract to sell one's whole output to one buyer. I would not attempt to define the dividing line between contracts which are and contracts which are not in restraint of trade, but in my view this contract must be held to be in restraint of trade. So it is necessary to consider whether its provisions can be justified.

[Lord Reid referred to Lord Macnaghten's statement in the *Nordenfelt* case (*page 581, 11.2.1*) and continued:]

So in every case it is necessary to consider first whether the restraint went farther than to afford adequate protection to the party in whose favour it was granted, secondly whether it can be justified as being in the interests of the party restrained, and, thirdly, whether it must be held contrary to the public interest. I find it difficult to agree with the way in which the court has in some cases treated the interests of the party restrained. Surely it can never be in the interest of a person to agree to suffer a restraint unless he gets some compensating advantage, direct or indirect. And Lord Macnaghten said: ' . . . of course the quantum of consideration may enter into the question of the reasonableness of the contract'.

Where two experienced traders are bargaining on equal terms and one has agreed to a restraint for reasons which seem good to him the court is in grave danger of stultifying itself if it says that it knows that trader's interest better than he does himself. But there may well be cases where, although the party to be restrained has deliberately accepted the main terms of the contract, he has been at a disadvantage as regards other terms: for example where a set of conditions has been incorporated which has not been the subject of negotiation—there the court may have greater freedom to hold them unreasonable . . . [W]hether or not a restraint is in the personal interests of the parties, it is I think well established that the court will not enforce a restraint which goes further than affording adequate protection to the legitimate interests of the party in whose favour it is granted. This must I think be because too wide a restraint is against the public interest . . . When petrol rationing came to an end in 1950 the large producers began to make agreements, now known as solus agreements, with garage owners under which the garage owner, in return for certain advantages, agreed to sell only the petrol of the producer with whom he made the agreement. Within a short time three-quarters of the filling stations in this country were tied in that way and by the dates of the agreements in this case over 90 per cent had agreed to ties. It appears that the garage owners were not at a disadvantage in bargaining with the large producing companies as there was intense competition between these companies to obtain these ties. So we can assume that both the garage owners and the companies thought that such ties were to their advantage. And it is not said in this case that all ties are either against the public interest or against the interests of the parties. The respondents' case is that the ties with which we are concerned are for too long periods.

The advantage to the garage owner is that he gets a rebate on the wholesale price of the petrol which he buys and also may get other benefits or financial assistance. The main advantages for the producing company appear to be that distribution is made easier and more economical and that it is assured of a steady outlet for its petrol over a period. As regards distribution, it appears that there were some 35,000 filling stations in this country at the relevant time, of which about a fifth were tied to the appellants. So they only have to distribute to some 7,000 filling stations instead of to a very much larger number if most filling stations sold several brands of petrol. But the main reason why the producing companies want ties for five years and more, instead of ties for one or two years only, seems to be that they can organise their business better if on the average only one-fifth or less of their ties come to an end in any one year. The appellants make a point of the fact that they have invested some £200 millions in refineries and other plant and that they could not have done that unless they could foresee a steady and assured level of sales of their petrol. Most of their ties appear to have been made for periods of between five and 20 years. But we have no evidence as to the precise additional advantage which they derive from a five-year tie as compared with a two-year tie or from a 20-year tie as compared with a five-year tie.

The Court of Appeal held that these ties were for unreasonably long periods. They thought that, if for any reason the respondents ceased to sell the appellants' petrol, the appellants could have found other suitable outlets in the neighbourhood within two or three years. I do not think that that is the right test. In the first place there was no evidence about this and I do not think that it would be practicable to apply this test in practice. It might happen that when the respondents ceased to sell their petrol, the appellants would find such an alternative outlet in a very short time. But, looking to the fact that well over 90 per cent of existing filling stations are tied and that there may be great difficulty in opening a new filling station, it might take a very long time to find an alternative. Any estimate of how long it might take to find suitable alternatives for the respondents' filling stations could be little better than guesswork.

I do not think that the appellants' interest can be regarded so narrowly. They are not so much concerned with any particular outlet as with maintaining a stable system of distribution throughout the country so as to enable their business to be run efficiently and economically. In my view there is sufficient material to justify a decision that ties of less than five years were insufficient, in the circumstances of the trade when these agreements were made, to afford adequate protection to the appellants' legitimate interests . . . A tie for 21 years stretches far beyond any period for which developments are reasonably foreseeable. Restrictions on the garage owner which might seem tolerable and reasonable in reasonably foreseeable conditions might come to have a very different effect in quite different conditions: the public interest comes in here more strongly. And, apart from a case where he gets a loan, a garage owner appears to get no greater advantage from a 20-year tie than he gets from a five-year tie. So I would think that there must at least be some clearly established advantage to the producing company—something to show that a shorter period would not be adequate—before so long a period could be justified. But in this case there is no evidence to prove anything of the kind . . . I would add that the decision in this case—particularly in view of the paucity of evidence—ought not, in my view, to be regarded as laying down any general rule as to the length of tie permissible in a solus agreement . . . I must not be taken as expressing any opinion as to the validity of ties for periods mid-way between the two periods with which the present case is concerned.

NOTE The majority of the House of Lords considered that the restraint of trade doctrine applied only where a person gave up a right that would otherwise have been enjoyed. Therefore, if an exclusive dealing transaction relating to land were to be inserted in a conveyance or lease of land, it would not be subject to the doctrine, since a person buying or leasing land has no previous right to trade there and would not be giving up any right previously held. In *Peninsula Securities Ltd v Dunnes Stores (Bangor) Ltd* *(Northern Ireland)* [2020] UKSC 36 that reasoning was overruled, and it was instead held that there was no difference in principle between a contract entered into by the owner of unencumbered land and a contract entered into as a condition of obtaining an interest in that land. The restraint of trade doctrine thus operates on any commercial tie applicable to the use of land, whether the tie was imposed on an existing landowner or as a condition of the transfer of the land.

11.2.4 Exclusive service agreements

A. Schroeder Music Publishing Co. Ltd v Macaulay
[1974] 1 WLR 1308 (HL)

M, an unknown 21-year-old songwriter, entered into a contract with S Ltd, music publishers, whereby they engaged his exclusive services for five years. Under the contract, M assigned full copyright for all of his compositions during the contractual period. However, S Ltd was not obliged to publish anything composed by M. If M's royalties exceeded £5,000 during the five-year period, the contract was to be automatically extended for another five years. Although S Ltd could terminate the agreement on one month's notice, M had no such rights. M alleged that the agreement was contrary to public policy.

Held: The agreement fell within the restraint of trade doctrine. It was unreasonable as between the parties, since it was one-sided.

LORD REID: I think that in a case like the present case two questions must be considered. Are the terms of the agreement so restrictive that either they cannot be justified at all or they must be justified by the party seeking to enforce the agreement? Then, if there is room for justification, has that party proved justification—normally by showing that the restrictions were not more than what was reasonably required to protect his legitimate interests? . . . The public interest requires in the interests both of the public and of the individual that everyone should be free so far as practicable to earn a livelihood and to give to the public the fruits of his particular abilities. The main question to be considered is whether and how far the operation of the terms of this agreement is likely to conflict with this objective. The respondent is bound to assign to the appellants during a long period the fruits of his musical talent. But what are the appellants bound to do with those fruits? Under the contract nothing. If they do use the songs which the respondent composes they must pay in terms of the contract. But they need not do so. As has been said they may put them in a drawer and leave them there.

No doubt the expectation was that if the songs were of value they would be published to the advantage of both parties. But if for any reason the appellants chose not to publish them the respondent would get no remuneration and he could not do anything. Inevitably the respondent must take the risk of misjudgment of the merits of his work by the appellants. But that is not the only reason which might cause the appellants not to publish. There is no evidence about this so we must do the best we can with common knowledge. It does not seem fanciful and it was not argued that it is fanciful to suppose that purely commercial consideration might cause a publisher to refrain from publishing and promoting promising material. He might think it likely to be more profitable to promote work by other composers with whom he had agreements and unwise or too expensive to try to publish and popularise the respondent's work in addition. And there is always the possibility that less legitimate reasons might influence a decision not to publish the respondent's work.

[I]t appears to me to be an unreasonable restraint to tie the composer for this period of years so that his work will be sterilised and he can earn nothing from his abilities as a composer if the publisher chooses not to publish. If there had been in clause 9 any provision entitling the composer to terminate the agreement in such an event the case might have had a very different appearance. But as the agreement stands not only is the composer tied but he cannot recover the copyright of work which the publisher refuses to publish.

It was strenuously argued that the agreement is in standard form, that it has stood the test of time, and that there is no indication that it ever causes injustice. Reference was made to passages in the speeches of Lord Pearce and Lord Wilberforce in *Esso Petroleum Co Ltd v Harper's Garage (Stourport) Ltd* [1968] AC 269 with which I wholly agree. Lord Pearce said, at p. 323:

> It is important that the court, in weighing the question of reasonableness, should give full weight to commercial practices and to the generality of contracts made freely by parties bargaining on equal terms.

and Lord Wilberforce said, at pp. 332–333:

> But the development of the law does seem to show that judges have been able to dispense from the necessity of justification under a public policy test of reasonableness such contracts or provisions of contracts as, under contemporary conditions, may be found to have passed into the accepted and normal currency of commercial or contractual or conveyancing relations. That such contracts have done so may be taken to show with at least strong prima force that, moulded under the pressures of negotiation, competition and public opinion, they have assumed a form which satisfies the test of public policy as understood by the courts at the time, or, regarding the matter from the point of view of the trade, that the trade in question has assumed such a form that for its health or expansion it requires a degree of regulation.

But those passages refer to contracts 'made freely by parties bargaining on equal terms' or 'moulded under the pressures of negotiation, competition and public opinion.' I do not find from any evidence in this case, nor does it seem probable, that this form of contract made between a publisher and an unknown composer has been moulded by any pressure of negotiation. Indeed, it appears that established composers who can bargain on equal terms can and do make their own contracts.

Any contract by which a person engages to give his exclusive services to another for a period necessarily involves extensive restriction during that period of the common law right to exercise any lawful activity he chooses in such manner as he thinks best. Normally the doctrine of restraint of trade has no application to such restrictions: they require no justification. But if contractual restrictions appear to be unnecessary or to be reasonably capable of enforcement in an oppressive manner, then they must be justified before they can be enforced.

In the present case the respondent assigned to the appellants 'the full copyright for the whole world' in every musical composition 'composed created or conceived' by him alone or in collaboration with any other person during a period of five or, it might be 10 years. He received no payment (apart from an initial £50) unless his work was published and the appellants need not publish unless they chose to do so. And if they did not publish he had no right to terminate the agreement or to have copyrights re-assigned to him. I need not consider whether in any circumstances it would be possible to justify such a one-sided agreement. It is sufficient to say that such evidence as there is falls far short of justification. It must therefore follow that the agreement so far as unperformed is unenforceable.

11.2.5 Severance of the objectionable parts of covenants

11.2.5.1 Striking out the objectionable part as it stands

Goldsoll v Goldman
[1915] 1 Ch 292 (CA)

The claimant and the defendant were both in business as dealers in imitation jewellery at Old Bond Street and New Bond Street in London. The defendant sold his business to the claimant and covenanted that for two years he would not:

> either solely or jointly with or as agent or employee for any person or persons or company directly or indirectly carry on or be engaged or concerned or interested in or render services (gratuitously or otherwise) to the business of a vendor of or dealer in real or imitation jewellery in the county of London, England, Scotland, Ireland, Wales, or any part of the United Kingdom of Great Britain and Ireland and the Isle of Man or in France, the United States of America, Russia, or Spain, or within twenty-five miles of Potsdamerstrasse, Berlin, or St. Stefans Kirche, Vienna.

Held: The covenant was too wide in terms of subject matter, since it referred to real jewellery when the defendant had not traded in real jewellery. It was also too wide in geographical area, since the defendant had not traded abroad. However, these restrictions were severable from the rest of the promise, leaving a covenant that the defendant would not carry on the business of dealing in imitation jewellery in the UK or the Isle of Man. This restriction was reasonably necessary for the claimant's protection and hence was enforceable.

NOTES

1. This is an example of severance in a covenant relating to the sale of a business. It may be that the courts are less likely to sever in the case of covenants between employer and employee, where the bargaining power may be unequal.

2. *Nordenfelt v Maxim Nordenfelt Guns & Ammunition Co. Ltd* [1894] AC 535 (*page 581, 11.2.1*) is another example of severance in the context of a covenant on the sale of a business. The second part of the covenant, relating to engaging in any business competing with that of the company, was void because it went further than was reasonably necessary to protect the business acquired. However, it could be severed from the first part because the two were clearly separable promises.

3. In *Mason v Provident Clothing & Supply Co. Ltd* [1913] AC 724 (*page 582, 11.2.2*), concerning a covenant between employer and employee, the House of Lords refused to redraft a clause so as to render it reasonable. Therefore, the whole promise was void and unenforceable.

LORD MOULTON: It would in my opinion be pessimi exempli if, when an employer had exacted a covenant deliberately framed in unreasonably wide terms, the Courts were to come to his assistance and, by applying their ingenuity and knowledge of the law, carve out of this void covenant the maximum of what he might validly have required. It must be remembered that the real sanction at the back of these covenants is the terror and expense of litigation, in which the servant is usually at a great disadvantage, in view of the longer purse of his master. It is sad to think that in this present case this appellant, whose employment is a comparatively humble one, should have had to go through four Courts before he could free himself from such unreasonable restraints as this covenant imposes, and the hardship imposed by the exaction of unreasonable covenants by employers would be greatly increased if they could continue the practice with the expectation that, having exposed the servant to the anxiety and expense of litigation, the Court would in the end enable them to obtain everything which they could have obtained by acting reasonably. It is evident that those who drafted this covenant aimed at making it a penal rather than a protective covenant, and that they hoped by means of it to paralyse the earning capabilities of the man if and when he left their service, and were not thinking of what would be a reasonable protection to their business, and having so acted they must take the consequences.

11.2.5.2 Severance must not alter the nature of the original covenant

Tillman v Egon Zehnder Ltd
[2019] UKSC 32

The claimant was employed by the defendant, the UK subsidiary in a worldwide group in the business of specialist executive search and recruitment. Clause 13 of the agreement, entitled COVENANTS, provided that the claimant would not, for a six-month period after the termination of her employment, 'without the prior written consent of the company directly or indirectly, either alone or jointly with or on behalf of any third party and whether as principal, manager, employee, contractor, consultant, agent or otherwise'. Her employment came to an end on 30 January 2017, and she informed the defendant that she intended to start working for a competing company on 1 May 2017. The claimant contended that the covenant was void for restraint of trade, in that the prohibition on her being 'interested' in any competing business was unreasonable and prohibited her from holding even a minority shareholding in a competing business. The Supreme Court agreed that the clause had that effect and fell within the doctrine of restraint of trade, and it was conceded that it was unreasonable. The question was whether the word 'interested' could be severed from the rest of the clause. The claimant relied upon *Attwood v Lamont* [1920] 3 KB 571 (CA) for the proposition that where there was a single covenant for the protection of the employer's entire business rather than several covenants for the protection of different businesses, severance was not possible without altering the nature of the covenant and so the entire covenant was void.

Held: The covenant was severable and the word 'interest' could be severed, leaving the remainder of the covenant in force so that the claimant could not be employed by a competitor within six months.

LORD WILSON (with whose judgment the rest of the Supreme Court agreed): 73. In *Beckett Investment Management Group Ltd v Hall* [2007] EWCA Civ 613, [2007] ICR 1539, the defendants, who had been employed by the claimant as independent financial advisers, covenanted that, for the year immediately following termination of their employment, they would not deal with any of the claimant's clients with whom they had dealt in the preceding year; and that, if they had then dealt with agents of its clients, the agents should be deemed to be its clients for this purpose. The Court of Appeal held that the deeming of agents as clients was unreasonable; that the covenant should be severed and the deeming provision removed; and that the remainder of the restraint should be enforced against the defendants . . .

79. A survey of the development in England and Wales of the severance principle, when applied to post-employment restraints of trade, would be deficient if it failed to note the current standing of the principle in other common law jurisdictions. In *Shafron v KRG Insurance Brokers (Western) Inc* [2009] 1 RCS 157 the Supreme Court of Canada, by a judgment delivered by Rothstein J, firmly adhered at para 36 to the historical approach directed by the *Attwood* case from the foot of the observations of Lord Moulton; and it even rejected the move in the *T Lucas* case to shed the second requirement of triviality or technicality. By contrast, in *Lee Gwee Noi v Humming Flowers and Gifts Pte Ltd* [2014] SGHC 64, a magisterial survey of the standing of the principle in Singapore, albeit conducted at first instance, concluded that its application there was subject to the three criteria approved in the *Beckett* case: paras 155 and 172. In New Zealand the legislature has relieved the courts altogether from the shackles of the severance principle by conferring on them a discretion actively to rewrite an unreasonable covenant in restraint of trade: see section 83(1)(b) of the Contract and Commercial Law Act 2017 . . .

84. It therefore becomes appropriate to analyse the effect of each of the three criteria indorsed in the *Beckett* case.

85. The first is that 'the unenforceable provision is capable of being removed without the necessity of adding to or modifying the wording of what remains'. This is the so-called 'blue pencil' test. Unfortunately it can work capriciously and, if the aspiration of our judgments today had been to discern in the common law a principle which can always be applied so as to produce a sensible outcome, we would have laboured in vain. In his judgment in the Divisional Court in [*Attwood v Lamont* [1920] 2 KB 146], Bailhache J said at p 155:

> . . . the courts will sever in a proper case where the severance can be performed by a blue pencil but not otherwise. To give an illustration, a covenant 'not to carry on business in Birmingham or within 100 miles' may be severed so as to reduce the area to Birmingham, but a covenant 'not to carry on business within 100 miles of Birmingham' will not be severed so as to read 'will not carry on business in Birmingham'. The distinction seems artificial, but is I think settled.

The distinction is indeed settled. It is inherent in the word 'severance' itself, which means cutting things up and does not extend to adding things in. The 'blue pencil' criterion is a significant brake on application of the principle; and, although it can work arbitrarily, it is in my view an appropriate brake on the ability of employers to secure severance of an unreasonable restraint customarily devised by themselves. Were it ever to be thought appropriate to confer on the court a power to rewrite a restraint so as to make it reasonable, it would surely have to be achieved by legislation along the lines of that in New Zealand which has been noticed in para 79 above.

86. The second criterion is that 'the remaining terms continue to be supported by adequate consideration'. It goes without saying that an employer who sues on a covenant made otherwise than under seal must show that he provided consideration for it. But why is it said to be a prerequisite of his ability to sever? The answer is surely to be found in the unusual circumstances of the *Sadler* and *Marshall* cases, which generated the criteria adopted in the *Beckett* case. In those two cases it was the claimant employee who secured severance of unreasonable obligations cast by the contract upon himself. In that situation the court needed to satisfy itself (and in each case it did so) that, were his unreasonable obligation to be removed, there would nevertheless remain consideration passing from him under the contract such as would support the obligation which he was seeking to enforce. In the usual post-employment situation, however, the need to do so does not arise. A claimant employer who asks the court to sever and remove part of a covenant made by the defendant employee is in no way proposing to diminish the consideration passing from himself under the contract such as is necessary to support the obligation which he seeks to enforce. In the usual situation the second requirement can be ignored.

87. The third criterion is that 'the removal of the unenforceable provision does not so change the character of the contract that it becomes "not the sort of contract that the parties entered into at all"'. This is the crucial criterion and I find it impossible to equate it with the *Attwood* requirement, as suggested by the Court of Appeal. In my view this third criterion was rightly imported into the general jurisprudence by the *Beckett* case and has rightly been applied by our courts ever since then, otherwise than in the decision under appeal. But I suggest, with respect, that the criterion would better be expressed as being whether removal of the provision would not generate any major change in the overall effect of all the post-employment restraints in the contract. It is for the employer to establish that its removal would not do so. The focus is on the legal effect of the restraints, which will remain constant, not on their perhaps changing significance for the parties and in particular for the employee.

88. Application of the severance principle to Ms Tillman's restraint covenants now becomes straight-forward. First, the words 'or interested' are capable of being removed from the non-competition covenant without the need to add to or modify the wording of the remainder. And, second, removal of the prohibition against her being 'interested' would not generate any major change in the overall effect of the restraints. So those words should be severed and removed

11.3 Money or property transferred under an illegal contract

11.3.1 General rule

Before the decision in *Patel v Mirza*, as a general principle, money or property transferred under an illegal contract could be recovered. For example, in *Parkinson v College of Ambulance Ltd & Harrison* [1925] 2 KB 1, it was not possible for the payer to recover the money paid in the belief that he was to receive a knighthood, even though he had been defrauded. The courts gradually developed a series of exceptions to the principle of no recovery, including: the parties were not of equal guilt (not *in pari delicto*); the contract was not performed and the guilty party withdrew (*locus poenitentia*); and no reliance on the illegal contract. Those exceptions were rendered redundant by *Patel v Mirza*, as there is now a generalized approach to recovery of benefits conferred under an illegal contract. The cases on these topics have accordingly been deleted from the present edition of this work, although for those wishing to investigate the history of the issue the most important of the cases can be found in the 14th edition.

Patel v Mirza
[2016] UKSC 42

A foreign exchange broker had agreed with the claimant that the broker would place a bet on the movement of Royal Bank of Scotland (RBS) shares based on advance information that he was to receive from insiders in the bank concerning a statement from the government relating to its investment in the bank and the claimant transferred £620,000 for this purpose. The bet was not placed because the government statement (i.e. the insider information) did not materialize. The claimant wanted the return of his money, but it was alleged that the contract was illegal as relying upon insider information, which was illegal under Part V of the Criminal Justice Act 1993. At first instance the judge held that the money could not be recovered because the claimant would need to plead the illegal purpose underpinning the payment of that money and the failure of that purpose. The claimant could not rely on the doctrine of the *locus poenitentiae* (voluntary withdrawal from the agreement before performance) because the reason the illegal agreement was not carried out was down to a change in circumstances which caused the purpose of the agreement to be frustrated for reasons other than the claimant's actions, i.e. the claimant 'never himself withdrew, and certainly did not do so voluntarily'. The Court of Appeal reversed the trial judge, holding that the agreement had not been wholly or partially performed and the reason for the claimant's withdrawal was irrelevant. The Supreme Court upheld the Court of Appeal, but there was a division on why that was the case. Lord Toulson (with whom Lady Hale and Lords Kerr, Wilson, and Hodge agreed), rested his decision on the flexible approach to illegality. Lord Neuberger held that the *locus poenitentia* principle applied, but that, more generally, Lord Toulson's flexible approach should be adopted.

LORD TOULSON: 120. The essential rationale of the illegality doctrine is that it would be contrary to the public interest to enforce a claim if to do so would be harmful to the integrity of the legal system (or, possibly, certain aspects of public morality, the boundaries of which have never been made entirely clear and which do not arise for consideration in this case). In assessing whether the public interest would be harmed in that way, it is necessary a) to consider the underlying purpose of the prohibition which has been transgressed and whether that purpose will be enhanced by denial of the claim, b) to consider any other relevant public policy on which the denial of the claim may have an impact and c) to consider whether denial of the claim would be a proportionate response to the illegality, bearing in mind that punishment is a matter for the criminal courts. Within that framework, various factors may be relevant, but it would be a mistake to suggest that the court is free to decide a case in an undisciplined way. The public interest is best served by a principled and transparent assessment of the considerations identified, rather by than the application of a formal approach capable of producing results which may appear arbitrary, unjust or disproportionate.

121. A claimant, such as Mr Patel, who satisfies the ordinary requirements of a claim for unjust enrichment, should not be debarred from enforcing his claim by reason only of the fact that the money which he seeks to recover was paid for an unlawful purpose. There may be rare cases where for some particular reason the enforcement of such a claim might be regarded as undermining the integrity of the justice system, but there are no such circumstances in this case. I would dismiss the appeal.

11.3.2 The Law Commission and reform

In its Consultation Paper No. 154, *Illegal Transactions: The effect of illegality on contracts and trusts* (1999), paras. 7.27–7.57, the Law Commission had proposed introducing a discretion (in cases other than those in which the contract is illegal as being contrary to public policy) enabling the courts to decide whether illegality should act as a defence to a claim to enforce a contract the formation, purpose, or performance of which is illegal. In the exercise of this discretion, the Law Commission had proposed that the courts should consider: the seriousness of the illegality; the knowledge and intention of the claimant; and whether denying relief would act as a deterrent, would be proportionate to the illegality, or would further the purpose of the rules rendering the contract illegal. The Law Commission recognized that, inevitably, such a proposed reform would introduce uncertainty, but it would give the courts the flexibility to examine the claimant's position on the individual facts of the case and ensure that the policy objectives lying behind the illegality rules are respected.

However, when the Law Commission published its long-awaited Consultative Report No. 189, *The Illegality Defence* (2009), whilst reaffirming its criticisms of the law, it retreated from its recommendation for a discretion (para. 3.122) and instead recommended that any improvement to the law 'can best be left to development through the case law'. The Law Commission noted (Part 2, para. 2.35) that:

The illegality defence should be allowed where its application can be firmly justified by the policies that underlie its existence. These include: (a) furthering the purpose of the rule which the illegal conduct has infringed; (b) consistency; (c) that the claimant should not profit from his or her own wrong; (d) deterrence; and (e) maintaining the integrity of the legal system.

There is one important exception, however: the Law Commission provisionally recommended legislation to implement a 'structured discretion to deprive a beneficial owner of his interest in the trust in limited circumstances' (para. 6.100). In other words, the intention was to deprive, in some circumstances, a *Tinsley v Milligan* party of the beneficial interest that they can currently establish based on a resulting trust.

A year later, the Law Commission published its final Report No. 320, *The Illegality Defence* (2010), which included a draft Bill: the Trusts (Concealment of Interests) Bill. In this report, the Law Commission recommended that where a trust has been set up to conceal the beneficiary's interest in order to commit a criminal offence, as in *Tinsley*, there should be legislative intervention to provide the courts with a discretion to deprive the beneficiary of their interest in limited circumstances. The draft Bill was intended to implement the recommendation. Pending implementation, however, *Tinsley v Milligan* remains good law.

In the context of the doctrine of *locus poenitentiae*, the Law Commission's 1999 Consultation Paper No. 154, paras. 7.58–7.69, had provisionally proposed that the courts should have a discretion to allow a party to withdraw from an illegal contract and to have any property or benefits restored where this would reduce the likelihood of the illegal act being completed or the illegal purpose being accomplished. The court would first need to be satisfied that the contract could not be enforced against that party and, in considering the exercise of this discretion, it was proposed that the court should consider: (i) whether the claimant genuinely repents of the illegality; and (ii) the seriousness of the illegality in question. However, as we have seen, in its 2009 Consultative Report No. 189, the Law Commission retreated from legislative reform in favour of 'development through case law'. The future of the doctrine of *locus poenitentiae* will therefore be a matter of balancing the competing policies at play in this area, which include a number that have direct relevance in terms of the situations in which the doctrine may be relied upon. For example, the named policies include 'deterrence', 'maintaining the integrity of the legal system', and ensuring that a claimant does not profit from his own wrong. The question of 'repentance' was not mentioned.

The Law Commission had also been concerned about the interaction of the presumption of advancement and the illegality principles. It recommended abolition of the presumption as discriminatory and the Equality Act 2010 contains a provision to this effect in s. 199—although, at the time of writing, it has yet to be brought into force and even the Law Commission considers that intervening case law developments in the law of trusts mean that this section might not achieve its objectives in any event. The Law Commission's Consultative Report had similarly recommended that any improvement to the law was best left to the courts. Although that report has not been implemented by Parliament, the Supreme Court has effectively done so in *Patel v Mirza*.

Performance and termination of contract

Part

4

Chapter 12

Discharge by frustration: subsequent impossibility

12.1 The frustration doctrine: discharge for subsequent impossibility

If, after the formation of the contract, events occur without the fault of either party that render further performance of the contract impossible, illegal, or radically different from what was originally envisaged, the contract may be automatically discharged on the grounds of frustration and the parties will be excused further performance of their contractual obligations. Statute also provides for adjustment of obligations arising before frustration.

However, the frustration doctrine applies only in the absence of an express provision in the contract allocating the risk. If the contract contains such a *force majeure* clause covering the event that has occurred, that clause will govern and not the frustration doctrine.

12.2 The contractual allocation of risk

12.2.1 Assuming the risk

If one party has assumed the risk of the event in question or has assumed the risk of the existence of the subject matter, in the event that the risk materializes or the subject matter ceases to exist, that party will be responsible and cannot rely on the legal doctrine of frustration. It is vital therefore to examine the scope of any such *force majeure* clause to determine whether it can be construed as applying to the event in question.

12.2.2 Event occurs as a result of the fault of one of the parties

The essence of frustration is that the extraneous event that renders the contract impossible to perform is not attributable to any act or fault of one of the parties. If it is, the impossibility is said to be 'self-induced' and the frustration doctrine cannot apply.

12

Maritime National Fish Ltd v Ocean Trawlers Ltd
[1935] AC 524 (PC)

The defendants (appellants in the appeal) chartered a steam trawler, the *St Cuthbert*, from the claimants solely for fishing use. It could operate as a trawler only with an otter trawl and both parties knew that a licence was required. The defendants applied to the minister for licences for five trawlers that they were operating (including the *St Cuthbert*). The minister indicated that only three licences would be granted and asked the defendants to name the three trawlers to which the licences would be applied. The defendants did not name the *St Cuthbert* as one of the three. The claimants claimed the charter hire, but the defendants pleaded that the charter was frustrated because it was impossible to perform, i.e. to use this vessel to fish.

Held: The charter contract was not frustrated because the defendants' own election had prevented this trawler from having a licence to fish. The defendants were liable for the hire.

LORD WRIGHT [delivering the judgment of the court]: The essence of 'frustration' is that it should not be due to the act or election of the party. There does not appear to be any authority which has been decided directly on this point. There is, however, a reference to the question in the speech of Lord Sumner in *Bank Line, Ltd v Arthur Capel & Co.* [1919] AC 435. What he says is: . . .

> . . . I think it is now well settled that the principle of frustration of an adventure assumes that the frustration arises without blame or fault on either side. Reliance cannot be placed on a self-induced frustration; indeed, such conduct might give the other party the option to treat the contract as repudiated . . .

If it be assumed that the performance of the contract was dependent on a licence being granted, it was [the appellants'] election which prevented performance, and on that assumption it was the appellants' own default which frustrated the adventure: the appellants cannot rely on their own default to excuse them from liability under the contract.

NOTES

1. In *Ocean Tramp Tankers Corporation v V/O Sovfracht, The Eugenia* [1964] 2 QB 226, *The Eugenia* was chartered for a voyage to India via the Black Sea. A clause in the charterparty provided that the vessel was not to be taken into a war zone without the owner's consent. The vessel entered the Suez Canal in breach of this war clause and became trapped when the Canal was blocked. The charterers claimed that the charterparty was frustrated. Lord Denning MR stated, at p. 237, that:

> One thing that is obvious is that the charterers cannot rely on the fact that the *Eugenia* was trapped in the canal; for that was their own fault. They were in breach of the war clause in entering it. They cannot rely on a self-induced frustration, see *Maritime National Fish Ltd v Ocean Trawlers Ltd* [1935] AC 524.

2. In *Great Peace Shipping Ltd v Tsavliris Salvage (International) Ltd* [2001] EWCA Civ 1407, [2003] QB 679, Lord Phillips MR considered that the question of assumption of risk and whether the impossibility is attributable to the fault of one of the parties to be similar in effect. In both cases, one party will assume the responsibility for the subsequent event and the doctrine of frustration cannot apply to excuse non-performance.

3. If one party wishes to argue that a particular event was caused by the other's fault, he must prove it on the balance of probabilities: *Joseph Constantine Steamship Line Ltd v Imperial Smelting Corporation Ltd* [1942] AC 154. The other will then be in breach of contract.

The mere existence of a choice may be sufficient to establish that what follows was self-induced.

J. Lauritzen AS v Wijsmuller BV, The Super Servant Two
[1990] 1 Lloyd's Rep 1 (CA)

The defendants agreed to carry the claimants' drilling rig (the *'Dan King* contract'), and to deliver it between 20 June and 20 August 1981, using either *Super Servant One* or *Super Servant Two*. The defendants had intended to use *Super Servant Two* for this contract and had entered into other contracts with third parties that they could perform only using *Super Servant One*. On 29 January 1981, the *Super Servant Two* sank and, in February 1981, the defendants informed the claimants that they would not perform. When the claimants alleged breach of contract, the defendants argued that they were not liable because the contract had been frustrated by the sinking of *Super Servant Two*.

Held: According to the contract terms, the defendants could have satisfied their obligation by using *Super Servant One* after *Super Servant Two* had sunk, but had elected not to do so. The frustration doctrine could only assist a party who had contracted to perform a contract with a vessel that, through no fault of its own, no longer existed. It therefore could not apply here, since there was an alternative, and the sinking of *Super Servant Two* did not automatically bring the contract to an end.

BINGHAM LJ: The argument in this case raises important issues on the English law of frustration . . . Certain propositions, established by the highest authority, are not open to question:

1. The doctrine of frustration was evolved to mitigate the rigour of the common law's insistence on literal performance of absolute promises (*Hirji Mulji v Cheong Yue Steamship Co. Ltd* . . . (1926) 24 Ll L Rep 209 at p. 213, col. 2; [1926] AC 497 at p. 510: *Denny, Mott & Dickson Ltd v James B. Fraser & Co. Ltd* [1944] AC 265 at p. 275; *Joseph Constantine Steamship Line Ltd v Imperial Smelting Corporation Ltd* (1941) 70 Ll L Rep 1 at p. 12, col. 2; [1942] AC 154 at p. 171). The object of the doctrine was to give effect to the demands of justice, to achieve a just and reasonable result, to do what is reasonable and fair, as an expedient to escape from injustice where such would result from enforcement of a contract in its literal terms after a significant change in circumstances (*Hirji Mulji*, . . . at p. 213, col. 2; p. 510; *Joseph Constantine Steamship Line Ltd* . . . at p. 18, col, 2; p. 23, col. 1; pp. 183, 193; *National Carriers Ltd v Panalpina (Northern) Ltd* [1981] AC 675 at p. 701).

2. Since the effect of frustration is to kill the contract and discharge the parties from further liability under it, the doctrine is not to be lightly invoked, must be kept within very narrow limits and ought not to be extended (*Bank Line Ltd v Arthur Capel & Co.* [1919] AC 435 at p. 459; *Davis Contractors Ltd* . . . at pp. 715, 727; *Pioneer Shipping Ltd v B.T.P. Tioxide Ltd (The Nema)* [1981] 2 Lloyd's Rep 239 at p. 253, col. 2; [1982] AC 724 at 752).

3. Frustration brings the contract to an end forthwith, without more and automatically (*Hirji Mulji*, . . . at pp. 211, 212; pp. 505, 509; *Maritime National Fish Ltd v Ocean Trawlers Ltd* (1935) 51 Lloyd's L Rep 299 at p. 302; [1935] AC 524 at p. 527; *Joseph Constantine Steamship Line Ltd* . . . at pp. 9, 11, 12, 20, 25; pp. 163, 170, 171, 187, 200; *Denny Mott & Dickson Ltd* . . . at p. 274).

4. The essence of frustration is that it should not be due to the act or election of the party seeking to rely on it (*Hirji Mulji* . . . at p. 213; p. 510; *Maritime National Fish Ltd* . . . at p. 303; p. 530; *Joseph Constantine Steamship Ltd* . . . at p. 12; p. 170; *Denny Mott & Dickson Ltd* . . . at p. 274; *Davis Contractors Ltd* . . . at p. 728). A frustrating event must be some outside event or extraneous change of situation (*Paal Wilson & Co. A/S v Partenreederi Hannah Blumenthal (The Hannah Blumenthal)* [1983] 1 Lloyd's Rep 103 at p. 112; [1983] 1 AC 854 at p. 909).

5. A frustrating event must take place without blame or fault on the side of the party seeking to rely on it (*Bank Line Ltd* . . . at 452; *Joseph Constantine Steamship Ltd* . . . at p. 12; p. 171; *Davis Contractors Ltd* . . . at p. 729; *The Hannah Blumenthal* [1982] 1 Lloyd's Rep 582 at p. 592; [1983] 1 Lloyd's Rep 103 at p. 112; [1983] 1 AC 854 at pp. 882, 909) . . .

Had the *Dan King* contract provided for carriage by *Super Servant Two* with no alternative, and that vessel had been lost before the time for performance, then assuming no negligence by Wijsmuller (as for purposes of this question we must), I feel sure the contract would have been frustrated. The doctrine must avail a party who contracts to perform a contract of carriage with a vessel which, through no fault of his, no longer exists. But that is not this case. The *Dan King* contract did provide an alternative. When that contract was made one of the contracts eventually performed by *Super Servant One* during the period of contractual carriage of *Dan King* had been made, the other had not, at any rate finally. Wijsmuller have not alleged that when the *Dan King* contract was made either vessel was earmarked for its performance. That, no doubt, is why an option was contracted for. Had it been foreseen when the *Dan King* contract was made that *Super Servant Two* would be unavailable for performance, whether because she had been deliberately sold or accidentally sunk, Lauritzen at least would have thought it no matter since the carriage could be performed with the other . . . [T]he present case does not fall within the very limited class of cases in which the law will relieve one party from an absolute promise he has chosen to make

. . . I cannot, furthermore, reconcile Wijsmuller's argument with the reasoning or the decision in *Maritime National Fish Ltd* . . . In that case the Privy Council declined to speculate why the charterers selected three of the five vessels to be licensed but, as I understand the case, regarded the interposition of human choice after the allegedly frustrating event as fatal to the plea of frustration. If Wijsmuller are entitled to succeed here, I cannot see why the charterers lost there. The cases on frustrating delay do not, I think, help Wijsmuller since it is actual and prospective delay (whether or not recognised as frustrating by a party at the time) which frustrates the contract, not a party's election or decision to treat the delay as frustrating . . . [I]t is in my view inconsistent with the doctrine of frustration as previously understood on high authority that its application should depend on any decision, however reasonable and commercial, of the party seeking to rely on it.

NOTES

1. Bingham LJ considered that the existence of a choice was fatal no matter how reasonable and commercial the decision to elect had been.

Treitel's view—that if the party acted reasonably in making the election, it could use such means as remained available to perform some of the contracts and claim that the others were frustrated by the supervening event—was rejected by the Court of Appeal. Dillon LJ stated, at pp. 13–14:

It is the view of Professor Treitel . . . that where a party has entered into a number of contracts with other parties and an uncontemplated supervening event has the result that he is deprived of the means of satisfying all those contracts, he can, provided he acts 'reasonably' in making his election, elect to use such means as remains available to him to perform some of the contracts, and claim that the others, which he does not perform, have been frustrated by the supervening event. The reasoning depends on the proposition that if it is

known to those concerned that the party will have entered into commitments with others and if he acts 'reasonably' in his allocation of his remaining means to his commitments, the chain of causation between the uncontemplated supervening event and the non-performance of those of his contracts which will not have been performed will not have been broken by the election to apply his remaining means in a 'reasonable' way . . . Such an approach is however inconsistent to my mind with the view expressed by Lord Wright in . . . *Maritime National Fish* . . . where he said:

It is immaterial to speculate why they preferred to put forward for licences the three trawlers which they actually selected.

It is also, as my Lord has pointed out, inconsistent with the long accepted view that frustration brings the contract to an end forthwith, without more ado automatically. Plainly the sinking of *Super Servant Two* did not do that, since even after that sinking the defendants could have used *Super Servant One* to perform the contract.

See the assessment in Peel, *Treitel's The Law of Contract*, 14th edn (Sweet & Maxwell, 2015), [19-086]–[19-088], and in Treitel, *Frustration and Force Majeure*, 3rd edn (Sweet & Maxwell, 2014), ch. 14.

2. It appears that the Court considered that the risk of the defendants being overcommitted had been placed on the defendants. If they had wished to alter this, an appropriately drafted *force majeure* clause could have been incorporated.

It is evident that the courts prefer the risk to be placed on one of the parties to the contract, thereby avoiding the application of the frustration doctrine.

3. See Swanton (1990) 2 JCL 206 and McKendrick [1990] LMCLQ 153.

12.3 The theoretical basis for the doctrine of frustration

12.3.1 The competing theories

It was originally considered that the doctrine of frustration was based on the implication of a term, e.g. an implied condition that if the subject matter of the contract were to cease to exist then the contract would be discharged.

Taylor v Caldwell
(1863) 3 B & S 826, 122 ER 309 (QB)

On 27 May 1862, the claimants entered into a contract with the defendants whereby the defendants agreed to let the claimants have the use of Surrey Gardens and Music Hall on 17 June, 15 July, and 5 and 19 August for the purpose of giving a series of four grand concerts and fêtes. On 11 June (before the first of these dates on which a concert was to be given), the Hall was destroyed by fire, without the fault of either party. The concerts could not be given as intended. The claimants argued that the defendants were in breach of contract in failing to supply the Hall and they sought damages for their wasted advertising expenditure.

Held: The continuation of the contract was subject to an implied condition that the parties would be excused if the subject matter was destroyed. Therefore the contract was discharged by frustration, both parties were released and no breach of contract had occurred.

BLACKBURN J [delivering the judgment of the court]: [W]here, from the nature of the contract, it appears that the parties must from the beginning have known that it could not be fulfilled unless when the time for the fulfilment of the contract arrived some particular specified thing continued to exist, so that, when entering into the contract, they must have contemplated such continuing existence as the foundation of what was to be done; there, in the absence of any express or implied warranty that the thing shall exist, the contract is not to be construed as a positive contract, but as subject to an implied condition that the parties shall be excused in case, before breach, performance becomes impossible from the perishing of the thing without default of the contractor.

There seems little doubt that this implication tends to further the great object of making the legal construction such as to fulfil the intention of those who entered into the contract. For in the course of affairs men in making such contracts in general would, if it were brought to their minds, say that there should be such a condition . . .

. . . [The] excuse is by law implied, because from the nature of the contract it is apparent that the parties contracted on the basis of the continued existence of the particular person or chattel. In the present case, looking at the whole contract, we find that the parties contracted on the basis of the continued existence of the Music Hall at the time when the concerts were to be given; that being essential to their performance . . . We think, therefore, that the Music Hall having ceased to exist, without fault of either party, both parties are excused, the plaintiffs from taking the gardens and paying the money, the defendants from performing their promise to give the use of the Hall and Gardens . . .

However, the implied term theory was rejected by the House of Lords in the context of frustration in *Davis Contractors v Fareham Urban District Council* [1956] AC 969, in which contractors agreed to build 78 houses for a local authority for £92,425 within a period of eight months. Without the fault of either party, adequate supplies of labour were not available and the work took 22 months to complete. The contractors argued that the contract was frustrated and that they could therefore claim on a *quantum meruit* basis (which would be more than the contract price) for the houses that they completed. It was held that the contract had not been frustrated. The shortage of labour had rendered the contract more onerous than expected, but had not altered the fundamental nature of the contractual performance. It will be seen that the contractors were seeking to profit from the frustration by using it to escape the contractual price that they had agreed, and instead to claim a larger sum on a *quantum meruit*. Not surprisingly, the Court denied that result. Lord Radcliffe's test was whether the frustrating event created 'a thing radically different from that which was undertaken by the contract'. The decision of the Court of Appeal in *Great Peace Shipping Ltd v Tsavliris Salvage (International) Ltd* [2002] EWCA Civ 1407, [2003] QB 679, has also since confirmed that the development of the doctrines of frustration and common mistake (initial impossibility) was linked, so that the implied term theory is also inappropriate as the theoretical basis for common mistake.

Much of the difficulty in reconciling the case law concerning the frustration doctrine stems from the fact that some of it is professed to be based on the implied theory in *Taylor v Caldwell*, e.g. *Krell v Henry* [1903] 2 KB 740. The earlier case law should now be considered in the light of the restatement of principle by Marcus Smith J in *Canary Wharf (BP4) T1 Ltd v European Medicines Agency* [2019] EWHC 921 (Ch).

Canary Wharf (BP4) T1 Ltd v European Medicines Agency
[2019] EWHC 921 (Ch)

In October 2014 Canary Wharf agreed to lease premises to EMA, an agency of the EU, for a period of 25 years. Following the UK's decision to leave the EU, EMA contended that the lease had been frustrated in that an EU agency could no longer use the premises as a matter of law or practicality and that if it was required to continue to pay rent then it would still have to rent premises elsewhere in the EU. At the time of the hearing the date and terms of withdrawal from the EU had not been determined, and the Court was required to consider a number of different scenarios.

Held: Even though the withdrawal of the UK from the EU had not been foreseeable, the lease had not been frustrated in that its terms dealt specifically with the consequences of early termination for any reason. EMA could either assign or sublet the premises, failing which the rent remained payable. The Court analysed the basis of frustration.

MARCUS SMITH J:

. . .

(2) The juridical basis for the doctrine of frustration

25. It is difficult to differentiate between subsequent events that do not, and subsequent events that do, cause a contract to be frustrated. Whilst it is clear that the object of the doctrine is to do justice as between the parties, where injustice would result from the literal enforcement of the contract, what is 'just' and what is 'unjust' is coloured by the nature of the doctrine and the juridical basis upon which it operates.

26. A number of juridical bases have been articulated:

(1) *The implied term or implied condition theory.* By this theory, the court must consider whether a term or condition can be implied into the contract, providing for the subsequent event. The problem with such an approach is that it turns on a test of what the parties would have said in response to the interjection of the 'officious bystander' at the moment of the parties' agreement. Given that the subsequent, frustrating, event is something in essence unanticipated, it is difficult to know what such a person would say. As Lord Hailsham noted in *National Carriers Ltd v. Panalpina (Northern) Ltd* [1981] 1 AC 675 at 700 'I have not the least idea what they would have said, or whether either would have entered into the lease at all'. Of course, where the legal test for the implication of a term is met, the term implied may very well be relevant to questions of frustration. But that is not the same as resolving all questions of frustration by reference to an implied term or condition.

(2) *The total failure of consideration theory.* By this theory, a contract can only be frustrated where the subsequent event causes one party to sustain a total failure of consideration. As an explanation for the doctrine of frustration, it is inadequate on two grounds:

(a) First, as Lord Hailsham noted in *Panalpina*, 'many, if not most, cases of frustration which have followed *Taylor v. Caldwell* have occurred during the currency of a contract executed on both sides, when no question of total failure of consideration can possibly arise'.

(b) Secondly, there will be cases of total failure of consideration, where there is no subsequent 'frustrating' event. Not every total failure of consideration ends in the contract being frustrated, and the total failure of consideration theory says nothing about what constitutes a 'frustrating' event.

(3) *The 'frustration of the adventure' or 'frustration of the foundation of the contract' theory.* Although attractively phrased, this theory is no more than a form of words, with no clear meaning behind it. As Lord Hailsham said in *Panalpina*:

This, of course, leaves open the question of what is, in any given case, the foundation of the contract or what is 'fundamental' to it or what is the 'adventure'.

(4) *Construction of the contract theory.* This involves ascertaining precisely which obligations each party did, and did not, assume. Plainly—and unsurprisingly—where the contract makes sufficient provision for the subsequent 'frustrating' event, the contract will prevail, and there will be no discharge. This is, quite simply, a matter of the due and proper construction of the contract. But, just as with the implied term or implied condition theory—of which this is a more sophisticated variant—whilst the true construction of the contract may be relevant to the question of frustration, it is not of itself the test for frustration. Just as the parties may not know how to respond to the officious bystander in the case of implied terms, so too even a sophisticated contract, carefully constructed, may be silent in the face of a subsequent, unanticipated, event. More to the point, even a sophisticated contract which, on its face, appears to make provision for all subsequent vicissitudes may find itself defeated by the truly unforeseen.

(5) *Performance rendered radically different by fundamental change in circumstances.* Lord Radcliffe's dictum, quoted in paragraph 22 above, is said to encapsulate this theory, which has found favour in the recent case law. In *Panalpina*, Lord Roskill said this:

> What is sometimes called the construction theory has found greater favour. But, my Lords, if I may respectfully say so, I think the most satisfactory explanation of the doctrine is that given by Lord Radcliffe in *Davis Contractors Ltd v. Fareham Urban District Council*, [1956] 1 AC 696, 728. There must have been by reason of some supervening event some such fundamental change of circumstances as to enable the court to say: 'this was not the bargain which these parties made and their bargain must be treated as at an end' – a view which Lord Radcliffe himself tersely summarised in a quotation of five words from the *Aeneid*: '*non haec in foedera veni*'. Since in such a case the crucial question must be answered as one of law . . . by reference to the particular contract which the parties made and to the particular facts of the case in question, there is, I venture to think, little difference between Lord Radcliffe's view and the so-called construction theory.

In many cases, Lord Roskill may be right: in many cases, there may be little difference in outcome between the construction of the contract theory and the 'performance is radically different' test. But there is, in my judgment, a very material difference in how these two theories work in their application. Under the former, the true construction of the contract resolves all; the latter theory recognises the importance of the true construction of the contract, but also recognises that even construction has its limits when faced with extreme and unforeseeable supervening events.

27. As I have noted, certainly since *Panalpina*, the prevailing wisdom is that the fifth approach that I have described best encapsulates the essence of the doctrine of frustration. Whether a contract is frustrated depends upon a consideration of the nature of the bargain of the parties when considered in the light of the supervening event said to frustrate that bargain. Only if the supervening event renders the performance of the bargain 'radically different', when compared to the considerations in play at the conclusion of the contract, will the contract be frustrated.

12.3.2 Foreseeability

In *Ocean Tramp Tankers Corporation v V/O Sovfracht, The Eugenia* [1964] 2 QB 226 (*page 599, 12.2.2*) Lord Denning advocated that the frustration doctrine should still apply where the event is foreseen, as long as no provision is included to deal with it. There is a similar *obiter* statement by Goddard J in *W. J. Tatem Ltd v Gamboa* [1939] 1 KB 132. However, it appears that greater flexibility is required in assessing the impact of foreseeability, as expressed in the multifactorial test adopted in *Edwinton Commercial Corporation v Tsavliris Russ (Worldwide Salvage & Towage) Ltd, The Sea Angel* [2007] EWCA Civ 547, [2007] 1 CLC 876, [2007] 2 Lloyd's Rep 517 (*page 608, 12.4.1.2*). It was there argued that the seizure of a salvage ship was foreseeable where there were pollution concerns relating to the stricken vessel so that the charterer could not allege that the seizure absolved it from financial responsibility for port charges. The Court of Appeal used foreseeability as an aid to the construction process for determining frustration and concluded that the charter was not frustrated on these facts.

RIX LJ [with whose judgment Wall and Hooper LJJ agreed]:

The foreseeability of the risk

127 . . . In a sense, most events are to a greater or lesser degree foreseeable. That does not mean that they cannot lead to frustration. Even events which are not merely foreseen but made the subject of express contractual provision may lead to frustration: as occurs when an event such as a strike, or a

restraint of prices, lasts for so long as to go beyond the risk assumed under the contract and to render performance radically different from that contracted for. However, as Treitel shows through his analysis of the cases, and as *Chitty* [*Chitty on Contracts*] summarises, the less that an event, in its type and its impact, is foreseeable, the more likely it is to be a factor which, depending on other factors in the case, may lead on to frustration.

128 . . . The foreseeability of this general risk, recognised within the industry, and provided for in its well-known terms of trade (SCOPIC), provides a special and highly relevant factor against which the issue of frustration needs to be assessed. However, like most factors in most cases, it must not be exaggerated into something critical . . .

12.4 Frustrating events

A contract may be automatically discharged by frustration where a *frustrating event* occurs without the fault of the contracting parties *after* the formation of the contract.

12.4.1 Impossibility

12.4.1.1 Destruction of the subject matter

See *Taylor v Caldwell* (1863) 3 B & S 826, 122 ER 309 (*page 603, 12.3.1*). This was a contract for the hire of both the Hall and gardens. Only the Hall was destroyed, but the court held the contract to be frustrated. Compare this with *Herne Bay Steam Boat Co. v Hutton* [1903] 2 KB 683 (*page 614, 12.4.3*).

In sale of goods contracts, there are special rules governing the perishing of the goods without the fault of the parties.

Sale of Goods Act 1979

7. *Goods perishing before sale but after agreements to sell*

Where there is an agreement to sell specific goods and subsequently the goods, without any fault on the part of the seller or buyer, perish before the risk passes to the buyer, the agreement is avoided.

20. *Risk prima facie passes with property*

(1) Unless otherwise agreed, the goods remain at the seller's risk until the property in them is transferred to the buyer, but when the property in them is transferred to the buyer the goods are at the buyer's risk whether delivery has been made or not.

NOTES

1. Section 20(1) of the Sale of Goods Act (SGA) 1979 applies only in the context of a commercial contract (s. 20(4)), since where the buyer is a consumer, the goods remain at the seller's risk until delivery, identified as physical possession by the consumer (Consumer Rights Act (CRA) 2015, s. 29(1) and (2)).

2. If the goods are destroyed after the risk has passed, the contract is not frustrated. If the goods are destroyed before the risk has passed, the contract is frustrated where the goods are specific (i.e. identified and agreed on at the time that the contract is made), or if, under the contract, they are to come from a particular source and the entire source is destroyed.

3. If, on the other hand, the goods were not specific, sellers are obliged to deliver goods of the contractual description and cannot argue that the goods they intended to use have been destroyed. In this situation, the contract cannot be frustrated. In *CTI Group Inc. v Transclear SA, The Mary Nour* [2008] EWCA Civ 856, [2008] Bus LR 1729, the seller found that it had no sources of supply and sought to argue that its contracts of sale had become 'commercially impossible' to perform. However, the Court of Appeal held that the supply risk rested with the seller.

This was a case of breach and not frustration. Moore-Bick LJ stated:

> [27] . . . In order to rely on the doctrine of frustration it is necessary for there to have been a supervening event which renders the performance of the seller's obligations impossible or fundamentally different in nature from that which was envisaged when the contract was made. In the present case, however, . . . the nature of the performance called for by the contract remained the same.

The seller could have contracted to protect itself by making delivery conditional on it securing supply.

12.4.1.2 Temporary Unavailability of the Subject Matter

The question in each case is whether the contractual performance, when resumed, would amount to performance of a fundamentally different contract.

Jackson v Union Marine Insurance Co. Ltd
(1874) LR 10 CP 125 (Exchequer Chamber)

A ship was chartered in November 1871. It was required to proceed 'with all possible dispatch (dangers and accidents of navigation excepted) from Liverpool to Newport, and there load a cargo for carriage to San Francisco'. The ship sailed from Liverpool on 2 January 1872, but ran aground on the way to Newport on 3 January. The ship was not repaired until the end of August. On 15 February, the charterers repudiated the charter and chartered another ship. The shipowner brought an action on his insurance policy. The question in the case was whether the shipowner could have maintained an action against the charterers for not loading. Only if no such action could have been maintained would this be a loss of freight by insured perils entitling the owners to recover under the policy. The jury found as facts that the delay owing to the repairs was so long as to make it unreasonable for the charterers to supply a cargo in August for the voyage to San Francisco.

Held: The contract was frustrated and the charterers were not bound to load. There was therefore a loss of the chartered freight by perils of the sea within the insurance policy.

> BRAMWELL B: [The jury have found that] the voyage the parties contemplated had become impossible; that a voyage undertaken after the ship was sufficiently repaired would have been a different voyage, not, indeed, different as to the ports of loading and discharge, but different as a different adventure,—a voyage for which at the time of the charter the plaintiff had not in intention engaged the ship, nor the charterers the cargo; a voyage as different as though it had been described as intended to be a spring voyage, while the one after the repair would be an autumn voyage.

NOTES

1. In *Bank Line Ltd v Arthur Capel & Co.* [1919] AC 435, a 12-month charter was to run from April 1915 to April 1916. The ship was requisitioned before delivery and not returned until September 1915. The House of Lords (Viscount Haldane dissenting) held the charterparty to have been frustrated because a September–September charter would be a substantially different charter from that which had been agreed.

2. In cases involving unavailability for a temporary period, the courts have traditionally applied the test enunciated by Bailhache J in *Anglo-Northern Trading Co. Ltd v Emlyn Jones & Williams* [1917] 2 KB 78, 84: 'The main consideration is the probable length of the total deprivation of use of the vessel as compared with the unexpired duration of the charterparty.' However, in *The Sea Angel*, the Court of Appeal criticized the general application of such a test.

Edwinton Commercial Corporation v Tsavliris Russ (Worldwide Salvage & Towage) Ltd, The Sea Angel
[2007] EWCA Civ 547, [2007] 1 CLC 876, [2007] 2 Lloyd's Rep 517 (CA)

The Sea Angel was chartered for up to 20 days to enable the salvage company to remove oil from a stricken vessel. However, it was detained by the local port authorities for a three-month period towards the end of that 20 days, when it had just unloaded its last shuttle cargo of retrieved oil.

Held (on appeal): The charter was not frustrated by this unlawful detention. This was very different from a supervening event that postponed or interrupted the purpose of the contract, since this purpose had been largely performed and the only consequences of the detention were financial, i.e. the liability to pay the hire continued for longer.

RIX LJ [with whose judgment Wall and Hooper LJJ agreed]: 111 In my judgment, the application of the doctrine of frustration requires a multifactorial approach. Among the factors which have to be considered are the terms of the contract itself, its matrix or context, the parties' knowledge, expectations, assumptions and contemplations, in particular as to risk, as at the time of contract, at any rate so far as these can be ascribed mutually and objectively, and then the nature of the supervening event, and the parties' reasonable and objectively ascertainable calculations as to the possibilities of future performance in the new circumstances. Since the subject matter of the doctrine of frustration is contract, and contracts are about the allocation of risk, and since the allocation and assumption of risk is not simply a matter of express or implied provision but may also depend on less easily defined matters such as 'the contemplation of the parties', the application of the doctrine can often be a difficult one. In such circumstances, the test of 'radically different' is important: it tells us that the doctrine is not to be lightly invoked; that mere incidence of expense or delay or onerousness is not sufficient; and that there has to be as it were a break in identity between the contract as provided for and contemplated and its performance in the new circumstances . . .

117 . . . I agree with [counsel] that the critical question was whether, as of 13 October (or 17 October, and for present purposes I am content to adopt either date), the delay which had already occurred and prospective further delay would have led the parties at that time to have reasonably concluded that the charter was frustrated . . . For these purposes, since on the facts a delay of some five weeks had already occurred and the prospective delay involved in a revised strategy involving litigating in the Pakistani courts would involve a further four to six weeks at least, the first question to consider is whether [counsel] is right in his submission that the Bailhache J test of comparing the probable length of the delay with the unexpired duration of the charter is the critical or main and in any event overbearing test to apply (see *Anglo-Northern, Bank Line, Tatem v Gamboa*).

118 In my judgment it is not. It may be an important consideration, but it is, on our facts, only the starting point. In the first place, the development of the law shows that such a single-factored approach is too blunt an instrument . . . Secondly, requisition, like seizure in *Tatem v Gamboa*, could not be rectified; whereas in our case, the consequences of the detention by the port authorities remained very much a matter for enquiry, negotiation, diplomacy, and, whatever the ordering of the tactics, legal pressure. Thirdly, where, as in our case, the supervening event comes at the very end of a charter, with redelivery as essentially the only remaining obligation, the effect of the detention on the performance of the charter is purely a question of the financial consequences of the delay, which will fall on one party or the other, depending on whether the charter binds or does not bind. It is not like the different situation where the supervening event either postpones or, which may be even worse, interrupts the heart of the adventure itself: as, for instance, in *Tatem v Gamboa* . . . [T]he purpose for which *Sea Angel* had been chartered, namely the lightening of the casualty, had been performed.

119 Fourthly, in general terms the contractual risk of such delay caused by detention by government authorities was firmly on the charterers, Tsavliris . . . [I]n essence it follows from their obligation to pay hire, subject to the off-hire clause, until redelivery. And even the off-hire clause itself expressly provided for 'detention by the authorities at home or abroad' but not in terms which were relied on as covering the particular event here. Fifthly, as was even common ground, the risk of detention by the littoral authorities arising out of a salvage situation where there was a concern about pollution was, at any rate in general terms, foreseeable . . . Sixthly, that general risk was foreseeable by the salvage industry as a whole, and was provided for by the terms of that industry . . .

120 Seventhly, it is now common ground, on the particular facts of this case, that, short as the charter was, a mere 20 days, and shorter still as the unexpired period of the charter was, a mere three days, there was no frustration until the strategy of commercial negotiation had initially failed (by 13 or 17 October), some five weeks after the detention began. So, in any event, this is not a case like *Anglo-Northern* and *Tatem v Gamboa*, where the charters were frustrated then and there by the supervening event. Ours is one of those 'wait and see' situations . . . In such situations, it is a matter for assessment, on all the circumstances of the case, whether by a particular date the tribunal of fact, putting itself in the position of the parties, and viewing the matter in the role of reasonable and well-informed men, concludes that those parties would or properly speaking should have formed the view that, in all fairness and consistently with the demands of justice, their contract, as something whose performance in the new circumstances, past and prospective, had become 'radically different', had ceased to bind.

NOTES

1. Rix LJ's 'multifactorial approach', at [111], was approved and applied in *Islamic Republic of Iran Shipping Lines v Steamship Mutual Underwriting Association (Bermuda) Ltd* [2010] EWHC 2661 (Comm), [2010] 2 CLC 534, [2011] 1 Lloyd's Rep 195. This case concerned a claim of frustration in relation to insurance cover for Iranian-owned ships when transactions and business relationships with Iranian entities had been made illegal by the UK government. However, a licence had been issued permitting insurance in respect of bunker oil pollution for three months. Nevertheless, the insurer had terminated the insurance, alleging frustration. Beatson J applied the 'multifactorial' approach and examined the purpose of the contract. The purpose of the contract had been to provide indemnity insurance and part of that purpose remained lawful. The nature of the cover was the same; only its scope was different. It followed that the illegality was incomplete and the contract was not frustrated.

2. The multifactorial approach was also accepted and applied by Teare J at first instance in *ACG Acquisition XX LLC v Olympic Airlines SA (in liquidation)* [2012] EWHC 1070 (Comm), [2012] 2 CLC 48. The case concerned an unsuccessful argument that a five-year lease of an aircraft by Olympic (as lessee) was frustrated a matter of weeks into the lease when the Greek aviation authority suspended the aircraft's airworthiness certificate following the discovery of certain defects with cables. Teare J took the broad approach and focused on the overall position, the risk allocation, and justice on the facts.

TEARE J:

The demands of justice

184 I am not persuaded that the demands of justice favour frustration of the contract. The lease was for 5 years. Only one of those years had elapsed. The alleged frustrating events (absent any question of breach) were events of which Olympic would have been expected to take the risk. Olympic had the opportunity to arrange for the required AD check, albeit (to use counsel's phrase) 'costly work, the extent of which was uncertain.' Such a course was impractical for Olympic given its impending liquidation and would have seemed unattractive even to a financially healthy operator of 737–300s in the Autumn of 2009. But to hold that the lease was frustrated would reverse the allocation of risk on which the parties (absent any question of breach) had agreed.

185 I therefore do not accept the submission that the lease had been frustrated.

3. The multifactorial approach was also accepted as correct by Flaux J at first instance in *Bunge SA v Kyla Shipping Co. Ltd* [2012] EWHC 3522 (Comm), [2012] 2 CLC 998 and it was considered by the Courts in in *Melli Bank plc v Holbud Ltd* [2013] EWHC 1506 (Comm), at [15] and *Canary Wharf (BP4) T1 Ltd v European Medicines Agency* [2019] EWHC 921 (Ch), at [39] as an accepted principle of the law governing frustration.

It was also applied in *Flying Music Co. Ltd v Theater Entertainment SA* [2017] EWHC 3192 (QB), where the first defendant, a Greek theatrical promoter, agreed by a contract dated 21 May 2010 to stage a series of performances by the claimant of Michael Jackson's *Thriller* in Thessalonika and Athens the following month. Only a small number of the performances took place by reason of the civil unrest in Greece at the time. The second and third defendants had guaranteed the liability of the first defendant, and they contested liability under the guarantee on the basis that the contract between the claimant and defendant had been frustrated. The defence was dismissed. The judge was (at para. 68):

not persuaded on the evidence that the Contract was frustrated. I find that, by the time it was signed, the difficulty was already sufficiently apparent, and it would not be correct in fact or law, applying the principles from the authorities which I have identified, to release the parties from their obligations under the Contract by reason of events after 21 May 2010. There was already unrest. How long it would last was uncertain. Ticket sales had already begun, and they were low. There were already road closures. There were already demonstrations. There was already violence. The Troika had already arrived. Thessaloniki and Athens had already erupted. The parties both knew enough about the risks that this posed to the success of the production for it to be wrong, now, with the benefit of hindsight, to re-allocate those risks by releasing the Theater Entertainment from its Contract obligations.

12.4.1.3 Impossibility of agreed method of performing

Nickoll & Knight v Ashton, Edridge & Co.
[1901] 2 KB 126 (CA)

By a contract made in October 1899, the defendants sold the claimants a cargo of cotton seed to be shipped by a steamship called *Orlando* from Alexandria during January 1900. In December 1899, the *Orlando* went aground and could not reach Alexandria in January. The claimants brought an action against the defendants for failure to ship the cargo. The majority of the Court of Appeal (Vaughan Williams LJ dissenting) followed the implied term approach in *Taylor v Caldwell* (*page 603, 12.3.1*).

Held: The contract must be construed as subject to an implied condition that if, at the time of performance, the *Orlando* was not fit to ship the cargo, the contract would be at an end. The use of the *Orlando* was regarded by the majority as the contractually agreed means of performance and the only means of performing.

NOTE It is not sufficient that the parties contemplated a particular method of performance that has now become impossible. It must actually have been expressly agreed that this was the exclusive method of performing, so that any other method would result in the performance being radically different from that which was envisaged.

Tsakiroglou & Co. Ltd v Noblee Thorl GmbH
[1962] AC 93 (HL)

On 4 October 1956, a written contract was made whereby the sellers agreed to sell Sudanese groundnuts to the buyers for shipment from Port Sudan to Hamburg during November and December 1956. Both parties expected that shipment would be made via the Suez Canal, but there was no express stipulation to this effect. On 2 November, the Canal was closed to navigation, but the goods could have been shipped to Hamburg via the Cape of Good Hope. This route was twice as long and the freightage was far more costly. The sellers failed to ship the goods.

Held: The contract was not frustrated by the closure of the Canal. The House of Lords refused to imply a term that shipment should be made via the Suez Canal. The sellers should have shipped the goods by the alternative route, which was not substantially different from that envisaged by the contract.

LORD REID: The question now is whether by reason of the closing of the Suez route the contract had been ended by frustration.

The appellants' first argument was that it was an implied term of the contract that shipment should be via Suez. It is found in the case that both parties contemplated that shipment would be by that route but I find nothing in the contract or in the case to indicate that they intended to make this a term of the contract or that any such term should be implied: they left the matter to the ordinary rules of law . . .

I turn then to consider the position after the Canal was closed, and to compare the rights and obligations of the parties thereafter, if the contract still bound them, with what their rights and obligations would have been if the Canal had remained open. As regards the sellers, the appellants, the only difference to which I find reference in the case—and indeed the only difference suggested in argument—was that they would have had to pay £15 per ton freight instead of £7 10s. They had no concern with the nature of the voyage. In other circumstances that might have affected the buyers, and it is necessary to consider the position of both parties because frustration operates without being invoked by either party and, if the market price of groundnuts had fallen instead of rising, it might have been the buyers who alleged frustration. There might be cases where damage to the goods was a likely result of the longer voyage which twice crossed the Equator, or perhaps the buyer could be prejudiced by the fact that the normal duration of the voyage via Suez was about three weeks whereas the normal duration via the Cape was about seven weeks. But there is no suggestion in the case that the longer voyage could damage the groundnuts or that the delay could have caused loss to these buyers of which they could complain. Counsel for the appellants rightly did not argue that this increase in the freight payable by the appellants was sufficient to frustrate the contract and I need not therefore consider what the result might be if the increase had reached an astronomical figure. The route by the Cape was certainly practicable. There could be, on the findings in the case, no objection to it by the buyers and the only objection to it from the point of view of the sellers was that it cost them more and it was not excluded by the contract. Where, then, is there any basis for frustration?

It appears to me that the only possible way of reaching a conclusion that this contract was frustrated would be to concentrate on the altered nature of the voyage. As I understood the argument it was based on the assumption that the voyage was the manner of performing the sellers' obligations and that therefore its nature was material. I do not think so. What the sellers had to do was simply to find a ship proceeding by what was a practicable and now a reasonable route—if perhaps not yet a usual route—to pay the freight and obtain a proper bill of lading, and to furnish the necessary documents to the buyers. That was their manner of performing their obligations, and for the reasons which I have given I think that such changes in these matters as were made necessary fell far short of justifying a finding of frustration . . .

NOTE It follows that it cannot be argued that a contract is frustrated if only one party contemplated its performance in a particular way: *Blackburn Bobbin Co. Ltd v T. W. Allen & Sons Ltd* [1918] 2 KB 467.

Ocean Tramp Tankers Corporation v V/O Sovfracht, The Eugenia
[1964] 2 QB 226 (CA)

Facts see *12.2.2.*

LORD DENNING MR:

[The charterers] seek to rely on the fact that the canal itself was blocked. They assert that even if the *Eugenia* had never gone into the canal, but had stayed outside (in which case she would not have been in breach of the war clause), nevertheless she would still have had to go round by the Cape. And that, they say, brings about a frustration, for it makes the venture fundamentally different from what they contracted for . . . I think the position is now reasonably clear. It is simply this: if it should happen, in the course of carrying out a contract, that a fundamentally different situation arises for which the parties made no provision—so much so that it would not be just in the new situation to hold them bound to its terms—then the contract is at an end.

. . .

We are thus left with the simple test that a situation must arise which renders performance of the contract 'a thing radically different from that which was undertaken by the contract,' see *Davis Contractors Ltd v Fareham Urban District Council* [1956] AC 696 by Lord Radcliffe. To see if the doctrine applies, you have first to construe the contract and see whether the parties have themselves provided for the situation that has arisen. If they have provided for it, the contract must govern. There is no frustration. If they have not provided for it, then you have to compare the new situation with the situation for which they did provide. Then you must see how different it is. The fact that it has become more onerous or more expensive for one party than he thought is not sufficient to bring about a frustration. It must be more than merely more onerous or more expensive. It must be positively unjust to hold the parties bound. It is often difficult to draw the line. But it must be done. And it is for the courts to do it as a matter of law: see *Tsakiroglou & Co. Ltd v Noblee Thorl GmbH* [1962] AC 93 by Lord Simonds and by Lord Reid.

Applying these principles to this case, I have come to the conclusion that the blockage of the canal did not bring about a 'fundamentally different situation' such as to frustrate the venture. My reasons are these: (1) The venture was the *whole* trip from delivery at Genoa, out to the Black Sea, there load cargo, thence to India, unload cargo, and redelivery. The time for this vessel from Odessa to Vizagapatam via the Suez Canal would be 26 days, and via the Cape, 56 days. But that is not the right comparison. You have to take the whole venture from delivery at Genoa to redelivery at Madras. We were told that the time for the whole venture via the Suez Canal would be 108 days and via the Cape 138 days. The difference over the whole voyage is not so radical as to produce a frustration. (2) The cargo was iron and steel goods which would not be adversely affected by the longer voyage, and there was no special reason for early arrival. The vessel and crew were at all times fit and sufficient to proceed via the Cape. (3) The cargo was loaded on board at the time of the blockage of the canal. If the contract was frustrated, it would mean, I suppose, that the ship could throw up the charter and unload the cargo wherever she was, without any breach of contract. (4) The voyage round the Cape made no great difference except that it took a good deal longer and was more expensive for the charterers than a voyage through the canal.

12.4.2 Supervening illegality

See *Fibrosa Spolka Akcyjna v Fairbairn Lawson Combe Barbour Ltd* [1943] AC 32 (*page 618, 12.5.1.1*).
The following case concerned temporary illegality.

National Carriers Ltd v Panalpina (Northern) Ltd
[1981] AC 675 (HL)

A warehouse was leased to the defendants for ten years from 1 January 1974. The lease contained a covenant that the premises should be used only as a warehouse. The only vehicular access to the warehouse was by a street, which the local authority closed on 16 May 1979 in order to demolish a dangerous building. The street was likely to be closed for 20 months and the defendants were not able to use the warehouse in that period. The claimants brought an action for unpaid rent, but the defendants claimed that the lease was frustrated, so that they were discharged.

Held: On the facts, having regard to the period of the lease that would remain after the interruption ceased, compared to the ten-year term of the lease, the defendants could not rely on frustration as a defence.

12.4.3 Frustration of the common purpose of the parties

Since this depends upon establishing that *both* parties had the same purpose in entering into the contract and that purpose can no longer be achieved, it will rarely succeed as a frustrating event. This is confirmed by *Canary Wharf (BP4) T1 Ltd v European Medicines Agency* [2019] EWHC 921 (Ch) (*page 603, 12.3.1*), where the court rejected the argument that the common purpose of the lease was to allow the EMA to have a permanent headquarters in the UK, and held instead held that the parties had different commercial objectives.

It will not be sufficient that the purpose has become more difficult to achieve: see *Davis Contractors v Fareham Urban District Council* [1956] AC 696 (*page 603, 12.3.1*) and *Tsakiroglou & Co. Ltd v Noblee Thorl* [1962] AC 93 (*page 611, 12.4.1.3*).

Krell v Henry
[1903] 2 KB 740 (CA)

On 20 June 1902, the defendant agreed to hire a flat in Pall Mall from the claimant for £75. The hire was for 26 and 27 June (days only), which were the days on which the Coronation procession of Edward VII was scheduled to take place and pass along Pall Mall. The £25 deposit was paid and the balance was due on 24 June. The contract contained no express reference to the Coronation procession or to any other purpose for which the flat was taken. It was announced on 24 June that the procession would not take place on those days because the Coronation had been postponed as a result of the King's illness. The defendant refused to pay the balance of the agreed rent. Darling J (at first instance), relying on *Taylor v Caldwell*, held that there was an implied condition in the contract that the procession should take place.

Held (on appeal): From the circumstances, it was clear that the procession actually taking place on these days along the advertised route was regarded by both contracting parties as being of the foundation of the contract, and hence the contract was frustrated.

VAUGHAN WILLIAMS LJ: I do not think that the principle of the civil law [frustration] as introduced into the English law is limited to cases in which the event causing the impossibility of performance is the destruction or non-existence of some thing which is the subject-matter of the contract or of some condition or state of things expressly specified as a condition of it. I think that you first have to ascertain, not necessarily from the terms of the contract, but, if required, from necessary inferences, drawn from surrounding circumstances recognised by both contracting parties, what is the substance of the contract, and then to ask the question whether that substantial contract needs for its foundation the assumption of the existence of a particular state of things. If it does, this will limit the operation of the general words, and in such case, if the contract becomes impossible of performance by reason of the non-existence of the state of things assumed by both contracting parties as the foundation of the contract, there will be no breach of the contract thus limited. Now what are the facts of the present case? The contract is contained in two letters of June 20 which passed between the defendant and the plaintiff's agent, Mr Cecil Bisgood. These letters do not mention the coronation, but speak merely of the taking of Mr Krell's chambers, or, rather, of the use of them, in the daytime of June 26 and 27, for the sum of 75l., 25l. then paid, balance

50l. to be paid on the 24th. But the affidavits, which by agreement between the parties are to be taken as stating the facts of the case, shew that the plaintiff exhibited on his premises, third floor, 56A, Pall Mall, an announcement to the effect that windows to view the Royal coronation procession were to be let, and that the defendant was induced by that announcement to apply to the housekeeper on the premises, who said that the owner was willing to let the suite of rooms for the purpose of seeing the Royal procession for both days, but not nights, of June 26 and 27. In my judgment the use of the rooms was let and taken for the purpose of seeing the Royal procession. It was not a demise of the rooms, or even an agreement to let and take the rooms. It is a licence to use rooms for a particular purpose and none other. And in my judgment the taking place of those processions on the days proclaimed along the proclaimed route, which passed 56A, Pall Mall, was regarded by both contracting parties as the foundation of the contract; and I think that it cannot reasonably be supposed to have been in the contemplation of the contracting parties, when the contract was made, that the coronation would not be held on the proclaimed days, or the processions not take place on those days along the proclaimed route . . . It was suggested in the course of the argument that if the occurrence, on the proclaimed days, of the coronation and the procession in this case were the foundation of the contract, and if the general words are thereby limited or qualified, so that in the event of the non-occurrence of the coronation and procession along the proclaimed route they would discharge both parties from further performance of the contract, it would follow that if a cabman was engaged to take some one to Epsom on Derby Day at a suitable enhanced price for such a journey, say 10l., both parties to the contract would be discharged in the contingency of the race at Epsom for some reason becoming impossible; but I do not think this follows, for I do not think that in the cab case the happening of the race would be the foundation of the contract. No doubt the purpose of the engager would be to go to see the Derby, and the price would be proportionately high; but the cab had no special qualifications for the purpose which led to the selection of the cab for this particular occasion. Any other cab would have done as well. Moreover, I think that, under the cab contract, the hirer, even if the race went off, could have said, 'Drive me to Epsom; I will pay you the agreed sum; you have nothing to do with the purpose for which I hired the cab,' and that if the cabman refused he would have been guilty of a breach of contract, there being nothing to qualify his promise to drive the hirer to Epsom on a particular day. Whereas in the case of the coronation, there is not merely the purpose of the hirer to see the coronation procession, but it is the coronation procession and the relative position of the rooms which is the basis of the contract as much for the lessor as the hirer; and I think that if the King, before the coronation day and after the contract, had died, the hirer could not have insisted on having the rooms on the days named. It could not in the cab case be reasonably said that seeing the Derby race was the foundation of the contract, as it was of the licence in this case. Whereas in the present case, where the rooms were offered and taken, by reason of their peculiar suitability from the position of the rooms for a view of the coronation procession, surely the view of the coronation procession was the foundation of the contract, which is a very different thing from the purpose of the man who engaged the cab—namely, to see the race—being held to be the foundation of the contract. Each case must be judged by its own circumstances. In each case one must ask oneself, first, what, having regard to all the circumstances, was the foundation of the contract? Secondly, was the performance of the contract prevented? Thirdly, was the event which prevented the performance of the contract of such a character that it cannot reasonably be said to have been in the contemplation of the parties at the date of the contract? If all these questions are answered in the affirmative (as I think they should be in this case), I think both parties are discharged from further performance of the contract. In the present case the condition which fails and prevents the achievement of that which was, in the contemplation of both parties, the foundation of the contract, is not expressly mentioned either as a condition of the contract or the purpose of it; but I think for the reasons which I have given that the principle of *Taylor v Caldwell* (1863) 3 B & S 826 ought to be applied.

> **? QUESTION**
>
> If a coach firm advertises a coach trip with entrance tickets to see the Derby on Derby day, and the race is cancelled, would the coach firm be able to escape liability for breach of contract by pleading frustration?

NOTES

1. In *Krell v Henry*, the defendant had responded to an advertisement in a window of the claimant's flat to the effect that windows to view the Coronation procession were to be let. In addition, since the flat was only at the defendant's disposal in the daytime, it was easier to establish that the claimant's purpose was to let rooms to view the procession.

2. The decision to cancel the procession took place after the hiring contract was made, but in *Griffith v Brymer* (1903) 19 TLR 434, a contract to hire a room to view the procession made at 11 a.m. on 24 June was held to be void for common mistake where,

unknown to both parties, the decision to cancel the procession had already been taken at 10 a.m. that day (initial impossibility). If the contract in *Griffith v Brymer* had been made at 9.30 a.m., the case would have turned on frustration.

3. The result in *Krell v Henry* would seem perfectly acceptable, since the claimant should not have been enriched at the defendant's expense and, assuming that the procession would be rearranged, the defendant would not have had to pay twice to view it. It was not a case in which the defendant was seeking to avoid an inconvenient contract.

Herne Bay Steam Boat Co. v Hutton
[1903] 2 KB 683 (CA)

The defendant hired a steamship from the claimants, which was to be at the disposal of the defendant to take passengers from Southampton for the purpose of viewing the naval review at Spithead on 28 and 29 June 1902, and to cruise round the fleet. The price was £250 and the defendant paid a £50 deposit. On 25 June, the review was cancelled as a result of the King's illness, although the fleet remained anchored at Spithead. The claimants informed the defendant that the ship was ready and asked for the balance of the price.

Held: The contract was not frustrated, since the naval review was not the sole basis of the contract. Consequently, there was no total failure of the consideration, because the cruise round the fleet could still have taken place.

VAUGHAN WILLIAMS LJ: [The defendant], in hiring this vessel, had two objects in view: first, of taking people to see the naval review, and, secondly, of taking them round the fleet. Those, no doubt, were the purposes of Mr Hutton, but it does not seem to me that because, as it is said, those purposes became impossible, it would be a very legitimate inference that the happening of the naval review was contemplated by both parties as the basis and foundation of this contract, so as to bring the case within the doctrine of *Taylor v Caldwell* (1863) 3 B & S 826. On the contrary, when the contract is properly regarded, I think the purpose of Mr Hutton, whether of seeing the naval review or of going round the fleet with a party of paying guests, does not lay the foundation of the contract within the authorities.

Having expressed that view, I do not know that there is any advantage to be gained by going on in any way to define what are the circumstances which might or might not constitute the happening of a particular contingency as the foundation of a contract. I will content myself with saying this, that I see nothing that makes this contract differ from a case where, for instance, a person has engaged a brake to take himself and a party to Epsom to see the races there, but for some reason or other, such as the spread of an infectious disease, the races are postponed. In such a case it could not be said that he could be relieved of his bargain. So in the present case it is sufficient to say that the happening of the naval review was not the foundation of the contract.

ROMER LJ: In my opinion . . . it is a contract for the hiring of a ship by the defendant for a certain voyage, though having, no doubt, a special object, namely, to see the naval review and the fleet; but it appears to me that the object was a matter with which the defendant, as hirer of the ship, was alone concerned, and not the plaintiffs, the owners of the ship.

The case cannot, in my opinion, be distinguished in principle from many common cases in which, on the hiring of a ship, you find the objects of the hiring stated. Very often you find the details of the voyage stated with particularity, and also the nature and details of the cargo to be carried. If the voyage is intended to be one of pleasure, the object in view may also be stated, which is a matter that concerns the passengers. But this statement of the objects of the hirer of the ship would not, in my opinion, justify him in saying that the owner of the ship had those objects just as much in view as the hirer himself. The owner would say, 'I have an interest in the ship as a passenger or cargo carrying machine, and I enter into the contract simply in that capacity; it is for the hirer to concern himself about the objects.' . . .

The view I have expressed with regard to the general effect of the contract before us is borne out by the following considerations. The ship (as a ship) had nothing particular to do with the review or the fleet except as a convenient carrier of passengers to see it: any other ship suitable for carrying passengers would have done equally as well. Just as in the case of the hire of a cab or other vehicle, although the object of the hirer might be stated, that statement would not make the object any the less a matter for the hirer alone, and would not directly affect the person who was letting out the vehicle for hire. In the present case I may point out that it cannot be said that by reason of the failure to hold the naval review there was a total failure of consideration. That cannot be so. Nor is there anything like a total destruction of the subject-matter of the contract. Nor can we, in my opinion, imply in this contract any condition in favour of the defendant which would enable him to escape liability. A condition ought only to be implied in order to carry out the presumed intention of the parties, and I cannot ascertain any such presumed intention here. It follows that, in my opinion, so far as the plaintiffs are concerned, the objects of the passengers on this voyage with regard to sight-seeing do not form the subject-matter or essence of this contract . . .

STIRLING LJ: It is said that, by reason of the reference in the contract to the 'naval review,' the existence of the review formed the basis of the contract, and that as the review failed to take place the parties became discharged from the further performance of the contract, in accordance with the doctrine of *Taylor v Caldwell* (1863) 3 B & S 826. I am unable to arrive at that conclusion. It seems to me that the reference in the contract to the naval review is easily explained; it was inserted in order to define more exactly the nature of the voyage, and I am unable to treat it as being such a reference as to constitute the naval review the foundation of the contract so as to entitle either party to the benefit of the doctrine in *Taylor v Caldwell*. I come to this conclusion the more readily because the object of the voyage is not limited to the naval review, but also extends to a cruise round the fleet. The fleet was there, and passengers might have been found willing to go round it. It is true that in the event which happened the object of the voyage became limited, but, in my opinion, that was the risk of the defendant whose venture the taking the passengers was.

NOTES

1. Arguably, in *Herne Bay Steamboat Co. v Hutton*, the purpose was simply to have the steamship at the defendant's disposal, whereas in *Krell v Henry* it was clearly to view the procession. However, in *Krell v Henry* there was no express term in the contract relating to viewing the procession, whereas in *Herne Bay Steamboat Co. v Hutton* the contract stated that the hire was for the purpose of viewing the naval review and cruising round the fleet.

2. In *Herne Bay Steamboat Co. v Hutton*, although seeing the review and the fleet was the defendant's purpose, it was not that of the claimants. In other words, it could be similar to the position when a taxi cab is hired to go to Epsom on Derby day: seeing the

Derby is not the taxi owner's purpose, even though it is clearly the hirer's.

This type of fine distinction is unsatisfactory in an area of the law in which certainty is vital.

3. The argument of Brownsword (1985) 129 SJ 860 has much to recommend it. He argued that, in *Herne Bay Steamboat Co. v Hutton*, there was an 'imprudent commercial bargain', in that the defendant had lost the commercial benefit of cashing in on the naval review. The courts will not allow frustration to be used to avoid the consequences of what turn out to be bad bargains. On the other hand, the defendant in *Krell v Henry* was a consumer and the court was being asked to prevent the unjust enrichment of the claimant at the defendant's request.

12.5 The effects of frustration

Frustration discharges contractual performance from the date of frustration, so that the parties are excused from future performance.

12.5.1 At common law

12.5.1.1 Recovering money paid in advance of frustration

Fibrosa Spolka Akcyjna v Fairbairn Lawson Combe Barbour Ltd
[1943] AC 32 (HL)

In July 1939, an English company agreed to sell machinery to a Polish company and to deliver it between three and four months later to Gdynia in Poland. The purchase price was £4,800, of which £1,600 was to be paid when the order was placed. In fact, only £1,000 of this advance sum was paid. War broke out between Germany and Britain on 3 September 1939, and Gdynia was occupied by the German army on 23 September.

Held: The contract was frustrated because performance would have amounted to trading with the enemy. The House of Lords also held that, since there was a total failure of consideration (i.e. the buyer got no part of what he bargained for), the buyer could recover the £1,000 advance payment and did not have to pay the outstanding balance on the advance payment of £600.

NOTES

1. *Fibrosa v Fairbairn* relaxed the previous common law rule that because the obligation to make the advance payment had arisen *before* the frustrating event, it had to be fulfilled: see *Chandler v Webster* [1904] 1 KB 493. Instead, the advance payment could be recovered, but only where there was a total failure of consideration. If some of the goods had been delivered before the frustrating event occurred, then the advance payment could not have been recovered.

2. On the facts of this case, the English sellers had already incurred expenses in making machines, but were not able to keep any part of the advance payment to cover this.

12.5.1.2 Benefit Provided Prior to the Frustrating Event

Appleby v Myers
(1867) LR 2 CP 651 (Exchequer Chamber)

The claimant contracted to install and maintain certain machinery in the defendant's factory for two years, payment to be made on completion. After some of the work of installation had been completed, the factory and the machinery were accidentally destroyed by fire.

Held: The contract was frustrated, so that the defendant was discharged from his obligation to pay, but the claimant was not entitled to recover any sum for the work that had been completed. Blackburn J referred to the normal assumption that the contract will be severable and not 'entire' and continued as follows.

> BLACKBURN J: But, though this is the prima facie contract between those who enter into contracts for doing work and supplying materials, there is nothing to render it either illegal or absurd in the workman to agree to complete the whole, and be paid when the whole is complete, and not till then: and we think that the plaintiffs in the present case had entered into such a contract. Had the accidental fire left the defendant's premises untouched, and only injured a part of the work which the plaintiffs had already done, we apprehend that it is clear the plaintiffs under such a contract as the present must have done that part over again, in order to fulfil their contract to complete the whole and 'put it to work for the sums above named respectively.' As it is, they are, according to the principle laid down in *Taylor v Caldwell* (1863) 3 B & S 826, excused from completing the work; but they are not therefore entitled to any compensation for what they have done, but which has, without any fault of the defendant, perished. The case is in principle like that of a shipowner who has been excused from the performance of his contract to carry goods to their destination, because his ship has been disabled by one of the excepted perils, but who is not therefore entitled to any payment on account of the part-performance of the voyage, unless there is something to justify the conclusion that there has been a fresh contract to pay freight pro rata.

NOTE The common law position is largely historical, but is of residual interest, since the Law Reform (Frustrated Contracts) Act 1943 was drafted to address the deficiencies of the common law position—namely, to allow recovery of advance payments (subject to the expenses discretion) (s. 1(2)) and providing for recovery, albeit in limited circumstances, in instances in which the payment obligation is discharged by frustration (s. 1(3)).

12.5.2 The Law Reform (Frustrated Contracts) Act 1943

See McKendrick, 'The consequences of frustration: The Law Reform (Frustrated Contracts) Act 1943' in *Force Majeure and Frustration of Contract*, 2nd edn (LLP Professional Publishing, 1995), and Stewart and Carter [1992] CLJ 66.

12.5.2.1 Recovering money paid in advance of frustration

Law Reform (Frustrated Contracts) Act 1943

1. Adjustment of rights and liabilities of parties to frustrated contracts

. . .

(2) All sums paid or payable to any party in pursuance of the contract before the time when the parties were so discharged (in this Act referred to as 'the time of discharge') shall, in the case of sums so paid, be recoverable from him as money received by him for the use of the party by whom the sums were paid, and, in the case of sums so payable, cease to be so payable:

Provided that, if the party to whom the sums were so paid or payable incurred expenses before the time of discharge in, or for the purpose of, the performance of the contract, the court may, if it considers it just to do so having regard to all the circumstances of the case, allow him to retain or, as the case may be, recover the whole or any part of the sums so paid or payable, not being an amount in excess of the expenses so incurred.

. . .

(4) In estimating, for the purposes of the foregoing provisions of this section, the amount of any expenses incurred by any party to the contract, the court may, without prejudice to the generality of the said provisions, include such sum as appears to be reasonable in respect of overhead expenses and in respect of any work or services performed personally by the said party.

NOTES

1. Money paid before the frustrating event is recoverable and money payable before the frustrating event ceases to be payable (irrespective of whether there has been a total failure of consideration).

2. The payee *may* be permitted by the court to set off any expenses that he incurred before the frustrating event in performing the contract against the advance payment.

3. The amount of expenses that can be recovered is limited in any event to the amount of the advance payment. This means that, if there was no advance payment, s. 1(2) cannot be used to recover expenses. Similarly, if the expenses are more than the advance payment amount, the amount of the advance payment is the maximum that can be recovered as expenses.

Gamerco SA v I.C.M./Fair Warning (Agency) Ltd
[1995] 1 WLR 1226

The claimants, Spanish pop group promoters, had agreed in a contract with the defendants that they would promote a rock concert by the group Guns N' Roses at a stadium in Madrid on 4 July 1992. However, on 1 July, the permit issued for the stadium was withdrawn because of safety concerns about the cement used in its construction, and the parties became aware of these events on 2 July. No other suitable venue could be found and the concert had to be cancelled. The claimants, the promoters, had already paid $412,500 on account and were under an obligation to pay, but had not yet paid, a further $362,500. Both parties had incurred expenses in preparation for the concert. The judge, Garland J, accepted that the defendants' expenses amounted to $50,000, and the undisputed evidence was that the claimants had also incurred expenses of $450,000 prior to the cancellation. The claimants claimed that the contract was frustrated and sought to recover their advance payment (the sum paid on account) under s. 1(2) of the Law Reform (Frustrated Contracts) Act 1943. The defendants counterclaimed for damages for breach of contract by the claimants in failing to hold the concert.

Held: The claimants were not in breach because the contract was frustrated when the permit for the stadium was revoked. Therefore the claimants were entitled to recover the advance payment of $412,500 and did not need to make the further payment of $362,500 already due (s. 1(2)). The court had a 'broad discretion' to allow the defendants to set off their expenses under the proviso to s. 1(2) so as to reduce the advance payment amount that would be recoverable by the claimants. In all of the circumstances, and having particular regard to the expenses incurred by the claimants, no deduction for the defendants' expenses was made under the proviso.

GARLAND J: The issue which I have to decide is whether and, if so, to what extent the defendants can set off against the US$412,500 expenses incurred before the time of discharge in or for the purpose of the performance of the contract. It is perhaps surprising that over a period of 50 years there is no reported case of the operation of section 1(2), although it was considered obiter by Robert Goff J in *B.P. Exploration Co. (Libya) Ltd v Hunt (No. 2)* [1979] 1 WLR 783, 800 . . .

The approach to the proviso

The following have to be established: (1) that the defendants incurred expenses paid or payable (2) before the discharge of the contract on 2 July (3) in performance of the contract (which is not applicable) or (4) for the purposes of the performance of the contract, and (5) that it is just in all the circumstances to allow them to retain the whole or any part of the sums so paid or payable.

The onus of establishing these matters must lie on the defendant . . . I have already dealt with (1), (2) and (4) so far as the evidence allows. I turn to (5). I take the following matters into consideration. (a) My assumption that the relevant expenses of US$50,000 was undisputed. (b) It was undisputed that the plaintiffs incurred expenses in excess of 52m. pesetas (approximately £285,000 or US$450,000). (c) Neither party conferred any benefit on the other or on a third party, so that subsections (3) and (6) did not apply. (d) The plaintiffs' expenditure was wholly wasted, as was the defendants. (e) The plaintiffs were concerned with one contract only. The defendants were concerned with the last of 20 similar engagements, neither party being left with any residual benefit or advantage. (f) As already stated, I entirely ignore any insurance recoveries in accordance with subsection (5).

Various views have been advanced as to how the court should exercise its discretion and these can be categorised as follows.

(1) *Total retention.* This view was advanced by the Law Revision Committee in 1939 (Cmd. 6009) on the questionable ground 'that it is reasonable to assume that in stipulating for prepayment the payee intended to protect himself from loss under the contract.' As the editor of *Chitty on Contracts*, 27th ed. (1994), vol. 1, p. 1141, para. 23–060, note 51, (Mr EG McKendrick) comments: 'He probably intends to protect himself against the possibility of the other party's insolvency or default in payment.' To this, one can add: 'and secure his own cash flow.'

In *B.P. Exploration Co. (Libya) Ltd v Hunt (No. 2)* [1979] 1 WLR 783 Robert Goff J considered the principle of recovery under subsections (2) and (3). He said, at pp. 799–800:

> The Act is *not* designed to do certain things: (i) It is not designed to apportion the loss between the parties. There is no general power under either section 1(2) or section 1(3) to make any allowance for expenses incurred by the plaintiff (except, under the proviso to section 1(2), to enable him to enforce pro tanto payment of a sum payable but unpaid before frustration); and expenses incurred by the defendant are only relevant in so far as they go to reduce the net benefit obtained by him and thereby limit any award to the plaintiff (ii) It is not concerned to put the parties in the position in which they would have been if the contract had been performed. (iii) It is not concerned to restore the parties to the position they were in before the contract was made. A remedy designed to prevent unjust enrichment may not achieve that result; for expenditure may be incurred by either party under the contract which confers no benefit on the other, and in respect of which no remedy is available under the Act.

He then turned to section 1(2) and said:

> There is no discretion in the court in respect of a claim under section 1(2), except in respect of the allowance for expenses; subject to such an allowance . . . the plaintiff is entitled to repayment of the money he has paid. The allowance for expenses is probably best rationalised as a statutory recognition of the defence of change of position. True, the expenses need not have been incurred by reason of the plaintiff's payments; but they must have been incurred in, or for the purpose of, the performance of the contract under which the plaintiff's payment has been made, and for that reason it is just that they should be brought into account.

I do not derive any specific assistance from the *B.P Exploration Co.* case. There was no question of any change of position as a result of the plaintiffs' advance payment.

(2) *Equal division*. This was discussed by Professor Treitel in *Frustration and Force Majeure*, pp. 555–556, paras 15–059 and 15–060. There is some attraction in splitting the loss, but what if the losses are very unequal? Professor Treitel considers statutory provisions in Canada and Australia but makes the point that unequal division is unnecessarily rigid and was rejected by the Law Revision Committee in the 1939 report to which reference has already been made. The parties may, he suggests have had an unequal means of providing against the loss by insurers, but he appears to overlook subsection (5). It may well be that one party's expenses are entirely thrown away while the other is left with some realisable or otherwise usable benefit or advantage. Their losses may, as in the present case, be very unequal. Professor Treitel therefore favours the third view.

(3) *Broad discretion*. It is self-evident that any rigid rule is liable to produce injustice. The words, 'if it considers it just to do so having regard to all the circumstances of the case,' clearly confer a very broad discretion. Obviously the court must not take into account anything which is not 'a circumstance of the case' or fail to take into account anything that is and then exercise its discretion rationally. I see no indication in the Act, the authorities or the relevant literature that the court is obliged to incline towards either total retention or equal division. Its task is to do justice in a situation which the parties had neither contemplated nor provided for, and to mitigate the possible harshness of allowing all loss to lie where it has fallen.

I have not found my task easy. As I have made clear, I would have welcomed assistance on the true measure of the defendants' loss and the proper treatment of overhead and non-specific expenditure. Because the defendants have plainly suffered some loss, I have made a robust assumption. In all the circumstances, and having particular regard to the plaintiffs' loss, I consider that justice is done by making no deduction under the proviso.

? QUESTION

Is this decision explicable on the basis that Garland J is compensating for the inadequacies of s. 1(3)—namely, the fact that a s. 1(3) claim by the claimants was not possible because they had conferred no benefit on the defendants at the date of the frustration, so that allowing the defendants to recover their expenses would have amounted to throwing all the loss on the claimants?

NOTES

1. Carter and Tolhurst (1996) 10 JCL 264 disagreed with the approach adopted by Garland J and argued that, given the wording of the proviso ('the whole or any part') and the restitutionary basis of the 1943 Act, 'there was no discretion to award a nil sum'. They appeared to prefer a 'total retention' approach.

2. The decision to revoke the permit was taken on 1 July, but Garland J treats 2 July as the point at which the contract was discharged by frustration. Although, on these facts, it can be argued that frustration would not occur until it was clear that an alternative venue could not be found, it must be the position that, where it is the decision itself that causes the contract to be frustrated, frustration will normally occur when the decision is made rather than when the parties are notified of it: see *Griffith v Brymer* (1903) 19 TLR 434 (*page 614, 12.4.3*). Although it is not clear from the judgment in *Gamerco v I.C.M.*, it appears that it was the decision to revoke the permit that was crucial and not merely the fact that the stadium was unsafe, thereby making performance at the agreed venue impossible, since presumably this construction problem pre-dated the contract.

12.5.2.2 Benefit provided prior to the frustrating event

Law Reform (Frustrated Contracts) Act 1943
1. Adjustment of rights and liabilities of parties to frustrated contracts

. . .

(3) Where any party to the contract has, by reason of anything done by any other party thereto in, or for the purpose of, the performance of the contract, obtained a valuable benefit (other than a payment of money to which the last foregoing subsection applies) before the time of discharge, there shall be recoverable from him by the said other party such sum (if any), not exceeding the value of the said benefit to the party obtaining it, as the court considers just, having regard to all the circumstances of the case and, in particular,—

  (a) the amount of any expenses incurred before the time of discharge by the benefited party in, or for the purpose of, the performance of the contract, including any sums paid or payable by him to any other party in pursuance of the contract and retained or recoverable by that party under the last foregoing subsection, and

  (b) the effect, in relation to the said benefit, of the circumstances giving rise to the frustration of the contract.

NOTES

1. Section 1(3) applies where one party (A) has conferred a non-monetary 'valuable benefit' on the other party (B) before the frustrating event. The court may award party A a 'just sum' to recompense him and this sum must not exceed the value of the benefit to party B, the party receiving that benefit.

2. The subsection also appears to state that, when calculating this 'just sum', the court must in particular consider the expenses incurred by the benefited party B, i.e. the fact that an advance payment was made to the provider of the benefit, party A, which party A was permitted to retain under s. 1(2). The provider of the benefit, party A, cannot recover twice for the same expenses under both s. 1(2) and (3).

3. By s. 1(3)(b), the court must also consider 'the effect of the frustrating event on the benefit received'.

BP Exploration Co. (Libya) Ltd v Hunt (No. 2)
[1979] 1 WLR 783

In December 1957, the Libyan government granted the defendant a concession to explore for, and extract, oil in a specified area in the Libyan desert. In June 1960, the defendant made an agreement with the claimant oil company whereby the defendant assigned a half-share in the oil concession to the claimant, and the claimant undertook to explore, develop, and operate the whole concession at its expense, and to make payments in cash and oil to the defendant. The agreement provided that if and when oil was discovered in commercial quantities, the operating expenses were to be shared and the claimant was to be entitled to three-eighths of the defendant's half-share of the oil produced for a particular period. The claimant spent considerable sums of money in exploration and development of the concession, and found oil in commercially worthwhile quantities. However, following a revolution in Libya, the Libyan government first expropriated the claimant's half-share in the concession on 7 December 1971, and then the defendant's half-share on 11 June 1973. The claimant brought an action against the defendant, alleging that the agreement was frustrated on 7 December 1971, and claiming a 'just sum' under s. 1(3) of the 1943 Act in respect of the benefit obtained by the defendant as a result of the claimant's performance of the contract prior to frustration.

Held: The contract was frustrated and the Act applied.

ROBERT GOFF J: The principle, which is common to both s. 1(2) and (3), and indeed is the fundamental principle underlying the Act itself, is prevention of the unjust enrichment of either party to the contract at the other's expense. It was submitted by [counsel], on behalf of BP, that the principle common to both subsections was one of restitution for net benefits received, the net benefit being the benefit less an appropriate deduction for expenses incurred by the defendant. This is broadly correct so far as s. 1(2) is concerned; but under s. 1(3) the net benefit of the defendant simply provides an upper limit to the award—it does not measure the amount of the award to be made to the plaintiff. This is because in s. 1(3) a distinction is drawn between the plaintiff's performance under the contract, and the benefit which the defendant has obtained by reason of that performance, . . . and the net benefit obtained by the defendant from the plaintiff's performance may be more than a just sum payable in respect of such performance, in which event a sum equal to the defendant's net benefit would not be an appropriate sum to award to the plaintiff. I therefore consider it better to state the principle underlying the Act as being the principle of unjust enrichment, which underlies the right of recovery in very many cases in English law, and indeed is the basic principle of the English law of restitution, of which the Act forms part.

[Robert Goff J then considered the process of calculating a s. 1(3) award. He continued:]

(a) *General* . . . First, it has to be shown that the defendant has, by reason of something done by the plaintiff in, or for the purpose of, the performance of the contract, obtained a valuable benefit (other than a payment of money) before the time of discharge. That benefit has to be identified, and valued, and such value forms the upper limit of the award. Secondly, the court may award to the plaintiff such sum, not greater than the value of such benefit, as it considers just having regard to all the circumstances of the case, including in particular the matters specified in s. 1(3)(a) and (b). In the case of an award under s. 1(3) there are, therefore, two distinct stages—the identification and valuation of the benefit, and the award of the just sum. The amount to be awarded is the just sum, unless the defendant's benefit is less, in which event the award will be limited to the amount of that benefit. The distinction between the identification and valuation of the defendant's benefit, and the assessment of the just sum, is the most controversial part of the Act. It represents the solution adopted by the legislature of the problem of restitution in cases where the benefit does not consist of a payment of money; but the solution so adopted has been criticised by some commentators as productive of injustice, and it certainly gives rise to considerable problems, to which I shall refer in due course.

(b) *Identification of the defendant's benefit.* In the course of the argument before me, there was much dispute whether, in the case of services, the benefit should be identified as the services themselves, or as the end product of the services. One example canvassed (because it bore some relationship to the facts of the present case) was the example of prospecting for minerals. If minerals are discovered, should the benefit be regarded (as counsel for Mr Hunt contended) simply as the services of prospecting, or (as counsel for BP contended) as the minerals themselves being the end product of the successful exercise? Now, I am satisfied that it was the intention of the legislature, to be derived from s. 1(3) as a matter of construction, that the benefit should in an appropriate case be identified as the end product of the services. This appears, in my judgment, not only from the fact that s. 1(3) distinguishes between the plaintiff's performance and the defendant's benefit, but also from s. 1(3)(b) which clearly relates to the product of the plaintiff's performance. Let me take the example of a building contract. Suppose that a contract for work on a building is frustrated by a fire which destroys the building and which, therefore, also destroys a substantial amount of work already done by the plaintiff. Although it might be thought just to award the plaintiff a sum assessed on a quantum meruit basis, probably a rateable part of the contract price, in respect of the work he has done, the effect of s. 1(3)(b) will be to reduce the award to nil, because of the effect, in relation to the defendant's benefit, of the circumstances giving rise to the frustration of the contract. It is quite plain that, in s. 1(3)(b), the word 'benefit' is intended to refer, in the example I have given, to the actual improvement to the building, because that is what will be affected by the frustrating event; the subsection therefore contemplates that, in such a case, the benefit is the end product of the plaintiff's services, not the services themselves. This will not be so in every case, since in some cases the services will have no end product; for example, where the services consist of doing such work as surveying, or transporting goods. In each case it is necessary to ask the question: what benefit has the defendant obtained by reason of the plaintiff's contractual performance? But it must not be forgotten that in s. 1(3) the relevance of the value of the benefit is to fix a ceiling to the award. If, for example, in a building contract, the building is only partially completed, the value of the partially completed building (i.e. the product of the services) will fix a ceiling for the award; the stage of the work may be such that the uncompleted building may be worth less than the value of the work and materials that have gone into it, particularly as completion by another builder may cost more than completion by the original builder would have cost. In other cases, however, the actual benefit to the defendant may be considerably more than the appropriate or just sum to be awarded to the plaintiff, in which event the value of the benefit will not in fact determine the quantum of the award. I should add, however, that, in a case of prospecting, it would usually be wrong to identify the discovered mineral as the benefit. In such a case there is always (whether the prospecting is successful or not) the benefit of the prospecting itself, ie of knowing whether or not the land contains any deposit of the relevant minerals; if the prospecting is successful, the benefit may include also the enhanced value of the land by reason of the discovery; if the prospector's contractual task goes beyond discovery and includes development and production, the benefit will include the further enhancement of the land by reason of the installation of the facilities, and also the benefit of in part transforming a valuable mineral deposit into a marketable commodity.

I add by way of footnote that all these difficulties would have been avoided if the legislature had thought it right to treat the services themselves as the benefit. In the opinion of many commentators, it would be more just to do so; after all, the services in question have been requested by the defendant, who normally takes the risk that they may prove worthless, from whatever cause. In the example I have given of the building destroyed by fire, there is much to be said for the view that the builder should be paid for the work he has done, unless he has (for example by agreeing to insure the works) taken on himself the risk of destruction by fire. But my task is to construe the Act as it stands. On the true construction of the Act, it is in my judgment clear that the defendant's benefit must, in an appropriate case, be identified as the end product of the plaintiff's services, despite the difficulties which this construction creates, difficulties which are met again when one comes to value the benefit . . .

(d) *Valuing the benefit.* Since the benefit may be identified with the product of the plaintiff's performance, great problems arise in the valuation of the benefit. First, how does one solve the problem which arises from the fact that a small service may confer an enormous benefit, and conversely, a very substantial service may confer only a very small benefit? The answer presumably is that at the stage of valuation of the benefit (as opposed to assessment of the just sum) the task of the court is simply to assess the value of the benefit to the defendant. For example, if a prospector after some very simple prospecting discovers a large and unexpected deposit of a valuable mineral, the benefit to the defendant (namely, the enhancement in the value of the land) may be enormous; it must be valued as such, always bearing in mind that the assessment of a just sum may very well lead to a much smaller amount being awarded to the plaintiff. But conversely, the plaintiff may have undertaken building work for a substantial sum which is, objectively speaking, of little or no value—for example, he may commence the redecoration, to the defendant's execrable taste, of rooms which are in good decorative order. If the contract is frustrated before the work is complete, and the work is unaffected by the frustrating event, it can be argued that the defendant has obtained no benefit, because the defendant's property has been reduced in value by the plaintiff's work; but the partial work must be treated as a benefit to the defendant, since he requested it, and valued as such. Secondly, at what point in time is the benefit to be valued? If there is a lapse of time between the date of the receipt of the benefit, and the date of frustration, there may in the meanwhile be a substantial variation in the value of the benefit. If the benefit had simply been identified as the services rendered, this problem would not arise; the court would simply award a reasonable remuneration for the services rendered at the time when they were rendered, the defendant taking the risk of any subsequent depreciation and the benefit of any subsequent appreciation in value. But that is not what the Act provides: s. 1(3)(b) makes it plain that the plaintiff is to take the risk of depreciation or destruction by the frustrating event. If the effect of the frustrating event upon the value of the benefit is to be measured, it must surely be measured upon the benefit as at the date of frustration. For example, let it be supposed that a builder does work which doubles in value by the date of frustration, and is then so severely damaged by fire that the contract is frustrated; the valuation of the residue must surely be made on the basis of the value as at the date of frustration.

But there is a further problem which I should refer to, before leaving this topic. Section 1(3)(a) requires the court to have regard to the amount of any expenditure incurred before the time of discharge by the benefited party in, or for the purpose of, the performance of the contract. The question arises—should this matter be taken into account at the stage of valuation of the benefit, or of assessment of the just sum? Take a simple example. Suppose that the defendant's benefit is valued at £150, and that a just sum is assessed at £100, but that there remain to be taken into account defendant's expenses of £75: is the award to be £75 or £25? The clue to this problem lies, in my judgment, in the fact that the allowance for expenses is a statutory recognition of the defence of change of position. Only to the extent that the position of the defendant has so changed that it would be unjust to award restitution, should the court make an allowance for expenses. Suppose that the plaintiff does work for the defendant which produces no valuable end product, or a benefit no greater in value than the just sum to be awarded in respect of the work: there is then no reason why the whole of the relevant expenses should not be set off against the just sum. But suppose that the defendant has reaped a large benefit from the plaintiff's work, far greater in value than the just sum to be awarded for the work. In such circumstances it would be quite wrong to set off the whole of the defendant's expenses against the just sum. The question whether the defendant has suffered a change of position has to be judged in the light of all the circumstances of the case. Accordingly, on the Act as it stands, under s. 1(3) the proper course is to deduct the expenses from the value of the benefit, with the effect that only in so far as they reduce the value of the benefit below the amount of the just sum which would otherwise be awarded will they have any practical bearing on the award . . .

(e) *Assessment of the just sum.* The principle underlying the Act is prevention of the unjust enrichment of the defendant at the plaintiff's expense. Where, as in cases under s. 1(2), the benefit conferred on the defendant consists of payment of a sum of money, the plaintiff's expense and the defendant's enrichment are generally equal; and, subject to other relevant factors, the award of restitution will consist simply of an order for repayment of a like sum of money. But where the benefit does not consist of money, then the defendant's enrichment will rarely be equal to the plaintiff's expense. In such cases, where (as in the case of a benefit conferred under a contract thereafter frustrated) the benefit has been requested by the defendant, the basic measure of recovery in restitution is the reasonable value of the plaintiff's performance—in a case of services, a quantum meruit or reasonable remuneration, and in a case of goods, a quantum valebat or reasonable price. Such cases are to be contrasted with cases where such a benefit has not been requested by the defendant. In the latter class of case, recovery is rare in restitution; but if the sole basis of recovery was that the defendant had been incontrovertibly benefited, it might be legitimate to limit recovery to the defendant's actual benefit—a limit which has (perhaps inappropriately) been imported by the legislature into s. 1(3) of the Act. However, under s. 1(3) as it stands, if the defendant's actual benefit is less than the just or reasonable sum which would otherwise be awarded to the plaintiff, the award must be reduced to a sum equal to the amount of the defendant's benefit.

? QUESTIONS

1. What is the effect of the Act on the factual scenario in *Appleby v Myers*?

2. Why was no s. 1(3) claim made by the claimants in *Gamerco v I.C.M.* (*page 619, 12.5.2.1*) in respect of their expenditure in preparing to perform?

3. At what point in time should the benefit be identified? The difficulty caused by identifying the benefit as the end product of the services results from s. 1(3)(b), which requires the court to consider the effect of the frustration on the benefit received. If a fire destroys that end product, then, according to Goff J, there is no benefit to value and there can be no s. 1(3) award. Thus, Goff J considers both s. 1(3)(a) and (b) when valuing the benefit to the party receiving it. However, the Act itself requires s. 1(3)(b) to be considered when assessing the 'just sum' and not when valuing the benefit. The benefit should be valued on the basis of circumstances existing *immediately before* the frustrating event, but the specified factors are to be taken into account when the court fixes the figure of the 'just sum' to award.

NOTES

1. See Peel, *Treitel's Law of Contract*, 14th edn (Sweet & Maxwell, 2015), [19-101]–[19-104].

2. It is very difficult to predict what the court will decide the reasonable value of the claimant's performance to be.

3. Haycroft and Waksman [1984] JBL 207 criticized Robert Goff J's identification of the benefit as the end product of the services, which Goff J insisted was inevitable given the wording of the Act. They preferred the benefit to be identified as the value of the services themselves.

4. The complexity in the section is caused by the need to assess two figures: the value of the benefit to the defendant; and the just sum to award the claimant. Robert Goff J considered that the purpose underlying the Act was to prevent unjust enrichment of one party at the expense of the other. His view is that if the frustration destroys the benefit, there is no benefit and no unjust enrichment to be remedied.

However, Haycroft and Waksman believe the real purpose of the Act to be to provide a mechanism for apportioning the loss caused by frustration between two innocent parties. See also the support for this view in relation to s. 1(3) in McKendrick, 'Frustration, restitution, and loss apportionment', in Burrows (ed.) *Essays on the Law of Restitution* (Oxford University Press, 1991), but compare Stewart and Carter [1992] CLJ 66, pp. 109–10.

Chapter 13

Breach of contract

The contractual terms determine the performance obligations of the parties. Since a failure, without lawful excuse, to comply in full with a performance obligation is a breach, it is vital to know the standard of performance required.

13.1 Absolute and qualified contractual obligations

If a contractual obligation is strict, non-compliance is a breach of contract irrespective of fault, e.g. the obligations imposed on sellers in B2B (business to business) sale of goods contracts by ss. 13–15 of the Sale of Goods Act 1979 are strict.

In the consumer context (B2C—trader and consumer contracts), the corresponding obligations (as to correspondence with description, satisfactory quality, fitness for purpose, correspondence with sample) in contracts to supply goods and digital content, are entrenched rights and therefore strict obligations (Part 1 of the Consumer Rights Act (CRA) 2015).

Qualified contractual obligations impose a duty to take reasonable care. For example, in *Liverpool City Council v Irwin* [1977] AC 239, the House of Lords held that the local authority owed a duty to take reasonable care to ensure that the common parts of a block of flats were in reasonable repair and in use. Since the local authority had taken reasonable care, there was no breach. Similarly, a surgeon owes a duty to exercise reasonable care and skill in the performance of an operation, but cannot guarantee the result: *Thake v Maurice* [1986] 1 All ER 497. The obligation in a contract for the supply of a service whereby the supplier owes a duty to perform the service with reasonable care and skill, e.g. s. 13 of the Supply of Goods and Services Act (SGSA) 1982 in the B2B context and s. 49 CRA 2015 in the B2C context.

Supply of Goods and Services Act 1982

13. Implied term about care and skill

In a contract for the supply of a service where the supplier is acting in the course of a business, there is an implied term that the supplier will carry out the service with reasonable care and skill.

Consumer Rights Act 2015

49. Service to be performed with reasonable care and skill

(1) Every contract to supply a service is to be treated as including a term that the trader must perform the service with reasonable care and skill.

13

However, some obligations in a contract to provide a service may well be strict, e.g. in *Platform Funding Ltd v Bank of Scotland plc* [2008] EWCA Civ 930, [2009] QB 426, the majority of the Court of Appeal (Sir Anthony Clarke MR dissenting) accepted that the normal duty owed by a surveyor was a duty of reasonable care and skill in carrying out the survey and checking for defects. It was, however, a strict undertaking that the surveyor would survey the correct property!

NOTE On standards of performance, see Peel, *Treitel's The Law of Contract*, 14th edn (Sweet & Maxwell, 2015), [17-065]–[17-069]; and *Poole's Textbook on Contract Law*, 15th edn (Oxford University Press, 2021), 13.2.1.1.

13.2 Consequences of breach

Subject to an enforceable exemption clause, a contract breach entitles the injured party to damages to compensate for the loss suffered following the breach.

Photo Production Ltd v Securicor Transport Ltd
[1980] AC 827 (HL)

For the facts, see *page 262*, 6.3.5.

Lord Diplock explained the effects of a breach of a contractual obligation.

LORD DIPLOCK: [B]reaches of primary obligations give rise to substituted or secondary obligations on the part of the party in default, and, in some cases, may entitle the other party to be relieved from further performance of his own primary obligations

. . . Every failure to perform a primary obligation is a breach of contract. The secondary obligation on the part of the contract breaker to which it gives rise by implication of the common law is to pay monetary compensation to the other party for the loss sustained by him in consequence of the breach; but, with two exceptions, the primary obligations of both parties so far as they have not yet been fully performed remain unchanged. This secondary obligation to pay compensation (damages) for non-performance of primary obligations I will call the 'general secondary obligation.' It applies in the cases of the two exceptions as well.

The exceptions are: (1) Where the event resulting from the failure by one party to perform a primary obligation has the effect of depriving the other party of substantially the whole benefit which it was the intention of the parties that he should obtain from the contract, the party not in default may elect to put an end to all primary obligations of both parties remaining unperformed. (If the expression 'fundamental breach' is to be retained, it should, in the interests of clarity, be confined to this exception.) (2) Where the contracting parties have agreed, whether by express words or by implication of law, that *any* failure by one party to perform a particular primary obligation ('condition' in the nomenclature of the Sale of Goods Act 1893), irrespective of the gravity of the event that has in fact resulted from the breach, shall entitle the other party to elect to put an end to all primary obligations of both parties remaining unperformed. (In the interests of clarity, the nomenclature of the Sale of Goods Act 1893, 'breach of condition' should be reserved for this exception.)

Where such an election is made (a) there is substituted by implication of law for the primary obligations of the party in default which remain unperformed a secondary obligation to pay monetary compensation to the other party for the loss sustained by him in consequence of their non-performance in the future and (b) the unperformed primary obligations of that other party are discharged. This secondary obligation is additional to the general secondary obligation; I will call it 'the anticipatory secondary obligation.'

NOTES

1. The primary obligations are the performance obligations in the contract. Breaches of these obligations give rise to secondary obligations to pay damages.

2. A breach of contract will not necessarily result in the termination of the contract, so that the primary obligations of both parties may continue. However, if there has been a repudiatory breach, the injured party has an option to terminate or affirm the contract. On termination, the primary obligations due in the future are discharged (i.e. no longer need to be performed). If the contract is affirmed, the contract continues and future obligations must be performed.

In *Decro-Wall International SA v Practitioners in Marketing Ltd* [1971] 1 WLR 361, 375, Sachs LJ stated:

The law on the effect of repudiation is settled. The point of reference is the speech of Viscount Simon LC in *Heyman v Darwins Ltd* [1942] AC 356, 361: 'But repudiation by one party standing alone does not terminate the contract. It takes two to end it, by repudiation, on the one side, and acceptance of the repudiation, on the other'. Whether the other party accepts is a matter for his option: if he does not, the contract remains alive . . .

3. Lord Diplock refers to two situations in which the primary obligations that have not yet been performed are discharged (come to an end for the future). They correspond to breaches of conditions (*13.3*) and breaches of non-conditions that deprive the injured party of substantially the whole benefit of the contract—see *Hongkong Fir Shipping v Kawasaki Kishen Kaisha* [1962] 2 QB 26 (*page 644, 13.3.2*)—i.e. repudiatory breaches that have been accepted as permitting the contract to be terminated.

13.2.1 Termination for repudiatory breach

For the contract to be terminated, the injured party must have 'accepted' the repudiatory breach as terminating the contract. Can the innocent party 'accept' the repudiation merely by failing to perform his own future obligations under the contract?

Vitol SA v Norelf Ltd, The Santa Clara
[1996] AC 800 (HL)

Under the contract for the sale of a cargo, the ship carrying the cargo was to arrive, berth, and leave Houston between 1 and 7 March 1991. During the loading of the cargo, the claimant buyer sent a telex (on 8 March) purporting to reject the cargo for breach of condition stating the loading would not be completed within the contractual period. The vessel completed loading and sailed on 9 March, but thereafter neither party took any steps to perform the contract; in particular, the seller did not tender the bill of lading, which would have been required to claim the price. The market price of the cargo fell and the seller resold it for a much reduced price. The arbitrator held that the buyer's telex constituted an anticipatory repudiatory breach (discussed and explained at *13.5*), which had been accepted by the seller as terminating the contract, since, to the knowledge of the buyer, it had not taken any steps thereafter to perform the contract. The buyer appealed on this point, arguing that mere inactivity could not constitute acceptance of the repudiation.

Whereas Phillips J, at first instance, upheld the arbitrator's decision and held that the seller's failure to perform its own contractual obligations constituted 'acceptance' of the buyer's repudiation, the Court of Appeal allowed the buyer's appeal and held that a mere failure to perform contractual obligations could not, as a matter of law, constitute such acceptance. The seller appealed.

Held (on appeal to the House of Lords): Although it was possible as a matter of law for an innocent party to accept a repudiatory breach as terminating the contract simply by failing to perform its own contractual obligations, whether it did so was a question of fact depending on the contractual relationship and the particular circumstances of the case.

LORD STEYN [with whose reasoning the other members of the House of Lords agreed]: For present purposes I would accept as established law the following propositions. (1) Where a party has repudiated a contract the aggrieved party has an election to accept the repudiation or to affirm the contract: *Fercometal SARL v Mediterranean Shipping Co. SA* [1989] AC 788. (2) An act of acceptance of a repudiation requires no particular form: a communication does not have to be couched in the language of acceptance. It is sufficient that the communication or conduct clearly and unequivocally conveys to the repudiating party that that aggrieved party is treating the contract as at an end. (3) It is rightly conceded by counsel for the buyers that the aggrieved party need not personally, or by an agent, notify the repudiating party of his election to treat the contract as at an end. It is sufficient that the fact of the election comes to the repudiating party's attention, e.g. notification by an unauthorised broker or other intermediary may be sufficient . . .

The arbitrator did not put forward any heterodox general theory of the law of repudiation. On the contrary he expressly stated that unless the repudiation was accepted by the sellers and the acceptance was communicated to the buyers the election was of no effect. It is plain that the arbitrator directed himself correctly in accordance with the governing general principle. The criticism of the arbitrator's reasoning centres on his conclusion that 'the failure of [the sellers] to take any further step to perform the contract which was apparent to [the buyers] constituted sufficient communication of acceptance'. By that statement the arbitrator was simply recording a finding that the buyers knew that the sellers were treating the contract as at an end. That interpretation is reinforced by the paragraph in his award read as a whole. The only question is whether the relevant holding of the arbitrator was wrong in law.

It is now possible to turn directly to the . . . issue posed, namely whether non-performance of an obligation is ever as a matter of law capable of constituting an act of acceptance. On this aspect I found the judgment of Phillips J entirely convincing. One cannot generalise on the point. It all depends on the particular contractual relationship and the particular circumstances of the case. But, like Phillips J, I am satisfied that a failure to perform may sometimes signify to a repudiating party an election by the aggrieved party to treat the contract as at an end. Postulate the case where an employer at the end of a day tells a contractor that he, the employer, is repudiating the contract and that the contractor need not return the next day. The contractor does not return the next day or at all. It seems to me that the contractor's failure to return may, in the absence of any other explanation, convey a decision to treat the contract as at an end. Another example may be an overseas sale providing for shipment on a named ship in a given month. The seller is obliged to obtain an export licence. The buyer repudiates the contract before loading starts. To the knowledge of the buyer the seller does not apply for an export licence with the result that the transaction cannot proceed. In such circumstances it may well be that an ordinary businessman, circumstanced as the parties were, would conclude that the seller was treating the contract as at an end. Taking the present case as illustrative, it is important to bear in mind that the tender of a bill of lading is the pre-condition to payment of the price. Why should an arbitrator not be able to infer that when, in the days and weeks following loading and the sailing of the vessel, the seller failed to tender a bill of lading to the buyer, he clearly conveyed to a trader that he was treating the contract as at an end? In my view therefore the passage from the judgment of Kerr LJ in the *Golodetz* case [*State Trading Corporation of India Ltd v M. Golodetz Ltd (now Transcontinental Affiliates Ltd)*] [1989] 2 Lloyd's Rep 277 at 286, if it was intended to enunciate a general and absolute rule, goes too far. It will be recalled, however, that Kerr LJ spoke of a *continuing* failure to perform. One can readily accept that a continuing failure to perform, i.e. a breach commencing before the repudiation and continuing thereafter, would necessarily be equivocal. In my view too much has been made of the observation of Kerr LJ. Turning to the observation of Nourse LJ [in the Court of Appeal] [1996] QB 108, 116–117 that a failure to perform a contractual obligation is necessarily and always equivocal I respectfully disagree. Sometimes in the practical world of businessmen an omission to act may be as pregnant with meaning as a positive declaration. While the analogy of offer and acceptance is imperfect it is not without significance that while the general principle is that there can be no acceptance of an offer by silence, our law does in exceptional cases recognise acceptance of an offer by silence. Thus in *Rust v Abbey Life Assurance Co. Ltd* [1979] 2 Lloyd's Rep 334 the Court of Appeal held that a failure by a proposed insured to reject a proffered insurance policy for seven months justified on its own an inference of acceptance . . . Similarly, in the different field of repudiation, a failure to perform may sometimes be given a colour by special circumstances and may only be explicable to a reasonable person in the position of the repudiating party as an election to accept the repudiation.

My Lords, I would answer the question posed by this case in the same way as Phillips J did. In truth the arbitrator inferred an election, and communication of it, from the tenor of the rejection telex and the failure *inter alia* to tender the bill of lading. That was an issue of fact within the exclusive jurisdiction of the arbitrator.

For these reasons I would allow the appeal of the sellers.

13.2.2 The meaning of 'termination'

By 'termination', we mean that performance of future obligations under the contract is no longer required. It does not mean that the contract is treated as if it never existed. (Care should therefore be taken with the expression 'rescission for breach of contract'.)

In *Johnson v Agnew* [1980] AC 367, 392–3, Lord Wilberforce stated:

[I]t is important to dissipate a fertile source of confusion and to make clear that although the vendor is sometimes referred to in the above situation as 'rescinding' the contract, this so-called 'rescission' is quite different from rescission ab initio, such as may arise for example in cases of mistake, fraud or lack of consent. In those cases, the contract is treated in law as never having come into existence . . . In the case of an accepted repudiatory breach the contract has come into existence but has been put an end to or discharged. Whatever contrary indications may be disinterred from old authorities, it is now quite clear, under the general law of contract, that acceptance of a repudiatory breach does not bring about 'rescission ab initio.' I need only quote one passage to establish these propositions.

In *Heyman v Darwins Ltd* [1942] AC 356, 399, Lord Porter said:

To say that the contract is rescinded or has come to an end or has ceased to exist may in individual cases convey the truth with sufficient accuracy, but the fuller expression that the injured party is thereby absolved from future performance of his obligations under the contract is a more exact description of the position. Strictly speaking, to say that on acceptance of the renunciation of a contract the contract is rescinded is incorrect. In such a case the injured party may accept the renunciation as a breach going to the root of the whole of the consideration. By that acceptance he is discharged from further performance and may bring an action for damages, but the contract itself is not rescinded.

13.2.3 Affirmation

If the contract is affirmed following a repudiatory breach, both parties must continue to perform their contractual obligations.

What will constitute affirmation?

Yukong Line Ltd of Korea v Rendsburg Investments Corporation of Liberia
[1996] 2 Lloyd's Rep 604 (Commercial Court)

In June 1995, the claimants chartered a vessel to the defendants, Rendsburg, for three years. However, on 23 January 1996, the charterers sent a message stating that they were 'unable to perform any further'. The following day, the claimants sent the following telex message in response:

[R]eally upset to receive notice of non-performance from charterers. Charterers' cancellation is totally unacceptable and charterers are strongly requested to honour their contractual obligations according to the charter party. . .In case of non-performance all damages, loss and any other costs incurred directly or indirectly to be for charterers' responsibility and liability.

Look forward to receiving honourable confirmation from charterers . . .

Having received no response to this message, on 1 February, the claimants advised the charterers that they were accepting the repudiation as terminating the contract.

As a preliminary question of law, Moore-Bick J had to determine whether the claimants' telex of 24 January amounted to an affirmation of the contract.

Held: It did not affirm the repudiatory breach. The judge stressed the need for very clear evidence of the intention to continue with the contract.

MOORE-BICK J: The injured party will not be treated as having elected to affirm the contract in the face of the renunciation unless it can be shown that he knew of the facts giving rise to his right to treat the contract as discharged and of his right to choose between affirming the contract and treating it as discharged

. . . A binding election requires the injured party to communicate his choice to the other party in clear and unequivocal terms. In particular, he will not be held bound by a qualified or conditional decision

. . . Election can be express or implied and will be implied where the injured party acts in a way which is consistent only with a decision to keep the contract alive or where he exercises rights which would only be available to him if the contract had been affirmed.

Two observations in the authorities cited to me strike me as being of particular significance in the context of this case in which the argument has turned mainly on the proper construction to be placed upon the owners' response to the charterers' original message that they could not perform. In *Johnson and another v Agnew* [[1980] AC 367] Lord Wilberforce said, at p. 398E of the report:

Election, though the subject of much learning and refinement, is in the end a doctrine based on simple considerations of common sense and equity.

And in *Peyman v Lanjani and others* [[1985] Ch 457], Lord Justice Slade, having held that actual knowledge of the right to choose is essential to support an election, pointed out, at p. 501B of the report, that the doctrine of estoppel will often operate to prevent any injustice in a case where the repudiating party has relied on an apparent election by the injured party.

These comments seem to me to provide strong support for the view that the Court should not adopt an unduly technical approach to deciding whether the injured party has affirmed the contract and should not be willing to hold that the contract has been affirmed without very clear evidence that the injured party has indeed chosen to go on with the contract notwithstanding the other party's repudiation. In my view, the Court should generally be slow to accept that the injured party has committed himself irrevocably to continuing with the contract in the knowledge that if, without finally committing himself, the injured party has made an unequivocal statement of some kind on which the party in repudiation has relied, the doctrine of estoppel is likely to prevent any injustice being done.

Considerations of this kind are perhaps most likely to arise when the injured party's initial response to the renunciation of the contract has been to call on the other to change his mind, accept his obligations and perform the contract. That is often the most natural response and one which, in my view, the Court should do nothing to discourage. It would be highly unsatisfactory, if, by responding in that way, the injured party were to put himself at risk of being held to have irrevocably affirmed the contract whatever the other's reaction might be, and in my judgment he does not do so. The law does not require an injured party to snatch at a repudiation and he does not automatically lose his right to treat the contract as discharged merely by calling on the other to reconsider his position and recognise his obligations.

[The judge then considered whether the telex of 24 January constituted an affirmation by the claimants:] . . . [Counsel for the defendants] reminded me of the passage in the speech of Lord Ackner in *The Simona* [[1988] 2 Lloyd's Rep 199] where he said at p. 203, col. 2; p. 799 of the reports [i.e. Appeal Cases, [1989] AC 788]:

> When one party wrongly refuses to perform obligations, this will not automatically bring the contract to an end. The innocent party has an option. He may either accept the wrongful repudiation as determining the contract and sue for damages, or he may ignore or reject the attempt to determine the contract and affirm its continued existence. Cockburn CJ in *Frost v Knight* [(1872) LR 7 Ex 111] put the matter thus: '. . .The promisee, if he pleases, may, treat the notice of intention as inoperative, and await the time when the contract is to be executed, and then hold the other party responsible for all the consequences of non-performance'.

He submitted that in their message the owners quite clearly rejected any cancellation of the charter and made it clear that as far as they were concerned the contract was going ahead. They demanded that the charterers should perform their obligations and threatened to hold them liable in damages if in the event they failed to do so. This, [counsel] submitted, was a plain case of the owners 'rejecting the attempt to determine the contract' in the words of Lord Ackner, and 'choosing to treat the charterers' notice as inoperative', to use the words of Cockburn, CJ. Accordingly, he said, they affirmed the charter.

[Counsel for the plaintiffs] submitted that the telex cannot properly be read in that way at all. What it amounted to, he said, was an expression of outrage and a demand that the charterers withdraw their repudiation and perform their obligations. The threat to hold them responsible in damages if they did not do so was, he said, wholly consistent with the retaining of the option to treat the contract as discharged, and the final sentence containing the request for 'an honourable confirmation' made it clear that their willingness to proceed with the contract depended on their receiving confirmation from the charterers that they would honour their obligations.

This telex, of course, has to be read as a whole. It would be quite wrong to take it apart and seek to attach a particular meaning to one section while ignoring what precedes and follows it. And it must also be remembered that it is not a formal document but one drafted by businessmen whose native language was not English.

In my view, this message, read as a whole, can only be read as a cry of protest at what the owners regarded as a dishonourable attempt by the charterers to abandon their obligations. Far from rejecting the idea that the charter might be discharged, as [counsel for the defendants] suggests, what the owners are here saying is that they regard the charterers' conduct in seeking to abandon it as totally unacceptable behaviour. Likewise, I cannot read the final sentence as simply inviting the charterers to confirm that if in due course their failure [*sic*] to perform the contract they would be liable in damages. The threat to report the charterers' attitude as well as their actions shows clearly that it is their present conduct which concerned the owners. The only meaning one can sensibly give to the final sentence of the telex is that the owners were asking the charterers to withdraw their repudiation and confirm their willingness to perform the contract. However one reads this telex, it is impossible, in my view, to find in it an unequivocal statement on the part of the owners that they will proceed with the contract and await performance in due course regardless of the position adopted by the charterers. That being so, the argument that the owners affirmed the contract by sending this message must fail.

. . . It follows that, in my judgment, the owners had not previously elected to affirm the contract when on Feb. 1 they accepted the charterers' repudiation as discharging it and that they were entitled to take that step. When doing so, they referred expressly to the charterers' failure to confirm that they would fulfil the contract. That, in my view, was an understandable reference back to their telex of Jan. 24 in which they had asked for an honourable confirmation of the charterers' intention to perform . . .

NOTES

1. *Yukong* is concerned with a particular type of repudiatory breach—namely, anticipatory repudiatory breach (a contractual renunciation before the time fixed for performance). It follows that affirmation will relate to *this* breach, giving the breaching party a further opportunity to perform on the date set for performance. If the breaching party were still not to perform on that date, this would constitute a fresh repudiatory breach and give rise to a fresh election to terminate or affirm.

2. This decision confirms that there must be an unequivocal affirmation of the contract that firmly commits the injured party to continuing with the contract. This decision on affirmation can usefully be compared with the approach taken by the House of Lords in *Vitol SA v Norelf Ltd, The Santa Clara* (*page 630, 13.2.1*) to what can constitute acceptance of a repudiatory breach as terminating the contract.

3. Moore-Bick J considers that this restrictive approach to affirmation is tempered by the fact that the doctrine of estoppel will prevent injustice to a defendant who has relied on unequivocal statements by the claimant that appeared to constitute affirmation of the repudiatory breach: *Fercometal v Mediterranean Shipping* (*page 664, 13.5.3.2.1*). However, it is necessary to distinguish clearly those actions that are not sufficiently unequivocal to constitute affirmations, but are sufficiently unequivocal to found an estoppel.

13.3 Identifying repudiatory breach and the classification of terms

See Brownsword (1992) 5 JCL 83.

The traditional distinction is between two types of promissory contractual term: conditions and warranties. A condition is an important term 'going to the root of the contract'; a warranty is a less important term not going to the substance of the contract, the breach of which is adequately compensated by damages (money).

As a general principle, a breach of condition is a repudiatory breach, and gives the injured party the option of terminating the performance and obtaining damages for its loss caused by the breach, or affirming the contract and recovering damages for the breach. However, a broken warranty is no repudiatory breach, and only allows the injured party to claim damages. On breach of a warranty, both parties must continue to perform their obligations under the contract.

13.3.1 Is the term a condition?

13.3.1.1 Statutory Classification

Does statute classify the term? In the context of B2B (business to business) contracts, the implied terms as to description, fitness for purpose, satisfactory quality, and correspondence with sample are classified as conditions under the Sales of Goods Act (SGA) 1979, ss. 13(1A), 14(6), and 15(3), as amended. In case of a breach, the buyer should be entitled to reject the goods (terminate the contract for repudiatory breach) or to affirm (as by acceptance of the goods: SGA 1979, s. 35). However, s. 15A(1) provides that, in the B2B context, such a breach *may* instead be treated as a breach of warranty (with the only remedy as damages) where the breach is so slight that it would be unreasonable to reject the goods (i.e. unreasonable to exercise the normal option of terminating the contract).

Sale of Goods Act 1979

15A Modification of remedies for breach of condition in non-consumer cases.

(1) Where in the case of a contract of sale—

  (a) the buyer would, apart from this subsection, have the right to reject goods by reason of a breach on the part of the seller of a term implied by section 13, 14 or 15 above, but

  (b) the breach is so slight that it would be unreasonable for him to reject them, the breach is not to be treated as a breach of condition but may be treated as a breach of warranty.

(2) This section applies unless a contrary intention appears in, or is to be implied from, the contract.

(3) It is for the seller to show that a breach fell within subsection (1)(b) above.

NOTES

1. See also the Supply of Goods (Implied Terms) Act 1973, s. 11A, and the Supply of Goods and Services Act 1982, ss. 5A and 10A, for the equivalent provisions for hire purchase, work and materials, and hire contracts.

2. This provision inevitably leads to uncertainty over whether the breach of a condition is treated as giving rise to the right to reject for ss. 13–15 breaches in a non-consumer contract. The consequences normally attributed to a breach of condition will not automatically follow.

While flexibility is welcome, this provision does not assist the clarity of the law in this area. Significantly, even if the breach is so slight that it would be unreasonable for the non-consumer buyer to reject, it does not necessarily follow that the only remedy will be damages, because the section is drafted so as to give the court a discretion. Section 15A(1) provides that although the breach is not to be treated as a breach of condition (with an automatic right to reject), it '*may* be treated as a breach of warranty' (damages only).

3. Section 15A(2), however, provides for the uncertainty to be excluded by the contract, e.g. by including an express provision that there is a right to reject.

4. In the consumer context, the Consumer Rights Act (CRA) 2015 (implementing the European Consumer Rights Directive (CRD) 2011/83/EU) does not make any distinction between conditions and warranties but classifies such obligations relating to the goods as 'terms' (and they are 'entrenched rights' so that the parties cannot exclude or restrict them). The CRA 2015 also specifies a broader range of possible remedies:

(a) an immediate short-term right to termination within 30 days (to reject the goods or part of the goods) for breaches of terms imposing obligations relating to the goods (e.g. satisfactory quality, fitness for purpose, correspondence with description, sample or model seen or examined) and to receive a refund (ss. 20, 21, and 22 CRA 2015);

(b) the ability to require the trader to repair or replace the goods unless this is impossible or disproportionate (s. 23 CRA 2015); and

(c) a right to a price reduction *or* a final right to reject where repair or replacement is impossible or disproportionate, or the repair or replacement has failed or not taken place within a reasonable time and without significant inconvenience to the consumer (s. 24 CRA 2015).

There may be a deduction from any refund for use of the goods by the consumer.

13.3.1.2 Effective classification by the parties as a condition?

Have the parties classified the term? If so, does it operate as a condition?

Lombard North Central plc v Butterworth
[1987] QB 527 (CA)

The claimants leased a computer to the defendant. Clause 2(a) of the agreement made punctual payment of each instalment of hire *of the essence* of the agreement, and under clause 5 failure to make due and punctual payment entitled the claimants to terminate the agreement. The defendant was late in paying the third, fourth, and fifth instalments, and when the sixth instalment was six weeks overdue, the claimants terminated the agreement and sought damages for breach of contract. The Court of Appeal stressed that the parties were free to classify the relative importance of the terms of their contract.

Held: Clause 2(a) made prompt payment a condition of the contract, so that if any payment were not made on time, there would be a breach of the agreement entitling the claimants to terminate the contract and recover damages for the loss of the transaction, even though the breach itself was not regarded as giving rise to serious consequences.

MUSTILL LJ: The reason why I am impelled to hold that the plaintiffs' contentions are well founded can most conveniently be set out in a series of propositions.

1. Where a breach goes to the root of the contract, the injured party may elect to put an end to the contract. Thereupon both sides are relieved from those obligations which remain unperformed.

2. If he does so elect, the injured party is entitled to compensation for (a) any breaches which occurred before the contract was terminated, and (b) the loss of his opportunity to receive performance of the promisor's outstanding obligations.

3. Certain categories of obligation, often called conditions, have the property that any breach of them is treated as going to the root of the contract. Upon the occurrence of any breach of condition, the injured party can elect to terminate and claim damages, whatever the gravity of the breach.

4. It is possible by express provision in the contract to make a term a condition, even if it would not be so in the absence of such a provision.

5. A stipulation that time is of the essence, in relation to a particular contractual term, denotes that timely performance is a condition of the contract. The consequence is that delay in performance is treated as going to the root of the contract, without regard to the magnitude of the breach.

6. It follows that where a promisor fails to give timely performance of an obligation in respect of which time is expressly stated to be of the essence, the injured party may elect to terminate and recover damages in respect of the promisor's outstanding obligations, without regard to the magnitude of the breach . . .

NOTES

1. Diplock LJ, in *Hongkong Fir Shipping v Kawasaki Kishen Kaisha* [1962] 2 QB 26 (*page 644, 13.3.2*) and Lord Wilberforce in *Bunge Corporation v Tradax SA* [1981] 1 WLR 711 (*page 640, 13.3.1.4*) also indicated that the parties were free to make a particular term a condition. *Lombard v Butterworth* appears to have provided a simple formulation with which to achieve this. This effect can also be achieved by expressly stipulating that the remedy is to be the right to terminate (or to reject the goods): see Ormrod LJ in *Cehave NV v Bremer Handelsgesellschaft GmbH, The Hansa Nord* [1976] QB 44 (*page 644, 13.3.2*).

2. *Union Eagle Ltd v Golden Achievement Ltd* [1997] AC 514 provides a further illustration of the effect of 'time is of the essence'. The claimant had agreed to buy a flat and had paid a deposit of 10 per cent of the purchase price. The purchase agreement specified the date, time, and place of completion, and stated

that time was of the essence of the contract, so that the vendor had the right to terminate the contract and forfeit the deposit if the purchaser failed to comply with any term of the agreement. The purchaser failed to complete by the stipulated time and was ten minutes late tendering the purchase price. The vendor therefore terminated the contract and forfeited the deposit. The claimant sought specific performance of the agreement. The Privy Council dismissed this claim on the basis that the purchaser had committed a repudiatory breach, which entitled the vendor to reject late performance and terminate the contract.

However, in the next case, the House of Lords considered that a term described as a 'condition' could not have been intended by the parties to have this effect.

L. Schuler AG v Wickman Machine Tool Sales
[1974] AC 235 (HL)

Wickman, an English company, was given the sole selling rights for the German company's panel presses for four-and-a-half years. Clause 7(b) of the distributorship contract provided that '[i]t shall be [a] condition of the agreement that (i) [Wickman] shall send its representative to visit (the six largest UK motor manufacturers) at least once in every week' to solicit orders. Wickman failed to make a number of these visits and Schuler terminated the agreement under clause 11(a) on the basis that Wickman had committed a material breach of its obligations, which it had failed to remedy within 60 days of being required in writing to do so. Wickman claimed damages for wrongful repudiation.

Held (Lord Wilberforce dissenting): Clause 7(b) was not a condition in the sense that a single breach, however trivial, would entitle the innocent party to terminate the contract.

LORD REID: Sometimes a breach of a term gives that option [to terminate for repudiatory breach] to the aggrieved party because it is of a fundamental character going to the root of the contract, sometimes it gives that option because the parties have chosen to stipulate that it shall have that effect. Blackburn J said in *Bettini v Gye* (1876) 1 QBD 183, 187: 'Parties may think some matter, apparently of very little importance, essential; and if they sufficiently express an intention to make the literal fulfilment of such a thing a condition precedent, it will be one. . .'

In the present case it is not contended that Wickman's failures to make visits amounted in themselves to fundamental breaches. What is contended is that the terms of clause 7 'sufficiently express an intention' to make any breach, however small, of the obligation to make visits a condition so that any breach shall entitle Schuler to rescind the whole contract if they so desire.

Schuler maintains that the use of the word 'condition' is in itself enough to establish this intention. No doubt some words used by lawyers do have a rigid inflexible meaning. But we must remember that we are seeking to discover intention as disclosed by the contract as a whole. Use of the word 'condition' is an indication—even a strong indication—of such an intention but it is by no means conclusive.

The fact that a particular construction leads to a very unreasonable result must be a relevant consideration. The more unreasonable the result the more unlikely it is that the parties can have intended it, and if they do intend it the more necessary it is that they shall make that intention abundantly clear.

Clause 7(b) requires that over a long period each of the six firms shall be visited every week by one or other of two named representatives. It makes no provision for Wickman being entitled to substitute others even on the death or retirement of one of the named representatives. Even if one could imply some right to do this, it makes no provision for both representatives being ill during a particular week. And it makes no provision for the possibility that one or other of the firms may tell Wickman that they cannot receive Wickman's representative during a particular week. So if the parties gave any thought to the matter at all they must have realised the probability that in a few cases out of the 1,400 required visits a visit as stipulated would be impossible. But if Schuler's contention is right, failure to make even one visit entitle [*sic*] them to terminate the contract however blameless Wickman might be.

This is so unreasonable that it must make me search for some other possible meaning of the contract. If none can be found then Wickman must suffer the consequences. But only if that is the only possible interpretation . . . If I have to construe clause 7 standing by itself then I do find difficulty in reaching any other interpretation. But if clause 7 must be read with clause 11 the difficulty disappears. The word 'condition' would make any breach of clause 7(b), however excusable, a material breach. That would then entitle Schuler to give notice under clause 11(a)(i) requiring the breach to be remedied. There would be no point in giving such a notice if Wickman were clearly not in fault but if it were given Wickman would have no difficulty in showing that the breach had been remedied. If Wickman were at fault then on receiving such a notice they would have to amend their system so that they could show that the breach had been remedied. If they did not do that within the period of the notice then Schuler would be entitled to rescind.

In my view, that is a possible and reasonable construction of the contract and I would therefore adopt it. The contract is so obscure that I can have no confidence that this is its true meaning but for the reasons which I have given I think that it is the preferable construction. It follows that Schuler was not entitled to rescind the contract as it purported to do . . .

? QUESTION

Could the majority of the House of Lords be accused of rewriting the parties' agreement?

NOTES

1. Lord Wilberforce (dissenting) was of the opinion that the term was clearly a condition because that was the word that the parties had used. He added that if it were not a condition, then Schuler would find itself in breach, having wrongfully repudiated.

2. The House of Lords majority, in interpreting what the parties intended, appears to have ignored the clear use of the word 'condition' on the basis that they considered this interpretation to be so unreasonable that it could not have been intended by the parties. This type of approach was criticized by the Supreme Court in *Arnold v Britton* [2015] UKSC 36, [2015] AC 1619, which placed the primary emphasis on the language chosen by the parties as the starting point for identifying the intended meaning from an objective perspective. The courts would not depart from the natural meaning of these words unless they were evidently ambiguous. Lord Neuberger made specific reference to the fact that *Schuler* would need to be read in this light. It was not the role of the court to remedy drafting errors or ill-thought-out provisions.

3. If the word 'condition' is not conclusive of the fact that a right to terminate was intended, then what form of wording will be effective to achieve this objective is unclear and it falls to the innocent party to judge whether it has the right to terminate for breach. As noted, it may later be decided that there was no such right because it was not a breach of a condition, so that the repudiating party will have wrongfully repudiated and find itself in breach of contract.

13.3.1.3 What if the parties have not made a successful classification?

The courts must seek to ascertain the parties' intentions by looking at the relative importance of the term on the contract as a whole to see whether it 'goes to the root of the contract', as the majority of the House of Lords did in *Schuler v Wickman Machine Tool Sales* (*page 637, 13.3.1.2*).

In *Couchman v Hill* [1947] KB 554 (*page 173, 5.1.2*), the term was considered a condition because the heifer being unserved was 'a substantial ingredient in the identity of the thing sold'. A similar principle can be seen in *Bannerman v White* (1861) 10 CB NS 844 (*page 173, 5.1.2*), since if the term was so important to the buyer that he would not have purchased without it, it is more likely to be construed as a condition.

In *Barber v NWS Bank plc* [1996] 1 All ER 906, the Court of Appeal held that, in a conditional sale agreement for the purchase of a car whereby the property in the car remained vested in the finance company until the hirer had paid the balance and all sums owing, it was a condition that the finance company was the owner of the car at the date of the agreement. The Court of Appeal ruled out the possibility that such a term was innominate (*page 644, 13.3.2*), because it was clearly fundamental to the transaction and could be broken in only one way, which would necessarily be serious. Sir Roger Parker stated, at p. 911, that: '[T]his term is not one which admits of different breaches, some of which are trivial, for which damages are an adequate remedy, and others of which are sufficiently serious to warrant rescission. There is here one breach only.'

13.3.1.4 Time stipulations in mercantile contracts: conditions?

Until comparatively recently, the need for certainty resulted in time stipulations in mercantile contracts being classified as conditions without it having to be established that they went to the root of the contract. Where the same term is used in a standard form, subsequent parties could then rely on it and know in advance what the remedies for breach would be.

Maredelanto Compania Naviera SA v Bergbau-Handel GmbH, The Mihalis Angelos
[1971] 1 QB 164 (CA)

By a charterparty dated 25 May 1965, the *Mihalis Angelos* was chartered to proceed to Haiphong and load a cargo there. The charterparty described the vessel as 'expected ready to load under this charter about 1 July 1965'. On 23 June, the vessel arrived at Hong Kong to discharge a cargo from the previous voyage; it was still there on 17 July 1965, when the charterers purported to cancel the charterparty. They did so on the grounds of *force majeure* (*page 599, 12.1*), because there was no cargo at Haiphong owing to war. The owners accepted this action as a repudiation of the contract and claimed damages for their loss of profit. The arbitrator had found that there were no grounds to terminate for *force majeure*, so the question was whether the charterers nevertheless had the right to terminate.

Held: The expected readiness to load clause was a condition that the owners had broken, since, on 25 May when the contract was made, they could not reasonably have expected that the ship would be ready to load in Haiphong on 1 July. Therefore, the charterers did have the right to terminate on 17 July.

MEGAW LJ: In my judgment, such a term in a charterparty ought to be regarded as being a condition of the contract, in the old sense of the word 'condition': that is, that when it has been broken, the other party can, if he wishes, by intimation to the party in breach, elect to be released from performance of his further obligations under the contract; and he can validly do so without having to establish that on the facts of the particular case the breach has produced serious consequences which can be treated as 'going to the root of the contract' or as being 'fundamental,' or whatever other metaphor may be thought appropriate for a frustration case . . .

. . . One of the essential elements of law is some measure of uniformity. One of the important elements of the law is predictability. At any rate in commercial law, there are obvious and substantial advantages in having, where possible, a firm and definite rule for a particular class of legal relationship: for example, as here, the legal categorisation of a particular, definable type of contractual clause in common use. It is surely much better, both for shipowners and charterers (and, incidentally, for their advisers), when a contractual obligation of this nature is under consideration, and still more when they are faced with the necessity for an urgent decision as to the effects of a suspected breach of it, to be able to say categorically: 'If a breach is proved, then the charterer can put an end to the contract,' rather than that they should be left to ponder whether or not the courts would be likely, in the particular case, when the evidence has been heard, to decide that in the particular circumstances the breach was or was not such as 'to go to the root of the contract.' Where justice does not require greater flexibility, there is everything to be said for, and nothing against, a degree of rigidity in legal principle.

Bunge Corporation v Tradax SA
[1981] 1 WLR 711 (HL)

The buyers agreed to purchase 15,000 tons of soya bean meal from the sellers. One shipment was to be made in June 1975 and the buyers were to provide a vessel at the nominated port. Clause 7 stated that the buyers were to 'give at least 15 consecutive days' notice' of their probable readiness to load the vessel. In order for the goods to be shipped in June, this notice had to be given by 13 June. The notice was not given until 17 June and the sellers claimed that the late notice was a breach, amounting to a repudiation of the contract. They claimed damages from the buyers on the basis that, by that time, the market price of the soya bean meal had fallen by more than US$60 a ton. The buyers contended that the term as to notice was an intermediate term and the effect of the breach was not sufficiently serious for the sellers to treat the contract as repudiated. At first instance, the judge had applied *Hongkong Fir* and concluded that the term was innominate. However, both the Court of Appeal and the House of Lords held it to be a condition, since it was a time stipulation in a mercantile contract.

LORD WILBERFORCE: As to such a clause there is only one kind of breach possible, namely to be late, and the questions which have to be asked are, first, what importance have the parties expressly ascribed to this consequence, and second, in the absence of expressed agreement, what consequence ought to be attached to it having regard to the contract as a whole.

The test suggested by the appellants was a different one. One must consider, they said, the breach actually committed and then decide whether that default would deprive the party not in default of substantially the whole benefit of the contract . . . One may observe in the first place that the introduction of a test of this kind would be commercially most undesirable. It would expose the parties, after a breach of one, two, three, seven and other numbers of days to an argument whether this delay would have left time for the seller to provide the goods. It would make it, at the time, at least difficult, and sometimes impossible, for the supplier to know whether he could do so. It would fatally remove from a vital provision in the contract that certainty which is the most indispensable quality of mercantile contracts, and lead to a large increase in arbitrations. It would confine the seller—perhaps after arbitration and reference through the courts—to a remedy in damages which might be extremely difficult to quantify. These are all serious objections in practice. But I am clear that the submission is unacceptable in law . . . It remains true, as Lord Roskill has pointed out in *Cehave NV v Bremer Handelsgesellschaft mbH (The Hansa Nord)* [1976] QB 44, that the courts should not be too ready to interpret contractual clauses as conditions. And I have myself commended, and continue to commend, the greater flexibility in the law of contracts to which *Hong Kong Fir* points the way (*Reardon Smith Line Ltd v Hansen-Tangen* [1976] 1 WLR 989 at 998). But I do not doubt that, in suitable cases, the courts should not be reluctant, if the intentions of the parties as shown by the contract so indicate, to hold that an obligation has the force of a condition, and that indeed they should usually do so in the case of time clauses in mercantile contracts. To such cases the 'gravity of the breach' approach of the *Hong Kong Fir* case would be unsuitable . . .

Breach of contract 13

NOTE This approach's drawback is that, once a term is classified as a condition, it always gives rise to a right to terminate if broken, even if the little or no damage ensues. *The Mihalis Angelos* illustrates how a party can escape from a bad bargain, simply on the ground that the other party has committed a breach of a condition.

More recently, the courts have tended to avoid drawing an automatic conclusion for such time stipulations. For example, the House of Lords has stated that timely redelivery of a vessel at the end of a time charterparty is not a condition, but an innominate term, despite the fact that it is essentially a time stipulation in a mercantile contract.

Torvald Klaveness A/S v Arni Maritime Corporation, The Gregos
[1994] 1 WLR 1465 (HL)

The time charterparty stipulated the last date for redelivery of the vessel by the charterers to the owners the 18 March 1988. On 9 February, the charterers ordered the vessel from Matanzas in Venezuela to the port of Palua to load a cargo for delivery to Fos in Italy prior to redelivery to the owners by 18 March. The order of readiness to load in Palua was given on 25 February, but the Orinoco River was blocked by another vessel, the owners therefore considered that if a cargo were loaded, the vessel would not be redelivered in time and requested fresh orders from the charterers. The charterers refused.

The owners claimed that the charterers' order was a repudiatory breach and accepted it as terminating the contract.

Held: The charterers had committed a repudiatory breach. The majority (Lord Mustill, with whom Lords Ackner, Slynn, and Woolf agreed) held that the obligation to redeliver on time was innominate, so that the issuing of the order for the voyage did not in itself constitute a repudiatory breach, but that the charterers' persistence in the order that had become illegitimate amounted to a renunciation of the contract, i.e. a repudiatory breach.

LORD MUSTILL: I find it hard to accept that timely redelivery is a condition of the contract. The classification of an obligation as a condition or an 'innominate' term is largely determined by its practical importance in the scheme of the contract, and this is not easily judged in relation to the obligation to redeliver, since the occasions for the cancellation of a charter on the ground of a few days' delay at the end of the chartered service are likely to be few. If the ship is laden when the final date arrives the shipowner will often have obligations to third party consignees which make it impossible for him to cut short the voyage, quite apart from the improbability that he will go to the trouble and expense of arranging for the discharge and receipt of the cargo at an alternative destination, just to save a few days' delay. These problems will not arise if the vessel is ballasting to the redelivery port, but even if the shipowner really wants the vessel back on time, rather than a few days late, he will not usually need to have recourse to a cancellation, since the charterer will have no motive to keep the charter in being, with its obligation to pay hire for an empty ship. Even acknowledging the importance given in recent years to time clauses in mercantile contracts (see, for example, *Bunge Corporation New York v Tradax Export SA Panama* [1981] 1 WLR 711 and *Compagnie Commerciale Sucres et Denrées v C Czarnikow Ltd* [1990] 1 WLR 1337). I would incline to the view that this particular obligation is 'innominate' and that a short delay in redelivery would not justify the termination of the contract.

However, Lord Templeman considered that the obligation to redeliver at the end of a time charter is of the essence of the contract and that, since the charterers had given an order that would prevent the vessel being redelivered on time, the owners could accept that repudiatory breach as terminating the contract.

LORD TEMPLEMAN: My Lords, in a time charter, the time for redelivery of the vessel by the charterer to the owner at the end of the charter is of the essence of the contract, absent any provision in the contract to the contrary. If the charterer in the course of the charterparty evinces an intention not to redeliver the vessel by the date or last date fixed for redelivery, the charterer will evince an intention no longer to be bound by the contract and will thus repudiate the contract. The owner may ignore the repudiation and claim damages resulting from breach of contract by any late delivery or accept the repudiation, withdraw the vessel from the control of the charterer and claim damages resulting from repudiation . . .

There was a good deal of discussion about legitimate and illegitimate last voyages but to my mind this appeal falls to be determined by the application of elementary principles of contract. The charterer agrees to redeliver on time and must therefore give orders which ensure that the vessel will be redelivered on time. If the charterer gives an order which will not enable the vessel to be redelivered on time, the owner may treat that order as a repudiatory breach of contract. If the owner complies with the order he loses his right to repudiate but is entitled to damages for any late delivery. In the present case, the crucial date was 25 February when the charterers could have given an order which would have enabled redelivery on time but insisted on an order which did not allow the vessel to be redelivered on time. The order to load at Palua on 25 February was a repudiatory breach of contract. If the *Gregos* had been loaded, pursuant to that order, the owners would have lost their right to repudiate but would have remained entitled to damages for late delivery. The owners accepted the repudiation and withdrew the vessel . . .

NOTES

1. This decision highlights the tension in this area between certainty and flexibility.

2. It is advisable to judge the decision of the majority in light of the background facts—namely, a rising market and evidence that the owners wished to recharter at the earliest possible opportunity to take advantage of such higher rates. Lord Mustill expressly commented on the dangers of concluding that this term was a condition when he stated, at p. 1475:

My Lords, although it is well established that certain obligations under charterparties do have the character of conditions I would not for my part wish to enlarge the category unduly, given the opportunity which this provides for a party to rely on an innocuous breach as a means of escaping from an unwelcome bargain.

3. It could still be that the courts prefer to classify terms in mercantile contracts as conditions. *Kuwait Rocks Co. v AMN BulkCarriers Inc., The Astra* [2013] EWHC 865 (Comm), [2013] 1 CLC 819, [2013] 2 All ER (Comm) 689, involved an unsurprising classification of a term in a mercantile contract as a 'condition'. The obligation to make punctual payment of hire included a right to withdraw the vessel in the event of any breach, and the judge held that this made time of the essence and was therefore a 'condition'. Any breach would be repudiatory. Flaux J also suggested that the flexible approach in *Torvald Klaveness A/S v Arni Maritime Corporation, The Gregos* [1994] 1 WLR 1465 may be fact-dependent and may not represent the general approach to all time stipulations in mercantile contracts.

FLAUX J: 117 . . . [I]t seems to me that this court need not show any reluctance to hold that the obligation is a condition.

The reluctance demonstrated by Lord Mustill in *The Gregos* was really limited to the particular provisions he was considering and did not extend to the obligation to make punctual payment of hire. Furthermore, as Lords Wilberforce and Roskill made clear in *Bunge v Tradax* . . . in the case of so-called time clauses in mercantile contracts, of which this obligation is one, the courts should not show any reluctance to find that such provisions are conditions and, indeed, should usually do so.

4. Subsequently, however, in *Spar Shipping AS v Grand China Logistics Holding (Group) Co. Ltd* [2015] EWHC 718 (Comm), [2015] 1 All ER (Comm) 879, [2015] 2 Lloyd's Rep 407, Popplewell J disagreed with Flaux J's analysis in *The Astra* and held that payment of hire was not a condition of the contract in circumstances where there was a similar right to withdraw provision. The inconsistencies in interpretation based on the importance attached by individual judges to certainty in commercial transactions are clear. Specifically, Popplewell J considered that for such a term to be a condition, the parties' agreement needed to entitle the non-breaching party to treat the contract as 'repudiated', rather than merely 'terminated for the breach'.

POPPLEWELL J: 97 A contractual term may, however, provide for termination in the case of breach without the parties intending the consequences to be the same as would arise at common law if the term breached were categorised as a condition. Parties may agree that in the event of breach the innocent party should have the right to terminate the contract, so as to put an end to future performance obligations under the contract, but without intending that the defaulting party should be liable for any consequences of the termination. Such provisions are concerned solely to provide the innocent party with an option to put an end to his performance obligations, but not to confer a right to claim damages flowing from the termination itself. In such cases it is the innocent party's election to exercise his option to terminate which is treated as the cause of the termination, and the cause of whatever loss flows from it, not the breach which triggers the innocent party's right to cancel. I shall use the expression 'option to cancel' to connote such a term, whilst recognising that contractual language couched in terms of cancellation may be equally consistent with an intention to treat the term breached as a condition with the full damages consequences which flow from that analysis.

98 Such an option to cancel leaves unaffected the innocent party's rights to claim damages, which remain governed by the common law principles . . . If there has been a repudiatory breach or renunciation, the right to damages is preserved; if there has been no repudiatory breach or renunciation, the option to cancel does not confer a right to damages, in the absence of clear language to the contrary, but merely confers a right to put an end to future performance obligations.

Following *Spar Shipping*, it is necessary for shipowners to demonstrate that the non-payment of hire is clear evidence of an intention on the part of the charterers not to be bound by that charter. Popplewell J's position is now upheld by the Court of Appeal in *Spar Shipping AS v Grand China Logistics Holding (Group) Co. Ltd* [2016] EWCA Civ 982, [2016] 2 Lloyd's Rep 447. And Flaux J's analysis in *The Astra* is, on that issue, considered as overruled. Popplewell's definition of a condition was unanimously endorsed by the Court of Appeal in

Ark Shipping Co. LLC v Silverburn Shipping (IoM) Ltd [2019] EWCA Civ 1161, [2019] 2 Lloyd's Rep 603 (at [40]). Also endorsing the Supreme Court in *Wood v Capita Insurance Services* [2017] UKSC 24, [2017] 2 WLR 1095, [2017] AC 765 (*page 243, 5.5.4*), Lord McCombe also clarified the position that this was a construction issue (at [40]) and therefore applies to all kinds of clauses in commercial contracts, not just payment clauses. The tension between certainty and flexibility was clearly at the centre of the decision. After recognizing that certainty was important, it was not an 'acceptable trade-off' against the 'risk of trivial breaches having disproportionate consequences' (at [78]).

5. Outside mercantile (or shipping) contracts, although express reference to 'time being of the essence' in relation to a payment obligation in a commercial contract will lead to classification as a 'condition' (*page 637, 13.3.1.2*), the time of payment will not necessarily be of the essence in the absence of party agreement that it should be. In *Valilas v Januzj* [2014] EWCA Civ 436, [2015] 1 All ER (Comm) 1047, 154 Con LR 38, a majority of the Court of Appeal (Arden and Floyd LJJ; Underhill LJ dissenting) considered that a failure by a dentist to make monthly payments under a facilities contract with the dental practice owner did not amount to a breach of condition which would have automatically given rise to a repudiatory breach.

13.3.2 More flexibility at a price: innominate or intermediate terms

Hongkong Fir Shipping Co. Ltd v Kawasaki Kisen Kaisha Ltd
[1962] 2 QB 26 (CA)

The charterers hired a ship for 24 months, 'being in every way fitted for ordinary cargo service'. The ship was delivered on 13 February 1957, and sailed that day to pick up a cargo in the United States and take it to Osaka. Because of the age of the ship's machinery, it needed to be maintained by an experienced, competent, careful, and adequate engine-room staff. There were insufficient numbers of staff and the chief engineer was incompetent. As a result, there were many serious breakdowns in the machinery. On the voyage at sea for eight-and-a-half weeks, the ship was off-hire for five weeks for repairs and, on reaching Osaka on 25 May, required 15 weeks of repairs to make her seaworthy. In June 1957, the charterers repudiated the charterparty (freight rates having fallen in the interim). There were no reasonable grounds for thinking that the ship would not be seaworthy in mid-September and, in fact, she was seaworthy on 15 September, which left 17 months of the original charter period. The owners sought damages for wrongful repudiation.

Held: Although there was a breach of the charterparty because the ship was unseaworthy, seaworthiness was not a condition of the charterparty entitling the charterer to terminate. The delay caused by the breakdowns and the repairs was not so great as to frustrate the commercial purpose of the charterparty.

DIPLOCK LJ: Every synallagmatic contract contains in it the seeds of the problem: in what event will a party be relieved of his undertaking to do that which he has agreed to do but has not yet done? The contract may itself expressly define some of these events, as in the cancellation clause in a charter-party; but, human prescience being limited, it seldom does so exhaustively and often fails to do so at all. In some classes of contracts such as sale of goods, marine insurance, contracts of affreightment evidenced by bills of lading and those between parties to bills of exchange, Parliament has defined by statute some of the events not provided for expressly in individual contracts of that class; but where an event occurs the occurrence of which neither the parties nor Parliament have expressly stated will discharge one of the parties from further performance of his undertakings, it is for the court to determine whether the event has this effect or not.

The test whether an event has this effect or not has been stated in a number of metaphors all of which I think amount to the same thing: does the occurrence of the event deprive the party who has further undertakings still to perform of substantially the whole benefit which it was the intention of the parties as expressed in the contract that he should obtain as the consideration for performing those undertakings?

This test is applicable whether or not the event occurs as a result of the default of one of the parties to the contract, but the consequences of the event are different in the two cases. Where the event occurs as a result of the default of one party, the party in default cannot rely upon it as relieving himself of the performance of any further undertakings on his part, and the innocent party, although entitled to, need not treat the event as relieving him of the further performance of his own undertakings. This is only a specific application of the fundamental legal and moral rule that a man should not be allowed to take advantage of his own wrong. Where the event occurs as a result of the default of neither party, each is relieved of the further performance of his own undertakings, and their rights in respect of undertakings previously performed are now regulated by the Law Reform (Frustrated Contracts) Act, 1943.

This branch of the common law has reached its present stage by the normal process of historical growth, and the fallacy in [counsel for the charterers'] contention that a different test is applicable when the event occurs as a result of the default of one party from that applicable in cases of frustration where the event occurs as a result of the default of neither party lies, in my view, from a failure to view the cases in their historical context. The problem: in what event will a party to a contract be relieved of his undertaking to do that which he has agreed to do but has not yet done? has exercised the English courts for centuries . . .

Once it is appreciated that it is the event and not the fact that the event is a result of a breach of contract which relieves the party not in default of further performance of his obligations, two consequences follow. (1) The test whether the event relied upon has this consequence is the same whether the event is the result of the other party's breach of contract or not, as Devlin J pointed out in *Universal Cargo Carriers Corporation v Citati* [1957] 2 QB 401. (2) The question whether an event which is the result of the other party's breach of contract has this consequence cannot be answered by treating all contractual undertakings as falling into one of two separate categories: 'conditions' the breach of which gives rise to an event which relieves the party not in default of further performance of his obligations, and 'warranties' the breach of which does not give rise to such an event.

Lawyers tend to speak of this classification as if it were comprehensive, partly for the historical reasons which I have already mentioned and partly because Parliament itself adopted it in the Sale of Goods Act, 1893, as respects a number of implied terms in contracts for the sale of goods and has in that Act used the expressions 'condition' and 'warranty' in that meaning. But it is by no means true of contractual undertakings in general at common law.

No doubt there are many simple contractual undertakings, sometimes express but more often because of their very simplicity ('It goes without saying') to be implied, of which it can be predicated that every breach of such an undertaking must give rise to an event which will deprive the party not in default of substantially the whole benefit which it was intended that he should obtain from the contract. And such a stipulation, unless the parties have agreed that breach of it shall not entitle the non-defaulting party to treat the contract as repudiated, is a 'condition.' So too there may be other simple contractual undertakings of which it can be predicated that *no* breach can give rise to an event which will deprive the party not in default of substantially the whole benefit which it was intended that he should obtain from the contract; and such a stipulation, unless the parties have agreed that breach of it shall entitle the non-defaulting party to treat the contract as repudiated, is a 'warranty.'

There are, however, many contractual undertakings of a more complex character which cannot be categorised as being 'conditions' or 'warranties,' if the late nineteenth-century meaning adopted in the Sale of Goods Act, 1893, and used by Bowen LJ in *Bentsen v Taylor, Sons & Co.* [1893] 2 QB 274 be given to those terms. Of such undertakings all that can be predicated is that some breaches will and others will not give rise to an event which will deprive the party not in default of substantially the whole benefit which it was intended that he should obtain from the contract; and the legal consequences of a breach of such an undertaking, unless provided for expressly in the contract, depend upon the nature of the event to which the breach gives rise and do not follow automatically from a prior classification of the undertaking as a 'condition' or a 'warranty.' For instance, to take Bramwell B's example in *Jackson v Union Marine Insurance Co. Ltd* (1874) LR 10 CP 125 itself, breach of an undertaking by a shipowner to sail with all possible dispatch to a named port does not necessarily relieve the charterer of further performance of his obligation under the charterparty, but if the breach is so prolonged that the contemplated voyage is frustrated it does have this effect . . .

As my brethren have already pointed out, the shipowners' undertaking to tender a seaworthy ship has, as a result of numerous decisions as to what can amount to 'unseaworthiness,' become one of the most complex of contractual undertakings. It embraces obligations with respect to every part of the hull and machinery, stores and equipment and the crew itself. It can be broken by the presence of trivial defects easily and rapidly remediable as well as by defects which must inevitably result in a total loss of the vessel.

Consequently the problem in this case is, in my view, neither solved nor soluble by debating whether the shipowner's express or implied undertaking to tender a seaworthy ship is a 'condition' or a 'warranty.' It is like so many other contractual terms an undertaking one breach of which may give rise to an event which relieves the charterer of further performance of his undertakings if he so elects and another breach of which may not give rise to such an event but entitle him only to monetary compensation in the form of damages . . .

What the judge had to do in the present case, as in any other case where one party to a contract relies upon a breach by the other party as giving him a right to elect to rescind the contract, and the contract itself makes no express provision as to this, was to look at the events which had occurred as a result of the breach at the time at which the charterers purported to rescind the charterparty and to decide whether the occurrence of those events deprived the charterers of substantially the whole benefit which it was the intention of the parties as expressed in the charterparty that the charterers should obtain from the further performance of their own contractual undertakings . . . The question which the judge had to ask himself was, as he rightly decided, whether or not at the date when the charterers purported to rescind the contract, namely, June 6, 1957, or when the shipowners purported to accept such rescission, namely, August 8, 1957, the delay which had already occurred as a result of the incompetence of the engine-room staff, and the delay which was likely to occur in repairing the engines of the vessel and the conduct of the shipowners by that date in taking steps to remedy these two matters, were, when taken together, such as to deprive the charterers of substantially the whole benefit which it was the intention of the parties they should obtain from further use of the vessel under the charterparty . . .

UPJOHN LJ: Why is this apparently basic and underlying condition of seaworthiness not, in fact, treated as a condition? It is for the simple reason that the seaworthiness clause is breached by the slightest failure to be fitted 'in every way' for service. Thus, to take examples from the judgments in some of the cases I have mentioned . . . , if a nail is missing from one of the timbers of a wooden vessel or if proper medical supplies or two anchors are not on board at the time of sailing, the owners are in breach of the seaworthiness stipulation. It is contrary to common sense to suppose that in such circumstances the parties contemplated that the charterer should at once be entitled to treat the contract as at an end for such trifling breaches . . .

It is open to the parties to a contract to make it clear either expressly or by necessary implication that a particular stipulation is to be regarded as a condition which goes to the root of the contract, so that it is clear that the parties contemplate that any breach of it entitles the other party at once to treat the contract as at an end. That matter has to be determined as a question of the proper interpretation of the contract . . . Where, however, upon the true construction of the contract, the parties have not made a particular stipulation a condition, it would in my judgment be unsound and misleading to conclude that, being a warranty, damages is necessarily a sufficient remedy.

In my judgment the remedies open to the innocent party for breach of a stipulation which is not a condition strictly so called, depend entirely upon the nature of the breach and its foreseeable consequences. Breaches of stipulation fall, naturally, into two classes. First there is the case where the owner by his conduct indicates that he considers himself no longer bound to perform his part of the contract; in that case, of course, the charterer may accept the repudiation and treat the contract as at an end. The second class of case is, of course, the more usual one and that is where, due to misfortune such as the perils of the sea, engine failures, incompetence of the crew and so on, the owner is unable to perform a particular stipulation precisely in accordance with the terms of the contract try he never so hard to remedy it. In that case the question to be answered is, does the breach of the stipulation go so much to the root of the contract that it makes further commercial performance of the contract impossible, or in other words is the whole contract frustrated? If yea, the innocent party may treat the contract as at an end. If nay, his claim sounds in damages only . . . The only unseaworthiness alleged, serious though it was, was the insufficiency and incompetence of the crew, but that surely cannot be treated as going to the root of the contract for the parties must have contemplated that in such an event the crew could be changed and augmented . . .

NOTES

1. Diplock LJ suggested the introduction of a third category of term: the intermediate, or innominate, term. However, Upjohn LJ's approach has more to commend it. Upjohn LJ argues that the crucial test is to see if the term is a condition; if it is not, then it should not be assumed that the remedy for breach of this non-condition is always damages. Instead, the effects of the breach should be examined, and if they were nevertheless serious effects, then the contract could be terminated. This approach avoids the uncomfortable task of distinguishing an intermediate term from a warranty. See Reynolds (1981) 97 LQR 541 and Peel, *Treitel's The Law of Contract*, 14th edn (Sweet & Maxwell, 2015), [18-051], on the question of whether there are two or three types of term and *Poole's Textbook on Contract Law*, 13.5.6.

2. Diplock LJ also suggested that a term would be a condition only if every breach of the particular term would deprive the innocent party of substantially the whole benefit of the contract. This was rejected by the House of Lords in *Bunge Corporation v Tradax SA*. It is, however, possible to say that a term will be a condition if it can be broken in only one way, which must inevitably be serious and is evidence that the term 'goes to the root of the contract'.

3. In *Wuhan Ocean Economic & Technical Cooperation Company Ltd v Schiffahrts-Gesellschaft 'Hansa Murcia' mbH & Co. KG* [2012] EWHC 3104 (Comm), [2013] 1 All ER (Comm) 1277, [2013] 1 Lloyd's Rep 273, the shipyard was in breach of contract in failing to renew a refund guarantee in favour of the buyer within a reasonable time. Since the contract had become unprofitable, the

buyers were looking to find an escape route, and two days before the guarantee was due to expire they commenced arbitration, alleging that this failure amounted to a repudiatory breach by the shipyard. It was held to be an innominate term, since it could be broken in a number of ways, not all of which would be serious. Although it was possible to identify breaches of the term that might have gone to the root of the contract, e.g. if the sellers had failed to procure the extension of the refund guarantee for a period of a year or more after the expiry of the guarantee, on the facts the buyers' security was not at risk because the refund guarantee was automatically extended if the buyers commenced arbitration, which they had done, against the shipyard. It followed that breach of the innominate term had not deprived the buyers of 'substantially the whole benefit of the contract'.

4. Thus, with the innominate term approach, a party cannot use a minor breach by the other party to justify terminating a contract that has become a bad bargain. For example, in *Reardon Smith Line Ltd v Hansen Tangen* [1976] 1 WLR 989, an error in stating the yard where a vessel was built did not enable the charterers to avoid the contract, which had become unprofitable.

5. Relying upon *Cehave NV v Bremer Handelsgesellschaft GmbH, The Hansa Nord*, Weir [1976] CLJ 33 argued that the *Hongkong Fir v Kawasaki* approach 'rewards incompetence'.

Cehave NV v Bremer Handelsgesellschaft GmbH, The Hansa Nord
[1976] QB 44 (CA)

The German sellers agreed to sell to Dutch buyers 12,000 tons of US citrus pulp pellets for use as animal feed. The contract provided 'shipment to be made in good condition'. Following payment of the price of £100,000 by the buyers and receipt of shipping documents, a shipment arrived at the destination port. By this time, the market price of citrus pulp pellets had fallen. Some of the cargo was found to be damaged. The buyers rejected the whole cargo and claimed the repayment of the price on the ground that shipment was not made in good condition. The goods had then been sold for £30,000 to an importer, who had resold them on the same day to the buyers at the same price of £30,000. The buyers then used the entire cargo to manufacture cattle feed (the original purpose).

Held: The term 'shipment in good condition' was an intermediate term, which did not give a right to reject unless the breach went to the root of the contract. Since the entire cargo was used for its intended purpose as animal feed, the breach did not go to the root of the contract and the buyers, although entitled to damages, were not entitled to reject the goods.

ORMROD LJ: [Counsel for the sellers] relying on s. 11(1)(b) [Sale of Goods Act 1893], argued that in a contract of sale, the court was required to categorise all relevant stipulations as conditions or warranties, that this must be done by way of construction of the contract, and that, once done, the buyer's remedy for breach was determined; if a condition, he could reject, subject to the other provisions of the Act; if a warranty, he had no right to reject in any circumstances, his only remedy being damages. Construction, at least in theory, means ascertaining the intention of the parties in accordance with the general rules. If this submission is right, it means that a buyer can always reject for breach of a condition, however trivial the consequences, subject only to the so-called de minimis rule, and never reject for breach of warranty, however serious the consequences. So, on a falling market the buyer can take advantage of a minor breach of condition and, on a rising market, waive the breach and sue for damages. It also means . . . that if breach of a stipulation could have potentially serious consequences for a buyer, the court may be obliged, whatever the results in the instant case, to construe the stipulation as a condition. Moreover, where the contract is in a standard form as in this case, a decision in one case will, in effect, categorise the stipulation for other cases in which the same form is used . . . If one asks oneself the question in the form, 'Did the parties intend that the buyer should be entitled to reject the goods if they were not shipped in good condition?' the answer must be that it depends on the nature and effects of the breach.

This is directly in line with Diplock LJ's approach in the *Hong Kong Fir Shipping Co.* case [1962] 2 QB 26, 69–70, not surprisingly, since there can be very little difference in principle between whether the ship is seaworthy and whether goods are in good condition. There is obviously a strong case for applying the general principle of the *Hong Kong Fir Shipping Co.* case to contracts for the sale of goods. The question remains, however and it is the kernel of [counsel for the sellers'] submission, whether it is open to the court to do so. The parties themselves, of course, can do it by express agreement . . . If it can be done expressly, it can be done by implication, unless it is in some way prohibited. [Counsel for the sellers] argues that s. 11(1)(b) compels the court to choose between condition and warranty. I do not think that the subsection was intended to have any prohibitory effect. It is essentially a definition section, defining 'condition' and 'warranty' in terms of remedies. Nor is the classification absolutely rigid, for it provides that a buyer may treat a condition as a warranty if he wishes, by accepting the goods. It does not, however, envisage the possibility that a breach of warranty might go to the root of the contract, and so, in certain circumstances, entitle the buyer to treat the contract as repudiated. But the law has developed since the Act was passed. It is now accepted as a general principle since the *Hong Kong Fir Shipping Co.* case [1962] 2 QB 26 that it is the events resulting from the breach, rather than the breach itself, which may destroy the consideration for the buyer's promise and so enable him to treat the contract as repudiated.

The problem is how to integrate this principle with s. 11(1)(b). In practice it may not arise very often. Faced with a breach which has had grave consequences for a buyer, the court may be disposed to hold that he was entitled ex post facto, to rescind, or reject the goods, without categorising the broken stipulation, applying the general principles of the law of contract. The difficulty only arises if the court had already categorised the stipulation as a warranty. The present case provides an example. If the relevant part of clause 7 is construed as a warranty in this case, and later, another dispute occurs in relation to another contract in the same form, between the same parties, for the sale of similar goods, in which the breach of clause 7 has produced much more serious consequences for the buyer, is the court bound by its decision in this case to hold that the buyer is precluded from rejecting the goods under the later contract because, as a matter of construction, it has already categorised the stipulation as a warranty? This is the converse of *The Mihalis Angelos* [1971] 1 QB 164 situation. If the answer is in the affirmative s. 11(1)(b) has, by implication, excluded one of the general common law rules of contract. It was clearly not intended to have this effect and I agree with Lord Denning MR, for the reasons that he has given in his judgment, that the Act should not, if it can be avoided, be construed in this way. Section 61(2) seems to provide an answer. If this view is correct it is bound to have important repercussions on the way in which courts in future will approach the construction of stipulations in contracts for the sale of goods. It will no longer be necessary to place so much emphasis on the potential effects of a breach on the buyer, and to feel obliged, as Mocatta J did in this case, to construe a stipulation as a condition because in other cases or in other circumstances the buyer ought to be entitled to reject. Consequently, the court will be freer to regard stipulations, as a matter of construction, as warranties, if what might be called the 'back-up' rule of the common law is available to protect buyers who ought to be able to reject in proper circumstances. I doubt whether, strictly speaking, this involves the creation of a third category of stipulations; rather, it recognises another ground for holding that a buyer is entitled to reject, namely, that, de facto, the consideration for his promise has been wholly destroyed.

The result may be summarised in this way. When a breach of contract has taken place the question arises: 'Is the party who is not in breach entitled in law to treat the contract as repudiated or, in the case of a buyer, to reject the goods? The answer depends on the answers to a series of other questions. Adopting Upjohn LJ's judgment in the *Hong Kong Fir Shipping Co.* case [1962] 2 QB 26, 64, the first question is: "Does the contract expressly provide that in the event of the breach of the term in question the other party is entitled to terminate the contract or reject the goods?" If the answer is No, the next question is: 'Does the contract when correctly construed so provide?' The relevant term, for example, may be described as a 'condition.' The question then arises whether this word is used as a code word for the phrase 'shall be entitled to repudiate the contract or reject the goods,' or in some other sense, as in *Wickman Machine Tool Sales Ltd v L. Schuler AG* [1972] 1 WLR 840. The next question is whether the breach of the relevant term creates a right to repudiate or reject. This may arise either from statute or as a result of judicial decision on particular contractual terms. For example, if the requirements of s. 14(1) or (2) of the Sale of Goods Act 1893 are fulfilled, the buyer will be entitled to reject the goods, as a result of this section, read with s. 11(2). In fact, in all those sections of the Sale of Goods Act 1893 which create implied conditions the word 'condition' is, by definition a code word for 'breach of this term will entitle the buyer to reject the goods,' subject to any other relevant provision of the Act. In other cases, the courts have decided that breach of some specific terms, such as, for example, an 'expected ready to load' stipulation, will ipso facto give rise to a right in the other party to repudiate the contract: *The Mihalis Angelos* [1971] 1 QB 164, 194, *per* Lord Denning MR. In these two classes of case the consequences of the breach are irrelevant or, more accurately, are assumed to go to the root of the contract, and to justify repudiation. There remains the non-specific class where the events produced by the breach are such that it is reasonable to describe the breach as going to the root of the contract and so justifying repudiation.

If this approach is permissible in the present case I would unhesitatingly hold that the stipulation in clause 7 that the goods were to be shipped in good condition was not a condition, and that on the facts of this case the breach did not go to the root of the contract, and that, consequently, the buyers were not entitled to reject the goods.

NOTE Weir's argument is that because the Court of Appeal did not want the buyers to get the cargo for substantially less than its true value, it made the buyers pay the true value of the spoilt cargo (and the sellers' profit) even though the initial breach was by the sellers in shipping goods that were not in good condition. The buyers were punished for wrongfully rejecting the goods. Weir argued that the guilty party gets all that he bargained for, unless there is a breach of a condition so that he gets no part of what he bargained for. (Since this is a B2B contract, Ormrod LJ's judgment must be read in the light of s. 15A of the SGA 1979: *page 636, 13.3.1.1.*)

The next case is a rare example of a breach of an innominate term being sufficiently serious to justify termination.

Federal Commerce & Navigation Co. Ltd v Molena Alpha Inc.
[1979] AC 757 (HL)

Clause 9 of a charter provided that the charterers were to sign bills of lading stating that the freight had been correctly paid. Following a dispute concerning deductions made by the charterers, the shipowners withdrew this authority, contrary to the terms of the charter. The master was instructed not to sign bills of lading with the indorsement 'freight pre-paid' or which did not contain an indorsement giving the owners a lien over the cargo for freight. This would put the charterers in an impossible position commercially. The charterers treated the owner's actions as a repudiation of the charter.

Held: Although the term broken was not a condition, the breach went to the root of the contract by depriving the charterers of virtually the whole benefit of the contract because the issue of such bills was essential to the charterers' trade.

Aerial Advertising Co. v Batchelors Peas Ltd (Manchester)
[1938] 2 All ER 788

The parties entered into a contract whereby the claimants were to advertise the defendants' goods by flying over various towns trailing a banner reading 'Eat Batchelors' Peas'. The pilot was to telephone the defendants each day to get their approval for what he proposed to do that day. He failed to do this on 11 November 1937 and flew over the main square in Salford during the two minutes' silence on Armistice Day, towing his banner, much to the indignation of the thousands of people there. The defendants received many letters announcing a boycott of their goods, and a marked drop in demand for their goods indeed followed. The defendants sought damages and a declaration that they would no longer be bound by the contract. Atkinson J released them on the ground that it was commercially wholly unreasonable to continue with the contract. However, this was based on the seriousness of the consequences of the breach.

NOTE This last case pre-dates *Hongkong Fir v Kawasaki*, but it is the type of term that ought to be innominate (i.e. it can be broken in a number of different ways, not all of which would be serious).

13.3.3 The timing of the test for repudiatory breach and the multi-factorial assessment

Ampurius NU Homes Holdings Ltd v Telford Homes (Creekside) Ltd
[2013] EWCA Civ 577, [2013] 4 All ER 377, [2013] BLR 400 (CA)

An agreement provided that Telford was to build four mixed-use blocks and lease them to Ampurius under a 999-year lease. A contractual term set out a target date for completion of the build, 'or as soon as reasonably possible' after this date. Following financial pressures, building work on two of the blocks were suspended while Telford sought additional funding. Ampurius had written to Telford stating that it considered the suspension to be a repudiatory breach and reserving its right to affirm or terminate at a later stage. A year after its initial letter to Telford, Ampurius sought to terminate on the basis of delay and to claim damages. By this stage, work had resumed on the remaining two blocks. The judge at first instance held that Telford had been in repudiatory breach.

Held (in the Court of Appeal, allowing the appeal): The test for determining whether a breach was repudiatory breach was whether the breach had deprived the injured party of substantially the whole benefit of the contract (the *Hongkong Fir* test). This test had to be applied at the time when the right to terminate was exercised and not at the date of the breach. It had to involve any steps taken by the guilty party by that date to remedy the accrued breach and any likely future events judged by reference to objective facts at the date of purported termination.

LEWISON LJ: 42 In *Hongkong Fir* Diplock LJ addressed the question: at what time should the seriousness and character of the breach be evaluated? He said:

> What the judge had to do in the present case, as in any other case where one party to a contract relies upon a breach by the other party as giving him a right to elect to rescind the contract, and the contract itself makes no express provision as to this, was to look at the events which had occurred as a result of the breach *at the time at which the charterers purported to rescind the charterparty* and to decide whether the occurrence of those events deprived the charterers of substantially the whole benefit which it was the intention of the parties as expressed in the charterparty that the charterers should obtain from the further performance of their own contractual undertakings. (Emphasis added)

43 Thus, turning to the facts, Diplock LJ said:

> The question which the judge had to ask himself was, as he rightly decided, whether or not at the date when the charterers purported to rescind the contract, namely, June 6, 1957, or when the shipowners purported to accept such rescission, namely, August 8, 1957, the delay which had already occurred as a result of the incompetence of the engine-room staff, and the delay which was likely to occur in repairing the engines of the vessel and the conduct of the shipowners by that date in taking steps to remedy these two matters, were, when taken together, such as to deprive the charterers of substantially the whole benefit which it was the intention of the parties they should obtain from further use of the vessel under the charterparty.

44 There are three points which emerge from this. First, the task of the court is to look at the position as at the date of purported termination of the contract even in a case of actual rather than anticipatory breach. Second, in looking at the position at that date, the court must take into account any steps taken by the guilty party to remedy accrued breaches of contract. Third, the court must also take account of likely future events, judged by reference to objective facts as at the date of purported termination . . .

51 Whatever test one adopts, it seems to me that the starting point must be to consider what benefit the injured party was intended to obtain from performance of the contract. In our case, the benefit that Ampurius was intended to obtain from performance of the contract was, first and foremost, a leasehold interest of 999 years duration in four blocks. In other words, what Ampurius bargained for was the right to possession of those units for 999 years, and the right for a like period to exploitation of the rents and profits to be derived from them . . . I do not think that the judge gave adequate weight to the ultimate objective of the contract, viz. the grant to Ampurius of 999 year leases. He concentrated on the expected effects on the marketing period. This, in my judgment, permeates his consideration of what practical effect the breaches of contract had.

52 The next thing to consider is the effect of the breach on the injured party. What financial loss has it caused? How much of the intended benefit under the contract has the injured party already received? Can the injured party be adequately compensated by an award of damages? Is the breach likely to be repeated? Will the guilty party resume compliance with his obligations? Has the breach fundamentally changed the value of future performance of the guilty party's outstanding obligations?

53 I agree with the judge that if Ampurius were only ever to be able to acquire interests in two out of the four blocks, then it would have been deprived of the benefit of a substantial part of the contract. That is because it would not have acquired two out of the four promised 999 year leases. But that is not this case.

At the date of the purported termination, work had restarted and the Court of Appeal concluded that it was therefore not possible to say at the date of termination that the actual and reasonably foreseeable effects of Telford's breach had deprived Ampurius of substantially the whole benefit of the contract—namely, the eventual leasehold interest in the four blocks. The delay was short in the context of the intended 999-year lease and any loss could be compensated in damages. It followed that Ampurius had put itself in repudiatory breach of contract by purporting to terminate when this option was not available.

NOTES

1. This decision is of great commercial significance for termination for delays in development building projects, since the 'benefit' of the contract will not be limited to keeping to the building schedule, but is likely to be linked to leases with lengthy terms. Without specific drafting, in this context, delays are unlikely to be 'bad enough' to be repudiatory unless the builder renounces the contract altogether.

2. These principles were applied in *Urban I (Blonk Street) Ltd v Ayres* [2013] EWCA Civ 816, [2014] 1 WLR 756, [2014] 1 P & CR 1. The Court of Appeal held that,

in the context of a development relating to a 125-year lease of property, a delay of only a month between the earliest possible date for completion and the purported termination of the contract did not deprive the purchasers of substantially the whole benefit of a contract.

3. The multi-factorial assessment of the innominate term to determine whether the breach was repudiatory was also adopted by the Court of Appeal majority (Arden and Floyd LJJ; Underhill LJ dissenting) in *Valilas v Januzj* [2014] EWCA Civ 436, [2015] 1 All ER (Comm) 1047, 154 Con LR 38. At [53] Floyd LJ stated:

Whether a breach or threatened breach does give rise to a right to terminate involves a multi-factorial assessment involving the nature of the contract and the relationship it creates, the nature of the term, the kind and degree of the breach and the consequences of the breach for the injured party.

On the facts, the effect of the breaches in failing to make monthly payments under the terms of a dental facilities contract did not deprive the practice owner of substantially the whole benefit of the contract since he knew that he would eventually be paid. Any loss therefore related to loss of use of the money in the meantime which is usually compensated by means of interest. However, since the practice owner had accepted the breaches as terminating the contract, it followed that he had wrongfully terminated.

13.4 Entire obligations

A contractual obligation may be construed as 'entire', meaning that it must be completely and precisely performed before the other party is obliged to perform its contractual obligations.

Cutter v Powell
(1795) 6 Term Rep 320, 101 ER 573 (Court of King's Bench)

Cutter was employed as second mate for a sea voyage from Jamaica to Liverpool. Ten days after the ship's arrival in Liverpool, Cutter was to receive 'thirty guineas, provided he proceeds, continues and does his duty as second mate in the said ship from hence to the port of Liverpool'. The ship sailed on 2 August 1793, but Cutter died on 20 September, before the ship arrived in Liverpool on 9 October. Cutter's widow sought wages for the work that he had completed before his death on a *quantum meruit* basis (i.e. reasonable value of work done). The usual wages of a second mate were £4 a month and this voyage usually took eight weeks.

Held: Cutter's obligation for the voyage was entire and the defendant's promise depended upon the condition precedent being performed. Emphasis was placed on the fact that a second mate would normally expect to earn £8 on such a voyage, whereas Cutter had been promised 30 guineas if he fulfilled these conditions.

ASHHURST J: This is a written contract, and it speaks for itself. And as it is entire, and as the defendant's promise depends on a condition precedent to be performed by the other party, the condition must be performed before the other party is entitled to receive any thing under it. It has been argued however that the plaintiff may now recover on a quantum meruit: but she has no right to desert the agreement; for wherever there is an express contract the parties must be guided by it; and one party cannot relinquish or abide by it as it may suit his advantage. Here the intestate was by the terms of his contract to perform a given duty before he could call upon the defendant to pay him any thing; it was a condition precedent, without performing which the defendant is not liable. And that seems to me to conclude the question: the intestate did not perform the contract on his part; he was not indeed to blame for not doing it; but still as this was a condition precedent, and as he did not perform it, his representative is not entitled to recover.

NOTES

1. As the promised sum was considerably in excess of the market rate for the job, it is unsurprising that the Court interpreted this express stipulation as meaning that Cutter was to receive 30 guineas if he performed and nothing if he did not. The contract placed the risk of non-completion on Cutter.

2. Entire obligations are the exception rather than the rule. If an obligation is severable or divisible, then the defaulting party can recover at the stipulated rate for each instalment provided, subject to a set-off or counterclaim for damages for breach (e.g. the Apportionment Act 1870 provides that 'rents' and 'periodical payments in the nature of income' are severable).

3. A contract can have both entire and severable obligations. For example, the obligation in the case of *Hoenig v Isaacs* [1952] 2 All ER 176 (*page 655, 13.4.1.2*) to complete the amount of work, specifically decorating and furnishing a flat, was entire in relation to payment of the balance. This work had been performed so that, although the quality obligation was not entire, the balance on completion still needed to be paid, albeit less a deduction in respect of the defective performance. By comparison the work in *Bolton v Mahadeva* [1972] 1 WLR 1009 (*page 655, 13.4.1.2*) was incomplete. This amounted to a breach of an entire obligation and the price was not payable.

4. Building contracts that provide for a lump-sum payment on completion will be construed as entire because it is not possible to apportion the price over the work completed. These are more common in the consumer context.

13.4.1 Avoiding the 'entire obligation rule'

13.4.1.1 Acceptance of the benefit by the non-breaching party

It is possible to recover on a *quantum meruit* for work done if the injured party had the option to accept or reject the partial performance and voluntarily accepted it.

Sumpter v Hedges
[1898] 1 QB 673 (CA)

The claimant builder contracted with the defendant to build two houses and stables on the defendant's land for a lump sum of £565. The claimant did work amounting to £333 in value, but then informed the defendant that he had no money and could not go on with the work. The defendant finished the building himself using building materials belonging to the claimant, which the claimant had left on the defendant's land.

Held: The obligation to do the building work was entire. The defendant had not voluntarily adopted the part performance, so there was no new implied contract to pay for the part performance on a *quantum meruit* basis.

COLLINS LJ: There are cases in which, though the plaintiff has abandoned the performance of a contract, it is possible for him to raise the inference of a new contract to pay for the work done on a quantum meruit from the defendant's having taken the benefit of that work, but, in order that that may be done, the circumstances must be such as to give an option to the defendant to take or not to take the benefit of the work done. It is only where the circumstances are such as to give that option that there is any evidence on which to ground the inference of a new contract. Where, as in the case of work done on land, the circumstances are such as to give the defendant no option whether he will take the benefit of the work or not, then one must look to other facts than the mere taking the benefit of the work in order to ground the inference of a new contract. In this case I see no other facts on which such an inference can be founded. The mere fact that a defendant is in possession of what he cannot help keeping, or even has done work upon it, affords no ground for such an inference.

He is not bound to keep unfinished a building which in an incomplete state would be a nuisance on his land. I am therefore of opinion that the plaintiff was not entitled to recover for the work which he had done . . .

NOTE The injured party must have the choice whether to accept the part performance. In cases of unfinished buildings on the injured party's land, there is no practical choice. However, the defendant did not have to accept the materials left on his land, but decided to do so. Bruce J, at first instance, held that the defendant had to pay for these materials.

13.4.1.2 Substantial performance

If the party in breach has 'substantially performed' their contractual obligations as to quality, then they can claim the price less damages in respect of the defective performance.

Hoenig v Isaacs
[1952] 2 All ER 176 (CA)

The defendant employed the claimant to decorate and furnish the defendant's flat for the sum of £750 'net cash as the work proceeds and the balance on completion'. The defendant refused to pay the balance of £350 on the ground that certain of the work done and articles supplied were defective. The defendant contended that the claimant could not recover the balance, since this was an entire obligation, which the claimant had not performed. The official referee found that a wardrobe door needed replacing and a bookcase required alterations, and assessed the cost of remedying the defects at £55.

Held: For an entire contract, the defendant cannot repudiate liability on the ground that the work, although substantially performed, is in some respects not in accordance with the contract. The defendant was therefore liable for the balance, less a deduction for the cost of putting right the defects.

SOMERVELL LJ: Each case turns on the construction of the contract. [*Cutter v Powell*] clearly decided that his continuing as mate during the whole voyage was a condition precedent to payment. It did not decide that if he had completed the main purpose of the contract, namely, serving as mate for the whole voyage, the defendant could have repudiated his liability by establishing that in the course of the voyage the sailor had, possibly through inadvertence, failed on some occasion in his duty as mate whereby some damage had been caused . . .

The principle that fulfilment of every term is not necessarily a condition precedent in a contract for a lump sum is usually traced back to a short judgment of Lord Mansfield CJ in *Boone v Eyre* (1779) 1 Hy Bl 273n—the sale of the plantation with its slaves. Lord Mansfield said:

. . . where mutual covenants go to the whole of the consideration on both sides, they are mutual conditions, the one precedent to the other. But where they go only to a part, where a breach may be paid for in damages, there the defendant has a remedy on his covenant, and shall not plead it as a condition precedent.

The learned official referee regarded *H. Dakin & Co. Ltd v Lee* [1916] 1 KB 566 as laying down that the price must be paid subject to set-off or counterclaim if there was a substantial compliance with the contract. I think on the face of this case where the work was finished in the ordinary sense, though in part defective, this is right. It expresses in a convenient epithet what is put from another angle in the Sale of Goods Act, 1893. The buyer cannot reject if he proves only the breach of a term collateral to the main purpose . . .

Breach of contract

13

DENNING LJ: In determining this issue the first question is whether, on the true construction of the contract, entire performance was a condition precedent to payment. It was a lump sum contract, but that does not mean that entire performance was a condition precedent to payment. When a contract provides for a specific sum to be paid on completion of specified work, the courts lean against a construction of the contract which would deprive the contractor of any payment at all simply because there are some defects or omissions. The promise to complete the work is, therefore, construed as a term of the contract, but not as a condition. It is not every breach of that term which absolves the employer from his promise to pay the price, but only a breach which goes to the root of the contract, such as an abandonment of the work when it is only half done. Unless the breach does go to the root of the matter, the employer cannot resist payment of the price. He must pay it and bring a cross-claim for the defects and omissions, or, alternatively, set them up in diminution of the price. It is, of course, always open to the parties by express words to make entire performance a condition precedent. A familiar instance is when the contract provides for progress payments to be made as the work proceeds, but for retention money to be held until completion. Then entire performance is usually a condition precedent to payment of the retention money, but not, of course, to the progress payments. The contractor is entitled to payment pro rata as the work proceeds, less a deduction for retention money. But he is not entitled to the retention money until the work is entirely finished, without defects or omissions. In the present case the contract provided for 'net cash, as the work proceeds; and balance on completion.' If the balance could be regarded as retention money, then it might well be that the contractor ought to have done all the work correctly, without defects or omissions, in order to be entitled to the balance. But I do not think the balance should be regarded as retention money. Retention money is usually only ten per cent, or fifteen per cent, whereas this balance was more than fifty per cent. I think this contract should be regarded as an ordinary lump sum contract. It was substantially performed. The contractor is entitled, therefore, to the contract price, less a deduction for the defects.

ROMER LJ: In certain cases it is right that the rigid rule for which the defendant contends should be applied, for example, if a man tells a contractor to build a ten foot wall for him in his garden and agrees to pay £x for it, it would not be right that he should be held liable for any part of the contract price if the contractor builds the wall to two feet and then renounces further performance of the contract, or builds the wall of a totally different material from that which was ordered, or builds it at the wrong end of the garden. The work contracted for has not been done and the corresponding obligation to pay consequently never arises. But when a man fully performs his contract in the sense that he supplies all that he agreed to supply but what he supplies is subject to defects of so minor a character that he can be said to have substantially performed his promise, it is, in my judgment, far more equitable to apply the *H. Dakin & Co. Ltd v Lee* [1916] 1 KB 566 principle than to deprive him wholly of his contractual rights and relegate him to such remedy (if any) as he may have on a quantum meruit . . .

NOTES

1. As discussed earlier, *Hoenig v Isaacs* concerned defective performance but the quality obligation was not the entire obligation. The entire obligation was the obligation to complete the specified work in order to receive the balance payment. By comparison, *Cutter v Powell* concerned the order of performance. In *Cutter v Powell*, the obligation to serve as second mate for the whole voyage was entire. Cutter could have recovered 30 guineas if he had completed the voyage, but, in not doing so (although he was not to blame for it), he had been guilty of a breach of duty.

2. In *Williams v Roffey Bros. & Nicholls (Contractors) Ltd* [1991] 1 QB 1 (*page 106, 3.1.3.7*), the defendants argued that the alteration provided that the claimant would be paid on completion of each of the flats. The Court of Appeal, relying on *Hoenig v Isaacs*, held that the claimant had 'substantially completed' and was entitled to the payment for the eight flats, less a deduction for defects and incomplete work.

? QUESTION

Was there any incomplete work in *Hoenig v Isaacs*? The Court may have viewed defective performance as a failure to complete the work, so that the obligation was entire.

Bolton v Mahadeva
[1972] 1 WLR 1009 (CA)

The claimant agreed to install central heating in the defendant's house for a lump sum of £560. Upon completion, the defendant complained that it was defective and refused to pay. The judge found that the flue was defective, so that it gave off fumes, making the rooms uncomfortable, and that the system was inefficient in that the amount of heat varied from one room to another. The cost of rectifying these defects was £174.

Held: The claimant was not entitled to recover, because there had been no substantial performance.

CAIRNS LJ: The main question in the case is whether the defects in workmanship found by the judge to be such as to cost £174 to repair—that is, between one third and one quarter of the contract price—were of such a character and amount that the plaintiff could not be said to have substantially performed his contract. That is, in my view, clearly the legal principle which has to be applied to cases of this kind . . . In considering whether there was substantial performance I am of opinion that it is relevant to take into account both the nature of the defects and the proportion between the cost of rectifying them and the contract price. It would be wrong to say that the contractor is only entitled to payment if the defects are so trifling as to be covered by the de minimis rule.

The main matters that were complained of in this case were that when the heating system was put on, fumes were given out which made some of the living rooms (to put it at the lowest) extremely uncomfortable and inconvenient to use; secondly, that by reason of there being insufficient radiators and insufficient insulation, the heating obtained by the central heating system was far below what it should have been . . . Now, certainly it appears to me that the nature and amount of the defects in this case were far different from those which the court had to consider in *H. Dakin & Co. Ltd v Lee* [1916] 1 KB 566 and *Hoenig v Isaacs* [1952] 2 All ER 176. For my part, I find it impossible to say that the judge was right in reaching the conclusion that in those circumstances the contract had been substantially performed. The contract was a contract to install a central heating system. If a central heating system when installed is such that it does not heat the house adequately and is such, further, that fumes are given out, so as to make living rooms uncomfortable, and if the putting right of those defects is not something which can be done by some slight amendment of the system, then I think that the contract is not substantially performed.

NOTES

1. This type of breach clearly goes to the root of the contract and it appears that, on that basis, the performance could not be 'substantial'. The approach is similar to the nature of the effects of the breach approach adopted in *Hongkong Fir v Kawasaki* (*page 644, 13.3.2*). If the actual defects are serious, the contract is repudiated; if they are trivial, it is not.

2. The Law Commission's Report No. 121, *Pecuniary Restitution for Breach of Contract* (1983)— see also Burrows (1984) 47 MLR 76—recommended that a party who part performs an entire contract should be permitted to recover in respect of benefits that he has conferred on the other as a result of that part performance. These recommendations have not been implemented.

13.5 Anticipatory breach

An anticipatory breach occurs where, before the time for performance, one party informs the other that he will not perform his contractual obligations. This type of breach will normally be repudiatory, since the contract is renounced or the party incapacitates himself from performing the obligations under the contract.

Renunciation of the contract in advance of the time for performance occurs where one party evinces an unconditional intention not to perform his contractual obligations or not to be bound by the contract.

13.5.1 What will constitute renunciation?

SK Shipping (S) Pte Ltd v Petroexport Ltd
[2009] EWHC 2974 (Comm), [2010] 2 Lloyd's Rep 158

The claimant shipowner claimed damages for the alleged repudiatory breach of a charterparty (contract to hire a ship) by the defendant charterer. Had the charterer had evinced an unequivocal intention not to be bound by the contract. A number of behaviours gave the impression that the charterer had been struggling to find a buyer for the cargo being shipped, e.g. attempting to renegotiate the charter; issuing an instruction that the usual notice of readiness should not be given to the port authorities and cargo suppliers; not setting up the letter of credit for the cargo; and instructing the ship's master to slow down on the voyage to the port where the cargo was to be collected. When the shipowner asked the charterer to confirm that it would load the cargo, the charterer had instead offered to agree a mutual cancellation. The shipowner treated this as a repudiatory breach and terminated the charter despite the fact that the laydays had not then expired (any breach was anticipatory). Had the charterer renounced the charter in sufficiently unequivocal terms?

Held: The shipowner had to show not only that the words or conduct were objectively evincing an intention not to perform, but also that the shipowner subjectively believed that to be the case. Particular words or conduct taken in isolation might appear equivocal in terms of amounting to a renunciation, but did mean that it was legitimate for the shipowner to enquire about the charterer's intention to perform. The charterer could easily have confirmed that intention. The fact that the charterer had not provided this reassurance, but had stated that it would perform only something different, meant that the charterer had indicated, through its words and conduct (objectively assessed), that it was renouncing the charter and the shipowners had subjectively believed this to be the case.

FLAUX J:

Renunciation

83. In the present case, both the grounds upon which the claimant seeks to justify its termination, renunciation and impossibility, are examples of anticipatory breach of contract, since at the time when the claimant purported to accept the defendant's repudiation as terminating the charterparty, the time for performance by the defendant had not yet expired. In particular, the laydays had not expired.

84. The contrast between these two modes of anticipatory breach and the principles of law applicable in determining whether there has been a renunciation by one party to the contract, entitling the other party to treat the contract as at an end, are discussed in the judgment of Devlin J in *Universal Cargo Carriers v Citati* [1957] 2 QB 401 at 436–7:

> . . .A renunciation can be made either by words or by conduct, provided it is clearly made. It is often put that the party renunciating must 'evince an intention' not to go on with the contract. The intention can be evinced either by words or by conduct. The test of whether an intention is sufficiently evinced by conduct is whether the party renunciating has acted in such a way as to lead a reasonable person to the conclusion that he does not intend to fulfil his part of the contract. . .
>
> Of the two modes, renunciation has since the decision in *Hochster v. De la Tour* (1853) 2 E&B 678 established itself as the favourite. The disadvantage of the other is that the party who elects to treat impossibility as an anticipatory breach may be running a serious risk. Suppose, for example, that a man promises to marry a woman on a future date, or to execute a lease or to deliver goods; and that before the day arrives he marries another, or executes the lease in favour of another, or delivers the goods to a third party. The aggrieved party may sue at once. 'One reason alleged in support of such an action,' Campbell C.J. observed in *Hochster v. De la Tour* [at 688] 'is, that the defendant has, before the day, rendered it impossible for him to perform the contract at the day: but this does not necessarily follow; for, prior to the day fixed for doing the act, the first wife may have died, a surrender of the lease executed might be obtained, and the defendant might have repurchased the goods so as to be in a situation to sell and deliver them to the plaintiff.' But if the plaintiff treats the defendant's conduct as amounting to renunciation and justifies his rescission on that ground, the defendant could not avail himself of this defence.
>
> I said that it was after *Hochster v. De la Tour* that renunciation established itself as the favourite, because until then it was not certain that a man who said 'I will not perform' would be held to his word. In *Hochster v. De la Tour* it was argued that he could change his mind, and that the fact that at one time he said he was not ready and willing did not necessarily mean that he would be unwilling when the time for performance came. *Hochster v. De la Tour* established that a renunciation, when acted upon, became final. Thus, if a man proclaimed by words or conduct an inability to perform, the other party could safely act upon it without having to prove that when the time for performance came the inability was still effective . . .

86. The critical question is . . . whether, by its words or conduct, a party has evinced an intention not to perform the contract, which a reasonable person in the position of the other, innocent, party would regard as clear and absolute . . .

88 . . . The court has to look at the totality of the relevant words and conduct relied upon, in the light of all the circumstances, including the history of the contractual relationship, to determine whether at the time that the claimant purports to accept the words and conduct as renunciatory, the defendant has evinced an intention not to perform, as at that time. Furthermore, particular words or conduct taken in isolation may appear equivocal, but taken with other words and conduct may become unequivocal in terms of amounting to a renunciation. That proposition is of some application in the present case . . . Since there must be an intention to abandon the contract, a party who relies on a contractual termination provision cannot be renouncing that contract.

Woodar Investment Development Ltd v Wimpey Construction UK Ltd
[1980] 1 WLR 277 (HL)

The full facts of this case appear at *page 330, 7.6.2.*

Wimpey sought to terminate the contract to purchase land on the ground that the Secretary of State for the Environment had commenced a compulsory acquisition procedure on the land. The contract expressly reserved the right to terminate in these circumstances. Woodar, the vendors, claimed that Wimpey had repudiated the contract.

Held (Lord Salmon and Lord Russell of Killowen dissenting): To constitute a renunciation of the contract, there had to be an intention to abandon the contract, and instead of abandoning the contract, Wimpey was relying on its terms as justifying its right to terminate.

> LORD WILBERFORCE: [I]t would be a regrettable development of the law of contract to hold that a party who bona fide relies upon an express stipulation in a contract in order to rescind or terminate a contract should, by that fact alone, be treated as having repudiated his contractual obligations if he turns out to be mistaken as to his rights. Repudiation is a drastic conclusion which should only be held to arise in clear cases of a refusal, in a matter going to the root of the contract, to perform contractual obligations. To uphold the respondents' contentions in this case would represent an undesirable extension of the doctrine.

13.5.2 The election

As with all repudiatory breaches, where an anticipatory breach occurs, the injured party has the option of affirming or terminating the contract.

Yukong Line Ltd of Korea v Rendsburg Investments Corporation of Liberia
[1996] 2 Lloyd's Rep 604 (Commercial Court)

The facts of this case are given at *page 633, 13.2.3.1.*

Moore-Bick J identified the following principles from the authorities that would be applicable where there had been an anticipatory repudiatory breach:

(1) A renunciation of the contract by one party, prior to the time for performance is not itself a breach but it gives the other party, the injured party, the right to treat it as a breach in anticipation and thus to treat the contract as discharged immediately. In other words, if a person says he will not perform, the law allows the other to take him at his word and act accordingly.

(2) In such a case the injured party is not ordinarily bound to treat the contract as discharged: the law gives him a choice. He may treat the contract as discharged or he may disregard the repudiation and treat the contract as continuing in full effect, notwithstanding what has occurred. He can, in other words, elect to affirm it.

(3) If the injured party elects to affirm the contract, both parties' rights and obligations under it remain completely unaffected; the renunciation is 'writ in water', to use the well-known expression of Lord Justice Asquith in *Howard v Pickford Tool Co. Ltd* [1951] 1 KB 417 at p. 421.

(4) The choice placed before the injured party is between inconsistent rights, and once the choice has been made and communicated to the other party to the contract, it is irrevocable. Unlike estoppel, election does not depend upon any change in position by the party to whom it is communicated.

(5) Although the injured party is bound by his election once it has been made, the fact that he has affirmed the contract does not of course preclude him from treating it as discharged on a subsequent occasion if the other party again repudiates it.

13.5.3 Affirmation

If the injured party chooses to affirm, the contract continues and the injured party awaits performance on the performance date. However, this does not mean that no damages will be recoverable by the injured party, since if the guilty party does not perform on the performance date, the injured party can seek damages for this *actual* breach of contract (subject to there being no subsequent frustration or breach by the injured party: *page 664, 13.5.3.2*).

13.5.3.1 Is the election to affirm following an anticipatory repudiatory breach irrevocable?

It is crucial to know whether, if revocable, the party, having first affirmed, can then accept the repudiation and bring the contract to an end before the date of an actual breach.

In *Yukong Line v Rendsburg* [1996] 2 Lloyd's Rep 604 (*page 633, 13.2.3.1*), whether the election to affirm was irrevocable did not arise for decision, since once the judge had concluded that there was no affirmation on 24 January, he did not then need to consider whether the claimants could terminate on 1 February. The judge's emphasis on the need for an unequivocal affirmation of the contract, which firmly commits the injured party to continuing with the contract (see *page 660, 13.5.2*), is based on the premise that the consequences of affirmation are viewed as being strict, i.e. the injured party cannot later change his mind and accept the repudiatory breach as terminating the contract. Thus, the implication is that the election to affirm is irrevocable. However, comments in the next case indicate that this cannot be the position where there is a continuing breach.

Stocznia Gdanska SA v Latvian Shipping Co. (Repudiation)

The claimants, a shipbuilding company ('the yard'), had entered into six contracts to build six refrigerated vessels. The contract terms provided that the price was payable by instalments, with 5 per cent becoming payable after receipt of the claimants' bank guarantee and the second instalment of 20 per cent of the purchase price becoming payable five banking days after the claimants had given the purchasers telex notice of the laying of the keel. The defendant purchasers repudiated the contracts after the first instalment had been paid by stating that they were financially unable to perform. The claimants carried on with performance and claimed the second instalment for each vessel, having given notice of keel-laying for all six vessels. In fact, keels had been laid only for vessels one and two, and the claimants had renumbered those vessels in order to serve notice of keel-laying for vessels three, four, five, and six.

Since the defendants did not pay any of the second instalments of 20 per cent on keel-laying, the claimants purported to terminate for non-payment. The defendants argued that the claimants had affirmed by tendering the keel-laying notices following the breach and that this election was irrevocable.

[2001] CLC 1290, [2001] 1 Lloyd's Rep 537 (Commercial Court)

Thomas J concluded that the tendering of the keel-laying notices did not amount to affirmation, but stated in *obiter* comments that the election to affirm was not irrevocable in relation to continuing or renewed anticipatory breach in the period between affirmation and the date set for contractual performance.

THOMAS J: Once the innocent party has affirmed, he must go on performing. He must then be able to point to behaviour that amounts to a repudiation after the affirmation either by way of some fresh conduct amounting to repudiation or by way of the continuing refusal to perform amounting to a repudiation. I cannot see any reason why the innocent party must wait until there is an actual repudiatory breach . . . To require an innocent party, who has by pressing for performance of the contract affirmed it, to wait until there is an actual breach by the party in breach before he can bring the contract to an end might well, as in this case, have required that innocent party to engage in performance that is entirely pointless and wasteful as the party in breach would, when he became under an obligation to accept performance, refuse to do so . . . The question therefore is whether the breach was a continuing one and amounted to repudiatory conduct. In my view it was. As I have set out, the yard pressed for performance on 19 April 1994 and 4 May 1994; there was no response. It does not seem to me that the failure to respond can make a difference; if, for example, Latreefers had replied and said that they were not going to perform, then there would clearly have been a new repudiatory act. Can it make a difference that they were silent in the face of a demand for performance, if the inference from silence was their continuing refusal to perform? As that is the inference I draw, I do not think it can make a difference, as by not responding in the circumstances of this case they were making clear that they were not going to perform. The matter can be tested by asking whether in such circumstances, the yard were meant to proceed to start to build the vessels and wait until such time as there was some act of Latreefers that amounted to a fresh actual breach. Had they done so, I am sure that it would be said rightly that they had failed to mitigate in circumstances where it was obvious that Latreefers were not going to take the vessels.

[2002] EWCA Civ 889, [2002] 2 All ER (Comm) 768, [2003] 1 CLC 282 (CA)

The Court of Appeal held that there was a middle ground between acceptance of the repudiation as terminating the contract and affirmation. This was the period prior to any election during which the innocent party was making up his mind what action to take. During this period, the contract was kept in being, but the right to treat it as repudiated was reserved.

RIX LJ [with whose judgment Tuckey and Aldous LJJ agreed]: 87 In my judgment, there is of course a middle ground between acceptance of repudiation and affirmation of the contract, and that is the period when the innocent party is making up his mind what to do. If he does nothing for too long, there may come a time when the law will treat him as having affirmed. If he maintains the contract in being for the moment, while reserving his right to treat it as repudiated if his contract partner persists in his repudiation, then he has not yet elected. As long as the contract remains alive, the innocent party runs the risk that a merely anticipatory repudiatory breach, a thing 'writ in water' until acceptance, can be overtaken by another event which prejudices the innocent party's rights under the contract—such as frustration or even his own breach. He also runs the risk, if that is the right word, that the party in repudiation will resume performance of the contract and thus end any continuing right in the innocent party to elect to accept the former repudiation as terminating the contract.

In the circumstances, the tendering of the keel-laying notices did not constitute affirmation, because the validity of these notices had always been disputed. As a result, the contracts remained in force until the exercise of the contractual mechanism to terminate.

Having concluded that there had been no affirmation, the Court of Appeal (*obiter*, since, given the decision on affirmation, it was not necessary to come to a conclusion on the point) appeared to agree with Thomas J that affirmation for anticipatory breach would not prevent the innocent party from terminating for continuing anticipatory breach in the period prior to the contractual date for performance.

> RIX LJ: 97 That means that it is unnecessary to rule on a further submission based on an article written by Professor Sir Gunther Treitel QC *'Affirmation after repudiatory breach'* (1998) 114 LQR 22 in response to the facts of this very case, to the effect that affirmation should not necessarily be regarded as irrevocable. In the House of Lords at [1998] 1 WLR 574 at 594 Lord Goff thought it right that . . . full consideration could be given at trial to the yard's argument on continuing repudiation . . .
>
> 98 Lord Goff had in mind a sentence in his own speech in *The Kanchenjunga* at 398 that 'Once an election is made, however, it is final'. Professor Treitel argues powerfully that such an election, if indeed the concept of election is the correct concept at all in this context, should not be final or binding, in the sense of irrevocable, in the face of a continuing *anticipatory* repudiation.
>
> 99 It seems to me that an affirmation of a repudiatory actual breach may differ from an affirmation of a merely anticipatory repudiatory breach in that the former breach is complete at the time it occurs whereas the latter breach looks to the future. An affirmation of an actual breach may therefore be said to leave nothing outstanding for the future, in that the worst has already occurred, whereas an affirmation of an anticipatory breach still leaves the future open. Prima facie an election or waiver looks to the past, even if it is possible, in a very clear case, to waive one's rights for the future too. Two views might therefore be taken as to the effect of an affirmation of an anticipatory breach. One is that it is a waiver for the future as well . . . The other is that the affirmation prima facie relates only to the past, leaving open the question of a continuing or renewed anticipatory breach. It seems to me that the latter view is to be preferred, and is inherent in the decision in the *Safehaven Investments Inc. v Springbok* and in the decision already taken in relation to this case. That would still leave open of course the question of how one tells whether an anticipatory breach is a continuing one, and the correct way of viewing silence. Professor Treitel highlights [(1998) 114 LQR 22 at 26] the undesirability of subverting considerations of substance or policy to the accidents of negotiation. I wonder whether each case does not in truth have to be decided on its own facts. However, substance and principle suggest that silence should not in this context be too readily regarded as equivocal; and that against the background of an earlier anticipatory repudiation it should not take much further to prove continuing repudiatory conduct.
>
> 100 It also occurs to me that even in the case of an actual repudiatory breach, where the breach is of a continuing nature, such as a failure to pay or to deliver, an affirmation at one stage is not necessarily an irrevocable affirmation for all time in the future. If it were otherwise, the law could not have developed the doctrine of *Charles Rickards Ltd v Oppenhaim*.
>
> 101 I express these thoughts in response to the interesting arguments deployed in this case, but it is not necessary to decide the issue and I refrain from doing so.

NOTES

1. Affirmation following an anticipatory repudiatory breach does not prevent the injured party from later accepting the *actual* repudiatory breach as terminating the contract (i.e. the failure to perform on the date set for contractual performance). See Carter (1998) 12 JCL 247, at p. 250: 'If the promisor fails to perform, and that failure gives rise to a right to terminate, there is a fresh right of termination not affected by the prior affirmation.'

2. The observations in *Stocznia* have resolved the question of whether an election to affirm is irrevocable between the affirmation and the date for contractual performance. At least in those instances in which there has been no change of position by the guilty party in reliance on the affirmation so that he would be prejudiced by the change of heart, the innocent party is entitled to go back on his affirmation where there has been a continuing or renewed anticipatory breach by the guilty party. This is the position advocated by Treitel (1998) 114 LQR 22, and has the support of Thomas J and Rix LJ giving the judgment of the Court of Appeal.

There is therefore a distinction between anticipatory breaches that cannot be remedied prior to the date set for performance, e.g. because the subject matter has been destroyed or sold to a third party, and anticipatory breaches that can be remedied, such as a statement that the party is unable to pay. Clearly, if the anticipatory breach can be remedied, but the guilty party expressly states that he will not do so, there will be a renewed repudiation and the innocent party should be able to terminate. However, the difficulties of analysis arise where the guilty party remains silent. Both Thomas J and Rix LJ considered that the inference from such silence was of a continuing refusal to perform. Rix LJ went further and considered that, where there was a clear duty to rectify the inferences from silence in the context of a continuing obligation to perform, such silence might be 'a speaking silence'. The adoption of this position reflects the commercial need for the yard to know whether it should continue with construction of the vessels, expenditure that might be 'entirely pointless and wasteful' (*per* Thomas J).

3. In *White Rosebay Shipping SA v Hong Kong Chain Glory Shipping Ltd, The Fortune Plum* [2013] EWHC 1355 (Comm), [2013] 2 CLC 884, [2013] 2 All ER (Comm) 449, approving the statements and approach of Rix LJ in the *Stocznia* case, Teare J stated:

> [53] . . . In a case of renunciation or anticipatory breach (as opposed to repudiation based upon an actual breach) it does not necessarily follow that a termination following an affirmation is a repudiatory breach. For if the renunciating party continues to renounce the contract after the affirmation then the acceptance of that continuing renunciation is not a repudiatory breach but a lawful termination of the contract with a right to damages caused by the renunciation.

On the facts, the owners had affirmed on 11 November and the judge noted that '[i]f the charterers' renunciation of the charterparty continued until 14 November when the owners purported to accept the charterers' renunciation as terminating the charterparty then that termination is likely to be lawful and not repudiatory'.

4. Crucially, if the injured party elects to affirm, the contract remains in force and any damages award will not be available until (at the earliest) the contractual date for performance. These damages will then be assessed on the basis of loss resulting from the actual breach at the date on which the contract ought to have been performed rather than the date of the anticipatory repudiatory breach.

13.5.3.2 Are there any risks in affirming for anticipatory repudiatory breach?

Following affirmation, the contract continues in force, which presents some risks to the injured party. The same risks exist in the 'middle ground' position prior to making the election: see Rix LJ in *Stocznia Gdanska SA v Latvian Shipping Co. (Repudiation)* [2002] EWCA Civ 889, [2002] 2 All ER (Comm) 768, [2003] 1 CLC 282, [87] (*page 661, 13.5.3.1*).

13.5.3.2.1 *Subsequent breach by the injured party*

If the injured party subsequently breaches the contract in the intervening period, the injured party is liable to pay damages for his breach and cannot argue that the guilty party's anticipatory breach excused further performance of the contractual obligations.

Fercometal SARL v Mediterranean Shipping Co. SA, The Simona
[1989] AC 788 (HL)

Under a charterparty for the carriage of steel coils from Durban to Bilbao, the charterers were entitled to cancel if the vessel was not ready to load on or before 9 July. On 2 July, the charterers committed an anticipatory repudiatory breach by chartering another vessel to carry the cargo when the owners had requested an extension to 13 July. Not accepting this repudiation, the owners notified the charterers that the vessel would start loading on 8 July. This notice was invalid because the vessel was not, in fact, ready to load. Consequently, the owners were committing a breach of contract. The charterers sought to cancel the charterparty, relying on the express cancellation provision.

Held: If the injured party elects to affirm the contract following an anticipatory repudiatory breach, then that party is not absolved from tendering further performance of its obligations under the contract. The charterers therefore retained the right to cancel the charterparty. The House of Lords did state, however, that if the charterers had indicated that the owner was no longer required to perform and the owner had relied upon that as excusing the performance, then the charterers would be estopped from relying on the breach and could not have cancelled the charterparty.

LORD ACKNER: When A wrongfully repudiates his contractual obligations in anticipation of the time for their performance, he presents the innocent party B with two choices. He may either affirm the contract by treating it as still in force or he may treat it as finally and conclusively discharged. There is no third choice, as a sort of via media, to affirm the contract and yet be absolved from tendering further performance unless and until A gives reasonable notice that he is once again able and willing to perform. Such a choice would negate the contract being kept alive for the benefit of *both* parties and would deny the party who unsuccessfully sought to rescind, the right to take advantage of any supervening circumstance which would justify him in declining to complete.

[Counsel for the owners] submitted that the charterers' conduct had induced or caused the owners to abstain from having the ship ready prior to the cancellation date. Of course, it is always open to A, who has refused to accept B's repudiation of the contract, and thereby kept the contract alive, to contend that in relation to a particular right or obligation under the contract, B is estopped from contending that he, B, is entitled to exercise that right or that he, A, has remained bound by that obligation. If B represents to A that he no longer intends to exercise that right or requires that obligation to be fulfilled by A and A acts upon that representation, then clearly B cannot be heard thereafter to say that he is entitled to exercise that right or that A is in breach of contract by not fulfilling that obligation. If, in relation to this option to cancel, the owners had been able to establish that the charterers had represented that they no longer required the vessel to arrive on time because they had already fixed the *Leo Tornado* and in reliance upon that representation, the owners had given notice of readiness only after the cancellation date, then the charterers would have been estopped from contending they were entitled to cancel the charterparty. There is, however, no finding of any such representation, let alone that the owners were induced thereby not to make the vessel ready to load by 9 July. On the contrary, the owners on 5 July on two occasions asserted that the vessel would start loading on 8 July and on 8 July purported to tender notice of readiness . . . The non-readiness of the vessel by the cancelling date was in no way induced by the charterers' conduct. It was the result of the owners' decision to load other cargo first.

In short in affirming the continued existence of the contract, the owners could only avoid the operation of the cancellation clause by tendering the vessel ready to load on time (which they failed to do), or by establishing (which they could not) that their failure was the result of the charterers' conduct in representing that they had given up their option, which representation the owners had acted on by not presenting the vessel on time . . .

13.5.3.2.2 *Frustration between affirmation and date for performance*

If the contract is frustrated between the date of affirmation and the date fixed for performance, then the injured party will lose its right to remedies for the breach.

Avery v Bowden
(1855) 5 E & B 714, 119 ER 647 (QB); affirmed (1856) 6 E & B 953 (Exchequer Chamber)

A ship was required to load cargo at Odessa within 45 days. The ship's master was told before the expiry of these laydays that no cargo would be available. He elected to affirm the contract and remained in port, hoping that a cargo would be provided. Before the expiry of the 45-day period, the contract was frustrated by the outbreak of war, which made it illegal to load a cargo at an enemy port.

Held: The shipowners could not recover damages for the anticipatory repudiatory breach in failing to provide a cargo, since the master had affirmed. If the master had sailed away on receiving that information, then not only could another cargo have been loaded at a friendly port, but the shipowner would also have had a right to claim damages for the loss caused by the breach.

13.5.3.3 Claiming the contract price as an alternative to damages

In some circumstances, the injured party can continue his performance of the contract and claim the contract price (as an action for a liquidated sum) rather than sue for damages for the breach. This is controversial, since the performance clearly is not required and the expenditure in performing is wasted.

White & Carter (Councils) Ltd v McGregor
[1962] AC 413 (HL)

The claimants, advertising contractors, had contracted with the defendant garage proprietor to display advertisements for the garage on litter bins for a three-year period. On the same day, the defendant requested that the agreement be cancelled, but the claimants refused. The claimants displayed the advertisements for 156 weeks and then claimed the contract price of £196 4s.

Held (Lords Morton and Keith dissenting): The claimants were entitled to carry out the contract and to claim the full contract price. They were not bound to accept the repudiation and sue for the lost profit on the contract as their damages. The minority were of the opinion that there could be no recovery of unwanted wasted expenditure and that the claimants should have mitigated (*page 730, 14.7*).

LORD REID: If one party to a contract repudiates it in the sense of making it clear to the other party that he refuses or will refuse to carry out his part of the contract, the other party, the innocent party, has an option. He may accept that repudiation and sue for damages for breach of contract, whether or not the time for performance has come; or he may if he chooses disregard or refuse to accept it and then the contract remains in full effect . . . I need not refer to the numerous authorities. They are not disputed by the respondent but he points out that in all of them the party who refused to accept the repudiation had no active duties under the contract. The innocent party's option is generally said to be to *wait* until the date of performance and then to claim damages estimated as at that date. There is no case in which it is said that he may, in face of the repudiation, go on and incur useless expense in performing the contract and then claim the contract price. The option, it is argued, is merely as to the date as at which damages are to be assessed.

Developing this argument, the respondent points out that in most cases the innocent party cannot complete the contract himself without the other party doing, allowing or accepting something, and that it is purely fortuitous that the appellants can do so in this case. In most cases by refusing cooperation the party in breach can compel the innocent party to restrict his claim to damages. Then it was said that, even where the innocent party can complete the contract without such co-operation, it is against the public interest that he should be allowed to do so. An example was developed in argument. A company might engage an expert to go abroad and prepare an elaborate report and then repudiate the contract before anything was done. To allow such an expert then to waste thousands of pounds in preparing the report cannot be right if a much smaller sum of damages would give him full compensation for his loss. It would merely enable the expert to extort a settlement giving him far more than reasonable compensation

. . . It may well be that, if it can be shown that a person has no legitimate interest, financial or otherwise, in performing the contract rather than claiming damages, he ought not to be allowed to saddle the other party with an additional burden with no benefit to himself. If a party has no interest to enforce a stipulation, he cannot in general enforce it: so it might be said that, if a party has no interest to insist on a particular remedy, he ought not to be allowed to insist on it. And, just as a party is not allowed to enforce a penalty, so he ought not to be allowed to penalise the other party by taking one course when another is equally advantageous to him. If I may revert to the example which I gave of a company engaging an expert to prepare an elaborate report and then repudiating before anything was done, it might be that the company could show that the expert had no substantial or legitimate interest in carrying out the work rather than accepting damages: I would think that the de minimis principle would apply in determining whether his interest was substantial, and that he might have a legitimate interest other than an immediate financial interest. But if the expert had no such interest then that might be regarded as a proper case for the exercise of the general equitable jurisdiction of the court. But that is not this case. Here the respondent did not set out to prove that the appellants had no legitimate interest in completing the contract and claiming the contract price rather than claiming damages; there is nothing in the findings of fact to support such a case, and it seems improbable that any such case could have been proved. It is, in my judgment, impossible to say that the appellants should be deprived of their right to claim the contract price merely because the benefit to them, as against claiming damages and re-letting their advertising space, might be small in comparison with the loss to the respondent: that is the most that could be said in favour of the respondent . . .

LORD MORTON OF HENRYTON [dissenting]: My Lords, I think that this is a case of great importance, although the claim is for a comparatively small sum. If the appellants are right, strange consequences follow in any case in which, under a repudiated contract, services are to be performed by the party who has not repudiated it, so long as he is able to perform these services without the cooperation of the repudiating party. Many examples of such contracts could be given. One, given in the course of the argument and already mentioned by my noble and learned friend, Lord Reid, is the engagement of an expert to go abroad and write a report on some subject for a substantial fee plus his expenses. If the appellants succeed in the present case, it must follow that the expert is entitled to incur the expense of going abroad, to write his unwanted report, and then to recover the fee and expenses, even if the other party has plainly repudiated the contract before any expense has been incurred.

It is well established that repudiation by one party does not put an end to a contract. The other party can say 'I hold you to your contract, which still remains in force.' What then is his remedy if the repudiating party persists in his repudiation and refuses to carry out his part of the contract? The contract has been broken. The innocent party is entitled to be compensated by damages for any loss which he has suffered by reason of the breach, and in a limited class of cases the court will decree specific implement. The law of Scotland provides no other remedy for a breach of contract, and there is no reported case which decides that the innocent party may act as the appellants have acted. The present case is one in which specific implement could not be decreed, since the only obligation of the respondent under the contract was to pay a sum of money for services to be rendered by the appellants. Yet the appellants are claiming a kind of inverted specific implement of the contract. They first insist on performing their part of the contract, against the will of the other party, and then claim that he must perform his part and pay the contract price for unwanted services. In my opinion, my Lords, the appellants' only remedy was damages, and they were bound to take steps to minimise their loss, according to a well-established rule of law. Far from doing this, having incurred no expense at the date of the repudiation, they made no attempt to procure another advertiser, but deliberately went on to incur expense and perform unwanted services with the intention of creating a money debt which did not exist at the date of the repudiation . . . The course of action followed by the appellants seems to me unreasonable and oppressive, but it is not on that ground that I would reject their claim. I would reject it for the reasons which I have already given.

NOTES

1. In effect, the majority was stating that the right to affirm includes the right to earn the contract price by performing the contract, as long as this can be achieved without the other party's cooperation. However, the actual result has been criticized, partly on the ground that it achieves the same effect as an order for specific performance where specific performance would not have been available.

2. The majority considered that there was no duty to mitigate because they felt that, on affirmation, there was no breach. However, if on the contractual date for performance there is no performance, there will inevitably be a breach, which on these facts the claimants affirmed. Arguably, therefore, the claimants should have mitigated as from this date.

3. It is true that the claim here was an action for an agreed sum, so that damages rules such as that relating to mitigation do not apply. This decision illustrates the unsatisfactory nature of the consequences that can follow from this distinction.

4. In *Reichman v Beveridge* [2006] EWCA Civ 1659, [2007] Bus LR 412 (*page 669, 13.5.3.3.2*, note 1), a tenant argued that, having left the premises three years into a five-year lease, there was a duty placed on the landlord to mitigate in a claim for rent arrears following the abandonment, e.g. by marketing the premises, finding a replacement tenant, and not rejecting offers from prospective tenants. However, the Court of Appeal accepted that there was no such duty to mitigate in an action in debt (i.e. the action for arrears of rent).

13.5.3.3.1 *Limitations on the ability to affirm and to claim the contract price*

White & Carter v McGregor has been limited in subsequent decisions by reference to two apparent restrictions placed upon it by Lord Reid. First, the claimants must have been able to perform without the cooperation of the defendant (i.e. a limitation on the ability to continue performance and hence claim the contract price), and the second, that the claimants must have a legitimate interest in continuing to perform rather than claiming damages (i.e. a limitation on the ability to affirm, as opposed to accepting the anticipatory breach as terminating the contract).

In *Clea Shipping Corporation v Bulk Oil International Ltd, The Alaskan Trader* [1984] 1 All ER 129, 133B–I (*page 669, 13.5.3.3.2*), Lloyd J explained these limitations:

Lord Reid agreed with Lord Hodson and Lord Tucker that on the facts the plaintiffs' claim in debt must succeed. But his speech contains two important observations on the law. First, he pointed out that it is only in rare cases that the innocent party will be able to complete performance of his side of the contract, without the assent or cooperation of the party in breach. Obviously, if the innocent party cannot complete performance, he is restricted to his claim for damages. A buyer who refuses to accept delivery of the goods, and thereby prevents property passing, cannot, in the ordinary case, be made liable for the price. The peculiarity of *White & Carter v McGregor* [1961] 3 All ER 1178 at 182, [1962] AC 413 at 429, as Lord Reid pointed out, was that the plaintiffs could completely fulfil their part of the contract without any cooperation from the defendant.

The second observation which Lord Reid made as to the law was that a party might well be unable to enforce his contractual remedy if 'he had no legitimate interest, financial or otherwise, in performing the contract rather than claiming damages'. Lord Reid did not go far in explaining what he meant by legitimate interest except to say that the de minimis principle would apply. Obviously it would not be sufficient to establish that the innocent party was acting unreasonably . . . It is clear that, on the facts, no attempt had been made by the defendant to establish absence of legitimate interest. Accordingly, counsel for the owners was right when he submitted that the two observations which I have mentioned were both, strictly speaking, *obiter*.

? QUESTION

Did the claimants in *White & Carter v McGregor* have a legitimate interest in performing the contract?

13.5.3.3.2 A legitimate interest to justify the election to affirm

---

Attica Sea Carriers Corporation v Ferrostaal Poseidon Bulk Reederei GmbH, The Puerto Buitrago
[1976] 1 Lloyd's Rep 250 (CA)

The question in the case was whether the shipowners could ignore a repudiation by the charterers in redelivering a vessel in breach of a repair obligation and sue for the charter hire until the repairs were completed (the evidence being that the repairs would cost $2 million, which would be greatly in excess of the value of the vessel).

ORR LJ [(with whose conclusion Browne LJ agreed) referred to the judgment of Lord Reid in *White & Carter Ltd v McGregor* and continued]: The present case differs from that case in that here it cannot be said that the owners could fulfil the contract without any cooperation from the charterers and also because in this case the charterers have set out to prove that the owners have no legitimate interest in claiming the charter hire rather than claiming damages . . . [I]f either or both of these factors had been present in *White & Carter v McGregor* Lord Reid might well have agreed with Lord Morton and Lord Keith as to the outcome of the appeal, with the result that there would have been a majority in favour of dismissing it.

LORD DENNING MR: [*White & Carter Ltd v McGregor*] has been criticized in a leading textbook (Cheshire & Fifoot, pp. 600 and 601). It is said to give a 'grotesque' result. Even though it was a Scots case, it would appear that the House of Lords, as at present constituted, would expect us to follow it in any case that is precisely on all fours with it. But I would not follow it otherwise. It has no application whatever in a case where the plaintiff ought, in all reason, to accept the repudiation and sue for damages—provided that damages would provide an adequate remedy for any loss suffered by him. The reason is because, by suing for the money, the plaintiff is seeking to enforce specific performance of the contract—and he should not be allowed to do so when damages would be an adequate remedy. Take a servant, who has a contract for six months certain, but is dismissed after one month. He cannot sue for his wages for each of the six months by alleging that he was ready and willing to serve. His only remedy is damages. Take a finance company which lets a machine or motor-car on hire purchase, but the hirer refuses to accept it. The finance company cannot sue each month for the instalments. Its only remedy is in damages: see *National Cash Register Co. v Stanley* [1921] 3 KB 292; *Karsales (Harrow) v Wallis* [1956] 1 WLR 936 (2nd point). So here, when the charterers tendered redelivery at the end of the period of the charter—in breach of the contract to repair—the shipowners ought in all reason to have accepted it. They cannot sue for specific performance—either of the promise to pay the charter hire, or of the promise to do the repairs—because damages are an adequate remedy for the breach. What is the alternative which the shipowners present to the charterers? Either the charterers must pay the charter hire for years to come, whilst the vessel lies idle and useless for want of repair. *Or* the charterers must do repairs which would cost twice as much as the ship would be worth when repaired—after which the shipowners might sell it as scrap, making the repairs a useless waste of money. In short, on either alternative, the shipowners seek to compel specific performance of one or other of the provisions of the charter—with most unjust and unreasonable consequences—when damages would be an adequate remedy. I do not think the law allows them to do this. I think they should accept redelivery and sue for damages . . .

Clea Shipping Corporation v Bulk Oil International Ltd, The Alaskan Trader
[1984] 1 All ER 129

After 12 months of a two-year charter, the vessel suffered a serious engine breakdown, necessitating several months of repair. The charterers indicated that they would not require the vessel, but the owners went ahead with repairs costing £800,000, which were completed in April 1981. They informed the charterers that the vessel was available, and maintained a full crew ready to sail between April and December 1981. The charterers sought repayment of the hire paid between April and December, alleging that the owners should have accepted the charterers' conduct as repudiating the contract and claimed damages. The owners argued that they were free to elect to affirm and to keep the vessel at the disposal of the charterers.

Held: Although, in general, there was an unfettered right to elect, in exceptional cases the court would exercise its general equitable jurisdiction to refuse to allow the injured party to affirm if there were no legitimate interest in performing the contract rather than claiming damages. The arbitrator had found that the claimants (the owners) had acted wholly unreasonably and Lloyd J upheld this finding. Therefore, although the charterers were liable in damages, they could recover the hire they had paid.

LLOYD J: Whether one takes Lord Reid's language, which was adopted by Orr and Browne LJJ in *The Puerto Buitrago*, or Lord Denning MR's language in that case ('in all reason'), or Kerr J's language in *The Odenfeld* ('wholly unreasonable. . .quite unrealistic, unreasonable and untenable'), there comes a point at which the court will cease, on general equitable principles, to allow the innocent party to enforce his contract according to its strict legal terms. How one defines that point is obviously a matter of some difficulty, for it involves drawing a line between conduct which is merely unreasonable (see per Lord Reid in *White & Carter v McGregor* [1961] 3 All ER 1178 at 1182, [1962] AC 413 at 429–430) and conduct which is wholly unreasonable (see per Kerr J in *The Odenfeld* [1978] 2 Lloyd's Rep 357 at 374). But however difficult it may be to define the point, that there is such a point seems to me to have been accepted both by the Court of Appeal in *The Puerto Buitrago* and by Kerr J in *The Odenfeld*.

I appreciate that the House of Lords has recently re-emphasised the importance of certainty in commercial contracts, when holding that there is no equitable jurisdiction to relieve against the consequences of the withdrawal clause in a time charter: see *Scandinavian Trading Tanker Co. AB v Flota Petrolera Ecuatoriana, The Scaptrade* [1983] 2 All ER 763, [1983] 3 WLR 203. I appreciate, too, that the importance of certainty was one of the main reasons urged by Lord Hodson in *White & Carter v McGregor* in upholding the innocent party's unfettered right to elect. But, for reasons already mentioned, it seems to me that this court is bound to hold that there is *some* fetter, if only in extreme cases; and, for want of a better way of describing that fetter, it is safest for this court to use the language of Lord Reid, which, as I have already said, was adopted by a majority of the Court of Appeal in *The Puerto Buitrago*.

NOTES

1. In *Reichman v Beveridge* [2006] EWCA Civ 1659, [2007] Bus LR 412 (*page 666, 13.5.3.3*, note 4), the Court of Appeal held that (i) it was not wholly unreasonable for an innocent landlord to refuse to take steps to find a new, replacement tenant, and (ii) damages might not be an adequate remedy, because if the landlords were to accept the action as forfeiting (terminating) the lease and relet, but at a lower market rent than that available under the terms of the lease, damages could not be recovered for loss of that rent, there being no authority in English law allowing a landlord to recover loss of *future* rent (i.e. from a forfeiture to the expiry of the lease) from a former tenant. The landlord would therefore not be acting unreasonably in concluding that he should not terminate the lease because, if the future rent were lower, he might not be able to recover the lost rent as damages. The tenant was the party in breach and should not be able to transfer the consequences to the landlord, i.e. a duty to forfeit and find new tenants.

Thus, while the Court of Appeal stressed the limited nature of the principle in *White & Carter (Councils) Ltd v McGregor* [1962] AC 413, i.e. affirmation and recovery in debt with no duty to mitigate, it found it to be applicable to this situation involving a relationship of landlord and tenant.

2. In *Ocean Marine Navigation Ltd v Koch Carbon Inc., The Dynamic* [2003] EWHC 1936 (Comm), [2003] 2 Lloyd's Rep 693, the owner of a vessel claimed to be entitled to rely on the right to hire, available in accordance with the terms of the charterparty, rather than being limited to damages for the charterers' repudiatory breach in not redelivering the vessel on time. The judge, Simon J, considered Lord Reid's limitation in *White & Carter* and its interpretation in subsequent cases.

SIMON J: 23. These cases establish the following exception to the general rule that the innocent party has an option whether or not to accept a repudiation: (i) The burden is on the *contract-breaker* to show that the innocent party has no legitimate interest in performing the contract rather than claiming damages. (ii) This burden is not discharged merely by showing that the benefit to the other party is small in comparison to the loss to the contract-breaker. (iii) The exception to the general rule applies only in extreme cases: where damages would be an adequate remedy and where an election to keep the contract alive would be unreasonable.

The word 'wholly' in 'wholly unreasonable' in the statement by Kerr J in *The Odenfeld* [1978] 2 Lloyd's Rep 357, 373 ('any fetter on the innocent party's right of election whether or not to accept a repudiation will only be applied in extreme cases, viz. where damages would be an adequate remedy and where an election to keep the contract alive would be wholly unreasonable') added nothing to the test itself and only made it clear that 'the rule is general and the exception only applies in extreme cases'.

3. This means that the innocent party's right to elect to affirm is not as restricted as might have been thought and that it requires an 'extreme case' for the ability to affirm to be lost. Nevertheless, having affirmed, the ability to continue performance and claim the contract price is limited by the need to be able to do this without the cooperation of the contract breaker. Thus, Lord Reid's two limitations relate to two different issues.

Isabella Shipowner SA v Shagang Shipping Co. Ltd, The Aquafaith
[2012] EWHC 1077 (Comm), [2012] 2 All ER (Comm) 461, [2012] 1 CLC 899

Shipowners refused to accept early delivery of the ship in anticipatory breach of the charterparty to render the charterers liable for the charter hire for the minimum term. The arbitrator had accepted the charterers' argument that the owners had no legitimate interest in performing rather than claiming damages, so that the owners were restricted to damages.

Held (on appeal): It was not sufficient to refuse affirmation simply because damages would be an available remedy on the facts. Affirmation had to be 'beyond all reason' or 'perverse' before there was no legitimate interest in maintaining the contract. That involved considering whether there was any benefit to the shipowners, however small, as compared to the loss to the charterers. On the facts, there were 94 days left of a five-year time charter in a market in which finding a substitute time charter would have been very difficult. Maintaining the hire was therefore neither 'unreasonable' nor 'wholly unreasonable', and this was not an 'extreme or unusual' case.

COOKE J:

Did the arbitrator err in law in finding that the exception to the White and Carter principle applied?

42 In my judgment it is clear that the arbitrator applied the wrong test when considering whether or not the owners had a legitimate interest in maintaining the charter for the balance of 94 days and claiming hire, as opposed to accepting the repudiatory breach of the charterers as bringing the charter to an end, trading on the spot market in mitigation of loss and claiming damages for the difference. The arbitrator concluded that because the owners could accept the repudiation, mitigate loss by trading on the spot market and claim damages representing the difference, the owners had no legitimate interest in keeping the charterparty alive. The arbitrator never directed his mind to the principles set out in The Puerto Buitrago, The Odenfeld [Gator Shipping Corp v Trans-Asiatic Oil SA, The Odenfeld [1978] 2 Lloyd's Rep 357], The Alaskan Trader, Stocznia, or The Dynamic. He never asked himself the question whether the owners should 'in all reason' accept the repudiation (or to put the point the other way, whether the owners' refusal to accept the repudiation was 'beyond all reason'): he never asked the question whether it would be 'wholly unreasonable' to keep the contract alive; he never asked whether it would be more than 'unreasonable' and 'wholly unreasonable' to do so, by reference to the language of the Court of Appeal in the various cases. If he had applied the principles set out by Simon J in The Dynamic, he would have asked himself whether the charterers had discharged the burden of showing that the owners had no legitimate interest in maintaining the charter and had done so by showing that this was an extreme case where damages would be an adequate remedy and where an election to keep the contract alive would be so unreasonable that the owners should not be allowed to do so. He should have explored whether there was any benefit to the owners, whether or not small in comparison to the loss to the charterers . . .

46 . . . The only financial interest to which he [the arbitrator] had regard was whether the owners would be 'worse off' by mitigating and claiming damages, as compared with maintaining the charter and claiming hire whilst the only other legitimate interest he considered was the ability of charterers to sublet the vessel, which he considered an irrelevance because the charterers had been clear and emphatic in maintaining their repudiatory stance. Whilst on a very generous reading of the award it might just be possible to read into it a decision that damages were an adequate remedy, because of the possibility of mitigating loss and claiming the balance in damages, he never looked at the degree of unreasonableness of the owners' conduct nor saw the need for it to be an extreme case before the exception could apply. He considered that the ability to accept the termination, to trade the vessel on the spot market and to claim the balance of actual loss, as against hire, was conclusive of the issue, when seen in the light of the charterers' emphatic insistent repudiatory stance.

47 . . . [T]he owners had submitted that damages were an inadequate remedy because the charterers were in financial difficulty. The owners were therefore at risk of the charterers directing their limited funds to meet obligations to other parties, whilst delaying payment of any sums owing to the owners until the end of the charterparty and the assessment of what was due in damages. Instead of paying hire up front, semi monthly in advance, with all the cashflow implications of that, the charterers wished to compel the owners to trade the vessel in mitigation of loss and leave themselves liberty to argue about the quantum of damages at the end of the relevant period and pay whatever they could at that stage . . . Should the charterers choose to do so, payment of any liability could be postponed until the conclusion of an arbitration, months away, by which time the charterers could conceivably have become insolvent or arguments used to secure a settlement discount on any loss claimed. The owners wished to guard against that by maintaining the charter with the ability to claim hire and sue/proceed in arbitration for it on any default, without the propensity for argument as to failure to mitigate damages. The arbitrator never appears to have grappled with this point at all.

48 Nor did he grapple with the argument that the contract breaker was seeking to foist upon the innocent party the burden of seeking to trade in a difficult spot market, where a substitute time charter was impossible, with all the management issues involved . . . The contract breaker was therefore seeking to be shot of the difficulties in trading the vessel by imposing that burden on the innocent party, as well as depriving him of the assured income of advance hire . . .

NOTE The movement towards favouring the ability to affirm (and concluding that there is a legitimate interest in keeping the contract alive) appears to have been limited by the decision of the Court of Appeal in *MSC Mediterranean Shipping Co. SA v Cottonex* [2016] EWCA Civ 789, [2017] 1 All ER (Comm) 483. A cargo had been delivered but was never collected by the buyer although ownership of the cargo had been transferred. Consequently, the seller could not unpack the containers and return them to the shipper. This constituted a repudiatory breach and, in accordance with the contract terms, the shipper was entitled to charge 'container demurrage' for every day that the containers were not returned following delivery of the cargo. In the High Court [2015] EWHC 283 (Comm), [2015] 2 All ER (Comm) 614, [2015] 1 Lloyd's Rep 359, Leggatt J was unhappy at the prospect of such an open-ended liability and held that the shipper had no legitimate interest in affirming following that breach and should be forced to accept the repudiatory breach as terminating the contract because it was clear that there was no reasonable prospect of redelivery of the containers and future performance.

This is a startling result since it limits the injured party's ability to act in its own commercial interests—and the exercise of the agreed 'container demurrage' provision ought to be seen as a legitimate interest in affirming and continuing with the contract. Leggatt J went further (at [97]), stating that the decision to terminate for repudiatory breach needed to be taken in 'good faith' although he recognized that the election for repudiatory breach arose by operation of law. Justification for the conclusion that there was no legitimate interest in affirming on these facts was provided by the conclusion that the 'container demurrage' was an unenforceable penalty rather than a liquidated damages amount.

LJ Moore-Bick, giving the leading judgment in the Court of Appeal, agreed that the delay by Cottonex in returning the container was a repudiation of the contract but stated, on the facts, this was not a case 'in which the *White and Carter* principle applies'.

40. It may be that the implications of Lord Reid's observation in *White & Carter* and the principles of law which underpin it have yet to be fully identified, but the existence of the broad principle towards which he pointed has been accepted in a number of cases, of which *The 'Puerto Buitrago'* is but one example. In *Clea Shipping Corp v Bulk Oil International Ltd (The 'Alaskan Trader')* [1984] 1 All E.R. 129 Lloyd J. upheld the decision of a commercial arbitrator that the owner of a vessel let under a time charter could not recover hire because it had no legitimate interest in affirming the charter following its repudiation by the charterer. The judge in that case described the principle as being that the court on equitable grounds refuses to allow the innocent party to enforce his full contractual *rights*, but I am inclined to think that the observations of Lord Reid himself in *White & Carter* and of Lord Wilson in *Geys v Société Générale* suggest that the true explanation may be that in an appropriate case the court in the exercise of its general equitable jurisdiction will decline to grant the innocent party the *remedy* to which he would normally be entitled. This may appear to be a distinction without a difference and in most cases that may be so, but in some cases, of which *Geys v Société Générale* is an example, it is a distinction of importance.

41 However, in my view the proposition that in the present case demurrage can continue to accrue indefinitely until the containers are redelivered to the carrier fails to take account of the fact that by 2nd February 2012 the remaining commercial purpose of the adventure had been frustrated, i.e., the performance of the contracts of carriage had become radically different from that which the parties had envisaged when they entered into them. That situation having been brought about by a breach of contract on the part of the shipper, two questions arise: can the carrier still insist on performance of the shipper's obligation to redeliver the containers; and if not, what damages flow from the breach of that obligation?

42 The fact that by 2nd February 2012 the point had been reached at which the commercial purposes of the adventure had become frustrated meant that in commercial terms the containers had been lost. They could no longer be redelivered in the context of the original adventure (if at all). Lord Reid's observations in *White & Carter* and the dicta the cases to which I have referred were directed to cases in which the party in breach was refusing to perform continuing obligations or obligations that fell due for performance at a future date. In such cases the existence of a legitimate interest in holding the defaulting party to its obligations may arise. Although the party in default may already be in breach of its obligations, the important question for these purposes is whether the innocent party has a legitimate interest in affirming the contract by insisting on performance in the future or is required to accept an anticipatory breach of all obligations remaining to be performed.

43 If it had been open to the carrier to affirm the contract I should have agreed with the judge that it had no legitimate

interest in continuing to insist on performance by the shipper of its remaining obligations under the contracts. The accrued demurrage already exceeded by a considerable amount the value of the containers. Replacement containers were readily available at Chittagong and the carrier had no interest in keeping the contract alive other than to earn demurrage pending their return. This is a classic case in which it would have been wholly unreasonable for the carrier to insist on further performance. The only reasonable course for it to take would have been to accept the shipper's failure to redeliver the containers as a repudiation of the contract. However, I do not think that the option of affirming the contracts remained open to the carrier once the adventure had become frustrated,

because at that point further performance became impossible, just as it would if the shipper or those for whom it was responsible had caused the containers to be destroyed. With respect to the judge, therefore, I do not think that this is a case in which the *White & Carter* principle applies. As at 2nd February 2012 the shipper could no longer redeliver the containers and, having brought about that situation by its breach, had become liable in damages for their loss.

The point was reinforced by Tomlinson LJ, who, at [63] simply stated that 'the innocent party simply cannot treat the contract as subsisting because it is no longer capable of performance as agreed'.

13.5.3.3.3 *The ability to perform without cooperation and so be in a position to claim the contract price*

In the following case, Megarry J considered that cooperation in this context meant passive, as well as active, cooperation.

Hounslow London Borough Council v Twickenham Garden Developments Ltd
[1971] Ch 233

Contractors were working on a site belonging to the local authority. The local authority 'repudiated' their contract, but the contractors refused to accept this and elected to proceed with the work on site. Did they have the right to insist on continuing to perform the contract?

Held: No, they did not.

MEGARRY J: The case before me is patently one in which the contractor cannot perform the contract without any co-operation by the borough. The whole machinery of the contract is geared to acts by the architect and quantity surveyor, and it is a contract that is to be performed on the borough's land. True, the contractor already has de facto possession or control of the land; there is no question of the borough being required to do the act of admitting the contractor into possession, and so in that respect the contractor can perform the contract without any 'co-operation' by the borough. But I do not think that the point can be brushed aside so simply. Quite apart from questions of active co-operation, cases where one party is lawfully in possession of property of the other seem to me to raise issues not before the House of Lords in *White and Carter (Councils) Ltd v McGregor* [1962] AC 413. Suppose that A, who owns a large and valuable painting, contracts with B, a picture restorer, to restore it over a period of three months. Before the work is begun, A receives a handsome offer from C to purchase the picture, subject to immediate delivery of the picture in its unrestored state, C having grave suspicions of B's competence. If the work of restoration is to be done in A's house, he can effectually exclude B by refusing to admit him to the house: without A's 'co-operation' to this extent B cannot perform his contract. But what if the picture stands in A's locked barn, the key of which he has lent to B so that he may come and go freely, or if the picture has been removed to B's premises? In these cases can B insist on performing his contract, even though this makes it impossible for A to accept C's offer? In the case of the barn, A's co-operation may perhaps be said to be requisite to the extent of not barring B's path to the barn or putting another lock on the door: but if the picture is on B's premises, no active co-operation by A is needed. Nevertheless, the picture is A's property, and I find it difficult to believe that Lord Reid intended to restrict the concept of 'co-operation' to active co-operation. In *White and Carter (Councils) Ltd v McGregor* no co-operation by the proprietor, either active or passive, was required: the contract could be performed by the agents wholly without reference to the proprietor or his property. The case was far removed from that of a property owner being forced to stand impotently aside while a perhaps ill-advised contract is executed on property of his which he has delivered into the possession of the other party, and is powerless to retrieve.

Accordingly, I do not think that *White and Carter (Councils) Ltd v McGregor* has any application to the case before me. I say this, first, because a considerable degree of active co-operation under the contract by the borough is requisite, and second, because the work is being done to property of the borough. I doubt very much whether the *White* case can have been intended to apply where the contract is to be performed by doing acts to property owned by the party seeking to determine it. I should add that it seems to me that the ratio of the *White* case involves acceptance of Lord Reid's limitations, even though Lord Tucker and Lord Hodson said nothing of them: for without Lord Reid there was no majority for the decision of the House. Under the doctrine of precedent, I do not think that it can be said that a majority of a bare majority is itself the majority.

? QUESTION

This interpretation has considerably diminished the scope of *White & Carter (Councils) Ltd v McGregor*, since the performance of many contracts will require at least passive cooperation from the other party. There appears to be a difference between a contractor working on the site of the owner and one working on the site of a third party. Should this make a difference?

NOTES

1. Where the anticipatory breach is of a contract for the sale or supply of unascertained or future goods and the buyer indicates that he does not want the goods, the seller will not be able to perform so as to be entitled to claim the price because the buyer will not accept the goods. See *Poole's Textbook on Contract Law*, 13.7, for a detailed explanation.

2. Lord Reid's comment on the need to establish a legitimate interest in continuing to perform rather than claim damages was not accepted by the other members of the House of Lords, but Megarry J appears to treat it as part of the *ratio* of the case.

3. The restriction in *White & Carter* that a claimant was limited to a remedy in damages where he could not perform without the cooperation of the contract breaker applies only where the performance that had been prevented by the breach was a precondition to the payment obligation, i.e. the performance obligation was entire (as in *White & Carter*): *Ministry of Sound (Ireland) Ltd v World Online Ltd* [2003] EWHC 2178 (Ch), [2003] 2 All ER (Comm) 823. In *Ministry of Sound*, the innocent party could perform only if CDs were supplied by the guilty party. However, since there was no link between the required performance and the right to receive the contractual payment, and since the contract had not been terminated for the repudiatory breach, in principle (although not on the facts) the contract term as to payment could be enforced via a claim in debt. Because there was no link between performance and payment, it did not matter whether performance was impossible without cooperation.

4. In *Isabella Shipowner SA v Shagang Shipping Co. Ltd, The Aquafaith* [2012] EWHC 1077 (Comm), [2012] 2 All ER (Comm) 461, [2012] 1 CLC 899 (*page 669, 13.5.3.3.2*), the judge rejected the charterers' argument that the owners could not claim the remaining hire following early redelivery because the charterer's operation involved the cooperation of the charterer.

COOKE J: 37 The question, to my mind, is very simple. Could the owners claim hire from the charterers under this time charter without the need for the charterers to do anything under the charter? The answer is yes. If the charterers failed to give any orders, the vessel would simply stay where it was, awaiting orders but earning hire. Although the master is under the orders of the charterer, the master and crew are the servants of the owners and the ship is available to the charterers for any order they wish to give. Hire continues to be earned. Although the charterers are obliged under the terms of the charter to provide and pay for fuel, should the bunkers run out whilst awaiting orders, it is open to the owners to stem the vessel and to charge that to the charterers' account. In order to complete their side of the bargain, the owners do not need the charterers to do anything in order for them to earn the hire in question. The earning of hire after purported redelivery was not dependent on any performance by the charterers of their obligations . . .

13.5.4 **Termination**

The injured party terminates by 'accepting' the other's repudiatory breach as terminating the contract. When the injured party accepts an anticipatory breach, then it can claim damages from that time and does not have to wait for the time fixed for performance.

Hochster v De La Tour
(1853) 2 E & B 678, 118 ER 922 (QB)

On 12 April 1852, the defendant agreed to employ the claimant as a courier for three months as from 1 June 1852. On 11 May, the defendant wrote to the claimant. stating that he had changed his mind and that the claimant's services were no longer required. On 22 May, the claimant commenced an action for breach of contract and the defendant argued that there could be no breach of contract before 1 June.

Held: The claimant was entitled to commence an action for damages on 22 May and did not have to wait until 1 June.

LORD CAMPBELL CJ: [I]t cannot be laid down as a universal rule that, where by agreement an act is to be done on a future day, no action can be brought for a breach of the agreement till the day for doing the act has arrived. If a man promises to marry a woman on a future day, and before that day marries another woman, he is instantly liable to an action for breach of promise of marriage. If a man contracts to execute a lease on and from a future day for a certain term, and, before that day, executes a lease to another for the same term, he may be immediately sued for breaking the contract. So, if a man contracts to sell and deliver specific goods on a future day, and before the day he sells and delivers them to another, he is immediately liable to an action at the suit of the person with whom he first contracted to sell and deliver them. One reason alleged in support of such an action is, that the defendant has, before the day, rendered it impossible for him to perform the contract at the day: but this does not necessarily follow; for, prior to the day fixed for doing the act, the first wife may have died, a surrender of the lease executed might be obtained, and the defendant might have repurchased the goods so as to be in a situation to sell and deliver them to the plaintiff . . . If the plaintiff has no remedy for breach of the contract unless he treats the contract as in force, and acts upon it down to the 1 June 1852, it follows that, till then, he must enter into no employment which will interfere with his promise 'to start with the defendant on such travels on the day and year,' and that he must then be properly equipped in all respects as a courier for a three months' tour on the continent of Europe. But it is surely much more rational, and more for the benefit of both parties, that, after the renunciation of the agreement by the defendant, the plaintiff should be at liberty to consider himself absolved from any future performance of it, retaining his right to sue for any damage he has suffered from the breach of it. Thus, instead of remaining idle and laying out money in preparations which must be useless, he is at liberty to seek service under another employer, which would go in mitigation of the damages to which he would otherwise be entitled for a breach of the contract. It seems strange that the defendant, after renouncing the contract, and absolutely declaring that he will never act under it, should be permitted to object that faith is given to his assertion, and that an opportunity is not left to him of changing his mind. If the plaintiff is barred of any remedy by entering into an engagement inconsistent with starting as a courier with the defendant on the 1 June, he is prejudiced by putting faith in the defendant's assertion: and it would be more consonant with principle, if the defendant were precluded from saying that he had not broken the contract when he declared that he entirely renounced it. Suppose that the defendant, at the time of his renunciation, had embarked on a voyage for Australia, so as to render it physically impossible for him to employ the plaintiff as a courier on the continent of Europe in the months of June, July and August 1852: according to decided cases, the action might have been brought before the 1 June; but the renunciation may have been founded on other facts, to be given in evidence, which would equally have rendered the defendant's performance of the contract impossible. The man who wrongfully renounces a contract into which he has deliberately entered cannot justly complain if he is immediately sued for a compensation in damages by the man whom he has injured: and it seems reasonable to allow an option to the injured party, either to sue immediately, or to wait till the time when the act was to be done, still holding it as prospectively binding for the exercise of this option, which may be advantageous to the innocent party, and cannot be prejudicial to the wrongdoer . . . If it should be held that, upon a contract to do an act on a future day, a renunciation of the contract by one party dispenses with a condition to be performed in the meantime by the other, there seems no reason for requiring that other to wait till the day arrives before seeking his remedy by action: and the only ground on which the condition can be dispensed with seems to be, that the renunciation may be treated as a breach of the contract.

NOTES

1. The injured party must mitigate (*14.7*) from the date of accepting the breach as terminating the contract. On the facts, the claimant had found another engagement to start later in June.

2. The right to this immediate remedy of damages turns on the fact of repudiation. However, the courts must therefore consider whether the repudiation has deprived the injured party of the anticipated performance, i.e. whether the performance depended upon a contingency that will not materialize. If it is clear beyond doubt that the contingency cannot materialize so that the repudiation cannot be said to deprive the other party of any reasonably expected performance, no remedy will be available. In *The Mihalis Angelos* [1971] 1 QB 164. Megaw LJ stated, at pp. 209H–210B:

In my view, where there is an anticipatory breach of contract, the breach is the repudiation once it has been accepted, and the other party is entitled to recover by way of damages the true value of the contractual rights which he has thereby lost; subject to his duty to mitigate. If the contractual rights which he has lost were capable by the terms of the contract of being rendered either less valuable or valueless in certain events, and if it can be shown that those events were, at the date of the acceptance of the repudiation, predestined to happen, then in my view the damages which he can recover are not more than the true value, if any, of the rights which he has lost, having regard to those predestined events. [Emphasis added]

Although *The Mihalis Angelos* is concerned with anticipatory breach and a predestined event judged at the date of the breach (said to be at the date of acceptance of the repudiation), in *Golden Strait Corporation v Nippon Yusen Kubishika Kaisha, The Golden Victory* [2007] UKHL 12, [2007] 2 AC 353 (for the facts and a discussion, *14.4*), this principle was extended to non-anticipatory breach in order to reduce the damages award in light of the occurrence of a contractual contingency, which was taken to have occurred at the date of judgment for the purposes of awarding 'actual loss', although it was arguably not 'predestined' at the date of the breach.

Chapter 14

Damages for breach of contract

14.1 The aim of contractual damages

The aim of contractual damages is to compensate the injured party for the loss suffered as a result of the other party's breach of contract.

Contractual damages are not punitive other than in exceptional circumstances: see the discussion of *Attorney-General v Blake* [2001] 1 AC 268 and *WWF World Wide Fund for Nature v World Wrestling Federation Entertainment Inc.* [2007] EWCA Civ 286, [2008] 1 WLR 445, [2007] Bus LR 1252 (*page 780, 15.4.1.1*). Where the injured party has suffered no loss, it is not generally considered possible to recover damages that transfer the benefit gained by the guilty party as a result of the breach of contract, even if that breach was deliberate. The injured party can recover only for his actual loss.

Surrey County Council v Bredero Homes Ltd
[1993] 1 WLR 1361 (CA)

The council had sold land to the defendant developer on the basis of a contract that required the developer to develop the land in accordance with planning permission for 72 houses, which had already been granted. After the sale, however, the defendant obtained a new planning permission allowing an additional five houses to be built on the site. The defendant then deliberately breached the contract term requiring it to abide by the original planning permission and constructed the extra houses. The council sought damages for the breach, based on the sum from the defendant's profits that the council argued the defendant would have had to pay to it in order to obtain a relaxation of the covenant restricting construction.

Held: The council was entitled to recover only nominal damages, since it had not suffered any loss as a result of the breach and, in financial terms, was already in the position in which it would have been had the covenant been performed.

14

NOTE That recovery based on compensation for actual loss is the governing principle for the award of contractual damages can be seen clearly in the speeches of the House of Lords in *Golden Strait Corporation v Nippon Yusen Kubishika Kaisha, The* *Golden Victory* [2007] UKHL 12, [2007] 2 AC 353 (for the facts and a discussion, see *page 698, 14.4*), and it was the factor governing the decision to permit subsequent events to be taken into account when assessing the measure of damages recoverable for breach.

Morris Garner v One Step (Support) Ltd
[2018] UKSC 20

In 1999 the first defendant established a business providing support for young people leaving care. In 2002 she sold a 50 per cent interest in the business to Mr and Mrs Costelloe. To give effect to their arrangements the parties established the claimant, One Step, in which the first defendant and Mrs Costelloe held equal shares. Relationships deteriorated and in December 2006 Mrs Costelloe acquired the first defendant's shares in One Step on terms that the first defendant would not compete with One Step. By August 2007 the first defendant had established Positive Living in competition to One Step, and One Step's business experienced a significant downturn. One Step sought an account of Positive Living's profits or, in the alternative, restitutionary damages, for breach of the non-competition covenant. The Court of Appeal, [2017] 1 QB 1, awarded damages based on the amount that would notionally have been agreed between the parties as the price for releasing the first defendant from her obligation not to compete.

Held: The Court of Appeal had erred in its assessment of damages, and the correct approach was to award damages by reference to what had been lost by One Step as a result of the breach.

LORD REED: 31 Damages in contract serve a different remedial purpose from damages in tort, reflecting the different nature of the obligation breached by the wrongdoer in each case. The law of tort is concerned with civil wrongs, that is to say with breaches of duties imposed by the law, sometimes generally and sometimes on those who are party to particular relationships or have assumed particular responsibilities, which protect the interests of others in respect of such matters as their bodily integrity, their liberty, their property, their privacy and their reputation. Damages in tort are generally intended to place the claimant as nearly as possible in the same position as he would have been in if the tort had not been committed. The law of contract, on the other hand, gives effect to consensual agreements entered into by particular individuals in their own interests. Remedies granted by the courts are designed to give effect to what was voluntarily undertaken by the parties. Damages in contract are therefore intended to place the claimant in the same position as he would have been in if the contract had been performed . . .

36 The objective of compensating the claimant for the loss sustained as a result of non-performance (an expression used here in a broad sense, so as to encompass delayed performance and defective performance) makes it necessary to quantify the loss which he sustained as accurately as the circumstances permit. What is crucial is first to identify the loss: the difference between the claimant's actual situation and the situation in which he would have been if the primary contractual obligation had been performed. Once the loss has been identified, the court then has to quantify it in monetary terms . . .

NOTES

1. This decision confirms the purely compensatory function of damages, so that the defendant's profit and also the defendant's motives are to be left out of account: the calculation—however difficult that might be—focuses on the claimant's loss.

2. Prior to *One Step*, there was a line of authority, beginning with *Wrotham Park Estate Co. Ltd v Parkside Homes Ltd* [1974] 1 WLR 798, in which the courts awarded damages based upon the amount that the claimant would have been willing to accept in order to release the defendant from its contractual obligations. The Supreme Court in *One Step* reclassified this form of compensation as 'negotiating damages' and limited its availability to cases where the claimant has been wrongfully deprived of his right to exploit an asset. All of this is discussed in detail in *Chapter 15*.

Damages for breach of contract

14

14.2 Expectation loss

Contractual damages are usually awarded to compensate for the injured party's loss of expectation, i.e. what the injured party would have received had the contract been properly performed.

In *Robinson v Harman* (1848) 1 Exch 850, p. 855, Parke B said:

> The rule of the common law is, that where a party sustains a loss by reason of a breach of contract, he is, so far as money can do it, to be placed in the same situation, with respect to damages, as if the contract had been performed.

14.2.1 Measurement: difference in value

One measure is the difference in value between what the injured party expected to receive and what he actually did receive, e.g. in relation to defective goods, the measure will be the difference in value between the goods as promised and the goods actually received.

> **Sale of Goods Act 1979**
>
> **50. Damages for non-acceptance**
>
> (1) Where the buyer wrongfully neglects or refuses to accept and pay for the goods, the seller may maintain an action against him for damages for non-acceptance.
>
> (2) The measure of damages is the estimated loss directly and naturally resulting, in the ordinary course of events, from the buyer's breach of contract.
>
> (3) Where there is an available market for the goods in question the measure of damages is prima facie to be ascertained by the difference between the contract price and the market or current price at the time or times when the goods ought to have been accepted or (if no time was fixed for acceptance) at the time of the refusal to accept.
>
> **51. Damages for non-delivery**
>
> (1) Where the seller wrongfully neglects or refuses to deliver the goods to the buyer, the buyer may maintain an action against the seller for damages for non-delivery.
>
> (2) The measure of damages is the estimated loss directly and naturally resulting, in the ordinary course of events, from the seller's breach of contract.
>
> (3) Where there is an available market for the goods in question the measure of damages is prima facie to be ascertained by the difference between the contract price and the market or current price of the goods at the time or times when they ought to have been delivered or (if no time was fixed) at the time of the refusal to deliver.
>
> (4) This section does not apply to a contract to which Chapter 2 of Part 1 of the Consumer Rights Act 2015 applies (but see the provision made about such contracts in section 19 of that Act).

NOTES

1. Both sections lay down a default rule of damages based on the difference between contract price and market price where there is an 'available market' for the goods not accepted or not supplied, as the case may be. If the goods in question cannot readily be resold (s. 50) or obtained from another source (s. 51)—as will be the case where the subject matter is unique—then there is no market price and the court must assess damages using evidence as to the value of the subject matter at the time and place of breach.

See *Hughes v Pendragon Sabre Ltd* [2016] EWCA Civ 18, where it was held there was no available market for a Porsche given the small number of such vehicles sold in the UK in any year.

2. Section 51(4) of the Sale of Goods Act (SGA) 1979, as amended by the Consumer Rights Act (CRA) 2105, provides that s. 51 no longer applies to a B2C (trader and consumer) contract. It makes reference to s. 19 CRA 2015 and s. 19(8) states: 'Section 28 makes provision about remedies for breach of a term about the time for delivery of goods.' Section 28 CRA 2015 is primarily concerned with the consumer's ability to terminate the contract on the grounds of non-delivery, and the point at which this ability arises. The section provides for the trader to reimburse the consumer for 'all payments made under the contract' in the event of non-delivery and s. 28(13) allows the consumer to seek other remedies (presumably a reference to damages for the extra cost of any substitute) 'where it is open to the consumer to do so'. There is no provision dealing with the measure of these damages and it seems that, given the non-applicability of s. 51 SGA 1979, the consumer buyer will have to establish their actual loss on the facts in each instance.

14.2.2 Measurement: cost of cure

14.2.2.1 When, if ever, can the cost of cure be recovered?

Ruxley Electronics & Construction Ltd v Forsyth
[1996] 1 AC 344 (HL)

The defendant contracted with the claimant for the construction of an enclosed swimming pool in his garden. The contract terms required that the maximum depth of the pool should be 7 feet 6 inches; in fact, it was later discovered to be only 6 feet 9 inches as a maximum, and only 6 feet at the diving point. When the claimants claimed the unpaid balance of the purchase price, the defendant counterclaimed for breach of contract. The trial judge found as a fact that the pool as constructed was perfectly safe to dive into, and that there was no difference in value between the swimming pool contracted for and that supplied. He refused to award the claimed cost of cure damages of £21,560 so that the specified depth could be achieved, on the basis that it would be unreasonable to award such damages, which were 'wholly disproportionate to the disadvantage' of having a pool of this depth, and he was not satisfied that the defendant intended to carry out the reconstruction work. Instead, the judge awarded £2,500 for loss of amenity.

The majority of the Court of Appeal (Staughton and Mann LJJs; Dillon LJ dissenting), allowing the appeal, awarded cost of cure damages on the basis that it was the only way in which to fulfil the defendant's contractual objective. Reasonableness was not a factor in its own right, but was relevant only to mitigation and, given that there was no cheaper way of compensating for the loss, it was not unreasonable to award such cost of cure damages. Although the defendant had given an undertaking to rebuild on the appeal, it was held that this was irrelevant.

Held (on appeal to the House of Lords, restoring the award of the trial judge): The cost of cure damages could be recovered only if it were reasonable to do so, and it would be reasonable to do so only if the cost were not out of all proportion to the benefit to be obtained. The intention to rebuild was relevant to the reasonableness of awarding cost of cure, because otherwise there would not be a substantial loss needing to be compensated. The House of Lords confirmed the award of £2,500 for loss of amenity.

LORD JAUNCEY: Damages are designed to compensate for an established loss and not to provide a gratuitous benefit to the aggrieved party, from which it follows that the reasonableness of an award of damages is to be linked directly to the loss sustained. If it is unreasonable in a particular case to award the cost of reinstatement it must be because the loss sustained does not extend to the need to reinstate. A failure to achieve the precise contractual objective does not necessarily result in the loss which is occasioned by a total failure. This was recognised by the High Court of Australia in the passage in *Bellgrove v Eldridge* [(1954) 90 CLR 613, 617–18], where it was stated that the cost of reinstatement work subject to the qualification of reasonableness was the extent of the loss, thereby treating reasonableness as a factor to be considered in determining what was that loss rather than, as the respondents argued, merely a factor in determining which of two alternative remedies were appropriate for a loss once established. Further support for this view is to be found in the following passage in the judgment of Sir Robert Megarry V-C in *Tito v Waddell (No. 2)* [1977] Ch 106, at 332:

> Per contra, if the plaintiff has suffered little or no monetary loss in the reduction of value of his land, and he has no intention of applying any damages towards carrying out the work contracted for, or its equivalent, I cannot see why he should recover the cost of doing work which will never be done. It would be a mere pretence to say that this cost was a loss and so should be recoverable as damages.

The Vice-Chancellor was as I understand it there saying that it would be unreasonable to treat as a loss the cost of carrying out work which would never in fact be done.

I take the example suggested during argument by my noble and learned friend Lord Bridge of Harwich. A man contracts for the building of a house and specifies that one of the lower courses of brick should be blue. The builder uses yellow brick instead. In all other respects the house conforms to the contractual specification. To replace the yellow bricks with blue would involve extensive demolition and reconstruction at a very large cost. It would clearly be unreasonable to award to the owner the cost of reconstructing because his loss was not the necessary cost of reconstruction of his house, which was entirely adequate for its design purpose, but merely the lack of aesthetic pleasure which he might have derived from the sight of blue bricks. Thus in the present appeal the respondent has acquired a perfectly serviceable swimming pool, albeit one lacking the specified depth. His loss is thus not the lack of a useable pool with consequent need to construct a new one. Indeed were he to receive the cost of building a new one and retain the existing one he would have recovered not compensation for loss but a very substantial gratuitous benefit, something which damages are not intended to provide.

What constitutes the aggrieved party's loss is in every case a question of fact and degree. Where the contract breaker has entirely failed to achieve the contractual objective it may not be difficult to conclude that the loss is the necessary cost of achieving that objective. Thus if a building is constructed so defectively that it is of no use for its designed purpose the owner may have little difficulty in establishing that his loss is the necessary cost of reconstructing. Furthermore in taking reasonableness into account in determining the extent of loss it is reasonableness in relation to the particular contract and not at large. Accordingly if I contracted for the erection of a folly in my garden which shortly thereafter suffered a total collapse it would be irrelevant to the determination of my loss to argue that the erection of such a folly which contributed nothing to the value of my house was a crazy thing to do . . .

However where the contractual objective has been achieved to a substantial extent the position may be very different.

It was submitted that where the objective of a building contract involved satisfaction of a personal preference the only measure of damages available for a breach involving failure to achieve such satisfaction was the cost of reinstatement. In my view this is not the case. Personal preference may well be a factor in reasonableness and hence in determining what loss has been suffered but it cannot per se be determinative of what that loss is.

My Lords, the trial judge found that it would be unreasonable to incur the cost of demolishing the existing pool and building a new and deeper one. In so doing he implicitly recognised that the respondent's loss did not extend to the cost of reinstatement. He was, in my view, entirely justified in reaching that conclusion. It therefore follows that the appeal must be allowed.

LORD MUSTILL: In my opinion there would indeed be something wrong if, on the hypothesis that cost of reinstatement and the depreciation in value were the only available measures of recovery, the rejection of the former necessarily entailed the adoption of the latter; and the court might be driven to opt for the cost of reinstatement, absurd as the consequence might often be, simply to escape from the conclusion that the promisor can please himself whether or not to comply with the wishes of the promisee which, as embodied in the contract, formed part of the consideration for the price. Having taken on the job the contractor is morally as well as legally obliged to give the employer what he stipulated to obtain, and this obligation ought not to be devalued. In my opinion, however, the hypothesis is not correct. There are not two alternative measures of damage, at opposite poles, but only one: namely, the loss truly suffered by the promisee. In some cases the loss cannot be fairly measured except by reference to the full cost of repairing the deficiency in performance. In others, and in particular those where the contract is designed to fulfil a purely commercial purpose, the loss will very often consist only of the monetary detriment brought about by the breach of contract. But these remedies are not exhaustive, for the law must cater for those occasions where the value of the promise to the promisee exceeds the financial enhancement of his position which full performance will secure. This excess, often referred to in the literature as the 'consumer surplus' (see for example the valuable discussion by Harris, Ogus and Phillips (1979) 95 LQR 581) is usually incapable of precise valuation in terms of money, exactly because it represents a personal, subjective and non-monetary gain. Nevertheless, where it exists the law should recognise it and compensate the promisee if the misperformance takes it away. The lurid bathroom tiles, or the grotesque folly instanced in argument by my noble and learned friend Lord Keith of Kinkel, may be so discordant with general taste that in purely economic terms the builder may be said to do the employer a favour by failing to install them. But this is too narrow and materialistic a view of the transaction. Neither the contractor nor the court has the right to substitute for the employer's individual expectation of performance a criterion derived from what ordinary people would regard as sensible. As my Lords have shown, the test of reasonableness plays a central part in determining the basis of recovery, and will indeed be decisive in a case such as the present when the cost of reinstatement would be wholly disproportionate to the non-monetary loss suffered by the employer. But it would be equally unreasonable to deny all recovery for such a loss. The amount may be small, and since it cannot be quantified directly there may be room for difference of opinion about what it should be. But in several fields the judges are well accustomed to putting figures to intangibles, and I see no reason why the imprecision of the exercise should be a barrier, if that is what fairness demands.

My Lords, once this is recognised the puzzling and paradoxical feature of this case, that it seems to involve a contest of absurdities, simply falls away. There is no need to remedy the injustice of awarding too little by unjustly awarding far too much. The judgment of the trial judge acknowledges that the employer has suffered a true loss and expresses it in terms of money. Since there is no longer any issue about the amount of the award, as distinct from the principle, I would simply restore his judgment by allowing the appeal.

LORD LLOYD [cited the judgment of Cardozo J in *Jacob & Youngs Inc. v Kent* (1921) 230 NY 239 and continued]: Cardozo J's judgment is important, because it establishes two principles which I believe to be correct and which are directly relevant to the present case: first, the cost of reinstatement is not the appropriate measure of damages if the expenditure would be out of all proportion to the benefit to be obtained, and secondly, the appropriate measure of damages in such a case is the difference in value, even though it would result in a nominal award.

The first of these principles is contrary to Staughton LJ's view [in the Court of Appeal] that the plaintiff is entitled to reinstatement, however expensive, if there is no cheaper way of providing what the contract requires. The second principle is contrary to the whole thrust of [counsel for the defendant's] argument that the judge had no alternative but to award the cost of reinstatement, once it became apparent that the difference in value produced a nil result.

[He then cited *Bellgrove v Eldridge* (1954) 90 CLR 613, *East Ham Borough Council v Bernard Sunley & Sons Ltd* [1966] AC 406, and *G. W. Atkins Ltd v Scott* (1991) 7 Const LJ 215, continuing:]

. . . It seems to me that in the light of these authorities . . . [counsel for the plaintiff] was right when he submitted, and Dillon LJ was right when he held, that mitigation is not the only area in which the concept of reasonableness has an impact on the law of damages.

If the court takes the view that it would be unreasonable for the plaintiff to insist on reinstatement, as where, for example, the expense of the work involved would be out of all proportion to the benefit to be obtained, then the plaintiff will be confined to the difference in value. If the judge had assessed the difference in value in the present case at, say, £5,000, I have little doubt that the Court of Appeal would have taken that figure rather than £21,560. The difficulty arises because the judge has, in the light of the expert evidence, assessed the difference in value as nil. But that cannot make reasonable what he has found to be unreasonable.

So I cannot accept that reasonableness is confined to the doctrine of mitigation. It has a wider impact . . .

How then does [counsel for the defendant] seek to support the majority judgment? It can only be, I think, by attacking the judge's finding of fact that the cost of rebuilding the pool would have been out of all proportion to the benefit to be obtained. [Counsel] argues that this was not an ordinary commercial contract but a contract for a personal preference . . .

I am far from saying that personal preferences are irrelevant when choosing the appropriate measure of damages ('predilections' was the word used by Ackner LJ in *G W Atkins Ltd v Scott* 7 Const LJ 215, 221, adopting the language of Oliver J in *Radford v De Froberville* [1977] 1 WLR 1262). But such cases should not be elevated into a separate category with special rules. If, to take an example mentioned in the course of argument, a landowner wishes to build a folly in his grounds, it is no answer to a claim for defective workmanship that many people might regard the presence of a well-built folly as reducing the value of the estate. The eccentric landowner is entitled to his whim, provided the cost of reinstatement is not unreasonable. But the difficulty of that line of argument in the present case is that the judge, as is clear from his judgment, took Mr Forsyth's personal preferences and predilections into account. Nevertheless, he found as a fact that the cost of reinstatement was unreasonable in the circumstances. The Court of Appeal ought not to have disturbed that finding . . .

Intention

I fully accept that the courts are not normally concerned with what a plaintiff does with his damages.

But it does not follow that intention is not relevant to reasonableness, at least in those cases where the plaintiff does not intend to reinstate. Suppose in the present case Mr Forsyth had died, and the action had been continued by his executors. Is it to be supposed that they would be able to recover the cost of reinstatement, even though they intended to put the property on the market without delay?

There is, as Staughton LJ observed, a good deal of authority to the effect that intention may be relevant to a claim for damages based on cost of reinstatement. The clearest decisions on the point are those of Sir Robert Megarry V-C in *Tito v Waddell (No. 2)* [1977] Ch 106 and Oliver J in *Radford v De Froberville* [1977] 1 WLR 1262 . . .

In the present case the judge found as a fact that Mr Forsyth's stated intention of rebuilding the pool would not persist for long after the litigation had been concluded. In these circumstances it would be 'mere pretence' to say that the cost of rebuilding the pool is the loss which he has in fact suffered. This is the critical distinction between the present case and the example given by Staughton LJ of a man who has had his watch stolen. In the latter case, the plaintiff is entitled to recover the value of the watch because that is the true measure of his loss. He can do what he wants with the damages. But if, as the judge found, Mr Forsyth had no intention of rebuilding the pool, he has lost nothing except the difference in value, if any . . .

Does Mr Forsyth's undertaking to spend any damages which he may receive on rebuilding the pool make any difference? Clearly not. He cannot be allowed to create a loss, which does not exist, in order to punish the defendants for their breach of contract. The basic rule of damages, to which exemplary damages are the only exception, is that they are compensatory not punitive.

NOTES

1. See Poole, 'Damages for breach of contract: compensation and "personal preferences"' (1996) 59 MLR 272.

2. Cost of cure damages are an example of compensation that takes account of the innocent party's subjective contractual preferences or subjective valuation of the contractual performance. This involves accepting that the innocent party's loss may be more than the objective difference in value measure and that the only way in which to compensate that party is to provide him with the means to fulfil that subjective requirement: see Harris, Ogus, and Phillips (1979) 95 LQR 581. In *Attorney-General v Blake* [2001] 1 AC 268, 282B, Lord Nicholls stated that 'the law recognises that a party to a contract may have an interest in performance which is not readily measured in terms of money'. See also Lord Goff (dissenting) in *Alfred McAlpine Construction v Panatown Ltd* [2001] 1 AC 518, 551 (extracted at *page 340, 7.6.2.1.1*).

3. The arguments in favour of awarding cost of cure damages on facts such as these are, first, that not to do so sends the wrong signals to the construction industry by indicating that builders will not have to pay substantial damages if they do not fulfil the subjective preferences of the other party specified in the contract where there is no difference in value, and, secondly, that it can be argued that, otherwise, the innocent party does not actually receive what he specifically requested under the contract. However, some limit on the ability to compensate for loss of subjective preferences is clearly called for in order to avoid windfall damages and unjust enrichment to the innocent party as a result of a damages award. The crucial factor in *Ruxley* appears to have been the relative triviality of the breach. Although Mr Forsyth's wishes were relevant, they could not dictate an award of cost of cure damages when reconstruction was not a reasonable course of action in the circumstances. However, the House of Lords did make it clear that there can be no objection in principle to fulfilling unusual tastes where these are contracted for.

4. The conclusion of Staughton and Mann LJJs in the Court of Appeal that there was no requirement to establish an intention to carry out the repair had also received support from Steyn and Dillon LJJ in *Darlington Borough Council v Wiltshier Northern Ltd* [1995] 1 WLR 68 (*page 338, 7.6.2.1*), but the intention to repair was revived by the House of Lords as being relevant to reasonableness and establishing the extent of the loss sustained (see the speech of Lord Lloyd in *Ruxley* at *page 736, 14.8.1.4*). Thus, there is a distinction between intention for the purposes of identifying a loss and the situation in which there is a clear loss, when it is no concern of the courts to assess what the claimant will do with his damages award: see Lord Clyde in *Alfred McAlpine v Panatown* (*page 340, 7.6.2.1.1*).

5. *Ruxley* was applied in *Birse Construction Ltd v Eastern Telegraph Co. Ltd* [2004] EWHC 2512 (TCC), [2004] 47 EG 164 (CS). The alleged breaches related to defective construction of a residential college. However, rather than seek to remedy these defects, the defendant had sought to sell the college, and there was no discount in the sale price to reflect the defects. The defendant sought substantial damages, but the judge, Humphrey Lloyd QC, held that it would be unreasonable to award cost of repair damages, particularly since there was no intention to repair. He confirmed the principle post-*Ruxley*, at [51]:

It is now clear from *Ruxley* . . . that the normal measure of damages for defective works is the cost of reinstatement (i.e., the cost of remedial works) but in every instance it has to be reasonable to apply it. Thus where that measure is out of proportion to the claimant's real loss then some other measure should be used.

On the facts, the judge also rejected a claim for loss of amenity damages on the basis that there was no evidence of that loss of amenity because the defendant had taken no steps to improve the appearance and comfort of the college in consequence of these breaches. This stems from his conclusion, which he described as 'pragmatic', that there was no 'real' loss.

This decision confirms the importance at the outset of clear identification of the loss. On the question of identification of loss, see the discussion of 'the broad ground' advocated by Lord Griffiths in *Linden Gardens Trust Ltd v Lenesta Sludge Disposals Ltd ('the St Martin's Property Appeal')* [1994] 1 AC 85 (*page 330, 7.6.2*).

The same principle of 'no loss' was applied in *Sunrock Aircraft Corporation Ltd v Scandinavian Airlines System Denmark-Norway-Sweden* [2007] EWCA Civ 882, [2007] 2 Lloyd's Rep 612. Two leased aircraft had been returned unrepaired and the normal measure of damages would be the cost of repair. No repair was carried out. Instead, the lessor had sold on the aircraft at a price that reflected the fact that there had been no diminution in the value of the aircraft. Nominal damages were therefore awarded.

6. It has been argued that the damages in a case like *Ruxley* should be restitutionary 'damages' to prevent unjust enrichment of the contractor by making him liable for the amount that he has saved by not performing the obligation in question. However, this was not argued in *Ruxley* and it was rejected in *Surrey v Bredero* [1993] 1 WLR 1361. For an outline of other suggested alternatives on damages, see Poole (1996) 59 MLR 272, pp. 284–5. Interestingly, in *Attorney-General v Blake* [1998] Ch 439, in the Court of Appeal, Lord Woolf MR identified the case of 'skimped performance', in which compensatory damages would be inadequate, as one of the situations in which restitutionary 'damages' for breach of contract ought to be available. However, this was rejected by the House of Lords in that case in relation to situations justifying the award of an account of profits. Lord Nicholls considered that 'skimped performance' might be addressed in other ways. It is therefore unlikely that this will be seen as a future solution.

7. For further discussion of the award for loss of amenity, *page 736, 14.8.1.4*.

? QUESTIONS

1. The example of the folly in the judgment of Lord Jauncey is a useful one in explaining why and where the line on recovery is likely to be drawn. What would the position be if the breach were that the folly had been constructed 6 inches to the right of the preferred spot?

2. Could counsel for Mr Forsyth have succeeded in an argument that Mr Forsyth would have been entitled to substantial damages had the pool been constructed to a depth of 7 feet 5 inches?

14.2.2.2 Cost of cure is not recoverable if there is a breach of a qualified contractual obligation

Watts v Morrow
[1991] 1 WLR 1421 (CA)

The claimants purchased a country house for £177,500 in reliance on the defendant's survey. When the claimants took possession, they discovered that there were substantial defects not mentioned in the report that required urgent repair, including renewal of the roof, windows, and floorboards. The true value of the house at the date of purchase was therefore only £162,500 (a difference in value of £15,000). The claimants carried out the repairs at a cost of nearly £34,000 and brought an action to recover those costs. At first instance, the cost of repairs was awarded.

Held: Although it was reasonable for the claimants to retain the property and carry out the repairs, the proper measure of damages was the difference in value, since this was the amount required to put the claimants in the position in which they would have been had the survey been carried out properly and the true value of the house paid. If they recovered the cost of repairs, they would be recovering damages for breach of warranty as to the condition of the house when no such warranty had been given.

RALPH GIBSON LJ: It was rightly acknowledged for [the plaintiffs] that proof that the plaintiff, properly advised, would not have bought the property does not by itself cause the diminution in value rule to be inapplicable. It was contended, however, that it becomes inapplicable if it is also proved that it is reasonable for the plaintiff to retain the property and to do the repairs. I cannot accept that submission for the following reasons.

(1) The fact that it is reasonable for the plaintiff to retain the property and to do the repairs seems to me to be irrelevant to determination of the question whether recovery of the cost of repairs is justified in order to put the plaintiff in the position in which he would have been if the contract, i.e. the promise to make a careful report, had been performed. The position is no different from that in *Philips v Ward* [1956] 1 WLR 471: the plaintiff would either have refused to buy or he would have negotiated a reduced price. Recovery of the cost of repairs after having gone into possession: that is to say in effect the acquisition of the house at the price paid less the cost of repairs at the later date of doing those repairs, is not a position into which the plaintiff could have been put as a result of proper performance of the contract. Nor is that cost recoverable as damages for breach of any promise by the defendant because, as stated above, there was no promise that the plaintiff would not incur any such cost.

(2) In the context of the contract proved in this case, I have difficulty in seeing when or by reference to what principle it would not be reasonable for the purchaser of a house to retain it and to do the repairs. He is free to do as he pleases. He can owe no duty to the surveyor to take any cheaper course. The measure of damages should depend, and in my view does depend, upon proof of the sum needed to put the plaintiff in the position in which he would have been if the contract was properly performed, and a reasonable decision by him to remain in the house and to repair it, upon discovery of the defects, cannot alter that primary sum, which remains the amount by which he was caused to pay more than the value of the house in its condition.

NOTE The surveyor owed a duty to exercise reasonable care and skill in carrying out the survey. He had not warranted that no repairs would be needed. To award the cost of repair would involve treating the surveyor's obligation as strict, when it was only qualified. Whereas the House of Lords in *Farley v Skinner* *(No. 2)* [2001] UKHL 49, [2002] 2 AC 732 (*page 738, 14.8.1.5*), disapproved of the distinction between strict and qualified obligations for the purposes of determining the availability of damages for distress and disappointment, it remains a relevant distinction in terms of recovery of the basic measure of damages.

14.3 Wasted expenditure

The injured party may wish to claim damages to compensate for wasted expenditure (often referred to as 'reliance loss'), i.e. the expenses incurred in preparing to perform or performing the contract that have now been wasted as a result of the breach. These damages are often termed 'reliance interest damages', but recent authority indicates that they are a species of expectation loss compensation: *Omak Maritime Ltd v Mamola Challenger Shipping Co.* [2010] EWHC 2026 (Comm), [2011] Bus LR 212. Had the breach not occurred, ordinarily these expenses would have been recovered as an integral element of the price paid.

When can such wasted expenditure damages be claimed?

14.3.1 Where expectation of profit is too speculative

Damages for wasted profits are available where that measure properly reflects the claimant's loss. *Morris-Garner v One Step (Support) Ltd* [2018] UKSC 20 makes it clear that the claimant does not have a right to elect between different measures of damages, but rather is entitled to damages which put the claimant in the same position as if the contract had been performed. An assessment based on loss of profit will be inappropriate where the claimant was not seeking to make a profit (as in *Royal Devon and Exeter NHS Foundation Trust v ATOS IT Services UK Ltd* [2017] EWHC 2197 (TCC)) or where profits are too speculative to be capable of assessment.

McRae v Commonwealth Disposals Commission
(1951) 84 CLR 377 (High Court of Australia)

The Commission invited tenders 'for the purchase of an oil tanker lying on Jourmaund Reef. The vessel is said to contain oil.' The claimant's tender of £285 was accepted. The claimant spent money in fitting out a salvage expedition, but there was no tanker at the location.

Held: The Commission was in breach of contract since it had promised that there was an oil tanker at the location given. However, since the Commission had not promised to deliver any oil or a tanker of any specified size, the claim for the loss of profit on the tanker and the oil was too speculative. The amount that the claimant was entitled to recover was £285 (the purchase price) and damages of £3,000 (being the cost of the salvage expedition, which was wasted as a result of the breach of promise that the oil tanker could be found at the stated location).

DIXON J and FULLAGER J [McTiernan J concurring]: [I]t is quite impossible to place any value on what the Commission purported to sell. The plaintiffs indeed, on one basis of claim which is asserted in their statement of claim, assessed their damages on the basis of an 'average-sized tanker, 8,000–10,000 ton oil tanker, valued at £1,000,000, allowing for the said tanker lying on Jourmaund Reef, valued at £250,000', and, for good measure, they added their 'estimated value of cargo of oil' at the figure of £50,000. But this, as a basis of damages, seems manifestly absurd. The Commission simply did not contract to deliver a tanker of any particular size or of any particular value or in any particular condition, nor did it contract to deliver any oil.

It was strongly argued for the plaintiffs that mere difficulty in estimating damages did not relieve a tribunal from the responsibility of assessing them as best it could. This is undoubtedly true. In the well-known case of *Chaplin v Hicks* [1911] 2 KB 786 Vaughan Williams LJ said:—'The fact that damages cannot be assessed with certainty does not relieve the wrongdoer of the necessity of paying damages for his breach of contract'. That passage, and others from the same case, are quoted by Street CJ in *Howe v Teefy* (1927) 27 SR (NSW) 301, but the learned Chief Justice himself states the position more fully. He says:—'The question in every case is: has there been any assessable loss resulting from the breach of contract complained of? There may be cases where it would be impossible to say that any assessable loss had resulted from a breach of contract, but, short of that, if a plaintiff has been deprived of something which has a monetary value, a jury is not relieved from the duty of assessing the loss merely because the calculation is a difficult one or because the circumstances do not admit of the damages being assessed with certainty' . . . It does not seem possible to say that 'any assessable loss has resulted from' non-delivery as such. In *Chaplin v Hicks* [1911] 2 KB 786, if the contract had been performed, the plaintiff would have had a real chance of winning the prize, and it seems proper enough to say that that chance was worth something. It is only in another and quite different sense that it could be said here that, if the contract had been performed, the plaintiffs would have had a chance of making a profit. The broken promise itself in *Chaplin v Hicks* [1911] 2 KB 786 was, in effect, 'to give the plaintiff a chance': here the element of chance lay in the nature of the thing contracted for itself. Here we seem to have something which cannot be assessed. If there were nothing more in this case than a promise to deliver a stranded tanker and a failure to deliver a stranded tanker, the plaintiffs would, of course, be entitled to recover the price paid by them, but beyond that, in our opinion, only nominal damages.

NOTE There is a distinction between a loss that is merely speculative and a 'real' loss of a chance, as in *Chaplin v Hicks*, where the court should seek to quantify the loss. See also *Allied Maples Group Ltd v Simmons & Simmons (a firm)* [1995] 1 WLR 1602, in which the claimant's loss resulting from the defendant's negligence depended on the hypothetical action of a third party. The Court of Appeal held that a claimant could succeed if it proved on the balance of probabilities that there was a substantial chance of the action being taken and not merely a speculative chance. This substantial chance could then be evaluated by the Court and would lie 'somewhere between something that just qualifies as real or substantial on the one hand and near certainty on the other'. In *Bank of Credit and Commerce International SA (in liquidation) v Ali (No. 3)* [2002] EWCA Civ 82, [2002] 3 All ER 750, the Court of Appeal confirmed the same principle and held, in relation to the loss of the chance of employment, that a claimant must show on the balance of probabilities that he had lost 'a substantial chance rather than a speculative one'.

Anglia Television Ltd v Reed
[1972] 1 QB 60 (CA)

The defendant, an American actor, contracted with the claimants to play the leading male role in a television play from 9 September to 11 October. On 3 September, the defendant repudiated. The claimants could not get a substitute and abandoned the production. The claimants sued the defendant for damages of £2,750, their total wasted expenditure on the production. The defendant argued that they could recover only the expenditure incurred after they made the contract with him (£854). The Court of Appeal awarded £2,750.

Held: Since the claimants had elected to claim their wasted expenditure instead of loss of profits, they could also recover pre-contract expenditure as long as it was reasonably in the contemplation of the parties as likely to be wasted if the contract was broken. (For a discussion of remoteness, *page 711, 14.6*).

LORD DENNING MR: Anglia Television do not claim their profit. They cannot say what their profit would have been on this contract if Mr Reed had come here and performed it. So, instead of claim for loss of profits, they claim for the wasted expenditure. They had incurred the director's fees, the designer's fees, the stage manager's and assistant manager's fees, and so on. It comes in all to £2,750. Anglia Television say that all that money was wasted because Mr Reed did not perform his contract.

Mr Reed's advisers take a point of law. They submit that Anglia Television cannot recover for expenditure incurred *before* the contract was concluded with Mr Reed. They can only recover the expenditure *after* the contract was concluded. They say that the expenditure *after* the contract was only £854.65, and that is all that Anglia Television can recover.

The master rejected that contention: he held that Anglia Television could recover the whole £2,750; and now Mr Reed appeals to this court.

. . . It seems to me that a plaintiff in such a case as this has an election: he can either claim for loss of profits; or for his wasted expenditure. But he must elect between them. He cannot claim both. If he has not suffered any loss of profits—or if he cannot prove what his profits would have been—he can claim in the alternative the expenditure which has been thrown away, that is, wasted, by reason of the breach. That is shown by *Cullinane v British 'Rema' Manufacturing Co. Ltd* [1954] 1 QB 292, 303, 308.

If the plaintiff claims the wasted expenditure, he is not limited to the expenditure incurred *after* the contract was concluded. He can claim also the expenditure incurred *before* the contract, provided that it was such as would reasonably be in the contemplation of the parties as likely to be wasted if the contract was broken. Applying that principle here, it is plain that, when Mr Reed entered into this contract, he must have known perfectly well that much expenditure had already been incurred on director's fees and the like. He must have contemplated—or, at any rate, it is reasonably to be imputed to him—that if he broke his contract, all that expenditure would be wasted, whether or not it was incurred before or after the contract. He must pay damages for all the expenditure so wasted and thrown away. This view is supported by the recent decision of Brightman J in *Lloyd v Stanbury* [1971] 1 WLR 535. There was a contract for the sale of land. In anticipation of the contract—and before it was concluded—the purchaser went to much expense in moving a caravan to the site and in getting his furniture there. The seller afterwards entered into a contract to sell the land to the purchaser, but afterwards broke his contract. The land had not increased in value, so the purchaser could not claim for any loss of profit. But Brightman J held, at p. 547, that he could recover the cost of moving the caravan and furniture, because it was 'within the contemplation of the parties when the contract was signed.' That decision is in accord with the correct principle, namely, that wasted expenditure can be recovered when it is wasted by reason of the defendant's breach of contract. It is true that, if the defendant had never entered into the contract, he would not be liable, and the expenditure would have been incurred by the plaintiff without redress: but, the defendant having made his contract and broken it, it does not lie in his mouth to say he is not liable, when it was because of his breach that the expenditure has been wasted.

NOTES

1. The expectation loss of lost profits on the television film was considered too speculative to be claimed since the film had not been sold to any television channel.

2. Although Lord Denning states that an election must be made between recovering loss of profits and wasted expenditure, the correct position is that the injured party cannot recover *gross* profit as expectation loss as well as the costs of performing the contract, since the gross profit figure includes those costs and it is not possible to recover twice for the same loss. There is no reason, however, why a claim could not be combined for net profit and wasted expenditure, since there would then be no double recovery.

14.3.2 Limitation on recovery of wasted expenditure damages

It is not possible to recover wasted expenditure damages to compensate the claimant for having made a 'bad bargain', since this would put an injured party in a better position than he would have been had the contract been performed.

C. & P. Haulage v Middleton
[1983] 1 WLR 1461 (CA)

The claimants granted the defendant a contractual licence to occupy their premises for the purposes of the defendant's work. The defendant spent money making the premises suitable by building an enclosing wall and putting in electricity, even though it was expressly provided that fixtures put in by him were not to be removed when the licence expired. The defendant was unlawfully ejected by the claimants, but the local authority allowed him to use his own garage for business purposes, which meant that he saved £60–£100 a week rent. The claimants claimed unpaid rent and the defendant counterclaimed for the expenditure on the improvements to the premises.

Held: The Court had to endeavour to put the defendant in the position in which he would have been had the contract been performed, and since the defendant had suffered no loss, his damages were nominal. To award him the wasted expenditure would have put him in a better position than he would have been in had the contract been properly performed.

ACKNER LJ: [The defendant] is not claiming for the loss of his bargain, which would involve being put in the position that he would have been in if the contract had been performed. He is not asking to be put in that position. He is asking to be put in the position he would have been in if the contract had never been made at all. If the contract had never been made at all, then he would not have incurred these expenses, and that is the essential approach he adopts in mounting this claim; because if the right approach is that he should be put in the position in which he would have been had the contract been performed, then it follows that he suffered no damage. He lost his entitlement to a further ten weeks of occupation after October 5, and during that period he involved himself in no loss of profit because he found other accommodation, and in no increased expense—in fact the contrary—because he returned immediately to his own garage, thereby saving whatever would have been the agreed figure which he would have to have paid the plaintiffs . . .

The case which I have found of assistance . . . is a case in the British Columbia Supreme Court: *Bowlay Logging Ltd v Domtar Ltd* [1978] 4 W.W.R. 105. Berger J., in a very careful and detailed judgment, goes through various English and American authorities and refers to the leading textbook writers, and I will only quote a small part of his judgment. At the bottom of p. 115 he refers to the work of Professor L.L. Fuller and William R. Perdue, Jr, in 'The Reliance Interest in Contract Damages: 1' (1936), 46 Yale Law Jour, 52 and their statement, at p. 79:

We will not in a suit for reimbursement for losses incurred in reliance on a contract knowingly put the plaintiff in a better position than he would have occupied had the contract been fully performed.

Berger J., at p. 116, then refers to *L. Albert & Son v Armstrong Rubber Co.* (1949) 178 F. 2d 182 in which Learned Hand C.J., speaking for the Circuit Court of Appeals, Second Circuit:

held that on a claim for compensation for expenses in part performance the defendant was entitled to deduct whatever he could prove the plaintiff would have lost if the contract had been fully performed.

What Berger J. had to consider was this, p. 105:

The parties entered into a contract whereby the plaintiff would cut timber under the defendant's timber sale, and the defendant would be responsible for hauling the timber away from the site of the timber sale. The plaintiff claimed the defendant was in breach of the contract as the defendant had not supplied sufficient trucks to make the plaintiff's operation, which was losing money, viable, and claimed not for loss of profits but for compensation for expenditures. The defendant argued that the plaintiff's operation lost money not because of a lack of trucks but because of the plaintiff's inefficiency, and, further, that even if the defendant had breached the contract the plaintiff should not be awarded damages because its operation would have lost money in any case.

This submission was clearly accepted because the plaintiff was awarded only nominal damages, and Berger J. said, at p. 117:

The law of contract compensates a plaintiff for damages resulting from the defendant's breach; it does not compensate a plaintiff for damages resulting from his making a bad bargain. Where it can be seen that the plaintiff would have incurred a loss on the contract as a whole, the expenses he has incurred are losses flowing from entering into the contract, not losses flowing from the defendant's breach. In these circumstances, the true consequence of the defendant's breach is that the plaintiff is released from his obligation to complete the contract—or in other words, he is saved from incurring further losses. If the law of contract were to move from compensating for the consequences of breach to compensating for the consequences of entering into contracts, the law would run contrary to the normal expectations of the world of

> commerce. The burden of risk would be shifted from the plaintiff to the defendant. The defendant would become the insurer of the plaintiff's enterprise. Moreover, the amount of the damages would increase not in relation to the gravity or consequences of the breach but in relation to the inefficiency with which the plaintiff carried out the contract. The greater his expenses owing to inefficiency, the greater the damages. The fundamental principle upon which damages are measured under the law of contract is restitutio in integrum. The principle contended for here by the plaintiff would entail the award of damages not to compensate the plaintiff but to punish the defendant . . .
>
> In my judgment, the approach of Berger J. is the correct one. It is not the function of the courts where there is a breach of contract knowingly, as this would be the case, to put a plaintiff in a better financial position than if the contract had been properly performed. In this case the defendant who is the plaintiff in the counterclaim, if he was right in his claim, would indeed be in a better position because, as I have already indicated, had the contract been lawfully determined as it could have been in the middle of December, there would have been no question of his recovering these expenses . . .

In *Omak Maritime Ltd v Mamola Challenger Shipping Co.* [2010] EWHC 2026 (Comm), [2011] Bus LR 212, Teare J explained that recovery of wasted expenditure was merely the appropriate means of giving effect to the party's expectation of performance and therefore was not different in nature from other expectation losses, although inevitably it is different in terms of the way in which its calculation is made.

Omak Maritime Ltd v Mamola Challenger Shipping Co.
[2010] EWHC 2026 (Comm), [2011] Bus LR 212

The owners of a supply vessel had chartered the vessel to the defendant time charterer. The terms of the charter contract required the owners to make expensive modifications to the vessel ahead of delivery to the charterer. Subsequently, the charterers repudiated and the owners terminated for this repudiatory breach. The owners were, in fact, able to earn considerably more post-repudiation when rechartering, since the market rate of hire was unusually much higher than the rate applicable to this charter. They had therefore not lost any profit as a result of the breach. The owners sought damages for the wasted expenditure that they had incurred for the modifications necessary to prepare the vessel ahead of the charter. They claimed that since such damages were designed to put them in the position in which they would have been had the charter contract not been made, the damages had nothing to do with the position in which the owners would have been had the charter contract been properly performed, so that the normal duty to mitigate in respect of the lost future hire did not apply. The arbitrators considered that the owners were entitled to succeed in the claim for wasted expenditure.

Held (on appeal, allowing the appeal): The claim for the modification expenses was for expenditure that had been incurred in the expectation that the contract would be performed (and so recovered as part of the cost of hire). It followed that this 'reliance loss' was a species of expectation loss and the aim was to secure the benefit for the claimant that it would have earned had the contract been properly performed (less the costs expended to earn that benefit), rather than to put the claimant in the position in which it would have been had the contract not been made at all. Overall, the owners had suffered no net loss as a result of the profits made on the recharter contracts and therefore could not recover the wasted expenditure. To allow this would have put them in a better position than that in which they would have been had the contract been performed.

TEARE J: 42 I consider that the weight of authority strongly suggests that reliance losses are a species of expectation losses and that they are neither, to use [counsel for the owners'] phrase, 'fundamentally different' nor awarded on a different 'juridical basis of claim'. That they are a species of expectation losses is supported by the decision of the Court of Appeal in *C & P Haulage v Middleton* and by very persuasive authorities in the United States, Canada and Australia . . .

44 It seems to me that the expectation loss analysis does provide a rational and sensible explanation for the award of damages in wasted expenditure cases. The expenditure which is sought to be recovered is incurred in expectation that that [*sic*] the contract will be performed. It therefore appears to me to be rational to have regard to the position that the claimant would have been in had the contract been performed.

45 If there were an independent principle pursuant to which expenditure incurred in expectation of the performance of a contract was recoverable without regard to what the position would have been had the contract been performed the defendant would in effect underwrite the claimant's decision to enter the contract. If the contract was unwise from his point of view, because his expenses were likely to exceed any gross profit, it is difficult to understand why the defendant should pay damages in an amount equal to that expenditure. His breach has not caused that loss. The claimant's expenditure should only be recoverable where the likely gross profit would at least cover that expenditure.

46 This was the approach of Chief Judge Learned Hand in *L Albert & Son v Armstrong Rubber Co* 178 F 2d 182 and of Berger J in *Bowlay Logging Ltd v Domtar Ltd* 87 DLR (3d) 325. That approach was followed and approved in *C & P Haulage v Middleton*.

47 The authorities therefore state a rational and sensible explanation for the view that the expectation loss principle underpins the award of damages in wasted expenditure cases. In some cases a contract can be shown to be a bad bargain. In other cases it may not be possible to show one way or the other whether the likely gross profits would at least equal the expenditure. In that latter type of case the question arises as to which party should bear the evidential burden of proof. Should the burden be on the claimant to show that the likely profits would at least equal his expenditure or on the defendant to show that the likely profits would not at least equal the claimant's expenditure? The authorities to which I have referred, in particular *L Albert & Son v Armstrong Rubber Co Ltd* and *CCC Films (London) Ltd v Impact Quadrant Films Ltd* [1985] QB 16 provide a rational and sensible explanation for the view that that burden should be on the defendant.

48 [Counsel for the owners] suggested several reasons why the expectation loss principle cannot provide a rational and sensible explanation for the award of damages in wasted expenditure cases.

49 First, he criticised the circumstance that it rests on an assumption (articulated in *Commonwealth of Australia v Amann Aviation Pty Ltd* 66 ALJR 123 by Deane J, in particular, at p 148, but by other judges in that case as well) that had the contract been performed the claimant would have recouped his expenditure out of profit. This criticism has been developed by Professor Treitel in an article ('Damages for Breach of Contract in the High Court of Australia') commenting on *Commonwealth of Australia v Amann Aviation* in (1992) 108 LQR 226. It is said that the assumption is not consistent with experience in that there are many unprofitable contracts, a point made by McHugh J in *Commonwealth of Australia v Amman* at pp 165–166. It is true that there are many unprofitable contracts. But it does not follow that the assumption leads to unrealistic results for the assumption is rebuttable by evidence. The important question is whether the defendant should bear the evidential burden of proof in this regard. The reasons why he should bear that burden have been explained by Chief Judge Learned Hand in *L Albert & Son v Armstrong Rubber Co* and by Hutchinson J in *CCC Films (London) Ltd v Impact Quadrant Films Ltd*. I am therefore not persuaded by [counsel's] first criticism, notwithstanding that it is supported by Professor Treitel.

50 I am however naturally troubled that Professor Treitel suggests, at p 229, that an award of reliance damages appears to be inconsistent with the principle in *Robinson v Harman* 1 Exch 850, that he suspects that the suggestion that such an award is consistent with that principle is a 'verbal trick' and that there are in reality two different principles, which are recognised by English law, which cannot be welded into one. Those principles are, firstly, that an award of damages on an expectancy basis is designed to put the claimant in the position he would have been in had the contract been performed and, secondly, that an award of damages on a reliance basis is designed to put the claimant in the position he would have been in had the contract not been made. This is [counsel's] argument.

51 [Counsel] illustrates this argument by observing that if a claim for reliance loss is to be explained as a claim for expectation loss it makes no sense to talk of a claimant having an *election* as to which loss he claims. And yet English law states that a claimant has such an election: see *Anglia Television Ltd v Reed* [1972] 1 QB 60 63–64, per Lord Denning MR. He submits that the need for an election shows that the two claims are fundamentally different.

52 However, the force of this criticism depends upon what is meant by an *election*. The criticism assumes that the right to elect between a claim for expectation losses and a claim for reliance losses is a right to elect between two inconsistent remedies or courses of action. An example of such an election is where, following a repudiatory breach, the innocent party must elect between affirming a contract and accepting the breach as terminating the contract. If, however, all that is meant is that a claimant may choose to frame his claim for damages on the reliance basis rather than on the expectancy basis, as suggested by Hutchinson J in *CCC Films (London) Ltd v Impact Quadrant Films Ltd* [1985] QB 16, 32, with the defendant having the opportunity to prove that the expenditure sought to be recovered would not in any event have been recouped because, for example, the contract was a loss making contract, then the right so to elect is not inconsistent with reliance losses being a form of expectation losses . . .

55 I am not therefore persuaded that the right to choose or elect between claiming damages on an expectancy basis or on a reliance basis indicates that there are two different principles at work. Both bases of damages are founded on, and are illustrations of, the fundamental principle in *Robinson v Harman* 1 Exch 850, for the reasons explained by Chief Judge Learned Hand in *L Albert & Son v Armstrong Rubber Co* 178 F 2d 182, by Berger J in *Bowlay Logging v Domtar Ltd* 87 DLR (3d) 325, by all members of the High Court of Australia in *Commonwealth of Australia v Amman Aviation Pty Ltd* 66 ALJR 123 and by the English courts in *C & P Haulage v Middleton* [1983] 1 WLR 1461 and *CCC Films (London) Ltd v Impact Quadrant Films Ltd* [1985] QB 16. Thus, notwithstanding my unfeigned respect for any opinion of Professor Treitel, I am unable to accept that there are two principles, rather than one, governing the law of damages for breach of contract.

56 [Counsel for the owners] has a further criticism, namely, that there are many contracts where a party does not expect or aim to make a profit, such as where purchases are made for pleasure or for charitable purposes. He suggests that the expectancy basis would deny recovery of wasted expenditure in such cases. I disagree. In such cases the defendant will usually be unable to show that the expenses exceeded the benefit expected to be obtained from the contract and thus the expense will be recoverable as damages. This was recognised by Deane J in *Commonwealth of Australia v Amman Aviation Pty Ltd*, at pp 148–149

> The presumption will not, however, be displaced . . . by the circumstance that the perceived 'benefit' which the plaintiff sought and for which [he] incurred the past expenditure is something which is of value only to the plaintiff or which, for some other reason, is not capable of being objectively valued in monetary terms . . .

57 I am therefore unpersuaded that the expectation loss principle cannot provide a rational and sensible explanation for the award of reliance losses . . .

Conclusion

64 . . . I am persuaded that the tribunal's decision was wrong in law . . .

65 The tribunal's error was to regard a claim for wasted expenses and a claim for loss of profits as two separate and independent claims which could not be 'mixed'. But the weight of authority clearly shows that both claims are illustrations of, and governed by, the fundamental principle stated by Parke B in *Robinson v Harman* 1 Exch 850. That principle requires the court to make a comparison between the claimant's position and what it would have been had the contract been performed. Where steps have been taken to mitigate the loss which would otherwise have been caused by a breach of contract that principle requires the benefits obtained by mitigation to be set against the loss which would otherwise have been sustained. To fail to do so would put the claimant in a better position than he would have been in had the contract been performed.

66 It follows that the appeal must be allowed and the award set aside.

NOTES

1. This judgment is important in clarifying the nature of wasted expenditure damages as expectation loss, rather than being based on the protection of 'reliance loss'. The result is compatible with previous case law, e.g. references to a claim for both net losses and wasted expenditure, or gross profit. It would seem preferable in future to use the term 'wasted expenditure' damages (as used in this book), since these damages can no longer be seen as 'reliance-based'. See also McLauchlan (2011) 127 LQR 23.

2. The significance of recognition of wasted expenditure as part of lost expectation is apparent when we look at the argument discussed at [58]–[59] of Teare J's judgment. In *Omak Maritime*, there was no 'net actual loss' overall as a result of the breach. In *C&P Haulage v Middleton*, the defendant was 'out of pocket' on the costs of the fixtures, although that was a loss that was not caused by the breach, but by the terms of the contract. *Omak Maritime* is significant, since the wasted expenditure loss was attributable to the breach—i.e. in the normal course, these expenses would have been recovered through the payment of the hire. This was a 'good bargain', whereas *C&P Haulage v Middleton* was clearly a 'bad bargain' case. It was important therefore to see the loss of expectation as a whole if the owner in *Omak Maritime* was not to recover wasted expenditure as a 'windfall' and so be in a better position than if the contract had been performed.

3. The *Omak* principle was considered in *Royal Devon and Exeter NHS Foundation Trust v ATOS IT Services UK Ltd* [2017] EWHC 2197 (TCC). The defendant agreed to provide an IT system for the claimant, designed for the provision of health record scanning, electronic document management, and associated services, at a price of just under £5 million. The claimant was dissatisfied from the outset, and after two years of the five-year contract served notice on the defendant alleging material breach as a result of the defendant's failure to remedy the alleged defects. The claimant sought damages of £7.9 million for wasted expenditure. O'Farrell J held that the loss suffered was in the form of expectation of a benefit, and there was a rebuttable presumption that such loss was at least equal to the expenditure, i.e. the amount which the claimant was prepared to pay for the benefit. In the present case the claimant had not sought to make a profit from the subject matter, so there was nothing to set off against the costs incurred. Characterizing the damages as compensation for loss of a functioning system rather than compensation for lost profits meant that an exclusion clause in the contract for loss of profits was inapplicable to the claim.

? QUESTION

Who bears the burden of proving whether the claimant has made a bad bargain, i.e. whether the expenditure would have been recouped?

14.3.3 Burden of proof in wasted expenditure claims

CCC Films (London) Ltd v Impact Quadrant Films Ltd
[1985] 1 QB 16

The claimant had been given a licence by the defendants to exploit, distribute, and exhibit films, but owing to the defendants' breach of contract, the claimant did not receive the tapes of the films and so could not exploit the licence.

Held: Where the claimant was claiming for wasted expenditure (here, the US$12,000 spent on the licence) and had been prevented by the defendant's breach of contract from recouping his expenditure, the onus was on the defendant to show that the expenditure would not have been recouped even if the claimant had been able to exploit the licence. On the facts, the defendants had not discharged this burden.

> HUTCHISON J (Hutchison J quoted from the judgment of Learned Hand CJ in *L. Albert & Son v Armstrong Rubber Co.* (1949) 178 F 2d 182, 189):
>
> > In cases where the venture would have proved profitable to the promisee there is no reason why he should not recover his expenses. On the other hand, on those occasions in which the performance would not have covered the promisee's outlay, such a result imposes the risk of the promisee's contract upon the promisor. We cannot agree that the promisor's default in performance should under this guise make him an insurer of the promisee's venture; yet it does not follow that the breach should not throw upon him the duty of showing that the value of the performance would in fact have been less than the promisee's outlay. It is often very hard to learn what the value of the performance would have been; and it is a common expedient, and a just one, in such situations to put the peril of the answer upon that party who by his wrong has made the issue relevant to the rights of the other. On principle, therefore, the proper solution would seem to be that the promisee may recover this outlay in preparation for the performance, subject to the privilege of the promisor to reduce it by as much as he can show that the promisee would have lost, if the contract had been performed.
>
> . . . It seems to me that at least in those cases where the plaintiff's decision to base his claim on abortive expenditure was dictated by the practical impossibility of proving loss of profit rather than by unfettered choice, any other rule would largely, if not entirely, defeat the object of allowing this alternative method of formulating the claim. This is because, notwithstanding the distinction to which I have drawn attention between proving a loss of net profit and proving in general terms the probability of sufficient returns to cover expenditure, in the majority of contested cases impossibility of proof of the first would probably involve like impossibility in the case of the second. It appears to me to be eminently fair that in such cases where the plaintiff has by the defendant's breach been prevented from exploiting the chattel or the right contracted for and, therefore, putting to the test the question of whether he would have recouped his expenditure, the general rule as to the onus of proof of damage should be modified in this manner.
>
> It follows that, the onus being on the defendants to prove that the expenditure incurred by the plaintiffs is irrecoverable because they would not have recouped their expenditure (and that onus admittedly not having been discharged), the plaintiffs are entitled to recover such expenditure as was wasted as a result of such breach or breaches of contract as they have proved.

Thus, where there is a claim for wasted expenditure, there is a presumption in favour of the innocent party to the effect that he would have recovered his wasted expenses had the contract been properly performed (and the breach not occurred). It is then for the guilty party to seek to bring evidence with a view to rebutting this. This is sensible, since it is the defendant's breach that undermines the ability to recover for these expenses.

NOTES

1. In *Omak Maritime Ltd v Mamola Challenger Shipping Co.* [2010] EWHC 2026 (Comm), [2011] Bus LR 212, Teare J had also relied on these authorities (see [45]–[47]) to conclude that the burden of proof lay on the defendant to establish that the claimant seeking to recover wasted expenditure would not have recovered that expenditure had the contract been properly performed.

2. In *Yam Seng Pte Ltd v International Trade Corporation Ltd* [2013] EWHC 111 (QB), [2013] 1 CLC 662, [2013] 1 All ER (Comm) 1321, Leggatt J rejected Yam Seng's claim for loss of the profits that it would allegedly have made had ITC performed its obligations under the distribution agreement for the whole of the contract period, because it had failed to prove what profit it would have made or even that it would have made a profit at all had ITC fully performed its obligations. However, Yam Seng was entitled to recover its net expenditure incurred in performing the agreement (wasted expenditure).

Yam Seng Pte Ltd v International Trade Corporation Ltd
[2013] EWHC 111 (QB), [2013] 1 CLC 662, [2013] 1 All ER (Comm) 1321

LEGGATT J:

Claim for wasted expenditure

186 ITC's alternative claim is for its net expenditure incurred as a result of entering into the agreement. The basis on which wasted expenditure can be recovered as damages for breach of contract was considered by Teare J in *Omak Maritime Ltd v Mamola Challenger Shipping Co* [2010] 2 CLC 194. In his masterly judgment Teare J has shown that awarding compensation for wasted expenditure is not an exception to the fundamental principle stated by Baron Parke in *Robinson v Harman* (1848) 1 Ex 850 at 855 that the aim of an award of damages for breach of contract is to put the injured party, so far as money can do it, in the same position as if the contract had been performed, but is a method of giving effect to that fundamental principle. That conclusion must logically follow once it is recognised, as it was by the Court of Appeal in *C & P Haulage v Middleton* [1983] 1 WLR 1461, that the court will not on a claim for reimbursement of losses incurred in reliance on the contract knowingly put the claimant in a better position than if the contract had been performed.

187 The advantage of claiming damages on the 'reliance' basis is not that the claimant can recover expenditure which would have been wasted even if the contract had been performed but that, where such a claim is made, the burden of proof lies on the defendant to show that the expenditure would not have been recouped and would have been wasted in any event: see *CCC Films (London) Ltd v Impact Quadrant Films* [1985] QB 16. In this regard the English courts have adopted the approach stated by Learned Hand CJ in *L Albert & Son v Armstrong Rubber Co* 178 F 2d 182 (1949):

> We cannot agree that the promisor's default in performance should under this guise make him the insurer of the promisee's venture; yet it does not follow that the breach should not throw upon him the duty of showing that the value of the performance would in fact have been less than the promisee's outlay. It is often very hard to learn what the value of the performance would have been; and it is a common expedient, and a just one, in such situations to put the peril of the answer upon that party who by his wrong has made the issue relevant to the rights of the other.

188 The 'common expedient' referred to by Chief Judge Learned Hand reflects a general theme which runs through the law of damages. On the one hand, the general rule that the burden lies on the claimant to prove its case applies to proof of loss just as it does to the other elements of the claimant's cause of action. But on the other hand, the attempt to estimate what benefit the claimant has lost as a result of the defendant's breach of contract or other wrong can sometimes involve considerable uncertainty; and courts will do the best they can not to allow difficulty of estimation to deprive the claimant of a remedy, particularly where that difficulty is itself the result of the defendant's wrongdoing. As Vaughan Williams LJ said in *Chaplin v Hicks* [1911] 2 KB 786 at 792: 'the fact that damages cannot be assessed with

certainty does not relieve the wrong-doer of the necessity of paying damages for his breach of contract.'
Accordingly the court will attempt so far as it reasonably can to assess the claimant's loss even where
precise calculation is impossible. The court is aided in this task by what may be called the principle of
reasonable assumptions—namely, that it is fair to resolve uncertainties about what would have happened but for the defendant's wrongdoing by making reasonable assumptions which err if anything on
the side of generosity to the claimant where it is the defendant's wrongdoing which has created those
uncertainties . . .

190 It seems to me that the (rebuttable) presumption that the claimant would have recouped expenditure incurred in reliance on the defendant's performance of the contract is an illustration of this approach.
Parties in normal circumstances contract and incur expenditure in pursuance of their contract in the
expectation of making a profit. Where money has been spent in that expectation but the defendant's
breach of contract has prevented that expectation from being put to the test, it is fair to assume that the
claimant would at least have recouped its expenditure had the contract been performed unless and to
the extent that the defendant can prove otherwise.

191 Applying this approach to the present case, ITC has not attempted to discharge the burden of
showing what financial return Yam Seng would have made if ITC had not been in breach of contract. It
is reasonable to suppose that if ITC had made all the Manchester United products available in accordance with the timetable promised and had shipped all orders promptly, Yam Seng would have made
more sales than it in fact did. What the proceeds of such sales would have been and whether they
would have been sufficient to defray Yam Seng's expenditure including its expenditure on marketing
and promoting the fragrance is impossible for me to determine. ITC has not put forward any estimate
of what loss, if any, Yam Seng would have suffered in those circumstances and I am unable to make
such an assessment.

192 I therefore conclude that Yam Seng is entitled to recover as damages for ITC's breach of contract
its net expenditure incurred in performing the agreement.

14.4 Time for assessment of loss and recovery for actual loss

The general principle is that damages are to be assessed at the time of breach (or when the loss
is suffered), which usually occurs at the time when performance became due: *Miliangos v George
Frank (Textiles) Ltd* [1976] AC 443, p. 468; and *Johnson v Agnew* [1980] AC 367, pp. 400–1. This
is because it is the earliest date on which the claimant could be expected to mitigate, i.e. to
find the substitute performance (*page 730, 14.7*), or to take other appropriate remedial action.
However, it is accepted that the breach date principle may not be appropriate in all cases, e.g.
Lord Wilberforce in *Johnson v Agnew*, at p. 400, stated: '[B]ut this is not an absolute rule: if
to follow it would give rise to injustice, the court has power to fix such other date as may be
appropriate in the circumstances.'

Golden Strait Corporation v Nippon Yusen Kubishika Kaisha, The Golden Victory
[2007] UKHL 12, [2007] 2 AC 353 (HL)

The charterer had chartered *The Golden Victory* from the shipowner under a time charterparty
commencing in July 1998. The earliest date for its termination was December 2005. Clause 33 of

the charter provided that if war were to break out between named countries, then both parties would be entitled to terminate. The charterer repudiated on 14 December 2001 by redelivering the ship and the shipowner accepted that repudiation on 17 December. The shipowner claimed to be entitled to damages measured by reference to the full remaining term of the repudiated time charter (four years). However, in the meantime, the second Gulf War broke out in March 2003, which was an event that would have justified the charterer terminating the charter under clause 33. The charterer claimed that a party in breach could rely on subsequent events to reduce the damages, so that no damages could be recovered after March 2003 (meaning that the damages would cover a period of 14 months instead of four years), whereas the shipowner alleged that, in the interests of commercial certainty and finality, the loss should be measured at the date of acceptance of the repudiation and that anything that might have happened afterwards was irrelevant.

Held (Lords Scott, Carswell, and Brown; Lords Bingham and Walker dissenting): Damages may be reduced where subsequent events are known to the court at the date of the hearing (when the assessment of quantum occurs) and those events *have reduced* the actual loss suffered. Since contractual principles required the innocent party (shipowner) to be placed in the position in which it would have been had the contract had been properly performed, the most important principle was to compensate for actual loss suffered rather than commercial certainty and finality, which is inherent in the breach date rule. It followed that a subsequent event *that occurred* before the assessment of damages was made could be taken into account when calculating damages for loss caused by the breach.

LORD SCOTT OF FOSCOTE: 28 . . . First, it is common ground that, if the charterparty had still been on foot when, in March 2003, hostilities between the United States of America and the United Kingdom on one side and Iraq on the other side began, the charterers would have exercised their clause 33 right to terminate the charterparty. Second, it is common ground that as at 17 December 2001 the chance that any hostilities triggering the clause 33 right of termination would break out was no more than a possibility and certainly not a probability.

29 My Lords, the answer to the question at issue must depend on principles of the law of contract. It is true that the context in this case is a charterparty, a commercial contract. But the contractual principles of the common law relating to the assessment of damages are no different for charterparties, or for commercial contracts in general, than for contracts which do not bear that description. The fundamental principle governing the quantum of damages for breach of contract is long established and not in dispute. The damages should compensate the victim of the breach for the loss of his contractual bargain. The principle was succinctly stated by Parke B in *Robinson v Harman* (1848) 1 Exch 850, 855 and remains as valid now as it was then:

> The rule of the common law is, that where a party sustains a loss by reason of a breach of contract, he is, so far as money can do it, to be placed in the same situation, with respect to damages, as if the contract had been performed.

If the contract is a contract for performance over a period, whether for the performance of personal services, or for supply of goods, or, as here, a time charter, the assessment of damages for breach must proceed on the same principle, namely, the victim of the breach should be placed, so far as damages can do it, in the position he would have been in had the contract been performed.

30 If a contract for performance over a period has come to an end by reason of a repudiatory breach but might, if it had remained on foot, have terminated early on the occurrence of a particular event, the chance of that event happening must, it is agreed, be taken into account in an assessment of the damages

payable for the breach. And if it is certain that the event will happen, the damages must be assessed on that footing. In *The Mihalis Angelos* [1971] 1 QB 164, 210, Megaw LJ referred to events 'predestined to happen'. He said that

> if it can be shown that those events were, at the date of acceptance of the repudiation, predestined to happen, then . . . the damages which [the claimant] can recover are not more than the true value, if any, of the rights which he has lost, having regard to those predestined events.

Another way of putting the point being made by Megaw LJ is that the claimant is entitled to the benefit, expressed in money, of the contractual rights he has lost, but not to the benefit of more valuable contractual rights than those he has lost. In *Wertheim v Chicoutimi Pulp Co* [1911] AC 301, 307, Lord Atkinson referred to

> the general intention of the law that, in giving damages for breach of contract, the party complaining should, so far as it can be done by money, be placed in the same position as he would have been in if the contract had been performed

and, in relation to a claim by a purchaser for damages for late delivery of goods where the purchaser had, after the late delivery, sold the goods for a higher price than that prevailing in the market on the date of delivery, observed, at p 308, that

> the loss he sustains must be measured by that price, unless he is, against all justice, to be permitted to make a profit by the breach of contract, be compensated for a loss he never suffered, and be put, as far as money can do it, not in the same position in which he would have been if the contract had been performed, but in a much better position.

31 The result contended for by the appellant in the present case is, to my mind, similar to that contemplated by Lord Atkinson in the passage last cited. If the charterparty had not been repudiated and had remained on foot, it would have been terminated by the charterers in or shortly after March 2003 when the Second Gulf War triggered the clause 33 termination option. But the owners are claiming damages up to 6 December 2005 on the footing, now known to be false, that the charterparty would have continued until then. It is contended that because the charterers' repudiation and its acceptance by the owners preceded the March 2003 event, the rule requiring damages for breach of contract to be assessed at the date of breach requires that event to be ignored.

32 That contention, in my opinion, attributes to the assessment of damages at the date of breach rule an inflexibility which is inconsistent both with principle and with the authorities. The underlying principle is that the victim of a breach of contract is entitled to damages representing the value of the contractual benefit to which he was entitled but of which he has been deprived. He is entitled to be put in the same position, so far as money can do it, as if the contract had been performed. The assessment at the date of breach rule can usually achieve that result. But not always. In *Miliangos v George Frank (Textiles) Ltd* [1976] AC 443, 468–469 Lord Wilberforce referred to 'the general rule' that damages for breach of contract are assessed as at the date of breach but went on to observe that

> It is for the courts, or for arbitrators, to work out a solution in each case best adapted to giving the injured plaintiff that amount in damages which will most fairly compensate him for the wrong which he has suffered

and, when considering the date at which a foreign money obligation should be converted into sterling, chose the date that 'gets nearest to securing to the creditor exactly what he bargained for'. If a money award of damages for breach of contract provides to the creditor a lesser or a greater benefit than the creditor bargained for, the award fails, in either case, to provide a just result.

[Lord Scott discussed *Dodd Properties (Kent) Ltd v Canterbury City Council* [1980] 1 WLR 433, *County Personnel (Employment Agency) Ltd v Alan R Pulver & Co* [1987] 1 WLR 916, *County Personnel (Employment Agency) Ltd v Alan R Pulver & Co* [1987] 1 WLR 916, *Lavarack v Woods of Colchester Ltd*

[1967] 1 QB 278 and *North Sea Energy Holdings NV v Petroleum Authority of Thailand* [1999] 1 Lloyd's Rep 483, and continued] . . .

34 The assessment at the date of breach rule is particularly apt to cater for cases where a contract for the sale of goods in respect of which there is a market has been repudiated. The loss caused by the breach to the seller or the buyer, as the case may be, can be measured by the difference between the contract price and the market price at the time of the breach. The seller can re-sell his goods in the market. The buyer can buy substitute goods in the market. Thereby the loss caused by the breach can be fixed. But even here some period must usually be allowed to enable the necessary arrangements for the substitute sale or purchase to be made: see, e g *Kaines (UK) Ltd v Österreichische Warrenhandelsgesellschaft* [1993] 2 Lloyd's Rep 1. The relevant market price for the purpose of assessing the quantum of the recoverable loss will be the market price at the expiration of that period.

35 In cases, however, where the contract for sale of goods is not simply a contract for a one-off sale, but is a contract for the supply of goods over some specified period, the application of the general rule may not be in the least apt. Take the case of a three-year contract for the supply of goods and a repudiatory breach of the contract at the end of the first year. The breach is accepted and damages are claimed but before the assessment of the damages an event occurs that, if it had occurred while the contract was still on foot, would have been a frustrating event terminating the contract, e g legislation prohibiting any sale of the goods. The contractual benefit of which the victim of the breach of contract had been deprived by the breach would not have extended beyond the date of the frustrating event. So on what principled basis could the victim claim compensation attributable to a loss of contractual benefit after that date? Any rule that required damages attributable to that period to be paid would be inconsistent with the overriding compensatory principle on which awards of contractual damages ought to be based.

36 The same would, in my opinion, be true of any anticipatory breach the acceptance of which had terminated an executory contract. The contractual benefit for the loss of which the victim of the breach can seek compensation cannot escape the uncertainties of the future. If, at the time the assessment of damages takes place, there were nothing to suggest that the expected benefit of the executory contract would not, if the contract had remained on foot, have duly accrued, then the quantum of damages would be unaffected by uncertainties that would be no more than conceptual. If there were a real possibility that an event would happen terminating the contract, or in some way reducing the contractual benefit to which the damages claimant would, if the contract had remained on foot, have become entitled, then the quantum of damages might need, in order to reflect the extent of the chance that that possibility might materialise, to be reduced proportionately. The lodestar is that the damages should represent the value of the contractual benefits of which the claimant had been deprived by the breach of contract, no less but also no more. But if a terminating event had happened, speculation would not be needed, an estimate of the extent of the chance of such a happening would no longer be necessary and, in relation to the period during which the contract would have remained executory had it not been for the terminating event, it would be apparent that the earlier anticipatory breach of contract had deprived the victim of the breach of nothing. In *Bwllfa and Merthyr Dare Steam Collieries (1891) Ltd v Pontypridd Waterworks Co* [1903] AC 426, the Earl of Halsbury LC, at p 429, rejected the proposition that 'because you could not arrive at the true sum when the notice was given, you should shut your eyes to the true sum now you do know it, because you could not have guessed it then' and Lord Robertson said, at p 432, that 'estimate and conjecture are superseded by facts as the proper media concludendi' and, at p 433, that 'as in this instance facts are available, they are not to be shut out' . . .

37 My noble and learned friend, Lord Bingham, in what has been rightly described as a strong dissent, has referred, in para 9, to the overriding compensatory principle that the injured party is entitled

to such damages as will put him in the same financial position as if the contract had been performed. On the facts of the present case, however, the contract contained clause 33 and would not have required any performance by the charterers after March 2003. It should follow that, in principle, the owners, the injured party, are not entitled to any damages in respect of the period thereafter. As at the date of the owners' acceptance of the charterers' repudiation of the charterparty, the proposition that what at that date the owners had lost was a charterparty with slightly less than four years to run requires qualification. The charterparty contained clause 33. The owners had lost a charterparty which contained a provision that would enable the charterers to terminate the charterparty if a certain event happened. The event did happen. It happened before the damages had been assessed. It was accepted in argument before your Lordships that the owners' charterparty rights would not, in practice, have been marketable for a capital sum. The contractual benefit of the charterparty to the owners, the benefit of which they were deprived by the repudiatory breach, was the right to receive the hire rate during the currency of the charterparty. The termination of the charterparty under clause 33 would necessarily have brought to an end that right.

38 The arguments of the owners offend the compensatory principle. They are seeking compensation exceeding the value of the contractual benefits of which they were deprived. Their case requires the assessor to speculate about what might happen over the period 17 December 2001 to 6 December 2005 regarding the occurrence of a clause 33 event and to shut his eyes to the actual happening of a clause 33 event in March 2003. The argued justification for thus offending the compensatory principle is that priority should be given to the so-called principle of certainty. My Lords, there is, in my opinion, no such principle. Certainty is a desideratum and a very important one, particularly in commercial contracts. But it is not a principle and must give way to principle. Otherwise incoherence of principle is the likely result. The achievement of certainty in relation to commercial contracts depends, I would suggest, on firm and settled principles of the law of contract rather than on the tailoring of principle in order to frustrate tactics of delay to which many litigants in many areas of litigation are wont to resort. Be that as it may, the compensatory principle that must underlie awards of contractual damages is, in my opinion, clear and requires the appeal in the case to be dismissed. I wish also to express my agreement with the reasons given by my noble and learned friends, Lord Carswell and Lord Brown of Eaton-under-Heywood, for coming to the same conclusion.

LORD BINGHAM OF CORNHILL [dissenting]:

22 The thrust of the charterers' argument was that the owners would be unfairly over-compensated if they were to recover as damages sums which, with the benefit of hindsight, it is now known that they would not have received had there been no accepted repudiation by the charterers. There are, in my opinion, several answers to this. The first is that contracts are made to be performed, not broken. It may prove disadvantageous to break a contract instead of performing it. The second is that if, on their repudiation being accepted, the charterers had promptly honoured their secondary obligation to pay damages, the transaction would have been settled well before the Second Gulf War became a reality. The third is that the owners were, as the arbitrator held . . . entitled to be compensated for the value of what they had lost on the date it was lost, and it could not be doubted that what the owners lost at that date was a charterparty with slightly less than four years to run. This was a clear and, in my opinion, crucial finding, but it was not mentioned in either of the judgments below, nor is it mentioned by any of my noble and learned friends in the majority. On the arbitrator's finding, it was marketable on that basis. I can readily accept that the value of a contract in the market may be reduced if terminable on an event which the market judges to be likely but not certain, but that was not what the arbitrator found to be the fact in this case. There is, with respect to those who think otherwise, nothing artificial in this approach. If a party is compensated

for the value of what he has lost at the time when he loses it, and its value is at that time for any reason depressed, he is fairly compensated. That does not cease to be so because adventitious later events reveal that the market at that time was depressed by the apprehension of risks that did not eventuate. A party is not, after all, obliged to accept a repudiation: he can, if he chooses, keep the contract alive, for better or worse. By describing the prospect of war in December 2001 as 'merely a possibility', the expression twice used by the arbitrator in para 59 of his reasons, the arbitrator can only have meant that it was seen as an outside chance, not affecting the marketable value of the charter at that time.

23 There is, however, a further answer which I, in common with the arbitrator, consider to be of great importance. He acknowledged the force of arguments advanced by the owners based on certainty ('generally important in commercial affairs'), finality ('the alternative being a running assessment of the state of play so far as the likelihood of some interruption to the contract is concerned'), settlement ('otherwise the position will remain fluid'), consistency ('the idea that a party's accrued rights can be changed by subsequent events is objectionable in principle') and coherence ('the date of repudiation is the date on which rights and damages are assessed'). Langley J [2005] 1 Lloyd's Rep 443 [first instance in *The Golden Victory*] was not greatly impressed by the charterers' argument along these lines, observing, at paras 13 and 35, that although certainty is a real and beneficial target, it is not easily achieved, and the charterparty contained within it the commercial uncertainty of the war clause. Lord Mance [Court of Appeal in this case] similarly said [2006] 1 WLR 533, 543–544, para 24:

> Certainty, finality and ease of settlement are all of course important general considerations. But the element of uncertainty, resulting from the war clause, meant that the owners were never entitled to absolute confidence that the charter would run for its full seven-year period. They never had an asset which they could bank or sell on that basis. There is no reason why the transmutation of their claims to performance of the charter into claims for damages for non-performance of the charter should improve their position in this respect.

I cannot, with respect, accept this reasoning. The importance of certainty and predictability in commercial transactions has been a constant theme of English commercial law at any rate since the judgment of Lord Mansfield CJ in *Vallejo v Wheeler* (1774) 1 Cowp 143, 153, and has been strongly asserted in recent years in cases such as *Scandinavian Trading Tanker Co AB v Flota Petrolera Ecuatoriana (The Scaptrade)* [1983] QB 529, 540–541, [1983] 2 AC 694, 703–704; *Homburg Houtimport BV v Agrosin Private Ltd (The Starsin)* [2004] 1 AC 715, 738; *Jindal Iron and Steel Co Ltd v Islamic Solidarity Shipping Co Jordan Inc (The Jordan II)* [2005] 1 WLR 1363, 1370. Professor Sir Guenter Treitel QC read the Court of Appeal's judgment as appearing to impair this quality of certainty ('Assessment of Damages for Wrongful Repudiation' (2007) 123 LQR 9–18) and I respectfully share his concern.

24 On my reading of *The Seaflower* [2000] 2 Lloyd's Rep 37 (see para 19 above), I do not think the arbitrator was bound by that decision to reach the conclusion he did. If he was, I respectfully think Timothy Walker J was wrong to analyse *The Mihalis Angelos* [1971] 1 QB 164 as he did in that case. But on the facts he was entitled to value the owners' charter in *The Seaflower* at two months' purchase as of the repudiation acceptance date. In the present case, by contrast, the arbitrator found four years' purchase (less a few days) as the true market value of the charterparty on the repudiation acceptance date.

NOTES

1. See Coote, 'Breach, anticipatory breach or the breach anticipated' (2007) 123 LQR 503.

2. This majority view of their Lordships followed the approach taken in the lower courts and is based on the principle that, where there is knowledge, speculation is not required. There was indeed knowledge of the fact that the Gulf War had broken out in March 2003. However, instead of judging the certainty of outcomes for the future assessed at the date of the acceptance of the repudiation (which would be

mitigating as from that date), the majority assumed something that was far from 'predestined to happen' at the date of repudiation.

3. This is a difficult decision for commercial lawyers, whose primary focus is commercial certainty and who regard breach, and its acceptance terminating the contract, as crystallizing the loss at that date: see the important dissenting speeches of Lord Bingham, particularly at [14], and of Lord Walker. It is important to remember that the shipowners had accepted the repudiatory breach; they had not affirmed it. Their duty was therefore to mitigate their loss, and that loss should be assessed at the acceptance date based on predestined losses at that time (not possibilities at that time). Indeed, the normal reaction and expectation in such instances would be for the owner to recharter the vessel in the market and to recover for any loss as the difference between this market rate and the rate under the charter for the remainder of the term.

4. The result of this decision is similar to treating termination for repudiatory breach as if the contract had been affirmed, and the risk of subsequent events would then fall on the party who chose to affirm: *Fercometal SARL v Mediterranean Shipping Co. SA* [1989] AC 788. It also has the unfortunate side-effect of implicitly encouraging the delay of the hearing for the assessment of quantum in such cases in the hope that a war clause or similar will be assumed to have been activated. On termination, the loss should have become fixed, subject only to mitigation, which might reduce the damages otherwise payable.

5. This principle seems to have acquired a life of its own in subsequent case law. At first instance in *Force India Formula One Team Ltd v Etihad Airways PJSC* [2009] EWHC 2768 (QB), [2010] ETMR 14, the judge allowed Force India to recover damages for wrongful termination, which included points gained in the championship in subsequent seasons. There was no need to speculate about the contingency of the points arising in subsequent seasons, i.e. to make a claim based on loss of the chance of acquiring a bonus based on those points, since there was evidence that the points had in fact been gained. The judge could see no reason not to apply the principle in *The Golden Victory* in order to assess damages in the light of events subsequent to the breach.

6. This principle was also applied in *Glory Wealth Shipping Pte Ltd v Korea Line Corporation, The Wren* [2011] EWHC 1819, [2011] 2 Lloyd's Rep 370, when, following an early repudiation of a time charter as a consequence of a collapse in the market, the owners terminated and claimed damages. Whereas the normal measure would be the difference between the contract rate and market rate for the remainder of the charter, in these circumstances there was no market for the entire period of the remainder of the charter. Nevertheless, the owner had obtained substitute fixtures in the spot market in the short term. This seems to be no more than the application of principles of mitigation for the purposes of assessing the measure of damages recoverable. The owner was under a duty to seek to minimize the loss.

7. In *Ageas (UK) Ltd v Kwik-Fit (GB) Ltd* [2014] EWHC 2178 (QB), [2014] Bus LR 1338, Popplewell J went as far as advocating a principle of 'hindsight' based on *The Golden Victory* as long as that application of 'hindsight' did not conflict with any contractual allocation of the risk of subsequent events. This was on the basis that, at [32], a judge should 'avail himself of all the information at hand at the time of making his award which may be laid before him' and refuse to 'listen to conjecture on a matter which has become an accomplished fact'.

The case concerned a claim for breach of warranty under a share purchase agreement. The defendant's insurer had argued that, in order to give effect to the compensatory principle, the assessment of damages should take into account developments after the valuation date of the target company (so-called 'hindsight'). Popplewell J accepted that, where the value of the target company depended on a future contingency, any relevant events after the valuation date relating to this contingency could be taken into account to give effect to the compensatory principle.

POPPLEWELL J: 36 This seems to me consistent with principle and justice. In the course of argument I posited an example of the sale of a racehorse, which the seller warranted to be free from disease; its value at the date of sale was to be measured by reference to an assessment of the races it might win and its consequent stud value; at the date of sale it had a latent disease which increased the risk of it suffering a career ending lameness at some stage; if the parties had known the true position at the date of sale the horse would have been valued at half the price because of this increased risk of lameness; by the time damages came to be assessed, however, the horse's racing days were over and it was known that there had been no incidence of career ending lameness despite the increased risk. Would the buyer still be able to claim half the price of the horse on the basis that its value without the benefit of hindsight was half what he paid? I am inclined to think not. By the time damages come to be assessed, it is known that the buyer received a horse which was every bit as valuable at the date of sale as the horse as warranted; with the benefit of hindsight it is known that the horse was as capable of winning the same number of races over its racing career as a horse without the latent disease. To award the buyer half the price of the horse would offend the compensatory principle and provide the buyer with a windfall.

However, this was subject to the limitation that it must not infringe the parties' own allocation of risk and, on the facts, the share purchase agreement had already allocated the risk of such events occurring—and allocated that risk to the purchaser.

8. There remained some doubt as to the application of the principle in *The Golden Victory* in the context of sales of goods following *obiter* comments by Hamblen J at first instance in *Bunge SA v Nidera BV (formerly Nidera Handelscompagnie BV)* [2013] EWHC 84 (Comm), [2013] 1 CLC 325, [2013] 1 Lloyd's Rep 621. The judge considered that since *The Golden Victory* was concerned with a charter over a period of time, such a contract over a period might be very different to a one-off sales contract where there is an available market for the goods and where the date of breach rule had traditionally been applied. At [55] he stated:

There is in such a case no difficulty about valuing what has been lost. The innocent party is compensated for the value of what he has lost at the time he loses it. Having had a mitigation opportunity which can be valued without difficulty by reference to the market there is no need or warrant to consider subsequent events. Fixing the damages by reference to market value promotes certainty and predictability, and helps inform the innocent party's decision whether or not to terminate.

However, the judge left this point open because it had not been fully argued and he did not need to decide it. The Court of Appeal took the same position on the appeal ([2013] EWCA Civ 1628). This question has now been resolved by the Supreme Court and it has been confirmed that the principle in *The Golden Victory* is both correct and of general application.

Bunge SA v Nidera BV (formerly Nidera Handelscompagnie BV)
[2015] UKSC 43, [2015] 3 All ER 1082, [2015] Bus LR 987 (SC)

The Supreme Court endorsed the principle in *The Golden Victory* on the basis that certainty did not justify a substantial damages award where no loss had in fact been suffered.

LORD SUMPTION JSC [(with whom Lord Neuberger of Abbotsbury PSC, Lord Mance, and Lord Clarke of Stone-Cum-Ebony JJSC agreed) explained the different approaches taken by the majority and minority in *The Golden Victory*]: 21 The reasoning has to some extent been obscured by the focus on the implications of the so-called 'breach-date rule' and on the competing demands of certainty and compensation. The real difference between the majority and the minority turned on the question what was being valued for the purpose assessing [*sic*] damages. The majority were valuing the chartered service that would actually have been performed if the charterparty had not been wrongfully brought to a premature end. On that footing, the notional substitute contract, whenever it was made and at whatever market rate, would have made no difference because it would have been subject to the same war clause as the original contract . . . The minority on the other hand considered that one should value not the chartered service which would actually have been performed, but the charterparty itself, assessed at the time that it was terminated, by reference to the terms of a notional substitute concluded as soon as possible after the termination of the original. That would vary, not according to the actual outcome, but according to the outcomes which were perceived as possible or probable at the time that the notional substitute contract was made. The possibility or probability of war would then be factored into the price agreed in the substitute contract . . . I think that the majority's view on this point was correct. Sections 50 and 51 of the Sale of Goods Act, like the corresponding principles of the common law, are concerned with the price of the goods or services which would have been delivered under the contract. They are not concerned with the value of the contract as an article of commerce in itself. As Lord Brown observed at paras 82–83, even if the charterparty rights could have been sold for a capital sum, this was not a proper basis for assessing loss, and an assessment which proceeded as if it were would 'extend the effect of the available market rule well beyond its proper scope'.

22 The leading speech for the majority, which was delivered by Lord Scott of Foscote, contains dicta which have sometimes been taken to suggest a distinction between a contract for a one-off sale and a contract for the supply of goods or services over a period of time: see paras 34–35. These dicta influenced both the board of appeal and Hamblen J in the present case. But I do not think that Lord Scott

was suggesting that the underlying principle was any different in the case of a one-off sale. Where the only question is the relevant date for taking the market price, the financial consequences of the breach may be said to 'crystallise' at that date. But where, after that date, some supervening event occurs which shows that that neither the original contract (had it continued) nor the notional substitute contract at the market price would ever have been performed, the concept of 'crystallising' the assessment of damages at that price is unhelpful. The occurrence of the supervening event would have reduced the value of performance, possibly to nothing, even if the contract had not been wrongfully terminated and whatever the relevant market price. The nature of that problem does not differ according to whether the contract provides for a single act of performance or several successive ones. Nor, as it seems to me, is there any principled reason why the majority's solution should be any different in the two cases. If a distinction were to be made between them, it is difficult to see how *The Mihalis Angelos* [1971] 1 QB 164, which concerned a contract for a single voyage, could have been decided as it was. As Lord Scott observed in *The Golden Victory* [2007] Bus LR 997, para 36, the compensatory principle would be equally offended by disregarding subsequent events serving to reduce or eliminate the loss under 'any anticipatory breach the acceptance of which had terminated an executory contract'. The most that can be said about one-off contracts of sale is that the facts may be different. In particular, if the injured party goes into the market and enters into a substitute contract by way of mitigation, it will not necessarily be subject to the same contingencies as the original contract.

23 The principle upheld in *The Golden Victory* has come in for a certain amount of academic criticism and judicial doubt. To my mind both the criticism and the doubt are unjustified. The most comprehensive and influential critic has been Professor Treitel. His views were set out in their fullest form in a case note on the decision of the Court of Appeal, which had reached the same conclusion as the majority of the Appellate Committee: see 'Assessment of Damages for Wrongful Repudiation' (2007) 123 LQR 9. Professor Treitel's case note was cited to the Appellate Committee but evidently did not move them. His main criticisms were, first, that the decision failed to distinguish between the different supervening events (successful mitigation by the defaulting party, inability of the innocent party to perform, cancellation under an express provision) which may serve to reduce or extinguish the loss; secondly, that it took no account of the collateral motives that might have moved the party who had repudiated the contract to cancel it lawfully at a later stage if it had continued; and, thirdly, that it attached insufficient weight to the commercial value of certainty. I am no more convinced by these criticisms than the Appellate Committee was in *The Golden Victory*. The principle which the Committee applied was neither new nor heterodox. There is no principled reason why, in order to determine the value of the contractual performance which has been lost by the repudiation, one should not consider what would have happened if the repudiation had not occurred. On the contrary, this seems to be fundamental to any assessment of damages designed to compensate the injured party for the consequences of the breach. If the contract had not been repudiated, it would have been lawfully cancellable. If it was lawfully cancellable, the charterer would have been entitled to avail himself of that right regardless of his motive. The only question is whether he would in fact have done so, a question which in practice would probably have been determined by his financial interest. Commercial certainty is undoubtedly important, although its significance will inevitably vary from one contract to another. But it can rarely be thought to justify an award of substantial damages to someone who has not suffered any. As Lord Mance pointed out in the Court of Appeal in *The Golden Victory* [2006] 1 WLR 533, para 24, the degree of uncertainty involved in that case was no greater than the uncertainty inherent in the contract itself. The parties' obligations were always defeasible in the uncertain event of war, just as their obligations under the contract presently in issue were always defeasible in the uncertain event of an export embargo.

NOTE Given the conclusive nature of the judgments in the Supreme Court, there can no longer be any doubt concerning the status of *The Golden Victory* as a central principle of the law relating to the measure of damages in the event of breach. However, it is to be borne in mind that the line of cases beginning with *The Golden Victory* concerns the measure of damages in the event of anticipatory breach, i.e. where the defendant has stated its intention not to perform future obligations. In that situation *The Golden Victory* provides that there is no need to guess what losses have been suffered when the answer is known by the time of trial. The position is quite different where there is an actual breach of an existing obligation. In that situation the loss accrues immediately and the claimant is entitled to recover that loss, subject to mitigation.

Classic Maritime Inc. v Limbungan Makmur SDN BHD
[2019] EWCA Civ 1102

The charterers of a vessel entered into a contract with the owners for the carriage of six cargoes of iron ore. The charterers failed to provide the ore, causing the owners to suffer loss of their carriage charges (freight). The charterers argued that even if they had been able to perform, the owners would still have suffered loss by reason of a dam burst that would have disrupted the carriage, and that *The Golden Victory* required the court to take note of the fact that independently of the breach there would have been a loss. The Court of appeal disagreed.

MALES LJ: 80. Both *The Golden Victory* and *Bunge v Nidera* were concerned with the assessment of damages for an anticipatory breach by renunciation which required the court to value the innocent party's right to future performance, in the former case the right to performance of what was in effect an instalment contract with monthly hire payments and in the latter case the right to performance of a single supply of goods. In both cases the compensatory principle operated to reduce or extinguish the innocent party's claim for damages. That was because the value of the performance to which that party was entitled was adversely affected by events which occurred after the acceptance of the repudiation. However, the fundamental principle is clear.

81. The present case is not concerned with an anticipatory breach, but with actual breaches as a result of the charterer's failure to supply cargoes for each of the five shipments in issue. It is common ground that, subject only to clause 32, the charterer's obligation to supply cargoes was an absolute obligation. Thus the performance to which the shipowner was entitled, once it was determined that clause 32 did not provide the charterer with a defence, was the supply of cargoes. The value of that performance was the freights which the shipowner would have earned if the cargoes had been supplied less the cost of earning them. In principle, therefore, the comparison which application of the compensatory principle required was between (1) the freights which the shipowner would have earned less the cost of earning them and (2) the actual position in which the shipowner found itself as a result of the breach. It is now agreed that this comparison would result in a damages award of over US$19 million.

82. The comparison which the judge carried out was different. It was between the shipowner's position if the charterer had been ready and willing to perform and the shipowner's actual position. The judge said at [146] that undertaking this comparison did not involve 'an impermissible sleight of hand' but I do not agree. The character's obligation was not to be ready and willing to supply a cargo in each case, but actually to supply one. The charterer was not in breach because it was unwilling to perform, but because it failed to do so, even if the reason why it failed to do so was because it was unwilling.

83. In the case of an anticipatory breach (i.e. a renunciation in advance of the time for performance), a party repudiates a contract if it demonstrates an unwillingness to perform, in which case (as in *The Golden Victory* and *Bunge v Nidera*) it may be necessary to consider whether, if it had not demonstrated that unwillingness, it would nevertheless have been excused from performance by later events. If so, that will affect the value of the rights which the innocent party has lost. But that is not so in the case of

an actual breach, as in the present case. In the present case, where there is an absolute obligation to supply a cargo, whether the charterer was ready and willing to supply is neither here nor there. Nor is it relevant whether performance is impossible as (in the absence of a defence such as frustration or illegality) impossibility is not a defence: *Taylor v Caldwell* (1863) 3 B&S 826 at page 833. The simple fact is that the charterer failed to do what it had promised to do and is thereby in breach.

14.5 Causation and contributory negligence

14.5.1 Causation

The injured party must establish a causal link between his loss and the defendant's breach of contract. In *Galoo Ltd v Bright Grahame Murray* [1994] 1 WLR 1360, the Court of Appeal held that, in a breach of contract claim, a claimant was entitled to claim damages where the breach was the effective or dominant cause of his loss. It was not sufficient that the breach merely provided the claimant with the opportunity to sustain loss. The 'but for' test governing causation in tort was not sufficient in contract.

In *County Ltd v Girozentrale Securities* [1996] 3 All ER 834, it was argued that a number of causes had combined to bring about the loss suffered by a bank in connection with the underwriting of an issue of shares. The Court of Appeal held that, in such a situation, a court was not required to choose which was the more effective cause. It was sufficient in a contractual claim that the cause in question (in this case, a breach of contract by the brokers engaged to approach potential investors) was an effective cause of the loss. However, if the claimant chooses to terminate a contract for reasons unconnected with the defendant's breach, e.g. on the defendant's insolvency, it is not later open to the claimant to seek damages for loss of bargain on the ground that there was a right to terminate for damages albeit one not exercised at the time: *Phones 4U Ltd v EE Ltd* [2018] EWHC 49 (Comm).

Assuming that the defendant has been in breach of contract, an intervening cause of loss may break the chain of causation.

Beoco Ltd v Alfa Laval Co. Ltd
[1994] 3 WLR 1179 (CA)

The first defendant installed a heat exchanger at the claimant company's premises. Later, a leak was discovered and the claimant employed the second defendant to repair it. Without inspecting the repair, which would have revealed that it was defective, the claimant put the heat exchanger back into use. Two months later, the heat exchanger exploded, damaging the claimant's plant and causing loss of production.

In a claim against the first defendant for breach of warranty, the claimant sought the loss of profits that would have been suffered because of the defect in the heat exchanger necessitating further repair or replacement. This was a purely hypothetical loss because of the intervening explosion (which was attributed to the claimant's failure to inspect the repair).

Held: The principles were the same as those applicable in tort—see e.g. *Jobling v Associated Dairies Ltd* [1982] AC 794—so that the claimant could not recover for the hypothetical loss of profits when the intervening event (resulting from the claimant's negligence) had caused greater damage.

14.5.2 Contributory negligence

If the injured party's negligent actions are not sufficient to break the chain of causation, but contribute to the loss, can the damages in contract be apportioned to take account of this contributory negligence? Is the Law Reform (Contributory Negligence) Act 1945 wide enough to cover claims in contract?

Law Reform (Contributory Negligence) Act 1945

1. Apportionment of liability in case of contributory negligence

(1) Where any person suffers damage as the result partly of his own fault and partly of the fault of any other person or persons, a claim in respect of that damage shall not be defeated by reason of the fault of the person suffering the damage, but the damages recoverable in respect thereof shall be reduced to such extent as the court thinks just and equitable having regard to the claimant's share in the responsibility of the damage: . . .

4. Interpretation

'fault' . . . means negligence, breach of statutory duty or other act or omission which gives rise to liability in tort or would, apart from this Act, give rise to the defence of contributory negligence

---

Forsikringsaktieselskapet Vesta v Butcher
[1989] AC 852 (CA)

The claimant insurers were seeking to place a contract of reinsurance through the defendant brokers. It was alleged that the brokers failed to ensure that the reinsurance coverage matched the claimants' own liabilities to their policyholder. Had that allegation been made out, there would have been a breach of the brokers' duty of care owed to the claimants in tort, and a breach of an implied term in their contract with the claimants that they would exercise reasonable care and skill. The defendant brokers alleged that the claimants had many opportunities to put the omission right and were therefore contributorily negligent. The claimants alleged that, by formulating their claim in contract, they could avoid apportionment of damages under the Law Reform (Contributory Negligence) Act 1945.

Held: Where the defendant's liability in contract is the same as the liability in the tort of negligence (independent of the existence of any contract), the Act applied to enable the Court to apportion damages even though the claim was made in contract.

O'CONNOR LJ: The important issue of law is whether on the facts of this case there is power to apportion under the Law Reform (Contributory Negligence) Act 1945 and thus reduce the damages recoverable by Vesta.

I start by pointing out that Vesta pleaded its claim against the brokers in contract and tort. This is but a recognition of what I regard as a clearly established principle that where under the general law a person owes a duty to another to exercise reasonable care and skill in some activity, a breach of that duty gives rise to a claim in tort notwithstanding the fact that the activity is the subject matter of a contract between them. In such a case the breach of duty will also be a breach of contract. The classic example of this situation is the relationship between doctor and patient.

Since the decision of the House of Lords in *Hedley Byrne & Co Ltd v Heller & Partners Ltd* [1964] AC 465 the relationship between the brokers and Vesta is another example. [Counsel] for Vesta accepts that this is so but he submits that if a claimant makes his claim in contract contributory negligence cannot be relied on by the defendant whereas it is available if the claim is made in tort. If this contention is sound then the law has been sadly adrift for a very long time for it would mean that in employers' liability cases an injured employee could debar the employer from relying on any contributory negligence by framing his action in contract.

. . . The judge [Hobhouse J] dealt with this submission and said [1986] 2 All ER 488, 508:

> The question whether the 1945 Act applies to claims brought in contract can arise in a number of classes of case. Three categories can conveniently be identified. (1) Where the defendant's liability arises from some contractual provision which does not depend on negligence on the part of the defendant. (2) Where the defendant's liability arises from a contractual obligation which is expressed in terms of taking care (or its equivalent) but does not correspond to a common law duty to take care which would exist in the given case independently of contract. (3) Where the defendant's liability in contract is the same as his liability in the tort of negligence independently of the existence of any contract.

The present case fell fairly and squarely within the judge's category (3). He said, at p. 509:

> The category (3) question has arisen in very many different types of case and the answer is treated as so obvious that it passes without any comment. It is commonplace that actions are brought by persons who have suffered personal injuries as the result of the negligence of the person sued and that there is a contractual as well as tortious relationship. In such cases apportionment of blame is invariably adopted by the court notwithstanding that the plaintiff could sue in contract as well as in tort. The example normally cited in the present context is the decision of the Court of Appeal in *Sayers v Harlow Urban District Council* [1958] 2 All ER 342, [1958] 1 WLR 623, which concerned a contractual visitor to premises (a lady who had paid to use a public lavatory). The Court of Appeal said it did not matter whether the cause of action was put in tort or in contract and proceeded to apportion blame awarding her three-quarters of her damages. This was a decision on a category (3) case. The power to make an apportionment was part of the ratio decidendi and is binding on me. There are innumerable similar decisions to the same effect which could be cited, very many by appellate courts . . .

In my judgment *Sayers v Harlow Urban District Council* is a category (3) case and the decision of the Court of Appeal that there is power to apportion was not only right but is binding on us just as the judge held it was binding on him . . . I am satisfied that the judge came to the right conclusion on this topic and in respect of it I would dismiss Vesta's appeal.

NOTES

1. This case fell within Hobhouse J's 'category (3)', so that the Act applied. Hobhouse J indicated that the Act did not apply to 'category (1)' cases, i.e. breaches of strict contractual obligations.

2. When the case went on appeal to the House of Lords, it was held that the reinsurance properly construed did match the insurance, so that although the brokers had been in breach of duty by failing to secure reinsurance that plainly matched the insurance, the claimants had not actually suffered any loss: *Vesta v Butcher* [1989] 1 All ER 402.

3. The Law Commission Working Paper No. 114 *Contributory Negligence as a Defence in Contract* (1990)—especially pp. 69–73—recommended that, unless the contract expressly declared to the contrary, the courts should be able to apportion damages in all three contractual cases in which the claimant's conduct contributed to his loss. However, in its subsequent Report No. 219, *Contributory Negligence as a Defence in Contract* (1993), the Law Commission recommended apportionment of damages where there is a breach of a qualified contractual obligation (contractual negligence), but not if the breach is of a strict contractual obligation. The report recommended a separate legislative provision for the contractual position and included a draft Bill. Under this proposed legislation, it would, however, have been possible to exclude apportionment for contributory negligence, either expressly or by implication, e.g. using a liquidated damages clause to fix the damages in advance. Nothing happened in terms of this proposed legislative solution and it now appears unlikely that it will. However, the courts appear to favour the approach indicated in the report as far as breaches of strict contractual obligations are concerned.

Barclays Bank plc v Fairclough Building Ltd
[1995] QB 214 (CA)

The defendant contractor was in breach of a contract to clean roofs containing asbestos and, in particular, had failed to comply with statutory requirements relating to asbestos. The defendant argued that the claimant had failed to supervise the work and therefore that damages should be reduced under the 1945 Act for this contributory negligence.

Held: Contributory negligence was not a defence to a claim for damages based on a breach of a strict contractual obligation, even where the defendant might have also had a parallel liability in tort.

SIMON BROWN LJ: [W]hen, as in a category (1) case, the contractual liability is by no means immaterial, when rather it is a strict liability arising independently of any negligence on the defendants' part, then there seem to me compelling reasons why the contract, even assuming it is silent as to apportionment, should be construed as excluding the operation of the Act of 1945. The very imposition of a strict liability on the defendant is to my mind inconsistent with an apportionment of the loss. And not least because of the absurdities that the contrary approach carries in its wake. Assume a defendant, clearly liable under a strict contractual duty. Is his position to be improved by demonstrating that besides breaching that duty he was in addition negligent? Take this very case. Is this contract really to be construed so that the defendant is advantaged by an assertion of its own liability in nuisance or trespass as well as in contract? Are we to have trials at which the defendant calls an expert to implicate him in tortious liability, whilst the plaintiffs' expert seeks paradoxically to exonerate him? The answer to all these questions is surely 'No'. Whatever arguments exist for apportionment in other categories of case—and these are persuasively deployed in the 1993 Law Commission Report, (Law Com No. 219)—to my mind there are none in the present type of case and I for my part would construe the contract accordingly.

NOTES

1. This decision indicates the importance of correct identification of the nature of the obligation broken.

2. In *Hi-Lite Electrical Ltd v Wolseley UK Ltd* [2011] EWHC 2153 (TCC), [2011] BLR 629, in which the defendant had breached s. 14(2) SGA 1979—a strict contractual obligation—there could be no apportionment for any contributory negligence by the claimant.

14.6 Remoteness of damage

Hadley v Baxendale
(1854) 9 Exch 341, 156 ER 145 (Exchequer)

The claimants, owners of a flour mill, contracted with the defendant carriers for the carriage of a crank shaft to Greenwich for use as a pattern for a new crank shaft. The carriage was delayed as a result of the negligence of the defendants, so that the new shaft was received late. The claimants claimed their loss of profits in operating the mill during the delay. The defendants argued that this loss was too remote for them to be liable for it.

Held: The loss of profits was not recoverable.

ALDERSON B: Now we think the proper rule in such a case as the present is this:—Where two parties have made a contract which one of them has broken, the damages which the other party ought to receive in respect of such breach of contract should be such as may fairly and reasonably be considered either arising naturally, i.e., according to the usual course of things, from such breach of contract itself, or such as may reasonably be supposed to have been in the contemplation of both parties, at the time they made the contract, as the probable result of the breach of it. Now, if the special circumstances under which the contract was actually made were communicated by the plaintiffs to the defendants, and thus known to both parties, the damages resulting from the breach of such a contract, which they would reasonably contemplate, would be the amount of injury which would ordinarily follow from a breach of contract under these special circumstances so known and communicated. But, on the other hand, if these special circumstances were wholly unknown to the party breaking the contract, he, at the most, could only be supposed to have had in his contemplation the amount of injury which would arise generally, and in the great multitude of cases not affected by any special circumstances, from such a breach of contract. For, had the special circumstances been known, the parties might have specially provided for the breach of contract by special terms as to the damages in that case; and of this advantage it would be very unjust to deprive them . . . Now, in the present case, if we are to apply the principles above laid down, we find that the only circumstances here communicated by the plaintiffs to the defendants at the time the contract was made, were, that the article to be carried was the broken shaft of a mill, and that the plaintiffs were the millers of that mill. But how do these circumstances shew reasonably that the profits of the mill must be stopped by an unreasonable delay in the delivery of the broken shaft by the carrier to the third person? Suppose the plaintiffs had another shaft in their possession put up or putting up at the time, and that they only wished to send back the broken shaft to the engineer who made it; it is clear that this would be quite consistent with the above circumstances, and yet the unreasonable delay in the delivery would have no effect upon the intermediate profits of the mill. Or, again, suppose that, at the time of the delivery to the carrier, the machinery of the mill had been in other respects defective, then, also, the same results would follow. Here it is true that the shaft was actually sent back to serve as a model for a new one, and that the want of a new one was the only cause of the stoppage of the mill, and that the loss of profits really arose from not sending down the new shaft in proper time, and that this arose from the delay in delivering the broken one to serve as a model. But it is obvious that, in the great multitude of cases of millers sending off broken shafts to third persons by a carrier under ordinary circumstances, such consequences would not, in all probability, have occurred; and these special circumstances were here never communicated by the plaintiffs to the defendants. It follows, therefore, that the loss of profits here cannot reasonably be considered such a consequence of the breach of contract as could have been fairly and reasonably contemplated by both the parties when they made this contract. For such loss would neither have flowed naturally from the breach of this contract in the great multitude of such cases occurring under ordinary circumstances, nor were the special circumstances, which, perhaps, would have made it a reasonable and natural consequence of such breach of contract, communicated to or known by the defendants . . .

? QUESTION

Is the size of the mill important to the imputed knowledge of the carrier? For example, if the mill is small, would the carrier be taken to know that there was no spare shaft?

NOTES

1. Traditionally, it has been accepted that there are two distinct limbs to this remoteness rule.

(a) Losses 'arising naturally' are inevitably within the parties' reasonable contemplation. The stoppage of the mill did not arise naturally from the carrier's delay, because there might have been a spare shaft, so that the mill could have kept working.

(b) 'Abnormal losses', dependent on special facts, will be within the parties' reasonable contemplation only if the special facts giving rise to the loss were known to both parties at the time of the contract. This is important to the ability to allocate known risks. The carriers had been told only that they were transporting a broken crank shaft to be used as a pattern for a new one. Had they been told that the mill would have to stop or that there was no spare shaft, then the loss of profits could have been recoverable.

2. However, Evans LJ in *Kpohraror v Woolwich Building Society* [1996] 4 All ER 119, at pp. 127–8, stated:

I would prefer to hold the starting point for any application of *Hadley v Baxendale* is the extent of shared knowledge of both parties when the contract was made . . . When that is established it may often be the case that the first and second parts of the rule overlap, or at least that it is unnecessary to draw a clear line of demarcation between them.

(The 'shared knowledge' is imputed knowledge of normal loss and actual knowledge of the special facts making a loss abnormal.) In *Jackson v Royal Bank of Scotland* [2005] UKHL 3, [2005] 1 WLR 377, Lord Hope recognized that there is a single principle underlying both limbs of 'what was in the contemplation of the parties at the time they made the contract'. However, the limbs are useful in terms of the application of that principle.

3. In *Jackson v Royal Bank of Scotland*, the House of Lords confirmed what should have been a clear matter of principle—namely, that what was in the contemplations of the parties was to be judged at the time of the contract and not at the time of the breach.

14.6.1 Normal and abnormal loss

Victoria Laundry (Windsor) Ltd v Newman Industries Ltd
[1949] 2 KB 528 (CA)

The claimants were launderers and dyers who wished to extend their business. They contracted with the defendants, an engineering firm, for the purchase of a boiler, which was to be delivered on 5 June. The boiler was not delivered until 8 November. The defendants were aware of the nature of the claimants' business and had been informed by letter that the claimants intended to put the boiler to immediate use in their business. In an action for breach of contract, the claimants claimed:

(a) the profit that they would have earned using the boiler between 5 June and 8 November from the expansion of their business; and

(b) the profit on a number of highly lucrative dyeing contracts, which they 'could and would have accepted' with the Ministry of Supply.

Held: Although the loss of normal business profits was a *reasonably foreseeable* consequence of the delayed delivery, the defendants had no knowledge of the highly lucrative dyeing contracts, so that this loss was too remote.

ASQUITH LJ [delivering the judgment of the Court]: What propositions applicable to the present case emerge from the authorities as a whole . . . We think they include the following:—

(1) It is well settled that the governing purpose of damages is to put the party whose rights have been violated in the same position, so far as money can do so, as if his rights had been observed: (*Sally Wertheim v Chicoutimi Pulp Company* [1911] AC 301). This purpose, if relentlessly pursued, would provide him with a complete indemnity for all loss de facto resulting from a particular breach, however improbable, however unpredictable. This, in contract at least, is recognised as too harsh a rule. Hence,

(2) In cases of breach of contract the aggrieved party is only entitled to recover such part of the loss actually resulting as was at the time of the contract reasonably foreseeable as liable to result from the breach.

(3) What was at that time reasonably so foreseeable depends on the knowledge then possessed by the parties or, at all events, by the party who later commits the breach.

(4) For this purpose, knowledge 'possessed' is of two kinds; one imputed, the other actual. Everyone, as a reasonable person, is taken to know the 'ordinary course of things' and consequently what loss is liable to result from a breach of contract in that ordinary course. This is the subject matter of the 'first rule' in *Hadley v Baxendale* (1854) 9 Exch 341. But to this knowledge, which a contract-breaker is assumed to possess whether he actually possesses it or not, there may have to be added in a particular case knowledge which he actually possesses, of special circumstances outside the 'ordinary course of things,' of such a kind that a breach in those special circumstances would be liable to cause more loss. Such a case attracts the operation of the 'second rule' so as to make additional loss also recoverable.

(5) In order to make the contract-breaker liable under either rule it is not necessary that he should actually have asked himself what loss is liable to result from a breach. As has often been pointed out, parties at the time of contracting contemplate not the breach of the contract, but its performance. It suffices that, if he had considered the question, he would as a reasonable man have concluded that the loss in question was liable to result.

(6) Nor, finally, to make a particular loss recoverable, need it be proved that upon a given state of knowledge the defendant could, as a reasonable man, foresee that a breach must necessarily result in that loss. It is enough if he could foresee it was likely so to result. It is indeed enough if the loss (or some factor without which it would not have occurred) is a 'serious possibility' or a 'real danger.' For short, we have used the word 'liable' to result. Possibly the colloquialism 'on the cards' indicates the shade of meaning with some approach to accuracy . . .

NOTES

1. The Court of Appeal applied a test of reasonable foreseeability, which suggested that the test for remoteness in contract was the same as that for recovery in tort. However, this approach was criticized by the House of Lords in *The Heron II* (see below).

2. Asquith LJ pointed out that the headnote to *Hadley v Baxendale* is misleading, since it suggests that the carrier knew that the mill had stopped. If that were so, then the loss should have been recoverable under the second limb of the rule.

3. It is argued that the second limb encourages the sharing of risks, and if a party is aware of the scope of likely liability, that party can take out insurance to cover it.

4. *Victoria Laundry* indicates that the critical distinction is between 'normal' and 'abnormal' loss in relation to the breach since the knowledge required is determined by this classification. In *Balfour Beatty Construction (Scotland) Ltd v Scottish Power plc* (1994) 71 BLR 20, the House of Lords had to consider whether knowledge of a construction process—namely, the need for a continuous pour of concrete—could be imputed to the electricity supplier, so that when the electricity supply failed, the consequential demolition and rebuilding costs could be recovered as 'a loss arising naturally'. The House of Lords held that there was no general rule that contracting parties were presumed to have knowledge of each other's business practices, but the simpler the activity, the easier it would be to infer knowledge of the practice. However, where, as here, it was a complicated construction technique, the supplier was not deemed to know about it.

5. The decision in *Victoria Laundry* was distinguished by the Court of Appeal in *Wellesley Partners LLP v Withers LLP* [2015] EWCA Civ 1146, [2016] CILL 3757 (*page* 719, later in this section). A similar decision is *125 OBA (Nominees) v Land Lease Construction (Europe) Ltd* [2017] EWHC (TCC), where the claimants sought to recover from builders the cost of replacing glass panes and also refinancing costs incurred by the claimants in the form of increased fees, increased interest payments, and associated legal costs. Those costs were held not to be too remote: although the defendants were unaware of the precise financing arrangements when the contract was made, the fact that some arrangements would have been in place was, in the words of Stuart-Smith J, 'absolutely basic' (para. 236) and, accordingly, the losses were reasonably foreseeable.

The decision of the House of Lords in *The Heron II* is helpful in terms of identifying 'normal loss' or 'loss arising naturally'. The default position is then that other loss (not arising naturally from that breach) will be 'abnormal' and require actual knowledge of the special facts leading to that loss in order to be recoverable.

Koufos v C. Czarnikow Ltd, The Heron II
[1969] 1 AC 350 (HL)

Charterers chartered a vessel from the owners for the carriage of sugar from Constanza to Basrah. The shipowners knew that the charterers were sugar merchants and that there was a sugar market at Basrah, but did not actually know that the charterers intended to sell the sugar promptly on arrival at Basrah. In breach of the charterparty, the vessel deviated from the voyage, so that instead of arriving at Basrah on 22 November, it did not arrive until 2 December. The market price of sugar at Basrah had fallen in this period from £32 10s. per ton to £31 2s. 9d. per ton.

Held: The charterers were entitled to recover the difference in price caused by the delay. Knowledge was imputed to them that it was *not unlikely* (to use the words of Lord Reid) that the sugar would be sold on arrival and that market prices fluctuate. Lord Reid rejected the reasonable foreseeability test used in *Victoria Laundry v Newman Industries* (*page 713, 14.6.1*), since the test in contract was different from that in tort.

LORD REID: So the question for decision is whether a plaintiff can recover as damages for breach of contract a loss of a kind which the defendant, when he made the contract, ought to have realised was not unlikely to result from a breach of contract causing delay in delivery. I use the words 'not unlikely' as denoting a degree of probability considerably less than an even chance but nevertheless not very unusual and easily foreseeable.

[Lord Reid referred to *Hadley v Baxendale*. He continued:]

Alderson B clearly did not and could not mean that it was not reasonably foreseeable that delay might stop the resumption of work in the mill. He merely said that in the great multitude—which I take to mean the great majority—of cases this would not happen. He was not distinguishing between results which were foreseeable or unforeseeable, but between results which were likely because they would happen in the great majority of cases, and results which were unlikely because they would only happen in a small minority of cases. He continued:

> It follows, therefore, that the loss of profits here cannot reasonably be considered such a consequence of the breach of contract as could have been fairly and reasonably contemplated by both the parties when they made this contract.

He clearly meant that a result which will happen in the great majority of cases should fairly and reasonably be regarded as having been in the contemplation of the parties, but that a result which, though foreseeable as a substantial possibility, would only happen in a small minority of cases should not be regarded as having been in their contemplation . . .

I am satisfied that the court did not intend that every type of damage which was reasonably foreseeable by the parties when the contract was made should either be considered as arising naturally, i.e., in the usual course of things, or be supposed to have been in the contemplation of the parties. Indeed the decision makes it clear that a type of damage which was plainly foreseeable as a real possibility but which would only occur in a small minority of cases cannot be regarded as arising in the usual course of things or be supposed to have been in the contemplation of the parties: the parties are not supposed to contemplate as grounds for the recovery of damage any type of loss or damage which on the knowledge available to the defendant would appear to him as only likely to occur in a small minority of cases.

In cases like *Hadley v Baxendale* (1854) 9 Exch 341 or the present case it is not enough that in fact the plaintiff's loss was directly caused by the defendant's breach of contract. It clearly was so caused in both. The crucial question is whether, on the information available to the defendant when the contract was made, he should, or the reasonable man in his position would, have realised that such loss was sufficiently likely to result from the breach of contract to make it proper to hold that the loss flowed naturally from the breach or that loss of that kind should have been within his contemplation.

The modern rule of tort is quite different and it imposes a much wider liability. The defendant will be liable for any type of damage which is reasonably foreseeable as liable to happen even in the most unusual case, unless the risk is so small that a reasonable man would in the whole circumstances feel justified in neglecting it. And there is good reason for the difference. In contract, if one party wishes to protect himself against a risk which to the other party would appear unusual, he can direct the other party's attention to it before the contract is made, and I need not stop to consider in what circumstances the other party will then be held to have accepted responsibility in that event. But in tort there is no opportunity for the injured party to protect himself in that way, and the tortfeasor cannot reasonably complain if he has to pay for some very unusual but nevertheless foreseeable damage which results from his wrongdoing. I have no doubt that today a tortfeasor would be held liable for a type of damage as unlikely as was the stoppage of Hadley's Mill for lack of a crankshaft: to anyone with the knowledge the carrier had that may have seemed unlikely but the chance of it happening would have been seen to be far from negligible. But it does not at all follow that *Hadley v Baxendale* (1854) 9 Exch 341 would today be differently decided.

[Lord Reid then referred to *Victoria Laundry v Newman Industries* [1949] 2 KB 528 and Asquith LJ's formulation.]

To bring in reasonable foreseeability appears to me to be confusing measure of damages in contract with measure of damages in tort. A great many extremely unlikely results are reasonably foreseeable: it is true that Lord Asquith may have meant foreseeable as a likely result, and if that is all he meant I would not object further than to say that I think that the phrase is liable to be misunderstood. For the same reason I would take exception to the phrase 'liable to result'. Liable is a very vague word but I think that one would usually say that when a person foresees a very improbable result he foresees that it is liable to happen.

. . . It has never been held to be sufficient in contract that the loss was foreseeable as 'a serious possibility' or 'a real danger' or as being 'on the cards'. It is on the cards that one can win £100,000 or more for a stake of a few pence—several people have done that. And anyone who backs a hundred to one chance regards a win as a serious possibility—many people have won on such a chance. And the *Wagon Mound (No. 2)* [1961] AC 388 could not have been decided as it was unless the extremely unlikely fire should have been foreseen by the ship's officer as a real danger. It appears to me that in the ordinary use of language there is wide gulf between saying that some event is not unlikely or quite likely to happen and saying merely that it is a serious possibility, a real danger, or on the cards. Suppose one takes a well-shuffled pack of cards, it is quite likely or not unlikely that the top card will prove to be a diamond: the odds are only 3 to 1 against. But most people would not say that it is quite likely to be the nine of diamonds for the odds are then 51 to 1 against. On the other hand I think that most people would say that there is a serious possibility or a real danger of its being turned up first and of course it is on the cards. If the tests of 'real danger' or 'serious possibility' are in future to be authoritative then the *Victoria Laundry* case [1949] 2 KB 528 would indeed be a landmark because it would mean that *Hadley v Baxendale* (1854) 9 Exch 341 would be differently decided today. I certainly could not understand any court deciding that, on the information available to the carrier in that case, the stoppage of the mill was neither a serious possibility nor a real danger. If those tests are to prevail in future then let us cease to pay lip service to the rule in *Hadley v Baxendale* (1854) 9 Exch 341. But in my judgement to adopt these tests would extend liability for breach of contract beyond what is reasonable or desirable. From the limited knowledge which I have of commercial affairs I would not expect such an extension to be welcomed by the business community and from the legal point of view I can find little or nothing to recommend it.

1. Do you agree with Lord Reid that if the test is reasonable foreseeability, then the carrier in *Hadley v Baxendale* would have been liable?

2. Is there a distinction between 'natural losses' and 'foreseeable losses'?

3. Lord Reid justified a stricter test of remoteness in contract because the parties will know each other and are therefore in a better position to assess the risk of loss due to the breach. If we accept Lord Reid's distinction, what should the position be if a claim on the facts could lie in both contract and tort? Can the injured party choose to formulate the claim in tort so that recovery of losses will be wider? The answer to this question may now have been provided by the decision of the Court of Appeal in *Wellesley Partners LLP v Withers LLP* [2015] EWCA Civ 1146, [2016] CILL 3757 (discussed at *page 719*, later in this section).

H. Parsons (Livestock) Ltd v Uttley Ingham & Co. Ltd
[1978] 1 QB 791 (CA)

The claimants, pig farmers, ordered a bulk food storage hopper for storing pig nuts from the defendants. When the defendants installed the hopper, they failed to ensure that the ventilator on the top was open. The pig nuts went mouldy, and when the pigs ate them, they became ill with E. coli (an intestinal disease). A total of 254 pigs died.

Held (Scarman and Orr LJJ): The death of the pigs was not too remote a loss, since the parties might reasonably have contemplated *some* illness to the pigs resulting from this breach and they did not have to foresee the actual illness that occurred. Lord Denning also held that the death of the pigs was within the remoteness rule. He thought that the same distinction should be drawn in contract as applied in tort between physical damage and economic loss (loss of profit), and that the tort test of remoteness should apply to physical damage.

LORD DENNING MR:

The law as to remoteness

Remoteness of damage is beyond doubt a question of law. In *C. Czarnikow Ltd v Koufos* [1969] AC 350 the House of Lords said that, in remoteness of damage, there is a difference between contract and tort. In the case of a *breach of contract*, the court has to consider whether the consequences were of such a kind that a reasonable man, at the time of making the contract, would *contemplate* them as being of a very substantial degree of probability. (In the House of Lords various expressions were used to describe this degree of probability, such as, not merely 'on the cards' because that may be too low: but as being 'not unlikely to occur' (see pp. 383 and 388); or 'likely to result or at least not unlikely to result' (see p. 406); or 'liable to result' (see p. 410); or that there was a 'real danger' or 'serious possibility' of them occurring (see p. 415).)

In the case of a *tort*, the court has to consider whether the consequences were of such a kind that a reasonable man, at the time of the tort committed, would *foresee* them as being of a much lower degree of probability. (In the House of Lords various expressions were used to describe this, such as, it is sufficient if the consequences are 'liable to happen in the most unusual case' (see p. 385); or in a 'very improbable' case (see p. 389); or that 'they may happen as a result of the breach, however unlikely it may be, unless it can be brushed aside as far-fetched' (see p. 422).)

I find it difficult to apply those principles universally to all cases of contract or to all cases of tort: and to draw a distinction between what a man 'contemplates' and what he 'foresees'. I soon begin to get out of my depth. I cannot swim in this sea of semantic exercises—to say nothing of the different degrees of probability—especially when the cause of action can be laid either in contract or in tort. I am swept under by the conflicting currents. I go back with relief to the distinction drawn in legal theory by Professors Hart and Honoré in their book *Causation in the Law* (1959), at pp. 281–287. They distinguish between those cases in contract in which a man has suffered no damage to person or property, but only *economic loss*, such as, loss of profit or loss of opportunities for gain in some future transaction: and those in which he claims damages for an *injury actually done* to his person or *damage actually done* to his property (including his livestock) or for ensuing expense (damnum emergens) to which he has actually been put. In the law of *tort*, there is emerging a distinction between economic loss and physical damage: see *Spartan Steel & Alloys Ltd v Martin & Co. (Contractors) Ltd* [1973] QB 27, 36–37.

It seems to me that in the law of *contract*, too, a similar distinction is emerging. It is between loss of profit consequent on a breach of contract and physical damage consequent on it.

Loss of profit cases

I would suggest as a solution that in the former class of case—loss of profit cases—the defaulting party is only liable for the consequences if they are such as, at the time of the contract, he ought reasonably to have *contemplated* as a *serious* possibility or real danger. You must assume that, at the time of the contract, he had the very kind of breach in mind—such a breach as afterwards happened, as for instance, delay in transit—and then you must ask: ought he reasonably to have *contemplated* that there was a *serious* possibility that such a breach would involve the plaintiff in loss of profit? If yes, the contractor is liable for the loss unless he has taken care to exempt himself from it by a condition in the contract—as, of course, he is able to do if it was the sort of thing which he could reasonably contemplate. The law on this class of case is now covered by the three leading cases of *Hadley v Baxendale*, 9 Exch 341; *Victoria Laundry (Windsor) Ltd v Newman Industries Ltd* [1949] 2 KB 528; and *C. Czarnikow Ltd v Koufos* [1969] 1 AC 350. These were all 'loss of profit' cases: and the test of 'reasonable contemplation' and 'serious possibility' should, I suggest, be kept to that type of loss or, at any rate, to economic loss.

Physical damage cases

In the second class of case—the physical injury or expense case—the defaulting party is liable for any loss or expense which he ought reasonably to have *foreseen* at the time of the breach as a possible consequence, even if it was only a *slight* possibility. You must assume that he was aware of his breach, and then you must ask: ought he reasonably to have foreseen, at the time of the breach, that something of this kind might happen in consequence of it? This is the test which has been applied in cases of tort ever since *The Wagon Mound* cases [1961] AC 388 and [1967] 1 AC 617. But there is a long line of cases which support a like test in cases of contract . . .

Coming to the present case, we were told that in some cases the makers of these hoppers supply them direct to the pig farmer under contract with him, but in other cases they supply them through an intermediate dealer—who buys from the manufacturer and resells to the pig farmer on the selfsame terms—in which the manufacturer delivers direct to the pig farmer. In the one case the pig farmer can sue the manufacturer in contract. In the other in tort. The test of remoteness should be the same. It should be the test in tort.

Conclusion

The present case falls within the class of case where the breach of contract causes physical damage. The test of remoteness in such cases is similar to that in tort. The contractor is liable for all such loss or expense as could reasonably have been foreseen at the time of the breach, as a possible consequence of it. Applied to this case, it means that the makers of the hopper are liable for the death of the pigs. They ought reasonably to have foreseen that, if the mouldy pignuts were fed to the pigs, there was a possibility that they might become ill. Not a serious possibility. Nor a real danger. But still a slight possibility. On that basis the makers were liable for the illness suffered by the pigs. They suffered from diarrhoea at the beginning. This triggered off the deadly E. coli. That was a far worse illness than could then be foreseen. But that does not lessen this liability. The type or kind of damage was foreseeable even though the extent of it was not: see *Hughes v Lord Advocate* [1963] AC 837 . . .

NOTES

1. Scarman and Orr LJJs expressly refused to adopt this distinction on the basis that the case law did not support it.

2. The decision of the majority means that if the type of loss is within the parties' reasonable contemplation, the extent of it need not be. See also *Brown v KMR Services Ltd* [1995] 4 All ER 598, in which this principle was applied. This principle came under scrutiny by some of their Lordships in *Transfield Shipping Inc. v Mercator Shipping Inc., The Achilleas* [2008] UKHL 48, [2009] 1 AC 61 (*page 722, 14.6.2*).

3. In *Victoria Laundry v Newman Industries* (*page 713, 14.6.1*), the type of loss appears to be loss of profits, but the profits on the dyeing contracts were not recoverable. Is it possible to explain this difference in treatment?

In the next case the Court of Appeal considered the applicable remoteness rule for instances of concurrent liability in contract and tort.

Wellesley Partners LLP v Withers LLP
[2015] EWCA Civ 1146, [2016] CILL 3757 (CA)

The defendant law firm was engaged by the claimant head-hunter to draft a partnership agreement to cover new partners. The claimant wanted the partnerships agreement to allow a withdrawal of half of the capital invested by a new partner after 42 months. However, the agreement as drafted allowed this to happen at any time within the first 41 months. The investment bank was a new partner which exercised this option to withdraw its capital. The judge had found that the defendant firm had been negligent in drafting this agreement and it was also clearly a breach of contract, i.e. there was concurrent liability. The appeal concentrated on the measure of damages. Part of the claimant's alleged loss was losses resulting from the loss of a chance to generate more profits by opening an office in New York. Did this loss fall within remoteness so that it could, in principle, be recoverable?

The Court of Appeal held that where there was concurrent liability, the remoteness test determining recovery for economic loss should be the same—and it should be the contractual test. Applying the contractual test, the Court of Appeal considered that this loss did fall within the parties' reasonable contemplations because the defendant firm knew that the partnership planned to expand into the US at the time of making the contract to draw up the agreement. This loss (the Nomura contract) was therefore of a 'kind' (or type) that fell within reasonable contemplations and the losses in respect of the US contract were recoverable.

FLOYD LJ: 80 . . . I am persuaded that where, as in the present case, contractual and tortious duties to take care in carrying out instructions exist side by side, the test for recoverability of damage for economic loss should be the same, and should be the contractual one. The basis for the formulation of the remoteness test adopted in contract is that the parties have the opportunity to draw special circumstances to each other's attention at the time of formation of the contract. Whether or not one calls it an implied term of the contract, there exists the opportunity for consensus between the parties, as to the type of damage (both in terms of its likelihood and type) for which it will be able to hold the other responsible. The parties are assumed to be contracting on the basis that liability will be confined to damage of the kind which is in their reasonable contemplation. It makes no sense at all for the existence of the concurrent duty in tort to upset this consensus, particularly given that the tortious duty arises out of the same assumption of responsibility as exists under the contract.

81 I am not, however, persuaded that this conclusion results in the appeal being allowed. The judge has held that the damage represented by the loss of the Nomura mandates was a type of damage that was reasonably foreseeable. In holding Withers liable in negligence he must have considered that the damage was of a kind which fell within the scope of the duty of care in tort. It seems to me to be plain that it does fall within the scope of that duty. Withers were given express instructions to draft a clause which would prevent Addax from withdrawing half its capital until November 2011. I see nothing unfair or unreasonable, or inconsistent with the purpose of the duty in holding that damage which is the consequence of the unavailability of that capital should be the responsibility of Withers. This is not a case like *SAAMCO* [*South Australia Asset Management Corp v York Montague Ltd* [1997] AC 191] where some of the damage arose from factors which had nothing to do with the incorrectness of information.

82 It is, I think, also clear that the damage must be taken to be of a kind for which Withers had assumed responsibility under their contract. Just as in *SAAMCO*, I would regard this as a case where the scope of duty in the two cases was the same. The damage awarded by the judge was not excluded by the principles enunciated by Lord Hoffmann and Lord Hope in *The Achilleas*. The special individual circumstances present in that case for holding that the charterer had not assumed responsibility for the loss are not, at least cumulatively, present here. The fact that the extent of loss cannot be predicted at the date of the formation of the contract cannot by itself amount to a sufficient reason for holding that the contract breaker has not assumed responsibility for it.

83 If the contractual test is to come to the assistance of Withers, it seems to me that it must be because the kind of damage, although reasonably foreseeable, cannot be regarded as within the contemplation of the parties as not unlikely to occur. In my judgment the damage was of a kind which was in the reasonable contemplation of the parties as not unlikely to result from a breach. Thus, whilst the judge only held that Withers knew sufficient for it to be reasonably foreseeable that if Addax were able to withdraw its capital WP might be prevented from earning profits in the US, it seems to me that, on the evidence which he summarised, it was equally within the reasonable contemplation of the parties that it was not unlikely that this would be so. Withers knew, on the judge's findings, that WP was thinking of expanding into the US and this was one of the ways in which the capital raised by the Addax investment was to be used to make profits from head hunting in the investment banking sector. Neither party knew at the stage of making the contract any more about how the profits would be made, other than that they would be made by carrying out head hunting services in the investment banking sector: the common contemplation must have been that they would exploit such opportunities as arose. I think it is quite unrealistic, and uncommercial, to suppose that a solicitor drafting an agreement would consider the Nomura opportunity to be a different sort of risk from other opportunities in the United States which they must be assumed to have contemplated.

84 Three reasons seem to have motivated the judge as to his provisional view as to why the Nomura contracts should be treated as damage of a different kind from that which the parties would have

contemplated as not unlikely: that the Nomura contract was a very particular contract, that it was very profitable, and that it was analogous to the forward charterparty in *The Achilleas* and the especially profitable government contract in *Victoria Laundry*.

85 It is true that the Nomura contract was a very particular one which arose through Mr Channing's connections. The damage caused to WP by its loss was not in my judgment different in any relevant way from other business which WP might obtain. Mr Channing was a highly successful and well-connected head hunter who could be expected to exploit such connections as he had. It would be otherwise if the services to be offered by WP were different in kind, or in some other way a departure from their known ways of doing business. In fact the services to be offered by WP were in all respects the same as those which the parties contemplated being offered in the US.

86 It is also true that the Nomura contract was a profitable one. However this is a factor which, it seems to me, goes to the quantum of the loss and not its kind. The fact that the scale of the losses was unforeseeable does not make them too remote if they are losses for which the contract breaker has otherwise assumed responsibility: see per Lord Hoffman in *The Achilleas* at paragraph 21 and per Rix LJ in *Rubenstein* [*Rubenstein v HSBC Bank plc* [2012] EWCA Civ 1184, [2013] 1 All ER (Comm) 915] at paragraph 107 citing *Brown v KMR Services* [1995] 4 All ER 598, [1995] 2 Lloyd's Rep 513.

87 I accept that there are factual analogies which can be drawn with the high value government contracts in *Victoria Laundry*. Factual analogies with other cases are, however, dangerous. The facts in *Victoria Laundry* justified the finding that a loss of a particular high value government contract unknown to the defendant was loss of a different kind from losses of the ordinary business of a laundry. The contract breaker had no knowledge that the laundry was proposing to undertake work of this kind. Lord Hoffmann explains this case in *The Achilleas* at paragraph 22 on the basis that the vendor of the boilers would have regarded the profits on these contracts as a different and higher form of risk than the general risk of loss of profits by the laundry. By contrast, it seems artificial to suppose that a firm of solicitors employed to draft a clause with the effect of preventing a withdrawal of capital would have regarded the loss of the Nomura contract as a different sort of risk. Moreover the expectations of the parties here were different. In *Victoria Laundry* the defendants had no reason to suppose that the laundry in question was anything other than an ordinary laundry. Here the defendants must be assumed to have been aware of Mr Channing's star qualities. The two cases could not be more different in this respect.

88 The analogy with the forward charterparty in *The Achilleas* is also not persuasive. That case also turned, at least in part, on the particular commercial circumstances known to the parties at the time of formation of the contract. These included the evidence of the general understanding in the shipping market that liability was restricted to the difference between the market rate and the charter rate for the overrun period, and that any departure from this rule was likely to give rise to a real risk of serious commercial uncertainty which the industry as a whole would regard as undesirable. We are not in that territory in the present case.

89 The damages awarded by the judge are therefore recoverable applying the test for remoteness in contract. I would therefore reject this ground of Withers' appeal.

NOTE This decision makes sense. As the judge at first instance, Nugee J ([2014] EWHC 556 (Ch), [2014] PNLR 22) had stated, at [212]: 'A rational system of law would only give one answer to that question [i.e. which losses should be recoverable in instances of professional negligence]. And . . . if there were only one answer, it seems far more satisfactory that parties in a contractual relationship should be governed by the contract rules rather than the tort ones.'

14.6.2 A new approach to remoteness in contract?

Transfield Shipping Inc. v Mercator Shipping Inc., The Achilleas
[2008] UKHL 48, [2009] 1 AC 61 (HL)

Time charterers were nine days late in redelivery of the vessel. The owners had rechartered the vessel and, when it was not redelivered on time, the owners had agreed an extension of the cancelling date under the new (follow-on) charter, but only on the basis that the new charterers received a reduction in the daily rate of the hire. The question was whether damages were limited by the remoteness principles to the difference between the charter rate and the market rate at the time of redelivery for the nine-day period of the overrun during which the owners did not have the vessel because of the breach (as argued by the charterers), or whether the owners could claim damages based on the loss of hire on the next charter ($8,000 a day for 191 days of the follow-on charter). The owners alleged that the latter measure was the only way in which they could be compensated for their actual loss, but the charterers argued that this was possible only where there was actual knowledge (i.e. the second limb of *Hadley v Baxendale*).

The arbitrator and judge had considered that this situation fell within the first limb (normal loss), so that the actual loss suffered was within reasonable contemplations. The Court of Appeal agreed on the basis that a time charterer would know that the owner was likely to have entered into a new charter to follow closely on from the redelivery of the vessel and impliedly took the risk of loss in relation to this if they were late in redelivering. They were therefore liable for the full extent of that type of loss.

Held (on appeal to the House of Lords, allowing the appeal): Damages were limited to the lower figure—namely, the difference between the charter rate and the market rate at the time of redelivery for the nine-day period of the overrun. Responsibility in contract needed to be undertaken voluntarily and the principles of remoteness were based on an objective assessment of the common basis on which the parties had contracted in the context of their agreement. The charterers had assumed responsibility for the nine-day delay in returning the vessel, but they had not assumed responsibility for the entirety of the follow-on charter, because they could neither control that loss nor quantify it.

Although this can be extracted as a *ratio*, their Lordships did not adopt a single line of reasoning to justify their conclusion as to the measure of recovery. An influencing factor seems to have been the general understanding in the shipping market that liability was restricted to the difference between the market rate and the charter rate for the overrun period. Lords Hoffmann and Hope referred to a principle of objective 'assumption of responsibility' for a loss of the type that has occurred and could find none. Lord Rodger and Baroness Hale adopted a more traditional approach, concluding that the loss was not normal loss, because it would not follow 'in the ordinary course of things', but was the product of market conditions that had led the owners to concede the discount. Lord Walker considered that the parties had simply not contracted on the basis that there should be unlimited recovery for losses associated with the follow-on charter, particularly because the charterers could have no control over the follow-on contract or the terms on which the owners had contracted.

LORD HOFFMANN: 9 The case . . . raises a fundamental point of principle in the law of contractual damages: is the rule that a party may recover losses which were foreseeable ('not unlikely') an external rule of law, imposed upon the parties to every contract in default of express provision to the contrary, or is it a prima facie assumption about what the parties may be taken to have intended, no doubt applicable in the great majority of cases but capable of rebuttal in cases in which the context, surrounding circumstances or general understanding in the relevant market shows that a party would not reasonably have been regarded as assuming responsibility for such losses? . . .

12 It seems to me logical to found liability for damages upon the intention of the parties (objectively ascertained) because all contractual liability is voluntarily undertaken. It must be in principle wrong to hold someone liable for risks for which the people entering into such a contract in their particular market, would not reasonably be considered to have undertaken.

13 The view which the parties take of the responsibilities and risks they are undertaking will determine the other terms of the contract and in particular the price paid. Anyone asked to assume a large and unpredictable risk will require some premium in exchange . . .

14 In their submissions to the House, the owners said that the 'starting point' was that damages were designed to put the innocent party, so far as it is possible, in the position as if the contract had been performed: see *Robinson v Harman* (1848) 1 Exch 850, 855. However, in *Banque Bruxelles Lambert SA v Eagle Star Insurance Co Ltd* (sub nom *South Australia Asset Management Corpn* [*SAAMCO*] *v York Montague Ltd*) [1997] AC 191, 211, I said (with the concurrence of the other members of the House):

> I think that this was the wrong place to begin. Before one can consider the principle on which one should calculate the damages to which a plaintiff is entitled as compensation for loss, it is necessary to decide for what kind of loss he is entitled to compensation. A correct description of the loss for which the valuer is liable must precede any consideration of the measure of damages.

15 In other words, one must first decide whether the loss for which compensation is sought is of a 'kind' or 'type' for which the contract-breaker ought fairly to be taken to have accepted responsibility . . .

16 What is true of an implied contractual duty (to take reasonable care in the valuation) is equally true of an express contractual duty (to redeliver the ship on the appointed day). In both cases, the consequences for which the contracting party will be liable are those which 'the law regards as best giving effect to the express obligations assumed' and '[not] extending them so as to impose on the [contracting party] a liability greater than he could reasonably have thought he was undertaking'.

17 The effect of the *South Australia* case was to exclude from liability the damages attributable to a fall in the property market notwithstanding that those losses were foreseeable in the sense of being 'not unlikely' (property values go down as well as up) and had been caused by the negligent valuation in the sense that, but for the valuation, the bank would not have lent at all and there was no evidence to show that it would have lost its money in some other way. It was excluded on the ground that it was outside the scope of the liability which the parties would reasonably have considered that the valuer was undertaking.

18 That seems to me in accordance with the careful way in which Robert Goff J stated the principle in *Satef-Huttenes Albertus SpA v Paloma Tercera Shipping Co SA (The Pegase)* [1981] 1 Lloyd's Rep 175, 183, where the emphasis is upon what a reasonable person would have considered to be the extent of his responsibility:

> the test appears to be: have the facts in question come to the defendant's knowledge in such circumstances that a reasonable person in the shoes of the defendant would, if he had considered the matter at the time of making the contract, have contemplated that, in the event of a breach by him, such facts were to be taken into account when considering his responsibility for loss suffered by the plaintiff as a result of such breach.

. . .

24 The findings of the majority arbitrators shows that they considered their decision to be contrary to what would have been the expectations of the parties, but dictated by the rules in *Hadley v Baxendale* as explained in *The Heron II* [1969] 1 AC 350. But in my opinion these rules are not so inflexible; they are intended to give effect to the presumed intentions of the parties and not to contradict them.

25 The owners submit that the question of whether the damage is too remote is a question of fact on which the arbitrators have found in their favour. It is true that the question of whether the damage was foreseeable is a question of fact: see *Monarch Steamship Co Ltd v Karlshamns Oljefabriker (A/B)* [1949] AC 196. But the question of whether a given type of loss is one for which a party assumed contractual responsibility involves the interpretation of the contract as a whole against its commercial background, and this, like all questions of interpretation, is a question of law.

26 . . . In my opinion, the findings of the arbitrators and the commercial background to the agreement are sufficient to make it clear that the charterer cannot reasonably be regarded as having assumed the risk of the owner's loss of profit on the following charter. I would therefore allow the appeal.

LORD RODGER OF EARLSFERRY: 46 In these circumstances the owners claim damages (agreed at US$1,364,584.17) for their loss of profit as a result of having to reduce the daily rate of hire under the Cargill fixture by US$8,000, when they obtained the extension of the cancelling date which they needed in order to accommodate the charterers' delay in redelivering the vessel. Clearly, the owners incurred that loss in the wake of the charterers' breach of contract. Nevertheless, in respectful disagreement with Christopher Clarke J and the Court of Appeal, I have come to the conclusion that the charterers are not liable in damages for the owners' loss of profit.

47 Today, as for more than 150 years, the starting-point for determining the measure of damages for breach of contract is the judgment of Alderson B in *Hadley v Baxendale* (1854) 9 Exch 341 . . .

52 In any event, amidst a cascade of different expressions, it is important not to lose sight of the basic point that, in the absence of special knowledge, a party entering into a contract can only be supposed to contemplate the losses which are likely to result from the breach in question—in other words, those losses which will generally happen in the ordinary course of things if the breach occurs. Those are the losses for which the party in breach is held responsible—the stated rationale being that, other losses not having been in contemplation, the parties had no opportunity to provide for them.

53 In the present case, the arbitrators found that—as conceded by counsel then acting for the charterers— missing a date for a subsequent fixture was a 'not unlikely' result of the late redelivery of a vessel . . . [W]hen they entered into the addendum, the parties could reasonably have contemplated that it was not unlikely that the owners would miss a date for a subsequent fixture if the *Achilleas* were redelivered late. The majority of the arbitrators also found that, at the time of contracting, the parties, who were both engaged in the business of shipping, would have known that market rates for tonnage go up and down, sometimes quite rapidly. Nevertheless, as Rix LJ himself pointed out [2007] 2 Lloyd's Rep 555, 577, para 120—when seeking to combat any criticism that the Court of Appeal's decision would throw the situation in general into confusion because late redelivery and changing market conditions are common occurrences—'It requires extremely volatile market conditions to create the situation which occurred here'. In other words, the extent of the relevant rise and fall in the market within a short time was actually unusual. The owners' loss stemmed from that unusual occurrence.

54 The obligation of the charterers was to redeliver the vessel to the owners by midnight on 2 May. Therefore, the charterers are taken to have had in contemplation, at the time when they entered into the addendum, the loss which would generally happen in the ordinary course of things if the vessel were deliv- ered some nine days late so that the owners missed the cancelling date for a follow-on fixture. Obviously, that would include loss suffered as a result of the owners not having been paid under the contract for the charterers' use of the vessel for the period after midnight on 2 May. So, as both sides agree, the owners had to be compensated for that loss by the payment of damages. But the parties would also have contemplated that, if the owners lost a fixture, they would then be in a position to enter the market for a substitute fixture. Of course, in some cases, the available market rate would be lower and, in some cases, higher, than the rate under the lost fixture. But the parties would reasonably contemplate that, for the

most part, the availability of the market would protect the owners if they lost a fixture. That I understand to be the thinking which lies behind the dicta to the effect that the appropriate measure of damages for late redelivery of a vessel is the difference between the charter rate and the market rate if the market rate is higher than the charter rate for the period between the final terminal date and redelivery: *Hyundai Merchant Marine Co Ltd v Gesuri Chartering Co Ltd (The Peonia)* [1991] 1 Lloyd's Rep 100, 108 . . .

57 . . . The implication . . . is that, ordinarily, the appropriate measure of damages will be that set out by Bingham LJ in *The Peonia* [1991] 1 Lloyd's Rep 100, since owners will be able to obtain substitute employment for their vessel.

58 I would enter two caveats. First, it may be that, at least in some cases, when concluding a charterparty, a charterer could reasonably contemplate that late delivery of a vessel of that particular type, in a certain area of the world, at a certain season of the year would mean that the market for its services would be poor. In these circumstances, the owners might have a claim for some general sum for loss of business, somewhat along the line of the damages for the loss of business envisaged by the Court of Appeal in *Victoria Laundry (Windsor) Ltd v Newman Industries Ltd* [1949] 2 KB 528, 542–543. Because of the agreement on figures, the matter was not explored in this case and I express no view on it. But, even if some such loss of business could have been reasonably contemplated, as *Victoria Laundry* shows, this would not mean that the owners' particular loss of profit as a result of the re-negotiation of the Cargill fixture should be recoverable. To hold otherwise would risk undermining the first limb of *Hadley v Baxendale*, which limits the charterers' liability to 'the amount of injury' that would arise 'ordinarily' or 'generally'.

59 Secondly, the position on damages might also be different, if, for example—when a charterparty was entered into—the owners drew the charterers' attention to the existence of a forward charter of many months' duration for which the vessel had to be delivered on a particular date. The charterers would know that a failure to redeliver the vessel in time to allow the owners to deliver it under that charter would be liable to result in the loss of that fixture. Then the second rule or limb in *Hadley v Baxendale* might well come into play. But the point does not arise in this case.

60 Returning to the present case, I am satisfied that, when they entered into the addendum in September 2003, neither party would reasonably have contemplated that an overrun of nine days would 'in the ordinary course of things' cause the owners the kind of loss for which they claim damages. That loss was not the 'ordinary consequence' of a breach of that kind. It occurred in this case only because of the extremely volatile market conditions which produced both the owners' initial (particularly lucrative) transaction, with a third party, and the subsequent pressure on the owners to accept a lower rate for that fixture. Back in September 2003, this loss could not have been reasonably foreseen as being likely to arise out of the delay in question. It was, accordingly, too remote to give rise to a claim for damages for breach of contract.

. . .

63 I have not found it necessary to explore the issues concerning *South Australia Asset Management Corpn v York Montague Ltd* [1997] AC 191 and assumption of responsibility, which my noble and learned friend, Lord Hoffmann, has raised. Nevertheless, I am otherwise in substantial agreement with his reasons as well as with those to be given by Lord Walker of Gestingthorpe. I would allow the appeal.

BARONESS HALE OF RICHMOND: 88 . . . Are the first charterers liable to pay only for the use of the ship for the number of days that they were late at the market rate then prevailing? Or are they liable to pay the difference between what the owners would have got from the new charter had the ship been returned in time and what the owners in fact got?

89 My Lords, this could be an examination question. Although the context is a specialised one, the answer has mainly to be found in the general principles to be derived from the well known authorities to

which your Lordships have all referred, principally *Hadley v Baxendale* (1854) 9 Exch 341; *Victoria Laundry (Windsor) Ltd v Newman Industries Ltd* [1949] 2 KB 528 and, above all, *C Czarnikow Ltd v Koufos (The Heron II)* [1969] 1 AC 350. There is no obviously right answer: two very experienced commercial judges have reached one answer, your Lordships have reached another. There is no obviously just answer: the charterer's default undoubtedly caused the owner's loss, but a loss for which no one has ever had to pay before. The examiners would surely have given first class marks to all the judges who have answered the question so far.

90 In common with my noble and learned friend, Lord Hope of Craighead, I was at first inclined to agree with the very full and thoughtful judgments in the courts below which arrived at the second answer. Their careful reviews of the shipping cases show that, although the normal measure of damages is undoubtedly the first, there is no case in which a claim to the second has been rejected. The fact that no one has thought to make such a claim before now does not mean that it is unfounded . . . It is not novel in principle. The object of damages for breach of contract is to put the claimants in the position in which they would have been had the contract been properly performed. Had this contract not been broken in the way that it was, the claimants would have had the benefit of the next fixture at the original rate. Putting them in the position in which they would have been had the contract been performed in accordance with its terms entails paying them the difference. No one has suggested that it was at all unusual or unlikely for the owners to commit their ship to a new fixture to begin as soon as possible after the ship was free from the first. It was conceded before the arbitrators that missing dates for a subsequent fixture was a 'not unlikely' result of late redelivery. Both parties would have been well aware of that at the time when the contract was made. They would also have been well aware that a new charter was likely to commit that particular ship rather than to allow the ship-owner to go into the market and find a substitute to fulfil his next commitment if his ship was late back. Charterparties allowing the owner to substitute a different vessel are unusual. Above all, if the parties wish to exclude liability for consequential loss of this kind then it will be very simple to insert such a clause into future charterparties. It would take a much more complicated piece of drafting, following some complicated negotiations, to impose liability for this sort of loss. To rule out a whole class of loss, simply because the parties had not previously thought about it, risks as much uncertainty and injustice as letting it in.

91 That argument cuts both ways. We are looking here at the general principles which limit a contract breaker's liability when the contract itself does not do so. The contract breaker is not inevitably liable for all the loss which his breach has caused. Loss of the type in question has to be 'within the contemplation' of the parties at the time when the contract was made. It is not enough that it should be foreseeable if it is highly unlikely to happen. It would not then arise 'in the usual course of things': see *The Heron II* [1969] 1 AC 350, 385, per Lord Reid. So one answer to our question, given as I understand it by my noble and learned friend, Lord Rodger of Earlsferry, is that these parties would not have had this particular type of loss within their contemplation. They would expect that the owner would be able to find a use for his ship even if it was returned late. It was only because of the unusual volatility of the market at that particular time that this particular loss was suffered. It is one thing to say, as did the majority arbitrators, that missing dates for a subsequent fixture was within the parties' contemplation as 'not unlikely'. It is another thing to say that the 'extremely volatile' conditions which brought about this particular loss were 'not unlikely'.

92 Another answer to the question, given as I understand it by my noble and learned friends, Lord Hoffmann and Lord Hope, is that one must ask, not only whether the parties must be taken to have had this type of loss within their contemplation when the contract was made, but also whether they must be taken to have had liability for this type of loss within their contemplation then. In other words, is the charterer to be taken to have undertaken legal responsibility for this type of loss? What should the unspoken terms of their contract be taken to be? If that is the question, then it becomes relevant

to ask what has been the normal expectation of parties to such contracts in this particular market. If charterers would not normally expect to pay more than the market rate for the days they were late, and ship-owners would not normally expect to get more than that, then one would expect something extra before liability for an unusual loss such as this would arise. That is essentially the reasoning adopted by the minority arbitrator.

93 My Lords, I hope that I have understood this correctly, for it seems to me that it adds an interesting but novel dimension to the way in which the question of remoteness of damage in contract is to be answered, a dimension which does not clearly emerge from the classic authorities. There is scarcely a hint of it in *The Heron II*, apart perhaps from Lord Reid's reference, at p 385, to the loss being 'sufficiently likely to result from the breach of contract *to make it proper* to hold that the loss flowed naturally from the breach or that loss of that kind should have been within his contemplation' (emphasis supplied). In general, *The Heron II* points the other way, as it emphasises that there are no special rules applying to charterparties and that the law of remoteness in contract is not the same as the law of remoteness in tort. There is more than a hint of it in the judgment of Waller LJ in *Mulvenna v Royal Bank of Scotland plc* [2003] EWCA Civ 1112, but in the context of the 'second limb' of *Hadley v Baxendale* where knowledge of an unusual risk is posited. To incorporate it generally would be to introduce into ordinary contractual liability the principle adopted in the context of liability for professional negligence in *South Australia Asset Management Corpn v York Montague Ltd* [1997] AC 191, 211. In an examination, this might well make the difference between a congratulatory and an ordinary first class answer to the question. But despite the excellence of counsels' arguments it was not explored before us, although it is explored in academic textbooks and other writings, including those cited by Lord Hoffmann in para 11 of his opinion. I note, however, that the most recent of these, Professor Robertson's article on 'The basis of the remoteness rule in contract' (2008) 28 Legal Studies 172 argues strongly to the contrary. I am not immediately attracted to the idea of introducing into the law of contract the concept of the scope of duty which has perforce had to be developed in the law of negligence. The rule in *Hadley v Baxendale* asks what the parties must be taken to have had in their contemplation, rather than what they actually had in their contemplation, but the criterion by which this is judged is a factual one. Questions of assumption of risk depend upon a wider range of factors and value judgments. This type of reasoning is, as Lord Steyn put it in *Aneco Reinsurance Underwriting Ltd v Johnson & Higgins Ltd* [2002] 1 Lloyd's Rep 157, 186, a 'deus ex machina'. Although its result in this case may be to bring about certainty and clarity in this particular market, such an imposed limit on liability could easily be at the expense of justice in some future case. It could also introduce much room for argument in other contractual contexts. Therefore, if this appeal is to be allowed, as to which I continue to have doubts, I would prefer it to be allowed on the narrower ground identified by Lord Rodger, leaving the wider ground to be fully explored in another case and another context.

NOTES

1. With the exception of Lord Walker, whose focus is direct and less concerned with tests and principle, the other members of the House of Lords were greatly influenced by the 'market understanding' of what the measure would be in these circumstances: see Lord Hoffmann (2010) 14 Edin, LR 47, accepting this extrajudicially. They therefore 'reason backwards' with differing degrees of allegiance to the limbs in *Hadley v Baxendale* and the perception that general loss of profits on a follow-on contract might otherwise be considered as contemplatable loss.

2. It must be considered unfortunate that there appears to be majority support for the 'assumption of responsibility' test divorced from the limbs in *Hadley v Baxendale*. It might just as effectively be argued that the parties assume responsibility for normal losses because these are expected (and fall within the scope of the duty or contractual promises made), whereas abnormal losses would not be assumed (and not fall

within the scope of the duty) without a more express assumption of the risk involved. This is a recovery and not a liability question; the breach was clear and identified—and existing principle is perfectly equipped to respond.

3. Their Lordships faced a problem. This appeared to be normal loss on the basis of *The Heron II*. The fact that there would be a follow-on charter would have been within reasonable contemplations as likely to occur. Therefore, on the 'type/extent' principle in *Parsons v Uttley Ingham* [1978] 1 QB 791 (*page 713, 14.6.1*), the full extent of the loss of profit should have been recoverable. That does not necessarily follow, since the identification of the loss is flexible and it could be more narrowly defined. Neither does it follow that the market context had to be ignored; on the contrary, it is a special fact that would have made the particular loss of profits better classified as abnormal loss (in the same way as type of profits had been distinguished by the Court of Appeal in *Victoria Laundry*). It would then have followed that, since the charterer had no knowledge of the special facts relating to the discounted follow-on charter at the date on which the original charter was made, this loss would have been too remote and could not be recovered. That would also have accorded with the outcome accepted as the commercial understanding of the position. In other words, the approach of Lord Rodger has rather more to recommend it.

It is then possible to give expression to that process by saying that the loss did not fall within the parties' reasonable contemplations or that the charterer did not assume responsibility for it. To remove this consequence as a 'loss' by adopting the approach in *South Australia Asset Management Corpn v York Montague Ltd* [1997] AC 191 is artificial, and risks a return to the days when contractual and tortious principles of recovery were confused.

4. The only result of adopting 'assumption of responsibility' as the test is that there are likely to be arguments denying an assumption of responsibility for all and any losses, because this has now become a question of fact in each instance. The clear market understanding in *The Achilleas* is likely to be a rarity. Defendants will need to establish all of the background facts on which they will rely as denying an assumption of responsibility. The result will be complex and unnecessary arguments that raise the possibility of assimilating remoteness in contract and tort. It is to be hoped that the rationale for the special contract test in *Hadley v Baxendale*, as explained and interpreted in *The Heron II*, will prevail.

5. The signs post-*The Achilleas* are encouraging. In *ASM Shipping Ltd of India v TTMI Ltd of England, The Amer Energy* [2009] 1 Lloyd's Rep 293, Flaux J stated, at [17]–[19]:

To the extent that Lord Hoffmann was purporting to lay down some new test as to recoverability of damages in contract, he was in a minority. Although Lord Hope adopts a similar analysis at paras 30 and 36, he does so essentially by way of application of established principles. In any event it is important to note that even Lord Hoffmann acknowledges in paras 9 and 11 of his opinion that departure from the normal principles of foreseeability would be unusual. Although he refers to shipping as a market where limitations on the extent of liability arising out of general expectations in that market might be more common, I do not consider that he was intending to say that in all shipping cases (as opposed to the type of time charter case then under consideration) the rule in *Hadley v Baxendale* as subsequently refined, will no longer apply. If he was saying that, it was not a view shared by the majority and it would be heterodox to say the least.

6. This interpretation also received some support from Cooke J in *Classic Maritime Inc. v Lion Diversified Holdings Berhad* [2009] EWHC 1142 (Comm), [2010] 1 Lloyd's Rep 59, [2010] 1 CLC 445, when he noted the disapproval of Flaux J and commented that it would be surprising if the House of Lords had altered the remoteness test for contract to 'assumption of responsibility'. Cooke J went on to apply the first limb in *Hadley v Baxendale* and to approve references to 'reasonable contemplations'. On the basis that the loss in question was within the parties' contemplations, Cooke J considered that none of their Lordships in *The Achilleas* had said that the full extent of such a loss should not be recoverable.

Thus, the crucial factor may not be that 'assumption of responsibility' and 'reasonable contemplations' are different tests, which Flaux J denied in *The Amer Energy*, but whether it is possible post-*The Achilleas* to retain the limbs of normal loss and abnormal loss to assist in reaching a conclusion on this outcome. The comments in *Classic Maritime* and the application in *GB Gas Holdings Ltd v Accenture (UK) Ltd* [2009] EWHC 2734 (Comm)—reversed in part on other grounds by the Court of Appeal [2010] EWCA Civ 912, but the judge's conclusions on the limbs were incorporated without question—and *Mayhaven Healthcare Ltd v Bothma (t/a DAB Builders)* [2009] EWHC 2634 (TCC), [2010] BLR 154, 127 Con LR 1, suggest that the limbs are not so easily overturned, since they provide an established and helpful route to a conclusion. In *Mayhaven*, the judge made express reference to the fact that he was not applying Lord Hoffmann's principle. He considered that loss of profits was not to be treated as a single 'type of loss', concluding that the particular loss of profit in relation to use of a care home for particular occupants was not recoverable under the first limb in *Hadley* and was also not recoverable under the second limb for lack of actual knowledge.

7. However, the Court of Appeal in *Supershield Ltd v Siemens Building Technologies FE Ltd* [2010] EWCA 7, [2010] 1 Lloyd's Rep 349, [2010] 1 CLC 241, was more willing to accept a reformulation of remoteness principles.

TOULSON LJ [with whom Richards and Mummery LJJ agreed]: 43. *Hadley v Baxendale* remains a standard rule but it has been rationalised on the basis that it reflects the expectation to be imputed to the parties in the ordinary case, i.e. that a contract breaker should ordinarily be liable to the other party for damage resulting from his breach if, but only if, at the time of making the contract a reasonable person in his shoes would have had damage of that kind in mind as not unlikely to result from a breach. However, *South Australia* and *Transfield Shipping* are authority that there may be cases where the court, on examining the contract and the commercial background, decides that the standard approach would not reflect the expectation or intention reasonably to be imputed to the parties. In those two instances the effect was exclusionary; the contract breaker was held not to be liable for loss which resulted from its breach although some loss of the kind was not unlikely. But logically the same principle may have an inclusionary effect. If, on the proper analysis of the contract against its commercial background, the loss was within the scope of the duty, it cannot be regarded as too remote, even if it would not have occurred in ordinary circumstances.

This suggests that if there is no assumption of responsibility for a loss (i.e. it is not within the scope of the contractual duty owed), the normal remoteness principles in *Hadley v Baxendale* can be overridden and the loss will be too remote (the 'exclusionary' effect), and vice versa (the 'inclusionary' effect). This approach and language were subsequently applied by Tomlinson J in *Pindell Ltd v AirAsia Berhad* [2010] EWHC 2516 (Comm), [2011] 2 All ER (Comm) 396, [2012] 2 CLC 1. This seems an uneasy 'fudge' and a recipe for commercial uncertainty, since this broad contextual approach seems to be applied ahead of, or in addition to, the principles and limbs in *Hadley v Baxendale*.

In *John Grimes Partnership Ltd v Gubbins* [2013] EWCA Civ 37, [2013] PNLR 17, [2013] BLR 126, a developer sought damages resulting from the fall in market value of a construction development as a result of the failure to complete the work on time. Was this loss too remote a consequence of the breach? The Court of Appeal held that the type of loss fell within the parties' reasonable contemplations within *Hadley v Baxendale*, which should be departed from only where 'the commercial background' to the agreement indicated that this 'would not reflect the expectation or intention reasonably to be imputed to the parties'.

SIR DAVID KEENE: 24 I too agree with the summary of the law provided by Toulson LJ in *Supershield*, although I would put it in slightly different language. It seems to me to be right to bear in mind, as Lord Hoffmann emphasised in *The Achilleas*, that one is dealing with the law of contract, where the situation is governed by what has been agreed between the parties. If there is no express term dealing with what types of losses a party is accepting potential liability for if he breaks the contract, then the law in effect implies a term to determine the answer. Normally, there is an implied term accepting responsibility for the types of losses which can reasonably be foreseen at the time of contract to be not unlikely to result if the contract is broken. But if there is evidence in a particular case that the nature of the contract and the commercial background, or indeed other relevant special circumstances, render that implied assumption of responsibility inappropriate for a type of loss, then the contract-breaker escapes liability. Such was the case in *The Achilleas*.

In *SC Confectia SA v Miss Mania Wholesale Ltd* [2014] EWCA Civ 1484, Beatson LJ (at [25]) concluded that case law subsequent to *The Achilleas* made it clear that '*Hadley v Baxendale* remains the standard rule and is grounded in policy' and that it could be displaced only in the circumstances referred to by Toulson LJ in *Supershield*.

8. In *Sylvia Shipping Co. Ltd v Progress Bulk Carriers Ltd* [2010] EWHC 542 (Comm), [2010] 2 Lloyd's Rep 81, [2010] 1 CLC 470, Hamblen J considered that assumption of responsibility would be relevant only in exceptional cases:

40 In my judgment, the decision in *The Achilleas* results in an amalgam of the orthodox and the broader approach. The orthodox approach remains the general test of remoteness applicable in the great majority of cases. However, there may be 'unusual' cases, such as *The Achilleas* itself, in which the context, surrounding circumstances or general understanding in the relevant market make it necessary specifically to consider whether there has been an assumption of responsibility. This is most likely to be in those relatively rare cases where the application of the general test leads or may lead to an unquantifiable, unpredictable, uncontrollable or disproportionate liability or where there is clear evidence that such a liability would be contrary to market understanding and expectations.

41 In the great majority of cases it will not be necessary specifically to address the issue of assumption of responsibility. Usually the fact that the type of loss arises in the ordinary course of things or out of special known circumstances will carry with it the necessary assumption of responsibility.

The loss on the facts (loss on a sub-charter, where the owners were late in delivering the vessel) clearly fell within the first limb as normal loss and the general market understanding was that such loss was recoverable. In Singapore, in *MFM Restaurants Pte Ltd v Fish & Co. Restaurants Pte Ltd* [2010] SGCA 36, Andrew Phang Boon Leong JA (delivering the judgment of the Singapore Court of Appeal) rejected 'assumption of responsibility' altogether, noting that the *Achilleas* situation could be accommodated within the existing scope of *Hadley v Baxendale*.

14.7 Mitigation

The injured party is prevented from recovering for losses that he failed to mitigate. Viscount Haldane LC, in *British Westinghouse Electric & Manufacturing Co. Ltd v Underground Electric Railways Co. of London Ltd* [1912] AC 673, at p. 689, said:

> I think that there are certain broad principles which are quite well settled. The first is that, as far as possible, he who has proved a breach of a bargain to supply what he contracted to get is to be placed, as far as money can do it, in as good a situation as if the contract had been performed.
>
> The fundamental basis is thus compensation for pecuniary loss naturally flowing from the breach; but this first principle is qualified by a second, which imposes on a plaintiff the duty of taking all reasonable steps to mitigate the loss consequent on the breach, and debars him from claiming any part of the damage which is due to his neglect to take such steps. In the words of James LJ in *Dunkirk Colliery Co v Lever* (1878) 9 Ch D 20, 'The person who has broken the contract is not to be exposed to additional cost by reason of the plaintiffs not doing what they ought to have done as reasonable men, and the plaintiffs not being under any obligation to do anything otherwise than in the ordinary course of business.'
>
> As James LJ indicates, this second principle does not impose on the plaintiff an obligation to take any step which a reasonable and prudent man would not ordinarily take in the course of his business. But when in the course of his business he has taken action arising out of the transaction, which action has diminished his loss, the effect in actual diminution of the loss he has suffered may be taken into account even though there was no duty on him to act.

NOTE Although the expression 'duty to mitigate' is used, it is not strictly accurate, since there is no liability if the injured party fails to mitigate. The effect of failure to mitigate is to reduce the damages that might otherwise have been payable.

14.7.1 Reasonable steps

Payzu Ltd v Saunders
[1919] 2 KB 581 (CA)

The defendant contracted to sell crêpe de Chine to the claimants, delivery as required within a nine-month period, and payment within one month of delivery. When the claimants failed to pay punctually for the first instalment, the defendant refused to deliver any more under the contract. (This amounted to a repudiatory breach by the defendant.) However, the defendant did offer to deliver the goods at the contract price if the claimants would agree to pay cash when ordering. The claimants refused this offer and sought damages for breach of contract. The market price of crêpe de Chine had risen, and damages of the difference between the market price and contract price were sought.

Held: The claimants should have mitigated their loss by accepting the defendant's offer. Damages were confined to the loss that the claimants would have suffered had they paid cash and acquired the goods at the contract price. The Court of Appeal also held that the question of whether the steps were reasonable was a question of fact in each case.

BANKES LJ: It is plain that the question what is reasonable for a person to do in mitigation of his damages cannot be a question of law but must be one of fact in the circumstances of each particular case. There may be cases where as matter of fact it would be unreasonable to expect a plaintiff to consider any offer made in view of the treatment he has received from the defendant. If he had been rendering personal services and had been dismissed after being accused in presence of others of being a thief, and if after that his employer had offered to take him back into his service, most persons would think he was justified in refusing the offer, and that it would be unreasonable to ask him in this way to mitigate the damages in an action of wrongful dismissal. But that is not to state a principle of law, but a conclusion of fact to be arrived at on a consideration of all the circumstances of the case . . . [Counsel for the appellants] complained that the respondent had treated his clients so badly that it would be unreasonable to expect them to listen to any proposition she might make. I do not agree. In my view each party was ready to accuse the other of conduct unworthy of a high commercial reputation, and there was nothing to justify the appellants in refusing to consider the respondent's offer.

? QUESTION

Who received the benefit of the rise in market price?

NOTES

1. It also appears that an injured party is not required to take action that will damage its reputation or public relations: *London & South of England Building Society v Stone* [1983] 1 WLR 1242.

2. In *Farley v Skinner (No. 2)* [2001] UKHL 49, [2002] 2 AC 732 (*page 738, 14.8.1.5*), the House of Lords considered that it was reasonable for a house purchaser not to sell and to remain in the property after discovering a breach of contract affecting his enjoyment of that property.

3. In *Pilkington v Wood* [1953] Ch 770, the claimant instructed the defendant solicitor to act for him in the purchase of a house. The defendant negligently advised that the title of the vendor was good, when in fact the vendor held as trustee of the property. The defendant argued that the claimant should have mitigated his loss by bringing legal proceedings against the vendor for having conveyed a defective title. It was held, however, that there was no duty to embark on 'a complicated and difficult piece of litigation' in order to protect the defendant from the consequences of his own carelessness.

14.7.2 What if the reasonable steps increase the loss?

Banco de Portugal v Waterlow & Sons Ltd
[1932] AC 452 (HL)

The claimant bank had engaged the defendant printers to print banknotes. In breach of contract, the defendants also delivered a large number of these notes to a criminal, who put them into circulation in Portugal. When the bank discovered this, it withdrew the complete issue of the particular note and undertook to exchange all such notes presented to it for other notes. The defendants argued that they were liable only for the cost of printing new notes and that the remaining loss was caused by the bank's action in exchanging those notes for others.

Held (Lord Warrington of Clyffe and Lord Russell of Killowen dissenting): Since the bank's actions had been reasonable, the value of the currency given in exchange was also recoverable.

LORD MACMILLAN: Where the sufferer from a breach of contract finds himself in consequence of that breach placed in a position of embarrassment the measures which he may be driven to adopt in order to extricate himself ought not to be weighed in nice scales at the instance of the party whose breach of contract has occasioned the difficulty. It is often easy after an emergency has passed to criticize the steps which have been taken to meet it, but such criticism does not come well from those who have themselves created the emergency. The law is satisfied if the party placed in a difficult situation by reason of the breach of a duty owed to him has acted reasonably in the adoption of remedial measures, and he will not be held disentitled to recover the cost of such measures merely because the party in breach can suggest that other measures less burdensome to him might have been taken.

14.7.3 Avoided loss and accounting for benefits

Globalia Business Travel SAU (formerly Travelplan SAU) v Fulton Shipping Inc.
of Panama, The New Flamenco
[2017] UKSC 43

This case concerned an early redelivery of a cruise vessel in November 2007 in breach of a time charter that was due to expire in November 2009. The owners immediately sold the vessel for a sum in excess of US$23.7 million. The vessel had then fallen in value between November 2007 and November 2009 due to the global financial crisis and was worth only US$7 million. Were the owners obliged to give credit for this substantially higher value in their damages claim for net loss of profits in the remaining two years of the charter? This would have extinguished the owners' claim. The judge had held that the owner's decision to sell the vessel was independent of the charterers' breach in redelivering the vessel two years early. The judge laid down 11 propositions, proposition 8 being that 'There is no requirement that the benefit must be of the same kind as the loss being claimed or mitigated.' The Court of Appeal, allowing the appeal held that if the claimant secured a benefit through actions in mitigation which had been caused by a breach of contract and which were actions taken 'in the ordinary course of business', the benefit would need to be brought into account when assessing the claimant's loss.

Held (on further appeal to the Supreme Court): The judge's decision was reinstated by the Supreme Court.

LORD CLARKE: 29. Viewed as a question of principle, most damages issues arise from the default rules which the law devises to give effect to the principle of compensation, while recognising that there may be special facts which show that the default rules will not have that effect in particular cases. On the facts here the fall in value of the vessel was in my opinion irrelevant because the owners' interest in the capital value of the vessel had nothing to do with the interest injured by the charterers' repudiation of the charterparty.

30. This was not because the benefit must be of the same kind as the loss caused by the wrongdoer. In this regard I agree in particular with the eighth proposition identified by the judge . . . As I see it, difference in kind is too vague and potentially too arbitrary a test. The essential question is whether there is a sufficiently close link between the two and not whether they are similar in nature. The relevant link is causation. The benefit to be brought into account must have been caused either by the breach of the charterparty or by a successful act of mitigation.

31. On the facts found by the arbitrator, the benefit that the charterers are seeking to have brought into account is the benefit of having avoided a loss of just under about US$17m by selling the vessel

in October 2007 for US$23,765,000 by comparison with the value of the vessel in November 2009, namely (as the arbitrator found) US$7m.

32. That difference or loss was, in my opinion, not on the face of it caused by the repudiation of the charterparty. The repudiation resulted in a prospective loss of income for a period of about two years. Yet, there was nothing about the premature termination of the charterparty which made it necessary to sell the vessel, either at all or at any particular time. Indeed, it could have been sold during the term of the charterparty. If the owners decide to sell the vessel, whether before or after termination of the charterparty, they are making a commercial decision at their own risk about the disposal of an interest in the vessel which was no part of the subject matter of the charterparty and had nothing to do with the charterers.

NOTE The Supreme Court did not review earlier decisions in reaching this conclusion, but the principles laid down by the Supreme Court can be seen in operation in earlier cases. In *Thai Airways International Public Company Ltd v KI Holdings Co. Ltd* [2015] EWHC 1250 (Comm) the breach involved a failure to deliver aircraft seats. Thai Airways sought to recover its expenses in mitigation, including the cost of leasing a third party aircraft (approx. $162 million) and the cost of purchasing alternative, more expensive, seats. Koito argued that Thai Airways's costs in mitigation should be offset against the financial benefits it had derived in the process, i.e. the profits made from operating the additional leased aircraft as well as fuel savings following from the lighter seats it had purchased, and that these eliminated the airline's losses. Leggatt J accepted that any increased profits or savings had to be deducted from the airline's losses despite the fact that this profitability resulted from acts of mitigation. He also considered that since a lease for two years would have been sufficient to mitigate, taking the lease for three years was commercially motivated and the airline could not recover the lease costs for the extra year.

The burden of identifying the benefits arising in mitigation to the injured party was held to lie on the party in breach by analogy with the burden of proof in the wasted expenditure cases: *Omak Maritime Ltd v Mamola Challenger Shipping Co.* [2010] EWHC 2026 (Comm), [2011] Bus LR 212 and *Yam Seng Pte Ltd v International Trade Corp Ltd* [2013] EWHC 111 (QB), [2013] 1 CLC 662, [2013] 1 All ER (Comm) 1321 (*page 696, 14.3.3*). Since Koito had failed to show that the increased profits covered the cost of the two-year lease, Thai Airways was awarded the full cost of $107 million. Koito had also failed to demonstrate fuel savings in relation to some of the alternative seats so that these savings could also not be offset.

14.8 Non-pecuniary loss

14.8.1 Damages for disappointment and distress

14.8.1.1 The general rule

In *Addis v Gramophone Co. Ltd* [1909] AC 488, the House of Lords held that any damages award for wrongful dismissal must not compensate for injured feelings—but see the attempt to circumvent this in *Johnson v Unisys Ltd* [2001] UKHL 13, [2001] 2 WLR 1076. The House of Lords in *Johnson v Gore Wood & Co. (a firm)* [2002] 2 AC 1 approved the general principle in *Addis* that damages for breach of contract should not generally include damages for disappointment and distress (non-pecuniary loss).

14.8.1.2 Limited exceptions

There are two exceptional cases in which such damages for distress can be recovered in contract. The authoritative statement of the law is the statement of Bingham LJ in *Watts v Morrow* [1991] 1 WLR 1421, at p. 1445.

BINGHAM LJ: A contract-breaker is not in general liable for any distress, frustration, anxiety, displeasure, vexation, tension or aggravation which his breach of contract may cause to the innocent party. This rule is not, I think, founded on the assumption that such reactions are not foreseeable, which they surely are or may be, but on considerations of policy.

But the rule is not absolute. Where the very object of a contract is to provide pleasure, relaxation, peace of mind or freedom from molestation, damages will be awarded if the fruit of the contract is not provided or if the contrary result is procured instead. If the law did not cater for this exceptional category of case it would be defective. A contract to survey the condition of a house for a prospective purchaser does not, however, fall within this exceptional category.

In cases not falling within this exceptional category, damages are in my view recoverable for physical inconvenience and discomfort caused by the breach and mental suffering directly related to that inconvenience and discomfort. If those effects are foreseeably suffered during a period when defects are repaired I am prepared to accept that they sound in damages even though the cost of the repairs is not recoverable as such. But I also agree that awards should be restrained . . .

NOTE This statement was cited with approval by Lord Cooke in *Johnson v Gore Wood & Co.* [2002] 2 AC 1, at p. 49, and by Lord Steyn in *Farley v Skinner* (*No. 2*) [2001] UKHL 49, [2002] 2 AC 732, [14]. It was also cited by Lord Bingham himself in *Johnson v Gore Wood & Co.*, at p. 37.

Bliss v South East Thames Regional Health Authority
[1987] ICR 700 (CA)

The claimant was employed by the defendant health authority as a consultant orthopaedic surgeon. Following a dispute with a colleague, the regional health authority required him to undergo a psychiatric examination, but the claimant refused to comply and was suspended. The claimant's solicitors alleged that the defendant had repudiated the claimant's employment contract. The claimant then brought an action against the defendant health authority for damages for breach of contract, and the judge's award included £2,000 damages for mental distress.

Held (on appeal): In contract, it was not possible to recover damages for distress in cases of wrongful dismissal. The Court of Appeal overruled *Cox v Philips Industries Ltd* [1976] 3 All ER 161, which had suggested that such damages were more widely available.

DILLON LJ: It remains to consider . . . the validity of the judge's award of £2,000 with interest by way of general damages for frustration and mental distress. In making such an award, the judge considered that he was justified by the decision of Lawson J in *Cox v Philips Industries Ltd* [1976] ICR 138. With every respect to them, however, the views of Lawson J in that case and of the judge in the present case are on this point, in my judgment, wrong.

The general rule laid down by the House of Lords in *Addis v Gramophone Co. Ltd* [1909] AC 488 is that where damages fall to be assessed for breach of contract rather than in tort it is not permissible to award general damages for frustration, mental distress, injured feelings or annoyance occasioned by the breach. Modern thinking tends to be that the amount of damages recoverable for a wrong should be the same whether the cause of action is laid in contract or in tort. But in the *Addis* case Lord Loreburn regarded the rule that damages for injured feelings cannot be recovered in contract for wrongful dismissal as too inveterate to be altered, and Lord James of Hereford supported his concurrence in the speech of Lord Loreburn by reference to his own experience at the Bar.

There are exceptions now recognised where the contract which has been broken was itself a contract to provide peace of mind or freedom from distress: see *Jarvis v Swans Tours Ltd* [1973] QB 233 and *Heywood v Wellers* [1976] QB 446. Those decisions, do not however cover this present case.

In *Cox v Philips Industries Ltd* [1976] ICR 138 Lawson J took the view that damages for distress, vexation and frustration, including consequent ill-health, could be recovered for breach of a contract of employment if it could be said to have been in the contemplation of the parties that the breach would cause such distress etc. For my part, I do not think that that general approach is open to this court unless and until the House of Lords has reconsidered its decision in the *Addis* case.

14.8.1.3 Contracts the object of which is to provide peace of mind or freedom from distress

Holiday contracts fall within the category of contracts 'to provide peace of mind' under which such damages are recoverable.

Jarvis v Swans Tours Ltd
[1973] QB 233 (CA)

As his annual fortnight's holiday, the claimant booked a Christmas skiing holiday with the defendants for £63.45. The defendants' brochure described the holiday as a 'house party', and stated that the hotel had its own bar and that various social activities were included in the price. There were only 13 people at the hotel in the first week; in the second week, the claimant was the only resident, so that there was no 'house party' at all. The skiing did not correspond to the claims in the brochure, and the social events were limited and not as the brochure would have led guests to expect. The claimant claimed damages for these breaches of contract.

Held: The claimant was entitled to be compensated for his disappointment and distress at the loss of his holiday, and for the loss of the facilities that had been promised in the brochure.

LORD DENNING MR: In a proper case damages for mental distress can be recovered in contract, just as damages for shock can be recovered in tort. One such case is a contract for a holiday, or any other contract to provide entertainment and enjoyment. If the contracting party breaks his contract, damages can be given for the disappointment, the distress, the upset and frustration caused by the breach. I know, that it is difficult to assess in terms of money, but it is no more difficult than the assessment which the courts have to make every day in personal injury cases for loss of amenities. Take the present case. Mr Jarvis has only a fortnight's holiday in the year. He books it far ahead, and looks forward to it all that time. He ought to be compensated for the loss of it.

A good illustration was given by Edmund Davies LJ in the course of the argument. He put the case of a man who has taken a ticket for Glyndebourne. It is the only night on which he can get there. He hires a car to take him. The car does not turn up. His damages are not limited to the mere cost of the ticket. He is entitled to general damages for the disappointment he has suffered and the loss of the entertainment which he should have had. Here, Mr Jarvis's fortnight's winter holiday has been a grave disappointment. It is true that he was conveyed to Switzerland and back and had meals and bed in the hotel. But that is not what he went for. He went to enjoy himself with all the facilities which the defendants said he would have. He is entitled to damages for the lack of those facilities and for his loss of enjoyment . . .

I think the judge was in error in taking the sum paid for the holiday £63.45 and halving it. The right measure of damages is to compensate him for the loss of entertainment and enjoyment which he was promised, and which he did not get.

Looking at the matter quite broadly, I think the damages in this case should be the sum of £125.

NOTES

1. An example of a contract the purpose of which is freedom from distress is provided by *Heywood v Wellers* [1976] QB 446. The claimant employed the defendant solicitors to secure a method of preventing a former male friend from pestering her. The solicitors sought a non-molestation injunction, but were negligent in making the application, so that the injunction was ineffective and the claimant was molested on three or four further occasions, causing her mental distress and upset. The Court of Appeal awarded damages, which included a sum to compensate her for the anxiety and distress that she had suffered in consequence of the continued molestation, since this was a direct and foreseeable consequence of the solicitors' failure to obtain the relief that it was the very purpose of the contract to secure.

In *Yearworth v North Bristol NHS Trust* [2009] EWCA Civ 37, [2009] 3 WLR 118, the Court of Appeal held that contractual arrangements for the storage of sperm amounted to a contract for the provision of peace of mind, in that the purpose of the contract was to preserve the ability for the men involved to become fathers when they were about to undergo cancer treatment, which would impact their fertility. It followed that modest recovery of damages for distress was possible when the storage equipment failed.

2. In these examples, it appears that damages for distress were available in order to compensate the claimant for loss of expectation under those contracts, thereby taking account of 'subjective' losses. The *very purpose* of the contracts had been lost.

3. The scope of this exception had always been limited by the need to show that this purpose was 'the very object' of the contract. This limitation necessarily resulted in the exclusion of commercial contracts from the scope of the exception.

14.8.1.4 The basis for a loss of amenity award

In *Ruxley Electronics v Forsyth* [1996] 1 AC 344 (*page 681, 14.2.2.1*), the House of Lords confirmed the trial judge's award of £2,500 for loss of pleasurable amenity. For tactical reasons, there was no substantial argument before the House of Lords regarding this figure or the basis for the award. The only speech dealing with the matter in any depth is that of Lord Lloyd.

LORD LLOYD:

Loss of amenity

I turn last to the head of damages under which the judge awarded £2,500 . . . In the Court of Appeal Mr Forsyth sought to increase the award under this head. According to Staughton LJ this led to an interesting argument. But the Court of Appeal did not find it necessary to deal with the point.

Before your Lordships, [counsel for the defendant] abandoned the point altogether, for what [counsel for the plaintiff] described as forensic reasons. It undermined the main theme of his argument that since difference in value gave Mr Forsyth nothing by way of damages, he must be entitled to the cost of reinstatement. So [counsel for the defendant] was contending that the judge's award of £2,500 was without precedent in the field of damages, and was fundamentally inconsistent with the decision of this House in *Addis v Gramophone Co. Ltd* [1909] AC 488. For obvious reasons, [counsel for the plaintiff] did not press the contrary argument. So your Lordships are placed in something of a difficulty. The House does not have the benefit of the views of the Court of Appeal on the point, and the submissions before your Lordships have been artificially restricted.

Addis v Gramophone Co. Ltd established the general rule that in claims for breach of contract, the plaintiff cannot recover damages for his injured feelings. But the rule, like most rules, is subject to exceptions. One of the well-established exceptions is when the object of the contract is to afford pleasure, as, for example, where the plaintiff has booked a holiday with a tour operator. If the tour operator is in breach of contract by failing to provide what the contract called for, the plaintiff may recover damages for his disappointment: see *Jarvis v Swans Tours Ltd* [1973] QB 233 and *Jackson v Horizon Holidays Ltd* [1975] 1 WLR 1468.

This was, as I understand it, the principle which Judge Diamond applied in the present case. He took the view that the contract was one 'for the provision of a pleasurable amenity'. In the event, Mr Forsyth's pleasure was not so great as it would have been if the swimming pool had been 7 feet 6 inches deep. This was a view which the judge was entitled to take. If it involves a further inroad on the rule in *Addis v Gramophone Co. Ltd* [1909] AC 488, then so be it. But I prefer to regard it as a logical application or adaptation of the existing exception to a new situation. I should, however, add this note of warning. Mr Forsyth was, I think, lucky to have obtained so large an award for his disappointed expectations. But as there was no criticism from any quarter as to the quantum of the award as distinct from the underlying principle, it would not be right for your Lordships to interfere with the judge's figure.

That leaves one last question for consideration. I have expressed agreement with the judge's approach to damages based on loss of amenity on the facts of the present case. But in most cases such an approach would not be available. What is then to be the position where, in the case of a new house, the building does not conform in some minor respect to the contract, as, for example, where there is a difference in level between two rooms, necessitating a step. Suppose there is no measurable difference in value of the complete house, and the cost of reinstatement would be prohibitive. Is there any reason why the court should not award by way of damages for breach of contract some modest sum, not based on difference in value, but solely to compensate the buyer for his disappointed expectations? Is the law of damages so inflexible, as I asked earlier, that it cannot find some middle ground in such a case? I do not give a final answer to that question in the present case. But it may be that it would have afforded an alternative ground for justifying the judge's award of damages. And if the judge had wanted a precedent, he could have found it in Sir David Cairns' judgment in *G W Atkins Ltd v Scott* 7 Const LJ 215, where, it will be remembered, the Court of Appeal upheld the judge's award of £250 for defective tiling. Sir David Cairns said, at p. 221:

> There are many circumstances where a judge has nothing but his common sense to guide him in fixing the quantum of damages, for instance, for pain and suffering, for loss of pleasurable activities or for inconvenience of one kind or another.

Nevertheless, it must be doubted whether an award of loss of amenity is generally available outside the context of the 'pleasure' exception to *Addis v Gramophone*—see Poole (1996) 59 MLR 272—so that if the main purpose of the contract is not the provision of pleasure, e.g. commercial contracts, *Ruxley* will not permit a loss of amenity award.

Regus (UK) Ltd v Epcot Solutions Ltd
[2007] EWHC 938 (Comm), [2007] 2 All ER (Comm) 766

This case concerned a contract for serviced office accommodation. The air-conditioning system was defective and a third party inspector had recommended urgent remedial work, costing £23,500, but this was not carried out. In its claim for damages for breach of contract, the accommodation user had sought, along with damages for loss of profits, damages for distress, inconvenience, and loss of amenity in connection with the defective air-conditioning system.

Held: There was no authority permitting recovery for loss of amenity where the purpose of the contract was not to provide pleasure and *Ruxley* could not apply here.

JUDGE MACKIE QC [referring to *Ruxley Electronics v Forsyth*]: 48 . . . As I read the decision however the House of Lords when reversing the decision of the Court of Appeal to overturn the judgment of the Mercantile Judge also upheld, for the most part in passing, an award of damages of £2,500 for loss of the pleasurable amenity (ie fun) of a swimming pool. This was on the basis that the contract was one to provide pleasure and amenity analogous to *Jarvis* and the holiday cases, and thus very different from the business purpose of the contract in this case. Epcot does not however appear to claim damages for loss of any subjective or idiosyncratic pleasure or amenity and it would be unusual, if not impossible for a company to do so. For the most part a company's advances and setbacks are measured in financial terms. I emphasise that I was taken to no authority on this issue.

14.8.1.5 'A major or important object'

The House of Lords has awarded distress damages for so-called 'loss of amenity' on the basis that the *major or important object* of the contract was to provide pleasure, relaxation, or peace of mind.

Farley v Skinner (No. 2)
[2001] UKHL 49, [2002] 2 AC 732 (HL)

The claimant was considering the purchase of a house situated 15 miles from Gatwick airport. He employed the defendant surveyor and specifically requested that the defendant should investigate whether the property would be affected by aircraft noise, since he did not wish to live on a flight path. The surveyor's report stated that it was unlikely that the property would suffer greatly from such noise. The claimant purchased the property and spent money on modernization. However, when he moved in, he discovered that the property was badly affected by aircraft noise because it was close to a navigation beacon where aircraft were 'stacked' at busy times awaiting clearance to land. He decided not to sell, but wanted to recover damages for the breach of contract. The judge at first instance found that there was no difference between the purchase price and the market value of the property (i.e. no difference in value), but awarded £10,000 as damages for distress consequent upon physical discomfort (*page 733, 14.8.1*), since the noise was 'a confounded nuisance'. The majority of the Court of Appeal allowed the defendant's appeal against this award on the basis that there was no physical inconvenience and the case did not fall within the exceptional category, since 'the very object' of the contract was to undertake the survey with reasonable care and skill rather than the provision of peace of mind. The obligation to investigate the aircraft noise was a minor aspect of the overall contract purpose.

Held (on appeal to the House of Lords, allowing the appeal and restoring the award of the trial judge): Although distress damages for breach of contract were not generally available, they could be awarded for distress and disappointment at the loss of a pleasurable amenity where the provision of that amenity was 'a major or important part of the contract rather than its sole object'. The obligation to investigate the aircraft noise was *a major or important* part of this contract, because the claimant had specifically asked for confirmation on this matter. Alternatively, and *obiter*, their Lordships considered that the claimant might have recovered damages for distress consequent on physical inconvenience.

LORD STEYN (with whose reasons Lord Browne-Wilkinson and Lord Scott agreed) [referred to the two exceptions identified by Bingham LJ in *Watts v Morrow* [1991] 1 WLR 1421, 1445 (*page 686, 14.2.2.2*) and continued]: 16 The scope of these exceptions is in issue in the present case. It is, however, correct, as counsel for the surveyor submitted, that the entitlement to damages for mental distress caused by a breach of contract is not established by mere foreseeability: the right to recovery is dependent on the case falling fairly within the principles governing the special exceptions. So far there is no real disagreement between the parties.

VI. The very object of the contract: the framework

17 I reverse the order in which the Court of Appeal considered the two issues. I do so because the issue whether the present case falls within the exceptional category governing cases where the very object of the contact is to give pleasure, and so forth, focuses directly on the terms actually agreed between the parties. It is concerned with the reasonable expectations of the parties under the specific terms of the contract. Logically, it must be considered first.

18 It is necessary to examine the case on a correct characterisation of the plaintiff's claim. Stuart-Smith LJ [in the Court of Appeal] [2000] Lloyd's Rep PN 516, 521 thought that the obligation undertaken by the surveyor was 'one relatively minor aspect of the overall instructions'. What Stuart-Smith and Mummery LJJ would have decided if they had approached it on the basis that the obligation was a major or important part of the contract between the plaintiff and the surveyor is not clear. But the Court of Appeal's characterisation of the case was not correct. The plaintiff made it crystal clear to the surveyor that the impact of aircraft noise was a matter of importance to him. Unless he obtained reassuring information from the surveyor he would not have bought the property. That is the tenor of the evidence. It is also what the judge found. The case must be approached on the basis that the surveyor's obligation to investigate aircraft noise was a major or important part of the contract between him and the plaintiff. It is also important to note that, unlike in *Addis v Gramophone Co Ltd* [1909] AC 488, the plaintiff's claim is not for injured feelings caused by the breach of contract. Rather it is a claim for damages flowing from the surveyor's failure to investigate and report, thereby depriving the buyer of the chance of making an informed choice whether or not to buy resulting in mental distress and disappointment.

19 The broader legal context of *Watts v Morrow* [1991] 1 WLR 1421 must be borne in mind. The exceptional category of cases where the very object of a contract is to provide pleasure, relaxation, peace of mind or freedom from molestation is not the product of Victorian contract theory but the result of evolutionary developments in case law from the 1970s. Several decided cases informed the description given by Bingham LJ of this category. The first was the decision of the sheriff court in *Diesen v Samson* 1971 SLT (Sh Ct) 49. A photographer failed to turn up at a wedding, thereby leaving the couple without a photographic record of an important and happy day. The bride was awarded damages for her distress and disappointment. In the celebrated case of *Jarvis v Swans Tours Ltd* [1973] QB 233, the plaintiff recovered damages for mental distress flowing from a disastrous holiday resulting from a travel agent's negligent representations: compare also *Jackson v Horizon Holidays Ltd* [1975] 1 WLR 1468. In *Heywood v Wellers* [1976] QB 446, the plaintiff instructed solicitors to bring proceedings to restrain a man from molesting her. The solicitors negligently failed to take appropriate action with the result that the molestation continued. The Court of Appeal allowed the plaintiff damages for mental distress and upset. While apparently not cited in *Watts v Morrow* [1991] 1 WLR 1421, *Jackson v Chrysler Acceptances Ltd* [1978] RTR 474 was decided before *Watts v Morrow*. In *Jackson's* case the claim was for damages in respect of a motor car which did not meet the implied condition of merchantability in section 14 of the Sale of Goods Act 1893 (56 & 57 Vict c 71). The buyer communicated to the seller that one of his reasons for buying the car was a forthcoming touring holiday in France. Problems with the car spoilt the holiday. The disappointment of a spoilt holiday was a substantial element in the award sanctioned by the Court of Appeal.

20 At their Lordships' request counsel for the plaintiff produced a memorandum based on various publications which showed the impact of the developments already described on litigation in the county courts. Taking into account the submissions of counsel for the surveyor and making due allowance for a tendency of the court sometimes not to distinguish between the cases presently under consideration and cases of physical inconvenience and discomfort, I am satisfied that in the real life of our lower courts non-pecuniary damages are regularly awarded on the basis that the defendant's breach of contract deprived

the plaintiff of the very object of the contract, viz pleasure, relaxation, and peace of mind. The cases arise in diverse contractual contexts, e g the supply of a wedding dress or double glazing, hire purchase transactions, landlord and tenant, building contracts, and engagements of estate agents and solicitors. The awards in such cases seem modest. For my part what happens on the ground casts no doubt on the utility of the developments since the 1970s in regard to the award of non-pecuniary damages in the exceptional categories. But the problem persists of the precise scope of the exceptional category of case involving awards of non-pecuniary damages for breach of contract where the very object of the contract was to ensure a party's pleasure, relaxation or peace of mind . . .

VII. The very object of the contract: the arguments against the plaintiff's claim

22 Counsel for the surveyor advanced three separate arguments each of which he said was sufficient to defeat the plaintiff's claim. First, he submitted that even if a major or important part of the contract was to give pleasure, relaxation and peace of mind, that was not enough. It is an indispensable requirement that the object of the entire contract must be of this type. Secondly, he submitted that the exceptional category does not extend to a breach of a contractual duty of care, even if imposed to secure pleasure, relaxation and peace of mind. It only covers cases where the promiser guarantees achievement of such an object . . .

23 The first argument fastened onto a narrow reading of the words 'the very object of [the] contract' as employed by Bingham LJ in *Watts v Morrow* [1991] 1 WLR 1421, 1445. Cases where a major or important part of the contract was to secure pleasure, relaxation and peace of mind were not under consideration in *Watts v Morrow*. It is difficult to see what the principled justification for such a limitation might be. After all, in 1978, the Court of Appeal allowed such a claim in *Jackson v Chrysler Acceptances Ltd* [1978] RTR 474 in circumstances where a spoiled holiday was only one object of the contract. Counsel was, however, assisted by the decision of the Court of Appeal in *Knott v Bolton* (1995) 11 Const LJ 375 which in the present case the Court of Appeal treated as binding on it. In *Knott v Bolton* an architect was asked to design a wide staircase for a gallery and impressive entrance hall. He failed to do so. The plaintiff spent money in improving the staircase to some extent and he recovered the cost of the changes. The plaintiff also claimed damages for disappointment and distress at the lack of an impressive staircase. In agreement with the trial judge the Court of Appeal disallowed this part of his claim. Reliance was placed on the dicta of Bingham LJ in *Watts v Morrow* [1991] 1 WLR 1421, 1445.

24 Interpreting the dicta of Bingham LJ in *Watts v Morrow* narrowly the Court of Appeal in *Knott v Bolton* ruled that the central object of the contract was to design a house, not to provide pleasure to the occupiers of the house. It is important, however, to note that *Knott v Bolton* was decided a few months before the decision of the House in *Ruxley Electronics and Construction Ltd v Forsyth* [1996] AC 344. In any event, the technicality of the reasoning in *Knott v Bolton*, and therefore in the Court of Appeal judgments in the present case, is apparent. It is obvious, and conceded, that if an architect is employed only to design a staircase, or a surveyor is employed only to investigate aircraft noise, the breach of such a distinct obligation may result in an award of non-pecuniary damages. Logically the same must be the case if the architect or surveyor, apart from entering into a general retainer, concludes a separate contract, separately remunerated, in respect of the design of a staircase or the investigation of aircraft noise. If this is so the distinction drawn in *Knott v Bolton* and in the present case is a matter of form and not substance. David Capper, 'Damages for Distress and Disappointment: The Limits of Watts v Morrow' (2000) 116 LQR 553, 556 has persuasively argued:

> A ruling that intangible interests only qualify for legal protection where they are the 'very object of the contract' is tantamount to a ruling that contracts where these interests are merely important, but not the central object of the contract, are in part unenforceable. It is very difficult to see what policy objection there can be to parties to a contract

agreeing that these interests are to be protected via contracts where the central object is something else. If the defendant is unwilling to accept this responsibility he or she can say so and either no contract will be made or one will be made but including a disclaimer.

There is no reason in principle or policy why the scope of recovery in the exceptional category should depend on the object of the contract as ascertained from all its constituent parts. It is sufficient if a major or important object of the contract is to give pleasure, relaxation or peace of mind. In my view, *Knott v Bolton* 11 Const LJ 375 was wrongly decided and should be overruled. To the extent that the majority in the Court of Appeal relied on *Knott v Bolton* their decision was wrong.

25 That brings me to the second issue, namely whether the plaintiff's claim is barred by reason of the fact that the surveyor undertook an obligation to exercise reasonable care and did not guarantee the achievement of a result. This was the basis upon which Hale LJ after the first hearing in the Court of Appeal thought that the claim should be disallowed. This reasoning was adopted by the second Court of Appeal and formed an essential part of the reasoning of the majority. This was the basis on which they distinguished *Ruxley Electronics and Construction Ltd v Forsyth* [1996] AC 344. Against the broad sweep of differently framed contractual undertakings, and the central purpose of contract law in promoting the observance of contractual promises, I am satisfied that this distinction ought not to prevail. It is certainly not rooted in precedent. I would not accept the suggestion that it has the pedigree of an observation of Ralph Gibson LJ in *Watts v Morrow* [1991] 1 WLR 1421, 1442b–d: his emphasis appears to have been on the fact that the contract did not serve to provide peace of mind, and so forth. As far as I am aware the distinction was first articulated in the present case. In any event, I would reject it. I fully accept, of course, that contractual guarantees of performance and promises to exercise reasonable care are fundamentally different. The former may sometimes give greater protection than the latter. Proving breach of an obligation of reasonable care may be more difficult than proving breach of a guarantee. On the other hand, a party may in practice be willing to settle for the relative reassurance offered by the obligation of reasonable care undertaken by a professional man. But why should this difference between an absolute and relative contractual promise require a distinction in respect of the recovery of non-pecuniary damages? Take the example of a travel agent who is consulted by a couple who are looking for a golfing holiday in France. Why should it make a difference in respect of the recoverability of non-pecuniary damages for a spoiled holiday whether the travel agent gives a guarantee that there is a golf course very near the hotel, represents that to be the case, or negligently advises that all hotels of the particular chain of hotels are situated next to golf courses? If the nearest golf course is in fact 50 miles away a breach may be established. It may spoil the holiday of the couple. It is difficult to see why in principle only those plaintiffs who negotiate guarantees may recover non-pecuniary damages for a breach of contract. It is a singularly unattractive result that a professional man, who undertakes a specific obligation to exercise reasonable care to investigate a matter judged and communicated to be important by his customer, can in Lord Mustill's words in *Ruxley Electronics and Construction Ltd v Forsyth* [1996] AC 344, 360 'please himself whether or not to comply with the wishes of the promise which, as embodied in the contract, formed part of the consideration for the price'. If that were the law it would be seriously deficient. I am satisfied that it is not the law. In my view the distinction drawn by Hale LJ and by the majority in the Court of Appeal between contractual guarantees and obligations of reasonable care is unsound . . .

VIII. Quantum

28 In the surveyor's written case it was submitted that the award of £10,000 was excessive. It was certainly high. Given that the plaintiff is stuck indefinitely with a position which he sought to avoid by the terms of his contract with the surveyor I am not prepared to interfere with the judge's evaluation on

the special facts of the case. On the other hand, I have to say that the size of the award appears to be at the very top end of what could possibly be regarded as appropriate damages. Like Bingham LJ in *Watts v Morrow* [1991] 1 WLR 1421, 1445h I consider that awards in this area should be restrained and modest. It is important that logical and beneficial developments in this corner of the law should not contribute to the creation of a society bent on litigation.

LORD SCOTT: 74 The reason why such an apparently straightforward issue has caused such division of opinion is because it has been represented as raising the question whether and when contractual damages for mental distress are available. It is highly desirable that your Lordships should resolve the present angst on this subject and avoid the need in the future for relatively simple claims, such as Mr Farley's, to have to travel to the appellate courts for a ruling.

75 In my opinion, the issue can and should be resolved by applying the well known principles laid down in *Hadley v Baxendale* (1854) 9 Exch 341 (as restated in *Victoria Laundry (Windsor) Ltd v Newman Industries Ltd* [1949] 2 KB 528) in the light of the recent guidance provided by Bingham LJ in *Watts v Morrow* [1991] 1 WLR 1421 and by this House in *Ruxley Electronics and Construction Ltd v Forsyth* [1996] AC 344.

76 The basic principle of damages for breach of contract is that the injured party is entitled, so far as money can do it, to be put in the position he would have been in if the contractual obligation had been properly performed. He is entitled, that is to say, to the benefit of his bargain: see *Robinson v Harman* (1848) 1 Exch 850, 855.

[Lord Scott then referred to *Ruxley Electronics v Forsyth* and continued:]

79 *Ruxley's* case establishes, in my opinion, that if a party's contractual performance has failed to provide to the other contracting party something to which that other was, under the contract, entitled, and which, if provided, would have been of value to that party, then, if there is no other way of compensating the injured party, the injured party should be compensated in damages to the extent of that value. Quantification of that value will in many cases be difficult and may often seem arbitrary. In *Ruxley's* case the value placed on the amenity value of which the pool owner had been deprived was £2,500. By that award, the pool owner was placed, so far as money could do it, in the position he would have been in if the diving area of the pool had been constructed to the specified depth.

80 In *Ruxley's* case the breach of contract by the builders had not caused any consequential loss to the pool owner. He had simply been deprived of the benefit of a pool built to the depth specified in the contract. It was not a case where the recovery of damages for consequential loss consisting of vexation, anxiety or other species of mental distress had to be considered.

81 In *Watts v Morrow* [1991] 1 WLR 1421, however, that matter did have to be considered. As in the present case, the litigation in *Watts v Morrow* resulted from a surveyor's report . . . [Lord Scott gave the facts of *Watts v Morrow* (*page 686, 14.2.2.2*) and continued:] As to the damages for 'distress and inconvenience' the Court of Appeal upheld the award in principle but held that the damages should be limited to a modest sum for the physical discomfort endured and reduced the award to £750 for each plaintiff . . .

86 In summary, the principle expressed in *Ruxley Electronics and Construction Ltd v Forsyth* [1996] AC 344 should be used to provide damages for deprivation of a contractual benefit where it is apparent that the injured party has been deprived of something of value but the ordinary means of measuring the recoverable damages are inapplicable. The principle expressed in *Watts v Morrow* [1991] 1 WLR 1421 should be used to determine whether and when contractual damages for inconvenience or discomfort can be recovered.

87 These principles, in my opinion, provide the answer, not only to the issue raised in the present case, but also to the issues raised in the authorities which were cited to your Lordships.

88 In *Hobbs v London and South Western Railway Co.* LR 10 QB 111 the claim was for consequential damage caused by the railway company's breach of contract. Instead of taking the plaintiff, his wife and two children to Hampton Court, their train dumped them at Esher and they had to walk five miles or so home in the rain. The plaintiff's wife caught a cold as a result of the experience. The plaintiff was awarded damages for the inconvenience and discomfort of his and his family's walk home but his wife's cold was held to be too remote a consequence. The plaintiff's recovery of damages attributable, in part, to the discomfort suffered by his wife and children was in accordance with principle. The contractual benefit to which he was entitled was the carriage of himself and his family to Hampton Court. It was reasonable in my opinion, to value that benefit, of which he had been deprived by the breach of contract, by reference to the discomfort to the family of the walk home. This was, in my view, a *Ruxley Electronics* case.

89 *Jarvis v Swans Tours Ltd* [1973] QB 233 was a case in which the plaintiff had contracted for a holiday with certain enjoyable qualities. He had been given a holiday which lacked those qualities. His holiday had caused him discomfort and distress. The trial judge awarded him £31.72, one-half of the price of the holiday. This must, I think have been the value attributed by the judge to the contractual benefit of which the plaintiff had been deprived. But on the plaintiff's appeal against so low an award, the Court of Appeal allowed him £125.

90 Somewhat different reasons were given by the three members of the court. Lord Denning MR said, at pp 237–238:

> In a proper case damages for mental distress can be recovered in contract . . . One such case is a contract for a holiday, or any other contract to provide entertainment and enjoyment. If the contracting party breaks his contract, damages can be given for the disappointment, the distress, the upset and frustration caused by the breach.

The reference in this passage to the 'contract for a holiday, or any other contract to provide entertainment and enjoyment' is consistent with an intention to compensate the plaintiff for the contractual benefit of which he had been deprived. The reference, however, to 'the disappointment, the distress' etc reads like a reference to consequential damage.

91 Edmund Davies LJ based his decision on the defendant's failure to provide a holiday of the contractual quality'. He held that the amount of damages was not limited by the price for the holiday. He said, at p 239: 'The court is entitled, and indeed bound, to contrast the overall quality of the holiday so enticingly promised with that which the defendants in fact provided'. He regarded the plaintiff's vexation and disappointment as relevant matters to take into account in 'determining what would be proper compensation for the defendants' marked failure to fulfil their undertaking'. This was a *Ruxley Electronics and Construction Ltd v Forsyth* [1996] AC 344 approach. Stephenson LJ, at p 240, based his decision on the 'reasonable contemplation of the parties . . . as a likely result of [the holiday contract] being so broken'. He said, at pp 240–241, that where there are contracts 'in which the parties contemplate inconvenience on breach which may be described as mental: frustration, annoyance, disappointment . . .' damages for breach should take that inconvenience into account. This was a *Watts v Morrow* [1991] 1 WLR 1421 approach . . .

93 *Knott v Bolton* 11 Const LJ 375 is, in my opinion, inconsistent with *Ruxley's* case and should now be regarded as having been wrongly decided. The plaintiffs had been deprived of the wide staircase and gallery and baronial entrance hall to which they were contractually entitled and had to put up with lesser facilities. A value should, in my opinion, have been placed on the benefit of which they had been deprived . . .

105 It is time for me to turn to the present case and apply the principles expressed in *Ruxley Electronics and Construction Ltd v Forsyth* [1996] AC 344 and *Watts v Morrow* [1991] 1 WLR 1421. In my judgment,

Mr Farley is entitled to be compensated for the 'real discomfort' that the judge found he suffered. He is so entitled on either of two alternative bases.

106 First, he was deprived of the contractual benefit to which he was entitled. He was entitled to information about the aircraft noise from Gatwick-bound aircraft that Mr Skinner, through negligence, had failed to supply him with. If Mr Farley had, in the event, decided not to purchase Riverside House, the value to him of the contractual benefit of which he had been deprived would have been nil. But he did buy the property. And he took his decision to do so without the advantage of being able to take into account the information to which he was contractually entitled. If he had had that information he would not have bought. So the information clearly would have had a value to him. Prima facie, in my opinion, he is entitled to be compensated accordingly.

107 In these circumstances, it seems to me, it is open to the court to adopt a *Ruxley Electronics and Construction Ltd v Forsyth* [1996] AC 344 approach and place a value on the contractual benefit of which Mr Farley has been deprived. In deciding on the amount, the discomfort experienced by Mr Farley can, in my view, properly be taken into account. If he had had the aircraft noise information he would not have bought Riverside House and would not have had that discomfort.

[Lord Scott then discussed the alternative basis for an award of distress damages (*page 748, 14.8.1.7*) and continued:]

109 I would add that if there had been an appreciable reduction in the market value of the property caused by the aircraft noise. Mr Farley could not have recovered both that difference in value and damages for discomfort. To allow both would allow double recovery for the same item.

110 Whether the approach to damages is on *Ruxley Electronics and Construction Ltd v Forsyth* [1996] AC 344 lines, for deprivation of a contractual benefit, or on *Watts v Morrow* [1991] 1 WLR 1421 lines, for consequential damage within the applicable remoteness rules, the appropriate amount should, in my opinion, be modest. The degree of discomfort experienced by Mr Farley, although 'real', was not very great. I think £10,000 may have been on the high side. But in principle, in my opinion, the judge was right to award damages and I am not, in the circumstances, disposed to disagree with his figure.

111 For the reasons I have given and for the reasons contained in the opinion of my noble and learned friend, Lord Steyn, I would allow the appeal and restore the judge's order.

NOTES

1. See McKendrick and Graham [2002] LMCLQ 161 and Capper (2002) 118 LQR 193.

2. Although Lord Scott stated that he was agreeing with the reasons given in the speech of Lord Steyn, his approach, although not the outcome, is quite different. Lord Scott considers that damages will be available in accordance with general principles for recovery, and particularly the principle in *Ruxley*, where the non-performance has resulted in the loss of contractual performance having a value to the claimant and the loss falls within remoteness. The damages award will represent that value. This seems to be a loss of amenity award and is not explicitly linked to distress damages or the exceptional cases in which such damages will be available. The principles deriving from the 'exceptional cases' are rejected in favour of the distinction between *Ruxley*

cases (loss of valuable contractual performance) and *Watts v Morrow* damages for inconvenience or discomfort (which is loss consequential on repair), as discussed at *page 686, 14.2.2.2*.

3. Lord Scott considered that an award of damages for distress would not arise at all if there were a difference in value as a result of the breach, on the basis that any other conclusion would involve double recovery. This is a product of his rather different analysis and it is difficult to see that this necessarily follows, since a claimant may suffer a reduction in the value of property *and* additional loss of satisfaction with the end product. In *Hamilton-Jones v David and Snape (a firm)* [2003] EWHC 3147 (Ch), [2004] 1 WLR 924, the Court awarded damages for distress as an additional element of the damages award. In addition, in the context of a holiday contract in *Milner v*

Carnival plc (t/a Cunard) [2010] EWCA Civ 389, [2010] 3 All ER 701, the Court of Appeal considered that it would technically be possible to award damages for diminution of value in the promised holiday, consequential loss, physical inconvenience and discomfort, and damages for distress, although noted the importance of ensuring that there was no duplication in relation to the different heads of loss, particularly the discomfort (physical) and distress (not turning on physical inconvenience). In *Herrmann v Withers LLP* [2012] EWHC 1492 (Ch), [2012] PNLR 28, the judge rejected an argument that the difference in value damages relating to the house would reflect the absence of access to a garden, so that it was inappropriate also to award damages for disappointment and distress. He considered that non-pecuniary loss was potentially separate and was suffered on these facts because the property had been purchased to live in rather than as an investment.

4. The Court of Appeal had followed the approach in *Watts v Morrow* that, since the surveyor had not guaranteed a particular result, and owed only a duty of reasonable care and skill, it was not possible to award damages for distress. This was also stated to be a factor distinguishing this case from *Ruxley Electronics*, in which there was an absolute obligation to construct a swimming pool of the required depth. The House of Lords has rejected such a distinction, at least in the context of awarding damages for distress. It cannot make a difference to the award of such damages that the obligation is expressed in absolute or qualified terms. It does, however, make a difference to the ability to award cost of cure damages rather than difference in value.

5. The significant factor in this case was that the claimant had specifically requested some reassurance on the question of aircraft noise and, given that the judge had found there to be no difference in value, awarding damages for distress ensured that the claimant had a remedy for breach of the defendant's undertaking on this matter.

Hamilton-Jones v David & Snape (a firm)
[2003] EWHC 3147 (Ch), [2004] 1 WLR 924

The claimant instructed the defendant solicitors to take action to ensure that her husband, from whom she was separated, was unable to remove the children from the country. Court orders were obtained for residence and to prevent this removal, and although the defendant notified the UK Passport Agency of these orders in 1994 and asked it not to issue a passport to the husband or in the names of the children, the defendant failed to renew the notification after 12 months, despite being warned by the Passport Agency that the notice would require this renewal. In 1996, the husband was able to obtain a passport and removed two of the children from the jurisdiction. The claimant brought an action for breach of contract, which included a claim for damages for distress.

Neuberger J adopted the traditional approach on the question of recovery of damages for mental distress, i.e. that the general rule is that such damages are not recoverable—*Addis v Gramophone Co. Ltd* [1909] AC 488—unless the case fell within one of the established exceptions stated by Bingham LJ in *Watts v Morrow*. Neuberger J considered that whilst Bingham LJ in *Watts v Morrow* had originally expounded the exception as requiring that '*the very object* of a contract is to provide pleasure, relaxation, peace of mind or freedom from molestation', Lord Steyn, and the majority, in *Farley v Skinner (No. 2)* had relaxed this requirement so that it required only that '*a major or important object* of the contract is to give pleasure, relaxation or peace of mind'.

Held: The claimant was awarded £20,000 as damages for the distress since *a major object* of the contract was to ensure that, for her peace of mind, the claimant should retain custody of her children.

NEUBERGER J: 61 . . . [O]n any view, it appears to me that both the claimant and the defendants would have had in mind that a significant reason for the claimant instructing the defendants was with a view to ensuring, so far as possible, that the claimant retained custody of her children for her own pleasure and peace of mind. It would, I think, be a relatively unusual parent who . . . would not have had, and would not be perceived by her solicitors to have had, her own peace of mind and pleasure in the company of her children as an important factor.

NOTES

1. Thus, given the purpose behind the instruction, peace of mind was at least 'an important' object of the contract and part of the reason for contracting, albeit that it was not the sole purpose, since the primary purpose under the relevant legislation was to protect the children. The solicitors had been engaged to minimize the inevitable distress associated with these circumstances, or the risk of that distress, and had failed to do so.

2. This case is similar to *Heywood v Wellers* [1976] QB 446 and *McLeish v Amoo-Gottfried & Co.* (1993) 10 PN 102, in that peace of mind and the avoidance of distress were integral to the performance contracted for. This contracted-for performance will, it seems, need to be quite specific. These cases can be compared with *Channon v Lindley Johnstone* [2002] EWCA Civ 353, [2002] Lloyd's Rep PN 342, in which the claimant alleged distress suffered in consequence of having to pay more in ancillary relief to his ex-wife as a result of the negligence of his solicitors. The claim failed because there was no particular undertaking by the solicitors as to his property or to achieve a particular result. It follows that, even in the context of a contract made with a consumer, something akin to the type of specific request in *Farley v Skinner* may be required in order to permit recovery of damages for distress within the exceptions in the context of contracts for the provision of a service. Such a position would fit with the policy considerations in relation to recovery of distress damages in the context of the exceptions.

3. The judge did not follow the approach advocated by Lord Scott in *Farley v Skinner* and it would seem unlikely that a first instance decision will do so.

Haysman v Mrs Rogers Films Ltd [2008] EWHC 2494 (QB) provides an illustration to demonstrate the liberality of the 'peace of mind' exception post-*Farley*. The judge considered that 'one' of the important objects of the contract to use the claimant's house for filming was the peace of mind to the homeowner, who was permitting this activity to take place. The film company had expressly promised to indemnify against damage to the property and to restore it to its original condition.

The more liberal approach to the exceptions is also evident in *Herrmann v Withers LLP* [2012] EWHC 1492 (Ch), [2012] PNLR 28. Solicitors acting for a couple in relation to a property purchase had incorrectly advised the couple that the property included a right to use the garden in the nearby square. Newey J considered that, because the garden was important to the couple when purchasing a house near a garden square, 'a major or important object' of the contract with the solicitors was 'to give pleasure, relaxation or peace of mind' and the couple would have suffered disappointment on discovering the truth. Rejecting the suggested damages award of £50,000 under this head, the judge settled on £2,000, on the basis that such damages involve modest awards.

14.8.1.6 No distress damages for breach of commercial contracts

Damages for distress will not be available in relation to a breach of a commercial contract, since, as Lord Cooke stated in *Johnson v Gore Wood & Co. (a firm)* [2002] 2 AC 1, 49: 'Contract-breaking is treated as an incident of commercial life which players in the game are expected to meet with mental fortitude.'

Hayes v James and Charles Dodd
[1990] 2 All ER 815 (CA)

The premises that the claimants wished to purchase for their motor repair business had only a narrow access through a tunnel at the front, but the claimants' solicitor negligently informed them that there was a right of way over land at the rear, so that there would be access to the garage. The claimants purchased the property, but the owner of the land at the rear blocked the access. This had a devastating effect on the claimants' business and, after 12 months, the business was closed down. At first instance, the damages award included £1,500 damages for each claimant for anguish and vexation. The Court of Appeal overturned this award.

Held: Such damages were not available if, as here, they arose out of a breach of a purely commercial contract.

STAUGHTON LJ: Like the judge, I consider that the English courts should be wary of adopting what he called 'the United States practice of huge awards'. Damages awarded for negligence or want of skill, whether against professional men or anyone else, must provide fair compensation, but no more than that. And I would not view with enthusiasm the prospect that every shipowner in the Commercial Court, having successfully claimed for unpaid freight or demurrage, would be able to add a claim for mental distress suffered while he was waiting for his money.

In a sense, the wrong done to the plaintiffs in this action, for which they seek compensation under this head, lay in the defendants' failure to admit liability at an early stage. On 6 July 1983 the defendants acknowledged that there was no right of way, but denied negligence. Had they on that very day admitted liability and tendered a sum on account of damages, or offered interim reparation in some other form, the anxiety of the plaintiffs, and their financial problems, could have been very largely relieved. But liability was not admitted until January 1987. I believe that in one or more American states damages are awarded for wrongfully defending an action. But there is no such remedy in this country so far as I am aware.

In *Perry v Sidney Phillips & Son (a firm)* [1982] 3 All ER 705, [1982] 1 WLR 1297 damages were awarded for the distress, worry, inconvenience and trouble which the plaintiff had suffered while living in the house he bought, owing to the defects which his surveyor had overlooked. Lord Denning MR considered that these consequences were reasonably foreseeable ([1982] 3 All ER 705 at 709, [1982] 1 WLR 1297 at 1302). Kerr LJ stated a narrower test ([1982] 3 All ER 705 at 712, [1982] 1 WLR 1297 at 1307):

> So far as the question of damages for vexation and inconvenience is concerned, it should be noted that the deputy judge awarded these not for the tension or frustration of a person who is involved in a legal dispute in which the other party refuses to meet its liabilities. If he had done so, it would have been wrong, because such aggravation is experienced by almost all litigants. He awarded these damages because of the physical consequences of the breach, which were all foreseeable at the time. The fact that in such cases damages under this head may be recoverable, if they have been suffered but not otherwise, is supported by the decision of this court in *Hutchinson v Harris* (1978) 10 Build LR 19.

I would emphasise the reference to physical consequences of the breach.

I am not convinced that it is enough to ask whether mental distress was reasonably foreseeable as a consequence, or even whether it should reasonably have been contemplated as not unlikely to result from a breach of contract. It seems to me that damages for mental distress in contract are, as a matter of policy, limited to certain classes of case. I would broadly follow the classification provided by Dillon LJ in *Bliss v South East Thames Regional Health Authority* [1987] ICR 700 at 718:

> . . . where the contract which has been broken was itself a contract to provide peace of mind or freedom from distress . . .

Damages for breach of contract

14

It may be that the class is somewhat wider than that. But it should not, in my judgment, include any case where the object of the contract was not comfort or pleasure, or the relief of discomfort, but simply carrying on a commercial activity with a view to profit. So I would disallow the item of damages for anguish and vexation.

NOTES

1. Staughton and Purchas LJJ stressed the fact that such damages could be recovered only for distress caused by the breach, rather than that caused by the litigation process. In this instance, the distress was primarily caused by the fact that the claimants had financial difficulties and the solicitors did not admit liability until 1987.

2. In *Alexander v Rolls Royce Motor Cars* [1996] RTR 95, the Court of Appeal rejected the argument that a contract to repair a car was akin to a contract to provide freedom from worry and anxiety, so that damages for distress or loss of enjoyment in the use of the car were not available if the car was not repaired in breach of contract.

3. The availability of damages for distress in relation to contracts that can be classified as commercial has changed little as a result of *Farley v Skinner*. Distress damages will not be available in the absence of a specific undertaking on a matter of importance that brings the contract within the peace of mind or pleasure exception.

14.8.1.7 Distress directly consequent on physical inconvenience caused by the defendant's breach of contract

Perry v Sidney Phillips & Son
[1982] 1 WLR 1297 (CA)

The claimant purchased a house in reliance on a survey report prepared by the defendants. This stated that the house was in good order. After moving in, the claimant discovered serious problems with the roof and the septic tank. The Court of Appeal awarded damages for discomfort caused by the repairs, since this was foreseeable.

NOTE This is the second exception discussed in the third paragraph of Bingham LJ's statement of principle in *Watts v Morrow* [1991] 1 WLR 1421, 1445 (*page 686, 14.2.2.2*). It was the basis for the award of damages for distress in *Watts v Morrow*, i.e. damages for the distress caused by the physical inconvenience of living in the house whilst repairs were carried out.

Farley v Skinner (No. 2)
[2001] UKHL 49, [2002] 2 AC 732

For the facts, see *page 738, 14.8.1.5*.

The House of Lords accepted that, as an alternative basis for its decision, it would have been possible for Mr Farley to have recovered damages for distress under this exception, although Lord Scott considered that this was not because it fell within one of the exceptions, but because it was normal consequential loss that could be recovered as long as it was not too remote a loss.

LORD SCOTT: 84 First, there will, in many cases, be an additional remoteness hurdle for the injured party to clear. Consequential damage, including damage consisting of inconvenience or discomfort, must, in order to be recoverable, be such as, at the time of the contract, was reasonably foreseeable as liable to result from the breach: see McGregor on Damages, 16th ed, pp 159–160, para 250.

85 Second, the adjective 'physical', in the phrase 'physical inconvenience and discomfort', requires, I think, some explanation or definition. The distinction between the 'physical' and the 'non-physical' is not

always clear and may depend on the context. Is being awoken at night by aircraft noise 'physical'? If it is, is being unable to sleep because of worry and anxiety 'physical'? What about a reduction in light caused by the erection of a building under a planning permission that an errant surveyor ought to have warned his purchaser-client about but had failed to do so? In my opinion, the critical distinction to be drawn is not a distinction between the different types of inconvenience or discomfort of which complaint may be made but a distinction based on the cause of the inconvenience or discomfort. If the cause is no more than disappointment that the contractual obligation has been broken, damages are not recoverable even if the disappointment has led to a complete mental breakdown. But, if the cause of the inconvenience or discomfort is a sensory (sight, touch, hearing, smell etc) experience, damages can, subject to the remoteness rules, be recovered . . .

108 [As an alternative basis for the decision] Mr Farley can, in my opinion, claim compensation for the discomfort as consequential loss. Had it not been for the breach of contract, he would not have suffered the discomfort. It was caused by the breach of contract in a causa sine qua non sense. Was the discomfort a consequence that should reasonably have been contemplated by the parties at the time of contract as liable to result from the breach? In my opinion, it was. It was obviously within the reasonable contemplation of the parties that, deprived of the information about aircraft noise that he ought to have had, Mr Farley would make a decision to purchase that he would not otherwise have made. Having purchased, he would, having become aware of the noise, either sell in which case at least the expenses of the resale would have been recoverable as damages or he would keep the property and put up with the noise. In the latter event, it was within the reasonable contemplation of the parties that he would experience discomfort from the noise of the aircraft. And the discomfort was 'physical' in the sense that Bingham LJ in *Watts v Morrow* [1991] 1 WLR 1421, 1445 had in mind. In my opinion, the application of *Watts v Morrow* principles entitles Mr Farley to damages for discomfort caused by the aircraft noise.

NOTE Lord Scott's emphasis on the cause of the inconvenience or discomfort reflects the true nature of this exception as *distress directly consequent on physical inconvenience*. If the distress results in physical consequences, there is no recovery of damages for distress within this exception, e.g. sleeplessness resulting from anxiety about the breach. This distress is the direct result of (caused by) the breach. On the other hand, if the breach causes a physical consequence, such as repairs, and this causes inconvenience and distress, the resultant distress is consequent on the physical inconvenience and is recoverable within the scope of the exception if it falls within the remoteness principle. This distress is caused by the physical inconvenience, rather than directly by the breach. Some confusion appears to have resulted from the failure to make this distinction clear.

14.8.2 Damages for loss of reputation

Addis v Gramophone Co. Ltd [1909] AC 488 has traditionally been regarded as House of Lords' authority for the fact that, in general, there can be no damages for loss sustained as a result of the fact that a wrongful dismissal makes it more difficult to obtain fresh employment (see Lord Loreburn LC at 491).

However, in the next case, the House of Lords accepted that, in some very limited circumstances, damages for loss of reputation might be awarded to former employees as damages for breach of their employment contracts, although this would be damages to compensate for financial loss caused by this breach.

For the facts, see *page 208, 5.4.1.1.*

The claimants, former employees of the bank, alleged breach of the implied term of trust and confidence owed to employees, and sought recovery for financial loss, arguing that, on the bank's liquidation, it had been made more difficult for them to obtain alternative employment because of alleged stigma associated with BCCI. The Court of Appeal had agreed with the liquidator and the judge at first instance that such a claim for damages could not succeed.

Held (on appeal): If an employer acted in breach of the employment contract by conducting the business in a dishonest and corrupt manner, and if it were reasonably foreseeable that such a breach would prejudice the future employment prospects of the employees, then damages for financial losses associated with loss of reputation could be recovered by employees who established that they had, in fact, been handicapped in the labour market as a result of this conduct by the bank.

LORD STEYN:

The availability of the remedy of damages

In considering the availability of the remedy of damages it is important to bear in mind that the applicants claim damages for financial loss. That is the issue. It will be recalled that the Court of Appeal decided the case against the applicants on the basis that there is a positive rule debarring the recovery of damages in contract for injury to an existing reputation, and that in truth the two applicants were claiming damages for injury to their previously existing reputations . . .

[Lord Steyn noted that *Addis v Gramophone Co. Ltd* [1909] AC 488 has been cited as authority for the decision reached by the Court of Appeal and continued:]

The true ratio decidendi of the House of Lords' decision in *Addis v Gramophone Co. Ltd* has long been debated. Some have understood it as authority for the proposition that an employee may not recover damages even for pecuniary loss caused by a breach of contract of the employer which damages the employment prospects of an employee. If *Addis's* case establishes such a rule it is an inroad on traditional principles of contract law. And any such restrictive rule has been criticised by distinguished writers: *Treitel, The Law of Contract*, 9th ed. (1995), p. 893, *Burrows, Remedies for Torts and Breach of Contract*, 2nd ed. (1994), pp. 221–225. Moreover, it has been pointed out that *Addis's* case was decided in 1909 before the development of modern employment law, and long before the evolution of the implied mutual obligation of trust and confidence. Nevertheless, it is necessary to take a closer look at *Addis's* case so far as it affects the issues in this case. A company had dismissed an overseas manager in a harsh and oppressive manner. The House of Lords held that the employee was entitled to recover his direct pecuniary loss, such as loss of salary and commission. But the jury had been allowed to take into account the manner in which the employee had been dismissed and to reflect this in their award. The House of Lords, with Lord Collins dissenting, held that this was wrong. The headnote to the case states that in a case of wrongful dismissal the award of damages may not include compensation for the manner of his dismissal, for his injured feelings, or for the loss he may suffer from the fact that the dismissal of itself makes it more difficult to obtain fresh employment . . .

I would accept . . . that Lord Loreburn LC and the other Law Lords in the majority apparently thought they were applying a special rule applicable to awards of damages for wrongful dismissal. It is, however, far from clear how far the ratio of *Addis's* case extends. It certainly enunciated the principle that an employee cannot recover exemplary or aggravated damages for wrongful dismissal. That is still sound law.

The actual decision is only concerned with wrongful dismissal. It is therefore arguable that as a matter of precedent the ratio is so restricted. But it seems to me unrealistic not to acknowledge that *Addis's* case is authority for a wider principle. There is a common proposition in the speeches of the majority. That proposition is that damages for breach of contract may only be awarded for breach of contract, and not for loss caused by the manner of the breach. No Law Lord said that an employee may not recover financial loss for damage to his employment prospects caused by a breach of contract. And no Law Lord said that in breach of contract cases compensation for loss of reputation can never be awarded, or that it can only be awarded in cases falling in certain defined categories. *Addis's* case simply decided that the loss of reputation in that particular case could not be compensated because it was not caused by a breach of contract: Nelson Enonchong, 'Contract Damages for Injury to Reputation' (1996) 59 MLR 592, 593. So analysed *Addis's* case does not bar the claims put forward in the present case . . .

[However, the present case] is based not on the manner of a wrongful dismissal but on a breach of contract which is separate from and independent of the termination of the contract of employment.

In my judgment therefore the authorities relied on by Morritt LJ [in the Court of Appeal] do not on analysis support his conclusion. Moreover, the fact that in appropriate cases damages may in principle be awarded for loss or reputation caused by breach of contract is illustrated by a number of cases which Morritt LJ discussed: *Aerial Advertising Co. v Batchelors Peas Ltd (Manchester)* [1938] 2 All ER 788; *Foaminol Laboratories Ltd v British Artid Plastics Ltd* [1941] 2 All ER 393 and *Anglo-Continental Holidays Ltd v Typaldos Lines (London) Ltd* [1967] 2 Lloyd's Rep 61. But, unlike Morritt LJ, I regard these cases not as exceptions but as the application of ordinary principles of contract law. Moreover, it is clear that a supplier who delivers contaminated meat to a trader can be sued for loss of commercial reputation involving loss of trade: see *Cointax v Myham & Son* [1913] 2 KB 220 and *G.K.N. Centrax Gears Ltd v Matbro Ltd* [1976] 2 Lloyd's Rep 555. Rhetorically, one may ask, why may a bank manager not sue for loss of professional reputation, if it causes financial loss flowing from a breach of the contract of employment? . . . The principled position is as follows. Provided that a relevant breach of contract can be established, and the requirements of causation, remoteness and mitigation can be satisfied, there is no good reason why in the field of employment law recovery of financial loss in respect of damage to reputation caused by breach of contract is necessarily excluded.

The effect of my conclusions

. . . [E]ven if the employee can establish a breach of this obligation, it does not follow that he will be able to recover damages for injury to his employment prospects. The Law Commission has pointed out that loss of reputation is inherently difficult to prove: Consultation Paper No. 132 on Aggravated, Exemplary and Restitutionary Damages, p. 22, para 2.15. It is, therefore, improbable that many employees would be able to prove 'stigma compensation'. The limiting principles of causation, remoteness and mitigation present formidable practical obstacles to such claims succeeding. But difficulties of proof cannot alter the legal principles which permit, in appropriate cases, such claims for financial loss caused by breach of contract being put forward for consideration.

NOTES

1. This is a very limited decision dependent on there being a breach of the implied term that the employer will not conduct its business in a manner likely to undermine the trust and confidence required of the employment relationship.

2. In practice, it will be extremely difficult to establish the necessary causal link between the breach and the financial loss. In *Bank of Credit and Commerce International SA (in liquidation) v Ali (No. 3)* [2002] EWCA Civ 82, [2002] 3 All ER 750, the Court of Appeal accepted the principle in *Mahmud*, but held that the employees in question had failed to prove that the stigma had caused them any financial loss.

3. The claim in *Mahmud* was for financial loss and the House of Lords was not dealing with a claim for damages for humiliation or distress.

4. As the speeches in *Mahmud* make clear, there are some recognized instances where damages for loss of reputation can be recovered. These relate to loss of publicity contemplated by the contract where an actor is wrongfully dismissed, breach of a contract under which the main purpose was to provide advertising or publicity, and damages for loss of credit reputation on the wrongful dishonouring of a cheque: *Marbe v George Edwardes (Daly's Theatre) Ltd* [1928] 1 KB 269, *Aerial Advertising Co. v Batchelors Peas Ltd (Manchester)* [1938] 2 All ER 788 (*page 644, 13.3.2*), and *Kpohraror v Woolwich Building Society* [1996] 4 All ER 119, respectively.

5. In addition, as has been confirmed in *Johnson v Unisys Ltd* [2003] UKHL 13, [2003] 1 AC 518, *Mahmud* applies to a breach of this duty only during the period for which the employees are employed. *Addis v Gramophone Co. Ltd* [1909] AC 488 remains the authority concerning damages for the *manner* of the dismissal, whether that relates to damages for distress associated with the manner of a dismissal or difficulties in obtaining future employment owing to the manner of a dismissal. The majority of the House of Lords (Lord Steyn dissenting) in *Johnson v Unisys Ltd* also considered that this position should be maintained in order to avoid undermining the statutory regime governing compensation for unfair dismissal (and, in particular, the maximum compensation awarded). This rationale also applies to recovery of damages for unfair dismissal where the breach is of an express term in the contract relating to the dismissal process, as opposed to breach of the implied term in *Mahmud*: *Edwards v Chesterfield Royal Hospital NHS Foundation Trust* [2011] UKSC 58, [2012] 2 WLR 55.

14.9 The special position of insurance contracts

The common law, as set out in *Sprung v Royal Insurance* [1999] Lloyd's Rep IR 111, did not recognize the right of a policyholder under an insurance contract to recover damages representing loss where the insurers failed to pay the claim within a reasonable time. That restriction resulted from the operation of a combination of different principles: the insurers' obligation to make payment arose as soon as the insured peril occurred, so that damages were payable from the outset and the law did not recognize an award of damages for not paying damages; if the policyholder suffered financial loss as a result of non-payment, the cause of that loss was the policyholder's own inability to raise funds from a separate source; and, as regards loss of amenity, a policy of insurance was not one designed to give peace of mind, particularly where the policyholder was a commercial organization. The common law was swept away by ss. 13A and 16A of the Insurance Act 2015, added by the Enterprise Act 2016.

Insurance Act 2015

13A Implied term about payment of claims

(1) It is an implied term of every contract of insurance that if the insured makes a claim under the contract, the insurer must pay any sums due in respect of the claim within a reasonable time.

(2) A reasonable time includes a reasonable time to investigate and assess the claim.

(3) What is reasonable will depend on all the relevant circumstances, but the following are examples of things which may need to be taken into account—

(a) the type of insurance,

(b) the size and complexity of the claim,

(c) compliance with any relevant statutory or regulatory rules or guidance,

(d) factors outside the insurer's control.

(4) If the insurer shows that there were reasonable grounds for disputing the claim (whether as to the amount of any sum payable, or as to whether anything at all is payable)—

(a) the insurer does not breach the term implied by subsection (1) merely by failing to pay the claim (or the affected part of it) while the dispute is continuing, but

(b) the conduct of the insurer in handling the claim may be a relevant factor in deciding whether that term was breached and, if so, when.

(5) Remedies (for example, damages) available for breach of the term implied by subsection (1) are in addition to and distinct from—

(a) any right to enforce payment of the sums due, and

(b) any right to interest on those sums (whether under the contract, under another enactment, at the court's discretion or otherwise).

By s. 16A any term in a consumer insurance contract which would put the consumer in a worse position is to that extent of no effect. As regards a non-consumer insurance contract, a term which seeks to limit or exclude s. 13A is of no effect unless it has been drawn to the policy-holder's attention at the outset and is clear and unambiguous. But even if those transparency requirements are satisfied the exclusion cannot be relied upon if the insurers' failure to pay within a reasonable time was deliberate or reckless in that the insurers were aware that they were in breach or did not care whether they were in breach.

14.10 Agreed damages clauses

The contract may provide that specified damages shall be payable in respect of particular types of breach, thus avoiding difficulties of quantification and disruptions to a continuing legal relationship.

14.10.1 Liquidated damages and penalty clauses

A distinction has been drawn between 'liquidated damages clauses', which are enforceable, and 'penalty clauses', which are not enforceable beyond the amount of the injured party's actual loss. A penalty has traditionally been defined as a clause designed as a threat to compel performance by penalizing the other for non-performance and as not amounting to genuine compensation because it was unrelated to the amount of the likely loss. It followed that a liquidated damages clause was generally defined as a clause which represented a genu-ine attempt to pre-estimate the loss so that it was in line with the compensatory principle. This has now been reformulated by the decision of the Supreme Court in the conjoined appeals in *Cavendish Square Holdings BV v Makdessi* and *ParkingEye Ltd v Beavis* [2015] UKSC 67, [2015] 3 WLR 1373.

14.10.1.1 Identifying penalties and the penalty rule test: secondary obligations and the protection of legitimate interest

Cavendish Square Holdings BV v Makdessi
[2015] UKSC 67, [2015] 3 WLR 1373 (SC)

Makdessi entered into an agreement with Cavendish whereby, following extensive negotiations over a six-month period that had been conducted through highly experienced lawyers, Makdessi agreed to sell a controlling stake in his marketing and communications company. The price was payable in instalments and reflected, to a large extent, the existing goodwill in this business. The terms of the agreement between the parties sought to protect this goodwill. In particular, breaches of the non-competition clause by Makdessi would mean that he would not be entitled to receive the interim and/or the final instalment payments (clause 5.1) and that he granted Cavendish an option to purchase his remaining shares at their net asset value price, i.e. at a price excluding any value for the goodwill (clause 5.6).

Makdessi admitted that he had committed a breach through his ongoing, although unpaid, involvement in a company called Carat. This invoked clauses 5.1 and 5.6 but he argued that both clauses were unenforceable penalties because the consequence of their application was extreme financial loss for him, e.g. the operation of clause 5.1 would cost him over $40 million and the price for the shares in the compulsory sale would be greatly reduced if no account was taken of the value of the goodwill. Cavendish, on the other hand, denied that the clauses were penal on the basis that the contract as a whole represented a negotiated, and freely entered into, commercial bargain and that the purpose of these clauses was to protect the goodwill in the marketing business being purchased which, as a major part of the price, would have been negatively impacted by any breach of covenant of the type contemplated.

Held: Neither clause constituted a penalty. Both constituted primary contractual obligations whereas 'agreed damages clauses' were designed to apply in place of the secondary obligation in the contract to pay damages for breach.

Clause 5.1 was a price adjustment clause so that it constituted a primary obligation, rather than a secondary provision. Cavendish had a legitimate interest in the observance of the restrictive covenants which extended beyond the recovery of its loss and, since the clause amounted to a carefully negotiated agreement between informed and legally advised parties at arm's length, the clause could not be regarded as extravagant, exorbitant, or unconscionable. It was not a penalty.

Clause 5.6, which contained a price formula for the sale of retained shares, was also a primary obligation. It did not represent the estimated loss attributable to the breach but it did reflect the reduced price with Cavendish would have been prepared to pay for the business in the event of competitive behaviour of the type undertaken by Makdessi. It was therefore justified by this legitimate interest and was also not a penalty.

LORD NEUBERGER OF ABBOTSBURY PSC and LORD SUMPTION JSC (with whom Lord Carnwath JSC agreed):

The law in relation to penalties

3 The penalty rule in England is an ancient, haphazardly constructed edifice which has not weathered well, and which in the opinion of some should simply be demolished, and in the opinion of others should be reconstructed and extended. For many years, the courts have struggled to apply standard tests formulated more than a century ago for relatively simple transactions to altogether more complex situations.

The application of the rule is often adventitious. The test for distinguishing penal from other principles is unclear. As early as 1801, in *Astley v Weldon* (1801) 2 Bos & P 346, 350 Lord Eldon CJ confessed himself, not for the first time, 'much embarrassed in ascertaining the principle upon which [the rule was] founded'. Eighty years later, in *Wallis v Smith* (1882) 21 Ch D 243, 256, Jessel MR, not a judge noted for confessing ignorance, observed that 'The ground of that doctrine I do not know'. In 1966 Diplock LJ, not a judge given to recognising defeat, declared that he could 'make no attempt, where so many others have failed, to rationalise this common law rule': *Robophone Facilities Ltd v Blank* [1966] 1 WLR 1428, 1446. The task is no easier today. But unless the rule is to be abolished or substantially extended, its application to any but the clearest cases requires some underlying principle to be identified.

. . .

9 The distinction between a clause providing for a genuine pre-estimate of damages and a penalty clause has remained fundamental to the modern law, as it is currently understood. The question whether a damages clause is a penalty falls to be decided as a matter of construction, therefore as at the time that it is agreed . . . This is because it depends on the character of the provision, not on the circumstances in which it falls to be enforced. It is a species of agreement which the common law considers to be by its nature contrary to the policy of the law. One consequence of this is that relief from the effects of a penalty is, as Hoffmann LJ put it in *Else (1982) Ltd v Parkland Holdings Ltd* [1994] 1 BCLC 130, 144, 'mechanical in effect and involves no exercise of discretion at all.' Another is that the penalty clause is wholly unenforceable: *Clydebank Engineering & Shipbuilding Co Ltd v Yzquierdo y Castaneda* [1905] AC 6, 9, 10 (the Earl of Halsbury LC); *Modern Engineering (Bristol) Ltd v Gilbert-Ash (Northern) Ltd* [1974] AC 689, 698 (Lord Reid), 703 (Lord Morris of Borth-y-Gest) and 723–724 (Lord Salmon); *Scandinavian Trading Tanker Co AB v Flota Petrolera Ecuatoriana (The Scaptrade)* [1983] 2 AC 694, 702 (Lord Diplock) . . . Deprived of the benefit of the provision, the innocent party is left to his remedy in damages under the general law. As Lord Diplock put it in *The Scaptrade*, at p 702:

> The classic form of penalty clause is one which provides that upon breach of a primary obligation under the contract a secondary obligation shall arise on the part of the party in breach to pay to the other party a sum of money which does not represent a genuine pre-estimate of any loss likely to be sustained by him as the result of the breach of primary obligation but is substantially in excess of that sum. The classic form of relief against such a penalty clause has been to refuse to give effect to it, but to award the common law measure of damages for the breach of primary obligation instead.

. . .

11 The penalty rule as it has been developed by the judges gives rise to two questions, both of which have a considerable bearing on the questions which arise on these appeals. In what circumstances is the rule engaged at all? And what makes a contractual provision penal?

In what circumstances is the penalty rule engaged?

12 In England, it has always been considered that a provision could not be a penalty unless it provided an exorbitant alternative to common law damages. This meant that it had to be a provision operating on a breach of contract. In *Moss Empires Ltd v Olympia (Liverpool) Ltd* [1939] AC 544, this was taken for granted by Lord Atkin (p 551) and Lord Porter: p 558. As a matter of authority the question is settled in England by the decision of the House of Lords in *Export Credits Guarantee Department v Universal Oil Products Co* [1983] 1 WLR 399 ('ECGD'). Lord Roskill, with whom the rest of the committee agreed, said, at p 403:

> perhaps the main purpose, of the law relating to penalty clauses is to prevent a plaintiff recovering a sum of money in respect of a breach of contract committed by a defendant which bears little or no relationship to the loss actually suffered by the plaintiff as a result of the breach by the defendant. But it is not and never has been for the courts to relieve a party from the consequences of what may in the event prove to be an onerous or possibly even a commercially imprudent bargain.

. . .

13 This principle is worth restating at the outset of any analysis of the penalty rule, because it explains much about the way in which it has developed. There is a fundamental difference between a jurisdiction to review the fairness of a contractual obligation and a jurisdiction to regulate the remedy for its breach. Leaving aside challenges going to the reality of consent, such as those based on fraud, duress or undue influence, the courts do not review the fairness of men's bargains either at law or in equity. The penalty rule regulates only the remedies available for breach of a party's primary obligations, not the primary obligations themselves. This was not a new concept in 1983, when ECGD was decided. It had been the foundation of the equitable jurisdiction, which depended on the treatment of penal defeasible bonds as secondary obligations . . . And it provided the whole basis of the classic distinction made at law between a penalty and a genuine pre-estimate of loss, the former being essentially a way of punishing the contract-breaker rather than compensating the innocent party for his breach. We shall return to that distinction below.

14 This means that in some cases the application of the penalty rule may depend on how the relevant obligation is framed in the instrument, ie whether as a conditional primary obligation or a secondary obligation providing a contractual alternative to damages at law. Thus, where a contract contains an obligation on one party to perform an act, and also provides that, if he does not perform it, he will pay the other party a specified sum of money, the obligation to pay the specified sum is a secondary obligation which is capable of being a penalty; but if the contract does not impose (expressly or impliedly) an obligation to perform the act, but simply provides that, if one party does not perform, he will pay the other party a specified sum, the obligation to pay the specified sum is a conditional primary obligation and cannot be a penalty.

15 However, the capricious consequences of this state of affairs are mitigated by the fact that, as the equitable jurisdiction shows, the classification of terms for the purpose of the penalty rule depends on the substance of the term and not on its form or on the label which the parties have chosen to attach to it. As Lord Radcliffe said in *Campbell Discount Co Ltd v Bridge* [1962] AC 600, 622, 'the intention of the parties themselves', by which he clearly meant the intention as expressed in the agreement, 'is never inclusive and may be overruled or ignored if the court considers that even its clear expression does not represent "the real nature of the transaction" or what "in truth" it is taken to be' (and cf per Lord Templeman in *Street v Mountford* [1985] AC 809, 819). This aspect of the equitable jurisdiction was inherited by the courts of common law, and has been firmly established since the earliest common law cases.

16 Payment of a sum of money is the classic obligation under a penalty clause and, in almost every reported case involving a damages clause, the provision stipulates for the payment of money. However, it seems to us that there is no reason why an obligation to transfer assets (either for nothing or at an under-value) should not be capable of constituting a penalty. While the penalty rule may be somewhat artificial, it would heighten its artificiality to no evident purpose if it were otherwise. Similarly, the fact that a sum is paid over by one party to the other party as a deposit, in the sense of some sort of surety for the first party's contractual performance, does not prevent the sum being a penalty, if the second party in due course forfeits the deposit in accordance with the contractual terms, following the first party's breach of contract: see the Privy Council decisions in *Comr of Public Works v Hills* [1906] AC 368, 375–376, and *Workers Trust & Merchant Bank Ltd v Dojap Investments Ltd* [1993] AC 573. By contrast, in the *Else (1982)* case [1994] 1 BCLC 130, 146, Hoffmann LJ, citing *Stockloser v Johnson* [1954] 1 QB 476 in support, said that, unlike a case where 'money has been deposited as security for due performance of [a] party's obligation', 'retention of instalments which have been paid under the contract so as to become the absolute property of the vendor does not fall within the penalty rule', although, he added that it was 'subject . . . to the jurisdiction for relief against forfeiture.'

17 The relationship between penalty clauses and forfeiture clauses is not entirely easy. Given that they had the same origin in equity, but that the law on penalties was then developed through common law while the law on forfeitures was not, this is unsurprising. Some things appear to be clear. Where a proprietary interest or a 'proprietary or possessory right' (such as a patent or a lease) is granted or transferred subject to revocation or determination on breach, the clause providing for determination or revocation is a forfeiture and cannot be a penalty, and, while it is enforceable, relief from forfeiture may be granted: see *BICC plc v Burndy Corpn* [1985] Ch 232, 246–247 and 252 (Dillon LJ) and *The Scaptrade* [1983] 2 AC 694, 701–703 (Lord Diplock). But this does not mean that relief from forfeiture is unavailable in cases not involving land: see *Çukurova Finance International Ltd v Alfa Telecom Turkey Ltd (No. 3)* [2015] 2 WLR 875, especially at paras 92–97, and the cases cited there.

18 What is less clear is whether a provision is capable of being both a penalty clause and a forfeiture clause. It is inappropriate to consider that issue in any detail in this judgment, as we have heard very little argument on forfeitures—unsurprisingly because in neither appeal has it been alleged that any provision in issue is a forfeiture from which relief could be granted. But it is right to mention the possibility that, in some circumstances, a provision could, at least potentially, be a penalty clause as well as a forfeiture clause . . .

What makes a contractual provision penal?

19 As we have already observed, until relatively recently this question was answered almost entirely by reference to straightforward liquidated damages clauses. It was in that context that the House of Lords sought to restate the law in two seminal decisions at the beginning of the 20th century, the *Clydebank case* [1905] AC 6 in 1904 and the *Dunlop case* [1915] AC 79 in 1915.

20 The *Clydebank case* [1905] AC 6 was a Scottish appeal about a shipbuilding contract with a provision (described as a 'penalty') for the payment of £500 per week for delayed delivery. The provision was held to be a valid liquidated damages clause, not a penalty. The Earl of Halsbury LC (p 10) said that the distinction between the two depended on:

> whether it is, what I think gave the jurisdiction to the courts in both countries to interfere at all in an agreement between the parties, unconscionable and extravagant, and one which no court ought to allow to be enforced.

The Earl of Halsbury LC declined to lay down any 'abstract rule' for determining what was unconscionable or extravagant, saying only that it must depend on 'the nature of the transaction—the thing to be done, the loss likely to accrue to the person who is endeavouring to enforce the performance of the contract, and so forth.' The Earl of Halsbury LC's formulation has proved influential, and the two other members of the Appellate Committee both delivered concurring judgments agreeing with it. It is, however, worth drawing attention to an observation of Lord Robertson (pp 19–20) which points to the principle underlying the contrasting expressions 'liquidated damages' and 'penalty':

> Now, all such agreements, whether the thing be called penalty or be called liquidate damage, are in intention and effect what Professor Bell calls 'instruments of restraint', and in that sense penal. But the clear presence of this element does not in the least degree invalidate the stipulation. The question remains, had the respondents no interest to protect by that clause, or was that interest palpably incommensurate with the sums agreed on? It seems to me that to put this question, in the present instance, is to answer it.

21 The *Dunlop* case [1915] AC 79 arose out of a contract for the supply of tyres, covers and tubes by a manufacturer to a garage. The contract contained a number of terms designed to protect the manufacturer's brand, including prohibitions on tampering with the marks, restrictions on the unauthorised export or exhibition of the goods, and on resales to unapproved persons. There was also a resale price maintenance clause, which would now be unlawful but was a legitimate restriction of competition according to

the notions prevailing in 1914. It was this clause which the purchaser had broken. The contract provided for the payment of £5 for every tyre, cover or tube sold in breach of any provision of the agreement. Once again, the provision was held to be a valid liquidated damages clause. In his speech, Lord Dunedin formulated four tests 'which if applicable to the case under consideration may prove helpful, or even conclusive': p 87. They were (a) that the provision would be penal if 'the sum stipulated for is extravagant and unconscionable in amount in comparison with the greatest loss that could conceivably be proved to have followed from the breach'; (b) that the provision would be penal if the breach consisted only in the non-payment of money and it provided for the payment of a larger sum; (c) that there was 'a presumption (but no more)' that it would be penal if it was payable in a number of events of varying gravity; and (d) that it would not be treated as penal by reason only of the impossibility of precisely pre-estimating the true loss.

22 Lord Dunedin's speech in the *Dunlop* case achieved the status of a quasi-statutory code in the subsequent case law. Some of the many decisions on the validity of damages clauses are little more than a detailed exegesis or application of his four tests with a view to discovering whether the clause in issue can be brought within one or more of them. In our view, this is unfortunate. In the first place, Lord Dunedin proposed his four tests not as rules but only as considerations which might prove helpful or even conclusive 'if applicable to the case under consideration'. He did not suggest that they were applicable to every case in which the law of penalties was engaged. Second, as Lord Dunedin himself acknowledged, the essential question was whether the clause impugned was 'unconscionable' or 'extravagant'. The four tests are a useful tool for deciding whether these expressions can properly be applied to simple damages clauses in standard contracts. But they are not easily applied to more complex cases. To deal with those, it is necessary to consider the rationale of the penalty rule at a more fundamental level. What is it that makes a provision for the consequences of breach 'unconscionable'? And by comparison wih [*sic*] what is a penalty clause said to be 'extravagant'? Third, none of the other three Law Lords expressly agreed with Lord Dunedin's reasoning, and the four tests do not all feature in any of their speeches. Indeed, it appears that, in his analysis at pp 101–102, Lord Parmoor may have taken a more restrictive view of what constituted a penalty than did Lord Dunedin. More generally, the other members of the Appellate Committee gave their own reasons for concurring in the result, and they also repay consideration. For present purposes, the most instructive is that of Lord Atkinson, who approached the matter on an altogether broader basis.

23 Lord Atkinson pointed (pp 90–91) to the critical importance to Dunlop of the protection of their brand, reputation and goodwill, and their authorised distribution network.

[Lord Neuberger then explained that Lord Atkinson was stressing that the provision was designed to protect Dunlop's legitimate commercial interests in avoiding under-cutting and the impact that this would have on Dunlop's trade].

Lord Atkinson went on to draw an analogy, which has particular resonance in the *Cavendish* appeal, with a clause dealing with damages for breach of a restrictive covenant on the canvassing of business by a former employee. In this context, he said, at pp 92–93:

> It is, I think, quite misleading to concentrate one's attention upon the particular act or acts by which, in such cases as this, the rivalry in trade is set up, and the repute acquired by the former employee that he works cheaper and charges less than his old master, and to lose sight of the risk to the latter that old customers, once tempted to leave him, may never return to deal with him, or that business that might otherwise have come to him may be captured by his rival. The consequential injuries to the trader's business arising from each breach by the employee of his covenant cannot be measured by the direct loss in a monetary point of view on the particular transaction constituting the breach.

Lord Atkinson was making substantially the same point as Lord Robertson had made in the *Clydebank case* [1905] AC 6. The question was: what was the nature and extent of the innocent party's interest in the performance of the relevant obligation. That interest was not necessarily limited to the mere recovery of compensation for the breach. Lord Atkinson considered that the underlying purpose of the resale price maintenance clause gave Dunlop a wider interest in enforcing the damages clause than pecuniary compensation. £5 per item was not incommensurate with that interest even if it was incommensurate with the loss occasioned by the wrongful sale of a single item.

24 Although the other members of the Appellate Committee did not express themselves in the same terms as Lord Atkinson, their approach was entirely consistent with his. Lord Parker of Waddington [1915] AC 79, 97, said that 'whether the sum agreed to be paid on the breach is really a penalty must depend on the circumstances of each particular case', and at p 99, echoing Lord Atkinson's fuller treatment of the point, as just set out, he described the damage which would result from any breach as 'consist[ing] in the disturbance or derangement of the system of distribution by means of which [Dunlop's] goods reach the ultimate consumer.' In their speeches, Lord Dunedin (p 87), Lord Parker (p 98) and Lord Parmoor (p 103) ultimately were content to rest their decision that the £5 was not a penalty on the ground that an exact pre-estimate of loss was impossible, whereas, in the passages quoted above, Lord Atkinson analysed why that was so. It seems clear that the actual result of the case was strongly influenced by Lord Atkinson's reasoning. The clause was upheld although, on the face of it, it failed all but the last of Lord Dunedin's tests. The £5 per item applied to breaches of very variable significance and it was impossible to relate the loss attributable to the sale of that item. It was justifiable only by reference to the wider interests identified by Lord Atkinson.

25 The great majority of cases decided in England since the *Dunlop* case have concerned more or less standard damages clauses in consumer contracts, and Lord Dunedin's four tests have proved perfectly adequate for dealing with those. More recently, however, the courts have returned to the possibility of a broader test in less straightforward cases, in the context of the supposed 'commercial justification' for clauses which might otherwise be regarded as penal. An early example is the decision of the House of Lords in *The Scaptrade* [1983] 2 AC 694, 702, where Lord Diplock, with whom the rest of the Appellate Committee agreed, observed that a right to withdraw a time-chartered vessel for non-payment of advance hire was not a penalty because its commercial purpose was to create a fund from which the cost of providing the chartered service could be funded.

26 In *Lordsvale Finance plc v Bank of Zambia* [1996] QB 752, Colman J was concerned with a common form provision in a syndicated loan agreement for interest to be payable at a higher rate during any period when the borrower was in default. There was authority that such provisions were penal . . . But Colman J held that the clause was valid because its predominant purpose was not to deter default but to reflect the greater credit risk associated with a borrower in default. At [1996] QB 752, 763–764, he observed that a provision for the payment of money on breach could not be categorised as a penalty simply because it was not a genuine pre-estimate of damages, saying that there would seem to be:

> no reason in principle why a contractual provision the effect of which was to increase the consideration payable under an executory contract upon the happening of a default should be struck down as a penalty if the increase could in the circumstances be explained as commercially justifiable, provided always that its dominant purpose was not to deter the other party from breach.

27 Colman J's approach was approved by Mance LJ, delivering the leading judgment in the Court of Appeal in *Cine Bes Filmcilik ve Yapimcilik AS v United International Pictures* [2004] 1 CLC 401, para 13. A similar view was taken by Arden LJ in *Murray v Leisureplay plc* [2005] IRLR 946, para 54, where she posed the question:

> Has the party who seeks to establish that the clause is a penalty shown that the amount payable under the clause was imposed in terrorem, or that it does not constitute a genuine pre-estimate of loss for the purposes of the *Dunlop* case,

and, if he has shown the latter, is there some other reason which justifies the discrepancy between [the amount payable under the clause and the amount payable by way of damages in common law]? (Emphasis added.)

She considered that the clause in question had advantages for both sides, and pointed out that no evidence had been adduced to show that the clause lacked commercial justification: see paras 70–76. But Buxton LJ put the matter on a wider basis for which Clarke LJ (para 105) expressed a preference. He referred to the speech of Lord Atkinson in the *Dunlop case* [1915] AC 79 and suggested [2005] IRLR 946, para 117 that the ratio of the actual decision in that case had been that 'an explanation of the clause in commercial rather than deterrent terms was available'. All three members of the court endorsed the approach of Colman J in the *Lordsvale case* [1996] QB 752 and Mance LJ in the *Cine Bes case* [2004] 1 CLC 401.

28 Colman J in the *Lordsvale* case and Arden LJ in the *Murray case* [2005] IRLR 946 were inclined to rationalise the introduction of commercial justification as part of the test, by treating it as evidence that the impugned clause was not intended to deter. Later decisions in which a commercial rationale has been held inconsistent with the application of the penalty rule, have tended to follow that approach: see, for example, *Euro London Appointments Ltd v Claessens International Ltd* [2006] 2 Lloyd's Rep 436, *General Trading Co (Holdings) Ltd v Richmond Corpn Ltd* [2008] 2 Lloyd's Rep 475. It had the advantage of enabling them to reconcile the concept of commercial justification with Lord Dunedin's four tests. But we have some misgivings about it. The assumption that a provision cannot have a deterrent purpose if there is a commercial justification, seems to us to be questionable. By the same token, we agree with Lord Radcliffe's observations in the *Campbell Discount case* [1962] AC 600, 622, where he said:

I do not myself think that it helps to identify a penalty, to describe it as in the nature of a threat 'to be enforced in terrorem' (to use Lord Halsbury's phrase in *Elphinstone v Monkland Iron & Coal Co Ltd* (1886) 11 App Cas 332, 348). I do not find that that description adds anything of substance to the idea conveyed by the word 'penalty' itself, and it obscures the fact that penalties may quite readily be undertaken by parties who are not in the least terrorised by the prospect of having to pay them and yet are, as I understand it, entitled to claim the protection of the court when they are called upon to make good their promises.

. . . A damages clause may properly be justified by some other consideration than the desire to recover compensation for a breach. This must depend on whether the innocent party has a legitimate interest in performance extending beyond the prospect of pecuniary compensation flowing directly from the breach in question.

[Lord Neuberger then referred to the legitimate interest requirement identified by Lord Reid in *White and Carter (Councils) Ltd v McGregor* [1962] AC 413, at p. 431 and the fact that the remedy of specific performance requires that damages should not be an adequate remedy and so requires identification of some other interest in performance extending beyond pecuniary compensation for breach.]

29 . . . In the *White and Carter* case the innocent party was entitled to ignore the repudiation of the contract-breaker and proceed to perform, claiming his remuneration in debt rather than limiting himself to damages, notwithstanding that this course might be a great deal more expensive for the contract-breaker. This, according to Lord Reid (p 431), was because the contract-breaker did not set out to prove that the appellants had no legitimate interest in completing the contract and claiming the contract price rather than claiming damages.

30 More generally, the attitude of the courts, reflecting that of the Court of Chancery, is that specific performance of contractual obligations should ordinarily be refused where damages would be an adequate remedy. This is because the minimum condition for an order of specific performance is that the innocent

party should have a legitimate interest extending beyond pecuniary compensation for the breach . . . As Lord Hoffmann put it in addressing a very similar issue 'the purpose of the law of contract is not to punish wrongdoing but to satisfy the expectations of the party entitled to performance': *Co-operative Insurance Society Ltd v Argyll Stores (Holdings) Ltd* [1998] AC 1, 15.

31 In our opinion, the law relating to penalties has become the prisoner of artificial categorisation, itself the result of unsatisfactory distinctions: between a penalty and genuine pre-estimate of loss, and between a genuine pre-estimate of loss and a deterrent. These distinctions originate in an over-literal reading of Lord Dunedin's four tests and a tendency to treat them as almost immutable rules of general application which exhaust the field . . . The real question when a contractual provision is challenged as a penalty is whether it is penal, not whether it is a pre-estimate of loss. These are not natural opposites or mutually exclusive categories. A damages clause may be neither or both. The fact that the clause is not a pre-estimate of loss does not therefore, at any rate without more, mean that it is penal. To describe it as a deterrent (or, to use the Latin equivalent, in terrorem) does not add anything. A deterrent provision in a contract is simply one species of provision designed to influence the conduct of the party potentially affected. It is no different in this respect from a contractual inducement. Neither is it inherently penal or contrary to the policy of the law. The question whether it is enforceable should depend on whether the means by which the contracting party's conduct is to be influenced are 'unconscionable' or (which will usually amount to the same thing) 'extravagant' by reference to some norm.

32 The true test is whether the impugned provision is a secondary obligation which imposes a detriment on the contract-breaker out of all proportion to any legitimate interest of the innocent party in the enforcement of the primary obligation. The innocent party can have no proper interest in simply punishing the defaulter. His interest is in performance or in some appropriate alternative to performance. In the case of a straightforward damages clause, that interest will rarely extend beyond compensation for the breach, and we therefore expect that Lord Dunedin's four tests would usually be perfectly adequate to determine its validity. But compensation is not necessarily the only legitimate interest that the innocent party may have in the performance of the defaulter's primary obligations . . .

33 The penalty rule is an interference with freedom of contract. It undermines the certainty which parties are entitled to expect of the law. Diplock LJ was neither the first nor the last to observe that 'The court should not be astute to descry a "penalty clause"': the *Robophone case* [1966] 1 WLR 1428, 1447. As Lord Woolf said, speaking for the Privy Council in *Philips Hong Kong Ltd v Attorney General of Hong Kong* (1993) 61 BLR 41, 59, 'the court has to be careful not to set too stringent a standard and bear in mind that what the parties have agreed should normally be upheld', not least because 'any other approach will lead to undesirable uncertainty especially in commercial contracts'.

34 Although the penalty rule originates in the concern of the courts to prevent exploitation in an age when credit was scarce and borrowers were particularly vulnerable, the modern rule is substantive, not procedural. It does not normally depend for its operation on a finding that advantage was taken of one party. As Lord Wright MR observed in *Imperial Tobacco Co (of Great Britain and Ireland) Ltd v Parslay* [1936] 2 All ER 515, 523:

> A millionaire may enter into a contract in which he is to pay liquidated damages, or a poor man may enter into a similar contract with a millionaire, but in each case the question is exactly the same, namely, whether the sum stipulated as damages for the breach was exorbitant or extravagant . . .

35 But for all that, the circumstances in which the contract was made are not entirely irrelevant. In a negotiated contract between properly advised parties of comparable bargaining power, the strong initial presumption must be that the parties themselves are the best judges of what is legitimate

in a provision dealing with the consequences of breach. In that connection, it is worth noting that in the *Philips Hong Kong case* 61 BLR 41, 57–59, Lord Woolf specifically referred to the possibility of taking into account the fact that 'one of the parties to the contract is able to dominate the other as to the choice of the terms of a contract' when deciding whether a damages clause was a penalty. In doing so, he reflected the view expressed by Mason and Wilson JJ in the *AMEV-UDC case* 162 CLR 170, 194 that the courts were thereby able to 'strike a balance between the competing interests of freedom of contract and protection of weak contracting parties' (citing Atiyah, *The Rise and Fall of Freedom of Contract* (1979), chapter 22). However, Lord Woolf was rightly at pains to point out that this did not mean that the courts could thereby adopt 'some broader discretionary approach'. The notion that the bargaining position of the parties may be relevant is also supported by Lord Browne-Wilkinson giving the judgment of the Privy Council in the *Workers Trust case* [1993] AC 573. At p 580, he rejected the notion that 'the test of reasonableness [could] depend upon the practice of one class of vendor, which exercises considerable financial muscle' as it would allow such people 'to evade the law against penalties by adopting practices of their own.' In his judgment, he decided that, in contracts for sale of land, a clause providing for a forfeitable deposit of 10% of the purchase price was valid, although it was an anomalous exception to the penalty rule. However, he held that the clause providing for a forfeitable 25% deposit in that case was invalid because 'in Jamaica, the customary deposit has been 10%' and '[a] vendor who seeks to obtain a larger amount by way of forfeitable deposit must show special circumstances which justify such a deposit', which the appellant vendor in that case failed to do.

Should the penalty rule be abrogated?

36 The primary case of [counsel for Cavendish] was that the penalty rule should now be regarded as antiquated, anomalous and unnecessary, especially in the light of the growing importance of statutory regulation in this field. It is the creation of the judges, and, she argued, the judges should now take the opportunity to abolish it. There is a case to be made for taking this course. It was expounded with considerable forensic skill by [counsel] and has some powerful academic support: see Sarah Worthington, 'Common Law Values: the Role of Party Autonomy in Private Law', in *The Common Law of Obligations: Divergence and Unity* (eds Andrew Robertson and Michael Tilbury) (2016), ch 14 (also Cambridge University Faculty of Law Legal Studies Research Paper No 33/2015 (June 2015)). We rather doubt that the courts would have invented the rule today if their predecessors had not done so three centuries ago. But this is not the way in which English law develops, and we do not consider that judicial abolition would be a proper course for this court to take.

37 The first point to be made is that the penalty rule is not only a long-standing principle of English law, but is common to almost all major systems of law, at any rate in the western world. It has existed in England since the 16th century . . . The researches of counsel have shown that it has been adopted with some variants in all common law jurisdictions, including those of the United States. A corresponding rule was derived from Roman law by Pothier, *Traité des Obligations*, No 346, which is to be found in the Civil Codes of France (article 1152), Germany (for non-commercial contracts only) (sections 343, 348), Switzerland (article 163.3), Belgium (article 1231) and Italy (article 1384). It is included in influential attempts to codify the law of contracts internationally, including the *Unidroit Principles of International Commercial Contracts* (2010) (article 7.4.13), and the *Uncitral Uniform Rules on Contract Clauses for an Agreed Sum Due upon Failure of Performance* (1983) (article 6). In January 1978 the Committee of Ministers of the Council of Europe recommended a number of common principles relating to penal clauses, including (article 7) that a stipulated sum payable on breach 'may be reduced by the court when it is manifestly excessive.'

38 It is true that statutory regulation, which hardly existed at the time that the penalty rule was developed, is now a significant feature of the law of contract. In England, the landmark legislation was the Unfair Contract Terms Act 1977. For most purposes, the Act was superseded by the Unfair Terms in Consumer Contracts Regulations 1994 (SI 1994/3159), which was in turn replaced by the 1999 Regulations, both of which give effect to European Directives . . . None the less, statutory regulation is very far from covering the whole field . . . There are major areas, notably non-consumer contracts, which are not regulated by statute. Some of those who enter into such contracts, for example professionals and small businesses, may share many of the characteristics of consumers which are thought to make the latter worthy of legal protection. The English Law Commission considered penalty clauses in 1975 (Working Paper No 61, *Penalty Clauses and Forfeiture of Moneys Paid*, April 1975), at a time when there was no relevant statutory regulation, and the Scottish Law Commission reported on them in May 1999 (Scot Law Com No 171). Neither of these reports recommended abolition of the rule. On the contrary, both recommended legislation which would have expanded its scope.

39 Further, although there are justified criticisms that can be made of the penalty rule, it is consistent with other well established principles which have been developed by judges (albeit mostly in the Chancery courts) and which involve the court in declining to give full force to contractual provisions, such as relief from forfeiture, the equity of redemption, and refusal to grant specific performance . . . Finally, the case for abolishing the rule depends heavily on anomalies in the operation of the law as it has traditionally been understood. Many, though not all of these are better addressed (i) by a realistic appraisal of the substance of contractual provisions operating on breach, and (ii) by taking a more principled approach to the interests that may properly be protected by the terms of the parties' agreement.

NOTES

1. The language of legitimate interest has therefore replaced that of commercial justification. These are not the same since the emphasis has now altered to focusing on the position and perspective of the injured party, rather than analysing the clause in the context of other provisions which may alter the initial interpretation of extravagance. Although the Supreme Court is correct to conclude that the penalty rule should regulate only the contractual remedy, that remedy is best understood in the context of the other contractual provisions rather than as a provision in the abstract.

2. The Supreme Court chose to evaluate the obligations to determine whether they were penal even though they had been identified as primary contractual obligations not capable of amounting to penalties. Care should be taken with this part of the judgment, as it merely constitutes guidance by the Supreme Court as to the type of considerations to be taken into account in determining when a secondary obligation may be regarded as penal: the Supreme Court was not suggesting that primary obligations had to be assessed in this way.

3. The Supreme Court considered that a provision could not be a penalty unless it provided an exorbitant alternative to common law damages. It followed that it had to be a provision operating on breach. The penalty rule only regulated the secondary remedy for breach of a primary obligation under the contract; it did not amount to a licence to review the fairness of primary contractual obligations. It follows that in so far as the penalty rule represents a control on contractual substance, that control should be restricted to remedial provisions only and this will substantially reduce the scope of its operation. In future it will be necessary to evaluate provisions in terms of their substance rather than their form to determine whether in substance they amount to a conditional primary obligation or a secondary obligation providing a contractual alternative to damages at common law. Future case law is likely to be preoccupied with the distinction between primary and secondary obligations; this is not necessarily as easy a distinction to make as might be supposed. In *Vivienne Westwood Ltd v Conduit Street Development Ltd* [2017] EWHC 350 (Ch) premises were leased to the claimant at a rent of £250,000 a year for the period November 2014 to November 2019. However, by a side letter, the defendant landlord agreed to a lower rent of £125,000 per year as long as the claimant did not— in breach of the terms of the lease—assign the lease or cease to trade from the premises. This was held to be a penalty clause.

4. In the context of secondary or remedial obligations, the position in the light of this decision of the Supreme Court is that the test is whether the clause is penal and that is not the same as whether it is a genuine pre-estimate of the likely loss or whether it operates as a deterrent. The real test of a penal clause turns on whether the means by which the contracting party's conduct was to be influenced were unconscionable or extravagant and this was formulated (at [32]) as a test of whether the clause 'amounts to a secondary obligation which imposes a detriment on the contract-breaker out of all proportion to the non-breaching party's legitimate interest in the enforcement of the primary obligation'. Thus, the emphasis is placed on the performance interest of the non-breaching (injured) party and the Supreme Court accepted that compensation was not necessarily the only legitimate interest that the innocent party might have in ensuring the other's performance of its primary obligations. The interest might be securing compensation for breach but there could be wider interests.

5. Where compensation for breach was the only legitimate interest, Lord Dunedin's guidelines in *Dunlop v New Garage* would usually suffice to determine whether the clause was penal. However, compensation might not be the only legitimate interest of the injured party and, in the commercial context where the contract was negotiated between parties of equal bargaining power, the natural assumption had to be that the parties were the best judges of their interests and had drafted the remedy provision to reflect these interests. In the commercial context this is likely to be confirmation of the continuing decline in the operation of the penalty rule, e.g. *Philips Hong Kong Ltd v A-G of Hong Kong* (1993) 61 BLR 41 and *Murray v Leisureplay plc* [2005] EWCA Civ 963, [2005] IRLR 946. In *Murray v Leisureplay plc* the Court of Appeal held that a clause providing for the payment of one year's gross salary in lieu of a year's notice was a liquidated damages clause. The employer had sought to argue that the clause was a penalty because it took no account of the fact that the employee would be expected to mitigate by finding alternative employment and so this figure could not be 'a genuine pre-estimate of the likely loss'. However, the Court of Appeal held that the employer had failed to discharge the burden of proof, particularly since the employer had freely agreed to this compensation figure in a commercial setting. There were balancing advantages to both parties in agreeing this figure as compensation, and the difference between the one year's gross salary and the amount of unliquidated damages (taking account of the amount likely to be earned when mitigating) could not therefore lead to the conclusion that the clause was penal. By contrast, in *Vivienne Westwood* the provisions of the lease were held to be penal because the side letter, properly construed, imposed an 'obligation to pay rent at a higher rate as from the rent commencement date of the lease, regardless of the nature and consequences of the breach and when it occurs' (at para. 63).

Dunlop Pneumatic Tyre Co. Ltd v New Garage & Motor Co. Ltd
[1915] AC 79 (HL)

For facts and discussion see Lord Neuberger's judgment in *Cavendish Square Holdings v Makdessi*, [21]–[24]. The guidelines suggested by Lord Dunedin for distinguishing liquidated damages and penalty clauses may remain of relevance following the Supreme Court's decision in circumstances where financial compensation for breach is the injured party's only legitimate interest in performance.

LORD DUNEDIN: I shall content myself with stating succinctly the various propositions which I think are deducible from the decisions which rank as authoritative:—

1. Though the parties to a contract who use the words 'penalty' or 'liquidated damages' may prima facie be supposed to mean what they say, yet the expression used is not conclusive. The Court must find out whether the payment stipulated is in truth a penalty or liquidated damages . . .

. . .

3. The question whether a sum stipulated is penalty or liquidated damages is a question of construction to be decided upon the terms and inherent circumstances of each particular contract, judged of as at the time of the making of the contract, not as at the time of the breach . . .

4. To assist this task of construction various tests have been suggested, which if applicable to the case under consideration may prove helpful, or even conclusive. Such are:

   (a) It will be held to be penalty if the sum stipulated for is extravagant and unconscionable in amount in comparison with the greatest loss that could conceivably be proved to have followed from the breach.

   (b) It will be held to be a penalty if the breach consists only in not paying a sum of money, and the sum stipulated is a sum greater than the sum which ought to have been paid (*Kemble v Farren* (1829) 6 Bing 141). This though one of the most ancient instances is truly a corollary to the last test . . .

   (c) There is a presumption (but no more) that it is penalty when 'a single lump sum is made payable by way of compensation, on the occurrence of one or more or all of several events, some of which may occasion serious and others but trifling damage'.

   On the other hand:

   (d) It is no obstacle to the sum stipulated being a genuine pre-estimate of damage, that the consequences of the breach are such as to make precise pre-estimation almost an impossibility. On the contrary, that is just the situation when it is probable that pre-estimated damage was the true bargain between the parties . . .

Turning now to the facts of the case, it is evident that the damage apprehended by the appellants owing to the breaking of the agreement was an indirect and not a direct damage. So long as they got their price from the respondents for each article sold, it could not matter to them directly what the respondents did with it. Indirectly it did. Accordingly, the agreement is headed 'Price Maintenance Agreement,' and the way in which the appellants would be damaged if prices were cut is clearly explained in evidence . . ., and no successful attempt is made to controvert that evidence. But though damage as a whole from such a practice would be certain, yet damage from any one sale would be impossible to forecast. It is just, therefore, one of those cases where it seems quite reasonable for parties to contract that they should estimate that damage at a certain figure, and provided that figure is not extravagant there would seem no reason to suspect that it is not truly a bargain to assess damages, but rather a penalty to be held in terrorem.

14.10.1.2 The penalty rule applied in the consumer context

ParkingEye Ltd v Beavis
[2015] UKSC 67, [2015] 3 WLR 1373 (SC)

Mr Beavis parked at a retail park. The car park operator for this retail park was paid a fixed weekly amount to oversee the car park and was obliged by the terms of its contract to keep it as a free parking facility. It was allowed to retain any parking charges collected for breaches of the car parking rules. Notices in the car park were clear about the charge imposed if the period of free parking was exceeded. Mr Beavis left his car in the car park for longer than the permitted two hours of free parking and was subject to the charge—£85, reduced to £50 for prompt payment. He refused to pay this sum and was sued by the parking company, ParkingEye, for breach of the parking contract. Mr Beavis argued that he did not need to pay the charge because it was an unenforceable penalty on the basis that car park operator had suffered no financial loss and therefore the £85 could not be a genuine pre-estimate of the likely loss due to his breach in overstaying and, in any event, it was not binding on him as an unfair contract term within the relevant consumer legislation (then the Unfair Terms in Consumer Contracts Regulations (UTCCR) 1999, *page 292, 6.5*).

Held: While the penalty rule was plainly engaged, the £85 charge was not a penalty. Although the claimant was not liable to suffer loss as a result of overstaying motorists, it had a legitimate interest in charging them which extended beyond the recovery of any loss. The Supreme Court looked at the purpose underpinning the imposition of the charge and concluded that there were two main objectives which the Court considered to be perfectly reasonable: (i) to manage the efficient use of parking space in the interests of the nearby retail outlets and of their customers, and (ii) to provide an income stream to enable ParkingEye to meet the costs of operating the scheme and make a profit. There was no reason to suppose that £85 was out of all proportion to the claimant's interests. Consumer motorists regularly used the car park knowing of the charge and took the risk that they would need to pay £85 if they overstayed. Similar parking charges applied elsewhere. The charge was therefore was neither extravagant nor unconscionable.

Six of the seven Justices also considered that the charge did not infringe the UTCCR 1999 as being an unfair term because any imbalance in the parties' positions was not 'contrary to the requirements of good faith' given Parking Eye's legitimate interest in managing the car park for the benefit of all users and the fact that the charge was not higher than was necessary to protect that interest.

NOTE Sch. 2, Part 1, para. 6, Consumer Rights Act 2015 provides that in a consumer contract, a term may be unfair and unenforceable if it requires 'any consumer who fails to fulfil his obligation to pay a disproportionately high sum in compensation'. However, it is necessary to determine what is meant by a 'disproportionately high sum' in the general context of unfairness and good faith. In *Munkenbeck & Marshall v Harold* [2005] EWHC 356 (TCC), a term providing for interest at 8 per cent over base to be payable in the event of late payment was held to be unfair as involving a significant imbalance in the parties' positions contrary to good faith and to the detriment of the consumer, because there was no similar term in respect of monies that might be payable to the consumer. However, although the term was unfair, it was held that it did not constitute a penalty because, in view of the late payment legislation, it could not be said that the figure itself was necessarily penal. Thus, a liquidated damages clause was held to be an unfair term within the UTCCR 1999 which were applicable to the contract.

14.10.1.3 The effect of each type of clause

The effect of a penalty clause on the contract is explained in Lord Neuberger's judgment in *Cavendish Square Holdings v Makdessi*, at [9]. The penalty is unenforceable and the injured party must seek to prove and recover its actual loss. On the other hand, if the clause is a liquidated damages clause, then the injured party recovers that amount irrespective of the actual loss sustained.

Cellulose Acetate Silk Co. Ltd v Widnes Foundry (1925) Ltd
[1933] AC 20 (HL)

In a contract for the delivery and erection of plant, if the work was not completed within a certain time, the contractors were to pay to the purchasers by way of 'penalty' a sum of £20 for every week during which they were in default. The contractors were 30 weeks late in completing the work. The contractors sought the purchase price, but the defendant purchasers counterclaimed for their actual loss caused by the delay (£5,850).

Held: The clause was a liquidated damages clause (even though it was set at *less* than the estimated loss). The claimants were therefore liable to pay only £600 (i.e. £20 × 30).

14.10.1.4 The penalty rule applies only where the sum specified is payable on breach

The penalty rule applies only where the sum specified is payable on breach. The clause will therefore be enforceable where it operates on an event other than breach even if it appears unconscionable or extravagant. This has traditionally been criticized as leading to unsatisfactory fine distinctions. However, it makes perfect sense in the light of the explanation of the Supreme Court in *Cavendish Square Holdings v Makdessi* that the penalty rule applies to secondary (or remedial) contractual obligations as opposed to primary contractual obligations (see the discussion of the decision in *Export Credits Guarantee Department v Universal Oil Products Co.* [1983] 1 WLR 399 at [12]–[13] of Lord Neuberger's judgment). It will therefore be the substance rather than the form of the clause that should determine whether it relates to a primary or secondary contractual obligation and decisions such as *Alder v Moore* should therefore be a thing of the past.

Alder v Moore
[1961] 2 QB 57 (CA)

The Association Football Players and Trainers Union took out a policy of insurance on behalf of its members. It provided that if a member of the union were to suffer permanent total disability that prevented him from playing as a professional footballer, he would be paid £500. The defendant received an eye injury in the course of a match and was certified totally disabled. He was paid £500 under the policy and signed a declaration required by the terms of the policy agreeing to 'take no part as a playing member in any form of professional football in the future and that in the event of an infringement of this condition I will be subject to a penalty of the amount stated above' (£500). Within four months of receiving this payment, the defendant began to play professional football on a part-time basis. The insurers claimed the return of the £500, and the defendant argued that it was a penalty and unenforceable.

Held (Devlin LJ dissenting): This declaration amounted to a promise to repay the £500 if the defendant played again, rather than a promise not to play, with a £500 penalty for breach of that promise. The penalty rule did not apply here to relieve the defendant and he had to repay the £500.

NOTES

1. In *Berg v Blackburn Rovers Football Club & Athletic plc* [2013] EWHC 1070 (Ch), [2013] IRLR 537, a sum payable under the provisions of a termination clause to a dismissed manager of a football club was not a penalty, since it was not payable on breach. Following the decision in *Cavendish Square Holdings v Makdessi*, such a clause would be regarded as a primary obligation of the contract rather than a secondary obligation that arises on breach. It would not be subject to the penalty rule on that basis.

2. In relation to the attempts to reclaim bank charges, it had been argued that since the charge applied when the customer became overdrawn, it amounted to an unenforceable penalty payable on breach. However, the argument put by the banks was that customers were not prohibited from becoming overdrawn, so that payment of this charge did not arise through breach; instead, the charge was imposed in relation to the overdraft as a charge for an ongoing banking service under the terms of the banking contract.

Office of Fair Trading v Abbey National plc
[2008] EWHC 2325 (Comm), [2009] 1 All ER (Comm) 717

Held: In general, the OFT arguments involved strained constructions of wording and, in many cases, the banks were entitled to declarations that the terms, and charges imposed under the terms, were not capable of amounting to penalties at common law.

ANDREW SMITH J: 18 The fact that a penalty is a sum payable upon breach does not mean that the law against penalties has no application whenever the wrongdoer receives some advantage from his wrong-doing, whether from and at the expense of the other party or otherwise, at least (and this is sufficient for present purposes) if the benefit to the wrongdoer and the corresponding expense to the other party is inherent in or intimately related to the wrongdoing, as when it involves the customer using a cheque guarantee card without the requisite funds or facility and thereby obtaining an overdraft. The payment levied for creating the overdraft would still be naturally referable to the breach: that, to my mind, would be the natural perception by the parties to the contract and the normal characterisation of the payment by the reasonable man . . .

19 Nor do I consider that the law of penalties applies only if the wrongdoing is a necessary and sufficient cause of the charge being payable. The contract need not provide that the penalty is payable whenever the term is broken in order for it to be payable upon breach. Some banks allow customers a 'buffer' so that charges are not levied if customers overdraw by a small amount, or do not levy a charge upon the first occasion that customers overdraw, or limit the number of charges levied in a month or other period. The fact that a payment is levied only if the breach is committed in particular circumstances or if other conditions are satisfied does not in itself mean that it is not paid on breach. Thus, a bank's terms might prohibit the customer from using his cheque guarantee card and provide for a Guaranteed Paid Item Charge, but allow the customer a 'buffer'. The Guaranteed Paid Item Charge imposed where the customer is not protected by the 'buffer' might still be penal. (If the customer used his card when its use is prohibited but he was protected by the 'buffer', it would depend upon the particular contract whether the bank would, in principle, be entitled to unliquidated damages, often nominal damages, or the provision of a 'buffer' impliedly excluded this.)

20 Further, a sum can be penal if it is payable upon events that may or may not be a breach of contract if in fact it becomes payable upon a breach. Although the law on this question has caused some difficulty (see *Chitty on Contracts* (2004) 29th ed., vol 2 para 38–314), the better view, it seems to me, is that 'where a sum is contractually payable on the happening of a number of events, including a breach of contract by the payer, the sum is capable of being a penalty when the circumstances giving rise to payment are the breach of contract, but not when the circumstances giving rise to payment are otherwise': Lewison, *The Interpretation of Contracts*, (2007) 3rd Ed para 16.04 p. 598, and see *Cooden Engineering Co Ltd v Stanford*, [1953] 1 QB 86.

NOTE The judge had already rejected a claim in previous proceedings that the UTCCR 1999 had removed the application of the common law penalty doctrine in the context of consumer contracts: [2008] EWHC 875 (Comm), [2008] 2 All ER (Comm) 625.

Chapter 15

Remedies providing for specific relief and restitutionary remedies

15.1 Claiming an agreed sum

If one party has performed its primary contractual obligations and the other party's breach consists of a failure to pay the contractual price or other agreed sum, the performing party can claim this agreed (liquidated) sum rather than damages.

In relation to an action for the price in a contract for the sale of goods, the Sale of Goods Act (SGA) 1979, s. 49(1), provides:

> Where, under a contract of sale, the property in the goods has passed to the buyer and he wrongfully neglects or refuses to pay for the goods according to the terms of the contract, the seller may maintain an action against him for the price of the goods.

Since it is a liquidated claim, the remoteness rules and duty to mitigate do not apply: see *White & Carter (Councils) Ltd v McGregor* [1962] AC 413 (*page 666, 13.5.3.3*), which was an action for an agreed sum where the claimants were able to continue with performance and claim the agreed sum without having to mitigate. In addition, because it is a liquidated claim, it has the procedural advantage that summary judgment can be applied for (i.e. early judgment).

15.2 Specific performance and injunctions

Specific performance is an order of the court requiring the party in breach to perform his primary obligations under the contract. The remedy is necessary where the claimant cannot be properly compensated for loss that might arise from the defendant's failure to perform, e.g. where the subject matter of the contract is unique (a building or a painting). In relation to the sale of goods, the remedy has been put into statutory form.

An injunction, meanwhile, is an order restraining a breach of a negative stipulation in a contract, e.g. breach of a restraint of trade stipulation (*page 586, 11.2.3*).

It is important to remember that, unlike damages, specific performance and injunctions are discretionary remedies.

Numerous restrictions are placed on the ability of the injured party to obtain an order for specific performance. These restrictions also apply to the grant of an injunction against the breach of a negative stipulation in the contract that would have the same effect as an order to perform the obligation.

15.2.1 If damages are an adequate remedy, specific performance is not available

In *Beswick v Beswick* [1968] AC 58 (*page 328, 7.6.1*), the loss to the estate caused by the nephew's failure to pay the widow the annuity was nominal, since it was the widow who suffered the loss. The House of Lords ordered specific performance of the contract on the ground that damages to compensate for the loss to the estate would not provide an adequate remedy.

In relation to sale of goods, damages will be an adequate remedy if it is possible for the injured party to purchase substitute goods: *Société des Industries Metallurgiques SA v The Bronx Engineering Co. Ltd* [1975] 1 Lloyd's Rep 465. If the goods are unique, then damages might not be adequate.

15.2.2 Supervision

Specific performance may not be granted where the contract extends over a period of time because of the difficulty of constant supervision: *Ryan v Mutual Tontine Westminster Chambers Association* [1893] 1 Ch 116. However, in *C. H. Giles & Co. Ltd v Morris* [1972] 1 WLR 307, Megarry J expressed dissatisfaction with any absolute restriction based on difficulties in supervision.

The House of Lords in the next case clarified the restrictions on the availability of the remedy of specific performance. In particular, the House of Lords clarified what is meant by 'supervision' and made clear that, in some circumstances, specific performance may still be refused even if damages would be inadequate.

Co-operative Insurance Society Ltd v Argyll Stores (Holdings) Ltd
[1997] 2 WLR 898 (HL)

The claimant, a developer of a shopping centre, had granted a 35-year lease of one of the major units in the centre to the defendant, a leading supermarket chain. The presence of a major supermarket was important to the success of the shopping centre, since it would attract customers and therefore make it easier to let smaller units. The claimant consequently included a covenant in the lease, which was designed to protect it against the possibility that the defendant would move out of the centre. The defendant had covenanted to keep the premises open for retail trade during the usual hours of business in the locality. The lease had commenced in August 1979, but in May 1995 the defendant closed the supermarket and moved out of the centre. The claimant sought specific performance of the covenant, compelling the defendant to continue to operate the supermarket. It was clear that damages would not be adequate, since it would be difficult to quantify the claimant's loss over the rest of the term of the lease. The judge had refused to order specific performance, but a majority of the Court of Appeal had overturned this decision.

Held (in the House of Lords, allowing the appeal): Specific performance should not be ordered in such circumstances. In particular, it would be difficult to formulate an order with sufficient precision to avoid wasteful litigation concerning compliance with it and, since the effect of such an order might be to order someone to carry on an uneconomic business, the loss might be out of all proportion to the loss being suffered by the claimant as a result of the breach of covenant.

LORD HOFFMANN (with whose judgment the other members of the House of Lords agreed): [Lord Hoffmann first referred to the 'settled practice' whereby the courts would not grant mandatory injunctions requiring the carrying on of a business and continued:] Specific performance is traditionally regarded in English law as an exceptional remedy, as opposed to the common law damages to which a successful plaintiff is entitled as of right. There may have been some element of later rationalisation of an untidier history, but by the 19th century it was orthodox doctrine that the power to decree specific performance was part of the discretionary jurisdiction of the Court of Chancery to do justice in cases in which the remedies available at common law were inadequate. This is the basis of the general principle that specific performance will not be ordered when damages are an adequate remedy. By contrast, in countries with legal systems based on civil law, such as France, Germany and Scotland, the plaintiff is prima facie entitled to specific performance. The cases in which he is confined to a claim for damages are regarded as the exceptions. In practice, however, there is less difference between common law and civilian systems than these general statements might lead one to suppose. The principles upon which English judges exercise the discretion to grant specific performance are reasonably well settled and depend upon a number of considerations, mostly of a practical nature, which are of very general application. I have made no investigation of civilian systems, but a priori I would expect that judges take much the same matters into account in deciding whether specific performance would be inappropriate in a particular case.

The practice of not ordering a defendant to carry on a business is not entirely dependent upon damages being an adequate remedy. In *Dowty Boulton Paul Ltd v Wolverhampton Corporation* [1971] 1 WLR 204, Sir John Pennycuick VC refused to order the corporation to maintain an airfield as a going concern because: 'It is very well established that the court will not order specific performance of an obligation to carry on a business:' see p. 211. He added: 'It is unnecessary in the circumstances to discuss whether damages would be an adequate remedy to the company:' see p. 212. Thus the reasons which underlie the established practice may justify a refusal of specific performance even when damages are not an adequate remedy.

The most frequent reason given in the cases for declining to order someone to carry on a business is that it would require constant supervision by the court. In *J. C. Williamson Ltd v Lukey and Mulholland* (1931) 45 CLR 282, 297–298, Dixon J said flatly: 'Specific performance is inapplicable when the continued supervision of the court is necessary in order to ensure the fulfilment of the contract.'

There has, I think, been some misunderstanding about what is meant by continued superintendence. It may at first sight suggest that the judge (or some other officer of the court) would literally have to supervise the execution of the order. In *C. H. Giles & Co. Ltd v Morris* [1972] 1 WLR 307, 318 Megarry J said that 'difficulties of constant superintendence' were a 'narrow consideration' because:

> there is normally no question of the court having to send its officers to supervise the performance of the order . . . Performance . . . is normally secured by the realisation of the person enjoined that he is liable to be punished for contempt if evidence of his disobedience to the order is put before the court; . . .

This is, of course, true but does not really meet the point. The judges who have said that the need for constant supervision was an objection to such orders were no doubt well aware that supervision would in practice take the form of rulings by the court, on applications made by the parties, as to whether there had been a breach of the order. It is the possibility of the court having to give an indefinite series of such rulings in order to ensure the execution of the order which has been regarded as undesirable.

Why should this be so? A principal reason is that, as Megarry J pointed out in the passage to which I have referred, the only means available to the court to enforce its order is the quasi-criminal procedure of punishment for contempt. This is a powerful weapon; so powerful, in fact, as often to be unsuitable as an instrument for adjudicating upon the disputes which may arise over whether a business is being run in accordance with the terms of the court's order. The heavy-handed nature of the enforcement mechanism is a consideration which may go to the exercise of the court's discretion in other cases as well, but its use to compel the running of a business is perhaps the paradigm case of its disadvantages and it is in this context that I shall discuss them.

The prospect of committal or even a fine, with the damage to commercial reputation which will be caused by a finding of contempt of court, is likely to have at least two undesirable consequences. First, the defendant, who ex hypothesi did not think that it was in his economic interest to run the business at all, now has to make decisions under a sword of Damocles which may descend if the way the business is run does not conform to the terms of the order. This is, as one might say, no way to run a business. In this case the Court of Appeal made light of the point because it assumed that, once the defendant had been ordered to run the business, self-interest and compliance with the order would thereafter go hand in hand. But, as I shall explain, this is not necessarily true.

Secondly, the seriousness of a finding of contempt for the defendant means that any application to enforce the order is likely to be a heavy and expensive piece of litigation. The possibility of repeated applications over a period of time means that, in comparison with a once-and-for-all inquiry as to damages, the enforcement of the remedy is likely to be expensive in terms of cost to the parties and the resources of the judicial system.

This is a convenient point at which to distinguish between orders which require a defendant to carry on an activity, such as running a business over or [*sic*] more or less extended period of time, and orders which require him to achieve a result. The possibility of repeated applications for rulings on compliance with the order which arises in the former case does not exist to anything like the same extent in the latter. Even if the achievement of the result is a complicated matter which will take some time, the court, if called upon to rule, only has to examine the finished work and say whether it complies with the order. This point was made in the context of relief against forfeiture in *Shiloh Spinners Ltd v Harding* [1973] AC 691. If it is a condition of relief that the tenant should have complied with a repairing covenant, difficulty of supervision need not be an objection. As Lord Wilberforce said, at p. 724:

> what the court has to do is to satisfy itself, ex post facto, that the covenanted work has been done, and it has ample machinery, through certificates, or by inquiry, to do precisely this.

This distinction between orders to carry on activities and to achieve results explains why the courts have in appropriate circumstances ordered specific performance of building contracts and repairing covenants: see *Wolverhampton Corporation v Emmons* [1901] 1 KB 515 (building contract) and *Jeune v Queens Cross Properties Ltd* [1974] Ch 97 (repairing covenant). It by no means follows, however, that even obligations to achieve a result will always be enforced by specific performance. There may be other objections, to some of which I now turn.

One such objection, which applies to orders to achieve a result and a fortiori to orders to carry on an activity, is imprecision in the terms of the order. If the terms of the court's order, reflecting the terms of the obligation, cannot be precisely drawn, the possibility of wasteful litigation over compliance is increased. So is the oppression caused by the defendant having to do things under threat of proceedings for contempt. The less precise the order, the fewer the signposts to the forensic minefield which he has to traverse. The fact that the terms of a contractual obligation are sufficiently definite to escape being void for uncertainty, or to found a claim for damages, or to permit compliance to be made a condition of relief against forfeiture, does not necessarily mean that they will be sufficiently precise to be capable of being specifically performed. So in *Wolverhampton Corporation v Emmons*, Romer LJ said, at p. 525, that the first condition for specific enforcement of a building contract was that the particulars of the work are so far definitely ascertained that the court can sufficiently see what is the exact nature of the work of which it is asked to order the performance.

Similarly in *Morris v Redland Bricks Ltd* [1970] AC 652, 666, Lord Upjohn stated the following general principle for the grant of mandatory injunctions to carry out building works:

> the court must be careful to see that the defendant knows exactly in fact what he has to do and this means not as a matter of law but as a matter of fact, so that in carrying out an order he can give his contractors the proper instructions.

Precision is of course a question of degree and the courts have shown themselves willing to cope with a certain degree of imprecision in cases of orders requiring the achievement of a result in which the plaintiffs' merits appeared strong; like all the reasons which I have been discussing, it is, taken alone, merely a discretionary matter to be taken into account: see Spry, *Equitable Remedies*, 4th ed. (1990), p. 112. It is, however, a very important one . . .

There is a further objection to an order requiring the defendant to carry on a business, which was emphasised by Millett LJ in the Court of Appeal. This is that it may cause injustice by allowing the plaintiff to enrich himself at the defendant's expense. The loss which the defendant may suffer through having to comply with the order (for example, by running a business at a loss for an indefinite period) may be far greater than the plaintiff would suffer from the contract being broken. As Professor R. J. Sharpe explains in 'Specific Relief for Contract Breach,' ch. 5 of *Studies in Contract Law* (1980), edited by Reiter and Swan, p. 129:

> In such circumstances, a specific decree in favour of the plaintiff will put him in a bargaining position vis-à-vis the defendant whereby the measure of what he will receive will be the value to the defendant of being released from performance. If the plaintiff bargains effectively, the amount he will set will exceed the value to him of performance and will approach the cost to the defendant to complete.

. . . It is true that the defendant has, by his own breach of contract, put himself in such an unfortunate position. But the purpose of the law of contract is not to punish wrongdoing but to satisfy the expectations of the party entitled to performance. A remedy which enables him to secure, in money terms, more than the performance due to him is unjust. From a wider perspective, it cannot be in the public interest for the courts to require someone to carry on business at a loss if there is any plausible alternative by which the other party can be given compensation. It is not only a waste of resources but yokes the parties together in a continuing hostile relationship. The order for specific performance prolongs the battle. If the defendant is ordered to run a business, its conduct becomes the subject of a flow of complaints, solicitors' letters and affidavits. This is wasteful for both parties and the legal system. An award of damages, on the other hand, brings the litigation to an end. The defendant pays damages, the forensic link between them is severed, they go their separate ways and the wounds of conflict can heal.

The cumulative effect of these various reasons, none of which would necessarily be sufficient on its own, seems to me to show that the settled practice is based upon sound sense. Of course the grant or refusal of specific performance remains a matter for the judge's discretion. There are no binding rules, but this does not mean that there cannot be settled principles, founded upon practical considerations of the kind which I have discussed, which do not have to be re-examined in every case, but which the courts will apply in all but exceptional circumstances . . .

NOTES

1. Until the decision of the Court of Appeal, it had been assumed that breach of such a covenant would give rise to a damages claim. The decision of the Court of Appeal had far-reaching implications for retailers who might well have been forced to operate uneconomic stores. It would also have had repercussions for property developers, since tenants would understandably have been reluctant to agree to covenants of this nature and would have been in a good bargaining position to negotiate reduced rents on leases.

2. Although the Court of Appeal had been influenced by what it regarded as the bad behaviour of the defendants, Lord Hoffmann made the following comment, at p. 18C–G:

> The principles of equity have always had a strong ethical content and nothing which I say is intended to diminish the influence of moral values in their application. I can envisage cases of gross breach of personal faith, or attempts to use the threat of non-performance as blackmail, in which the needs of justice will override all the considerations which support the settled practice. But although any breach of covenant is regrettable, the exercise of the discretion as to whether or not to grant specific performance starts from the fact that the covenant has been broken. Both landlord and tenant in this case are large sophisticated commercial organisations and I have no doubt that both were perfectly aware that the remedy for breach of the covenant was likely to be limited to an award of damages. The interests of both were purely financial: there was no element of personal breach of faith, as in the Victorian cases of railway companies which refused to honour obligations to build stations for landowners whose property they had taken: compare *Greene v West Cheshire Railway Co* (1871) LR 13 Eq 44. No doubt there was an effect on the businesses of other traders in the Centre, but Argyll had made no promises to them and it is not suggested that C.I.S. warranted to other tenants that Argyll would remain. Their departure, with or without the consent of C.I.S., was a commercial risk which the tenants were able to deploy in negotiations for the next rent review. On the scale of broken promises, I can think of worse cases, but the language of the Court of Appeal left them with few adjectives to spare.

3. The Court of Appeal's order had been suspended pending assignment of the lease to another tenant. Such a tenant had been found by the time of the final appeal to the House of Lords. Therefore, in practical terms, the order would never have been enforced. Nevertheless, this factor could not determine the outcome of the exercise of the discretion to award specific performance.

4. An example of the application of *Co-operative Society v Argyll* is provided by the decision in *Vertex Data Science Ltd v Powergen Retail Ltd* [2006] EWHC 1340 (Comm), [2006] 2 Lloyd's Rep 591. V had agreed to supply P, the electricity supply company, with outsourcing services. The parties had not got on and P had issued a notice of termination, alleging a number of persistent and material breaches. V sought an injunction to prevent P from acting on its notice, which would be equivalent to an order for specific performance. Tomlinson J held that it would not be appropriate to grant this relief, since the agreement required extensive mutual cooperation, and it would have the effect of compelling parties whose relationship had broken down to continue in a contractual relationship. In addition, the court would struggle to enforce such an order given that the contract did not indicate precisely the action required if P were to avoid preventing or hindering V from performing its contractual obligations.

5. In *Rainbow Estates Ltd v Tokenhold Ltd* [1998] 2 All ER 860, it was held that the courts had the power in appropriate circumstances to order specific performance of a tenant's covenant to repair. This would be an order to achieve a result (as opposed to an order to carry on an activity). Accordingly, there would not be the same difficulties regarding the need for constant supervision as long as what needed to be done in order to comply with the order of specific performance was sufficiently defined by the court.

15.2.3 **Contracts for personal services**

Generally, a court will not order specific performance of a contract requiring personal services, e.g. where there is a negative stipulation in the contract whereby one party must render exclusive services to the other, and will not grant an injunction to restrain the breach, since this would have the same effect as specific performance and would compel one person to work for another.

Page One Records Ltd v Britton
[1968] 1 WLR 157

The claimants were the managers and publishers of pop group, 'The Troggs'. The contract between them provided that the group would not 'engage any other person firm or corporation to act as [their] managers or agents or act themselves in such capacity'. The claimants sought an interlocutory (interim) injunction to restrain the group from engaging Harvey Block Associates Ltd as their manager in breach of contract, and from publishing music performed by them. The claimants also sought an injunction against Harvey Block Associates Ltd restraining any inducement to the defendants to break their contract with the claimants.

Held: Enforcement of these negative covenants would be tantamount to ordering specific performance of the contract of personal services by the claimants. It would be wrong to put pressure on the defendants to continue to employ in the fiduciary capacity of a manager and agent someone in whom they had lost confidence.

STAMP J: [T]his present case, in my judgment, fails, on the facts at present before me, on a more general principle, the converse of which was conveniently stated in the judgment of Branson J in *Warner Brothers Pictures Inc v Nelson* [1937] 1 KB 209. Branson J stated the converse of the proposition and the proposition, correctly stated, is, I think, this, that where a contract of personal service contains negative covenants the enforcement of which will amount either to a decree of specific performance of the positive covenants of the contract or to the giving of a decree under which the defendant must either remain idle or perform those positive covenants, the court will not enforce those negative covenants.

In the *Warner Brothers* case Branson J felt able to find that the injunction sought would not force the defendant to perform his contract or remain idle . . .

So it was said in this case that if an injunction is granted the Troggs could, without employing any other manager or agent, continue as a group on their own or seek other employment of a different nature. So far as the former suggestion is concerned, in the first place I doubt whether consistently with the terms of the agreements which I have read, the Troggs could act as their own managers; and, in the second place, I think I can, and should, take judicial notice of the fact that these groups, if they are to have any great success, must have managers. Indeed, it is the plaintiffs' own case that the Troggs are simple persons, of no business experience, and could not survive without the services of a manager. As a practical matter on the evidence before me, I entertain no doubt that they would be compelled, if the injunction was granted, on the terms that the plaintiffs seek, to continue to employ the first plaintiff as their manager and agent and it is, I think, on this point that this case diverges from *Lumley v Wagner* (1852) 1 De GM & G 604 and the cases which have followed it, including the *Warner Brothers* case [1937] 1 KB 209: for it would be a bad thing to put pressure upon these four young men to continue to employ as a manager and agent in a fiduciary capacity one who, unlike the plaintiff in those cases (who had merely to pay the defendant money) has duties of a personal and fiduciary nature to perform and in whom the Troggs, for reasons good, bad or indifferent, have lost confidence and who may, for all I know, fail in its duty to them.

On the facts before me on this interlocutory motion, I should, if I granted the injunction, be enforcing a contract for personal services in which personal services are to be performed by the first plaintiff. In *Lumley v Wagner* Lord St Leonards, in his judgment, disclaimed doing indirectly what he could not do directly; and in the present case, by granting an injunction I would, in my judgment, be doing precisely that. I must, therefore, refuse the injunction which the first plaintiff seeks.

NOTES

1. Particular stress was placed on the fact that this relationship was one requiring mutual trust and confidence. As *Vertex Data Science Ltd v Powergen Retail Ltd* [2006] EWHC 1340 (Comm), [2006] 2 Lloyd's Rep 591, illustrates, even where the parties are in a commercial and not a personal relationship, the courts are unlikely to order specific performance where the mutual confidence in the relationship has broken down. In *Ashworth v Royal National Theatre* [2014] EWHC 1176 (QB), [2014] 4 All ER 238, Cranston J stressed the loss of confidence argument when refusing an application by musicians for specific performance (or a mandatory injunction) which would require the theatre to re-engage them after the theatre had decided to use recorded music in place of live music for the theatre production. The judge referred, at [23], to this as 'a standard case where on a traditional analysis loss of confidence is the primary block to this type of relief'. He added: 'Loss of confidence is fact specific . . . The plain fact is that the production of a play necessarily entails close cooperation between all those involved, the actors and those directing and producing the play.'

2. An injunction may be granted where there is an express term of the contract preventing the party in question from taking up *specified* alternative employment. For example, in *Lumley v Wagner* (1852)

1 De GM & G 604, the claimant engaged the defendant to sing at his theatre and the contract contained an express clause forbidding the defendant from singing anywhere else for the period of the contract. The defendant then entered another contract to sing elsewhere and refused to perform under her contract with the claimant. Specific performance was not available to the claimant because the contract was for personal service, but the express negative covenant could be enforced by injunction, thereby preventing the defendant from singing elsewhere. This also explains the decision in *Warner Brothers Pictures Inc. v Nelson* [1937] 1 KB 209, in which an injunction was granted to prevent the film actress, Bette Davis, appearing in any film or stage production for anyone other than Warner Brothers without its consent. Warner Brothers did not seek enforcement of a positive performance obligation, which would have been refused.

3. In *Araci v Fallon* [2011] EWCA Civ 668, [2011] LLR 440, the Court of Appeal granted an interim injunction to prevent the jockey, Kieren Fallon, from breaching a negative obligation in the contract that prevented him from riding any rival horse in the Epsom Derby. There was also a positive obligation to ride the particular owner's horse, but this could not be compelled, and Fallon ended up without a ride in the race.

15.2.4 Damages in lieu of, or in addition to, injunction or specific performance

> **Senior Courts Act 1981**
>
> ***50 Power to award damages as well as, or in substitution for, injunction or specific performance.***
> Where the Court of Appeal or the High Court has jurisdiction to entertain an application for an injunction or specific performance, it may award damages in addition to, or in substitution for, an injunction or specific performance.

NOTES

1. The Supreme Court in *Morris Garner v One Step (Support) Ltd* [2018] UKSC 20 made it clear that damages under Lord Cairns' Act are not necessarily assessed on ordinary common law principles, and that their purpose is to compensate for the absence of an equitable remedy: that may relate to future as well as past losses.

LORD REED: 41. Historically, the Court of Chancery could provide remedies in aid of equitable rights, including restitution if the right was violated. It could also provide remedies

which were not available at common law, such as an injunction or specific performance, in aid of common law rights. Its jurisdiction was wider than that of the common law courts, for it could give relief where there was no cause of action at common law, for example by granting an injunction to prevent a threatened wrong. However, one form of relief which it could not grant (except, according to some authorities, where it was granted in addition to specific performance) was damages, ie monetary relief for the breach of a common law obligation. If the plaintiff wished to claim damages in addition to equitable relief, it was normally necessary to apply to the common law courts. The damages which could then be claimed were restricted to compensation for loss in respect of which there was a cause of action at common law.

42. That inconvenience was addressed by section 2 of the Chancery Amendment Act 1858, commonly known as Lord Cairns' Act . . . Equivalent provision is now contained in section 50 of the Senior Courts Act 1981.

43. Lord Cairns' Act enabled the Court of Chancery to award damages in the circumstances specified 'in addition to' an injunction. That power enabled the Court of Chancery to award damages which could otherwise have been awarded by the common law courts, and has lost its significance since the fusion of the administration of law and equity. The Act also enabled the Court of Chancery to award damages 'in substitution for' an injunction: a statutory power to award damages in circumstances in which they could not be awarded at common law. [Lord Reed considered *Jaggard v Sawyer* [1995] 1 WLR 269 and continued] . . .

44. Damages awarded in substitution for an injunction are, as one might expect, a monetary substitute for an injunction. As Viscount Finlay stated in *Leeds Industrial Co-operative Society Ltd v Slack* [1924] AC 851, p 859, 'the power to give damages in lieu of an injunction must in all reason import the power to give an equivalent for what is lost by the refusal of the injunction'. Where it is likely that the refusal of an injunction will result in the claimant's sustaining loss and damage as a consequence of the tort, breach of contract or other wrongful act which the court has declined to prevent, the damages should provide compensation for that loss and damage, as Sir Thomas Bingham MR and Millett LJ explained in *Jaggard v Sawyer* at pp 276–277 and 286 respectively.

45. The power to award damages in substitution for an injunction is dependent on the court's having jurisdiction to grant an injunction, determined as at the commencement of the proceedings. The provision that damages can be awarded 'in substitution for such injunction' might be thought to imply that the court must also have before it an application for an injunction, which it has decided to withhold. The point does not arise for decision in these proceedings . . .

46. Like the jurisdiction to grant an injunction, the jurisdiction to grant damages in lieu is equitable in nature, as Millett LJ explained in *Jaggard v Sawyer* at p 287:

When the plaintiff claims an injunction and the defendant asks the court to award damages instead, the proper approach for the court to adopt cannot be in doubt. Clearly the plaintiff must first establish a case for equitable relief, not only by proving his legal right and an actual or threatened infringement by the defendant, but also by overcoming all equitable defences such as laches, acquiescence or estoppel.

2. Lord Reed in para. 45 expressly stated his hesitation in endorsing the view of Lord Walker in *Pell Frischmann Ltd v Bow Valley Iran Ltd* [2009] UKPC 45, [2011] 1 WLR 2370 that 'Although damages under Lord Cairns's Act are awarded in lieu of an injunction it is not necessary that an injunction should actually have been claimed in the proceedings, or that there should have been any prospect, on the facts, of it being granted' (para. 48). Lord Reed is here implying that Lord Cairns' Act and its successor in the Senior Courts Act 1981 are narrow in their scope and do not provide a stand-alone assessment of damages even where no equitable relief has been sought.

15.3 Restitutionary remedies: no agreement

Restitution allows the injured party to recover money paid or the value of benefits conferred on the party in breach where it would be unjust to allow the guilty party to retain that benefit. The cases discussed in this section are concerned with the restitution of benefits conferred where there is no binding contract.

15.3.1 Total failure of consideration

If the benefit consisted of a payment of money, it can be recovered where there has been a total failure of consideration (i.e. the injured party has received no part of the contractual performance), but not if the failure of consideration is only partial, since the courts would then have to calculate whether the contractual performance was equivalent to the sum paid. Bovill CJ, in *Whincup v Hughes* (1871) LR 6 CP 78, 81, explained this difficulty of apportionment:

This is an action brought to recover a part of the premium paid upon the execution of an apprenticeship deed, on the ground of failure of consideration. The general rule of law is, that where a contract has been in part performed no part of the money paid under such contract can be recovered back. There may be some cases of partial performance which form exceptions to this rule, as, for instance, if there were a contract to deliver ten sacks of wheat and six only were delivered, the price of the remaining four might be recovered back. But there the consideration is clearly severable. The general rule being what I have stated, is there anything in the present case to take it out of such rule? The master instructed the apprentice under the deed for the period of a year, and then died. It is clear law that the contract being one of a personal nature, the death of the master, in the absence of any stipulation to the contrary, puts an end to it for the future. The further performance of it has been prevented by the act of God, and there is thus no breach of contract upon which any action will lie against the executor. That being so, can any action be maintained otherwise than upon the contract? The contract having been in part performed, it would seem that the general rule must apply unless the consideration be in its nature apportionable. I am at a loss to see on what principle such apportionment could be made. It could not properly be made with reference to the proportion which the period during which the apprentice was instructed bears to the whole term. In the early part of the term the teaching would be most onerous, and the services of the apprentice of little value; as time went on his services would probably be worth more, and he would require less teaching . . .

In *Stocznia Gdanska SA v Latvian Shipping Co.* [1998] 1 WLR 574 (for the facts, *page 661, 13.5.3.1*), the defendants argued that because they had not received anything under the contract, there had been a total failure of consideration. However, the House of Lords held that, for there to be a total failure of consideration, the test was not whether the purchasers had received anything under the contract, but whether the shipbuilders had performed any part of their contractual duties. It was therefore a matter of determining what the shipbuilders had promised to do under the contract; since the contract imposed an obligation for design and construction in addition to delivery, there was no total failure of consideration. Lord Goff stated, at p. 588:

I find myself to be in agreement with [counsel for the yard's] submission on this point. I start from the position that failure of consideration does not depend upon the question whether the promisee has or has not *received* anything under the contract like, for example, the property in the ships being built under contracts 1 and 2 in the present case. Indeed, if that were so, in cases in which the promisor undertakes to do work or render services which confer no direct benefit on the promisee, for example where he undertakes to paint the promisee's daughter's house, no consideration would ever be furnished for the promisee's payment. In truth, the test is not whether the promisee has received a specific benefit, but rather whether the promisor has performed any part of the contractual duties in respect of which the payment is due. The present case cannot, therefore, be approached by asking the simple question whether the property in the vessel or any part of it has passed to the buyers. That test would be apposite if the contract in question was a contract for the sale of goods (or indeed a contract for the sale of land) simpliciter under which the consideration for the price would be the passing of the property in the goods (or land). However before that test can be regarded as appropriate, the anterior question has to be asked: is the contract in question simply a contract for the sale of a ship? Or is it rather a contract under which the design and construction of the vessel formed part of the yard's contractual duties, as well as the duty to transfer the finished object to the buyers? If it is the latter, the design and construction of the vessel form part of the consideration for which the price is to be paid, and the fact that the contract has been brought to an end before the property in the vessel or any part of it has passed to the buyers does not prevent the yard from asserting that there has been no total failure of consideration in respect of an instalment of the price which has been paid before the contract was terminated, or that an instalment which has then accrued due could not, if paid, be recoverable on that ground.

I am satisfied that the present case falls into the latter category. This was what the contracts provided in their terms. Moreover, consistently with those terms, payment of instalments of the price was geared to progress in the construction of the vessel. That this should be so is scarcely surprising in the case of a shipbuilding contract, under which the yard enters into major financial commitments at an early stage, in the placing of orders for machinery and materials, and in reserving and then occupying a berth for the construction of the vessel. Indeed if [counsel for the buyer's] argument is right, it would follow that no consideration would have been furnished by the yard when instalments of the price fell due before the moment of delivery, notwithstanding all the heavy and irreversible financial commitments then undertaken by the yard.

15.3.2 *Quantum meruit*

If the benefit consists of services and there is no contractual provision for remuneration, the injured party can claim their reasonable value on a *quantum meruit*: *Planche v Colburn* (1831) 8 Bing 14, 131 ER 305. See also *British Steel Corporation v Cleveland Bridge & Engineering Co. Ltd* [1984] 1 All ER 504 (*page 82, 2.6.4*), in which the services were requested by the benefited party, and compare *Regalian Properties plc v London Dockland Development Corporation* [1995] 1 WLR 212 (*page 82, 2.6.4*).

15.4 Negotiating damages

15.4.1 The *Wrotham Park* principle

Where the parties have entered into an agreement and the claim is for damages for breach, the rather different question arises as to whether the measure of damages is based on the claimant's loss or the defendant's gain. Although the former is clearly correct, there will be situations in which the defendant's gain is obvious but the claimant's loss is not. In a series of cases beginning with *Wrotham Park Estate Co. Ltd v Parkside Homes Ltd* [1974] 1 WLR 798 the English courts developed the principle that if the defendant's breach of contract deprived the claimant of the ability to enjoy a property right, damages were to be assessed on the basis of implied licence. The question to be asked was, what price would the claimant have demanded had a licence been granted to the defendant to use the right? The notional implied licence is a familiar approach in cases involving the infringement of intellectual property rights and also of rights over land, but the effect of *Wrotham Park* was to extend the implied licence concept to contract claims where the defendant had broken the contract and thereby deprived the claimant of benefits under the contract. *Wrotham Park* was given new impetus by the decision of the House of Lords in *Attorney-General v Blake* [2001] 1 AC 268 (HL), in which, in rather unique circumstances, an account of profits was awarded against a government official who had, in breach of contract, written a book about his experiences. In the aftermath of *Blake*, the distinct notions of *Wrotham Park* damages and account of profits became intertwined until the necessary separation was effected by the Supreme Court in *Morris-Garner v One Step (Support) Ltd* [2018] UKSC 20.

In this and the following section the development of the two ideas, and the effects of *One Step* are considered. Some of the post-*Blake* judgments deal with both matters, and in the following extracts the two are kept separate.

15.4.1.1 The development of *Wrotham Park* damages

In *Wrotham Park* itself, the owners of land forming part of an estate conveyed it to developers but subject to a restrictive covenant that it would be developed only in accordance with the agreement of the estate owners. The developers erected houses without the consent of the estate owners, and the latter sought mandatory injunctions ordering the developers to remove the houses and also damages. The injunctive relief was refused in the discretion of the court, in that estate owners had been aware of the infringement of their rights but had not sought to intervene. As for damages, the estate owners were unable to prove that they had suffered any loss, but Brightman J held that it was appropriate to award damages to the estate owners based upon the amount that they would have charged to the developers for permission to build. The case was concerned solely with the award of damages under Lord Cairns' Act, but the decision was subsequently taken to lay down a general principle that damages based on a notional licence are awardable for breach of contract.

In *Experience Hendrix LLC v PPX Enterprises Inc.* [2003] EWCA Civ 323 there had been breaches of a 1973 settlement agreement relating to masters of titles and licences of the music of Jimi Hendrix. Injunctions had been issued to prevent these breaches, but Buckley J at first instance dismissed a claim for damages relating to past breaches. The claimant appealed to the Court of Appeal on the question of damages. There was no evidence to establish the financial loss suffered by the claimant as a result of the breaches, so it sought the amount that it could reasonably have demanded to relax the prohibitions in the settlement agreement (i.e. the *Wrotham Park* principle) or the profit attributable to the exploitation of the material. Damages were awarded on that basis, Peter Gibson LJ stating (para. 58) that damages should be available under *Wrotham Park* where: '(1) there was a deliberate breach by the defendant of its contractual obligations for its own reward; (2) the claimant would have difficulty in establishing financial loss therefrom; and (3) the claimant had a "legitimate interest" in preventing the defendant's profit-making activity in breach of contract'.

It will be seen from this reasoning that the key criteria for the award of *Wrotham Park* damages were that the defendant had deliberately broken the contract for its own reward and that the claimant's loss could not easily be quantified. *Wrotham Park* thus became a potential means for awarding damages to a claimant who could not prove actual loss by reason of the defendant's breach but was instead able to seek what was essentially a restitutionary basis by depriving the defendant of wrongfully obtained profits. The question whether *Wrotham Park* damages were akin to an account of profits under *Blake* was considered in the next case.

WWF World Wide Fund for Nature v World Wrestling Federation Entertainment Inc.
[2007] EWCA Civ 286, [2008] 1 WLR 445, [2007] Bus LR 1252 (CA)

A dispute had arisen between the parties concerning the initials 'WWF', which were used by the Wrestling Federation, but had long been associated with the World Wide Fund for Nature. The parties had entered into an agreement to compromise their litigation and to regulate the future use of these initials. The agreement had restricted the use that could be made of the initials by the Wrestling Federation. This action arose out of various breaches of this agreement by the Wrestling Federation. Peter Smith J [2006] EWHC 184 (Ch), [2006] FSR 38, granting the application for summary judgment in respect of these breaches, refused the claimant's application for an account of the defendant's profits resulting from these breaches of the restrictions. The Fund then sought to recast its claim in the form of *Wrotham Park* damages. The Wrestling Federation argued that the *Wrotham Park* remedy was a juridically similar remedy to the account of profits that had been refused earlier on in the proceedings. If this were the case, it would follow that the matter of the remedy had already been decided and could not be reopened in later proceedings on the *res judicata* principle. The argument was that both were 'gains-based awards'.

Held: Since the account of profits had been refused, it would be an abuse of process to give permission to seek damages on the *Wrotham Park* basis, because these claims were juridically 'highly similar', although this was because they were both compensatory in nature (albeit compensation where there was no identifiable financial loss) and not because they were both restitutionary (or gains-based) remedies.

CHADWICK LJ [with whose judgment Maurice Kay and Wilson LJJ agreed]: 53 In the light of the judgments in the *Experience Hendrix* case [2003] EWCA Civ 323, it must now be regarded as settled in this court that, on a claim by a covenantee for an injunction and damages against a covenantor who has acted in breach of a restrictive covenant, the court may, in addition to granting an injunction to restrain further breaches, award damages in respect of past breaches notwithstanding that the covenantee cannot establish actual financial loss. In such a case the damages in respect of past breaches may be in an amount assessed as the sum which the court considers it would have been reasonable for the covenantor to pay and the covenantee to accept for the hypothetical release of the covenant . . .

54 I should add, for completeness, that (if it were necessary to decide the point) I would hold that, in a case where a covenantor has acted in breach of a restrictive covenant, the court may award damages on the *Wrotham Park* basis, notwithstanding that there is no claim for an injunction—and notwithstanding that there could be no claim for an injunction. In my view, the analysis in the speech of Lord Nicholls in *Blake's* case compels that conclusion. The power to award damages on a *Wrotham Park* basis does not depend on Lord Cairns's Act: it exists at common law. Further, as it seems to me, the power to award damages on the basis of what it would have been reasonable for the covenantor to pay for a hypothetical release does not depend on the covenantee establishing (as a factual premise) that, absent a release, the covenant could have been enforced by injunction. That, I think, is what Mance LJ had in mind when he said in the *Experience Hendrix* case [2003] EWCA Civ 323, para 16, that the decision in *Blake's* case had freed this court from constraints imposed by the reasoning in the *Bredero Homes* case and 'some of the reasoning in *Jaggard v Sawyer*'. But it is not necessary to decide that point on this appeal. As I have said, this is a case in which—as in the *Experience Hendrix* case—the claimant was in a position to, and did, seek an injunction to restrain further breaches. In this case the claimant could rely on the jurisdiction conferred by Lord Cairns' Act—as Peter Gibson LJ explained [2003] 1 All ER (Comm) 830, para 56.

55 In the *Experience Hendrix* case this court rejected the claimant's invitation to order an account of profits; it ordered that the defendant pay 'a reasonable sum for its use of material in breach of the settlement agreement'—paras 45 and 58. It indicated that the defendant should pay to the claimant 'by way of damages, a proportion of each of the advances received to date and (subject to deduction of such proportion) an appropriate royalty rate on retail selling prices': para 45. But that formula, as it seems to me, was informed by the view, at para 45, that the circumstances led inexorably to the conclusion that, had there been any negotiated release from the restrictions imposed by the settlement agreement, it would have been 'on terms requiring payment of a royalty'. The formula reflected the court's view as to the basis upon which the hypothetical bargain between the parties, acting reasonably, would have been made.

56 I am not persuaded that, on a true analysis, the outcome in the *Experience Hendrix* case provides support for the proposition that an award of damages on the *Wrotham Park* basis is to

be characterised as a gains-based remedy . . . The rationale which underlies the outcome in the *Experience Hendrix* case is, I think, helpfully summarised in the final sentences of para 26 in the judgment of Mance LJ . . .:

> In such a context [where the instinctive reaction is that, whether or not the claimant would have been better off if the wrong had not been committed, the wrongdoer should make some reasonable recompense] it is natural to pay regard to any profit made by the wrongdoer . . . The law can in such cases act either by ordering payment over of a percentage of any profit or, in some cases, by taking the cost which the wrongdoer would have had to incur to obtain (if feasible) equivalent benefit from another source.

In the *Experience Hendrix* case there were compelling reasons why the appropriate order was for payment over of a percentage of turnover (by way of royalty); but that outcome does not lead to the conclusion that this court saw the remedy as other than compensatory in nature.

57 It follows that I would hold that the premise on which the contentions in . . . the . . . application notice are based—that an award of damages on the *Wrotham Park* basis is not an award of compensatory damages, but is properly to be characterised as a gains-based award—is not made out . . .

58 Having said that, I should add that the real question, as it seems to me, is not whether an award of damages on the *Wrotham Park* basis is to be characterised as a gain-based award, but whether (as the law stands following the decision of the House of Lords in *Blake's* case [2001] 1 AC 268) an order for an account of profits, in a case where the claim is based on breach of contract rather than on infringement of proprietary rights, is to be characterised as an award of compensatory damages. That, of course, is an inversion of the argument in the present appeal. But support for that view is, I think, found in the observations of Lord Nicholls in *Blake's* case (with which, with the exception of Lord Hobhouse, the other members of the House of Lords agreed) when drawing together his analysis under the section of his speech headed 'Breach of contract'. He said, at pp 284–285:

> My conclusion is that there seems to be no reason, *in principle*, why the court must in all circumstances rule out an account of profits as a remedy for breach of contract. I prefer to avoid the unhappy expression 'restitutionary damages'. Remedies are the law's response to a wrong (or, more precisely, to a cause of action). When, exceptionally, a just response to a breach of contract so requires, the court should be able to grant the discretionary remedy of requiring a defendant to account to the plaintiff for the benefits he has received from his breach of contract. In the same way as a plaintiff's interest in performance of a contract may render it just and equitable for the court to make an order for specific performance or grant an injunction, so the plaintiff's interest in performance may make it just and equitable that the defendant should retain no benefit from his breach of contract. The state of the authorities encourages me to reach this conclusion, rather than the reverse. The law recognises that damages are not always a sufficient remedy for breach of contract. This is the foundation of the court's jurisdiction to grant the remedies of specific performance and injunction. Even when awarding damages, the law does not adhere slavishly to the concept of compensation for financially measurable loss. When the circumstances require, damages are measured by reference to the benefit obtained by the wrongdoer . . . With the established authorities going thus far, I consider it would be only a modest step for the law to recognise openly that, exceptionally, an account of profits may be the most appropriate remedy for breach of contract.

59 When the court makes an award of damages on the *Wrotham Park* basis it does so because it is satisfied that that is a just response to circumstances in which the compensation which is the claimant's due cannot be measured (or cannot be measured solely) by reference to identifiable financial loss. Lord Nicholls's analysis in *Blake's* case demonstrates that there are exceptional cases in which the just response to circumstances in which the compensation which is the claimant's due cannot be measured by reference to identifiable financial loss is an order which deprives the wrongdoer of all the fruits of his wrong. The circumstances in which an award of damages on the *Wrotham Park* basis may be an appropriate response, and those in which the appropriate response is an account of profits, may differ in degree. But the underlying feature, in both cases, is that the court recognises the need to compensate the claimant

in circumstances where he cannot demonstrate identifiable financial loss. To label an award of damages on the *Wrotham Park* basis as a 'compensatory' remedy and an order for an account of profits as a 'gains-based' remedy does not assist an understanding of the principles on which the court acts. The two remedies should, I think, each be seen as a flexible response to the need to compensate the claimant for the wrong which has been done to him.

60 It follows, therefore, that although I would reject the premise on which the contentions in . . . the . . . application notice are based (that an award of damages on the *Wrotham Park* basis is not an award of compensatory damages, but is properly to be characterised as a gains-based award), I would accept that, on a true analysis, the allegation . . . (that the remedy now sought by the fund (an award of damages on the *Wrotham Park* basis) is 'a juridically highly similar remedy to, the relief'—an account of profits—'previously sought') is well founded . . .

NOTE Thus, although the *Wrotham Park* award was unavailable in this case, the Court of Appeal made it clear that, in a claim for an injunction and damages for past breaches of a restrictive covenant, the court might award damages of the price for the release of the negative covenant (as the sum that the court considered would be reasonable for the covenantor to pay and the covenantee to accept for the hypothetical release of the covenant) in addition to an injunction, or *Wrotham Park* damages alone, despite the fact that the claimant (covenantee) was unable to establish any identifiable financial loss. This sum was to be assessed as at the date immediately before the breaches occurred and would cover the period until the injunction (covering future breaches) began to operate. The Court of Appeal was clear that this remedy was separate from the remedy of the injunction and not dependent on it in any way. In other words, the decision in *Experience Hendrix* was confirmed as providing the most appropriate remedy in these circumstances.

Lane v O'Brien Homes Ltd
[2004] EWHC 303 (QB)

Lane had sold a site to O'Brien on which O'Brien was to build houses. The sale was subject to an oral collateral contract limiting the number of houses to be built to three. O'Brien built four houses in breach of this oral collateral contract and damages of £150,000 had been awarded, representing the value of the 'loss of chance of the bargaining position' that Lane possessed when negotiating any release from the undertaking to build only three houses.

Held (on appeal): *Wrotham Park Estate Co. v Parkside Homes* was the proper basis for the award, rather than damages for loss of chance. This principle required the court to consider hypothetical negotiations for the release from the restriction to build three houses at the time of the grant of planning permission in order to build four houses on the land and to award damages to represent the amount reasonably required to secure relaxation of the 'covenant' (or undertaking in this case). (There was no restrictive covenant in this case, but only an oral collateral undertaking to build no more than three houses.)

Clarke J considered that the case law did not provide that such damages were limited to a small percentage of the purchaser's potential profit arising from the breach of the undertaking (although only 5 per cent had been awarded in *Wrotham Park*). Indeed, he did not think that the judge had acted erroneously in awarding damages of £150,000. Thus, it is clear that the potential profit is the starting point for any assessment of such damages and the actual award in *Lane* represents a sizeable proportion of the profit made on the sale of the fourth house— around £280,000. Counsel had argued that the decision in *Blake* suggested that the law was moving to a position of accepting awards of the entire profit rather than a share of it. However, the judge considered that 'the factual context of that case . . . is so far from the present case that I do not find it helpful in my task'.

In *Lunn Poly Ltd v Liverpool & Lancashire Properties Ltd* [2006] EWCA Civ 430 Neuberger J referred to such damages as 'negotiating damages'. In *Pell Frischmann Engineering Ltd v Bow Valley Iran Ltd* [2009] UKPC 45, [2011] 1 WLR 2370, Lord Walker confirmed the principles applicable to a *Wrotham Park* award and noted, in particular:

> 49 . . . It is a negotiation between a willing buyer (the contract breaker) and a willing seller (the party claiming damages) in which the subject matter of the negotiation is the release of the relevant contractual obligation. Both parties are to be assumed to act reasonably. The fact that one or both parties would in practice have refused to make a deal is therefore to be ignored.

In *Abbar v Saudi Economic & Development Co. (SEDCO) Real Estate Ltd* [2013] EWHC 1414 (Ch), [226], David Richards J rejected an argument advocating that 'the lack of an identifiable financial loss was not a precondition to an award of negotiating damages', on the basis that:

> 225 Negotiating damages have not, however, replaced the usual compensatory damages as the primary remedy in damages for breach of contract. It is a basis of assessment available where a breach of contract has been established but the claimant cannot establish any financial loss, assessed on the usual basis, flowing from the breach. In those circumstances, and where the defendant has proceeded to act without the consent of the claimant, justice requires that there should nonetheless be an award of substantial as opposed to nominal damages.

15.4.2 The replacement of *Wrotham Park* damages with negotiating damages

The possible development of *Wrotham Park* damages into a restitutionary remedy was halted by the Supreme Court in *Morris-Garner v One Step (Support) Ltd* [2018] UKSC 20, where *Wrotham Park* damages were formally reclassified as 'negotiating damages' and were held to be awardable in limited circumstances only. The facts of the case were set out at *page 678, 14.1*. In outline, the claimant sought damages from the defendant for breach of a non-competition clause following the transfer of the claimant's business to the defendant. The Court of Appeal awarded *Wrotham Park* damages, with Longmore LJ adopting the reasoning of Peter Gibson LJ in *Experience Hendrix LLC v PPX Enterprises Inc.* [2003] EWCA Civ 323: the defendant was in deliberate breach; the claimant could not easily quantify its own loss; and the claimant had a legitimate interest in preventing the defendant from making profits. That reasoning was rejected by the Supreme Court. Lord Reed, giving the leading judgment, held that damages were to be assessed on conventional grounds by reference to the claimant's loss. The judgment in *Morris-Garner* put the matter in the following way:

> LORD REED: 90. In particular, in so far as the reasoning [in *WWF*] might convey the impression that the fact that loss or damage may be difficult to measure renders it unnecessary to identify such loss or damage, or that it is relevant to an award of damages that the breach of contract was deliberate or the party in breach benefited from his conduct, or that it is relevant to an award of damages that the claimant has a 'legitimate interest' in preventing an activity carried out in breach of contract, or that damages for breach of contract and an account of profits are similar remedies at different points along a continuum, that impression would be mistaken.

91. The use of an imaginary negotiation can give the impression that negotiation damages are fundamentally incompatible with the compensatory purpose of an award of contractual damages. Damages for breach of contract depend on considering the outcome if the contract had been performed, whereas an award based on a hypothetical release fee depends on considering the outcome if the contract had not been performed but had been replaced by a different contract. That impression of fundamental incompatibility is, however, potentially misleading. There are certain circumstances in which the loss for which compensation is due is the economic value of the right which has been breached, considered as an asset. The imaginary negotiation is merely a tool for arriving at that value. The real question is as to the circumstances in which that value constitutes the measure of the claimant's loss.

92. As the foregoing discussion has demonstrated, such circumstances can exist in cases where the breach of contract results in the loss of a valuable asset created or protected by the right which was infringed, as for example in cases concerned with the breach of a restrictive covenant over land, an intellectual property agreement or a confidentiality agreement. Such cases share an important characteristic with the cases in which Lord Shaw's 'second principle' and Nicholls LJ's 'user principle' were applied. The claimant has in substance been deprived of a valuable asset, and his loss can therefore be measured by determining the economic value of the asset in question. The defendant has taken something for nothing, for which the claimant was entitled to require payment.

93. It might be objected that there is a sense in which any contractual right can be described as an asset, or indeed as property. In the present context, however, what is important is that the contractual right is of such a kind that its breach can result in an identifiable loss equivalent to the economic value of the right, considered as an asset, even in the absence of any pecuniary losses which are measurable in the ordinary way. That is something which is true of some contractual rights, such as a right to control the use of land, intellectual property or confidential information, but by no means of all. For example, the breach of a non-compete obligation may cause the claimant to suffer pecuniary loss resulting from the wrongful competition, such as a loss of profits and goodwill, which is measurable by conventional means, but in the absence of such loss, it is difficult to see how there could be any other loss.

94. It is not easy to see how, in circumstances other than those of the kind described in paras 91–93, a hypothetical release fee might be the measure of the claimant's loss. It would be going too far, however, to say that it is only in those circumstances that evidence of a hypothetical release fee can be relevant to the assessment of damages. If, for example, in other circumstances, the parties had been negotiating the release of an obligation prior to its breach, the valuations which the parties had placed on the release fee, adjusted if need be to reflect any changes in circumstances, might be relevant to support, or to undermine, a subsequent quantification of the losses claimed to have resulted from the breach. It would be a matter for the judge to decide whether, in the particular circumstances, evidence of a hypothetical release fee was relevant and, if so, what weight to place upon it. However, the hypothetical release fee would not itself be a quantification of the loss caused by a breach of contract, other than in circumstances of the kind described in paras 91–93 above.

95 The foregoing discussion leads to the following conclusions:

(1) Damages assessed by reference to the value of the use wrongfully made of property (sometimes termed 'user damages') are readily awarded at common law for the invasion of rights to tangible moveable or immoveable property (by detinue, conversion or trespass). The rationale of such awards is that the person who makes wrongful use of property, where its use is commercially valuable, prevents the owner from exercising a valuable right to control its use, and should therefore compensate him for the loss of the value of the exercise of that right. He takes something for nothing, for which the owner was entitled to require payment.

(2) Damages are also available on a similar basis for patent infringement and breaches of other intellectual property rights.

(3) Damages can be awarded under Lord Cairns' Act in substitution for specific performance or an injunction, where the court had jurisdiction to entertain an application for such relief at the time when the proceedings were commenced. Such damages are a monetary substitute for what is lost by the withholding of such relief.

(4) One possible method of quantifying damages under this head is on the basis of the economic value of the right which the court has declined to enforce, and which it has consequently rendered worthless. Such a valuation can be arrived at by reference to the amount which the claimant might reasonably have demanded as a quid pro quo for the relaxation of the obligation in question. The rationale is that, since the withholding of specific relief has the same practical effect as requiring the claimant to permit the infringement of his rights, his loss can be measured by reference to the economic value of such permission.

(5) That is not, however, the only approach to assessing damages under Lord Cairns' Act. It is for the court to judge what method of quantification, in the circumstances of the case before it, will give a fair equivalent for what is lost by the refusal of the injunction.

(6) Common law damages for breach of contract are intended to compensate the claimant for loss or damage resulting from the non-performance of the obligation in question. They are therefore normally based on the difference between the effect of performance and non-performance upon the claimant's situation.

(7) Where damages are sought at common law for breach of contract, it is for the claimant to establish that a loss has been incurred, in the sense that he is in a less favourable situation, either economically or in some other respect, than he would have been in if the contract had been performed.

(8) Where the breach of a contractual obligation has caused the claimant to suffer economic loss, that loss should be measured or estimated as accurately and reliably as the nature of the case permits. The law is tolerant of imprecision where the loss is incapable of precise measurement, and there are also a variety of legal principles which can assist the claimant in cases where there is a paucity of evidence.

(9) Where the claimant's interest in the performance of a contract is purely economic, and he cannot establish that any economic loss has resulted from its breach, the normal inference is that he has not suffered any loss. In that event, he cannot be awarded more than nominal damages.

(10) Negotiating damages can be awarded for breach of contract where the loss suffered by the claimant is appropriately measured by reference to the economic value of the right which has been breached, considered as an asset. That may be the position where the breach of contract results in the loss of a valuable asset created or protected by the right which was infringed. The rationale is that the claimant has in substance been deprived of a valuable asset, and his loss can therefore be measured by determining the economic value of the right in question, considered as an asset. The defendant has taken something for nothing, for which the claimant was entitled to require payment.

(11) Common law damages for breach of contract cannot be awarded merely for the purpose of depriving the defendant of profits made as a result of the breach, other than in exceptional circumstances . . .

(12) Common law damages for breach of contract are not a matter of discretion. They are claimed as of right, and they are awarded or refused on the basis of legal principle.

NOTES

1. Although the members of the Supreme Court were unanimous in concluding that damages were to be assessed by reference to the claimant's loss, there was some difference in the reasoning of Lord Reed (with whom Lady Hale and Lords Wilson and Carnwath agreed) and Lord Sumption. Lord Reed confined negotiating damages to the situations where there had been an invasion of property rights

or where damages were awarded under the successor to Lord Cairns' Act, whereas Lord Sumption saw a wider role for the idea negotiating damages, commenting (at para. 124) that 'Its use is appropriate only if there is material on which the notional release fee can be assessed and then only so far as the trial judge finds it helpful, in the light of such other evidence as may be before him.' Lord Sumption's broader analysis was criticized by Lord Carnwath for extending property concepts to contract and for giving rise to uncertainty as to exactly when negotiating damages might be awarded.

2. In *Priyanka Shipping Ltd v Glory Bulk Carriers Pte Ltd* [2019] EWHC 2804 (Comm) a contract for the sale of a vessel provided that it was sold for the purpose of demolition only, in order to protect the seller's profits in the shipping market where there was existing overcapacity. The buyer resold the vessel and the seller claimed damages under point (10) in *One Step*. David Edwards QC, sitting as a Deputy High Court Judge, rejected the claim, holding that (para. 193): 'The present case is not one which is concerned with breach of a restrictive covenant over land or of a contractual right to control the use of land, or with breach of an intellectual property agreement or a confidentiality agreement. It is not, therefore, concerned with breaches of any of specific types of agreement or covenant that Lord Reed JSC mentioned.'

15.5 Account of profits

15.5.1 Damages are to compensate, not to punish

Where the innocent party has suffered no loss, it is not generally considered possible to recover damages that transfer the benefit gained by the guilty party as a result of the breach of contract, even if that breach was deliberate. The innocent party can recover only for his actual loss: *Surrey County Council v Bredero Homes Ltd* [1993] 1 WLR 1361 (*page 678, 14.1*), in which the Court of Appeal held that the council could recover only nominal damages for the developer's breach of covenant in building the extra five houses and could not recover damages based on the developer's profit on the extra houses.

It has been argued that the law should be prepared to award damages to reverse enrichment gained by a breach of contract: see Birks (1993) 109 LQR 518. The argument is that this would counter deliberate breaches of contract in these circumstances, since there would then be no advantage to the party in breach. In *Surrey County Council v Bredero Homes Ltd* [1993] 1 WLR 1361, p. 1370F–H, such an argument was rejected by Steyn LJ, partly on the basis that the motive of the party committing the breach is not a factor in assessing damages for breach of contract and also because of reasons of policy.

STEYN LJ: The introduction of restitutionary remedies to deprive cynical contract breakers of the fruits of their breaches of contract will lead to greater uncertainty in the assessment of damages in commercial and consumer disputes. It is of paramount importance that the way in which disputes are likely to be resolved by the courts must be readily predictable. Given the premise that the aggrieved party has suffered no loss, is such a dramatic extension of restitutionary remedies justified in order to confer a windfall in each case on the aggrieved party? I think not. In any event such a widespread availability of restitutionary remedies will have a tendency to discourage economic activity in relevant situations. In a range of cases such liability would fall on underwriters who have insured relevant liability risks. Inevitably underwriters would have to be compensated for the new species of potential claims. Insurance premiums would have to go up. That, too, is a consequence which militates against the proposed extension. The recognition of the proposed extension will in my view not serve the public interest. It is sound policy to guard against extending the protection of the law of obligations too widely. For these substantive and policy reasons I regard it as undesirable that the range of restitutionary remedies should be extended in the way in which we have been invited to do so.

NOTES

1. The Law Commission Consultation Paper No. 132, *Aggravated, Exemplary and Restitutionary Damages* (1993), suggested that gain-based damages should be available if the gain were attributable to an interference with a proprietary or analogous right, or to deliberate wrongdoing that could have been restrained by injunction. If this were accepted, much would depend on the meaning of 'proprietary interest'. However, Steyn LJ expressly stated that he considered the link with the availability of a remedy of injunction to be unsatisfactory, since this was a 'wholly different and discretionary' remedy.

2. In its Report No. 247, *Aggravated, Exemplary and Restitutionary Damages* (1997), paras. 3.38–3.47, the Law Commission recommended that there should be no legislation on the question of restitutionary damages for breach of contract, because it would be dangerous to attempt to 'freeze' the position in legislative form. Instead, it recommended that the availability of such damages should be left to common law development, following support for such a position from those responding to the Consultation Paper. In response to its own consultation on this question, *The Law of Damages* (CP 9/07, 2009), the Ministry of Justice also considered legislation to be unnecessary.

15.5.2 An account of profits in an exceptional case

The House of Lords in *Attorney-General v Blake* [2001] 1 AC 268 (HL) held that, in very exceptional circumstances, it may be possible to obtain an order that the party in breach has to account for a profit made as a result of that breach of contract. This decision had, in principle at least, the potential to revolutionize the basis on which damages were awarded in contract by introducing a punitive element. In doing so it relied heavily upon *Wrotham Park*. The principle was devised against a very specific and limited factual background and it was envisaged that the scope of this remedy would be tightly circumscribed. The narrowness of *Blake* has been confirmed by the Supreme Court in *One Step*.

Attorney-General v Blake
[2001] 1 AC 268 (HL)

The defendant was a former member of the intelligence services, but had become an agent for the Soviet Union. He had been tried and imprisoned for treason, but had escaped from prison and fled to Moscow, where he had written his autobiography. The autobiography had been published in England in breach of a term of the defendant's former employment contract that he would not divulge official information. The Attorney-General wished to prevent payment of the book royalties to the defendant. A number of arguments were put at various stages of the action, including an argument that the defendant owed a fiduciary duty to the Crown not to use information gained in his former position (rejected at first instance) and a claim in public law to prevent the receipt of any benefit resulting from criminal conduct (rejected by the House of Lords). The Court of Appeal had accepted that the defendant was in breach of contract, but held that, since the Crown could not establish that it had suffered loss as a result of this breach, it was limited to the recovery of nominal damages. The Court of Appeal did, however, indicate its support for the availability of 'restitutionary damages' for breach of contract in some circumstances, which Lord Woolf MR (giving the judgment of the Court of Appeal) identified as instances of 'skimped performance' (i.e. charging the full price, but not providing the full performance contracted for) and instances in which the profit is obtained by doing the very thing that the person in question contracted not to do. A claim for disgorgement of profits was argued on appeal to the House of Lords.

Held (Lord Hobhouse dissenting): In an exceptional case in which the normal remedies for breach of contract provided inadequate compensation, the court could grant the discretionary remedy of requiring the defendant to account to the claimant for the benefits received from the breach of contract even where the breach of contract did not involve the use of, or interference with, a property interest of the plaintiff. Such a remedy would give effect to *the claimant's interest in performance* and, on these facts, it was just that such an account of profits be ordered.

LORD NICHOLLS [with whom Lords Goff, Browne-Wilkinson, and Steyn agreed]: The basic remedy [for breach of contract] is an award of damages. In the much quoted words of Baron Parke, the rule of the common law is that where a party sustains a loss by reason of a breach of contract, he is, so far as money can do it, to be placed in the same position as if the contract had been performed: *Robinson v Harman* (1848) 1 Exch 850, 855. Leaving aside the anomalous exception of punitive damages, damages are compensatory. That is axiomatic. It is equally well established that an award of damages, assessed by reference to financial loss, is not always 'adequate' as a remedy for a breach of contract. The law recognises that a party to a contract may have an interest in performance which is not readily measurable in terms of money. On breach the innocent party suffers a loss. He fails to obtain the benefit promised by the other party to the contract. To him the loss may be as important as financially measurable loss, or more so. An award of damages, assessed by reference to financial loss, will not recompense him properly. For him a financially assessed measure of damages is inadequate.

The classic example of this type of case, as every law student knows, is a contract for the sale of land. The buyer of a house may be attracted by features which have little or no impact on the value of the house. An award of damages, based on strictly financial criteria, would fail to recompense a disappointed buyer for this head of loss. The primary response of the law to this type of case is to ensure, if possible, that the contract is performed in accordance with its terms. The court may make orders compelling the party who has committed a breach of contract, or is threatening to do so, to carry out his contractual obligations. To this end the court has wide powers to grant injunctive relief. The court will, for instance, readily make orders for the specific performance of contracts for the sale of land, and sometimes it will do so in respect of contracts for the sale of goods. In *Beswick v Beswick* [1968] AC 58 the court made an order for the specific performance of a contract to make payments of money to a third party. The law recognised that the innocent party to the breach of contract had a legitimate interest in having the contract performed even though he himself would suffer no financial loss from its breach. Likewise, the court will compel the observance of negative obligations by granting injunctions. This may include a mandatory order to undo an existing breach, as where the court orders the defendant to pull down building works carried out in breach of covenant.

All this is trite law. In practice, these specific remedies go a long way towards providing suitable protection for innocent parties who will suffer loss from breaches of contract which are not adequately remediable by an award of damages. But these remedies are not always available. For instance, confidential information may be published in breach of a non-disclosure agreement before the innocent party has time to apply to the court for urgent relief. Then the breach is irreversible. Further, these specific remedies are discretionary. Contractual obligations vary infinitely. So do the circumstances in which breaches occur, and the circumstances in which remedies are sought. The court may, for instance, decline to grant specific relief on the ground that this would be oppressive.

An instance of this nature occurred in *Wrotham Park Estate Co. Ltd v Parkside Homes Ltd* [1974] 1 WLR 798.

[Lord Nicholls then considered *Wrotham Park Estate Co. Ltd v Parkside Homes Ltd* [1974] 1 WLR 798 and *Surrey County Council v Bredero Homes Ltd* and continued:]

[*Surrey v Bredero*] is a difficult decision. It has attracted criticism from academic commentators and also in judgments of Sir Thomas Bingham MR and Millett LJ in *Jaggard v Sawyer* [1995] 1 WLR 269. I need not pursue the detailed criticisms. In the *Bredero* case Dillon LJ himself noted, at p. 1364, that had the covenant been worded differently, there could have been provision for payment of an increased price if a further planning permission were forthcoming. That would have been enforceable. But, according to the *Bredero* decision, a covenant not to erect any further houses without permission, intended to achieve the same result, may be breached with impunity. That would be a sorry reflection on the law. Suffice to say, in so far as the *Bredero* decision is inconsistent with the approach adopted in the *Wrotham Park* case, the latter approach is to be preferred.

The *Wrotham Park* case, therefore, still shines, rather as a solitary beacon, showing that in contract as well as tort damages are not always narrowly confined to recoupment of financial loss. In a suitable case damages for breach of contract may be measured by the benefit gained by the wrongdoer from the breach. The defendant must make a reasonable payment in respect of the benefit he has gained. In the present case the Crown seeks to go further. The claim is for all the profits of Blake's book which the publisher has not yet paid him. This raises the question whether an account of profits can ever be given as a remedy for breach of contract. The researches of counsel have been unable to discover any case where the court has made such an order on a claim for breach of contract. In *Tito v Waddell (No. 2)* [1977] Ch 106, 332, a decision which has proved controversial, Sir Robert Megarry VC said that, as a matter of fundamental principle, the question of damages was 'not one of making the defendant disgorge' his gains, in that case what he had saved by committing the wrong, but 'one of compensating the plaintiff.' In *Occidental Worldwide Investment Corporation v Skibs A/S Avanti* [1976] 1 Lloyd's Rep 293, 337, Kerr J summarily rejected a claim for an account of profits when ship owners withdrew ships on a rising market.

. . .

My conclusion is that there seems to be no reason, *in principle*, why the court must in all circumstances rule out an account of profits as a remedy for breach of contract. I prefer to avoid the unhappy expression 'restitutionary damages'. Remedies are the law's response to a wrong (or, more precisely, to a cause of action). When, exceptionally, a just response to a breach of contract so requires, the court should be able to grant the discretionary remedy of requiring a defendant to account to the plaintiff for the benefits he has received from his breach of contract. In the same way as a plaintiff's interest in performance of a contract may render it just and equitable for the court to make an order for specific performance or grant an injunction, so the plaintiff's interest in performance may make it just and equitable that the defendant should retain no benefit from his breach of contract.

The state of the authorities encourages me to reach this conclusion rather than the reverse. The law recognises that damages are not always a sufficient remedy for breach of contract. This is the foundation of the court's jurisdiction to grant the remedies of specific performance and injunction. Even when awarding damages, the law does not adhere slavishly to the concept of compensation for financially measurable loss. When the circumstances require, damages are measured by reference to the benefit obtained by the wrongdoer. This applies to interference with property rights. Recently, the like approach has been adopted to breach of contract. Further, in certain circumstances an account of profits is ordered in preference to an award of damages. Sometimes the injured party is given the choice: either compensatory damages or an account of the wrongdoer's profits. Breach of confidence is an instance of this. If confidential information is wrongfully divulged in breach of a non-disclosure agreement, it would be nothing short of sophistry to say that an account of profits may be ordered in respect of the equitable wrong but not in respect of the breach of contract which governs the relationship between the parties. With the established authorities going thus far, I consider it would be only a modest step for the law to recognise openly that, exceptionally, an account of profits may be the most appropriate remedy for breach of contract. It is not as though this step would contradict some recognised principle applied consistently throughout the law to the grant or withholding of the remedy of an account of profits. No such principle is discernible . . .

The present case

The present case is exceptional. The context is employment as a member of the security and intelligence services. Secret information is the lifeblood of these services. In the 1950s Blake deliberately committed repeated breaches of his undertaking not to divulge official information gained as a result of his employment. He caused untold and immeasurable damage to the public interest he had committed himself to serve. In 1990 he published his autobiography, a further breach of his express undertaking. By this time the information disclosed was no longer confidential. In the ordinary course of commercial dealings the disclosure of non-confidential information might be regarded as venial. In the present case disclosure was also a criminal offence under the Official Secrets Acts, even though the information was no longer confidential . . .

In considering what would be a just response to a breach of Blake's undertaking the court has to take these considerations into account. The undertaking, if not a fiduciary obligation, was closely akin to a fiduciary obligation, where an account of profits is a standard remedy in the event of breach. Had the information which Blake has now disclosed still been confidential, an account of profits would have been ordered, almost as a matter of course. In the special circumstances of the intelligence services, the same conclusion should follow even though the information is no longer confidential. That would be a just response to the breach . . .

NOTES

1. This decision inevitably led to intense debate, particularly over the circumstances in which this principle might be applicable. The comments of Lord Nicholls on this matter are far too general to be of much assistance, although it seems that he envisaged that it will be necessary for a claimant to establish that he has 'a legitimate interest in preventing the defendant's profit-making activity and, hence, in depriving him of his profit'. It may also be significant that, as Lord Nicholls noted, the defendant's position in *Blake* was closely analogous to that of a fiduciary, which was itself a potentially limiting factor.

2. It is important to note that the House of Lords did not accept the categories for any restitutionary remedy of disgorgement that had been identified by Lord Woolf in the Court of Appeal.

3. Only Lord Hobhouse dissented on the issue of liability to account for profits. He emphasized the essential distinction between remedies in restitution (property-based) and contract (based on the compensation principle). He regarded the essence of restitutionary remedies, at p. 297B–C, as:

the procuring by the courts of the *performance* by the defendant of his obligations. The plaintiff recovers what he is actually entitled to, not some monetary substitute for it. If what the plaintiff is entitled to is wealth expressed in monetary terms, the order will be for the payment of money, but this does not alter the character of the remedy or of the right being recognised. He gets the money because it was his property or he was in some other way entitled to it. It is still the enforced performance of an obligation.

Lord Hobhouse did not see how this could be relevant on the facts, since the Crown no longer had any right to enforce against the defendant. The remedy being awarded by the majority was 'a remedy based on proprietary principles when the necessary proprietary principles are absent'.

4. The decision in *WWF World Wide Fund for Nature v World Wrestling Federation Entertainment Inc.* [2007] EWCA Civ 286, [2008] 1 WLR 445, [2007] Bus LR 1252, subsequently confirmed that the account of profits is a compensatory remedy and not one based on restitutionary principles. It is merely one method of recognizing a claimant's interest in the performance of the contract where compensatory damages would be inadequate (no loss), so as to compensate the claimant for the non-performance of a contractual obligation. More generally, the law has been most flexible of late in terms of providing a method of protecting this performance interest.

5. In *Blake*, at p. 299D–E, Lord Hobhouse (dissenting) expressed some concern that the principle formulated by the majority should not be extended in the context of commercial contracts without a full appreciation of the consequences:

I must also sound a further note of warning that if some more extensive principle of awarding non-compensatory damages for breach of contract is to be introduced into our commercial law the consequences will be very far reaching and disruptive. I do not believe that such is the intention of your Lordships but if others are tempted to try to extend the decision of the present exceptional case to commercial situations so as to introduce restitutionary rights beyond those presently recognised by the law of restitution, such a step will require very careful consideration before it is acceded to.

In the event of a breach of a commercial contract, the innocent party would be expected to mitigate and would recover damages to compensate only for losses on this basis. The remedy of an account of profits would bypass mitigation, and would almost certainly involve causation questions and complex and difficult calculations in arriving at the appropriate profit figure.

6. In the immediate aftermath of the decision in *Blake*, there was evidence of an account of profits being claimed as a potential remedy in the commercial context. In *Esso Petroleum Co. Ltd v Niad Ltd* [2001] All ER (D) 324 (Nov)—noted by Beatson (2002) 118 LQR 377—Morritt VC applied the principle in *Blake* in concluding that an account of profits was an available remedy on the facts, which involved a breach of a commercial contract.

Esso Petroleum Co. Ltd v Niad Ltd
[2001] All ER (D) 324 (Nov)

The defendant was the owner of a petrol service station and had a solus agreement (for the exclusive supply of petrol) with the claimant oil company. In 1996, the claimant had introduced a marketing scheme, 'Pricewatch', which the defendant had agreed to implement. This involved the owners of petrol stations reporting prices charged by local competitors, which the claimant then took into account in setting the price to be charged by its petrol stations. In return for implementing the scheme and agreeing to charge the price specified, the defendant received a discount on the price that it paid the claimant for petrol. The evidence was that, in breach of contract, the defendant had failed to implement the scheme, despite repeated assurances that he would do so, and had kept the discount received from the claimant. The claimant therefore wished to determine whether, in principle, it was entitled to an account of profits or 'restitution' of the amount charged by the defendant in excess of the price recommended by the claimant.

Held: In principle, alternative remedies of an account of profits or restitution of the amount by which the charges for petrol exceeded the claimant's recommended prices were available. On the basis of the decision in *Blake*, an account of profits would be granted only in exceptional circumstances under which the usual remedies for breach of contract were inadequate and the claimant had a legitimate interest in preventing the defendant from profiting from the breach. This was such an exceptional case, since damages were inadequate: the claimant was unable to recover damages for this breach because it could not establish the lost sales attributable to the individual defendant's failure to implement the scheme. Since the defendant's breach threatened to undermine the 'Pricewatch' scheme, the claimant had the necessary legitimate interest in preventing the defendant from profiting from the breach to allow an account of profits to be ordered.

NOTE It is difficult to see how the facts of *Esso Petroleum v Niad* are 'exceptional' in the commercial context, and the real issue seems to have been the deliberate and repeated breaches, coupled with difficulties of causation and proof of loss.

The decision of the Court of Appeal in the next case provided some assistance in setting the limits for the use of the *Blake* principle in the commercial context and explaining its relationship with the principle in *Wrotham Park Estate Co. Ltd v Parkside Homes Ltd* [1974] 1 WLR 798 (discussed by Lord Nicholls in *Blake*, extracted at *page 788, 15.5.2*).

Experience Hendrix LLC v PPX Enterprises Inc.
[2003] EWCA Civ 323, [2003] 1 All ER (Comm) 830 (CA)

There had been breaches of a 1973 settlement agreement relating to masters of titles and licences of the music of Jimi Hendrix. Injunctions had been issued to prevent these breaches, but Buckley J at first instance had dismissed a claim for damages and an account of profits relating to past breaches. The claimant had therefore appealed on this question to the Court of Appeal. There was no evidence to establish the financial loss suffered by the appellant as a result of the breaches, so it sought the amount that it could reasonably have demanded to relax the prohibitions in the settlement agreement (i.e. the *Wrotham Park* principle) or the profit attributable to the exploitation of the material.

Held: The claimant could recover the amount that might reasonably be demanded by the Hendrix estate to release the prohibition (*Wrotham Park*). This was not an appropriate case in which to award an account of profits. Mance LJ (with whose judgment Peter Gibson LJ and Hooper J agreed) noted the exceptional features of *Blake* as:

(a) the context of Blake's employment in the security and intelligence service, the operation of which was dependent on secret information;

(b) the deliberate and repeated breaches, and the fact that Blake's notoriety meant that he could command considerable sums for his publication; and

(c) that the contractual undertaking that he had given was closely akin to a fiduciary obligation for which an account of profits is a common remedy.

The Court of Appeal concluded that *Hendrix* was not an exceptional case within the principle in *Blake*. Mance LJ noted that features (a) and (c) were missing on these facts (and, of course, they were also missing in *Esso v Niad*), although the fact that an injunction had been issued in relation to future breaches established that the appellant had a legitimate interest in preventing this profit-making activity. *Niad* was distinguished on the basis that, in that case, the defendant's breaches were fundamental to the scheme and questioned its viability.

Mance LJ added, at [44], as a practical point:

> Here, the breaches, though deliberate, took place in a commercial context. PPX, though knowingly and deliberately breaching its contract, acted as it did in the course of a business, to which it no doubt gave some expenditure of time and effort and probably the use of connections and some skill . . . An account of profits would involve a detailed assessment of such matters, which, as is very clear from *Blake*, should not lightly be ordered.

Accordingly, he concluded that PPX should pay the sum that might reasonably be demanded by the Hendrix estate to release the prohibition (*Wrotham Park*). Such an assessment would allow such commercial considerations and the broader context to be taken into account, and, it is submitted, will often be a more appropriate remedy in this context than an account of profits.

Peter Gibson LJ agreed that this was not an appropriate case for ordering an account of profits, adding, at [53]:

> No doubt deliberate breaches of contract occur frequently in the commercial world; yet something more is needed to make the circumstances exceptional enough to justify ordering an account of profits, particularly when another remedy is available.

15.5.3 The effect of *One Step*

The Supreme Court in *One Step* made important comments on *Blake* although without reaching definitive conclusions on its scope. Lord Reed in *One Step* was highly critical of the reasoning of Lord Nicholls in *Blake*:

LORD REED: 66. Lord Nicholls' first stepping stone towards his conclusion was that the user damages awarded for interferences with rights of property in the cases considered earlier 'cannot be regarded as conforming to the strictly compensatory measure of damage . . . unless loss is given a strained and artificial meaning', since 'the injured person's rights were invaded but, in financial terms, he suffered no loss' (p 279). However, as explained at para 30 above, a compensatory analysis need not be regarded as strained or artificial. The person who makes wrongful use of property, in breach of another person's valuable right to control its use, prevents that person from exercising his right to obtain the economic value of the use in question, and should therefore compensate him for the consequent loss.

67. The second stepping stone was a consideration of remedies for breach of fiduciary duty, which established the availability in equity of an order for an account of profits. That is in a context where the fiduciary owes his principal a duty of unqualified loyalty, and a consequent duty to account for all profits made from his position. The nature of the remedy reflects the nature of the obligation which has been infringed.

68. The third stepping stone was a consideration of cases under Lord Cairns' Act, such as *Bracewell v Appleby* and *Jaggard v Sawyer*, and pre-1858 cases which could now be brought under the Act, such as 'the case of a continuing wrong, such as maintaining overhanging eaves and gutters', as in *Battishill v Reed* (1856) 18 CB 696, 139 ER 1544. These were said to show that 'in the same way as damages at common law for violations of a property right may be measured by reference to the benefits wrongfully obtained by a defendant, so under Lord Cairns' Act damages may include damages measured by reference to the benefits likely to be obtained in future by the defendant' ([2001] 1 AC 268, 281).

69. A gains-based analysis of awards under Lord Cairns' Act was rejected in *Jaggard v Sawyer*, as explained at para 58 above. The damages awarded in that case, and in *Bracewell v Appleby*, were measured according to the amount which the claimant could fairly and reasonably have charged for the voluntary relinquishment of a valuable right of which he had effectively been deprived by the refusal of an injunction. In the absence of any reasons of fairness requiring its modification, the award was based on the economic value of the right: a value which was necessarily equivalent to that of the wrongful use which the claimant had to tolerate, since they were two sides of the same coin. That is consistent with Lord Nicholls' approval of the analysis of the measure of damages awarded in this type of case as 'the price payable for the compulsory acquisition of a right' (ibid). The claimant does not literally lose the right in question, but, as Lord Nicholls stated, 'the court's refusal to grant an injunction means that in practice the defendant is thereby permitted to perpetuate the wrongful state of affairs he has brought about' (ibid).

70. In the case of the overhanging eaves and gutters, on the other hand, the best measure of damages in the event of an injunction being refused might be found to be the consequent reduction in the value of the claimant's property. It was only because that measure would have produced 'nil or purely nominal damages' that Brightman J adopted a different measure in *Wrotham Park* (p 812). Under Lord Cairns' Act, as under the common law, the situations in which damages are awarded are so various on their facts that the courts cannot adopt a uniform approach.

71. Those three disparate types of award (damages for interferences with property, an account of profits made through a breach of fiduciary duty, and damages in substitution for an injunction), each reflecting the characteristics of the obligation which had been breached or the jurisdiction being exercised, formed the stepping stones to the fourth, namely damages for breach of contract. Lord Nicholls began by stating

that such damages are compensatory: 'that', he said, 'is axiomatic' (p 282). But 'a party to a contract may have an interest in performance which is not readily measurable in terms of money' (ibid). In such cases, 'a financially assessed measure of damages is inadequate' (ibid). The primary response of the law to this type of case was to provide specific relief, such as an injunction, so as to ensure that the contractual obligation was performed. These specific remedies, it was said, 'go a long way towards providing suitable protection for innocent parties who will suffer loss from breaches of contract which are not adequately remediable by an award of damages' (p 282). But they were not always available.

72. Lord Nicholls then cited *Wrotham Park* as an example of a case in which specific relief had been refused. The judge had been right to apply by analogy the cases concerning interferences with property rights, since 'it is not easy to see why, as between the parties to a contract, a violation of a party's contractual rights should attract a lesser degree of remedy than a violation of his property rights' (p 283). *Wrotham Park* was said at pp 283–284 to shine as a solitary beacon, showing:

> . . . that in contract as well as tort damages are not always narrowly confined to recoupment of financial loss. In a suitable case damages for breach of contract may be measured by the benefit gained by the wrongdoer from the breach. The defendant must make a reasonable payment in respect of the benefit he has gained.

73. This part of Lord Nicholls' speech is not altogether easy to interpret. A few observations can however be made. First, the fact that 'a party to a contract may have an interest in performance which is not readily measurable in terms of money' (p 282) has long been recognised by the law of damages. The law normally responds to inherent difficulties of measurement, and to difficulties arising from a paucity of evidence in a particular case, in the ways discussed at paras 37–38 above. Such difficulties do not justify the abandonment of any attempt to measure loss, and the use of the benefit gained by the wrongdoer as an alternative basis for an award of contractual damages, since that alternative is inconsistent with the logic of contractual damages, as explained at paras 31–35 above.

74. It is also necessary to recognise that the assessment of a hypothetical release fee is itself a difficult and uncertain exercise. In cases such as *Wrotham Park*, *Bracewell v Appleby* and *Jaggard v Sawyer*, judges estimated in a rough and ready way the amount which the claimant might fairly and reasonably have demanded as a quid pro quo for the relaxation of the obligation in question. More recently, the practice has developed of instructing forensic accountants to give expert evidence about a hypothetical negotiation between a reasonable person in the position of the claimant and a reasonable person in the position of the defendant. Such imaginary negotiations have become increasingly elaborate, and a host of questions can emerge as to the basis on which they should be hypothesised. This is well illustrated by Mr Grantham's report in the present case.

75. The artificiality of the exercise can be a further problem. Since the aim is to arrive at an objective valuation, the fact that the claimant might in reality have been unwilling to release the defendant from the obligation is not necessarily a problem, as Brightman J recognised in *Wrotham Park*. But the premise of the hypothetical negotiation—that a reasonable person in the claimant's position would have been willing to release the defendant from the obligation in return for a fee—breaks down in a situation where any reasonable person in the claimant's position would have been unwilling to grant a release, as was found to be the position in *Marathon Asset Management LLP v Seddon* [2017] EWHC 300 (Comm); [2017] ICR 791. The result of the exercise may be an appearance of precision, but as Hildyard J commented in *CF Partners (UK) LLP v Barclays Bank plc* [2014] EWHC 3049 (Ch), para 1199, 'the exercise is artificial; and, despite the apparent precision of the figures and calculations deployed typically (and necessarily) on each side, it necessarily involves a question of impression . . . it is to some considerable extent a "broad brush"'.

76. Secondly, although it is not clear what Lord Nicholls meant by 'a lesser degree of remedy' (p 283), it is not surprising that damages for breach of contract are generally assessed differently from damages for the invasion of a proprietary right, since the rights and obligations in question are generally of a different character. It is only in circumstances where they are analogous that it would be reasonable to expect

some consistency of approach. As has been explained, damages for breach of contract are based on the difference to the claimant between the outcome of performance and non-performance. That is not generally the same as the economic value of the right to performance, considered as an asset (which is not to deny that they may be the same, or similar, in some circumstances) . . .

77. Thirdly, as Lord Walker remarked in *Pell Frischmann* at para 48, it is a little surprising that Lord Nicholls should have described *Wrotham Park* as a beacon in relation to common law damages for breach of contract. In the first place, the proceedings were not based on a contractual right: there was no contract between the parties. They were concerned with the invasion of a property right, as Lord Walker observed. Furthermore, *Wrotham Park* was not concerned with common law damages, but with damages awarded in substitution for an injunction. In the circumstances of the case, these were not merely arbitrary matters of legal categorisation, but bore directly on the damages awarded, as has been explained. That is not to say that common law damages for a particular breach of contract are necessarily different from damages for analogous breaches of other types of obligation. As was said earlier, in circumstances where the rights and obligations are analogous, it would be reasonable to expect some consistency of approach.

78. Fourthly, it is plainly true that 'in contract as well as tort damages are not always narrowly confined to recoupment of financial loss'. However, that proposition does not depend on the *Wrotham Park* line of cases. It is illustrated, in relation to breach of contract, by cases concerned with the award of damages at common law for breaches causing non-economic loss, such as *Ruxley Electronics* and *Milner v Carnival plc (trading as Cunard)* [2010] EWCA Civ 389; [2010] 3 All ER 701.

79. Fifthly, since the assessment of damages in the property cases was based on the value of the right to control the use of the property as it had been wrongfully used, there is a sense in which it can be said that the damages in those cases 'may be measured by reference to the benefit gained by the wrongdoer from the breach', provided the 'benefit' is taken to be the objective value of the wrongful use. The same can be said of the *Wrotham Park* line of cases, subject to the same proviso, and subject also to the role of equitable considerations in the making of awards under Lord Cairns' Act. The courts did not, however, adopt a benefits-based approach, but conceived of the awards as compensating for loss.

80. For the avoidance of doubt, the award of damages for skimped performance, based on the difference between the value of the goods or services contracted for and those actually provided, is not excluded by the principle in *Robinson v Harman,* but is an example of its application. That was recognised by Lord Nicholls in *Blake* at p 286. This is worth mentioning, as it was submitted on behalf of the defendants in the present case, under reference to the Canadian case of *Smith v Landstar Properties Inc* [2011] BCCA 44, that such awards amounted to *Wrotham Park* damages.

81. Finally, in relation to Lord Nicholls' speech, the connection which he drew between *Wrotham Park* and an account of profits has had consequences in the later case law which are unlikely to have been intended. One has been a view that damages assessed on the basis of a hypothetical release fee, and an account of profits, are similar remedies (partial and total disgorgement of profits, respectively), at different points along a sliding scale, calibrated according to the degree of disapproval with which the court regards the defendant's conduct: see, for example, *Experience Hendrix*, paras 36–37 and 44. Related to this has been a view, illustrated by the present case, that damages assessed on the basis of a hypothetical release fee, like an account of profits in some circumstances, are available at the election of the claimant, and can be awarded by the court at its discretion whenever they might appear to be a just response. Neither view can be justified on an orthodox analysis of damages for breach of contract.

NOTE The precise status of *Blake* and the availability of the remedy of account of profits for breach of contract remain uncertain after *One Step*. However, the Supreme Court confirmed the primacy of the compensatory function of damages, and it may be that the award of an account of profits in *Blake* is to be confined to the almost unique situation that arose in that case.

Index